W9-ARF-168

Statistical Techniques in

Business & Economics

Eleventh Edition

A Note to Instructors

If you used previous editions of this textbook, thank you. If you are looking at it for the first time, we appreciate your consideration.

The amount of information available and the speed at which calculations are made have changed the way we do statistics. We have tried to capture these changes in this revision. We emphasize the interpretation of data and minimize calculations. We suggest the use of computer software. It does the work faster and more accurately.

New in the Eleventh Edition

Major Content Changes

We take a great deal of pride in the success and reputation established in the previous ten editions. We believe that the revisions in this edition further improve the text. Major revisions in this edition are:

- Sampling and confidence intervals are now covered in separate chapters, 8 and 9. Separating the topics makes the chapter sizes more manageable and the additional exercises will help students understand the concepts.
- The breakdown of hypothesis testing is now based on populations sampled rather than the size of the sample. This allows the better coverage and emphasis on the assumptions required for various tests.
- There is increased coverage of skewness. The additional explanation shows the students how to produce the same results as Excel.
- A new improved version of the MegaStat for Excel add-in software, along with a User Manual is included on the Student CD-ROM. We have also integrated MegaStat into the text where appropriate.
- There are many new data sets built into examples and problems.
- More Excel and MINITAB integration within the text.

Retained Pedagogical Features

- Computer examples using Excel, MegaStat, and MINITAB software have been interspersed throughout the text. The explanations of the software commands are placed at the end of the chapters to allow the students to focus first on the statistical concepts as they are introduced and explained.
- A pronunciation key lists each mathematical symbol, its meaning, and how to pronounce it. We believe this will help the student retain the meaning of the symbol and generally enhance course communications.
- Almost all of the chapters include references to Internet websites for companies, government organizations, or university data sets. These websites contain information to enhance the exercises at the end of the chapters and can be used for projects or for keeping your course up to date.

Text Features

As in previous editions, we continue to make every effort to support student learning and provide motivation. We present the concepts as clearly as we can for students, and we support those immediately with examples and exercises to make the text as useful as possible for students. The basic structure of each chapter is as follows:

Describing Data: Frequency Distributions and Graphic Presentation

2

GOALS

When you have completed this chapter, you will be able to:

1 Organize data into a *frequency distribution.*

2 Portray a frequency distribution in a *histogram, frequency polygon,* and *cumulative frequency polygon.*

3 Develop and interpret a *stem-and-leaf display.*

4 Present data using such graphical techniques as *line charts, bar charts,* and *pie charts.*

Merrill Lynch completed a study regarding the size of investment portfolios for a sample of clients in the 40- to 50-age group. Create a histogram and frequency distribution based on the sample (see Goal 2 and Exercise 43).

Goals

Each chapter begins with a set of learning objectives designed to provide focus for the chapter and motivate student learning. These objectives indicate what the student should be able to do after completing the chapter. The photo on the first page of each chapter ties to one of the exercises in the chapter.

Introduction

At the start of each chapter, we review the important concepts of the previous chapter(s) and provide a link from those into what concepts the current chapter will cover.

Color Photographs

There are color photographs interspersed throughout the text. We hope these help students see statistics with imagination and enthusiasm and help overcome the intimidation some students have of statistics.

Introduction

Rob Whitner is the owner of Whitner Pontiac in Columbia, South Carolina. Rob's father founded the dealership in 1964, and for more than 30 years they sold exclusively Pontiacs. In the early 1990s Rob's father's health began to fail, and Rob took over more of the day-to-day operation of the dealership. At this same time, the automobile business began to change—dealers began to sell vehicles from several manufacturers—and Rob was faced with some major decisions. The first came when another local dealer, who handled Volvos, Saabs, and Volkswagens, approached Rob about purchasing his dealership. After considerable thought and analysis, Rob purchased that dealership. More recently, the local Jeep Eagle dealership got into difficulty and Rob bought them out. So now, on the same lot, Rob sells the complete line of Pontiacs, the expensive Volvos, Saabs, Volkswagens, and the Chrysler products, including the popular Jeep line. Whitner Pontiac employs 83, including 23 full-time salespeople. Because of the diverse product line, there is quite a bit of variation in the selling price of the vehicles. A top-of-the-line Volvo sells for more than twice that of a Pontiac Grand Am. Rob would like to develop some charts and graphs that he could review monthly to see where the selling prices tend to cluster, to see the variation in the selling prices, and to note any trends. In this chapter we present techniques that will be useful to Rob or someone like him in managing his business.

Example/Solution

After important concepts are introduced, we always provide a solved example in a straightforward student oriented style. In our experience, these are a key-learning tool for students as they serve two purposes. First they provide a "how to" illustration for students. Second, they show a relevant business or economics based application which helps answer the "what will I use this for" question. In all examples, we have attempted to strike the appropriate balance for students, providing a realistic scenario or application, but also making the size and scale of the math reasonable for introductory students.

Self-Reviews

Self-Reviews are interspersed throughout the chapter and closely patterned after the preceding Examples. They help the student monitor their progress and provide immediate reinforcement for that particular technique. The worked-out solutions are provided at the end of each chapter.

EXAMPLE

The variation in the annual incomes of executives is to be compared with the variation in incomes of unskilled employees. For a sample of executives, $\bar{X} = \$500,000$ and $s = \$50,000$. For a sample of unskilled employees, $\bar{X} = \$32,000$, and $s = \$3,200$. We are tempted to say that there is more dispersion in the annual incomes of the executives because $\$50,000 > \$3,200$. The means are so far apart, however, that we need to convert the statistics to coefficients of variation to make a meaningful comparison of the variations in annual incomes.

For the executives:

$$CV = \frac{s}{\bar{X}}(100) = \frac{\$50,000}{\$500,000}(100) = 10 \text{ percent}$$

For the unskilled employees:

$$CV = \frac{s}{\bar{X}}(100) = \frac{\$3,200}{\$32,000}(100) = 10 \text{ percent}$$

There is no difference in the relative dispersion of the two groups.

Self-Review 4–6

A large group of Air Force inductees was given two experimental tests—a mechanical aptitude test and a finger dexterity test. The arithmetic mean score on the mechanical aptitude test was 200, with a standard deviation of 10. The mean and standard deviation for the finger dexterity test were: $\bar{X} = 30$, $s = 6$. Compare the relative dispersion in the two groups.

Definitions

Definitions of new terms or terms unique to the study of statistics are set apart from the text and highlighted for easy reference and review.

Margin Notes

There are more than 300 concise notes in the margin. Each is aimed at reemphasizing the key concepts presented immediately adjacent to it.

Formulas

Formulas used for the first time are boxed and numbered for reference. In addition a formula card is bound into the text, which lists these key formulas.

Variance and Standard Deviation

Variance and standard deviation are based on squared deviations from the mean.

The **variance** and **standard deviation** are also based on the deviations from the mean.

VARIANCE The arithmetic mean of the squared deviations from the mean.

Note that the variance is non-negative, and it is zero only if all observations are the same.

STANDARD DEVIATION The square root of the variance.

Population Variance The formulas for the population variance and the sample variance are slightly different. The population variance is considered first. (Recall that a population is the totality of all observations being studied.) The **population variance** for ungrouped data, that is, data not tabulated into a frequency distribution, is found by:

POPULATION VARIANCE $$\sigma^2 = \frac{\Sigma(X - \mu)^2}{N} \qquad [4\text{–}3]$$

Statistics in Action

Statistics in Action articles are scattered throughout the text, usually about two per chapter. They provide unique and interesting applications and historical insights into the field of statistics.

Statistics in Action

In 1788, James Madison, John Jay, and Alexander Hamilton anonymously published a series of essays entitled *The Federalist.* These Federalist papers were an attempt to convince the people of New York that they should ratify the Constitution. In the course of history, the authorship of most of these papers became known, but 12 remained contested. Through the use of statistical analysis, and particularly the study of the frequency of the use of various words, we can now conclude that James Madison is the likely author of the 12 papers. In fact, the statistical evidence that Madison is the author is overwhelming.

$21,000. The actual range is $20,379, found by $32,925 − $12,546. Comparing that value to $21,000 we have an excess of $621. Because we need to cover only the distance ($H - L$), it is natural to put approximately equal amounts of the excess in each of the two tails. Of course, we should also select convenient multiples of ten for the class limits. So here are the classes we could use for this data.

$12,000 up to 15,000
15,000 up to 18,000
18,000 up to 21,000
21,000 up to 24,000
24,000 up to 27,000
27,000 up to 30,000
30,000 up to 33,000

Step 4: Tally the vehicle selling prices into the classes. To begin, the selling price of the first vehicle in Table 2–1 is $20,197. It is tallied in the $18,000 up to $21,000 class. The second selling price in the first column of Table 2–1 is $16,587. It is tallied in the $15,000 up to $18,000 class. The other selling prices are tallied in a similar manner. When all the selling prices are tallied, the table would appear as:

Class	Tallies
$12,000 up to $15,000	𝍸 III
$15,000 up to $18,000	𝍸 𝍸 𝍸 𝍸 III
$18,000 up to $21,000	𝍸 𝍸 𝍸 II
$21,000 up to $24,000	𝍸 𝍸 𝍸 III
$24,000 up to $27,000	𝍸 III
$27,000 up to $30,000	IIII
$30,000 up to $33,000	II

Step 5: Count the number of items in each class. The number of observations in each class is called the **class frequency.** In the $12,000 up to $15,000 class there are 8 observations, and in the $15,000 up to $18,000 class there are 23 observations. Therefore, the class frequency in the first class is 8 and the class frequency in the second class is 23. There is a total of 80 observations or frequencies in the entire set of data.

Often it is useful to express the data in thousands, or some convenient units,

Pronunciation Key

This tool lists the mathematical symbol, its meaning, and how to pronounce it. We believe this will help the student retain the meaning of the symbol and generally enhance course communications.

Pronunciation Key

SYMBOL	MEANING	PRONUNCIATION
μ	Population mean	*mu*
Σ	Operation of adding	*sigma*
ΣX	Adding a group of values	*sigma X*
$\overline{X}$	Sample mean	*X bar*
$\overline{X}_w$	Weighted mean	*X bar sub w*
GM	Geometric mean	*G M*
ΣfX	Adding the product of the frequencies and the class midpoints	*sigma f X*

Exercises

We include exercises within the chapter and at the end of the chapter. Generally, the end-of-chapter exercises are the most challenging and integrative of the chapter concepts. The answers and worked-out solutions for all odd-numbered exercises appear at the end of the book in an appendix. For exercises with more than twenty observations, the data can be found on the CD-ROM included with the text. These files are in three formats: Excel, MINITAB, and ASCII. This Instructor's Edition includes answers to all even-numbered exercises printed next to the problem in color for your convenience.

Chapter Exercises

29. A data set consists of 83 observations. How many classes would you recommend for a frequency distribution?

30. 60

30. A data set consists of 145 observations that range from 56 to 490. What size class interval would you recommend?

31. The following is the number of minutes to commute from home to work for a group of automobile executives.

28	25	48	37	41	19	32	26	16	23	23	29	36
31	26	21	32	25	31	43	35	42	38	33	28	

a. How many classes would you recommend?
b. What class interval would you suggest?
c. What would you recommend as the lower limit of the first class?
d. Organize the data into a frequency distribution.
e. Comment on the shape of the frequency distribution.

Computer Output

We added computer examples using Excel spreadsheets, including the use of MegaStat and MINITAB software in the text where appropriate. Over 100 screen captures are highlighted with either a MINITAB of Excel logo in the margin.

Computer Solution

We can use a computer software package to find many measures of central tendency.

EXAMPLE

Table 2–1 on page 23 shows the prices of the 80 vehicles sold last month at Whitner Pontiac. Determine the mean and the median selling price.

SOLUTION

EXCEL

The mean and the median selling prices are reported in the following Excel output. (Remember: The instructions to create the output appear in the **Computer Commands** section at the end of the chapter.) There are 80 vehicles in the study, so the calculations with a calculator would be tedious and prone to error.

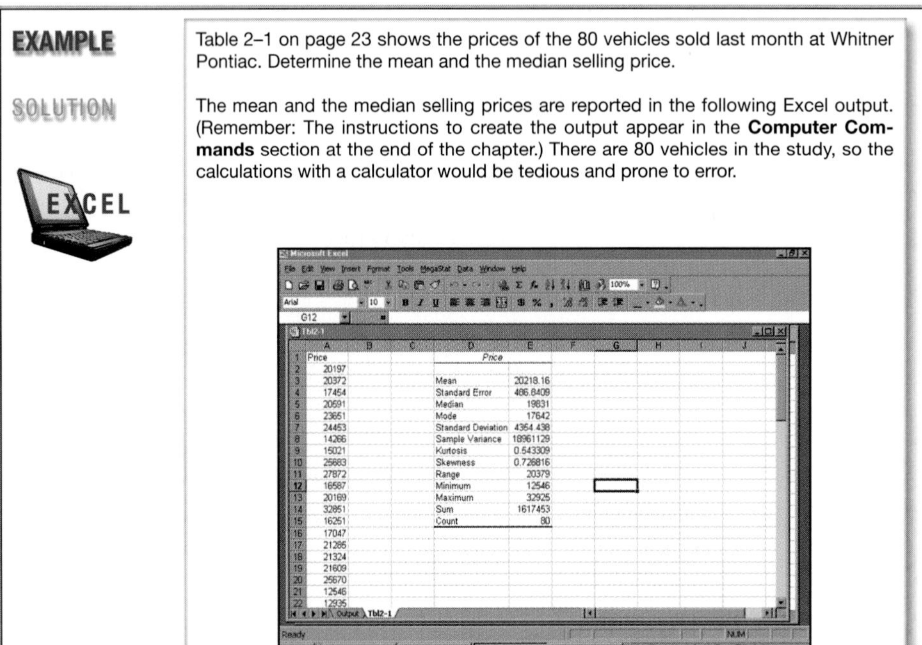

With a computer software package, it is quite easy to sort the data from smallest to largest and to locate percentiles and deciles. Both MINITAB and Excel output summary statistics. Listed below is the MINITAB output. It includes the first and third quartiles, as well as the mean, median, standard deviation, and coefficient of skewness for the Whitner Pontiac data (see Table 2–1). We conclude that 25 percent of the vehicles sold for less than $17,074 and that 75 percent sold for less than $22,795.

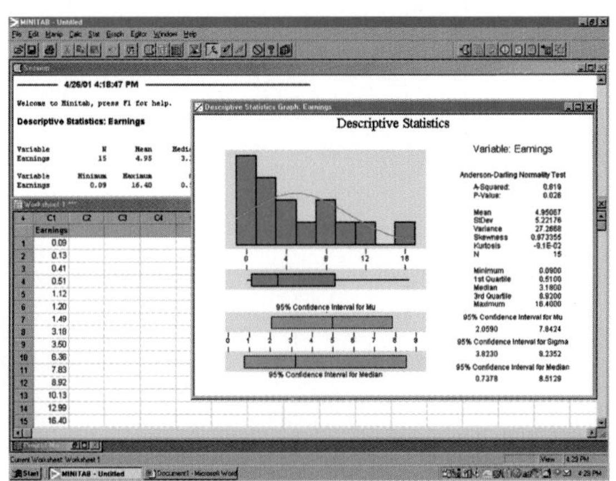

Computer Commands

In addition, the explanations of the computer commands are placed at the end of the chapter allowing students to focus on the statistical techniques and the explanation rather than how to input commands.

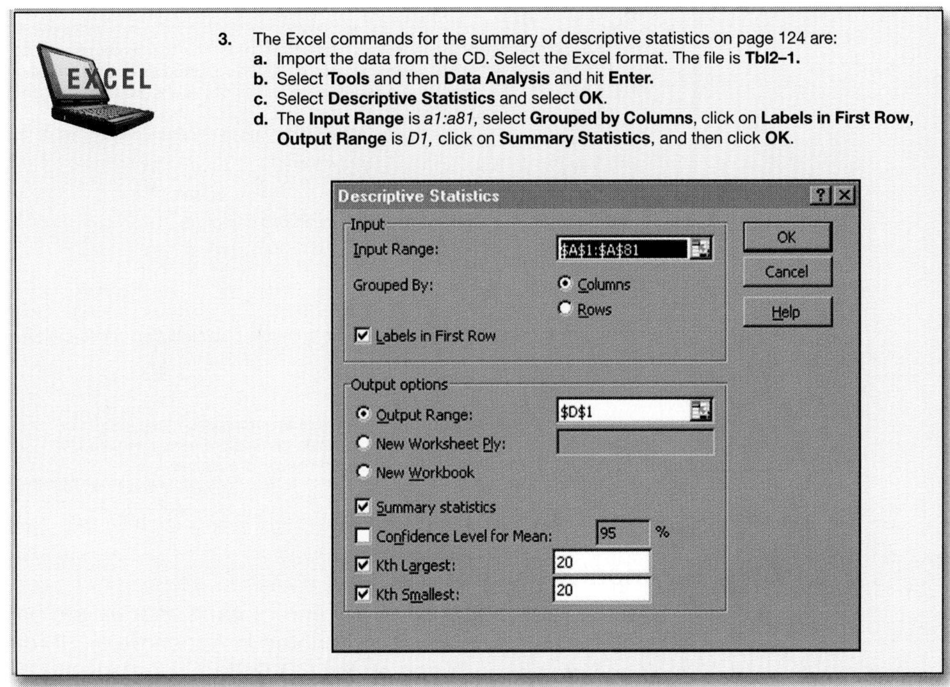

3. The Excel commands for the summary of descriptive statistics on page 124 are:
   a. Import the data from the CD. Select the Excel format. The file is **Tbl2–1.**
   b. Select **Tools** and then **Data Analysis** and hit **Enter.**
   c. Select **Descriptive Statistics** and select **OK.**
   d. The **Input Range** is *a1:a81,* select **Grouped by Columns**, click on **Labels in First Row, Output Range** is *D1,* click on **Summary Statistics**, and then click **OK.**

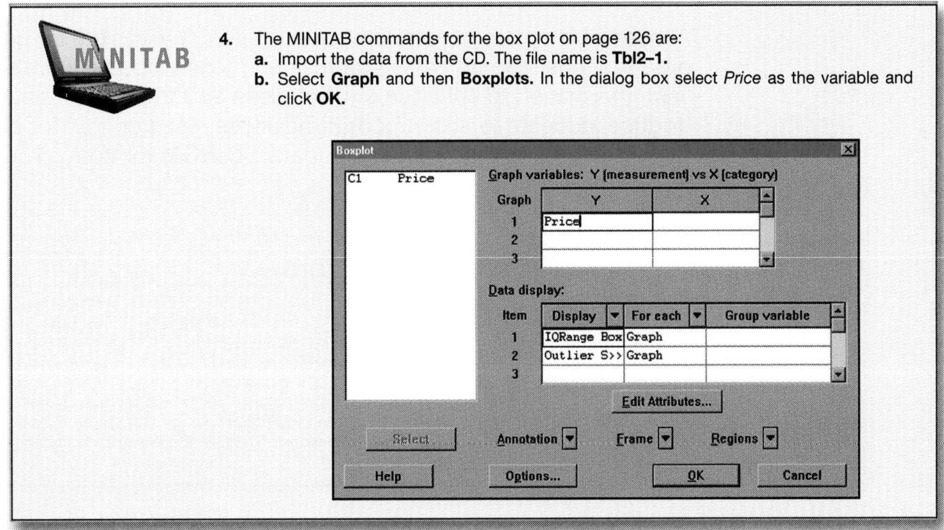

4. The MINITAB commands for the box plot on page 126 are:
   a. Import the data from the CD. The file name is **Tbl2–1.**
   b. Select **Graph** and then **Boxplots.** In the dialog box select *Price* as the variable and click **OK.**

Chapter Outline

As a summary, each chapter includes a Chapter Outline. This learning aid provides an opportunity for students to review material, particularly vocabulary, and see the critical formulas again.

Chapter Outline

I. A measure of location is a value used to describe the center of a set of data.
 A. The arithmetic mean is the most widely reported measure of location.
  1. It is calculated by adding the values of the observations and dividing by the total number of observations.
   a. The formula for a population mean of ungrouped or raw data is:

$$\mu = \frac{\Sigma X}{N} \qquad \textbf{[3–1]}$$

   b. The formula for the mean of a sample is

$$\overline{X} = \frac{\Sigma X}{n} \qquad \textbf{[3–2]}$$

   c. For data grouped into a frequency distribution, the formula is:

$$\overline{X} = \frac{\Sigma fX}{n} \qquad \textbf{[3–6]}$$

  2. The major characteristics of the arithmetic mean are:
   a. At least the interval scale of measurement is required.
   b. All the data values are used in the calculation.

Computer Data Exercises

The last several exercises at the end of each chapter are based on four large data sets. These data sets are found printed in Appendixes J through N at the end of the book and are also included on the CD-ROM packaged with the text. These data sets present the student with real-world applications of statistics and with more complex applications of the concepts.

Web Exercises

Almost all chapters have references to Internet websites for companies, government organizations, and university data sets. These websites contain interesting and relevant information to enhance the exercises and the end of the chapters. They also introduce students to this important business research tool for data. The addresses for these sites are included on the student CD-ROM for convenience.

exercises.com

15. Bill Clegg is a financial consultant for Paine Webber Financial Services. He must recommend to one of his clients whether to purchase stock in Johnson and Johnson, Inc. (a pharmaceutical company) or Pepsico (the parent company of Pepsi and Frito Lay). He checks the Internet for each and finds that 23 brokers have evaluated each stock. Brokers rate a stock a "1" if it is a strong buy and a "5" if it is a strong sell. Go to the following web site: http://quote.yahoo.com. To the left of "Get Quotes" type the two stock symbols, which are JNJ and PEP, then click on **Get Quote.** Finally, in the column headed "More Info" click on **Research.** What level is the data? Compare the results. Which stock would you recommend?

Computer Data Exercises

16. a. township is qualitative, others are quantitative.
b. township is nominal, others are ratio

16. Refer to the Real Estate data at the back of the text, which reports information on homes sold in the Venice, Florida, area last year. Consider the following variables: selling price, number of bedrooms, township, and distance from the center of the city.
    a. Which of the variables are qualitative and which are quantitative?
    b. Determine the level of measurement for each of the variables.
17. Refer to the Baseball 2000 data, which reports information on the 30 Major League Baseball teams for the 2000 season. Consider the following variables: number of wins, team salary, team attendance, whether the team played its home games on a grass or a turf field, and the number of home runs hit.
    a. Which of these variables are quantitative and which are qualitative?
    b. Determine the level of measurement for each of the variables.

Section Reviews

After selected logical groups of chapters (1–4, 5–7, 8 and 9, 10–12, 13 and 14, and 15 and 16), a Section Review is included. Much like a review before an exam, these include a brief overview of the chapters, a glossary of the key terms, and a practice examination of the material covered. The review also includes continuing cases and several small cases that let students make decisions using tools and techniques from a variety of chapters.

A Review of Chapters 1–4

This section is a review of the major concepts and terms introduced in Chapters 1 through 4. These chapters were concerned with describing a set of data by organizing it into a *frequency distribution* and then portraying the distribution in the form of a *histogram,* a *frequency polygon,* and a *cumulative frequency polygon.* The purpose of these graphs is to visually reveal the important characteristics of the data.

Computing a central value to represent the data is a numerical way of summarizing a mass of observations. Chapter 3 looked at several measures of central tendency, including the *mean, weighted mean, geometric mean, median,* and *mode.* Chapter 4 described the *dispersion,* or *spread,* in the data by computing the *range, standard deviation,* and other measures. Further, *skewness,* or lack of symmetry in the data, was described by determining the *coefficient of skewness.*

We stressed the importance of computer software packages, including Excel and Minitab. Several computer outputs in these chapters demonstrated how quickly and accurately a mass of raw data can be organized into a frequency distribution and a histogram. Also, we noted that the computer outputs present a large number of descriptive measures, including the mean, the variance, and the standard deviation.

Glossary

Chapter 1

Descriptive statistics The techniques used to describe the important characteristics of a set of data. These may include organizing the values into a frequency distribution and computing measures of central tendency and measures of spread and skewness.

Exhaustive Each observation must fall into one of the categories.

Inferential statistics, also called **statistical inference** or **inductive statistics** This facet of statistics deals with estimating a population parameter based on a sample statistic. For example, if 2 out of the 10 hand calculators sampled are defective, we might infer that 20 percent of the production is defective.

example, consumer response to the sound of a new speaker might be excellent, very good, fair, or poor.

Population The collection, or set, of all individuals, objects, or measurements whose properties are being studied.

Ratio measurement If the distances between numbers are of a known constant size and *there is a true zero point,* and the ratio of two values is meaningful, the measurement is ratio scale. For example, the distance between \$200 and \$300 is \$100, and in the case of money there is a true zero point. If you have zero dollars, there is an absence of money (you have none). Also the ratio between \$200 and \$300 is meaningful.

Sample A portion, or subset, of the population being studied.

Cases

A. Century National Bank

The following case will appear in the review sections. Assume that you work in the Planning Department of the Century National Bank and report to Ms. Lamberg. You will need to do some data analysis and prepare a short written report. Remember, Mr. Selig is the president of the bank, so you will want to ensure that your report is complete and accurate. A copy of the data appears in Appendix N.

The Century National Bank has offices in several cities in the Midwest and the southeastern part of the United States. Mr. Dan Selig, president and CEO, would like to know the characteristics of his checking account customers. What is the balance of a typical customer? How many other bank services do the checking account customers use? Do the customers use the ATM service and, if so, how often? What about debit cards? Who uses them, and how often are they used?

To better understand the customers, Mr. Selig asked Ms. Wendy Lamberg, Director of Planning, to select a sample of customers and prepare a report. To begin, she has appointed a team from her staff. You are the head of the team and responsible for preparing the report. You select a random sample of 60 customers. In addition to the balance in each account at the end of last month, you determine: (1) the number of ATM (automatic teller machine) transactions in the last month; (2) the number of other bank services (a savings account, a certificate of deposit, etc.) the customer uses; (3) whether the customer has a debit card (this is a relatively new bank service in which charges are made directly to the customer's account); and (4) whether or not interest is paid on the checking account. The sample includes customers from the branches in Cincinnati, Ohio; Atlanta, Georgia; Louisville, Kentucky; and Erie, Pennsylvania.

1. Develop a graph or table that portrays the checking balances. What is the balance of a typical customer? Do many customers have more than $2,000 in their accounts? Does it appear that there is a difference in the distribution of the accounts among the four branches? Around what value do the account balances tend to cluster?
2. Determine the mean and median of the checking account balances. Compare the mean and the median balances for the four branches. Is there a difference among the branches? Be sure to explain the difference between the mean and the median in your report.
3. Determine the range and the standard deviation of the checking account balances. What do the first and third quartiles show? Determine the coefficient of skewness and indicate what it shows. Because Mr. Selig does not deal with statistics daily, include a brief description and interpretation of the standard deviation and other measures.

B. Wildcat Plumbing Supply, Inc.: Do We Have Gender Differences?

Wildcat Plumbing Supply has served the plumbing needs of Southwest Arizona for more than 40 years. The company was founded by Mr. Terrence St. Julian and is run today by his son Cory. The company has grown from a handful of employees to more than 500 today. Cory is concerned about several positions within the company where he has men and women doing essentially the same job but at different pay. To investigate, he collected the information below. Suppose you are a student intern in the Accounting Department and have been given the task to write a report summarizing the situation.

Yearly Salary ($000)	Women	Men
Less than 30	2	0
30 up to 40	3	1
40 up to 50	17	4
50 up to 60	17	24
60 up to 70	8	21
70 up to 80	3	7
80 or more	0	3

To kick off the project, Mr. Cory St. Julian held a meeting with his staff and you were invited. At this meeting it was suggested that you calculate several measures of location, draw charts, such as a more-than cumulative frequency distribution, and determine the quartiles for both men and women. Develop the charts and write the report summarizing the yearly salaries of employees at Wildcat Plumbing Supply. Does it appear that there are gender differences?

Ancillary Materials

A **Student CD-ROM,** packaged free with all copies of the text, features chapter quizzes, PowerPoint slides, data files (in MINITAB, Excel, and ASCII formats) for the large data sets and exercises, video clips, practice problems, electronic tutorials, and Internet links to the text website and other online statistics resources. Also included is **MegaStat for Excel** by J. B. Orris of Butler University. **MegaStat version 8.9,** an Excel add-in, includes new routines for nonparametrics, time series, regression modeling, control charts, and box plots. Help files are built in and an introductory users manual is also included on the CD-ROM.

Also included *free* on the student CD-ROM is **Visual Statistics, 2.0,** by Doane, Mathieson, and Tracy. This package of 21 software programs and hundreds of data files and examples is designed for teaching and learning basic statistics. The modules of Visual Statistics provide an interactive, highly graphical, experimental format in which to explore statistics. The software and worktext promote active learning through competency building exercises, individual and team projects, and built-in databases. Over 400 data sets from business settings are included within the package, and the Visual Statistics CD includes the worktext in electronic files.

A comprehensive **Study Guide** (0-07-248163-3) written by Walter Lange, is organized much like the textbook. Each chapter includes objectives, a brief summary, a glossary, problems and their solutions, self-review exercises, and assignments. The Study Guide is set up in an easy-to-use format so that instructors can grade assignments easily if they choose. The assignment answers are in the Instructor's Manual.

An **Instructor's Manual** (0-07-248164-1) prepared by Denise Heban and the authors contains the complete solutions to all exercises, the cases, and the review problems, as well as the exercises in the Study Guide. Also included are syllabi for a one-semester, two-semester, or two-quarter course.

PowerPoint Electronic Slides developed by Jane Lind are included on both the student and instructor CD-ROMS. Over 450 full-color slides include chapter objectives, definitions of key terms, graphics, and additional examples. Students may use them as a chapter review tool, or as a source of additional solved examples. Instructors can use them to enhance their lectures and add additional material of their own.

A **Test Bank** (0-07-248166-8), developed by Samuel Wathen, contains over 1,900 multiple-choice, true/false, and short answer questions and problems. The answers to all questions are given, along with a rating of the level of difficulty and what chapter goal the question tests. An electronic version of the Test Bank is available on the Instructor's CD-ROM.

The **Instructor's Presentation CD-ROM** (0-07-248160-9) lets instructors access PowerPoint slides, text exhibits, the Diploma Test Bank: an easy-to-use test generating software system, and the Instructor's Manual with a click of the mouse. Drawing from this immense set of resources, instructors can easily prepare custom lectures, even editing and importing their own material. The Presentation Manager allows easy preparation of lectures using materials drawn from PowerPoint, video files, text figures, and more.

Basic Statistics Using Excel for Office 2000 (0-07-248161-7) by Merchant, Goffinet, and Koehler is a workbook that introduces students to Excel and shows how to apply it to introductory statistics. This manual presumes no prior familiarity with Excel or statistics and provides step-by-step directions in a how-to style using Excel '97 or 2000 and text examples and problems.

With the eleventh edition of *Statistical Techniques in Business and Economics*, special discounts are available for combination packages. Check with your sales representative or bookstore for pricing:

Text with MINITAB Student Version (0-07-413374-8)

Text with Basic Statistics Using Excel for Office 2000 (0-07-415245-9)

Text with Study Guide (0-07-413373-X)

Text with PowerWeb (0-07-415384-6)

Text with McGraw-Hill Pocket Dictionary of Statistics by Sahai and Khurshid (0-07-415246-7)

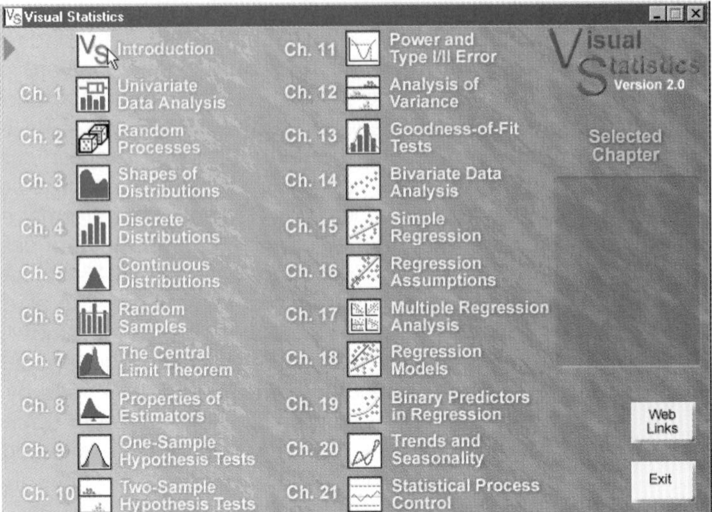

Online Learning Center

The Online Learning Center includes online content for both instructors and students. Based on the Study Guide, the site provides text specific resources for student reference and assistance. This site includes a summary, glossary, solved problems, data files, web links, and more. The Instructor's Center provides updates, the Instructor's Manual, and other teaching support materials (http://www.mhhe.com/lind11e).

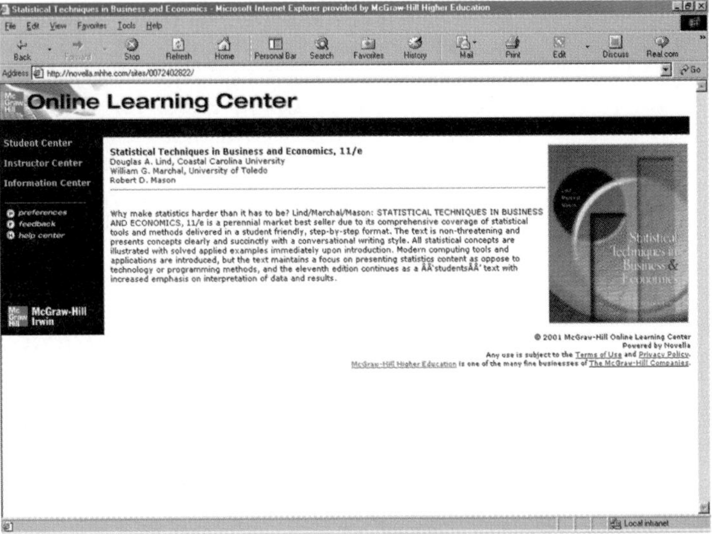

Pageout

Pageout is an exclusive McGraw-Hill product that allows instructors to quickly create a professional course website. You simply fill in the template provided with your specific course information, click on one of the designs, and the website is complete. The interactive course syllabus allows you to post content to coincide with your lectures and assignments. When students visit the site, they are directed to McGraw-Hill web content or your own specific material. The online grade book automatically stores quiz and test grades and allows scores to be posted to the entire class or individually. The discussion board allows for exchange of ideas, questions, or discussion of topic.

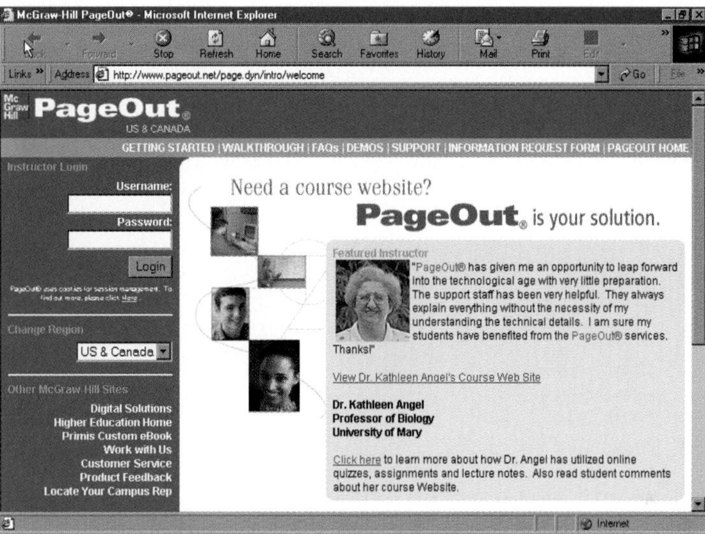

Business Statistics Center

The McGraw-Hill Business Statistics Center of BSC is a comprehensive collection of Internet-based resources for teaching and learning about statistics. This site is located at http://www.mhhe.com/bstat.

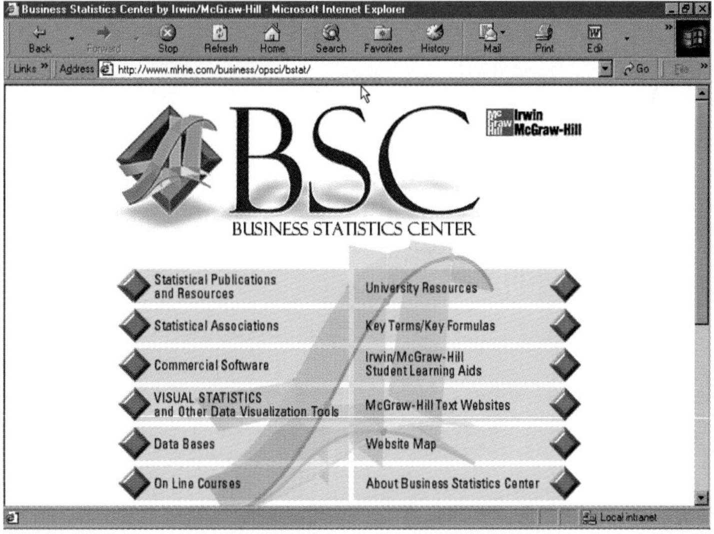

Statistical Techniques in

Business & Economics

MCGRAW-HILL/IRWIN SERIES
Operations and Decision Sciences

BUSINESS STATISTICS

Alwan
Statistical Process Analysis
First Edition

Aczel
Complete Business Statistics
Fourth Edition

Bowerman, O'Connell, and Hand
Business Statistics in Practice
Second Edition

Bryant and Smith
Practical Data Analysis: Case Studies in Business Statistics
Volumes I and II, Second Edition; Volume III, First Edition

Butler
Business Research Sources
First Edition

Cooper and Schindler
Business Research Methods
Seventh Edition

Delurgio
Forecasting Principles and Applications
First Edition

Doane, Mathieson, and Tracy
Visual Statistics
Second Edition, 2.0

Doane, Mathieson, and Tracy
Visual Statistics: Statistical Process Control
First Edition, 1.0

Gitlow, Oppenheim, and Oppenheim
Quality Management: Tools and Methods for Improvement
Second Edition

Lind, Mason, and Marchal
Basic Statistics for Business and Economics
Third Edition

Lind, Marchal, and Mason
Statistical Techniques in Business and Economics
Eleventh Edition

Merchant, Goffinet, and Koehler
Basic Statistics Using Excel for Office 2000
Third Edition

Neter, Kutner, Nachtsheim, and Wasserman
Applied Linear Statistical Models
Fourth Edition

Neter, Kutner, Nachtsheim, and Wasserman
Applied Linear Regression Models
Third Edition

Siegel
Practical Business Statistics
Fourth Edition

Webster
Applied Statistics for Business and Economics: An Essentials Version
Third Edition

Wilson and Keating
Business Forecasting
Third Edition

Statistical Techniques in Business & Economics

Eleventh Edition

Douglas A. Lind
Coastal Carolina University and The University of Toledo

William G. Marchal
The University of Toledo

Robert D. Mason
Late of The University of Toledo

Boston Burr Ridge, IL Dubuque, IA Madison, WI New York San Francisco St. Louis
Bangkok Bogotá Caracas Kuala Lumpur Lisbon London Madrid Mexico City
Milan Montreal New Delhi Santiago Seoul Singapore Sydney Taipei Toronto

McGraw-Hill Higher Education

A Division of The ***McGraw-Hill*** *Companies*

STATISTICAL TECHNIQUES IN BUSINESS AND ECONOMICS

Published by McGraw-Hill, an imprint of The McGraw-Hill Companies, Inc. 1221 Avenue of the Americas, New York, NY, 10020.

Some ancillaries, including electronic and print components, may not be available to customers outside the United States.

This book is printed on acid-free paper.

domestic 1 2 3 4 5 6 7 8 9 0 DOW/DOW 0 9 8 7 6 5 4 3 2 1
international 1 2 3 4 5 6 7 8 9 0 DOW/DOW 0 9 8 7 6 5 4 3 2 1

ISBN 0-07-240284-9

Vice president and editor-in-chief: *Robin J. Zwettler*
Executive editor: *Richard T. Hercher, Jr.*
Developmental editor: *Christina A. Sanders*
Senior marketing manager: *Zina Craft*
Project manager: *Jim Labeots*
Senior production supervisor: *Lori Koetters*
Media producer: *Greg Bates*
Senior designer: *Jennifer McQueen*
Cover image: *© Photodisc, Inc. All Rights Reserved.*
Interior design: *Maureen McCutcheon*
Senior supplement coordinator: *Rose M. Range*
Printer: *R. R. Donnelley & Sons Company*
Typeface: *9.5/11 Helvetica Neue 55*
Compositor: *GAC/Indianapolis*

Library of Congress Cataloging-in-Publication Data

Lind, Douglas A.
Statistical techniques in business and economics / Douglas A. Lind, William G. Marchal, Robert D. Mason.—11th ed.
p. cm.
Mason's name appears first on the earlier edition.
Includes bibliographical references and index.
ISBN 0-07-240282-2 (alk. paper)
1. Social sciences—Statistical methods. 2. Economics—Statistical methods. 3. Commercial statistics. I. Marchal, William G. II. Mason, Robert Deward, 1919- III. Title.
HA29.M268 2002
519.5—dc21

2001030664

INTERNATIONAL EDITION ISBN 0-07-112318-0

www.mhhe.com

To Jane, my wife and best friend, and to our sons,
Mike, Steve, and Mark

Douglas A. Lind

To Andrea, my heart and the mother of my children:
Rachel Anne (and Eric), Joseph Andrew, Sarah Louise,
Christopher Brophy, and Mary Bridget

William G. Marchal

Preface

As the name implies, the objective of *Statistical Techniques in Business and Economics* is to provide students majoring in economics, finance, marketing, accounting, management, and other fields of business administration, with an introductory survey of the many business applications of descriptive and inferential statistics. While we have focused on business applications, we have also attempted to use examples and problems that are student oriented and that do not require previous business courses.

When Bob Mason wrote the first edition of this text in 1967, locating relevant data was difficult. That has changed! Today, locating data is not a problem. The number of items you purchase at the grocery store is automatically recorded at the checkout stand. Phone companies keep track of the length of a call, the time it was made, and the number of the person called. Medical devices can automatically monitor and record our heart rate, blood pressure, and temperature. A large amount of business information is recorded and reported almost instantly. CNN, *USA Today,* and Yahoo!, for example, have websites where you can track stock prices with a delay of less than 20 minutes.

Today, skills are needed to deal with all this numerical information. First, we need to be critical consumers of information presented by others. Second, we need to be able to reduce large amounts of data into a meaningful form so that we can make effective interpretations, judgments, and decisions.

Today, all students not only have calculators, but many have their own computers or at least have access to a computer in a campus lab. Statistical software is also widely available, as is electronically-stored data. In response to these changes, we include screen captures from Excel and MINITAB within the chapters. This enables the student to actually view the output. The commands necessary to achieve the software results are at the end of the chapter. We have replaced many of the calculation examples with interpretation ones, to aid the student in communicating the statistical results.

While making these changes, we have not moved away from presenting, as best we can, the key concepts, along with supporting examples. The eleventh edition of *Statistical Techniques in Business and Economics* is the product of many people: students, colleagues reviewers, and the staff at McGraw-Hill/Irwin. We thank them all. We wish to express our sincere gratitude to the reviewers:

Douglas Barrett
University of North Alabama

Darl Bien
University of Denver

Wendy Brown
Southern Alberta Institute of Technology

Mary Elizabeth Camp
Indiana University

Sharad Chitgopekar
Illinois State University

Giopal Dorai
William Paterson University

Bernice Evans
Morgan State University

Burdette Hansen
University of Phoenix

Clifford B. Hawley
West Virginia University

Lloyd R. Jaisingh
Morehead State University

Valerie M. Jones
Tidewater Community College

Creig Kronstedt
Cardinal Stritch University

Denise Kummer
St. Louis Community College
Jack Muryn
Cardinal Stritch University
Julia A. Norton
California State University — Hayward
Louis A. Patille
University of Phoenix — Colorado
Christopher W. Rogers
Miami-Dade Community College
Charlene Robert
Louisiana State University
Linda Stephanchick
DeVry Institute of Technology
Andrew Welki
John Carroll University
Kathleen Whitcomb
University of South Carolina
Charles W. Williams
Troy State University

Their suggestions and thorough review of the previous edition and the manuscript for this edition made this a better text.

A special thanks goes to a number of people. Dr. Leonard Presby, of William Paterson University, Dr. Jerzy Kamburowski, of The University of Toledo, and Dr. Roberta Thomas, of The University of Phoenix, reviewed the manuscript and checked the exercises for accuracy. Professor Walter H. Lange, of The University of Toledo, prepared the Study Guide, and Dr. Samuel Wathen, of Coastal Carolina University, prepared the test bank and checked the text for accuracy. Ms. Denise Heban and the text authors prepared the Instructor's Manual, and Ms. Jane Lind the PowerPoint Presentation. We appreciate their efforts on the project.

We also would like to thank the staff at McGraw-Hill/Irwin. This includes Richard T. Hercher, Jr., Executive Editor; Christina Sanders, Development Editor; Zina Craft, Marketing Manager, Jim Labeots, Project Manager; and others who we don't know personally, but who we know made valuable contributions.

A Note to the Student

We have tried to make this material "no more difficult than it needs to be." By that we mean we always keep the explanations practical without oversimplifying. We have used examples similar to those you will encounter in the business world. When you have completed this book, you will understand how to apply statistical tools to help make business decisions. In addition, you will find that many of the topics and methods you learn can be used in other courses in your business education, and that they are consistent with what you encounter in other quantitative or statistics electives.

There is no doubt that today there is more data available to a business than ever. However, people who can convert data in useful information and interpret it well are in short supply. If you thoughtfully work through this text, you will be well prepared to contribute to the success and development of your company. Remember, as one of the authors read recently in a fortune cookie, "None of the secrets of success will work unless you do."

Learning Aids

We have designed the text to assist you in taking this course without the anxiety often associated with statistics. These learning aids are all intended to help you in your study.

Objectives Each chapter begins with a set of learning objectives. They are designed to provide focus for the chapter and to motivate learning. These objectives indicate what you should be able to do after completing the chapter. We include a photo that ties these chapter objectives to one of the exercises within the chapter.

Introduction At the start of each chapter, we review the important concepts of the previous chapter(s) and describe how they link to what the current chapter will cover.

Definitions Definitions of new terms or terms unique to the study of statistics are set apart from the text and highlighted. This allows easy reference and review.

Formulas Whenever a formula is used for the first time it is boxed and numbered for easy reference. In addition, a formula card that summarizes the key formulas is bound into the text. This can be removed and carried for quick reference as you do homework or review for exams.

Margin Notes There are more than 300 concise notes in the margin. Each emphasizes the key concept being presented immediately adjacent to it.

Examples/Solutions We include numerous examples with solutions. These are designed to show you immediately in detail, how the concepts can be applied to business situations.

Statistics in Action Statistics in Action articles are scattered throughout the text, usually about two per chapter. They provide unique and interesting applications and historical insights into statistics.

Self-Reviews Self-reviews are interspersed throughout the chapter and each is closely patterned after the preceding **Example/Solution.** They will help you monitor your progress and provide immediate reinforcement for that particular technique. The answers and methods of solution are located at the end of the chapter.

Exercises We include exercises within the chapter, after the **Self-Reviews,** and at the end of the chapter. The answers and method of solution for all odd-numbered exercises are at the end of the book. For most exercises with more than 20 observations, the data is on the CD-ROM in the text.

Chapter Outline As a summary, each chapter includes a chapter outline. This learning aid provides an opportunity to review material, particularly vocabulary, and to see and review the formulas again.

Web Exercises Almost all chapters have references to the Internet for companies, government organizations, and university data sets. These sites contain interesting and relevant information to enhance the exercises at the end of the chapters.

Computer Data Exercises In most chapters, the last four exercises refer to four large business data sets. A complete listing of the data is available in the back of the text and on the CD-ROM included with the text.

Section Reviews After selected groups of chapters, a section review is included. This includes a brief review of the chapters, a glossary of the key terms, and a practice examination of the material covered. This review also includes cases that let you make decisions using tools and techniques from a variety of chapters.

Supplements

The **Student CD** packaged free with all copies of the text, features self-graded practice quizzes. Software tutorials, PowerPoint slides, the data files (in MINITAB, Excel, and ASCII formats) for the end of chapter data and for exercises having 20 or more data values. As well as an Internet link to the text web site and to the web sites listed in the Web exercises in the text. Also included is MegaStat for Excel, by J. B. Orris, software that enhances the power of Excel in statistical analysis. Visual Statistics 20, written by Doanne, Tracy, and Mathieson, is also included. Visual Statistics is a software program for teaching and learning statistics through interactive experimentation and visualization.

A comprehensive **Study Guide,** written by Professor Walter Lange of The University of Toledo, is organized much like the textbook. Each chapter includes objectives, a brief summary of the chapter, problems and their solution, self-review exercises, and assignment problems.

Douglas A. Lind
William G. Marchal

Brief Contents

Contents

1

What Is Statistics?

Forbes publishes annually a list of the richest Americans. William Gates, founder of Microsoft Corporation, is the richest. His net worth is estimated at $60 billion. (See Goal 5 and Statistics in Action box on page 3.)

GOALS

When you have completed this chapter you will be able to:

1. **Understand why we study statistics.**
2. **Explain what is meant by *descriptive statistics* and *inferential statistics.***
3. **Distinguish between a *qualitative variable* and a *quantitative variable.***
4. **Distinguish between a *discrete variable* and a *continuous variable.***
5. **Distinguish among the *nominal, ordinal, interval,* and *ratio* levels of measurement.**
6. **Define the terms *mutually exclusive* and *exhaustive.***

Introduction

More than 100 years ago H. G. Wells, an English author and historian, noted that "statistical thinking will one day be as necessary for efficient citizenship as the ability to read." He made no mention of business because the Industrial Revolution was just beginning. Were he to comment on statistical thinking today, he would probably say that "statistical thinking is necessary not only for effective citizenship but also for effective decision making in various facets of business."

The late W. Edwards Deming, a noted statistician and quality-control expert, insisted that statistics education should begin before high school. He liked to tell the story of an 11-year-old who devised a quality-control chart to track the on-time performance of his school bus. Deming commented, "He's got a good start in life." We hope that this book will give you a solid foundation in statistics for your future life in marketing, management, accounting, sales, or some other facet of business.

Almost daily we apply statistical concepts in our lives. For example, to start the day you turn on the shower and let it run for a few moments. Then you put your hand in the shower to sample the temperature and decide to add more hot water or more cold water, or you conclude that the temperature is just right and enter the shower. As a second example, suppose you are at the grocery store looking to buy a frozen pizza. One of the pizza makers has a stand, and they offer a small wedge of their pizza. After sampling the pizza, you decide whether to purchase the pizza or not. In both the shower and pizza examples, you make a decision and select a course of action based on a sample.

Businesses are faced with similar problems. The Kellogg Company must ensure that the mean amount of Raisin Bran in the 25.5 gram package meets the label specifications. To do so, they select periodic random samples from the production area and weigh the contents.

On a national level, a candidate for the office of President of the United States wants to know what percent of the voters in Illinois will support him or her in the upcoming election. There are several ways he could go about answering this question. He could have his staff call all those people in Illinois who plan to vote in the upcoming election and ask for whom they plan to vote. He could go out on a street in Chicago, stop 10 people that look to be of voting age, and ask them for whom they plan to vote. He could select a random sample of about 2,000 voters from the state, contact these voters and, based on this cross-section, make an estimate of the percent who will vote for him in the upcoming election. In this text we will show you why the third choice is the best course of action.

What Is Meant by Statistics?

How do we define the word *statistics*? We encounter it frequently in our everyday language. It really has two meanings. In the more common usage, statistics refers to numerical information. Examples include the average starting salary of college graduates, the average number of Fords sold per month at Kistler Ford over the last year, the percentage of undergraduates attending Harvard who will attend graduate school, the number of deaths due to alcoholism last year, the change in the Dow Jones Industrial

Statistics in Action

We want to call your attention to a feature we call *Statistics in Action.* Read each one carefully to get an appreciation of the wide application of statistics in management, economics, nursing, law enforcement, sports, and other disciplines. Following is an assortment of statistical information, from surveys published in *USA Today, Forbes, Time,* and other magazines and newspapers.

- *Forbes* publishes annually a list of the richest Americans. William Gates, founder of Microsoft Corporation, is the richest. His net worth is estimated at $60 billion.
- The four largest American companies, ranked by sales are General Motors, Wal-Mart Stores, Ford, and General Electric.
- The typical American earns $1,235,720 and pays $178,364 in taxes in his or her lifetime.

Average from yesterday to today, or the number of home runs hit by the Chicago Cubs during the 2000 season. In these examples statistics are a value or a percentage. Other examples include:

- The typical automobile in the United States travels 11,099 miles per year, the typical bus 9,353 miles per year, and the typical truck 13,942 miles per year. In Canada the corresponding information is 10,371 miles for automobiles, 19,823 miles for busses, and 7,001 miles for trucks.
- The mean time waiting for technical support is 17 minutes.
- The Bureau of the Census projects the population of the United States to be 335,050,000 by the year 2025.
- The mean length of the business cycle since 1945 (measured from peak to peak) is 61 months.

The above are all examples of **statistics.** A collection of numerical information is called **statistics** (plural).

Statistics can appear in graphic as well as sentence form. A graph is often useful for capturing reader attention and to portray a large amount of information. For example, Chart 1-1 shows Frito-Lay volume and market share for the major snack and potato chip categories in supermarkets in the United States for 1999. It requires only a quick glance to discover there were nearly 800 million pounds of potato chips sold in 1999 and that Frito-Lay sold 64 percent of that total. Also note that Frito-Lay has 82 percent of the corn chip market.

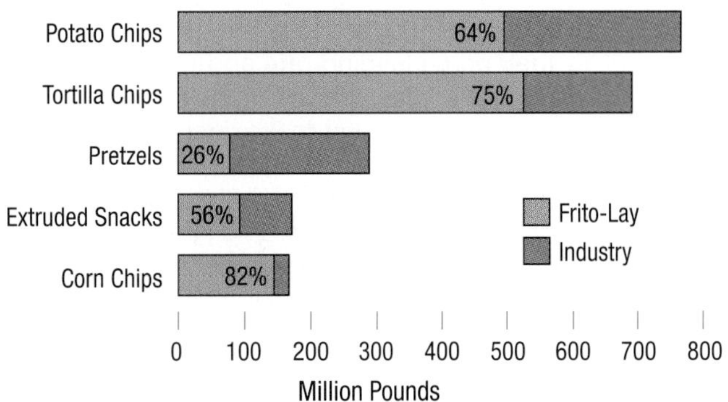

CHART 1–1 Frito-Lay Volume and Share of Major Snack Chip Categories in U.S. Supermarkets.
Source: 1999 Annual Report, p. 6.

The subject of statistics, as we will explore it in this text, has a much broader meaning than just collecting and publishing numerical information. We define statistics as:

> **STATISTICS** The science of collecting, organizing, presenting, analyzing, and interpreting data to assist in making more effective decisions.

As the definition suggests, the first step in investigating a problem is to collect relevant data. It must be organized in some way and perhaps presented in a chart, such as Chart 1–1. Only after the data have been organized are we then able to analyze and interpret it. Here are some examples of the need for data collection.

- Research analysts for Merrill Lynch evaluate many facets of a particular stock before making a "buy" or "sell" recommendation. They collect the past sales data of the company and estimate future earnings. Other factors, such as the projected worldwide demand for the company's products, the strength of the competition, and the effect of the new union-management contract, are also considered before making a recommendation.

- The marketing department at Lever Brothers, a manufacturer of soap products, has the responsibility of making recommendations regarding the potential profitability of a newly developed group of face soaps having fruit smells, such as grape, orange, and pineapple. Before making a final decision, they will test it in several markets. That is, they may advertise and sell it in Topeka, Kansas, and Tampa, Florida. Based on the test marketing in these two regions, Lever Brothers will make a decision whether to market the soaps in the entire country.
- The United States government is concerned with the present condition of our economy and with predicting future economic trends. The government conducts a large number of surveys to determine consumer confidence and the outlook of management regarding sales and production for the next 12 months. Indexes, such as the Consumer Price Index (described in Chapter 18), are constructed each month to assess inflation. Information on department store sales, housing starts, money turnover, and industrial production are just a few of the hundreds of items used to form the basis of the projections. These evaluations are used by banks to decide their prime lending rate and by the Federal Reserve Board to decide the level of control to place on the money supply.
- Management must make decisions on the quality of production. For example, automatic drill presses do not produce a perfect hole that is always 1.30 inches in diameter each time the hole is drilled (because of drill wear, vibration of the machine, and other factors). Slight tolerances are permitted, but when the hole is too small or too large, production is defective and the products cannot be used. The Quality Assurance Department is charged with continually monitoring production by using sampling techniques (described in Chapter 17).

Why Study Statistics?

If you look through your university catalog, you will find that statistics is required for many college programs. Why is this so? What are the differences in the statistics courses taught in the Engineering College, Psychology or Sociology Departments in the Liberal Arts College, and that of the College of Business? The biggest difference is the examples used. The course content is basically the same. In the College of Business we are interested in such things as profits, hours worked, and wages. In the Psychology Department they are interested in test scores, and in Engineering they may be interested in how many units are manufactured on a particular machine. However, all three are interested in what is a typical value and how much variation there is in the data. There may also be a difference in the level of mathematics required. An engineering statistics course usually requires calculus. Statistics courses in colleges of business and education usually teach the course at a more applied level. You should be able to handle the mathematics in this text if you have completed high school algebra.

So why is statistics required in so many majors? The first reason is that numerical information is everywhere. Look in the newspapers (*USA Today*), news magazines

Examples of why we study statistics

(*Time, Newsweek,* and *U.S. News and World Report*), business magazines (*Business Week* or *Forbes*), or general interest magazines (*People*), women's magazines (*Home and Garden*), or sports magazines (*Sports Illustrated, ESPN The Magazine)*, and you will be bombarded with numerical information.

Here are some examples:

- The General Electric Company reported revenues of $111,630,000 in 1999, up from $100,469,000 in 1998. The 1999 year end closing price for a share of common stock was $154.75, up from $102.00 at the end of 1998.
- Graduates of the University of Notre Dame Master of Business Administration Program had a mean starting salary of $54,000 and 91 percent were employed within three months of graduation.
- There are 26.4 million golfers age 12 and over in the United States. Approximately 6.1 million are avid golfers, i.e. they play 25 or more rounds in a year. The typical golfer is male, 40 years old, has a household income of $68,209, and plays 21.3 rounds per year.
- The USA drinks more coffee than any other country, an average of 1.75 cups per person per day.

How are we to determine if the conclusions reported are reasonable? Was the sample large enough? How were the sampled units selected? To be an educated consumer of this information, we need to be able to read the charts and graphs and understand the discussion of the numerical information. An understanding of the concepts of basic statistics will be a big help.

The second reason for taking a statistics course is that statistical techniques are used to make decisions that affect our daily lives. That is, they affect our personal welfare. Here are a few examples:

- Insurance companies use statistical analysis to set rates for home, automobile, life, and health insurance. Tables are available that summarize the probability that a 25-year-old woman will survive the next year, the next 5 years, and so on. On the basis of these probabilities, life insurance premiums can be established.
- The Environmental Protection Agency is interested in the water quality of Lake Erie. They periodically take water samples to establish the level of contamination and maintain the level of quality.
- Medical researchers study the cure rates for diseases, based on the use of different drugs and different forms of treatment. For example, what is the effect of treating a certain type of knee injury surgically or with physical therapy? If you take an aspirin each day, does that reduce your risk of a heart attack?

A third reason for taking a statistics course is that the knowledge of statistical methods will help you understand why decisions are made and give you a better understanding of how they affect you.

No matter what line of work you select, you will find yourself faced with decisions where an understanding of data analysis is helpful. In order to make an informed decision, you will need to be able to:

1. Determine whether the existing information is adequate or additional information is required.
2. Gather additional information, if it is needed, in such a way that it does not provide misleading results.
3. Summarize the information in a useful and informative manner.
4. Analyze the available information.
5. Draw conclusions and make inferences while assessing the risk of an incorrect conclusion.

The statistical methods presented in the text will provide you with a framework for the decision-making process.

In summary, there are at least three reasons for studying statistics: (1) data is everywhere, (2) statistical techniques are used to make many decisions that affect our lives, and (3) no matter what your future line of work, you will make decisions that involve data. An understanding of statistical methods will help you make these decisions more effectively.

Types of Statistics

Descriptive Statistics

The study of statistics is usually divided into two categories: descriptive statistics and inferential statistics. The definition of statistics given earlier referred to "organizing, presenting, analyzing . . . data." This facet of statistics is usually referred to as **descriptive statistics.**

> **DESCRIPTIVE STATISTICS** Methods of organizing, summarizing, and presenting data in an informative way.

For instance, the United States government reports the population of the United States was 179,323,000 in 1960, 203,302,000 in 1970, 226,542,000 in 1980, 248,709,000 in 1990, and 265,000,000 in 2000. This information is descriptive statistics. It is descriptive statistics if we calculate the percentage growth from one decade to the next. However, it would **not** be descriptive statistics if we used the data to forecast the population of the United States in the year 2010 or the percentage growth from 1990 to 2010.The following are some other examples of descriptive statistics.

- There are a total of 42,796 miles of interstate highways in the United States. The interstate system represents only 1 percent of the nation's total roads but carries more than 20 percent of the traffic. The longest is I-90, which stretches from Boston to Seattle, a distance of 3,081 miles. The shortest is I-878 in New York City, which is 0.70 of a mile in length. Alaska does not have any interstate highways, Texas has the most interstate miles at 3,232, and New York has the most interstate routes with 28.
- According to the Bureau of Labor Statistics, the average weekly earnings rose by 3.7 percent, seasonally adjusted, from March 1999 to March 2000. After deflation by the Consumer Price Index, average weekly earnings decreased by 0.2 percent. Before adjustment for seasonal change and inflation, average weekly earnings were $465.80 in March 2000, compared with $448.70 a year earlier.
- The Internal Revenue Service reports that the mean time to file Form 1040EZ is 2 hours and 46 minutes. This compares with 7 hours and 34 minutes for Form 1040A, and 10 hours and 53 minutes for Form 1040. The average time to complete a return via the TeleFile system is 37 minutes.

Masses of unorganized data—such as the census of population, the weekly earnings of thousands of computer programmers, and the individual responses of 2,340 registered voters regarding their choice for President of the United States—are of little value as is. However, statistical techniques are available to organize this type of data into a meaningful form. Some data can be organized into a **frequency distribution.** (The procedure for doing this is covered in Chapter 2.) Various **charts** may be used to describe data; several basic chart forms are also presented in Chapter 2.

Specific measures of central tendency, such as the mean, may be computed to describe the central value of a group of numerical data. These averages are presented in Chapter 3. A number of statistical measures may be used to describe how closely the data are clustered about an average. These measures are examined in Chapter 4.

Inferential Statistics

Another facet of statistics is **inferential statistics**—also called **statistical inference** and **inductive statistics.** Our main concern regarding inferential statistics is finding something about a population based on a sample taken from that population. For example, based on a sample survey by the federal government reported in *USA Today,* only 46 percent of high school seniors can solve problems involving fractions, decimals, and percentages. And only 77 percent of high school seniors correctly totaled the cost of soup, a burger, fries, and a cola on a restaurant menu. Since these are inferences about the population (all high school seniors) based on sample data, we refer to them as inferential statistics.

> **INFERENTIAL STATISTICS** The methods used to determine something about a population, based on a sample.

Note the words "population" and "sample" in the definition of inferential statistics. We often make reference to the population living in the United States or the 1 billion population of China. However, in statistics the word *population* has a broader meaning. A *population* may consist of *individuals*—such as all the students enrolled at Utah State University, all the students in Accounting 201, or all the inmates at Attica prison. A population may also consist of *objects,* such as all the XB-70 tires produced during the week at Cooper Tire and Rubber Company in Findlay, Ohio, or all the trout in a stock pond. A population may also consist of a group of *measurements,* such as all the weights of the defensive linemen on the Penn State University football team or all the heights of the basketball players in the Southeastern Conference. Thus, a population in the statistical sense of the word does not necessarily refer to people.

> **POPULATION** A collection of all possible individuals, objects, or measurements of interest.

To infer something about a population, we usually take a **sample** from the population.

> **SAMPLE** A portion, or part, of the population of interest.

Reasons for sampling

Why take a sample instead of studying every member of the population? A sample of registered voters is necessary because of the prohibitive cost of contacting millions of voters before an election. Testing wheat for moisture content destroys the wheat, thus making a sample imperative. If the wine tasters tested all the wine, none would be available for sale. It would be physically impossible for a few marine biologists to capture and tag all the seals in the ocean. (These and other reasons for sampling are discussed in Chapter 8.)

As noted, taking a sample to learn something about a population is done extensively in business, agriculture, politics, and government, as cited in the following examples:

- Television networks constantly monitor the popularity of their programs by hiring Nielsen and other organizations to sample the preferences of TV viewers. These program ratings are used to set advertising rates and to cancel programs.
- A public accounting firm selects a random sample of 100 invoices and checks each invoice for accuracy. There were errors on five of the invoices; hence the accounting firm estimates that 5 percent of the entire population of invoices contain an error.
- A random sample of 1,260 accounting graduates from four-year schools showed their mean starting salary was $32,694. We therefore estimate the mean starting salary for all accounting graduates of four-year institutions to be $32,694.

The relationship between a sample and a population is portrayed below.

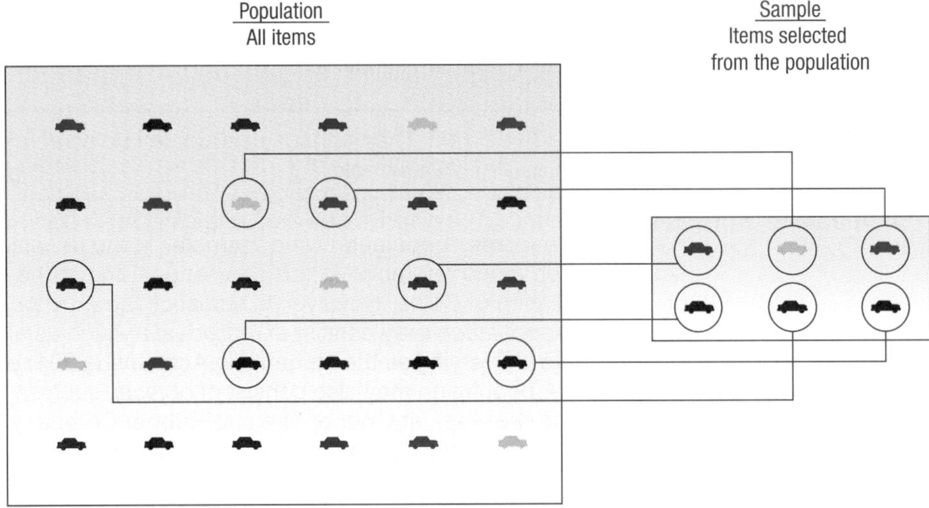

We strongly suggest you do the Self-Review exercises

Following is a self-review problem. There are a number of them interspersed throughout each chapter. They test your comprehension of the preceding material. The answer and method of solution are given at the end of the chapter. We recommend that you solve each one and then check your answer.

Self-Review 1–1

The answers are at the end of the chapter.

Chicago-based Market Facts asked a sample of 1,960 consumers to try a newly developed frozen fish dinner by Morton called Fish Delight. Of the 1,960 sampled, 1,176 said they would purchase the dinner if it is marketed.

(a) What would Market Facts report to Morton Foods regarding acceptance of Fish Delight in the population?

(b) Is this an example of descriptive statistics or inferential statistics? Explain.

Types of Variables

Qualitative variable

There are two basic types of data: (1) those obtained from a qualitative population and (2) those obtained from a quantitative population. When the characteristic or variable being studied is nonnumeric, it is called a **qualitative variable** or an **attribute.** Examples of qualitative variables are gender, religious affiliation, type of automobile owned, state of birth, and eye color. When the data being studied are qualitative, we are usually interested in how many or what proportion fall in each category. For example, what percent of the population has blue eyes? How many Catholics and how many Protestants are there in the United States? What percent of the total number of cars sold last month were Buicks? Qualitative data are often summarized in charts and bar graphs (Chapter 2).

Quantitative variable

When the variable studied can be reported numerically, the variable is called a **quantitative variable,** and the population is called a quantitative population. Examples of quantitative variables are the balance in your checking account, the ages of company presidents, the life of a battery (such as 42 months), the speeds of automobiles traveling along Interstate 5 near Seattle, and the number of children in a family.

Statistics in Action

Where did statistics get its start? In 1662 John Graunt published an article called "Natural and Political Observations Made upon Bills of Mortality." The author's "observations" were the result of his study and analysis of a weekly church publication called "Bill of Mortality," which listed births, christenings, and deaths and their causes. This analysis and interpretation of social and political data are thought to mark the start of statistics.

Quantitative variables are either discrete or continuous. **Discrete variables** can assume only certain values, and there are usually "gaps" between the values. Examples of discrete variables are the number of bedrooms in a house (1, 2, 3, 4, etc.), the number of cars arriving at the exit on I-75 at Berea, Kentucky, over an hour (16, 19, 30, etc.), and the number of students in each section of a statistics course (25 in section A, 42 in section B, and 18 in section C). We count, for example, the number of cars arriving at the Berea exit on I-75, and we count the number of statistics students in each section. Notice that a home can have 3 or 4 bedrooms, but it cannot have 3.56 bedrooms. Thus, there is a "gap" between possible values. Typically, discrete variables result from counting.

Observations of a **continuous variable** can assume any value within a specific range. Examples of continuous variables are the air pressure in a tire and the weight of a shipment of grain (which, depending on the accuracy of the scales, could be 15.0 tons, 15.01 tons, 15.013 tons, etc.). The amount of raisin bran in a box and the time it took to fly from Orlando to San Diego are other variables of a continuous nature. The Orlando–San Diego flight could take 7 hours and 30 minutes; or 7 hours, 30 minutes, and 45 seconds; or 7 hours, 30 minutes, and 45.1 seconds, depending on the accuracy of the timing device. Typically, continuous variables result from measuring something.

Levels of Measurement

Data can be classified according to levels of measurement. The level of measurement of the data often dictates the calculations that can be done to summarize and present the data. It will also determine the statistical tests that should be performed. For example, there are six colors of candies in a bag of M&M's candies. Suppose we assign the brown a value of 1, yellow 2, blue 3, orange 4, green 5, and red 6. From a bag of candies, we add the assigned color values and divide by the number of candies and report that the mean color is 3.56. Does this mean that the average color is blue or orange? As a second example, in a high school track meet there are eight competitors in the 400 meter run. We report the order of finish and that the mean finish is 4.5. What does the mean finish tell us? In both of these instances, we have not properly used the level of measurement.

There are actually four levels of measurement: nominal, ordinal, interval, and ratio. The "lowest," or the most primitive, measurement is the nominal level. The highest, or the level that gives us the most information about the observation, is the ratio level of measurement.

Nominal Level Data

In the **nominal level** of measurement, the observations can only be classified and counted. There is no particular order to the labels. The classification of the six colors of M&M's candies is an example of the nominal level of measurement. We simply classify the candies by color. There is no natural order. That is, we could report the brown

candies first, the orange first, or any of the colors first. Gender is another example of the nominal level of measurement. Suppose we count the number of students entering a football game with a student ID and report how many are men and how many are women. We could report either the men or the women first. For the nominal level the only measurement involved consists of counts. Table 1–1 shows a breakdown of U.S. long distance telephone usage. This is the nominal level of measurement because we recorded which carrier each customer used. Do not be distracted by the fact that we then summarized the data by reporting how many times each carrier was used.

TABLE 1–1 Long Distance Telephone Usage by Carrier

Carrier	Number of Calls	Percent
AT&T	108,115,800	75
MCI	20,577,310	14
Sprint	8,238,740	6
Other	7,130,620	5
Total	144,062,470	100

The arrangement of the carriers in Table 1–1 could have been changed. That is, we could have reported MCI first, Sprint second, and so on. This essentially indicates the major feature of the nominal level of measurement: there is no particular order to the categories.

These categories are **mutually exclusive,** meaning, for example, that a particular phone call cannot originate with both AT&T and MCI.

MUTUALLY EXCLUSIVE A property of a set of categories such that an individual, object, or measurement is included in only one category.

The categories in Table 1–1 are also **exhaustive,** meaning that every member of the population or sample must appear in one of the categories. So if a call did not originate with AT&T, MCI, or Sprint, it is classified as Other.

EXHAUSTIVE A property of a set of categories such that each individual, object, or measurement must appear in a category.

In order to process data on telephone usage, gender, employment by industry, and so forth, the categories are often numerically coded 1, 2, 3, and so on, with 1 representing AT&T, 2 representing MCI, for example. This facilitates counting by the computer. However, because we have assigned numbers to the various companies, this does not give us license to manipulate the numbers. For example, 1 + 2 does not equal 3, that is, AT&T + MCI does not equal Sprint. To summarize, the nominal level data have the following properties:

1. Data categories are mutually exclusive and exhaustive.
2. Data categories have no logical order.

Ordinal Level Data

The next higher level of data is the **ordinal level.** Table 1–2 lists the student ratings of Professor James Brunner in an Introduction to Finance course. Each student in the class answered the question "Overall how did you rate the instructor in this class?" This illustrates the use of the ordinal scale of measurement. One classification is "higher" or "better" than the next one. That is, "Superior" is better than "Good," "Good" is better than "Average," and so on. However, we are not able to distinguish the magnitude of the differences between groups. Is the difference between "Superior" and "Good" the same as the difference between "Poor" and "Inferior"? We cannot tell. If we substitute a 5 for "Superior" and a 4 for "Good," we can conclude that the rating of "Superior" is better than the rating of "Good," but we cannot add a ranking of "Superior" and a ranking of "Good," with the result being meaningful. Further we cannot conclude that a rating of "Good" (rating is 4) is necessarily twice as good as a "Poor" (rating is 2). We can only conclude that a rating of "Good" is better than a rating of "Poor." We cannot conclude how much better the rating is.

TABLE 1–2 Rating of a Finance Professor

Rating	Frequency
Superior	6
Good	28
Average	25
Poor	12
Inferior	3

In summary, the properties of ordinal level data are:

1. The data classifications are mutually exclusive and exhaustive.
2. Data classifications are ranked or ordered according to the particular trait they possess.

Interval Level Data

The **interval level** of measurement is the next highest level. It includes all the characteristics of the ordinal level, but in addition, the difference between values is a constant size. An example of the interval level of measurement is temperature. Suppose the high temperatures on three consecutive winter days in Boston are 28, 31, and 20 degrees Fahrenheit. These temperatures can be easily ranked, but we can also determine the difference between temperatures. This is possible because 1 degree Fahrenheit represents a constant unit of measurement. Equal differences between two temperatures are the same, regardless of their position on the scale. That is, the difference between 10 degrees Fahrenheit and 15 degrees is 5, the difference between 50 and 55 degrees is also 5 degrees. It is also important to note that 0 is just a point on the scale. It does not represent the absence of the condition. Zero degrees Fahrenheit does not represent the absence of heat, just that it is cold! In fact 0 degrees Fahrenheit is about -18 degrees on the Celsius scale.

The properties of the interval level data are:

1. Data classifications are mutually exclusive and exhaustive.
2. Data classifications are scaled according to the amount of the characteristic they possess.
3. Equal differences in the characteristic are represented by equal differences in the measurements.

There are few examples of the interval scale of measurement. Temperature, which was just cited, is one example. Another is shoe size.

Ratio Level Data

Practically all quantitative data are the ratio level of measurement. The **ratio level** is the "highest" level of measurement. It has all the characteristics of the interval level, but in addition, the 0 point is meaningful and the ratio between two numbers is meaningful. Examples of the ratio scale of measurement include: wages, units of production, weight, changes in stock prices, distance between branch offices, and height. Money is a good illustration. If you have zero dollars, then you have no money. Weight is another example. If the dial on the scale is at zero, then there is a complete absence of weight. The ratio of two numbers is also meaningful. If Jim earns $30,000 per year selling insurance and Rob earns $60,000 per year selling cars, then Rob earns twice as much as Jim.

The properties of the ratio level data are:

1. Data classifications are mutually exclusive and exhaustive.
2. Data classifications are scaled according to the amount of the characteristics they possess.
3. Equal differences in the characteristic are represented by equal differences in the numbers assigned to the classifications.
4. The zero point is the absence of the characteristic.

Table 1–3 illustrates the use of the ratio scale of measurement. It shows the incomes of four father and son combinations.

TABLE 1–3 Father–Son Income Combinations

Name	Father	Son
Lahee	$80,000	$ 40,000
Nale	90,000	30,000
Rho	60,000	120,000
Steele	75,000	130,000

Observe that the senior Lahee earns twice as much as his son. In the Rho family the son makes twice as much as the father.

Chart 1–2 summarizes the major characteristics of the various levels of measurement.

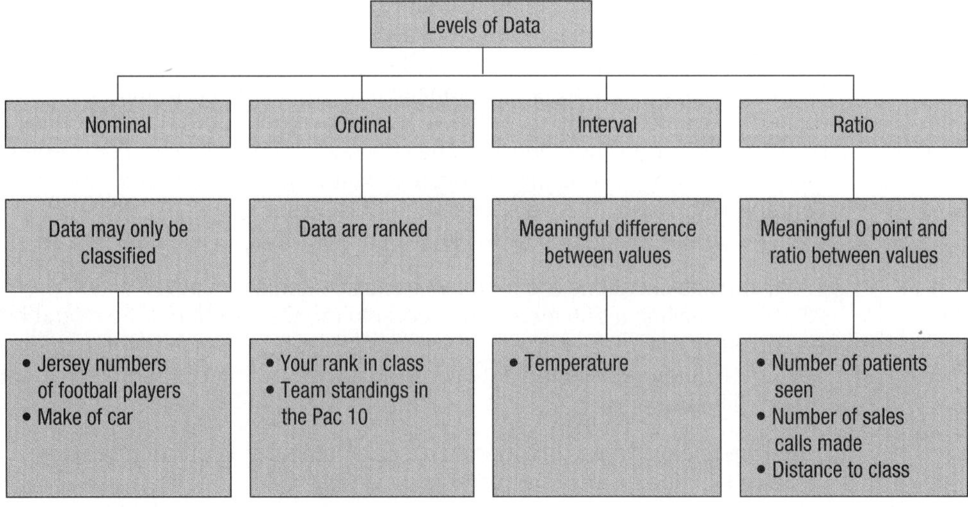

CHART 1-2 Summary of the Characteristics for Levels of Measurement

Self-Review 1–2

What is the level of measurement reflected by the following data?

(a) The age of a sample of 50 adults who listen to the nearly 700 Oldies radio stations in the United States is:

35	29	41	34	44	46	42	42	37	47
30	36	41	39	44	39	43	43	44	40
47	37	41	27	33	33	39	38	43	22
44	39	35	35	41	42	37	42	38	43
35	37	38	43	40	48	42	31	51	34

(b) In a survey of 200 luxury-car owners, 100 were from California, 50 from New York, 30 from Illinois, and 20 from Ohio.

Exercises

The answers to the odd-numbered exercises are at the end of the book.

1. What is the level of measurement for each of the following variables?
   a. Student IQ ratings.
   b. Distance students travel to class.
   c. Student scores on the first statistics test.
   d. A classification of students by state of birth.
   e. A ranking of students by freshman, sophomore, junior, and senior.
   f. Number of hours students study per week.
2. What is the level of measurement for these items related to the newspaper business?
   a. The number of papers sold each Sunday during 1998.
   b. The number of employees in each of the departments, such as editorial, advertising, sports, etc.
   c. A summary of the number of papers sold by county.
   d. The number of years with the paper for each employee.

2. a. Ratio
   b. Nominal
   c. Ratio
   d. Ratio

3. Look in the latest edition of *USA Today* or your local newspaper and find examples of each level of measurement. Write a brief memo summarizing your findings.
4. For each of the following, determine whether the group is a sample or a population.
   a. The participants in a study of a new diabetes drug.
   b. The drivers who received a speeding ticket in Kansas City last month.
   c. Those on welfare in Cook County (Chicago), Illinois.
   d. The 30 stocks reported as a part of the Dow Jones Industrial Average.

4. a. Sample
   b. Population
   c. Population
   d. Sample

Uses and Abuses of Statistics

You have probably heard the old saying that there are three kinds of lies: lies, damn lies, and statistics. This saying is attributable to Benjamin Disraeli and is over a century old. It has also been said that "figures don't lie: liars figure." Both of these statements refer to the abuses of statistics in which data are presented in ways that are misleading. Many abusers of statistics are simply ignorant or careless, while others have an objective to mislead the reader by emphasizing data that support their position while leaving out data that may be detrimental to their position. One of our major goals in this text is to make you a more critical consumer of information. When you see charts or data in a newspaper, in a magazine, or on TV, always ask yourself: What is the person trying to tell me? Does that person have an agenda? Following are several examples of the abuses of statistical analysis.

An average may not be representative of all the data.

The term *average* refers to several different measures of central tendency that we discuss in Chapter 3. To most people, an average is found by adding the values involved and dividing by the number of values. So if a real estate developer tells a client that the average home in a particular subdivision sold for $150,000, we assume that $150,000 is a representative selling price for all the homes. But suppose there are only 5 homes in the subdivision and they sold for $50,000, $50,000, $60,000, $90,000, and $500,000. We can correctly claim that the average selling price is $150,000, but does $150,000 really seem like a "typical" selling price? Would you like to also know that the same number of homes sold for more than $60,000 as less than $60,000? Or that $50,000 is the selling price that occurred most frequently? So what selling price really is the most "typical"? This example illustrates that a reported average can be misleading, because it can be one of several numbers that could be used to represent the data. There is really no objective set of criteria that states what average should be reported on each occasion. We want to educate you as a consumer of data about how a person or group might report one value that favors their position and exclude other values. We will discuss averages, or measures of central tendency, in Chapter 3.

Charts and graphs can also be used to visually mislead. Suppose school taxes for the Corry Area Exempted School District increased from $100 in 1990 to $200 in the year 2000. That is, the taxes doubled during the ten-year period. To show this change, the dollar sign on the right is twice as tall as the one on the left. However, it is also twice as wide! Therefore the area of the dollar sign on the right is 4 times (not twice) that on the left.

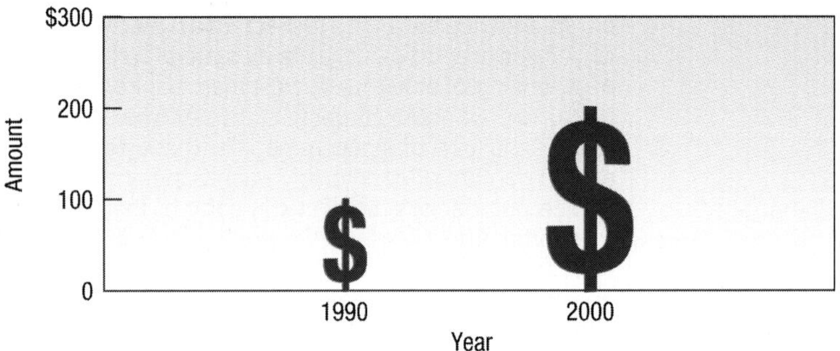

CHART 1-3 School Taxes for 1990 and 2000, Corry Exempted School District

The figure is misleading because visually the increase is much larger than it really is. We discuss the construction of tables and charts in Chapter 2.

Study the sampling methods.

Several years ago, a series of TV advertisements reported that "2 out of 3 dentists surveyed indicated they would recommend Brand X toothpast to their patients." The implication is that 67 percent of all dentists would recommend the product to their patients. The trick is that the manufacturer of the toothpaste could take *many* surveys of 3 dentists and report *only* the survey of 3 dentists that had 2 indicating they would recommend Brand X. Undoubtedly, a survey of more than 3 is needed, and it must be unbiased and representative of the population of all dentists. We discuss sampling methods in Chapter 8.

Another area where there can be a misrepresentation of data is the association between variables. In statistical analysis often we find there is a strong *association* between variables. We find there is a strong association between the number of hours a student studies for an exam and the score he or she receives. Does this mean that studying causes the higher score? No. It means the two variables are related, that is, they tend to act together in a predictable fashion. We study the association between variables in Chapter 13 and 14.

Sometimes numbers themselves can be deceptive. The mean price of homes sold last month in the Tampa, Florida, area is $134,891.58. This sounds like a very precise value and may instill a high degree of confidence in its accuracy. To report that the mean selling price is $135,000 doesn't convey the same precision and accuracy. However, a statistic that is very precise and carries 5 or even 10 decimal places is not necessarily accurate.

There are many other ways that statistical information can be deceiving. Entire books have been written about the subject. The most famous of these is *How to Lie with Statistics* by Darrell Huff. Understanding these practices will make you a better consumer of statistical information and help you defend yourself against those who might wish to mislead.

Computer Applications

Computers are now available to students at most colleges and universities. Spreadsheets, such as Microsoft Excel, and statistical software packages, such as MINITAB, are available in most computer labs. The Microsoft Excel package is bundled with many home computers. In this text we used both Excel and MINITAB for the applications. We also use an Excel add-in called MegaStat. This add-in gives Excel the capability to produce additional statistical reports.

The following example shows the application of computers in statistical analysis. In Chapters 2, 3, and 4 we illustrate methods for summarizing and describing data. An example used in those chapters refers to the selling price of 80 vehicles sold last month at Whitner Pontiac. The following Excel output reveals, among other things, that (1) 80 vehicles were sold last month, (2) the mean (average) selling price was $20,218, and (3) the selling prices ranged from a minimum of $12,546 to a maximum of $32,925.

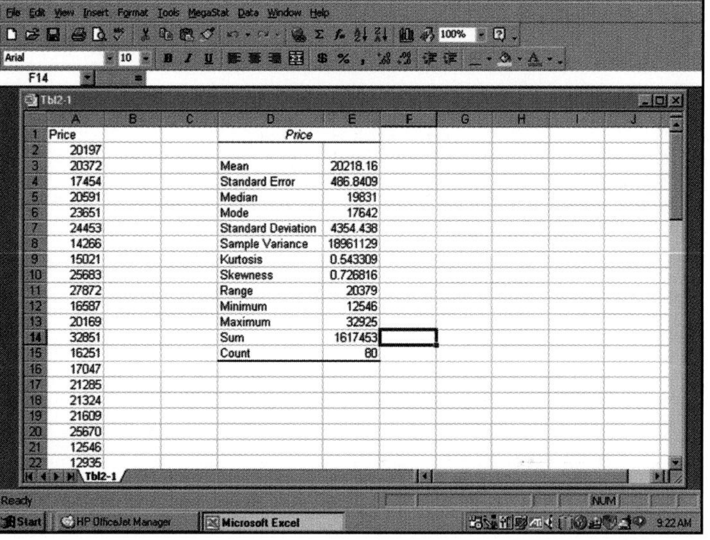

	A	D	E
1	Price	Price	
2	20197		
3	20372	Mean	20218.16
4	17454	Standard Error	486.8409
5	20591	Median	19831
6	23651	Mode	17642
7	24453	Standard Deviation	4354.438
8	14266	Sample Variance	18961129
9	15021	Kurtosis	0.543309
10	25683	Skewness	0.726816
11	27872	Range	20379
12	16587	Minimum	12546
13	20169	Maximum	32925
14	32851	Sum	1617453
15	16251	Count	80
16	17047		
17	21285		
18	21324		
19	21609		
20	25670		
21	12546		
22	12935		

The following output is from the MINITAB system. It contains much of the same information.

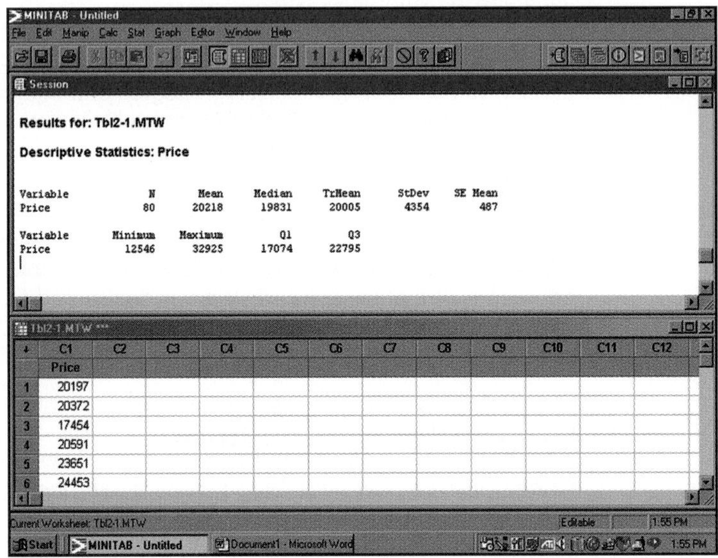

Had we used a calculator to arrive at these measures and others needed to fully analyze the selling prices, hours of calculations would have been required. The likelihood of an error in arithmetic is high when a large number of values are concerned. On the other hand, statistical software packages and spreadsheets can provide accurate information in seconds.

At the option of your instructor, and depending on the operating system available, we urge you to apply a computer package to the exercises in the **Computer Data Exercises** section in each chapter. It will relieve you of the tedious calculations and allow you to concentrate on data analysis.

Chapter Outline

I. Statistics is the science of collecting, organizing, presenting, analyzing, and interpreting data to assist in making more effective decisions.

II. There are two types of statistics.

- **A.** Descriptive statistics are procedures used to organize and summarize data.
- **B.** Inferential statistics involve taking a sample from a population and making estimates about a population based on the sample results.
  - **1.** A population is the total collection of individuals or objects.
  - **2.** A sample is a part of the population.

III. There are two types of variables.

- **A.** A qualitative variable is nonnumeric.
  - **1.** Usually we are interested in the number or percent of the observations in each category.
  - **2.** Qualitative data are usually summarized in graphs and bar charts.
- **B.** There are two types of quantitative variables and they are usually reported numerically.
  - **1.** Discrete variables can assume only certain values, and there are usually gaps between values.
  - **2.** A continuous variable can assume any value within a specified range.

IV. There are four levels of measurement.

- **A.** With the nominal level, the data are sorted into categories with no particular order to the categories.
  - **1.** The categories are mutually exclusive. An individual or object appears in only one category.
  - **2.** The categories are exhaustive. An individual or object appears in at least one of the categories.
- **B.** The ordinal level of measurement presumes that one classification is ranked higher than another.
- **C.** The interval level of measurement has the ranking characteristic of the ordinal level of measurement plus the characteristic that the distance between values is a constant size.
- **D.** The ratio level of measurement has all the characteristics of the interval level, plus there is a meaningful zero point and the ratio of two values is meaningful.

Chapter Exercises

5. Explain the difference between qualitative and quantitative data. Give an example of qualitative and quantitative data.
6. Explain the difference between a sample and a population.
7. List the four levels of measurement and give an example (different from those used in the book) of each level of measurement.
8. Define the term *mutually exclusive.*
9. Define the term *exhaustive.*
10. Using data from such publications as the *Statistical Abstract of the United States,* the *World Almanac, Forbes,* or your local newspaper, give examples of the nominal, ordinal, interval, and ratio level of measurement.
11. A random sample of 300 executives out of 2,500 employed by a large firm showed that 270 would move to another location if it meant a substantial promotion. Based on these findings, write a brief note to management regarding all executives in the firm.
12. A random sample of 500 customers was asked to test a new toothpaste. Of the 500, 400 said it was excellent, 32 thought it was fair, and the remaining customers had no opinion. Based on these sample findings, make an inference about the reaction of all customers to the new toothpaste.
13. Explain the difference between a discrete and a continuous variable. Give an example of each not included in the text.

6\. Population—entire group. Sample—subset of population.
8\. Included in only one class.
10\. Answers will vary.
12\. 80% believe it is excellent.

14. In June 1999 fell to lowest level, 50.6.

14. A survey of U.S. households regarding satisfaction with public school performance revealed the following data, which is portrayed graphically. Note that 1993 = 100. A value of 100 suggests an "average" satisfaction of Americans during the given year. A value of 75 would indicate that consumer satisfaction with school performance for that year is 25 percent below normal. Write an analysis of the level of satisfaction from 1988 to 1999.

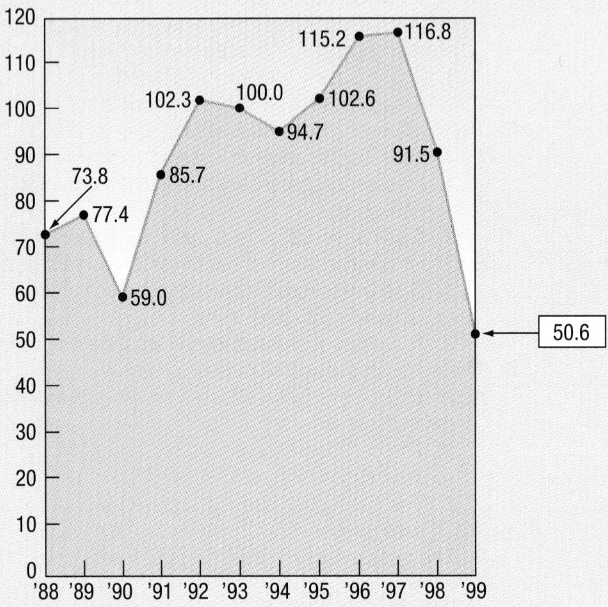

School Performance Survey, 1993 = 100

exercises.com

15. Bill Clegg is a financial consultant for Paine Webber Financial Services. He must recommend to one of his clients whether to purchase stock in Johnson and Johnson, Inc. (a pharmaceutical company) or Pepsico (the parent company of Pepsi and Frito Lay). He checks the Internet for each and finds that 23 brokers have evaluated each stock. Brokers rate a stock a "1" if it is a strong buy and a "5" if it is a strong sell. Go to the following web site: http://quote.yahoo.com. To the left of "Get Quotes" type the two stock symbols, which are JNJ and PEP, then click on **Get Quote.** Finally, in the column headed "More Info" click on **Research.** What level is the data? Compare the results. Which stock would you recommend?

Computer Data Exercises

16. a. township is qualitative, others are quantitative.
b. township is nominal, others are ratio

16. Refer to the Real Estate data at the back of the text, which reports information on homes sold in the Venice, Florida, area last year. Consider the following variables: selling price, number of bedrooms, township, and distance from the center of the city.
a. Which of the variables are qualitative and which are quantitative?
b. Determine the level of measurement for each of the variables.

17. Refer to the Baseball 2000 data, which reports information on the 30 Major League Baseball teams for the 2000 season. Consider the following variables: number of wins, team salary, team attendance, whether the team played its home games on a grass or a turf field, and the number of home runs hit.
a. Which of these variables are quantitative and which are qualitative?
b. Determine the level of measurement for each of the variables.

18. a. G7 is qualitative, others are quantitative
b. G7 is nominal, others are ratio.

18. Refer to the OECD data, which reports information on census, economic, and business data for 29 countries. Consider the following variables: total area, population, exchange rate, size of the labor force, and whether or not the country is a G7 country.
a. Which of these variables are quantitative and which are qualitative?
b. Determine the level of measurement for each of the variables.

19. Refer to the School District Data Set, which reports information on 94 school districts in Northwest Ohio. Consider the following variables: number of students in the district, the name of the school district, amount spent per pupil, and the mean salary of the teachers.
a. Which of the variables are qualitative and which are quantitative?
b. Determine the level of measurement for each of the variables.

Chapter 1 Answers to Self-Review

1–1 **a.** Based on the sample of 1,960 consumers, we estimate that, if it is marketed, 60 percent of all consumers will purchase Fish Delight (1,176/1,960) × 100 = 60 percent.

b. Inferential statistics, because a sample was used to draw a conclusion about how all consumers in the population would react if Fish Delight were marketed.

1–2 **a.** Age is a ratio scale variable. A 40-year-old is twice as old as someone 20 years old.

b. Nominal scale. We could arrange the states in any order.

Describing Data: Frequency Distributions and Graphic Presentation

2

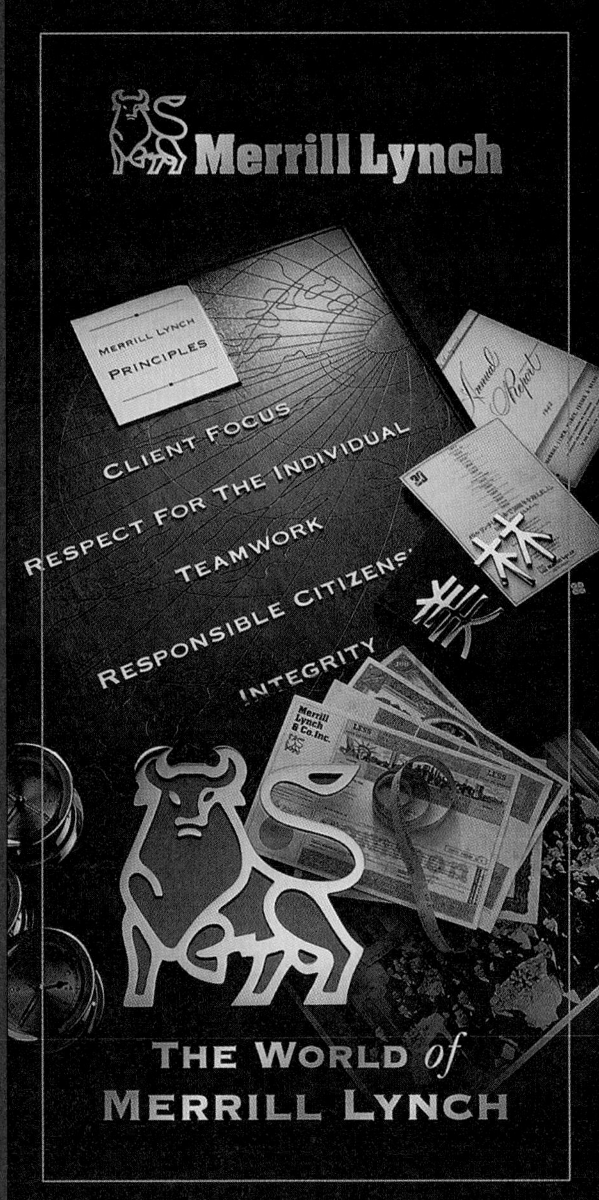

Merrill Lynch completed a study regarding the size of investment portfolios for a sample of clients in the 40- to 50-age group. Create a histogram and frequency distribution based on the sample. (See Exercise 43 and Goal 2.)

GOALS

When you have completed this chapter, you will be able to:

1 **Organize data into a *frequency distribution.***

2 **Portray a frequency distribution in a *histogram, frequency polygon,* and *cumulative frequency polygon.***

3 **Develop and interpret a *stem-and-leaf display.***

4 **Present data using such graphical techniques as *line charts, bar charts,* and *pie charts.***

Introduction

Rob Whitner is the owner of Whitner Pontiac in Columbia, South Carolina. Rob's father founded the dealership in 1964, and for more than 30 years they sold exclusively Pontiacs. In the early 1990s Rob's father's health began to fail, and Rob took over more of the day-to-day operation of the dealership. At this same time, the automobile business began to change—dealers began to sell vehicles from several manufacturers—and Rob was faced with some major decisions. The first came when another local dealer, who handled Volvos, Saabs, and Volkswagens, approached Rob about purchasing his dealership. After considerable thought and analysis, Rob purchased that dealership. More recently, the local Jeep Eagle dealership got into difficulty and Rob bought them out. So now, on the same lot, Rob sells the complete line of Pontiacs, the expensive Volvos, Saabs, Volkswagens, and the Chrysler products, including the popular Jeep line. Whitner Pontiac employs 83, including 23 full-time salespeople. Because of the diverse product line, there is quite a bit of variation in the selling price of the vehicles. A top-of-the-line Volvo sells for more than twice that of a Pontiac Grand Am. Rob would like to develop some charts and graphs that he could review monthly to see where the selling prices tend to cluster, to see the variation in the selling prices, and to note any trends. In this chapter we present techniques that will be useful to Rob or someone like him in managing his business.

Constructing a Frequency Distribution

Recall from Chapter 1 that we refer to techniques used to describe a set of data as *descriptive statistics.* To put it another way, we use descriptive statistics to organize data in various ways to point out where the data values tend to concentrate and help distinguish the largest and the smallest values. The first procedure we use to describe a set of data is a **frequency distribution.**

> **FREQUENCY DISTRIBUTION** A grouping of data into mutually exclusive classes showing the number of observations in each.

How do we develop a frequency distribution? The first step is to tally the data into a table that shows the classes (categories) and the number of observations in each category. The steps in constructing a frequency distribution are best described using an example. Remember, our goal is to make a table that will quickly reveal the shape of the data.

EXAMPLE

In the Introduction we describe a case where Rob Whitner, owner of Whitner Pontiac, is interested in collecting information on the selling prices of vehicles sold at his dealership. What is the typical selling price? What is the largest selling price? What is the smallest selling price? Around what value do the selling prices tend to cluster? In order to answer these questions, we need to collect data. According to sales records, Whitner Pontiac sold 80 vehicles last month. The price paid by the customer for each vehicle is shown in Table 2–1. Summarize the selling prices of the vehicles sold last month. Around what value do the selling prices tend to cluster?

TABLE 2–1 Prices of Vehicles Sold Last Month at Whitner Pontiac

$20,197	$20,372	$17,454	$20,591	$23,651	$24,453	$14,266	$15,021	$25,683	$27,872	
16,587	20,169	32,851	16,251	17,047	21,285	21,324	21,609	25,670	12,546	Lowest
12,935	16,873	22,251	22,277	25,034	21,533	24,443	16,889	17,004	14,357	
17,155	16,688	20,657	23,613	17,895	17,203	20,765	22,783	23,661	29,277	
17,642	18,981	21,052	22,799	12,794	15,263	32,925	14,399	14,968	17,356	
18,442	18,722	16,331	19,817	16,766	17,633	17,962	19,845	23,285	24,896	
26,076	29,492	15,890	18,740	19,374	21,571	22,449	25,337	17,642	20,613	
21,220	27,655	19,442	14,891	17,818	23,237	17,445	18,556	18,639	21,296	
						Highest				

SOLUTION

We refer to the unorganized information in Table 2–1 as **raw data** or **ungrouped data.** With a little searching, we can find the lowest selling price ($12,546) and the highest selling price ($32,925), but that is about all. It is difficult to determine a typical selling price. It is also difficult to visualize where the selling prices tend to occur. The raw data are more easily interpreted if organized into a frequency distribution.

The steps for organizing data into a frequency distribution.

Step 1: Decide on the number of classes. The goal is to use just enough groupings or **classes** to reveal the shape of the distribution. Some judgment is needed here. Too many classes or too few classes might not reveal the basic shape of the set of data. In the vehicle selling price problem, for example, three classes would not give much insight into the pattern of the data (see Table 2–2).

TABLE 2–2 An Example of Too Few Classes

Vehicle Selling Price ($)	Number of Vehicles
12,000 up to 21,000	48
21,000 up to 30,000	30
30,000 up to 39,000	2
Total	80

A useful recipe to determine the number of classes is the "2 to the *k* rule." This guide suggests you select the smallest number (k) for the number of classes such that 2^k (in words, 2 raised to the power of k) is greater than the number of observations (n).

In the Whitner Pontiac example, there were 80 vehicles sold. So $n = 80$. If we try $k = 6$, which means we would use 6 classes, then $2^6 = 64$, somewhat less than 80. Hence, 6 is not enough classes. If we let $k = 7$, then $2^7 = 128$, which is greater than 80. So the recommended number of classes is 7.

Step 2: Determine the class interval or width. Generally the class interval or width should be the same for all classes. The classes all taken together must cover at least the distance from the lowest value in the raw data up to the highest value. Expressing these words in a formula:

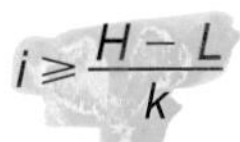

$$i \geq \frac{H - L}{k}$$

where i is the class interval, H is the highest observed value, L is the lowest observed value, and k is the number of classes.

In the Whitner Pontiac case, the lowest value is $12,546 and the highest value is $32,925. If we need 7 classes, the interval should be at least ($32,925−$12,546)/7 = $2,911. In practice this interval size is usually rounded up to some convenient number, such as a multiple of 10 or 100. The value of $3,000 might readily be used in this case.

Unequal class intervals present problems in graphically portraying the distribution and in doing some of the computations which we will see in later chapters. Unequal class intervals, however, may be necessary in certain situations to avoid a large number of empty, or almost empty, classes. Such is the case in Table 2–3. The Internal Revenue Service used unequal-sized class intervals to report the adjusted gross income on individual tax returns. Had they used an equal-sized interval of, say, $1,000, more than 1,000 classes would have been required to describe all the incomes. A frequency distribution with 1,000 classes would be difficult to interpret. In this case the distribution is easier to understand in spite of the unequal classes. Note also that the number of income tax returns or "frequencies"is reported in thousands in this particular table. This also makes the information easier to understand.

TABLE 2–3 Adjusted Gross Income for Individuals Filing Income Tax Returns

Adjusted Gross Income	Number of Returns (in thousands)
Under $ 2,000	135
$ 2,000 up to 3,000	3,399
3,000 up to 5,000	8,175
5,000 up to 10,000	19,740
10,000 up to 15,000	15,539
15,000 up to 25,000	14,944
25,000 up to 50,000	4,451
50,000 up to 100,000	699
100,000 up to 500,000	162
500,000 up to 1,000,000	3
$1,000,000 and over	1

Step 3: Set the individual class limits. State clear class limits so you can put each observation into only one category. This means you must avoid overlapping or unclear class limits. For example, classes such as $1,300 − $1,400 and $1,400 − $1,500 should not be used because it is not clear whether the value $1,400 is in the first or second class. Classes stated as $1,300 − $1,400 and $1,500 − $1,600 are frequently used, but may also be confusing without the additional common convention of rounding all data at or above $1,450 up to the second class and data below $1,450 down to the first class. In this text we will generally use the format $1,300 up to $1,400 and $1,400 up to $1,500 and so on. With this format it is clear that $1,399 goes into the first class and $1,400 in the second.

Because we round the class interval up to get a convenient class size, we cover a larger than necessary range. For example, 7 classes of width $3,000 in the Whitner Pontiac case result in a range of 7($3,000) =

Statistics in Action

In 1788, James Madison, John Jay, and Alexander Hamilton anonymously published a series of essays entitled *The Federalist.* These Federalist papers were an attempt to convince the people of New York that they should ratify the Constitution. In the course of history, the authorship of most of these papers became known, but 12 remained contested. Through the use of statistical analysis, and particularly the study of the frequency of the use of various words, we can now conclude that James Madison is the likely author of the 12 papers. In fact, the statistical evidence that Madison is the author is overwhelming.

$21,000. The actual range is $20,379, found by $32,925 − $12,546. Comparing that value to $21,000 we have an excess of $621. Because we need to cover only the distance ($H - L$), it is natural to put approximately equal amounts of the excess in each of the two tails. Of course, we should also select convenient multiples of ten for the class limits. So here are the classes we could use for this data.

$12,000 up to 15,000
15,000 up to 18,000
18,000 up to 21,000
21,000 up to 24,000
24,000 up to 27,000
27,000 up to 30,000
30,000 up to 33,000

Step 4: Tally the vehicle selling prices into the classes. To begin, the selling price of the first vehicle in Table 2–1 is $20,197. It is tallied in the $18,000 up to $21,000 class. The second selling price in the first column of Table 2–1 is $16,587. It is tallied in the $15,000 up to $18,000 class. The other selling prices are tallied in a similar manner. When all the selling prices are tallied, the table would appear as:

<table>
<tr><th>Class</th><th>Tallies</th></tr>
<tr><td>$12,000 up to $15,000</td><td>卌 |||</td></tr>
<tr><td>$15,000 up to $18,000</td><td>卌 卌 卌 卌 |||</td></tr>
<tr><td>$18,000 up to $21,000</td><td>卌 卌 卌 ||</td></tr>
<tr><td>$21,000 up to $24,000</td><td>卌 卌 卌 |||</td></tr>
<tr><td>$24,000 up to $27,000</td><td>卌 |||</td></tr>
<tr><td>$27,000 up to $30,000</td><td>||||</td></tr>
<tr><td>$30,000 up to $33,000</td><td>||</td></tr>
</table>

Step 5: Count the number of items in each class. The number of observations in each class is called the **class frequency.** In the $12,000 up to $15,000 class there are 8 observations, and in the $15,000 up to $18,000 class there are 23 observations. Therefore, the class frequency in the first class is 8 and the class frequency in the second class is 23. There is a total of 80 observations or frequencies in the entire set of data.

Often it is useful to express the data in thousands, or some convenient units, rather than the actual data. Table 2–4, for example, reports the vehicle selling prices in thousands of dollars, rather than dollars.

Now that we have organized the data into a frequency distribution, we can summarize the pattern in the selling prices of the vehicles for Rob Whitner. Observe the following:

1. The selling prices ranged from about $12,000 up to about $33,000.
2. The selling prices are concentrated between $15,000 and $24,000. A total of 58, or 72.5 percent, of the vehicles sold within this range.
3. The largest concentration is in the $15,000 up to $18,000 class. The middle of this class is $16,500, so we say that a typical selling price is $16,500.
4. Two of the vehicles sold for $30,000 or more, and 8 sold for less than $15,000.

By presenting this information to Mr. Whitner, we give him a clear picture of the distribution of selling prices for last month.

TABLE 2–4 Frequency Distribution of Selling Prices at Whitner Pontiac Last Month

Selling Prices ($ thousands)	Frequency
12 up to 15	8
15 up to 18	23
18 up to 21	17
21 up to 24	18
24 up to 27	8
27 up to 30	4
30 up to 33	2
Total	80

We admit that arranging the information on selling prices into a frequency distribution does result in the loss of some detailed information. That is, by organizing the data into a frequency distribution, we cannot pinpoint the exact selling price, such as $20,197 or $23,372. Or, we cannot tell that the actual selling price for the least expensive vehicle was $12,546 and for the most expensive $32,925. However, the lower limit of the first class and the upper limit of the largest class convey essentially the same meaning. Rob will make the same judgment if he knows the lowest price is about $12,000 that he will if he knows the exact price is $12,546. The advantages of condensing the data into a more understandable form more than offset this disadvantage.

Self-Review 2–1

The answers are at the end of the chapter.

The commissions earned for the first quarter of last year by the eleven members of the sales staff at Master Chemical Company are:

$1,650	$1,475	$1,510	$1,670	$1,595	$1,760	$1,540	$1,495	$1,590	$1,625	$1,510.

(a) What are the values such as $1,650 and $1,475 called?
(b) Using $1,400 up to $1,500 as the first class, $1,500 up to $1,600 as the second class, and so forth, organize the quarterly commissions into a frequency distribution.
(c) What are the numbers in the right column of your frequency distribution called?
(d) Describe the distribution of monthly commissions, based on the frequency distribution. What is the largest amount of commission earned? What is the smallest? What is the typical amount earned?

Class Intervals and Class Midpoints

We will use two other terms frequently: **class midpoint** and **class interval.** The midpoint, also called the **class mark,** is halfway between the lower limits of two consecutive classes. It can be computed by adding the lower class limit to the upper class limit and dividing by 2. Referring to Table 2–4, for the first class the lower class limit is

$12,000 and the next limit is $15,000. The class midpoint is $13,500, found by ($12,000 + $15,000)/2. The midpoint of $13,500 best represents, or is typical of, the selling price of the vehicles in that class.

To determine the class interval, subtract the lower limit of the class from the lower limit of the next class. The class interval of the vehicle selling price data is $3,000, which we find by subtracting the lower limit of the first class, $12,000, from the lower limit of the next class; that is, $15,000 − $12,000 = $3,000. You can also determine the class interval by finding the difference between consecutive midpoints. The midpoint of the first class is $13,500 and the midpoint of the second class is $16,500. The difference is $3,000.

A Software Example

As we mentioned in Chapter 1, there are many software packages that perform statistical calculations and output the results. Throughout this text we will show the output from Microsoft Excel; from MegaStat, which is an add-in to Microsoft Excel; and from MINITAB. The commands necessary to generate the outputs are given in the **Computer Commands** section at the end of each chapter.

The following is a frequency distribution, produced by MegaStat, showing the prices of the 80 vehicles sold last month at Whitner Pontiac. The form of the output is somewhat different than the frequency distribution of Table 2–4, but the overall conclusions are the same.

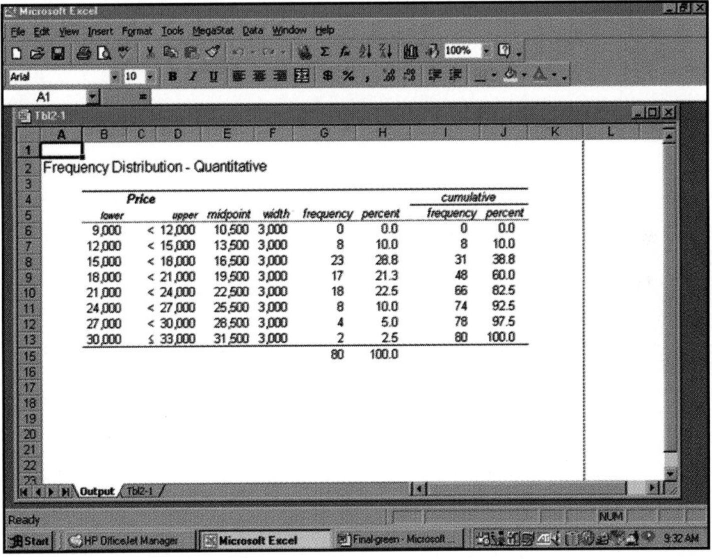

Frequency Distribution - Quantitative

Price						cumulative	
lower	upper	midpoint	width	frequency	percent	frequency	percent
9,000	< 12,000	10,500	3,000	0	0.0	0	0.0
12,000	< 15,000	13,500	3,000	8	10.0	8	10.0
15,000	< 18,000	16,500	3,000	23	28.8	31	38.8
18,000	< 21,000	19,500	3,000	17	21.3	48	60.0
21,000	< 24,000	22,500	3,000	18	22.5	66	82.5
24,000	< 27,000	25,500	3,000	8	10.0	74	92.5
27,000	< 30,000	28,500	3,000	4	5.0	78	97.5
30,000	≤ 33,000	31,500	3,000	2	2.5	80	100.0
				80	100.0		

Self-Review 2–2

During the 1998 baseball season, Mark McGuire broke the home run record by hitting 70 home runs. The longest was 550 feet and the shortest was 340 feet. It may also be interesting to note that the home run that actually broke the record was "only" 341 feet. You need to construct a frequency distribution for these home run lengths.

(a) How many classes would you use?
(b) How wide would you make the classes?
(c) What are the actual classes you would use?

Relative Frequency Distribution

A relative frequency distribution converts the frequency to a percent.

It may be desirable to convert class frequencies to **relative class frequencies** to show the fraction of the total number of observations in each class. In our vehicle sales example, we may want to know what percent of the vehicle prices are in the $18,000 up to $21,000 class. In another study, we may want to know what percent of the employees are absent between one and three days per year due to illness.

To convert a frequency distribution to a *relative* frequency distribution, each of the class frequencies is divided by the total number of observations. Using the distribution of vehicle sales again (Table 2–4, where the selling price is reported in thousands of dollars), the relative frequency for the $12,000 up to $15,000 class is 0.10, found by dividing 8 by 80. That is, the price of 10 percent of the vehicles sold at Whitner Pontiac is between $12,000 and $15,000. The relative frequencies for the remaining classes are shown in Table 2–5.

TABLE 2–5 Relative Frequency Distribution of the Prices of Vehicles Sold Last Month at Whitner Pontiac

Selling Price ($ thousands)	Frequency	Relative Frequency	Found by
12 up to 15	8	0.1000 ←	8/80
15 up to 18	23	0.2875	23/80
18 up to 21	17	0.2125	17/80
21 up to 24	18	0.2250	18/80
24 up to 27	8	0.1000	8/80
27 up to 30	4	0.0500	4/80
30 up to 33	2	0.0250	2/80
Total	80	1.0000	

Self-Review 2–3

Refer to Table 2–5, which shows the relative frequency distribution for the vehicles sold last month at Whitner Pontiac.
(a) How many vehicles sold for $15,000 up to $18,000?
(b) What percent of the vehicles sold for a price between $15,000 and $18,000?
(c) What percent of the vehicles sold for $27,000 or more?

Exercises

The answers to the odd-numbered exercises are at the end of the book.

1. A set of data consists of 38 observations. How many classes would you recommend for the frequency distribution?
2. A set of data consists of 45 observations between $0 and $29. What size would you recommend for the class interval?

2. $k = 6, i = 5$

3. A set of data consists of 230 observations between $235 and $567. What class interval would you recommend?
4. A set of data contains 53 observations. The lowest value is 42 and the largest is 129. The data are to be organized into a frequency distribution.
   a. How many classes would you suggest?
   b. What would you suggest as the lower limit of the first class?

4. **a.** 6
   b. 40

5. The Wachesaw Outpatient Center, designed for same-day minor surgery, opened last month. Following is the number of patients served the first 16 days.

27	27	27	28	27	25	25	28
26	28	26	28	31	30	26	26

The information is to be organized into a frequency distribution.

a. How many classes would you recommend?
b. What class interval would you suggest?
c. What lower limit would you recommend for the first class?
d. Organize the information into a frequency distribution and determine the relative frequency distribution.
e. Comment on the shape of the distribution.

6. The Quick Change Oil Company has a number of outlets in the metropolitan Seattle area. The numbers of oil changes at the Oak Street outlet in the past 20 days are:

65	98	55	62	79	59	51	90	72	56
70	62	66	80	94	79	63	73	71	85

6. **a.** 5 classes
b. $i = 10$
c. 50
d. See IM.
e. See IM.

The data are to be organized into a frequency distribution.

a. How many classes would you recommend?
b. What class interval would you suggest?
c. What lower limit would you recommend for the first class?
d. Organize the number of oil changes into a frequency distribution.
e. Comment on the shape of the frequency distribution. Also determine the relative frequency distribution.

7. The local manager of Food Queen is interested in the number of times a customer shops at her store during a two-week period. The responses of 51 customers were:

5	3	3	1	4	4	5	6	4	2	6	6	6	7	1
1	14	1	2	4	4	4	5	6	3	5	3	4	5	6
8	4	7	6	5	9	11	3	12	4	7	6	5	15	1
1	10	8	9	2	12									

a. Starting with 0 as the lower limit of the first class and using a class interval of 3, organize the data into a frequency distribution.
b. Describe the distribution. Where do the data tend to cluster?
c. Convert the distribution to a relative frequency distribution.

8. Moore Travel Agency, a nationwide travel agency, offers special rates on certain Caribbean cruises to senior citizens. The president of Moore Travel wants additional information on the ages of those people taking cruises. A random sample of 40 customers taking a cruise last year revealed these ages.

77	18	63	84	38	54	50	59	54	56	36	26	50	34	44
41	58	58	53	51	62	43	52	53	63	62	62	65	61	52
60	60	45	66	83	71	63	58	61	71					

8. **a.** 10
b. Cluster between 45 and 65.
c. See IM.
d. See IM.

a. Organize the data into a frequency distribution, using seven classes and 15 as the lower limit of the first class. What class interval did you select?
b. Where do the data tend to cluster?
c. Describe the distribution.
d. Determine the relative frequency distribution.

Stem-and-Leaf Displays

In the previous section, we showed how to organize data into a frequency distribution so we could summarize the raw data into a meaningful form. The major advantage to organizing the data into a frequency distribution is that we get a quick visual picture of the shape of the distribution without doing any further calculation. That is, we can see where the data are concentrated and also determine whether there are any extremely large or small values. There are two disadvantages, however, to organizing the data into a frequency distribution: (1) we lose the exact identity of each value and (2) we are not sure how the values within each class are distributed. To explain, the following frequency distribution shows the number of advertising spots purchased by the 45 members of the Greater Buffalo Automobile Dealers Association in the year 2000. We observe that 7 of the 45 dealers purchased between 90 and 99 spots (but less than 100). However, is the number of spots purchased within this class clustered about 90, spread evenly throughout the class, or clustered near 99? We cannot tell.

Number of Spots Purchased	Frequency
80 up to 90	2
90 up to 100	7
100 up to 110	6
110 up to 120	9
120 up to 130	8
130 up to 140	7
140 up to 150	3
150 up to 160	3
Total	45

One technique that is used to display quantitative information in a condensed form is the **stem-and-leaf display.** An advantage of the stem-and-leaf display over a frequency distribution is that we do not lose the identity of each observation. In the above example, we would not know the identity of the values in the 90 up to 100 class. To illustrate the construction of a stem-and-leaf display using the number of advertising spots purchased, suppose the seven observations in the 90 up to 100 class are: 96, 94, 93, 94, 95, 96, and 97. The **stem** value is the leading digit or digits, in this case 9. The **leaves** are the trailing digits. The stem is placed to the left of a vertical line and the leaf values to the right.

The values in the 90 up to 100 class would appear as follows:

9 | 6 4 3 4 5 6 7

Finally, we sort the values within each stem from smallest to largest. Thus, the second row of the stem-and-leaf display would appear as follows:

9 | 3 4 4 5 6 6 7

With the stem-and-leaf display, we can quickly observe that there were two dealers who purchased 94 spots and that the number of spots purchased ranged from 93 to 97. A stem-and-leaf display is similar to a frequency distribution with more information, i.e., data values instead of tallies.

STEM-AND-LEAF DISPLAY A statistical technique to present a set of data. Each numerical value is divided into two parts. The leading digit(s) becomes the stem and the trailing digit the leaf. The stems are located along the vertical axis, and the leaf values are stacked against each other along the horizontal axis.

The following example will explain the details of developing a stem-and-leaf display.

Listed in Table 2–6 is the number of 30-second radio advertising spots purchased by each of the 45 members of the Greater Buffalo Automobile Dealers Association last year. Organize the data into a stem-and-leaf display. Around what values do the number of advertising spots tend to cluster? What is the fewest number of spots purchased by a dealer? The largest number purchased?

TABLE 2–6 Number of Advertising Spots Purchased by Members of the Greater Buffalo Automobile Dealers Association

96	93	88	117	127	95	113	96	108	94	148	156
139	142	94	107	125	155	155	103	112	127	117	120
112	135	132	111	125	104	106	139	134	119	97	89
118	136	125	143	120	103	113	124	138			

SOLUTION

From the data in Table 2–6 we note that the smallest number of spots purchased is 88. So we will make the first stem value 8. The largest number is 156, so we will have the stem values begin at 8 and continue to 15. The first number in Table 2–6 is 96, which will have a stem value of 9 and a leaf value of 6. Moving across the top row, the second value is 93 and the third is 88. After the first 3 data values are considered, your chart is as follows.

Stem	Leaf
8	8
9	6 3
10	
11	
12	
13	
14	
15	

Organizing all the data, the stem-and-leaf chart looks as follows.

Stem	Leaf
8	8 9
9	6 3 5 6 4 4 7
10	8 7 3 4 6 3
11	7 3 2 7 2 1 9 8 3
12	7 5 7 0 5 5 0 4
13	9 5 2 9 4 6 8
14	8 2 3
15	6 5 5

The usual procedure is to sort the leaf values from the smallest to largest. The last line, the row referring to the values in the 150s, would appear as:

15 | 5 5 6

The final table would appear as follows, where we have sorted all of the leaf values.

Stem	Leaf
8	8 9
9	3 4 4 5 6 6 7
10	3 3 4 6 7 8
11	1 2 2 3 3 7 7 8 9
12	0 0 4 5 5 5 7 7
13	2 4 5 6 8 9 9
14	2 3 8
15	5 5 6

You can draw several conclusions from the stem-and-leaf display. First the lowest number of spots purchased is 88 and the largest is 156. Two dealers purchased less than 90 spots, and three purchased 150 or more. You can observe, for example, that the three dealers who purchased more than 150 spots actually purchased 155, 155, and 156 spots. The concentration of the number of spots is between 110 and 130. There were 9 dealers who purchased between 110 and 119 spots and 8 who purchased between 120 and 129 spots. We can also tell that within the 120 to 129 group the actual number of spots purchased was spread evenly throughout. That is, two dealers purchased 120 spots, one dealer purchased 124 spots, three dealers purchased 125 spots, and two purchased 127 spots.

We can also generate this information on the MINITAB software system. We have named the variable *Spots.* The MINITAB output is below. You can find the MINITAB commands that will produce this output at the end of the chapter.

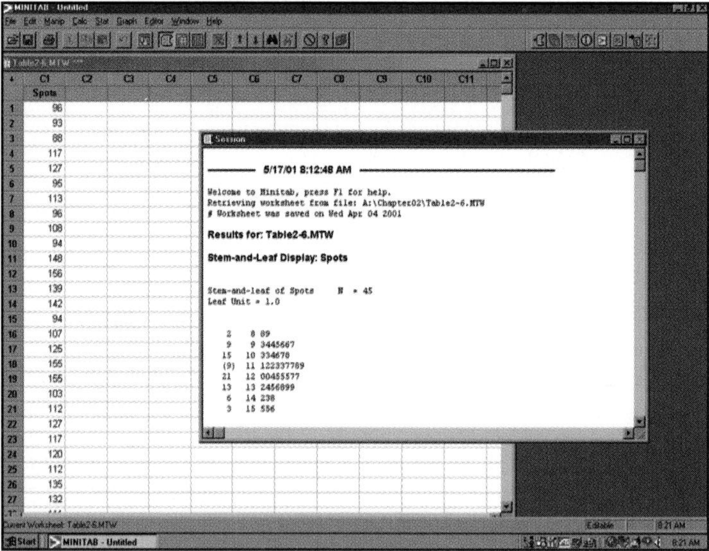

The MINITAB solution provides some additional information regarding cumulative totals. In the column to the left of the stem values are numbers such as 2, 9, 15, and so on. The number 9 indicates that there are 9 observations that have occurred before the value of 100. The number 15 indicates that 15 observations have occurred prior to 110. About halfway down the column the number 9 appears in parentheses. The parentheses indicate that the middle value appears in that row. In this case, we describe the middle value as the value below which half of the observations occur. There are a total of 45 observations, so the middle value, if the data were arranged from smallest, would be the 23rd observation. After the median row, the values begin to decline. These values represent the "more than" cumulative totals. There are 21 observations of 120 or more, 13 of 130 or more, and so on.

Self-Review 2–4

The price-earnings ratios for 21 stocks in the retail trade category are:

8.3	9.6	9.5	9.1	8.8	11.2	7.7	10.1	9.9	10.8	
10.2	8.0	8.4	8.1	11.6	9.6	8.8	8.0	10.4	9.8	9.2

Organize this information into a stem-and-leaf display.
(a) How many values are less than 9.0?
(b) List the values in the 10.0 up to 11.0 category.
(c) What is the middle value?
(d) What are the largest and the smallest price-earnings ratios?

Exercises

9. The first row of a stem-and-leaf chart appears as follows: 62 | 1 3 3 7 9. Assume whole number values.
a. What is the "possible range" of the values in this row?
b. How many data values are in this row?
c. List the actual values in this row of data.

10. The third row of a stem-and-leaf chart appears as follows: 21 | 0 1 3 5 7 9. Assume whole number values.
a. What is the "possible range" of the values in this row?
b. How many data values are in this row?
c. List the actual values in this row of data.

10. a. 210 to 219
b. 6
c. 210, 211, 213, 215, 217, 219

11. The following stem-and-leaf chart shows the number of units produced per day in a factory.

1	3	8
1	4	
2	5	6
9	6	0133559
(7)	7	0236778
9	8	59
7	9	00156
2	10	36

a. How many days were studied?
b. How many observations are in the first class?
c. What are the smallest value and the largest value?
d. List the actual values in the fourth row.
e. List the actual values in the second row.
f. How many values are less than 70?
g. How many values are 80 or more?
h. What is the middle value?
i. How many values are between 60 and 89, inclusive?

12. The following stem-and-leaf chart reports the number of movies rented per day at Video Connection.

3	12	689
6	13	123
10	14	6889
13	15	589
15	16	35
20	17	24568
23	18	268
(5)	19	13456
22	20	034679
16	21	2239
12	22	789
9	23	00179
4	24	8
3	25	13
1	26	
1	27	0

12. **a.** 50
b. One
c. 126, 270
d. 155, 158, 159
e. No values
f. 13
g. 12
h. 193 or 194
i. 19

a. How many days were studied?
b. How many observations are in the last class?
c. What are the largest and the smallest values in the entire set of data?
d. List the actual values in the fourth row.
e. List the actual values in the next to the last row.
f. On how many days were less than 160 movies rented?
g. On how many days were 220 or more movies rented?
h. What is the middle value?
i. On how many days were between 170 and 210 movies rented?

13. A survey of the number of calls received by a sample of Southern Phone Company subscribers last week revealed the following information. Develop a stem-and-leaf chart. How many calls did a typical subscriber receive? What were the largest and the smallest number of calls received?

52	43	30	38	30	42	12	46	39
37	34	46	32	18	41	5		

14. See IM.

14. Aloha Banking Co. is studying the number of times their automatic teller, located in Loblaws Supermarket, is used each day. The following is the number of times it was used during each of the last 30 days. Develop a stem-and-leaf chart. Summarize the data on the number of times the automatic teller was used: How many times was the teller used on a typical day? What were the largest and the smallest number of times the teller was used? Around what values did the number of times the teller was used tend to cluster?

83	64	84	76	84	54	75	59	70	61
63	80	84	73	68	52	65	90	52	77
95	36	78	61	59	84	95	47	87	60

Graphic Presentation of a Frequency Distribution

Sales managers, stock analysts, hospital administrators, and other busy executives often need a quick picture of the trends in sales, stock prices, or hospital costs. These trends can often be depicted by the use of charts and graphs. Three charts that will help portray a frequency distribution graphically are the histogram, the frequency polygon, and the cumulative frequency polygon.

Histogram

One of the most common ways to portray a frequency distribution is a **histogram**.

> **HISTOGRAM** A graph in which the classes are marked on the horizontal axis and the class frequencies on the vertical axis. The class frequencies are represented by the heights of the bars, and the bars are drawn adjacent to each other.

Thus, a histogram describes a frequency distribution using a series of adjacent rectangles, where the height of each rectangle is proportional to the frequency the class represents. The construction of a histogram is best illustrated by reintroducing the prices of the 80 vehicles sold last month at Whitner Pontiac.

Below is the frequency distribution.

Selling Prices ($ thousands)	Frequency
12 up to 15	8
15 up to 18	23
18 up to 21	17
21 up to 24	18
24 up to 27	8
27 up to 30	4
30 up to 33	2
Total	80

Construct a histogram. What conclusions can you reach based on the information presented in the histogram?

SOLUTION

The class frequencies are scaled along the vertical axis (*Y*-axis) and either the class limits or the class midpoints along the horizontal axis. To illustrate the construction of the histogram, the first three classes are shown in Chart 2–1.

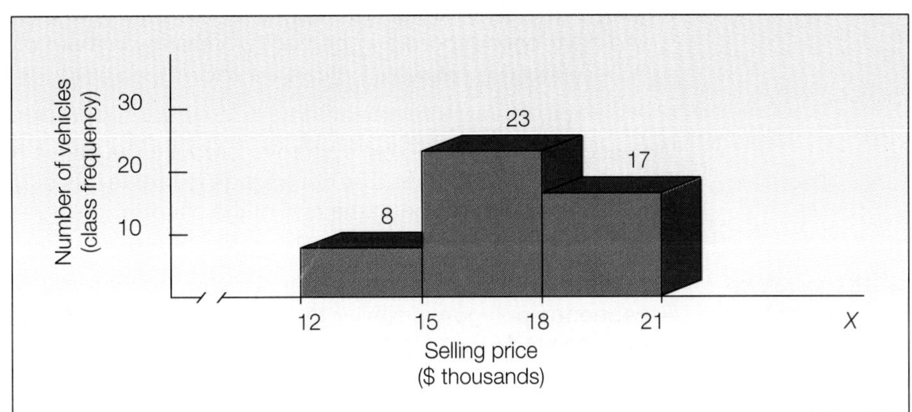

CHART 2–1 Construction of a Histogram

From Chart 2–1 we note that there are eight vehicles in the $12,000 up to $15,000 class. Therefore, the height of the column for that class is 8. There are 23 vehicles in the $15,000 up to $18,000 class, so, logically, the height of that column is 23. The height of the bar represents the number of observations in the class.

This procedure is continued for all classes. The complete histogram is shown in Chart 2–2. Note that there is no space between the bars. This is a feature of the histogram. In bar charts, which are described in a later section, the vertical bars are separated.

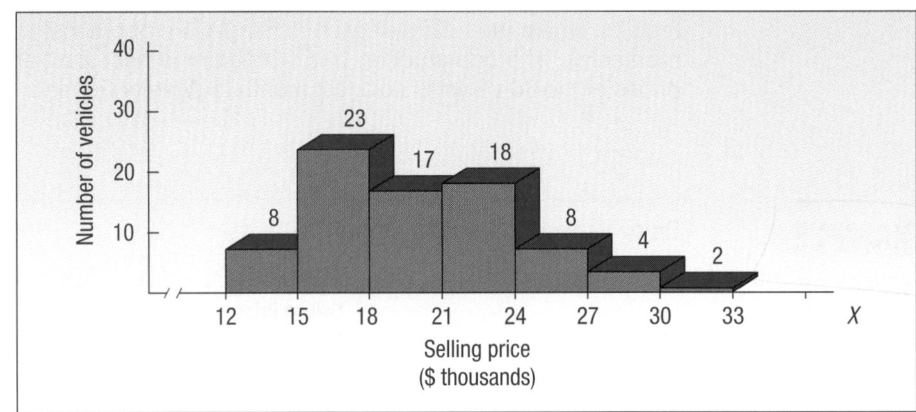

CHART 2–2 Histogram of the Selling Prices of 80 Vehicles at Whitner Pontiac

Based on the histogram in Chart 2–2, we conclude:

1. The lowest selling price is about $12,000, and the largest is about $33,000.
2. The largest class frequency is the $15,000 up to $18,000 class. A total of 23 of the 80 vehicles sold are within this price range.
3. Fifty-eight of the vehicles, or 72.5 percent, had a selling price between $15,000 and $24,000.

Thus, the histogram provides an easily interpreted visual representation of a frequency distribution. We should also point out that we would have reached the same conclusions and the shape of the histogram would have been the same had we used a relative frequency distribution instead of the actual frequencies. That is, if we had used the relative frequencies of Table 2–5, found on page 28, we would have had a histogram of the same shape as Chart 2–2. The only difference is that the vertical axis would have been reported in percent of vehicles instead of the number of vehicles.

We used the Microsoft Excel system to produce the above histogram for the Whitner Pontiac vehicle sales data. The commands to create this output are given in the Computer Commands section at the end of the chapter.

Frequency Polygon

In a frequency polygon the class midpoints are connected with a line segment.

A **frequency polygon** is similar to a histogram. It consists of line segments connecting the points formed by the intersections of the class midpoints and the class frequencies. The construction of a frequency polygon is illustrated in Chart 2–3 on the

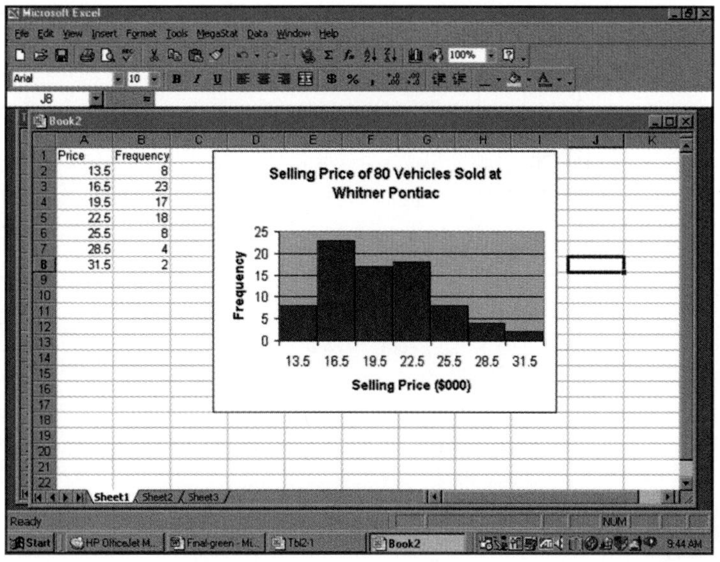

Statistics in Action

Florence Nightingale is known as the founder of the nursing profession. However, she also saved many lives by using statistical analysis. When she encountered an unsanitary condition or an undersupplied hospital, she improved the conditions and then used statistical data to document the improvement. Thus, she was able to convince others of the need for medical reform, particularly in the area of sanitation. She developed original graphs to demonstrate that, during the Crimean War, more soldiers died from unsanitary conditions than were killed in combat.

next page. We use the vehicle prices for the cars sold last month at Whitner Pontiac. The midpoint of each class is scaled on the *X*-axis and the class frequencies on the *Y*-axis. Recall that the class midpoint is the value at the center of a class and represents the values in that class. The class frequency is the number of observations in a particular class. The vehicle selling prices at Whitner Pontiac are:

Selling Price ($ thousands)	Midpoint	Frequency
12 up to 15	13.5	8
15 up to 18	16.5	23
18 up to 21	19.5	17
21 up to 24	22.5	18
24 up to 27	25.5	8
27 up to 30	28.5	4
30 up to 33	31.5	2
Total		80

As noted previously, the $12,000 up to $15,000 class is represented by the midpoint $13,500. To construct a frequency polygon, move horizontally on the graph to the midpoint, $13.5, and then vertically to 8, the class frequency, and place a dot. The *X* and the *Y* values of this point are called the *coordinates.* The coordinates of the next point are X = $16.5 and Y = 23. The process is continued for all classes. Then the points are connected in order. That is, the point representing the lowest class is joined to the one representing the second class and so on.

Note in Chart 2–3 that, to complete the frequency polygon, midpoints of $10.5 and $34.5 are added to the *X*-axis to "anchor" the polygon at zero frequencies. These two values, $10.5 and $34.5, were derived by subtracting the class interval of $3.0 from the lowest midpoint ($13.5) and by adding $3.0 to the highest midpoint ($31.5) in the frequency distribution.

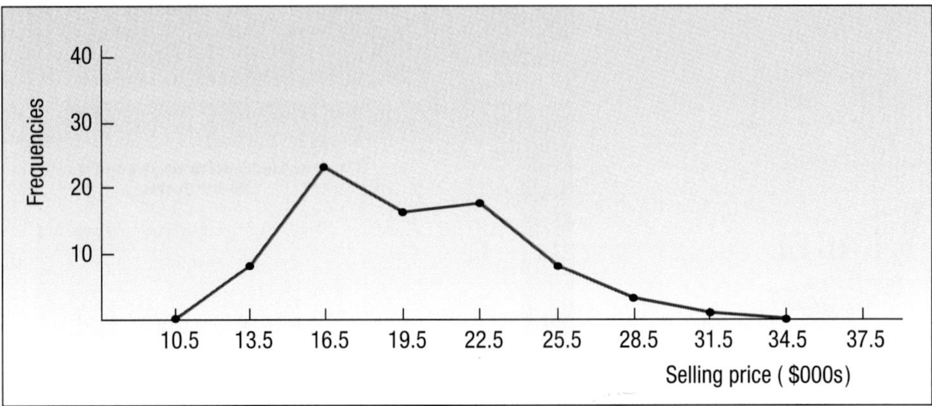

CHART 2–3 Frequency Polygon of the Selling Prices of 80 Vehicles at Whitner Pontiac

Both the histogram and the frequency polygon allow us to get a quick picture of the main characteristics of the data (highs, lows, points of concentration, etc.). Although the two representations are similar in purpose, the histogram has the advantage of depicting each class as a rectangle, with the height of the rectangular bar representing the number of frequencies in each class. The frequency polygon, in turn, has an advantage over the histogram. It allows us to compare directly two or more frequency distributions. Suppose that Rob Whitner, the owner of Whitner Pontiac, wants to compare the sales last month at his dealership with those at Midtown Cadillac. To do this, two frequency polygons are constructed, one on top of the other, as in Chart 2–4. It is clear from Chart 2–4 that the typical vehicle selling price is higher at the Cadillac dealership.

The total number of frequencies at Whitner Pontiac and at Midtown Cadillac are about the same, so a direct comparison is possible. If the difference in the total number of frequencies is quite large, converting the frequencies to relative frequencies and then plotting the two distributions would allow a clearer comparison.

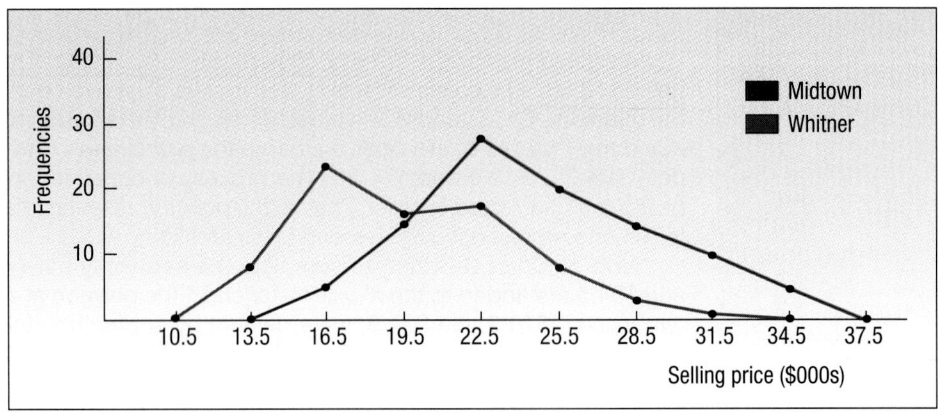

CHART 2–4 Distribution of Vehicle Selling Prices at Whitner Pontiac and Midtown Cadillac

Self-Review 2–5

The annual imports of a selected group of electronic suppliers are shown in the following frequency distribution.

Imports ($ millions)	Number of Suppliers
2 up to 5	6
5 up to 8	13
8 up to 11	20
11 up to 14	10
14 up to 17	1

(a) Portray the imports as a histogram.
(b) Portray the imports as a relative frequency polygon.
(c) Summarize the important facets of the distribution (such as low and high, concentration, etc.)

Exercises

15. Molly's Candle Shop has several retail stores in the coastal areas of North and South Carolina. Many of Molly's customers ask her to ship their purchases. The following chart shows the number of packages shipped per day for the last 100 days.

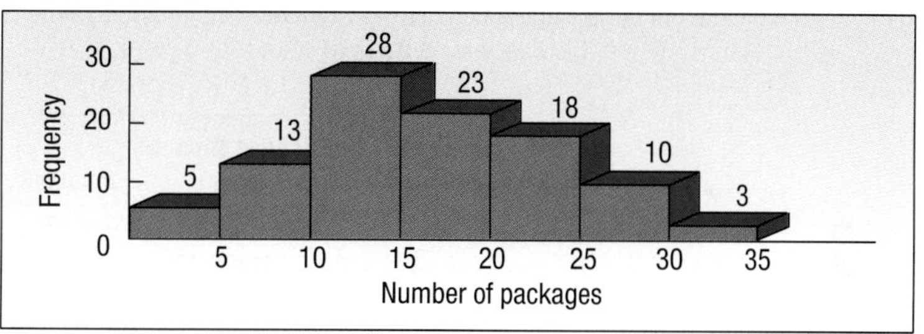

a. What is this chart called?
b. What is the total number of frequencies?
c. What is the class interval?
d. What is the class frequency for the 10 up to 15 class?
e. What is the relative frequency of the 10 up to 15 class?
f. What is the midpoint of the 10 up to 15 class?
g. On how many days were there 25 or more packages shipped?

16. The following chart shows the number of patients admitted daily to Memorial Hospital through the emergency room.

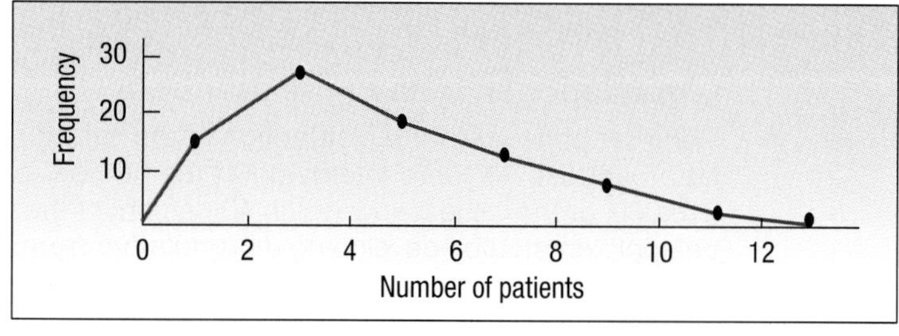

16. a. 3
b. About 26
c. 76
d. 2
e. Frequency polygon

a. What is the midpoint of the 2 up to 4 class?
b. How many days were 2 up to 4 patients admitted?
c. Approximately how many days were studied?
d. What is the class interval?
e. What is this chart called?

17. The following frequency distribution represents the number of days during a year that employees at the E. J. Wilcox Manufacturing Company were absent from work due to illness.

Number of Days Absent	Number of Employees
0 up to 3	5
3 up to 6	12
6 up to 9	23
9 up to 12	8
12 up to 15	2
Total	50

a. Assuming that this is a sample, what is the sample size?
b. What is the midpoint of the first class?
c. Construct a histogram.
d. A frequency polygon is to be drawn. What are the coordinates of the plot for the first class?
e. Construct a frequency polygon.
f. Interpret the rate of employee absenteeism using the two charts.

18. A large retailer is studying the lead time (elapsed time between when an order is placed and when it is filled) for a sample of recent orders. The lead times are reported in days.

Lead Time (days)	Frequency
0 up to 5	6
5 up to 10	7
10 up to 15	12
15 up to 20	8
20 up to 25	7
Total	40

18. a. 40
b. 2.5
c. 2.5, 6
d. See IM.
e. See IM.
f. See IM.

a. How many orders were studied?
b. What is the midpoint of the first class?
c. What are the coordinates of the first class for a frequency polygon?
d. Draw a histogram.
e. Draw a frequency polygon.
f. Interpret the lead times using the two charts.

Cumulative Frequency Distributions

Consider once again the distribution of the selling prices of vehicles at Whitner Pontiac. Suppose we were interested in the number of vehicles that sold for less than \$18,000, or the value below which 40 percent of the vehicles sold. These numbers can be approximated by developing a **cumulative frequency distribution** and portraying it graphically in a **cumulative frequency polygon.**

The frequency distribution of the vehicle selling prices at Whitner Pontiac is repeated from Table 2–4.

Selling Price ($ thousands)	Frequency
12 up to 15	8
15 up to 18	23
18 up to 21	17
21 up to 24	18
24 up to 27	8
27 up to 30	4
30 up to 33	2
Total	80

Construct a cumulative frequency polygon. Fifty percent of the vehicles were sold for less than what amount? Twenty-five of the vehicles were sold for less than what amount?

SOLUTION

As the name implies, a cumulative frequency distribution and a cumulative frequency polygon require *cumulative frequencies*. To construct a cumulative frequency distribution, refer to the preceding table and note that there were eight vehicles sold for less than $15,000. Those 8 vehicles, plus the 23 in the next higher class, for a total of 31, were sold for less than $18,000. The cumulative frequency for the next higher class is 48, found by 8 + 23 + 17. This process is continued for all the classes. All the vehicles were sold for less than $33,000. (See Table 2–7.)

TABLE 2–7 Cumulative Frequency Distribution for Vehicle Selling Price

Selling Price ($ thousands)	Frequency	Cumulative Frequency	Found by
12 up to 15	8	8	
15 up to 18	23	31 ←	8 + 23
18 up to 21	17	48	8 + 23 + 17
21 up to 24	18	66	8 + 23 + 17 + 18
24 up to 27	8	74	
27 up to 30	4	78	
30 up to 33	2	80	
Total	80		

To plot a cumulative frequency distribution, scale the upper limit of each class along the X-axis and the corresponding cumulative frequencies along the Y-axis. To provide additional information, you can label the vertical axis on the left in units and the vertical axis on the right in percent. In the Whitner Pontiac example, the vertical axis on the left is labeled from 0 to 80 and on the right from 0 to 100 percent. The value of 50 percent corresponds to 40 vehicles sold.

To begin the plotting, 8 vehicles sold for less than $15,000, so the first plot is at $X = 15$ and $Y = 8$. The coordinates for the next plot are $X = 18$ and $Y = 31$. The rest of the points are plotted and then the dots connected to form the chart (see Chart 2–5). To find the selling price below which half the cars sold, we draw a line from the 50 percent mark on the right-hand vertical axis over to the polygon, then drop down to the X-axis and read the selling price. The value on the X-axis is about 19.5, so we estimate that 50 percent of the vehicles sold for less than $19,500.

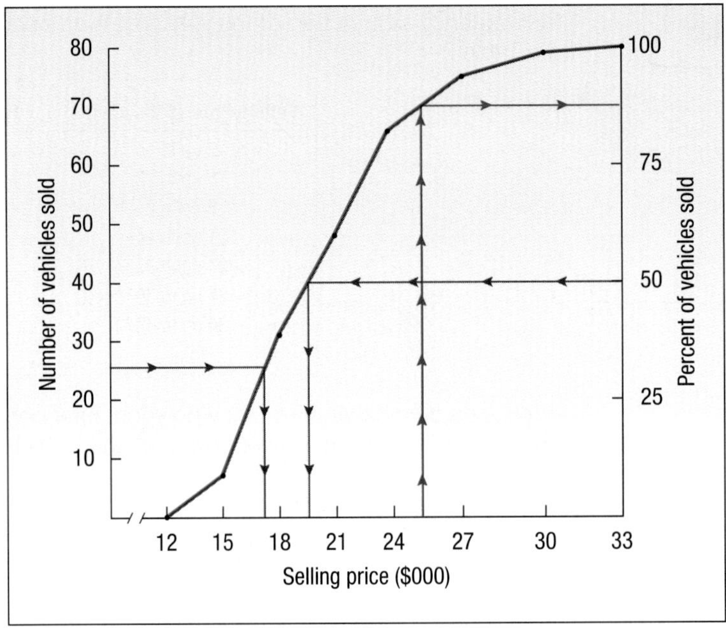

CHART 2–5 Cumulative Frequency Distribution for Vehicle Selling Price

To find the price below which 25 of the vehicles sold, we locate the value of 25 on the left-hand vertical axis. Next, we draw a horizontal line from the value of 25 to the polygon, and then drop down to the X-axis and read the price. It is about 17.5, so we estimate that 25 of the vehicles sold for less than $17,500. We can also make estimates of the percent of vehicles that sold for less than a particular amount. To explain, suppose we want to estimate the percent of vehicles that sold for less than $25,500. We begin by locating the value of 25.5 on the X-axis, move vertically to the polygon, and then horizontally to the vertical axis on the right. The value is about 87 percent, so we conclude that 87 percent of the vehicles sold for less than $25,500.

Self-Review 2–6

A sample of the hourly wages of 15 employees at Food City Supermarkets was organized into the following table.

Hourly Wages	Number of Employees
$ 6 up to $ 8	3
8 up to 10	7
10 up to 12	4
12 up to 14	1

(a) What is the table called?
(b) Develop a cumulative frequency distribution and portray the distribution in a cumulative frequency polygon.
(c) Based on the cumulative frequency polygon, how many employees earn $9 an hour or less? Half of the employees earn an hourly wage of how much more? Four employees earn how much less?

Exercises

19. The following chart shows the hourly wages of certified welders in the Atlanta, Georgia, area.

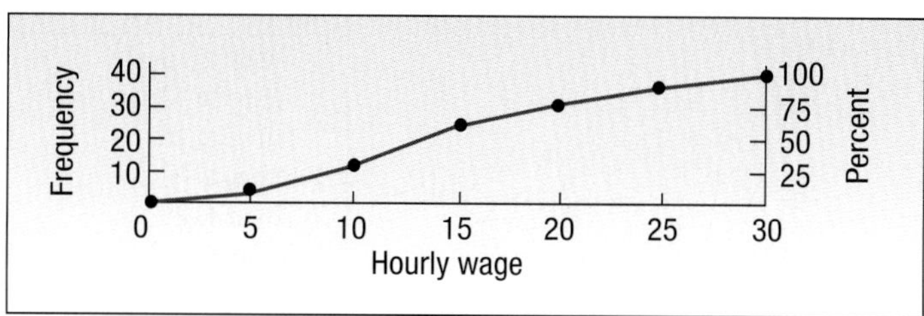

a. How many welders were studied?
b. What is the class interval?
c. About how many welders earn less than $10.00 per hour?
d. About 75 percent of the welders make less than what amount?
e. Ten of the welders studied made less than what amount?
f. What percent of the welders make less than $20.00 per hour?

20. The following chart shows the selling price ($000) of houses sold in the Billings, Montana, area.

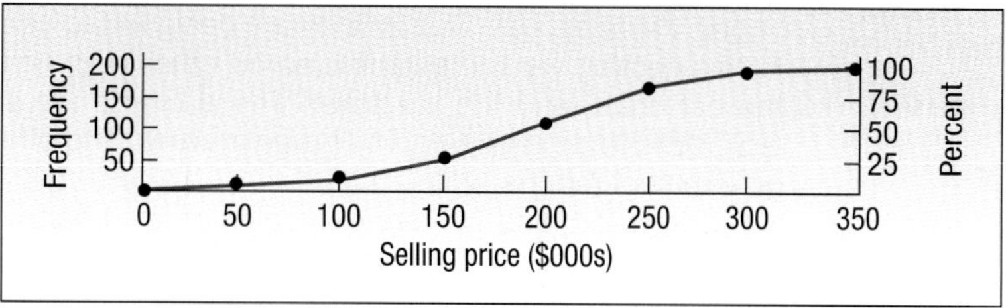

a. How many homes were studied?
b. What is the class interval?
c. One hundred homes sold for less than what amount?
d. About 75 percent of the homes sold for less than what amount?
e. Estimate the number of homes in the $150 up to $200 class.
f. About how many homes sold for less than $225?

20. **a.** 200
b. $50,000
c. About $180,000.
d. About $240,000.
e. About 60.
f. About 130.

21. The frequency distribution representing the number of days annually the employees at the E. J. Wilcox Manufacturing Company were absent from work due to illness is repeated from Exercise 17.

Number of Days Absent	Frequency
0 up to 3	5
3 up to 6	12
6 up to 9	23
9 up to 12	8
12 up to 15	2
Total	50

a. How many employees were absent less than three days annually? How many were absent less than six days due to illness?
b. Convert the frequency distribution to a cumulative frequency distribution.
c. Portray the cumulative distribution in the form of a cumulative frequency polygon.
d. Based on the cumulative frequency polygon, about three out of four employees were absent for how many days or less due to illness?

22. The frequency distribution of the lead time to fill an order from Exercise 18 is repeated below.

Lead Time (days)	Frequency
0 up to 5	6
5 up to 10	7
10 up to 15	12
15 up to 20	8
20 up to 25	7
Total	40

22. a. 13, 25
b. See IM.
c. See IM.
d. 14

a. How many orders were filled in less than 10 days? In less than 15 days?
b. Convert the frequency distribution to a cumulative frequency distribution.
c. Develop a cumulative frequency polygon.
d. About 60 percent of the orders were filled in less than how many days?

Other Graphic Presentations of Data

The histogram, the frequency polygon, and the cumulative frequency polygon all have strong visual appeal. That is, they are designed to capture the attention of the reader. In this section we will examine some other graphical forms, namely the line chart, the bar chart, and the pie chart. These charts are seen extensively in *USA Today, U.S. News and World Report, Business Week,* and other newspapers, magazines, and government reports.

Charts 2–6 and 2–7 are examples of line charts. Line charts are particularly effective for business because we can show the change in a variable over time. The variable, such as the number of units sold or the total value of sales, is scaled along the vertical axis and time along the horizontal axis. Chart 2–6 shows the Dow Jones Industrial Average and the Nasdaq, the two most widely reported measures of business activity, on Tuesday, June 6, 2000. Both measures were down for the day. The Dow closed at 10,735.57, down 79.73, and the Nasdaq at 3,756.39, down 65.37, for the day.

CHART 2–6 Market Summary on June 6, 2000

Chart 2–7 is also a line chart. It shows the circulation of *Sun Times* newspaper beginning with 1995 through the year 2000. It shows the newspaper's sales are increasing, but the growth rate of sales since 1997 seems to be slowing down.

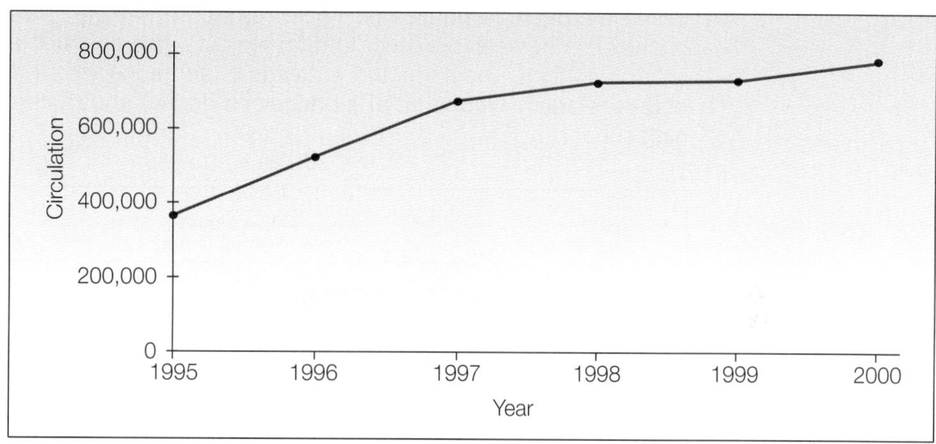

CHART 2–7 The *Sun Times* Circulation from 1995 to 2000

Quite often two or more series of figures are plotted on the same line chart. Thus, one chart can show the trend of several series. This allows for a comparison of several series over a period of time. Chart 2–8 shows the domestic and international sales (in millions of dollars) of Johnson and Johnson, Inc., for the years 1990 through 2000. We can easily see that the sales in both segments are growing, with the domestic component staying ahead of international sales in most years.

A **bar chart** can be used to depict any of the levels of measurement—nominal, ordinal, interval, or ratio. (Recall, we discussed the levels of data beginning on page 9 in Chapter 1.) Suppose we want to show the difference in earnings based on the level of education. From the Census Bureau *Current Population Reports,* the average earnings for someone over the age of 18 are $22,895 if a high school diploma is the highest degree earned. With a bachelor's degree the average earnings increase to $40,478

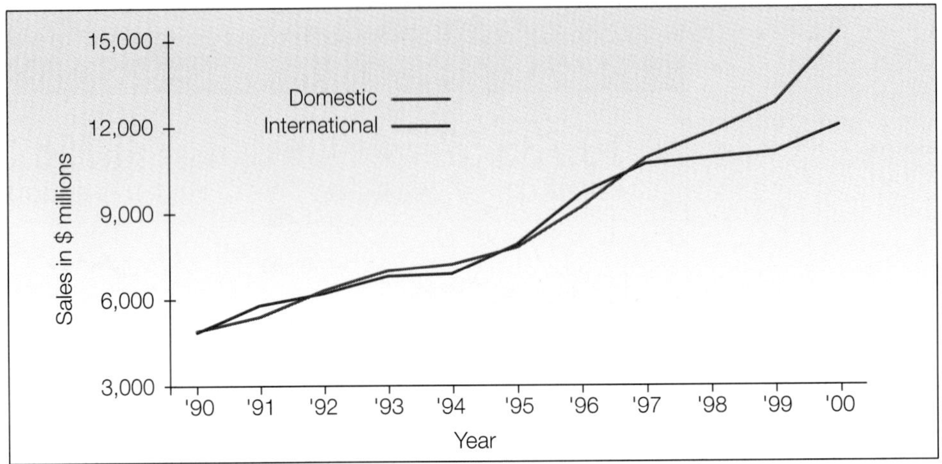

CHART 2–8 Domestic and International Sales for Johnson and Johnson, Inc.

and with a professional or master's degree the amount increases to $73,165. This information is summarized in Chart 2–9. We call this chart a **horizontal bar chart** because the bars are horizontal. With the chart it is easy to see that a person with a bachelor's degree can expect to earn almost twice as much as someone with a high school diploma. The expected earnings of someone with a master's or professional degree is nearly twice that of a bachelor's degree and more than three times that of high school.

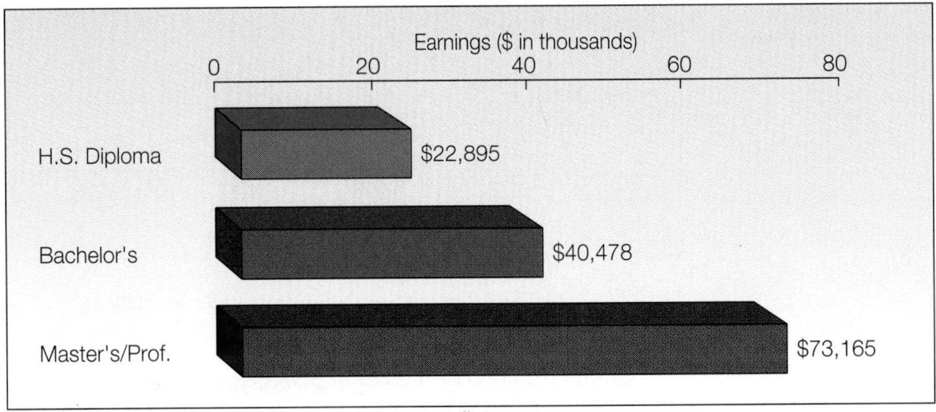

CHART 2–9 Average Earnings Based on Educational Level

A chart in *U.S. News and World Report* showed that Americans today are embracing new technology at a faster pace. Chart 2–10, a **vertical bar chart,** shows the number of years it took for five key technologies, after their introduction, to enter one-quarter of American homes. From the chart, it took only 7 years for the Internet to reach one-quarter of American homes, but it took the telephone 35 years. The years correspond to the height of the bars.

Note that there is space between the bars representing the various technologies. This is one way in which a histogram differs from a bar chart. There is no space

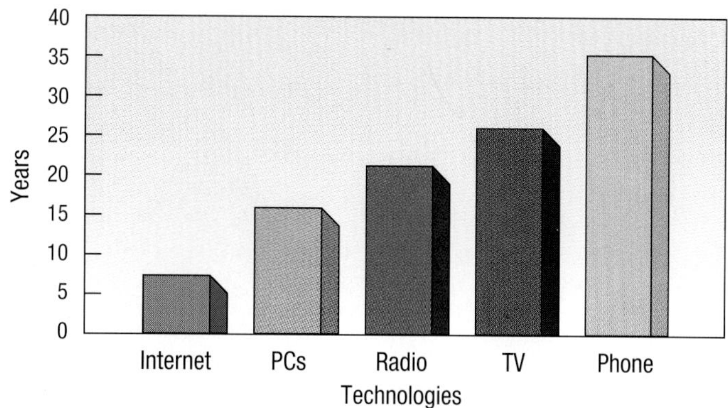

CHART 2–10 Time for Key Technologies to Reach One-Quarter of American Homes

Source: *US News and World Report.* November 13, 2000, page 16.

between the bars in a histogram (see Chart 2–2 on page 36), because the data are interval or ratio scale. This is not the case in a bar chart. The various technologies are measured on the nominal scale; therefore, the bars are separated.

A **pie chart** is especially useful for depicting nominal level data. We will use the information in Table 2–8, which shows a breakdown of state lottery proceeds since 1964, to explain the details of constructing a pie chart.

TABLE 2–8 State Lottery Proceeds

Use of Profits	Percent Share
Education	56
General fund	23
Cities	10
Senior citizens	9
Other	2
Total	100

The first step is to record the percentages 0, 5, 10, 15, and so on evenly around the circumference of a circle. To plot the 56 percent share for education, draw a line from 0 to the center of the circle and then another line from the center to 56 percent on the circle. The area of this "slice" represents the lottery proceeds that were given to education. Next, add the 56 percent transferred to education to the 23 percent transferred to the general fund; the result is 79 percent. Draw a line from the center of the circle to 79 percent, so the area between 56 percent and 79 percent represents the percent of the lottery proceeds transferred to the general fund of the state. Continuing, add 10, the component given to the cities, which gives us a total of 89 percent. Draw a line from the center out to the value 89, so the area between 79 and 89 represents the share transferred to cities. Continue the same process for the senior citizen programs and "Other." Because the areas of the pie represent the relative shares of each category, we can quickly compare them: The largest percent of the proceeds goes to education; this amount is more than half the total, and it is more than twice the amount given to the next largest category.

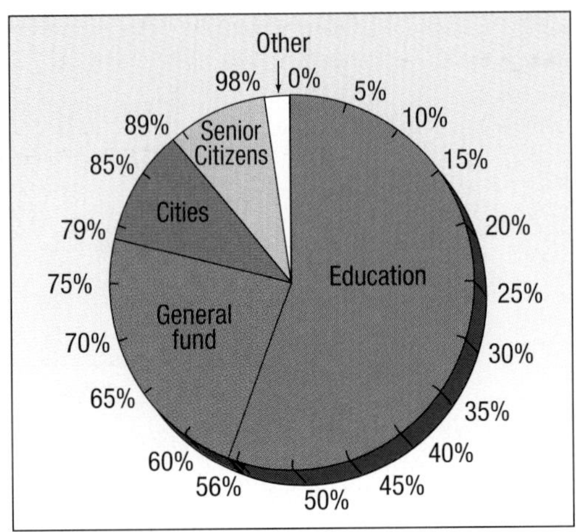

Percent of State Lottery Proceeds

The Excel system will develop a pie chart and output the result. Following is an Excel chart showing the percentage of viewers watching each of the major television networks during prime time.

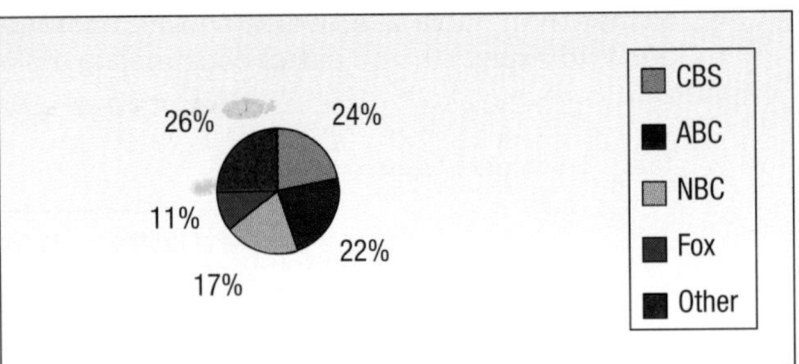

Share of Prime-Time Viewing for Major Networks

Self-Review 2–7

The Clayton County Commissioners want a chart to show taxpayers attending the forthcoming meeting what happens to their tax dollars. The total amount of taxes collected is $2 million. Expenditures are: $440,000 for schools, $1,160,000 for roads, $320,000 for administration, and $80,000 for supplies. A pie chart seems ideal to show the portion of each tax dollar going for schools, roads, administration, and supplies. Convert the dollar amounts to percents of the total and portray the percents in the form of a pie chart.

Misleading Graphs

When you create graphic illustrations you must be careful not to mislead or misrepresent. In this section we present several examples of charts and graphs that are misleading. Whenever you see a chart or graph, study it carefully. Ask yourself: What is the writer trying to show me? Could the writer have any bias?

One of the easiest ways to mislead the reader is to make the range of the *Y*-axis very small in terms of the units used for that axis. A second method is to begin at some value other than 0 on the *Y*-axis. In the chart below, it appears there has been a dramatic increase in sales from 1989 to 2000. However, during the period, sales increased only 2 percent (from $5.0 million to $5.1 million)! In addition, observe that the *Y*-axis does not begin at 0. To be clear, it is not wrong to begin the vertical or the horizontal axis at some value other than zero, but the reader should be alert to the effect.

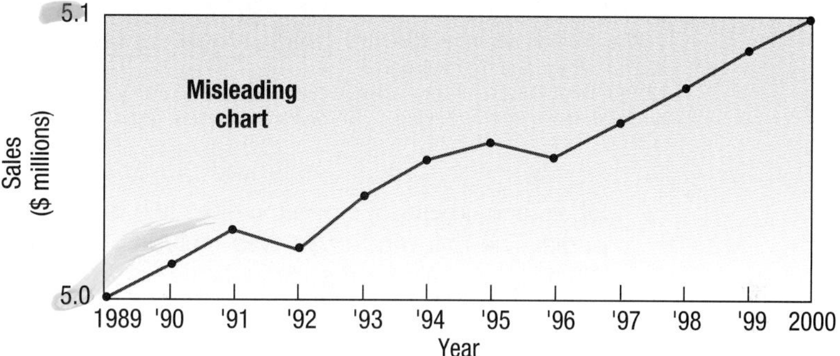

Sales of Matsui Nine-Passenger Vans, 1989–2000

The chart below gives the correct impression of the trend in sales. Sales are almost flat from 1989 to 2000; that is, there has been practically no change in sales during the 10-year period.

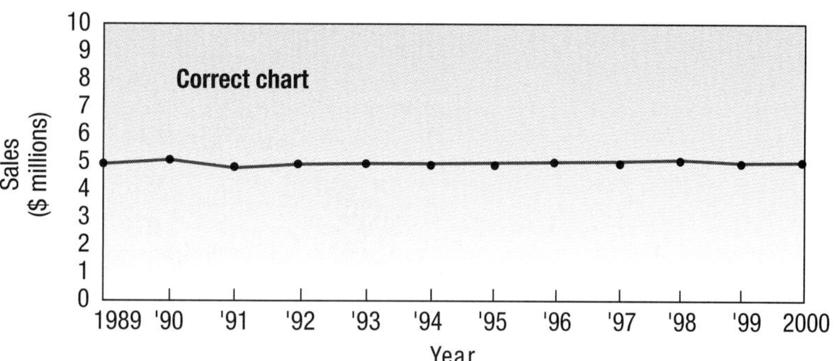

Sales of Matsui Nine-Passenger Vans, 1989–2000

Without much comment, we ask you to look at each of the following charts and carefully decide whether the intended message is accurate.

1. The following chart was adapted from an advertisement for the new Wilson ULTRA DISTANCE golf ball. The chart shows that the new ball gets the longest distance, but what is the scale for the horizontal axis? How was the test conducted?

Maybe everybody can't hit a ball like John Daly. But everybody wants to. That's why Wilson© is introducing the new ULTRA© DISTANCE ball. ULTRA DISTANCE is the longest, most accurate ball you'll ever hit.

Wilson has totally redesigned this ball from the inside out, making ULTRA DISTANCE a major advancement in golf technology.

ULTRA© DISTANCE	591.2 Yds.
DUNLOP© DDH IV	584.6 Yds.
MAXFLI MD©	571.2 Yds.
TITLEIST© HVC	569.3 Yds.
TOP-FLITE© Tour 90	565.9 Yds.
TOP-FLITE© MAGNA	564.3 Yds.

Combined yardage with a driver, #5 iron and #9 iron, ULTRA DISTANCE is clearly measurably longer.

2. Fibre Tech, in Largo, Florida, makes and installs fiberglass coatings for swimming pools. The following chart was included in a brochure. Is the comparison fair? What is the scale for the vertical axis? Is the scale in dollars or in percent?

Fibre Tech Reduces Chemical Use, Saving You Time and Money.

- Saves up to 60% on chemical costs alone.
- Reduces water loss, which means less need to replace chemicals and up to 10% warmer water (reducing heating costs, too).
- Fibre Tech pays for itself in reduced maintenance and chemical costs.

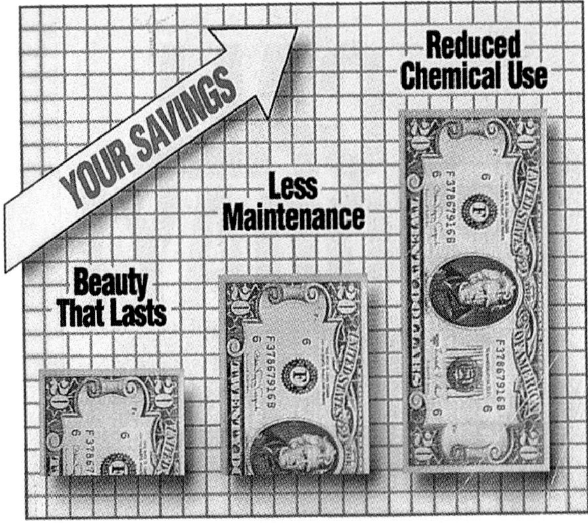

Again, we caution you. When you see a chart or graph, particularly as part of an advertisement, be careful. Look at the scales used on the X-axis and the Y-axis.

Exercises

23. A small business consultant is investigating the performance of several companies. The sales in 2000 (in thousands of dollars) for the selected companies were:

Corporation	Fourth-Quarter Sales ($ thousands)
Hoden Building Products	$ 1,645.2
J & R Printing, Inc.	4,757.0
Long Bay Concrete Construction	8,913.0
Mancell Electric and Plumbing	627.1
Maxwell Heating and Air Conditioning	24,612.0
Mizelle Roofing & Sheet Metals	191.9

The consultant wants to include a chart in his report comparing the sales of the six companies. Use a bar chart to compare the fourth quarter sales of these corporations and write a brief report summarizing the bar chart.

24. See IM.

24. The Blair Corporation, located in Warren, Pennsylvania, sells fashion apparel for men and women plus a broad range of home products. It services its customers by mail. Listed below are the net sales for Blair from 1995 through 1999. Draw a line chart depicting the net sales over the time period and write a brief report.

Year	Net Sales ($ millions)
1995	500.0
1996	519.2
1997	526.5
1998	550.7
1999	562.9

25. A headline in the *Toledo Blade* reported that crime was on the decline. Listed below are the number of homicides from 1986 to 1999. Draw a line chart to summarize the data and write a brief summary of the homicide rates for the last 14 years.

Year	Homicides	Year	Homicides
1986	21	1993	45
1987	34	1994	40
1988	26	1995	35
1989	42	1996	30
1990	37	1997	28
1991	37	1998	25
1992	44	1999	21

26. See IM.

26. A report prepared for the governor of a western state indicated that 56 percent of the state's tax revenue went to education, 23 percent to the general fund, 10 percent to the counties, 9 percent to senior programs, and the remainder to other social programs. Develop a pie chart to show the breakdown of the budget.

27. The following table, in millions, shows the population of the United States in 5-year intervals from 1950 to 1995. Develop a line chart depicting the population growth and write a brief report summarizing your findings.

Year	Population (millions)	Year	Population (millions)
1950	152.30	1975	216.00
1955	165.90	1980	227.70
1960	180.70	1985	238.50
1965	194.30	1990	249.90
1970	205.10	1995	263.00

28. St. Louis is largest; Washington, DC, smallest.

28. Shown below are the military and civilian personnel expenditures for the eight largest military locations in the United States. Develop a bar chart and summarize the results in a brief report.

Location	Amount Spent (millions)	Location	Amount Spent (millions)
St. Louis, MO	$6,087	Norfolk, VA	$3,228
San Diego, CA	4,747	Marietta, GA	2,828
Pico Rivera, CA	3,272	Fort Worth, TX	2,492
Arlington, VA	3,284	Washington, DC	2,347

Chapter Outline

I. A frequency distribution is a grouping of data into mutually exclusive classes showing the number of observations in each class.
  - **A.** The steps in constructing a frequency distribution are:
    1. Decide how many classes you wish.
    2. Determine the class interval or width.
    3. Set the individual class limits.
    4. Tally the raw data into the classes.
    5. Count the number of tallies in each class.
  - **B.** The class frequency is the number of observations in each class.
  - **C.** The class interval is the difference between the limits of two consecutive classes.
  - **D.** The class midpoint is halfway between the limits of two consecutive classes.

II. A relative frequency distribution shows the percent of the observations in each class.

III. A stem-and-leaf display is an alternative to a frequency distribution.
  - **A.** The leading digit is the stem and the trailing digit the leaf.
  - **B.** The advantages of the stem-and-leaf chart over a frequency distribution include:
    1. The identity of each observation is not lost.
    2. The digits themselves give a picture of the distribution.
    3. The cumulative frequencies are also reported.

IV. There are two methods for graphically portraying a frequency distribution.
  - **A.** A histogram portrays the number of frequencies in each class in the form of rectangles.
  - **B.** A frequency polygon consists of line segments connecting the points formed by the intersections of the class midpoints and the class frequencies.

V. A cumulative frequency polygon shows the number of observations below a certain value.

VI. There are many charts used in newspapers and magazines.
  - **A.** A line chart is ideal for showing the trend of sales or income over time.
  - **B.** Bar charts are similar to line charts and are useful for showing changes in nominal scale data.
  - **C.** Pie charts are useful for showing the percent that various components are of the total.

Chapter Exercises

29. A data set consists of 83 observations. How many classes would you recommend for a frequency distribution?

30. 60

30. A data set consists of 145 observations that range from 56 to 490. What size class interval would you recommend?
31. The following is the number of minutes to commute from home to work for a group of automobile executives.

28	25	48	37	41	19	32	26	16	23	23	29	36
31	26	21	32	25	31	43	35	42	38	33	28	

   a. How many classes would you recommend?
   b. What class interval would you suggest?
   c. What would you recommend as the lower limit of the first class?
   d. Organize the data into a frequency distribution.
   e. Comment on the shape of the frequency distribution.
32. The following data give the weekly amounts spent on groceries for a sample of households.

$271	$363	$159	$ 76	$227	$337	$295	$319	$250
279	205	279	266	199	177	162	232	303
192	181	321	309	246	278	50	41	335
116	100	151	240	474	297	170	188	320
429	294	570	342	279	235	434	123	325

32. a. 6
b. 100
c. 0
d. See IM.

   a. How many classes would you recommend?
   b. What class interval would you suggest?
   c. What would you recommend as the lower limit of the first class?
   d. Organize the data into a frequency distribution.
33. The following stem-and-leaf display shows the number of minutes of daytime TV viewing for a sample of college students.

2	0	05
3	1	0
6	2	137
10	3	0029
13	4	499
24	5	00155667799
30	6	023468
(7)	7	1366789
33	8	01558
28	9	1122379
21	10	022367899
12	11	2457
8	12	4668
4	13	249
1	14	5

   a. How many college students were studied?
   b. How many observations are in the second class?
   c. What are the smallest value and the largest value?
   d. List the actual values in the fourth row.
   e. How many students watched less than 60 minutes of TV?
   f. How many students watched 100 minutes or more of TV?

g. What is the middle value?
h. How many students watched at least 60 minutes but less than 100 minutes?

34. The following stem-and-leaf display reports the number of orders received per day by a mail-order firm.

1	9	1
2	10	2
5	11	235
7	12	69
8	13	2
11	14	135
15	15	1229
22	16	2266778
27	17	01599
(11)	18	00013346799
17	19	03346
12	20	4679
8	21	0177
4	22	45
2	23	17

34. a. 55
b. 2
c. 91, 237
d. 141, 143, 145
e. 8
f. 12
g. 3
h. 180

a. How many days were studied?
b. How many observations are in the fourth class?
c. What are the smallest value and the largest value?
d. List the actual values in the sixth class.
e. How many days did the firm receive less than 140 orders?
f. How many days did the firm receive 200 or more orders?
g. On how many days did the firm receive 180 orders?
h. What is the middle value?

35. The following histogram shows the scores on the first statistics exam.

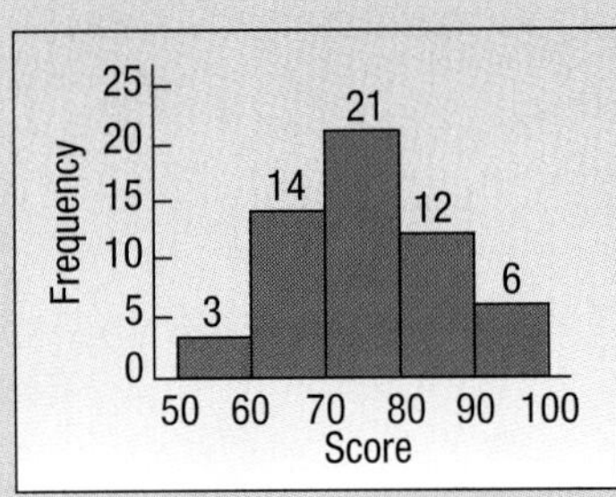

a. How many students took the exam?
b. What is the class interval?
c. What is the class midpoint for the first class?
d. How many students earned a score of less than 70?

36. The following chart summarizes the selling price of homes sold last month in the Sarasota, Florida, area.

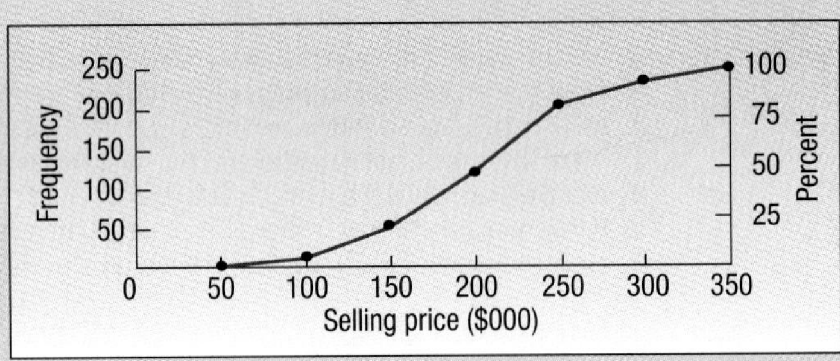

36. a. Cumulative frequency polygon.
b. 250
c. 50
d. 240
e. 230

a. What is the chart called?
b. How many homes were sold during the last month?
c. What is the class interval?
d. About 75 percent of the houses sold for less than what amount?
e. One hundred seventy-five of the homes sold for less than what amount?

37. A chain of sport shops catering to beginning skiers, headquartered in Aspen, Colorado, plans to conduct a study of how much a beginning skier spends on his or her initial purchase of equipment and supplies. Based on these figures, they want to explore the possibility of offering combinations, such as a pair of boots and a pair of skis, to induce customers to buy more. A sample of their cash register receipts revealed these initial purchases:

$140	$ 82	$265	$168	$ 90	$114	$172	$230	$142
86	125	235	212	171	149	156	162	118
139	149	132	105	162	126	216	195	127
161	135	172	220	229	129	87	128	126
175	127	149	126	121	118	172	126	

a. Arrive at a suggested class interval. Use five classes, and let the lower limit of the first class be $80.
b. What would be a better class interval?
c. Organize the data into a frequency distribution using a lower limit of $80.
d. Interpret your findings.

38. See IM.

38. The numbers of shareholders for a selected group of large companies (in thousands) are:

Company	Number of Shareholders (thousands)	Company	Number of Shareholders (thousands)
Pan American World Airways	144	Northeast Utilities	200
General Public Utilities	177	Standard Oil (Indiana)	173
Occidental Petroleum	266	Home Depot	195
Middle South Utilities	133	Detroit Edison	220
DaimlerChrysler	209	Eastman Kodak	251
Standard Oil of California	264	Dow Chemical	137
Bethlehem Steel	160	Pennsylvania Power	150
Long Island Lighting	143	American Electric Power	262
RCA	246	Ohio Edison	158
Greyhound Corporation	151	Transamerica Corporation	162
Pacific Gas & Electric	239	Columbia Gas System	165
Niagara Mohawk Power	204	International Telephone &	
E. I. du Pont de Nemours	204	Telegraph	223
Westinghouse Electric	195	Union Electric	158
Union Carbide	176	Virginia Electric and Power	162
BankAmerica	175	Public Service Electric & Gas	225
		Consumers Power	161

The numbers of shareholders are to be organized into a frequency distribution and several graphs drawn to portray the distribution.

a. Using seven classes and a lower limit of 130, construct a frequency distribution.
b. Portray the distribution as a frequency polygon.
c. Portray the distribution in a cumulative frequency polygon.
d. Based on the polygon, three out of four (75 percent) of the companies have how many shareholders or less?
e. Write a brief analysis of the number of shareholders based on the frequency distribution and graphs.

39. A recent survey showed that the typical American car owner spends $2,950 per year on operating expenses. Below is a breakdown of the various expenditure items. Draw an appropriate chart to portray the data and summarize your findings in a brief report.

Expenditure Item	Amount
Fuel	$ 603
Interest on car loan	279
Repairs	930
Insurance and license	646
Depreciation	492
Total	$2,950

40. The Midland National Bank selected a sample of 40 student checking accounts. Below are their end-of-the-month balances.

$404	$ 74	$234	$149	$279	$215	$123	$ 55	$ 43	$321
87	234	68	489	57	185	141	758	72	863
703	125	350	440	37	252	27	521	302	127
968	712	503	489	327	608	358	425	303	203

40. a. See IM.
b. See IM.
c. About 33%.
d. Less than $50.

a. Tally the data into a frequency distribution using $100 as a class interval and $0 as the starting point.
b. Draw a cumulative frequency polygon.
c. The bank considers any student with an ending balance of $400 or more a "preferred customer." Estimate the percentage of preferred customers.
d. The bank is also considering a service charge to the lowest 10 percent of the ending balances. What would you recommend as the cutoff point between those who have to pay a service charge and those who do not?

41. The United States Department of Transportation keeps track of the percentage of flights that arrive within 15 minutes of the scheduled time, by airline. Below is the latest information. Construct a stem-and-leaf chart from these data. Summarize your conclusion.

Airline	Percent on Time	Airline	Percent on Time
Pan Am	82.7	American	78.1
America West	82.7	United	76.4
Northwest	81.0	Delta	76.1
USAir	80.1	Continental	76.9
Southwest	79.7	British Airways	80.4
Alaska	79.7	Japan Airlines	81.4

42. See IM.

42. A recent study of home technologies reported the number of hours of personal computer usage per week for a sample of 60 persons. Excluded from the study were people who worked out of their home and used the computer as a part of their work.

9.3	5.3	6.3	8.8	6.5	0.6	5.2	6.6	9.3	4.3
6.3	2.1	2.7	0.4	3.7	3.3	1.1	2.7	6.7	6.5
4.3	9.7	7.7	5.2	1.7	8.5	4.2	5.5	5.1	5.6
5.4	4.8	2.1	10.1	1.3	5.6	2.4	2.4	4.7	1.7
2.0	6.7	1.1	6.7	2.2	2.6	9.8	6.4	4.9	5.2
4.5	9.3	7.9	4.6	4.3	4.5	9.2	8.5	6.0	8.1

a. Organize the data into a frequency distribution. How many classes would you suggest? What value would you suggest for a class interval?
b. Draw a histogram. Interpret your result.

43. Merrill Lynch recently completed a study regarding the size of investment portfolios (stocks, bonds, mutual funds, and certificates of deposit) for a sample of clients in the 40 to 50 age group. Listed below is the value of all the investments for the 70 participants in the study.

669.9	7.5	77.2	7.5	125.7	516.9	219.9	645.2
301.9	235.4	716.4	145.3	26.6	187.2	315.5	89.2
136.4	616.9	440.6	408.2	34.4	296.1	185.4	526.3
380.7	3.3	363.2	51.9	52.2	107.5	82.9	63.0
228.6	308.7	126.7	430.3	82.0	227.0	321.1	403.4
39.5	124.3	118.1	23.9	352.8	156.7	276.3	23.5
31.3	301.2	35.7	154.9	174.3	100.6	236.7	171.9
221.1	43.4	212.3	243.3	315.4	5.9	1002.2	171.7
295.7	437.0	87.8	302.1	268.1	899.5		

a. Organize the data into a frequency distribution. How many classes would you suggest? What value would you suggest for a class interval?

b. Draw a histogram. Interpret your result.

44. See IM.

44. In its annual report ExxonMobil reported its total worldwide earnings as $5,886 million. Of this total (all reported in millions of dollars), $1,541 were in the United States, $1,757 in Europe, $1,219 in Asia-Pacific, $439 in Canada, and $930 in other parts of the world. Develop a bar chart depicting this information.

45. The American Heart Association reported the following percentage breakdown of expenses. Draw a pie chart depicting the information. Interpret.

Category	Percent
Research	32.3
Public Health Education	23.5
Community Service	12.6
Fund Raising	12.1
Professional and Educational Training	10.9
Management and General	8.6

46. See IM.

46. In their 1999 annual report Schering-Plough Corporation reported their income, in millions of dollars, for the years 1995 to 1999 as follows. Develop a line chart depicting the results and comment on your findings.

Year	Income ($ million)
1995	1,053
1996	1,213
1997	1,444
1998	1,756
1999	2,110

47. Annual revenues, by type of tax, for the state of Georgia are as follows. Develop an appropriate chart or graph and write a brief report summarizing the information.

Type of Tax	Amount (000)
Sales	$2,812,473
Income (Individual)	2,732,045
License	185,198
Corporate	525,015
Property	22,647
Death and Gift	37,326
Total	$6,314,704

48. See IM, use a pie chart.

48. Annual imports from selected Canadian trading partners are listed below. Develop an appropriate chart or graph and write a brief report summarizing the information.

Partner	Annual Imports (million)
Japan	$9,550
United Kingdom	4,556
South Korea	2,441
China	1,182
Australia	618

49. Farming has changed from the early 1900s. In the early 20th century, machinery gradually replaced animal power. For example, in 1910 U.S. farms used 24.2 million horses and mules and only about 1,000 tractors. By 1960, 4.6 million tractors were used and only 3.2 million horses and mules. In 1920 there were over 6 million farms in the United States. Today there are less than 2 million. Listed below is the number of farms, in thousands, for each of the 50 states. Write a paragraph summarizing your findings.

47	1	8	46	76	26	4	3	39	45
4	21	80	63	100	65	91	29	7	15
7	52	87	39	106	25	55	2	3	8
14	38	59	33	76	71	37	51	1	24
35	86	185	13	7	43	36	20	79	9

50. See IM, use a pie chart or bar graph.

50. One of the most popular candies in the United States is M&M's, which is produced by the Mars Company. For many years the M&M's plain candies were produced in six colors: red, green, orange, tan, brown, and yellow. Recently, tan was replaced by blue. Did you ever wonder how many candies were in a bag, or how many of each color? Are there about the same number of each color, or are there more of some colors than others? Here is some information for a one-pound bag of M&M's plain candies. It contained a total of 544 candies. There were 135 brown, 156 yellow, 128 red, 22 green, 50 blue, and 53 orange. Develop a chart depicting this information and a brief report summarizing the information.

51. The following graph compares the average selling prices of the Ford Taurus and the Toyota Camry from 1993 to 2000. Write a brief report summarizing the information in the graph. Be sure to include the selling price of the two cars, the change in the selling price, and the direction of the change in the eight-year period.

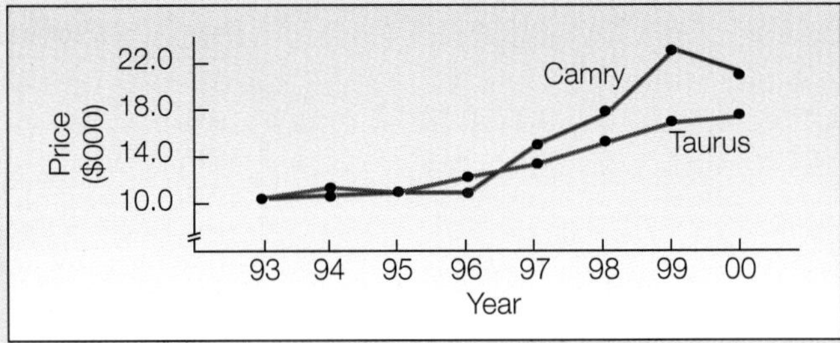

exercises.com

W W W

52. Monthly and year-to-date truck sales are available at the website: http://www.pickuptruck.com. Go to this site and under **Features** click on **News** to obtain the most recent information. Make a pie chart or a bar chart showing the most recent information. What is the best selling truck? What are the four or five best selling trucks? What is their market share? You may wish to group some of the trucks into a category called "Other" to get a better picture of market share. Comment on your findings.

52. See IM.

53. Go to an employment website such as http://jobsearch.monster.com. Click on Jobs and select a geographic region and an area of specialization of interest to you. For example, you might select the Orlando, Florida region and Banking as your area of interest. Make a stem-and-leaf display of the salaries offered for the various jobs. To make valid comparisons convert all wages to a yearly basis (assume 40 hours per week and 50 weeks in a year). Where a range is given for salaries, use the center of the range. Then write a brief summary describing the typical salary and the shape of the distribution.

Computer Data Exercises

54. See IM.

54. Refer to the Real Estate data, which reports information on homes sold in the Venice, Florida area during the last year.

a. Select an appropriate class interval and organize the selling prices into a frequency distribution.
 1. Around what values do the data tend to cluster?
 2. What is the largest selling price? What is the smallest selling price?

b. Draw a cumulative frequency distribution based on the frequency distribution developed in Part a.
 1. How many homes sold for less than $200,000?
 2. Estimate the percent of the homes that sold for more than $220,000.
 3. What percent of the homes sold for less than $125,000?

c. Write a report summarizing the selling prices of the homes.

55. Refer to the Baseball 2000 data, which reports information on the 30 Major League Baseball teams for the 2000 season.

a. Organize the information on the team salaries into a frequency distribution. Select an appropriate class interval.
 1. What is a typical team salary? What is the range of salaries?
 2. Comment on the shape of the distribution. Does it appear that any of the team salaries are out of line with the others?

b. Draw a cumulative frequency distribution based on the frequency distribution developed in Part a.
 1. Forty percent of the teams are paying less than what amount in total team salary?
 2. About how many teams have total salaries of less than $50,000,000?
 3. Below what amount do the lowest five teams pay in total salary?

c. Organize the information on the size of the various stadiums into a frequency distribution.
 1. What is a typical stadium size? Where do the stadium sizes tend to cluster?
 2. Comment on the shape of the distribution. Does it appear that any of the stadium sizes are out of line with the others?

d. Organize the information on the year in which the 30 major league stadiums were built into a frequency distribution. (You could also create a new variable called AGE by subtracting the year in which the stadium was built from the current year.)
 1. What is the year in which the typical stadium was built? Where do these years tend to cluster?
 2. Comment on the shape of the distribution. Does it appear that any of the stadium ages are out of line with the others? If so, which ones?

56. See IM, range is from 4.8% to 17.3%.

56. Refer to the OECD data, which reports information on census, economic, and business data for 29 countries. Develop a stem-and-leaf chart for the variable regarding the percent of the workforce that is over 65 years of age. Are there any outliers? Briefly describe the data.

57. Refer to the Schools data set, which reports information on the 94 school districts in Northwest Ohio. Organize the teachers' salaries into a stem-and-leaf display.

a. What is the highest salary among the 94 districts? What is the lowest salary among the districts?

b. What is a typical salary?

c. How many districts have average salaries of $30,000 or more?

d. Write a brief report summarizing your findings.

Computer Commands

1. The MegaStat commands for the frequency distribution on page 27 are:
   a. Open Excel and from the CD provided, select **Go to the Data Sets,** and select the Excel format; go to Chapter 2, and select **Tbl2-1.** Click on **MegaStat, Frequency Distribution, Quantitative,** and then hit **Enter**.
   b. In the dialog box, input the range from *A1:A81,* select **Equal width intervals,** use *3,000* as the interval width, *12,000* as the lower boundary of the first interval, select **Histogram,** and then click **OK.**

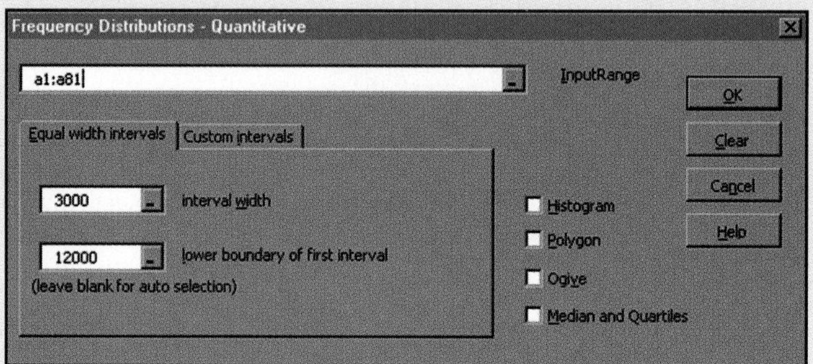

2. The MINITAB commands for the stem-and-leaf display on page 32 are:
   a. Import the data from the CD. The file name Is Tbl 2-6. Use the MINITAB format.
   b. Select **Stat, EDA, Stem-and-leaf,** and then hit **Enter.**
   c. Select the variable **Spots,** enter *10* for the **Increment,** and then click **OK.**

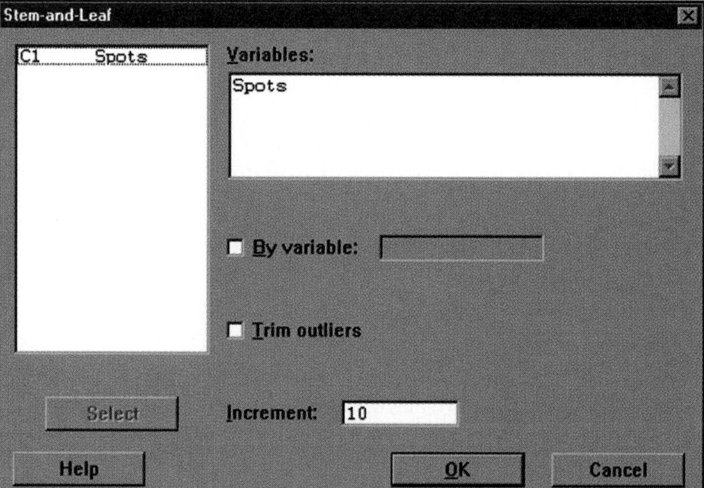

3. The Excel commands for the histogram on page 37 are:
   a. In cell A1 indicate that the column of data is the selling price and in B1 that it is the frequency. In columns A2 to A8 insert the midpoints of the selling prices in $000. In B2 to B8 record the class frequencies.
   b. With your mouse arrow on A1, click and drag to highlight the cells A1:B8.
   c. From the **Tool bar** select **Chart Wizard,** under **Chart type** select **Column,** under **Chart sub-type** select the vertical bars in the upper left corner, and finally click on **Next** in the lower right corner.
   d. At the top select the **Series** tab. Under the Series list box, **Price** is highlighted. Select **Remove.** (We do not want Price to be a part of the values.) At the bottom, in the

Category (X) axis labels text box, click the icon at the far right. Put your cursor on cell A2, click and drag to cell A8. There will be a running box around cells A2 to A8. Touch the **Enter** key. This identifies the column of **Prices** as the *X*-axis labels. Click on **Next.**

e. At the top of the dialog box click on **Titles.** Click on the **Chart title** box and key in *Selling Price of 80 Vehicles Sold at Whitner Pontiac.* Tab to the **Category (X)** axis box and key in the label *Selling Price in ($000).* Tab to the **Category (Y)** axis box and key in *Frequency.* At the top select **Legend** and remove the check from the **Show legend** box. Click **Finish.**

f. To make the chart larger, click on the middle handle of the top line and drag the line to row 1. Make sure the handles show on the chart box. With your right mouse button, click on one of the columns. Select **Format Data Series.** At the top select the **Options** tab. In the **Gap width** text box, click the down arrow until the gap width reads 0, and click **OK.**

4. Excel commands for the pie chart on page 48 are:

a. Set cell A1 as the active cell and type the words *Market Share.* In cells A2 through A6 enter the major networks: CBS, ABC, NBC, Fox, and Other.

b. Set cell B1 as the active cell and type the word *Percent.* In cells B2 through B6 enter the values 24, 22, 26, 17, and 11.

c. From the **Tool Bar** select the **Chart Wizard.** Select **Pie** as the chart type, select the chart type in the upper left corner, and then click on **Next.**

d. For the Data Range type *A1:B6,* indicate that the data are in a column, and finally click on **Next.**

e. Click on the chart title area and type *Share of Prime-Time Viewing for the Major Networks.* Then click **Finish.**

Chapter 2 Answers to Self-Review

2–1 **a.** The raw data.

b.

Commission	Number of Salespeople
$1,400 up to $1,500	2
1,500 up to 1,600	5
1,600 up to 1,700	3
1,700 up to 1,800	1
Total	11

c. Class frequencies.

d. The largest concentration of commissions is $1,500 up to $1,600. The smallest commission is about $1,400 and the largest is about $1,800.

2–2 **a.** $2^6 = 64 < 70 < 128 = 2^7$. So 7 classes are recommended.

b. The interval width should be at least $(550 - 340)/7 = 30$. So 35 feet would be a reasonable interval width.

c. Classes: 325 up to 360 feet, 360 up to 395 feet, 395 up to 430 feet, 430 up to 465 feet, 465 up to 500 feet, 500 up to 535 feet, and 535 up to 570 feet.

2–3 **a.** 23

b. 28.75%, found by $(23/80) \times 100$

c. 7.5%, found by $(6/80) \times 100$.

2–4

7	7
8	0013488
9	1256689
10	1248
11	26

a. 8

b. 10.1, 10.2, 10.4, 10.8

c. 9.5

d. 7.7, 11.6

2–5 **a.**

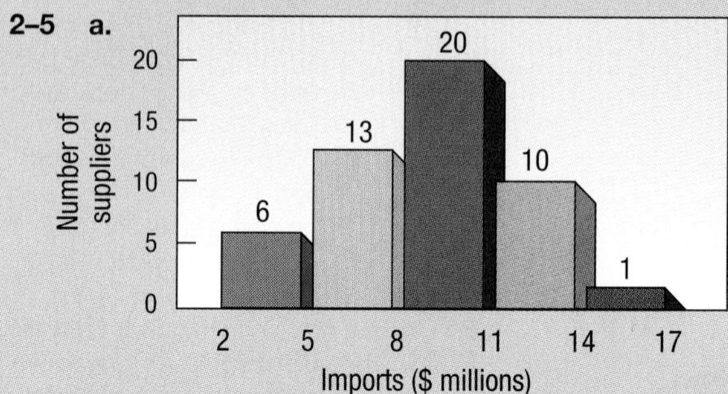

b.

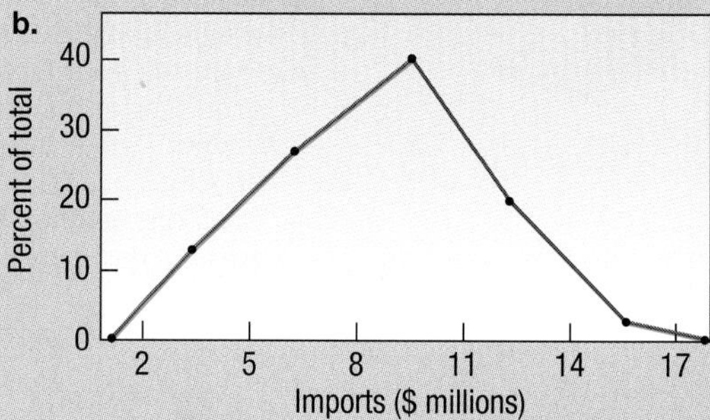

c. The smallest annual sales volume of imports by a supplier is about $2 million, the highest about $17 million. The concentration is between $8 million and $11 million.

2–6 **a.** A frequency distribution.

b.

Hourly Wages	Cumulative Number
Less than $6	0
Less than $8	3
Less than $10	10
Less than $12	14
Less than $14	15

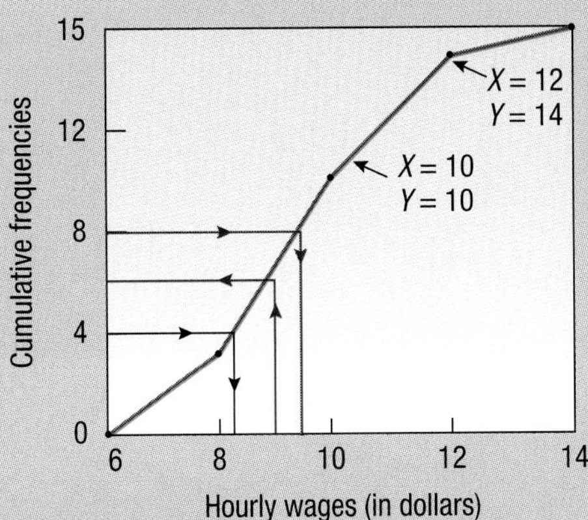

c. About 7 employees earn \$9.00 or less. About half the employees earn \$9.25 or more. About 4 employees earn \$8.25 or less.

2–7

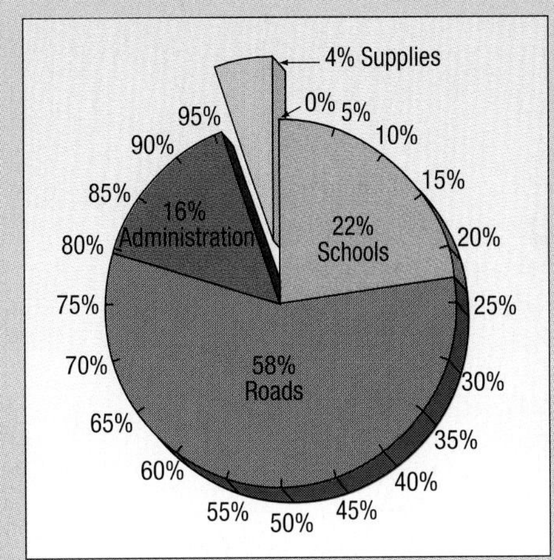

3

Describing Data:

Measures of Central Tendency

GOALS

When you have completed this chapter, you will be able to:

1. **Calculate the *arithmetic mean, weighted mean, median, mode,* and the *geometric mean.***

2. **Explain the characteristics, uses, advantages, and disadvantages of each measure.**

3. **Identify the positions of the arithmetic mean, median, and mode for both *symmetric* and *skewed* distributions.**

There are about 1.2 million enlisted men and women on active duty in the United States Armed Forces. What is the median age of enlisted personnel on active duty? (See Goal 1 and Exercise 36.)

Introduction

Chapter 2 began our study of descriptive statistics. In order to transform raw or ungrouped data into a meaningful form, we organized the data into a frequency distribution and portrayed it graphically in a histogram or a frequency polygon. We also described other tools for describing data, such as stem-and-leaf displays, line charts, bar charts, and pie charts.

In this chapter we continue to develop methods to describe data by finding a typical single value to describe a set of data. We refer to this single value as a **measure of central tendency.**

Statistics in Action

Did you ever meet the "average" American man? Well, his name is Robert (that is the nominal level of measurement), he is 31 years old (that is the ratio level), he is 69.5 inches tall (again the ratio level of measurement), weighs 172 pounds, wears a size 9½ shoe, has a 34-inch waist, and wears a size 40 suit. In addition, the average man eats 4 pounds of potato chips, watches 2,567 hours of TV, receives 598 pieces of mail, and eats 26 pounds of bananas each year. Also, he sleeps 7.7 hours per night. Is this really an "average" man or would it be better to refer to him as a "typical" man? Would you expect to find a man with all these characteristics?

> **MEASURE OF CENTRAL TENDENCY** A single value that summarizes a set of data. It locates the center of the values.

You are familiar with the concept of an average. The sports world is full of them. During the 2000 National Football League season, Torry Holt, of the St. Louis Rams, averaged 19.9 yards per reception. Alan Iverson, of the Philadelphia 76ers, led the NBA in scoring during the 2000–2001 season with an average of 31.4 points per game. Some other averages include:

- The average cost to drive a mile in Los Angeles is 55.8 cents, in Boston it is 49.8 cents, and it is 49.0 cents in Philadelphia. This includes the cost of insurance, depreciation, license, fees, fuel, oil, tires, and maintenance.
- Each person receives an average of 598 pieces of mail per year.
- Hertz Corporation reports that the average annual maintenance expense is $269 for a new car and $565 for a car more than one year old.
- The average U.S. home changes ownership every 11.8 years. The fastest turnarounds are in Arizona, where the average for the state is 6.2 years. For other selected states the averages are: Nevada 6.5 years, North Carolina 7.4 years, Utah 8.4 years, and Tennessee 8.8 years.

There is not just one measure of central tendency; in fact, there are many. We will consider five: the arithmetic mean, the weighted mean, the median, the mode, and the geometric mean. We will begin by discussing the most widely used and widely reported measure of central tendency, the arithmetic mean.

The Population Mean

Many studies involve all the values in a population. If we report that the mean ACT score of all students entering the University of Toledo in the Fall of 2000 is 19.6, this is an example of a population mean because we have a score for *all* students who entered in the fall of 2000. There are 12 sales associates employed at the Reynolds Road outlet of Carpets by Otto. The mean amount of commission they earned last month was $1,345. We consider this a population value because we considered *all* the sales associates. Other examples of a population mean would be: the mean closing price for Johnson and Johnson stock for the last five days is $98.75; the mean annual rate of return for the last 10 years for Berger Funds is 8.67 percent; and the mean number of hours of overtime worked last week by the six welders in the welding department of the Struthers Wells Corp. is 6.45 hours.

For raw data, that is, data that has not been grouped in a frequency distribution or a stem-and-leaf display, the population mean is the sum of all the values in the population divided by the number of values in the population. To find the population mean, we use the following formula.

$$\text{Population mean} = \frac{\text{Sum of all the values in the population}}{\text{Number of values in the population}}$$

Instead of writing out in words the full directions for computing the population mean (or any other measure), it is more convenient to use the shorthand symbols of mathematics. The mean of a population using mathematical symbols is:

POPULATION MEAN $$\mu = \frac{\Sigma X}{N}$$ **[3–1]**

where:

- μ represents the population mean. It is the Greek lowercase letter "mu."
- N is the number of items in the population.
- X represents any particular value.
- Σ is the Greek capital letter "sigma" and indicates the operation of adding.
- ΣX is the sum of the X values.

Any measurable characteristic of a population is called a **parameter.** The mean of a population is a parameter.

PARAMETER A characteristic of a population.

EXAMPLE

There are 12 automobile companies in the United States. Listed below is the number of patents granted by the United States government to each company last year.

Company	Number of Patents Granted	Company	Number of Patents Granted
General Motors	511	Mazda	210
Nissan	385	Chrysler	97
DaimlerChrysler	275	Porsche	50
Toyota	257	Mitsubishi	36
Honda	249	Volvo	23
Ford	234	BMW	13

Is this information a sample or a population? What is the arithmetic mean number of patents granted?

SOLUTION

This is a population because we are considering all the automobile companies obtaining patents. We add the number of patents for each of the 12 companies. The total number of patents for the 12 companies is 2,340. To find the arithmetic mean, we divide this total by 12. So the arithmetic mean is 195, found by 2340/12. Using formula (3–1):

$$\mu = \frac{511 + 385 + \cdots + 13}{12} = \frac{2340}{12} = 195$$

How do we interpret the value of 195? The typical number of patents received by an automobile company is 195. Because we considered all the companies receiving patents, this value is a population parameter.

The Sample Mean

As explained in Chapter 1, frequently we select a sample from the population in order to find something about a specific characteristic of the population. The quality assurance department, for example, needs to be assured that the ball bearings being produced have an acceptable outside diameter. It would be very expensive and time consuming to check the outside diameter of all the bearings being produced. Therefore, a sample of five bearings might be selected and the mean outside diameter of the five bearings calculated in order to estimate the mean diameter of all the bearings produced.

For raw data, that is, ungrouped data, *the mean is the sum of all the values divided by the total number of values.* To find the mean for a sample:

Mean of ungrouped sample data.

$$\text{Sample mean} = \frac{\text{Sum of all the values in the sample}}{\text{Number of all the values in the sample}}$$

The mean of a sample and the mean of a population are computed in the same way, but the shorthand notation used is different. The formula for the mean of a *sample* is:

SAMPLE MEAN $$\overline{X} = \frac{\Sigma X}{n}$$ **[3–2]**

where $\overline{X}$ stands for the sample mean. It is read "X bar." The lower case n is the number in the sample.

The mean of a sample, or any other measure based on sample data, is called a **statistic**. If the mean outside diameter of a sample of ball bearings is 0.625 inches, this is an example of a statistic.

STATISTIC A characteristic of a sample.

EXAMPLE

The Merrill Lynch Global Fund specializes in long-term obligations of foreign countries. We are interested in the interest rate on these obligations. A random sample of six bonds revealed the following.

Issue	Interest Rate
Australian government bonds	9.50%
Belgian government bonds	7.25
Canadian government bonds	6.50
French government "B-TAN"	4.75
Buoni Poliennali de Tesora (Italian government bonds)	12.00
Bonos del Estado (Spanish government bonds)	8.30

What is the arithmetic mean interest rate on this sample of long-term obligations?

SOLUTION

Using formula (3–2), the sample mean is:

$$\text{Sample mean} = \frac{\text{Sum of all the values in the sample}}{\text{Number of all the values in the sample}}$$

$$\overline{X} = \frac{\Sigma X}{n} = \frac{9.50\% + 7.25\% + \cdots + 8.30\%}{6} = \frac{48.3\%}{6} = 8.05\%$$

The arithmetic mean interest rate of the sample of long-term obligations is 8.05 percent.

The Properties of the Arithmetic Mean

The arithmetic mean is a widely used measure of central tendency. It has several important properties:

1. Every set of interval-level data has a mean. (Recall from Chapter 1 that interval-level data include such data as ages, incomes, and weights, with the distance between numbers being constant.)
2. All the values are included in computing the mean.
3. A set of data has only one mean. The mean is unique. (Later in the chapter we will discover an average that might appear twice, or more than twice, in a set of data.)
4. The mean is a useful measure for comparing two or more populations. It can, for example, be used to compare the performance of the production employees on the first shift at the Chrysler transmission plant with the performance of those on the second shift.
5. The arithmetic mean is the only measure of central tendency where *the sum of the deviations of each value from the mean will always be zero.* Expressed symbolically:

$$\Sigma(X - \overline{X}) = 0$$

As an example, the mean of 3, 8, and 4 is 5. Then:

$$\begin{aligned}\Sigma(X - \overline{X}) &= (3 - 5) + (8 - 5) + (4 - 5)\\ &= -2 + 3 - 1\\ &= 0\end{aligned}$$

Mean as a balance point

Thus, we can consider the mean as a balance point for a set of data. To illustrate, suppose we had a long board with the numbers 1, 2, 3, . . . , *n* evenly spaced on it. Suppose three bars of equal weight were placed on the board at numbers 3, 4, and 8, and the balance point was set at 5, the mean of the three numbers. We would find that the board balanced perfectly! The deviations below the mean (−3) are equal to the deviations above the mean (+3). Shown schematically:

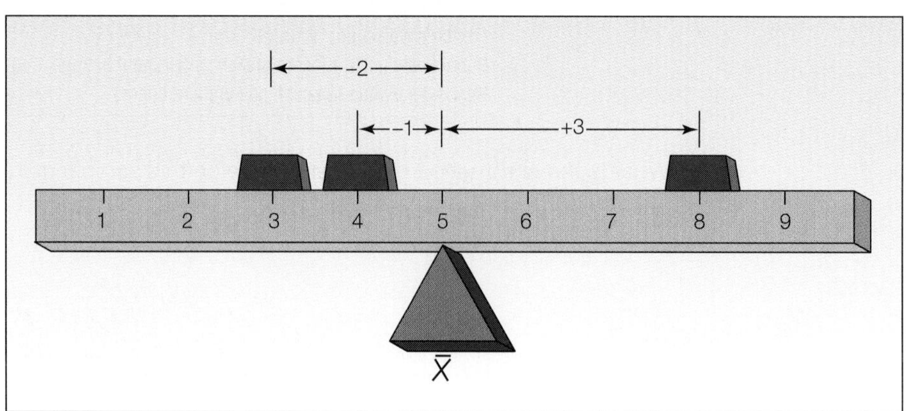

Mean unduly affected by unusually large or small values

The mean does have several disadvantages, however. Recall that the mean uses the value of every item in a sample, or population, in its computation. If one or two of these values are either extremely large or extremely small, the mean might not be an appropriate average to represent the data. For example, suppose the annual incomes of a small group of stockbrokers at Merrill Lynch are $62,900, $61,600, $62,500, $60,800, and $1.2 million. The mean income is $289,560. Obviously, it is not representative of this group, because all but one broker has an income in the $60,000 to $63,000 range. One income ($1.2 million) is unduly affecting the mean.

Cannot determine mean for open-ended data

The mean is also inappropriate if there is an *open-ended class* for data tallied into a frequency distribution. If a frequency distribution has the open-ended class "$100,000 and more," and there are 10 persons in that class, we really do not know whether their incomes are close to $100,000, $500,000, or $16 million. Since we lack information about their incomes, the arithmetic mean income for this distribution cannot be determined.

Self-Review 3–1

1. The annual incomes of a sample of several middle-management employees at Westinghouse are: $62,900, $69,100, $58,300, and $76,800.
   (a) Give the formula for the sample mean.
   (b) Find the sample mean.
   (c) Is the mean you computed in (b) a statistic or a parameter? Why?
   (d) What is your best estimate of the population mean?
2. All the students in advanced Computer Science 411 are considered the population. Their course grades are 92, 96, 61, 86, 79, and 84.
   (a) Give the formula for the population mean.
   (b) Compute the mean course grade.
   (c) Is the mean you computed in (b) a statistic or a parameter? Why?

Exercises

The answers to the odd-numbered exercises are at the end of the book.

1. Compute the mean of the following population values: 6, 3, 5, 7, 6.
2. Compute the mean of the following population values: 7, 5, 7, 3, 7, 4.
3. **a.** Compute the mean of the following sample values: 5, 9, 4, 10.
   b. Show that $\Sigma(X - \overline{X}) = 0$.
4. **a.** Compute the mean of the following sample values: 1.3, 7.0, 3.6, 4.1, 5.0.
   b. Show that $\Sigma(X - \overline{X}) = 0$.
5. Compute the mean of the following sample values: 16.25, 12.91, 14.58.
6. Compute the mean hourly wage paid to carpenters who earned the following wages: $15.40, $20.10, $18.75, $22.76, $30.67, $18.00.

2. 5.5
4. **a.** 4.2 **b.** $-3.6 + 3.6 = 0$
6. $20.95

For questions 7–10, (a) compute the arithmetic mean and (b) indicate whether it is a statistic or a parameter.

7. There are 10 salespeople employed by Midtown Ford. The numbers of new cars sold last month by the respective salespeople were: 15, 23, 4, 19, 18, 10, 10, 8, 28, 19.
8. The accounting department at a mail-order company counted the following numbers of incoming calls per day to the company's toll-free number during the first seven days in May 2001: 14, 24, 19, 31, 36, 26, 17.
9. The Cambridge Power and Light Company selected 20 residential customers at random. Following are the amounts to the nearest dollar, the customers were charged for electrical service last month:

8. **a.** 23.9 **b.** Parameter.

54	48	58	50	25	47	75	46	60	70
67	68	39	35	56	66	33	62	65	67

10. a. 10.73
b. Statistic.

10. The personnel director of Mercy Hospital began a study of the overtime hours of the registered nurses. Fifteen RNs were selected at random, and these overtime hours during June were noted:

13	13	12	15	7	15	5	12
6	7	12	10	9	13	12	

The Weighted Mean

The weighted mean is a special case of the arithmetic mean. It occurs when there are several observations of the same value which might occur if the data have been grouped into a frequency distribution. To explain, suppose the nearby Wendy's Restaurant sold medium, large, and Biggie-sized soft drinks for \$.90, \$1.25, and \$1.50, respectively. Of the last ten drinks sold, 3 were medium, 4 were large, and 3 were Biggie-sized. To find the mean amount of the last ten drinks sold, we could use formula (3–2).

$$\overline{X} = \frac{\$.90 + \$.90 + \$.90 + \$1.25 + \$1.25 + \$1.25 + \$1.25 + \$1.50 + \$1.50 + \$1.50}{10}$$

$$= \frac{\$12.20}{10} = \$1.22$$

The mean selling price of the last ten drinks is \$1.22.

An easier way to find the mean selling price is to determine the weighted mean. That is, we multiply each observation by the number of times it happens. We will refer to the weighted mean as $\overline{X}_w$. This is read "X bar sub w."

$$\overline{X}_w = \frac{3(\$0.90) + 4(\$1.25) + 3(\$1.50)}{10} = \frac{\$12.20}{10} = \$1.22$$

In general the weighted mean of a set of numbers designated $X_1, X_2, X_3, \ldots, X_n$ with the corresponding weights $w_1, w_2, w_3, \ldots, w_n$ is computed by:

WEIGHTED MEAN
$$\overline{X}_w = \frac{w_1X_1 + w_2X_2 + w_3X_3 + \cdots + w_nX_n}{w_1 + w_2 + w_3 + \cdots + w_n} \qquad \textbf{[3–3]}$$

This may be shortened to:

$$\overline{X}_w = \frac{\Sigma(wX)}{\Sigma w}$$

EXAMPLE

The Carter Construction Company pays its hourly employees \$6.50, \$7.50, or \$8.50 per hour. There are 26 hourly employees, 14 are paid at the \$6.50 rate, 10 at the \$7.50 rate, and 2 at the \$8.50 rate. What is the mean hourly rate paid the 26 employees?

SOLUTION

To find the mean hourly rate, we multiply each of the hourly rates by the number of employees earning that rate. Using formula (3–3), the mean hourly rate is

$$\overline{X}_w = \frac{14(\$6.50) + 10(\$7.50) + 2(\$8.50)}{14 + 10 + 2} = \frac{\$183.00}{26} = \$7.038$$

The weighted mean hourly wage is rounded to \$7.04.

Self-Review 3–2

Springers sold 95 Antonelli men's suits for the regular price of $400. For the spring sale the suits were reduced to $200 and 126 were sold. At the final clearance, the price was reduced to $100 and the remaining 79 suits were sold.

(a) What was the weighted mean price of an Antonelli suit?
(b) Springers paid $200 a suit for the 300 suits. Comment on the store's profit per suit if a salesperson receives a $25 commission for each one sold.

Exercises

11. In June an investor purchased 300 shares of Oracle stock at $20 per share. In August she purchased an additional 400 shares at $25 per share. In November she purchased an additional 400 shares, but the stock declined to $23 per share. What is the weighted mean price per share?

12. $1.50

12. A specialty bookstore concentrates mainly on used books. Paperbacks are $1.00 each, and hardcover books are $3.50. Of the 50 books sold last Tuesday morning, 40 were paperback and the rest were hardcover. What was the weighted mean price of a book?

13. Metropolitan Hospital employs 200 persons on the nursing staff. Fifty are nurse's aides, 50 are practical nurses, and 100 are registered nurses. Nurse's aides receive $8 an hour, practical nurses $10 an hour, and registered nurses $14 an hour. What is the weighted mean hourly wage?

14. $143.75

14. Andrews and Associates specialize in corporate law. They charge $100 an hour for researching a case, $75 an hour for consultations, and $200 an hour for writing a brief. Last week one of the associates spent 10 hours consulting with her client, 10 hours researching the case, and 20 hours writing the brief. What was the weighted mean hourly charge for her legal services?

The Median

It has been pointed out that for data containing one or two very large or very small values, the arithmetic mean may not be representative. The center point for such data can be better described using a measure of central tendency called the **median.**

To illustrate the need for a measure of central tendency other than the arithmetic mean, suppose you are seeking to buy a condominium in Palm Aire. Your real estate agent says that the average price of the units currently available is $110,000. Would you still want to look? If you had budgeted your maximum purchase price between $60,000 and $75,000, you might think they are out of your price range. However, checking the individual prices of the units might change your mind. They are $60,000, $65,000, $70,000, $80,000, and a superdeluxe penthouse costs $275,000. The arithmetic mean price is $110,000, as the real estate agent reported, but one price ($275,000) is pulling the arithmetic mean upward, causing it to be an unrepresentative average. It does seem that a price between $65,000 and $75,000 is a more typical or representative average, and it is. In cases such as this, the median provides a more accurate measure of central tendency.

> **MEDIAN** The midpoint of the values after they have been ordered from the smallest to the largest, or the largest to the smallest. Fifty percent of the observations are above the median and 50 percent below the median. The data must be at least ordinal level of measurement.

The median price of the units available is \$70,000. To determine this, we ordered the prices from low (\$60,000) to high (\$275,000) and selected the middle value (\$70,000).

Prices Ordered from Low to High		Prices Ordered from High to Low
\$ 60,000		\$275,000
65,000		80,000
70,000	← Median →	70,000
80,000		65,000
275,000		60,000

Median unaffected by extreme values

Note that there are the same number of prices below the median of \$70,000 as above it. The median is, therefore, unaffected by extremely low or high observations. Had the highest price been \$90,000, or \$300,000, or even \$1 million, the median price would still be \$70,000. Likewise, had the lowest price been \$20,000 or \$50,000, the median price would still be \$70,000.

In the previous illustration there is an *odd* number of observations (five). How is the median determined for an *even* number of observations? As before, the observations are ordered. Then the usual practice is to find the arithmetic mean of the two middle observations. Note that for an even number of observations, the median may not be one of the given values.

EXAMPLE

The five-year annualized total returns of the six top-performing stock mutual funds with emphasis on aggressive growth are listed below. What is the median annualized return?

Name of Fund	Annualized Total Return
PBHG Growth	28.5%
Dean Witter Developing Growth	17.2
AIM Aggressive Growth	25.4
Twentieth Century Giftrust	28.6
Robertson Stevens Emerging Growth	22.6
Seligman Frontier A	21.0

SOLUTION

Note that the number of returns is *even* (6). As before, the returns are first ordered from low to high. Then the two middle returns are identified. The arithmetic mean of the two middle observations gives us the median return. Arranging from low to high:

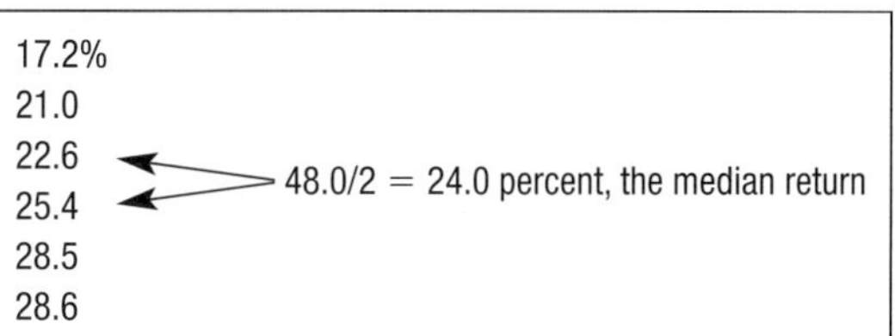

Notice that the median is not one of the values. Also, half of the returns are below the median and half are above it.

The major properties of the median are:

1. The median is unique; that is, like the mean, there is only one median for a set of data.
2. It is not affected by extremely large or small values and is therefore a valuable measure of central tendency when such values do occur.
3. It can be computed for a frequency distribution with an open-ended class if the median does not lie in an open-ended class. (We will show the computations for the median of data grouped in a frequency distribution shortly.)
4. It can be computed for ratio-level, interval-level, and ordinal-level data. (Recall from Chapter 1 that ordinal-level data can be ranked from low to high — such as the responses "excellent," "very good," "good," "fair," and "poor" to a question on a marketing survey.) To use a simple illustration, suppose five people rated a new fudge bar. One person thought it was excellent, one rated it very good, one called it good, one rated it fair, and one considered it poor. The median response is "good." Half of the responses are above "good"; the other half are below it.

Median can be determined for all levels of data except nominal

The Mode

The **mode** is another measure of central tendency.

> **MODE** The value of the observation that appears most frequently.

The mode is especially useful in describing nominal and ordinal levels of measurement. As an example of its use for nominal-level data, a company has developed five bath oils. Chart 3–1 shows the results of a marketing survey designed to find which bath oil consumers prefer. The largest number of respondents favored Lamoure, as evidenced by the highest bar. Thus, Lamoure is the mode.

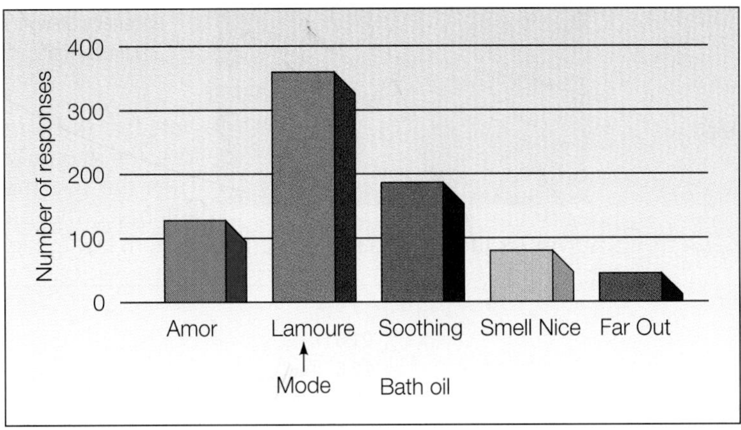

CHART 3–1 Number of Respondents Favoring Various Bath Oils

EXAMPLE

The annual salaries of quality-control managers in selected states are shown below. What is the modal annual salary?

State	Salary	State	Salary	State	Salary
Arizona	$35,000	Illinois	$58,000	Ohio	$50,000
California	49,100	Louisiana	60,000	Tennessee	60,000
Colorado	60,000	Maryland	60,000	Texas	71,400
Florida	60,000	Massachusetts	40,000	West Virginia	60,000
Idaho	40,000	New Jersey	65,000	Wyoming	55,000

SOLUTION

A perusal of the salaries reveals that the annual salary of $60,000 appears more often (six times) than any other salary. The mode is, therefore, $60,000.

In summary, we can determine the mode for all levels of data—nominal, ordinal, interval, and ratio. The mode also has the advantage of not being affected by extremely high or low values. Like the median, it can be used as a measure of central tendency for distributions with open-ended classes.

Disadvantages of the mode

The mode does have a number of disadvantages, however, that cause it to be used less frequently than the mean or median. For many sets of data, there is no mode because no value appears more than once. For example, there is no mode for this set of price data: \$19, \$21, \$23, \$20, and \$18. Since every value is different, however, it could be argued that every value is the mode. Conversely, for some data sets there is more than one mode. Suppose the ages of a group are 22, 26, 27, 27, 31, 35, and 35. Both the ages 27 and 35 are modes. Thus, this grouping of ages is referred to as *bimodal* (having two modes). One would question the use of two modes to represent the central tendency of this set of age data.

Self-Review 3–3

1. A sample of single persons in Towson, Texas, receiving Social Security payments revealed these monthly benefits: \$426, \$299, \$290, \$687, \$480, \$439, and \$565.
   (a) What is the median monthly benefit?
   (b) How many observations are below the median? Above it?
2. The numbers of work stoppages in the automobile industry for selected months are 6, 0, 10, 14, 8, and 0.
   (a) What is the median number of stoppages?
   (b) How many observations are below the median? Above it?
   (c) What is the modal number of work stoppages?

Exercises

15. What would you report as the modal value for a set of observations if there were a total of:
a. 10 observations and no two values were the same?
b. 6 observations and they were all the same?
c. 6 observations and the values were 1, 2, 3, 3, 4, and 4?

For exercises 16–19, (a) determine the median and (b) the mode.

16. Median = 33. Mode = 15

16. The following is the number of oil changes for the last seven days at the Jiffy Lube located at the corner of Elm Street and Pennsylvania Ave.

41	15	39	54	31	15	33

17. The following is the percent change in net income from 2000 to 2001 for a sample of 12 construction companies in Denver.

5	1	−10	−6	5	12	7	8	2	5	−1	11

18. Median = 10.5. Mode = 8.

18. The following are the ages of the 10 people in the video arcade at the Southwyck Shopping Mall at 10 A.M. this morning.

12	8	17	6	11	14	8	17	10	8

19. Listed below are several indicators of long-term economic growth in the United States. The projections are through the year 2005.

Economic Indicator	Percent Change	Economic Indicator	Percent Change
Inflation	4.5	Real GNP	2.9
Exports	4.7	Investment (residential)	3.6
Imports	2.3	Investment (nonresidential)	2.1
Real disposable income	2.9	Productivity (total)	1.4
Consumption	2.7	Productivity (manufacturing)	5.2

a. What is the median percent change?
b. What is the modal percent change?

20. Median = 9.2. Modes are 8.2, 8.5, and 10.3.

20. Listed below are the total automobile sales (in millions) in the United States for the last 14 years. During this period, what was the median number of automobiles sold? What is the mode?

9.0	8.5	8.0	9.1	10.3	11.0	11.5	10.3	10.5	9.8	9.3	8.2	8.2	8.5

Computer Solution

We can use a computer software package to find many measures of central tendency.

EXAMPLE

Table 2–1 on page 23 shows the prices of the 80 vehicles sold last month at Whitner Pontiac. Determine the mean and the median selling price.

SOLUTION

The mean and the median selling prices are reported in the following Excel output. (Remember: The instructions to create the output appear in the **Computer Commands** section at the end of the chapter.) There are 80 vehicles in the study, so the calculations with a calculator would be tedious and prone to error.

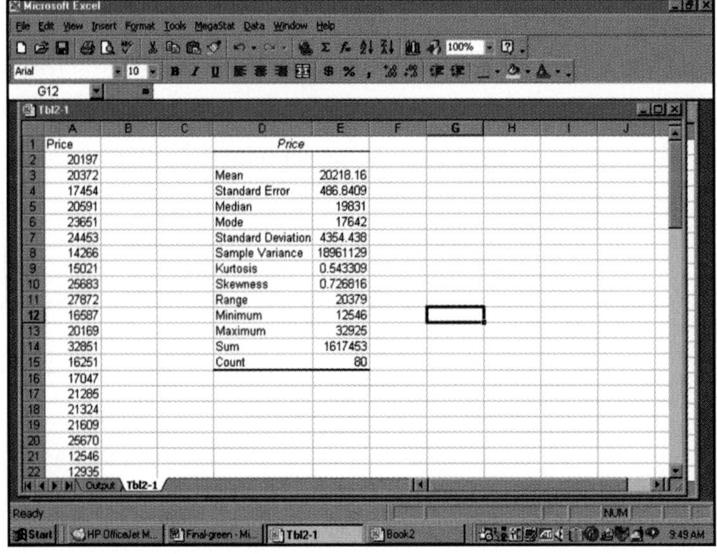

The mean selling price is \$20,218 and the median is \$19,831. These two values are less than \$400 apart. So either value is reasonable. We can also see from the Excel output that there were 80 vehicles sold and their total price is \$1,617,453.

What can we conclude? The typical vehicle sold for about \$20,000. Mr. Whitner might use this value in his revenue projections. For example, if the dealership could increase the number sold in a month from 80 to 90, this would result in an additional \$200,000 of revenue, found by 10 × \$20,000.

The Geometric Mean

The geometric mean is never greater than the arithmetic mean.

The geometric mean is useful in finding the average of percentages, ratios, indexes, or growth rates. It has a wide application in business and economics because we are often interested in finding the percentage changes in sales, salaries, or economic figures, such as the Gross National Product, which compound or build on each other. The geometric mean of a set of n positive numbers is defined as the nth root of the product of n values. The formula for the geometric mean is written:

GEOMETRIC MEAN

$$GM = \sqrt[n]{(X_1)(X_2)\cdots(X_n)} \qquad \textbf{[3–4]}$$

The geometric mean will always be less than or equal to (never more than) the arithmetic mean. Note also that all the data values must be positive to determine the geometric mean.

As a brief example of the interpretation of the geometric mean, suppose you receive a 5 percent increase in salary this year and a 15 percent increase next year. The average percent increase is 9.886, not 10.0. Why is this so? We begin by calculating the geometric mean. Recall, for example, that a 5 percent increase in salary is 105 or 1.05. We will write it as 1.05.

$$GM = \sqrt{(1.05)(1.15)} = 1.09886$$

This can be verified by assuming that your monthly earning was \$3,000 to start and you received two increases of 5 percent and 15 percent.

$$\text{Raise 1} = \$3{,}000\,(.05) = \$150.00$$
$$\text{Raise 2} = \$3{,}150\,(.15) = \underline{472.50}$$
$$\text{Total} \qquad \$622.50$$

Your total salary raise is \$622.50. This is equivalent to:

$$\$3{,}000.00\,(.09886) = \$296.58$$
$$\$3{,}296.58\,(.09886) = \underline{325.90}$$
$$\$622.48 \text{ is about } \$622.50$$

The following example shows the geometric mean of several percentages.

EXAMPLE

The profits earned by Atkins Construction Company on four recent projects were 3 percent, 2 percent, 4 percent, and 6 percent. What is the geometric mean profit?

SOLUTION

The geometric mean is 3.46 percent, found by

$$GM = \sqrt[n]{(X_1)(X_2)\cdots(X_n)} = \sqrt[4]{(3)(2)(4)(6)} = \sqrt[4]{144}$$

The geometric mean is the fourth root of 144 or 3.46.[1] The geometric mean profit is 3.46 percent.

The arithmetic mean profit is 3.75 percent, found by (3 + 2 + 4 + 6)/4. Although the profit of 6 percent is not extremely large, it draws the arithmetic mean upward. The geometric mean of 3.46 gives a more conservative profit figure because it is not being drawn by the large value. It will always, in fact, be less than or equal to the arithmetic mean.

A second application of the geometric mean is to find an average percent increase over a period of time. For example, if you earned $30,000 in 1990 and $50,000 in the year 2000, what is your annual rate of increase over the period? The rate of increase is determined from the following formula.

AVERAGE PERCENT INCREASE OVER TIME

$$GM = \sqrt[n]{\frac{\text{Value at end of period}}{\text{Value at beginning of period}}} - 1 \quad [3\text{–}5]$$

In the above box n is the number of periods. An example will show the details of finding the average annual percent increase.

EXAMPLE

The population of Haarlan, Alaska, in 1990 was 2 persons, by 2000 it was 22. What is the average annual rate of percentage increase during the period?

SOLUTION

There are 10 years between 1990 and 2000 so $n = 10$. The formula (3–5) for the geometric mean as applied to this type of problem is:

$$GM = \sqrt[n]{\frac{\text{Value at end of period}}{\text{Value at beginning of period}}} - 1$$

$$= \sqrt[10]{\frac{22}{2}} - 1 = 1.271 - 1 = 0.271$$

The final value is .271. So the annual rate of increase is 27.1 percent. This means that the rate of population growth in Haarlan is 27.1 percent per year.[2]

[1]Finding the nth root using a hand calculator is quite easy, but the details vary among calculator brands. Check the operating instructions of your particular calculator for the details. For a Texas Instruments TI-35X, first multiply 3(2)(4)(6), so that 144 appears. Next hit the 2nd, then $\sqrt[x]{y}$, then 4, and finally the "=" sign. The result is 3.464101615. We would round this value to 3.46.

[2]Again, the method of solution will depend on the calculator used. For the Texas Instruments TI-35X, the first step is to divide 22 by 2. The result is 11. Next hit 2nd, then $\sqrt[x]{y}$, then 10, and finally "=." The value is 1.270981615. We subtract 1.00 from this value, which leaves 0.270981615. We round this value to .271, or 27.1 percent.

Self-Review 3–4

1. The annual dividends, in percent, of four oil stocks are: 4.91, 5.75, 8.12, and 21.60.
   (a) Find the geometric mean dividend.
   (b) Find the arithmetic mean dividend.
   (c) Is the arithmetic mean equal to or greater than the geometric mean?
2. Production of Cablos trucks increased from 23,000 units in 1980 to 120,520 units in 2000. Find the geometric mean annual percent increase.

Exercises

21. Compute the geometric mean of the following values: 8, 12, 14, 26, and 5.

22. 5.413 **22.** Compute the geometric mean of the following values: 2, 8, 6, 4, 10, 6, 8, and 4.

23. Listed below is the percent increase in sales for the MG Corporation over the last 5 years. Determine the geometric mean increase in sales over the period.

9.4	13.8	11.7	11.9	14.7

24. 54.48 **24.** In 1998 revenue from gambling was \$651 million. In 2001 the revenue increased to \$2.4 billion. What is the geometric mean annual increase for the period?

25. In 1988 hospitals spent 3.9 billion on computer systems. In 2001 this amount increased to \$14.0 billion. What is the geometric mean annual increase for the period?

26. 19.56 **26.** In 1990 there were 9.19 million cable TV subscribers. By 2000 the number of subscribers increased to 54.87 million. What is the geometric mean annual increase for the period?

27. In 1996 there were 42.0 million pager subscribers. By 2001 the number of subscribers increased to 70.0 million. What is the geometric mean annual increase for the period?

28. 5.49, 5.70. About the same. **28.** The information below shows the cost for a year of college in public and private colleges in 1990 and 1998. What is the geometric mean annual increase for the period for the two types of colleges? Compare the rates of increase.

Type of College	1990	1998
Public	\$ 4,975	\$ 7,628
Private	12,284	19,143

The Mean, Median, and Mode of Grouped Data

Quite often data on incomes, ages, and so on are grouped and presented in the form of a frequency distribution. It is usually impossible to secure the original raw data. Thus, if we are interested in a typical value to represent the data, we must *estimate* it based on the frequency distribution.

The Arithmetic Mean

To approximate the arithmetic mean of data organized into a frequency distribution, we begin by assuming the observations in each class are represented by the *midpoint* of the class. The mean of a sample of data organized in a frequency distribution is computed by:

ARITHMETIC MEAN OF GROUPED DATA $$\overline{X} = \frac{\Sigma fX}{n}$$ **[3–6]**

where:

$\overline{X}$ is the designation for the arithmetic mean.
X is the midpoint of each class.
f is the frequency in each class.
fX is the frequency in each class times the midpoint of the class.
ΣfX is the sum of these products.
n is the total number of frequencies.

EXAMPLE

The computations for the arithmetic mean of data grouped into a frequency distribution will be shown based on the Whitner Pontiac data. Recall in Chapter 2, in Table 2–4 on page 26 we constructed a frequency distribution for the vehicle selling prices. The information is repeated below. Determine the arithmetic mean vehicle selling price.

Selling Price ($ thousands)	Frequency
12 up to 15	8
15 up to 18	23
18 up to 21	17
21 up to 24	18
24 up to 27	8
27 up to 30	4
30 up to 33	2
Total	80

SOLUTION

The mean vehicle selling price can be estimated from data grouped into a frequency distribution. To find the estimated mean, assume the midpoint of each class is representative of the data values in that class. Recall that the midpoint of a class is halfway between the upper and the lower class limits. To find the midpoint of a particular class, we add the upper and the lower class limits and divide by 2. Hence, the midpoint of the first class is \$13.5, found by (\$12 + \$15)/2. We assume that the value of \$13.5 is representative of the eight values in that class. To put it another way, we assume the sum of the eight values in this class is \$108, found by 8(\$13.5). We continue the process of multiplying the class midpoint by the class frequency for each class and then sum these products. The results are summarized in Table 3–1.

TABLE 3–1 Price of 80 New Vehicles Sold Last Month at Whitner Pontiac

Selling Price ($ thousands)	Frequency (f)	Midpoint (X)	fX
12 up to 15	8	$13.5	$ 108.0
15 up to 18	23	16.5	379.5
18 up to 21	17	19.5	331.5
21 up to 24	18	22.5	405.0
24 up to 27	8	25.5	204.0
27 up to 30	4	28.5	114.0
30 up to 33	2	31.5	63.0
Total	80		$1,605.0

Solving for the arithmetic mean using formula (3–6), we get:

$$\bar{X} = \frac{\Sigma fX}{n} = \frac{\$1,605}{80} = \$20.1 \text{ (thousands)}$$

So we conclude that the mean vehicle selling price is about $20,100.

The mean of data grouped into a frequency distribution may be different from that of raw data. The grouping results in some loss of information. In the vehicle selling price problem, the mean of the raw data, reported in the Excel output on page 76 is $20,218. This value is quite close to that estimated mean just computed. The difference is $118 or about 0.58 percent.

Self-Review 3–5

The net incomes of a sample of large importers of antiques were organized into the following table:

Net Income ($ millions)	Number of Importers
2 up to 6	1
6 up to 10	4
10 up to 14	10
14 up to 18	3
18 up to 22	2

(a) What is the table called?
(b) Based on the distribution, what is the estimate of the arithmetic mean net income?

Exercises

29. When we compute the mean of a frequency distribution, why do we refer to this as an *estimated* mean?

30. 12.67

30. Determine the estimated mean of the following frequency distribution.

Class	Frequency
0 up to 5	2
5 up to 10	7
10 up to 15	12
15 up to 20	6
20 up to 25	3

31. Determine the estimated mean of the following frequency distribution.

Class	Frequency
20 up to 30	7
30 up to 40	12
40 up to 50	21
50 up to 60	18
60 up to 70	12

32. $100.17

32. The selling prices of a sample of 60 antiques sold in Erie, Pennsylvania, last month were organized into the following frequency distribution. Estimate the mean selling price.

Selling Price ($ thousands)	Frequency
70 up to 80	3
80 up to 90	7
90 up to 100	18
100 up to 110	20
110 up to 120	12

33. FM radio station WLQR recently changed its format from easy listening to contemporary. A recent sample of 50 listeners revealed the following age distribution. Estimate the mean age of the listeners.

Age	Frequency
20 up to 30	1
30 up to 40	15
40 up to 50	22
50 up to 60	8
60 up to 70	4

34. 52

34. Advertising expenses are a significant component of the cost of goods sold. Listed below is a frequency distribution showing the advertising expenditures for 60 manufacturing companies located in the Southwest. Estimate the mean advertising expense.

Advertising Expenditure ($ millions)	Number of Companies
25 up to 35	5
35 up to 45	10
45 up to 55	21
55 up to 65	16
65 up to 75	8
Total	60

The Median

Median: Half the values are above it, half below

Recall that the median is defined as the value below which half of the values lie and above which the other half of the values lie. Since the raw data have been organized into a frequency distribution, some of the information is not identifiable. As a result we cannot determine the exact median. It can be estimated, however, by (1) locating the class in which the median lies and then (2) interpolating within that class to arrive at the median. The rationale for this approach is that the members of the median class are assumed to be evenly spaced throughout the class. The formula is:

MEDIAN OF GROUPED DATA

$$\text{Median} = L + \frac{\frac{n}{2} - CF}{f}(i) \quad [3\text{–}7]$$

where:

- L is the lower limit of the class containing the median.
- n is the total number of frequencies.
- f is the frequency in the median class.
- CF is the cumulative number of frequencies in all the classes preceding the class containing the median.
- i is the width of the class in which the median lies.

First, we shall estimate the median by locating the class in which it falls and interpolating. Then the formula for the median will be applied to check our answer.

EXAMPLE

The data involving the selling prices of vehicles at Whitner Pontiac is again used to show the procedure for estimating the median (see Table 3–2). The cumulative frequencies in the right column will be used shortly. What is the median selling price for a new vehicle sold by Whitner Pontiac?

TABLE 3–2 Prices of 80 New Vehicles Sold Last Month at Whitner Pontiac

Price ($ thousands)	Number Sold (f)	Cumulative Frequency (CF)
12 up to 15	8	8
15 up to 18	23	31
18 up to 21	17	48
21 up to 24	18	66
24 up to 27	8	74
27 up to 30	4	78
30 up to 33	2	80
Total	80	

SOLUTION

To find the median selling price we need to locate the 40th observation (there are a total of 80) when the data are arranged from smallest to largest. Why the 40th? Recall that half the observations in a set of data are less than the median and half are more than the median. So if we thought of arranging all the vehicle selling prices from smallest to largest, the one in the middle, the 40th, would be the median. To be technically correct, and consistent with how we found the median for ungrouped data, we should use $(n + 1)/2$ instead of $n/2$. However, because the number of observations is usually large for data grouped into a frequency distribution, we usually ignore this small difference.

The class containing the selling price of the 40th vehicle is located by referring to the right-hand column of Table 3–2, which is the cumulative frequency. There were 31 vehicles that sold for less than $18,000 and 48 that sold for less than $21,000. Hence, the 40th vehicle must be in the range of $18,000 up to $21,000. We have, therefore, located the median selling price as somewhere between the limits of $18,000 and $21,000.

To locate the median more precisely, we need to interpolate in this class containing the median. Recall that there are 17 vehicles in the "$18,000 up to $21,000" class. Assume the selling prices are evenly distributed between the lower ($18,000) and the upper ($21,000) class limits. There are nine vehicle selling prices between the 31st and the 40th vehicle, found by 40 − 31. The median is, therefore, 9/17 of the distance between $18,000 and $21,000. See Chart 3–2. The class width is $3,000 and 9/17 of $3,000 is $1,588. We add $1,588 to the lower class limit of $18,000, so the estimated median vehicle selling price is $19,588.

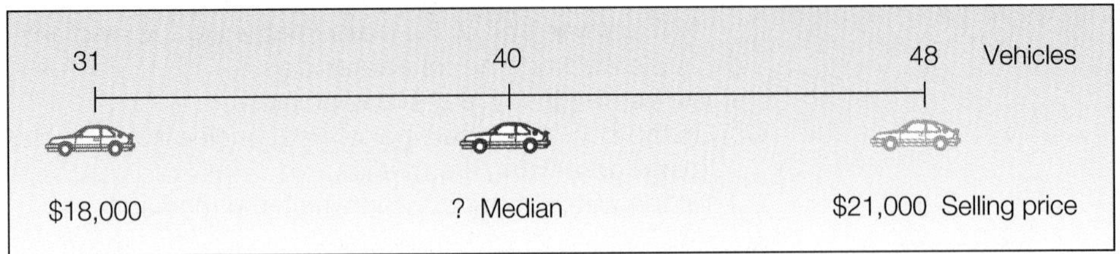

CHART 3–2 Location of the Median

We could also use formula 3–7 to determine the median of data grouped into a frequency distribution, where L is the lower limit of the class containing the median, which is $18,000. There are 80 vehicles sold, so $n = 80$. CF is the cumulative number of vehicles sold preceding the median class (31), f is the frequency of the number of observations in the median class (17), and i is the interval of the class containing the median ($3,000). Substituting these values:

$$\text{Median} = L + \frac{\frac{n}{2} - CF}{f}(i)$$

$$= \$18{,}000 + \frac{\frac{80}{2} - 31}{17}(\$3{,}000)$$

$$= \$18{,}000 + \$1{,}588 = \$19{,}588$$

The assumption underlying the approximation of the median, that the frequencies in the median class are evenly distributed between $18,000 and $21,000, may not be exactly correct. Therefore, it is safer to say that *about half* of the selling prices are less than $19,588 and about half are more. The median estimated from grouped data and the median determined from raw data are usually not exactly equal. In this case, the median computed from raw data using Excel is $19,831 and the median estimated from the frequency distribution is $19,588. The difference in the two estimates is $243 or about 1 percent.

Median can be determined for distributions having open ends.

A final note: The median is based only on the frequencies and the class limits of the median class. The open-ended classes that occur at the extremes are rarely needed. Therefore, the median of a frequency distribution having open ends can be determined. The arithmetic mean of a frequency distribution with an open-ended class cannot be accurately computed — unless, of course, the midpoints of the open-ended classes are estimated. Further, the median can be determined if *percentage frequencies* are given instead of the actual frequencies. This is because the median is the value with 50 percent of the distribution above it and 50 percent below it and does not depend on actual counts. The percents are considered substitutes for the actual frequencies. In a sense, they are actual frequencies whose total is 100.0.

The Mode

Class midpoint of the modal class is the estimated mode.

Recall that the mode is defined as the value that occurs most often. For data grouped into a frequency distribution, the mode can be approximated by the *midpoint of the class containing the largest number of class frequencies*. For Exercise 2 in Self-Review 3–6, the modal net sales are found by first locating the class containing the greatest number of percents. It is the $7 up to $10 million class because it has the largest percentage (40). The midpoint of that class ($8.5 million) is the estimated mode. This indicates that more stamping plants had net sales of $8.5 million than any other amount.

Two values may occur a large number of times. The distribution is then called *bimodal.* Suppose the ages of a sample of workers are 22, 27, 30, 30, 30, 30, 34, 58, 60, 60, 60, 60, and 65. The two modes are 30 years and 60 years. Often two points of concentration develop because the population being sampled is probably not homogeneous. In this illustration, the population might be composed of two distinct groups—one a group of relatively young employees who have been recently hired to meet the increased demand for a product, and the other a group of older employees who have been with the company a long time.

If the set of data has more than two modes, the distribution is referred to as being *multimodal.* In such cases we would probably not consider any of the modes as being representative of the central value of the data.

Self-Review 3–6

1. A sample of the daily production of transceivers at Scott Electronics was organized into the following distribution. Estimate the median daily production.

Daily Production	Frequency
80 up to 90	5
90 up to 100	9
100 up to 110	20
110 up to 120	8
120 up to 130	6
130 up to 140	2

2. The net sales of a sample of small stamping plants were organized into the following percentage frequency distribution. What is the estimated median net sales?

Net Sales ($ millions)	Percent of Total
1 up to 4	13
4 up to 7	14
7 up to 10	40
10 up to 13	23
13 and greater	10

Exercises

35. Refer to Exercise 30. Compute the median. What is the modal value?

36. 47.62; 45

36. Refer to Exercise 31. Compute the median. What is the modal value?

37. The chief accountant at Betts Machine, Inc. wants to prepare a report on the company's accounts receivable. Below is a frequency distribution showing the amounts outstanding.

Amount	Frequency
$ 0 up to $ 2,000	4
$ 2,000 up to $ 4,000	15
$ 4,000 up to $ 6,000	18
$ 6,000 up to $ 8,000	10
$ 8,000 up to $10,000	4
$10,000 up to $12,000	3

a. Determine the median amount.
b. What is the modal amount owed?

38. 25.53, 22.5

38. At the present time there are about 1.2 million enlisted men and women on active duty in the United States Army, Navy, Marines, and Air Force. Shown below is a percent breakdown by age. Determine the median age of enlisted personnel on active duty. What is the mode?

Age (years)	Percent
Up to 20	15
20 up to 25	33
25 up to 30	19
30 up to 35	17
35 up to 40	11
40 up to 45	4
45 or more	1

39. The following graphic appeared in *USA Today* and is available at the Website: http://www.usatoday.com/snapshot/news/snapmdex.htm. It reports the number of pages printed per day by office workers. Based on this information, what is the median number of pages printed per day per employee?

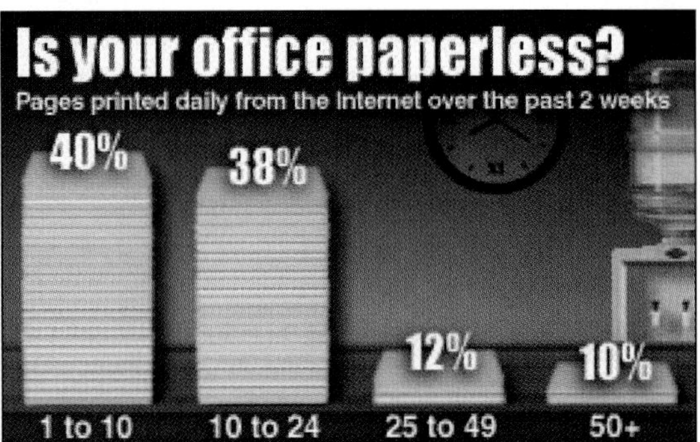

40. Church/ synagogue. Nominal.

40. The following graphic appeared in *USA Today* and is available at the Website: http://www.usatoday.com/snapshot/money/snapmdex.htm. What is the mode of this information? What level of measurement are the data? Tell why you cannot compute the mean or the median.

The Relative Positions of the Mean, Median, and Mode

For a symmetric, mound-shaped distribution, mean, median, and mode are equal.

Refer to the frequency polygon in Chart 3–3. It is a symmetric mound-shaped distribution, meaning it *has the same shape on either side of the center*. If the polygon were folded in half, the two halves would be identical. For a symmetric distribution, the mode, median, and mean are located at the center and are always equal. They are all 20 years in Chart 3–3.

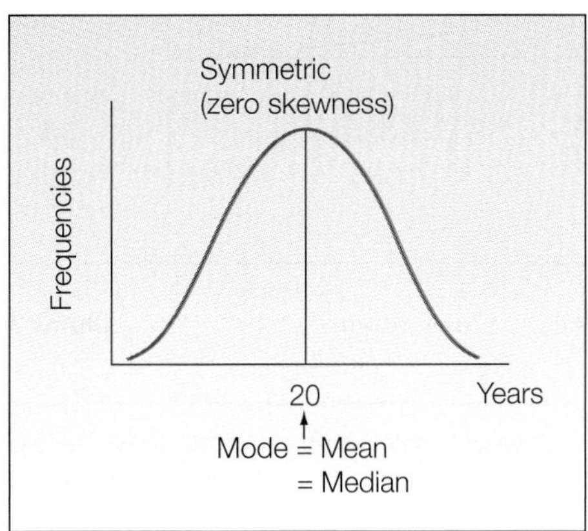

CHART 3–3 A Symmetric Distribution

The number of years corresponding to the highest point of the curve is the *mode* (20 years). Because the frequency curve is symmetrical, the *median* corresponds to the point where the distribution is cut in half (20 years). The total number of frequencies representing many years is offset by the total number representing few years, resulting in an *arithmetic mean* of 20 years. Logically, any of the three measures would be appropriate to represent this distribution.

A skewed distribution is not symmetrical.

If a set of data is nonsymmetrical, or **skewed,** the relationship among the three measures changes. In a **positively skewed distribution,** the arithmetic mean is the largest of the three measures. Why? Because the mean is influenced more than the median or mode by a few extremely high values. The median is generally the next largest measure in a positively skewed frequency distribution. The mode is the smallest of the three measures.

If the distribution is highly skewed, such as the weekly incomes in Chart 3–4, the mean would not be a good measure to use. The median and mode would be more representative.

Conversely, in a distribution that is **negatively skewed,** the mean is the lowest of the three measures. The mean is, of course, influenced by a few extremely low observations. The median is greater than the arithmetic mean, and the modal value is the largest of the three measures. Again, if the distribution is highly skewed, such as the distribution of tensile strengths shown in Chart 3–5, the mean should not be used to represent the data.

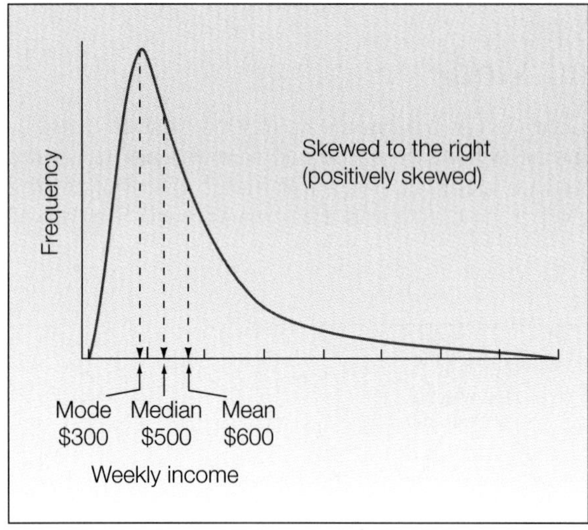

CHART 3–4 A Positively Skewed Distribution

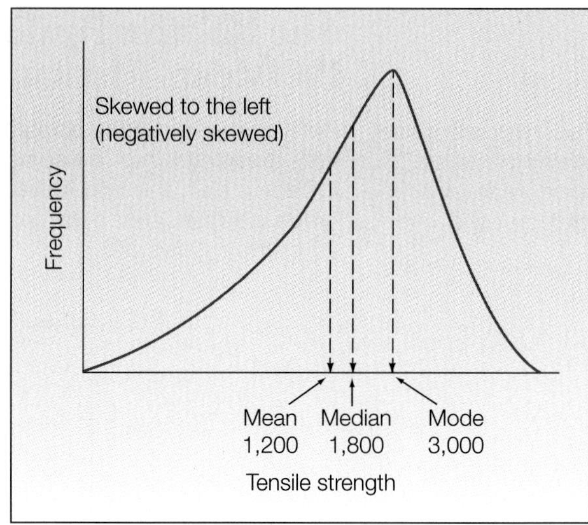

CHART 3–5 A Negatively Skewed Distribution

Self-Review 3–7

The weekly sales from a sample of Hi-Tec electronic supply stores were organized into a frequency distribution. The mean of weekly sales was computed to be $105,900, the median $105,000, and the mode $104,500.

(a) Sketch the sales in the form of a smoothed frequency polygon. Note the location of the mean, median, and mode on the X-axis.
(b) Is the distribution symmetrical, positively skewed, or negatively skewed? Explain.

Chapter Outline

I. A measure of location is a value used to describe the center of a set of data.
   A. The arithmetic mean is the most widely reported measure of location.
      1. It is calculated by adding the values of the observations and dividing by the total number of observations.
         a. The formula for a population mean of ungrouped or raw data is:

$$\mu = \frac{\Sigma X}{N} \qquad [3\text{–}1]$$

         b. The formula for the mean of a sample is

$$\overline{X} = \frac{\Sigma X}{n} \qquad [3\text{–}2]$$

         c. For data grouped into a frequency distribution, the formula is:

$$\overline{X} = \frac{\Sigma fX}{n} \qquad [3\text{–}6]$$

      2. The major characteristics of the arithmetic mean are:
         a. At least the interval scale of measurement is required.
         b. All the data values are used in the calculation.

Statistics in Action

Most colleges report the "average class size." This information can be misleading because average class size can be found several ways. If we find the number of students *in each class* at a particular university, the result is the mean number of students per class. If we compiled a list of the class sizes for each student and find the mean class size, we might find the mean to be quite different. One school found the mean number of students in each of their 747 classes to be 40. But when they found the mean from a list of the class sizes of each student it was 147. Why the disparity? Because there are few students in the small classes and a larger number of students in the larger class, which has the effect of increasing the mean class size when it is calculated this way. A school could reduce this mean class size for each student by reducing the number of students in each class. That is, cut out the large freshman lecture classes.

   c. A set of data has only one mean. That is, it is unique.
   d. The sum of the deviations from the mean equals 0.

B. The weighted mean is found by multiplying each observation by its corresponding weight.

   1. The formula for determining the weighted mean is:

$$\bar{X}_w = \frac{w_1X_1 + w_2X_2 + w_3X_3 + \cdots + w_nX_n}{w_1 + w_2 + w_3 + \cdots + w_n} \quad \textbf{[3–3]}$$

   2. It is a special case of the arithmetic mean.

C. The geometric mean is the nth root of the product of n values.

   1. The formula for the geometric mean is:

$$GM = \sqrt[n]{(X_1)(X_2)(X_3)\cdots(X_n)} \quad \textbf{[3–4]}$$

   2. The geometric mean is also used to find the rate of change from one period to another.

$$GM = \sqrt[n]{\frac{\text{Value at end of period}}{\text{Value at beginning of period}}} - 1 \quad \textbf{[3–5]}$$

   3. The geometric mean is always equal to or less than the arithmetic mean.

D. The median is the value in the middle of a set of ordered data.

   1. To find the median, sort the observations from smallest to largest and identify the middle value.
   2. The formula for estimating the median from grouped data is:

$$\text{Median} = L + \frac{\frac{n}{2} - CF}{f}(i) \quad \textbf{[3–7]}$$

   3. The major characteristics of the median are:
      a. At least the ordinal scale of measurement is required.
      b. It is not influenced by extreme values.
      c. Fifty percent of the observations are larger than the median.
      d. It is unique to a set of data.

E. The mode is the value that occurs most often in a set of data.

   1. The mode can be found for nominal level data.
   2. A set of data can have more than one mode.

Pronunciation Key

SYMBOL	MEANING	PRONUNCIATION
μ	Population mean	*mu*
Σ	Operation of adding	*sigma*
ΣX	Adding a group of values	*sigma X*
$\bar{X}$	Sample mean	*X bar*
$\bar{X}_w$	Weighted mean	*X bar sub w*
GM	Geometric mean	*G M*
ΣfX	Adding the product of the frequencies and the class midpoints	*sigma f X*

Chapter Exercises

41. The accounting firm of Crawford and Associates has five senior partners. Yesterday the senior partners saw six, four, three, seven, and five clients, respectively.

a. Compute the mean number and median number of clients seen by a partner.
b. Is the mean a sample mean or a population mean?
c. Verify that $\Sigma(X - \mu) = 0$.

42. a. $\bar{X} = 21.71$, median = 22.00.

42. Owens Orchards sells apples in a large bag by weight. A sample of seven bags contained the following numbers of apples: 23, 19, 26, 17, 21, 24, 22.
a. Compute the mean number and median number of apples in a bag.
b. Verify that $\Sigma(X - \bar{X}) = 0$.

43. A sample of households that subscribe to the United Bell Phone Company revealed the following numbers of calls received last week. Determine the mean and the median number of calls received.

52	43	30	38	30	42	12	46	39	37
34	46	32	18	41	5				

44. $\bar{X} = 70.53$.

44. The Citizens Banking Company is studying the number of times the ATM, located in a Loblaws Supermarket, is used per day. Following are the numbers of times the machine was used over each of the last 30 days. Determine the mean number of times the machine was used per day.

83	64	84	76	84	54	75	59	70	61
63	80	84	73	68	52	65	90	52	77
95	36	78	61	59	84	95	47	87	60

45. Listed below is the number of lampshades produced during the last 50 days at the American Lampshade Company in Rockville, GA. Compute the mean.

348	371	360	369	376	397	368	361	374
410	374	377	335	356	322	344	399	362
384	365	380	349	358	343	432	376	347
385	399	400	359	329	370	398	352	396
366	392	375	379	389	390	386	341	351
354	395	338	390	333				

46. 4.84, 4

46. Trudy Green works for the True-Green Lawn Company. Her job is to solicit lawn-care business via the telephone. Listed below are the number of appointments she made in each of the last 25 hours of calling. What is the arithmetic mean number of appointments she made per hour? What is the median number of appointments per hour? Write a brief report summarizing the findings.

9	5	2	6	5	6	4	4	7	2	3	6	3
4	4	7	8	4	4	5	5	4	8	3	3	

47. The Split-A-Rail Fence Company sells three types of fence to homeowners in suburban Seattle, Washington. Grade A costs \$5.00 per running foot to install, Grade B costs \$6.50 per running foot, and Grade C, the premium quality, costs \$8.00 per running foot. Yesterday, Split-A-Rail installed 270 feet of Grade A, 300 feet of Grade B, and 100 feet of Grade C. What was the mean cost per foot of fence installed?

48. 3.5

48. Rolland Poust is a sophomore in the College of Business at Scandia Tech. Last semester he took courses in statistics and accounting, 3 hours each, and earned an A in both. He earned a B in a five-hour history course and a B in a two-hour history of jazz course. In addition, he took a one-hour course dealing with the rules of basketball so he could get his

license to officiate high school basketball games. He got an A in this course. What was his GPA for the semester? Assume that he receives 4 points for an A, 3 for a B, and so on. What measure of central tendency did you just calculate?

49. The table below shows the percent of the labor force that is unemployed and the size of the labor force for three counties in Northwest Ohio. Jon Elsas is the Regional Director of Economic Development. He must present a report to several companies that are considering locating in Northwest Ohio. What would be an appropriate unemployment rate to show for the entire region?

County	Percent Unemployed	Size of Workforce
Wood	4.5	15,300
Ottawa	3.0	10,400
Lucas	10.2	150,600

50. $59.1

50. *Modern Healthcare* reported the average patient revenues (in $millions) for five types of hospitals. What is the median patient revenue?

Hospital Type	Patient Revenue (millions)
Catholic	$46.6
Other church	59.1
Nonprofit	71.7
Public	93.1
For profit	32.4

51. The *Bank Rate Monitor* reported the following savings rates. What is the median savings rate?

Instrument	Savings Rate (percent)	Instrument	Savings Rate (percent)
Money market mutual fund	3.01	1-year CD	3.51
Bank money market account	2.96	2.5-year CD	4.25
6-month CD	3.25	5-year CD	5.46

52. a. $1.438
b. $1.44
c. $1.49

52. The American Automobile Association checks the prices of gasoline before many holiday weekends. Listed below are the self-service prices for a sample of 15 retail outlets during the May 2000 Memorial Day weekend in the Detroit, Michigan, area.

1.44	1.42	1.35	1.39	1.49	1.49	1.41	1.46
1.41	1.49	1.45	1.48	1.39	1.46	1.44	

a. What is the arithmetic mean selling price?
b. What is the median selling price?
c. What is the modal selling price?

53. The following table shows major earthquakes by country between 1983 and 1995. Also reported is the size of the earthquake, as measured on the Richter Scale, and the number of deaths reported. Compute the mean and the median for both the size of the earthquake as measured on the Richter scale and the number of deaths. Which measure of central tendency would you report for each of the variables? Tell why.

Country	Richter	Deaths	Country	Richter	Deaths
Colombia	5.5	250	Iran	7.7	40,000
Japan	7.7	81	Philippines	7.7	1,621
Turkey	7.1	1,300	Pakistan	6.8	1,200
Chile	7.8	146	Turkey	6.2	4,000
Mexico	8.1	4,200	USA	7.5	1
Ecuador	7.3	4,000	Indonesia	7.5	2,000
India	6.5	1,000	India	6.4	9,748
China	7.3	1,000	Indonesia	7.0	215
Armenia	6.8	55,000	Colombia	6.8	1,000
USA	6.9	62	Algeria	6.0	164
Peru	6.3	114	Japan	7.2	5,477
Romania	6.5	8	Russia	7.6	2,000

54. .0094

54. The metropolitan area of Los Angeles–Long Beach, California, is the area expected to show the largest increase in the number of jobs between 1989 and 2010. The number of jobs is expected to increase from 5,164,900 to 6,286,800. What is the geometric mean expected yearly rate of increase?

55. Wells Fargo Mortgage and Equity Trust gave these occupancy rates in their annual report for various office income properties the company owns. What is the geometric mean occupancy rate?

Pleasant Hills, California	100%
Lakewood, Colorado	90
Riverside, California	80
Scottsdale, Arizona	20
San Antonio, Texas	62

56. .03

56. A recent article suggested that if you earn $25,000 a year today and the inflation rate continues at 3 percent per year, you'll need to make $33,598 in 10 years to have the same buying power. You would need to make $44,771 if the inflation rate jumped to 6 percent. Confirm that these statements are accurate by finding the geometric mean rate of increase.

57. Wells Fargo Mortgage and Equity Trust also reported these occupancy rates for some of its industrial income properties. What is the geometric mean occupancy rate?

Tucson, Arizona	81%
Irvine, California	100
Carlsbad, California	74
Dallas, Texas	80

58. $\overline{X} = 60.1$, GM = 55.209

58. The 12-month returns on five aggressive-growth mutual funds were 32.2 percent, 35.5 percent, 80.0 percent, 60.9 percent, and 92.1 percent. Determine the arithmetic mean and the geometric mean rates of return.

59. A major cost factor in the purchase of a home is the monthly loan payment. There are many Websites where prospective home buyers can shop the interest rates and determine their monthly payment. Capital Bank of Virginia is considering offering home loans on the Web. Before making a final decision, a sample of recent loans is selected and the monthly payment noted. The information is organized into the following frequency distribution.

Monthly Mortgage Payment	Number of Homeowners
\$ 100 up to \$ 500	1
500 up to 900	9
900 up to 1,300	11
1,300 up to 1,700	23
1,700 up to 2,100	11
2,100 up to 2,500	4
2,500 up to 2,900	1
Total	60

a. Determine the mean monthly payment.
b. Determine the median monthly payment.

60. The Department of Commerce, Bureau of the Census, reported the following information on the number of wage earners in more than 56 million American homes.

Number of Earners	Number (in thousands)
0	7,083
1	18,621
2	22,414
3	5,533
4 or more	2,797

60. a. 1.61
b. 2
c. open-ended class

a. What is the median number of wage earners per home?
b. What is the modal number of wage earners per home?
c. Explain why you cannot compute the mean number of wage earners per home.

61. ARS Services, Inc. employs 40 electricians, providing service to both residential and commercial accounts. ARS has been in business since the early 60s and has always advertised prompt and reliable service. Of concern in recent years is the number of days employees are absent. Below is a frequency distribution of the number of days missed by the 40 electricians last year.

Number of Days Missed	Number of Electricians
0 up to 3	17
3 up to 6	13
6 up to 9	7
9 up to 12	3
Total	40

a. Determine the mean number of days missed.
b. Determine the median number of days missed.

62. a. $\overline{X} = 10.71$.
b. 10.65

62. In recent years there has been intense competition for the long distance phone service of residential customers. In an effort to study the actual phone usage of residential customers, an independent consultant gathered the following data on the number of long distance phone calls per household for a sample of 70 households.

Number of Phone Calls	Frequency
3 up to 6	5
6 up to 9	19
9 up to 12	20
12 up to 15	20
15 up to 18	4
18 up to 21	2
Total	70

a. Determine the mean number of phone calls per household.
b. Determine the median number of phone calls per household.

63. A sample of 50 American cities with a population between 100,000 and 1,000,000 revealed the following frequency distribution for the cost per day for a double occupancy hospital room.

Cost of Hospital Room	Frequency
$100 up to $200	1
200 up to 300	9
300 up to 400	20
400 up to 500	15
500 up to 600	5
Total	50

a. Determine the mean cost per day.
b. Determine the median cost per day.

64. a. 161.2
b. 165.0
c. 170.0

64. A sample of 50 antique dealers in the southeast United States revealed the following sales last year:

Sales ($ thousands)	Number of Firms
100 up to 120	5
120 up to 140	7
140 up to 160	9
160 up to 180	16
180 up to 200	10
200 up to 220	3

a. Estimate the mean sales.
b. Estimate the median sales.
c. What is the modal sales amount?

65. Following are the mean hourly age for full-time and part-time registered nurses by size of the hospital, location of the hospital, and type of hospital.

	Full-time	Part-time
Number of beds:		
Under 100	$17.05	$17.10
100 up to 300	18.35	19.40
300 up to 500	18.50	20.15
500 or more	19.40	20.10
Location of hospital:		
Suburban	19.20	20.15
Urban	18.70	20.25
Rural	16.80	16.70
Type of hospital:		
Private, nonprofit	18.80	*
University	18.70	19.85
Community, nonprofit	18.50	19.10
Private, for profit	17.90	18.85
Public	17.45	*

*Insufficient data

Write a paragraph summarizing the results. Be sure to include information on the difference in the wages of full-time versus part-time nurses as well as among the categories of hospitals.

66. Answers will vary.

66. The information below profiles the typical home buyer in the United States for 1999 and 2000. Write a brief report summarizing the results. What changes do you note between 1999 and 2000? What are some of the differences between first-time buyers and repeat buyers?

	First-Time Buyers		Repeat Buyers	
	1999	2000	1999	2000
Mean cost of single-family home	$156,400	$147,400	$195,300	$212,700
Homes visited before buying	12.9	12.5	15.6	15.7
Mean monthly mortgage payment	$950	$945	$1,076	$1,114
Mean age	31.6	31.6	41.0	41.7

exercises.com

67. John Hardy is an investment advisor to several individuals in the Richmond, Virginia, area. He has been asked to compare the profitability of banks in the northeast to those in the southeast. The Yahoo Website allows him to do quick research on the entire industry. Go to http://www.yahoo.com, click on **Stock Quotes,** under **Research** select **By Industry,** select **Banks,** and again under **Banks** select the **Northeast Region.** Obtain the earnings per share for the most recent quarter for banks in the northeast. Compute the mean earnings per share for the region. Repeat the process for the southeast. That is, in the last step select **Southeast** as the region. Compute the mean earnings per share for banks in this region. Compare the two regions. Which region seems to be more profitable?

68. Answers will vary. See IM.

68. One of the most famous averages, the Dow Jones Industrial Average (DJIA), is not really an average. Following is a listing of the 30 stocks that make up the DJIA and their selling prices on July 11, 2000. Compute the mean of the 30 stocks. Compare this to the closing price on July 11, 2000 of 10,727.19. Then go to the Dow Jones Website and read about the history of this average and the stocks that are currently included in its calculation. To obtain this information go to: http://www.dowjones.com, in the bottom left corner click on **About Dow Jones,** click **on Dow Jones Industrial Average,** and finally click on **Stocks.** The output is below. Compute the mean of the 30 stocks included in the DJIA today and the DJIA with that of July 11, 2000. Has there been a change?

Company Name	Symbol	Price	Weighting %
Alcoa Inc.	(AA)	31.6875	1.677
American Express Co.	(AXP)	53.5625	2.835
AT & T Corp.	(T)	31.8750	1.687
Boeing Co.	(BA)	44.1250	2.335
Caterpillar Inc.	(CAT)	35.9375	1.902
Citigroup Inc.	(C)	65.8750	3.487
Coca-Cola Co.	(KO)	56.0000	2.964
DuPont Co.	(DD)	46.5625	2.464
Eastman Kodak Co.	(EK)	60.6250	3.209
Exxon Mobil Corp.	(XOM)	80.4375	4.258
General Electric Co.	(GE)	52.7500	2.792
General Motors Corp.	(GM)	62.0625	3.285
Home Depot Inc.	(HD)	57.1875	3.027
Honeywell International Inc.	(HON)	35.8125	1.895
Hewlett-Packard Co.	(HWP)	124.8125	6.607
International Business Machines Corp.	(IBM)	101.3750	5.366
Intel Corp.	(INTC)	138.8125	7.348
International Paper Co.	(IP)	34.8125	1.842
J.P. Morgan & Co.	(JPM)	117.9375	6.243
Johnson & Johnson	(JNJ)	99.6250	5.273
McDonald's Corp.	(MCD)	32.3750	1.713
Merck & Co.	(MRK)	74.3750	3.937
Microsoft Corp.	(MSFT)	78.8750	4.175
Minnesota Mining & Manufacturing Co.	(MMM)	88.4375	4.681
Philip Morris Cos.	(MO)	25.9375	1.373
Procter & Gamble Co.	(PG)	54.5625	2.888
SBC Communications Inc.	(SBC)	44.2500	2.342
United Technologies Corp.	(UTX)	59.3125	3.139
Wal-Mart Stores Inc.	(WMT)	61.8125	3.272
Walt Disney Co.	(DIS)	37.4375	1.981

Computer Data Exercises

69. Refer to the Real Estate data, which reports information on homes sold in the Venice, Florida, area during the last year.

a. Determine the mean and the median selling price of the homes. Does one measure of central tendency seem better, or more representative, than the other?

b. Determine the mean and the median number of bedrooms in a typical house. Does one measure of central tendency seem better, or more representative, than the other?

c. Determine the mean and the median number of bathrooms in a typical house. Does one measure of central tendency seem better, or more representative, than the other?

d. Determine the mean and the median distance from the center of the city. Does one measure of central tendency seem better, or more representative, than the other?

70. a. $\overline{X} = 56.67$, Median = 54.95
b. $\overline{X}$ = 2,419,737, Median = 2,581,633

70. Refer to the Baseball 2000 data, which reports information for the 30 Major League Baseball teams for the 2000 season.

a. Determine the mean and the median team salary. Does one measure of central tendency seem better, or more representative, than the other?

b. Determine the mean and the median attendance per team. Does one measure of central tendency seem better, or more representative, than the other?

c. $\overline{X} = 189.77$, Median = 181.0
d. Rate for players is 13.57%, CPI is 3.18%

c. Determine the mean and the median number of home runs per team. Does one measure of central tendency seem better, or more representative, than the other?
d. Determine the rate of increase in players' salaries from 1989 to 2000. As a basis of comparison, in 1988 the Consumer Price Index was 118.3, in 2000 it was 166.9. Compute the rate of inflation in the Consumer Price Index and compare it to the rate of increase in baseball players' salaries.

71. Refer to the OECD data, which reports information on census, economic, and business data for 29 selected countries.
   a. Compute the mean, median, and mode for the variable employment. Which measure of central tendency seems to be most representative of the data?
   b. Compute the mean, median, and mode of the percentage of the population over the age of 65. Which measure of central tendency is most representative of the data?

72. a. $\overline{X} = 33{,}181$, Median = 32,708
b. $\overline{X} = 2134$, Median = 1227
c. $\overline{X} = \$24{,}069$, Median = $23,690

72. Refer to the Schools data, which refers to the 94 school districts in Northwest Ohio.
   a. Determine the mean and the median teacher salary for this group of school districts. Does one measure of central tendency seem to be more representative than the others?
   b. Determine the mean and the median number of students for this group of school districts. Does one measure of central tendency seem to be more representative than the others?
   c. Determine the mean and the median income group of school districts. Does one measure of central tendency seem to be more representative than the others?

Computer Commands

The Excel Commands for the descriptive statistics on page 76 are:

1. From the CD retrieve the Whitner data file, which is called **Tbl2-1.**
2. From the menu bar select **Tools** and then **Data Analysis.** Select **Descriptive Statistics** and then click **OK.**
3. For the **Input Range,** type *A1:A81,* indicate that the data are grouped by column and that the labels are in the first row. Click on **Output Range,** indicate that the output should go in D1 (or any place you wish), click on **Summary statistics,** then click **OK.**
4. After you get your results, double-check the count in the output to be sure it contains the correct number of items.

Descriptive Statistics
Input
Input Range: $A$1:$A$81
Grouped By: Columns / Rows
Labels in First Row
Output options
Output Range: $D$1
New Worksheet Ply:
New Workbook
Summary statistics
Confidence Level for Mean: 95 %
Kth Largest: 1
Kth Smallest: 1
OK
Cancel
Help

Chapter 3 Answers to Self-Review

3–1 **1.** **(a)** $\overline{X} = \frac{\Sigma X}{n}$

(b) $\overline{X} = \frac{\$267,100}{4} = \$66,775.$

(c) Statistic, because it is a sample value.

(d) \$66,775. The sample mean is our best estimate of the population mean.

2. **(a)** $\mu = \frac{\Sigma X}{N}$

(b) $\mu = \frac{498}{6} = 83$

(c) Parameter, because it was computed using all the population values.

3–2 **(a)** \$237, found by:

$$\frac{(95 \times \$400) + (126 \times \$200) + (79 \times \$100)}{95 + 126 + 79} = 237$$

(b) The profit per suit is \$12, found by \$237 − \$200 cost − \$25 commission. The total profit for the 300 suits is \$3,600, found by 300 × \$12.

3–3 **1.** **(a)** \$439.

(b) 3, 3.

2. **(a)** 7, found by (6 + 8)/2 = 7.

(b) 3, 3.

(c) 0.

3–4 **1.** **(a)** About 8.39 percent.

(b) About 10.095 percent.

(c) Greater than, because 10.095 > 8.39.

2. 8.63 percent found by, $\sqrt[20]{\frac{120,520}{23,000}} - 1 = 1.0863 - 1.$

3–5 **1.** **(a)** Frequency distribution.

(b)

f	*X*	*fX*
1	4	4
4	8	32
10	12	120
3	16	48
2	20	40
20		244

$$\overline{X} = \frac{\Sigma fX}{n} = \frac{\$244}{20} = \$12.2$$

3–6 **1.**

Production	Frequency	CF
80 up to 90	5	5
90 up to 100	9	14
100 up to 110	20	34
110 up to 120	8	42
120 up to 130	6	48
130 up to 140	2	50
	50	

$$\text{Median} = 100 + \frac{25 - 14}{20}(10)$$
$$= 100 + 5.5 = 105.5$$

2.

Net Sales ($ Millions)	Cumulative Percent
\$ 1 up to \$ 4	13
4 up to 7	27
7 up to 10	67
10 up to 13	90
13 or greater	100

$$\text{Median} = \$7 + \frac{50 - 27}{40}(\$3)$$
$$= \$8.725$$

3–7 **(a)**

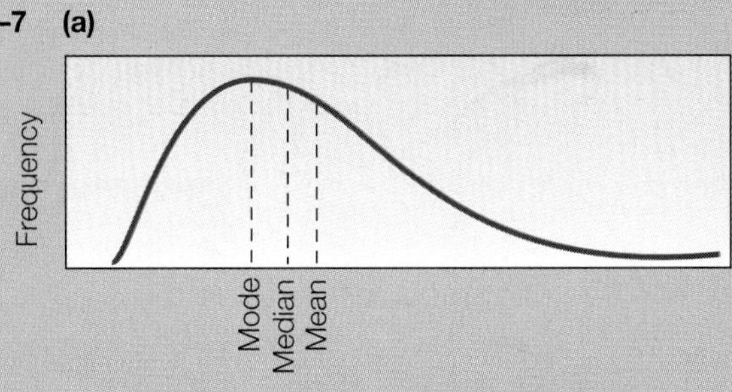

(b) Positively skewed, because the mean is the largest average and the mode is the smallest.

Other Descriptive Measures

4

'he distribution weight of a sample of 1,400 cargo containers is normally distributed. Based on the Empirical ule, what percent of the weight will lie between the mean to 2 standard deviations? See Goal 5 and Exercise 26.)

GOALS

When you have completed this chapter, you will be able to:

1 Compute and interpret the *range*, the *mean deviation*, the *variance*, and the *standard deviation* of ungrouped data.

2 Compute and interpret the range, the variance, and the standard deviation of grouped data.

3 Explain the characteristics, uses, advantages, and disadvantages of each measure.

4 Understand *Chebyshev's theorem* and the *Normal*, or *Empirical*, *Rule* as it relates to a set of observations.

5 Compute and interpret *quartiles* and the *interquartile range.*

6 Construct and interpret *box plots.*

7 Compute and understand the *coefficient of skewness* and the *coefficient of variation.*

Introduction

Chapter 2 began our study of descriptive statistics. We organized raw data into a table called a frequency distribution and then portrayed the distribution graphically in a histogram or a frequency polygon. This allowed us to visualize where the data tended to cluster and the general shape of the distribution. In Chapter 3 we computed several measures of central tendency, or averages, as they are commonly called. This allowed us to define a typical value in a set of observations. In this chapter we continue to develop measures to describe a set of data, concentrating on measures that describe the dispersion or variability of the data.

Why Study Dispersion?

An average, such as the mean or the median, only locates the center of the data. It is valuable from that standpoint, but an average does not tell us anything about the spread of the data. For example, if your nature guide told you that the river ahead averaged 3 feet in depth, would you cross it without additional information? Probably not. You would want to know something about the variation in the depth. Is the maximum depth of the river 3.25 feet and the minimum 2.75 feet? If that is the case, you would probably agree to cross. What if you learned the river depth ranged from 0.50 feet to 5.5 feet? Your decision would probably be not to cross. Before making a decision about crossing the river, you want information on both the typical depth and the variation in the depth of the river.

A small value for a measure of dispersion indicates that the data are clustered closely, say, around the arithmetic mean. The mean is therefore considered representative of the data. Conversely, a large measure of dispersion indicates that the mean is not reliable. Refer to Chart 4–1. The 100 employees of Struthers and Wells, Inc., a steel fabricating company, are organized into a histogram based on the number of years of employment with the company. The mean is 4.9 years, but the spread of the data is from 6 months to 16.8 years. The mean of 4.9 years is not very representative of all the employees.

The average is not representative because of the large spread.

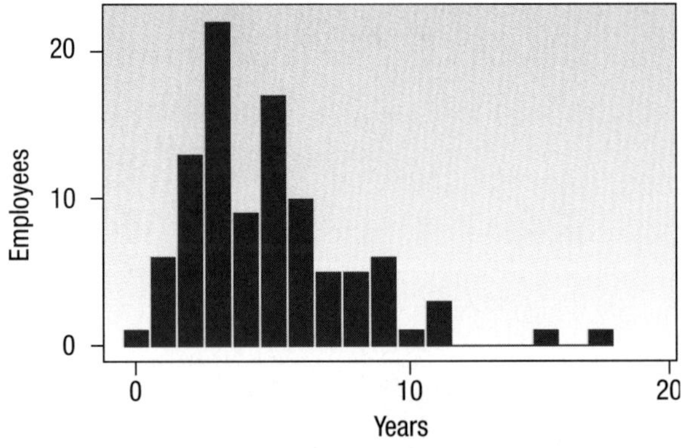

CHART 4–1 Histogram of Years of Employment at Struthers and Wells, Inc.

A second reason for studying the dispersion in a set of data is to compare the spread in two or more distributions. Suppose, for example, that the new PDM/3 computer is assembled in Baton Rouge and also in Tucson. The arithmetic mean daily output in the Baton Rouge plant is 50, and in the Tucson plant the mean output is also 50.

Based on the two means, one might conclude that the distributions of the daily outputs are identical. Production records for nine days at the two plants, however, reveal that this conclusion is not correct (see Chart 4–2). Baton Rouge production varies from 48 to 52 assemblies per day. Production at the Tucson plant is more erratic, ranging from 40 to 60 per day.

A measure of dispersion can be used to evaluate the reliability of two or more averages.

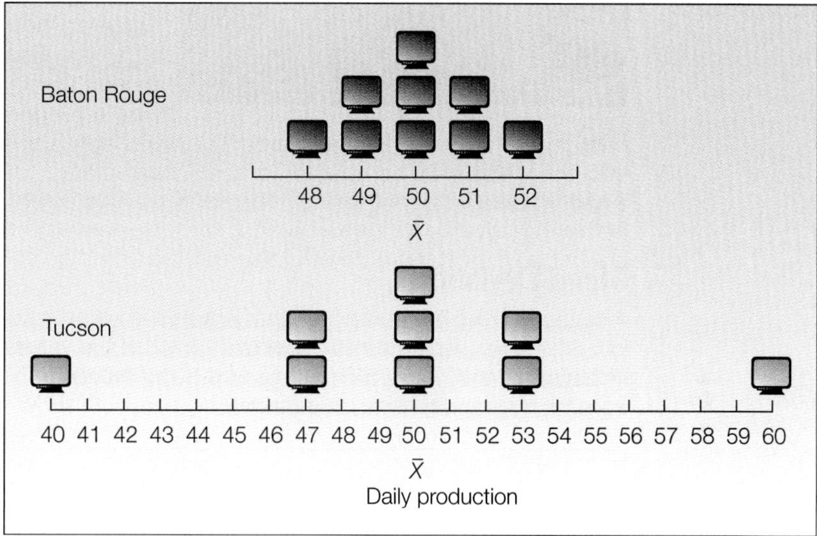

CHART 4–2 Daily Production of Computers at the Baton Rouge and Tucson Plants

Measures of Dispersion

We will consider several measures of dispersion. The range is based on the location of the largest and the smallest values in the data set. The mean deviation, the variance, and the standard deviation are all based on deviations from the mean.

Range

The simplest measure of dispersion is the **range.** It is the difference between the highest and the lowest values in a data set. In the form of an equation:

RANGE Range = Highest value − Lowest value **[4–1]**

The range is widely used in statistical process control (SPC) applications. For these applications, see Chapter 17.

EXAMPLE

Refer to Chart 4–2. Find the range in the number of computers produced for the Baton Rouge and the Tucson plants. Interpret the two ranges.

SOLUTION

The range of the daily production of computers at the Baton Rouge plant is 4, found by the difference between the largest daily production of 52 and the smallest of 48. The range in the daily production for the Tucson plant is 20 computers, found by

Statistics in Action

The United States Postal Service has not only turned a profit in the last several years but has also tried to become more "user friendly." A recent survey showed that customers were interested in more *consistency* in the time it takes to make a delivery. Under the old conditions, a local letter might take only one day to deliver, or it might take several. "Just tell me how many days ahead I need to mail the birthday card to Mom so it gets there on her birthday, not early, not late," was a common complaint. The level of consistency is measured by the standard deviation of the delivery times. A smaller standard deviation indicates more consistency.

60 − 40. We therefore conclude that (1) there is less dispersion in the daily production in the Baton Rouge plant than in the Tucson plant because the range of 4 computers is less than a range of 20 computers, and (2) the production is clustered more closely around the mean of 50 at the Baton Rouge plant than at the Tucson plant (because a range of 4 is less than a range of 20). Thus, the mean production in the Baton Rouge plant (50 computers) is a more representative average than the mean of 50 computers for the Tucson plant.

Mean Deviation

A serious defect of the range is that it is based on only two values, the highest and the lowest; it does not take into consideration all of the values. The **mean deviation** does. It measures the mean amount by which the values in a population, or sample, vary from their mean. In terms of a definition:

MEAN DEVIATION The arithmetic mean of the absolute values of the deviations from the arithmetic mean.

In terms of a formula, the mean deviation, designated *MD,* is computed for a sample by:

MEAN DEVIATION
$$MD = \frac{\Sigma|X - \overline{X}|}{n} \qquad [4\text{–}2]$$

where:

- X is the value of each observation.
- $\overline{X}$ is the arithmetic mean of the values.
- n is the number of observations in the sample.
- $||$ indicates the absolute value. In other words, the signs of the deviations from the mean are disregarded.

Why do we ignore the signs of the deviations from the mean? If we didn't, the positive and negative deviations from the mean would exactly offset each other, and the mean deviation would always be zero. Such a measure (zero) would be a useless statistic. Because we use absolute deviations, the mean deviation is also called the **mean absolute deviation,** or **MAD.** It is usually written **MD.**

EXAMPLE

The number of patients seen in the emergency room at St. Luke's Memorial Hospital for a sample of 5 days last year were: 103, 97, 101, 106, and 103. Determine the mean deviation and interpret.

SOLUTION

The mean deviation is the mean of the amounts that individual observations differ from the arithmetic mean. To find the mean deviation of a set of data, we begin by finding the arithmetic mean. The mean number of patients is 102, found by (103 + 97 + 101 + 106 + 103) / 5. Next we find the amount by which each observation differs from the mean. Then we sum these differences, ignoring the signs, and divide the sum by the number of observations. The result is the mean amount the observations differ from the mean. A small value for the mean deviation indicates the mean is representative of the data, whereas a large value for the mean deviation indicates dispersion in the data. Below are the details of the calculations using formula (4–2).

Number of Cases	$(X - \bar{X})$	Absolute Deviation
103	(103 − 102) = 1	1
97	(97 − 102) = −5	5
101	(101 − 102) = −1	1
106	(106 − 102) = 4	4
103	(103 − 102) = 1	1
	Total	12

$$MD = \frac{\Sigma|X - \bar{X}|}{n} = \frac{12}{5} = 2.4$$

The mean deviation is 2.4 patients per day. The number of patients deviates, on average, by 2.4 patients from the mean of 102 patients per day.

The mean deviation has two advantages. First, it uses all the values in the computation. Recall that the range uses only the highest and the lowest values. Second, it is easy to understand—it is the average amount by which values deviate from the mean. However, its major drawback is the use of absolute values. Generally, absolute values are difficult to work with, so the mean deviation is not used as frequently as other measures of dispersion, such as the standard deviation.

Self-Review 4–1

The weights of a group of crates being shipped to Ireland are (in pounds):

95	103	105	110	104	105	112	90

(a) What is the range of the weights?
(b) Compute the arithmetic mean weight.
(c) Compute the mean deviation of the weights.

Exercises

For questions 1 through 6 calculate the (a) range, (b) arithmetic mean, and (c) mean deviation, and (d) interpret the range and the mean deviation.

1. There were five customer service representatives on duty at the Electronic Super Store during last Friday's sale. The numbers of VCRs these representatives sold are: 5, 8, 4, 10, and 3.

2. The Department of Statistics at Western State University offers eight sections of basic statistics. Following are the numbers of students enrolled in these sections: 34, 46, 52, 29, 41, 38, 36, and 28.

2. a. 24
b. 38
c. 6.25
d. See IM.

4. a. 7.6%
   b. 13.85%
   c. 2.0%
   d. Mean difference of 2.0%.
6. a. 10
   b. 3.5
   c. 2.375
   d. See IM.

3. Dave's Automatic Door installs automatic garage door openers. The following list indicates the number of minutes needed to install a sample of 10 doors: 28, 32, 24, 46, 44, 40, 54, 38, 32, and 42.
4. A sample of eight companies in the aerospace industry was surveyed as to their return on investment last year. The results are (in percent): 10.6, 12.6, 14.8, 18.2, 12.0, 14.8, 12.2, and 15.6.
5. Ten experts rated a newly developed pizza on a scale of 1 to 50. The ratings were: 34, 35, 41, 28, 26, 29, 32, 36, 38, and 40.
6. A sample of the personnel files of eight male employees employed by Acme Carpet revealed that, during a six-month period, they lost the following numbers of days due to illness: 2, 0, 6, 3, 10, 4, 1, and 2.

Variance and Standard Deviation

Variance and standard deviation are based on squared deviations from the mean.

The **variance** and **standard deviation** are also based on the deviations from the mean.

VARIANCE The arithmetic mean of the squared deviations from the mean.

Note that the variance is non-negative, and it is zero only if all observations are the same.

STANDARD DEVIATION The square root of the variance.

Population Variance The formulas for the population variance and the sample variance are slightly different. The population variance is considered first. (Recall that a population is the totality of all observations being studied.) The **population variance** for ungrouped data, that is, data not tabulated into a frequency distribution, is found by:

POPULATION VARIANCE $$\sigma^2 = \frac{\Sigma(X - \mu)^2}{N} \qquad [4\text{–}3]$$

where:

σ^2 is the symbol for the population variance (σ is the lower-case Greek letter sigma). It is usually referred to as "sigma squared."
X is the value of an observation in the population.
μ is the arithmetic mean of the population.
N is the number of observations in the population.

EXAMPLE

The ages of all the patients in the isolation ward of Yellowstone Hospital are 38, 26, 13, 41, and 22 years. What is the population variance?

SOLUTION

Age (X)	$X - \mu$	$(X - \mu)^2$
38	+10	100
26	−2	4
13	−15	225
41	+13	169
22	−6	36
140	0*	534

$$\mu = \frac{\Sigma X}{N} = \frac{140}{5} = 28$$

$$\sigma^2 = \frac{\Sigma(X - \mu)^2}{N} = \frac{534}{5} = 106.8$$

*Sum of the deviations from mean must equal zero.

Like the range and the mean deviation, the variance can be used to compare the dispersion in two or more sets of observations. For example, the variance for the ages of the patients in isolation was just computed to be 106.8. If the variance in the ages of the cancer patients in the hospital is 342.9, we conclude that (1) there is less dispersion in the distribution of the ages of patients in isolation than in the age distribution of all cancer patients (because 106.8 is less than 342.9); and (2) the ages of the patients in isolation are clustered more closely about the mean of 28 years than are the ages of those in the cancer ward. Thus, the mean age for the patients in isolation is a more representative average than the mean for all cancer patients.

Variance is difficult to interpret because the units are squared.

Population Standard Deviation Both the range and the mean deviation are easy to interpret. The range is the difference between the high and low values of a set of data, and the mean deviation is the mean of the deviations from the mean. However, the variance is difficult to interpret for a single set of observations. The variance of 106.8 for the ages of the patients in isolation is not in terms of years, but rather "years squared."

Standard deviation is in the same units as the data.

There is a way out of this dilemma. By taking the square root of the population variance, we can transform it to the same unit of measurement used for the original data. The square root of 106.8 years-squared is 10.3 years. The square root of the population variance is called the **population standard deviation.** In terms of a formula for ungrouped data:

POPULATION STANDARD DEVIATION

$$\sigma = \sqrt{\frac{\Sigma(X - \mu)^2}{N}} \qquad [4–4]$$

Self-Review 4–2

The Philadelphia office of Price Waterhouse Coopers LLP hired five accounting trainees this year. Their monthly starting salaries were: $2,536; $2,173; $2,448; $2,121; and $2,622.

(a) Compute the population mean.
(b) Compute the population variance.
(c) Compute the population standard deviation.
(d) The Pittsburgh office hired 6 trainees. Their mean monthly salary was $2,550, and the standard deviation was $250. Compare the two groups.

Exercises

7. Consider these five values a population: 8, 3, 7, 3, and 4.
   a. Determine the mean of the population.
   b. Determine the variance.

8. a. 8
   b. 9.67

8. Consider these six values a population: 13, 3, 8, 10, 8, and 6.
   a. Determine the mean of the population.
   b. Determine the variance.
9. The annual report of Dennis Industries cited these primary earnings per common share for the past five years: \$2.68, \$1.03, \$2.26, \$4.30, and \$3.58. If we assume these are population values, what is:
   a. The arithmetic mean primary earnings per share of common stock?
   b. The variance?
10. Referring to Exercise 9, the annual report of Dennis Industries also gave these returns on stockholder equity for the same five-year period (in percent): 13.2, 5.0, 10.2, 17.5, and 12.9.
   a. What is the arithmetic mean return?
   b. What is the variance?

10. a. 11.76%
    b. 16.89%

11. Plywood, Inc. reported these returns on stockholder equity for the past five years: 4.3, 4.9, 7.2, 6.7, and 11.6. Consider these as population values.
   a. Compute the range, the arithmetic mean, the variance, and the standard deviation.
   b. Compare the return on stockholder equity for Plywood, Inc. with that for Dennis Industries cited in Exercise 10.

12. a. \$18,000
    b. \$79,600
    c. \$40,240,000; \$6,343.50
    d. Mean about the same, more dispersion in the other firm.

12. The annual incomes of the five vice presidents of TMV Industries are: \$75,000; \$78,000; \$72,000; \$83,000; and \$90,000. Consider this a population.
   a. What is the range?
   b. What is the arithmetic mean income?
   c. What is the population variance? The standard deviation?
   d. The annual incomes of officers of another firm similar to TMV Industries were also studied. The mean was \$79,000 and the standard deviation \$8,612. Compare the means and dispersions in the two firms.

Sample Variance The formula for the population mean given in Chapter 3 is $\mu = \Sigma X/N$. We just changed the symbols for the sample mean, that is $\overline{X} = \Sigma X/n$. Unfortunately, the conversion from the population variance to the sample variance is not as direct. It requires a change in the denominator. Instead of substituting n (number in the sample) for N (number in the population), the denominator is $n - 1$. Thus the formula for the **sample variance** is:

SAMPLE VARIANCE, DEVIATION FORMULA

$$s^2 = \frac{\Sigma(X - \overline{X})^2}{n - 1} \qquad [4\text{-}5]$$

where:

s^2 is the sample variance.
X is the value of each observation in the sample.
$\overline{X}$ is the mean of the sample.
n is the number of observations in the sample.

Why is this seemingly insignificant change made in the denominator? Although the use of n is logical, it tends to underestimate the population variance, σ^2. The use of $(n - 1)$ in the denominator provides the appropriate correction for this tendency. Because the primary use of sample statistics like s^2 is to estimate population parameters like σ^2, $(n - 1)$ is preferred to n when defining the sample variance. We will also use this convention when computing the sample standard deviation.

We can show that

$$\Sigma(X - \overline{X})^2 = \Sigma X^2 - \frac{(\Sigma X)^2}{n}$$

The second term is much easier to use, even with a hand calculator, because it avoids all but one subtraction. Hence, we recommend formula (4–6) for calculating a sample variance.

SAMPLE VARIANCE, DIRECT FORMULA

$$s^2 = \frac{\Sigma X^2 - \dfrac{(\Sigma X)^2}{n}}{n-1} \qquad \textbf{[4–6]}$$

EXAMPLE

The hourly wages for a sample of part-time employees at Fruit Packers, Inc. are: \$2, \$10, \$6, \$8, and \$9. What is the sample variance?

SOLUTION

The sample variance is computed using two methods. On the left is the deviation method, using formula (4–5). On the right is the direct method, using formula (4–6).

$$\bar{X} = \frac{\Sigma X}{n} = \frac{\$35}{5} = \$7$$

Using squared deviations from the mean:

Hourly Wage (X)	$X - \bar{X}$	$(X - \bar{X})^2$
\$ 2	−\$5	25
10	3	9
6	−1	1
8	1	1
9	2	4
\$35	0	40

$$s^2 = \frac{\Sigma(X - \bar{X})^2}{n-1} = \frac{40}{5-1}$$

$= 10$ in dollars squared

Using the direct formula:

Hourly Wage (X)	X^2
\$ 2	4
10	100
6	36
8	64
9	81
\$35	285

$$s^2 = \frac{\Sigma X^2 - \dfrac{(\Sigma X)^2}{n}}{n-1}$$

$$= \frac{285 - \dfrac{(35)^2}{5}}{5-1} = \frac{40}{5-1}$$

$= 10$ in dollars squared

Sample Standard Deviation The sample standard deviation is used as an estimator of the population standard deviation. As noted previously, the population standard deviation is the square root of the population variance. Likewise, the *sample standard deviation is the square root of the sample variance.* The sample standard deviation for ungrouped data is most easily determined by:

STANDARD DEVIATION, DIRECT FORMULA

$$s = \sqrt{\frac{\Sigma X^2 - \dfrac{(\Sigma X)^2}{n}}{n-1}} \qquad \textbf{[4–7]}$$

EXAMPLE

The sample variance in the previous example involving hourly wages was computed to be 10. What is the sample standard deviation?

SOLUTION

The sample standard deviation is $3.16, found by $\sqrt{10}$. Note again that the sample variance is in terms of dollars squared, but taking the square root of 10 gives us $3.16, which is in the same units (dollars) as the original data.

Self-Review 4–3

The weights of the contents of several small aspirin bottles are (in grams): 4, 2, 5, 4, 5, 2, and 6. What is the sample variance? Compute the sample standard deviation.

Exercises

For questions 13–17, do the following:

a. Compute the variance using the deviation formula.
b. Compute the variance using the direct formula.
c. Determine the sample standard deviation.

13. Consider these values a sample: 7, 2, 6, 2, and 3.

14. The following five values are a sample: 11, 6, 10, 6, and 7.

15. Dave's Automatic Door, referred to in Exercise 3, installs automatic garage door openers. Based on a sample, following are the times, in minutes, required to install 10 doors: 28, 32, 24, 46, 44, 40, 54, 38, 32, and 42.

16. The sample of eight companies in the aerospace industry, referred to in Exercise 4, was surveyed as to their return on investment last year. The results are: 10.6, 12.6, 14.8, 18.2, 12.0, 14.8, 12.2, and 15.6.

17. Trout, Inc. feeds fingerling trout in special ponds and markets them when they attain a certain weight. A sample of 10 trout were isolated in a pond and fed a special food mixture, designated RT-10. At the end of the experimental period, the weights of the trout were (in grams): 124, 125, 125, 123, 120, 124, 127, 125, 126, and 121.

18. Refer to Exercise 17. Another special mixture, AB-4, was used in another pond. The mean of a sample was computed to be 126.9 grams, and the standard deviation 1.2 grams. Which food results in a more uniform weight?

14. a. 5.5
b. 5.5
c. 2.3452

16. a. 6.0086
b. 6.0086
c. 2.4512

18. AB-4 standard deviation is smaller.

Measures of Dispersion for Data Grouped into a Frequency Distribution

Range

Recall that the range is the difference between the highest and lowest values. To estimate the range from data already grouped into a frequency distribution, subtract the lower limit of the lowest class from the upper limit of the highest class. For example, suppose a sample of 47 hourly wages was grouped into this frequency distribution:

Hourly Earnings	Frequency
$ 5 up to $10	6
10 up to 15	12
15 up to 20	19
20 up to 25	7
25 up to 30	3

The range is $25, found by $30 − $5.

Standard Deviation

Recall that for *ungrouped* data, one formula for the sample standard deviation is:

$$s = \sqrt{\frac{\Sigma X^2 - \frac{(\Sigma X)^2}{n}}{n - 1}}$$

If the data of interest are in *grouped* form (in a frequency distribution), the sample standard deviation can be approximated by substituting $\Sigma f X^2$ for ΣX^2 and $\Sigma f X$ for ΣX. The formula for the *sample standard deviation* then converts to:

STANDARD DEVIATION, GROUPED DATA

$$s = \sqrt{\frac{\Sigma f X^2 - \frac{(\Sigma f X)^2}{n}}{n - 1}} \quad \textbf{[4–8]}$$

where:

- s is the symbol for the sample standard deviation.
- X is the midpoint of a class.
- f is the class frequency.
- n is the total number of sample observations.

EXAMPLE

A sample of the semimonthly amounts invested in the Dupree Paint Company's profit-sharing plan by employees was organized into a frequency distribution for further study. (See Table 4–1.) What is the standard deviation of the data? What is the sample variance?

TABLE 4–1 A Sample of Semimonthly Amounts Invested by Employees in the Profit-Sharing Plan

Amount Invested	Number of Employees
\$30 up to \$35	3
35 up to 40	7
40 up to 45	11
45 up to 50	22
50 up to 55	40
55 up to 60	24
60 up to 65	9
65 up to 70	4

SOLUTION

Following the same practice used earlier for computing the arithmetic mean of data grouped into a frequency distribution, X represents the midpoint of each class. For example, the midpoint of the "\$30 up to \$35" class is \$32.50. (See Table 4–2.) It is assumed that the amounts invested in the "\$30 up to \$35" class average about \$32.50. Similarly, the seven amounts in the "\$35 up to \$40" class are assumed to average about \$37.50, and so on.

TABLE 4–2 Calculations Needed for the Sample Standard Deviation

Amount Invested	Number, f	Midpoint, X	fX	$fX \times X$ or fX^2
\$30 up to \$35	3	\$32.50	\$ 97.50	3,168.75
35 up to 40	7	37.50	262.50	9,843.75
40 up to 45	11	42.50	467.50	19,868.75
45 up to 50	22	47.50	1,045.00	49,637.50
50 up to 55	40	52.50	2,100.00	110,250.00
55 up to 60	24	57.50	1,380.00	79,350.00
60 up to 65	9	62.50	562.50	35,156.25
65 up to 70	4	67.50	270.00	18,225.00
Total	120		\$6,185.00	325,500.00

To find the standard deviation of these data grouped into a frequency distribution:

Step 1: Each class frequency is multiplied by its class midpoint. That is, multiply f times X. Thus, for the first class $3 \times \$32.50 = \$97.50$, for the second class $fX = 7 \times \$37.50 = \$262.50$, and so on.

Step 2: Calculate fX^2. This could be written $fX \times X$. For the first class it would be $\$97.50 \times \$32.50 = 3{,}168.75$, for the second class $\$262.50 \times \$37.50 = 9{,}843.75$, and so on.

Step 3: Sum the fX and the fX^2 columns. The totals are \$6,185 and 325,500, respectively.

Inserting these sums in formula (4–8) and solving for the sample standard deviation:

$$s = \sqrt{\frac{\Sigma fX^2 - \frac{(\Sigma fX)^2}{n}}{n-1}} = \sqrt{\frac{325{,}500 - 318{,}785.2}{119}} = \$7.51$$

The sample standard deviation is \$7.51. The sample variance is $(\$7.51)^2$, or about 56.40 (in dollars squared).

Self-Review 4–4

The ages of a sample of quarter-inch drills available for rental at Tool Rental, Inc. were organized into the following frequency distribution.

Age (months)	Frequency
2 up to 4	2
4 up to 6	5
6 up to 8	10
8 up to 10	4
10 up to 12	2

(a) Estimate the range.
(b) Estimate the sample standard deviation.
(c) Estimate the sample variance.

Exercises

For exercises 19–22 compute the range, the standard deviation, and the variance.

19. Refer to the following frequency distribution.

Class	Frequency
0 up to 5	2
5 up to 10	7
10 up to 15	12
15 up to 20	6
20 up to 25	3

20. Refer to the following frequency distribution.

Class	Frequency
20 up to 30	7
30 up to 40	12
40 up to 50	21
50 up to 60	18
60 up to 70	12

21. Each person who applies for an assembly job at Carolina Furniture, Inc. is given a mechanical aptitude test. One part of the test involves assembling a dresser based on numbered instructions. A sample of the lengths of time it took 42 persons to assemble the dresser was organized into the following frequency distribution.

Length of Time (minutes)	Frequency
2 up to 4	4
4 up to 6	8
6 up to 8	14
8 up to 10	9
10 up to 12	5
12 up to 14	2

22. A sample of the amounts paid for parking on Saturday at the Downtown Parking Garage in Toronto was organized into the following frequency distribution.

Amount Paid	Frequency
\$0.50 up to \$0.75	2
0.75 up to 1.00	7
1.00 up to 1.25	15
1.25 up to 1.50	28
1.50 up to 1.75	14
1.75 up to 2.00	9
2.00 up to 2.25	3
2.25 up to 2.50	2

Statistics in Action

Todd Helton of the Colorado Rockies and Nomar Garciaparra of the Boston Red Sox tied for the highest batting average during the 2000 Major League Baseball season. Each had a batting average of .372. The highest batting average in recent times was by Tony Gwynn, .394 in 1994, but this was during a strike-shortened season. Ted Williams batted .406 in 1941, and nobody has hit over .400 since. It is interesting to note that the mean batting average for all players has remained constant at about .260 for more than 100 years. The standard deviation of that average, however, has declined from .049 to .031. This indicates that there is less dispersion in the batting averages today and helps explain the lack of any .400 hitters in recent times.

20. 50, 12.179, and 148.32.
22. \$2.00, \$0.3641, and .1326.

Statistics in Action

In the previous chapter, we found that the average is a value used to represent all the data. However, often an average does not give the full picture. Stockbrokers are often faced with this problem when they are considering two investments, where the mean rate of return is the same. They usually calculate the standard deviation of the rates of return to assess the risk associated with the two investments. The investment with the larger standard deviation is considered to have the greater risk. In this context the standard deviation plays a vital part in making critical decisions regarding the composition of an investor's portfolio.

Interpretation and Uses of the Standard Deviation

The standard deviation is commonly used as a measure to compare the spread in two or more sets of observations. For example, the standard deviation of the semimonthly amounts invested in the Dupree Paint Company profit-sharing plan was just computed to be \$7.51. Suppose these employees are located in Georgia. If the standard deviation for a group of employees in Texas is \$10.47, and the means are about the same, it indicates that the amounts invested by the Georgia employees are not dispersed as much as those in Texas (because $\$7.51 < \$10.47$). Since the amounts invested by the Georgia employees are clustered more closely about the mean, the mean for the Georgia employees is a more reliable measure than the mean for the Texas group.

Chebyshev's Theorem

We have stressed that a small standard deviation for a set of values indicates that these values are located close to the mean. Conversely, a large standard deviation reveals that the observations are widely scattered about the mean. The Russian mathematician P. L. Chebyshev (1821–1894) developed a theorem that allows us to determine the minimum proportion of the values that lie within a specified number of standard deviations of the mean. For example, based on **Chebyshev's theorem,** at least three of four values, or 75 percent, must lie between the mean plus two standard deviations and the mean minus two standard deviations. This relationship applies regardless of the shape of the distribution. Further, at least eight of nine values, or 88.9 percent, will lie between plus three standard deviations and minus three standard deviations of the mean. At least 24 of 25 values, or 96 percent, will lie between plus and minus five standard deviations of the mean.

Chebyshev's theorem states:

CHEBYSHEV'S THEOREM For any set of observations (sample or population), the proportion of the values that lie within k standard deviations of the mean is at least $1 - 1/k^2$, where k is any constant greater than 1.

EXAMPLE

In the previous example and solution, the arithmetic mean semimonthly amount contributed by the Dupree Paint employees to the company's profit-sharing plan was \$51.54, and the standard deviation was computed to be \$7.51. At least what percent of the contributions lie within plus 3.5 standard deviations and minus 3.5 standard deviations of the mean?

SOLUTION

About 92 percent, found by

$$1 - \frac{1}{k^2} = 1 - \frac{1}{(3.5)^2} = 1 - \frac{1}{12.25} = 0.92$$

The Empirical Rule

Empirical Rule applies only to symmetrical, bell-shaped distributions.

Chebyshev's theorem is concerned with any set of values; that is, the distribution of values can have any shape. However, for a symmetrical, bell-shaped distribution such as the one in Chart 4–3, we can be more precise in explaining the dispersion about the mean. These relationships involving the standard deviation and the mean are the **Empirical Rule,** sometimes called the **Normal Rule.**

> **EMPIRICAL RULE** For a symmetrical, bell-shaped frequency distribution, approximately 68 percent of the observations will lie within plus and minus one standard deviation of the mean; about 95 percent of the observations will lie within plus and minus two standard deviations of the mean; and practically all (99.7 percent) will lie within plus and minus three standard deviations of the mean.

These relationships are portrayed graphically in Chart 4–3 for a bell-shaped distribution with a mean of 100 and a standard deviation of 10.

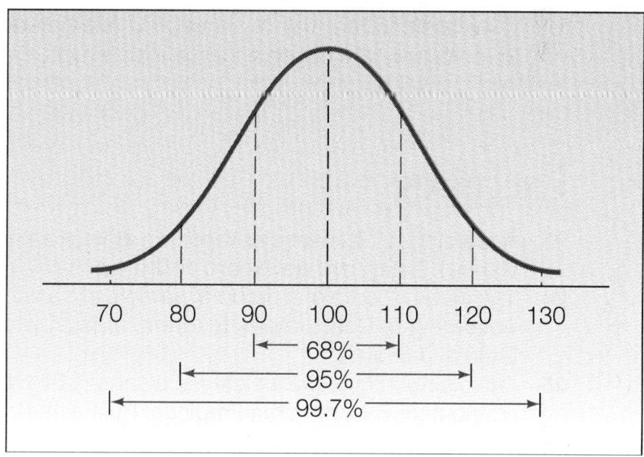

CHART 4–3 A Symmetrical, Bell-Shaped Curve Showing the Relationships between the Standard Deviation and the Mean

It has been noted that if a distribution is symmetrical and bell-shaped, practically all of the observations lie between the mean plus and minus three standard deviations. Thus, if $\overline{X} = 100$ and $s = 10$, practically all the observations lie between $100 + 3(10)$ and $100 - 3(10)$, or 70 and 130. The range is therefore 60, found by $130 - 70$.

Conversely, if we know that the range is 60, we can approximate the standard deviation by dividing the range by 6. For this illustration: range $\div$ 6 = 60 $\div$ 6 = 10, the standard deviation.

EXAMPLE

A sample of the monthly amounts spent for food by a senior citizen living alone approximates a symmetrical, bell-shaped frequency distribution. The sample mean is \$150; the standard deviation is \$20. Using the empirical rule:

1. About 68 percent of the monthly food expenditures are between what two amounts?

2. About 95 percent of the monthly food expenditures are between what two amounts?
3. Almost all of the monthly expenditures are between what two amounts?

SOLUTION

1. About 68 percent are between \$130 and \$170, found by $\overline{X} \pm 1s$ = \$150 ± 1(\$20).
2. About 95 percent are between \$110 and \$190, found by $\overline{X} \pm 2s$ = \$150 ± 2(\$20).
3. Almost all (99.7 percent) are between \$90 and \$210, found by $\overline{X} \pm 3s$ = \$150 ± 3(\$20).

Self-Review 4–5

The Pitney Pipe Company is one of several domestic manufacturers of PVC pipe. The quality control department sampled 600 10-foot lengths. At a point 1 foot from the end of the pipe they measured the outside diameter. The mean was 14.0 inches and the standard deviation 0.1 inches.

(a) If the shape of the distribution is not known, at least what percent of the observations will be between 13.85 inches and 14.15 inches?
(b) If we assume that the distribution of diameters is symmetrical and bell-shaped, about 95 percent of the observations will be between what two values?

Exercises

23. According to Chebyshev's theorem, at least what percent of any set of observations will be within 1.8 standard deviations of the mean?

24. 84%

24. The mean income of a group of sample observations is \$500; the standard deviation is \$40. According to Chebyshev's theorem, at least what percent of the incomes will lie between \$400 and \$600?

25. The distribution of the weights of a sample of 1,400 cargo containers is somewhat normally distributed. Based on the Empirical Rule, what percent of the weights will lie?

a. Between $\overline{X} - 2s$ and $\overline{X} + 2s$?
b. Between $\overline{X}$ and $\overline{X} + 2s$? Below $\overline{X} - 2s$?

26. The following figure portrays the symmetrical appearance of a sample distribution of efficiency ratings.

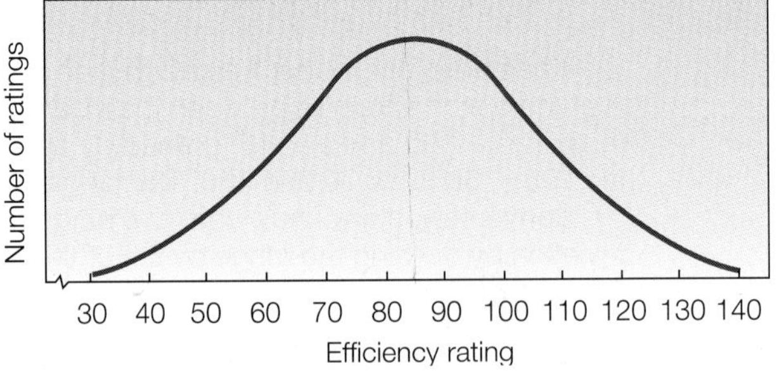

26. a. About 85.
b. About 18.
c. 67,103
d. 49,121

a. Estimate the mean efficiency rating.
b. Estimate the standard deviation to the nearest whole number.
c. About 68 percent of the efficiency ratings are between what two values?
d. About 95 percent of the efficiency ratings are between what two values?

Relative Dispersion

A direct comparison of two or more measures of dispersion—say, the standard deviation for a distribution of annual incomes and the standard deviation of a distribution of absenteeism for this same group of employees—is impossible. Can we say that the standard deviation of $1,200 for the income distribution is greater than the standard deviation of 4.5 days for the distribution of absenteeism? Obviously not, because we cannot directly compare dollars and days absent from work. In order to make a meaningful comparison of the dispersion in incomes and absenteeism, we need to convert each of these measures to a *relative* value—that is, a percent. Karl Pearson (1857–1936), pictured at left, who contributed significantly to the science of statistics, developed a relative measure called the **coefficient of variation** (CV). It is a very useful measure when:

When to use CV

1. The data are in different units (such as dollars and days absent).
2. The data are in the same units, but the means are far apart (such as the incomes of the top executives and the incomes of the unskilled employees).

COEFFICIENT OF VARIATION The ratio of the standard deviation to the arithmetic mean, expressed as a percent.

In terms of a formula for a sample:

COEFFICIENT OF VARIATION $CV = \frac{s}{\overline{X}}(100) \longleftarrow$ Multiplying by 100 converts the decimal to a percent **[4–9]**

EXAMPLE

A study of the amount of bonus paid and the years of service of employee resulted in these statistics: The mean bonus paid was $200; the standard deviation was 40. The mean number of years of service was 20 years; the standard deviation was 2 years. Compare the relative dispersion in the two distributions using the coefficient of variation.

SOLUTION

The distributions are in different units (dollars and years of service). Therefore, they are converted to coefficients of variation.

For the bonus paid:

$$CV = \frac{s}{\overline{X}}(100) = \frac{\$40}{200}(100) = 20 \text{ percent}$$

For years of service:

$$CV = \frac{s}{\overline{X}}(100) = \frac{2}{20}(100) = 10 \text{ percent}$$

Interpreting, there is more dispersion relative to the mean in the distribution of bonus paid compared with the distribution of years of service (because 20 percent > 10 percent).

The same procedure is used when the data are in the same units but the means are far apart. (See the following example.)

EXAMPLE

The variation in the annual incomes of executives is to be compared with the variation in incomes of unskilled employees. For a sample of executives, $\overline{X} = \$500{,}000$ and $s = \$50{,}000$. For a sample of unskilled employees, $\overline{X} = \$32{,}000$, and $s = \$3{,}200$. We are tempted to say that there is more dispersion in the annual incomes of the executives because \$50,000 > \$3,200. The means are so far apart, however, that we need to convert the statistics to coefficients of variation to make a meaningful comparison of the variations in annual incomes.

SOLUTION

For the executives:

$$CV = \frac{s}{\overline{X}}(100) = \frac{\$50{,}000}{\$500{,}000}(100) = 10 \text{ percent}$$

For the unskilled employees:

$$CV = \frac{s}{\overline{X}}(100) = \frac{\$3{,}200}{\$32{,}000}(100) = 10 \text{ percent}$$

There is no difference in the relative dispersion of the two groups.

Self-Review 4–6

A large group of Air Force inductees was given two experimental tests—a mechanical aptitude test and a finger dexterity test. The arithmetic mean score on the mechanical aptitude test was 200, with a standard deviation of 10. The mean and standard deviation for the finger dexterity test were: $\overline{X} = 30$, $s = 6$. Compare the relative dispersion in the two groups.

Exercises

27. For a sample of students in the College of Business Administration at Mid-Atlantic University, the mean grade point average is 3.10 with a standard deviation of 0.25. Compute the coefficient of variation.

28. Domestic 21.28%. Overseas 19.23%.

28. United Airlines is studying the weight of luggage for each passenger. For a large group of domestic passengers, the mean is 47 pounds with a standard deviation of 10 pounds. For a large group of overseas passengers, the mean is 78 pounds and the standard deviation is 15 pounds. Compute the relative dispersion of each group. Comment on the difference in relative dispersion.

29. The research analyst for the Sidde Financial stock brokerage firm wants to compare the dispersion in the price-earnings ratios for a group of common stocks with the dispersion of their return on investment. For the price-earnings ratios, the mean is 10.9 and the standard deviation 1.8. The mean return on investment is 25 percent and the standard deviation 5.2 percent.
    a. Why should the coefficient of variation be used to compare the dispersion?
    b. Compare the relative dispersion for the price-earnings ratios and return on investment.

30. a. Large difference in means.
    b. 28.95%, 5.71%

30. The spread in the annual prices of stocks selling for under $10 and the spread in prices of those selling for over $60 are to be compared. The mean price of the stocks selling for under $10 is $5.25 and the standard deviation $1.52. The mean price of those stocks selling for over $60 is $92.50 and the standard deviation $5.28.
    a. Why should the coefficient of variation be used to compare the dispersion in the prices?
    b. Compute the coefficients of variation. What is your conclusion?

Skewness

Chapter 3 numerically describes the central tendency of a set of observations using the mean, median, and mode. This chapter describes measures that show the amount of spread or variation in a set of data, such as the range and the standard deviation.

Another characteristic of a set of data is the shape. There are four shapes commonly observed: symmetric, positively skewed, negatively skewed, and bimodal. In a **symmetric** set of observations the mean and median are equal and the data values are evenly spread around these values. The data values below the mean and median are a mirror image of those above. A set of values is **skewed to the right** or **positively skewed** if there is a single peak and the values extend much further to the right of the peak than to the left of the peak. In this case the mean is larger than the median. In a **negatively skewed** distribution there is a single peak but the observations extend further to the left, in the negative direction, than to the right. In a negatively skewed distribution the mean is smaller than the median. Positively skewed distributions are more common. Salaries often follow this pattern. Think of the salaries of those employed in a small company of about 100 people. The president and a few top executives would have very large salaries relative to the other workers and hence the distribution of salaries would exhibit positive skewness. A bimodal distribution will have two or more peaks. This is often the case when the values are from two or more populations. This information is summarized in Chart 4–4.

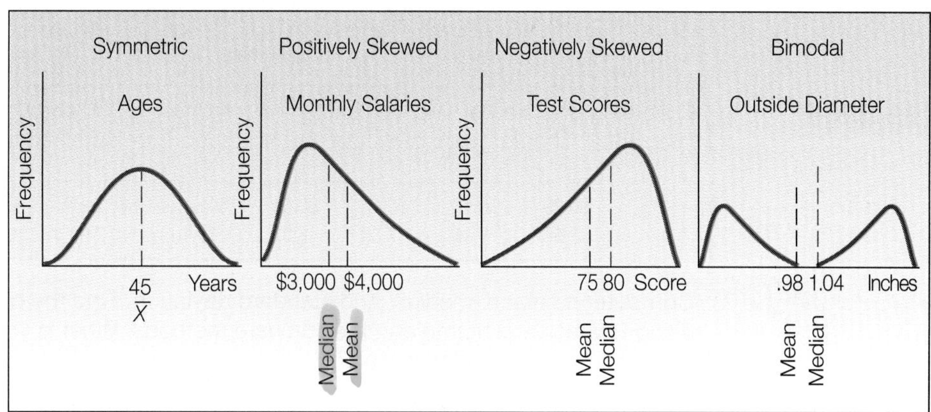

CHART 4–4 Shapes of Frequency Polygons

There are several formulas in the statistical literature used to calculate skewness. The simplest, developed by Professor Karl Pearson, is based on the difference between the mean and the median.

PEARSON'S COEFFICIENT OF SKEWNESS $$sk = \frac{3(\text{Mean} - \text{Median})}{s}$$ **[4–10]**

Using this relationship the coefficient of skewness can range from −3 up to 3. A value near −3, such as −2.57, indicates considerable negative skewness. A value such as 1.63 indicates moderate positive skewness. A value of 0, which will occur when the mean and median are equal, indicates the distribution is symmetrical and that there is no skewness present.

In this text we present output from the statistical software packages MINITAB and Excel. Both of these software packages will output a value for the coefficient of skewness that is based on the cubed deviations from the mean. The formula is:

SOFTWARE COEFFICIENT OF SKEWNESS $$sk = \frac{n}{(n-1)(n-2)}\left[\sum\left(\frac{X-\overline{X}}{s}\right)^3\right]$$ **[4–11]**

Formula 4-11 offers an insight into skewness. The right-hand side of the formula is the difference between each value and the mean, divided by the standard deviation. That is the portion $(X - \overline{X})/s$ of the formula. This idea is called **standardizing.** We will discuss the idea of standardizing a value in more detail in Chapter 7 when we describe the normal probability distribution. At this point, observe that the result is to report the difference between each value and the mean in units of the standard deviation. If this difference is positive, the particular value is larger than the mean; if it is negative, it is smaller than the mean. When we cube these values, we retain the information on the direction of the difference. Recall that in the formula for the standard deviation (see formula 4–7) we squared the difference between each value and the mean, so that result was all positive values.

If the set of data values under consideration is symmetric, when we cube the standardized values and sum over all the values the result would be near zero. If there are several large values, clearly separate from the others, the sum of the cubed differences would be a large positive value. Several values much smaller will result in a negative cubed sum.

An example will illustrate the idea of skewness.

EXAMPLE

Following are the earning per share for a sample of 15 software companies for the year 2000. The earnings per share are arranged from smallest to largest.

\$0.09	\$0.13	\$0.41	\$0.51	\$ 1.12	\$ 1.20	\$ 1.49	\$3.18
3.50	6.36	7.83	8.92	10.13	12.99	16.40	

Compute the mean, median, and standard deviation. Find the coefficient of skewness using Pearson's estimate and the software methods. What is your conclusion regarding the shape of the distribution?

SOLUTION

These are ungrouped sample data, so we use formula 3–2 to determine the mean

$$\overline{X} = \frac{\Sigma X}{n} = \frac{\$74.26}{15} = \$4.95$$

The median is the middle value in a set of data, arranged from smallest to largest. In this case the middle value is \$3.18, so the median earnings per share is \$3.18.

We use formula 4–7 to determine the sample standard deviation.

$$s = \sqrt{\frac{\Sigma X^2 - \frac{(\Sigma X)}{n}}{n-1}} = \sqrt{\frac{749.372 - \frac{(74.26)^2}{15}}{15-1}} = 5.22$$

Pearson's coefficient of skewness is 1.017, found by

$$sk = \frac{3(\text{Mean} - \text{Median})}{s} = \frac{3(\$4.95 - \$3.18)}{\$5.22} = 1.017$$

This indicates there is moderate positive skewness in the earnings per share data.

We obtain a similar, but not exactly the same, value from the software method. The details of the calculations are shown in Table 4–3. To begin we find the difference between each earnings per share value and the mean and divide this result by the standard deviation. Recall that we referred to this as standardizing. Next, we cube, that is, raise it to the third power, the result of the first step. Finally, we sum the cubed values. The details of the first row, that is, the company with an earnings per share of $0.09, are:

$$\left(\frac{X - \overline{X}}{s}\right)^3 = \left(\frac{0.09 - 4.95}{5.22}\right)^3 = (-0.9310)^3 = -0.8070$$

When we sum the 15 cubed values the result is 11.8274. That is, the term $\Sigma[(X - \overline{X})/s]^3 = 11.8274$. To find the coefficient of skewness, we use formula 4–11, with $n = 15$.

$$sk = \frac{n}{(n-1)(n-2)} \Sigma\left(\frac{X - \overline{X}}{s}\right)^3 = \frac{15}{(15-1)(15-2)}(11.8274) = 0.975$$

TABLE 4–3 Calculation of the Coefficient of Skewness.

Earnings per Share	$\frac{(X - \overline{X})}{s}$	$\left(\frac{X - \overline{X}}{s}\right)^3$
0.09	−0.9310	−0.8070
0.13	−0.9234	−0.7873
0.41	−0.8697	−0.6579
0.51	−0.8506	−0.6154
1.12	−0.7337	−0.3950
1.20	−0.7184	−0.3708
1.49	−0.6628	−0.2912
3.18	−0.3391	−0.0390
3.50	−0.2778	−0.0214
6.36	0.2701	0.0197
7.83	0.5517	0.1679
8.92	0.7605	0.4399
10.13	0.9923	0.9772
12.99	1.5402	3.6539
16.40	2.1935	10.5537
		11.8274

We conclude that the earnings per share values are somewhat positively skewed. The following chart, from MINITAB, reports the descriptive measures, such as the mean, median, and standard deviation of the earnings per share data. Also included are the coefficient of skewness and a histogram with a bell-shaped curve superimposed.

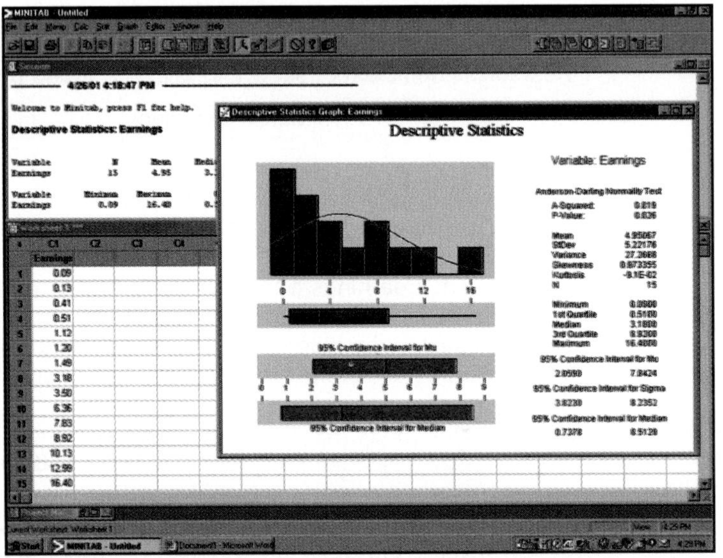

Self-Review 4–7

A sample of 5 data entry clerks employed in the Horry County Tax Office revised the following number of tax records last hour: 73, 98, 60, 92, and 84.

(a) Find the mean, median, and the standard deviation.
(b) Compute the coefficient of skewness using Pearson's method.
(c) Calculate the coefficient of skewness using the software method.
(d) What is your conclusion regarding the skewness of the data?

Exercises

For exercises 31–34, do the following:

a. Determine the mean, median, and the standard deviation.
b. Determine the coefficient of skewness using Pearson's method.
c. Determine the coefficient of skewness using the software method.

31. The following values are the starting salaries, in $000, for a sample of five accounting graduates who accepted positions in public accounting last year.

36.0	26.0	33.0	28.0	31.0

32. a. 542, 546, 25.083
b. −0.478
c. −0.375

32. Listed below are the salaries, in $000, for a sample of 15 executives in the electronics industry.

$516.0	$548.0	$566.0	$534.0	$586.0	$529.0
546.0	523.0	538.0	523.0	551.0	552.0
486.0	558.0	574.0			

33. Listed below are the commissions earned ($000) last year by the sales representatives at the Furniture Patch.

$ 3.9	$ 5.7	$ 7.3	$10.6	$13.0	$13.6	$15.1	$15.8	$17.1
17.4	17.6	22.3	38.6	43.2	87.7			

34. **a.** 3.046, 2,000, 2.963 **b.** 1.059 **c.** 0.877

34. Listed below are the salaries for the New York Yankees for the year 2000. The salary information is reported in millions of dollars.

$9.86	$9.50	$8.25	$6.25	$6.00	$5.95
5.25	5.00	4.33	4.30	4.25	3.40
3.13	2.02	2.00	1.90	1.85	1.82
0.80	0.38	0.35	0.35	0.20	0.20
0.20	0.20	0.20	0.20	0.20	

Other Measures of Dispersion

The standard deviation is the most widely used measure of dispersion. However, there are other ways of describing the variation or spread in a set of data. One method is to determine the *location* of values that divide a set of observations into equal parts. These measures include *quartiles, deciles,* and *percentiles.*

Quartiles divide a set of observations into four equal parts. To explain further, think of any set of values arranged from smallest to largest. In Chapter 3 we called the middle value of a set of data arranged from smallest to largest the median. That is, 50 percent of the observations are larger than the median and 50 percent are smaller. The median is a measure of location because it pinpoints the center of the data. In a similar fashion quartiles divide a set of observations into four equal parts. The first quartile, usually labeled Q_1, is the value below which 25 percent of the observations occur and the third quartile, usually labeled Q_3, is the value below which 75 percent of the observations occur. Logically, Q_2 is the median. The values corresponding to Q_1, Q_2, and Q_3 divide a set of data into four equal parts. Q_1 can be thought of as the "median" of the lower half of the data and Q_3 the "median" of the upper half of the data.

In a similar fashion deciles divide a set of observations into 10 equal parts and percentiles into 100 equal parts. So if you found that your GPA was in the 8th decile at your university, you could conclude that 80 percent of the students had a GPA lower than yours and 20 percent had a higher GPA. A GPA in the 33rd percentile means that 33 percent of the students have a lower GPA and 67 percent have a higher GPA. Percentile scores are frequently used to report results on such national standardized tests as the SAT, ACT, GMAT (used to judge entry into many Master of Business Administration programs), and LSAT (used to judge entry into law school).

Quartiles, Deciles, and Percentiles

To formalize the computational procedure, let L_p refer to the location of a desired percentile. So if we wanted to find the 33rd percentile we would use L_{33} and if we wanted the median, the 50th percentile, then L_{50}. The number of observations is n, so if we want to locate the middle observation, its position is at $(n + 1)/2$, or we could write this as $(n + 1)(P/100)$, where P is the desired percentile.

LOCATION OF A PERCENTILE

$$L_p = (n + 1)\frac{P}{100} \qquad \textbf{[4–12]}$$

An example will help to explain further.

EXAMPLE

Listed below are the commissions earned last month by a sample of 15 brokers at Salomon Smith Barney's Oakland, California, office. Salomon Smith Barney is an investment company with offices located throughout the United States.

\$2,038	\$1,758	\$1,721	\$1,637	\$2,097	\$2,047	\$2,205	\$1,787	\$2,287
1,940	2,311	2,054	2,406	1,471	1,460			

Locate the median, the first quartile, and the third quartile for the commissions earned.

SOLUTION

The first step is to organize the data from the smallest commission to the largest.

\$1,460	\$1,471	\$1,637	\$1,721	\$1,758	\$1,787	\$1,940	\$2,038
2,047	2,054	2,097	2,205	2,287	2,311	2,406	

The median value is the observation in the center. The center value or L_{50} is located at $(n + 1)/2$, where n is the number of observations. In this case that is position number 8, found by $(15 + 1)/2$. The eighth largest commission is \$2,038. So we conclude this is the median and that half the brokers earned commissions more than \$2,038 and half earned less than \$2,038.

Recall the definition of a quartile. Quartiles divide a set of observations into four equal parts. Hence 25 percent of the observations will be less than the first quartile. Seventy-five percent of the observations will be less than the third quartile. To locate the first quartile, we use formula (4–12), where $n = 15$ and $P = 25$:

$$L_{25} = (n + 1)\frac{P}{100} = (15 + 1)\frac{25}{100} = 4$$

and to locate the third quartile, $n = 15$ and $P = 75$:

$$L_{75} = (n + 1)\frac{P}{100} = (15 + 1)\frac{75}{100} = 12$$

Therefore, the first and third quartile values are located at positions 4 and 12. The fourth value in the ordered array is \$1,721 and the twelfth is \$2,205. These are the first and third quartiles, respectively.

In the above example the location formula yielded a whole number result. That is, we were looking to find the first quartile and there were 15 observations, so the location formula indicated we should look to the fourth ordered value. What if there were 20 observations in the sample, that is $n = 20$, and we wanted to locate the first quartile? From the location formula (4–12):

$$L_{25} = (n + 1)\frac{P}{100} = (20 + 1)\frac{25}{100} = 5.25$$

We would locate the fifth value in the ordered array and then move .25 of the distance between the 5th and 6th values and report that as the first quartile. Like the median, the quartile does not need to be one of the actual values in the data set.

To explain further, suppose a data set contained the six values: 91, 75, 61, 101, 43, and 104. We want to locate the first quartile. We order the values from smallest to largest: 43, 61, 75, 91, 101, and 104. The first quartile is located at

$$L_{25} = (n + 1)\frac{P}{100} = (6 + 1)\frac{25}{100} = 1.75$$

The position formula tells us that the first quartile is located between the first and the second value and that it is .75 of the distance between the first and the second values. The first value is 43 and the second is 61. So the distance between these two values is 18. To locate the first quartile, we need to move .75 of the distance between the first and second values, so .75(18) = 13.5. To complete the procedure, we add 13.5 to the first value and report that the first quartile is located at 56.5.

We can extend the idea to include both deciles and percentiles. If we wanted to locate the 23rd percentile in a sample of 80 observations, we would look for the 18.63 position.

$$L_{23} = (n + 1)\frac{P}{100} = (80 + 1)\frac{23}{100} = 18.63$$

To find the value corresponding to the 23rd percentile, we would locate the 18th value and the 19th value and determine the distance between the two values. Next, we would multiply this difference by 0.63 and add the result to the smaller value. The result would be the 23rd percentile.

With a computer software package, it is quite easy to sort the data from smallest to largest and to locate percentiles and deciles. Both MINITAB and Excel output summary statistics. Listed below is the MINITAB output. It includes the first and third quartiles, as well as the mean, median, standard deviation, and coefficient of skewness for the Whitner Pontiac data (see Table 2–1). We conclude that 25 percent of the vehicles sold for less than \$17,074 and that 75 percent sold for less than \$22,795.

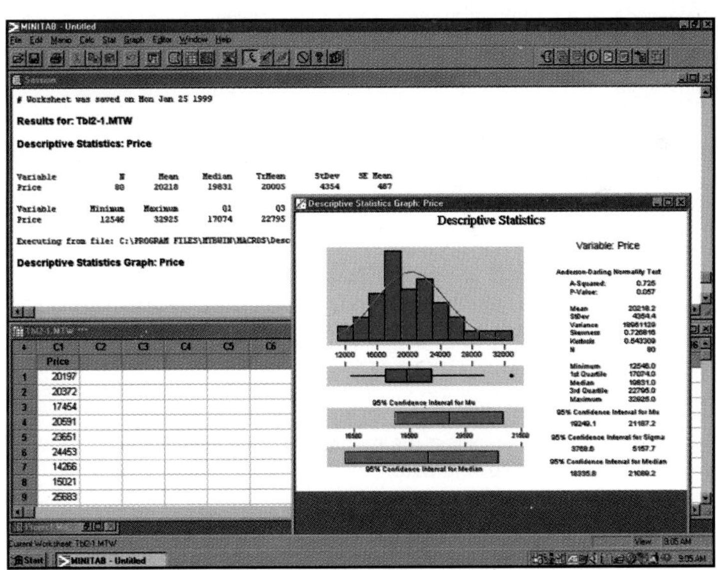

The Excel output on the following page includes the same information regarding the mean, median, standard deviation, and coefficient of skewness. It will also output the quartiles, but the method of calculation is not as precise. To find the quartiles, we multiply the sample size by the desired percentile and report the integer of that value. To explain, in the Whitner Pontiac data there are 80 observations, and we wish to locate the 25th percentile. We multiply 80 by .25; the result is 20.25. Excel will not allow us to enter a fractional value, so we use 20 and request the location of the largest 20 values and the smallest 20 values. The result is a good approximation of the 25th and 75th percentiles.

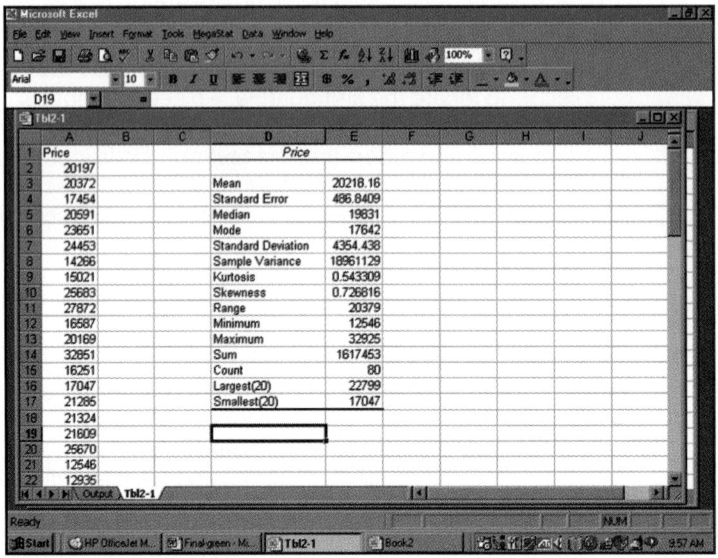

	A	B	C	D	E
1	Price			*Price*	
2	20197				
3	20372			Mean	20218.16
4	17454			Standard Error	486.8409
5	20591			Median	19831
6	23651			Mode	17642
7	24453			Standard Deviation	4354.438
8	14266			Sample Variance	18961129
9	15021			Kurtosis	0.543309
10	25683			Skewness	0.726816
11	27872			Range	20379
12	16587			Minimum	12546
13	20169			Maximum	32925
14	32851			Sum	1617453
15	16251			Count	80
16	17047			Largest(20)	22799
17	21285			Smallest(20)	17047
18	21324				
19	21609				
20	25670				
21	12546				
22	12935				

Self-Review 4–8

The quality control department of the Plainsville Peanut Company is responsible for checking the weight of the 8-ounce jar of peanut butter. The weights of a sample of 9 jars produced last hour are:

7.69	7.72	7.8	7.86	7.90	7.94	7.97	8.06	8.09

(a) What is the median weight?
(b) Determine the weights corresponding to the first and third quartiles.

Exercises

35. Determine the median and the values corresponding to the first and third quartiles in the following data.

46	47	49	49	51	53	54	54	55	55	59

36. Median = 9.53, Q_1 = 7.69, Q_3 = 12,59

36. Determine the median and the values corresponding to the first and third quartiles in the following data.

5.24	6.02	6.67	7.30	7.59	7.99	8.03	8.35	8.81	9.45
9.61	10.37	10.39	11.86	12.22	12.71	13.07	13.59	13.89	15.42

37. Anderson, Inc., is a distributor of small electrical motors. As with any business, the length of time customers take to pay their invoices is important. Listed below, arranged from smallest to largest, is the time, in days, for a sample of Anderson, Inc., invoices.

13	13	13	20	26	27	31	34	34	34	35	35	36	37	38
41	41	41	45	47	47	47	50	51	53	54	56	62	67	82

a. Determine the first and third quartiles.
b. Determine the 2nd decile and the 8th decile.
c. Determine the 67th percentile.

38. a. 58
b. 51.25, 66.0
c. 45.3, 76.4
d. 53.53

38. Wendy Hagel is the national sales manager for National Textbooks, Inc. She has a sales staff of 40 who visit college professors all over the United States. Each Saturday morning she requires her sales staff to send her a report. This report includes, among other things, the number of professors visited during the previous week. Listed below, ordered from smallest to largest, are the number of visits last week.

38	40	41	45	48	48	50	50	51	51	52	52	53	54	55	55	55	56	56	57
59	59	59	62	62	62	63	64	65	66	66	67	67	69	69	71	77	78	79	79

a. Determine the median number of calls.
b. Determine the first and third quartiles.
c. Determine the 1st decile and the 9th decile.
d. Determine the 33rd percentile.

Box Plots

A **box plot** is a graphical display, based on quartiles, that helps us picture a set of data. To construct a box plot, we need only five statistics: the minimum value, Q_1 (the first quartile), the median, Q_3 (the third quartile), and the maximum value. An example will help to explain.

EXAMPLE

Alexander's Pizza offers free delivery of its pizza within 15 miles. Alex, the owner, wants some information on the time it takes for delivery. How long does a typical delivery take? Within what range of times will most deliveries be completed? For a sample of 20 deliveries, he determined the following information:

$$\text{Minimum value} = 13 \text{ minutes}$$
$$Q_1 = 15 \text{ minutes}$$
$$\text{Median} = 18 \text{ minutes}$$
$$Q_3 = 22 \text{ minutes}$$
$$\text{Maximum value} = 30 \text{ minutes}$$

Develop a box plot for the delivery times. What conclusions can you make about the delivery times?

SOLUTION

The first step in drawing a box plot is to create an appropriate scale along the horizontal axis. Next, we draw a box that starts at Q_1 (15 minutes) and ends at Q_3 (22 minutes). Inside the box we place a vertical line to represent the median (18 minutes). Finally, we extend horizontal lines from the box out to the minimum value (13 minutes) and the maximum value (30 minutes). These horizontal lines outside of the box are sometimes called "whiskers" because they look a bit like a cat's whiskers.

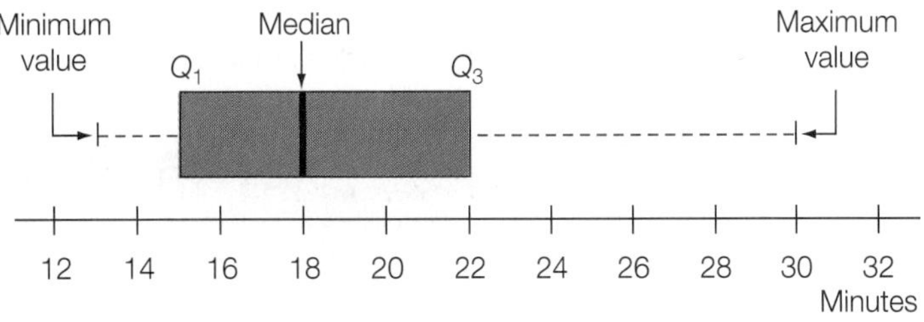

The box plot shows that the middle 50 percent of the deliveries take between 15 minutes and 22 minutes. The distance between the ends of the box, 7 minutes, is the **interquartile range.** The interquartile range is the distance between the first and the third quartile.

The box plot also reveals that the distribution of delivery times is positively skewed. How do we know this? In this case there are actually two pieces of information that suggest that the distribution is positively skewed. First, the dashed line to the right of the box from 22 minutes (Q_3) to the maximum time of 30 minutes is longer than the dashed line from the left of 15 minutes (Q_1) to the minimum value of 13 minutes. To put it another way, the 25 percent of the data larger than the third quartile is more spread out than the 25 percent less than the first quartile. A second indication of positive skewness is that the median is not in the center of the box. The distance from the first quartile to the median is smaller than the distance from the median to the third quartile. We know that the number of delivery times between 15 minutes and 18 minutes is the same as the number of delivery times between 18 minutes and 22 minutes.

EXAMPLE

Refer to the Whitner Pontiac data in Table 2–1. Develop a box plot of the data. What can we conclude about the distribution of the vehicle selling prices?

SOLUTION

The MINITAB statistical software system was used to develop the following chart.

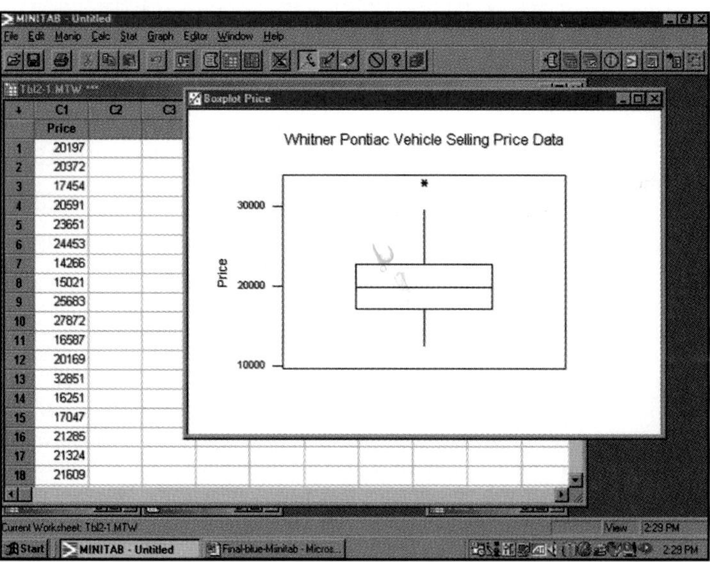

We conclude that the median vehicle selling price is about $20,000, that about 25 percent of the vehicles sell for less than $17,000, and that about 25 percent sell for more than $23,000. About 50 percent of the vehicles sell for between $17,000 and $23,000. The distribution is positively skewed because the solid line above $23,000 is somewhat longer than the line below $17,000.

There is an asterisk (*) above the $30,000 selling price. An asterisk indicates an outlier. An **outlier** is a value that is inconsistent with the rest of the data. The standard definition of an outlier is a value that is more than 1.5 times the interquartile range smaller than Q_1 or larger than Q_3. In this example, an outlier would be a value larger than $32,000, found by

$$\text{Outlier} > Q_3 + 1.5(Q_3 - Q_1) = \$23{,}000 + 1.5(\$23{,}000 - \$17{,}000) = \$32{,}000$$

A value less than $8,000 is also an outlier.

$$\text{Outlier} < Q_1 - 1.5(Q_3 - Q_1) = \$17{,}000 - 1.5(\$23{,}000 - \$17{,}000) = \$8{,}000$$

The MINITAB box plot indicates that there is only one value larger than $32,000. However, if you look at the actual data in Table 2–1 on page 23 you will notice that there are actually two values ($32,851 and $32,925). The software was not able to graph two data points so close together, so it shows only one asterisk.

Self-Review 4–9

The following box plot is given.

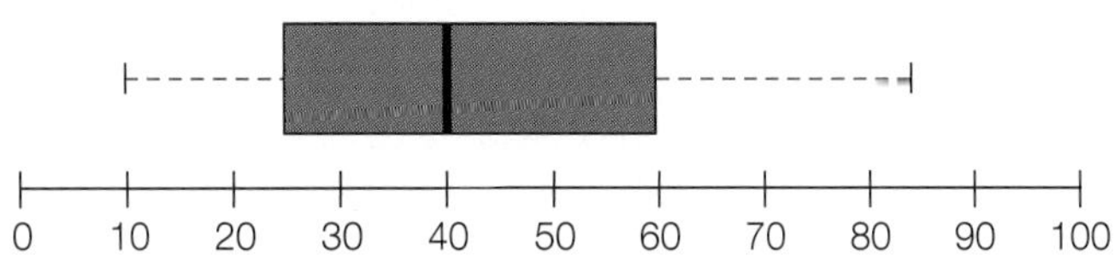

What are the median, the largest and smallest values, and the first and third quartiles? Would you agree that the distribution is symmetrical?

Exercises

39. Refer to the box plot below.

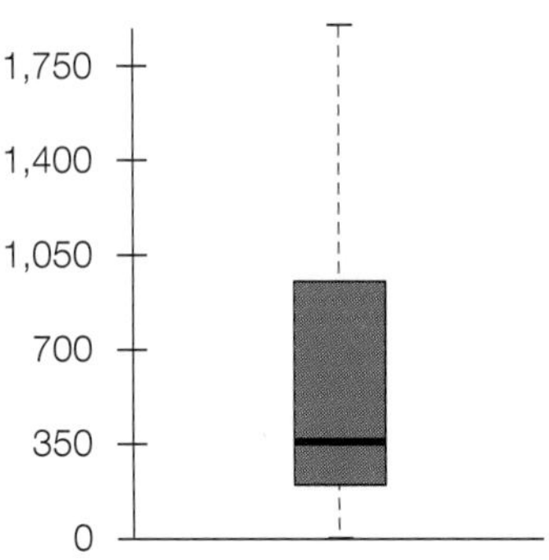

a. Estimate the median.
b. Estimate the first and third quartiles.
c. Determine the interquartile range.
d. Beyond what point is a value considered an outlier?
e. Identify any outliers and estimate their value.
f. Is the distribution symmetrical or positively or negatively skewed?

40. Refer to the following box plot.

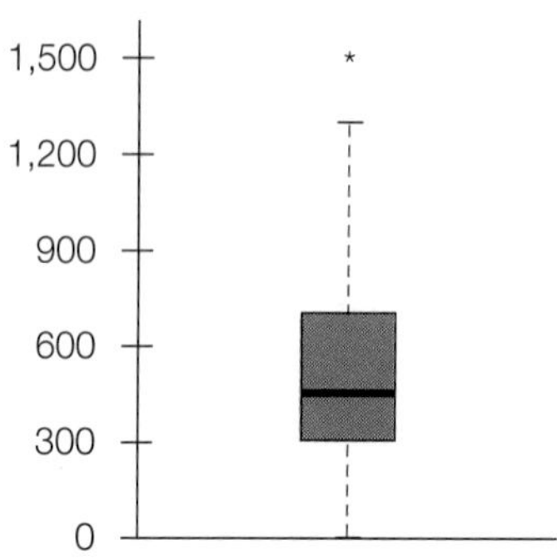

40. **a.** 450
b. 300, 700
c. 400
d. 1300
e. About 1500
f. Positive.

a. Estimate the median.
b. Estimate the first and third quartiles.
c. Determine the interquartile range.
d. Beyond what point is a value considered an outlier?
e. Identify any outliers and estimate their value.
f. Is the distribution symmetrical or positively or negatively skewed?

41. In a study of the mileage of automobiles manufactured in 2000, the mean number of miles per gallon was 27.5 and the median was 26.8. The smallest value in the study was 12.70 miles per gallon, and the largest was 50.20. The first and third quartiles were 17.95 and 35.45 miles per gallon, respectively. Develop a box plot and comment on the distribution. Is it a symmetric distribution?

42. See IM.

42. A sample of 28 hospitals in Florida revealed the following daily charges for a semiprivate room. For convenience the data are ordered from smallest to largest. Construct a box plot to represent the data. Comment on the distribution. Be sure to identify the first and third quartiles and the median.

$116	$121	$157	$192	$207	$209	$209
229	232	236	236	239	243	246
260	264	276	281	283	289	296
307	309	312	317	324	341	353

Chapter Outline

I. The dispersion is the variation in a set of data.
  A. The range is the difference between the largest and the smallest value in a set of data.
    1. The formula for the range is:

$$\text{Range} = \text{Highest value} - \text{Lowest value} \quad [4\text{–}1]$$

    2. The major characteristics of the range are:
      a. Only two values are used in its calculation.
      b. It is influenced by extreme values.
      c. It is easy to compute and to understand.
  B. The mean absolute deviation is the sum of the absolute deviations from the mean divided by the number of observations.
    1. The formula for computing the mean absolute deviation is

$$MD = \frac{\Sigma|X - \overline{X}|}{n} \quad [4\text{–}2]$$

2. The major characteristics of the absolute deviation are:
   a. It is not unduly influenced by large or small values.
   b. All observations are used in the calculation.
   c. The absolute values are somewhat difficult to work with.

C. The variance is the mean of the squared deviations from the arithmetic mean.
1. The major characteristics of the variance are:
   a. All observations are used in the calculation.
   b. It is not unduly influenced by extreme observations.
   c. The units are somewhat difficult to work with; they are the original units squared.
2. The formula for the population variance is:

$$\sigma^2 = \frac{\Sigma(X - \mu)^2}{N} \qquad \text{[4–3]}$$

3. The formula for the sample variance is

$$s^2 = \frac{\Sigma(X - \bar{X})^2}{n - 1} \qquad \text{[4-5]}$$

D. The standard deviation is the square root of the variance.
1. The following two formulas are for the sample standard deviation.

$$s = \sqrt{\frac{\Sigma(X - \bar{X})^2}{n - 1}} = \sqrt{\frac{\Sigma X^2 - \frac{(\Sigma X)^2}{n}}{n - 1}} \qquad \text{[4–5], [4–7]}$$

2. The major characteristics of the standard deviation are:
   a. It is in the same units as the original data.
   b. It is the square root of the average squared distance from the mean.
   c. It cannot be negative.
   d. It is the most widely reported measure of dispersion.

II. Chebyshev's theorem states that regardless of the shape of the distribution, at least $1 - 1/k^2$ of the observations will be within k standard deviations of the mean.

III. The coefficient of variation is a measure of relative dispersion.
A. The formula for the coefficient of variation is:

$$CV = \frac{s}{\bar{X}}(100) \qquad \text{[4–9]}$$

B. It reports the variation relative to the mean.
C. It is useful for comparing distributions with different units.

IV. The coefficient of skewness measures the symmetry of a distribution.
A. In a positively skewed set of data the long tail is to the right.
B. In a negatively skewed distribution the long tail is to the left.

V. Measures of location also describe the spread in a set of observations.
A. A quartile divides a set of observations into four equal parts.
1. Twenty-five percent of the observations are less than the first quartile, 50 percent are less than the second quartile (the median), and 75 percent are less than the third quartile.
2. The interquartile range is the difference between the third and the first quartile.

B. Deciles divide a set of observations into 10 equal parts.
C. Percentiles divide a set of observations into 100 equal parts.
D. A box plot is a graphic display of a set of data.
1. A box is drawn enclosing the first and third quartiles.
   a. A line through the inside of the box shows the median.
   b. Dotted line segments from the third quartile to the largest value and from the first quartile to the smallest value show the range of the largest 25 percent of the observations and the smallest 25 percent.

2. A box plot is based on five statistics: the largest and smallest observation, the first and third quartiles, and the median.

Pronunciation Key

SYMBOL	MEANING	PRONUNCIATION
σ^2	Population variance	*sigma squared*
σ	Population standard deviation	*sigma*
ΣfX^2	Sum of the product of the class midpoints squared and the class frequency	*sigma f X squared*
L_p	Location of percentile	*L sub p*
Q_1	First quartile	*Q sub 1*
Q_3	Third quartile	*Q sub 3*

Chapter Exercises

Exercises 43 through 51 are based on the following data. The quality control department at Clegg Industries constantly monitors three assembly lines producing ovens for private homes. The oven is designed to preheat to 240 degrees Fahrenheit in four minutes and then shut off. However, the oven may not reach 240 in the allotted time because of improper installation of the insulation and other reasons. Likewise, the temperature might go beyond 240 degrees during the four-minute preheating cycle. A large sample from each of the three production lines revealed the following information.

	Temperature (°F)		
Statistical Measure	**Line 1**	**Line 2**	**Line 3**
Arithmetic mean	238.1	240.0	242.9
Median	240.0	240.0	240.0
Mode	241.5	240.0	239.1
Standard deviation	3.0	0.4	3.9
Mean deviation	1.9	0.2	2.2
Interquartile range	2.0	0.2	3.4

43. Which of the lines has a bell-shaped distribution?

44. Line 3.

44. Which line has the most variation in the temperature? How do you know?

45. According to the Empirical Rule, about 95 percent of the temperature readings for line 2 are between what values?

46. Line 3.

46. The distribution of temperatures for which lines is positively skewed?

47. For line 2, approximate the first and the third quartiles.

48. 231.2, 254.6.

48. For line 3, according to Chebyshev's theorem, about 89 percent of the temperatures will be between what two values?

49. Determine the coefficient of variation for line 3.

50. −1.9

50. Determine the direction of the skewness for line 1.

51. Determine the variance for line 1.

52. Amount earned has more relative dispersion.

52. In a study of data from the personnel files of a large company, the coefficient of variation for the number of years with the company is 20 percent and the coefficient of variation for the amount of commission earned last year is 30 percent. Comment on the relative dispersion of the two variables.

53. In the same study discussed in exercise 52, the coefficient of skewness for the age of the employees is −2.25. Comment on the shape of the distribution. Which measure of central tendency is the largest? Which direction is the longer tail? What would you conclude about the ages of the employees?

54. a. 4
b. 1
c. 1.3093

54. The hourly outputs of a group of employees assembling plug-in units at Zenith were selected at random. The sample outputs were: 8, 9, 8, 10, 9, 10, 12, and 10.
- a. Compute the range.
- b. Compute the mean deviation.
- c. Compute the standard deviation.

55. The ages of a sample of Canadian tourists flying from Toronto to Hong Kong were: 32, 21, 60, 47, 54, 17, 72, 55, 33, and 41.
- a. Compute the range.
- b. Compute the mean deviation.
- c. Compute the standard deviation.

56. a. 9
b. 2.72
c. 3.5071

56. The weights (in pounds) of a sample of five boxes being sent by UPS are: 12, 6, 7, 3, and 10.
- a. Compute the range.
- b. Compute the mean deviation.
- c. Compute the standard deviation.

57. A southern state has seven state universities in its system. The numbers of volumes (in thousands) held in their libraries are 83, 510, 33, 256, 401, 47, and 23.
- a. Is this a sample or a population?
- b. Compute the standard deviation.
- c. Compute the coefficient of variation. Interpret.

58. a. 30
b. 6.514

58. A recent report in *Woman's World* magazine suggested that the typical family of four with an intermediate budget spends about $96 per week on food. The following frequency distribution was included in the report. Compute (a) the range and (b) the standard deviation.

Amount Spent	Frequency
$ 80 up to $ 85	6
85 up to 90	12
90 up to 95	23
95 up to 100	35
100 up to 105	24
105 up to 110	10

59. Bidwell Electronics, Inc., recently surveyed a sample of employees to determine how far they lived from corporate headquarters. The results are shown below. Compute the range and the standard deviation.

Distance (miles)	Frequency
0 up to 5	4
5 up to 10	15
10 up to 15	27
15 up to 20	18
20 up to 25	6

60. 30,6.09

60. Health issues are a concern of managers, especially as they evaluate the cost of medical insurance. In a recent survey of 150 executives at Elvers Industries, a large insurance and financial firm located in the Southwest, the number of pounds by which the executives were overweight was reported. Compute the range and the standard deviation.

Pounds Overweight	Frequency
0 up to 6	14
6 up to 12	42
12 up to 18	58
18 up to 24	28
24 up to 30	8

61. A major airline wanted some information on those enrolled in their "frequent flyer" program. A sample of 48 members resulted in the following number of miles flown, to the nearest 1,000 miles, by each participant. Develop a box plot of the data and comment on the information.

22	29	32	38	39	41	42	43	43	43	44	44
45	45	46	46	46	47	50	51	52	54	54	55
56	57	58	59	60	61	61	63	63	64	64	67
69	70	70	70	71	71	72	73	74	76	78	88

62. The National Muffler Company claims they will change your muffler in less than 30 minutes. An undercover consumer reporter for WTOL Channel 11 monitored 30 consecutive muffler changes at the National outlet on Liberty Street. The number of minutes to perform changes is reported below.

44	12	22	31	26	22	30	26	18	28	12
40	17	13	14	17	25	29	15	30	10	28
16	33	24	20	29	34	23	13			

62. a. See IM.
b. None.
c. Positive.

a. Develop a box plot for the time to change a muffler.
b. Does the distribution show any outliers?
c. Summarize your findings in a brief report.

63. The Walter Gogel Company is an industrial supplier of fasteners, tools, and springs. The amounts of their invoices vary widely, from less than $20.00 to over $400.00. During the month of January they sent out 80 invoices. Here is a box plot of these invoices. Write a brief report summarizing the amounts of their invoices. Be sure to include information on the values of the first and third quartile, the median, and whether there is any skewness. If there are any outliers, approximate the value of these invoices.

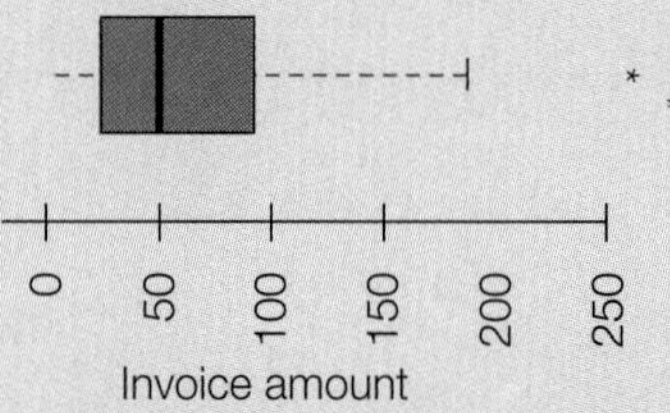

64. Median = 20.
Q_1 = 10,
Q_3 = 40,
positive.

64. The following box plot shows the number of daily newspapers published in each state and the District of Columbia. Write a brief report summarizing the number published. Be sure to include information on the values of the first and third quartiles, the median, and whether there is any skewness. If there are any outliers, estimate their value.

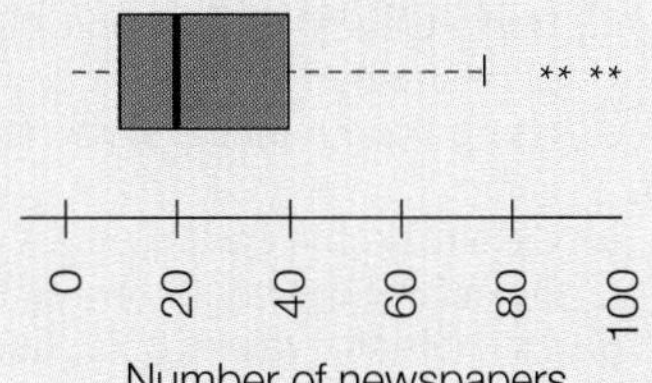

65. The previous problem presented a box plot of the number of daily newspapers by state and the District of Columbia. Listed below is a summary from Excel showing statistics for the same data set.

Number of Papers	
Mean	30.05882
Standard Error	3.409837
Median	23
Mode	22
Standard Deviation	24.35111
Sample Variance	592.9765
Kurtosis	0.933851
Skewness	1.271859
Range	96
Minimum	2
Maximum	98
Sum	1533
Count	51

a. Chebyshev's theorem states that at least 75 percent of the observations will be within two standard deviations of the mean. What are these limits?

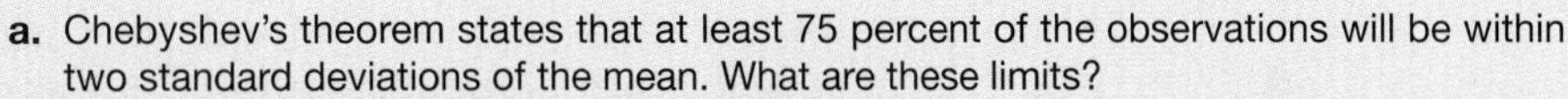

b. Determine the coefficient of variation. Interpret.

c. Do the values tend to show a positive or a negative skewness? How do you know?

66. Danfoss Electronics, Inc., has 150 suppliers throughout the United States and Canada. Listed below are MINITAB summary statistics on the sales volume to its suppliers.

```
Variable      N      Mean     Median    Tr Mean    StDev    SE Mean
Sales       150     128.1       81.0      102.2    162.7       13.3

Variable    Min       Max         Q1         Q3
Sales       2.0    1019.0       38.7      138.2
```

66. a. 1017
b. 99.5
c. 127%
d. .86 positive
e. See IM.

a. What is the range?

b. Determine the interquartile range.

c. Determine the coefficient of variation.

d. Determine the direction of the skewness.

e. Draw a box plot.

67. The following data are the estimated market values (in $millions) of 50 companies in the auto parts business.

26.8	8.6	6.5	30.6	15.4	18.0	7.6	21.5	11.0	10.2
28.3	15.5	31.4	23.4	4.3	20.2	33.5	7.9	11.2	1.0
11.7	18.5	6.8	22.3	12.9	29.8	1.3	14.1	29.7	18.7
6.7	31.4	30.4	20.6	5.2	37.8	13.4	18.3	27.1	32.7
6.1	0.9	9.6	35.0	17.1	1.9	1.2	16.6	31.1	16.1

a. Determine the mean and the median of the market values.

b. Determine the standard deviation of the market values.

c. Using Chebyshev's theorem, between what values would you expect about 56 percent of the market values to occur?
d. Using the Empirical Rule, about 95 percent of the values would occur between what values?
e. Determine the coefficient of variation.
f. Determine the coefficient of skewness.
g. Estimate the values of Q_1 and Q_3. Draw a box plot.
h. Write a brief report summarizing the results.

68. Listed below are the 20 largest mutual funds as of November 21, 2000, their assets in millions of dollars, their five-year rate of return, and their one-year rate of return. Assume the data is a sample.

Fund	Assets ($Mil)	Return-5yr	Return-1yr
Vanguard Index Fds: 500	104357	143.5	−4.4
Fidelity Invest: Magellan	101625	118.8	−3.9
American Funds A: ICAA	56614	129.8	3.1
American Funds A: WshA	46780	108.1	−2.4
Janus: Fund	46499	177.5	−2.2
Fidelity Invest: Contra	42437	133.4	1.6
Fidelity Invest: GroInc	42059	127.7	0.1
American Funds: Growth A	39400	202.8	−6.4
American Century: Ultra	38559	128.2	−5.8
Janus: WorldWide	37780	187.3	2.2
Fidelity Invest: GroCo	34255	202.1	13.2
American Funds A: EupacA	32826	98.0	−2.8
American Funds A: PerA	32308	122.8	−2.0
Janus: Twen	31023	264.3	−12.9
Fidelity Invest: Blue Chip	29708	132.0	−1.2
Vanguard Instl Fds: Instidx	28893	145.0	−4.3
PIMCO Funds Instl: TotRt	28201	41.4	7.7
Putman Funds A: VovA	24262	144.7	−0.5
Vanguard Funds: WndsII	24069	105.7	4.6
Vanguard Funds: Prmcp	22742	203.0	10.9

68. a. 42,220, 36,018, 22,495, 145.8, 132.7, 48.8, −0.27, −1.60, 6.10
b. 53.3, 33.4, −2259.3
c. 2.17, .454, .485
d. See IM.
e. See IM.

a. Compute the mean, median, and standard deviation for each of the variables. Compare the standard deviations for the one-year and five-year rates of return. Comment on your findings.
b. Compute the coefficient of variation for each of the above variables. Comment on the relative variation of the three variables.
c. Compute the coefficient of skewness for each of the above variables. Comment on the skewness of the three variables.
d. Compute the first and third quartiles for the one-year and five-year rates of return.
e. Draw a box plot for the one-year and five-year rates of return. Comment on the results. Are there any outliers?

69. The Apollo space program lasted from 1967 until 1972 and included 13 missions. The missions lasted from as little as 7 hours to as long as 301 hours. The duration of each flight is listed below.

9	195	241	301	216	260	7	244	192	147
10	295	142							

a. Find the mean, median, and standard deviation of the duration for the Apollo flights.
b. Compute the coefficient of variation and the coefficient of skewness. Comment on your findings.
c. Find the 45th and 82nd percentiles.
d. Draw a box plot and comment on your findings.

70. Listed below is the average daily circulation for the 50 U. S. newspapers with the largest circulation.

Newspaper	Circulation	Newspaper	Circulation
Wall Street Journal (New York, N.Y.)	1,740,450	Star Tribune (Minneapolis)	334,751
USA Today (Arlington, Va.)	1,653,428	Rocky Mountain News (Denver)	331,978
Times (Los Angeles)	1,067,540	Post-Dispatch (St. Louis)	329,582
Times (New York, N.Y.)	1,066,658	Sun (Baltimore)	314,033
Post (Washington, D.C.)	759,122	Constitution (Atlanta)	303,698
Daily News (New York, N.Y.)	723,143	Mercury News (San Jose, Calif.)	290,885
Tribune (Chicago)	673,508	Journal Sentinel (Milwaukee)	285,776
Newsday (Long Island, N.Y.)	572,444	Bee (Sacramento, Calif.)	283,589
Chronicle (Houston)	550,763	Star (Kansas City, Mo.)	281,596
Sun-Times (Chicago)	485,666	Herald (Boston)	271,425
Morning News (Dallas)	479,863	Times-Picayune (New Orleans)	259,317
Chronicle (San Francisco)	475,324	Sun-Sentinel (Fort Lauderdale, Fla.)	258,726
Globe (Boston)	470,825	Sentinel (Orlando, Fla.)	258,726
Post (New York, N.Y.)	437,467	Investor's Business Daily (Los Angeles)	251,172
Arizona Republic (Phoenix)	435,330	Dispatch (Columbus, Ohio)	246,528
Inquirer (Philadelphia)	428,895	News (Detroit)	245,351
Star-Ledger (Newark, N.J.)	407,026	Observer (Charlotte, N.C.)	243,818
Plain Dealer (Cleveland)	382,933	Post-Gazette (Pittsburgh, Pa.)	243,453
Free Press (Detroit)	378,256	News (Buffalo, N.Y.)	237,229
Union-Tribune (San Diego)	378,112	Tribune (Tampa, Fla.)	235,786
Register (Orange County, Calif.)	356,953	Star-Telegram (Fort Worth, Tex.)	232,112
Herald (Miami)	349,114	Star (Indianapolis)	230,223
Oregonian (Portland)	346,593	Courier-Journal (Louisville, Ky.)	228,144
Times (St. Petersburg, Fla.)	344,784	Times (Seattle)	227,715
Post (Denver)	341,554	World-Herald (Omaha, Neb.)	219,891

a. 439,025; 338,153; 256,838; 471,950
b. 241,274.6, 755,524.1
c. 2.82, large positive.
d. See IM.

a. Find the mean, median, Q_1, and Q_3.
b. Find the 15th and the 90th percentiles.
c. Find the coefficient of skewness and interpret the result.
d. Develop a box plot and interpret the result.

71. Listed below are the populations of the 50 states.

State	Population	State	Population	State	Population
Alabama	4,369,862	Louisiana	4,372,035	Ohio	11,256,654
Alaska	619,500	Maine	1,253,040	Oklahoma	3,858,044
Arizona	4,778,332	Maryland	5,171,634	Oregon	3,316,154
Arkansas	25,551,373	Massachusetts	6,175,169	Pennsylvania	11,994,016
California	33,145,121	Michigan	9,863,775	Rhode Island	990,819
Colorado	4,056,133	Minnesota	4,775,508	South Carolina	3,885,736
Connecticut	3,282,031	Mississippi	2,768,619	South Dakota	733,133
Delaware	753,538	Missouri	5,468,338	Tennessee	5,483,535
Florida	15,111,244	Montana	882,779	Texas	20,044,141
Georgia	7,788,240	Nebraska	1,666,028	Utah	2,129,836
Hawaii	1,185,497	Nevada	1,809,253	Vermont	593,740
Idaho	1,251,700	New Hampshire	1,201,134	Virginia	6,872,912
Illinois	12,128,370	New Jersey	8,143,412	Washington	5,756,361
Indiana	5,942,901	New Mexico	1,739,844	West Virginia	1,806,928
Iowa	2,869,413	New York	18,196,601	Wisconsin	5,250,446
Kansas	2,654,052	North Carolina	7,650,789	Wyoming	479,602
Kentucky	3,960,825	North Dakota	633,666		

a. Find the mean, median, Q_1, and Q_3.
b. Find the 15th and the 90th percentiles.
c. Find the coefficient of skewness and interpret the result.
d. Develop a box plot and interpret the result.

exercises.com

72. See IM.

72. The National Center for Health Statistics maintains a Website at: http://www.cdc.gov/nchs. Under the section labeled **Tabulated State Data**, click on **Births**. Go to that page and locate the table "Live Births by Race and Hispanic Origin of Mother: U.S., Each State, Puerto Rico, Virgin Islands, and Guam." Suppose you are interested in birth rates for the 50 states. Develop a box plot of the data. Compute the mean, median, standard deviation, and coefficient of skewness. What can you conclude about the shape of the distribution?

73. In Exercise 68 in Chapter 3, we presented information on the Dow Jones Industrial Average on July 11, 2000. That information is repeated below.

a. Develop a box plot for these 30 observations and write a brief report. Is the distribution symmetric? What are your estimates of the first and third quartiles and the median? Are there any outliers?

b. Determine the standard deviation of these stock prices. Do the prices show much variation?

c. You may want to go to the following Website to find current information about the DJIA: http://foxnews.com/news/features/dow/. Has there been much of a change since the above data were collected? You might want to check to see whether any of the companies included in the DJIA have changed.

Company Name	Symbol	Price	Weighting %
Alcoa Inc.	(AA)	31.6875	1.677
American Express Co.	(AXP)	53.5625	2.835
AT&T Corp.	(T)	31.8750	1.687
Boeing Co.	(BA)	44.1250	2.335
Caterpillar Inc.	(CAT)	35.9375	1.902
Citigroup Inc.	(C)	65.8750	3.487
Coca-Cola Co.	(KO)	56.0000	2.964
DuPont Co.	(DD)	46.5625	2.464
Eastman Kodak Co.	(EK)	60.6250	3.209
Exxon Mobil Corp.	(XOM)	80.4375	4.258
General Electric Co.	(GE)	52.7500	2.792
General Motors Corp.	(GM)	62.0625	3.285
Home Depot Inc.	(HD)	57.1875	3.027
Honeywell International Inc.	(HON)	35.8125	1.895
Hewlett-Packard Co.	(HWP)	124.8125	6.607
International Business Machines Corp.	(IBM)	101.3750	5.366
Intel Corp.	(INTC)	138.8125	7.348
International Paper Co.	(IP)	34.8125	1.842
J.P. Morgan & Co.	(JPM)	117.9375	6.243
Johnson & Johnson	(JNJ)	99.6250	5.273
McDonald's Corp.	(MCD)	32.3750	1.713
Merck & Co.	(MRK)	74.3750	3.937
Microsoft Corp.	(MSFT)	78.8750	4.175
Minnesota Mining & Manufacturing Co.	(MMM)	88.4375	4.681
Philip Morris Cos.	(MO)	25.9375	1.373
Procter & Gamble Co.	(PG)	54.5625	2.888
SBC Communications Inc.	(SBC)	44.2500	2.342
United Technologies Corp.	(UTX)	59.3125	3.139
Wal-Mart Stores Inc.	(WMT)	61.8125	3.272
Walt Disney Co.	(DIS)	37.4375	1.981

Computer Data Exercises

74. a. 1. 221.103; 213.6; 47.105
2. .474
3. See IM. Q_1 = 186.85, Q_3 = 251.85.
4. See IM.
b. 1. 2223.81; 2200; 248.66
2. .323
3. See IM.
4. See IM.

74. Refer to the Real Estate data, which reports information on homes sold in the Venice, Florida, area last year.
- **a.** For the variable selling price:
  1. Find the mean, median, and standard deviation.
  2. Determine the coefficient of skewness. Is the distribution positively or negatively skewed?
  3. Develop a box plot. Are there any outliers? Estimate the first and third quartiles.
  4. Write a brief summary of the distribution of selling prices.
- **b.** For the variable "area of the home in square feet":
  1. Find the mean, median, and the standard deviation.
  2. Determine the coefficient of skewness. Is the distribution positively or negatively skewed?
  3. Develop a box plot. Are there any outliers? Estimate the first and third quartiles.
  4. Write a brief summary of the distribution of the area of homes.

75. Refer to the Baseball 2000 data, which reports information on the 30 Major League Baseball teams for the 2000 baseball season.
- **a.** For the variable team salary:
  1. Find the mean, median, and standard deviation.
  2. Determine the coefficient of skewness. Is the distribution positively or negatively skewed?
  3. Develop a box plot. Are there any outliers? Estimate the first and third quartiles.
  4. Write a brief summary of the distribution of team salaries.
- **b.** For the variable that refers to the year in which the stadium was built (Hint: Subtract the current year from the year in which the stadium was built to find the stadium age and work with that variable):
  1. Find the mean, median, and standard deviation.
  2. Determine the coefficient of skewness. Is the distribution positively or negatively skewed?
  3. Develop a box plot. Are there any outliers? Estimate the first and third quartiles.
  4. Write a brief summary of the distribution of the age of the stadium.

76. a. 1. 17,543.7; 5175; 27,175.8
2. 3.288
3. See IM.
4. See IM.
b. 1. 13.3, 14.4, 3.2326
2. −1.616
3. See IM.
4. See IM.

76. Refer to the OECD data, which reports information on the census, economic, and business data for 29 countries.
- **a.** For the variable employment:
  1. Find the mean, median, and standard deviation.
  2. Determine the coefficient of skewness. Is the distribution positively or negatively skewed?
  3. Develop a box plot. Are there any outliers? Estimate the first and third quartiles.
  4. Write a brief summary of the distribution of employment.
- **b.** For the variable percent of the population over the age of 65:
  1. Find the mean, median, and standard deviation.
  2. Determine the coefficient of skewness. Is the distribution positively or negatively skewed?
  3. Develop a box plot. Are there any outliers? Estimate the first and third quartiles.
  4. Write a brief summary of the distribution of percent of population over 65.

77. Refer to the Schools data, which reports information on 94 school districts in Northwest Ohio.
- **a.** For the variable teacher salary:
  1. Find the mean, median, and standard deviation.
  2. Determine the coefficient of skewness. Is the distribution positively or negatively skewed?
  3. Develop a box plot. Are there any outliers? Estimate the first and third quartiles.
  4. Write a brief summary of the distribution.
- **b.** For the variable number of students in the school district:
  1. Find the mean, median, and standard deviation.
  2. Determine the coefficient of skewness. Is the distribution positively or negatively skewed?
  3. Develop a box plot. Are there any outliers? Estimate the first and third quartiles.
  4. Write a brief summary of the distribution.

Computer Commands

1. The MINITAB commands for the descriptive summary on page 120 are:
   a. Enter the earnings reported in the Example on page 118 in column C1 of the spreadsheet. Name the variable **Earnings**.
   b. Select **Stat**, **Basic Statistics**, and then **Display Descriptive Statistics**. In the dialog box select Earnings as the variable and then click on **Graphs** in the lower right corner. Within this dialog box select **Graphic summary** and click **OK**. Click **OK** in the next dialog box.

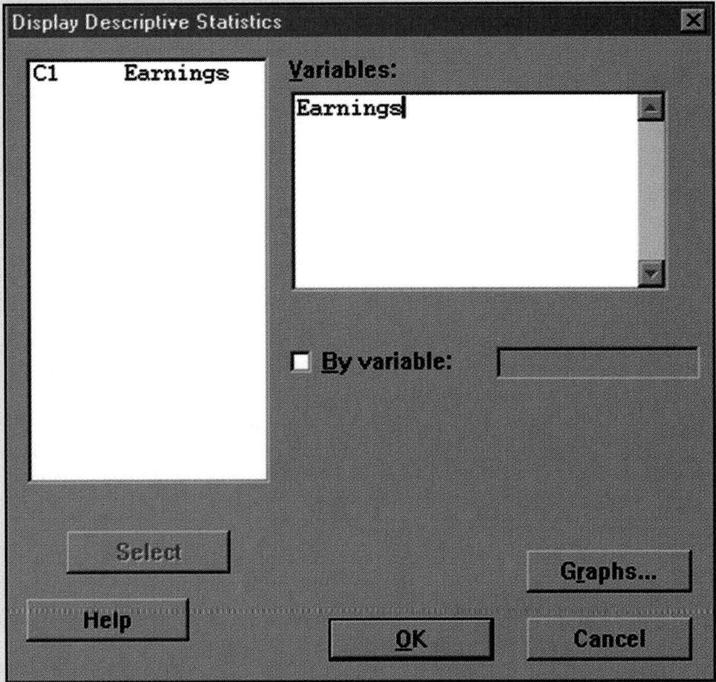

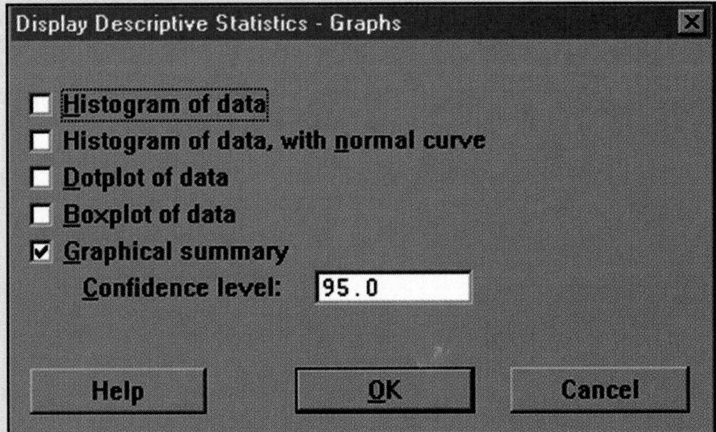

2. The MINITAB Commands for the summary of the Whitner Pontiac data on page 123 are:
   a. Import the data from the CD. The file name is **Tbl2–1.**
   b. Use the same commands as in the previous description. The dialog boxes will appear the same.

3. The Excel commands for the summary of descriptive statistics on page 124 are:
   a. Import the data from the CD. Select the Excel format. The file is **Tbl2–1.**
   b. Select **Tools** and then **Data Analysis** and hit **Enter.**
   c. Select **Descriptive Statistics** and select **OK**.
   d. The **Input Range** is *a1:a81*, select **Grouped by Columns**, click on **Labels in First Row**, **Output Range** is *D1*, click on **Summary Statistics**, and then click **OK**.

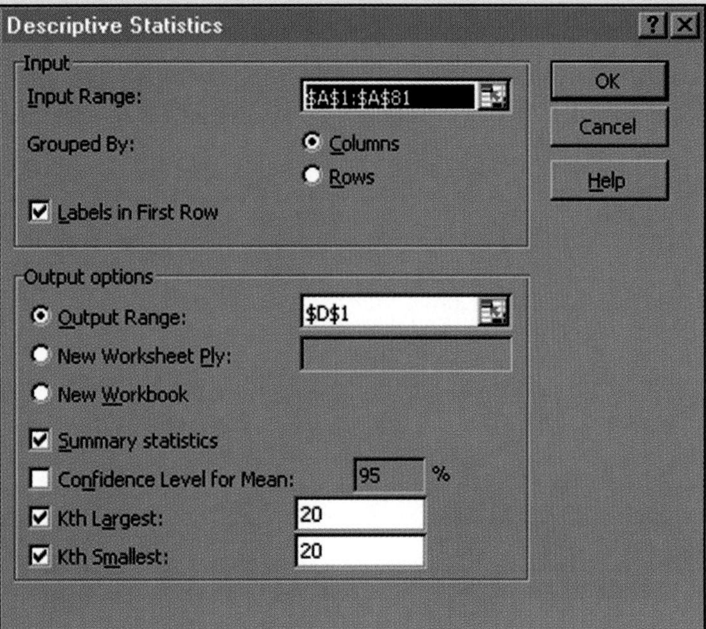

4. The MINITAB commands for the box plot on page 126 are:
   a. Import the data from the CD. The file name is **Tbl2–1.**
   b. Select **Graph** and then **Boxplots.** In the dialog box select *Price* as the variable and click **OK.**

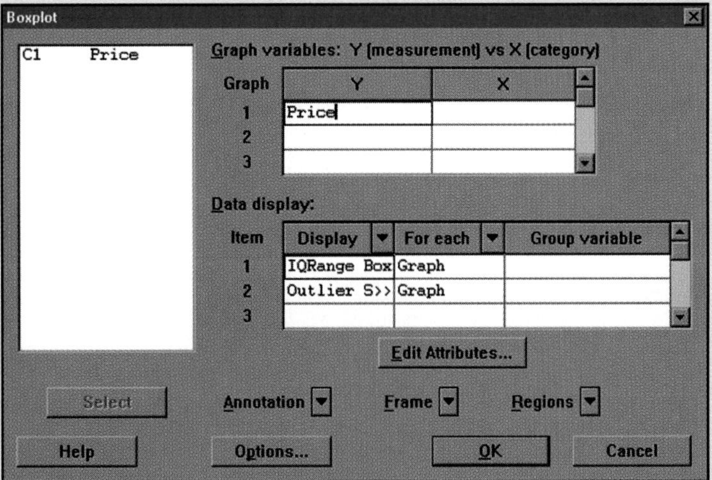

Chapter 4 Answers to Self-Review

4–1 **(a)** 22, found by 112 − 90.

(b) $\bar{X} = \frac{824}{8} = 103$

(c)

X	$\lvert X - \bar{X} \rvert$	Absolute Deviation
95	$\lvert -8 \rvert$	8
103	$\lvert 0 \rvert$	0
105	$\lvert +2 \rvert$	2
110	$\lvert +7 \rvert$	7
104	$\lvert +1 \rvert$	1
105	$\lvert +2 \rvert$	2
112	$\lvert +9 \rvert$	9
90	$\lvert -13 \rvert$	13
	Total	42

$$MD = \frac{42}{8} = 5.25 \text{ pounds}$$

4–2 **(a)** $\mu = \frac{\$11,900}{5} = \$2380$

(b) $\sigma^2 = \frac{(2536 - 2380)^2 + \cdots + (2622 - 2380)^2}{5}$

$$= \frac{(156)^2 + (-207)^2 + (68)^2 + (-259)^2 + (242)^2}{5}$$

$$= \frac{197,454}{5} = 39,490.8$$

(c) $\sigma = \sqrt{39,490.8} = 198.72$

(d) There is more variation in the Pittsburgh office because the standard deviation is larger. The mean is also larger in the Pittsburgh office.

4–3 2.33, found by:

$$\bar{X} = \frac{\Sigma X}{n} = \frac{28}{7} = 4$$

X	$X - \bar{X}$	$(X - \bar{X})^2$	X^2
4	0	0	16
2	−2	4	4
5	1	1	25
4	0	0	16
5	1	1	25
2	−2	4	4
6	2	4	36
28	0	14	126

$$s^2 = \frac{\Sigma(X - \bar{X})^2}{n - 1} \quad \text{or} \quad s^2 = \frac{\Sigma X^2 - \frac{(\Sigma X)^2}{n}}{n - 1}$$

$$= \frac{14}{7 - 1} \qquad = \frac{126 - \frac{(28)^2}{7}}{7 - 1}$$

$$= 2.33 \qquad = \frac{126 - 112}{6}$$

$$= 2.33$$

$$s = \sqrt{2.33} = 1.53$$

4–4 **(a)** 12 − 2 = 10 months

(b) 2.130 months, found by:

Months	f	X	fX	fX^2
2 up to 4	2	3	6	18
4 up to 6	5	5	25	125
6 up to 8	10	7	70	490
8 up to 10	4	9	36	324
10 up to 12	2	11	22	242
	23		159	1,199

$$s = \sqrt{\frac{1,199 - \frac{(159)^2}{23}}{23 - 1}}$$

$$= \sqrt{\frac{1,199 - 1,099.1739}{23}}$$

$$= \sqrt{4.53755}$$

$$= 2.130 \text{ months}$$

(c) $s^2 = (2.130)^2 = 4.5369.$

4–5 **(a)** $k = \frac{14.15 - 14.00}{.10} = 1.5$

$$1 - \frac{1}{(1.5)^2} = 1 - .44 = .56$$

(b) 13.8 and 14.2

4–6 *CV* for mechanical is 5 percent, found by (10/200)(100). For finger dexterity, *CV* is 20 percent, found by (6/30)(100). Thus, relative dispersion in finger dexterity scores is greater than relative dispersion in mechanical, because 20 percent > 5 percent.

4–7 **(a)** $\bar{X} = \frac{407}{5} = 81.4$, Median = 84

$$s = \sqrt{\frac{34{,}053 - \frac{(407)^2}{5}}{5-1}} = 15.19$$

(b) $sk = \frac{3(81.4 - 84.0)}{15.19} = -0.51$

(c)

X	$\frac{X-\bar{X}}{s}$	$\left[\frac{(X-\bar{X})^3}{s}\right]$
73	−0.5530	−0.1691
98	1.0928	1.3050
60	−1.4088	−2.7961
92	0.6978	0.3398
84	0.1712	0.0050
		−1.3154

$$sk = \frac{5}{(4)(3)}[-1.3154]$$

$$= -0.5481$$

(d) The distribution is somewhat negatively skewed.

4–8 **(a)** 7.90

(b) $Q_1 = 7.76$, $Q_2 = 8.015$

4–9 The smallest value is 10 and the largest 85; the first quartile is 25 and the third 60. About 50 percent of the values are between 25 and 60. The median value is 40. The distribution is somewhat positively skewed.

A Review of Chapters 1–4

This section is a review of the major concepts and terms introduced in Chapters 1 through 4. These chapters were concerned with describing a set of data by organizing it into a *frequency distribution* and then portraying the distribution in the form of a *histogram,* a *frequency polygon,* and a *cumulative frequency polygon.* The purpose of these graphs is to visually reveal the important characteristics of the data.

Computing a central value to represent the data is a numerical way of summarizing a mass of observations. Chapter 3 looked at several measures of central tendency, including the *mean, weighted mean, geometric mean, median,* and *mode.* Chapter 4 described the *dispersion,* or *spread,* in the data by computing the *range, standard deviation,* and other measures. Further, *skewness,* or lack of symmetry in the data, was described by determining the *coefficient of skewness.*

We stressed the importance of computer software packages, including Excel and MINITAB. Several computer outputs in these chapters demonstrated how quickly and accurately a mass of raw data can be organized into a frequency distribution and a histogram. Also, we noted that the computer outputs present a large number of descriptive measures, including the mean, the variance, and the standard deviation.

Glossary

Chapter 1

Descriptive statistics The techniques used to describe the important characteristics of a set of data. These may include organizing the values into a frequency distribution and computing measures of central tendency and measures of spread and skewness.

Exhaustive Each observation must fall into one of the categories.

Inferential statistics, also called **statistical inference** or **inductive statistics** This facet of statistics deals with estimating a population parameter based on a sample statistic. For example, if 2 out of the 10 hand calculators sampled are defective, we might infer that 20 percent of the production is defective.

Interval measurement If one observation is greater than another by a certain amount, and the zero point is arbitrary, the measurement is on an interval scale. For example, the difference between temperatures of 70 degrees and 80 degrees is 10 degrees. Likewise, a temperature of 90 degrees is 10 degrees more than a temperature of 80 degrees, and so on.

Mutually exclusive A property of a set of categories such that an individual, object, or measurement is included in only one category.

Nominal measurement The "lowest" level of measurement. If data are classified into categories and the order of those categories is not important, it is the nominal level of measurement. Examples are gender (male, female) and political affiliation (Republican, Democrat, Independent, all others). If it makes no difference whether male or female is listed first, the data are nominal level.

Ordinal measurement Data that can be logically ranked are referred to as ordinal measures. For example, consumer response to the sound of a new speaker might be excellent, very good, fair, or poor.

Population The collection, or set, of all individuals, objects, or measurements whose properties are being studied.

Ratio measurement If the distances between numbers are of a known constant size and *there is a true zero point,* and the ratio of two values is meaningful, the measurement is ratio scale. For example, the distance between $200 and $300 is $100, and in the case of money there is a true zero point. If you have zero dollars, there is an absence of money (you have none). Also the ratio between $200 and $300 is meaningful.

Sample A portion, or subset, of the population being studied.

Statistics The science of collecting, organizing, analyzing, and interpreting numerical data for the purpose of making more effective decisions.

Chapter 2

Charts Special graphical formats used to portray a frequency distribution, including histograms, frequency polygons, and cumulative frequency polygons. Other graphical devices used to portray data are line charts, bar charts, and pie charts. They are very useful, for example, for depicting the trend in long-term debt or percent changes in profit from last year to this year.

Class The interval in which the data are tallied. For example, $4 up to $7 is a class; $7 up to $11 is another class.

Class frequency The number of observations in each class. If there are 16 observations in the "$4 up to $6" class, 16 is the class frequency.

Frequency distribution A grouping of data into classes showing the number of observations in each

of the nonoverlapping classes. For example, data are organized into classes, such as $1,000 up to $2,000, $2,000 up to $3,000 and so on to summarize the information.
Midpoint The value that divides the class into two equal parts. For the classes $10 up to $20 and $20 up to $30, the midpoints are $15 and $25, respectively.

Chapter 3

Arithmetic mean The sum of the values divided by the number of values. The symbol for the mean of a sample is $\overline{X}$ and the symbol for a population mean is μ.
Geometric mean The *n*th root of the product of all the values. It is especially useful for averaging rates of change and index numbers. It minimizes the importance of extreme values. A second use of the geometric mean is to find the mean annual percent change over a period of time. For example, if gross sales were $245 million in 1985 and $692 million in 2000, what is the average annual percent increase?
Measure of central tendency A number that describes the central tendency of the data. There are several such measures, including the arithmetic mean, weighted mean, median, mode, and geometric mean.
Median The value of the middle observation after all the observations have been arranged from low to high. For example, if observations 6, 9, 4 are rearranged to read 4, 6, 9, the middle value is 6, the median.
Mode The value that appears most frequently in a set of data. For grouped data, it is the *midpoint* of the class containing the largest number of values.
Weighted mean Each value is weighted according to its relative importance. For example, if 5 shirts cost $10 each and 20 shirts cost $8 each, the weighted mean price is $8.40: [(5 × $10) + (20 × $8)]/25 = $210/25 = $8.40.

Chapter 4

Coefficient of skewness A measure of the lack of symmetry in a distribution. For a symmetrical distribution there is no skewness, so the coefficient of skewness is zero. Otherwise, it is either positive or negative, with the limits at ±3.0.
Coefficient of variation The standard deviation divided by the mean, expressed as a percent. It is especially useful for comparing the relative dispersion in two or more sets of data where (1) they are in different units or (2) one mean is much larger than the other mean.
Dispersion or spread A measure of central tendency pinpoints a single value that is typical of the data. A measure of dispersion indicates how close or far apart the values are from the mean or other measure of central tendency.
Interquartile range The distance between the third quartile and the first quartile.
Mean deviation The mean of the deviations from the mean, disregarding signs. It is abbreviated as *MD.*
Range Difference between the highest and lowest values.
Standard deviation Square root of the variance.
Variance Mean of the squared deviations from the mean.
Quartiles Values that divide a set of data into four equal parts.

Exercises

The answers to the odd-numbered exercises are at the end of the book.

1. A small number of employees were selected from all the employees at NED Electronics and their hourly rates recorded. The rates were: $9.50, $9.00, $11.70, $14.80, and $13.00.
   a. Are the hourly rates a sample or a population?
   b. What is the level of measurement?
   c. What is the arithmetic mean hourly rate?
   d. What is the median hourly rate? Interpret.
   e. What is the variance?
   f. What is the coefficient of skewness? Interpret.
2. The weekly overtime hours worked by all the employees at the Publix Market are: 1, 4, 6, 12, 5, and 2.
   a. Is this a sample or a population?
   b. What is the mean number of overtime hours worked?
   c. What is the median? Interpret.
   d. What is the mode?
   e. What is the mean deviation?
   f. What is the standard deviation?
   g. What is the coefficient of variation?

2. a. Population.
   b. 5.0 hours.
   c. 4.5 hours.
   d. No mode.
   e. 2.67 hours.
   f. 3.56 hours.
   g. 71%.

3. The Tourist Bureau of St. Thomas surveyed a sample of tourists as they left to return to the United States. One of the questions was: How many rolls of film did you expose when visiting our island? The responses were:

8	6	3	11	14	8	9	16	9	10
5	11	7	8	8	10	9	12	13	9

a. Using five classes, organize the sample data into a frequency distribution.
b. Portray the distribution in the form of a frequency polygon.
c. What is the mean number of rolls exposed? Use the actual raw data.
d. What is the median? Use the actual raw data.
e. What is the mode? Use the actual raw data.
f. What is the range? Use the actual raw data.
g. What is the sample variance? Use the actual raw data.
h. What is the sample standard deviation? Use the actual raw data.
i. Assuming that the distribution is symmetrical and bell-shaped, about 95 percent of the tourists exposed between ________ and ________ rolls.

4. The annual amounts spent on research and development for a sample of electronic component manufacturers are (in $ millions):

8	34	15	24	15	28	12	20	22	23
14	26	18	23	10	21	16	17	22	31
13	25	20	28	6	20	19	27	16	22

4. a. Ratio.
b. See IM.
c. See IM.
d. See IM.
e. $20 million.
f. $19.83.
g. About $9.

a. What is the level of measurement?
b. Using six classes, organize the expenditures into a frequency distribution.
c. Portray the distribution in the form of a histogram.
d. Portray the distribution in the form of a less-than cumulative frequency polygon.
e. Based on the less-than cumulative frequency polygon, what is the *estimated* median amount spent on research and development? Interpret.
f. What is the mean amount spent on research and development?
g. Based on the less-than cumulative frequency polygon, what is the interquartile range?

5. The rates of growth of Bardeen Chemicals for the past five years are 5.2 percent, 8.7 percent, 3.9 percent, 6.8 percent, and 19.5 percent.
a. What is the arithmetic mean annual growth rate?
b. What is the geometric mean annual growth rate?
c. Should the arithmetic mean or geometric mean be used to represent the average annual growth rate? Why?

6. 9.65%

6. The Currin Manufacturing Co. noted in its 2000 second-quarter report that as of June 30, 2000, notes payable amounted to $284.0 million. For the same date in 1990, they were $113.0 million. What is the geometric mean yearly percent increase (June to June) from June 1990 to June 2000?

7. BFI in its annual report revealed that working capital was (in billions) $4.4, $3.4, $3.0, $4.8, $7.8, and $8.3 consecutively for the years 1995–2000. Present these figures in either a simple line chart or a simple bar chart.

8. Refer to the following diagram.

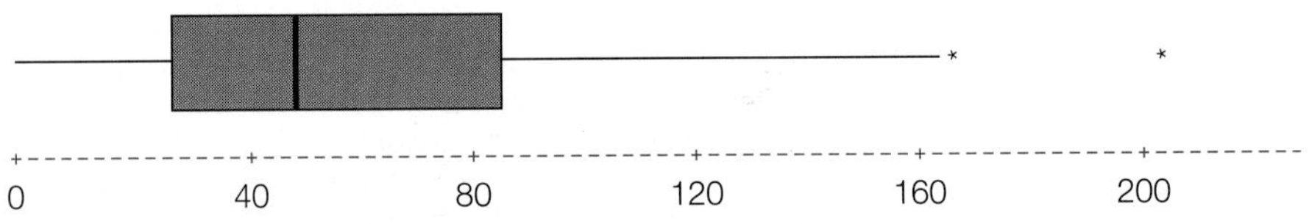

8. a. Box plot.
b. Median = 48, $Q_1 = 24$, $Q_3 = 84$.
c. Positively skewed.

a. What is the graph called?
b. What are the median, and first and third quartile values?
c. Is the distribution positively skewed. Tell how you know.

d. Yes, 168, 204.
e. No.

d. Are there any outliers? If yes, estimate these values.
e. Can you determine the number of observations in the study?

For exercises 9–18, fill in the blanks.

10. Statistic.

9. Employees in a company training course were asked to rate it as either outstanding, very good, good, fair, or poor. The level of measurement is ________.

10. A sample of senior citizens revealed that their mean annual retirement income is $16,900. Since the mean is based on a sample, the $16,900 is called a ________.

11. Refer to the following picture. It is called a ________. The third quartile is about ________, the first quartile ________, the interquartile range ________, and the range ________.

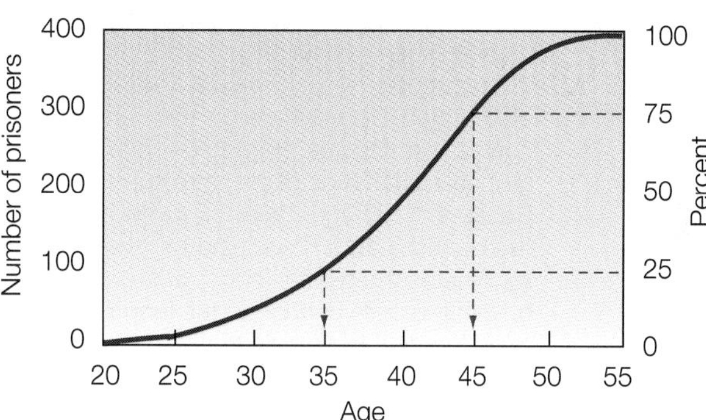

12. Frequency polygon, positive skewness.

12. Refer to the following picture, which is based on a frequency distribution. It is called a ________. Describe the skewness in the distribution. Explain.

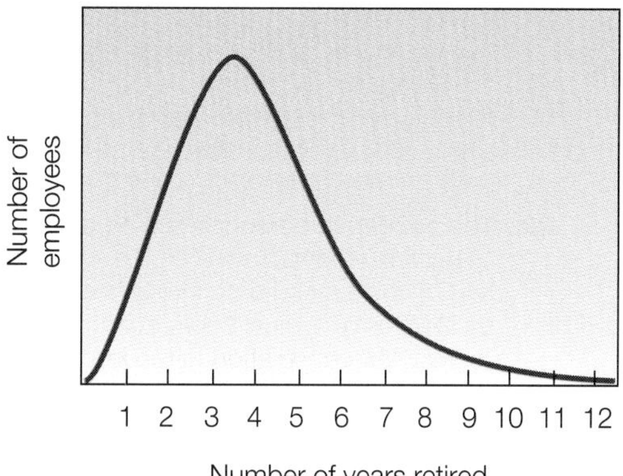

13. For a set of observations we have the following information: mean = $64, median = $61, mode = $60, standard deviation = $6, and range = $40. The coefficient of variation is ________.

14. 1.5

14. Refer to Exercise 13. The coefficient of skewness is ________.

15. A useful measure to compare the relative dispersion in two or more distributions, if they are in different units, is the ________.

16. 24

16. For a set of observations we have the following information: mean = 100, median = 100, mode = 100, and s = 4. The range is about ________.

17. Refer to Exercise 16. About 95 percent of the values lie between ________ and ________.

18. Geometric mean.

18. Fine Furniture, Inc. produced 2,460 desks in 1990 and 6,520 in 2000. To find the average annual percent increase in production, the ________ should be used.

19. A sample of the amounts of funds customers first deposited in First Federal's MCA (miniature checking account) revealed the following.

$124	$14	$150	$289	$52	$156	$203	$82	$27	$248
39	52	103	58	136	249	110	298	251	157
186	107	142	185	75	202	119	219	156	78
116	152	206	117	52	299	58	153	219	148
145	187	165	147	158	146	185	186	149	140

Using the preceding raw data and a statistical package (such as MINITAB):

a. Organize the data into a frequency distribution.

b. Calculate the mean, median, and other descriptive measures. Include charts, if available. You decide on the class interval.

c. Interpret the computer output; that is, describe the central tendency, spread, skewness, and other measures.

20. $\overline{X} = 147.90$; $s = 69.24$.

20. If a computer is not available, organize the miniature checking accounts into a frequency distribution. You decide on the class interval. Portray the distribution in chart form, and compute measures of central tendency, spread, and skewness. Then interpret the important characteristics of the miniature checking accounts.

21. Between 1789 and 1996, 85 judges served as associate justices of the Supreme Court of the United States. Their lengths of service are given below. Analyze the data.

a. What is the typical length of service?

b. What is the variation in the lengths of service?

c. Is the distribution skewed?

d. Develop a stem-and-leaf chart.

8	1	20	5	9	0	13	15	30	3
30	16	18	23	33	20	2	31	14	32
4	28	14	18	27	5	23	5	8	23
18	28	14	34	10	21	9	33	6	7
20	11	5	20	15	10	2	16	13	26
29	19	3	4	5	26	4	10	26	22
5	15	16	7	16	15	6	34	19	23
36	9	1	13	6	13	17	7	16	5
23	2	3	15	14					

22. **a.** See IM.
b. $13.767, 13.60
c. $s = 2.305$
d. See IM.
See IM.

22. The per capita personal income by state (including the District of Columbia), in thousands of dollars, follows.

a. Organize these data into a frequency distribution.

b. What is a "typical" per capita income for a state?

c. How much variation in the income data is there?

d. Is the distribution symmetrical?

e. Summarize your findings.

11.1	17.7	13.2	10.7	16.8	15.1	19.2	15.1
18.9	14.3	13.2	14.7	11.4	15.4	12.9	13.2
14.4	11.1	11.2	12.7	16.6	17.5	14.1	14.7
9.5	13.6	11.9	13.8	15.1	15.9	18.3	11.1
17.1	12.2	12.3	13.7	12.4	12.2	13.9	14.7
11.1	11.9	11.8	13.5	10.7	12.8	15.4	14.5
10.5	13.8	13.2					

23. Following are the ages at which the 42 U.S. presidents began their terms in office. Organize the data into a stem-and-leaf chart. Determine a typical age at the time of inauguration. Comment on the variation in age.

57	61	57	57	58	57	61	54	68	51
49	64	50	48	65	52	56	46	54	49
50	47	55	55	54	42	51	56	55	51
54	51	60	62	43	55	56	61	52	69
64	46								

Cases

A. Century National Bank

The following case will appear in the review sections. Assume that you work in the Planning Department of the Century National Bank and report to Ms. Lamberg. You will need to do some data analysis and prepare a short written report. Remember, Mr. Selig is the president of the bank, so you will want to ensure that your report is complete and accurate. A copy of the data appears in Appendix N.

The Century National Bank has offices in several cities in the Midwest and the southeastern part of the United States. Mr. Dan Selig, president and CEO, would like to know the characteristics of his checking account customers. What is the balance of a typical customer? How many other bank services do the checking account customers use? Do the customers use the ATM service and, if so, how often? What about debit cards? Who uses them, and how often are they used?

To better understand the customers, Mr. Selig asked Ms. Wendy Lamberg, Director of Planning, to select a sample of customers and prepare a report. To begin, she has appointed a team from her staff. You are the head of the team and responsible for preparing the report. You select a random sample of 60 customers. In addition to the balance in each account at the end of last month, you determine: (1) the number of ATM (automatic teller machine) transactions in the last month; (2) the number of other bank services (a savings account, a certificate of deposit, etc.) the customer uses; (3) whether the customer has a debit card (this is a relatively new bank service in which charges are made directly to the customer's account); and (4) whether or not interest is paid on the checking account. The sample includes customers from the branches in Cincinnati, Ohio; Atlanta, Georgia; Louisville, Kentucky; and Erie, Pennsylvania.

1. Develop a graph or table that portrays the checking balances. What is the balance of a typical customer? Do many customers have more than $2,000 in their accounts? Does it appear that there is a difference in the distribution of the accounts among the four branches? Around what value do the account balances tend to cluster?
2. Determine the mean and median of the checking account balances. Compare the mean and the median balances for the four branches. Is there a difference among the branches? Be sure to explain the difference between the mean and the median in your report.
3. Determine the range and the standard deviation of the checking account balances. What do the first and third quartiles show? Determine the coefficient of skewness and indicate what it shows. Because Mr. Selig does not deal with statistics daily, include a brief description and interpretation of the standard deviation and other measures.

B. Wildcat Plumbing Supply, Inc.: Do We Have Gender Differences?

Wildcat Plumbing Supply has served the plumbing needs of Southwest Arizona for more than 40 years. The company was founded by Mr. Terrence St. Julian and is run today by his son Cory. The company has grown from a handful of employees to more than 500 today. Cory is concerned about several positions within the company where he has men and women doing essentially the same job but at different pay. To investigate, he collected the information below. Suppose you are a student intern in the Accounting Department and have been given the task to write a report summarizing the situation.

Yearly Salary ($000)	Women	Men
Less than 30	2	0
30 up to 40	3	1
40 up to 50	17	4
50 up to 60	17	24
60 up to 70	8	21
70 up to 80	3	7
80 or more	0	3

To kick off the project, Mr. Cory St. Julian held a meeting with his staff and you were invited. At this meeting it was suggested that you calculate several measures of location, draw charts, such as a more-than cumulative frequency distribution, and determine the quartiles for both men and women. Develop the charts and write the report summarizing the yearly salaries of employees at Wildcat Plumbing Supply. Does it appear that there are gender differences?

C. Kimble Products: Is There a Difference in the Commissions?

At the January national sales meeting, the CEO of Kimble Products was questioned extensively regarding the company policy for paying commissions to its sales representatives. The company sells sporting goods to two major markets. There are 40 sales representatives who call directly on large volume customers, such as the athletic departments at major colleges and universities and professional sports franchises. There are 30 sales representatives who represent the company to retail stores located in shopping malls and large discounters such as Kmart and Target.

Upon his return to corporate headquarters, the CEO asked the sales manager for a report comparing the commissions earned last year by the two parts of the sales team. The information is reported on the right. Write a brief report. Would you conclude that there is a difference? Be sure to include information in the report on both the central tendency and dispersion of the two groups.

Commissions Earned by Sales Representatives Calling on Athletic Departments ($)

354	87	1,676	1,187	69	3,202	680	39	1,683	1,106
883	3,140	299	2,197	175	159	1,105	434	615	149
1,168	278	579	7	357	252	1,602	2,321	4	392
416	427	1,738	526	13	1,604	249	557	635	527

Commissions Earned by Sales Representatives Calling on Large Retailers ($)

1,116	681	1,294	12	754	1,206	1,448	870	944	1,255
1,213	1,291	719	934	1,313	1,083	899	850	886	1,556
886	1,315	1,858	1,262	1,338	1,066	807	1,244	758	918

5

A Survey of Probability Concepts

GOALS

When you have completed this chapter you will be able to:

1 **Define *probability.***

2 **Describe the *classical, empirical,* and *subjective* approaches to probability.**

3 **Understand the terms *experiment, event, outcome, permutations,* and *combinations.***

4 **Define the terms *conditional probability* and *joint probability.***

5 **Calculate probabilities using the *rules of addition* and *rules of multiplication.***

6 **Use a tree diagram to organize and compute probabilities.**

7 **Calculate a probability using Bayes' theorem.**

A study found that 60 percent of the tourists to China visited historical sites in or near Beijing. Forty percent visited sites in Xian, 30 percent of the tourists went to both Beijing and Xian. What is the probability that a tourist visited at least one of these locations? (See Goal 5 and Exercise 82.)

Introduction

The emphasis in Chapters 2 through 4 is on descriptive statistics. In Chapter 2 we organized the prices of 80 vehicles sold last month at Whitner Pontiac into a frequency distribution. This frequency distribution shows the lowest and the highest selling prices and where the largest concentration of data occur. In Chapters 3 and 4 we use a number of measures of central tendency and dispersion to locate a typical selling price (about $20,000) and to examine the spread in the data. We describe the spread in the selling prices with such measures of dispersion as the range and the standard deviation. Descriptive statistics is concerned with summarizing that which has already happened. For example, we described the vehicle selling prices last month at Whitner Pontiac.

We now turn to the second facet of statistics, namely, *computing the chance that something will occur in the future.* This facet of statistics is called **statistical inference** or **inferential statistics.**

Seldom does a decision maker have complete information from which to make a decision. For example:

- Toys and Things, a toy and puzzle manufacturer, recently developed a new game based on sports trivia. They want to know whether sports buffs will purchase the game. "Slam Dunk" and "Home Run" are two of the names under consideration. One way to minimize the risk of making a wrong decision is to hire pollsters to take a sample of, say, 2,000 from the population and ask each respondent for a reaction to the new game and its proposed titles.
- The quality assurance department of a Bethlehem Steel mill must assure management that the quarter-inch wire being produced has an acceptable tensile strength. Obviously, not all the wire produced can be tested for tensile strength because testing requires the wire to be stretched until it breaks—thus destroying it. So a random sample of 10 pieces is selected and tested. Based on the test results, all the wire produced is deemed to be either satisfactory or unsatisfactory.

- Other questions involving uncertainty are: Should the daytime drama *Days of Our Lives* be discontinued immediately? Should the New York Giants select Sammy Uwea or Clint Murray in the first round of the college draft? Will a newly developed mint-flavored cereal be profitable if marketed? Should I marry Jean? Should I buy a new Rolls Royce? Should I vote for Charles Linden for town commissioner?

Statistical inference deals with conclusions about a population based on a sample taken from that population. (The populations for the preceding illustrations are: all consumers who like sports trivia games, all the quarter-inch steel wire produced, all television viewers who watch soaps, all the college football players to be drafted by the professional teams, and so on.)

Because there is uncertainty in decision making, it is important that all the known risks involved be scientifically evaluated. Helpful in this evaluation is *probability theory,* which has often been referred to as the science of uncertainty. The use of probability theory allows the decision maker with only limited information to analyze the risks and minimize the gamble inherent, for example, in marketing a new product or accepting an incoming shipment possibly containing defective parts.

Because probability concepts are so important in the field of statistical inference (to be discussed starting with Chapter 8), this chapter introduces the basic language of probability, including such terms as *experiment, event, subjective probability,* and *addition* and *multiplication rules.*

What Is a Probability?

No doubt you are familiar with terms such as *probability, chance,* and *likelihood.* They are often used interchangeably. The weather forecaster announces that there is a 70 percent chance of rain for Super Bowl Sunday. Based on a survey of consumers who tested a newly developed pickle with a banana taste, the probability is .03 that, if marketed, it will be a financial success. (This means that the chance of the banana-tasting pickle being accepted by the public is rather remote.) What is a probability? In general, it is a number that describes the chance that something will happen.

PROBABILITY A value between zero and one, inclusive, describing the relative possibility (chance or likelihood) an event will occur.

Three key words are used in the study of probability: **experiment, outcome,** and **event.** These terms are used in our everyday language, but in statistics they have specific meanings.

EXPERIMENT A process that leads to the occurrence of one and only one of several possible observations.

This definition is more general than the one used in the physical sciences, where we picture someone manipulating test tubes or microscopes. In reference to probability, an experiment has two or more possible results, and it is uncertain which will occur.

OUTCOME A particular result of an experiment.

For example, the tossing of a coin is an experiment. You may observe the toss of the coin, but you are unsure whether it will come up "heads" or "tails." Similarly, asking 500 college students whether they would purchase a new Dell computer system at a particular price is an experiment. If the coin is tossed, one particular outcome is a "head." The alternative outcome is a "tail." In the computer purchasing experiment, one possible outcome is that 273 students indicate they would purchase the computer. Another outcome is that 317 students would purchase the computer. Still another outcome is that 423 students indicate that they would purchase it. When one or more of the experiment's outcomes are observed, we call this an event.

EVENT A collection of one or more outcomes of an experiment.

Examples to clarify the definitions of the terms *experiment, outcome,* and *event* are on the next several pages.

In the die-rolling experiment there are six possible outcomes, but there are many possible events. When counting the number of members of the board of directors for

Experiment	Roll a die	Count the number of members of the board of directors for Fortune 500 companies who are over 60 years of age
All possible outcomes	Observe a 1 Observe a 2 Observe a 3 Observe a 4 Observe a 5 Observe a 6	None are over 60 One is over 60 Two are over 60 ... 29 are over 60 ... ... 48 are over 60 ...
Some possible events	Observe an even number Observe a number greater than 4 Observe a number 3 or less	More than 13 are over 60 Fewer than 20 are over 60

Fortune 500 companies over 60 years of age, the number of possible outcomes can be anywhere from zero to the total number of members. There are an even larger number of possible events in this experiment.

A probability is frequently expressed as a decimal, such as .70, .27, or .50. However, it may be given as a fraction such as 7/10, 27/100, or 1/2. It can assume any number from 0 to 1, inclusive. If a company has only five sales regions, and each region's name or number is written on a slip of paper and the slips put in a hat, the probability of selecting one of the five regions is 1. The probability of selecting from the hat a slip of paper that reads "Pittsburgh Steelers" is 0. Thus, the probability of 1 represents something that is certain to happen, and the probability of 0 represents something that cannot happen.

The closer a probability is to 0, the more improbable it is the event will happen. The closer the probability is to 1, the more sure we are it will happen. The relationship is shown in the following diagram along with a few of our personal beliefs. You might, however, select a different probability for Slo Poke's chances to win the Kentucky Derby or for an increase in federal taxes.

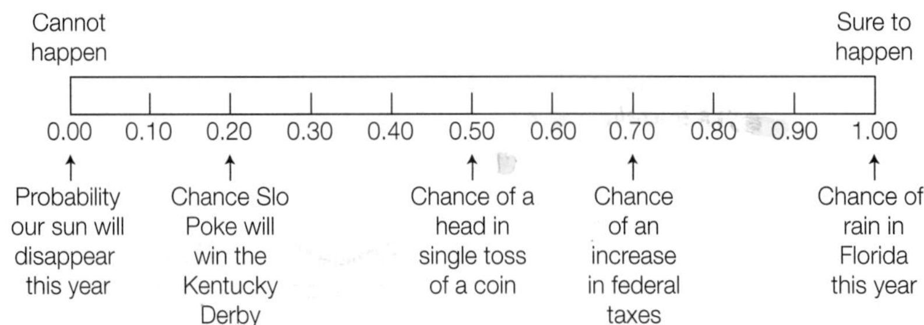

Self-Review 5–1

Video Games, Inc. recently developed a new video game. Its market potential is to be tested by 80 veteran game players.

(a) What is the experiment?
(b) What is one possible outcome?
(c) Suppose 65 players tried the new game and said they liked it. Is 65 a probability?
(d) The probability that the new game will be a success is computed to be −1. Comment.
(e) Specify one possible event.

What role does probability have in decision making? This question can be answered by citing two cases that will be discussed in forthcoming chapters.

Case 1

Based on past experience, a publishing company determined that at least 20 percent of a group, such as musicians, must subscribe to a monthly magazine to make it a financial success. The company is considering a monthly magazine for bird-watchers. A special copy was designed and mailed to a sample of 1,000 bird-watchers. In response, 190 out of 1,000, or 19 percent, said they would subscribe to the magazine if it were published. Should we state that this proportion is less than 20 percent and make an immediate decision not to publish the magazine? Or could the difference between the required percent (20) and the sample percent (19) be attributed to sampling, that is, chance? Probability will help us arrive at a decision for this type of situation, which will be discussed in Chapter 10.

Case 2

A large construction project requires thousands of concrete blocks. Specifications state that the blocks must stand up to the pressures of 1,050 pounds per square inch (psi). Two firms manufacturing these blocks submitted samples for testing. The arithmetic mean strength of the Strong Block Company blocks was 1,070 psi; those from the Taylor Company tested at 1,062 psi. Strong Block thinks it should be awarded the contract because its blocks have a higher mean strength. Taylor disagrees, saying that the difference of only 8 psi could be due to sampling (chance). If Strong Block's claim is correct, it will be awarded the contract. If Taylor's statement is correct, the contract will be divided between the two companies. Probability will help us reach a decision for a case such as this in Chapter 11.

Approaches to Probability

Two approaches to probability will be discussed, namely, the *objective* and the *subjective* viewpoints. **Objective probability** is subdivided into (1) *classical probability* and (2) *empirical probability.*

Classical Probability

Classical probability is based on the assumption that the outcomes of an experiment are *equally likely.* Using the classical viewpoint, the probability of an event happening is computed by dividing the number of favorable outcomes by the number of possible outcomes:

DEFINITION OF CLASSICAL PROBABILITY

$$\text{Probability of an event} = \frac{\text{Number of favorable outcomes}}{\text{Total number of possible outcomes}} \qquad [5\text{–}1]$$

EXAMPLE

Consider an experiment of rolling a six-sided die. What is the probability of the event "an even number of spots appear face up"?

SOLUTION

The possible outcomes are:

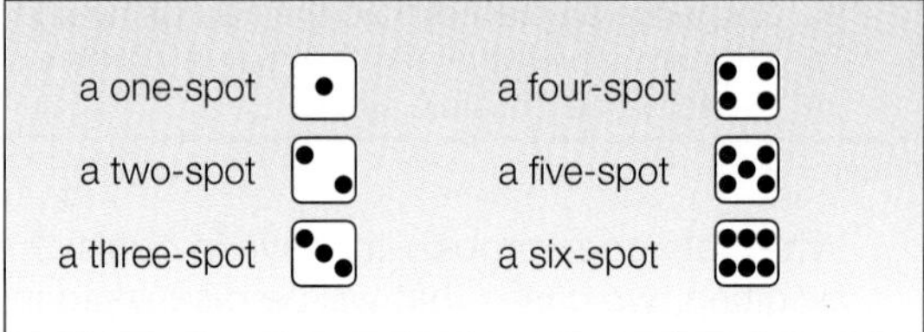

There are three "favorable" outcomes (a two, a four, and a six) in the collection of six equally likely possible outcomes. Therefore:

$$\text{Probability of an even number} = \frac{3}{6} \begin{array}{l} \leftarrow \\ \leftarrow \end{array} \boxed{\frac{\text{Number of favorable outcomes}}{\text{Total number of possible outcomes}}}$$

$$= .5$$

If *only one* of several events can occur at one time, we refer to the events as **mutually exclusive.**

MUTUALLY EXCLUSIVE The occurrence of one event means that none of the others can occur at the same time.

In the die-tossing experiment, the event "an even number" and the event "an odd number" are mutually exclusive. If an even number occurred, it could not also be an odd number.

If an experiment has a set of events that includes every possible outcome, such as the events "an even number" and "an odd number" in the die-tossing experiment, then the set of events is **collectively exhaustive.**

COLLECTIVELY EXHAUSTIVE At least one of the events must occur when an experiment is conducted.

For the die-tossing experiment, every outcome will be either even or odd. So the set is collectively exhaustive.

Sum of probabilities = 1

If the set of events is collectively exhaustive and the events are mutually exclusive, the sum of the probabilities equals 1. For a coin-tossing experiment:

	Probability
Event: Head	.5
Event: Tail	.5
Total	1.0

For the classical approach to be applied, the events must have the same chance of occurring (called *equally likely* events). Also, the set of events must be mutually exclusive and collectively exhaustive.

Historically, the classical approach to probability was developed and applied in the 17th and 18th centuries to games of chance, such as cards and dice. Note that it is unnecessary to do an experiment to determine the probability of an event occurring using the classical approach; we can logically arrive, for example, at the probability of getting a tail on the toss of one coin or three heads on the toss of three coins. Nor do we have to conduct an experiment to determine the probability that your income tax return will be audited if there are 2 million returns mailed to your district office and 2,400 are to be audited. Assuming that each return has an equal chance of being audited, your probability is .0012—found by 2,400 divided by 2 million. Obviously, the chance of your return being audited is rather remote.

Empirical Concept

Another way to define probability is based on **relative frequencies.** The probability of an event happening is determined by observing what fraction of the time similar events happened in the past. In terms of a formula:

$$\text{Probability of event happening} = \frac{\text{Number of times event occurred in past}}{\text{Total number of observations}}$$

EXAMPLE

A study of 751 business administration graduates of the University of Toledo revealed 383 of the 751 were *not* employed in their major area of study in college. For illustration, a person who majored in accounting is now the marketing manager of a tomato-processing firm. What is the probability that a particular business graduate will be employed in an area other than his or her college major?

SOLUTION

$$\text{Probability of event happening} = \frac{\text{Number of times event occurred in past}}{\text{Total number of observations}}$$

$$P(A) = \frac{383}{751}$$

$$= .51$$

To simplify, letters or numbers may be used. *P* stands for probability, and in this case *P*(*A*) stands for the probability a graduate is not employed in his or her major area of college study.

Since 383 out of 751, or .51 in terms of a probability, are in a different field of employment from their major in college, we can use this as an estimate of the probability. In other words, based on past experience, the probability is .51 that a new business graduate will be employed in a field other than his or her college major.

Subjective Probability

If there is little or no past experience on which to base a probability, it may be arrived at subjectively. Essentially, this means evaluating the available opinions and other information and then estimating or assigning the probability. This probability is aptly called a **subjective probability.**

SUBJECTIVE CONCEPT OF PROBABILITY The likelihood (probability) of a particular event happening that is assigned by an individual based on whatever information is available.

Illustrations of subjective probability are:

1. Estimating the likelihood the New England Patriots will play in the Super Bowl next year.
2. Estimating the probability General Motors Corp. will lose its number 1 ranking in total units sold to Ford Motor Co. or DaimlerChrysler within two years.
3. Estimating the likelihood you will earn an *A* in this course.

In summary, there are two viewpoints regarding probability—the objective and the subjective viewpoints. We noted that a probability statement always constitutes an estimate of an unknown value that will govern an event that has not yet occurred. There is, of course, a considerable latitude in the degree of uncertainty that surrounds this estimate, based primarily on the knowledge possessed by the individual concerning the underlying process. The individual possesses a great deal of knowledge about the toss of a die and can state that the probability that a one-spot will appear face up on the toss of a true die is one sixth. But we know very little concerning the acceptance in the marketplace of a new and untested product. For example, even though a market research director tests a newly developed product in 40 retail stores and states that there is a 70 percent chance that the product will have sales of more than 1 million units, she still has little knowledge of how consumers will react when it is marketed nationally. In both cases (the case of the person rolling a die and the testing of a new product) the individual is assigning a probability value to an event of interest, and a difference exists only in the predictor's confidence in the precision of the estimate. However, regardless of the viewpoint, the same laws of probability (presented in the following sections) will be applied.

Self-Review 5–2

1. One card will be randomly selected from a standard 52-card deck. What is the probability the card will be a queen? Which approach to probability did you use to answer this question?
2. The National Center for Health Statistics reports that of 883 deaths, 24 resulted from an automobile accident, 182 from cancer, and 333 from heart disease. What is the probability that a particular death is due to an automobile accident? Which approach to probability did you use to answer this question?
3. What is the probability that the Dow Jones Industrial Average will exceed 12,000? Which approach to probability did you use to answer this question?

Exercises

1. Some people are in favor of reducing Social Security benefits in order to achieve a balanced budget and others are against it. Two persons are selected and their opinions are recorded. List the possible outcomes.

2. See IM.

2. A quality control inspector selects a part to be tested. The part is then declared acceptable, repairable, or scrapped. Then another part is tested. List the possible outcomes of this experiment regarding two parts.

3. A survey of 34 students at the Wall College of Business showed the following majors:

Major	Count
Accounting	10
Finance	5
Info. Systems	3
Management	6
Marketing	10

Suppose you select a student and observe his or her major.

a. What is the probability he or she is a management major?
b. Which concept of probability did you use to make this estimate?

4. A large company that must hire a new president prepares a final list of five candidates, all of whom are equally qualified. Two of these candidates are members of a minority group. The company decides to select the president by lottery.
   a. What is the probability one of the minority is hired?
   b. Which concept of probability did you use to make this estimate?

4. a. .40
   b. Classical.

5. The Streets Department in Whitehouse, Illinois, is considering widening Indiana Avenue to three lanes. Before a final decision is made, 500 citizens are asked if they support the widening.
   a. What is the experiment?
   b. What are some of the possible events?
   c. List two possible outcomes.
6. The chairman of the board of Rudd Industries is delivering a speech to the company stockholders tomorrow explaining his position that the company should merge with Zimmerman Plastics. He has received six pieces of mail on the issue and is interested in the number of writers who agree with him.
   a. What is the experiment?
   b. What are some of the possible events?
   c. List two possible outcomes.

6. a. Counting stockholders in favor.
   b. 5 of 6 favor.
   c. One possibility is more than half favor merger.

7. In each of the following cases, indicate whether classical, empirical, or subjective probability is used.
   a. A basketball player makes 30 out of 50 foul shots. The probability is .6 that she makes the next foul shot attempted.
   b. A seven-member committee of students is formed to study environmental issues. What is the likelihood that any one of the seven is chosen as the spokesperson?
   c. You purchase one of 5 million tickets sold for Lotto Canada. What is the likelihood you win the $1 million jackpot?
   d. The probability of an earthquake in northern California in the next 10 years is .80.
8. A firm will promote two employees out of a group of six men and three women.
   a. List the outcomes of this experiment if there is particular concern about gender equity.
   b. Which concept of probability would you use to estimate these probabilities?

8. a. See IM.
   b. Classical.

9. There are 52 cards in a standard deck.
   a. What is the probability that the first card selected is a spade?
   b. What is the probability that the first card selected is the jack of spades?
   c. What concept of probability do a. and b. illustrate?
10. A single die is rolled.
   a. What is the probability that a two-spot will show face up?
   b. What concept of probability does this illustrate?
   c. Are the outcomes for the numbers 1 through 6 equally likely and mutually exclusive? Explain.

10. a. .167
   b. Classical.
   c. Yes.

11. A sample of forty minority executives were selected to test a questionnaire. One question about environmental issues required a yes or no answer.
   a. What is the experiment?
   b. List one possible event.
   c. Ten of the 40 executives responded "yes." Based on these sample responses, what is the probability an executive responded "yes"?
   d. What concept of probability does this illustrate?
   e. Are each of the possible outcomes equally likely and mutually exclusive?
12. A sample of 2000 licensed drivers revealed the following number of violations.

Number of Violations	Number of Drivers
0	1,910
1	46
2	18
3	12
4	9
5 or more	5
Total	2,000

12. a. Recording violations.
   b. One or more violations.
   c. .009
   d. Empirical.

a. What is the experiment?
b. List one possible event.
c. What is the probability that a particular driver had exactly two violations?
d. What concept of probability does this illustrate?

13. Bank of America customers select their own three-digit personal identification number (PIN) for use at ATMs.
a. Think of this as an experiment and list four possible outcomes.
b. What is the probability Mr. Jones and Mrs. Smith select the same PIN?
c. Which concept of probability did you use to answer the question above?

14. a. For example, up 1/16, down to 1/8.
b. .01, .02, .01
c. Subjective.

14. An investor buys 100 shares of AT&T stock and records its price change daily.
a. List several possible events for this experiment.
b. Estimate the probability for each event you described in a.
c. Which concept of probability did you use in b.?

Some Rules of Probability

Now that we have defined probability and described the different approaches to probability, we turn our attention to combining events by applying rules of addition and multiplication.

Rules of Addition

Mutually exclusive events cannot both happen.

Special Rule of Addition To apply the **special rule of addition,** the events must be mutually exclusive. Recall that *mutually exclusive* means that when one event occurs, none of the other events can occur at the same time. An illustration of mutually exclusive events in the die-tossing experiment is the events "a number 4 or larger" and "a number 2 or smaller." If the outcome is in the first group {4, 5, and 6}, then it cannot also be in the second group {1 and 2}. And a product coming off the assembly line cannot be defective and satisfactory at the same time.

If two events *A* and *B* are mutually exclusive, the special rule of addition states that the probability of one *or* the other event's occurring equals the sum of their probabilities. This rule is expressed in the following formula:

SPECIAL RULE OF ADDITION $P(A \text{ or } B) = P(A) + P(B)$ **[5–2]**

For three mutually exclusive events designated *A, B,* and *C,* the rule is written:

$$P(A \text{ or } B \text{ or } C) = P(A) + P(B) + P(C)$$

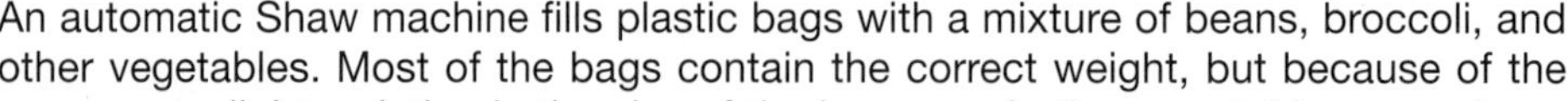

EXAMPLE

An automatic Shaw machine fills plastic bags with a mixture of beans, broccoli, and other vegetables. Most of the bags contain the correct weight, but because of the slight variation in the size of the beans and other vegetables, a package might be slightly underweight or overweight. A check of 4,000 packages filled in the past month revealed:

Weight	Event	Number of Packages	Probability of Occurrence	
Underweight	*A*	100	.025	← $\frac{100}{4,000}$
Satisfactory	*B*	3,600	.900	
Overweight	*C*	300	.075	
		4,000	1.000	

What is the probability that a particular package will be either underweight or overweight?

SOLUTION

The outcome "underweight" is the event *A*. The outcome "overweight" is the event *C*. Applying the special rule of addition:

$$P(A \text{ or } C) = P(A) + P(C) = .025 + .075 = .10$$

Note that the events are mutually exclusive, meaning that a package of mixed vegetables cannot be underweight, satisfactory, and overweight at the same time. They are also collectively exhaustive, that is, a selected package must be either underweight, satisfactory, or overweight.

A Venn diagram is a useful tool to depict addition or multiplication rules.

English logician J. Venn (1835–1888) developed a diagram to portray graphically the outcome of an experiment. The *mutually exclusive* concept and various other rules for combining probabilities can be illustrated using this device. To construct a Venn diagram, a space is first enclosed representing the total of all possible outcomes. This space is usually in the form of a rectangle. An event is then represented by a circular area which is drawn inside the rectangle proportional to the probability of the event. The following Venn diagram represents the *mutually exclusive* concept. There is no overlapping of events, meaning that the events are mutually exclusive.

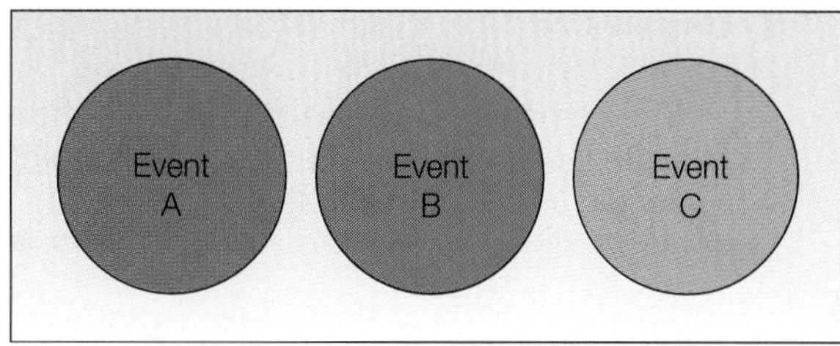

The probability that a bag of mixed vegetables selected is underweight, $P(A)$, plus the probability that it is not an underweight bag, written $P(\sim A)$ and read "not *A*," must logically equal 1. This is written:

$$P(A) + P(\sim A) = 1$$

This can be revised to read:

COMPLEMENT RULE	$P(A) = 1 - P(\sim A)$	**[5–3]**

This is the **complement rule.** Notice that the events *A* and $\sim A$ are mutually exclusive and collectively exhaustive.

The complement rule is used to determine the probability of an event occurring by subtracting the probability of the event *not* occurring from 1. A Venn diagram illustrating the complement rule might appear as:

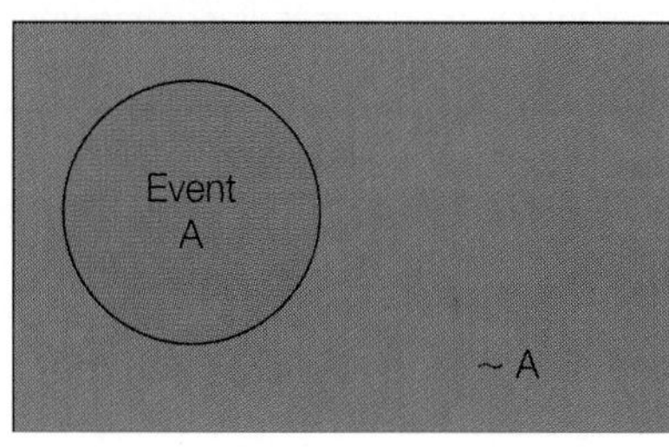

EXAMPLE

Recall the probability a bag of mixed vegetables is underweight is .025 and the probability of an overweight bag is .075. Use the complement rule to show the probability of a satisfactory bag is .900. Show the solution using a Venn diagram.

SOLUTION

The probability the bag is unsatisfactory equals the probability the bag is overweight plus the probability it is underweight. That is, $P(A \text{ or } C) = P(A) + P(C) = .025 + .075 = .100$. The bag is satisfactory if it is not underweight or overweight, so $P(B) = 1 - [P(A) + P(C)] = 1 - [.025 + .075] = 0.900$. The Venn diagram portraying this situation is:

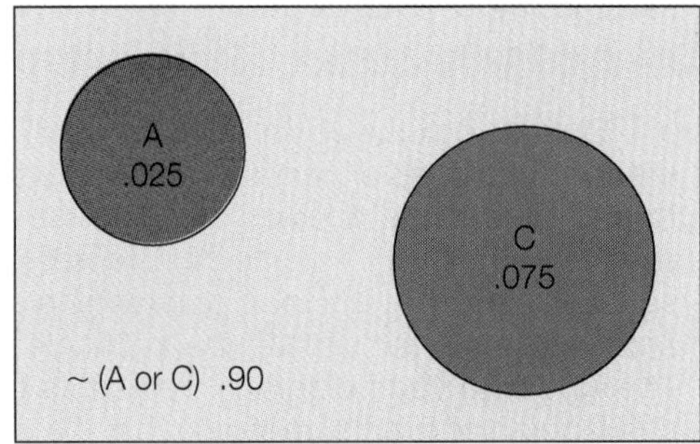

The complement rule is important in the study of probability. Often it is easier to calculate the probability of an event happening by determining the probability of it not happening and subtracting the result from 1.

Self-Review 5–3

A selected group of employees of Worldwide Enterprises is to be surveyed about a new pension plan. In-depth interviews are to be conducted with each employee selected in the sample. The employees are classified as follows:

Classification	Event	Number of Employees
Supervisors	*A*	120
Maintenance	*B*	50
Production	*C*	1,460
Management	*D*	302
Secretarial	*E*	68

(a) What is the probability that the first person selected is:
  (i) either in maintenance or a secretary?
  (ii) not in management?
(b) Draw a Venn diagram illustrating your answers to part (a).
(c) Are the events in part (a)(i) complementary or mutually exclusive or both?

The General Rule of Addition The outcomes of an experiment may not be mutually exclusive. Suppose, for illustration, that the Florida Tourist Commission selected a sample of 200 tourists who visited the state during the year. The survey revealed that 120 tourists went to Disney World and 100 went to Busch Gardens near Tampa. What

Statistics in Action

If you wish to get some attention at the next gathering you attend, announce that you believe that at least two people present were born on the same date—that is, the same day of the year but not necessarily the same year. If there are 30 people in the room, the probability of a duplicate is .706. If there are 60 people in the room, the probability is .994 that at least two people share the same birthday. With as few as 23 people the chances are even, that is .50, that at least two people share the same birthday.

is the probability that a person selected visited either Disney World or Busch Gardens? If the special rule of addition is used, the probability of selecting a tourist who went to Disney World is .60, found by 120/200. Similarly, the probability of a tourist going to Busch Gardens is .50. The sum of these probabilities is 1.10. We know, however, that this probability cannot be greater than 1. The explanation is that many tourists visited both attractions and are being counted twice! A check of the survey responses revealed that 60 out of 200 sampled did, in fact, visit both attractions.

To answer our question, "What is the probability a selected person visited either Disney World or Busch Gardens?" (1) add the probability that a tourist visited Disney World and the probability he/she visited Busch Gardens, and (2) subtract the probability of visiting both. Thus:

$$P(\text{Disney or Busch}) = P(\text{Disney}) + P(\text{Busch}) - P(\text{both Disney and Busch})$$
$$= .60 + .50 - .30 = .80$$

When two events both occur, the probability is called a **joint probability.** The probability that a tourist visits both attractions (.30) is an example of a joint probability.

JOINT PROBABILITY A probability that measures the likelihood two or more events will happen concurrently.

In summary, the general rule of addition refers to events that are not mutually exclusive. This rule for two events designated A and B is written:

GENERAL RULE OF ADDITION $$P(A \text{ or } B) = P(A) + P(B) - P(A \text{ and } B) \quad \textbf{[5–4]}$$

For the expression $P(A \text{ or } B)$, the word *or* suggests that *A* may occur or *B* may occur. This also includes the possibility that *A* and *B* may occur. This use of *or* is sometimes called an **inclusive.** To put it another way, you are happy when both *A* and *B* occur or when either one occurs.

EXAMPLE

What is the probability that a card chosen at random from a standard deck of cards will be either a king or a heart?

SOLUTION

We may be inclined to add the probability of a king and the probability of a heart. But this creates a problem. If we do that, the king of hearts is counted with the kings and also with the hearts. So, if we simply add the probability of a king (there are 4 in a deck of 52 cards) to the probability of a heart (there are 13 in a deck of 52 cards) and report that 17 out of 52 cards meet the requirement, we have counted the king of hearts twice. We need to subtract 1 card from the 17 so the king of hearts is counted only once. Thus, there are 16 cards that are either hearts or kings. So the probability is 16/52 = .3077.

Card	Probability	Explanation
King	$P(A) = 4/52$	4 kings in a deck of 52 cards
Heart	$P(B) = 13/52$	13 hearts in a deck of 52 cards
King of hearts	$P(A \text{ and } B) = 1/52$	1 king of hearts in a deck of 52 cards

Using formula (5–4):

$$\begin{aligned} P(A \text{ or } B) &= P(A) + P(B) - P(A \text{ and } B) \\ &= 4/52 + 13/52 - 1/52 \\ &= 16/52, \text{ or } .3077 \end{aligned}$$

A Venn diagram portrays these outcomes, which are not mutually exclusive.

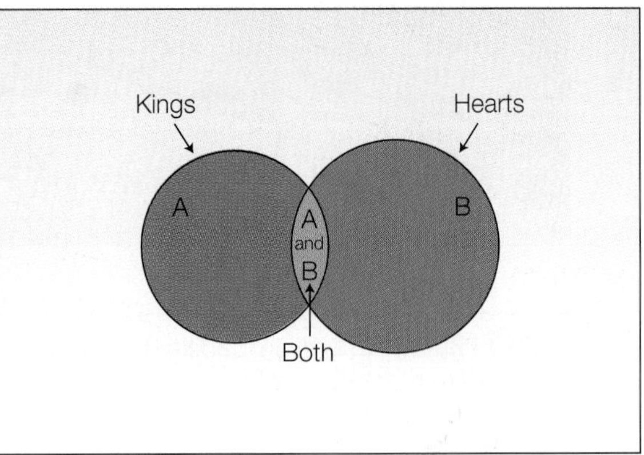

Self-Review 5–4

Routine physical examinations are conducted annually as part of a health service program for General Concrete, Inc. employees. It was discovered that 8 percent of the employees need corrective shoes, 15 percent need major dental work, and 3 percent need both corrective shoes and major dental work.

(a) What is the probability that an employee selected at random will need either corrective shoes or major dental work?
(b) Show this situation in the form of a Venn diagram.

Exercises

15. The events A and B are mutually exclusive. Suppose $P(A) = .30$ and $P(B) = .20$. What is the probability of either A or B occurring? What is the probability that neither A nor B will happen?

16. .07, .93

16. The events X and Y are mutually exclusive. Suppose $P(X) = .05$ and $P(Y) = .02$. What is the probability of either X or Y occurring? What is the probability that neither X nor Y will happen?

17. A study of 200 grocery chains revealed these incomes after taxes:

Income after Taxes	Number of Firms
Under $1 million	102
$1 million to $20 million	61
$20 million or more	37

   a. What is the probability a particular chain has under $1 million in income after taxes?
   b. What is the probability a grocery chain selected at random has either an income between $1 million and $20 million, or an income of $20 million or more? What rule of probability was applied?

18. a. Recording opinions
b. Any color but red, for example
c. .4575
d. .885

18. A study of the opinions of designers with respect to the primary color most desirable for use in executive offices showed:

Primary Color	Number of Opinions	Primary Color	Number of Opinions
Red	92	Blue	37
Orange	86	Indigo	46
Yellow	46	Violet	2
Green	91		

   a. What is the experiment?
   b. What is one possible event?
   c. What is the probability of selecting a particular response and discovering that the designer prefers red or green?
   d. What is the probability that a designer does not prefer yellow?

19. The chair of the board of directors says, "There is a 50% chance this company will earn a profit, a 30% chance it will break even, and a 20% chance it will lose money next quarter."
   a. Use an addition rule to find the probability they will not lose money next quarter.
   b. Use the complement rule to find the probability they will not lose money next quarter.

20. .75

20. Suppose the probability you will get a grade of A in this class is .25 and the probability you will get a B is .50. What is the probability your grade will be above C?

21. A single die is rolled. Let A be the event "the die shows 4," B be the event "the die shows an even number," and C be the event "the die shows an odd number." Consider each pair of these events and describe whether they are mutually exclusive. Then identify whether they are complementary.

22. Yes, no.

22. Two coins are tossed. If A is the event "two heads" and B is the event "two tails," are A and B mutually exclusive? Are they complements?

23. The probabilities of the events A and B are .20 and .30, respectively. The probability that both A and B occur is .15. What is the probability of either A or B occurring?

24. .70

24. Let $P(X) = .55$ and $P(Y) = .35$. Assume the probability that they both occur is .20. What is the probability of either X or Y occurring?

25. Suppose the two events A and B are mutually exclusive. What is the probability of their joint occurrence?

26. .80

26. A student is taking two courses, history and math. The probability the student will pass the history course is .60, and the probability of passing the math course is .70. The probability of passing both is .50. What is the probability of passing at least one?

27. A survey of top executives revealed that 35 percent of them regularly read *Time* magazine, 20 percent read *Newsweek,* and 40 percent read *U.S. News and World Report.* Ten percent read both *Time* and *U.S. News and World Report.*

- **a.** What is the probability that a particular top executive reads either *Time* or *U.S. News and World Report* regularly?
- **b.** What is the probability .10 called?
- **c.** Are the events mutually exclusive? Explain.

28. a. .55
b. Joint.
c. No.

28. A study by the National Park Service revealed that 50 percent of vacationers going to the Rocky Mountain region visit Yellowstone Park, 40 percent visit the Tetons, and 35 percent visit both.

- **a.** What is the probability a vacationer will visit at least one of these attractions?
- **b.** What is the probability .35 called?
- **c.** Are the events mutually exclusive? Explain.

Rules of Multiplication

Special Rule of Multiplication The special rule of multiplication requires that two events A and B be **independent.** Two events are independent if the occurrence of one does not alter the probability of the other. So if the events A and B are independent, the occurrence of A does not alter the probability of B.

> **INDEPENDENT** The occurrence of one event has no effect on the probability of the occurrence of any other event.

For two independent events A and B, the probability that A and B will both occur is found by multiplying the two probabilities. This is the **special rule of multiplication** and is written symbolically as:

SPECIAL RULE OF MULTIPLICATION $P(A \text{ and } B) = P(A)P(B)$ **[5–5]**

This rule for combining probabilities presumes that a second event is *not* affected by the first event. To illustrate what is meant by independence of events, suppose two coins are tossed. The outcome of one coin (head or tail) is unaffected by the outcome of the other coin (head or tail). To put it another way, two events are independent if the outcome of the second event does not depend on the outcome of the first event.

For three independent events A, B, and C, the special rule of multiplication used to determine the probability that all three events will occur is:

$$P(A \text{ and } B \text{ and } C) = P(A)P(B)P(C)$$

EXAMPLE

A survey by the American Automobile Association (AAA) revealed 60 percent of its members made airline reservations last year. Two members are selected at random. What is the probability both made airline reservations last year?

SOLUTION

The probability the first member made an airline reservation last year is .60, written $P(R_1) = .60$, where R_1 refers to the fact that the first member made a reservation. The probability that the second member selected made a reservation is also .60, so $P(R_2) = .60$. Since the number of AAA members is very large, you may assume that R_1 and R_2 are independent. Consequently, using formula 5–5, the probability they both make a reservation is .36, found by:

$$P(R_1 \text{ and } R_2) = P(R_1)P(R_2) = (.60)(.60) = .36$$

All possible outcomes can be shown as follows. R means a reservation is made, and NR means no reservation was made.

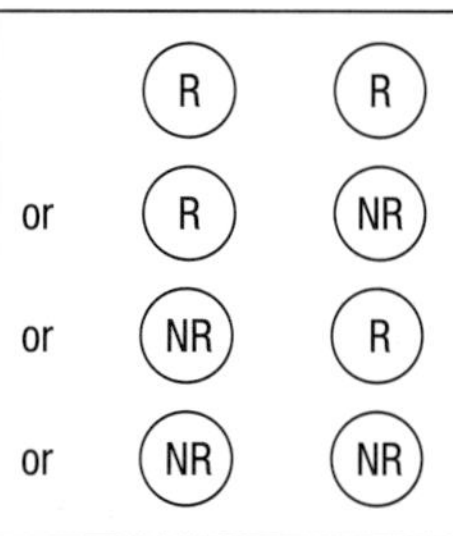

Self-Review 5–5

1. From long experience, Teton Tire knows the probability is .80 that their XB-70 will last 60,000 miles before it becomes bald or fails. An adjustment is made on any tire that does not last 60,000 miles. You purchase four XB-70s. What is the probability all four tires will last at least 60,000 miles?
2. As cited in an earlier example, an automatic Shaw machine inserts mixed vegetables into a plastic bag. Past experience revealed some packages were underweight and some overweight, but most of them had satisfactory weight.

Weight	Probability
Underweight	.025
Satisfactory	.900
Overweight	.075

(a) What is the probability of selecting three packages from the food processing line today and finding all three of them are underweight?
(b) What does this probability mean?

If two events are not independent, they are referred to as *dependent.* To illustrate dependency, suppose there are 10 rolls of film in a box, and it is known that 3 are defective. A roll of film is selected from the box. Obviously, the probability of selecting a defective roll is $3/10$, and the probability of selecting a good roll is $7/10$. Then a second roll is selected from the box without the first one being returned to the box. The probability this second roll is defective *depends* on whether the first roll selected was defective or good. The probability that the second roll is defective is:

$\frac{2}{9}$, if the first roll was defective. (Only two defective rolls remain in the box containing nine rolls.)

$\frac{3}{9}$, if the first roll selected was good. (All three defective rolls are still in the box containing nine rolls.)

The fraction $\frac{2}{9}$ (or $\frac{3}{9}$) is aptly called a **conditional probability** because its value is conditional on (dependent on) whether a defective or a good roll of film is chosen in the first selection from the box.

> **CONDITIONAL PROBABILITY** The probability of a particular event occurring, given that another event has occurred.

General Rule of Multiplication We use the **general rule of multiplication** to find the *joint probability* that two events will occur, such as selecting 2 defective rolls from the box of 10 rolls, one after the other. In general, the rule states that for two events *A* and *B*, the joint probability that both events will happen is found by multiplying the probability event *A* will happen by the conditional probability of event *B* occurring. Symbolically, the joint probability $P(A \text{ and } B)$ is found by:

> **GENERAL RULE OF MULTIPLICATION** $P(A \text{ and } B) = P(A)P(B \mid A)$ **[5–6]**

where $P(B \mid A)$ stands for the probability *B* will occur *given that A has already occurred.* The vertical line means "given that."

EXAMPLE

To illustrate the formula, let's use the problem with 10 rolls of film in a box, 3 of which are defective. Two rolls are to be selected, one after the other. What is the probability of selecting a defective roll followed by another defective roll?

SOLUTION

The first roll of film selected from the box being found defective is event *A*. $P(A) = \frac{3}{10}$ because 3 out of the 10 are defective. The second roll selected being found defective is event *B*. Therefore, $P(B \mid A) = \frac{2}{9}$, because after the first selection was found to be defective, only 2 defective rolls of film remained in the box containing 9 rolls. Determining the probability of two defectives [see formula (5–6)]:

$$P(A \text{ and } B) = P(A)P(B \mid A) = \left(\frac{3}{10}\right)\left(\frac{2}{9}\right) = \frac{6}{90}, \text{ or about } .07$$

Incidentally, it is assumed that this experiment was conducted *without replacement*—that is, the first defective roll of film was not thrown back in the box before the next roll was selected. It should also be noted that the general rule of multiplication can be extended to more than two events. For three events, *A*, *B*, and *C*, the formula would be:

$$P(A \text{ and } B \text{ and } C) = P(A)P(B \mid A)P(C \mid A \text{ and } B)$$

For illustration, the probability the first three rolls chosen from the box will all be defective is .00833, found by:

$$\begin{aligned} P(A \text{ and } B \text{ and } C) &= P(A)P(B \mid A)P(C \mid A \text{ and } B) \\ &= \left(\frac{3}{10}\right)\left(\frac{2}{9}\right)\left(\frac{1}{8}\right) = \frac{6}{720} = .00833 \end{aligned}$$

Self-Review 5–6

The board of directors of Tarbell Industries consists of eight men and four women. A four-member search committee is to be chosen at random to recommend a new company president.

(a) What is the probability all four members of the search committee will be women?
(b) What is the probability all four members will be men?
(c) Does the sum of the probabilities for the events described in parts (*a*) and (*b*) equal 1? Explain.

Another application of the general rule of multiplication follows. A survey of executives dealt with their loyalty to the company. One of the questions was, "If you were given an offer by another company equal to or slightly better than your present position, would you remain with the company or take the other position?" The responses of the 200 executives in the survey were cross-classified with their length of service with the company. (See Table 5–1.) The type of table that resulted is usually referred to as a **contingency table.**

TABLE 5–1 Loyalty of Executives and Length of Service with Company

	Length of Service				
Loyalty	Less than 1 Year	1–5 Years	6–10 Years	More than 10 Years	Total
Would remain	10	30	5	75	120
Would not remain	25	15	10	30	80
					200

EXAMPLE

What is the probability of randomly selecting an executive who is loyal to the company (would remain) and who has more than 10 years of service?

SOLUTION

Note that two events occur at the same time—the executive would remain with the company, and he or she has more than 10 years of service.

1. Event A happens if a randomly selected executive will remain with the company despite an equal or slightly better offer from another company. To find the probability that event A will happen, refer to Table 5–1. Note that there are 120 executives out of the 200 in the survey who would remain with the company, so $P(A) = 120/200$, or .60.
2. Event B_4 happens if a randomly selected executive has more than 10 years of service with the company. Thus, $P(B_4 \mid A)$ is the conditional probability that an executive with more than 10 years of service would remain with the company despite an equal or slightly better offer from another company. Referring to the contingency table, Table 5–1, 75 of the 120 executives who would remain have more than 10 years of service, so $P(B_4 \mid A) = 75/120$.

Solving for the probability that an executive randomly selected will be one who would remain with the company and who has more than 10 years of service with the company, using the general rule of multiplication in formula (5–6):

$$P(A \text{ and } B_4) = P(A)P(B_4 \mid A) = \left(\frac{120}{200}\right)\left(\frac{75}{120}\right) = \frac{9{,}000}{24{,}000} = .375$$

Self-Review 5–7

Refer to Table 5–1. Using the general rule of multiplication, what is the probability of selecting at random an executive who would not remain with the company and has less than one year of service?

Tree Diagrams

The **tree diagram** is a graph that is helpful in organizing calculations that involve several stages. Each segment in the tree is one stage of the problem. The branches of a tree diagram are weighted by probabilities. We will use the data in Table 5–1 to show the construction of a tree diagram.

Steps in constructing a tree diagram

1. To construct a tree diagram, we begin by drawing a heavy dot on the left to represent the root of the tree (see Chart 5–1).

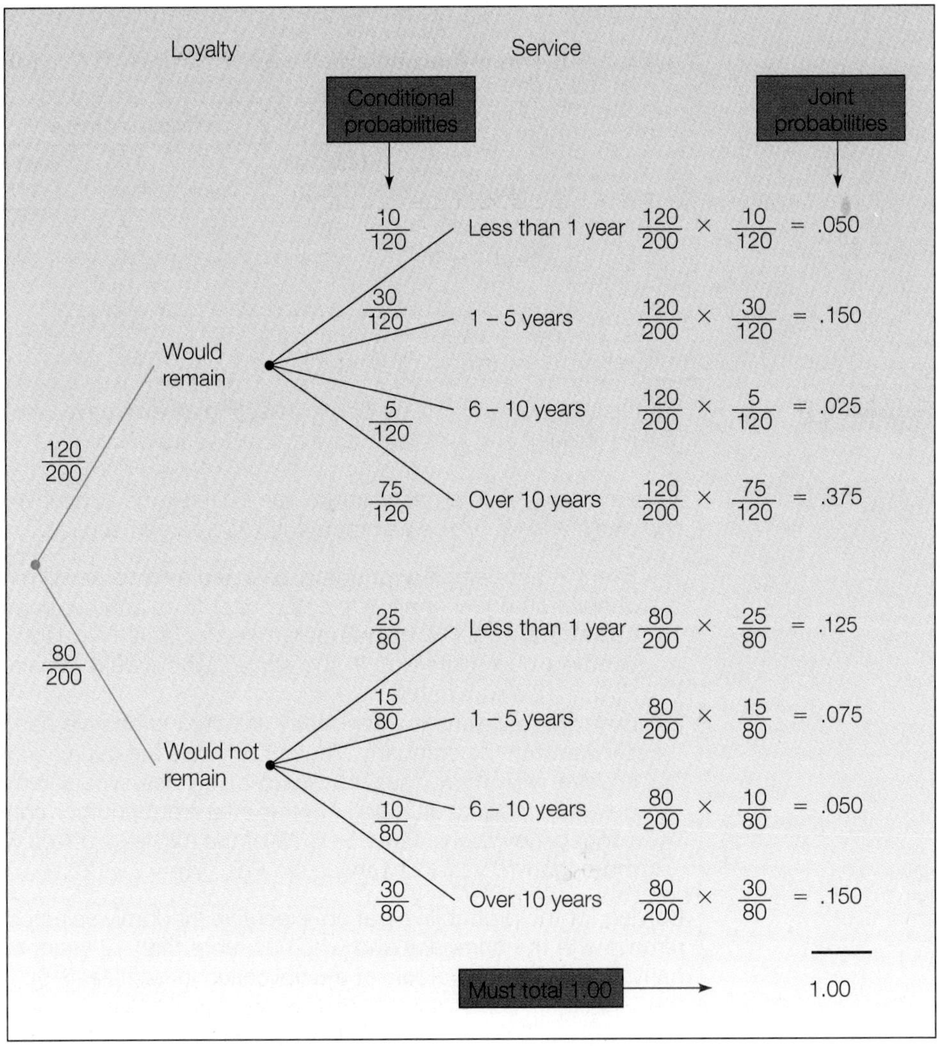

Loyalty

Service

Conditional probabilities

Joint probabilities

Loyalty		Conditional probabilities	Service	Joint probabilities
Would remain	$\frac{120}{200}$	$\frac{10}{120}$	Less than 1 year	$\frac{120}{200} \times \frac{10}{120} = .050$
		$\frac{30}{120}$	1 – 5 years	$\frac{120}{200} \times \frac{30}{120} = .150$
		$\frac{5}{120}$	6 – 10 years	$\frac{120}{200} \times \frac{5}{120} = .025$
		$\frac{75}{120}$	Over 10 years	$\frac{120}{200} \times \frac{75}{120} = .375$
Would not remain	$\frac{80}{200}$	$\frac{25}{80}$	Less than 1 year	$\frac{80}{200} \times \frac{25}{80} = .125$
		$\frac{15}{80}$	1 – 5 years	$\frac{80}{200} \times \frac{15}{80} = .075$
		$\frac{10}{80}$	6 – 10 years	$\frac{80}{200} \times \frac{10}{80} = .050$
		$\frac{30}{80}$	Over 10 years	$\frac{80}{200} \times \frac{30}{80} = .150$

Must total 1.00 → 1.00

CHART 5–1 Tree Diagram Showing Loyalty and Length of Service

2. For this problem, two main branches go out from the root, the upper one representing "would remain" and the lower one "would not remain." Their probabilities are written on the branches, namely, 120/200 and 80/200. These probabilities could also be denoted $P(A)$ and $P(\sim A)$.
3. Four branches "grow" out of each of the two main branches. These branches represent the length of service—less than 1 year, 1–5 years, 6–10 years, and more than 10 years. The conditional probabilities for the upper branch of the tree, 10/120, 30/120, 5/120, and so on are written on the appropriate branches. These are $P(B_1 \mid A)$, $P(B_2 \mid A)$, $P(B_3 \mid A)$, and $P(B_4 \mid A)$, where B_1 refers to less than 1 year of service, B_2 1 to 5 years, B_3 6 to 10 years, and B_4 more than 10 years. Next, write the conditional probabilities for the lower branch.
4. Finally, joint probabilities, that the events A and B_i, or the events $\sim A$ and B_i will occur together, are shown on the right side. For example, the joint probability of randomly selecting an executive who would remain with the company and who has less than one year of service, using formula (5–6), is:

$$P(A \text{ and } B_1) = P(A)P(B_1 \mid A) = \left(\frac{120}{200}\right)\left(\frac{10}{120}\right) = .05$$

Because the joint probabilities represent all possible selections (would remain, 6–10 years service; would not remain, more than 10 years of service; etc.), they must sum to 1.00. (See Chart 5–1.)

Self-Review 5–8

1. Refer to the tree diagram in Chart 5–1. Explain the path you would follow to find the joint probability of selecting an executive at random who has 6–10 years' service and who would not remain with the company upon receipt of an equal or slightly better offer from another company.
2. A random sample of the employees of the Hardware Manufacturing Company was chosen to determine their retirement plans after age 65. Those selected in the sample were divided into management and production. The results were:

	Plans after Age 65		
Employee	Retire	Not Retire	Total
Management	5	15	20
Production	30	50	80
			100

(a) What is the table called?
(b) Draw a tree diagram, and determine the joint probabilities.
(c) Do the joint probabilities total 1.00? Why?

Exercises

29. Suppose $P(A) = .40$ and $P(B \mid A) = .30$. What is the joint probability of A and B?

30. .30

30. Suppose $P(X_1) = .75$ and $P(Y_2 \mid X_1) = .40$. What is the joint probability of X_1 and Y_2?

31. A local bank reports that 80 percent of its customers maintain a checking account, 60 percent have a savings account, and 50 percent have both. If a customer is chosen at random, what is the probability the customer has either a checking or a savings account? What is the probability the customer does not have either a checking or a savings account?

32. .05

32. All Seasons Plumbing has two service trucks which frequently break down. If the probability the first truck is available is .75, the probability the second truck is available is .50, and the probability that both trucks are available is .30, what is the probability neither truck is available?

33. Refer to the following table.

Second Event	First Event A_1	A_2	A_3	Total
B_1	2	1	3	6
B_2	1	2	1	4
Total	3	3	4	10

a. Determine $P(A_1)$.
b. Determine $P(B_1 \mid A_2)$.
c. Determine $P(B_2 \text{ and } A_3)$.

34. a. .01579
b. .7158

34. Three defective electric toothbrushes were accidentally shipped to a drugstore by Cleanbrush Products along with 17 nondefective ones.
a. What is the probability the first two electric toothbrushes sold will be returned to the drugstore because they are defective?
b. What is the probability the first two electric toothbrushes sold will not be defective?

35. Each salesperson at Stiles-Compton is rated either below average, average, or above average with respect to sales ability. Each salesperson is also rated with respect to his or her potential for advancement — either fair, good, or excellent. These traits for the 500 salespeople were cross-classified into the following table.

Sales Ability	Potential for Advancement: Fair	Good	Excellent
Below average	16	12	22
Average	45	60	45
Above average	93	72	135

a. What is this table called?
b. What is the probability a salesperson selected at random will have above average sales ability and excellent potential for advancement?
c. Construct a tree diagram showing all the probabilities, conditional probabilities, and joint probabilities.

36. See IM.

36. An investor owns three common stocks. Each stock, independently of the other, has equally likely chances of (1) increasing in value, (2) decreasing in value, or (3) remaining the same value. List the possible outcomes of this experiment. Estimate the probability at least two of the stocks increase in value.

37. The board of directors of a small company consists of five people. Three of those are "strong leaders." If they buy an idea, the entire board will agree. The other "weak" members have no influence. Three salesmen are scheduled, one after the other, to make sales presentations to a board member of the salesman's choice. The salesmen are convincing but do not know who the "strong leaders" are. However, they will know who the previous salesmen spoke to. The first salesman to find a strong leader will win the account. Do the three salesmen have the same chance of winning the account? If not, find their respective probabilities of winning.

38. a. .0029
b. .612
c. .630

38. If you ask three strangers on campus, what is the probability: (a) All were born on Wednesday? (b) All were born on different days of the week? (c) None were born on Saturday?

Bayes' Theorem

In the 18th century Reverend Thomas Bayes, an English Presbyterian minister, pondered this question: Does God really exist? Being interested in mathematics, he attempted to develop a formula to arrive at the probability God does exist based on evidence available to him on earth. Later Laplace refined Bayes' work and gave it the name "Bayes' theorem." In a workable form, **Bayes' theorem** is:

BAYES' THEOREM

$$P(A_i \mid B) = \frac{P(A_i)P(B \mid A_i)}{P(A_1)P(B \mid A_1) + P(A_2)P(B \mid A_2)} \quad \textbf{[5–7]}$$

Assume in formula 5–7 that the events A_1 and A_2 are mutually exclusive and collectively exhaustive, and A_i refers to either event A_1 or A_2. The meaning of the symbols used is illustrated by the following example.

Suppose 5 percent of the population of Umen, a fictional Third World country, have a disease that is peculiar to that country. We will let A_1 refer to the event "has the disease" and A_2 refer to the event "does not have the disease." Thus, we know that if we select a person from Umen at random, the probability the individual chosen has the disease is .05, or $P(A_1) = .05$. This probability, $P(A_1) = P(\text{has the disease}) = .05$, is called the **prior probability.** It is given this name because the probability is assigned before any empirical data are obtained.

Statistics in Action

A recent study by the National Collegiate Athletic Association (NCAA) reported that of 150,000 senior boys playing on their high school basketball team, 64 would make a professional team. To put it another way, the odds of a high school senior basketball player making a professional team are 1 in 2,344. From the same study:

1. The odds of a high school senior playing some college basketball are about 1 in 40.
2. The odds of a high school senior playing college basketball as a senior in college are about 1 in 60.
3. If you play as a senior in college, the odds of making a professional team are about 1 in 37.5.

PRIOR PROBABILITY The initial probability based on the present level of information.

The prior probability a person is not afflicted with the disease is therefore .95, or $P(A_2) = .95$, found by $1 - .05$.

There is a diagnostic technique to detect the disease, but it is not very accurate. Let B denote the event "test shows the disease is present." Assume that historical evidence shows that if a person actually has the disease, the probability that the test will indicate the presence of the disease is .90. Using the conditional probability definitions developed earlier in this chapter, this statement is written as:

$$P(B \mid A_1) = .90$$

Assume the probability is .15 that for a person who actually does not have the disease the test will indicate the disease is present.

$$P(B \mid A_2) = .15$$

Let's randomly select a person from Umen and perform the test. The test results indicate the disease is present. What is the probability the person actually has the disease? In symbolic form, we want to know $P(A_1 \mid B)$, which is interpreted as: $P(\text{has the disease}) \mid (\text{the test results are positive})$. The probability $P(A_1 \mid B)$ is called a **posterior probability.**

POSTERIOR PROBABILITY A revised probability based on additional information.

With the help of Bayes' theorem, formula (5–7), we can determine the posterior probability.

$$P(A_1 \mid B) = \frac{P(A_1)P(B \mid A_1)}{P(A_1)P(B \mid A_1) + P(A_2)P(B \mid A_2)}$$

$$= \frac{(.05)(.90)}{(.05)(.90) + (.95)(.15)} = \frac{.0450}{.1875} = .24$$

So the probability that a person has the disease, given that he or she tested positive, is .24. How is the result interpreted? If a person is selected at random from the population, the probability that he or she has the disease is .05. If the person is tested and the test result is positive, the probability that the person actually has the disease is increased about fivefold, from .05 to .24.

In the preceding problem we had only two mutually exclusive and collectively exhaustive events A_1 and A_2. If there are n such events, $A_1, A_2, \ldots A_n$, Bayes' theorem, formula (5–7), becomes

$$P(A_i \mid B) = \frac{P(A_i)P(B \mid A_i)}{P(A_1)P(B \mid A_1) + P(A_2)P(B \mid A_2) + \cdots + P(A_n)P(B \mid A_n)}$$

Using the preceding notation, the calculations for the Umen problem are summarized in the following table.

Event, A_i	Prior Probability, $P(A_i)$	Conditional Probability, $P(B \mid A_i)$	Joint Probability, $P(A_i$ and $B)$	Posterior Probability, $P(A_i \mid B)$
Disease, A_1	.05	.90	.0450	.0450/.1875 = .24
No disease, A_2	.95	.15	.1425	.1425/.1875 = .76
			$P(B)$ = .1875	1.00

Another illustration of Bayes' theorem follows.

EXAMPLE

A manufacturer of VCRs purchases a particular microchip, called the LS-24, from three suppliers: Hall Electronics, Schuller Sales, and Crawford Components. Thirty percent of the LS-24 chips are purchased from Hall Electronics, 20 percent from Schuller Sales, and the remaining 50 percent from Crawford Components. The manufacturer has extensive histories on the three suppliers and knows that 3 percent of the LS-24 chips from Hall Electronics are defective, 5 percent of chips from Schuller Sales are defective, and 4 percent of the chips purchased from Crawford Components are defective.

When the LS-24 chips arrive at the manufacturer, they are placed directly in a bin and not inspected or otherwise identified by supplier. A worker selects a chip for installation in a VCR and finds it defective. What is the probability that it was manufactured by Schuller Sales?

SOLUTION

As a first step, let's summarize some of the information given in the problem statement.

- There are three mutually exclusive and collectively exhaustive events, that is, three suppliers.

  A_1 The LS-24 was purchased from Hall Electronics
  A_2 The LS-24 was purchased from Schuller Sales
  A_3 The LS-24 was purchased from Crawford Components

- The prior probabilities are:

  $P(A_1) = .30$ The probability the LS-24 was manufactured by Hall Electronics
  $P(A_2) = .20$ The probability the LS-24 was manufactured by Schuller Sales
  $P(A_3) = .50$ The probability the LS-24 was manufactured by Crawford Components

- The additional information can be either:

  B_1 The LS-24 appears defective, or
  B_2 The LS-24 appears not to be defective.

- The following conditional probabilities are given.

  $P(B_1 \mid A_1) = .03$ The probability that an LS-24 chip produced by Hall Electronics is defective
  $P(B_1 \mid A_2) = .05$ The probability that an LS-24 chip produced by Schuller Sales is defective
  $P(B_1 \mid A_3) = .04$ The probability that an LS-24 chip produced by Crawford Components is defective

- A chip is selected from the bin. Because the chips are not identified by supplier, we are not certain which supplier manufactured the chip. We want to determine the probability that the defective chip was purchased from Schuller Sales. The probability is written $P(A_2 \mid B_1)$.

Look at Schuller's quality record. It is the worst of the three suppliers. Now that we have found a defective LS-24 chip, we suspect that $P(A_2 \mid B_1)$ is greater than $P(A_2)$. That is, we expect the revised probability to be greater than .20. But how much greater? Bayes' theorem can give us the answer. As a first step, consider the tree diagram in Chart 5–2.

The events are dependent, so the prior probability in the first branch is multiplied by the conditional probability in the second branch to obtain the joint probability. The joint probability is reported in the last column of Chart 5–2. To construct the tree diagram of Chart 5–2, we used a time sequence that moved from the supplier to the determination of whether the chip was acceptable or unacceptable.

What we need to do is reverse the time process. That is, instead of moving from left to right in Chart 5–2, we need to move from right to left. We have a defective chip, and we want to determine the likelihood that it was purchased from Schuller Sales. How is that accomplished? We first look at the joint probabilities as relative frequencies out of 1,000 cases. For example, the likelihood of a defective LS-24 chip that was produced by Hall Electronics is .009. So of 1,000 cases we would expect to find 9 defective chips produced by Hall Electronics. We observe that in 39 of 1,000 cases the LS-24 chip selected for assembly will be defective, found by $9 + 10 + 20$. Of these 39 defective chips, 10 were produced by Schuller Sales. Thus, the probability that the defective LS-24 chip was purchased from Schuller Sales is $10/39 = .2564$. We have now determined the revised probability of $P(A_2 \mid B_1)$. Before we found the defective chip, the likelihood that it was purchased from Schuller Sales was .20. This likelihood has been increased to .2564.

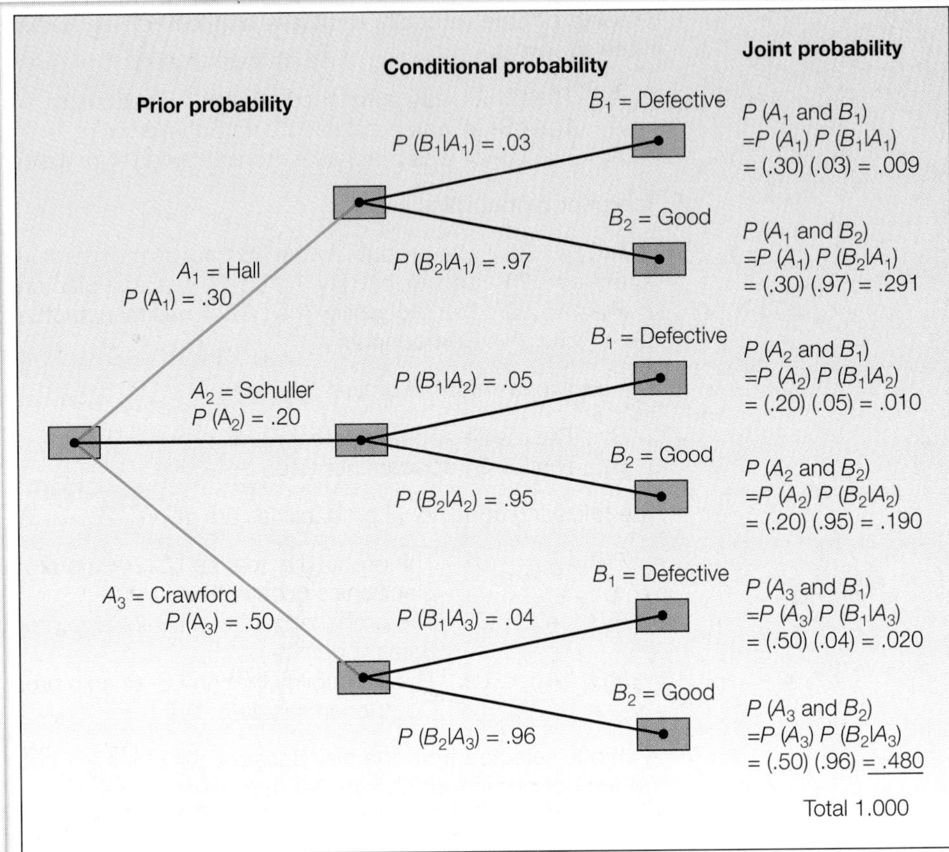

CHART 5–2 Tree Diagram of VCR Manufacturing Problem

This information is summarized in the following table.

Event, A_i	Prior Probability, $P(A_i)$	Conditional Probability, $P(B_1 \mid A_i)$	Joint Probability, $P(A_i \text{ and } B_1)$	Posterior Probability, $P(A_i \mid B_1)$
Hall	.30	.03	.009	.009/.039 = .2308
Schuller	.20	.05	.010	.010/.039 = .2564
Crawford	.50	.04	.020	.020/.039 = .5128
			$P(B_1)$ = .039	1.0000

The probability the defective LS-24 chip came from Schuller Sales can be formally found by using Bayes' theorem. We compute $P(A_2 \mid B_1)$, where A_2 refers to Schuller Sales and B_1 to the fact that the selected LS-24 chip was defective.

$$P(A_2 \mid B_1) = \frac{P(A_2)P(B_1 \mid A_2)}{P(A_1)P(B_1 \mid A_1) + P(A_2)P(B_1 \mid A_2) + P(A_3)P(B_1 \mid A_3)}$$

$$= \frac{(.20)(.05)}{(.30)(.03) + (.20)(.05) + (.50)(.04)} = \frac{.010}{.039} = .2564$$

This is the same result obtained from Chart 5–2 and from the conditional probability table.

Self-Review 5–9

Refer to the preceding example and solution.
(a) Design a formula to find the probability the part selected came from Crawford Components, given that it was a good chip.
(b) Compute the probability using Bayes' theorem.

Exercises

39. $P(A_1) = .60$, $P(A_2) = .40$, $P(B_1 \mid A_1) = .05$, and $P(B_1 \mid A_2) = .10$. Use Bayes' theorem to determine $P(A_1 \mid B_1)$.

40. .3636

40. $P(A_1) = .20$, $P(A_2) = .40$, and $P(A_3) = .40$. $P(B_1 \mid A_1) = .25$. $P(B_1 \mid A_2) = .05$, and $P(B_1 \mid A_3) = .10$. Use Bayes' theorem to determine $P(A_3 \mid B_1)$.

41. The Ludlow Wildcats baseball team, a minor league team in the Cleveland Indians organization, plays 70 percent of their games at night and 30 percent during the day. The team wins 50 percent of their night games and 90 percent of their day games. According to today's newspaper, they won yesterday. What is the probability the game was played at night?

42. .8571

42. Dr. Stallter has been teaching basic statistics for many years. She knows that 80 percent of the students will complete the assigned problems. She has also determined that among those who do their assignments, 90 percent will pass the course. Among those students who do not do their homework, 60 percent will pass. Mike Fishbaugh took statistics last semester from Dr. Stallter and received a passing grade. What is the probability that he completed the assignments?

43. The credit department of Lion's Department Store in Anaheim, California, reported that 30 percent of their sales are cash, 30 percent are paid for by check at the time of the purchase, and 40 percent are charged. Twenty percent of the cash purchases, 90 percent of the checks, and 60 percent of the charges are for more than \$50. Ms. Tina Stevens just purchased a new dress that cost \$120. What is the probability that she paid cash?

44. .625

44. One-fourth of the residents of the Burning Ridge Estates leave their garage doors open when they are away from home. The local chief of police estimates that 5 percent of the garages with open doors will have something stolen, but only 1 percent of those closed will have something stolen. If a garage is robbed, what is the probability the doors were left open?

Principles of Counting

If the number of possible outcomes in an experiment is small, it is relatively easy to count them. There are six possible outcomes, for example, resulting from the roll of a die, namely:

If, however, there are a large number of possible outcomes, such as the number of boys and girls for families with 10 children, it would be tedious to count all the possibilities. They could have all boys, one boy and nine girls, two boys and eight girls, and so on. To facilitate counting, three counting formulas will be examined: the **multiplication formula** (not to be confused with the multiplication *rule* described earlier in the chapter), the **permutation formula,** and the **combination formula.**

The Multiplication Formula

MULTIPLICATION FORMULA If there are m ways of doing one thing and n ways of doing another thing, there are $m \times n$ ways of doing both.

In terms of a formula:

MULTIPLICATION FORMULA Total number of arrangements $= (m)(n)$ **[5–8]**

This can be extended to more than two events. For three events m, n, and o:

$$\text{Total number of arrangements} = (m)(n)(o)$$

EXAMPLE

An automobile dealer wants to advertise that for $29,999 you can buy a convertible, a two-door, or a four-door model with your choice of either wire wheel covers or solid wheel covers. How many different arrangements of models and wheel covers can the dealer offer?

SOLUTION

Of course the dealer could determine the total number of arrangements by picturing and counting them. There are six.

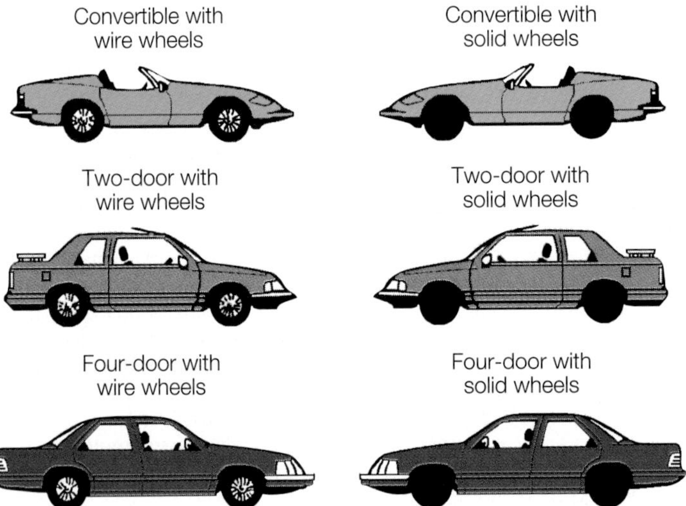

We can employ the multiplication formula as a check (where m is the number of models and n the wheel cover type). Using formula (5–8):

$$\text{Total possible arrangements} = (m)(n) = (3)(2) = 6$$

It was not difficult to count all the possible model and wheel cover combinations in this example. Suppose, however, that the dealer decided to offer eight models and six types of wheel covers. It would be tedious to picture and count all the possible alternatives. Instead, the multiplication formula can be used. In this case, there are $(m)(n) = (8)(6) = 48$ possible arrangements.

Note in the preceding applications of the multiplication formula that there were *two or more groupings from which you made selections.* The automobile dealer, for example, offered a choice of models and a choice of wheel covers. If a home builder offered you four different exterior styles of a home to choose from and three interior floor plans, the multiplication formula would be used to find how many different arrangements were possible.

Self-Review 5–10

1. Stiffin Lamps has developed five lamp bases and four lamp shades that can be used together. How many different arrangements of base and shade can be offered?
2. Pioneer manufactures three models of stereo receivers, two cassette decks, four speakers, and three CD carousels. When the four types of components are sold together, they form a "system." How many different systems can the electronics firm offer?

The Permutation Formula

As noted, the multiplication formula is applied to find the number of possible arrangements for two or more groups. The **permutation formula** is applied to find the possible number of arrangements when there is only *one* group of objects. As illustrations of this type of problem:

- Three electronic parts are to be assembled into a plug-in unit for a television set. The parts can be assembled in any order. The question involving counting is: In how many different ways can the three parts be assembled?
- A machine operator must make four safety checks before starting his machine. It does not matter in which order the checks are made. In how many different ways can the operator make the checks?

One order for the first illustration might be: the transistor first, the LEDs second, and the synthesizer third. This arrangement is called a **permutation.**

PERMUTATION Any arrangement of r objects selected from a single group of n possible objects.

Note that the arrangements *a b c* and *b a c* are different permutations. The formula to count the total number of different permutations is:

PERMUTATION FORMULA
$$_nP_r = \frac{n!}{(n-r)!} \qquad \textbf{[5–9]}$$

where:

n is the total number of objects.
r is the number of objects selected.

Before we solve the two problems illustrated, note that permutations and combinations (to be discussed shortly) use a notation called *n factorial.* It is written $n!$ and means the product of $n(n-1)(n-2)(n-3)\ldots(1)$. For instance, $5! = 5 \cdot 4 \cdot 3 \cdot 2 \cdot 1 = 120$.

As shown below, numbers can be canceled when the same numbers are included in the numerator and denominator.

$$\frac{6!3!}{4!} = \frac{6 \cdot 5 \cdot \not{4} \cdot \not{3} \cdot \not{2} \cdot \not{1}(3 \cdot 2 \cdot 1)}{\not{4} \cdot \not{3} \cdot \not{2} \cdot \not{1}} = 180$$

$0! = 1$

By definition, zero factorial, written 0!, is 1. That is, $0! = 1$.

EXAMPLE

Referring to the group of three electronic parts that are to be assembled in any order, in how many different ways can they be assembled?

SOLUTION

$n = 3$ because there are three electronic parts to be assembled. $r = 3$ because all three are to be inserted in the plug-in unit. Solving using formula (5–9):

$$_nP_r = \frac{n!}{(n-r)!} = \frac{3!}{(3-3)!} = \frac{3!}{0!} = \frac{3!}{1} = 6$$

A check can be made to the number of permutations arrived at using the permutation formula. To check, we merely determine how many "spaces" have to be filled and the possibilities for each "space" and apply the multiplication formula. In the problem involving three electronic parts, there are three locations in the plug-in unit for the three parts. There are three possibilities for the first place, two for the second (one has been used up), and one for the third, as follows:

$$(3)(2)(1) = 6 \text{ permutations}$$

The six ways in which the three electronic parts, lettered A, B, C, can be arranged are:

ABC	*BAC*	*CAB*	*ACB*	*BCA*	*CBA*

In the previous example we selected and arranged all the objects, that is $n = r$. In many cases, only some objects are selected and arranged from the n possible objects. We explain the details of this application in the following example.

EXAMPLE

The Betts Machine Shop, Inc., has eight screw machines but only three spaces available in the production area for the machines. In how many different ways can the eight machines be arranged in the three spaces available?

SOLUTION

There are eight possibilities for the first available space in the production area, seven for the second space (one has been used up), and six for the third space. Thus:

$$(8)(7)(6) = 336, \text{ that is,}$$

there are a total of 336 different possible arrangements. This could also be found using formula 5–9. If $n = 8$ machines, and $r = 3$ spaces available, the formula leads to

$$_nP_r = \frac{n!}{(n-r)!} = \frac{8!}{(8-3)!} = \frac{8!}{5!} = \frac{(8)(7)(6)5!}{5!} = 336$$

The Combination Formula

If the order of the selected objects is not important, any selection is called a *combination.* The formula to count the number of r object combinations from a set of n objects is:

COMBINATION FORMULA

$$_nC_r = \frac{n!}{r!(n-r)!} \qquad \textbf{[5–10]}$$

For example, if executives Able, Baker, and Chauncy are to be chosen as a committee to negotiate a merger, there is only one possible combination of these three; the committee of Able, Baker, and Chauncy is the same as the committee of Baker, Chauncy, and Able. Using the combination formula:

$$_nC_r = \frac{n!}{r!(n-r)!} = \frac{3 \cdot 2 \cdot 1}{3 \cdot 2 \cdot 1(1)} = 1$$

EXAMPLE

The marketing department has been given the assignment of designing color codes for the 42 different lines of compact discs sold by Goody Records. Three colors are to be used on each CD, but a combination of three colors used for one CD cannot be rearranged and used to identify a different CD. This means that if green, yellow, and violet were used to identify one line, then yellow, green, and violet (or any other combination of these three colors) cannot be used to identify another line. Would seven colors taken three at a time be adequate to color code the 42 lines?

SOLUTION

Using formula (5–10), there are 35 combinations, found by

$$_7C_3 = \frac{n!}{r!(n-r)!} = \frac{7!}{3!(7-3)!} = \frac{7!}{3!4!} = 35$$

The seven colors taken three at a time (i.e., three colors to a line) would not be adequate to color code the 42 different lines because they would provide only 35 combinations. Eight colors taken three at a time would give 56 different combinations. This would be more than adequate to color code the 42 different lines.

Self-Review 5–11

1. A musician wants to write a score based on only five chords: B-flat, C, D, E, and G. However, only three chords out of the five will be used in succession, such as C, B-flat, and E. Repetitions, such as B-flat, B-flat, and E, will not be permitted.
   (a) How many permutations of the five chords, taken three at a time, are possible?
   (b) Using formula (5–9), how many permutations are possible?
2. Recall that a machine operator must make four safety checks before starting to machine a part. It does not matter in which order the checks are made. In how many different ways can the operator make the checks?
3. The 10 numbers 0 through 9 are to be used in code groups of four to identify an item of clothing. Code 1083 might identify a blue blouse, size medium; the code group 2031 might identify a pair of pants, size 18; and so on. Repetitions of numbers are not permitted. That is, the same number cannot be used twice (or more) in a total sequence. For example, 2256, 2562, or 5559 would not be permitted. How many different code groups can be designed?
4. In the above example involving Goody Records, we said that eight colors taken three at a time would give 56 different combinations.
   (a) Use formula (5–10) to show this is true.
   (b) As an alternative plan for color coding the 42 different lines, it has been suggested that only two colors be placed on a disc. Would 10 colors be adequate to color code the 42 different lines? (Again, a combination of two colors could be used only once — that is, if pink and blue were coded for one line, blue and pink could not be used to identify a different line.)

Exercises

45. Solve the following:
a. 40!/35!
b. ${}_7P_4$
c. ${}_5C_2$

46. Solve the following:
a. 20!/17!
b. ${}_9P_3$
c. ${}_7C_2$

46. a. 6840
b. 504
c. 21

47. A pollster randomly selected 4 of 10 available people. How many different groups of 4 are possible?

48. A telephone number consists of seven digits, the first three representing the exchange. How many different telephone numbers are possible within the 537 exchange?

48. 10,000

49. An overnight express company must include five cities on its route. How many different routes are possible, assuming that it does not matter in which order the cities are included in the routing?

50. A representative of the Environmental Protection Agency (EPA) wants to select samples from 10 landfills. The director has 15 landfills from which she can collect samples. How many different samples are possible?

50. 3003

51. A national pollster has developed 15 questions designed to rate the performance of the President of the United States. The pollster will select 10 of these questions. How many different arrangements are there for the order of the 10 selected questions?

52. A company is creating three new divisions and seven managers are eligible to be appointed head of a division. How many different ways could the three new heads be appointed?

52. 210

Chapter Outline

I. A probability is a value between 0 and 1 inclusive that represents the likelihood a particular event will happen.
  A. An experiment is the observation of some activity or the act of taking some measurement.
  B. An outcome is a particular result of an experiment.
  C. An event is the collection of one or more outcomes of an experiment.

II. There are three definitions of probability.
  A. The classical definition applies when there are *n* equally likely outcomes to an experiment.
  B. The empirical definition occurs when the number of times an event happens is divided by the number of observations.
  C. A subjective probability is based on whatever information is available.

III. Two events are mutually exclusive if by virtue of one event happening the other cannot happen.

IV. Events are independent if the occurrence of one event does not affect the occurrence of another event.

V. The rules of addition refer to the union of events.
  A. The special rule of addition is used when events are mutually exclusive.

$$P(A \text{ or } B) = P(A) + P(B) \quad \textbf{[5–2]}$$

  B. The general rule of addition is

$$P(A \text{ or } B) = P(A) + P(B) - P(A \text{ and } B) \quad \textbf{[5–4]}$$

  C. The complement rule is used to determine the probability of an event happening by subtracting the probability of the event not happening from 1.

$$P(A) = 1 - P(\sim A) \quad \textbf{[5–3]}$$

Statistics in Action

Many states, such as Ohio, Michigan, California, and Florida, have lotteries in which a player buys a single ticket, often for only a dollar, and may win a large sum of money. In some states the amount of money to be won exceeds \$20 million. In order to win, the player must match all six numbers randomly drawn from a pool of 49 numbers. The odds of winning such a lottery are 1 in 13,983,816. The odds of obtaining 23 heads in a row while flipping a coin are 1 in 8,388,608. To put it another way, you have a better chance of flipping a coin 23 times and getting all heads than you do of winning the lottery.

VI. The rules of multiplication refer to the product of events.

A. The special rule of multiplication refers to events that are independent.

$$P(A \text{ and } B) = P(A)P(B) \quad \textbf{[5–5]}$$

B. The general rule of multiplication refers to events that are not independent.

$$P(A \text{ and } B) = P(A)P(B \mid A) \quad \textbf{[5–6]}$$

C. A joint probability is the likelihood that two or more events will happen at the same time.

D. A conditional probability is the likelihood that an event will happen, given that another event has already happened.

E. Bayes' theorem is a method of revising a probability, given that additional information is obtained. For two mutually exclusive and collectively exhaustive events:

$$P(A_1 \mid B) = \frac{P(A_1)P(B \mid A_1)}{P(A_1)P(B \mid A_1) + P(A_2)P(B \mid A_2)} \quad \textbf{[5–7]}$$

VII. There are three counting rules that are useful in determining the number of outcomes in an experiment.

A. The multiplication rule states that if there are m ways one event can happen and n ways another event can happen, then there are mn ways the two events can happen.

$$\text{Number of arrangements} = (m)(n) \quad \textbf{[5–8]}$$

B. A permutation is an arrangement in which the order of the objects selected from a specific pool of objects is important.

$${}_nP_r = \frac{n!}{(n-r)!} \quad \textbf{[5–9]}$$

C. A combination is an arrangement where the order of the objects selected from a specific pool of objects is not important.

$${}_nC_r = \frac{n!}{r!(n-r)!} \quad \textbf{[5–10]}$$

Pronunciation Key

SYMBOL	MEANING	PRONUNCIATION
$P(A)$	Probability of A	P of A
$P(\sim A)$	Probability of not A	P of not A
$P(A \text{ and } B)$	Probability of A and B	P of A and B
$P(A \text{ or } B)$	Probability of A or B	P of A or B
$P(A \mid B)$	Probability of A given B has happened	P of A given B
${}_nP_r$	Permutation of n items selected r at a time	Pnr
${}_nC_r$	Combination of n items selected r at a time	Cnr

Chapter Exercises

53. The marketing research department at Vernors plans to survey teenagers about a newly developed soft drink. Each will be asked to compare it with his or her favorite soft drink.

a. What is the experiment?

b. What is one possible event?

54. The number of times a particular event occurred in the past is divided by the number of occurrences. What is this approach to probability called?

54. Empirical.

55. The probability that the cause and the cure for all cancers will be discovered before the year 2010 is .20. What viewpoint of probability does this statement illustrate?

56. No.

56. Is it true that, if there is absolutely no chance a person will recover from 50 bullet wounds, the probability assigned to this event is −1.00? Why?
57. On the throw of one die, what is the probability that a one-spot or a two-spot or a six-spot will appear face up? What definition of probability is being used?
58. Berdine's Chicken Factory has several stores in the Hilton Head, South Carolina, area. When interviewing applicants for server positions, the owner would like to include information on the amount of tip a server can expect to earn per check (or bill). A study of 500 recent checks indicated the server earned the following tip.

Amount of Tip	Number
$ 0 up to $ 5	200
5 up to 10	100
10 up to 20	75
20 up to 50	75
50 or more	50
Total	500

58. a. .10
b. Yes.
c. 1.00
d. .60
e. .90

a. What is the probability of a tip of $50 or more?
b. Are the categories "$0 up to $5," "$5 up to $10," and so on considered mutually exclusive?
c. If the probabilities associated with each outcome were totaled, what would that total be?
d. What is the probability of a tip of up to $10?
e. What is the probability of a tip of less than $50?

59. Define each of these items:
a. Conditional probability.
b. Event.
c. Joint probability.

60. a. .077
b. .059
c. .0045

60. The first card selected from a standard 52-card deck was a king.
a. If it is returned to the deck, what is the probability that a king will be drawn on the second selection?
b. If the king is not replaced, what is the probability that a king will be drawn on the second selection?
c. What is the probability that a king will be selected on the first draw from the deck and another king on the second draw (assuming that the first king was not replaced)?

61. Armco, a manufacturer of traffic light systems, found that under accelerated-life tests, 95 percent of the newly developed systems lasted three years before failing to change signals properly.
a. If a city purchased four of these systems, what is the probability all four systems would operate properly for at least three years?
b. Which rule of probability does this illustrate?
c. Using letters to represent the four systems, write an equation to show how you arrived at the answer to part a.

62. Refer to the following picture.

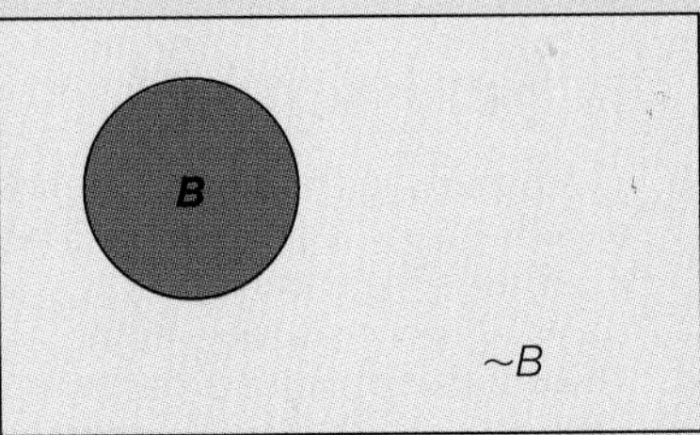

62. a. Venn Diagram.
b. Complement Rule.
c. Yes

a. What is the picture called?
b. What rule of probability is illustrated?
c. B represents the event of choosing a family that receives welfare payments. What does $P(B) + P(\sim B)$ equal?

63. In a management trainee program at Claremont Enterprises, 80 percent of the trainees are female and 20 percent male. Ninety percent of the females attended college, and 78 percent of the males attended college.
a. A management trainee is selected at random. What is the probability that the person selected is a female who did not attend college?
b. Construct a tree diagram showing all the probabilities, conditional probabilities, and joint probabilities.
c. Do the joint probabilities total 1.00? Why?

64. Assume the likelihood that any flight on American Airlines arrives within 15 minutes of the scheduled time is .90. We select four flights from yesterday for study.

64. a. .6561
b. .0001
c. .3439

a. What is the likelihood all four of the selected flights arrived within 15 minutes of the scheduled time?
b. What is the likelihood that none of the selected flights arrived within 15 minutes of the scheduled time?
c. What is the likelihood at least one of the selected flights did not arrive within 15 minutes of the scheduled time?

65. There are 100 employees at Kiddie Carts International. Fifty-seven of the employees are production workers, 40 are supervisors, 2 are secretaries, and the remaining employee is the president. Suppose an employee is selected:
a. What is the probability the selected employee is a production worker?
b. What is the probability the selected employee is either a production worker or a supervisor?
c. Refer to part b. Are these events mutually exclusive?
d. What is the probability the selected employee is neither a production worker nor a supervisor?

66. Todd Helton of the Colorado Rockies and Nomar Garciaparra of the Boston Red Sox tied for the highest batting average in the 2000 Major League Baseball season. Each had an average of .372. So assume the probability of their getting a hit is .372 for each time either batted. In a particular game assume either batted three times.

66. a. Empirical.
b. .051
c. .248
d. .752

a. This is an example of what type of probability?
b. What is the probability of getting three hits in a particular game?
c. What is the probability of not getting any hits in a game?
d. What is the probability of getting at least one hit?

67. The probability that a bomber hits its target on any particular mission is .80. Four bombers are sent after the same target. What is the probability:
a. They all hit the target?
b. None hit the target?
c. At least one hits the target?

68. Ninety students will graduate from Lima Shawnee High School this spring. Of the 90 students, 50 are planning to attend college. Two students are to be picked at random to carry flags at the graduation.

68. a. .3059
b. .4994

a. What is the probability both of the selected students plan to attend college?
b. What is the probability one of the two selected students plans to attend college?

69. Brooks Insurance, Inc. wishes to offer life insurance to men age 60 via the Internet. Mortality tables indicate the likelihood of a 60-year-old man surviving another year is .98. If the policy is offered to five men age 60:
a. What is the probability all five men survive the year?
b. What is the probability at least one does not survive?

70. Forty percent of the homes constructed in the Quail Creek area include a security system. Three homes are selected at random:

70. a. .064
b. .216
c. .784
d. Independent.

a. What is the probability all three of the selected homes have a security system?
b. What is the probability none of the three selected homes have a security system?
c. What is the probability at least one of the selected homes has a security system?
d. Did you assume the events to be dependent or independent?

71. Refer to Exercise 70, but assume there are ten homes in the Quail Creek area and four of them have a security system. Three homes are selected at random:
a. What is the probability all three of the selected homes have a security system?
b. What is the probability none of the three selected homes have a security system?
c. What is the probability at least one of the selected homes has a security system?
d. Did you assume the events to be dependent or independent?

72. .0889

72. A juggler has a bag containing three green balls, two yellow balls, one red ball, and four blues. The juggler picks a ball at random Then, without replacing it, he chooses a second ball. What is the probability the juggler first draws a yellow ball followed by a blue ball?

73. The board of directors of Saner Automatic Door Company consists of 12 members, 3 of whom are women. A new policy and procedures manual is to be written for the company. A committee of 3 is randomly selected from the board to do the writing.
a. What is the probability that all members of the committee are men?
b. What is the probability that at least 1 member of the committee is a woman?

74. A survey of undergraduate students in the School of Business at Northern University revealed the following regarding the gender and majors of the students:

	Major			
Gender	**Accounting**	**Management**	**Finance**	**Total**
Male	100	150	50	300
Female	100	50	50	200
Total	200	200	100	500

74. a. .40
b. .60
c. .60; general rule
d. .33
e. .1595

a. What is the probability of selecting a female student?
b. What is the probability of selecting a finance or accounting major?
c. What is the probability of selecting a female or an accounting major? Which rule of addition did you apply?
d. What is the probability of selecting an accounting major, given that the person selected is a male?
e. Suppose two students are selected randomly to attend a lunch with the president of the university. What is the probability that both of those selected are accounting majors?

75. The Wood County sheriff classifies crimes by age (in years) of the criminal and whether the crime is violent or nonviolent. As shown below, a total of 150 crimes were reported by the sheriff last year.

	Age (in years)			
Type of Crime	**Under 20**	**20 to 40**	**Over 40**	**Total**
Violent	27	41	14	82
Nonviolent	12	34	22	68
Total	39	75	36	150

a. What is the probability of selecting a case to analyze and finding it involved a violent crime?
b. What is the probability of selecting a case to analyze and finding the crime was committed by someone less than 40 years old?
c. What is the probability of selecting a case that involved a violent crime or an offender less than 20 years old? Which rule of addition did you apply?
d. Given that a violent crime is selected for analysis, what is the probability the crime was committed by a person under 20 years old?
e. Two crimes are selected for review by Judge Tybo. What is the probability that both are violent crimes?

76. Mr. and Mrs. Wilhelms are both retired and living in a retirement community in Arizona. Suppose the probability that a retired man will live another 10 years is .60. The probability that a retired woman will live another 10 years is .70.

76. a. .42 b. .28 c. .88

a. What is the probability that both Mr. and Mrs. Wilhelms will be alive 10 years from now?
b. What is the probability that in 10 years Mr. Wilhelms is not living and Mrs. Wilhelms is living?
c. What is the probability that in 10 years at least one is living?

77. Flashner Marketing Research, Inc. specializes in providing assessments of the prospects for women's apparel shops in shopping malls. Al Flashner, president, reports that he assesses the prospects as good, fair, or poor. Records from previous assessments show that 60 percent of the time the prospects were rated as good, 30 percent of the time fair, and 10 percent of the time poor. Of those rated good, 80 percent made a profit the first year; of those rated fair, 60 percent made a profit the first year; and of those rated poor, 20 percent made a profit the first year. Connie's Apparel was one of Flashner's clients. Connie's Apparel made a profit last year. What is the probability that it was given an original rating of poor?

78. There are 400 employees at G. G. Greene Manufacturing Co., and 100 of them smoke. There are 250 males working for the company, and 75 of them smoke. What is the probability that an employee selected at random:

78. a. .625 b. .250 c. .1875 d. .6875

a. Is a male?
b. Smokes?
c. Is male and smokes?
d. Is male or smokes?

79. With each purchase of a large pizza at Tony's Pizza, the customer receives a coupon that can be scratched to see if a prize will be awarded. The odds of winning a free soft drink are 1 in 10, and the odds of winning a free large pizza are 1 in 50. You plan to eat lunch tomorrow at Tony's. What is the probability:
a. That you will win either a large pizza or a soft drink?
b. That you will not win a prize?
c. That you will not win a prize on three consecutive visits to Tony's?
d. That you will win at least one prize on one of your next three visits to Tony's?

80. For the daily lottery game in Illinois, participants select three numbers between 0 and 9. A number cannot be selected more than once, so a winning ticket could be, say, 307. Purchasing one ticket allows you to select one set of numbers. The winning numbers are announced on TV each night.

80. a. 720 b. .00139 c. .99583

a. How many different outcomes (three-digit numbers) are possible?
b. If you purchase a ticket for the game tonight, what is the likelihood you will win?
c. Suppose you purchase three tickets for tonight's drawing and select a different number for each ticket. What is the probability that you will not win with any of the tickets?

81. A new job consists of assembling four different parts. All four have different color codes, and they can be assembled in any order. The production department wants to determine the most efficient way to assemble the four parts. The supervisors are going to conduct some experiments to solve the problem. First, they plan to assemble the parts in this order — green, black, yellow, and blue — and record the time. Then the assembly will be accomplished in a different order. In how many different ways can the four parts be assembled?

82. .70

82. It was found that 60 percent of the tourists to China visited the Forbidden City, the Temple of Heaven, the Great Wall, and other historical sites in or near Beijing. Forty percent visited Xi'an with its magnificent terracotta soldiers, horses, and chariots, which lay buried for over 2,000 years. Thirty percent of the tourists went to both Beijing and Xi'an. What is the probability that a tourist visited at least one of these places?

83. Two boxes of men's Old Navy shirts were received from the factory. Box 1 contained 25 mesh polo shirts and 15 Super-T shirts. Box 2 contained 30 mesh polo shirts and 10 Super-T shirts. One of the boxes was selected at random, and a shirt was chosen at random from that box to be inspected. The shirt was a mesh polo shirt. Given this information, what is the probability that the mesh polo shirt came from box 1?

84. 4,320, 4104

84. The operators of Riccardo's Restaurant want to advertise that they have a large number of different meals. They offer 4 soups, 3 salads, 12 entrees, 6 vegetables, and 5 desserts. How many different meals do they offer? In addition, Riccardo's has an "early bird" special: You may omit any part of the meal except the entrees for a reduced price. How many different meals do they have for the "early birds"?

85. Several years ago Wendy's Hamburgers advertised that there are 256 different ways to order your hamburger. You may choose to have, or omit, any combination of the following on your hamburger: mustard, ketchup, onion, pickle, tomato, relish, mayonnaise, and lettuce. Is the advertisement correct? Show how you arrive at your answer.

86. 15

86. Reynolds Construction Company has agreed not to erect all "look-alike" homes in a new subdivision. Five exterior designs are offered to potential home buyers. The builder has standardized three interior plans that can be incorporated in any of the five exteriors. How many different ways can the exterior and interior plans be offered to potential home buyers?

87. A small rug weaver has decided to use seven compatible colors in her new line of rugs. However, in weaving a rug, only five spindles can be used. In her advertising she wants to indicate the number of different color groupings for sale. How many color groupings using the seven colors taken five at a time are there? (This assumes that five different colors will go into each rug — i.e., there are no repetitions of color.)

88. 45

88. Consideration is being given to forming a Super Ten football conference. The top 10 football teams in the country, based on past records, would be members of the Super Ten conference. Each team would play every other team in the conference during the season. The team winning the most games would be declared the national champion. How many games would the conference commissioner have to schedule each year? (Remember, Oklahoma versus Michigan is the same as Michigan versus Oklahoma.)

89. A new chewing gum has been developed that is helpful to those who want to stop smoking. If 60 percent of those people chewing the gum are successful in stopping smoking, what is the probability that in a group of four smokers using the gum at least one quits smoking?

90. 17,576,000

90. The state of Maryland has license plates with three numbers followed by three letters. How many different license plates are possible?

91. A new sports car model has defective brakes 15 percent of the time and a defective steering mechanism 5 percent of the time. Let's assume (and hope) that these problems occur independently. If one or the other of these problems is present, the car is called a "lemon." If both of these problems are present, the car is a "hazard." Your instructor purchased one of these cars yesterday. What is the probability it is:
   a. A lemon?
   b. A hazard?

92. Tim Bleckie is the owner of Bleckie Investment and Real Estate Company. The company recently purchased four tracts of land in Holly Farms Estates and six tracts in Newburg Woods. The tracts are all equally desirable and sell for about the same amount.

92. a. .333
b. .9286
c. Dependent.

   a. What is the probability that the next two tracts sold will be in Newburg Woods?
   b. What is the probability that of the next four sold at least one will be in Holly Farms?
   c. Are these events independent or dependent?

93. There are four people being considered for the position of chief executive officer of Dalton Enterprises. Three of the applicants are over 60 years of age. Two are female, of which only one is over 60.
   a. What is the probability that a candidate is over 60 and female?
   b. Given that the candidate is male, what is the probability he is less than 60?
   c. Given that the person is over 60, what is the probability the person is female?

94. A case of 24 cans contains 1 can that is contaminated. Three cans are to be chosen randomly for testing.

94. a. 2,024
b. .125

   a. How many different combinations of 3 cans could be selected?
   b. What is the probability that the contaminated can is selected for testing?

95. A computer password consists of four characters. The characters can be one of the 26 letters of the alphabet. Each character may be used more than once. How many different passwords are possible?

96. Horwege Electronics, Inc. purchases TV picture tubes from four different suppliers. Tyson Wholesale supplies 20 percent of the tubes, Fuji Importers 30 percent, Kirkpatricks 25 percent, and Parts, Inc. 25 percent. Tyson Wholesale tends to have the best quality, as only 3 percent of their tubes arrive defective. Fuji Importers tubes are 4 percent defective, Kirkpatricks 7 percent, and Parts, Inc. 6.5 percent defective.

96. a. 5.175
b. .1159

   a. What is the overall percent defective?
   b. A defective picture tube was discovered in the latest shipment. What is the probability that it came from Tyson Wholesale?

c. .2319, .3382, .3140

c. What is the probability that the defective tube came from Fuji Importers? From Kirkpatricks? From Parts, Inc.?

97. The following diagram represents a system of two components, *A* and *B*, which are in series. (Being in series means that for the system to operate, both components *A* and *B* must work.) Suppose that the probability that *A* functions is .90, and the probability that *B* functions is also .90. Assume that these two components are independent. What is the probability that the system operates?

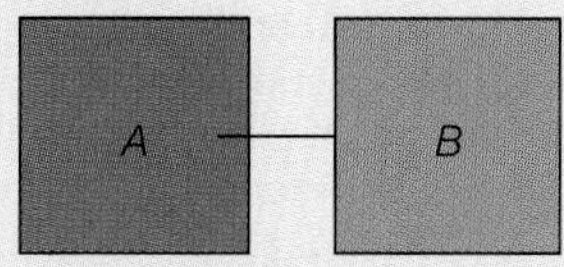

98. .99

98. Refer to the system diagram above, but suppose the system works if *either A* or *B* works. What is the probability the system works under these conditions?

99. A puzzle in the newspaper presents a matching problem. The names of 10 U.S. presidents are listed in one column, and their vice presidents are listed in random order in the second column. The puzzle asks the reader to match each president with his vice president. If you make the matches randomly, how many matches are possible? What is the probability all 10 of your matches are correct?

100. a. .14 b. .3214 c. .0058 d. Not effective. About ⅔ of those who are fired are innocent.

100. To reduce theft, the Meredeth Company screens all its employees with a lie detector test that is known to be correct 90 percent of the time (for both guilty and innocent subjects). George Meredeth decides to fire all employees who fail the test. Suppose 5 percent of the employees are guilty of theft.

a. What proportion of the workers are fired?
b. Of the workers fired, what proportion are actually guilty?
c. Of the workers not fired, what proportion are guilty?
d. What do you think of George's policy?

101. Peterson's Vitamins, an advertiser in the magazine *Healthy Living,* estimates that 1 percent of the subscribers will buy vitamins from Peterson's. They also estimate that 0.5 percent of nonsubscribers will buy the product and that there is one chance in 20 that a person is a subscriber.

a. Find the probability that a randomly selected person will buy the vitamins.
b. If a person buys the vitamins, what is the probability he subscribes to *Healthy Living*?
c. If a person does not buy the vitamins, what is the probability she subscribes to *Healthy Living*?

102. a. .0789 b. .3947 c. .5263

102. ABC Auto Insurance classifies drivers as good, medium, or poor risks. Drivers who apply to them for insurance fall into these three groups in the proportions: 30%, 50%, and 20%, respectively. The probability a "good" driver will have an accident is 0.01, the probability a "medium" risk driver will have an accident is 0.03, and the probability a "poor" driver will have an accident is 0.10. The company sells Mr. Brophy an insurance policy and he has an accident. What is the probability Mr. Brophy is:

a. A "good" driver? **b.** A "medium" risk driver? **c.** A "poor" driver?

exercises.com

WWW

103. During the 1970s the game show *Let's Make a Deal* had a long run on TV. In the show a contestant was given a choice of three doors, behind one of which was a prize. The other two doors contained a gag gift of some type. After the contestant selected a door, the host of the show then revealed to them one of the doors from among the two not selected. The host asked the contestant if they wished to switch doors to one of those not chosen. Should the contestant switch? Are the odds of winning increased by switching doors?

Go to the following Website, which is administered by the Department of Statistics at the University of South Carolina, and try your strategy: http://www.stat.sc.edu/~west/applets/LetsMakeaDeal.html. Go to the following Website and read about the odds for the game: http://www.stat.sc.edu/~west/javahtml/LetsMakeaDeal.html. Was your strategy correct?

Computer Data Exercises

104. Refer to the Real Estate data, which reports information on homes sold in the Venice, Florida, area during the last year.

a. Sort the data into a table that shows the number of homes that have a pool versus the number that don't have a pool in each of the five townships. If a home is selected at random, compute the following probabilities.

104. a. (1) .7238 **(1)** The home is in Township 1 or has a pool.

(2) .72 **(2)** Given that it is in Township 3, that it has a pool.

(3) .1714 **(3)** Has a pool and is in Township 3.

b. Sort the data into a table that shows the number of homes that have a garage versus those that don't have a garage in each of the five townships. If a home is selected at random, compute the following probabilities:

b. (1) .6762 **(1)** The home has a garage.

(2) .25 **(2)** Given that it is in Township 5, that it does not have a garage.

(3) .1429 **(3)** The home has a garage and is in Township 3.

(4) .4667 **(4)** Does not have a garage or is in Township 2.

105. Refer to the Baseball 2000 data, which reports information on the 30 Major League Baseball teams for the 2000 season. Set up a variable that divides the teams into two groups, those that had a winning season and those that did not. That is, create a variable to count the teams that won 81 games or more, and those that won 80 or less. Next create a new variable for attendance, using three categories: attendance less than 1,500,000, attendance of 1,500,000 up to 2,500,000, and attendance of 2,500,000 or more.

a. Create a table that shows the number of teams with a winning season versus those with a losing season by the three categories of attendance. If a team is selected at random, compute the following probabilities:

(1) Having a winning season.

(2) Having a winning season or attendance of more than 2.5 million.

(3) Given attendance of more than 2.5 million, having a winning season.

(4) Having a losing season and drawing less than 1.5 million.

b. Create a table that shows the number of teams that play on artificial surfaces and natural surfaces by winning and losing records. If a team is selected at random, compute the following probabilities:

(1) Selecting a team with a home field that has a natural surface.

(2) Is the likelihood of selecting a team with a winning record larger for teams with natural or artificial surfaces?

(3) Having a winning record or playing on an artificial surface.

106. Refer to the Schools data, which refers to 94 school districts in Northwest Ohio.

a. Group the districts based on the percent of students on welfare: "low" (less than 5 percent), "moderate" (between 5 and 10 percent, inclusive), and "high" (more than 10 percent).

106. a. (1) .66 **(1)** A school district is randomly selected. Then a student within that district is chosen. What is the probability the student passed the proficiency exam? Hint: Find the mean percent passing and use that value as the probability of passing the exam.

(2) .72 **(2)** If it is a "low" welfare district, what is the probability the student passed the exam?

(3) .54 **(3)** What is the probability the student is from a "high" welfare district and passes the exam?

(4) .56 **(4)** Find the probability the student is either from a "moderate" welfare district or failed the exam.

b. Now arrange the districts by size: "small" (less than 1,000 students), "medium" (between 1,000 and 3,000 students), or "large" (more than 3,000 students).

b. (1) 38% **(1)** What percent of the districts are "small"?

(2) 61% **(2)** If a district is "small," estimate the probability it is a "low" welfare district.

(3) 23% **(3)** What percent of the districts are both "small" and "low" welfare?

(4) 61% **(4)** What percent are either "small" or "low" welfare?

(5) .0856 **(5)** If three districts are randomly chosen, what is the probability they are all "medium" sized?

Chapter 5 Answers to Self-Review

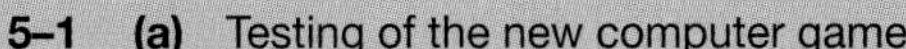

5–1 **(a)** Testing of the new computer game.
(b) Seventy-three players liked the game.
(c) No. Probability cannot be greater than 1. The probability that the game, if put on the market, will be successful is 65/80, or .8125.
(d) Cannot be less than 0. Perhaps a mistake in arithmetic.
(e) More than half of the persons testing the game liked it. (Of course, other answers are possible.)

5–2 **1.** $\frac{\text{4 queens in deck}}{\text{52 cards total}} = \frac{4}{52} = .0769$
Classical.

2. $\frac{24}{883} = .027$ Empirical.

3. The author's view when writing the text of the chance that the DJIA will climb to 12,000 is .25. You may be more optimistic or less optimistic.
Subjective.

5–3 **(a)** **(i)** $\frac{(50 + 68)}{2{,}000} = .059$

(ii) $1 - \frac{302}{2{,}000} = .849$

(b)

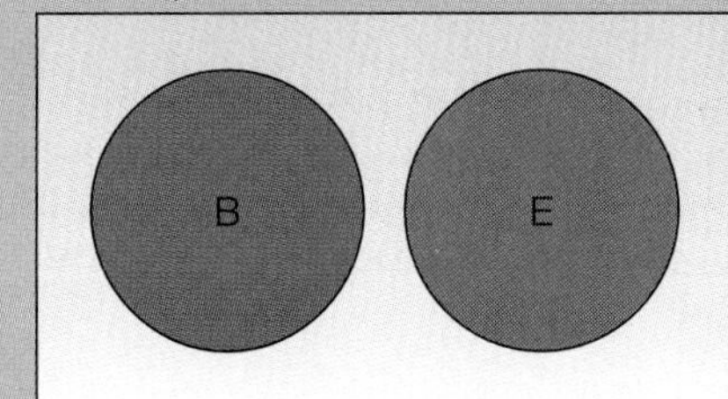

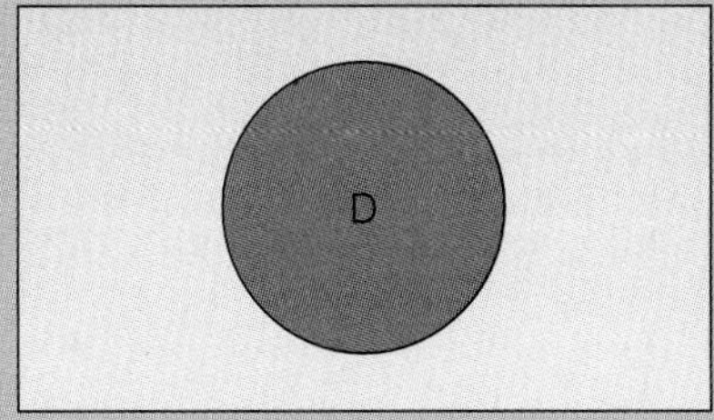

(c) They are not complementary, but are mutually exclusive.

5–4 **(a)** Need for corrective shoes is event *A*. Need for major dental work is event *B*.

$$P(A \text{ or } B) = P(A) + P(B) - P(A \text{ and } B)$$
$$= .08 + .15 - .03$$
$$= .20$$

(b) One possibility is:

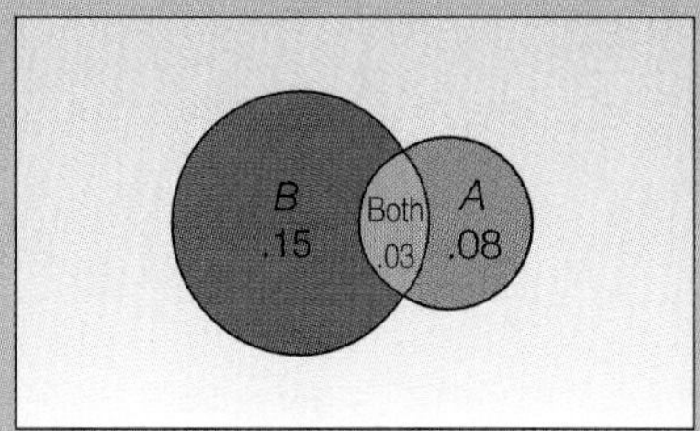

5–5 **1.** (.80)(.80)(.80)(.80) = .4096.

2. **(a)** .0000156, found by: (.025)(.025)(.025).
(b) The chance of selecting three bags and finding them all underweight is rather remote.

5–6 **(a)** .002, found by:

$$\left(\frac{4}{12}\right)\left(\frac{3}{11}\right)\left(\frac{2}{10}\right)\left(\frac{1}{9}\right) = \frac{24}{11{,}880} = .002$$

(b) .14, found by:

$$\left(\frac{8}{12}\right)\left(\frac{7}{11}\right)\left(\frac{6}{10}\right)\left(\frac{5}{9}\right) = \frac{1{,}68}{11{,}880} = .1414$$

(c) No, because there are other possibilities, such as three women and one man.

5–7 $P(A \text{ and } B) = P(A)P(B \mid A)$

$$= \left(\frac{80}{200}\right)\left(\frac{25}{80}\right) = .125$$

5–8 **1.** Go out from the tree trunk on the lower branch, "would not remain." The probability of that event is 80/200. Continuing on the same path, find the branch labeled "6–10 years." The conditional probability is 10/80. To get the joint probability:

$$P(A \text{ and } B) = \left(\frac{80}{200}\right)\left(\frac{10}{80}\right)$$
$$= \frac{800}{16{,}000} = .05$$

2. **(a)** Contingency table.

(b)

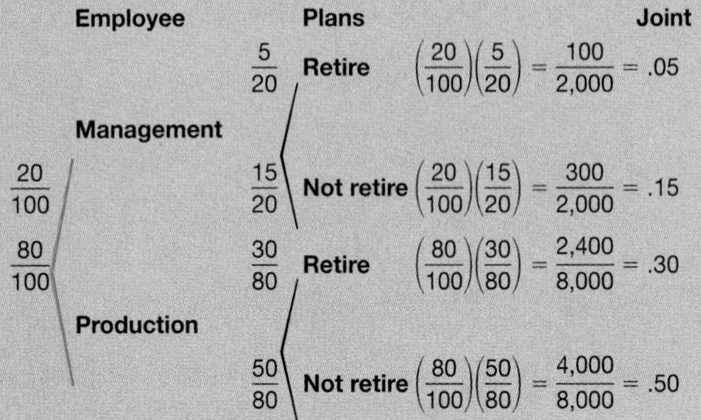

Employee		Plans	Joint
Management $\frac{20}{100}$	$\frac{5}{20}$	Retire	$\left(\frac{20}{100}\right)\left(\frac{5}{20}\right) = \frac{100}{2{,}000} = .05$
	$\frac{15}{20}$	Not retire	$\left(\frac{20}{100}\right)\left(\frac{15}{20}\right) = \frac{300}{2{,}000} = .15$
Production $\frac{80}{100}$	$\frac{30}{80}$	Retire	$\left(\frac{80}{100}\right)\left(\frac{30}{80}\right) = \frac{2{,}400}{8{,}000} = .30$
	$\frac{50}{80}$	Not retire	$\left(\frac{80}{100}\right)\left(\frac{50}{80}\right) = \frac{4{,}000}{8{,}000} = .50$

(c) Yes, all possibilities are included.

5–9 **(a)**

$$P(A_3 \mid B_2) = \frac{P(A_3)P(B_2 \mid A_3)}{P(A_1)P(B_2 \mid A_1) + P(A_2)P(B_2 \mid A_2) + P(A_3)P(B_2 \mid A_3)}$$

$$= \frac{.50(.96)}{(.30)(.97) + (.20)(.95) + (.50)(.96)}$$

$$= \frac{.480}{.961} = .499$$

5–10 **1.** There are 20, found by (5)(4)

2. There are 72, found by (3)(2)(4)(3)

5–11 **1.** **(a)** 60, found by (5)(4)(3).

(b) 60, found by:

$$\frac{5!}{(5-3)!} = \frac{5 \cdot 4 \cdot 3 \cdot \not{2} \cdot \not{1}}{\not{2} \cdot \not{1}}$$

2. 24, found by:

$$\frac{4!}{(4-4)!} = \frac{4!}{0!} = \frac{4!}{1} = \frac{4 \cdot 3 \cdot 2 \cdot 1}{1}$$

3. 5,040, found by:

$$\frac{10!}{(10-4)!} = \frac{10 \cdot 9 \cdot 8 \cdot 7 \cdot \not{6} \cdot \not{5} \cdot \not{4} \cdot \not{3} \cdot \not{2} \cdot \not{1}}{\not{6} \cdot \not{5} \cdot \not{4} \cdot \not{3} \cdot \not{2} \cdot \not{1}}$$

4. **(a)** 56 is correct, found by:

$$_8C_3 = \frac{n!}{r!(n-r)!} = \frac{8!}{3!(8-3)!} = 56$$

(b) Yes. There are 45 combinations, found by:

$$_{10}C_2 = \frac{n!}{r!(n-r)!} = \frac{10!}{2!(10-2)!} = 45$$

6

Discrete Probability Distributions

GOALS

When you have completed this chapter, you will be able to:

1 **Define the terms *probability distribution* and *random variable*.**

2 **Distinguish between discrete and continuous probability distributions.**

3 **Calculate the mean, variance, and standard deviation of a discrete probability distribution.**

4 **Describe the characteristics of and compute probabilities using the binomial probability distribution.**

5 **Describe the characteristics of and compute probabilities using the hypergeometric probability distribution.**

6 **Describe the characteristics of and compute probabilities using the Poisson probability distribution.**

An American Society of Investors survey found 30 percent of individual investors have used a discount broker. In a random sample of nine individuals, what is the probability that exactly two of the sampled individuals have used a discount broker? (See Goal 4 and Exercise 13.)

Introduction

Chapters 2 through 4 are devoted to descriptive statistics. We describe raw data by organizing them into a frequency distribution and portraying the distribution in charts. Also, we compute a measure of central tendency—such as the arithmetic mean, median, or mode—to locate a typical value near the center of the distribution. The range and the standard deviation are used to describe the spread in the data. These chapters focus on describing *something that has already happened.*

Starting with Chapter 5, the emphasis changes—we begin examining *something that would probably happen.* We note that this facet of statistics is called *statistical inference.* The objective is to make inferences (statements) about a population based on a number of observations, called a sample, selected from the population. In Chapter 5, we state that a probability is a value between 0 and 1 inclusive, and we examine how probabilities can be combined using rules of addition and multiplication.

This chapter will begin the study of **probability distributions.** A probability distribution gives the entire range of values that can occur based on an experiment. A probability distribution is similar to a relative frequency distribution. However, instead of describing the past, it describes how likely some future event is. For example, a drug manufacturer may claim a treatment will cause weight loss for 80 percent of the population. A consumer protection agency may test the treatment on a sample of six people. If the manufacturer's claim is true, it is *almost impossible* to have an outcome where no one in the sample loses weight and it is *most likely* that 5 out of the 6 do lose weight.

The mean, variance, and standard deviation for probability distributions as well as three frequently occurring families of probability distributions (the binomial, hypergeometric, and Poisson) are also presented in this chapter.

What Is a Probability Distribution?

A probability distribution shows the possible outcomes of an experiment and the probability of each of these outcomes.

PROBABILITY DISTRIBUTION A listing of all the outcomes of an experiment and the probability associated with each outcome.

How can we generate a probability distribution?

EXAMPLE

Suppose we are interested in the number of heads showing face up on three tosses of a coin. This is the experiment. The possible results are: zero heads, one head, two heads, and three heads. What is the probability distribution for the number of heads?

SOLUTION

There are eight possible outcomes. A tail might appear face up on the first toss, another tail on the second toss, and another tail on the third toss of the coin. Or we might get a tail, tail, and head, in that order. Listed below are the possible results.

Possible Result	Coin Toss First	Second	Third	Number of Heads
1	T	T	T	0
2	T	T	H	1
3	T	H	T	1
4	T	H	H	2

Possible Result	Coin Toss First	Second	Third	Number of Heads
5	H	T	T	1
6	H	T	H	2
7	H	H	T	2
8	H	H	H	3

Note that the outcome "zero heads" occured only once, "one head" occured three times, "two heads" occured three times, and the outcome "three heads" occured only once. That is, "zero heads" happened one out of eight times. Thus, the probability of zero heads is one eighth, the probability of one head is three eighths, and so on. The probability distribution is shown in Table 6–1. Note that, since one of these outcomes must happen, the total of the probabilities of all possible events is 1.000. This is always true. The same information is shown in Chart 6–1.

TABLE 6–1 Probability Distribution for the Events of Zero, One, Two, and Three Heads Showing Face Up on Three Tosses of a Coin

Number of Heads, x	Probability of Outcome, $P(x)$
0	$\frac{1}{8} = .125$
1	$\frac{3}{8} = .375$
2	$\frac{3}{8} = .375$
3	$\frac{1}{8} = .125$
Total	$\frac{8}{8} = 1.000$

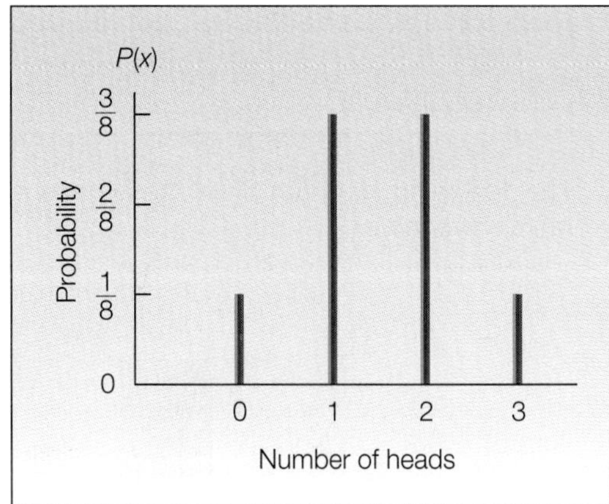

CHART 6–1 Graphical Presentation of the Number of Heads Resulting from Three Tosses of a Coin and the Corresponding Probability

Characteristics of a probability distribution

Before continuing, we should note two important characteristics of a probability distribution.

1. The probability of a particular value is between 0 and 1, inclusive. (The probabilities of x, written $P(x)$ in the coin tossing example, were .125, .375, etc.)
2. The sum of the probabilities of all mutually exclusive values is 1.000. (Referring to Table 6–1, .125 + .375 + .375 + .125 = 1.000.)

Self-Review 6–1

The possible outcomes of an experiment involving the roll of a six-sided die are: a one-spot, a two-spot, a three-spot, a four-spot, a five-spot, and a six-spot.

(a) Develop a probability distribution for the number of possible spots.
(b) Portray the probability distribution graphically.
(c) What is the sum of the probabilities?

Random Variables

In any experiment of chance, the outcomes occur randomly. So it is often called a *random variable.* For example, rolling a single die is an experiment: any one of six possible outcomes can occur. Some experiments result in outcomes that are quantitative (such as dollars, weight, or number of children), and others result in qualitative outcomes (such as color or religious preference). A few examples will further illustrate what is meant by a **random variable.**

- If we count the number of employees absent from the day shift on Monday, the number might be 0, 1, 2, 3, ... The number absent is the random variable.
- If we weigh a steel ingot, it might be 2,500 pounds, 2,500.1 pounds, 2,500.13 pounds, and so on, depending on the accuracy of the scale. The weight is the random variable.
- If we toss two coins and count the number of heads, there could be zero, one, or two heads. Because the number of heads resulting from this experiment is due to chance, the number of heads appearing is the random variable.
- Other random variables might be: the number of defective light bulbs produced during the week, the heights of the members of the girls' basketball team, the number of runners in the Boston Marathon, and the daily number of drivers charged with driving under the influence of alcohol in Texas.

RANDOM VARIABLE A quantity resulting from an experiment that, by chance, can assume different values.

The following diagram illustrates these three related terms: *outcome, event,* and *random variable.*

Possible *outcomes* for three coin tosses

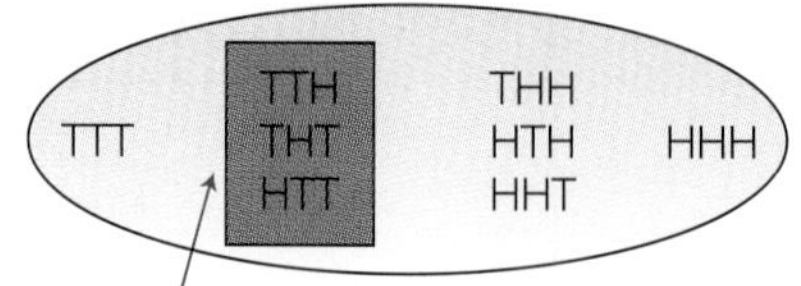

The *event* {one head} occurs and the *random variable* $x = 1$.

A random variable may be either *discrete* or *continuous.*

Discrete Random Variable

A discrete random variable can assume only a certain number of separated values. If there are 100 employees, then the count of the number absent on Monday can only be 0, 1, 2, 3, . . . , 100. A discrete random variable is usually the result of counting something. By way of definition:

> **DISCRETE RANDOM VARIABLE** A variable that can assume only certain clearly separated values.

A discrete variable can, in some cases, assume fractional or decimal values. These values must be separated, that is, have distance between them. As an example, the scores awarded by judges for technical competence and artistic form in figure skating are decimal values, such as 7.2, 8.9, and 9.7. Such values are discrete because there is distance between scores of, say, 8.3 and 8.4. A score cannot be 8.34 or 8.347, for example.

Continuous Random Variable

On the other hand, if the random variable is continuous, then the distribution is a continuous probability distribution. If we measure something such as the width of a room, the height of a person, or the pressure in an automobile tire, the variable is a *continuous random variable.* It can assume one of an infinitely large number of values, within certain limitations. As examples:

- The distance between Atlanta and Los Angeles could be measured as 2,254 miles, 2,254.1 miles, 2,254.162 miles, and so on, depending on the accuracy of our measuring device.
- Tire pressure could be measured as 28 pounds per square inch (psi), 28.6 psi, 28.62 psi, 28.624 psi, and so on, depending on the accuracy of the gauge.

Logically, if we organize a set of possible values of a discrete random variable in a probability distribution, the distribution is a **discrete probability distribution.**

The tools used, as well as the probability interpretations, are different for discrete and continuous random variables. This chapter is limited to discrete probability distributions. The next chapter will address an important example of continuous probability distributions.

The Mean, Variance, and Standard Deviation of a Probability Distribution

In Chapters 3 and 4, measures of location and variation are discussed for a frequency distribution. The mean reports the central location of the data, and the variance describes the spread in the data. In a similar fashion, a probability distribution is summarized by its mean and variance. We identify the mean of a probability distribution by the lower-case Greek letter mu (μ) and the standard deviation by the lower-case Greek letter sigma (σ).

Mean

The mean is a typical value used to represent a probability distribution. It also is the long-run average value of the random variable. The mean of a probability distribution is also referred to as its "expected value." It is a weighted average where the possible values are weighted by their corresponding probabilities of occurrence.

The mean of a discrete probability distribution is computed by the formula:

MEAN OF A PROBABILITY DISTRIBUTION	$\mu = \Sigma[xP(x)]$	**[6–1]**

where $P(x)$ is the probability of taking on a particular value x. In other words, multiply each x value by its probability of occurrence, and then add these products.

Variance and Standard Deviation

As noted, the mean is a typical value used to summarize a discrete probability distribution. However, it does not describe the amount of spread (variation) in a distribution. The variance does this. The formula for the variance of a probability distribution is:

VARIANCE OF A PROBABILITY DISTRIBUTION	$\sigma^2 = \Sigma[(x - \mu)^2P(x)]$	**[6–2]**

The computational steps are:

1. Subtract the mean from each value, and square this difference.
2. Multiply each squared difference by its probability.
3. Sum the resulting products to arrive at the variance.

The standard deviation, σ, is found by taking the square root of σ^2; that is, $\sigma = \sqrt{\sigma^2}$.

EXAMPLE

John Ragsdale sells new cars for Pelican Ford. John usually sells the largest number of cars on Saturday. He has the following probability distribution for the number of cars he expects to sell on a particular Saturday.

Number of Cars Sold, x	Probability, $P(x)$
0	.10
1	.20
2	.30
3	.30
4	.10
Total	1.00

1. What type of distribution is this?
2. On a typical Saturday, how many cars does John expect to sell?
3. What is the variance of the distribution?

SOLUTION

1. This is a discrete probability distribution. Note that John expects to sell only within a certain range of cars; he does not expect to sell 5 cars or 50 cars. Further, he cannot sell half a car. He can sell only 0, 1, 2, 3, or 4 cars. Also, the outcomes are mutually exclusive—he cannot sell a total of both 3 and 4 cars on the same Saturday.

2. The mean number of cars sold is computed by weighting the number of cars sold by the probability of selling that number and totaling the products using formula (6–1):

$$\begin{aligned}\mu &= \Sigma[xP(x)]\\ &= 0(.10) + 1(.20) + 2(.30) + 3(.30) + 4(.10)\\ &= 2.1\end{aligned}$$

These calculations are summarized in the following table.

Number of Cars Sold, x	Probability, $P(x)$	$x \cdot P(x)$
0	.10	0.00
1	.20	0.20
2	.30	0.60
3	.30	0.90
4	.10	0.40
Total	1.00	$\mu = 2.10$

How do we interpret a mean of 2.1? This value indicates that, over a large number of Saturdays, John Ragsdale expects to sell a mean of 2.1 cars a day. (Of course, it is not possible for him to sell *exactly* 2.1 cars on any particular Saturday.) Thus, the mean is sometimes called the expected value.

3. Again, a table is useful for systemizing the computations for the variance, which is 1.290.

Number of Cars Sold, x	Probability, $P(x)$	$(x - \mu)$	$(x - \mu)^2$	$(x - \mu)^2P(x)$
0	.10	0 − 2.1	4.41	0.441
1	.20	1 − 2.1	1.21	0.242
2	.30	2 − 2.1	0.01	0.003
3	.30	3 − 2.1	0.81	0.243
4	.10	4 − 2.1	3.61	0.361
				$\sigma^2 = 1.290$

Recall that the standard deviation, σ, is the square root of the variance. In this example, $\sqrt{\sigma^2} = \sqrt{1.290} = 1.136$ cars. How do we interpret a standard deviation of 1.136 cars? If salesperson Rita Kirsch also sold a mean of 2.1 cars on Saturdays, and the standard deviation in her sales was 1.91 cars, we would conclude that there is more variability in the Saturday sales of Ms. Kirsch than in those of Mr. Ragsdale (because $1.91 > 1.136$).

Here is an alternative formula for the variance of a discrete probability distribution. It has the advantage that it avoids most of the subtractions:

$$\sigma^2 = \Sigma x^2P(x) - \mu^2$$

For the Ragsdale data, we have:

x	x^2	$P(x)$	$x^2P(x)$
0	0	.1	0.00
1	1	.2	0.20
2	4	.3	1.20
3	9	.3	2.70
4	16	.1	1.60
			5.70

The variance using the above formula is: $\sigma^2 = \Sigma x^2P(x) - \mu^2 = 5.70 - (2.1)^2 = 1.29$, which is the same value we found before.

Self-Review 6–2

The Pizza Palace offers three sizes of cola—small, medium, and large—to go with its pizza. The colas are sold for $0.80, $0.90, and $1.20, respectively. Thirty percent of the orders are for small, 50 percent are for medium, and 20 percent are for the large sizes. Organize the size of the colas and the probability of a sale into a probability distribution.

(a) Is this a discrete probability distribution? Indicate why or why not.
(b) Compute the mean amount charged for a cola.
(c) What is the variance in the amount charged for a cola? The standard deviation?

Exercises

1. Compute the mean and variance of the following discrete probability distribution.

x	$P(x)$
0	.20
1	.40
2	.30
3	.10

2. $\mu = 5.4$
$\sigma^2 = 12.04$

2. Compute the mean and variance of the following discrete probability distribution.

x	$P(x)$
2	.50
8	.30
10	.20

3. Three tables listed below show "random variables" and their "probabilities." However, only one of these is actually a probability distribution.
a. Which is it?

x	$P(x)$
5	.3
10	.3
15	.2
20	.4

x	$P(x)$
5	.1
10	.3
15	.2
20	.4

x	$P(x)$
5	.5
10	.3
15	−.2
20	.4

b. Using the correct probability distribution, find the probability that x is:
(1) Exactly 15. **(2)** No more than 10. **(3)** More than 5.
c. Compute the mean, variance, and standard deviation of this distribution.

4. a. Discrete.
b. Continuous.
c. Discrete.
d. Continuous.
e. Discrete.
f. Continuous.

4. Which of these variables are discrete and which are continuous random variables?
a. The number of new accounts established by a salesperson in a year.
b. The time between customer arrivals to a bank ATM.
c. The number of customers in Big Nick's barber shop.
d. The amount of fuel in your car's gas tank.
e. The number of minorities on a jury.
f. The outside temperature today.

5. Dan Woodward is the owner and manager of Dan's Truck Stop. Dan offers free refills on all coffee orders. He gathered the following information on coffee refills. Compute the mean, variance, and standard deviation for the distribution of number of refills.

Refills	Percent
0	30
1	40
2	20
3	10

6. $\mu = 1110$
$\sigma^2 = 24{,}900$
$\sigma = 157.8$

6. The director of admissions at Kinzua University in Nova Scotia estimated the distribution of student admissions for the fall semester based on past experience. What is the expected number of admissions for the fall semester? Compute the variance and the standard deviation.

Admissions	Probability
1,000	.60
1,200	.30
1,500	.10

7. The following table lists the probability distribution for cash prizes in a lottery conducted at Lawson's Department Store.

Prize ($)	Probability
0	.45
10	.30
100	.20
500	.05

If you buy a single ticket, what is the probability that you win:
a. Exactly $100? **b.** At least $10? **c.** No more than $100?
d. Compute the mean, variance, and standard deviation of this distribution.

8. You are asked to match three songs with the performers who made those songs famous. If you guess, the probability distribution for the number of correct matches is:

Probability	.333	.500	0	.167
Number correct	0	1	2	3

8. a. .5
b. .6667
c. 0
d. 1, 1, 1

What is the probability you get:
a. Exactly one correct? **b.** At least one correct? **c.** Exactly two correct?
d. Compute the mean, variance, and standard deviation of this distribution.

Binomial Probability Distribution

The **binomial probability distribution** is a widely occurring discrete probability distribution. One characteristic of a binomial distribution is that there are only two possible outcomes on a particular trial of an experiment. For example, the statement in a true/false question is either true or false. The outcomes are *mutually exclusive,* meaning that the answer to a true/false question cannot be both true and false at the same time. As other examples, a product is classified as either acceptable or not acceptable by the quality control department, a worker is classified as employed or unemployed, and a sales call results in the customer either purchasing the product or not purchasing the product. Frequently, we classify the two possible outcomes as "success" and "failure." However, this classification does *not* imply that one outcome is good and the other is bad.

Another characteristic of the binomial distribution is that the random variable is the result of counts. That is, we count the number of successes in the total number of trials. We flip a fair coin five times and count the number of times a head appears; we select 10 workers and count the number who are over 50 years of age, or we select 20 boxes of Kellogg's Raisin Bran and count the number that weigh more than the amount indicated on the package.

Another characteristic of a binomial distribution is that the probability of a success remains the same from one trial to another. Two examples are:

- The probability you will guess the first question of a true/false test correctly (a success) is one half. This is the first "trial." The probability that you will guess right on the second question (the second trial) is also one half, the probability of success on the third trial is one half, and so on.
- If past experience revealed the drawbridge over the Gulf Intracoastal Waterway was raised one out of every five times you approach it, then the probability is one fifth that it will be raised (a "success") the next time you approach it, one fifth the following time, and so on.

The final characteristic of a binomial probability distribution is that each trial is *independent* of any other trial. This means that there is no pattern with respect to the outcomes. As an example, the answers to a true/false test are not arranged T, T, T, F, F, F, T, T, T, and so forth.

In summary, a binomial distribution has these characteristics:

A binomial distribution has these characteristics.

BINOMIAL PROBABILITY DISTRIBUTION

1. An outcome on each trial of an experiment is classified into one of two mutually exclusive categories—a success or a failure.
2. The random variable counts the number of successes in a fixed number of trials.
3. The probability of a success stays the same for each trial. So does the probability of a failure.
4. The trials are independent, meaning that the outcome of one trial does not affect the outcome of any other trial.

How Is a Binomial Probability Distribution Computed?

To construct a particular binomial probability distribution, we use (1) the number of trials and (2) the probability of success on each trial. For example, if an examination at the conclusion of a management seminar consists of 20 multiple-choice questions, the number of trials is 20. If each question has five choices and only one choice is correct, the probability of success for a person with no knowledge of the subject on each trial is .20. Thus, the probability is .20 that a person with no knowledge of the subject matter will guess the answer to a question correctly. So the conditions of the binomial distribution just noted are met.

The binomial probability distribution is computed by the formula:

BINOMIAL PROBABILITY DISTRIBUTION $P(x) = {}_nC_x \pi^x(1 - \pi)^{n-x}$ **[6–3]**

where:

- C denotes a combination.
- n is the number of trials.
- x is the number of successes.
- π is the probability of a success on each trial.

We use the Greek letter π (pi) to denote a binomial population parameter. Do not confuse it with the mathematical constant 3.1416.

EXAMPLE

There are five flights daily from Pittsburgh via Allegheny Airlines into the Bradford, Pennsylvania Regional Airport. Suppose the probability that any flight arrives late is .20. What is the probability that none of the flights are late today? What is the probability that exactly one of the flights is late today?

SOLUTION

We can use Formula (6–3). The probability that a particular flight is late is .20, so let $\pi = .20$. There are five flights, so $n = 5$, and x refers to the number of successes. In this case a "success" is a plane that arrives late. Because there are no late arrivals $x = 0$.

$$P(0) = {}_nC_x(\pi)^x(1 - \pi)^{n-x}$$
$$= {}_5C_0(.20)^0(1 - .20)^{5-0} = (1)(1)(.3277) = .3277$$

The probability that exactly one of the five flights will arrive late today is .4096 found by

$$P(1) = {}_nC_x(\pi)^x(1 - \pi)^{n-x}$$
$$= {}_5C_1(.20)^1(1 - .20)^{5-1} = (5)(.20)(.4096) = .4096$$

The entire probability distribution is shown in Table 6–2.

TABLE 6–2 Binomial Probability Distribution for $n = 5$, $\pi = .20$

Number of Late Flights	Probability
0	.3277
1	.4096
2	.2048
3	.0512
4	.0064
5	.0003
Total	1.000

The random variable in Table 6–2 is plotted in Chart 6–2. Note that the distribution of late arriving flights is positively skewed.

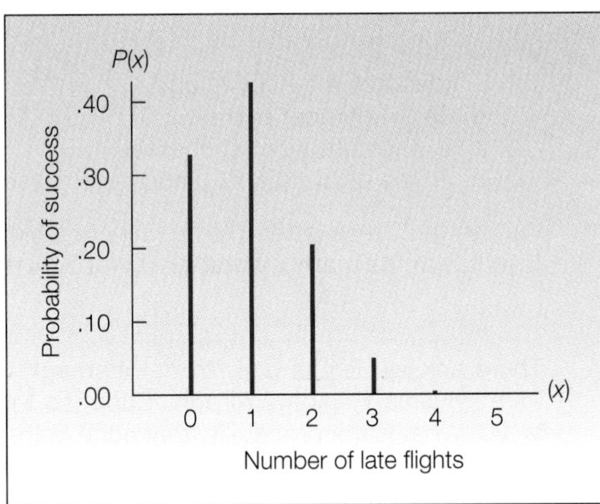

CHART 6–2 Binomial Probability Distribution for $n = 5$, $\pi = .20$

Binomial Probability Tables

Binomial table: Quick way of determining a probability

A binomial probability distribution, as has been shown, can be expressed by a formula. However, except for problems involving small n (say, $n = 3$ or 4), the calculations are rather tedious. As an aid, an extensive table has been developed that gives the probabilities of 0, 1, 2, 3, . . . , n successes for various values of n and π. This table is in Appendix A, and a small portion of the table for the following example is shown in Table 6–3.

TABLE 6–3 Binomial Probabilities for $n = 6$ and Selected Values of π

x	.05	.1	.2	.3	.4	.5	.6	.7	.8	.9	.95
0	.735	.531	.262	.118	.047	.016	.004	.001	.000	.000	.000
1	.232	.354	.393	.303	.187	.094	.037	.010	.002	.000	.000
2	.031	.098	.246	.324	.311	.234	.138	.060	.015	.001	.000
3	.002	.015	.082	.185	.276	.313	.276	.185	.082	.015	.002
4	.000	.001	.015	.060	.138	.234	.311	.324	.246	.098	.031
5	.000	.000	.002	.010	.037	.094	.187	.303	.393	.354	.232
6	.000	.000	.000	.001	.004	.016	.047	.118	.262	.531	.735

EXAMPLE

Five percent of the worm gears produced by an automatic, high-speed Carter-Bell milling machine are defective. What is the probability that out of six gears selected at random none will be defective? Exactly one? Exactly two? Exactly three? Exactly four? Exactly five? Exactly six out of six?

SOLUTION

The binomial conditions are met: (a) There is a constant probability of success (.05), (b) there is a fixed number of trials (6), (c) the trials are independent, and (d) there are only two possible outcomes (a particular gear is either defective or acceptable).

Refer to Table 6–3 for the probability of exactly zero defective gears. Go down the left margin to an x of 0. Now move horizontally to the column headed by a π of .05 to find the probability. It is .735.

The probability of exactly one defective in a sample of six worm gears is .232. The complete binomial probability distribution for $n = 6$ and $\pi = .05$ is:

Number of Defective Gears, x	Probability of Occurrence, $P(x)$	Number of Defective Gears, x	Probability of Occurrence, $P(x)$
0	.735	4	.000
1	.232	5	.000
2	.031	6	.000
3	.002		

Of course, there is a slight chance of getting exactly five defective gears out of six random selections. It is .00000178, found by inserting the appropriate values in the binomial formula:

$$P(5) = {}_6C_5(.05)^5(.95)^1 = (6)(.05)^5(.95) = .00000178$$

For six out of the six, the exact probability is .000000016. Thus, the probability is very small that five or six defective gears will be selected in a sample of six.

Self-Review 6–3

The Florida Department of Highways reports the drawbridge over the Gulf Intracoastal Waterway in Siesta Key, near Sarasota, is in the raised position, blocking vehicular traffic, 20 percent of the time. You are going to drive this route once each day for the next seven days.

(a) Does this situation fit the assumptions of the binomial probability distribution?
(b) Determine the probability the bridge will be raised each time you approach it.
(c) Use formula 6–3 to find the probability it will be raised three of the seven times you approach the bridge.
(d) Use formula 6–3 to find the probability it will be raised once.
(e) Use the binomial probability table in Appendix A to verify your answers to parts b, c, and d.

The MegaStat software will also compute the binomial distribution. Here is the output from the previous example. Note that in MegaStat p is used for π.

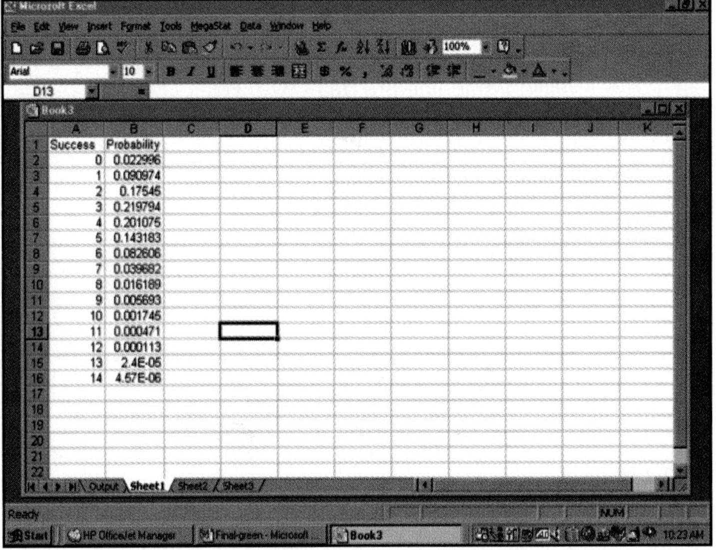

Success	Probability
0	0.022996
1	0.090974
2	0.17546
3	0.219794
4	0.201075
5	0.143183
6	0.082606
7	0.039682
8	0.016189
9	0.005693
10	0.001745
11	0.000471
12	0.000113
13	2.4E-05
14	4.57E-06

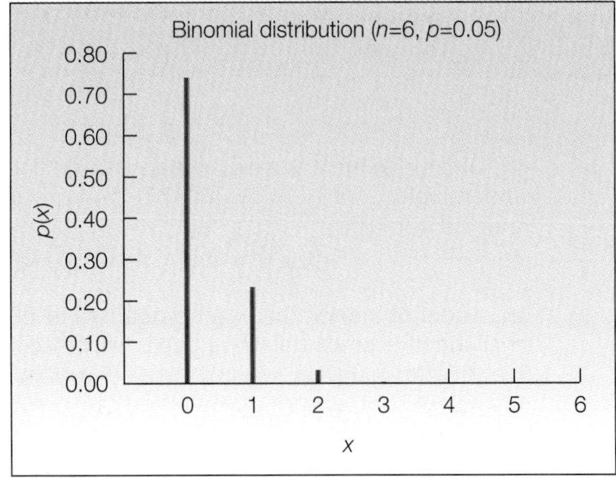

Statistics in Action

According to the Annals of Internal Medicine, a blood test on a normal person has a 5 percent chance of being read as abnormal by a laboratory computer. If this is true, and your physician submits a profile of 12 independent tests on you, the chance that your tests all appear normal to the computer is only 54 percent.

Appendix A is limited. It gives probabilities only for n values from 1 through 20 and 25 and π values of .05, .10, .20, . . . , .90, .95. A computer can generate the probabilities for a specified number of successes, given an n and π. The Excel output below shows the probability distribution when $n = 40$ and $\pi = .09$.

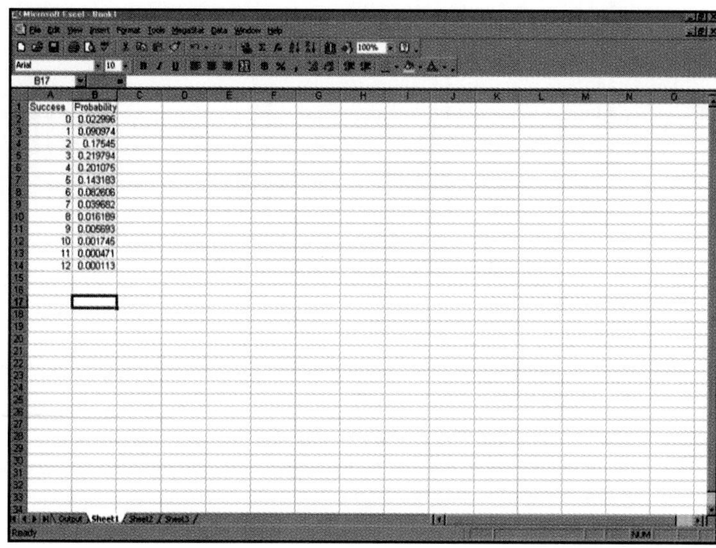

Success	Probability
0	0.022996
1	0.090974
2	0.17545
3	0.219794
4	0.201075
5	0.143183
6	0.082606
7	0.039682
8	0.016189
9	0.005693
10	0.001745
11	0.000471
12	0.000113

Several additional points should be made regarding the binomial probability distribution.

1. If n remains the same but π increases from .05 to .95, the shape of the distribution changes. Look at Table 6–4 and Chart 6–3. The probabilities for a π of.05 are positively skewed. As π approaches .50, the distribution becomes symmetrical. As π goes beyond .50 and moves toward .95, the probability distribution becomes negatively skewed. Table 6–4 highlights probabilities for $n = 10$ and π of .05, .10, .20, .50, and .70. The graphs of these probability distributions are shown in Chart 6–3.

TABLE 6–4 Probability of 0, 1, 2, . . . Successes for a π of .05, .10, .20, .50, and .70 and an n of 10

x	.05	.1	.2	.3	.4	.5	.6	.7	.8	.9	.95
0	.599	.349	.107	.028	.006	.001	.000	.000	.000	.000	.000
1	.315	.387	.268	.121	.040	.010	.002	.000	.000	.000	.000
2	.075	.194	.302	.233	.121	.044	.011	.001	.000	.000	.000
3	.010	.057	.201	.267	.215	.117	.042	.009	.001	.000	.000
4	.001	.011	.088	.200	.251	.205	.111	.037	.006	.000	.000
5	.000	.001	.026	.103	.201	.246	.201	.103	.026	.001	.000
6	.000	.000	.006	.037	.111	.205	.251	.200	.088	.011	.001
7	.000	.000	.001	.009	.042	.117	.215	.267	.201	.057	.010
8	.000	.000	.000	.001	.011	.044	.121	.233	.302	.194	.075
9	.000	.000	.000	.000	.002	.010	.040	.121	.268	.387	.315
10	.000	.000	.000	.000	.000	.001	.006	.028	.107	.349	.599

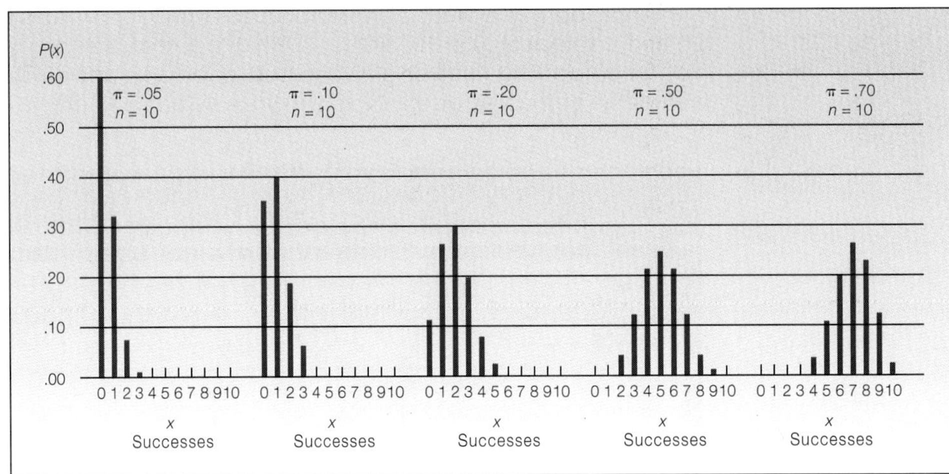

CHART 6–3 Graphing the Binomial Probability Distribution for a π of .05, .10, .20, .50, and .70 and an n of 10

2. If π, the probability of success, remains the same but n becomes larger, the shape of the binomial distribution becomes more symmetrical. Chart 6–4 shows a situation where π remains constant at .10 but n increases from 7 to 40.

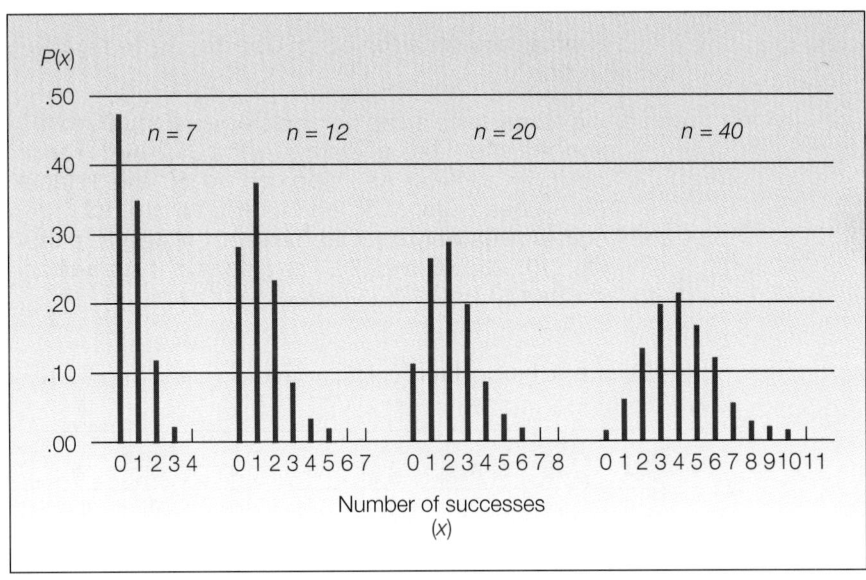

CHART 6–4 Chart Representing the Binomial Probability Distribution for a π of .10 and an n of 7, 12, 20, and 40

3. The mean (μ) and the variance (σ^2) of a binomial distribution can be computed in a "shortcut" fashion by:

MEAN OF A BINOMIAL DISTRIBUTION	$\mu = n\pi$	**[6–4]**

VARIANCE OF A BINOMIAL DISTRIBUTION	$\sigma^2 = n\pi(1 - \pi)$	[6–5]

For the example on page 203 regarding defective worm gears, recall that $\pi = .05$ and $n = 6$. Hence:

$$\mu = n\pi = 6(.05) = .30$$
$$\sigma^2 = n\pi(1 - \pi) = 6(.05)(1 - .05) = .285$$

The mean of .30 and the variance of .285 can be verified from formulas (6–1) and (6–2). The probability distribution from Table 6–3 and detailed calculations are shown below.

Number of Defects, x	$P(x)$	$xP(x)$	$x - \mu$	$(x - \mu)^2$	$(x - \mu)^2P(x)$
0	.735	0	−0.30	0.09	0.06615
1	.232	0.232	0.70	0.49	0.11368
2	.031	0.062	1.70	2.89	0.08959
3	.002	0.006	2.70	7.29	0.01458
4	.000	0	3.70	13.69	0
5	.000	0	4.70	22.09	0
6	.000	0	5.70	32.49	0
		0.30			0.284*

*The slight discrepancy between .285 and .284 is due to rounding.

Exercises

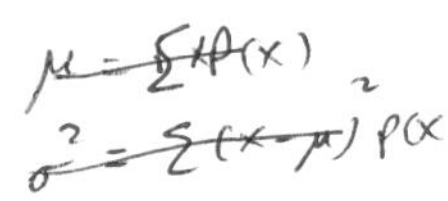

9. In a binomial situation $n = 4$ and $\pi = .25$. Determine the probabilities of the following events using the binomial formula.
   a. $x = 2$
   b. $x = 3$
10. In a binomial situation $n = 5$ and $\pi = .40$. Determine the probabilities of the following events using the binomial formula.
   a. $x = 1$
   b. $x = 2$

10. a. .2592
    b. .3456

11. Assume a binomial distribution where $n = 3$ and $\pi = .60$.
   a. Refer to Appendix A, and list the probabilities for values of x from 0 to 3.
   b. Determine the mean and standard deviation of the distribution from the general definitions given in formulas (6–1) and (6–2).
12. Assume a binomial distribution where $n = 5$ and $\pi = .30$.
   a. Refer to Appendix A, and list the probabilities for values of x from 0 to 5.
   b. Determine the mean and standard deviation of the distribution from the general definitions given in formulas (6–1) and (6–2).

12. a. See IM.
    b. $\mu = 1.5$
    $\sigma = 1.0247$

13. An American Society of Investors survey found 30 percent of individual investors have used a discount broker. In a random sample of nine individuals, what is the probability:
   a. Exactly two of the sampled individuals have used a discount broker?
   b. Exactly four of them have used a discount broker?
   c. None of them have used a discount broker?
14. The United States Postal Service reports 95 percent of first class mail within the same city is delivered within two days of the time of mailing. Six letters are randomly sent to different locations.

14. a. .7351
b. .2321
c. 5.7
d. $\sigma^2 = .2850$
$\sigma = .5339$

a. What is the probability that all six arrive within two days?
b. What is the probability that exactly five arrive within two days?
c. Find the mean number of letters that will arrive within two days.
d. Compute the variance and standard deviation of the number that will arrive within two days.

15. The industry standards suggest that 10 percent of new vehicles require warranty service within the first year. Jones Nissan in Sumter, South Carolina, sold twelve Nissans yesterday.
a. What is the probability that none of these vehicles requires warranty service?
b. What is the probability exactly one of these vehicles requires warranty service?
c. Determine the probability that exactly two of these vehicles require warranty service.
d. Compute the mean and standard deviation of this probability distribution.

16. A telemarketer makes six phone calls per hour and is able to make a sale on 30 percent of these contacts. During the next two hours, find:

16. a. .2311
b. .0138
c. .1678
d. 3.6

a. The probability of making exactly four sales.
b. The probability of making no sales.
c. The probability of making exactly two sales.
d. The mean number of sales in the two-hour period.

17. A recent survey by the American Accounting Association revealed 23 percent of students graduating with a major in accounting select public accounting. Suppose we select a sample of 15 recent graduates.
a. What is the probability two select public accounting?
b. What is the probability five select public accounting?
c. How many graduates would you expect to select public accounting?

18. Suppose 60 percent of all people prefer Coke to Pepsi. We select 18 people for further study.

18. a. 10.8
b. .1734
c. .0246

a. How many would you expect to prefer Coke?
b. What is the probability 10 of those surveyed will prefer Coke?
c. What is the probability 15 prefer Coke?

Cumulative Probability Distributions

We may wish to know the probability of correctly guessing the answers to 6 *or more* true/false questions out of 10. Or we may be interested in the probability of *selecting less than two* defectives at random from production during the previous hour. In these cases we need cumulative frequency distributions similar to the ones developed in Chapter 2. The following example will illustrate.

EXAMPLE

A recent study by the American Highway Patrolman's Association revealed that 60 percent of American drivers use their seat belts. A sample of 10 drivers on the Florida Turnpike is selected.

1. What is the probability that exactly 7 are wearing seat belts?
2. What is the probability that 7 or fewer of the drivers are wearing seat belts?

SOLUTION

This situation meets the binomial requirements, namely:

- A particular driver either is wearing a seat belt or is not. There are only two possible outcomes.
- The probability of "success" (wearing a seat belt) is the same from driver to driver: 60 percent.
- The trials are independent. If the fourth driver selected in the sample is wearing a seat belt, for example, it has no effect on whether the fifth driver selected is wearing a seat belt.
- There is a fixed number of trials — 10 in this case, because 10 drivers are checked.

1. To find the likelihood of *exactly* 7 drivers, we use Appendix A. Locate the page for $n = 10$. Next find the column for $\pi = .60$ and the row for $x = 7$. The value is .215. Thus, the probability of finding 7 out of 10 drivers in the sample wearing their seat belts is .215. This is often written as follows:

$$P(x = 7 \mid n = 10 \text{ and } \pi = .60) = .215$$

where x refers to the number of successes, n the number of trials, and π the probability of a success. The bar "|" means "given that."

2. To find the probability that 7 or fewer of the drivers will be wearing seat belts, we apply the special rule of addition, formula (5–2), from Chapter 5. Because the events are mutually exclusive, we determine the probability that of the 10 drivers stopped, none was wearing a seat belt, 1 was wearing a seat belt, 2 were wearing a seat belt, and so on up to 7 drivers. The probabilities of the eight possible outcomes are then totaled. From Appendix A, $n = 10$, and $\pi = .60$.

$$\begin{aligned} P(x \le 7 \mid n = 10 \text{ and } \pi = .60) &= P(x = 0) + P(x = 1) + P(x = 2) + P(x = 3) \\ &\quad + P(x = 4) + P(x = 5) + P(x = 6) + P(x = 7) \\ &= .000 + .002 + .011 + .042 + .111 + .201 \\ &\quad + .251 + .215 \\ &= .833 \end{aligned}$$

So the probability of stopping 10 cars at random and finding 7 or fewer of the drivers wearing their seat belts is .833.

This value may also be determined, with less computation, using the complement rule. First, find $P(x > 7)$ given that $n = 10$ and $\pi = .60$. This probability is .167, found by $P(x = 8) + P(x = 9) + P(x = 10) = .121 + .040 + .006$. The probability that $x \le 7$ is equal to $1 - P(x > 7)$, so $P(x \le 7) = 1 - .167 = .833$, the same as computed above.

Self-Review 6–4

For a case where $n = 4$ and $\pi = .60$, determine the probability that:

(a) $x = 2$.
(b) $x \le 2$.
(c) $x > 2$.

Exercises

19. In a binomial distribution $n = 8$ and $\pi = .30$. Find the probabilities of the following events.
a. $x = 2$.
b. $x \le 2$ (the probability that x is equal to or less than 2).
c. $x \ge 3$ (the probability that x is equal to or greater than 3).

20. In a binomial distribution $n = 12$ and $\pi = .60$. Find the following probabilities.
a. $x = 5$.
b. $x \le 5$.
c. $x \ge 6$.

20. a. .101
b. .157
c. .843

21. In a recent study 90 percent of the homes in the United States were found to have color TVs. In a sample of nine homes, what is the probability that:
a. All nine have color TVs?
b. Less than five have color TVs?
c. More than five have color TVs?
d. At least seven homes have color TVs?

22. A manufacturer of window frames knows from long experience that 5 percent of the production will have some type of minor defect that will require an adjustment. What is the probability that in a sample of 20 window frames:
    a. None will need adjustment?
    b. At least one will need adjustment?
    c. More than two will need adjustment?

22. a. .358
b. .642
c. .076

23. The speed with which utility companies can resolve problems is very important. GTC, the Georgetown Telephone Company, reports they can resolve customer problems the same day they are reported in 70 percent of the cases. Suppose the 15 cases reported today are representative of all complaints.
    a. How many of the problems would you expect to be resolved today? What is the standard deviation?
    b. What is the probability 10 of the problems can be resolved today?
    c. What is the probability 10 or 11 of the problems can be resolved today?
    d. What is the probability more than 10 of the problems can be resolved today?
24. Steele Electronics, Inc. sells expensive brands of stereo equipment in several shopping malls throughout the northwest section of the United States. The Marketing Research Department of Steele reports that 30 percent of the customers entering the store that indicate they are browsing will, in the end, make a purchase. Let the last 20 customers who enter the store be a sample.
    a. How many of these customers would you expect to make a purchase?
    b. What is the probability that exactly five of these customers make a purchase?
    c. What is the probability ten or more make a purchase?
    d. Does it seem likely at least one will make a purchase?

24. a. 6
b. .1789
c. .0479
d. Yes, $P(x \geq 1) =$ .9992

Hypergeometric Probability Distribution

For the binomial distribution to be applied, the probability of a success must stay the same for each trial. For example, the probability of guessing the correct answer to a true/false question is .50. This probability remains the same for each question on an examination. Likewise, suppose that 40 percent of the registered voters in a precinct are Republicans. If 27 registered voters are to be selected at random, the probability of choosing a Republican on the first selection is .40. The chance of choosing a Republican on the next selection is also .40, assuming that the sampling is done *with replacement,* meaning that the person selected is put back in the population before the next person is selected.

Most sampling, however, is done *without replacement.* Thus, if the population is small, the probability for each observation will change. For example, if the population consists of 20 items, the probability of selecting a particular item from that population is 1/20. If the sampling is done without replacement, after the first selection there are only 19 items remaining; the probability of selecting a particular item on the second selection is only 1/19. For the third selection, the probability is 1/18, and so on. This assumes that the population is **finite**—that is, the number in the population is known and relatively small in number. Examples of a finite population are 2,842 Republicans in the precinct, 9,241 applications for medical school, and the 18 Pontiac Sunbirds currently in stock at North Pontiac.

Recall that one of the criteria for the binomial distribution is that the probability of success remain the same from trial to trial. Since the probability of success does not remain the same from trial to trial when sampling is from a relatively small population without replacement, the binomial distribution should not be used. Instead, the **hypergeometric distribution** should be applied. Therefore, (1) if a sample is selected from a finite population without replacement and (2) if the size of the sample n is more than

5 percent of the population N, then the hypergeometric distribution is used to determine the probability of a specified number of successes or failures. It is especially appropriate when the size of the population is small.

The formula for the hypergeometric distribution is:

HYPERGEOMETRIC DISTRIBUTION $$P(x) = \frac{({}_SC_x)({}_{N-S}C_{n-x})}{{}_NC_n} \qquad \textbf{[6–6]}$$

where:

- N is the size of the population.
- S is the number of successes in the population.
- x is the number of successes in the sample. It may be 0, 1, 2, 3, ...
- n is the size of the sample or the number of trials.
- C is the symbol for a combination.

The following example illustrates the details of determining a probability using the hypergeometric distribution.

EXAMPLE

PlayTime Toys, Inc. employs 50 people in the Assembly Department. Forty of the employees belong to a union and ten do not. Five employees are selected at random to form a committee to meet with management regarding shift starting times. What is the probability that four of the five selected for the committee belong to a union?

SOLUTION

The population in this case is the 50 Assembly Department employees. An employee can be selected for the committee only once. Hence, the sampling is done without replacement. Thus, the probability of selecting a union employee, for example, changes from one trial to the next. The hypergeometric distribution is appropriate for determining the probability. In this problem,

- N is 50, the number of employees.
- S is 40, the number of union employees.
- x is 4, the number of union employees selected.
- n is 5, the number of employees selected.

We wish to find the probability 4 of the 5 committee members belong to a union. Inserting these values into formula 6–6:

$$P(4) = \frac{({}_{40}C_4)({}_{50-40}C_{5-4})}{{}_{50}C_5} = \frac{\left(\dfrac{40!}{4!36!}\right)\left(\dfrac{10!}{1!9!}\right)}{\dfrac{50!}{5!45!}} = \frac{(91{,}390)(10)}{2{,}118{,}760} = .431$$

Thus, the probability of selecting 5 assembly workers at random from the 50 workers and finding 4 of the 5 are union members is .431.

Table 6–5 shows the hypergeometric probabilities of finding 0, 1, 2, 3, 4, and 5 union members on the committee.

TABLE 6–5 Hypergeometric Probabilities ($n = 5$, $N = 50$, and $S = 40$) for the Number of Union Members on the Committee

Union Members	Probability
0	.000
1	.004
2	.044
3	.210
4	.431
5	.311
	1.000

In order for you to compare the two probability distributions, Table 6–6 shows the hypergeometric and binomial probabilities for the PlayTime Toys, Inc. example. Because 40 of the 50 Assembly Department employees belong to the union, we let $\pi = .80$ for the binomial distribution. The binomial probabilities for Table 6–6 come from the binomial table in Appendix A, with $n = 5$ and $\pi = .80$.

TABLE 6–6 Hypergeometric and Binomial Probabilities for PlayTime Toys, Inc. Assembly Department

Number of Union Members on Committee	Hypergeometric Probability, $P(x)$	Binomial Probability ($n = 5$ and $\pi = .80$)
0	.000	.000
1	.004	.006
2	.044	.051
3	.210	.205
4	.431	.410
5	.311	.328
	1.000	1.000

When the binomial requirement of a constant probability of success cannot be met, the hypergeometric distribution should be used. However, as Table 6–6 shows, under many conditions the results of the binomial distribution approximate those of the hypergeometric. This leads to a rule of thumb: if the selected items are not returned to the population and the sample size is less than 5 percent of the population, the binomial distribution can be used to approximate the hypergeometric distribution. That is, when $n < .05N$, the binomial should suffice.

A hypergeometric distribution can be created using Excel. See the following output. The necessary steps are given in the Computer Commands section.

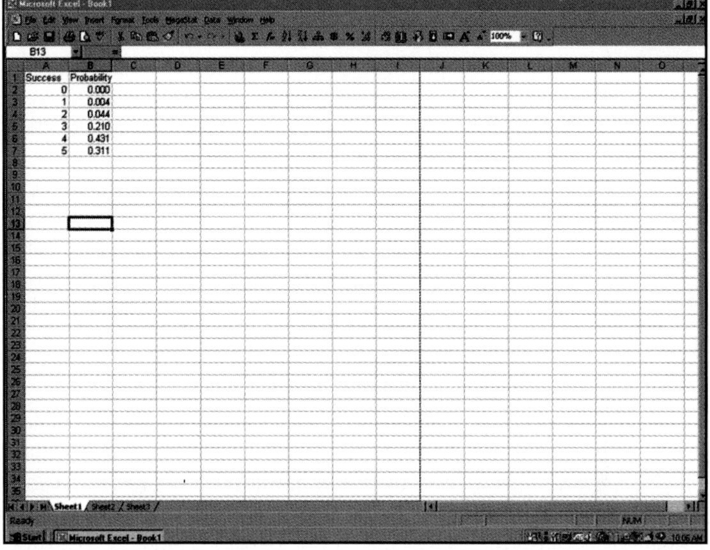

Self-Review 6–5

Horwege Discount Brokers plans to hire 5 new financial analysts this year. There is a pool of 12 approved applicants, and George Horwege, the owner, decides to randomly select those who will be hired. There are 8 men and 4 women among the approved applicants. What is the probability that 3 of the 5 hired are men?

Exercises

25. A population consists of ten items, six of which are defective. In a sample of three items, what is the probability that exactly two are defective?

26. .4396 **26.** A population consists of 15 items, 10 of which are acceptable. In a sample of 4 items, what is the probability that exactly 3 are acceptable?

27. Kolzak Appliance Outlet just received a shipment of ten TV sets. Shortly after they were received, the manufacturer called to report that he had inadvertently shipped three defective sets. Ms. Kolzak, the owner of the outlet, decided to test two of the ten sets she received. What is the probability that neither of the two sets tested is defective?

28. The Computer Systems Department has eight faculty, six of whom are tenured. Dr. Vonder, the chairman, wants to establish a committee of three department faculty members to review the curriculum. If she selects the committee at random:

28. a. .3571 **a.** What is the probability all members of the committee are tenured?

b. .6429 **b.** What is the probability that at least one member is not tenured? (Hint: For this question, use the complement rule.)

29. Keith's Florists has 15 delivery trucks, used mainly to deliver flowers and flower arrangements in the Greenville, South Carolina, area. Of these 15 trucks, 6 have brake problems. A sample of 5 trucks is randomly selected. What is the probability that 2 of those tested have defective brakes?

30. .8462 **30.** Professor Jon Hammer has a pool of 15 multiple-choice questions regarding probability distributions. Four of these questions involve the hypergeometric distribution. What is the probability at least one of these hypergeometric questions will appear on the five-question quiz on Monday?

Statistics in Action

Near the end of World War II, the Germans developed rocket bombs, which were fired at the city of London. The Allied military command did not know whether these bombs were fired at random or whether they had some type of aiming device. To investigate, the city of London was divided into 576 square regions. The distribution of the number of hits in each square was recorded as follows:

Hits	0	1	2	3	4	5
Regions	229	221	93	35	7	1

To interpret, the above chart indicates that 229 regions were not hit with one of the bombs. Seven regions were hit four times. Using the Poisson distribution, with a mean of 0.93 hits per region, the expected number of hits is as follows:

Hits	0	1	2	3	4	5 or more
Regions	227.3	211.3	98.3	30.5	7.1	1.6

Because the actual number of hits was close to the expected number of hits, the military command concluded that the bombs were falling at random. The Germans had not developed a bomb with an aiming device.

Poisson Probability Distribution

The **Poisson probability distribution** describes the number of times some event occurs during a specified interval. The interval may be time, distance, area, or volume. The distribution is based on two assumptions. The first assumption is that the probability is proportional to the length of the interval. The second assumption is that the intervals are independent. To put it another way, the longer the interval the larger the probability, and the number of occurrences in one interval does not affect the other intervals. This distribution is also a limiting form of the binomial distribution when the probability of a success is very small and n is large. It is often referred to as the "law of improbable events," meaning that the probability, π, of a particular event's happening is quite small. The Poisson distribution is a discrete probability distribution because it is formed by counting.

This distribution has many applications. It is used as a model to describe the distribution of errors in data entry, the number of scratches and other imperfections in newly painted car panels, the number of defective parts in outgoing shipments, the number of customers waiting to be served at a restaurant or waiting to get into an attraction at Disney World, and the number of accidents on I–75 during a three-month period.

The Poisson distribution can be described mathematically using the formula:

POISSON DISTRIBUTION $$P(x) = \frac{\mu^x e^{-\mu}}{x!} \qquad \textbf{[6–7]}$$

where:

- μ (mu) is the mean number of occurrences (successes) in a particular interval.
- e is the constant 2.71828 (base of the Naperian logarithmic system).
- x is the number of occurrences (successes).
- $P(x)$ is the probability for a specified value of x.

The mean number of successes, μ, can be determined in binomial situations by $n\pi$, where n is the total number of trials and π the probability of success.

MEAN OF A POISSON DISTRIBUTION $$\mu = n\pi \qquad \textbf{[6–8]}$$

The variance of the Poisson is also equal to its mean. If, for example, the probability that a check cashed by a bank will bounce is .0003, and 10,000 checks are cashed, the mean and the variance for the number of bad checks is 3.0, found by $\mu = n\pi = 10{,}000(.0003) = 3.0$.

Recall that for a binomial distribution there is a fixed number of trials. For example, for a four-question multiple-choice test there can only be zero, one, two, three, or four successes (correct answers). The random variable, x, for a Poisson distribution, however, can assume an *infinite number of values*—that is, 0, 1, 2, 3, 4, 5, ... However, *the probabilities become very small after the first few occurrences* (successes).

To illustrate the Poisson probability computation, assume baggage is rarely lost by Northwest Airlines. Most flights do not experience any mishandled bags; some have one bag lost; a few have two bags lost; rarely a flight will have three lost bags; and so on. Suppose a random sample of 1,000 flights shows a total of 300 bags were lost. Thus, the arithmetic mean number of lost bags per flight is 0.3, found by 300/1,000. If the number of lost bags per flight follows a Poisson distribution with $\mu = 0.3$, we can compute the various probabilities by the formula:

$$P(x) = \frac{\mu^x e^{-\mu}}{x!}$$

For example, the probability of not losing any bags is:

$$P(0) = \frac{(0.3)^0(e^{-0.3})}{0!} = 0.7408$$

In other words, 74 percent of the flights will have no lost baggage. The probability of exactly one lost bag is:

$$P(1) = \frac{(0.3)^1(e^{-0.3})}{1!} = 0.2222$$

Thus, we would expect to find exactly one lost bag on 22 percent of the flights.

Poisson probabilities can also be found in the table in Appendix C.

EXAMPLE

Recall from the previous illustration that the number of lost bags follows a Poisson distribution with a mean of 0.3. Use Appendix C to find the probability that no bags will be lost on a particular flight. What is the probability exactly one bag will be lost on a particular flight? When should the supervisor become suspicious that a flight is having too many lost bags?

SOLUTION

Part of Appendix C is repeated as Table 6–7. To find the probability of no lost bags, locate the column headed "0.3" and read down that column to the row labeled "0." The probability is .7408. That is the probability of no lost bags. The probability of one lost bag is .2222, which is in the next row of the table, in the same column. The probability of two lost bags is .0333, in the row below; for three lost bags it is .0033; and for four lost bags it is .0003. Thus, a supervisor should not be surprised to find one lost bag but should expect to see more than one lost bag infrequently.

TABLE 6–7 Poisson Table for Various Values of μ (from Appendix C)

	μ								
x	0.1	0.2	0.3	0.4	0.5	0.6	0.7	0.8	0.9
0	0.9048	0.8187	0.7408	0.6703	0.6065	0.5488	0.4966	0.4493	0.4066
1	0.0905	0.1637	0.2222	0.2681	0.3033	0.3293	0.3476	0.3595	0.3659
2	0.0045	0.0164	0.0333	0.0536	0.0758	0.0988	0.1217	0.1438	0.1647
3	0.0002	0.0011	0.0033	0.0072	0.0126	0.0198	0.0284	0.0383	0.0494
4	0.0000	0.0001	0.0003	0.0007	0.0016	0.0030	0.0050	0.0077	0.0111
5	0.0000	0.0000	0.0000	0.0001	0.0002	0.0004	0.0007	0.0012	0.0020
6	0.0000	0.0000	0.0000	0.0000	0.0000	0.0000	0.0001	0.0002	0.0003
7	0.0000	0.0000	0.0000	0.0000	0.0000	0.0000	0.0000	0.0000	0.0000

These probabilities can also be found using the MINITAB system. The commands necessary are reported at the end of the chapter. The output appears on page 216. A graph of the distribution of the number of lost bags is shown in Chart 6–5. Note that the distribution is severely skewed in the positive direction.

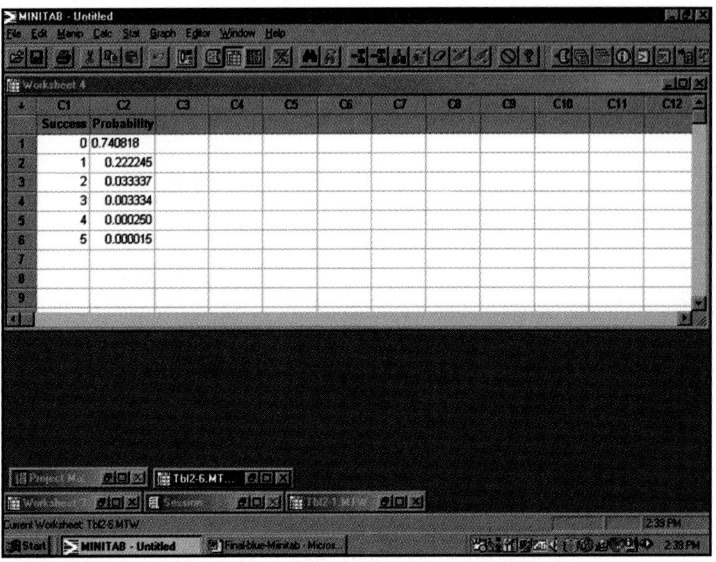

	C1	C2
	Success	Probability
1	0	0.740818
2	1	0.222245
3	2	0.033337
4	3	0.003334
5	4	0.000250
6	5	0.000015

CHART 6–5 Poisson Probability Distribution for $\mu = 0.3$

The Poisson probability distribution is always positively skewed. Also, the Poisson random variable has no specific upper limit. The Poisson distribution for the lost bags illustration, where $\mu = 0.3$ is highly skewed. As μ becomes larger, the Poisson distribution becomes more symmetrical. For example, Chart 6–6 shows the distributions of the number of transmission services, muffler replacements, and oil changes per day at Avellino's Auto Shop. They follow Poisson distributions with means of 0.7, 2.0, and 6.0, respectively.

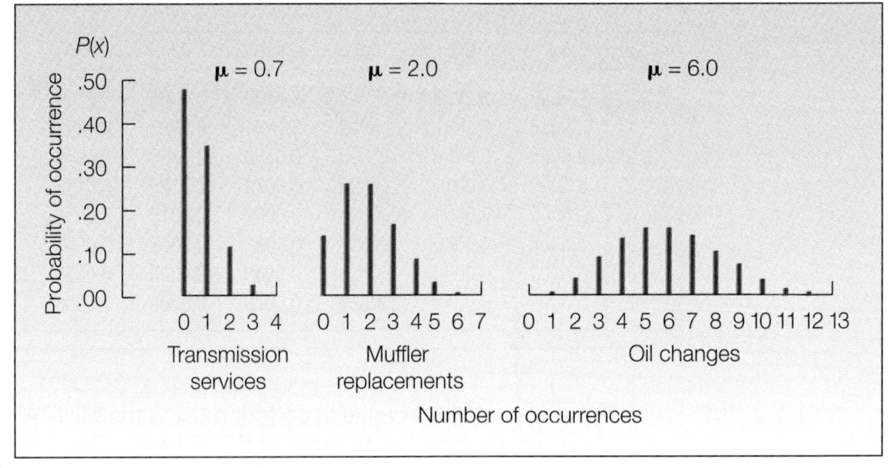

CHART 6–6 Poisson Probability Distributions for Means of 0.7, 2.0, and 6.0

Only μ needed to construct Poisson

In summary, the Poisson distribution is actually a family of discrete distributions. All that is needed to construct a Poisson probability distribution is the mean number of defects, errors, and so on—designated as μ.

Self-Review 6–6

From actuary tables the Washington Insurance Company determined the likelihood that a man age 25 will die within the next year is .0002. If Washington Insurance sells 4,000 policies to 25-year-old men this year, what is the probability they will pay on exactly one policy?-

Exercises

31. In a Poisson distribution $\mu = 0.4$.
   a. What is the probability that $x = 0$?
   b. What is the probability that $x > 0$?

32. In a Poisson distribution $\mu = 4$.
   a. What is the probability that $x = 2$?
   b. What is the probability that $x \leq 2$?
   c. What is the probability that $x > 2$?

32. a. .1465 b. .2381 c. .7619

33. Ms. Bergen is a loan officer at Coast Bank and Trust. Based on her years of experience, she estimates that the probability is .025 that an applicant will not be able to repay his or her installment loan. Last month she made 40 loans.
   a. What is the probability that 3 loans will be defaulted?
   b. What is the probability that at least 3 loans will be defaulted?

34. Automobiles arrive at the Elkhart exit of the Indiana Toll Road at the rate of two per minute. The distribution of arrivals approximates a Poisson distribution.
   a. What is the probability that no automobiles arrive in a particular minute?
   b. What is the probability that at least one automobile arrives during a particular minute?

34. a. .1353 b. .8647

35. It is estimated that 0.5 percent of the callers to the billing department of the U.S. West Telephone Company will receive a busy signal. What is the probability that of today's 1,200 callers at least 5 received a busy signal?

36. Textbook authors and publishers work very hard to minimize the number of errors in a text. However, some errors are unavoidable. Mr. J. A. Carmen, statistics editor, reports that the mean number of errors per chapter is 0.8. What is the probability that there are less than 2 errors in a particular chapter?

36. .8088

Chapter Outline

I. A random variable is a numerical value determined by the outcome of an experiment.

II. A probability distribution is a listing of all possible outcomes of an experiment and the probability associated with each outcome.
   A. A discrete probability distribution can assume only certain values. The main features are:
      1. The sum of the probabilities is 1.00.
      2. The probability of a particular outcome is between 0.00 and 1.00.
      3. The outcomes are mutually exclusive.
   B. A continuous distribution can assume an infinite number of values within a specific range.

III. The mean and variance of a probability distribution are computed as follows.
   A. The mean is equal to:

$$\mu = \Sigma[xP(x)] \quad \textbf{[6–1]}$$

   B. The variance is equal to:

$$\sigma^2 = \Sigma[(x - \mu)^2 P(x)] \quad \textbf{[6–2]}$$

IV. The binomial distribution has the following characteristics.

A. Each outcome is classified into one of two mutually exclusive categories.
B. The probability of a success remains the same from trial to trial.
C. Each trial is independent.
D. The distribution results from a count of the number of successes in a fixed number of trials.
E. A binomial probability is determined as follows:

$$P(x) = {}_xC_n\, \pi^x\, (1 - \pi)^{n-x} \quad [6\text{–}3]$$

F. The mean is computed as:

$$\mu = n\pi \quad [6\text{–}4]$$

G. The variance is

$$\sigma^2 = n\pi(1 - \pi) \quad [6\text{–}5]$$

V. The hypergeometric distribution has the following characteristics.

A. There are only two possible outcomes.
B. The probability of a success is not the same on each trial.
C. The distribution results from a count of the number of successes in a fixed number of trials.
D. A hypergeometric probability is computed from the following equation.

$$P(x) = \frac{({}_SC_x)({}_{N-S}C_{n-x})}{({}_NC_n)} \quad [6\text{–}6]$$

VI. The Poisson distribution has the following characteristics.

A. It describes the number of times some event occurs during a specified interval.
B. The probability of a "success" is proportional to the length of the interval.
C. Nonoverlapping intervals are independent.
D. It is a limiting form of the binomial distribution when n is large and π is small.
E. A Poisson probability is determined from the following equation:

$$P(x) = \frac{\mu^x e^{-\mu}}{x!} \quad [6\text{–}7]$$

F. The mean and the variance of a Poisson distribution are the same and are equal to $n\pi$.

Chapter Exercises

37. What is the difference between a random variable and a probability distribution?

38. See IM.

38. What is the difference between a discrete and a continuous random variable? For each of the following indicate whether the random variable is discrete or continuous random variable.

a. The length of time to get a haircut.
b. The number of cars a jogger passes each morning while running.
c. The number of hits for a team in a high school girls' softball game.
d. The number of patients treated at the South Strand Medical Center between 6 and 10 P.M. each night.
e. The number of miles your car traveled on the last fill up.
f. The number of customers at the Oak Street Wendy's who used the drive-through facility.
g. The distance between Gainesville, Florida, and all Florida cities of at least 50,000.

39. What are the requirements for the binomial distribution?

40. See IM.

40. Under what conditions will the binomial and the Poisson distributions give roughly the same results?

41. Samson Apartments has a large number of units available to rent each month. A concern of management is the number of vacant apartments each month. A recent study revealed the percent of the time that a given number of apartments are vacant. Compute the mean and standard deviation of the number of vacant apartments.

Number of Vacant Units	Probability
0	.10
1	.20
2	.30
3	.40

42. μ = \$2,200
σ^2 = \$1,560,000

42. An investment will be worth \$1,000, \$2,000, or \$5,000 at the end of the year. The probabilities of these values are .25, .60, and .15, respectively. Determine the mean and variance of the worth of the investment.

43. The personnel manager of the Cumberland Pig Iron Company is studying the number of on-the-job accidents over a period of one month. He developed the following probability distribution. Compute the mean, variance, and standard deviation of the number of accidents in a month.

Number of Accidents	Probability
0	.40
1	.20
2	.20
3	.10
4	.10

44. μ = 13.2
σ^2 = .86
σ = .9274

44. Croissant Bakery, Inc. offers special decorated cakes for birthdays, weddings, and other occasions. They also have regular cakes available in their bakery. The following table gives the total number of cakes sold per day and the corresponding probability. Compute the mean, variance, and standard deviation of the number of cakes sold per day.

Number of Cakes Sold in a Day	Probability
12	.25
13	.40
14	.25
15	.10

45. A Tamiami shearing machine is producing 10 percent defective pieces, which is abnormally high. The quality control engineer has been checking the output by almost continuous sampling since the abnormal condition began. What is the probability that in a sample of 10 pieces:
   a. Exactly 5 will be defective?
   b. 5 or more will be defective?

46. .168

46. Thirty percent of the population in a southwestern community are Spanish-speaking Americans. A Spanish-speaking person is accused of killing a non-Spanish-speaking American. Of the first 12 potential jurors, only 2 are Spanish-speaking Americans, and 10 are not. The defendant's lawyer challenges the jury selection, claiming bias against her client. The government lawyer disagrees, saying that the probability of this particular jury composition is common. What do you think?

47. An auditor for Health Maintenance Services of Georgia reports 40 percent of the policyholders 55 years or older submit a claim during the year. Fifteen policyholders are randomly selected for company records.
   a. How many of the policyholders would you expect to have filed a claim within the last year?
   b. What is the probability that ten of the selected policyholders submitted a claim last year?
   c. What is the probability that ten or more of the selected policyholders submitted a claim last year?
   d. What is the probability that more than ten the selected policyholders submitted a claim last year?

48. .1294

48. Tire and Auto Supply is considering a 2-for-1 stock split. Before the transaction is finalized, at least two thirds of the 1,200 company stockholders must approve the proposal. To evaluate the likelihood the proposal will be approved, the director of finance selected a sample of 18 stockholders. He contacted each and found 14 approved of the proposed split. What is the likelihood of this event, assuming two thirds of the stockholders approve?

49. A Federal study reported that 7.5 percent of the U.S. workforce has a drug problem. A drug enforcement official for the State of Indiana wished to investigate this statement. In his sample of 20 employed workers:

a. How many would you expect to have a drug problem? What is the standard deviation?
b. What is the likelihood that *none* of the workers sampled has a drug problem?
c. What is the likelihood *at least one* has a drug problem?

50. The Bank of Hawaii reports that 7 percent of its credit card holders will default at some time in their life. The Hilo branch just mailed out 12 new cards today.

50. a. 0.84, 0.884
b. .4186
c. .5814

a. How many of these new cardholders would you expect to default? What is the standard deviation?
b. What is the likelihood that *none* of the cardholders will default?
c. What is the likelihood *at least one* will default?

51. Recent statistics suggest that 15 percent of those who visit a retail site on the World Wide Web make a purchase. A local retailer wished to verify this claim. To do so, she selected a sample of 16 "hits" to her site and found that 4 had actually made a purchase.

a. What is the likelihood of exactly four purchases?
b. How many purchases should she expect?
c. What is the likelihood that four or more "hits" result in a purchase?

52. In Chapter 17 we discuss the *acceptance sample.* Acceptance sampling is used to monitor the quality of incoming raw materials. Suppose a purchaser of electronic components allows 1 percent of the components to be defective. To ensure the quality of incoming parts, they normally sample 20 parts and allow 1 defect.

52. a. .9831
b. .9401
c. .7359

a. What is the likelihood of accepting a lot that is 1 percent defective?
b. If the quality of the incoming lot was actually 2 percent, what is the likelihood of accepting it?
c. If the quality of the incoming lot was actually 5 percent, what is the likelihood of accepting it?

53. Colgate-Palmolive, Inc. recently developed a new toothpaste flavored by honey. They tested a group of ten people. Six of the group said they liked the new flavor, and the remaining four indicated they definitely did not. Four of the ten are selected to participate in an in-depth interview. What is the probability that of those selected for the in-depth interview two liked the new flavor and two did not?

54. a. See IM.
b. 4.5, 1.5732
c. .2384
d. .5044

54. Dr. Richmond, a psychologist, is studying the daytime television viewing habits of college students. She believes 45 percent of college students watch soap operas during the afternoon. To further investigate, she selects a sample of ten.

a. Develop a probability distribution for the number of students in the sample who watch soap operas.
b. Find the mean and the standard deviation of this distribution.
c. What is the probability of finding exactly four watch soap operas?
d. What is the probability less than half of the students selected watch soap operas?

55. A recent study conducted by Penn, Shone, and Borland, on behalf of LastMinute.com, revealed that 52 percent of business travelers plan their trips less than two weeks before departure. The study is to be replicated in the tri-state area with a sample of 12 frequent business travelers.

a. Develop a probability distribution for the number of travelers who plan their trips within two weeks of departure.
b. Find the mean and the standard deviation of this distribution.
c. What is the probability exactly 5 of the 12 selected business travelers plan their trips within two weeks of departure?
d. What is the probability 5 or fewer of the 12 selected business travelers plan their trips within two weeks of departure?

56. Suppose 5 of 25 Ford subcompact automobiles require adjustment of some kind. Four subcompacts are selected at random. We are interested in the probability that exactly one will require adjustment.

56. a. .4506 **a.** Solve the problem assuming that of the 25 subcompacts, the samples are drawn without replacement.
b. .410
c. .3595 **b.** Solve the problem assuming the sampling is done with replacement.
d. See IM. **c.** Assuming replacement, work the problem using the Poisson distribution.
d. Compare the results in parts a, b, and c. Comment on your findings.

57. The law firm of Hagel and Hagel is located in downtown Cincinnati. There are ten partners in the firm; seven live in Ohio and three in northern Kentucky. Ms. Wendy Hagel, the managing partner, wants to appoint a committee of three partners to look into moving the firm to northern Kentucky. If the committee is selected at random from the ten partners, what is the probability that:
a. One member of the committee lives in northern Kentucky and the others live in Ohio?
b. At least one member of the committee lives in northern Kentucky?

58. Recent information published by the U.S. Environmental Protection Agency indicates that Honda is the manufacturer of four of the top nine vehicles in terms of fuel economy.
58. a. .See IM. **a.** Determine the probability distribution for the number of Hondas in a sample of three cars chosen from the top nine.
b. .881 **b.** What is the likelihood that in the sample of three at least one Honda is included?

59. The position of chief of police in the city of Corry, Pennsylvania, is vacant. A search committee of Corry residents is charged with the responsibility of recommending a new chief to the city council. There are 12 applicants, 4 of which are either female or members of a minority. The search committee decides to interview all 12 of the applicants. To begin, they randomly select four applicants to be interviewed on the first day, and none of the four is female or a member of a minority. The local newspaper, the Corry *Press,* suggests discrimination in an editorial. What is the likelihood of this occurrence?

60. A box of six electric hair trimmers includes two that do not operate properly. Three trimmers are selected from the box.
60. a. .60 **a.** What is the probability that one does not operate properly?
b. .20 **b.** What is the probability that two trimmers of the three selected do not operate properly?

61. The sales of Lexus automobiles in the Detroit area follow a Poisson distribution with a mean of 3 per day.
a. What is the probability that no Lexus is sold on a particular day?
b. What is the probability that for five consecutive days at least one Lexus is sold?

62. a. .0498 **62.** Suppose 1.5 percent of the antennas on new Nokia cell phones are defective. For a random
b. .5768 sample of 200 antennas, find the probability that:
a. None of the antennas is defective.
b. Three or more of the antennas are defective.

63. A study of the checkout lines at the Safeway Supermarket in the South Strand area revealed that between 4 and 7 P.M. on weekdays there is an average of four customers waiting in line. What is the probability that you visit Safeway today during this period and find:
a. No customers are waiting?
b. Four customers are waiting?
c. Four or fewer are waiting?
d. Four or more are waiting?

64. An internal study at Lahey Electronics, a large software development company, revealed the mean time for an internal e-mail message to arrive at its destination was 2 seconds. Further, the distribution of the arrival times followed the Poisson distribution.
64. a. .2707 **a.** What is the probability a message takes exactly 1 second to arrive at its destination?
b. .0526 **b.** What is the probability it takes more than 4 seconds to arrive at its destination?
c. .1353 **c.** What is the probability it takes virtually no time, i.e., "zero" seconds?

65. Recent crime reports indicate that 3.1 motor vehicle thefts occur each minute in the United States. Assume that the distribution of thefts per minute can be approximated by the Poisson probability distribution.

a. Calculate the probability exactly *four* thefts occur in a minute.
b. What is the probability there are *no* thefts in a minute?
c. What is the probability there is *at least one* theft in a minute?

66. New Process, Inc., a large mail-order supplier of women's fashions, advertises same-day service on every order. Recently the movement of orders has not gone as planned, and there were a large number of complaints. Bud Owens, director of customer service, has completely redone the method of order handling. The goal is to have fewer than five unfilled orders on hand at the end of 95 percent of the working days. Frequent checks of the unfilled orders at the end of the day revealed that the distribution of the unfilled orders follows a Poisson distribution with a mean of two orders.

66. a. .9473
b. See IM.

a. Has New Process, Inc. lived up to its internal goal? Cite evidence.
b. Draw a histogram representing the Poisson probability distribution of unfilled orders.

67. On January 29, 1986, the space shuttle *Challenger* exploded 46,000 feet above the Atlantic Ocean, resulting in the death of all seven astronauts. A 1985 study published by the National Aeronautics and Space Administration (NASA) suggested that the probability of such a catastrophic occurrence was 1 in 60,000. A similar report by the Air Force set the likelihood of a catastrophe at 1 in 35. The *Challenger* flight was the 25th mission in the shuttle program. Use the Poisson distribution to compare the probabilities of at least one disaster in a sample of 25 missions using both estimates of the probability of occurrence.

68. .1899

68. According to the "January theory," if the stock market is up for the month of January, it will be up for the year. If it is down in January, it will be down for the year. According to an article in *The Wall Street Journal,* this theory held for 29 out of the last 34 years. Suppose there is no truth to this theory. What is the probability this could occur by chance? (You will probably need a software package such as Excel or MINITAB.)

69. During the second round of the 1989 U.S. Open golf tournament, four golfers scored a hole in one on the sixth hole. The odds of a professional golfer making a hole in one are estimated to be 3,708 to 1, so the probability is 1/3,708. There were 155 golfers participating in the second round that day. Estimate the probability that four golfers would score a hole in one on the sixth hole.

Computer Data Exercises

70. Refer to the Real Estate data, which reports information on homes sold in the Venice, Florida, area last year.

70. a. $\mu = 3.8$, $\sigma = 1.4954$
b. $\mu = 0.208$, $\sigma = .3912$

a. Create a probability distribution for the number of bedrooms. Compute the mean and the standard deviation of this distribution.
b. Create a probability distribution for the number of bathrooms. Compute the mean and the standard deviation of this distribution.

71. Refer to the Baseball 2000 data, which contains information on the 2000 Major League Baseball season. There are 30 teams in the major leagues, and 7 of them have home fields with artificial playing surfaces. As part of the negotiations with the players' union, a study regarding injuries on grass versus artificial surfaces will be conducted. Five teams will be selected to participate in the study, and the teams will be selected at random. What is the likelihood that two of the five teams selected for study play their home games on artificial surfaces?

Computer Commands

1. The Excel MegaStat commands to create the binomial probability distribution on page 204 are:
   a. Select the **MegaStat** option on the toolbar, click on **Probability**, and **Discrete Probability Distributions**.
   b. In the dialog box select **Binomial**, the number of trials is *6*, the probability of a success is *.05*. If you wish to see a graph click on **display graph**.

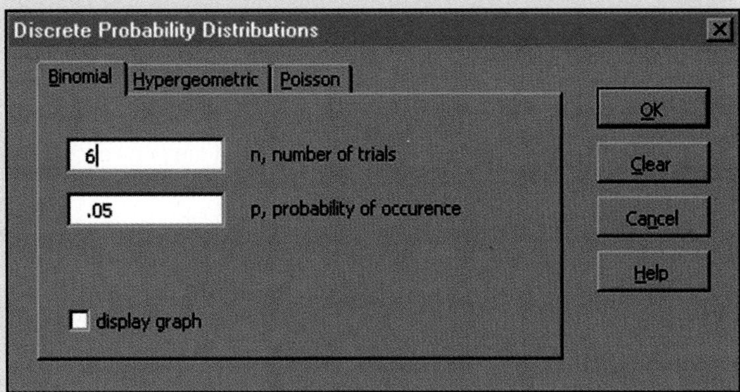

2. The Excel commands necessary to determine the binomial probability distribution on page 205 are:
   - **a.** On a blank Excel worksheet write the word *Success* in cell A1 and the word *Probability* in B1. In cells A2 through A14 write the integers *0* to *12*. Enter *B2* as the active cell.
   - **b.** From the toolbar select **Insert** and **Function Wizard**.
   - **c.** In the first dialog box select **Statistical** in the function category and **BINOMDIST** in the function name category, then click **OK.**
   - **d.** In the second dialog box enter the four items necessary to compute a binomial probability. Make sell B2 the active cell.
     1. Enter *0* for the number of successes.
     2. Enter *40* for the number of trials.
     3. Enter *.09* for the probability of a success.
     4. Enter the word *false* or the number *0* for the individual probabilities.
     5. Excel will compute the probability of 0 successes in 40 trials, with a .09 probability of success. The result, .02299618, is stored in cell B2.
   - **e.** To find the complete probability distribution, go to the formula bar and replace the *0* to the right of the open parentheses with *A2:A14.*
   - **f.** Move the mouse to the lower right corner of cell B2 and highlight the B column to cell B14. The probability of a success for the various values of the random variable will appear.

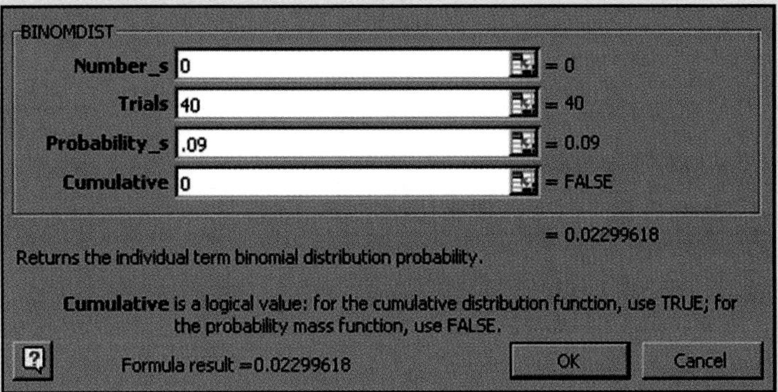

3. The Excel commands necessary to determine the hypergeometric distribution on page 213 are:
   - **a.** On a blank Excel worksheet write the word *Members* in cell A1 and the word *Probability* in B1. In cells A2 to A7 write the integers 0 to 5. Enter *B2* as the active cell.
   - **b.** From the toolbar choose **Insert** and **Function**.
   - **c.** In the first dialog box select **Statistical** and **HYPGEOMDIST**, and then click **OK**.

d. In the second dialog box enter the four items necessary to compute a hypergeometric probability.
   1. Enter *0* for the number of successes.
   2. Enter *5* for the number of trials.
   3. Enter *40* for the number of successes in the population.
   4. Enter *50* for the size of the population.
   5. Excel will compute the probability of 0 successes in 5 trials (.000118937) and store that result in cell B2.

e. To find the complete probability distribution, go to the formula bar and replace the 0 to the right of the open parentheses with *A2:A7*.

f. Move the mouse to the lower right corner of cell B2 and highlight the B column to cell B7. The probability of a success for the various outcomes will appear.

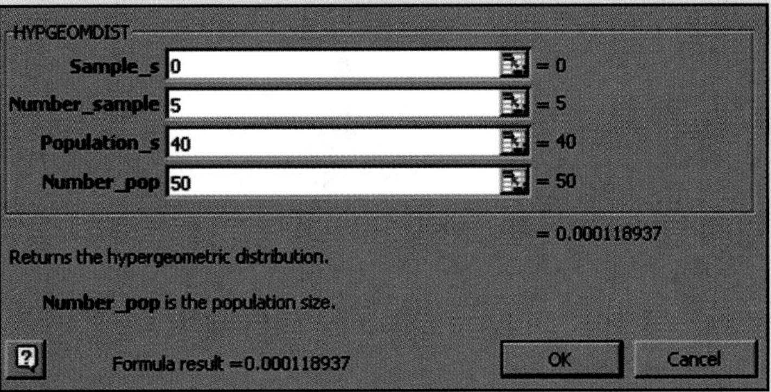

4. The MINITAB commands to generate the Poisson distribution on page 216 are:

a. Label column C1 as *Successes* and C2 as *Probability.* Enter the integers 0 though 5 in the first column.

b. Select **Calc**, then **Probability Distributions,** and **Poisson.**

c. In the dialog box click on **Probability,** set the mean equal to *.3,* and select *C1* as the Input column. Designate *C2* as Optional storage, and then click **OK.**

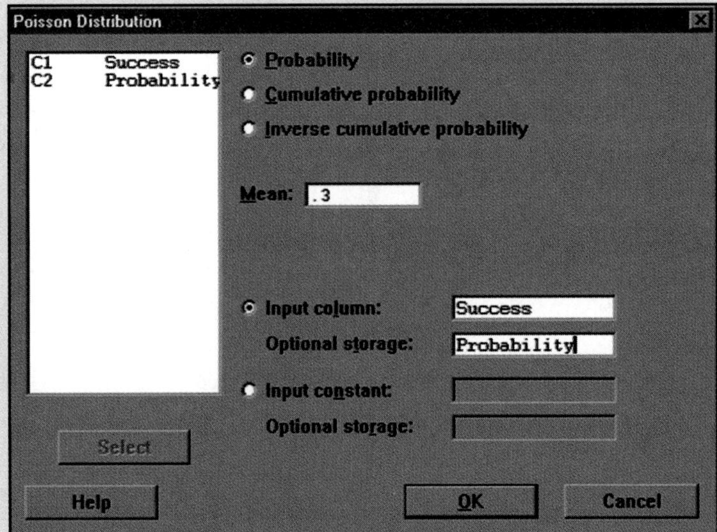

Chapter 6 Answers to Self-Review

6–1 (a)

Number of Spots	Probability
1	$\frac{1}{6}$
2	$\frac{1}{6}$
3	$\frac{1}{6}$
4	$\frac{1}{6}$
5	$\frac{1}{6}$
6	$\frac{1}{6}$
Total	$\frac{6}{6} = 1.00$

(b)

Probability: $\frac{1}{6}$, 0

Number of spots: 1 2 3 4 5 6

(c) $\frac{6}{6}$, or 1.

6–2 (a) It is discrete, because the values .80, .90, and 1.20 are clearly separated from each other, the sum of the probabilities is 1.00, and the outcomes are mutually exclusive.

(b)

x	$P(x)$	$xP(x)$
\$ .80	.30	0.24
.90	.50	0.45
1.20	.20	0.24
		0.93

The mean is 93 cents.

(c)

x	$P(x)$	$(x - \mu)$	$(x - \mu)^2 P(x)$
\$0.80	.30	−0.13	.00507
0.90	.50	−0.03	.00045
1.20	.20	0.27	.01458
			.02010

The variance is .02010, and the standard deviation is .14 cents.

6–3 (a) It would appear reasonable because: each day the bridge is either raised or not, we are only counting how many days the bridge is raised, the probability is .2 each day, and the days are independent of each other.

(b) $(.2)^7 = .0000128$

(c) $\frac{7!}{3!(7-3)!}(.2)^3(.8)^4 = .1147$

(d) $\frac{7!}{1!(7-1)!}(.2)^1(.8)^6 = .3670$

(e) They are all in agreement.

6–4 $n = 4, \pi = .60$

(a) $P(x = 2) = .346$

(b) $P(x \leq 2) = .526$

(c) $P(x > 2) = 1 - .526$
$= .474$

6–5
$$P(3) = \frac{{}_8C_3\,{}_4C_2}{{}_{12}C_5} = \frac{\left(\frac{8!}{3!5!}\right)\left(\frac{4!}{2!2!}\right)}{\frac{12!}{5!7!}} = \frac{(56)(6)}{792} = .424$$

6–6 $\mu = 4{,}000(.0002) = 0.8$

$$P(1) = \frac{0.8^1 e^{-0.8}}{1!} = .3595$$

7 The Normal Probability Distribution

GOALS

When you have completed this chapter, you will be able to:

1. List the characteristics of the normal probability distribution.
2. Define and calculate *z* values.
3. Determine the probability that an observation is between two points on a normal distribution using the standard normal distribution.
4. Determine the probability that an observation is above (or below) a point on a normal distribution using the standard normal distribution.
5. Compare two or more observations that are on different probability distributions.
6. Use the normal probability distribution to approximate the binomial probability distribution.

If 95 percent of the international flights in U.S. airports are cleared in 45 minutes, we can assume 5 percent take longer to clear. Assuming that the distribution is approximately normal and the standard deviation of the time to clear an international flight is 5 minutes, what is the mean time to clear a flight? (See Goal 5 and Exercise 51.)

Introduction

Chapter 6 deals with three families of *discrete* probability distributions: the binomial distribution, the hypergeometric distribution, and the Poisson distribution. Recall that these distributions are based on discrete random variables, which can assume only specified values. For example, the number of correct answers on a 10-question examination can only be 0, 1, 2, 3, . . . , 10. There cannot be a negative number of correct answers, such as −7, nor can there be 7¼ or 15 correct answers.

We will continue our study of probability distributions in this chapter by examining a very important *continuous* probability distribution, namely, the **normal probability distribution.** As noted in the preceding chapter, a continuous random variable is one that can assume an *infinite* number of possible values within a specified range. It usually results from measuring something, such as the weight of an individual. The weight might be 162.0 pounds, 162.1 pounds, 162.12 pounds, and so on, depending on the accuracy of the scale. Other continuous random variables are the life expectancy of alkaline batteries, the volume of a shipping container, and the weight of impurities in a steel ingot.

The probability distributions of the life expectancies of some products, such as batteries, tires, and light bulbs, tend to follow a "normal" pattern. So do the weights of boxes of Kellogg's Special K cereal, the lengths of rolls of aluminum, and other variables measured on a continuous scale.

In this chapter the main characteristics of a normal probability distribution and the normal curve are examined first. Then the **standard normal distribution** and its uses are presented. Finally, we look at how the normal distribution is used to estimate binomial probabilities.

The Family of Normal Probability Distributions

The normal probability distribution and its accompanying normal curve have the following characteristics:

1. The normal curve is **bell-shaped** and has a single peak at the center of the distribution. The arithmetic mean, median, and mode of the distribution are equal and located at the peak. Thus, half the area under the curve is above this center point, and the other half is below it.
2. The normal probability distribution is **symmetrical** about its mean. If we cut the normal curve vertically at this central value, the two halves will be mirror images.
3. The normal curve falls off smoothly in either direction from the central value. It is **asymptotic,** meaning that the curve gets closer and closer to the X-axis but never actually touches it. That is, the "tails" of the curve extend indefinitely in both directions.

These characteristics are shown graphically in Chart 7–1, on the following page.

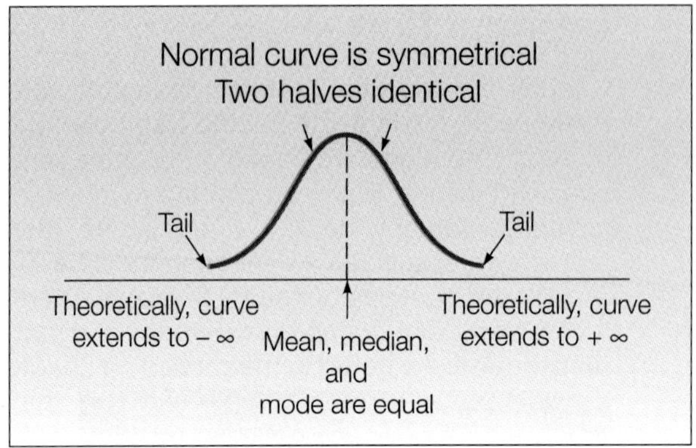

CHART 7–1 Characteristics of a Normal Distribution

There is not just one normal probability distribution, but rather a "family" of them. There is one normal probability distribution for the lengths of service of the employees in our Camden plant, where the mean is 20 years and the standard deviation is 3.1 years. There is another normal probability distribution for the lengths of service in our Dunkirk plant, where $\mu = 20$ years and $\sigma = 3.9$ years. Chart 7–2 portrays three normal distributions, where the means are the same but the standard deviations are different.

Equal means, unequal standard deviations

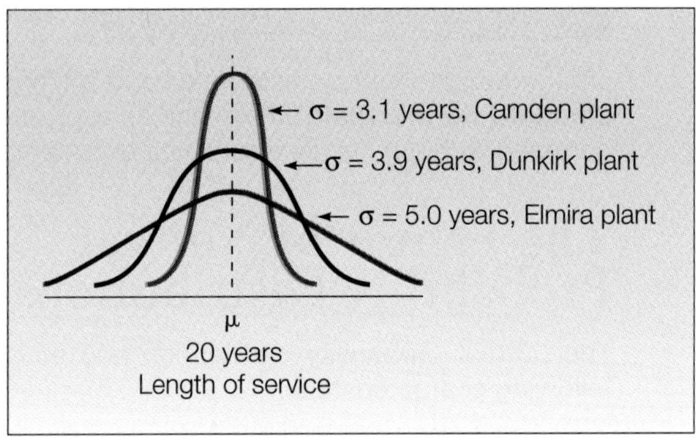

CHART 7–2 Normal Probability Distributions with Equal Means but Different Standard Deviations

Chart 7–3 shows the distribution of weights of three different cereals. The weights are normally distributed with different means but identical standard deviations.

Unequal means, equal standard deviations

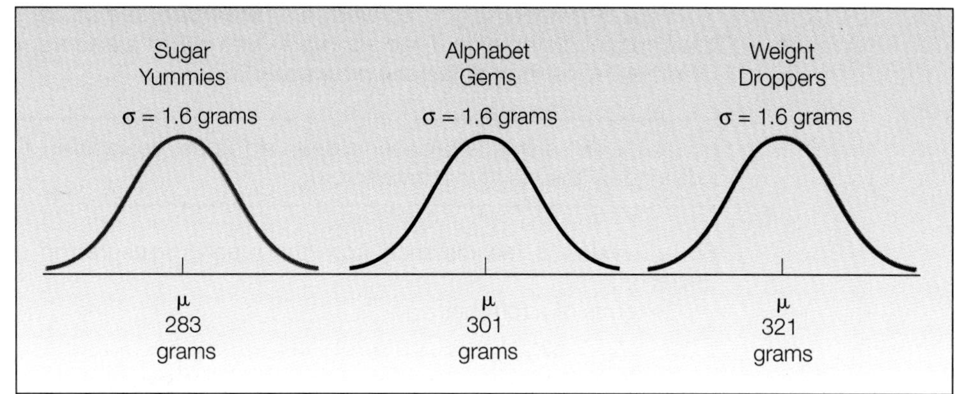

CHART 7–3 Normal Probability Distributions Having Different Means but Equal Standard Deviations

Finally, Chart 7–4 shows three normal distributions having different means and standard deviations. They show the distribution of tensile strengths, measured in pounds per square inch (psi), for three types of cables.

Unequal means, unequal standard deviations

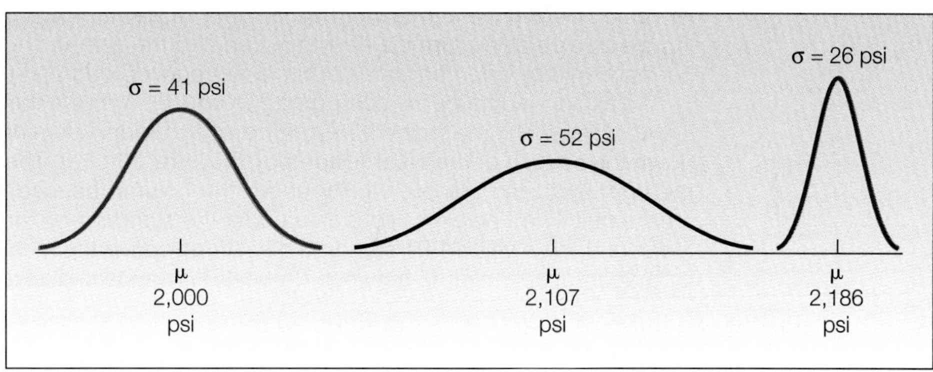

CHART 7–4 Normal Probability Distributions with Different Means and Standard Deviations

The Standard Normal Probability Distribution

There is a family of normal distributions. Each distribution may have a different mean (μ) or standard deviation (σ). The number of normal distributions is therefore unlimited. It would be physically impossible to provide a table of probabilities (such as for the binomial and Poisson) for each combination of μ and σ. Fortunately, one member of the family of normal distributions can be used for all cases where the normal distribution is applicable. It has a mean of 0 and a standard deviation of 1 and is called the **standard normal distribution.** Any normal distribution can be converted into the "standard normal distribution" by subtracting the mean from each observation and dividing by the standard deviation.

First, it is necessary to convert, or *standardize,* the actual distribution to a standard normal distribution using a *z value,* also called a *z score,* a *z statistic,* the *standard normal deviate,* or just the *normal deviate.*

> **z VALUE** The distance between a selected value, designated *X,* and the mean, μ, divided by the standard deviation, σ.

So, a *z* value is the distance from the mean, measured in units of the standard deviation.

In terms of a formula:

STANDARD NORMAL VALUE

$$z = \frac{X - \mu}{\sigma} \quad [7\text{–}1]$$

where:

- X is the value of any particular observation or measurement.
- μ is the mean of the distribution.
- σ is the standard deviation of the distribution.

As noted in the above definition, a *z* value measures the distance between a particular value of *X* and the arithmetic mean in units of the standard deviation. By determining the *z* value using formula (7–1), we can find the area or the probability under any normal curve by referring to the table in Appendix D (also on the inside back cover).

To explain, suppose we computed *z* to be 1.91. What is the area under the normal curve between the mean and *X*? A portion of Appendix D is repeated as Table 7–1. Go down the column of the table headed by the letter *z* to 1.9. Then move horizontally to the right and read the probability under the column headed 0.01. It is .4719. This means that 47.19 percent of the area under the standard normal curve is between the mean and the *X* value 1.91 standard deviations above the mean. This is the *probability* that an observation is between 0 and 1.91 standard deviations above the mean.

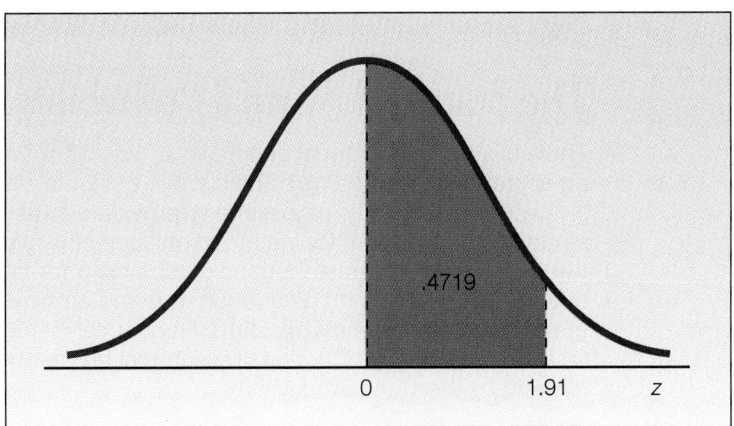

TABLE 7–1 Areas under the Normal Curve

z	0.00	0.01	0.02	0.03	0.04	0.05	...
⋮							
1.5	0.4332	0.4345	0.4357	0.4370	0.4382	0.4394	
1.6	0.4452	0.4463	0.4474	0.4484	0.4495	0.4505	
1.7	0.4554	0.4564	0.4573	0.4582	0.4591	0.4599	
1.8	0.4641	0.4649	0.4656	0.4664	0.4671	0.4678	
1.9	0.4713	0.4719	0.4726	0.4732	0.4738	0.4744	
⋮							

Applications of the Standard Normal Distribution

What is the area under the curve between the mean and X for the following z values? Check your answers against those given. Not all the values are available in Table 7–1. You will need to use Appendix D or the table located in the back endpapers of the text.

Computed z Value	Area under Curve
2.84	.4977
1.00	.3413
0.49	.1879

Now we will compute the z value given the population mean, μ, the population standard deviation, σ, and a selected X.

EXAMPLE

The weekly incomes of shift foremen in the glass industry are normally distributed with a mean of $1,000 and a standard deviation of $100. What is the z value for the income X of a foreman who earns $1,100 per week? For a foreman who earns $900 per week?

SOLUTION

Using formula (7–1), the z values for the two X values ($1,100 and $900) are:

For $X = \$1{,}100$:

$$z = \frac{X - \mu}{\sigma} = \frac{\$1{,}100 - \$1{,}000}{\$100} = 1.00$$

For $X = \$900$:

$$z = \frac{X - \mu}{\sigma} = \frac{\$900 - \$1{,}000}{\$100} = -1.00$$

The z of 1.00 indicates that a weekly income of $1,100 is one standard deviation above the mean, and a z of -1.00 shows that a $900 income is one standard deviation below the mean. Note that both incomes ($1,100 and $900) are the same distance ($100) from the mean.

SELF-REVIEW 7–1

Using the same information as in the preceding example (μ = \$1,000, σ = \$100), convert:

(a) The weekly income of \$1,225 to a standard unit (*z* value).
(b) The weekly income of \$775 to a *z* value.

Areas under the Normal Curve

Statistics in Action

An individual's skills depend on a combination of many hereditary and environmental factors, each having about the same amount of weight or influence on the skills. Thus, much like a binomial distribution with a large number of trials, many skills and attributes follow the normal distribution. For example, scores on the Scholastic Aptitude Test (SAT) are normally distributed with a mean of 1,000 and a standard deviation of 140.

Before examining various applications of the standard normal probability distribution, we will consider three areas under the normal curve that will be used extensively in the following chapters. They are also called the Empirical Rule in Chapter 4.

1. About 68 percent of the area under the normal curve is within one standard deviation of the mean. This can be written as $\mu \pm 1\sigma$.
2. About 95 percent of the area under the normal curve is within two standard deviations of the mean, written $\mu \pm 2\sigma$.
3. Practically all of the area under the normal curve is within three standard deviations of the mean, written $\mu \pm 3\sigma$.

Shown diagrammatically, using more precise percentages:

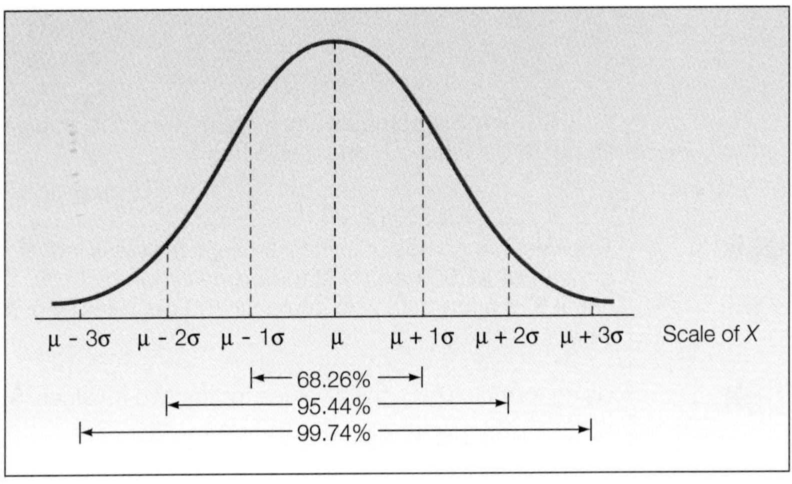

Transforming measurements to standard normal deviates changes the scale. The conversions are shown in the following graph. For example, $\mu + 1\sigma$ is converted to a *z* value of +1.00. Likewise, $\mu - 2\sigma$ is transformed to a *z* value of −2.00. Note that the center of the *z* distribution is zero, indicating no deviation from the mean, μ

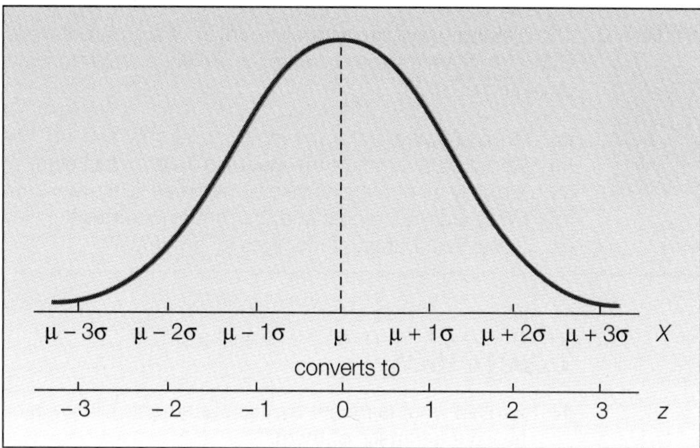

EXAMPLE

As part of their quality assurance program, the Autolite Battery Company conducts tests on battery life. For a particular D cell alkaline battery, the mean life is 19 hours. The useful life of the battery follows a normal distribution with a standard deviation of 1.2 hours. Answer the following questions.

1. About 68 percent of the batteries failed between what two values?
2. About 95 percent of the batteries failed between what two values?
3. Virtually all of the batteries failed between what two values?

SOLUTION

We can use the results of the Empirical Rule to answer these questions.

1. About 68 percent of the batteries will fail between 17.8 and 20.2 hours, found by $19.0 \pm 1(1.2)$ hours.
2. About 95 percent of the batteries will fail between 16.6 and 21.4 hours, found by $19.0 \pm 2(1.2)$ hours.
3. Virtually all failed between 15.4 and 22.6 hours, found by $19.0 \pm 3(1.2)$ hours.

This information is summarized on the following chart.

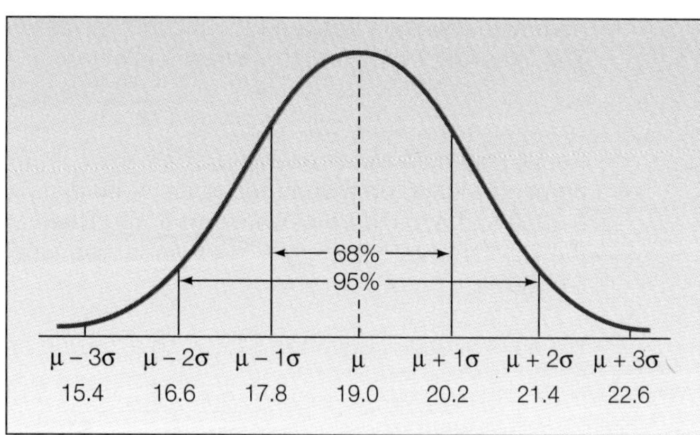

SELF–REVIEW 7–2 The distribution of the annual incomes of a group of middle-management employees at Compton Plastics approximates a normal distribution with a mean of $37,200 and a standard deviation of $800.

(a) About 68 percent of the incomes lie between what two amounts?
(b) About 95 percent of the incomes lie between what two amounts?
(c) Virtually all of the incomes lie between what two amounts?
(d) What are the median and the modal incomes?
(e) Is the distribution of incomes symmetrical?

Exercises

1. Explain what is meant by this statement: "There is not just one normal probability distribution but a 'family' of them."
2. List the major characteristics of a normal probability distribution.
3. The mean of a normal probability distribution is 500; the standard deviation is 10.
   a. About 68 percent of the observations lie between what two values?
   b. About 95 percent of the observations lie between what two values?
   c. Practically all of the observations lie between what two values?
4. The mean of a normal probability distribution is 60; the standard deviation is 5.
   a. About what percent of the observations lie between 55 and 65?
   b. About what percent of the observations lie between 50 and 70?
   c. About what percent of the observations lie between 45 and 75?
5. The Kamp family has twins, Rob and Rachel. Both Rob and Rachel graduated from college two years ago, and each is now earning $50,000 per year. Rachel works in the retail industry, where the mean salary for executives with less than 5 years' experience is $35,000 with a standard deviation of $8,000. Rob is an engineer. The mean salary for engineers with less than 5 years' experience is $60,000 with a standard deviation of $5,000. Compute the z values for both Rob and Rachel and comment on your findings.
6. A recent article in the Myrtle Beach *Sun Times* reported that the mean labor cost to repair a color TV is $90 with a standard deviation of $22. Monte's TV Sales and Service completed repairs on two sets this morning. The labor cost for the first was $75 and it was $100 for the second. Compute z values for each and comment on your findings.

(Margin answers:)
2. Bell-shaped, symmetrical, asymptotic, family of curves.
4. **a.** 68% **b.** 95% **c.** 99.7%
6. −0.68, 0.45

Finding Areas under the Normal Curve

The first application of the standard normal distribution involves finding the area in a normal distribution between the mean and a selected value, which we identify as X. The following example will illustrate the details.

EXAMPLE

Recall that in an earlier example (see page 231) we reported that the mean weekly income of a shift foreman in the glass industry is normally distributed with a mean of $1,000 and a standard deviation of $100. That is, $\mu = \$1,000$ and $\sigma = \$100$. What is the likelihood of selecting a foreman whose weekly income is between $1,000 and $1,100?

SOLUTION

We have already converted $1,100 to a z value of 1.00 using formula 7–1. To repeat:

$$z = \frac{X - \mu}{\sigma} = \frac{\$1,100 - \$1,000}{\$100} = 1.00$$

Statistics in Action

Many processes, such as filling soda bottles and canning fruit, are normally distributed. Manufacturers must guard against both over- and underfilling. If they put too much in the can or bottle, they are giving away their product. If they put too little in, the customer may feel cheated and the government may question the label description. "Control Charts," described in Chapter 17, with limits drawn three standard deviations above and below the mean, are routinely used to monitor this type of production process.

The probability associated with a z of 1.00 is available in Appendix D. A portion of Appendix D follows. To locate the probability, go down the left column to 1.0, and then move horizontally to the column headed .00. The value is .3413.

z	.00	.01	.02
⋮	⋮	⋮	⋮
0.7	.2580	.2611	.2642
0.8	.2881	.2910	.2939
0.9	.3159	.3186	.3212
1.0	.3413	.3438	.3461
1.1	.3643	.3665	.3686
⋮	⋮	⋮	⋮

The area under the normal curve between $1,000 and $1,100 is .3413. We could also say 34.13 percent of the shift foremen in the glass industry earn between $1,000 and $1,100 weekly, or the likelihood of selecting a foreman and finding his or her income is between $1,000 and $1,100 is .3413.

This information is summarized in the following chart.

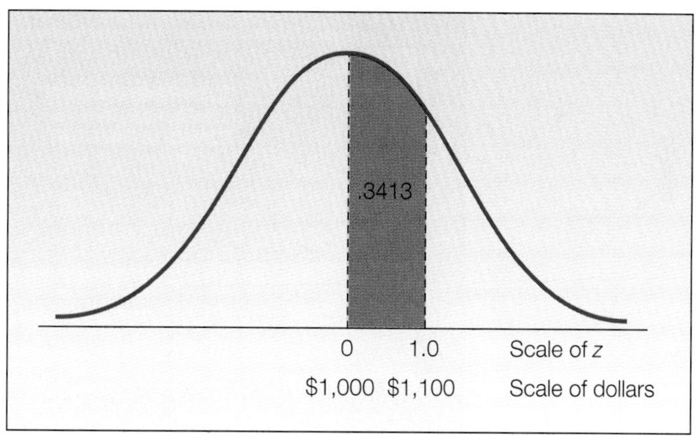

In the example just completed, we are interested in the probability between the mean and a given value. Let's change the question. Instead of wanting to know the probability of selecting a foreman who earned between $1,000 and $1,100, suppose we wanted the probability of selecting a foreman who earned less than $1,100. The method of solution is the same. We find the probability of selecting a foreman who earns between $1,000, the mean, and $1,100. This probability is .3413. Next, recall that half the area, or probability, is above the mean and half is below. So the probability of selecting a foreman earning less than $1,000 is .5000. Finally, we add the two probabilities, so .3413 + .5000 = .8413. About 84 percent of the foremen in the glass industry earn less than $1,100 per month. See the following diagram.

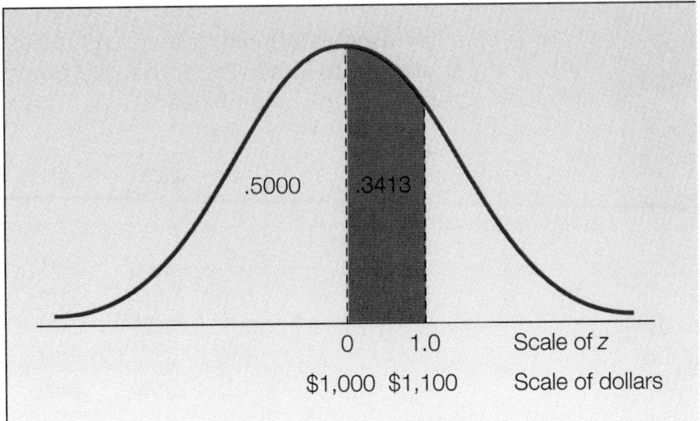

Excel will calculate this probability. See the following output. The necessary steps are shown in the **Computer Commands** section at the end of the chapter.

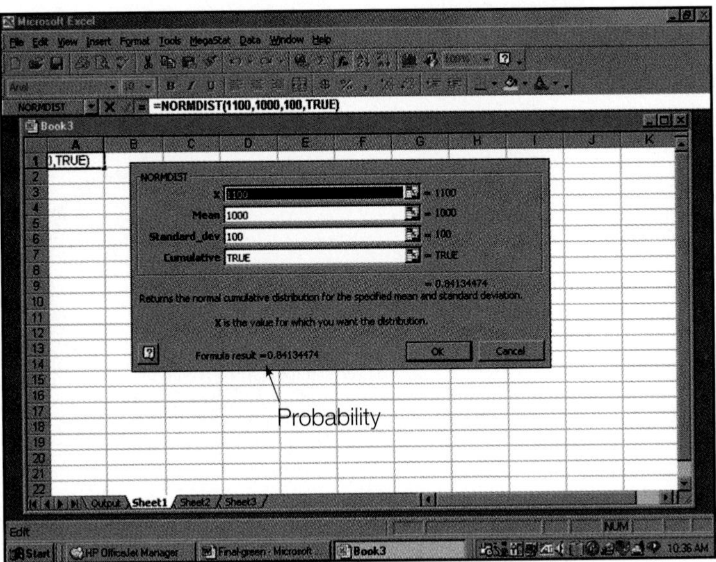

EXAMPLE

Refer to the information regarding the weekly income of shift foremen in the glass industry. The distribution of weekly incomes follows the normal distribution, with a mean of $1,000 and a standard deviation of $100. What is the probability of selecting a shift foreman in the glass industry whose income is:

1. Between $790 and $1,000?
2. Less than $790?

SOLUTION

We begin by finding the z value corresponding to a weekly income of $790. From formula 7–1:

$$z = \frac{X - \mu}{\sigma} = \frac{\$790 - \$1,000}{\$100} = -2.10$$

See Appendix D. Move down the left margin to the row 2.1 and across that row to the column headed 0.00. The value is .4821. So the area under a normal curve corresponding to a z value of 2.10 is .4821. However, because the normal distribution is symmetric, the area between 0 and a negative z is the same as that between 0 and z. The likelihood of finding a foreman earning between $790 and $1,000 is .4821.

z	0.00	0.01	0.02
⋮	⋮	⋮	⋮
2.0	.4772	.4778	.4783
2.1	.4821	.4826	.4830
2.2	.4861	.4864	.4868
2.3	.4893	.4896	.4898
⋮	⋮	⋮	⋮

The mean divides the normal curve into two identical halves. The area under the half to the left of the mean is .5000, and the area to the right is also .5000. Because the area under the curve between $790 and $1,000 is .4821, the area below $790 is .0179, found by .5000 − .4821.

This means that about 48 percent of the foremen have weekly incomes between $790 and $1,000. Further, we can anticipate that somewhat fewer than 2 percent earn less than $790 per week. This information is summarized in the following diagram.

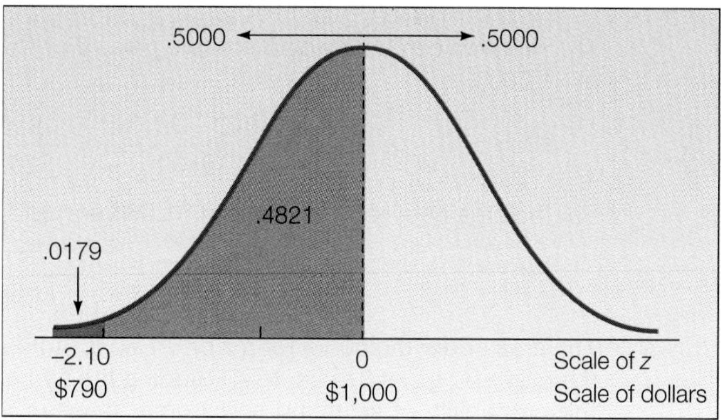

SELF-REVIEW 7–3 The employees of Cartwright Manufacturing are awarded efficiency ratings. The distribution of the ratings approximates a normal distribution. The mean is 400, the standard deviation 50.

(a) What is the area under the normal curve between 400 and 482?
(b) What is the area under the normal curve for ratings greater than 482?
(c) Show the facets of this problem in a chart.

Exercises

7. A normal population has a mean of 20.0 and a standard deviation of 4.0.
   a. Compute the z value associated with 25.0.
   b. What proportion of the population is between 20.0 and 25.0?
   c. What proportion of the population is less than 18.0?

8. A normal population has a mean of 12.2 and a standard deviation of 2.5.
   a. Compute the z value associated with 14.3.
   b. What proportion of the population is between 12.2 and 14.3?
   c. What proportion of the population is less than 10.0?

8. a. .84
   b. .2995
   c. .1894

9. A recent study of the hourly wages of maintenance crews for major airlines showed that the mean hourly salary was \$16.50, with a standard deviation of \$3.50. If we select a crew member at random, what is the probability the crew member earns:
   a. Between \$16.50 and \$20.00 per hour?
   b. More than \$20.00 per hour?
   c. Less than \$15.00 per hour?
10. The mean of a normal distribution is 400 pounds. The standard deviation is 10 pounds.
   a. What is the area between 415 pounds and the mean of 400 pounds?
   b. What is the area between the mean and 395 pounds?
   c. What is the probability of selecting a value at random and discovering that it has a value of less than 395 pounds?

10. a. .4332
    b. .1915
    c. .3085

A second application of the standard normal distribution involves combining two areas, or probabilities. One of the areas is to the right of the mean and the other to the left.

EXAMPLE

Recall the distribution of weekly incomes of shift foremen in the glass industry. The weekly incomes follow the normal distribution, with a mean of \$1,000 and a standard deviation of \$100. What is the area under this normal curve between \$840 and \$1,200?

SOLUTION

The problem can be divided into two parts. For the area between \$840 and the mean of \$1,000:

$$z = \frac{\$840 - \$1{,}000}{\$100} = \frac{-\$160}{\$100} = -1.60$$

For the area between the mean of \$1,000 and \$1,200:

$$z = \frac{\$1{,}200 - \$1{,}000}{\$100} = \frac{\$200}{\$100} = 2.00$$

The area under the curve for a z of -1.60 is .4452 (from Appendix D). The area under the curve for a z of 2.00 is .4772. Adding the two areas: $.4452 + .4772 = .9224$. Thus, the probability of selecting an income between \$840 and \$1,200 is .9224. In other words, 92.24 percent of the foremen have weekly incomes between \$840 and \$1,200. Shown in a diagram:

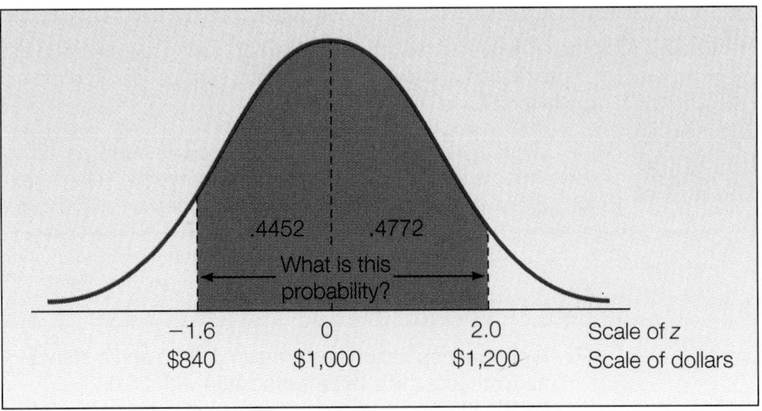

Another application of the normal distribution involves determining area between values on the *same* side of the mean.

EXAMPLE

Returning to the weekly incomes of shift foremen in the glass industry example ($\mu = \$1{,}000$, $\sigma = \$100$), what is the area under the normal curve between \$1,150 and \$1,250?

SOLUTION

The problem is again separated into two parts, and formula (7–1) is used. First, we find the z value associated with a weekly salary of \$1,250:

$$z = \frac{\$1{,}250 - \$1{,}000}{\$100} = 2.50$$

Next we find the z value for a weekly salary of \$1,150:

$$z = \frac{\$1{,}150 - \$1{,}000}{\$100} = 1.50$$

From Appendix D the area associated with a z value of 2.50 is .4938. So the probability of a weekly salary between \$1,000 and \$1,250 is .4938. Similarly, the area associated with a z value of 1.50 is .4332, so the probability of a weekly salary between \$1,000 and \$1,150 is .4332. The probability of a weekly salary between \$1,150 and \$1,250 is found by subtracting the area associated with a z value of 1.50 (.4332) from that associated with a z of 2.50 (.4938). Thus, the probability of a weekly salary between \$1,150 and \$1,250 is .0606. Shown in a diagram:

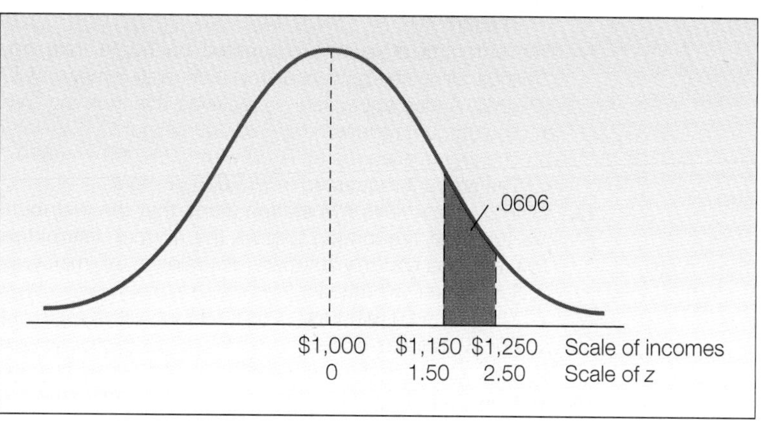

In brief, there are only four situations in which you may wish to find the area under the standard normal distribution.

1. If you wish to find the area between 0 and z (or $-z$), then you can look up the value directly in the table.
2. If you wish to find the area beyond z or ($-z$), then locate the probability of z in the table and subtract that value from .5000.
3. If you wish to find the area between two points on different sides of the mean, determine the z values and add the corresponding areas.
4. If you wish to find the area between two points on the same side of the mean, determine the z values and subtract the smaller area from the larger.

SELF-REVIEW 7–4 Refer to the previous example, where the distribution of weekly incomes follows the normal distribution with a mean of $1,000 and the standard deviation is $100.

(a) What percent of the shift foremen earn a weekly income between $750 and $1,225? Draw a normal curve and shade the desired area on your diagram.
(b) What percent of the shift foremen earn a weekly income between $1,100 and $1,225? Draw a normal curve and shade the desired area on your diagram.

Exercises

11. A normal distribution has a mean of 50 and a standard deviation of 4.
    a. Compute the probability of a value between 44.0 and 55.0.
    b. Compute the probability of a value greater than 55.0.
    c. Compute the probability of a value between 52.0 and 55.0.
12. A normal population has a mean of 80.0 and a standard deviation of 14.0.
    a. Compute the probability of a value between 75.0 and 90.0.
    b. Compute the probability of a value 75.0 or less.
    c. Compute the probability of a value between 55.0 and 70.0.

12. a. .4017
b. .3594
c. .2022

13. A cola-dispensing machine is set to dispense on average 7.00 ounces of cola per cup. The standard deviation is 0.10 ounces. The distribution amounts dispensed follows a normal distribution.
    a. What is the probability that the machine will dispense between 7.10 and 7.25 ounces of cola?
    b. What is the probability that the machine will dispense 7.25 ounces of cola or more?
    c. What is the probability that the machine will dispense between 6.80 and 7.25 ounces of cola?
14. The amounts of money requested on home loan applications at Down River Federal Savings follow the normal distribution, with a mean of $70,000 and a standard deviation of $20,000. A loan application is received this morning. What is the probability:
    a. The amount requested is $80,000 or more?
    b. The amount requested is between $65,000 and $80,000?
    c. The amount requested is $65,000 or more?

14. a. .3085
b. .2902
c. .5987

15. WNAE, an all-news AM station, finds that the distribution of the lengths of time listeners are tuned to the station follows the normal distribution. The mean of the distribution is 15.0 minutes and the standard deviation is 3.5 minutes. What is the probability that a particular listener will tune in:
    a. More than 20 minutes?
    b. For 20 minutes or less?
    c. Between 10 and 12 minutes?
16. The mean starting salary for college graduates in the spring of 2000 was $31,280. Assume that the distribution of starting salaries follows the normal distribution with a standard deviation of $3,300. What percent of the graduates have starting salaries:
    a. Between $30,000 and $35,000?
    b. More than $40,000?
    c. Between $35,000 and $40,000?

16. a. .5225
b. .0041
c. .1251

Previous examples require finding the percent of the observations located between two observations or the percent of the observations above, or below, a particular observation X. A further application of the normal distribution involves finding the value of the observation X when the percent above or below the observation is given.

EXAMPLE

A tire manufacturer wishes to set a minimum mileage guarantee on its new MX100 tire. Tests reveal the mean mileage is 67,900 with a standard deviation of 2,050 miles and a normal distribution. The manufacturer wants to set the minimum guaranteed mileage so that no more than 4 percent of the tires will have to be replaced. What minimum guaranteed mileage should the manufacturer announce?

SOLUTION

The facets of this case are shown in the following diagram, where X represents the minimum guaranteed mileage.

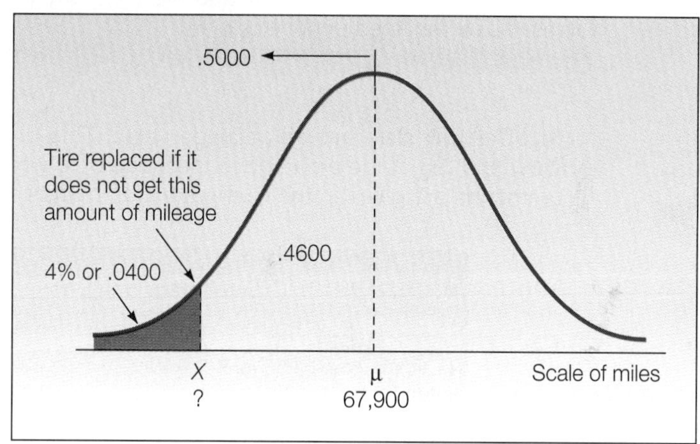

Inserting these values in formula (7–1) for z:

$$z = \frac{X - \mu}{\sigma} = \frac{X - 67{,}900}{2{,}050}$$

There are two unknowns, z and X. To find z, notice the area under the normal curve to the left of μ is .5000. The area between μ and X is .4600, found by .5000 − .0400. Now refer to Appendix D. Search the body of the table for the area closest to .4600. The closest area is .4599. Move to the margins from this value and read the z value of 1.75. Because the value is to the left of the mean, it is actually −1.75. These steps are summarized in Table 7–2.

TABLE 7–2 Selected Areas under the Normal Curve

z	.03	.04	.05	.06
⋮				
1.5	.4370	.4382	.4394	.4406
1.6	.4484	.4495	.4505	.4515
1.7	.4582	.4591	.4599	.4608
1.8	.4664	.4671	.4678	.4686

Knowing that the distance between μ and X is -1.75σ, we can now solve for X (the minimum guaranteed mileage):

$$z = \frac{X - 67{,}900}{2{,}050}$$

$$-1.75 = \frac{X - 67{,}900}{2{,}050}$$

$$-1.75(2{,}050) = X - 67{,}900$$

$$X = 67{,}900 - 1.75(2{,}050) = 64{,}312$$

So the manufacturer can advertise that it will replace for free any tire that wears out before it reaches 64,312 miles, and the company will know that only 4 percent of the tires will be replaced under this plan.

MegaStat will also find the mileage value. This output indicates .04 of the area is below and .96 of the area above the value of x, which is highlighted. The necessary commands are given in the Computer Commands section at the end of the chapter.

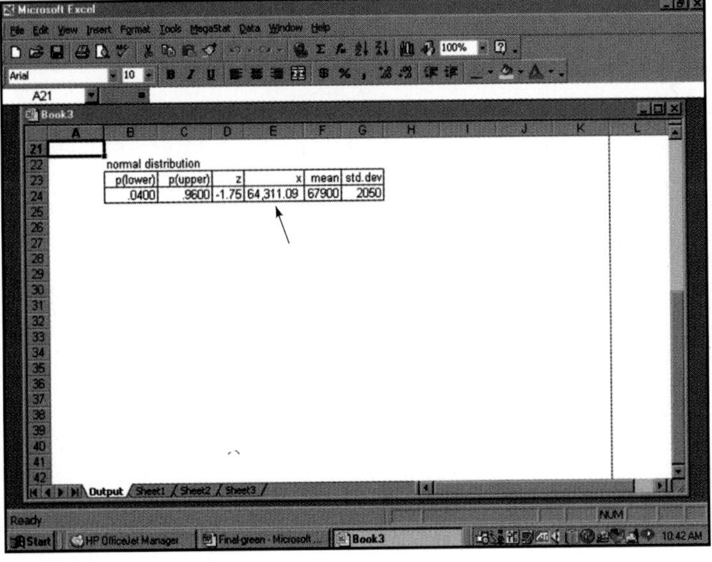

SELF-REVIEW 7–5 An analysis of the final test scores for Introduction to Business reveals the scores follow the normal distribution. The mean of the distribution is 75 and the standard deviation is 8. The professor wants to award an A to students whose score is in the highest 10 percent. What is the dividing point for those students who earn an A and those earning a B?

Exercises

17. A normal distribution has a mean of 50 and a standard deviation of 4. Determine the value below which 95 percent of the observations will occur.

18. 68.24

18. A normal distribution has a mean of 80 and a standard deviation of 14. Determine the value above which 80 percent of the values will occur.

19. The amounts dispensed by a cola machine follow the normal distribution with a mean of 7 ounces and a standard deviation of 0.10 ounces per cup. How much cola is dispensed in the largest 1 percent of the cups?

20. Refer to Exercise 14, where the amount requested for home loans followed the normal distribution with a mean of $70,000 and a standard deviation of $20,000.

20. a. $107,600
b. $44,400

a. How much is requested on the largest 3 percent of the loans?
b. How much is requested on the smallest 10 percent of the loans?

21. Assume that the mean hourly cost to operate a commercial airplane follows the normal distribution with a mean $2,100 per hour and a standard deviation of $250. What is the operating cost for the lowest 3 percent of the airplanes?

22. 1571

22. The monthly sales of mufflers in the Richmond, VA area follow the normal distribution with a mean of 1200 and a standard deviation of 225. The manufacturer would like to establish inventory levels such that there is only a 5 percent chance of running out of stock. Where should the manufacturer set the inventory levels?

The Normal Approximation to the Binomial

Chapter 6 describes the binomial probability distribution, which is a discrete distribution. The table of binomial probabilities in Appendix A goes successively from an n of 1 to an n of 20, and then to $n = 25$. If a problem involved taking a sample of 60, generating a binomial distribution for that large a number would be very time consuming. A more efficient approach is to apply the *normal approximation to the binomial.*

Using the normal distribution (a continuous distribution) as a substitute for a binomial distribution (a discrete distribution) for large values of n seems reasonable because, as n increases, a binomial distribution gets closer and closer to a normal distribution. Chart 7–5 depicts the change in the shape of a binomial distribution with $\pi = .50$ from an n of 1, to an n of 3, to an n of 20. Notice how the case where $n = 20$ approximates the shape of the normal distribution. That is, compare the case where $n = 20$ to the normal curve in Chart 7–1 on page 228.

When to use the normal approximation

When can we use the normal approximation to the binomial? The normal probability distribution is a good approximation to the binomial probability distribution when $n\pi$ and $n(1 - \pi)$ are both at least 5. However, before we apply the normal approximation, we must make sure that our distribution of interest is in fact a binomial distribution. Recall from Chapter 6 that four criteria must be met:

1. There are only two mutually exclusive outcomes to an experiment: a "success" and a "failure."

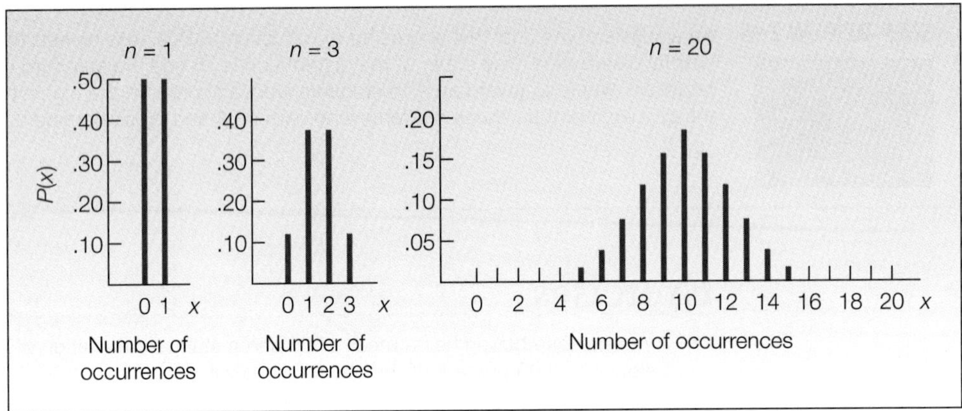

CHART 7–5 Binomial Distributions for an n of 1, 3, and 20, Where $\pi = .50$

2. The distribution results from counting the number of successes in a fixed number of trials.
3. Each trial is independent.
4. The probability, π, remains the same from trial to trial.

Continuity Correction Factor

To show the application of the normal approximation to the binomial and the need for a correction factor, suppose the management of the Santoni Pizza Restaurant found that 70 percent of their new customers return for another meal. For a week in which 80 new (first-time) customers dined at Santoni's, what is the probability that 60 or more will return for another meal?

Notice the binomial conditions are met: (1) There are only two possible outcomes—a customer either returns for another meal or does not return. (2) We can count the number of successes, meaning, for example, that 57 of the 80 customers return. (3) The trials are independent, meaning that if the 34th person returns for a second meal, that does not affect whether the 58th person returns. (4) The probability of a customer returning remains at .70 for all 80 customers.

Therefore, we could use the binomial formula (6–3)

$$P(x) = {}_nC_x\,(\pi)^x\,(1 - \pi)^{n-x}$$

To find the probability 60 or more customers return for another pizza, we need to first find the probability exactly 60 customers return. That is:

$$P(x = 60) = {}_{80}C_{60}\,(.70)^{60}\,(1 - .70)^{20} = .063$$

Next we find the probability that exactly 61 customers return. It is:

$$P(x = 61) = {}_{80}C_{61}\,(.70)^{61}\,(1 - .70)^{19} = .048$$

We continue this process until we have the probability all 80 customers return. Finally, we add the probabilities from 60 to 80. Solving the above problem in this manner is tedious. We can also use a computer software package such as MINITAB or Excel to find the various probabilities. Listed on the next page are the binomial probabilities for $n = 80$, $\pi = .70$, and x, the number of customers returning, ranging from 43 to 68. The probability of any number of customers less than 43 or more than 68 returning is less than .001.

Number Returning	Probability	Number Returning	Probability
43	0.001	56	0.097
44	0.002	57	0.095
45	0.003	58	0.088
46	0.006	59	0.077
47	0.009	60	0.063
48	0.015	61	0.048
49	0.023	62	0.034
50	0.033	63	0.023
51	0.045	64	0.014
52	0.059	65	0.008
53	0.072	66	0.004
54	0.084	67	0.002
55	0.093	68	0.001

We can find the probability of 60 or more returning by summing 0.063 + 0.048 + · · · + 0.001, which is 0.197. However, a look at the plot below shows the similarity of this distribution to a normal distribution. All we need do is "smooth out" the discrete probabilities into a continuous distribution. Furthermore, working with a normal distribution will involve far fewer calculations than working with the binomial.

The trick is to let the discrete probability for 56 customers be represented by an area under the continuous curve between 55.5 and 56.5. Then let the probability for 57 customers be represented by an area between 56.5 and 57.5 and so on. This is just the opposite of rounding off the numbers to a whole number.

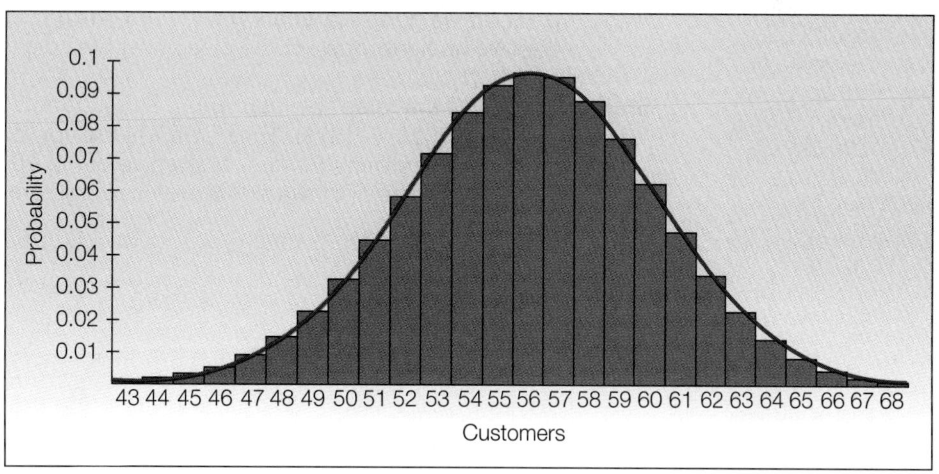

Because we use the normal distribution to determine the binomial probability of 60 or more successes, we must subtract, in this case, .5 from 60. The value .5 is called the **continuity correction factor.** This small adjustment must be made because a continuous distribution (the normal distribution) is being used to approximate a discrete distribution (the binomial distribution). Subtracting, $60 - .5 = 59.5$.

Statistics in Action

The heights of adults approximate a normal distribution, but those individuals who are very tall can cause design problems. For example, Shaquille O'Neal, a professional basketball player with the Los Angeles Lakers, is 7′2″ tall. The height of the standard doorway is 6′8″, so Shaquille and most other NBA players duck to get into most rooms.

As another example, the driver's seat in most vehicles is set to comfortably fit a person who is at least 159 cm (62.5″) tall. The distribution of heights of adult women is approximately a normal distribution with a mean of 161.5 cm and a standard deviation of 6.3 cm. Thus about 35 percent of adult women will not fit comfortably in the driver's seat.

CONTINUITY CORRECTION FACTOR The value .5 subtracted or added, depending on the question, to a selected value when a discrete probability distribution is approximated by a continuous probability distribution.

How to Apply the Correction Factor

Only four cases may arise. These cases are:

1. For the probability *at least* X occur, use the area *above* $(X - .5)$.
2. For the probability that *more than* X occur, use the area *above* $(X + .5)$.
3. For the probability that X *or fewer* occur, use the area *below* $(X + .5)$.
4. For the probability that *fewer than* X occur, use the area below $(X - .5)$.

To use the normal distribution to approximate the probability that 60 or more first-time Santoni customers out of 80 will return, follow the procedure shown below.

Step 1. Find the z corresponding to an X of 59.5 using formula (7–1), and formulas (6–4) and (6–5) for the mean and the variance of a binomial distribution:

$$\mu = n\pi = 80(.70) = 56$$

$$\sigma^2 = n\pi(1 - \pi) = 80(.70)(1 - .70) = 16.8$$

$$\sigma = \sqrt{16.8} = 4.10$$

$$z = \frac{X - \mu}{\sigma} = \frac{59.5 - 56}{4.10} = 0.85$$

Step 2. Determine the area under the normal curve between a μ of 56 and an X of 59.5. From step 1, we know that the z value corresponding to 59.5 is 0.85. So we go to Appendix D and read down the left margin to 0.8, and then we go horizontally to the area under the column headed by .05. That area is .3023.

Step 3. Calculate the area beyond 59.5 by subtracting .3023 from .5000 (.5000 − .3023 = .1977). Thus, .1977 is the approximate probability that 60 or more first-time Santoni customers out of 80 will return for another meal. The facets of this problem are shown graphically:

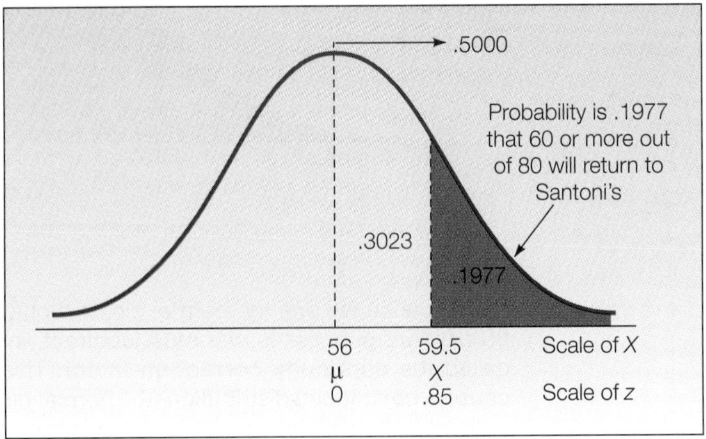

No doubt you will agree that using the normal approximation to the binomial is a more efficient method of estimating the probability of 60 or more first-time customers returning. The result compares favorably with that computed on page 245, using the exact distribution. The probability using the binomial distribution is .197, whereas the probability using the normal approximation is .1977.

SELF-REVIEW 7–6

A study by Great Southern Home Insurance revealed that none of the stolen goods were recovered by the homeowners in 80 percent of reported thefts.

(a) During a period in which 200 thefts occurred, what is the probability that no stolen goods were recovered in 170 or more of the robberies?
(b) During a period in which 200 thefts occurred, what is the probability that no stolen goods were recovered in 150 or more robberies?

Exercises

23. Assume a binomial probability distribution with $n = 50$ and $\pi = .25$. Compute the following:
  a. The mean and standard deviation of the random variable.
  b. The probability that x is 15 or more.
  c. The probability that x is 10 or less.

24. Assume a binomial probability distribution with $n = 40$ and $\pi = .55$. Compute the following:
  a. The mean and standard deviation of the random variable.
  b. The probability that x is 25 or greater.
  c. The probability that x is 15 or less.
  d. The probability that x is between 15 and 25 inclusive.

24. a. $\mu = 22$, $\sigma = 3.15$
b. .2148
c. .0197
d. .8578

25. Dottie's Tax Service specializes in federal tax returns for professional clients, such as physicians, dentists, accountants, and lawyers. A recent audit by the IRS of the returns she prepared indicated that an error was made on 5 percent of the returns she prepared last year. Assuming this rate continues into this year and she prepares 60 returns, what is the probability that she makes errors on:
  a. More than six returns?
  b. At least six returns?
  c. Exactly six returns?

26. Shorty's Muffler advertises they can install a new muffler in 30 minutes or less. However, the work standards department at corporate headquarters recently conducted a study and found that 20 percent of the mufflers were not installed in 30 minutes or less. The Maumee branch installed 50 mufflers last month. If the corporate report is correct:
  a. How many of the installations at the Maumee branch would you expect to take more than 30 minutes?
  b. What is the likelihood that fewer than eight installations took more than 30 minutes?
  c. What is the likelihood that eight or fewer installations took more than 30 minutes?
  d. What is the likelihood that exactly 8 of the 50 installations took more than 30 minutes?

26. a. 10
b. .1894
c. .2981
d. .1087

27. A study conducted by the nationally known Taurus Health Club revealed that 30 percent of its new members are significantly overweight. A membership drive in a metropolitan area resulted in 500 new members.
  a. It has been suggested that the normal approximation to the binomial be used to determine the probability that 175 or more of the new members are significantly overweight. Does this problem qualify as a binomial problem? Explain.
  b. What is the probability that 175 or more of the new members are significantly overweight?
  c. What is the probability that 140 or more new members are significantly overweight?

28. Research on new juvenile delinquents revealed that 38 percent of them committed another crime.
  a. What is the probability that of the last 100 new juvenile delinquents put on probation, 30 or more will commit another crime?
  b. What is the probability that 40 or fewer of the delinquents will commit another crime?
  c. What is the probability that between 30 and 40 of the delinquents will commit another crime?

28. a. .9599
b. .6985
c. .6584

Chapter Outline

I. The normal distribution is a continuous probability distribution with the following characteristics.
   A. It is bell-shaped and the mean, median, and mode are equal.
   B. It is symmetrical.
   C. It is asymptotic, meaning the curve approaches but never touches the *X*-axis.
   D. It is completely described by the mean and standard deviation.
   E. There is a family of normal distributions. Each time the mean or standard deviation changes, a new distribution is created.

II. The standard normal distribution is a particular normal distribution.
   A. It has a mean of 0 and a standard deviation of 1.
   B. Any normal distribution can be converted to the standard normal distribution by the following formula.

$$z = \frac{X - \mu}{\sigma} \qquad \textbf{[7–1]}$$

   C. By standardizing a normal distribution, we can report the distance from the mean in units of the standard deviation.

III. The normal distribution can approximate a binomial distribution under certain conditions.
   A. $n\pi$ and $n(1 - \pi)$ must both be at least 5.
      1. n is the number of observations.
      2. π is the probability of a success.
   B. The four conditions for a binomial distribution are:
      1. There are only two possible outcomes.
      2. π remains the same from trial to trial.
      3. The trials are independent.
      4. The distribution results from a count of the number of successes in a fixed number of trials.
   C. The mean and variance of a binomial distribution are computed as follows:

$$\mu = n\pi$$

$$\sigma^2 = n\pi(1 - \pi)$$

   D. The continuity correction factor of .5 is used to extend the continuous value of *X* one-half unit in either direction. This correction compensates for estimating a discrete distribution by a continuous distribution.

Chapter Exercises

29. The net sales and the number of employees for aluminum fabricators with similar characteristics are organized into frequency distributions. Both are normally distributed. For the net sales, the mean is $180 million and the standard deviation is $25 million. For the number of employees, the mean is 1,500 and the standard deviation is 120. Clarion Fabricators had sales of $170 million and 1,850 employees.
   a. Convert Clarion's sales and number of employees to *z* values.
   b. Locate the two *z* values.
   c. Compare Clarion's sales and number of employees with those of the other fabricators.

30. The accounting department at Weston Materials, Inc., a national manufacturer of unattached garages, reports that it takes two construction workers a mean of 32 hours and a standard deviation of 2 hours to erect the Red Barn model. Assume the assembly times follow the normal distribution.
   a. Determine the *z* values for 29 and 34 hours. What percent of the garages take between 32 hours and 34 hours to erect?
   b. What percent of the garages take between 29 hours and 34 hours to erect?
   c. What percent of the garages take 28.7 hours or less to erect?
   d. Of the garages, 5 percent take how many hours or more to erect?

30. a. −1.5, 1.0, .3413
b. .7745
c. .0495
d. 35.3

31. A recent report in *USA Today* indicated a typical family of four spends \$490 per month on food. Assume the distribution of food expenditures for a family of four follows the normal distribution, with a mean of \$490 and a standard deviation of \$90.

a. What percent of the families spend more than \$30 but less than \$490 per month on food?

b. What percent of the families spend less than \$430 per month on food?

c. What percent spend between \$430 and \$600 per month on food?

d. What percent spend between \$500 and \$600 per month on food?

32. A study of long distance phone calls made from the corporate offices of a large company reveals the calls follow the normal distribution. The mean length of time per call was 4.2 minutes and the standard deviation was 0.60 minutes.

a. What fraction of the calls last between 4.2 and 5 minutes?

b. What fraction of the calls last more than 5 minutes?

c. What fraction of the calls last between 5 and 6 minutes?

d. What fraction of the calls last between 4 and 6 minutes?

e. As part of her report to the president the Director of Communications would like to report the length of the longest (in duration) 4 percent of the calls. What is this time?

32. a. .4082
b. .0918
c. .0905
d. .6280
e. 5.25

33. Shaver Manufacturing, Inc. offers dental insurance to its employees. A recent study by the Human Resource Director shows the annual cost per employee per year followed the normal distribution, with a mean of \$1,280 and a standard deviation of \$420 per year.

a. What fraction of the employees cost more than \$1,500 per year for dental expenses?

b. What fraction of the employees cost between \$1,500 and \$2,000 per year?

c. Estimate the percent that did not have any dental expense.

d. What was the cost for the 10 percent of employees that incurred the highest dental expense?

34. The Director of Emergency Medicine at Big Mountain Medical Services is studying patient waiting time. Waiting time is defined as the time from when a patient enters the facility until seen by a physician. The study indicates the waiting time follows a normal distribution with a mean of 22 minutes and a standard deviation of 8 minutes.

a. What fraction of the patients is seen in between 15 and 22 minutes?

b. What fraction is seen in less than 15 minutes?

c. What fraction is seen in more than 15 minutes but less than 32 minutes?

d. What fraction is seen in more than 25 minutes but less than 32 minutes?

e. Five percent of the patients are seen in how many minutes or less? That is, how quickly are 5 percent of the patients seen?

34. a. .3106
b. .1894
c. .7050
d. .2464
e. 8.8

35. A study of Furniture Wholesales, Inc. regarding the payment of invoices reveals the time from billing until payment is received follows the normal distribution. The mean time until payment is received is 20 days and the standard deviation is 5 days.

a. What percent of the invoices are paid within 15 days of receipt?

b. What percent of the invoices are paid in more than 28 days?

c. What percent of the invoices are paid in more than 15 days but less than 28 days?

d. The management of Furniture Wholesales wants to encourage their customers to pay their monthly invoices as soon as possible. Therefore, it announced that a 2 percent reduction in price would be in effect for customers who pay within 7 working days of the receipt of the invoice. What percent of customers will earn this discount?

36. The annual commissions earned by sales representatives of Machine Products Inc., a manufacturer of light machinery, follow the normal distribution. The mean yearly amount earned is \$40,000 and the standard deviation is \$5,000.

a. What percent of the sales representatives earn more than \$42,000 per year?

b. What percent of the sales representatives earn between \$32,000 and \$42,000?

c. What percent of the sales representatives earn between \$32,000 and \$35,000?

d. The sales manager wants to award the sales representatives who earn the largest commissions a bonus of \$1,000. He can award a bonus to 20 percent of the representatives. What is the cutoff point between those who earn a bonus and those who do not?

36. a. .3446
b. .6006
c. .1039
d. \$44,200

37. The weights of cans of Monarch pears follow the normal distribution with a mean of 1,000 grams and a standard deviation of 50 grams. Calculate the percentage of the cans that weigh:

a. Less than 860 grams.

b. Between 1,055 and 1,100 grams.

c. Between 860 and 1,055 grams.

38. a. 39.44%
b. 10.56%
c. 3.36%
d. 1739.6

40. a. .47%
b. 12.41%
c. 84.13%
d. No trucks traveled more than 70,000.

42. a. 26.43%
b. 26.43%
c. Continuous distribution.
d. About 4.26%.
e. 45.24

44. a. .0262
b. .9441
c. .0297
d. .8882

38. The number of passengers on the *Queen Elizabeth II* during one-week cruises in the Caribbean follows the normal distribution. The mean number of passengers per cruise is 1,820 and the standard deviation is 120.
   a. What percent of the cruises will have between 1,820 and 1,970 passengers?
   b. What percent of the cruises will have 1,970 passengers or more?
   c. What percent of the cruises will have 1,600 or fewer passengers?
   d. How many passengers are on the cruises with the fewest 25 percent of passengers?
39. Management at Gordon Electronics is considering adopting a bonus system to increase production. One suggestion is to pay a bonus on the highest 5 percent of production based on past experience. Past records indicate weekly production follows the normal distribution. The mean of this distribution is 4,000 units per week and the standard deviation is 60 units per week. If the bonus is paid on the upper 5 percent of production, the bonus will be paid on how many units or more?
40. Fast Service Truck Lines uses the Ford Super 1310 exclusively. Management made a study of the maintenance costs and determined the number of miles traveled during the year followed the normal distribution. The mean of the distribution was 60,000 miles and the standard deviation 2,000 miles.
   a. What percent of the Ford Super 1310s logged 65,200 miles or more?
   b. What percent of the trucks logged more than 57,060 but less than 58,280 miles?
   c. What percent of the Fords traveled 62,000 miles or less during the year?
   d. Is it reasonable to conclude that any of the trucks were driven more than 70,000 miles? Explain.
41. The annual income of a large group of supervisors at Belco Industries follows the normal distribution. The mean amount earned yearly is $48,000 and the standard deviation is $1,200. The length of service of the same supervisors also follows the normal distribution, with a mean of 20 years and a standard deviation of 5 years. John McMaster earns $50,400 annually and has 10 years of service.
   a. Compare his income with those of the other supervisors.
   b. Compare his length of service with those of the other supervisors.
   c. The president of Belco wants to give a bonus to those supervisors at the lower end of the income distribution. If he gives a bonus to the lowest 8 percent, what is the cutoff point between those who receive the bonus and those who do not?
42. An executive at Westinghouse drives from his home in the suburbs near Pittsburgh to his office in the center of the city. The driving times can be approximated by the normal distribution, with a mean of 35 minutes and a standard deviation of 8 minutes.
   a. What percent of the days will it take him 30 minutes or less to drive to work?
   b. In what percent of the days will it take 40 minutes or more to drive to work?
   c. Explain to the executive why the probability is nearly 0 that it will take him exactly 40 minutes to get to work.
   d. The executive didn't understand your answer to part c. How would you estimate the percent of days it takes 40 minutes to drive to work? (Hint: Within what range of values would the times be rounded to 40?)
   e. Some days there will be accidents or other delays, so the trip will take longer than usual. How long will the longest 10 percent of the trips take?
43. A large retailer offers a "no hassle" returns policy. The number of items returned per day follows the normal distribution. The mean number of customer returns is 10.3 per day and the standard deviation is 2.25 per day.
   a. In what percent of the days are there 8 or fewer customers returning items?
   b. In what percent of the days are between 12 and 14 customers returning items?
   c. Is there any chance of a day with no returns?
44. A recent study shows that 20 percent of all employees steal from their company each year. If a company employs 50 people, what is the probability that:
   a. Fewer than 5 employees steal?
   b. More than 5 employees steal?
   c. Exactly 5 employees steal?
   d. More than 5 but fewer than 15 employees steal?
45. The Myrtle Beach *Sun Times* reported that 64 percent of American men over the age of 18 consider nutrition a top priority in their lives. Suppose we select a sample of 60 men. What is the likelihood that:

a. 32 or more consider nutrition important?
b. 44 or more consider nutrition important?
c. More than 32 but fewer than 43 consider nutrition important?
d. Exactly 44 consider diet important?

46. Two-liter plastic bottles used for bottling cola are shipped in lots of 100. Suppose the lots are 5 percent defective. Some bottles leak, some are too small, and so forth.

46. a. 5, 2.18
b. See IM.
c. .1251
d. .1192
e. .0714
f. .0197

a. In the sample of 100, how many of the bottles would you expect to be defective? What is the standard deviation?
b. Tell why this situation meets the binomial assumptions.
c. What is the probability that a shipment of plastic bottles contains 8 or more defectives?
d. What is the probability that between 8 and 10 bottles are defective?
e. What is the probability that there are exactly 8 defectives?
f. What is the probability of no defectives?

47. At Casper State College 20 percent of the students drop basic statistics the first time they enroll. There are 50 students enrolled in Dr. Ard's statistics class this semester. Compute the following probabilities.
a. How many students would you expect to drop the class? What is the standard deviation?
b. Tell why this situation meets the binomial assumptions.
c. What is the probability that at least 8 drop?
d. What is the probability that 8 or fewer drop?
e. What is the probability exactly 8 drop?

48. It is estimated that 10 percent of those taking the quantitative methods portion of the CPA examination fail that section. Sixty students are taking the exam this Saturday.

48. a. 6, 2.32
b. .0393
c. .9738

a. How many would you expect to fail? What is the standard deviation?
b. What is the probability that exactly two students will fail?
c. What is the probability at least two students will fail?

49. The Georgetown, South Carolina, Traffic Division reported 40 percent of the high-speed chases involving automobiles result in a minor or major accident. During a month in which 50 high-speed chases occur, what is the probability that 25 or more will result in a minor or major accident?

50. .0150

50. Cruise ships of the Royal Viking line report that 80 percent of their rooms are occupied during September. For a cruise ship having 800 rooms, what is the probability that 665 or more are occupied in September?

51. The goal at U.S. airports handling international flights is to clear these flights within 45 minutes. Let's interpret this to mean that 95 percent of the flights are cleared in 45 minutes, so 5 percent of the flights take longer to clear. Let's also assume that the distribution is approximately normal.
a. If the standard deviation of the time to clear an international flight is 5 minutes, what is the mean time to clear a flight?
b. Suppose the standard deviation is 10 minutes, not the 5 minutes suggested in part a. What is the new mean?
c. A customer has 30 minutes from the time her flight landed to catch her limousine. Assuming a standard deviation of 10 minutes, what is the likelihood that she will be cleared in time?

52. An Air Force study indicates that the probability of a disaster such as the January 28, 1986, explosion of the space shuttle *Challenger* was 1 in 35. The *Challenger* flight was the 25th mission.

52. a. .714
b. .6026

a. How many disasters would you expect in the first 25 flights?
b. Use the normal approximation to estimate the probability of at least one disaster in 25 missions.

53. The registrar at Elmwood University studied the grade point averages (GPAs) of students over many years. Assume the GPA distribution follows a normal distribution with a mean of 3.10 and a standard deviation of 0.30.
a. What is the probability that a randomly selected Elmwood student has a GPA between 2.00 and 3.00?
b. What percent of the students are on probation, that is, have a GPA less than 2.00?
c. The student population at EU is 10,000. How many students are on the dean's list, that is, have GPAs of 3.70 or higher?

d. To qualify for a Bell scholarship, a student must be in the top 10 percent. What GPA must a student attain to qualify for a Bell scholarship?

54. 5.71, 88% tile, 48% tile

54. Jon Molnar will graduate from Carolina Forest High School this year. He took the American College Test (ACT) for college admission and received a score of 30. The high school principal informed him that only 2 percent of the students taking the exam receive a higher score. The mean score for all students taking the exam is 18.3. Jon's friends Karrie and George also took the test but were not given any information by the principal other than their scores. Karrie scored 25 and George 18. Based on this information, what were Karrie's and George's percentile ranks? Assume that the distribution of scores follows the normal distribution.

55. The weights of canned hams processed at the Henline Ham Company follow the normal distribution, with a mean of 9.20 pounds and a standard deviation of 0.25 pounds. The label weight is given as 9.00 pounds.

a. What proportion of the hams actually weigh less than the amount claimed on the label?

b. The owner, Glen Henline, is considering two proposals to reduce the proportion of hams below label weight. He can increase the mean weight to 9.25 and leave the standard deviation the same, or he can leave the mean weight at 9.20 and reduce the standard deviation from 0.25 pounds to 0.15. Which change would you recommend?

56. The Cincinnati *Enquirer* (October 12, 2000) reported that the mean number of hours worked per week by those employed full time is 43.9. The article further indicated that about one third of those employed full time work less than 40 hours per week.

56. a. 9.07
b. 6.07, not normal.

a. Given this information and assuming that number of hours worked follows the normal distribution, what is the standard deviation of the number of hours worked?

b. The article also indicated that 20 percent of those working full time work more than 49 hours per week. Determine the standard deviation with this information. Are the two estimates of the standard deviation similar? What would you conclude?

57. Most four-year automobile leases allow up to 60,000 miles. If the lessee goes beyond this amount, a penalty of 10 cents per mile is added to the lease cost. Suppose the distribution of miles driven on four-year leases follows the normal distribution. The mean is 52,000 miles and the standard deviation is 5,000 miles.

a. What percent of the leases will yield a penalty because of excess mileage?

b. If the automobile company wanted to change the terms of the lease so that 25 percent of the leases went over the limit, where should the new upper limit be set?

c. One definition of a low-mileage car is one that is four years old and has been driven less than 45,000 miles. What percent of the cars returned are considered low-mileage?

58. The price of shares of Bank of Florida at the end of trading each day for the last year followed the normal distribution. Assume there were 240 trading days in the year. The mean price was $42.00 per share and the standard deviation was $2.25 per share.

58. a. 9.18%
22 days.
b. 14.92%
c. $44.34

a. What percent of the days was the price over $45.00? How many days would you estimate?

b. What percent of the days was the price between $38.00 and $40.00?

c. What was the stock's price on the *highest 15* days of the year?

59. The annual sales of romance novels follow the normal distribution. However, the mean and the standard deviation are unknown. Forty percent of the time sales are more than 470,000, and 10 percent of the time sales are more than 500,000. What are the mean and the standard deviation?

60. 32.56

60. In establishing warranties on TV sets, the manufacturer wants to set the limits so that few will need repair at manufacturer expense. On the other hand, the warranty period must be long enough to make the purchase attractive to the buyer. For a new TV the mean number of months until repairs are needed is 36.84 with a standard deviation of 3.34 months. Where should the warranty limits be set so that only 10 percent of the TVs need repairs at the manufacturer's expense?

61. DeKorte Tele-Marketing Inc. is considering purchasing a machine that randomly selects and automatically dials telephone numbers. DeKorte Tele-Marketing makes most of its calls during the evening, so calls to business phones are wasted. The manufacturer of the machine claims that their programming reduces the calling to business phones to 15 percent of all calls. To test this claim the Director of Purchasing at DeKorte programmed the machine to select a sample of 150 phone numbers. What is the likelihood that more than 30 of the phone numbers selected are that of a business, assuming the manufacturer's claim is correct?

Computer Data Exercises

62. Refer to the Real Estate data set, which reports information on homes sold in the Venice, Florida, area during the last year.

62. a. 10.56% versus 13.33%

a. The mean selling price (in $ thousands) of the homes was computed earlier to be $221.10, with a standard deviation of $47.11. Use the normal distribution to estimate the percent of homes selling for more than $280.0. Compare this to the actual results. Does the normal distribution yield a good approximation of the actual results?

b. 17.96% versus 23.0%

b. The mean distance from the center of the city is 14.629 miles with a standard deviation of 4.874 miles. Use the normal distribution to estimate the number of homes 18 or more miles but less than 22 miles from the center of the city. Compare this to the actual results. Does the normal distribution yield a good approximation of the actual results?

63. Refer to the Baseball 2000 data set, which reports information on the 30 Major League Baseball teams for the 2000 season.

a. The mean attendance per team for the season was 2.42 (in millions) with a standard deviation of 0.777 (in millions). Use the normal distribution to estimate the number of teams with attendance of more than 3.5 million. Compare that estimate with the actual number. Comment on the accuracy of your estimate.

b. The mean team salary was $56.67 million with a standard deviation of $24.54 million. Use the normal distribution to estimate the number of teams with a team salary of more than $50 million. Compare that estimate with the actual number. Comment on the accuracy of the estimate.

64. Refer to the Schools data set, which reports information on 94 school districts in Northwest Ohio.

64. a. 40.13% versus 8.5%

a. The mean amount spent on instruction is $2,725 with a standard deviation of $1,095. Use the normal distribution to estimate the percentage of school districts that spend more than $3,000 on instruction. Compare this estimate with the actual proportion. Does the normal distribution appear accurate in this case? Explain.

b. 51.2% versus 32.0%

b. The mean number of students per school district is 2,134 with a standard deviation of 3,895. Use the normal distribution to estimate the percentage of school districts with more than 2,000 students enrolled. Compare this estimate with the actual proportion.

Computer Commands

1. The Excel commands necessary to produce the output on page 236 are:

a. Select **Insert** and **Function**, then from the box select **Statistical** and **NORMDIST** and click *OK*.

b. In the dialog box put *1100* in the box for X, *1000* for the **Mean**, *100* for the **Standard_dev**, *True* in the **Cumulative** box, and click **OK**.

c. The result will appear in the dialog box. If you click OK, the answer appears in your spreadsheet.

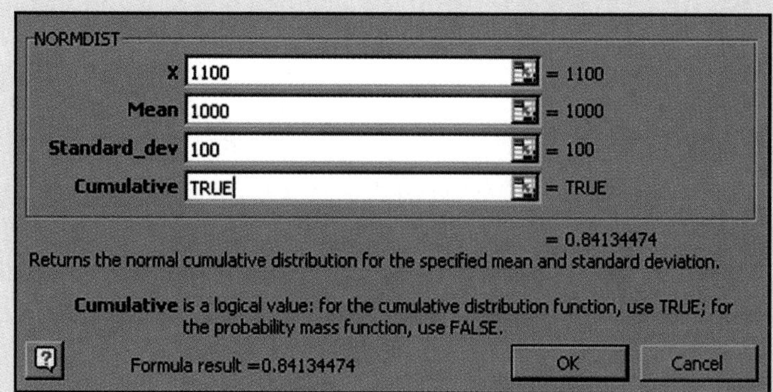

2. The Excel commands necessary to produce the MegaStat output on page 242 are:
   a. On the toolbar select **MegaStat**, **Probability**, and **Continuous Probability Distributions**.
   b. In the dialog box click on **x given probability**, insert *.96* to the right of the word **probability**, insert *67900* for the **mean,** and *2050* for the **standard deviation**. You can preview the results by clicking on the word **Preview**.

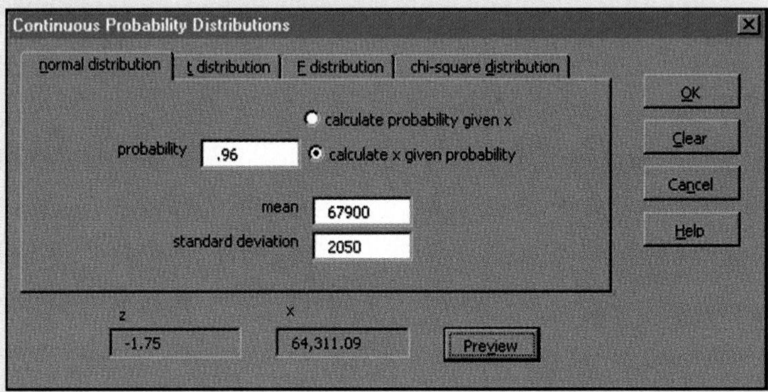

Chapter 7 Answers to Self-Review

7–1 **(a)** 2.25, found by:

$$z = \frac{\$1{,}225 - \$1{,}000}{\$100} = \frac{\$225}{\$100} = 2.25$$

(b) −2.25, found by:

$$z = \frac{\$775 - \$1{,}000}{\$100} = \frac{-\$225}{\$100} = -2.25$$

7–2 **(a)** \$36,400 and \$38,000, found by \$37,200 ± 1(\$800).

(b) \$35,600 and \$38,800, found by \$37,200 ± 2(\$800).

(c) \$34,800 and \$39,600, found by \$37,200 ± 3(\$800).

(d) \$37,200. Mean, median, and mode are equal for a normal distribution.

(e) Yes, a normal distribution is symmetrical.

7–3 **(a)** Computing z:

$$z = \frac{482 - 400}{50} = +1.64$$

Referring to Appendix D, the area is .4495.

(b) .0505, found by .5000 − .4495

(c)

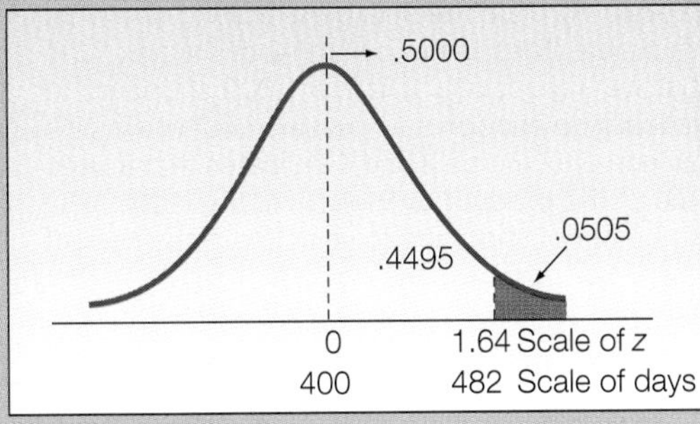

7–4 **(a)** 98.16%, found by 0.4938 + 0.4878.

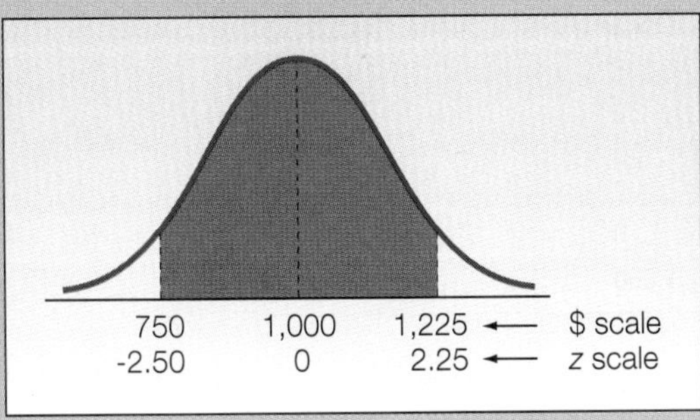

(b) 14.65%, found by 0.4878 − 0.3413.

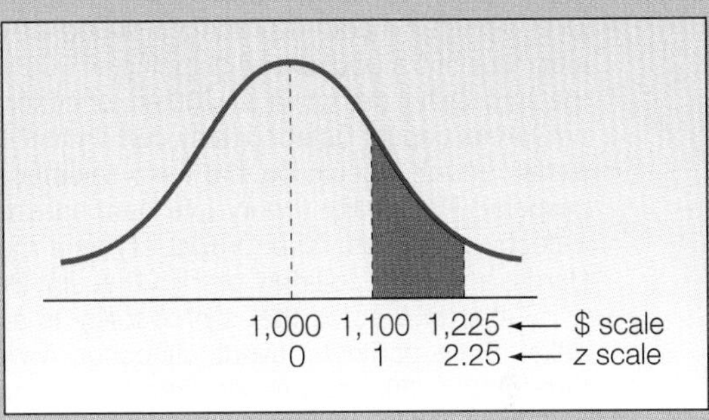

7–5 85.24 (instructor would no doubt make it 85). The closest area to .4000 is .3997; z is 1.28. Then:

$$1.28 = \frac{X - 75}{8}$$

$$10.24 = X - 75$$

$$X = 85.24$$

7–6 **(a)** .0465, found by $\mu = n\pi = 200(.80) = 160$, and $\sigma^2 = n\pi(1 - \pi) = 200(.80)(1 - .80) = 32$. Then,

$$\sigma = \sqrt{32} = 5.66$$

$$z = \frac{169.5 - 160}{5.66} = 1.68$$

Area from Appendix D is .4535. Subtracting from .5000 gives .0465.

(b) .9686, found by .4686 + .5000. First calculate z:

$$z = \frac{149.5 - 160}{5.66} = -1.86$$

Area from Appendix D is .4686.

A Review of Chapters 5–7

This section is a review of the major concepts, terms, symbols, and equations introduced in Chapters 5, 6, and 7. These three chapters are concerned with methods of dealing with uncertainty. As an example of the uncertainty in business, consider the role of the quality assurance department in most mass-production firms. Usually, the department has neither the personnel nor the time to check, say, all 200 plug-in modules produced during a two-hour period. Standard procedure may call for selecting a sample of 5 modules and shipping all 200 modules if the 5 operate correctly. However, if 1 or more in the sample are defective, all 200 are checked. Assuming that all 5 function correctly, quality assurance personnel cannot be absolutely certain that their action (allowing shipment of the modules) will prove to be correct. It could be that the 5 selected at random are the only ones out of the 200 that function properly! Probability theory lets us measure the uncertainty involved, in this case, of shipping out defective modules. Also, probability as a measurement of uncertainty comes into play when Gallup, Harris, and other pollsters predict that Jim Barstow will win the vacant senatorial seat in Georgia.

Chapter 5 notes that a *probability* is a value between 0 and 1, inclusive, that expresses one's belief that a particular event will occur. A weather forecaster might state that the probability of rain tomorrow is .20. The project director of a firm bidding on a subway station in Bangkok might assess the firm's chance of being awarded the contract at .50. We looked at the ways probabilities can be combined using rules of addition and multiplication, some principles of counting, and the importance of Bayes' theorem.

Chapter 6 presents *discrete* probability distributions — the *binomial distribution,* the *hypergeometric distribution,* and the *Poisson distribution.* Other probability distributions will be discussed in forthcoming chapters (*t* distribution, chi-square distribution, etc.). Probability distributions are listings of all the possible outcomes of an experiment and the probability associated with each outcome. A probability distribution allows us to evaluate sample results.

As an example, a consumer research firm, such as National Family Opinion (NFO), conducted a survey to find whether grocery shoppers can identify the brand name of a product if the name does not appear on the can, box, or package. For question 1, NFO deleted the name of a soup and gave the shopper five choices: (1) Campbell's, (2) Knorr, (3) Progresso, (4) Chalet Suzanne, and (5) Heinz.

There were six similar questions, and 1,000 shoppers participated in the experiment. There is a possibility that shoppers unfamiliar with various labels and brand names would select a name at random — that is, guess the brand name. So a binomial probability distribution is generated to see what a random distribution of choices would look like. These probabilities are in column 2 of the following table; the numbers expected are in column 3. Note that we expect only 2 of the 1,000 shoppers to *guess* five of the six questions correctly. We expect practically no shoppers to guess six out of six. The actual distribution of responses is in column 4. A comparison of columns 3 and 4 indicates that a large percentage of the shoppers can identify the brand name of the product by looking at the label. NFO would conclude that it is highly unlikely for such a large number of shoppers to select so many correct brand names by chance.

1 Number of Correct Identifications	2 Probability*	3 Expected Number by Chance	4 Actual Number in Survey
0	.262	262	5
1	.393	393	16
2	.246	246	10
3	.082	82	27
4	.015	15	81
5	.002	2	346
6	.000	0	515
	1.000	1,000	1,000

*Probabilities from Appendix A.

Chapter 7 describes the *normal probability distribution,* which is a continuous distribution. Some phenomena, such as the tensile strength of wires and the weights of the contents of cans and bottles, approximate a normal, bell-shaped distribution. Actually, there is a family of normal distributions — each with its own mean and standard deviation. There is a normal distribution, for example, for a mean of $100 and a standard deviation of $5, another for a mean of $149 and a standard deviation of $5.26, and so on. It was noted that a normal probability distribution is bell-shaped and symmetrical about its mean and that the tails of the normal curve extend in either direction infinitely. Since there is an unlimited number of normal distributions, it is difficult to compare two or more distributions directly. Instead, the distributions of interest are *standardized.* The distribution of these standardized values is called the *standard normal distribution.* The standard normal distribution has a mean of 0 and a standard deviation of 1. It is very useful, for example, for comparing distributions in different units. The distribution of the incomes of middle managers and the distribution of their efficiency ratings is an example of distributions in different units. It is also used to compute the probability that various events will happen.

Glossary

Chapter 5

Bayes' theorem Developed by Reverend Bayes in the 1700s, it is designed to find the probability of one event, A, occurring, given that another event, B, has already occurred.

Classical probability Probability based on the assumption that each of the outcomes is equally likely. Using this concept of probability, if there are n possible outcomes, the probability of a particular outcome is $1/n$. Thus, on the toss of a coin, the probability of a head is $1/n = ½$.

Combination formula A formula to count the number of possible outcomes. If the order a, b, c is considered the same as b, a, c, or c, b, a, and so on, the number of arrangements is found by:

$$_nC_r = \frac{n!}{r!(n-r)!}$$

Conditional probability The likelihood that an event will occur given that another event has already occurred.

Event A collection of one or more outcomes of an experiment. For example, an event may be three defective valves in an incoming shipment of valves for a 351 cu. in. Ford V8 engine.

Empirical probability A concept of probability based on past experience. For example, the Metropolitan Life Insurance Company reported that during the year, 100.2 of every 100,000 persons in Wyoming died of accidental death (motor vehicle accidents, falls, drowning, firearms, etc.). Based on this experience, Metropolitan can estimate the probability of accidental death for a particular person in Wyoming: 100.2/100,000 = .001002.

Experiment An activity that is either observed or measured. An experiment may be counting the number of correct responses to a question, for example.

General rule of addition Used to find the probabilities of complex events made up of A or B.

$$P(A \text{ or } B) = P(A) + P(B) - P(A \text{ and } B)$$

General rule of multiplication Used to find the probabilities of complex events made up of A and B. Example: It is known that there are 3 defective radios in a box containing 10 radios. What is the probability of selecting 2 defective radios on the first two selections from the box?

$$P(A \text{ and } B) = P(A)P(B \mid A) = \frac{3}{10} \times \frac{2}{9} = \frac{6}{90} = .067$$

Where $P(B \mid A)$ means "the probability of B occurring given that A has already occurred."

Independent The occurrence of one event has no effect on the probability of the occurrence of another event.

Multiplication formula One of the formulas used to count the number of possible outcomes of an experiment. It states that if there are m ways of doing one thing and n ways of doing another, there are $m \times n$ ways of doing both. Example: A sports shop offers two sport coats and three contrasting pants for $400. How many different outfits can there be? Answer: $m \times n = 2 \times 3 = 6$.

Outcome A particular result of an experiment.

Permutation formula A formula to count the number of possible outcomes. If a, b, c is one arrangement, b, a, c another, c, a, b another; and so on, the total number of arrangements is determined by

$$_nP_r = \frac{n!}{(n-r)!}$$

Probability A value between 0 and 1, inclusive, that reports the likelihood that a specific event will occur.

Special rule of addition For this rule to apply, the events must be mutually exclusive. For two events, the probability of A or B occurring is found by:

$$P(A \text{ or } B) = P(A) + P(B)$$

Example: The probability of a one-spot or a two-spot occurring on the toss of one die.

$$P(A \text{ or } B) = \frac{1}{6} + \frac{1}{6} = \frac{2}{6} = \frac{1}{3}$$

Special rule of multiplication If two events are not related — that is, they are independent — this rule can be applied to determine the probability of their joint occurrence.

$$P(A \text{ and } B) = P(A)P(B)$$

Example: The probability of two heads on two tosses of a coin is:

$$P(A \text{ and } B) = P(A)P(B) = \frac{1}{2} \times \frac{1}{2} = \frac{1}{4}$$

Subjective probability The chance of an event happening based on whatever information is available — hunches, personal opinion, opinions of others, rumors, and so on.

Chapter 6

Binomial probability distribution A discrete random variable with the following characteristics:

1. Each outcome can be classified into one of two mutually exclusive categories.
2. The distribution is the result of counting the number of successes.
3. Each trial is independent, meaning that the answer to trial 1 (correct or wrong) in no way affects the answer to trial 2.
4. The probability of a success stays the same from trial to trial.

Continuous random variable A random variable that may assume an infinite number of values within a given range.

Discrete random variable A random variable that can assume only certain separate values.

Hypergeometric probability distribution A probability distribution based on a discrete random variable. Its major characteristics are:

1. There is a fixed number of trials.
2. The probability of success is not the same from trial to trial.

Poisson distribution A distribution often used to approximate binomial probabilities when n is large and π is small. What is considered "large" or "small" is not precisely defined, but a general rule is that n should be equal to or greater than 20 and π equal to or less than .05.

Probability distribution A listing of the possible outcomes of an experiment and the probability associated with each outcome.

Random variable A quantity obtained from an experiment that may, by chance, result in different values. For example, a count of the number of accidents (the experiment) on I-75 during a week might be 10, or 11, or 12, or some other number.

Chapter 7

Continuity correction factor Used to improve the accuracy of the approximation of a discrete distribution (binomial) by a continuous distribution (normal).

Normal probability distribution A continuous distribution that is bell-shaped, with the mean dividing the distribution into two equal parts. Further, the normal curve extends infinitely in either direction; that is, it never touches the X-axis. By converting a normal distribution to a *standard normal distribution,* we can, for example, compare two or more distributions having significantly different means or that are in different units (such as incomes and years of service).

***z* value** The distance between a selected value and the population mean measured in units of the standard deviation.

Exercises

Part I — Fill in the Blanks

1. Based on your assessment of the stock market, you state that chances are 50-50 that stock prices will start to go down within two months. This concept of probability based on your belief is called ________.

2. Experiment.

2. A study of absenteeism from the classroom is being conducted. In our study of probability, this particular activity is called ________.

3. Refer to Exercise 2. It was found that 126 students were absent from Monday morning classes. This number (126) is called ________.

4. Mutually exclusive.

4. To apply this rule of addition:

$$P(A \text{ or } B \text{ or } C) = P(A) + P(B) + P(C)$$

the events must be ________

5. Management claims that the probability of a defective relay is only .001.The name of the rule used for finding the probability of the relay *not* being defective is________. The formula for that rule is ________. The probability of a particular relay not being defective is ________.

6. 1.00

6. For a probability distribution, the sum or the probabilities of all possible outcomes must equal ________.
7. Is the binomial distribution a discrete or continuous probability distribution? ________.

8. 2 outcomes, result of counts, independent trials, constant probability of success.

8. The characteristics of a binomial probability distribution are: ________, ________, ________, ________.
9. The Poisson probability distribution is (discrete or continuous)? ________.

10. μ

10. To construct a Poisson distribution, you need________.
11. The characteristics of a normal probability distribution and its accompanying normal curve are: ________, ________, ________.

12. Standard normal.

12. If we convert values of a normal distribution to a distribution that has a mean of 0 and a standard deviation of 1, this probability distribution is called the ________.

Part II — Problems

13. A self-study course on management principles was offered to all employees of TMC Electronics. At the end of the time period, the employees were tested, with the following results:

Course Grade	Number of Employees
A	20
B	35
C	90
D	40
F	10
Withdrew	5

What is the probability that an employee selected at random:

a. Earned an A?
b. Earned a C or better?
c. Did not fail or withdraw?

14. a. .035
b. .018
c. .648

14. It is claimed that Aldradine, a new medicine for acne, is 80 percent effective — that is, of every 100 persons who apply it, 80 show significant improvement. It is applied to the affected area of a group of 15 people. What is the probability that:

a. All 15 will show significant improvement?
b. Fewer than 9 of 15 will show significant improvement?
c. That 12 or more people will show significant improvement?

15. First National Bank thoroughly investigates its applicants for small home-improvement loans. Their default record is very impressive: the probability that a homeowner will default is only .005. The bank has approved 400 small home-improvement loans. Assuming the Poisson probability distribution applies to this problem:

a. What is the probability that no homeowners out of the 400 will default?
b. How many of the 400 are expected not to default?
c. What is the probability that 3 or more homeowners will default on their small home-improvement loans?

16. a. .0401
b. .6147
c. 7440

16. A study of the attendance at the University of Alabama's basketball games revealed that the distribution of attendance is normally distributed with a mean of 10,000 and a standard deviation of 2,000.

a. What is the probability a particular game has an attendance of 13,500 or more?
b. What percent of the games have an attendance between 8,000 and 11,500?
c. Ten percent of the games have an attendance of how many or less?

17. The following table shows a breakdown of the U.S. Congress by party affiliation.

	Party		
	Democrats	Republicans	Others
House	210	223	2
Senate	50	50	0

a. A member of Congress is selected at random. What is the probability of selecting a Republican member of Congress?
b. Given that the person selected is a member of the House of Representatives, what is the probability he or she is a Republican?
c. What is the probability of selecting a member of the House of Representatives or a Democrat?

18. .345
.579.

18. The Internal Revenue Service has set aside 200 tax returns where the amount of charitable contributions seemed excessive. A sample of six returns is selected from the group. If two or more of this sampled group have "excessive" amounts deducted for charitable contributions, the entire group will be audited. What is the probability the entire group will be audited, if the true proportion of "excessive" deductions is 20 percent? What if the true proportion is 30 percent?

19. The Daniel-James Insurance Company will insure an offshore Mobil Oil production platform against weather losses for one year. The president of Daniel-James estimates the following losses for that platform (in millions of dollars) with the accompanying probabilities:

Amount of Loss ($ millions)	Probability of Loss
0	.98
40	.016
300	.004

a. What is the expected amount Daniel-James will have to pay to Mobil in claims?
b. What is the likelihood that Daniel-James will actually lose less than the expected amount?
c. Given that Daniel-James suffers a loss, what is the likelihood that it is for $300 million?
d. Daniel-James has set the annual premium at $2.0 million. Does that seem like a fair premium? Will it cover their risk?

20. The distribution of the number of school-age children per family in the Whitehall Estates area of Boise, Idaho, is:

Number of children	0	1	2	3	4
Percent of families	40	30	15	10	5

20. a. $\mu = 1.10$, $\sigma = 1.18$
b. About 550.
c. $\mu = 1.833$

a. Determine the mean and standard deviation of the number of school-age children per family in Whitehall Estates.
b. A new school is planned in Whitehall Estates. An estimate of the number of school-age children is needed. There are 500 family units. How many children would you estimate?
c. Some additional information is needed about only the families having children. Convert the preceding distribution to one for families with children. What is the mean number of children among families that have children?

Cases

A. Century National Bank

Refer to the Century National Bank data. Is it reasonable that the distribution of checking account balances approximates a normal distribution? Determine the mean and the standard deviation for the sample of 60 customers. Compare the actual distribution with the theoretical distribution. Cite some specific examples and comment on your findings.

Divide the account balances into three groups, of about 20 each, with the smallest third of the balances in the first group, the middle third in the second group, and those with the largest balances in the third group. Next, develop a table that shows the number in each of the categories of the account balances by branch. Does it appear that account balances are related to the branch? Cite some examples and comment on your findings.

B. Elections Auditor

An item such as an increase in taxes, recall of elected officials, or an expansion of public services can be placed on the ballot if a required number of valid signatures are collected on the petition. Unfortunately, many people will sign the petition even though they are not registered to vote in that particular district, or they will sign the petition more than once.

Sara Ferguson, the elections auditor in Venango County, must certify the validity of these signatures after the petition is officially presented. Not surprisingly, her staff is overloaded, so she is considering using statistical methods to validate the pages of 200 signatures, instead of validating each individual signature. At a recent professional meeting, she found that in some communities in the state, election officials were checking only five signatures on each page, rejecting the entire page if two or more signatures were invalid. Some people are concerned that five may not be enough to make a good decision. They suggest that you should check 10 signatures and reject the page if three or more are invalid.

In order to investigate these methods, Sara asks her staff to pull the results from the last election and sample 30 pages. It happens that the staff selected 14 pages from the Avondale district, 9 pages from the Midway district, and 7 pages from the Kingston district. Each page had 200 signatures, and the data below show the number of invalid signatures on each.

Use the data to evaluate Sara's two proposals. Calculate the probability of rejecting a page under each of the approaches. Would you get about the same results by examining every single signature? Offer a plan of your own, and discuss how it might be better or worse than the two plans proposed by Sara.

Avondale	Midway	Kingston
9	19	38
14	22	39
11	23	41
8	14	39
14	22	41
6	17	39
10	15	39
13	20	
8	18	
8		
9		
12		
7		
13		

C. Geoff "Applies" His Education

Geoff Brown is the manager for a small telemarketing firm and is evaluating the sales rate of experienced workers in order to set minimum standards for new hires. During the past few weeks, he has recorded the number of successful calls per hour for the staff. These data appear below along with some summary statistics he worked out with a statistical software package. Geoff has been a student at the local community college and has heard of what seem like many different kinds of probability distributions (binomial, normal, hypergeometric, Poisson, etc.). Could you give Geoff some advice on which distribution to use to fit these data as well as possible and how to decide when a probationary employee should be accepted as having reached full production status? This is important because it means a pay raise for the employee, and there have been some probationary employees in the past who have quit because of discouragement that they would never meet the standard.

Successful sales calls per hour during the week of August 14:

4	2	3	1	4	5	5	2	3	2	2	4	5	2	5	3	3	0
1	3	2	8	4	5	2	2	4	1	5	5	4	5	1	2	4	

Descriptive statistics:

```
N     MEAN    MEDIAN   TRMEAN   STDEV   SEMEAN
35    3.229   3.000    3.194    1.682   0.284
MIN   MAX     Q1       Q3
0.0   8.000   2.000    5.000
```

Which distribution do you think Geoff should use for his analysis?

D. CNP Bank Card

Before banks issue a credit card, they usually rate or score the customer in terms of his or her projected probability of being a profitable customer. A typical scoring table appears below.

Age	Under 25 (12 pts.)	25-29 (5 pts.)	30-34 (0 pts.)	35+ (18 pts.)
Time at same address	< 1 yr. (9 pts.)	1–2 yrs. (0 pts.)	3–4 yrs. (13 pts.)	5+ yrs. (20 pts.)
Auto age	None (18 pts.)	0–1 yr. (12 pts.)	2–4 yrs. (13 pts.)	5+ yrs. (3 pts.)
Monthly car payment	None (15 pts.)	$1–$99 (6 pts.)	$100–299 (4pts.)	$300+ (0 pts.)
Housing cost	$1–$199 (0 pts.)	$200–$399 (10 pts.)	Owns (12 pts.)	Lives with relatives (24 pts.)
Checking/ savings accounts	Both (15 pts.)	Checking only (3 pts.)	Savings only (2 pts.)	Neither (0 pts.)

The score is the sum of the points on the six items. For example, Sushi Brown is under 25 years old (12 pts.), has lived at the same address for 2 years (0 pts.), owns a 4-year-old car (13 pts.), with car payments of $75 (6 pts.), housing cost of $200 (10 pts.), and a checking account (3 pts.). She would score 44.

A second chart is then used to convert scores into the probability of being a profitable customer. A sample chart of this type appears below.

Score	30	40	50	60	70	80	90
Probability	.70	.78	.85	.90	.94	.95	.96

Sushi's score of 44 would translate into a probability of being profitable of approximately .81. In other words 81 percent of customers like Sushi will make money for the bank card operations.

Here are the interview results for three potential customers.

Name	David Born	Edward Brendan	Ann McLaughlin
Age	42	23	33
Time at same address	9	2	5
Auto age	2	3	7
Monthly car payment	$140	$99	$175
Housing cost	$300	$200	Owns clear
Checking/savings accounts	Both	Checking only	Neither

a. Score each of these customers and estimate their probability of being profitable.
b. What is the probability that all three are profitable?
c. What is the probability that none of them are profitable?
d. Find the entire probability distribution for the number of profitable customers among this group of three.

8

Sampling Methods and the Central Limit Theorem

GOALS

When you have completed this chapter you will be able to:

1. **Explain why a sample is often the only feasible way to learn something about a population.**
2. **Describe methods to select a sample.**
3. **Define and construct a sampling distribution of the sample mean.**
4. **Explain the *central limit theorem.***
5. **Use the central limit theorem to find probabilities of selecting possible sample means from a specified population.**

Plastic Products is concerned about the inside diameter of the plastic PVC pipe it produces. About 720 pipes are produced per machine during a two-hour period. How would you go about taking a sample from the two-hour production period? (See Goal 2 and Exercise 30.)

Introduction

Chapters 1 through 4 emphasize techniques to describe data. To illustrate these techniques, we organize the prices for the 80 vehicles sold last month at Whitner Pontiac into a frequency distribution and compute various measures of location, position, and dispersion. Such measures as the mean and the standard deviation describe the typical selling price and the spread in the selling prices. In these chapters the emphasis is on describing the condition of the data. That is, we describe something that has already happened.

Chapter 5 starts to lay the foundation for statistical inference with the study of probability. Recall that in statistical inference our goal is to determine something about a *population* based only on the *sample.* The population is the entire group of individuals or objects under consideration, and the sample is a part or subset of that population. Chapter 6 extends the probability concepts by describing three discrete probability distributions: the binomial, the hypergeometric, and the Poisson. Chapter 7 describes the normal probability distribution, a widely applicable continuous probability distribution. Probability distributions encompass all possible outcomes of an experiment and the probability associated with each outcome. We use probability distributions to evaluate something that might occur in the future.

This chapter begins our study of sampling. A sample is a tool to infer something about a population. We begin this chapter by discussing methods of selecting a sample from a population. Next, we construct a distribution of the sample mean to understand how the sample means tend to cluster around the population mean. Finally, we show that the shape of this distribution tends to follow the normal probability distribution.

Sampling the Population

In many cases sampling is the only way to determine something about the population. Some of the major reasons for sampling are:

Reasons for sampling.

1. **The destructive nature of certain tests.** If the wine tasters at the Sutter Home Winery in California drank all the wine to evaluate the vintage, they would consume the entire crop, and none would be available for sale. In the area of industrial production, steel plates, wires, and similar products must have a certain minimum tensile strength. To ensure that the product meets the minimum standard, the Quality Assurance Department selects a sample from the current production. Each piece is stretched until it breaks, and the breaking point (usually measured in pounds per square inch) recorded. Obviously, if all the wire or all the plates were tested for tensile strength, none would be available for sale or use. For the same reason, only a sample of photographic film is selected and tested by Kodak to determine the quality of all the film produced, and only a few seeds are tested for germination by Burpee prior to the planting season.

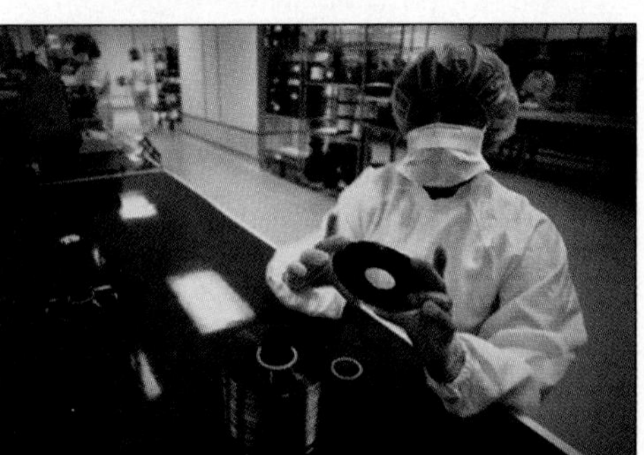

2. **The physical impossibility of checking all items in the population.** The populations of fish, birds, snakes, mosquitoes, and the like are large and are constantly moving, being born, and dying. Instead of even attempting to count all the ducks in Canada or all the fish in Lake Erie, we make estimates using various techniques—such as counting all the ducks on a pond picked at random, making creel checks, or setting nets at predetermined places in the lake.

3. **The cost of studying all the items in a population is often prohibitive.** Public opinion polls and consumer testing organizations, such as Gallup Polls and Marketing Facts, usually contact fewer than 2,000 families of the nearly 60 million families in the United States. One consumer panel-type organization charges about $40,000 to mail samples and tabulate responses in order to test a product (such as breakfast cereal, cat food, or perfume). The same product test using all 60 million families would cost about $1 billion.
4. **The adequacy of sample results.** Even if funds were available, it is doubtful the additional accuracy of a 100 percent sample — that is, studying the entire population — is essential in most problems. For example, the federal government uses a sample of grocery stores scattered throughout the United States to determine the monthly index of food prices. The prices of bread, beans, milk, and other major food items are included in the index. It is unlikely that the inclusion of all grocery stores in the United States would significantly affect the index, since the prices of milk, bread, and other major foods usually do not vary by more than a few cents from one chain store to another.
5. **To contact the whole population would often be time consuming.** A candidate for a national office may wish to determine her chances for election. A sample poll using the regular staff and field interviews of a professional polling firm would take only one or two days. By using the same staff and interviewers and working seven days a week, it would take nearly 200 years to contact all the voting population! Even if a large staff of interviewers could be assembled, the benefit of contacting all of the voters would probably not be worth the expense. If the candidate were extremely popular, the sample poll might indicate that she would most certainly receive between 79 percent and 81 percent of the popular vote. The additional expense and time needed to find she might receive exactly 80 percent of the popular vote does not seem justified.

Probability Sampling Methods

In general, there are two types of samples: a *probability sample* and a *nonprobability sample.* What is a probability sample?

PROBABILITY SAMPLE A sample selected in such a way that each item or person in the population has a known (nonzero) likelihood of being included in the sample.

There is no one "best" method of selecting a probability sample from a population of interest. A method used to select a sample of invoices in a file drawer might not be the most appropriate method for choosing a national sample of voters. However, all probability sampling methods have a similar goal, namely, *to allow chance to determine the items or persons to be included in the sample.*

Simple Random Sampling

The most widely used type of sampling is a **simple random sample.**

> **SIMPLE RANDOM SAMPLE** A sample selected so that each item or person in the population has the same chance of being included.

To illustrate simple random sampling and selection, suppose a population consists of 845 employees of Nitra Industries. A sample of 52 employees is to be selected from that population. One way of ensuring that every employee in the population has the same chance of being chosen is to first write the name of each one on a small slip of paper and deposit all of the slips in a box. After they have been thoroughly mixed, the first selection is made by drawing a slip out of the box without looking at it. This process is repeated until the sample size of 52 is chosen.

A table of random numbers is an efficient way to select members of the sample

A more convenient method of selecting a random sample is to use the identification number of each employee and a **table of random numbers** such as the one in Appendix E. As the name implies, these numbers have been generated by a random process (in this case, by a computer). For each digit of a number, the probability of 0, 1, 2, . . . , 9 is the same. Thus, the probability that employee number 011 will be selected is the same as for employee 722 or employee 382. Bias is eliminated from the selection process.

A portion of a table of random numbers is shown in the following illustration. To use this table to select a sample of employees, you must first choose a starting point in the table. Any starting point will do. Suppose the time is 3:04. You might look at the third column and then move down to the fourth set of numbers. The number is 03759. Since there are only 845 employees, we will use the first three digits of a five-digit random number. Thus, 037 is the number of the first employee to be a member of the sample. To continue selecting employees, you could move in any direction. Suppose you move right. The first three digits of the number to the right of 03759 are 447 — the number of the employee selected to be the second member of the sample. The next three-digit number to the right is 961. You skip 961 because there are only 845 employees. You continue to the right and select employee 784, then 189, and so on. Another way of selecting the starting point is to close your eyes and point at a number in the table.

50525	57454	28455	68226	34656	38884	39018
72507	53380	53827	42486	54465	71819	91199
34986	74297	00144	38676	89967	98869	39744
68851	27305	03759	44723	96108	78489	18910
06738	62879	03910	17350	49169	03850	18910
11448	10734	05837	24397	10420	16712	94496
		Starting point	Second employee		Third employee	

A study conducted by Marion Bryson and Robert Mason further illustrates the use of a table of random numbers and simple random sampling.

> Located in 18 warehouses on a U.S. Army depot were 186,810 different military supply items, such as tires, nuts, bolts, tank treads, and tire irons. In each warehouse there were bays, and in each bay were bins. For example, in warehouse 17, motor vehicle parts were stored. Bay 260, bin 2, contained Jeep cranks. Bay 260, bin 3, had Jeep radiator caps.

Statistics in Action

Is discrimination taking a bite out of your paycheck? Before you answer, consider a recent article in *Personnel Journal.* These findings indicate that attractive men and women earn about 5 percent more than average lookers, who in turn earn about 5 percent more than their plain counterparts. This is true for both men and women. It is also true for a wide range of occupations, from construction workers to auto repair to telemarketing, occupations for which it would seem that looks would not matter.

The problem involved selecting a bin at random from a warehouse and counting the items found in the bin. This physical count was compared with the count that computer inventory records indicated should be on hand. Thus, the problem was essentially a physical inventory problem involving sampling methods. The objective of the project was to verify the accuracy of the computer records.

To ensure that each bin had an equal chance of being selected, a table of random numbers was used to choose the warehouse, bay, and bin.

If warehouse 5, bay 455, and bin 6 were selected, a checker went to that location and counted the number of items in that bin.

Using a table of random numbers to prevent bias.

Why was such a time-consuming method used to select the bins to sample? The alternative would have been to allow the checkers to count the items in any bins they wished. No doubt the checkers would have avoided counting the items in bins containing heavy or greasy parts. And they probably would have shunned the top bins, 20 feet from the floor of the warehouse. The omission of the items in these bins from this physical inventory research project might have biased the results—that is, their omission might have given a false picture of the accuracy of the computer records.

Self-Review 8–1

The class roster, found below, lists the students enrolling in an introductory course in business statistics. Three students are to be randomly selected and asked various questions regarding course content and method of instruction.

(a) The numbers 00 through 45 are handwritten on slips of paper and placed in a bowl. The three numbers selected are 31, 7, and 25. Which students would be included in the sample?
(b) Now use the table of random digits, Appendix E, to select your own sample.
(c) What would you do if you encountered the number 59 in the table of random digits?

CSPM 264 01 BUSINESS & ECONOMIC STAT

8:00 AM 9:40 AM MW ST 118 LIND D

RANDOM NUMBER	NAME	CLASS RANK	RANDOM NUMBER	NAME	CLASS RANK
00	ANDERSON, RAYMOND	SO	23	MEDLEY, CHERYL ANN	SO
01	ANGER, CHERYL RENEE	SO	24	MITCHELL, GREG R	FR
02	BALL, CLAIRE JEANETTE	FR	25	MOLTER, KRISTI MARIE	SO
03	BERRY, CHRISTOPHER G	FR	26	MULCAHY, STEPHEN ROBERT	SO
04	BOBAK, JAMES PATRICK	SO	27	NICHOLAS, ROBERT CHARLES	JR
05	BRIGHT, M. STARR	JR	28	NICKENS, VIRGINIA	SO
06	CHONTOS, PAUL JOSEPH	SO	29	PENNYWITT, SEAN PATRICK	SO
07	DETLEY, BRIAN HANS	JR	30	POTEAU, KRIS E	JR
08	DUDAS, VIOLA	SO	31	PRICE, MARY LYNETTE	SO
09	DULBS, RICHARD ZALFA	JR	32	RISTAS, JAMES	SR
10	EDINGER, SUSAN KEE	SR	33	SAGER, ANNE MARIE	SO
11	FINK, FRANK JAMES	SR	34	SMILLIE, HEATHER MICHELLE	SO
12	FRANCIS, JAMES P	JR	35	SNYDER, LEISHA KAY	SR
13	GAGHEN, PAMELA LYNN	JR	36	STAHL, MARIA TASHERY	SO
14	GOULD, ROBYN KAY	SO	37	ST. JOHN, AMY J	SO
15	GROSENBACHER, SCOTT ALAN	SO	38	STURDEVANT, RICHARD K	SO
16	HEETFIELD, DIANE MARIE	SO	39	SWETYE, LYNN MICHELE	SO
17	KABAT, JAMES DAVID	JR	40	WALASINSKI, MICHAEL	SO
18	KEMP, LISA ADRIANE	FR	41	WALKER, DIANE ELAINE	SO
19	KILLION, MICHELLE A	SO	42	WARNOCK, JENNIFER MARY	SO
20	KOPERSKI, MARY ELLEN	SO	43	WILLIAMS, WENDY A	SO
21	KOPP, BRIDGETTE ANN	SO	44	YAP, HOCK BAN	SO
22	LEHMANN, KRISTINA MARIE	JR	45	YODER, ARLAN JAY	JR

Systematic Random Sampling

The simple random sampling procedure may be awkward in certain research situations. For example, suppose the population of interest consists of 2,000 invoices located in file drawers. Drawing a simple random sample would first require numbering the invoices from 0000 to 1999. Using a table of random numbers, a sample of, say, 100 numbers would then have to be selected. An invoice to match each of these 100 numbers would have to be located in the file drawers. This would be a very time-consuming task. Instead, a **systematic random sample** could be selected by going through the file drawers and selecting every 20th invoice for study. The first invoice should be chosen using a random process—a table of random numbers, for example. If the 10th invoice were chosen as the starting point the sample would consist of the 10th, 30th, 50th, 70th, . . . invoices. Since the first item is chosen at random, all items have the same likelihood of being selected for the sample. Thus, it is a probability sample.

In a systematic sample the first item is chosen at random.

SYSTEMATIC RANDOM SAMPLE The items or individuals of the population are arranged in some way—alphabetically, in a file drawer by date received, or by some other method. A random starting point is selected, and then every *k*th member of the population is selected for the sample.

A systematic sample should not be used, however, if there is a pattern to the population. For example, in the physical inventory study mentioned previously, some of the warehouses in the depot have bays six bins high. In the bottom row of bins are fast-moving items, such as grease, touch-up spray paint, and hardware. These items are stored on the floor-level bins to speed the work of the pickers who must fill the requisitions. In the top row of bins are slow-moving items, such as tire rims, half-track treads, and firing pins. The middle four rows are stocked with moderately fast-moving items, such as tires, headlights, and cotter pins. If a systematic sample is used to check the inventory, then it is quite possible that a biased sample will be selected. Suppose the sampling procedure called for a selection of every third bin, and bin 1 is selected first. Then bins 1, 4, 7, 10, 13, 16, 19, and 22 would be selected systematically.

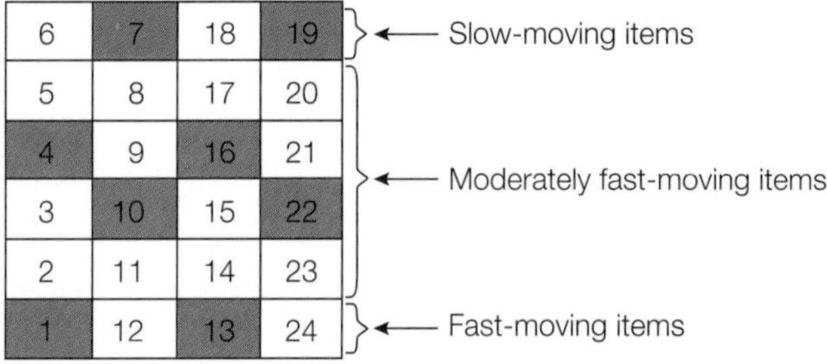

Under certain conditions a systematic sample may produce biased results.

The systematic procedure automatically selected 4 bins filled with moderately fast-moving items and a total of 4 bins filled with either fast-moving or slow-moving items. This 50-50 division of the sample does not coincide with the actual population characteristics. The population consists of 16 bins of moderately fast-moving items, 4 bins of fast-moving items, and 4 bins of slow-moving items. The sample results would undoubtedly be biased toward the slow- and fast-moving items.

Stratified Random Sampling

Another type of probability sampling is referred to as **stratified random sampling.**

> **STRATIFIED RANDOM SAMPLE** A population is divided into subgroups, called strata, and a sample is selected from each stratum.

A stratified sample guarantees representation of each subgroup.

After the population has been divided into strata, either a *proportional* or a *nonproportional* sample is selected. As the name implies, a proportional sampling procedure requires that the number of items in each stratum be in the same proportion as in the population. For instance, the problem might be to study the advertising expenditures of the 352 largest companies in the United States. Suppose the objective of the study is to determine whether firms with high returns on equity (a measure of profitability) spent more of each sales dollar on advertising than firms with a low return or a deficit. Assume that the 352 firms were divided into five strata. (See Table 8–1.) If, say, 50 firms are to be selected for intensive study, then 1 firm with a level of profitability of 30 percent or more would be included, 5 firms in the 20–30 percent stratum would be selected at random, and so on.

TABLE 8–1 Number Selected for a Proportional Stratified Random Sample

Stratum	Profitability (return on equity)	Number of Firms	Percent of Total	Number Sampled
1	30 percent and over	8	2	1*
2	20 up to 30 percent	35	10	5*
3	10 up to 20 percent	189	54	27
4	0 up to 10 percent	115	33	16
5	Deficit	5	1	1
Total		352	100	50

*2 percent of 50 = 1; 10 percent of 50 = 5; etc.

In a *nonproportional* stratified sample, the number of items chosen in each stratum is disproportionate to the respective numbers in the population. We then weight the sample results according to the stratum's proportion of the total population. For example, if nonproportional sampling were used in the preceding case, we would weight the results of stratum 1 by 2/100, stratum 2 by 10/100, stratum 3 by 54/100, and so on. Regardless of whether a proportional or a nonproportional sampling procedure is used, every item or person in the population has a chance of being selected for the sample.

Stratified sampling has the advantage, in some cases, of more accurately reflecting the characteristics of the population than does simple random or systematic random sampling. Note in Table 8–1 that 2 percent of the firms have a return on equity of 30 percent or more (stratum 1), and 1 percent have a deficit (stratum 5). If a simple random sample of 50 were taken, we might not *by chance* select any firms in stratum 1 or 5. A stratified random sample, however, would ensure that at least one firm in stratum 1 and one firm in stratum 5 are represented in the sample.

Cluster Sampling

Cluster sampling reduces sampling cost.

Another common type of sampling is **cluster sampling.** It is often employed to reduce the cost of sampling a population scattered over a large geographic area. Suppose you want to determine the views of industrialists in a state about state and federal environmental protection policies. Selecting a random sample of industrialists in the state and personally contacting each one would be time consuming and very expensive. Instead, you could employ cluster sampling by subdividing the state into small units — either counties or regions. These are often called *primary units.* Suppose you divided the state into 12 primary units, then selected at random four regions — 2, 7, 4, and 12 — and concentrated your efforts in these primary units. You could take a random sample of the industrialists in each of these regions and interview them. (Note that this is a combination of cluster sampling and simple random sampling.)

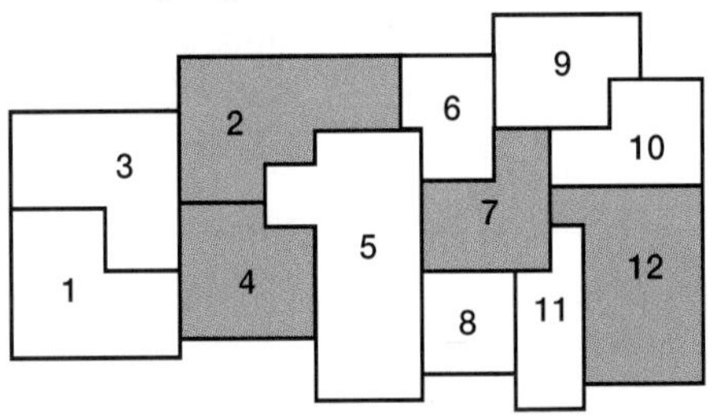

Many other sampling methods

The discussion of sampling methods in the preceding sections did not include all the sampling methods available to a researcher. Should you become involved in a major research project in marketing, finance, accounting, or other areas, you would need to consult books devoted solely to sample theory and sample design.

Self-Review 8–2

Refer to Self-Review 8–1 and the class roster on page 267. Suppose a sample is to consist of every ninth student enrolled in the class. Initially, the fourth student on the list was selected at random. That student is numbered 03. Remembering that the random numbers start with 00, which students will be chosen to be members of the sample?

Exercises

1. The following is a list of Marco's Pizza stores in Lucas County. Also noted is whether the store is corporate-owned (C) or manager-owned (M). A sample of four locations is to be selected and inspected for customer convenience, safety, cleanliness, and other features.

ID No.	Address	Type	ID No.	Address	Type
00	2607 Starr Av	C	12	2040 Ottawa River Rd	C
01	309 W Alexis Rd	C	13	2116 N Reynolds Rd	C
02	2652 W Central Av	C	14	3678 Rugby Dr	C
03	630 Dixie Hwy	M	15	1419 South Av	C
04	3510 Dorr St	C	16	1234 W Sylvania Av	C
05	5055 Glendale Av	C	17	4624 Woodville Rd	M
06	3382 Lagrange St	M	18	5155 S Main	M
07	2525 W Laskey Rd	C	19	106 E Airport Hwy	C
08	303 Louisiana Av	C	20	6725 W Central	M
09	149 Main St	C	21	4252 Monroe	C
10	835 S McCord Rd	M	22	2036 Woodville Rd	C
11	3501 Monroe St	M	23	1316 Michigan Av	M

a. The random numbers selected are 08, 18, 11, 54, 02, 41, and 54. Which stores are selected?

b. Use the table of random numbers to select your own sample of locations.

c. A sample is to consist of every seventh location. The number 03 is the starting point. Which locations will be included in the sample?

d. Suppose a sample is to consist of three locations, of which two are corporate-owned and one is manager-owned. Select a sample accordingly.

2. See IM.

2. The following is a list of hospitals in the Cincinnati (Ohio) and Northern Kentucky Region. Also included is whether the hospital is a general medical/surgical hospital (M/S) or a specialty hospital (S).

ID Number	Name	Address	Type	ID Number	Name	Address	Type
00	Bethesda North	10500 Montgomery Cincinnati, Ohio 45242	M/S	15	Providence Hospital	2446 Kipling Avenue Cincinnati, Ohio 45239	M/S
01	Ft. Hamilton-Hughes	630 Eaton Avenue Hamilton, Ohio 45013	M/S	16	St. Francis- St. George Hospital	3131 Queen City Avenue Cincinnati, Ohio 45238	M/S
02	Jewish Hospital- Kenwood	4700 East Galbraith Rd. Cincinnati, Ohio 45236	M/S	17	St. Elizabeth Medical Center, North Unit	401 E. 20th Street Covington, Kentucky 41014	M/S
03	Mercy Hospital- Fairfield	3000 Mack Road Fairfield, Ohio 45014	M/S	18	St. Elizabeth Medical Center, South Unit	One Medical Village Edgewood, Kentucky 41017	M/S
04	Mercy Hospital- Hamilton	100 Riverfront Plaza Hamilton, Ohio 45011	M/S	19	St. Luke's Hospital West	7380 Turfway Dr. Florence, Kentucky 41075	M/S
05	Middletown Regional	105 McKnight Drive Middletown, Ohio 45044	M/S	20	St. Luke's Hospital East	85 North Grand Avenue Ft. Thomas, Kentucky 41042	M/S
06	Clermont Mercy Hospital	3000 Hospital Dr. Batavia, Ohio 45103	M/S	21	Care Unit Hospital Cinti.	3156 Glenmore Avenue Cincinnati, Ohio 45211	S
07	Mercy Hospital- Anderson	7500 State Road Cincinnati, Ohio 45255	M/S	22	Emerson Behavioral Science	2446 Kipling Avenue Cincinnati, Ohio 45239	S
08	Bethesda Oak Hospital	619 Oak Street Cincinnati, Ohio 45206	M/S	23	Pauline Warfield Lewis Center for Psychiatric Treat.	1101 Summit Rd. Cincinnati, Ohio 45237	S
09	Children's Hospital Medical Center	3333 Burnet Avenue Cincinnati, Ohio 45229	M/S	24	Children's Psychiatric No. Kentucky	502 Farrell Drive Covington, Kentucky 41011	S
10	Christ Hospital	2139 Auburn Avenue Cincinnati, Ohio 45219	M/S	25	Drake Center Rehab— Long Term	151 W. Galbraith Road Cincinnati, Ohio 45216	S
11	Deaconess Hospital	311 Straight Street Cincinnati, Ohio 45219	M/S	26	No. Kentucky Rehab Hospital—Short Term	201 Medical Village Edgewood, Kentucky	S
12	Good Samaritan Hospital	375 Dixmyth Avenue Cincinnati, Ohio 45220	M/S	27	Shriners Burns Institute	3229 Burnet Avenue Cincinnati, Ohio 45229	S
13	Jewish Hospital	3200 Burnet Avenue Cincinnati, Ohio 45229	M/S	28	VA Medical Center	3200 Vine Cincinnati, Ohio 45220	S
14	University Hospital	234 Goodman Street Cincinnati, Ohio 45267	M/S				

a. A sample of five hospitals is to be randomly selected. The random numbers are 09, 16, 00, 49, 54, 12, and 04. Which hospitals are included in the sample?
b. Use a table of random numbers to develop your own sample of five hospitals.
c. A sample is to consist of every fifth location. We select 02 as the starting point. Which hospitals will be included in the sample?
d. A sample is to consist of four medical and surgical hospitals and one specialty hospital. Select an appropriate sample.

3. Listed below are the 35 members of the Metro Toledo Automobile Dealers Association.

ID Number	Dealer	ID Number	Dealer	ID Number	Dealer
00	Dave White Acura	12	Spurgeon Chevrolet Motor Sales, Inc.	24	Lexus of Toledo
01	Autofair Nissan	13	Dunn Chevrolet	25	Mathews Ford Oregon, Inc.
02	Autofair Toyota-Suzuki	14	Don Scott Chevrolet-Pontiac-Geo, Inc.	26	Northtowne Chevrolet-GEO
03	George Ball's Buick GMC Truck	15	Dave White Chevrolet Co.	27	Quality Ford Sales, Inc.
04	Yark Automotive Group	16	Dick Wilson Pontiac	28	Rouen Chrysler Jeep Eagle
05	Bob Schmidt Chevrolet	17	Doyle Pontiac Buick	29	Saturn of Toledo
06	Bowling Green Lincoln Mercury Jeep Eagle	18	Franklin Park Lincoln Mercury	30	Ed Schmidt Pontiac Jeep Eagle
07	Brondes Ford	19	Genoa Motors	31	Southside Lincoln Mercury
08	Brown Honda	20	Great Lakes Ford Nissan	32	Valiton Chrysler
09	Brown Mazda	21	Grogan Towne Chrysler	33	Vin Divers
10	Charlie's Dodge	22	Hatfield Motor Sales	34	Whitman Ford
11	Thayer Chevrolet Geo Toyota	23	Kistler Ford, Inc.		

a. We want to select a random sample of five dealers. The random numbers are: 05, 20, 59, 21, 31, 28, 49, 38, 66, 08, 29, and 02. Which dealers would be included in the sample?
b. Use the table of random numbers to select your own sample of five dealers.
c. A sample is to consist of every 7th dealer. The number 04 is selected as the starting point. Which dealers are included in the sample?

4. See IM.

4. Listed below are the 27 Nationwide Insurance agents in the Toledo, Ohio, metropolitan area.

ID Number	Agent	ID Number	Agent	ID Number	Agent
00	**Bly Scott** 3332 W Laskey Rd	09	**Harris Ev** 2026 Albon Rd	18	**Priest Harvey** 5113 N Summit St
01	**Coyle Mike** 5432 W Central Av	10	**Heini Bernie** 7110 W Central	19	**Riker Craig** 2621 N Reynolds Rd
02	**Denker Brett** 7445 Airport Hwy	11	**Hinckley Dave** 14 N Holland Sylvania Rd	20	**Schwab Dave** 572 W Dussel Dr
03	**Denker Rollie** 7445 Airport Hwy			21	**Seibert John** H 201 S Main
04	**Farley Ron** 1837 W Alexis Rd	12	**Joehlin Bob** 3358 Navarre Av	22	**Smithers Bob** 229 Superior St
05	**George Mark** 7247 W Central Av	13	**Keisser David** 3030 W Sylvania Av	23	**Smithers Jerry** 229 Superior St
06	**Gibellato Carlo** 6616 Monroe St 3521 Navarre Av	14	**Keisser Keith** 5902 Sylvania Av	24	**Wright Steve** 105 S Third St
		15	**Lawrence Grant** 342 W Dussel Dr	25	**Wood Tom** 112 Louisiana Av
07	**Glemser Cathy** 5602 Woodville Rd	16	**Miller Ken** 2427 Woodville Rd	26	**Yoder Scott** 6 Willoughby Av
08	**Green Mike** 4149 Holland Sylvania Rd	17	**O'Donnell Jim** 7247 W Central Av		

a. We want to select a random sample of four agents. The random numbers are: 02, 59, 51, 25, 14, 29, 77, 69, and 18. Which dealers would be included in the sample?
b. Use the table of random numbers to select your own sample of four agents.
c. A sample is to consist of every 5th dealer. The number 02 is selected as the starting point. Which agents will be included in the sample?

Sampling "Error"

The previous discussion stressed the importance of selecting a sample so that every item or individual in the population has a known chance of being selected. To accomplish this, we could choose a simple random sample, a systematic sample, a stratified sample, a cluster sample, or a combination of these methods. However, it is unlikely that the mean of a sample would be *identical* to the population mean. Likewise, the sample standard deviation or other measures computed from a sample would probably not be *exactly* equal to the corresponding population value. We can therefore expect some difference between a *sample statistic,* such as the sample mean or sample standard deviation, and the corresponding *population parameter.* The difference between a sample statistic and a population parameter is called **sampling error.**

> **SAMPLING ERROR** The difference between a sample statistic and its corresponding population parameter.

Suppose a population of five production employees had efficiency ratings of 97, 103, 96, 99, and 105. Further suppose that a sample of two ratings — 97 and 105 — is selected to estimate the population mean rating. The mean of that sample would be 101, found by (97 + 105)/2. Another sample of two is selected: 103 and 96, with a sample mean of 99.5. The mean of all the ratings (the population mean) is 100, found by: (97 + 103 + 96 + 99 + 105)/5 = 500/5 = 100. The sampling error for the first sample is 1.0, determined by $\bar{X} - \mu = 101 - 100$. The second sample has a sampling error of −0.5. Each of these differences, 1.0 and −0.5, is the error made in estimating the population mean based on a sample mean, and these sampling errors are due to chance. The amount of these errors will vary from one sample to the next.

Now that we have discovered the possibility of a sampling error when sample results are used to estimate a population parameter, how can we make an accurate prediction about the possible success of a newly developed toothpaste or other product, based only on sample results? How can the quality-assurance department in a mass-production firm release a shipment of microchips based only on a sample of 10 chips? How can Gallup or Harris polls make an accurate prediction about a presidential race based on a sample of 2,000 registered voters out of a voting population of nearly 90 million? To answer these questions, we first develop a *sampling distribution of the sample mean.*

Sampling Distribution of the Sample Mean

Sample means vary from sample to sample.

The efficiency rating example showed the means for samples of a specified size vary from sample to sample. The mean efficiency rating of the first sample of two employees was 101, and the second sample mean was 99.5. A third sample would probably result in a different mean. The population mean was 100. If we organized the means of all possible samples of 2 ratings into a probability distribution, we would obtain the **sampling distribution of the sample mean.**

> **SAMPLING DISTRIBUTION OF THE SAMPLE MEAN** A probability distribution of all possible sample means of a given sample size.

The following example illustrates the construction of a sampling distribution of the sample mean.

EXAMPLE

Tartus Industries has seven production employees (considered the population). The hourly earnings of each employee are given in Table 8–2.

TABLE 8–2 Hourly Earnings of the Production Employees of Tartus Industries

Employee	Hourly Earnings
Joe	$7
Sam	7
Sue	8
Bob	8
Jan	7
Art	8
Ted	9

1. What is the population mean?
2. What is the sampling distribution of the sample mean for samples of size 2?
3. What is the mean of the sampling distribution?
4. What observations can be made about the population and the sampling distribution?

SOLUTION

1. The population mean is $7.71, found by:

$$\mu = \frac{\$7 + \$7 + \$8 + \$8 + \$7 + \$8 + \$9}{7}$$

We identify the population mean with the Greek letter μ. Our policy, stated in Chapters 1, 3, and 4, is to identify population parameters with Greek letters.

2. To arrive at the sampling distribution of the sample mean, all possible samples of 2 were selected without replacement from the population, and their means were computed. There are 21 possible samples, found by using formula 5–10 on page 178.

$$_{N}C_{n} = \frac{N!}{n!(N-n)!} = \frac{7!}{2!(7-2)!} = 21$$

where $N = 7$ is the number of items in the population and $n = 2$ is the number of items in the sample.

The 21 distinct sample means from all possible samples of 2 that can be drawn from the population are shown in Table 8–3. This probability distribution is the sampling distribution of the sample mean and is summarized in Table 8–4.

TABLE 8–3 Sample Means for All Possible Samples of 2 Employees

Sample	Employees	Hourly Earnings	Sum	Mean	Sample	Employees	Hourly Earnings	Sum	Mean
1	Joe, Sam	$7, $7	$14	$7.00	12	Sue, Bob	$8, $8	$16	$8.00
2	Joe, Sue	7, 8	15	7.50	13	Sue, Jan	8, 7	15	7.50
3	Joe, Bob	7, 8	15	7.50	14	Sue, Art	8, 8	16	8.00
4	Joe, Jan	7, 7	14	7.00	15	Sue, Ted	8, 9	17	8.50
5	Joe, Art	7, 8	15	7.50	16	Bob, Jan	8, 7	15	7.50
6	Joe, Ted	7, 9	16	8.00	17	Bob, Art	8, 8	16	8.00
7	Sam, Sue	7, 8	15	7.50	18	Bob, Ted	8, 9	17	8.50
8	Sam, Bob	7, 8	15	7.50	19	Jan, Art	7, 8	15	7.50
9	Sam, Jan	7, 7	14	7.00	20	Jan, Ted	7, 9	16	8.00
10	Sam, Art	7, 8	15	7.50	21	Art, Ted	8, 9	17	8.50
11	Sam, Ted	7, 9	16	8.00					

TABLE 8–4 Sampling Distribution of the Sample Mean for $n = 2$

Sample Mean	Number of Means	Probability
$7.00	3	.1429
7.50	9	.4285
8.00	6	.2857
8.50	3	.1429
	21	1.0000

3. The mean of the sampling distribution of the sample mean is obtained by summing the various sample means and dividing the sum by the number of samples. The mean of all the sample means is usually written $\mu_{\bar{X}}$. The μ reminds us that it is a population value because we have considered all possible samples. The subscript $\bar{X}$ indicates that it is the sampling distribution of the sample mean.

Population mean is equal to the mean of the sample means

$$\mu_{\bar{X}} = \frac{\text{Sum of all sample means}}{\text{Total number of samples}} = \frac{\$7.00 + \$7.50 + \cdots + \$8.50}{21}$$

$$= \frac{\$162}{21} = \$7.71$$

4. Refer to Chart 8–1, which shows both the population distribution and the distribution of the sample mean. These observations can be made:
   a. The mean of the distribution of the sample mean ($7.71) is equal to the mean of the population: $\mu = \mu_{\bar{X}}$.
   b. The spread in the distribution of the sample mean is less than the spread in the population values. The sample mean ranges from $7.00 to $8.50, while the population values vary from $7.00 up to $9.00. In fact, the standard deviation of the distribution of the sample mean is equal to the population standard deviation divided by the square root of the sample size. So the formula for the standard deviation of the distribution of the sample mean is $\sigma/\sqrt{n}$. Notice, as we increase the size of the sample, the spread of the distribution of the sample mean becomes smaller.
   c. The shape of the sampling distribution of the sample mean and the shape of the frequency distribution of the population values are different. The distribution of the sample mean tends to be more bell-shaped and to approximate the normal probability distribution.

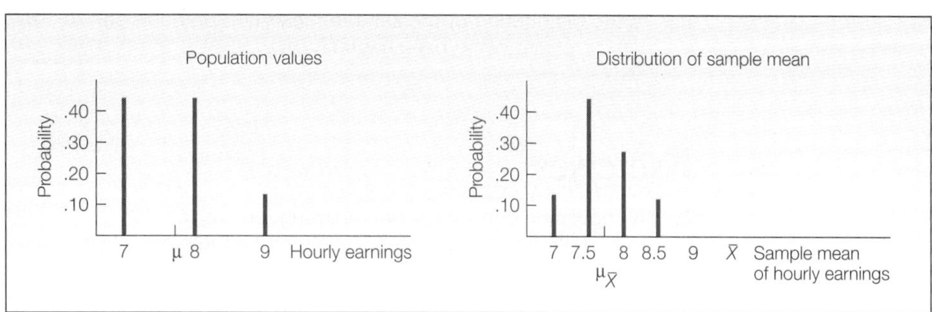

CHART 8–1 Distributions of Population Values and Sample Mean

In summary, we took all possible random samples from a population and for each sample calculated a sample statistic (the mean amount earned). Because each possible sample has a chance of being selected, the probability that the mean amount earned will be values such as $7.27, $8.50, $6.50, and so on can be determined. The distribution of the mean amounts earned is called the sampling distribution of the sample mean.

Even though in practice we see only one particular random sample, in theory any of the samples could arise. Consequently, we view the sampling process as repeated sampling of the statistic from its sampling distribution. This sampling distribution is then used to measure how likely a particular outcome might be.

Self-Review 8–3

The lengths of service of all the executives employed by Standard Chemicals are:

Name	Years
Mr. Snow	20
Ms. Tolson	22
Mr. Kraft	26
Ms. Irwin	24
Mr. Jones	28

(a) Using the combination formula, how many samples of size 2 are possible?
(b) List all possible samples of 2 executives from the population and compute their means.
(c) Organize the means into a sampling distribution.
(d) Compare the population mean and the mean of the sample means.
(e) Compare the dispersion in the population with that in the distribution of the sample mean.
(f) A chart portraying the population values follows. Is the distribution of population values normally distributed (bell-shaped)?

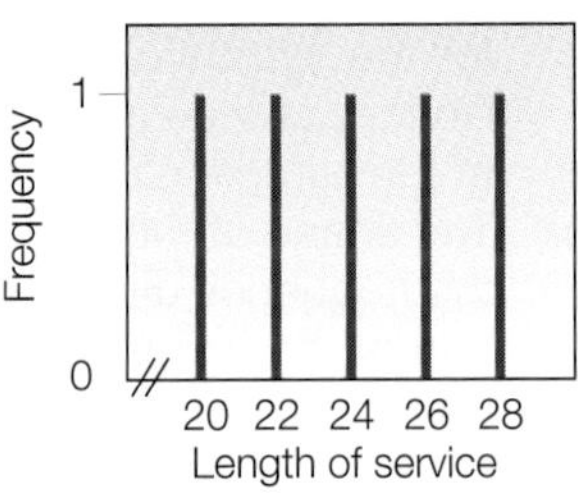

(g) Is the distribution of the sample mean computed in part (c) starting to show some tendency toward being bell-shaped?

Exercises

5. A population consists of the following four values: 12, 12, 14, and 16.
   a. List all samples of size 2, and compute the mean of each sample.
   b. Compute the mean of the distribution of the sample mean and the population mean. Compare the two values.
   c. Compare the dispersion in the population with that of the sample mean.

6. a. See IM.
b. $\mu = 4$, $\mu_{\bar{X}} = 4$
c. Less dispersion in samples.

8. a. See IM.
b. $\mu = 2$, $\mu_{\bar{X}} = 2$
c. Less dispersion in samples.

10. a. 10
b. See IM.
c. $\mu = 6.8$, $\mu_{\bar{X}} = 6.8$
d. More dispersion in the population.

6. A population consists of the following five values: 2, 2, 4, 4, and 8.
   a. List all samples of size 2, and compute the mean of each sample.
   b. Compute the mean of the distribution of the sample mean and the population mean. Compare the two values.
   c. Compare the dispersion in the population with that of the sample means.

7. A population consists of the following five values: 12, 12, 14, 15, and 20.
   a. List all samples of size 3, and compute the mean of each sample.
   b. Compute the mean of the distribution of the sample mean and the population mean. Compare the two values.
   c. Compare the dispersion in the population with that of the sample means.

8. A population consists of the following five values: 0, 0, 1, 3, 6.
   a. List all samples of size 3, and compute the mean of each sample.
   b. Compute the mean of the distribution of the sample mean and the population mean. Compare the two values.
   c. Compare the dispersion in the population with that of the sample means.

9. In the law firm Tybo and Associates, there are six partners. Listed below is the number of cases each associate actually tried in court last month.

Associate	Number of Cases
Ruud	3
Austin	6
Sass	3
Palmer	3
Wilhelms	0
Schueller	1

   a. How many different samples of 3 are possible?
   b. List all possible samples of size 3, and compute the mean number of cases in each sample.
   c. Compare the mean of the distribution of the sample mean to the population mean.
   d. On a chart similar to Chart 8–1, compare the dispersion in the population with that of the sample means.

10. There are five sales representatives at Mid-Motors Ford. The five representatives and the number of cars they sold last week are:

Sales Representative	Cars Sold
Peter Hankish	8
Connie Stallter	6
Ron Eaton	4
Ted Barnes	10
Peggy Harmon	6

   a. How many different samples of size 2 are possible?
   b. List all possible samples of size 2, and compute the mean of each sample.
   c. Compare the mean of the sampling distribution of the sample mean with that of the population.
   d. On a chart similar to Chart 8–1, compare the dispersion in the sample mean with that of the population.

The Central Limit Theorem

In this section, we examine the **central limit theorem.** Its application to the sampling distribution of the sample mean, introduced in the previous section, allows us to use the normal probability distribution to create confidence intervals for the population mean (described in Chapter 9) and perform tests of hypothesis (described in Chapter 10). The central limit theorem states that, for large random samples, the shape of the sampling distribution of the sample mean is close to a normal probability distribution. The approximation is more accurate for large samples than for small samples. This is one of the most useful conclusions in statistics. We can reason about the distribution of the sample mean with absolutely no information about the shape of the original distribution from which the sample is taken. In other words, the central limit theorem is true for all distributions.

A formal statement of the central limit theorem follows.

CENTRAL LIMIT THEOREM If all samples of a particular size are selected from any population, the sampling distribution of the sample mean is approximately a normal distribution. This approximation improves with larger samples.

If the population follows a normal probability distribution, then for any sample size the sampling distribution of the sample mean will also be normal. If the population distribution is symmetrical (but not normal), you will see the normal shape of the distribution of the sample mean emerge with samples as small as 10. On the other hand, if you start with a distribution that is skewed or has thick tails, it may require samples of 30 or more to observe the normality feature. This concept is summarized in Chart 8–2. Observe the convergence to a normal distribution regardless of the shape of the population distribution. Most statisticians consider a sample of 30 or more to be large enough for the central limit theorem to be employed.

The idea that the distribution of the sample means from a population that is not normal will converge to normality is illustrated in Charts 8–3, 8–4, and 8–5. We will discuss this example in more detail shortly, but Chart 8–3 is a graph of a discrete probability distribution that is positively skewed. There are many possible samples of 5 that might be selected from this population. Suppose we randomly select 25 samples of 5 each and compute the mean of each sample. These results are shown in Chart 8–4. Notice that the shape of the distribution of the sample mean has changed from the original population even though we selected only 25 of the many possible samples. To put it another way, we selected 25 random samples of 5 each from a population that is positively skewed and found the distribution of the sample mean has changed from the shape of the population. As we take larger samples, that is, $n = 20$ instead of $n = 5$, we will find the distribution of the sample mean will approach the normal distribution. Chart 8–5 shows the results of 25 random samples of 20 observations each from the same population. Observe the clear trend toward the normal probability distribution. This is the point of the central limit theorem. The following example will underscore this condition.

EXAMPLE

Ed Spence began his sprocket business 20 years ago. The business has grown over the years and now employs 40 people. Spence Sprockets, Inc. faces some major decisions regarding health care for these employees. Before making a final decision on what health care plan to purchase, Ed decides to form a committee of five representative employees. The committee will be asked to study the health care issue carefully and make a recommendation as to what plan best fits the employees' needs. Ed feels the views of newer employees toward health care may differ from those of more experienced employees. If Ed randomly selects this committee, what can he expect in terms of the mean years with Spence Sprockets for those on the committee? How does the shape of the distribution of years of experience of all employees (the population) compare with the shape of the sampling distribution of the mean? The lengths

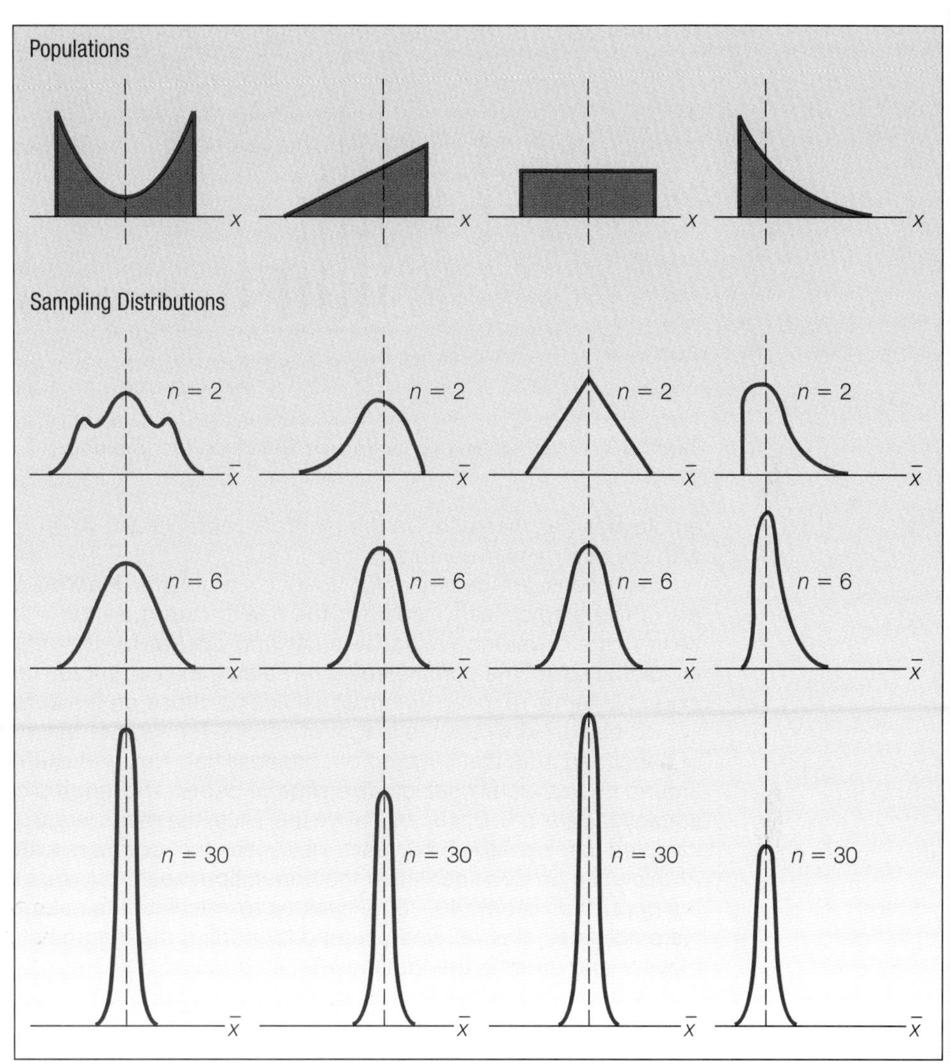

CHART 8–2 Results of the Central Limit Theorem for Several Populations

of service (rounded to the nearest year) of the 40 employees currently on the Spence Sprockets, Inc. payroll are as follows.

11	4	18	2	1	2	0	2	2	4
3	4	1	2	2	3	3	19	8	3
7	1	0	2	7	0	4	5	1	14
16	8	9	1	1	2	5	10	2	3

SOLUTION

Chart 8–3 shows the distribution of the years of experience for the population of 40 current employees. This distribution of lengths of service is positively skewed because there are a few employees who have worked at Spence Sprockets for a longer period of time. Specifically, six employees have been with the company 10 years or more. However, because the business has grown, the number of

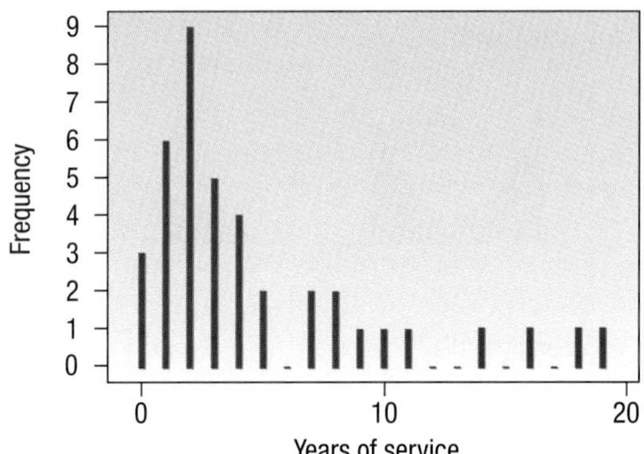

CHART 8–3 Length of Service for Spence Sprockets, Inc. Employees

employees has increased in the last few years. Of the 40 employees, 18 have been with the company two years or less.

Let's consider the first of Ed Spence's problems. He would like to form a committee of five employees to look into the health care question and suggest what type of health care coverage would be most appropriate for the majority of workers. How should he select the committee? If he selects the committee randomly, what might he expect in terms of mean length of service for those on the committee?

To begin, Ed writes the length of service for each of the 40 employees on pieces of paper and puts them into an old baseball hat. Next, he shuffles the pieces of paper around and randomly selects five slips of paper. The lengths of service for these five employees are 1, 9, 0, 19, and 14 years. Thus, the mean length of service for these five sampled employees is 8.60 years. How does that compare with the population mean? At this point Ed does not know the population mean, but the number of employees in the population is only 40, so he decides to calculate the mean length of service for *all* his employees. It is 4.8 years, found by adding the lengths of service for *all* the employees and dividing the total by 40.

$$\mu = \frac{11 + 4 + 18 + \cdots + 2 + 3}{40} = 4.80$$

The difference between the sample mean ($\bar{X}$) and the population mean (μ) is called **sampling error.** In other words, the difference of 3.80 years between the population mean of 4.80 and the sample mean of 8.60 is the sampling error. It is due to chance. Thus, if Ed selected these five employees to constitute the committee, their mean length of service would be larger than the population mean.

What would happen if Ed put the five pieces of paper back into the baseball hat and selected another sample? Would you expect the mean of this second sample to be exactly the same as the previous one? Suppose he selects another sample of five employees and finds the lengths of service in this sample to be 7, 4, 4, 1, and 3. This sample mean is 3.80 years. The result of selecting 25 samples of five employees each is shown in Table 8–5 and Chart 8–4. There are actually 658,008 possible samples of 5 from the population of 40 employees, found by the combination formula (5–10) for 40 things taken 5 at a time. Notice the difference in the shape of the population and the distribution of these sample means. The population of the lengths of service for employees (Chart 8–3) is positively skewed, but the distribution of these 25 sample means does not reflect the same positive skew. There is also a difference in the range of the sample means versus the range of the population. The population ranged from 0 to 19 years, whereas the sample means range from 1.6 to 8.6 years.

TABLE 8–5 Twenty-five Random Samples of Five Employees

Sample I.D.	Sample Data					Sample Mean
A	1	9	0	19	14	8.6
B	7	4	4	1	3	3.8
C	8	19	8	2	1	7.6
D	4	18	2	0	11	7.0
F	4	2	4	7	18	7.0
G	1	2	0	3	2	1.6
F	2	3	2	0	2	1.8
H	11	2	9	2	4	5.6
I	9	0	4	2	7	4.4
J	1	1	1	11	1	3.0
K	2	0	0	10	2	2.8
L	0	2	3	2	16	4.6
M	2	3	1	1	1	1.6
N	3	7	3	4	3	4.0
0	1	2	3	1	4	2.2
P	19	0	1	3	8	6.2
Q	5	1	7	14	9	7.2
R	5	4	2	3	4	3.6
S	14	5	2	2	5	5.6
T	2	1	1	4	7	3.0
U	3	7	1	2	1	2.8
V	0	1	5	1	2	1.8
W	0	3	19	4	2	5.6
X	4	2	3	4	0	2.6
Y	1	1	2	3	2	1.8

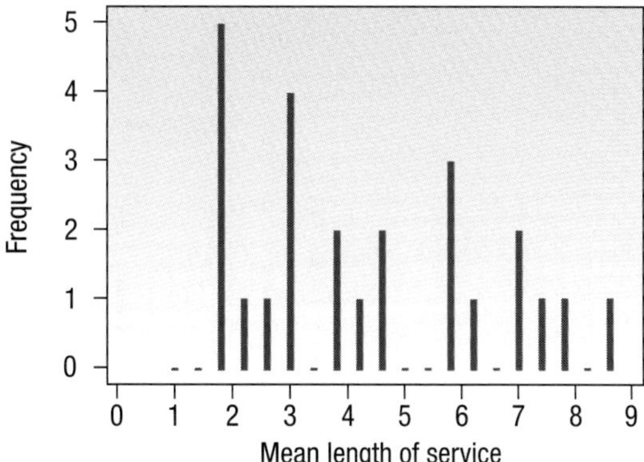

CHART 8–4 Histogram of Mean Lengths of Service for 25 Samples of Five Employees

Table 8–6 reports the result of selecting 25 samples of 20 employees each and computing their sample means. These sample means are shown graphically in Chart 8–5. Compare the shape of this distribution to the population (Chart 8–3) and to the distribution of sample means where the sample is $n = 5$ (Chart 8–4). You should observe two important features:

1. The shape of the distribution of the sample mean is different from that of the population. In Chart 8–3 the distribution of all employees is positively skewed.

TABLE 8–6 Random Samples and Sample Means of 25 Samples of 20 Spence Sprocket, Inc. Employees

Sample Number										Sample Data (Length of Service)											Sample Mean
A	3	8	3	0	2	1	2	3	11	5	1	3	4	2	7	1	1	2	4	16	3.95
B	2	3	8	2	1	5	2	0	3	1	0	7	1	4	3	11	4	4	3	1	3.25
C	14	5	0	3	2	14	11	9	2	2	1	2	19	1	0	1	4	2	19	8	5.95
D	9	2	1	1	4	10	0	8	4	3	2	1	0	8	1	14	5	10	1	3	4.35
E	18	1	2	2	4	3	2	8	2	1	0	19	4	19	0	1	4	0	3	14	5.35
F	10	4	4	18	3	3	1	0	0	2	2	4	7	10	2	0	3	4	2	1	4.00
G	5	7	11	8	11	18	1	1	16	2	2	16	2	3	2	16	2	2	2	4	6.55
H	3	0	2	0	5	4	5	3	8	3	2	5	1	1	2	9	8	3	16	5	4.25
I	0	0	18	2	1	7	4	1	3	0	3	2	11	7	2	8	5	1	2	3	4.00
J	2	7	2	4	1	3	3	2	5	10	0	1	1	2	9	3	2	19	3	2	4.05
K	7	4	5	3	3	0	18	2	0	4	2	7	2	7	4	2	10	1	1	2	4.20
L	0	3	10	5	9	2	1	4	1	2	1	8	18	1	4	3	3	2	0	4	4.05
M	4	1	2	1	7	3	9	14	8	19	4	4	1	2	0	3	1	2	1	2	4.40
N	3	16	1	2	4	4	4	2	1	5	2	3	5	3	4	7	16	1	11	1	4.75
O	2	19	2	0	2	2	16	2	3	11	9	2	8	0	8	2	7	3	2	2	5.10
P	2	18	16	5	2	2	19	0	1	2	11	4	2	2	1	4	2	0	4	3	5.00
Q	3	2	3	11	10	1	1	5	19	16	7	10	3	1	1	1	2	2	3	1	5.10
R	2	3	1	2	7	4	3	19	9	2	2	1	1	2	2	2	1	8	0	2	3.65
S	2	14	19	1	19	2	8	4	2	2	14	2	8	16	4	7	2	9	0	7	7.10
T	0	1	3	3	2	2	3	1	1	0	3	2	3	5	2	10	14	4	2	0	3.05
U	1	0	1	2	16	1	1	2	5	1	4	1	2	2	2	2	2	8	9	3	3.25
V	1	9	4	4	2	8	7	1	14	18	1	5	10	11	19	0	3	7	2	11	6.85
W	8	1	9	19	3	19	0	5	2	1	5	3	3	4	1	5	3	1	8	7	5.35
X	4	2	0	3	1	16	1	11	3	3	2	18	2	0	1	5	0	7	2	5	4.30
Y	1	2	1	2	0	2	7	2	4	8	19	2	5	3	3	0	19	2	1	18	5.05

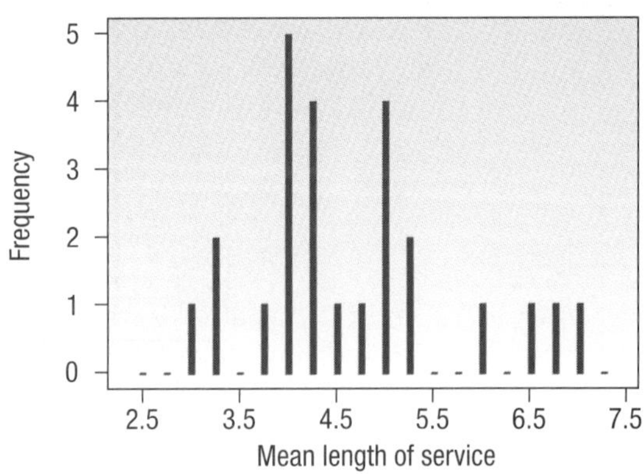

CHART 8–5 Histogram of Mean Lengths of Service for 25 Samples of 20 Employees

However, as we select random samples from this population, the shape of the distribution of the sample mean changes. As we increase the size of the sample, the distribution of the sample mean approaches the normal probability distribution. This illustrates the central limit theorem.

2. There is less dispersion in the sampling distribution of sample mean than in the population distribution. In the population the lengths of service ranged from 0 to 19 years. When we selected samples of 5, the sample means ranged from 1.6 to 8.6 years, and when we selected samples of 20, the means ranged from 3.05 to 7.10 years.

We can also compare the mean of the sample means to the population mean. The mean of the 25 samples reported in Table 8–6 is 4.676 years.

$$\mu_{\bar{X}} = \frac{3.95 + 3.25 + \cdots + 4.30 + 5.05}{25} = 4.676$$

We use the symbol $\mu_{\bar{X}}$ to identify the mean of the distribution of the sample mean. The subscript reminds us that the distribution is of the sample mean. It is read "mu sub X bar." We observe that the mean of the sample means, 4.676 years, is very close to the population mean of 4.80.

What should we conclude from this example? The central limit theorem indicates that, regardless of the shape of the population distribution, the sampling distribution of the sample mean will move toward the normal probability distribution. The larger the number of observations in each sample, the stronger the convergence. The Spence Sprockets, Inc. example shows how the central limit theorem works. We began with a positively skewed population (Chart 8–3). Next, we selected 25 random samples of 5 observations, computed the mean of each sample, and finally organized these 25 sample means into a graph (Chart 8–4). We observe a change in the shape of the sampling distribution of sample mean from that of the population. The movement is from a positively skewed distribution to a distribution that has the shape of the normal probability distribution.

To further illustrate the effects of the central limit theorem, we increased the number of observations in each sample from 5 to 20. We selected 25 samples of 20 observations each and calculated the mean of each sample. Finally, we organized these sample means into a graph (Chart 8–5). The shape of the histogram in Chart 8–5 is clearly moving toward the normal probability distribution.

The central limit theorem itself (reread the definition on page 278) does not say anything about the dispersion of the sampling distribution of sample mean or about the comparison of the mean of the sampling distribution of sample mean to the mean of the population. However, in our Example we did observe that there was less dispersion in the distribution of the sample mean than in the population distribution by noting the difference in the range in the population and the range of the sample means. We observe that the mean of the sample means is close to the mean of the population. It can be demonstrated that the mean of the sampling distribution is the population mean and if the standard deviation in the population is σ, the standard deviation of the sample means is $\sigma/\sqrt{n}$, where n is the number of observations in each sample. We refer to $\sigma/\sqrt{n}$ as the **standard error of the mean**. Its longer name is actually the *standard deviation of the sampling distribution of the sample mean.*

STANDARD ERROR OF THE MEAN

$$\sigma_{\bar{X}} = \frac{\sigma}{\sqrt{n}} \qquad \textbf{[8–1]}$$

In this section we also came to other important conclusions.

1. The mean of the distribution of the sample mean will be *exactly* equal to the population mean if we are able to select all possible samples of a particular size from a given population. That is:

$$\mu = \mu_{\bar{X}}$$

Even if we do not select all samples, we can expect the mean of the distribution of the sample mean to be close to the population mean.
2. There will be less dispersion in the sampling distribution of the distribution sample mean than in the population. If the standard deviation of the population is σ, the standard deviation of the distribution of the sample mean is $\sigma/\sqrt{n}$. Note that when we increase the size of the sample the standard error of the mean decreases.

Self-Review 8–4

Refer to the Spence Sprockets, Inc. data on page 278. Select 10 random samples of 5 employees each. Use the methods described earlier in the chapter and the Table of Random Numbers (Appendix E) to find the employees to include in the sample. Compute the mean of each sample and plot the sample means on a chart similar to Chart 8–3.

Exercises

11. Appendix E is a table of random numbers. Hence, each digit from 0 to 9 has the same likelihood of occurrence.
  a. Draw a graph showing the population distribution. What is the population mean?
  b. Below are the first 10 rows of five digits from Appendix E. Assume that these are 10 random samples of five values each. Determine the mean of each sample and plot the means on a chart similar to Chart 8–3. Compare the mean of the sampling distribution of the sample mean with the population mean.

0	2	7	1	1
9	4	8	7	3
5	4	9	2	1
7	7	6	4	0
6	1	5	4	5
1	7	1	4	7
1	3	7	4	8
8	7	4	5	5
0	8	9	9	9
7	8	8	0	4

12. The Scrapper Elevator Company has 20 sales representatives who sell their product throughout the United States and Canada. The number of units sold by each representative is listed below. Assume these sales figures to be the population values.

2	3	2	3	3	4	2	4	3	2	2	7	3	4	5	3	3	3	3	5

12. a. See IM.
b. $\mu = 3.3$
c. Answers will vary.

  a. Draw a graph showing the population distribution.
  b. Compute the mean of the population.
  c. Select five random samples of 5 each. Compute the mean of each sample. Use the methods described in this chapter and Appendix E to determine the items to be included in the sample.

d. See IM.

e. See IM.

d. Compare the mean of the sampling distribution of the sample mean to the population mean. Would you expect the two values to be about the same?

e. Draw a histogram of the sample means. Do you notice a difference in the shape of the distribution of sample means compared to the population distribution?

Using the Sampling Distribution of the Sample Mean

The previous discussion is important because most business decisions are made on the basis of sampling results. Here are some examples.

1. The Arm and Hammer Company wants to ensure that their laundry detergent actually contains 100 fluid ounces, as indicated on the label. Historical summaries from the filling process indicate the mean amount per container is 100 fluid ounces and the standard deviation is 2 fluid ounces. The quality technician in her 10 A.M. check of 40 containers finds the mean amount per container is 99.8 fluid ounces. Should the technician shut down the filling operation or is the sampling error reasonable?
2. The A. C. Nielsen Company provides information to companies advertising on television. Prior research indicates that adult Americans watch an average of 6.0 hours per day of television. The standard deviation is 1.5 hours. For a sample of 50 adults in the Greater Boston area, would it be reasonable that we could randomly select a sample and find that they watch an average of 6.5 hours of television per day?
3. The Haughton Elevator Company wishes to develop specifications for the number of people who can ride in a new oversized elevator. Suppose the mean weight for an adult is 160 pounds and the standard deviation is 15 pounds. However, the distribution of weights does not follow the normal probability distribution. It is positively skewed. What is the likelihood that for a sample of 30 adults their mean weight is 170 pounds or more?

In each of these situations we have a population about which we have some information. We take a sample from that population and wish to conclude whether the sampling error, that is, the difference between the population parameter and the sample statistic, is due to chance.

Using ideas discussed in the previous section, we can compute the probability that a sample mean will fall within a certain range. We know that the sampling distribution of the sample mean will follow the normal probability distribution under two conditions:

1. When the samples are taken from populations known to follow the normal distribution. In this case the size of the sample is not a factor.
2. When the shape of the population distribution is not known or the shape is known to be nonnormal, but our sample contains at least 30 observations.

We can use formula 7–1, from the previous chapter, to convert any normal distribution to the standard normal distribution. We also refer to this as a z value. Then we can use the standard normal table, Appendix D, to find the probability of selecting an observation that would fall within a specific range. The formula for finding a z value is:

$$z = \frac{X - \mu}{\sigma}$$

In this formula X is the value of the random variable, μ is the population mean, and σ the population standard deviation.

However, most business decisions refer to a sample—not just one observation. So we are interested in the distribution of $\bar{X}$, the sample mean, instead of X, the value of one observation. That is the first change we make in formula 7–1. The second is that we use the standard error of the mean of n observations instead of the population standard deviation. That is, we use $\sigma/\sqrt{n}$ in the denominator rather than σ. Therefore, to find the likelihood of a sample mean with a specified range, we first use the following formula to find the corresponding z value. Then we use Appendix D to locate the probability.

FINDING THE z VALUE OF $\bar{X}$ WHEN THE POPULATION STANDARD DEVIATION IS KNOWN

$$z = \frac{\bar{X} - \mu}{\sigma/\sqrt{n}} \qquad [8\text{–}2]$$

The following example will show the application.

EXAMPLE

The Quality Assurance Department for Cola, Inc. maintains records regarding the amount of cola in their "Jumbo" bottle. The actual amount of cola in each bottle is critical, but varies a small amount from one bottle to the next. Cola, Inc. does not wish to underfill the bottles, because they will have a problem with truth in labeling. On the other hand, they cannot overfill each bottle, because they would be giving cola away, hence reducing their profits. Their records indicate that the amount of cola follows the normal probability distribution. The mean amount per bottle is 31.2 ounces and the population standard deviation is 0.4 ounces. At 8 A.M. today the quality technician randomly selected 16 bottles from the filling line. The mean amount of cola contained in the bottles is 31.38 ounces. Is this an unlikely result? Is it likely the process is putting too much soda in the bottles? To put it another way, is the sampling error of 0.18 ounces unusual?

SOLUTION

We can use the results of the previous section to find the likelihood that we could select a sample of 16 (n) bottles from a normal population with a mean of 31.2 (μ) ounces and a population standard deviation of 0.4 (σ) ounces and find the sample mean to be 31.38 ($\bar{X}$). We use formula 8–2 to find the value of z.

$$z = \frac{\bar{X} - \mu}{\sigma/\sqrt{n}} = \frac{31.38 - 31.20}{0.4/\sqrt{16}} = 1.80$$

The numerator of this equation, $\bar{X} - \mu = 31.38 - 31.20 = .18$, is the sampling error. The denominator, $\sigma/\sqrt{n} = 0.40/\sqrt{16} = 0.1$, is the standard error of the sampling distribution of the sample mean. So the z values express the sampling error in standard units, in other words, the standard error.

Next, we compute the likelihood of a z value greater than 1.80. In Appendix D locate the probability corresponding to a z value of 1.80. It is .4641. The likelihood of a z value greater than 1.80 is .0359, found by $.5000 - .4641$.

What do we conclude? It is unlikely, less than a 4 percent chance, we could select a sample of 16 observations from a normal population with a mean of 31.2 ounces and a population standard deviation of 0.4 ounces and find the sample mean equal to or greater than 31.38 ounces. The process is putting too much cola in the bottles. The quality technician should see the production supervisor about reducing the amount of soda in each bottle. This information is summarized in Chart 8–6.

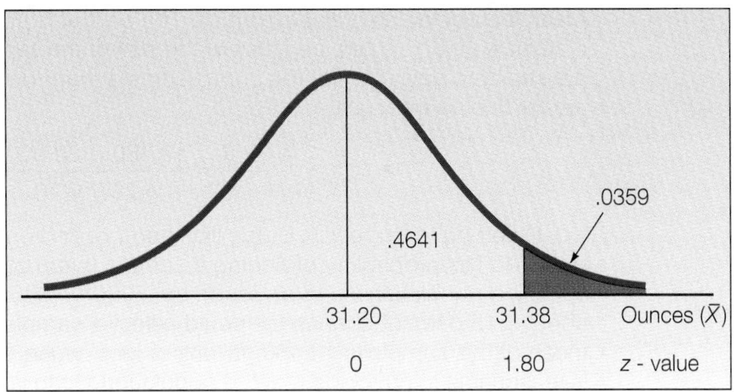

CHART 8–6 Sampling Distribution of the Mean Amount of Cola in a Jumbo Bottle

Self-Review 8–5

Refer to the Cola, Inc. information. Compute the probability that a sample of 16 Jumbo bottles would have a mean of 31.08 ounces or more.

There are many sampling situations in business for which we wish to make a statement about the population, but we do not have much knowledge about the population. Here the power of the central limit theorem helps. We know that, for any shape of the population distribution, if we select a sample sufficiently large, the sampling distribution of the sample mean will follow the normal distribution. Statistical theory has shown that samples of at least 30 are sufficiently large to allow us to assume that the sampling distribution follows the normal distribution.

Often we do not know the value of the population standard deviation, σ. Again, if the sample is at least 30, we estimate the population standard deviation with the sample standard deviation. When we use s to replace σ, the new formula for finding the value of z is:

FINDING THE z VALUE OF $\bar{X}$ WHEN THE POPULATION STANDARD DEVIATION IS UNKNOWN

$$z = \frac{\bar{X} - \mu}{s/\sqrt{n}} \quad \textbf{[8–3]}$$

EXAMPLE

The Metropolitan New York Gas Station Dealers' Association estimates that the mean number of gallons of gasoline sold per day at a gas station is 20,000. The shape of this distribution is unknown. A sample of 70 dealers yesterday revealed the mean number of gallons sold was 19,480. The standard deviation of the sample of 70 dealers was 4,250 gallons. Is the assertion that the population mean is 20,000 gallons reasonable? What is the likelihood of finding a sample with the given statistics from the proposed population? What assumptions do you need to make?

SOLUTION

We are unsure of the shape of the population of gallons sold. However, the sample is sufficiently large to allow us to assume that the sampling distribution of the sample mean follows the normal distribution. The central limit theorem provides the necessary statistical theory. Again, because of the size of the sample, we can substitute the sample standard deviation for the population standard deviation. Formula 8–3 is appropriate for finding the z value.

$$z = \frac{\bar{X} - \mu}{s/\sqrt{n}} = \frac{19{,}480 - 20{,}000}{4{,}250/\sqrt{70}} = -1.02$$

Referring to Appendix D, the likelihood of finding a z value between 0 and -1.02 is .3461. The probability of finding a sample mean of 19,480 gallons or less from the specified population is .1539, found by .5000 − .3461. To put it another way, there is about a 15 percent chance we could select a sample of 70 gas stations and find the mean of this sample is 19,480 gallons or less, when the population mean is 20,000. It is reasonable to conclude that the population mean is 20,000 gallons. This information is summarized in Chart 8–7.

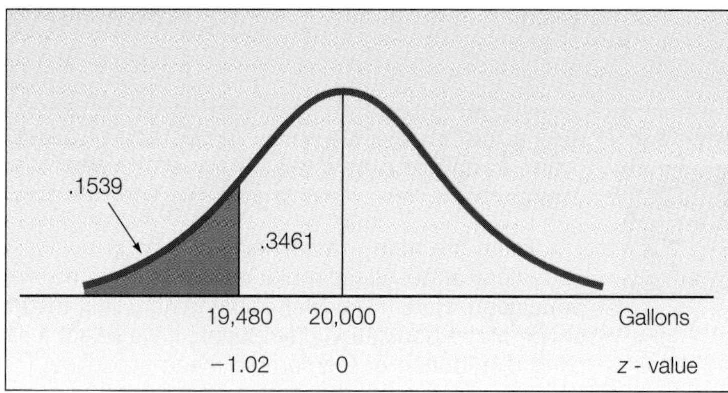

CHART 8–7 Sampling Distribution for the Sample Mean of the Number of Gallons Sold per Day

Self-Review 8–6

The mean hourly wage for plumbers in the Atlanta, Georgia, region is $28.00. What is the likelihood that we could select a sample of 50 plumbers with a mean wage of $28.50 or more? The standard deviation of the sample is $2.00 per hour.

Exercises

13. A normal population has a mean of 60 and a standard deviation of 12. You select a random sample of 9. Compute the probability the sample mean is:
a. Greater than 63.
b. Less than 56.
c. Between 56 and 63.

14. A population of unknown shape has a mean of 75. You select a sample of 40. The standard deviation of the sample is 5. Compute the probability the sample mean is:
a. Less than 74.
b. Between 74 and 76.
c. Between 76 and 77.
d. Greater than 77.

14. a. .1038
b. .7924
c. .0981
d. .0057

15. The mean rent for a one-bedroom apartment in Southern California is $1,200 per month. The distribution of the monthly costs does not follow the normal distribution. In fact, it is positively skewed. What is the probability of selecting a sample of 50 one-bedroom apartments and finding the mean to be at least $950 per month. The standard deviation of the sample is $250.

16. According to an IRS study, it takes an average of 330 minutes for taxpayers to prepare, copy, and mail a 1040 tax form. A consumer watchdog agency selects a random sample of 40 taxpayers and finds the standard deviation of the time to prepare, copy, and mail form 1040 is 80 minutes.

a. What assumption or assumptions do you need to make about the shape of the population?
b. What is the standard error of the mean in this example?
c. What is the likelihood the sample mean is greater than 320 minutes?
d. What is the likelihood the sample mean is between 320 and 350 minutes?
e. What is the likelihood the sample mean is greater than 350 minutes?

16. a. none.
b. 12.649
c. .7852
d. .7281
e. .0571

Chapter Outline

I. There are many reasons for sampling a population.
  A. Often testing destroys the sampled item and it cannot be returned to the population.
  B. It may be impossible to check or locate all the members of the population.
  C. The cost of studying all the items in the population may be prohibitive.
  D. The results of a sample may adequately estimate the value of the population parameter, thus saving time and money.
  E. It may be too time consuming to contact all members of the population.

II. There are probability and nonprobability samples.
  A. In a probability sample all members of the population have a chance of being selected for the sample. There are several probability sampling methods.
    1. In a simple random sample all members of the population have the same chance of being selected for the sample.
    2. In a systematic sample a random starting point is selected, and then every *k*th item thereafter is selected for the sample.
    3. In a stratified sample the population is divided into several groups, called strata, and then a random sample is selected from each stratum.
    4. In cluster sampling the population is divided into primary units, then samples are drawn from the primary units.
  B. In nonprobability sampling, inclusion in the sample is based on the judgment of the person conducting the sample. Nonprobability sampling can lead to biased results.

III. The sampling error is the difference between a population parameter and a sample statistic.

IV. The sampling distribution of the sample mean is a probability distribution of all possible sample means of a given size.
  A. For a given sample size, the mean of all possible sample means selected from a population is equal to the population mean.
  B. There is less variation in the distribution of the sample mean than in the population distribution.
    1. The standard error of the mean measures the variation in the sampling distribution of the sample mean.
      a. If we know the population standard deviation, the standard error is

$$\sigma_{\bar{X}} = \frac{\sigma}{\sqrt{n}} \quad \textbf{[8–1]}$$

      b. If we do not know the population standard deviation, the standard error is estimated by

$$s_{\bar{X}} = \frac{s}{\sqrt{n}}$$

C. If the population follows the normal distribution, the sampling distribution of the sample mean will also follow the normal distribution for samples of any size. Assume the population standard deviation is known. To determine the probability that a sample mean falls in a particular region, use the following formula.

$$z = \frac{\bar{X} - \mu}{\sigma/\sqrt{n}} \quad \textbf{[8–2]}$$

D. If the population is not normally distributed but the sample is of at least 30 observations, the sampling distribution of the sample mean is approximately normal. Assume the population standard deviation is not known. To determine the probability that a sample mean falls in a particular region, use the normal distribution and the following standardizing formula:

$$z = \frac{\bar{X} - \mu}{s/\sqrt{n}} \quad \textbf{[8–3]}$$

Pronunciation Key

SYMBOL	MEANING	PRONUNCIATION
$\mu_{\bar{X}}$	Mean of the sampling distribution of the sample mean	*mu sub X bar*
$\sigma_{\bar{X}}$	Population standard error of the sample mean	*sigma sub X bar*
$s_{\bar{X}}$	Estimate of the standard error of the sample mean	*s sub X bar*

Chapter Exercises

17. The retail stores located in the North Towne Square Mall are:

00	Elder-Beerman	09	Lion Store	18	County Seat
01	Montgomery Ward	10	Bootleggers	19	Kid Mart
02	Deb Shop	11	Formal Man	20	Lerner
03	Frederick's of Hollywood	12	Leather Ltd.	21	Coach House Gifts
04	Petries	13	B Dalton Bookseller	22	Spence Gifts
05	Easy Dreams	14	Pat's Hallmark	23	CPI Photo Finish
06	Summit Stationers	15	Things Remembered	24	Regis Hairstylists
07	E. B. Brown Opticians	16	Pearle Vision Express		
08	Kay-Bee Toy & Hobby	17	Dollar Tree		

a. If the following random numbers are selected, which retail stores should be contacted for a survey? 11, 65, 86, 62, 06, 10, 12, 77, and 04

b. Select a random sample of four retail stores. Use Appendix E.

c. A systematic sampling procedure is to be used. The first store is to be contacted and then every third store. Which stores will be contacted?

18. Medical Mutual Insurance is investigating the cost of a routine office visit to family-practice physicians in the Rochester, New York, area. The following is a list of family-practice physicians in the region. Physicians are to be randomly selected and contacted regarding their charges. The 39 physicians have been coded from 00 to 38. Also noted is whether they are in practice by themselves (S), have a partner (P), or are in a group practice (G).

Number	Physician	Type of Practice	Number	Physician	Type of Practice
00	R. E. Scherbarth, M.D.	S	20	Gregory Yost, M.D.	P
01	Crystal R. Goveia, M.D.	P	21	J. Christian Zona, M.D.	P
02	Mark D. Hillard, M.D.	P	22	Larry Johnson, M.D.	P
03	Jeanine S. Huttner, M.D.	P	23	Sanford Kimmel, M.D.	P
04	Francis Aona, M.D.	P	24	Harry Mayhew, M.D.	S
05	Janet Arrowsmith, M.D.	P	25	Leroy Rodgers, M.D.	S
06	David DeFrance, M.D.	S	26	Thomas Tafelski, M.D.	S
07	Judith Furlong, M.D.	S	27	Mark Zilkoski, M.D.	G
08	Leslie Jackson, M.D.	G	28	Ken Bertka, M.D.	G
09	Paul Langenkamp, M.D.	S	29	Mark DeMichiei, M.D.	G
10	Philip Lepkowski, M.D.	S	30	John Eggert, M.D.	P
11	Wendy Martin, M.D.	S	31	Jeanne Fiorito, M.D.	P
12	Denny Mauricio, M.D.	P	32	Michael Fitzpatrick, M.D.	P
13	Hasmukh Parmar, M.D.	P	33	Charles Holt, D.O.	P
14	Ricardo Pena, M.D.	P	34	Richard Koby, M.D.	P
15	David Reames, M.D.	P	35	John Meier, M.D.	P
16	Ronald Reynolds, M.D.	G	36	Douglas Smucker, M.D.	S
17	Mark Steinmetz, M.D.	G	37	David Weldy, M.D.	P
18	Geza Torok, M.D.	S	38	Cheryl Zaborowski, M.D.	P
19	Mark Young, M.D.	P			

18. See IM.

a. The random numbers obtained from Appendix E are: 31, 94, 43, 36, 03, 24, 17, and 09. Which physicians should be contacted?
b. Select a random sample of four physicians using the random numbers of Appendix E.
c. A sample is to consist of every fifth physician. The number 04 is selected as the starting point. Which physicians will be contacted?
d. A sample is to consist of two physicians in solo practice (S), two in partnership (P), and one in group practice (G). Select a sample accordingly. Explain your procedure.

19. What is sampling error? Could the value of the sampling error be zero? If it were zero, what would this mean?

20. See IM.

20. List the reasons for sampling. Give an example of each reason for sampling.

21. The commercial banks in Region III are to be surveyed. Some of them are very large, with assets of more than $500 million; others are medium-sized, with assets between $100 million and $500 million; and the remaining banks have assets of less than $100 million. Explain how you would select a sample of these banks.

22. See IM.

22. Plastic Products is concerned about the inside diameter of the plastic PVC pipe it produces. A machine extrudes the pipe, which is then cut into 10-foot lengths. About 720 pipes are produced per machine during a two-hour period. How would you go about taking a sample from the two-hour production period?

23. A study of motel facilities in a metropolitan area showed there were 25 facilities. The city's convention and visitors bureau is studying the number of rooms at each location. The results are as follows:

90	72	75	60	75	72	84	72	88	74	105	115	68	74	80	64	104	82	48	58	60	80	48	58	100

a. Using a table of random numbers (Appendix E), select a random sample of five motels from this population.
b. Obtain a systematic sample by selecting a random starting point among the first five motels and then select every fifth motel.
c. Suppose the last five motels are "cut-rate" motels. Describe how you would select a random sample of three regular motels and two cut-rate motels.

24. See IM.

24. As a part of their customer-service program, United Airlines randomly selected ten passengers from today's 9 A.M. Chicago–Tampa flight. Each sampled passenger is to be interviewed in depth regarding airport facilities, service, food, and so on. To identify the sample, each passenger was given a number as they boarded the aircraft. The numbers started with 001 and ended with 250.

- **a.** Select 10 usable numbers at random using Appendix E.
- **b.** The sample of 10 could have been chosen using a systematic sample. Choose the first number using Appendix E, and then list the numbers to be interviewed.
- **c.** Evaluate the two methods by giving the advantages and possible disadvantages.
- **d.** In what other way could a random sample be selected from the 250 passengers?

25. Suppose your statistics instructor gave six examinations during the semester. You received the following grades (percent correct): 79, 64, 84, 82, 92, and 77. Instead of averaging the six scores, the instructor indicated he would randomly select two grades and report that grade to the student records office.

- **a.** How many different samples of two test grades are possible?
- **b.** List all possible samples of size two and compute the mean of each.
- **c.** Compute the mean of the sample means and compare it to the population mean.
- **d.** If you were a student, would you like this arrangement? Would the result be different from dropping the lowest score? Write a brief report.

26. At the downtown office of First National Bank there are five tellers. Last week the tellers made the following number of errors each: 2, 3, 5, 3, and 5.

- **a.** How many different samples of 2 tellers are possible?
- **b.** List all possible samples of size 2 and compute the mean of each.
- **c.** Compute the mean of the sample means and compare it to the population mean.

26. a. 10
b. See IM.
c. $\mu = 3.6$, $\mu_{\bar{X}} = 3.6$

27. The quality control department employs five technicians during the day shift. Listed below is the number of times each technician instructed the production foreman to shut down the manufacturing process last week.

Technician	Shutdowns
Taylor	4
Hurley	3
Fowler	5
Rousche	3
Telatko	2

- **a.** How many different samples of two technicians are possible from this population?
- **b.** List all possible samples of two observations each and compute the mean of each sample.
- **c.** Compare the mean of the sample means with the population mean.
- **d.** Compare the shape of the population distribution with the shape of the distribution of the sample means.

28. The Appliance Center has six sales representatives at their North Jacksonville outlet. Listed below is the number of refrigerators sold by each last month.

Sales Representative	Number Sold
Zina Craft	54
Woon Junge	50
Ernie DeBrul	52
Jan Niles	48
Molly Camp	50
Rachel Myak	52

28. a. 15
b. See IM.
c. See IM.
d. 51, 51
e. See IM.
f. See IM.

a. How many samples of size two are possible?
b. Select all possible samples of two and compute the mean number sold.
c. Organize the sample means into a frequency distribution.
d. What is the mean of the population? What is the mean of the sample means?
e. What is the shape of the population distribution?
f. What is the shape of the distribution of the sample mean?

29. The Sony Corporation produces an AM/FM Walkman that requires two AA batteries. The mean life of these batteries in this product is 35.0 hours. The distribution of the battery lives closely follows the normal probability distribution with a standard deviation of 5.5 hours. As a part of their testing program Sony tests samples of 25 batteries.
a. What can you say about the shape of the distribution of sample mean?
b. What is the standard error of the distribution of the sample mean?
c. What fraction of the samples will have a mean useful life of more than 36 hours?
d. What fraction of the sample will have a mean useful life greater than 34.5 hours?
e. What fraction of the sample will have a mean useful life between 34.5 and 36.0 hours?

30. CRA CDs, Inc. wants the mean lengths of the "cuts" on a CD to be 135 seconds (2 minutes and 15 seconds). This will allow the disk jockeys to have plenty of time for commercials within each 10-minute segment. Assume the distribution of the length of the cuts follows the normal distribution with a standard deviation of 8 seconds. Suppose we select a sample of 16 cuts from various CDs sold by CRA CDs, Inc.

30. a. Normal.
b. 2
c. .0062
d. Almost all.
e. About .9938

a. What can we say about the shape of the distribution of the sample mean?
b. What is the standard error of the mean?
c. What percent of the sample means will be greater than 140 minutes?
d. What percent of the sample means will be greater than 128 minutes?
e. What percent of the sample means will be greater than 128 but less than 140 minutes?

31. Recent studies indicate that the typical 50-year-old woman spends $350 per year for personal-care products. The distribution of the amounts spent is positively skewed. We select a random sample of 40 women. The mean amount spent for those sampled is $335, and the standard deviation of the sample is $45. What is the likelihood of finding a sample mean this large or larger from the specified population?

32. Information from the American Institute of Insurance indicates the mean amount of life insurance per household in the United States is $110,000. This distribution is positively skewed. The standard deviation of the population is not known.

32. a. $s_{\bar{x}} = 5657$
b. Normal.
c. .3632
d. .9616
e. .5984

a. A random sample of 50 households revealed a mean of $112,000 and a standard deviation of $40,000. What is the standard error of the mean?
b. Suppose that you selected 50 samples of households. What is the expected shape of the distribution of the sample mean?
c. What is the likelihood of selecting a sample with a mean of at least $112,000?
d. What is the likelihood of selecting a sample with a mean of more than $100,000?
e. Find the likelihood of selecting a sample with a mean of more than $100,000 but less than $112,000.

33. The mean age at which men in the United States marry for the first time is 24.8 years. The shape and the standard deviation of the population are both unknown. For a random sample of 60 men, what is the likelihood that the age at which they were married for the first time is less than 25.1 years? Assume that the standard deviation of the sample is 2.5 years.

34. A recent study by the Greater Los Angeles Taxi Drivers Association showed that the mean fare charged for service from Hermosa Beach to the Los Angeles International Airport is $18.00 and the standard deviation is $3.50. We select a sample of 15 fares.

34. a. .8529
b. Normal population.

a. What is the likelihood that the sample mean is between $17.00 and $20.00?
b. What must you assume to make the above calculation?

35. The Crossett Trucking Company claims that the mean weight of their delivery trucks when they are fully loaded is 6,000 pounds and the standard deviation is 150 pounds. Assume that the population follows the normal distribution. Forty trucks are randomly selected and weighed. Within what limits will 95 percent of the sample means occur?

36. The mean amount purchased by each customer at Churchill's Grocery Store is $23.50. The population is positively skewed and the standard deviation is not known. For a sample of 50 customers, answer the following questions.

36. a. .0170
b. .9037
c. 22.33, 24.67

a. If the standard deviation of the sample is $5.00, what is the likelihood the sample mean is at least $25.00?
b. Again, assume the sample standard deviation is $5.00. What is the likelihood the sample mean is greater than $22.50 but less than $25.00?
c. Again, assume the sample standard deviation is $5.00. Within what limits will 90 percent of the sample means occur?

37. The mean SAT score for Division I student-athletes is 947 with a standard deviation of 205. If you select a random sample of 60 of these students, what is the probability the mean is below 900?

38. a. 36
b. See IM.
c. See IM.
d. $\mu = 3.5$, $\mu_{\bar{X}} = 3.5$, $\sigma_{\bar{X}} = 1.2076$, $\sigma = 1.7078$

38. Suppose we roll a fair die two times.
a. How many different samples are there?
b. List each of the possible samples and compute the mean.
c. On a chart similar to Chart 8–1, compare the distribution of sample means with the distribution of the population.
d. Compute the mean and the standard deviation of each distribution and compare them.

39. The following table lists the most recent data available on per capita personal income (in dollars) for each of the 50 states.

Number	State	Income	Number	State	Income	Number	State	Income
	New England			**Plains**			**Southwest**	
01	Connecticut	$39,300	17	Iowa	25,615	36	Arizona	25,189
02	Maine	24,603	18	Kansas	26,824	37	New Mexico	21,853
03	Massachusetts	35,551	19	Minnesota	30,793	38	Oklahoma	22,953
04	New Hampshire	31,114	20	Missouri	26,376	39	Texas	26,858
05	Rhode Island	29,377	21	Nebraska	27,049		**Rocky Mountain**	
06	Vermont	25,889	22	North Dakota	23,313	40	Colorado	31,546
	Mideast		23	South Dakota	25,045	41	Idaho	22,835
07	Delaware	30,778		**Southeast**		42	Montana	22,019
08	Maryland	32,465	24	Alabama	22,987	43	Utah	23,288
09	New Jersey	35,551	25	Arkansas	22,244	44	Wyoming	26,396
10	New York	33,890	26	Florida	27,780		**Far West**	
11	Pennsylvania	28,605	27	Georgia	27,340	45	Alaska	28,577
	Great Lakes		28	Kentucky	23,237	46	California	29,910
12	Illinois	31,145	29	Louisiana	22,847	47	Hawaii	27,544
13	Indiana	26,143	30	Mississippi	20,688	45	Nevada	31,022
14	Michigan	28,113	31	North Carolina	26,003	49	Oregon	27,023
15	Ohio	27,152	32	South Carolina	23,545	50	Washington	30,392
16	Wisconsin	27,390	33	Tennessee	25,574			
			34	Virginia	29,789			

a. You wish to select a sample of eight from this list. The selected random numbers are 45, 15, 81, 09, 39, 43, 90, 26, 06, 45, 01, and 42. Which states are included in the sample?
b. You wish to use a systematic sample of every sixth item and the digit 02 is chosen as the starting point. Which states are included?
c. A sample of one state from each region is to be selected. Describe how you would perform the sampling process in detail. That is, show the random numbers you selected and the corresponding states that are included in your sample.

exercises.com

40. See IM.

40. You need to find the “typical” earnings per share for “an airline.” You decide to sample six airlines from information available on the Internet. In its industry profile section, Yahoo lists the following airline companies.

AMR Corporation
Air Canada, Inc.
AirTran Holdings, Inc.
Alaska Air Group, Inc.
America West Holdings
Amtran, Inc.
Atlantic Coast Airl Hldgs.
British Airways, plc
China Eastern Airlines
China Southern Airlines
Continental Airlines, Inc.
Delta Air Lines, Inc.
Deutsche Lufthansa AG
Frontier Airlines, Inc.
Great Lakes Aviation, Ltd.
Hawaiian Airlines, Inc.
Japan Airlines Co., Ltd.
KLM Royal Dutch Airlines
Lan Chile S.A.
Mesa Air Group, Inc.
Mesaba Holdings, Inc.
Midway Airlines Corp.
Midwest Express Holdings
Northwest Airlines Corp.
Ryanair Holdings, Inc.
SkyWest, Inc.
Southwest Airlines Co.
Tower Air, Inc.
Trans World Airlines, Inc.
UAL Corporation
US Airways Group, Inc.
Vanguard Airlines
Virgin Express Holdings
Western Pacific Airlines

Number the above airlines from 01 to 34.

a. Which airlines would be included in a sample if the random numbers were 14, 08, 42, 25, 05, 44, 02, and 22? Go to the following Website: *http://biz.yahoo.com/p/_transp-airlin.* Find the current earnings per share for each, and determine the mean for the group of six airlines.

b. Which airlines are included if you use a systematic sample of every fifth item and the digit 04 is the starting point?

41. There are several Websites that will output the 30 stocks that make up the Dow Jones Industrial Average (DJIA). One site is *www.dbc.com/dbcfiles/dowt.html.* Compute the mean of the 30 stocks.

a. Use a random number table, such as Appendix E, to select a random sample of five companies that make up the DJIA. Compute the sample mean. Compare the sample mean to the population mean. What did you find? What did you expect to find?

b. You should not expect to find that the mean of these 30 stocks is the same as the current DJIA. Go to the Dow Jones Website at *www.djia.com* and read the reasons.

Computer Data Exercises

42. Refer to the Real Estate data, which reports information on the homes sold in the Venice, Florida, area last year.

42. a. See IM

a. Compute the mean and the standard deviation of the distribution of the selling prices for the homes. Assume this to be the population. Develop a histogram of the data. Would it seem reasonable from this histogram to conclude that the population of selling prices follows the normal distribution?

b. See IM

b. Let's assume a normal population. Select a sample of 10 homes. Compute the mean and the standard deviation of the sample. Determine the likelihood of finding a sample mean this large or larger from the population.

Chapter 8 Answers to Self-Review

8–1 **(a)** Students selected are Price, Detley, and Molter.
(b) Answers will vary.
(c) Skip it and move to the next random number.

8–2 The students selected are Berry, Francis, Kopp, Poteau, and Swetye.

8–3 **(a)** 10, found by:

$$_5C_2 = \frac{5!}{2!(5-2)!}$$

(b)

	Service	Sample Mean
Snow, Tolson	20, 22	21
Snow, Kraft	20, 26	23
Snow, Irwin	20, 24	22
Snow, Jones	20, 28	24
Tolson, Kraft	22, 26	24
Tolson, Irwin	22, 24	23
Tolson, Jones	22, 28	25
Kraft, Irwin	26, 24	25
Kraft, Jones	26, 28	27
Irwin, Jones	24, 28	26

(c)

Mean	Number	Probability
21	1	.10
22	1	.10
23	2	.20
24	2	.20
25	2	.20
26	1	.10
27	1	.10
	10	1.00

(d) Identical: population mean, μ, is 24, and mean of sample means, $\mu_{\bar{X}}$, is also 24.
(e) Sample means range from 21 to 27. Population values go from 20 to 28.
(f) Nonnormal.
(g) Yes.

8–4 The answers will vary. Here is one solution.

	Sample Number									
	1	2	3	4	5	6	7	8	9	10
	8	2	2	19	3	4	0	4	1	2
	19	1	14	9	2	5	8	2	14	4
	8	3	4	2	4	4	1	14	4	1
	0	3	2	3	1	2	16	1	2	3
	2	1	7	2	19	18	18	16	3	7
Total	37	10	29	35	29	33	43	37	24	17
$\bar{X}$	7.4	2	5.8	7.0	5.8	6.6	8.6	7.4	4.8	3.4

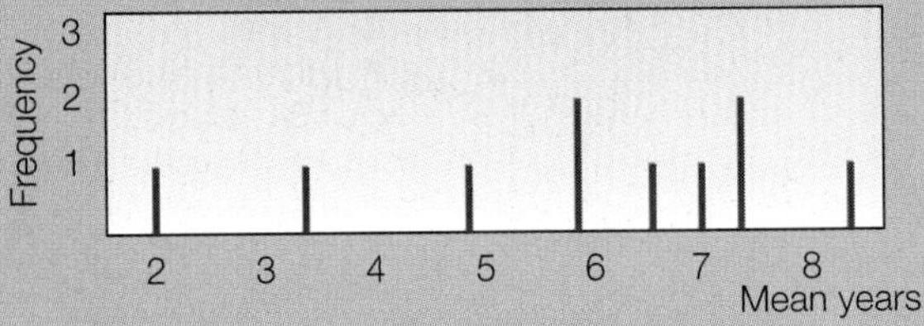

8–5 $z = \dfrac{31.08 - 31.20}{0.4/\sqrt{16}} = -1.20$

The probability that z is greater than -1.20 is $.5000 + .3849 = .8849$.

8–6 $z = \dfrac{\$28.50 - \$28.00}{\$2.00/\sqrt{50}} = 1.77$

The probability that z is greater than 1.77 is $.5000 - .4616 = .0394$.

9

Estimation and Confidence Intervals

GOALS

When you have completed this chapter you will be able to:

1. **Define a *point estimate.***
2. **Define *level of confidence.***
3. **Construct a confidence interval for the population mean when the population standard deviation is known.**
4. **Construct a confidence interval for a population mean when the population standard deviation is unknown.**
5. **Construct a confidence interval for a population proportion.**
6. **Determine the sample size for attribute and variable sampling.**

Past surveys revealed that 30 percent of tourists going to Las Vegas to gamble during a weekend spend more than $1,000. An update of this study is to use the .90 confidence level. The estimate is to be written within 1 percent of the population proportion. What is the necessary sample size? (See Goal 6 and Exercise 30.)

Introduction

The previous chapter introduces sampling. We stress that frequently it is not feasible to inspect the entire population. The reasons include: it may be too time consuming to examine the entire population, testing may destroy the product, the cost to examine the entire population is too large, or the results of a sample may be adequate. We introduce several methods of sampling. Simple random sampling is the most widely used method. With this type of sampling, each member of the population has the same chance of being selected to be a part of the sample.

Chapter 8 assumes information about the population, such as the mean, the standard deviation, or the shape of the population. In most business situations, such information is not available. In fact, the purpose of sampling may be to estimate some of these values. So, for example, you select a sample from a population and use the mean of the sample to estimate the mean of the population.

This chapter considers several important aspects of sampling. We begin by studying point estimates. A point estimate is a particular value used to estimate a population value. For example, select a sample of 50 junior executives and ask the number of hours they worked last week. Compute the mean of this sample of 50 and use the value of the sample mean as a point estimate of the unknown population mean. However, a point estimate is a single value. A more informative estimate is to present a range of values in which we expect the population parameter to occur. Such a range of values is called a confidence interval.

Frequently in business we need to determine the size of a sample. How many voters should a polling organization contact to forecast the election outcome? How many products do we need to examine to ensure our quality level? This chapter also develops a strategy for determining the size of the sample.

Point Estimates and Confidence Intervals

Known σ or a Large Sample

In the previous chapter, the data on the length of service of Spence Sprockets employees, presented in the example on page 280, is a population because we present the length of service for all 40 employees. In that case we can easily compute the population mean. We have all the data and the population is not too large. In most situations, however, the population is large or it is difficult to identify all members of the population, so we need to rely on sample information. In other words, we do not know the population parameter and we therefore want to estimate the value from a sample statistic. Consider the following business situations.

1. Tourism is a major source of income for many Caribbean countries, such as Barbados. Suppose the Bureau of Tourism for Barbados wants an estimate of the mean amount spent by tourists visiting the country. It would not be feasible to contact each tourist. So 500 tourists are randomly selected as they depart the country and asked in detail about their spending while visiting the island. The mean amount spent by the sample of 500 tourists is an estimate of the unknown population parameter. That is, we let $\overline{X}$, the sample mean, serve as an estimate of μ, the population mean.

2. Centex Home Builders, Inc. builds quality homes in the southeastern region of the United States. One of the major concerns of new buyers is the date on which the home will be completed. In recent times Centex has been telling customers, "Your home will be completed 45 working days from the date we begin installing drywall." The customer relations department at Centex wishes to compare this

pledge with recent experience. A sample of 50 homes completed this year revealed the mean number of working days from the start of drywall to the completion of the home was 46.7 days. Is it reasonable to conclude that the population mean is still 45 days and that the difference between the sample mean (46.7 days) and the proposed population mean is sampling error?

3. Recent medical studies indicate that exercise is an important part of a person's overall health. The director of human resources at OCF, a large glass manufacturer, wants an estimate of the number of hours per week employees spend exercising. A sample of 70 employees reveals the mean number of hours of exercise last week is 3.3. The sample mean of 3.3 hours is an estimate of the unknown population mean, the mean hours of exercise for all employees.

A point estimate is a single statistic used to estimate a population parameter. Suppose Best Buy, Inc. wants to estimate the mean age of buyers of stereo equipment. They select a random sample of 50 recent purchasers, determine the age of each purchaser, and compute the mean age of the buyers in the sample. The mean of this sample is a point estimate of the mean of the population. The sample mean is not the only value we could use to estimate the population mean. We could use the sample median. However, the sample median is not as efficient, meaning there is more dispersion in the distribution of the sample medians than of the sample means.

POINT ESTIMATE The statistic, computed from sample information, which is used to estimate the population parameter.

The sample mean, $\bar{X}$, is a point estimate of the population mean, μ; p, a sample proportion, is a point estimate of π, the population proportion; and s, the sample standard deviation, is a point estimate of σ, the population standard deviation.

A point estimate, however, tells only part of the story. While we expect the point estimate to be close to the population parameter, we would like to measure how close it really is. A confidence interval serves this purpose.

CONFIDENCE INTERVAL A range of values constructed from sample data so the parameter occurs within that range at a specified probability. The specified probability is called the *level of confidence.*

For example, we estimate the mean yearly income for construction workers in the New York–New Jersey area is $65,000. The range of this estimate might be from $61,000 to $69,000. We can describe how confident we are that the population parameter is in the interval by making a probability statement. We might say, for instance, that we are 90 percent sure that the mean yearly income of construction workers in the New York–New Jersey area is between $61,000 and $69,000.

The information developed about the shape of a sampling distribution of the sample mean, that is, the sampling distribution of $\bar{X}$, allows us to locate an interval that has a specified probability of containing the population mean, μ. For reasonably large samples, the results of the central limit theorem allow us to state the following:

1. Ninety-five percent of the sample means selected from a population will be within 1.96 standard deviations of the population mean μ.
2. Ninety-nine percent of the sample means will lie within 2.58 standard deviations of the population mean.

The standard deviation discussed here is the standard deviation of the sampling distribution of the sample mean. It is usually called the "standard error." Intervals computed in this fashion are called the **95 percent confidence interval** and the **99 percent confidence interval.** How are the values of 1.96 and 2.58 obtained? The *95 percent* and *99 percent* refer to the percent of the time that similarly constructed intervals would include the parameter being estimated. The *95 percent,* for example, refers to the middle 95 percent of the observations. Therefore, the remaining 5 percent are equally divided between the two tails.

See the following diagram.

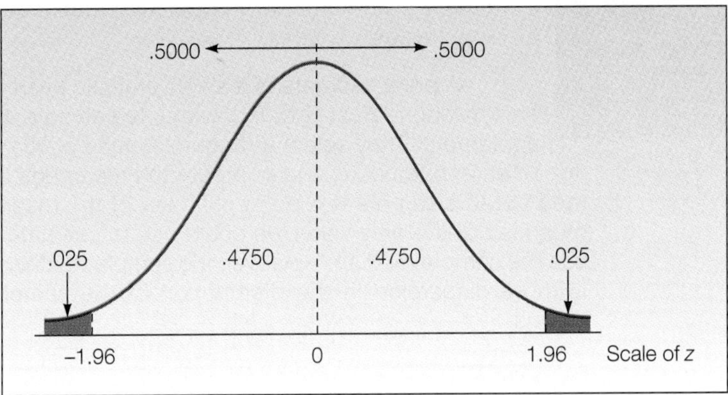

The central limit theorem, discussed in the previous chapter, states that the sampling distribution of the sample means is approximately normal when the sample contains at least 30 observations. Therefore, we can use Appendix D to find the appropriate z values. Locate .4750 in the body of the table. Read the corresponding row and column values. The value is 1.96. Thus, the probability of finding a z value between 0 and 1.96 is .4750. Likewise, the probability of being in the interval between −1.96 and 0 is also .4750. When we combine these two, the probability of being in the interval −1.96 to 1.96 is .9500. On the next page is a portion of Appendix D. The z value for the 90 percent level of confidence is determined in a similar manner. It is 1.65. For a 99 percent level of confidence the z value is 2.58.

How do you compute a 95 percent confidence interval? Assume your research involves the annual starting salary of business school graduates. You compute the sample mean to be $27,000 and the standard deviation (that is, the "standard error") of the sample mean to be $200. Assume your sample contains at least 30 observations. The 95 percent confidence interval is between $26,608 and $27,392, found by $27,000 ± 1.96($200). If 100 samples of the same size were selected from the population of interest and the corresponding 100 confidence intervals determined, you expect to find the population mean in 95 of the 100 confidence intervals.

In the above example, the standard error of the sampling distribution of the sample mean was $200. This is, of course, the standard error of the sample means, discussed in the previous chapter. See Formula 8–1 for the case when the population standard deviation is available. In most applied situations, the population standard deviation is not available, so we estimate it as follows:

$$s_{\bar{X}} = \frac{s}{\sqrt{n}}$$

The size of the standard error is affected by two values. The first is the standard deviation. If the standard deviation is large, then the standard error will also be large.

z	**0.00**	**0.01**	**0.02**	**0.03**	**0.04**	**0.05**	**0.06**	**0.07**	**0.08**	**0.09**
0.0	0.0000	0.0040	0.0080	0.0120	0.0160	0.0199	0.0239	0.0279	0.0319	0.0359
0.1	0.0398	0.0438	0.0478	0.0517	0.0557	0.0596	0.0636	0.0675	0.0714	0.0753
0.2	0.0793	0.0832	0.0871	0.0910	0.0948	0.0987	0.1026	0.1064	0.1103	0.1141
0.3	0.1179	0.1217	0.1255	0.1293	0.1331	0.1368	0.1406	0.1443	0.1480	0.1517
0.4	0.1554	0.1591	0.1628	0.1664	0.1700	0.1736	0.1772	0.1808	0.1844	0.1879
0.5	0.1915	0.1950	0.1985	0.2019	0.2054	0.2088	0.2123	0.2157	0.2190	0.2224
0.6	0.2257	0.2291	0.2324	0.2357	0.2389	0.2422	0.2454	0.2486	0.2517	0.2549
0.7	0.2580	0.2611	0.2642	0.2673	0.2704	0.2734	0.2764	0.2794	0.2823	0.2852
0.8	02881	0.2910	0.2939	0.2967	0.2995	0.3023	0.3051	0.3078	0.3106	0.3133
0.9	0.3159	0.3186	0.3212	0.3238	0.3264	0.3289	0.3315	0.3340	0.3365	0.3389
1.0	0.3413	0.3438	0.3461	0.3485	0.3508	0.3531	0.3554	0.3577	0.3599	0.3621
1.1	0.3643	0.3665	0.3686	0.3708	0.3729	0.3749	0.3770	0.3790	0.3810	0.3830
1.2	0.3849	0.3869	0.3888	0.3907	0.3925	0.3944	0.3962	0.3980	0.3997	0.4015
1.3	0.4032	0.4049	0.4066	0.4082	0.4099	0.4115	0.4131	0.4147	0.4162	0.4177
1.4	0.4192	0.4207	0.4222	0.4236	0.4251	0.4265	0.4279	0.4292	0.4306	0.4319
1.5	0.4332	0.4345	0.4357	0.4370	0.4382	0.4394	0.4406	0.4418	0.4429	0.4441
1.6	0.4452	0.4463	0.4474	0.4484	0.4495	0.4505	0.4515	0.4525	0.4535	0.4545
1.7	0.4554	0.4564	0.4573	0.4582	0.4591	0.4599	0.4608	0.4616	0.4625	0.4633
1.8	0.4641	0.4649	0.4656	0.4664	0.4671	0.4678	0.4686	0.4693	0.4699	0.4706
1.9	0.4713	0.4719	0.4726	0.4732	0.4738	0.4744	0.4750	0.4756	0.4761	0.4767
2.0	0.4772	0.4778	0.4783	0.4788	0.4793	0.4798	0.4803	0.4808	0.4812	0.4817
2.1	0.4821	0.4826	0.4830	0.4834	0.4838	0.4842	0.4846	0.4850	0.4854	0.4857
2.2	0.4861	0.4864	0.4868	0.4871	0.4875	0.4878	0.4881	0.4884	0.4887	0.4890
2.3	0.4893	0.4896	0.4898	0.4901	0.4904	0.4906	0.4909	0.4911	0.4913	0.4916
2.4	0.4918	0.4920	0.4922	0.4925	0.4927	0.4929	0.4931	0.4932	0.4934	0.4936

However, the standard error is also affected by the sample size. As the sample size is increased, the standard error decreases, indicating that there is less variability in the sampling distribution of the sample mean. This conclusion is logical, because an estimate made with a large sample should be more precise than one made from a small sample.

As we state in Chapter 8, when the sample size, *n*, is at least 30, it is generally agreed that the central limit theorem will ensure that the sample mean follows the normal distribution. This is an important consideration. If the sample mean is normally distributed, we can use the standard normal distribution, that is, *z*, in our calculations.

The 95 percent confidence interval is computed as follows, when the number of observations in the sample is at least 30.

$$\bar{X} \pm 1.96 \frac{s}{\sqrt{n}}$$

Similarly, the 99 percent confidence interval is computed as follows. Again we assume that the sample size is at least 30.

$$\bar{X} \pm 2.58 \frac{s}{\sqrt{n}}$$

As we discussed earlier, the values 1.96 and 2.58 are the *z* values corresponding to the middle 95 percent and the middle 99 percent of the observations, respectively.

We can use other levels of confidence. For those cases the value of z changes accordingly. In general, a confidence interval for the population mean is computed by:

CONFIDENCE INTERVAL FOR THE POPULATION MEAN ($n \geq 30$)

$$\bar{X} \pm z\frac{s}{\sqrt{n}} \quad [9\text{–}1]$$

where z depends on the level of confidence. Thus, for a 92 percent level of confidence, the value of z in formula 9–1 is 1.75. The value of z is from Appendix D. This table is based on half the normal distribution, so .9200/2 = .4600. The closest value in the body of the table is .4599 and the corresponding z value is 1.75.

Frequently, we also use the 90 percent level of confidence. In this case, we want the area between 0 and z to be .4500, found by .9000/2. To find the z value for this level of confidence, move down the left column of Appendix D to 1.6 and then over to the columns headed 0.04 and 0.05. The area corresponding to a z value of 1.64 is .4495, and for 1.65 it is .4505. To be conservative, we use 1.65. Try looking up the following levels of confidence and check your answers with the corresponding z values given on the right.

Confidence Level	Nearest Probability	z Value
80 percent	.3997	1.28
94 percent	.4699	1.88
96 percent	.4798	2.05

The following example shows the details for calculating a confidence interval and interpreting the result.

EXAMPLE

The American Management Association wishes to have information on the mean income of middle managers in the retail industry. A random sample of 256 managers reveals a sample mean of $45,420. The standard deviation of this sample is $2,050. The association would like answers to the following questions:

1. What is the population mean?
2. What is a reasonable range of values for the population mean?
3. What do these results mean?

SOLUTION

Generally, distributions of salary and income are positively skewed, because a few individuals earn considerably more than others, thus skewing the distribution in the positive direction. Fortunately, the central limit theorem stipulates that if we select a large sample the distribution of the sample means will follow the normal distribution, regardless of the shape of the population. So, in this instance, with a sample of 256 middle managers (remember, at least 30 is usually large enough), we can be assured that the sampling distribution will follow the normal distribution.

Another issue is that the population standard deviation is not known. Again, it is sound practice to use the sample standard deviation when we have a large sample. Now to answer the questions posed in the problem.

1. **What is the population mean?** In this case, we do not know. We do know the sample mean is $45,420. Hence, our best estimate of the unknown population

value is the corresponding sample statistic. Thus the sample mean of \$45,420 is a *point estimate* of the unknown population mean.

2. **What is a reasonable range of values for the population mean?** The Association decides to use the 95 percent level of confidence. To determine the corresponding confidence interval we use formula 9–1.

$$\bar{X} \pm z\frac{s}{\sqrt{n}} = \$45{,}420 \pm 1.96\frac{\$2{,}050}{\sqrt{256}} = \$45{,}420 \pm \$251$$

The usual practice is to round these endpoints to \$45,169 and \$45,671. These endpoints are the called the *confidence limits*. The degree of confidence or the *level of confidence* is 95 percent and the confidence interval is from \$45,169 to \$45,671.

3. **What do these results mean?** Suppose we select many samples of 256 managers, perhaps several hundred. For each sample, we compute the mean and the standard deviation and then construct a 95 percent confidence interval, such as we did in the previous section. We could expect about 95 percent of these confidence intervals to contain the *population* mean. About 5 percent of the intervals would not contain the population mean annual income, which is μ. However, a particular confidence interval either contains the population parameter or it does not. The following diagram shows the results of selecting samples from the population of middle managers in the retail industry, computing the mean and standard deviation of each, and then, using formula 9–1, determining a 95 percent confidence interval for the population mean. Note that not all intervals include the population mean. Both the endpoints of the fifth sample are less than the population mean. We attribute this to sampling error, and it is the risk we assume when we select the level of confidence.

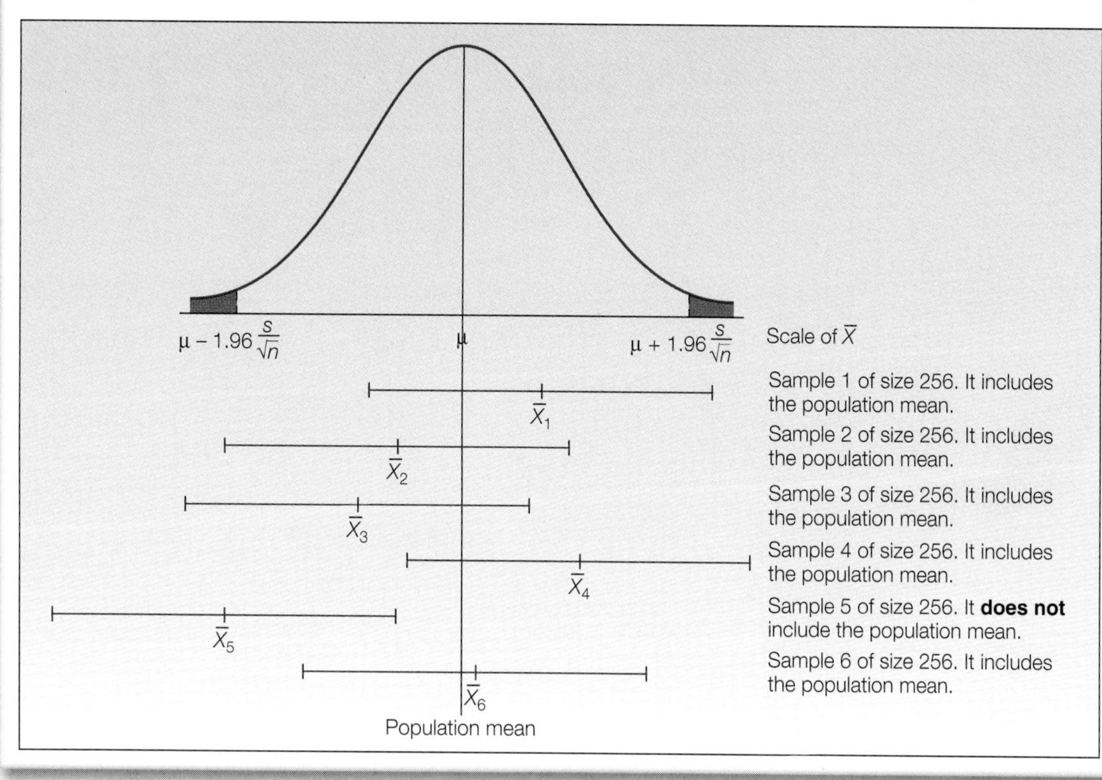

A Computer Simulation

With the aid of a computer, we can randomly select samples from a population, quickly compute the confidence interval, and show how confidence intervals usually, but not always, include the population parameter. The following Example will help to explain.

EXAMPLE

From many years in the automobile leasing business, Town Bank knows the mean distance driven on a four-year lease is 50,000 miles and the standard deviation is 5,000. Suppose, using the MINITAB statistical software system, we want to find what proportion of the 95 percent confidence intervals will include the population mean of 50. To make the calculations easier to understand, we'll conduct the study in thousands of miles, instead of miles. We select 60 random samples of size 30 from a population with a mean of 50 and a standard deviation of 5.

SOLUTION

The results of 60 random samples of 30 are in the table below. Of the 60 confidence intervals with a 95 percent confidence level, 2, or 3.33 percent, did not include the population mean of 50. The intervals (C3 and C59) that do *not* include the population mean are highlighted. 3.33 percent is close to the estimate that 5 percent of the intervals will not include the population mean, and the 58 of 60, or 96.67 percent, is close to 95 percent.

To explain the first calculation in more detail: MINITAB began by selecting a random sample of 30 observations from a population with a mean of 50 and a standard deviation of 5. The mean of these 30 observations is 50.053. The sampling error is 0.053, found by $\bar{X} - \mu = 50.053 - 50.000$. The endpoints of the confidence interval are 48.264 and 51.842. These endpoints are determined by using formula 9–1, but using σ instead of s.

$$\bar{X} \pm 1.96 \frac{\sigma}{\sqrt{n}} = 50.053 \pm 1.96 \frac{5}{\sqrt{30}} = 50.053 \pm 1.789$$

One-Sample Z:

The assumed sigma = 5

Variable	N	Mean	StDev	SE Mean	95.0% CI
C1	30	50.053	5.002	0.913	(48.264, 51.842)
C2	30	49.025	4.450	0.913	(47.236, 50.815)
C3	30	52.023	5.918	0.913	(50.234, 53.812)
C4	30	50.056	3.364	0.913	(48.267, 51.845)
C5	30	49.737	4.784	0.913	(47.948, 51.526)
C6	30	51.074	5.495	0.913	(49.285, 52.863)
C7	30	50.040	5.930	0.913	(48.251, 51.829)
C8	30	48.910	3.645	0.913	(47.121, 50.699)
C9	30	51.033	4.918	0.913	(49.244, 52.822)
C10	30	50.692	4.571	0.913	(48.903, 52.482)
C11	30	49.853	4.525	0.913	(48.064, 51.642)
C12	30	50.286	3.422	0.913	(48.497, 52.076)
C13	30	50.257	4.317	0.913	(48.468, 52.046)
C14	30	49.605	4.994	0.913	(47.816, 51.394)
C15	30	51.474	5.497	0.913	(49.685, 53.264)
C16	30	48.930	5.317	0.913	(47.141, 50.719)
C17	30	49.870	4.847	0.913	(48.081, 51.659)
C18	30	50.739	6.224	0.913	(48.950, 52.528)
C19	30	50.979	5.520	0.913	(49.190, 52.768)
C20	30	48.848	4.130	0.913	(47.059, 50.638)
C21	30	49.481	4.056	0.913	(47.692, 51.270)
C22	30	49.183	5.409	0.913	(47.394, 50.973)

Variable	N	Mean	StDev	SE Mean	95.0% CI
C23	30	50.084	4.522	0.913	(48.294, 51.873)
C24	30	50.866	5.142	0.913	(49.077, 52.655)
C25	30	48.768	5.582	0.913	(46.979, 50.557)
C26	30	50.904	6.052	0.913	(49.115, 52.694)
C27	30	49.481	5.535	0.913	(47.691, 51.270)
C28	30	50.949	5.916	0.913	(49.160, 52.739)
C29	30	49.106	4.641	0.913	(47.317, 50.895)
C30	30	49.994	5.853	0.913	(48.205, 51.784)
C31	30	49.601	5.064	0.913	(47.811, 51.390)
C32	30	51.494	5.597	0.913	(49.705, 53.284)
C33	30	50.460	4.393	0.913	(48.671, 52.249)
C34	30	50.378	4.075	0.913	(48.589, 52.167)
C35	30	49.808	4.155	0.913	(48.019, 51.597)
C36	30	49.934	5.012	0.913	(48.145, 51.723)
C37	30	50.017	4.082	0.913	(48.228, 51.806)
C38	30	50.074	3.631	0.913	(48.285, 51.863)
C39	30	48.656	4.833	0.913	(46.867, 50.445)
C40	30	50.568	3.855	0.913	(48.779, 52.357)
C41	30	50.916	3.775	0.913	(49.127, 52.705)
C42	30	49.104	4.321	0.913	(47.315, 50.893)
C43	30	50.308	5.467	0.913	(48.519, 52.097)
C44	30	49.034	4.405	0.913	(47.245, 50.823)
C45	30	50.399	4.729	0.913	(48.610, 52.188)
C46	30	49.634	3.996	0.913	(47.845, 51.424)
C47	30	50.479	4.881	0.913	(48.689, 52.268)
C48	30	50.529	5.173	0.913	(48.740, 52.318)
C49	30	51.577	5.822	0.913	(49.787, 53.366)
C50	30	50.403	4.893	0.913	(48.614, 52.192)
C51	30	49.717	5.218	0.913	(47.927, 51.506)
C52	30	49.796	5.327	0.913	(48.007, 51.585)
C53	30	50.549	4.680	0.913	(48.760, 52.338)
C54	30	50.200	5.840	0.913	(48.410, 51.989)
C55	30	49.138	5.074	0.913	(47.349, 50.928)
C56	30	49.667	3.843	0.913	(47.878, 51.456)
C57	30	49.603	5.614	0.913	(47.814, 51.392)
C58	30	49.441	5.702	0.913	(47.652, 51.230)
C59	30	47.873	4.685	0.913	(46.084, 49,662)
C60	30	51.087	5.162	0.913	(49.297, 52.876)

Self-Review 9–1

The mean daily sales are $2,000 for a sample of 40 days at a fast-food restaurant. The standard deviation of the sample is $300.

(a) What is the estimated mean daily sales of the population? What is this estimate called?
(b) What is the 99 percent confidence interval?
(c) Interpret your findings.

Exercises

1. A sample of 49 observations is taken from a normal population. The sample mean is 55, and the sample standard deviation is 10. Determine the 99 percent confidence interval for the population mean.

2. (38.911, 41.089)

2. A sample of 81 observations is taken from a normal population. The sample mean is 40, and the sample standard deviation is 5. Determine the 95 percent confidence interval for the population mean.
3. A sample of 10 observations is selected from a normal population for which the population standard deviation is known to be 5. The sample mean is 20.

a. Determine the standard error of the mean.
b. Explain why we can use formula 9–1 to determine the 95 percent confidence interval even though the sample is less than 30.
c. Determine the 95 percent confidence interval for the population mean.

4. 1.44

4. Suppose you want an 85 percent confidence level. What value would you use to multiply the standard error of the mean?
5. A research firm conducted a survey to determine the mean amount steady smokers spend on cigarettes during a week. A sample of 49 steady smokers revealed that $\bar{X} = \$20$ and $s = \$5$.
   a. What is the point estimate of the population mean? Explain what it indicates.
   b. Using the 95 percent level of confidence, determine the confidence interval for μ. Explain what it indicates.

6. a. (18.775, 21.225) b. Smaller standard error.

6. Refer to the previous exercise. Suppose that 64 smokers (instead of 49) were sampled. Assume the sample mean and the sample standard deviation remained the same ($20 and $5, respectively).
   a. What is the 95 percent confidence interval estimate of μ?
   b. Explain why this confidence interval is narrower than the one determined in the previous exercise.
7. Bob Nale is the owner of Nale's Texaco GasTown. Bob would like to estimate the mean number of gallons of gasoline sold to his customers. From his records, he selects a random sample of 60 sales and finds the mean number of gallons sold is 8.60 and the standard deviation is 2.30 gallons.
   a. What is the point estimate of the population mean?
   b. Develop a 99 percent confidence interval for the population mean.
   c. Interpret the meaning of part b.

8. (5.29, 6.81)

8. Dr. Patton is a Professor of English. Recently he counted the number of misspelled words in a group of student essays. For his class of 40 students, the mean number of misspelled words was 6.05 and the standard deviation 2.44 per essay. Construct a 95 percent confidence interval for the mean number of misspelled words in the population of students.

Unknown *s* and a Small Sample

In the previous section we used the standard normal distribution to express the level of confidence. We assumed either:

1. The population followed the normal distribution and the sample standard deviation was known, or
2. The shape of the population was not known, but the number of observations in the sample was at least 30.

What do we do if the sample is less than 30 and we do not know the population standard deviation? This situation is not covered by the results of the central limit theorem but exists in many cases. Often we can reason that the population is normal or reasonably close to a normal distribution. Under these conditions, the correct statistical procedure is to replace the standard normal distribution with the *t* distribution. The *t* distribution is a continuous distribution with many similarities to the standard normal distribution. William Gosset, an English brewmaster, was the first to study the *t* distribution. He did his work in the early 1900s. The brewery that employed Gosset preferred its employees to use pen names when publishing papers. For this reason Gosset's work was published under the pen name "Student." Hence, you will frequently see this distribution referred to as Student's *t*.

Gosset was concerned with the behavior of the following term:

$$t = \frac{\bar{X} - \mu}{s/\sqrt{n}}$$

s is an estimate of σ. He was especially worried about the discrepancy between s and σ when s was calculated from a very small sample. The *t* distribution and the standard normal distribution are shown graphically in Chart 9–1. Note particularly that the *t* distribution is flatter, more spread out, than the standard normal distribution. This is because the standard deviation of the t distribution is larger than that of the standard normal distribution.

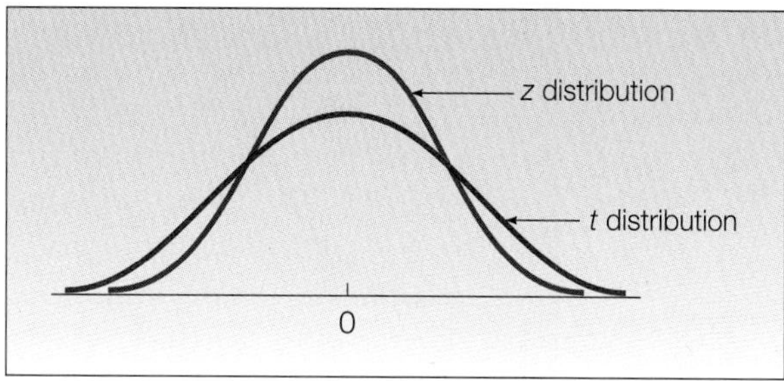

CHART 9–1 The Standard Normal Distribution and Student's t Distribution

Statistics in Action

William Gosset was born in England in 1876 and died there in 1937. He worked for many years at Arthur Guinness & Sons Brewery. In fact, in his later years he was in charge of Guinness Brewery in London. Guinness preferred their employees to use pen names when publishing papers, so in 1908, when Gosset wrote "The Probable Error of a Mean," he used the name "Student." In this paper he first described the properties of the t distribution.

The following characteristics of the t distribution are based on the assumption that the population of interest is normal, or nearly normal.

1. It is, like the z distribution, a continuous distribution.
2. It is, like the z distribution, bell-shaped and symmetrical.
3. There is not one t distribution, but rather a "family" of t distributions. All t distributions have a mean of 0, but their standard deviations differ according to the sample size, n. There is a t distribution for a sample size of 20, another for a sample size of 22, and so on. The standard deviation for a t distribution with 5 observations is larger than for a t distribution with 20 observations.
4. The t distribution is more spread out and flatter at the center than is the standard normal distribution (see Chart 9–1). As the sample size increases, however, the t distribution approaches the standard normal distribution, because the errors in using s for σ decrease with larger samples.

Because Student's t distribution has a greater spread than the z distribution, the value of t for a given level of confidence is larger in magnitude than the corresponding z values. Chart 9–2 shows the values of z and of t for a 95 percent level of confidence when the sample size is $n = 5$. How we obtained the actual value of t will be explained shortly. For now, observe that for the same level of confidence the t distribution is flatter or more spread out than the standard normal distribution.

To develop a confidence interval for the population mean using the t distribution, we adjust formula 9–1 as follows.

CONFIDENCE INTERVAL FOR THE POPULATION MEAN, σ UNKNOWN

$$\bar{X} \pm t \frac{s}{\sqrt{n}} \qquad \textbf{[9–2]}$$

To put it another way, to develop a confidence interval for the population mean with an unknown population standard deviation we:

1. Assume the samples are from a normal population.
2. Estimate the population standard deviation (σ) with the sample standard deviation (s).
3. Use the t distribution rather than the z distribution.

We should be clear at this point. We usually employ the standard normal distribution when the sample size is at least 30. We should, strictly speaking, make the decision whether to use z or t based on whether σ is known or not. When σ is known, we use

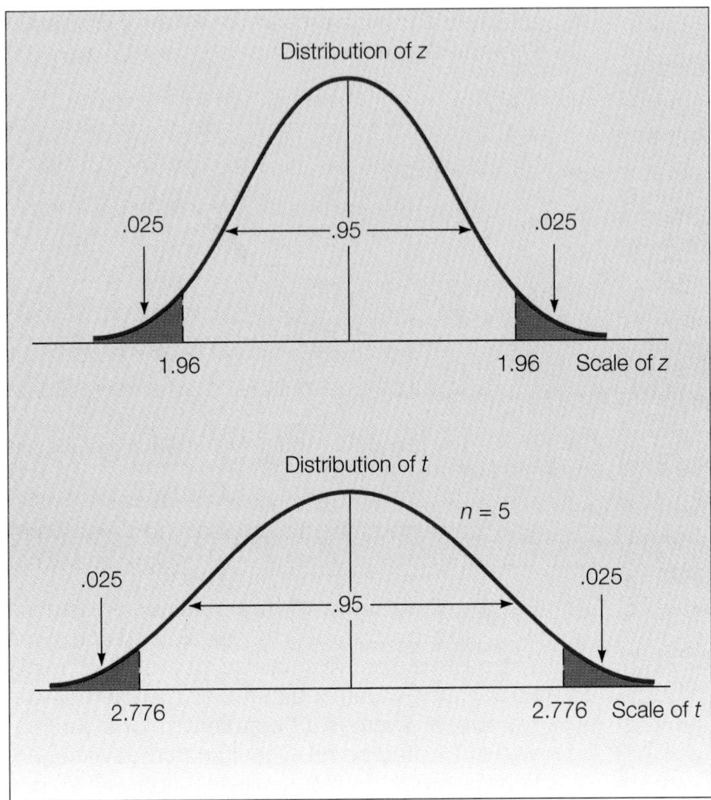

CHART 9–2 Values of z and t for the 95 Percent Level of Confidence

z; when it is not, we use t. The rule of using z when the sample is 30 or more is based on the fact that the t distribution approaches the normal distribution as the sample size increases. When the sample reaches 30, there is little difference between the z and t values, so we ignore the difference and use z. We will show this when we discuss the details of the t distribution and how to find values in a t distribution. Chart 9–3 summarizes the decision-making process.

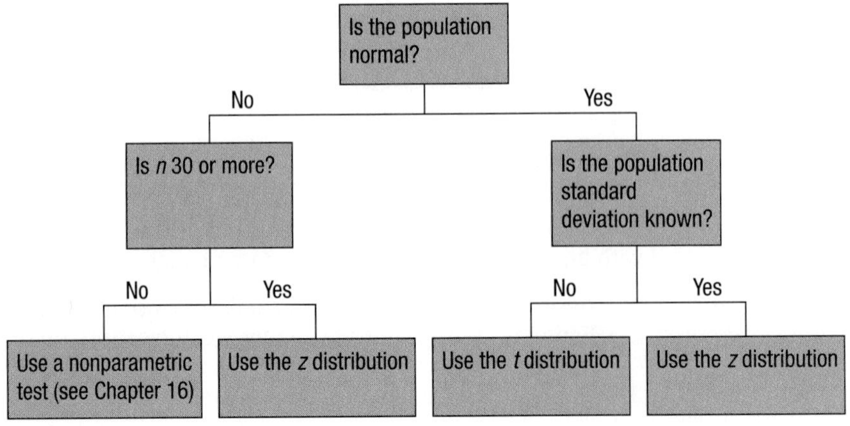

CHART 9–3 Determining When to Use the z Distribution or the t Distribution

The following example will illustrate a confidence interval for a population mean when the population standard deviation is unknown and how to find the appropriate value of *t* in a table.

EXAMPLE

A tire manufacturer wishes to investigate the tread life of its tires. A sample of 10 tires driven 50,000 miles revealed a sample mean of 0.32 inch of tread remaining with a standard deviation of 0.09 inch. Construct a 95 percent confidence interval for the population mean. Would it be reasonable for the manufacturer to conclude that after 50,000 miles the population mean amount of tread remaining is 0.30 inches?

SOLUTION

To begin, we assume the population distribution is normal. In this case, we don't have a lot of evidence, but the assumption is probably reasonable. We do not know the population standard deviation, but we know the sample standard deviation, which is .09 inches. To use the central limit theorem, we need a large sample, that is, a sample of 30 or more. In this instance there are only 10 observations in the sample. Hence, we cannot use the central limit theorem. That is, formula 9–1 is not applicable. We use formula 9–2:

$$\bar{X} \pm t\frac{s}{\sqrt{n}}$$

From the information given, $\bar{X} = 0.32$, $s = 0.09$, and $n = 10$. To find the value of *t* we use Appendix F, a portion of which is reproduced below as Chart 9–4. Appendix F is also reproduced on the back inside cover of the text. The first step for locating *t* is to move across the row identified for "Confidence Intervals" to the level of confidence requested. In this case we want the 95 percent level of confidence, so we move to the row headed "95%." The column on the left margin is identified as "*df.*" This refers to the number of degrees of freedom. The number of degrees of freedom is the number

	Confidence Intervals				
	80%	90%	95%	98%	99%
	Level of Significance for One-Tailed Test				
df	0.100	0.050	0.025	0.010	0.005
	Level of Significance for Two-Tailed Test				
	0.20	0.10	0.05	0.02	0.01
1	3.078	6.314	12.706	31.821	63.657
2	1.886	2.920	4.303	6.965	9.925
3	1.638	2.353	3.182	4.541	5.841
4	1.533	2.132	2.776	3.747	4.604
5	1.476	2.015	2.571	3.365	4.032
6	1.440	1.943	2.447	3.143	3.707
7	1.415	1.895	2.365	2.998	3.499
8	1.397	1.860	2.306	2.896	3.355
9	1.383	1.833	2.262	2.821	3.250
10	1.372	1.812	2.228	2.764	3.169

CHART 9–4 A Portion of the *t* Distribution.

of observations in the sample minus the number of samples, written $n - 1$.[1] In this case it is $10 - 1 = 9$. The value of t is 2.262.

To determine the confidence interval we substitute the values in formula 9–2.

$$\bar{X} \pm t \frac{s}{\sqrt{n}} = 0.32 \pm 2.262 \frac{0.09}{\sqrt{10}} = 0.32 \pm .064$$

The endpoints of the confidence interval are 0.256 and 0.384. How do we interpret this result? It is reasonable to conclude that the population mean is in this interval. The manufacturer can be reasonably sure (95 percent confident) that the mean remaining tread depth is between 0.256 and 0.384 inches. Because the value of 0.30 is in this interval, it is possible that the mean of the population is 0.30.

[1]In brief summary, because sample statistics are being used, it is necessary to determine the number of variables that are *free to vary.* To illustrate: assume that the mean of four numbers is known to be 5. The four numbers are 7, 4, 1, and 8. The deviations of these numbers from the mean must total 0. The deviations of +2, −1, −4, and +3 do total 0. If the deviations of +2, −1, and −4 are known, then the value of +3 is fixed (restricted) in order to satisfy the condition that the sum of the deviations must equal 0. Thus, 1 degree of freedom is lost in a sampling problem involving the standard deviation of the sample because one number (the arithmetic mean) is known.

Here is another example to clarify the use of confidence intervals. Suppose an article in your local newspaper reported that the mean time to sell a residential property in the area is 60 days. You select a random sample of 20 homes sold in the last year and find the mean selling time is 65 days. Based on the sample data, you develop a 95 percent confidence interval for the population mean. You find that the endpoints of the confidence interval are 62 days and 68 days. How do you interpret this result? You can be reasonably confident the population mean is within this range. The value proposed for the population mean, that is, 60 days, is not included in the interval. It is not likely that the population mean is 60 days. The evidence indicates the statement by the local newspaper is not correct. To put it another way, it is unreasonable to select the sample you did from a population that had a mean selling time of 60 days.

The following Example will show additional details for determining and interpreting a confidence interval. We used MINITAB to perform the calculations.

EXAMPLE

The manager of the Inlet Square Mall, just north of Ft. Meyers, Florida, wants to estimate the mean amount spent per shopping visit by customers. A sample of 20 customers reveals the following amounts spent.

$48.16	$42.22	$46.82	$51.45	$23.78	$41.86	$54.86
37.92	52.64	48.59	50.82	46.94	61.83	61.69
49.17	61.46	51.35	52.68	58.84	43.88	

What is the best estimate of the population mean? Determine a 95 percent confidence interval. Interpret the result. Would it be reasonable to conclude that the population mean is $50? What about $60?

SOLUTION

The mall manager assumes that the population of the amounts spent follows the normal distribution. This is a reasonable assumption in this case. Additionally, the confidence interval technique is quite powerful and tends to commit any errors on the conservative side if the population is not normal. We should not make the normality assumption when the population is severely skewed or when the distribution has "thick tails." In Chapter 16 we present methods for handling this problem if we cannot make the normality assumption. In this case, the normality assumption is reasonable.

The population standard deviation is not known and the size of the sample is less than 30. Hence, it is appropriate to use the t distribution and formula 9–2 to find the confidence interval. We use the MINITAB system to find the mean and standard deviation of this sample. The results are shown below.

```
Welcome to Minitab, press F1 for help.

Descriptive Statistics: Amount

Variable          N      Mean    Median    TrMean     StDev   SE Mean
Amount           20     49.35     50.00     50.08      9.01      2.02

Variable    Minimum   Maximum        Q1        Q3
Amount        23.78     61.83     44.62     54.32
```

	C1 Amount
1	48.16
2	42.22
3	46.82
4	51.45
5	23.78
6	41.86

The mall manager does not know the population mean. The sample mean is the best estimate of that value. From the above MINITAB output, the mean is \$49.35, which is the best estimate, the *point estimate*, of the unknown population mean.

We use formula 9–2 to find the confidence interval. The value of t is available from Appendix F. There are $n - 1 = 20 - 1 = 19$ degrees of freedom. We move across the row with 19 degrees of freedom to the column for the 95% confidence level. The value at this intersection is 2.093. We substitute these values into formula 9–2 to find the confidence interval.

$$\bar{X} \pm t\frac{s}{\sqrt{n}} = \$49.35 \pm 2.093\frac{\$9.01}{\sqrt{20}} = \$49.35 \pm \$4.22$$

The endpoints of the confidence interval are \$45.13 and \$53.57. It is reasonable to conclude that the population mean is in that interval. Following is another output from the MINITAB system. The confidence interval is reported on the right-hand side.

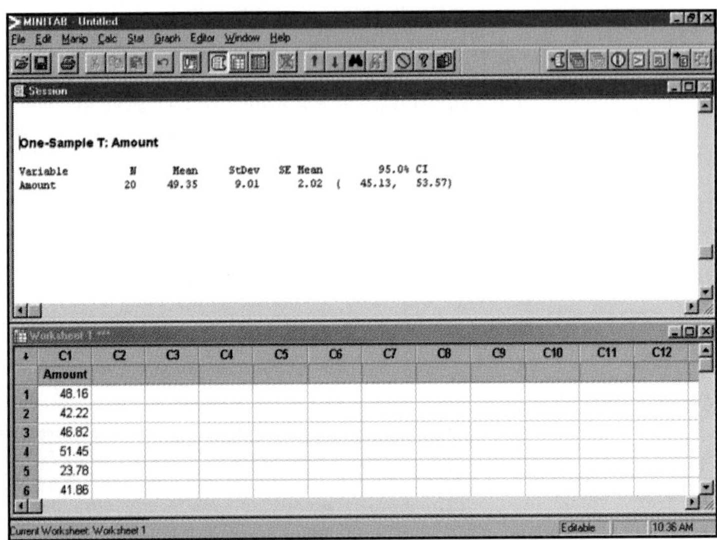

The manager of Inlet Square wondered whether the population mean could have been \$50 or \$60. The value of \$50 is within the confidence interval. It is reasonable that the population mean could be \$50. The value of \$60 is not in the confidence interval. Hence, we conclude that the population mean is not \$60.

Self-Review 9–2

Dottie Kleman is the "Cookie Lady." She bakes and sells cookies at 50 different locations in the Philadelphia area. Ms. Kleman is concerned about absenteeism among her workers. The information below reports the number of days absent for a sample of 10 workers during the last two-week pay period.

4	1	2	2	1	2	2	1	0	3

(a) Determine the mean and the standard deviation of the sample.
(b) What is the population mean? What is the best estimate of that value?
(c) Develop a 95 percent confidence interval for the population mean.
(d) Explain why the t distribution is used as a part of the confidence interval.
(e) Is it reasonable to conclude that the typical worker does not miss any days during a pay period?

Exercises

9. Use Appendix F to locate the value of t under the following conditions.
  a. The sample size is 12 and the level of confidence is 95 percent.
  b. The sample size is 20 and the level of confidence is 90 percent.
  c. The sample size is 8 and the level of confidence is 99 percent.

10. **a.** 2.145 **b.** 2.500 **c.** 1.796

10. Use Appendix F to locate the value of t under the following conditions.
  a. The sample size is 15 and the level of confidence is 95 percent.
  b. The sample size is 24 and the level of confidence is 98 percent.
  c. The sample size is 12 and the level of confidence is 90 percent.

11. The owner of Britten's Egg Farm wants to estimate the mean number of eggs laid per chicken. A sample of 20 chickens shows they laid an average of 20 eggs per month with a standard deviation of 2 eggs per month.

a. What is the value of the population mean? What is the best estimate of this value?
b. Explain why we need to use the *t* distribution. What assumption do you need to make?
c. For a 95 percent confidence interval, what is the value of *t*?
d. Develop the 95 percent confidence interval for the population mean.
e. Would it be reasonable to conclude that the population mean is 21 eggs? What about 25 eggs?

12. a. Unknown, 60. b. Small sample, unknown σ. c. 1.753 d. 51.235, 68.765 e. Yes.

12. The American Sugar Producers Association wants to estimate the mean yearly sugar consumption. A sample of 16 people reveals the mean yearly consumption to be 60 pounds with a standard deviation of 20 pounds.
a. What is the value of the population mean? What is the best estimate of this value?
b. Explain why we need to use the *t* distribution. What assumption do you need to make?
c. For a 90 percent confidence interval, what is the value of *t*?
d. Develop the 90 percent confidence interval for the population mean.
e. Would it be reasonable to conclude that the population mean is 63 pounds?

13. Merrill Lynch Securities and Health Care Retirement, Inc. are two large employers in downtown Toledo, Ohio. They are considering jointly offering child care for their employees. As a part of the feasibility study, they wish to estimate the mean weekly child-care cost of their employees. A sample of 10 employees who use child care reveals the following amounts spent last week.

$107	$92	$97	$95	$105	$101	$91	$99	$95	$104

Develop a 90 percent confidence interval for the population mean. Interpret the result.

14. 30.99, 39.15

14. The Greater Pittsburgh Area Chamber of Commerce wants to estimate the mean time workers who are employed in the downtown area spend getting to work. A sample of 15 workers reveals the following number of minutes traveled.

29	38	38	33	38	21	45	34
40	37	37	42	30	29	35	

Develop a 98 percent confidence interval for the population mean. Interpret the result.

A Confidence Interval for a Proportion

The material presented so far in this chapter uses the ratio scale of measurement. That is, we use such variables as incomes, weights, distances, and ages. We now want to consider situations such as the following:

- The career services director at Southern Technical Institute reports that 80 percent of its graduates enter the job market in a position related to their field of study.
- A company representative claims that 45 percent of Burger King sales are made at the drive-through window.
- A survey of homes in the Chicago area indicated that 85 percent of the new construction had central air conditioning.
- A recent survey of married men between the ages of 35 and 50 found that 63 percent felt that both partners should earn a living.

These examples illustrate the nominal scale of measurement. In the nominal scale an observation is classified into one of two or more mutually exclusive groups. For example, a graduate of Southern Tech either entered the job market in a position related to his or her field of study or not. A particular Burger King customer either made a purchase at the drive-through window or did not make a purchase at the drive-through window. There are only two possibilities, and the outcome must be classified into one of the two groups.

PROPORTION The fraction, ratio, or percent indicating the part of the sample or the population having a particular trait of interest.

As an example of a proportion, a recent survey indicated that 92 out of 100 surveyed favored the continued use of daylight savings time in the summer. The sample proportion is 92/100, or .92, or 92 percent. If we let p represent the sample proportion, X the number of successes, and n the number of items sampled, we can determine a sample proportion as follows.

SAMPLE PROPORTION $$p = \frac{X}{n}$$ **[9–3]**

The population proportion is identified by π. Therefore, π refers to the percent of successes in the population. Recall from Chapter 6 that π is the proportion of successes in a binomial distribution. This continues our policy of using Greek letters to identify population parameters and Roman letters to identify sample statistics.

To develop a confidence interval for a proportion, we need to meet the following assumptions.

1. The binomial conditions, discussed in Chapter 6, have been met. Briefly, these conditions are:
   a. The sample data is the result of counts.
   b. There are only two possible outcomes. (We usually label one of the outcomes a "success" and the other a "failure.")
   c. The probability of a success remains the same from one trial to the next.
   d. The trials are independent. This means the outcome on one trial does not affect the outcome on another.
2. The values $n\pi$ and $n(1 - \pi)$ should both be greater than or equal to 5. This condition allows us to invoke the central limit theorem and employ the standard normal distribution, that is, z, as a part of the confidence interval.

Statistics In Action

Many survey results reported in newspapers, in news magazines, and on TV use confidence intervals. For example, a recent survey of 800 TV viewers in Toledo, Ohio, found 44 percent watched the evening news on the local CBS affiliate. The article went on to indicate the margin of error was 3.4 percent. The margin of error is actually the amount that is added and subtracted from the point estimate to find the endpoints of a confidence interval. Using formula 9–6 and the 95 percent level of confidence:

$$z\sqrt{\frac{p(1-p)}{n}}$$

$$= 1.96\sqrt{\frac{.44(1-.44)}{800}}$$

$$= 0.034$$

Developing a point estimate for a population proportion and a confidence interval for a population proportion is similar to doing so for a mean. To illustrate, John Gail is running for Congress from the third district of Nebraska. From a random sample of 100 voters in the district, 60 indicate they plan to vote for him in the upcoming election. The sample proportion is .60, but the population proportion is unknown. That is, we do not know what proportion of votes in the *population* will vote for Mr. Gail. The sample value, .60, is the best estimate we have of the unknown population parameter. So we let p, which is .60, be an estimate of π, which is not known.

To develop a confidence interval for a population proportion, we change formula 9–1 slightly:

CONFIDENCE INTERVAL FOR A POPULATION PROPORTION $$p \pm z\sigma_p$$ **[9–4]**

The term σ_p is the "standard error" of the proportion. It measures the variability in the sampling distribution of the sample proportion.

STANDARD ERROR OF THE SAMPLE PROPORTION

$$\sigma_p = \sqrt{\frac{p(1-p)}{n}} \quad [9\text{–}5]$$

We can then construct a confidence interval for a population proportion from the following formula.

CONFIDENCE INTERVAL FOR A POPULATION PROPORTION

$$p \pm z\sqrt{\frac{p(1-p)}{n}} \quad [9\text{–}6]$$

EXAMPLE

The union representing the Bottle Blowers of America (BBA) is considering a proposal to merge with the Teamsters Union. According to BBA union bylaws, at least three-fourths of the union membership must approve any merger. A random sample of 2,000 current BBA members reveals 1,600 plan to vote for the merger proposal. What is the estimate of the population proportion? Develop a 95 percent confidence interval for the population proportion. Interpret the results. Basing your decision on this sample information, can you conclude that the necessary proportion of BBA members favor the merger?

SOLUTION

First, calculate the sample proportion from formula 9–3. It is .80, found by

$$p = \frac{X}{n} = \frac{1{,}600}{2{,}000} = .80$$

Thus, we estimate that 80 percent of the population favor the merger proposal. We determine the 95 percent confidence interval using formula 9–6. The z value corresponding to the 95 percent level of confidence is 1.96.

$$p \pm z\sqrt{\frac{p(1-p)}{n}} = .80 \pm 1.96\sqrt{\frac{.80(1-.80)}{2000}} = .80 \pm .018$$

The endpoints of the confidence interval are .782 and .818. The lower endpoint is greater than .75. Hence, we conclude that the merger proposal will pass.

Self-Review 9–3

A market survey was conducted to estimate the proportion of homemakers who would recognize the brand name of a cleanser based on the shape and the color of the container. Of the 1,400 homemakers sampled, 420 were able to identify the brand by name.

(a) Estimate the value of the population proportion.
(b) Compute the standard error of the proportion.
(c) Develop a 99 percent confidence interval for the population proportion.
(d) Interpret your findings.

Exercises

15. The owner of the West End Kwick Fill Gas Station wished to determine the proportion of customers who use his new pay-at-the-pump feature. This feature allows customers to use a credit card at the pump and never enter the station. He surveys 100 customers and finds that 80 paid at the pump.

a. Estimate the value of the population proportion.
b. Compute the standard error of the proportion.
c. Develop a 95 percent confidence interval for the population proportion.
d. Interpret your findings.

16. Ms. Maria Wilson is considering running for mayor of the town of Bear Gulch, Montana. Before completing the petitions, she decides to conduct a survey of voters in Bear Gulch. A sample of 400 voters reveals that 300 would support her in the November election.

a. Estimate the value of the population proportion.
b. Compute the standard error of the proportion.
c. Develop a 99 percent confidence interval for the population proportion.
d. Interpret your findings.

16. a. 0.75
b. .0217
c. .694, .806
d. See IM.

17. The Fox TV network is considering replacing one of its prime-time crime investigation shows with a new family-oriented comedy show. Before a final decision is made, network executives commission a sample of 400 viewers. After viewing the comedy, 250 indicated they would watch the new show and suggested it replace the crime investigation show.

a. Estimate the value of the population proportion.
b. Compute the standard error of the proportion.
c. Develop a 99 percent confidence interval for the population proportion.
d. Interpret your findings.

18. Schadek Silkscreen Printing, Inc. purchases plastic cups on which to print logos for sporting events, proms, birthdays, and other special occasions. Zack Schadek, the owner, received a large shipment this morning. To ensure the quality of the shipment, he selected a random sample of 300 cups. He found 15 to be defective.

a. What is the estimated proportion defective in the population?
b. Develop a 95 percent confidence interval for the proportion defective.
c. Zack has an agreement with his supplier that he is to return lots that are 10 percent or more defective. Should he return this lot? Explain your decision.

18. a. 0.05
b. .025, .075
c. Lot not 10% defective.

Finite-Population Correction Factor

The populations we have sampled so far have been very large or infinite. What if the sampled population is not very large? We need to make some adjustments in the way we compute the standard error of the sample means and the standard error of the sample proportions.

A population that has a fixed upper bound is *finite.* For example, there are 21,376 students enrolled at Eastern Illinois University, there are 40 employees at Spence Sprockets, DaimlerChrysler assembled 917 Jeep Wranglers at the Alexis Avenue plant yesterday, or there were 65 surgical patients at St. Rose Memorial Hospital in Sarasota yesterday. A finite population can be rather small; it could be all the students registered for this class. It can also be very large, such as all senior citizens living in Florida.

For a finite population, where the total number of objects is N and the size of the sample is n, the following adjustment is made to the standard errors of the sample means and proportions:

STANDARD ERROR OF THE SAMPLE MEAN, USING A CORRECTION FACTOR

$$\sigma_{\bar{X}} = \frac{\sigma}{\sqrt{n}}\sqrt{\frac{N-n}{N-1}} \quad [9\text{–}7]$$

STANDARD ERROR OF THE SAMPLE PRC
USING A CORRECTION FACTOR

This adjustment is called the **finit** to apply a factor, and what is it centage of the population, the $(N - n)/(N - 1)$. Suppose the tio is $(1{,}000 - 100)/(1{,}000 -$ tion factor, .9492. Multiplyin standard error by about 5 p standard error yields a sm the population proportion. If the ing that the standard error has been shows the effects of various sample sizes. No about 5 percent of the population, the impact of the The usual rule is if the ratio of n/N is less than .05, the correcti

TABLE 9–1 Finite-Population Correction Factor for Selected Sample When the Population Is 1,000

Sample Size	Fraction of Population	Correction Factor
10	.010	.9955
25	.025	.9879
50	.050	.9752
100	.100	.9492
200	.200	.8949
500	.500	.7075

EXAMPLE

There are 250 families in Scandia, Pennsylvania. A poll of 40 families reveals the mean annual church contribution is \$450 with a standard deviation of \$75. Construct a 90 percent confidence interval for the mean annual contribution.

SOLUTION

First, note that the population is finite. That is, there is a limit to the number of people in Scandia. Second, note that the sample constitutes more than 5 percent of the population; that is, $n/N = 40/250 = .16$. Hence, we use the finite-population correction factor. The 90 percent confidence interval is constructed as follows, using formulas 9–1 and 9–7.

$$\bar{X} \pm z\frac{s}{\sqrt{n}}\left(\sqrt{\frac{N-n}{N-1}}\right) = \$450 \pm 1.65\frac{\$75}{\sqrt{40}}\left(\sqrt{\frac{250-40}{250-1}}\right) = \$450 \pm \$19.57(\sqrt{.8434})$$
$$= \$450 \pm \$17.97$$

The endpoints of the confidence interval are \$432.03 and \$467.97. It is likely that the population mean falls within this interval.

Self-Review 9–4

The same study of church contributions in Scandia revealed that 15 of the 40 families sampled attend church regularly. Construct the 95 percent confidence interval for the proportion of families attending church regularly. Should the finite-population correction factor be used? Why or why not?

rcises

Thirty-six items are randomly selected from a population of 300 items. The sample mean is 35 and the sample standard deviation 5. Develop a 95 percent confidence interval for the population mean.

20. Forty-nine items are randomly selected from a population of 500 items. The sample mean is 40 and the sample standard deviation 9. Develop a 99 percent confidence interval for the population mean.

21. The attendance at the Durham Bulls minor league baseball game last night was 400. A random sample of 50 of those in attendance revealed that the mean number of soft drinks consumed per person was 1.86 with a standard deviation of 0.50. Develop a 99 percent confidence interval for the mean number of soft drinks consumed per person.

.77) **22.** There are 300 welders employed at the Maine Shipyards Corporation. A sample of 30 welders revealed that 18 graduated from a registered welding course. Construct the 95 percent confidence interval for the proportion of all welders who graduated from a registered welding course.

Choosing an Appropriate Sample Size

A concern that usually arises when designing a statistical study is "How many items should be in the sample?" If a sample is too large, money is wasted collecting the data. Similarly, if the sample is too small, the resulting conclusions will be uncertain. The necessary sample size depends on three factors:

1. The level of confidence desired.
2. The margin of error the researcher will tolerate.
3. The variability in the population being studied.

The first factor is the *level of confidence*. Those conducting the study select the level of confidence. The 95 percent and the 99 percent levels of confidence are the most common, but any value between 0 and 100 percent is possible. The 95 percent level of confidence corresponds to a z value of 1.96, and a 99 percent level of confidence corresponds to a z value of 2.58. The higher the level of confidence selected, the larger the size of the corresponding sample.

The second factor is the *allowable error*. The maximum allowable error, designated as E, is the amount that is added and subtracted to the sample mean (or sample proportion) to determine the endpoints of the confidence interval. It is the amount of error those conducting the study are willing to tolerate. It is also one-half the width of the corresponding confidence interval. A small allowable error will require a large sample. A large allowable error will permit a smaller sample.

The third factor in determining the size of a sample is the *population standard deviation*. If the population is widely dispersed, a large sample is required. On the other hand, if the population is concentrated (homogeneous), the required sample size will be smaller. However, it may be necessary to use an estimate for the population standard deviation. Here are three suggestions for finding that estimate.

1. **Use a comparable study.** Use this approach when there is an estimate of the dispersion available from another study. Suppose we want to estimate the number of hours worked per week by refuse workers. Information from certain state or federal agencies who regularly sample the workforce might be useful to provide an estimate of the standard deviation. If a standard deviation observed in a previous

study is thought to be reliable, it can be used in the current study to help provide an approximate sample size.

2. **Use a range-based approach.** To use this approach we need to know or have an estimate of the largest and smallest values in the population. Recall from Chapter 4, where we described the Empirical Rule, that virtually all the observations could be expected to be within plus or minus 3 standard deviations of the mean, assuming that the distribution was approximately normal. Thus, the distance between the largest and the smallest values is 6σ. We could estimate the standard deviation as one-sixth of the range. For example, the director of operations at University Bank wants an estimate of the number of checks written per month by college students. She believes that the distribution is approximately normal, the minimum number of checks written is 2 per month, and the most is 50 per month. The range of the number of checks written per month is 48, found by $50 - 2$. The estimate of the standard deviation then would be 8 checks per month, 48/6.
3. **Conduct a pilot study**. This is the most common method. Suppose we want an estimate of the number of hours per week worked by students enrolled in the College of Business at the University of Texas. To test the validity of our questionnaire, we use it on a small sample of students. From this small sample we compute the standard deviation of the number of hours worked and use this value to determine the appropriate sample size.

We can express the interaction among these three factors and the sample size in the following formula.

$$E = z\frac{s}{\sqrt{n}}$$

Solving this equation for n yields the following result.

SAMPLE SIZE FOR ESTIMATING THE POPULATION MEAN

$$n = \left(\frac{zs}{E}\right)^2 \qquad [9\text{–}9]$$

where:

- n is the size of the sample.
- z is the standard normal value corresponding to the desired level of confidence.
- s is an estimate of the population standard deviation.
- E is the maximum allowable error.

The result of this calculation is not always a whole number. When the outcome is not a whole number, the usual practice is to round up *any* fractional result. For example, 201.22 would be rounded up to 202.

EXAMPLE

A student in public administration wants to determine the mean amount members of city councils in large cities earn per month as remuneration for being a council member. The error in estimating the mean is to be less than $100 with a 95 percent level of confidence. The student found a report by the Department of Labor that estimated the standard deviation to be $1,000. What is the required sample size?

SOLUTION

The maximum allowable error, E, is \$100. The value of z for a 95 percent level of confidence is 1.96, and the estimate of the standard deviation is \$1,000. Substituting these values into formula 9–9, the required sample size is:

$$n = \left(\frac{zs}{E}\right)^2 = \left(\frac{(1.96)(\$1{,}000)}{\$100}\right)^2 = (19.6)^2 = 384.16$$

The computed value of 384.16 is rounded up to 385. A sample of 385 is required to meet the specifications. If the student wants to increase the level of confidence, for example to 99 percent, this will require a larger sample. The z value corresponding to the 99 percent level of confidence is 2.58.

$$n = \left(\frac{zs}{E}\right)^2 = \left(\frac{(2.58)(\$1{,}000)}{\$100}\right)^2 = (25.8)^2 = 665.64$$

We recommend a sample of 666. Observe how much the change in the confidence level changed the size of the sample. An increase from the 95 percent to the 99 percent level of confidence resulted in an increase of 281 observations. This could greatly increase the cost of the study, both in terms of time and money. Hence, the level of confidence should be considered carefully.

The procedure just described can be adapted to determine the sample size for a proportion. Again, three items need to be specified:

1. The desired level of confidence.
2. The margin of error in the population proportion.
3. An estimate of the population proportion.

The formula to determine the sample size of a proportion is:

SAMPLE SIZE FOR THE POPULATION PROPORTION

$$n = p(1 - p)\left(\frac{z}{E}\right)^2 \qquad \textbf{[9–10]}$$

If an estimate of π is available from a pilot study or some other source, it can be used. Otherwise, .50 is used because the term $p(1 - p)$ can never be larger than when $p = .50$. For example, if $p = .30$, then $p(1 - p) = .3(1 - 3) = .21$, but when $p = .50$, $p(1 - p) = .5(1 - 5) = .25$

EXAMPLE

The study in the previous example also estimates the proportion of cities that have private refuse collectors. The student wants the estimate to be within .10 of the population proportion, the desired level of confidence is 90 percent, and no estimate is available for the population proportion. What is the required sample size?

SOLUTION

The estimate of the population proportion is to be within .10, so $E = .10$. The desired level of confidence is .90, which corresponds to a z value of 1.65. Because no estimate of the population proportion is available, we use .50. The suggested number of observations is

$$n = (.5)(1 - .5)\left(\frac{1.65}{.10}\right)^2 = 68.0625$$

The student needs a random sample of 69 cities.

Self-Review 9–5

Will you assist the college registrar in determining how many transcripts to study? The registrar wants to estimate the arithmetic mean grade point average (GPA) of all graduating seniors during the past 10 years. GPAs range between 2.0 and 4.0. The mean GPA is to be estimated within plus or minus .05 of the population mean. The standard deviation is estimated to be 0.279. Use the 99 percent level of confidence.

Exercises

23. A population is estimated to have a standard deviation of 10. We want to estimate the population mean within 2, with a 95 percent level of confidence. How large a sample is required?

24. We want to estimate the population mean within 5, with a 99 percent level of confidence. The population standard deviation is estimated to be 15. How large a sample is required?

24. 60

25. The estimate of the population proportion is to be within plus or minus .05, with a 95 percent level of confidence. The best estimate of the population proportion is .15. How large a sample is required?

26. The estimate of the population proportion is to be within plus or minus .10, with a 99 percent level of confidence. The best estimate of the population proportion is .45. How large a sample is required?

26. 165

27. A survey is being planned to determine the mean amount of time corporation executives watch television. A pilot survey indicated that the mean time per week is 12 hours, with a standard deviation of 3 hours. It is desired to estimate the mean viewing time within one-quarter hour. The 95 percent level of confidence is to be used. How many executives should be surveyed?

28. A processor of carrots cuts the green top off each carrot, washes the carrots, and inserts six to a package. Twenty packages are inserted in a box for shipment. To test the weight of the boxes, a few were checked. The mean weight was 20.4 pounds, the standard deviation 0.5 pounds. How many boxes must the processor sample to be 95 percent confident that the sample mean does not differ from the population mean by more than 0.2 pounds?

28. 25

29. Suppose the President wants an estimate of the proportion of the population who support his current policy toward gun control. The President wants the estimate to be within .04 of the true proportion. Assume a 95 percent level of confidence. The President's political advisors estimated the proportion supporting the current policy to be .60.

a. How large a sample is required?

b. How large a sample would be necessary if no estimate were available for the proportion that support current policy?

30. Past surveys reveal that 30 percent of tourists going to Las Vegas to gamble during a weekend spend more than $1,000. Management wants to update this percentage.

a. The new study is to use the 90 percent confidence level. The estimate is to be within 1 percent of the population proportion. What is the necessary sample size?

b. Management said that the sample size determined above is too large. What can be done to reduce the sample? Based on your suggestion recalculate the sample size.

30. a. 5718
b. Change E to .05; then $n = 229$.

Chapter Outline

I. A point estimate is a single value (statistic) used to estimate a population value (parameter).

II. A confidence interval is a range of values within which the population parameter is expected to occur.

A. The factors that determine the width of a confidence interval for a mean are:

1. The number of observations in the sample, n.

2. The variability in the population, usually estimated by the sample standard deviation, s.

3. The level of confidence.
   a. To determine the value to represent the level of confidence when the population standard deviation is known or the sample is 30 or more, we use the z distribution. The formula is

$$\bar{X} \pm z \frac{s}{\sqrt{n}} \qquad \textbf{[9–1]}$$

   b. To determine the value to represent the level of confidence when the population standard deviation is unknown and the sample is less than 30, we use the t distribution. The formula is

$$\bar{X} \pm t \frac{s}{\sqrt{n}} \qquad \textbf{[9–2]}$$

III. The major characteristics of the t distribution are:

A. It is a continuous distribution.

B. It is mound-shaped and symmetrical.

C. It is flatter, or more spread out, than the standard normal distribution.

D. There is a family of t distributions, depending on the number of degrees of freedom.

IV. A proportion is a ratio, fraction, or percent that indicates the part of the sample or population that has the particular characteristic.

A. A sample proportion is found by X, the number of successes, divided by n, the number of observations.

B. The standard error of the sample proportion reports the variability in the distribution of sample proportions. It is found by

$$\sigma_p = \sqrt{\frac{p(1-p)}{n}} \qquad \textbf{[9–5]}$$

C. We construct a confidence interval for a sample proportion from the following formula.

$$p \pm z\sqrt{\frac{p(1-p)}{n}} \qquad \textbf{[9–6]}$$

V. We can determine the sample size for both means and proportions.

A. There are three factors that determine the sample size when we wish to estimate the mean.

1. The desired level of confidence, which is usually expressed by z.
2. The maximum allowable error, E.
3. The variation in the population, expressed by s.
4. The formula to determine the sample size for the mean is

$$n = \left(\frac{zs}{E}\right)^2 \qquad \textbf{[9–9]}$$

B. There are three factors that determine the sample size when we wish to estimate a proportion.

1. The desired level of confidence, which is usually expressed by z.
2. The maximum allowable error, E.
3. An estimate of the population proportion. If no estimate is available, use .50.
4. The formula to determine the sample size for a proportion is

$$n = p(1-p)\left(\frac{z}{E}\right)^2 \qquad \textbf{[9–10]}$$

Pronunciation Key

SYMBOL	MEANING	PRONUNCIATION
$\sigma_{\bar{X}}$	The standard error of the sample means	*sigma sub X bar*
σ_p	Standard error of the sample proportion	*sigma sub p*

Chapter Exercises

31. A random sample of 85 group leaders, supervisors, and similar personnel at General Motors revealed that, on the average, they spent 6.5 years on the job before being promoted. The standard deviation of the sample was 1.7 years. Construct a 95 percent confidence interval.

32. The Iowa state meat inspector has been given the assignment of estimating the mean net weight of packages of ground chuck labeled "3 pounds." Of course, he realizes that the weights cannot be precisely 3 pounds. A sample of 36 packages reveals the mean weight to be 3.01 pounds, with a standard deviation of 0.03 pounds.
   a. What is the estimated population mean?
   b. Determine a 95 percent confidence interval for the population mean.

32. a. 3.01
b. 3.0002, 3.0198

33. A recent study of 50 self-service gasoline stations in the Greater Cincinnati–North Kentucky metropolitan area revealed that the mean price of unleaded gas was $1.179 per gallon. The sample standard deviation was $0.03 per gallon.
   a. Determine a 99 percent confidence interval for the population mean price.
   b. Would it be reasonable to conclude that the population mean was $1.20? Why or why not?

34. A recent survey of 50 unemployed male executives showed that it took an average of 26 weeks for them to find another position. The standard deviation of the sample was 6.2 weeks. Construct a 95 percent confidence interval for the population mean. Is it reasonable that the population mean is 28 weeks? Justify your answer.

34. 24.28, 27.72
28 outside is interval

35. The Badik Construction Company limits its business to constructing decks. The mean time to construct one of their standard decks is 8 hours for a two-person construction crew. The information is based on a sample of 40 decks recently constructed. The standard deviation of the sample was 3 hours.
   a. Determine a 90 percent confidence interval for the population mean.
   b. Would it be reasonable to conclude that the population mean is actually 9 hours? Justify your answer.

36. The American Restaurant Association collected information on the number of meals eaten outside the home per week by young married couples. A survey of 60 couples showed the sample mean number of meals eaten outside the home was 2.76 meals per week, with a standard deviation of 0.75 meals per week. Construct a 97 percent confidence interval for the population mean.

36. 2.55, 2.97

37. The National Collegiate Athletic Association (NCAA) reported that the mean number of hours spent per week on coaching and recruiting by college football assistant coaches during the season is 70. A random sample of 50 assistant coaches showed the sample mean to be 68.6 hours, with a standard deviation of 8.2 hours.
   a. Using the sample data, construct a 99 percent confidence interval for the population mean.
   b. Does the 99 percent confidence interval include the value suggested by the NCAA? Interpret this result.
   c. Suppose you decided to switch from a 99 to a 95 percent confidence interval. Without performing any calculations, will the interval increase, decrease, or stay the same? Which of the values in the formula will change?

38. The Human Relations Department of Electronics, Inc. would like to include a dental plan as part of the benefits package. The question is: How much does a typical employee and his or her family spend per year on dental expenses? A sample of 45 employees reveals the mean amount spent last year was $1,820, with a standard deviation of $660.
   a. Construct a 95 percent confidence interval for the population mean.
   b. The information from part (a) was given to the president of Electronics, Inc. He indicated he could afford $1,700 of dental expenses per employee. Is it possible that the population mean could be $1,700? Justify your answer.

38. a. $1,627, $2,013
b. $1,700 possible

39. A student conducted a study and reported that the 95 percent confidence interval for the mean ranged from 46 to 54. He was sure that the mean of the sample was 50, that the standard deviation of the sample was 16, and that the sample was at least 30, but could not remember the exact number. Can you help him out?

40. A recent study by the American Automobile Dealers Association revealed the mean amount of profit per car sold for a sample of 20 dealers was $290, with a standard deviation of $125. Develop a 95 percent confidence interval for the population mean.

40. 231.5, 348.50

41. A study of 25 graduates of four-year colleges by the American Banker's Association revealed the mean amount owed by a student was $14,381. The standard deviation of the sample was $1,892. Construct a 90 percent confidence interval for the population mean. Is it reasonable to conclude that the mean of the population is actually $15,000? Tell why or why not.

42. 20.61, 27.39

42. An important factor in selling a residential property is the number of people who look through the home. A sample of 15 homes recently sold in the Buffalo, New York, area revealed the mean number looking through each home was 24 and the standard deviation of the sample was 5 people. Develop a 98 percent confidence interval for the population mean.

43. The Warren County Telephone Company claims in its annual report that "the typical customer spends $60 per month on local and long distance service." A sample of 12 subscribers revealed the following amounts spent last month.

$64	$66	$64	$66	$59	$62	$67	$61	$64	$58	$54	$66

a. What is the point estimate of the population mean?
b. Develop a 90 percent confidence interval for the population mean.
c. Is the company's claim that the "typical customer" spends $60 per month reasonable? Justify your answer.

44. The manufacturer of a new line of ink jet printers would like to include as part of their advertising the number of pages a user can expect from a print cartridge. A sample of 10 cartridges revealed the following number of pages printed.

2698	2028	2474	2395	2372	2475	1927	3006	2334	2379

44. a. 2408.8
b. 2191.06, 2626.54

a. What is the point estimate of the population mean?
b. Develop a 95 percent confidence interval for the population mean.

45. Dr. Susan Benner is an industrial psychologist. She is currently studying stress among executives of Internet companies. She has developed a questionnaire that she believes measures stress. A score above 80 indicates stress at a dangerous level. A random sample of 15 executives revealed the following stress level scores.

94	78	83	90	78	99	97	90	97	90	93	94	100	75	84

a. Find the mean stress level for this sample. What is the point estimate of the population mean?
b. Construct a 95 percent confidence level for the population mean.
c. Is it reasonable to conclude that Internet executives have a mean stress level in the dangerous level, according to Dr. Benner's test?

46. .641, .739

46. Furniture Land South surveyed 600 consumers and found that 414 were enthusiastic about a new home décor they plan to show in their store in High Point, North Carolina. Construct the 99 percent confidence interval for the population proportion.

47. There are 20,000 eligible voters in York County, South Carolina. A random sample of 500 York County voters revealed 350 plan to vote to return Louella Miller to the state senate. Construct a 99 percent confidence interval for the proportion of voters in the county who plan to vote for Ms. Miller. From this sample information, can you confirm she will be reelected?

48. In a poll to estimate presidential popularity, each person in a random sample of 1,000 voters was asked to agree with one of the following statements:
1. The President is doing a good job.
2. The President is doing a poor job.
3. I have no opinion.

A total of 560 respondents selected the first statement, indicating they thought the President was doing a good job.

48. a. .53, .59

b. Yes, 50 percent not in interval.

a. Construct a 95 percent confidence interval for the proportion of respondents who feel the President is doing a good job.

b. Based on your interval in part (a), is it reasonable to conclude that a majority (more than half) of the population believes the President is doing a good job?

49. Police Chief Aaron Ard of River City reports 500 traffic citations were issued last month. A sample of 35 of these citations showed the mean amount of the fine was $54, with a standard deviation of $4.50. Construct a 95 percent confidence interval for the mean amount of a citation in River City.

50. .345, .695

50. The First National Bank of Wilson has 650 checking account customers. A recent sample of 50 of these customers showed 26 to have a Visa card with the bank. Construct the 99 percent confidence interval for the proportion of checking account customers who have a Visa card with the bank.

51. It is estimated that 60 percent of U.S. households now subscribe to cable TV. You would like to verify this statement for your class in mass communications. If you want your estimate to be within 5 percentage points, with a 95 percent level of confidence, how large of a sample is required?

52. 134

52. You need to estimate the mean number of travel days per year for outside salespeople. The mean of a small pilot study was 150 days, with a standard deviation of 14 days. If you must estimate the population mean within 2 days, how many outside salespeople should you sample? Use the 90 percent confidence level.

53. You are to conduct a sample survey to determine the mean family income in a rural area of central Florida. The question is, how many families should be sampled? In a pilot sample of 10 families, the standard deviation of the sample was $500. The sponsor of the survey wants you to use the 95 percent confidence level. The estimate is to be within $100. How many families should be interviewed?

54. 865

54. You plan to conduct a survey to find what proportion of the workforce has two or more jobs. You decide on the 95 percent confidence level and state that the estimated proportion must be within 2 percent of the population proportion. A pilot survey reveals that 5 of the 50 sampled hold two or more jobs. How many in the workforce should be interviewed to meet your requirements?

55. The proportion of public accountants who have changed companies within the last three years is to be estimated within 3 percent. The 95 percent level of confidence is to be used. A study conducted several years ago revealed that the percent of public accountants changing companies within three years was 21.

a. To update this study, the files of how many public accountants should be studied?

b. How many public accountants should be contacted if no previous estimates of the population proportion are available?

56. The Hunington National Bank, like most other large banks, found that using automatic teller machines (ATMs) reduces the cost of routine bank transactions. Hunington installed an ATM in the corporate offices of the Fun Toy Company. The ATM is for the exclusive use of Fun's 605 employees. After several months of operation, a sample of 100 employees revealed the following use of the ATM machine by Fun employees in a month.

Number of Times ATM Used	Frequency
0	25
1	30
2	20
3	10
4	10
5	5

56. a. 0.25

b. .172, .328 40 percent not in interval

a. What is the estimate of the proportion of employees who do not use the ATM in a month?

b. Develop a 95 percent confidence interval for this estimate. Can Hunington be sure that at least 40 percent of the employees of Fun Toy Company will use the ATM?

c. 1.65
d. 1.387, 1.913
e. No.

c. How many transactions does the average Fun employee make per month?

d. Develop a 95 percent confidence interval for the mean number of transactions per month.

e. Is it possible that the population mean is 0? Explain.

57. In a recent Zogby poll of 1,000 adults nationwide, 613 said they believe other forms of life exist elsewhere in the universe. Construct the 99 percent confidence interval for the population proportion of those believing life exists elsewhere in the universe. Does your result imply that a majority of Americans believe life exists outside of Earth?

58. 29,745, 34,255

58. As part of an annual review of its accounts, a discount brokerage selects a random sample of 36 customers. Their accounts are reviewed for total account valuation, which showed a mean of $32,000, with a sample standard deviation of $8,200. What is a 90 percent confidence interval for the mean account valuation of the population of customers?

59. A sample of 352 subscribers to *Wired* magazine shows the mean time spent using the Internet is 13.4 hours per week, with a sample standard deviation of 6.8 hours. Find the 95 percent confidence interval for the mean time *Wired* subscribers spend on the Internet.

60. 2,185

60. The Tennessee Tourism Institute (TTI) plans to sample information center visitors entering the state to learn the fraction of visitors who plan to camp in the state. Current estimates are that 35 percent of visitors are campers. How large a sample would you take to estimate at a 95 percent confidence level the population proportion with an allowable error of 2 percent?

exercises.com

61. Hoover is an excellent source of business information. It includes daily summaries as well as information about various industries and specific companies. Go to the site at *www.hoovers.com*. Click on **Companies and Industries**, select one of the industries, such as chemicals or retail, and then within that industry select a sector. This should give you a list of companies. Use a table of random numbers, such as Appendix E, to randomly select 5 to 10 companies in the list. Click on **Capsule** and **Stock chart** to get information about the selected companies. One suggestion is to find the price earnings ratio (P/E ratio) for each of the selected companies. Compute the mean of each, and then develop a confidence interval for the mean P/E ratio. Because the sample is a large part of the population, you will want to include the correction factor. Interpret the result.

62. See IM.

62. The online edition of the *Information Please Almanac* is a valuable source of business information. Go to the Website at *www.infoplease.com*. Click on **Finance and Business**, and then click on **State Taxes on Individuals**. The result is a listing of the 50 states and the District of Columbia. Use a table of random numbers to randomly select 5 to 10 states. Compute the mean state tax rate on individuals. Develop a confidence interval for the mean amount. Because the sample is a large part of the population, you will want to include the correction factor. Interpret your result. You might, as an additional exercise, download all the information and use Excel or MINITAB to compute the population mean. Compare that value with the results of your confidence interval.

Computer Data Exercises

63. Refer to the Real Estate data, which reports information on the homes sold in Venice, Florida, last year.

a. Develop a 95 percent confidence interval for the mean selling price of the homes.

b. Develop a 95 percent confidence interval for the mean distance the home is from the center of the city.

c. Develop a 95 percent confidence interval for the proportion of homes with an attached garage.

64. Refer to the Baseball 2000 data, which reports information on the 30 Major League Baseball teams for the 2000 season.

64. a. 177.43, 202.11
b. 108.68, 121.12
c. 178.89, 210.85

a. Develop a 95 percent confidence interval for the mean number of home runs per team.
b. Develop a 95 percent confidence interval for the mean number of errors committed by each team.
c. Develop a 95 percent confidence interval for the mean number of stolen bases for each team.

65. Refer to the OECD data, which reports information on census, economic, and business data for 29 countries.
a. Develop a 90 percent confidence interval for the mean percent of the population over 65 years.
b. Develop a 90 percent confidence interval for the mean energy use.

66. See IM.

66. Refer to the Schools data, which reports information on the 94 school districts in northwest Ohio. Assume that these data are a sample. Select the variable referring to the percent of the students who come from a family on welfare. Compute the mean and the standard deviation for this variable, *but do not include Lima, Sandusky, Toledo, and Fostoria in the calculation of the sample mean*. Develop a 99 percent confidence interval for the mean percent on welfare. Is the percent of students on welfare in the excluded school districts in this interval? Does it appear that the percent on welfare in the omitted districts is different from the others? Why or why not?

Computer Commands

1. The MINITAB commands to generate the 60 columns of 30 random numbers used in the Example 1 solution on page 304 are:
   a. Select **Calc**, **Random Data**, and then click on **Normal**.
   b. From the dialog box click on **Generate** and type *30* for the number of rows of data, **Store** in *C1-C60,* the **Mean** is *50,* the **Standard Deviation** is *5.0,* and finally click **OK.**

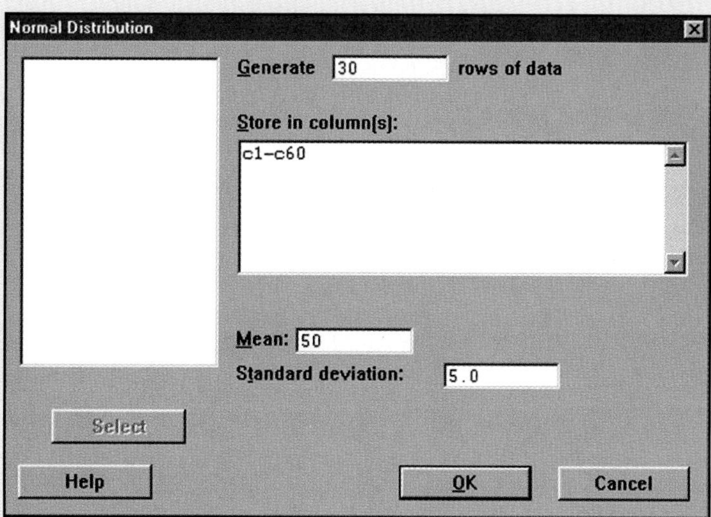

2. The MINITAB commands to create 60 confidence intervals on page 304 follow.
   a. Select **Stat**, **Basic Statistics**, and then click on **1-Sample-z**.
   b. In the dialog box indicate that the **Variables** are *C1-C60* and that **Sigma** is *5.0.* Next click on **Options** in the lower right corner, in the next dialog box indicate that the **Confidence level** is *95.0,* and then click **OK**. Click **OK** in the main dialog box.

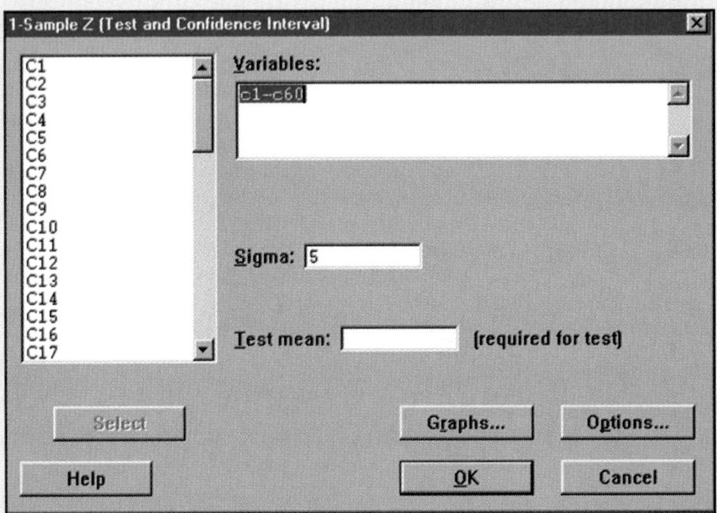

3. The MINITAB commands to create the descriptive statistics on page 311 are the same as those used on page 120 in Chapter 4. Enter the data in the first column and label this column *Amount*. On the Toolbar select **Stat**, **Basic Statistics**, and **Display Basic Statistics**. In the dialog box select *Amount* as the **Variable** and click **OK**.
4. The MINITAB commands to create the confidence interval for the amount spent at the Inlet Square Mall are:
   a. Enter the 20 amounts spent in column c1 and name the variable *Amounts*, or locate the data on the student data disk. It is named "Shopping" and is found in the folder for Chapter 9.
   b. On the Toolbar select **Stat**, **Basic Statistics**, and click on **1-Sample t**.
   c. Select *Amount* as the **Variable** and click **OK**.

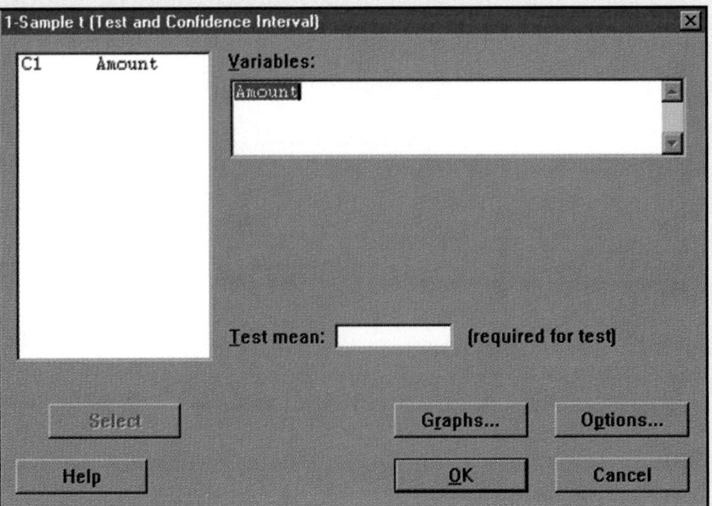

Chapter 9 Answers to Self-Review

9–1 **(a)** \$2,000. This is called the point estimate.

(b) $\$2{,}000 \pm 2.58 \dfrac{\$300}{\sqrt{40}} = \$2{,}000 \pm 122$

(c) The endpoints of the confidence interval are \$1,878 and \$2,122. About 99 percent of the intervals similarly constructed would include the population mean.

9–2 **(a)** $\bar{X} = \dfrac{18}{10} = 1.8 \quad s = \sqrt{\dfrac{44 - \dfrac{(18)^2}{10}}{10 - 1}} = 1.1353$

(b) The population mean is not known. The best estimate is the sample mean, 1.8 days.

(c) $1.80 \pm 2.262 \dfrac{1.1353}{\sqrt{10}} = 1.80 \pm 0.81$

(d) t is used because the population standard deviation is unknown and the sample contains less than 30 observations.

(e) The value of 0 is not in the interval. It is unreasonable to conclude that the mean number of days of work missed is 0 per employee.

9–3 **(a)** $p = \dfrac{420}{1400} = .30$

(b) $\sigma_p = \sqrt{\dfrac{.30(1 - .30)}{1400}} = .0122$

(c) $.30 \pm 2.58(.0122) = .30 \pm .03$

(d) The interval is between .27 and .33. About 99 percent of the similarly constructed intervals would include the population mean.

9–4 $.375 \pm 1.96 \sqrt{\dfrac{.375(1 - .375)}{40}} \sqrt{\dfrac{250 - 40}{250 - 1}} = .375 \pm$
$1.96(.0765)(.9184) = .375 \pm .138$
The correction factor should be applied because $40/240 > .05$.

9–5 $n = \left(\dfrac{2.58(.279)}{.05}\right)^2 = 207.26$ The sample should be rounded to 208.

A Review of Chapters 8 and 9

Chapter 8 began by describing the reasons sampling is necessary. We sample because it is often impossible to study every item, or individual, in some populations. It would be too expensive and time consuming, for example, to contact and record the annual incomes of all U.S. bank officers. Also, sampling often destroys the product. A drug manufacturer cannot test the properties of each tablet manufactured, because there would be none left to sell. To estimate a population parameter, therefore, we sample the population. A sample is a part of the population. Care must be taken to ensure that every member of our population has a chance of being selected; otherwise, the conclusions might be biased. A number of probability-type sampling methods can be used, including *simple random, systematic, stratified,* and *cluster sampling.*

Regardless of the sampling method selected, a sample statistic is seldom equal to the corresponding population parameter. For example, the mean of a sample is seldom exactly the same as the mean of the population. The difference between this sample statistic and the population parameter is the *sampling error.*

In Chapter 8 we demonstrated that if we selected all possible samples of a specified size from a population and calculated the mean of these samples, it would be exactly equal to the population mean. We also showed that the dispersion in the distribution of the sample means was equal to the population standard deviation divided by the square root of the sample size. Hence, we concluded that there was less dispersion in the distribution of the sample means than in the population. Also, as we increased the number of observations in each sample, we decreased the variation in the sampling distribution.

The central limit theorem is the foundation of statistical inference. It states that if the population from which we select the samples follows the normal probability distribution, the distribution of the sample means will also follcw the normal distribution. If the population is not normal, it will approach the normal probability distribution as we increase the size of the sample. From a practical standpoint, when the sample contains at least 30 observations, we conclude that the distribution of the sample means will follow the normal distribution.

Our focus in Chapter 9 was point estimates and interval estimates. A point estimate is a single value used to estimate a population parameter. An interval estimate is a range of values within which we expect the population parameter to occur. For example, based on a sample, we estimate that the mean annual income of all professional house painters in Atlanta, Georgia (the population), is $45,300. That estimate is called a *point estimate.* If we state that the population mean is probably in the interval between $45,200 and $45,400, that estimate is called an *interval estimate.* The two endpoints ($45,200 and $45,400) are the *confidence limits* for the population mean. We described the procedure for establishing a confidence interval for both large and small sample means as well as for sample proportions. In this chapter we also provided a method to determine the necessary sample size based on the dispersion in the population, the level of confidence desired, and the desired precision of the estimate.

Glossary

Bias A possible consequence if certain members of the population are denied the chance to be selected for the sample. As a result, the sample may not be representative of the population.

Central limit theorem If the size of the sample is sufficiently large, the sampling distribution of the sample mean will approach a normal distribution regardless of the shape of the population.

Cluster sampling A method often used to lower the cost of sampling if the population is dispersed over a wide geographic area. The area is divided into smaller units (counties, precincts, blocks, etc.) called primary units. Then a few primary units are chosen, and a random sample is selected from each unit.

Interval estimate The interval within which a population parameter probably lies, based on sample information. Example: Based on sample data, the population mean is in the interval between 1.9 and 2.0 pounds.

Point estimate A single value computed from a sample and used to estimate a population parameter. Example: If the sample mean is 1,020 psi, it is the best estimate of the mean tensile strength of the population.

Probability sample A sample of items or individuals chosen so that each member of the population has a chance of being included in the sample.

Sampling distribution of the sample mean A probability distribution consisting of all possible means of samples of a given size selected from the population.

Sampling error The difference between a sample statistic and the corresponding population parameter. Example: The sample mean income is \$22,100; the population mean is \$22,000. The sampling error is \$22,100 − \$22,000 = \$100. This error can be attributed to sampling, that is, chance.

Simple random sampling A sampling scheme such that each member of the population has the *same* chance of being selected as part of the sample.

Stratified random sampling A population is first divided into subgroups called strata. A sample is then chosen from each stratum. If, for example, the population of interest consisted of all undergraduate students, the sample design might call for sampling 62 freshmen, 51 sophomores, 40 juniors, and 39 seniors.

Systematic random sampling Assuming the population is arranged in some way, such as alphabetically, by height, or in a file drawer. A random starting point is selected, then every *k*th item becomes a member of the sample. If a sample design called for interviewing every ninth household on Main Street starting with 932 Main, the sample would consist of households at 932 Main, 941 Main, 950 Main, and so on.

Exercises

Part I — Multiple Choice

1. Each new employee is given an identification number. The personnel files are arranged sequentially starting with employee number 0001. To sample the employees, the number 0153 was first selected. Then numbers 0253, 0353, 0453, and so on became members of the sample. This type of sampling is called:
- **a.** Simple random sampling.
- **b.** Systematic sampling.
- **c.** Stratified random sampling.
- **d.** Cluster sampling.

2. d. **2.** You divide a precinct into blocks. Then you select 12 blocks at random and concentrate your sampling efforts in those 12 blocks. This type of sampling is called:
- **a.** Simple random sampling.
- **b.** Systematic sampling.
- **c.** Stratified random sampling.
- **d.** Cluster sampling.

3. The sampling error is:
- **a.** Equal to the population mean.
- **b.** A population parameter.
- **c.** Always positive.
- **d.** The difference between the sample statistic and the population parameter.

4. d. **4.** Which of the following are correct statements about confidence intervals?
- **a.** They cannot contain negative numbers.
- **b.** They are always based on the *z* distribution.
- **c.** They must always include the population parameter.
- **d.** None of the above are always correct.

5. The endpoints of a confidence interval are called:
- **a.** Confidence levels.
- **b.** The test statistics.
- **c.** The degrees of confidence.
- **d.** The confidence limits.

6. c. **6.** We compute the mean and the standard deviation of a sample of 50 observations from a population that is positively skewed. We wish to develop a confidence interval for the mean. Which of the following statements is correct?
- **a.** We cannot develop a confidence interval because the population is not normal.
- **b.** We cannot use *z* because we do not know the population standard deviation.
- **c.** We can use *z* because the central limit theorem shows that the distribution of the sample means will approximate the normal distribution.
- **d.** None of the above statements are correct.

7. Which of the following is *not* a correct statement about the *t* distribution?
a. It is positively skewed.
b. It is a continuous distribution.
c. It has a mean of 0.
d. There is a family of *t* distributions.

8. a.

8. As the number of degrees of freedom increases in the *t* distribution:
a. It approaches the standard normal distribution.
b. The level of confidence increases.
c. It becomes a continuous distribution.
d. It becomes flatter.

9. The degrees of freedom are:
a. The total number of observations.
b. The number of observations minus the number of samples.
c. The number of samples.
d. The number of samples minus one.

10. c.

10. We select a sample of 15 observations from a normal population and wish to develop a 98 percent confidence interval for the mean. The appropriate value of *t* is:
a. 2.947
b. 2.977
c. 2.624
d. None of the above.

Part II—Problems

11. A recent study indicated that women took an average of 8.6 weeks of unpaid leave from their jobs after the birth of a child. Assume that this distribution follows the normal probability distribution with a standard deviation of 2.0 weeks. We select a sample of 35 women who recently returned to work after the birth of a child. What is the likelihood that the mean of this sample is at least 8.8 weeks?

12. .0455

12. The manager of the Tee Shirt Emporium reports that the mean number of shirts sold per week is 1,210, with a standard deviation of 325. The distribution of sales follows the normal distribution. What is the likelihood of selecting a sample of 25 weeks and finding the sample mean to be 1,100 or less?

13. The owner of the Gulf Stream Café wished to estimate the mean number of lunch customers per day. A sample of 40 days revealed a mean of 160 per day, with a standard deviation of 20 per day. Develop a 92 percent confidence interval for the mean number of customers per day.

14. 2.58, 2.72

14. The manager of the local Hamburger Express wishes to estimate the mean time customers spend in the drive-through window. A sample of 80 customers experienced a mean waiting time of 2.65 minutes, with a standard deviation of 0.45 minutes. Develop an 85 percent confidence interval for the mean waiting time.

15. The office manager for a large company is studying the usage of its copy machines. A random sample of six copy machines revealed the following number of copies (reported in 000s) made yesterday.

826	931	1126	918	1011	1101

Develop a 95 percent confidence interval for the mean number of copies per machine.

16. John Kleman is the host of KXYZ Radio 55 AM drive-time news in Chicago. During his morning program, John asks listeners to call in and discuss current local and national news. This morning, John was concerned with the number of hours children under 12 years of age watch TV per day. The last 5 callers reported that their children watched the following number of hours of TV last night.

3.0	3.5	4.0	4.5	3.0

16. No, not a random sample.

Would it be reasonable to develop a confidence interval from these data to show the mean number of hours of TV watched? If yes, construct an appropriate confidence interval and interpret the result. If no, why would a confidence interval not be appropriate?

17. Historically, Widgets Manufacturing, Inc. produces 250 widgets per day. Recently the new owner bought a new machine to produce more widgets per day. A sample of 16 days production revealed a mean of 240 units with a standard deviation of 35. Construct a confidence interval for the mean number of widgets produced per day. Does it seem reasonable to conclude that the mean daily widget production has increased? Justify your conclusion.

18. 312

18. The manufacturer of a power chip used in expensive stereo equipment wishes to estimate the useful life of the chip (in thousands of hours). The estimate is to be within 0.10 (100) hours. Assume a 95 percent level of confidence and that the standard deviation of the useful life of the chip is 0.90 (900 hours).

19. The manager of a home improvement store wishes to estimate the mean amount of money spent in the store. The estimate is to be within $4.00 with a 95 percent level of confidence. The manager does not know the standard deviation of the amounts spent. However, he does estimate that the range is from $5.00 up to $155.00. How large of a sample is needed?

20. 0.532, .668

20. In a sample of 200 residents of Georgetown County, 120 reported they believed the county real estate taxes were too high. Develop a 95 percent confidence interval for the proportion of residents who believe the tax rate is too high. Would it be reasonable to conclude that the majority of the taxpayers feel that the taxes are too high?

21. In recent times, the percent of buyers purchasing a new vehicle via the Internet has been large enough that local automobile dealers are concerned about its impact on their business. The information needed is an estimate of the proportion of purchases via the Internet. How large of a sample of purchasers is necessary for the estimate to be within 2 percentage points with a 98 percent level of confidence? Current thinking is that about 8 percent of the vehicles are purchased via the Internet.

22. .205, .295

22. Historically, the proportion of adults over the age of 24 who smoke has been .30. In recent years, much information has been published and aired on radio and TV that smoking is not good for one's health. A sample of 500 adults revealed only 25 percent of those sampled smoked. Develop a 98 percent confidence interval for the proportion of adults who currently smoke. Would you agree that the proportion is less than 30 percent?

23. The auditor of the State of Ohio needs an estimate of the proportion of residents who regularly play the state lottery. Historically, about 40 percent regularly play, but the auditor would like some current information. How large a sample is necessary for the estimate to be within 3 percentage points, with a 98 percent level of confidence?

Case

Century National Bank

Refer to the description of the Century National Bank at the end of the Review of Chapters 1–4 on page 147. When Mr. Selig took over as president of Century several years ago, the use of debit cards was just beginning. He would like an update on the use of these cards. Develop a 95 percent confidence interval for the proportion of customers using these cards. On the basis of the confidence interval, is it reasonable to conclude that more than half of the customers use a debit card? Interpret the results.

With many other options available, customers no longer let their money sit in a checking account. For many years the mean checking balance has been $1,600. Does the sample data indicate that the mean account balance has declined from this value?

Recent years have also seen an increase in the use of ATM machines. When Mr. Selig took over the bank, the mean number of transactions per month per customer was 8; now he believes it has increased to more than 10. In fact, the advertising agency that prepares TV commercials for Century would like to use this on the new commercial being designed. Is there sufficient evidence to conclude that the mean number of transactions per customer is more than 10 per month? Could the advertising agency say the mean is more than 9 per month?

10

One-Sample Tests of Hypothesis

GOALS

When you have completed this chapter you will be able to:

1 **Define a *hypothesis* and *hypothesis testing.***

2 **Describe the five-step hypothesis-testing procedure.**

3 **Distinguish between a one-tailed and a two-tailed test of hypothesis.**

4 **Conduct a test of hypothesis about a population mean.**

5 **Conduct a test of hypothesis about a population proportion.**

6 **Define *Type I* and *Type II* errors.**

7 **Compute the probability of a Type II error.**

Dole Pineapple, Inc. is concerned that the 16-ounce can of sliced pineapples is being overfilled. A random sample of 50 cans found that the arithmetic mean weight was 16.05 ounces, with a sample standard deviation of 0.03 ounces. At the 5 percent level of significance, can we conclude that the mean weight is greater than 16 ounces? (See Goal 4 and Exercise 30.)

Introduction

Chapter 8 began our study of statistical inference. We described how we could select a random sample and from this sample estimate the value of a population parameter. For example, we selected a sample of 5 employees at Spence Sprockets, found the number of years of service for each sampled employee, computed the mean years of service, and used the sample mean to estimate the mean years of service for all employees. In other words, we estimated a population parameter from a sample statistic.

Chapter 9 continued the study of statistical inference by developing a confidence interval. A confidence interval is a range of values within which we expect the population parameter to occur. In this chapter, rather than develop a range of values within which we expect the population parameter to occur, we develop a procedure to test the validity of a statement about a population parameter. Some examples of statements we might want to test are:

- The mean speed of automobiles passing milepost 150 on the West Virginia Turnpike is 68 miles per hour.

- The mean number of miles driven by those leasing a Chevy Blazer for three years is 32,000 miles.
- The mean time an American family lives in a particular single-family dwelling is 11.8 years.
- The mean starting salary for graduates of four-year business schools is $2,200 per month.
- Thirty-five percent of retirees in the upper Midwest sell their home and move to a warm climate within 1 year of their retirement.
- Eighty percent of those who play the state lotteries regularly never win more than $100 in any one play.

This chapter and several of the following chapters are concerned with statistical hypothesis testing. We begin by defining what we mean by a statistical hypothesis and statistical hypothesis testing. Next, we outline the steps in statistical hypothesis testing. Then we conduct tests of hypothesis for means and proportions. In the last section of the chapter, we describe possible errors due to sampling in hypothesis testing.

What Is a Hypothesis?

A hypothesis is a statement about a population parameter.

A hypothesis is a statement about a population. Data are then used to check the reasonableness of the statement. To begin we need to define the word *hypothesis.* In the United States legal system, a person is innocent until proven guilty. A jury hypothesizes that a person charged with a crime is innocent and subjects this hypothesis to verification by reviewing the evidence and hearing testimony before reaching a verdict. In a similar sense, a patient goes to his or her physician and reports various symptoms. Based on the symptoms, the physician will order certain diagnostic tests, then based on the symptoms and the test results, determine the treatment to be followed.

In statistical analysis we make a claim, that is, state a hypothesis, then follow up with tests to verify the assertion or to determine that it is untrue. We define a statistical hypothesis as follows.

HYPOTHESIS A statement about a population parameter developed for the purpose of testing.

In most cases the population is so large that it is not feasible to study all the items, objects, or persons in the population. For example, it would not be possible to contact every systems analyst in the United States to find his or her monthly income. Likewise, the quality assurance department cannot check the breaking strength of each ampul produced to determine whether it is between 5 and 20 psi.

As noted in Chapter 8, an alternative to measuring or interviewing the entire population is to take a sample from the population. We can, therefore, test a statement to determine whether the sample does or does not support the statement concerning the population.

What Is Hypothesis Testing?

The terms *hypothesis testing* and *testing a hypothesis* are used interchangeably. Hypothesis testing starts with a statement, or assumption, about a population parameter — such as the population mean. As noted, this statement is referred to as a *hypothesis.* A hypothesis might be that the mean monthly commission of salespeople in retail computer stores, such as Computerland, is $2,000. We cannot contact all these salespeople to ascertain that the mean is in fact $2,000. The cost of locating and interviewing every computer salesperson in the United States would be exorbitant. To test the validity of the assumption (μ = $2,000), we must select a sample from the population of all computer salespeople, calculate sample statistics, and based on certain decision rules accept or reject the hypothesis. A sample mean of $1,000 for the computer salespeople would certainly cause rejection of the hypothesis. However, suppose the sample mean is $1,995. Is that close enough to $2,000 for us to accept the assumption that the population mean is $2,000? Can we attribute the difference of $5 between the two means to sampling error, or is that difference statistically significant?

HYPOTHESIS TESTING A procedure based on sample evidence and probability theory to determine whether the hypothesis is a reasonable statement.

Five-Step Procedure for Testing a Hypothesis

A systematic procedure

There is a five-step procedure that systematizes hypothesis testing; when we get to step 5, we are ready to reject or not reject the hypothesis. However, hypothesis testing as used by statisticians does not provide proof that something is true, in the manner in which a mathematician "proves" a statement. It does provide a kind of "proof

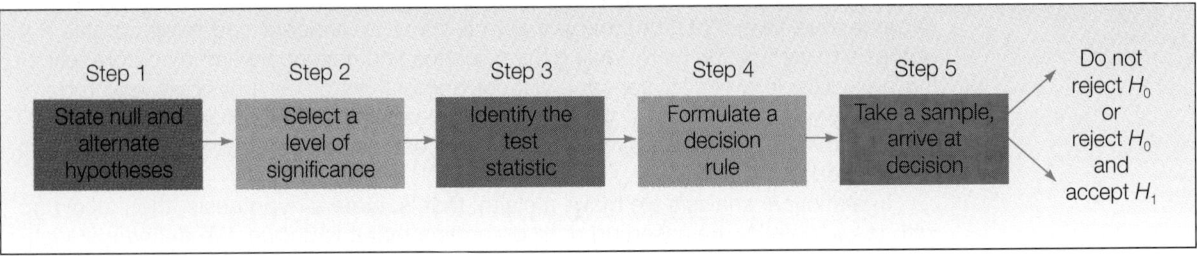

beyond a reasonable doubt," in the manner of the court system. Hence, there are specific rules of evidence, or procedures, that are followed. The steps are shown in the diagram at the bottom of the previous page. We will discuss in detail each of the steps.

Step 1: State the Null Hypothesis (H_0) and the Alternate Hypothesis (H_1)

The first step is to state the hypothesis being tested. It is called the **null hypothesis,** designated H_0, and read "*H sub zero*." The capital letter *H* stands for hypothesis, and the subscript zero implies "no difference." There is usually a "not" or a "no" term in the null hypothesis, meaning that there is "no change." For example, the null hypothesis is that the mean number of miles driven on the steel belted tire is not different from 60,000. The null hypothesis would be written H_0: $\mu = 60{,}000$. Generally speaking, the null hypothesis is developed for the purpose of testing. We either reject or fail to reject the null hypothesis. The null hypothesis is a statement that is not rejected unless our sample data provide convincing evidence that it is false.

We should emphasize that if the null hypothesis is not rejected based on the sample data, we cannot say that the null hypothesis is true. To put it another way, failing to reject the null hypothesis does not prove that H_0 is true, it means we have *failed to disprove* H_0. To prove without any doubt the null hypothesis is true, the population parameter would have to be known. To actually determine it, we would have to test, survey, or count every item in the population. This is usually not feasible. The alternative is to take a sample from the population.

State the null hypothesis and the alternative hypothesis.

It should also be noted that we often begin the null hypothesis by stating, "There is no *significant* difference between . . . ," or "The mean impact strength of the glass is not *significantly* different from. . . ." When we select a sample from a population, the sample statistic is usually numerically different from the hypothesized population parameter. As an illustration, suppose the hypothesized impact strength of a glass plate is 70 psi, and the mean impact strength of a sample of 12 glass plates is 69.5 psi. We must make a decision about the difference of 0.5 psi. Is it a true difference, that is, a significant difference, or is the difference between the sample statistic (69.5) and the hypothesized population parameter (70.0) due to chance (sampling)? As noted, to answer this question we conduct a test of significance, commonly referred to as a test of hypothesis. To define what is meant by a null hypothesis:

> **NULL HYPOTHESIS** A statement about the value of a population parameter.

The **alternate hypothesis** describes what you will conclude if you reject the null hypothesis. It is written H_1 and is read "*H sub one.*" It is also referred to as the research hypothesis. The alternate hypothesis is accepted if the sample data provide us with enough statistical evidence that the null hypothesis is false.

> **ALTERNATE HYPOTHESIS** A statement that is accepted if the sample data provide enough evidence that the null hypothesis is false.

The following example will help clarify what is meant by the null hypothesis and the alternate hypothesis. A recent article indicated the mean age of U.S. commercial aircraft is 15 years. To conduct a statistical test regarding this statement, the first step is to determine the null and the alternate hypotheses. The null hypothesis represents the current or reported condition. It is written H_0: $\mu = 15$. The alternate hypothesis is that the statement is not true, that is, H_1: $\mu \neq 15$. It is important to remember that no matter how the problem is stated, *the null hypothesis will always contain the equal sign.* The equality sign (=) will never appear in the alternate hypothesis. Why? Because the null hypothesis is the statement being tested, and we need a specific value to include in our calculations. We turn to the alternate hypothesis only if we prove the null hypothesis to be untrue.

Step 2: Select a Level of Significance

Select a level of significance or risk.

After setting up the null hypothesis and alternate hypothesis, the next step is to state the level of significance.

> **LEVEL OF SIGNIFICANCE** The probability of rejecting the null hypothesis when it is true.

The level of significance is designated α, the Greek letter alpha. It is also sometimes called the level of risk. This may be a more appropriate term because it is the risk you take of rejecting the null hypothesis when it is really true.

There is no one level of significance that is applied to all tests. A decision is made to use the .05 level (often stated as the 5 percent level), the .01 level, the .10 level, or any other level between 0 and 1. Traditionally, the .05 level is selected for consumer research projects, .01 for quality assurance, and .10 for political polling. You, the researcher, must decide on the level of significance *before* formulating a decision rule and collecting sample data.

To illustrate how it is possible to reject a true hypothesis, suppose a firm manufacturing personal computers uses a large number of printed circuit boards. Suppliers bid on the boards, and the one with the lowest bid is awarded a sizable contract. Suppose the contract specifies that the computer manufacturer's quality-assurance department will sample all incoming shipments of circuit boards. If more than 6 percent of the boards sampled are substandard, the shipment will be rejected. The null hypothesis is that the incoming shipment of boards contains 6 percent or less substandard boards. The alternate hypothesis is that more than 6 percent of the boards are defective.

A sample of 50 circuit boards received July 21 from Allied Electronics revealed that 4 boards, or 8 percent, were substandard. The shipment was rejected because it exceeded the maximum of 6 percent substandard printed circuit boards. If the shipment was actually substandard, then the decision to return the boards to the supplier was correct. However, suppose the 4 substandard printed circuit boards selected in the sample of 50 were the only substandard boards in the shipment of 4,000 boards. Then only $\frac{1}{10}$ of 1 percent were defective (4/4,000 = .001). In that case, less than 6 percent of the entire shipment was substandard and rejecting the shipment was an error. In terms of hypothesis testing, we rejected the null hypothesis that the shipment was not substandard when we should have accepted the null hypothesis. By rejecting a true null hypothesis, we committed a Type I error. The probability of committing a Type I error is α.

TYPE I ERROR Rejecting the null hypothesis, H_0, when it is true.

The probability of committing another type of error, called a Type II error, is designated by the Greek letter beta (β).

TYPE II ERROR Accepting the null hypothesis when it is false.

The firm manufacturing personal computers would commit a Type II error if, unknown to the manufacturer, an incoming shipment of printed circuit boards from Allied Electronics contained 15 percent substandard boards, yet the shipment was accepted. How could this happen? Suppose 2 of the 50 boards in the sample (4 percent) tested were substandard, and 48 of the 50 were good boards. According to the stated procedure, because the sample contained less than 6 percent substandard boards, the shipment was accepted. It could be that *by chance* the 48 good boards selected in the sample were the only acceptable ones in the entire shipment consisting of thousands of boards!

In retrospect, the researcher cannot study every item or individual in the population. Thus, there is a possibility of two types of error — a Type I error, wherein the null hypothesis is rejected when it should have been accepted, and a Type II error, wherein the null hypothesis is accepted when it should have been rejected.

We often refer to the probability of these two possible errors as *alpha*, α, and *beta*, β. Alpha (α) is the probability of making a Type I error, and beta (β) is the probability of making a Type II error.

The following table summarizes the decisions the researcher could make and the possible consequences.

	Researcher	
Null Hypothesis	**Accepts H_0**	***Rejects* H_0**
H_0 is true	Correct decision	Type I error
H_0 is false	Type II error	Correct decision

Step 3: Select the Test Statistic

There are many test statistics. In this chapter we use both z and t as the test statistic. In other chapters we will use such test statistics as F and χ^2, called chi-square.

TEST STATISTIC A value, determined from sample information, used to determine whether to reject the null hypothesis.

In hypothesis testing for the mean (μ) when σ is known or the sample size is large, the test statistic z is computed by:

z DISTRIBUTION AS A TEST STATISTIC

$$z = \frac{\bar{X} - \mu}{\sigma/\sqrt{n}} \qquad [10\text{–}1]$$

The z value is based on the sampling distribution of $\bar{X}$, which is normally distributed when the sample is reasonably large with a mean ($\mu_{\bar{X}}$) equal to μ, and a standard deviation $\sigma_{\bar{X}}$, which is equal to $\sigma/\sqrt{n}$. We can thus determine whether the difference between $\bar{X}$ and μ is statistically significant by finding the number of standard deviations $\bar{X}$ is from μ using formula 10–1.

Step 4: Formulate the Decision Rule

The decision rule states the conditions when H_0 is rejected.

A decision rule is a statement of the specific conditions under which the null hypothesis is rejected and the conditions under which it is not rejected. The region or area of rejection defines the location of all those values that are so large or so small that the probability of their occurrence under a true null hypothesis is rather remote.

Chart 10–1 portrays the rejection region for a test of significance that will be conducted later in the chapter.

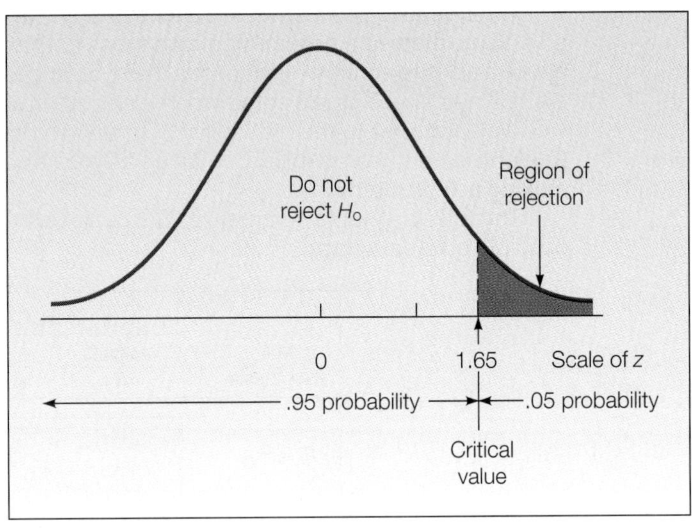

CHART 10–1 Sampling Distribution of the Statistic z, a Right-Tailed Test, .05 Level of Significance

Note in the chart that:

1. The area where the null hypothesis is not rejected is to the left of 1.65. We will explain how to get the 1.65 value shortly.
2. The area of rejection is to the right of 1.65.
3. A one-tailed test is being applied. (This will also be explained later.)
4. The .05 level of significance was chosen.
5. The sampling distribution of the statistic z is normally distributed.
6. The value 1.65 separates the regions where the null hypothesis is rejected and where it is not rejected.
7. The value 1.65 is the **critical value.**

Statistics in Action

During World War II, allied military planners needed estimates of the number of German tanks. The information provided by traditional spying methods was not reliable, but statistical methods proved to be valuable. For example, espionage and reconnaissance led analysts to estimate that 1,550 tanks were produced during June of 1941. However, using the serial numbers of captured tanks and statistical analysis, military planners estimated 244. The actual number produced, as determined from German production records, was 271. The estimate using statistical analysis turned out to be much more accurate. A similar type of analysis was used to estimate the number of Iraqi tanks destroyed during Desert Storm.

CRITICAL VALUE The dividing point between the region where the null hypothesis is rejected and the region where it is not rejected.

Step 5: Make a Decision

The fifth and final step in hypothesis testing is computing the test statistic, comparing it to the critical value, and making a decision to reject or not to reject the null hypothesis. Referring to Chart 10–1, if, based on sample information, z is computed to be 2.34, the null hypothesis is rejected at the .05 level of significance. The decision to reject H_0 was made because 2.34 lies in the region of rejection, that is, beyond 1.65. We would reject the null hypothesis, reasoning that it is highly improbable that a computed z value this large is due to sampling variation (chance).

Had the computed value been 1.65 or less, say 0.71, the null hypothesis would not be rejected. It would be reasoned that such a small computed value could be attributed to chance, that is, sampling variation.

As noted, only one of two decisions is possible in hypothesis testing — either accept or reject the null hypothesis. Instead of "accepting" the null hypothesis, H_0, some researchers prefer to phrase the decision as: "Do not reject H_0," "We fail to reject H_0," or "The sample results do not allow us to reject H_0."

It should be reemphasized that there is always a possibility that the null hypothesis is rejected when it should not be rejected (a Type I error). Also, there is a definable chance that the null hypothesis is accepted when it should be rejected (a Type II error).

Before actually conducting a test of hypothesis, we will differentiate between a one-tailed test of significance and a two-tailed test.

One-Tailed and Two-Tailed Tests of Significance

Refer to Chart 10–1. It depicts a one-tailed test. The region of rejection is only in the right (upper) tail of the curve. To illustrate, suppose that the packaging department at General Foods Corporation is concerned that some boxes of Grape Nuts are significantly overweight. The cereal is packaged in 453-gram boxes, so the null hypothesis is H_0: $\mu \leq 453$. This is read, "the population mean (μ) is equal to or less than 453." The alternate hypothesis is, therefore, H_1: $\mu > 453$. This is read, "μ is greater than 453." Note that the inequality sign in the alternate hypothesis $>$ points to the region of rejection in the upper tail. (See Chart 10–1.) Also note that the null hypothesis includes the equal sign. That is, H_0: $\mu \leq 453$. The equality condition always appears in H_0, never in H_1.

Chart 10–2 portrays a situation where the rejection region is in the left (lower) tail of the normal distribution. As an illustration, consider the problem of automobile manufacturers, large automobile leasing companies, and other organizations that purchase large quantities of tires. They want the tires to average, say, 60,000 miles of wear under normal usage. They will, therefore, reject a shipment of tires if tests reveal that the life of the tires is significantly below 60,000 miles on the average. They gladly accept a shipment if the mean life is greater than 60,000 miles! They are not concerned with this possibility, however. They are concerned only if they have sample evidence to conclude that the tires will average less than 60,000 miles of useful life. Thus, the test is set up to satisfy the concern of the automobile manufacturers that *the mean life of the tires is less than 60,000 miles.* The null and alternate hypotheses in this case are written H_0: $\mu \geq 60{,}000$ and H_1: $\mu < 60{,}000$.

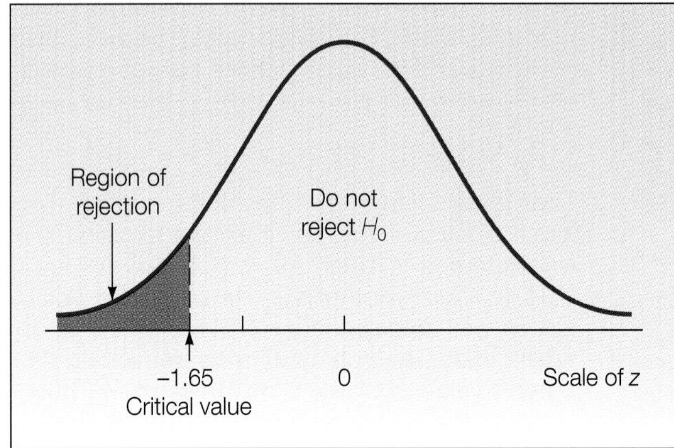

CHART 10–2 Sampling Distribution for the Statistic z, Left-Tailed Test, .05 Level of Significance

Test is one-tailed if H_1 states $\mu >$ or $\mu <$.

If H_1 states a direction, test is one-tailed.

One way to determine the location of the rejection region is to look at the direction in which the inequality sign in the alternate hypothesis is pointing (either $<$ or $>$). In this problem it is pointing to the left, and the rejection region is therefore in the left tail.

In summary, a test is *one-tailed* when the alternate hypothesis, H_1, states a direction, such as:

H_0: The mean income of women stockbrokers is $65,000 per year.
H_1: The mean income of women stockbrokers is *greater* than $65,000 per year.

If no direction is specified in the alternate hypothesis, we use a *two-tailed* test. Changing the previous problem to illustrate:

H_0: The mean income of women stockbrokers is $65,000 per year.
H_1: The mean income of women stockbrokers is *not equal to* $65,000 per year.

If the null hypothesis is rejected and H_1 accepted in the two-tailed case, the mean income could be significantly greater than $65,000 per year, or it could be significantly less than $65,000 per year. To accommodate these two possibilities, the 5 percent area of rejection is divided equally into the two tails of the sampling distribution (2.5 percent each). Chart 10-3 shows the two areas and the critical values. Note that the total area in the normal distribution is 1.0000, found by .9500 + .0250 + .0250.

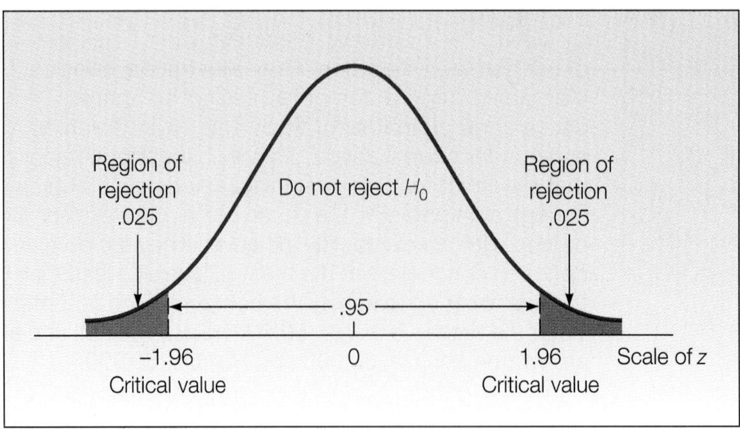

CHART 10–3 Regions of Nonrejection and Rejection for a Two-Tailed Test, .05 Level of Significance

Testing for a Population Mean with a Known Population Standard Deviation

A Two-Tailed Test

An example will show the details of the five-step hypothesis testing procedure. We also wish to use a two-tailed test. That is, we are *not* concerned whether the sample results are larger or smaller than the proposed population mean. Rather, we are interested in whether it is *different from* the proposed value for the population mean. We begin, as we did in the previous chapter, with a situation in which we have historical information about the population and in fact know its standard deviation.

EXAMPLE

The Jamestown Steel Company manufactures and assembles desks and other office equipment at several plants in western New York State. The weekly production of the Model A325 desk at the Fredonia Plant is normally distributed, with a mean of 200 and a standard deviation of 16. Recently, due to market expansion, new production methods have been introduced and new employees hired. The vice president of manufacturing would like to investigate whether there has been a change in the weekly production of the Model A325 desk. To put it another way, is the mean number of desks produced at the Fredonia Plant different from 200 at the .01 significance level?

SOLUTION

We use the statistical hypothesis testing procedure to investigate whether the production rate has changed from 200 per week.

Step 1: The null hypothesis is "The population mean is 200." The alternate hypothesis is "The mean is different from 200" or "The mean is not 200." These two hypotheses are written:

$$H_0\text{: } \mu = 200$$
$$H_1\text{: } \mu \neq 200$$

This is a *two-tailed test* because the alternate hypothesis does not state a direction. In other words, it does not state whether the mean production is greater than 200 or less than 200. The vice president only wants to find out whether the production rate is different from 200.

Step 2: As noted, the .01 level of significance is used. This is α, the probability of committing a Type I error, and it is the probability of rejecting a true hypothesis.

Step 3: The large sample test statistic for a mean is z. It was discussed at length in Chapter 7. Transforming the production data to standard units (z values) permits their use not only in this problem but also in other hypothesis-testing problems. Formula 10–1 for z is repeated below with the various letters identified.

Formula for the test statistic

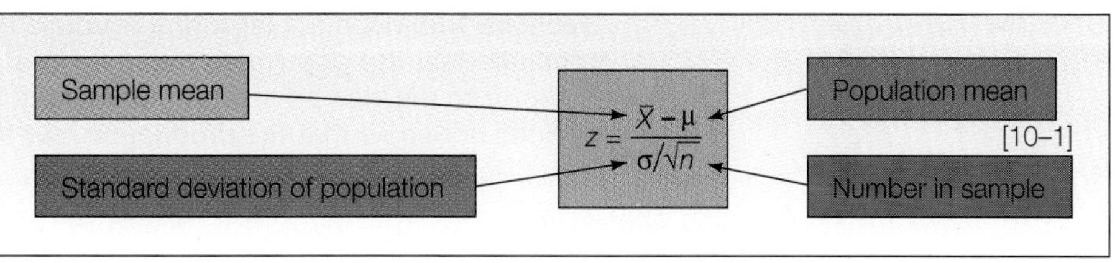

Step 4: The decision rule is formulated by finding the critical values of z from Appendix D. Since this is a two-tailed test, half of .01, or .005, is in each tail. The area where H_0 is not rejected, located between the two tails, is therefore .99. Appendix D is based on half of the area under the curve, or .5000. Then, .5000 − .005 is .4950, so .4950 is the area between 0 and the critical value. Locate .4950 in the body of the table. The value nearest to .4950 is .4951. Then read the critical value in the row and column corresponding to .4951. It is 2.58. For your convenience Appendix D, Areas under the Normal Curve, is repeated in the inside back cover.

All the facets of this problem are shown in the diagram in Chart 10–4.

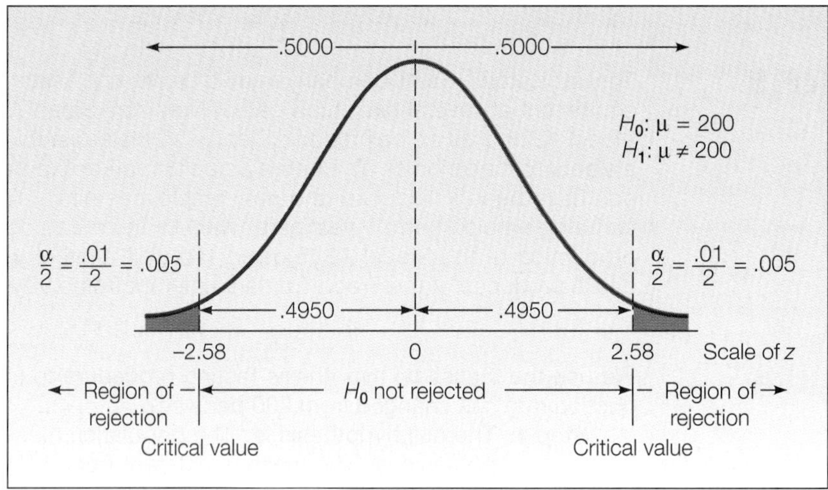

CHART 10–4 Decision Rule for the .01 Significance Level

The decision rule is, therefore: Reject the null hypothesis and accept the alternate hypothesis (which states that the population mean is not 200) if the computed value of z is not between −2.58 and +2.58. Do not reject the null hypothesis if z falls between −2.58 and +2.58.

Step 5: Take a sample from the population (weekly production), compute z, apply the decision rule, and arrive at a decision to reject H_0 or not to reject H_0. The mean number of desks produced last year (50 weeks, because the plant was shut down 2 weeks for vacation) is 203.5. The standard deviation of the population is 16 desks per week. Computing the z value from formula 10–1:

$$z = \frac{\bar{X} - \mu}{\sigma/\sqrt{n}} = \frac{203.5 - 200}{16/\sqrt{50}} = 1.55$$

Because 1.55 does not fall in the rejection region, H_0 is not rejected. We conclude that the population mean is *not* different from 200. So we would report to the vice president of manufacturing that the sample evidence does not show that the production rate at the Fredonia Plant has changed from 200 per week. The difference of 3.5 units between the historical weekly production rate and that last year can reasonably be attributed to chance. This information is summarized in the following chart.

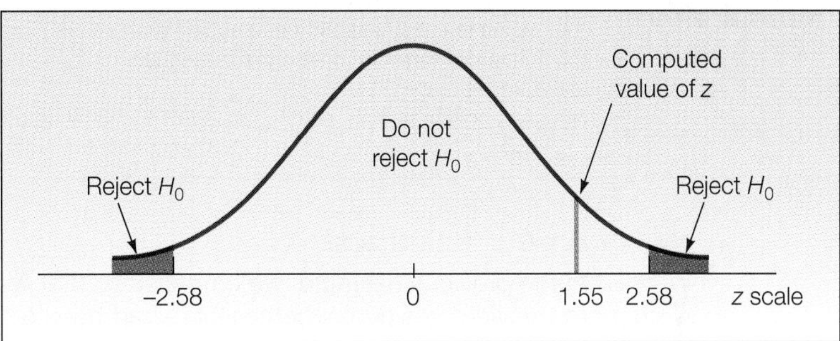

Did we prove that the assembly rate is still 200 per week? Not really. What we did, technically, was *fail to disprove the null hypothesis.* Failing to disprove the hypothesis that the population mean is 200 is not the same thing as proving it to be true. As we suggested in the chapter introduction, the conclusion is analogous to the American judicial system. To explain, suppose a person is accused of a crime but is acquitted by a jury. If a person is acquitted of a crime, the conclusion is that there was not enough evidence to prove the person guilty. The trial did not prove that the individual was innocent, only that there was not enough evidence to prove the defendant guilty. That is what we do in statistical hypothesis testing when we do not reject the null hypothesis. The correct interpretation is that we have failed to disprove the null hypothesis.

We selected the significance level, .01 in this case, before setting up the decision rule and sampling the population. This is the appropriate strategy. The significance level should be set by the investigator, but it should be determined *before* gathering the sample evidence and not changed based on the sample evidence.

How does the hypothesis testing procedure just described compare with that of confidence intervals discussed in the previous chapter? When we conducted the test of hypothesis regarding the production of desks we changed the units from desks per week to a z value. Then we compared the computed value of the test statistic (1.55) to that of the critical values (-2.58 and 2.58). Because the computed value was in the region where the null hypothesis was not rejected, we concluded that the population mean could be 200. To use the confidence interval approach, on the other hand, we would develop a confidence interval, based on formula 9–1. See page 302. The interval would be from 197.66 to 209.34, found by $203.5 \pm 2.58(16/\sqrt{50})$. Note that the proposed population value, 200, is within this interval. Hence, we would conclude that the population mean could reasonably be 200.

In general, H_0 is rejected if the confidence interval does not include the hypothesized value. If the confidence interval includes the hypothesized value, then H_0 is not rejected. So the "do not reject region" for a test of hypothesis is equivalent to the proposed population value occurring in the confidence interval. The primary difference lies in whether the interval is centered around the sample statistic, such as $\bar{X}$, or around 0, as in the test of hypothesis.

SELF-REVIEW 10–1 The mean annual turnover rate of the 200-count bottle of Bayer Aspirin is 6.0 with a standard deviation of 0.50. (This indicates that the stock of Bayer turns over on the pharmacy shelves an average of 6 times per year.) It is suspected that the mean turnover has changed and is not 6.0. Use the .05 significance level.

(a) State the null hypothesis and the alternate hypothesis.
(b) What is the probability of a Type I error?
(c) Give the formula for the test statistic.
(d) State the decision rule.
(e) A random sample of 64 bottles of the 200-count size Bayer Aspirin showed a mean of 5.84. Shall we reject the hypothesis that the population mean is 6.0? Interpret the result.

A One-Tailed Test

In the previous example, we emphasized that we were only concerned with reporting to the vice president whether there had been a change in the mean number of desks assembled at the Fredonia Plant. We were not concerned with whether the change was an increase or a decrease in the production.

To illustrate a one-tailed test, let's change the problem. Suppose the vice president wants to know whether there has been an *increase* in the number of units assembled. To put it another way, can we conclude, because of the improved production methods, that the mean number of desks assembled in the last 50 weeks was more than 200? Look at the difference in the way the problem is formulated. In the first case we wanted to know whether there was a *difference* in the mean number assembled, but now we want to know whether there has been an *increase.* Because we are investigating different questions, we will set our hypotheses differently. The biggest difference occurs in the alternate hypothesis. Before, we stated the alternate hypothesis as "different from"; now we want to state it as "greater than." In symbols:

A two-tailed test:	A one-tailed test:
H_0: $\mu = 200$	H_0: $\mu \leq 200$
H_1: $\mu \neq 200$	H_1: $\mu > 200$

The critical values for a one-tailed test are different from a two-tailed test at the same significance level. In the previous example, we split the significance level in half and put half in the lower tail and half in the upper tail. In a one-tailed test we put all the rejection region in one tail. See Chart 10–5.

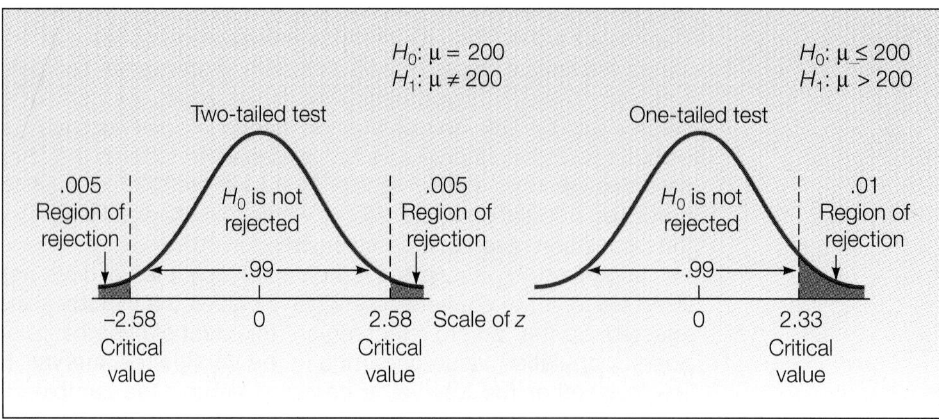

CHART 10-5 Rejection Regions for Two-Tailed and One-Tailed Tests, $\alpha = .01$

For the one-tailed test, the critical value is 2.33, found by: (1) subtracting .01 from .5000 and (2) finding the *z* value corresponding to .4900.

p-Value in Hypothesis Testing

In testing a hypothesis, we compared the test statistic to a critical value. A decision is made to either reject the null hypothesis or not to reject it. So, for example, if the critical value is 1.96 and the computed value of the test statistic is 2.19, the decision is to reject the null hypothesis.

In recent years, spurred by the availability of computer software, additional information is often reported on the strength of the rejection or acceptance. That is, how confident are we in rejecting the null hypothesis? This approach reports the probability (assuming that the null hypothesis is true) of getting a value of the test statistic at least as extreme as the value actually obtained. This process compares the probability, called the ***p*-value,** with the significance level. If the p-value is smaller than the significance level, H_0 is rejected. If it is larger than the significance level, H_0 is not rejected.

***p*-VALUE** The probability of observing a sample value as extreme as, or more extreme than, the value observed, given that the null hypothesis is true.

Determining the p-value not only results in a decision regarding H_0, but it gives us additional insight into the strength of the decision. A very small p-value, such as .0001, indicates that there is little likelihood the H_0 is true. On the other hand, a p-value of .2033 means that H_0 is not rejected, and there is little likelihood that it is false.

How do we compute the p-value? To illustrate we will use the example in which we tested the null hypothesis that the mean number of desks produced per week at Fredonia was 200. We did not reject the null hypothesis, because the value of z of 1.55 fell in the region between -2.58 and 2.58. We agreed not to reject the null hypothesis if the computed value of z fell in this region. The probability of finding a z value of 1.55 or more is .0606, found by $.5000 - .4394$. That is, the probability of obtaining an $\bar{X}$ greater than 203.5 if $\mu = 200$ is .0606. To compute the p-value, we need to be concerned with the region less than -1.55 as well as the values greater than 1.55 (because the rejection region is in both tails). The p-value is .1212, found by 2(.0606). The p-value of .1212 is greater than the significance level of .01 decided upon initially, so H_0 is not rejected. The details are shown in the following graph.

Statistics in Action

There is a difference between *statistically significant* and *practically significant.* To explain, suppose we develop a new diet pill and test it on 100,000 people. We conclude that the typical person taking the pill for two years lost one pound. Do you think many people would be interested in taking the pill to lose one pound? The results of using the new pill were statistically significant but not practically significant.

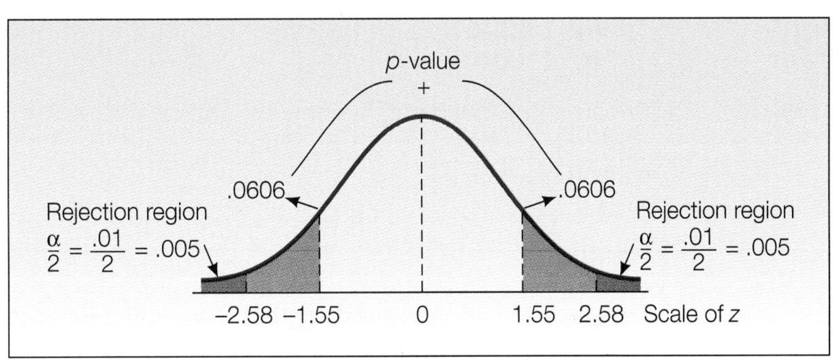

A p-value is a way to express the likelihood that H_0 is not true. But how do we interpret a p-value? We have already said that if the p-value is less than the significance level, then we reject H_0; if it is greater than the significance level, then we do not reject H_0. Also, if the p-value is very large then it is likely that H_0 is true. If the p-value is small, then it is likely that H_0 is not true. The following box will help to interpret p-values.

INTERPRETING THE WEIGHT OF EVIDENCE AGAINST H_0

If the p-value is less than
(a) .10, we have *some* evidence that H_0 is not true.
(b) .05, we have *strong* evidence that H_0 is not true.
(c) .01, we have *very strong* evidence that H_0 is not true.
(d) .001, we have *extremely strong* evidence that H_0 is not true.

Testing for a Population Mean: Large Sample, Population Standard Deviation Unknown

In the preceding example, we knew σ, the population standard deviation. In most cases, however, the population standard deviation is unknown. Thus, σ must be based on prior studies or estimated by the sample standard deviation, s. The population standard deviation in the following example is not known, so the sample standard deviation is used to estimate σ. As long as the sample size, n, is greater than 30, s can be substituted for σ, as illustrated in the following formula:

z STATISTIC, σ UNKNOWN

$$z = \frac{\bar{X} - \mu}{s/\sqrt{n}} \qquad \textbf{[10–2]}$$

EXAMPLE

The Thompson's Discount Appliance Store issues its own credit card. The credit manager wants to find whether the mean monthly unpaid balance is more than $400. The level of significance is set at .05. A random check of 172 unpaid balances revealed the sample mean is $407 and the standard deviation of the sample is $38. Should the credit manager conclude the population mean is greater than $400, or is it reasonable that the difference of $7 ($407 − $400 = $7) is due to chance?

SOLUTION

The null and alternate hypotheses are:

H_0: $\mu \leq \$400$
H_1: $\mu > \$400$

Because the alternate hypothesis states a direction, a one-tailed test is applied. The critical value of z is 1.65. The computed value of z is 2.42, found by using formula 10–2:

$$z = \frac{\bar{X} - \mu}{s/\sqrt{n}} = \frac{\$407 - \$400}{\$38/\sqrt{172}} = \frac{\$7}{\$2.8975} = 2.42$$

The decision rule is portrayed graphically in the following chart.

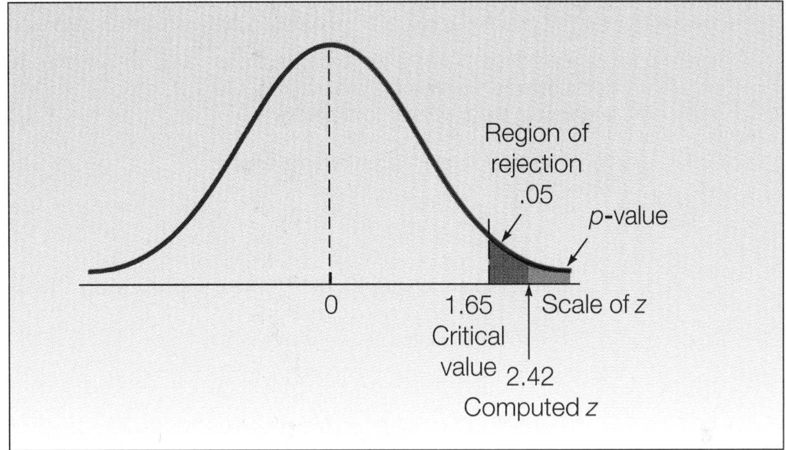

Because the computed value of the test statistic (2.42) is larger than the critical value (1.65), the null hypothesis is rejected. The credit manager can conclude the mean unpaid balance is greater than $400.

The *p*-value provides additional insight into the decision. Recall the *p*-value is the probability of finding a test statistic as large as or larger than that obtained, when the null hypothesis is true. So we find the probability of a *z* value greater than 2.42. From Appendix D the probability of a *z* value between 0 and 2.42 is .4922. We want to determine the likelihood of a value *greater than* 2.42, so $.5000 - .4922 = .0078$. We conclude that the likelihood of finding a *z* value of 2.42 or larger when the null hypothesis is true is 0.78 percent. It is unlikely, therefore, that the null hypothesis is true.

SELF-REVIEW 10–2 Refer to Self-Review 10–1.

(a) Suppose the hypothesis-testing problem was changed to a one-tailed test. How would the null hypothesis be written symbolically if it read, "The population mean is equal to or greater than 6.0"?
(b) How would the alternate hypothesis be written symbolically if it read, "The population mean is less than 6.0"?
(c) Show the decision rule graphically. Show the rejection region and indicate the critical value.

Exercises

For Exercises 1–4 answer the questions: (a) Is this a one- or two-tailed test? (b) What is the decision rule? (c) What is the value of the test statistic? (d) What is your decision regarding H_0? (e) What is the p-value? Interpret it.

1. The following information is available.

$$H_0: \mu = 50$$
$$H_1: \mu \neq 50$$

The sample mean is 49, and the sample size is 36. The population standard deviation is 5. Use the .05 significance level.

2. The following information is available.

$$H_0: \mu \leq 10$$
$$H_1: \mu > 10$$

The sample mean is 12 for a sample of 36. The population standard deviation is 3. Use the .02 significance level.

2. a. One-tailed.
b. Reject if $z > 2.05$.
c. $z = 4.00$
d. Reject.
e. 0.0000

3. A sample of 36 observations is selected from a normal population. The sample mean is 21, and the sample standard deviation is 5. Conduct the following test of hypothesis using the .05 significance level.

$$H_0: \mu \leq 20$$
$$H_1: \mu > 20$$

4. A sample of 64 observations is selected from a normal population. The sample mean is 215, and the sample standard deviation is 15. Conduct the following test of hypothesis using the .03 significance level.

$$H_0: \mu \geq 220$$
$$H_1: \mu < 220$$

4. a. One-tailed.
b. Reject if $z < -1.88$.
c. $z = -2.67$
d. Reject H_1.
e. .0038

For Exercises 5–8: (a) State the null hypothesis and the alternate hypothesis. (b) State the decision rule. (c) Compute the value of the test statistic. (d) What is your decision regarding H_0? (e) What is the p-value? Interpret it.

5. The manufacturer of the X-15 steel-belted radial truck tire claims that the mean mileage the tire can be driven before the tread wears out is 60,000 miles. The standard deviation of the mileage is 5,000 miles. The Crosset Truck Company bought 48 tires and found that the mean mileage for their trucks is 59,500 miles. Is Crosset's experience different from that claimed by the manufacturer at the .05 significance level?

6. The MacBurger restaurant chain claims that the waiting time of customers for service is normally distributed, with a mean of 3 minutes and a standard deviation of 1 minute. The quality-assurance department found in a sample of 50 customers at the Warren Road MacBurger that the mean waiting time was 2.75 minutes. At the .05 significance level, can we conclude that the mean waiting time is less than 3 minutes?

6. a. H_0: $\mu \geq 3$, H_1 $\mu < 3$
b. Reject H_0 if $z < -1.65$.
c. $z = -1.77$
d. Reject H_0.
e. p-value = .0384

7. A recent national survey found that high school students watched an average (mean) of 6.8 videos per month. A random sample of 36 college students revealed that the mean number of videos watched last month was 6.2, with a standard deviation of 0.5. At the .05 significance level, can we conclude that college students watch fewer videos a month than high school students?

8. At the time she was hired as a server at the Grumney Family Restaurant, Beth Brigden was told, "You can average more than $20 a day in tips." Over the first 35 days she was employed at the restaurant, the mean daily amount of her tips was $24.85, with a standard deviation of $3.24. At the .01 significance level, can Ms. Brigden conclude that she is earning an average of more than $20 in tips?

8. a. H_0: $\mu \leq 20$, H_1: $\mu > 20$
b. Reject if $z > 2.33$.
c. $z = 8.86$
d. Reject H_0.
e. 0.0000

Testing for a Population Mean: Small Sample, Population Standard Deviation Unknown

We are able to use the standard normal distribution, that is z, under two conditions:

1. The population is known to follow a normal distribution and the population standard deviation is known, or
2. The shape of the population is not known, but the number of observations in the sample is at least 30.

What do we do when the sample is less than 30 and the population standard deviation is not known? We encountered this same situation when constructing confidence intervals in the previous chapter. See pages 306–307 in Chapter 9. We summarized this problem in Chart 9–3 on page 308. Under these conditions the correct statistical procedure is to replace the standard normal distribution with the t distribution. To review, the major characteristics of the t distribution are:

1. It is a continuous distribution.
2. It is bell-shaped and symmetrical.
3. There is a family of t distributions. Each time the degrees of freedom change, a new distribution is created.
4. As the number of degrees of freedom increases the shape of the t distribution approaches that of the standard normal distribution.
5. The t distribution is flatter, or more spread out, than the standard normal distribution.

To conduct a test of hypothesis using the t distribution, we adjust formula 10–2 as follows.

TEST OF MEAN, SMALL SAMPLE

$$t = \frac{\bar{X} - \mu}{s/\sqrt{n}} \quad \textbf{[10–3]}$$

with $n - 1$ degrees of freedom, where:

$\bar{X}$ is the mean of the sample.
μ is the hypothesized population mean.
s is the standard deviation of the sample.
n is the number of observations in the sample.

The following example shows the details

EXAMPLE

The McFarland Insurance Company Claims Department reports that the mean cost to process a claim is \$60. An industry comparison showed this amount to be larger than most other insurance companies, so they instituted cost-cutting measures. To evaluate the effect of the cost-cutting measures, McFarland selected a random sample of 26 recent claims. The mean cost per claim was \$57 and the standard deviation was \$10. Can they conclude that the cost-cutting measures were effective? Or should they conclude that the difference between the sample mean (\$57) and the population mean (\$60) is due to chance? Use the .01 significance level.

SOLUTION

We will use the five-step hypothesis testing procedure.

Step 1: State the Null Hypothesis and the Alternate Hypothesis The null hypothesis is that the population mean is at least \$60. The alternate hypothesis is that the population mean is less than \$60. We can express the null and alternate hypotheses as follows:

H_0: $\mu \geq \$60$
H_1: $\mu < \$60$

The test is *one*-tailed because we want to determine whether there has been a *reduction* in the cost. The inequality in the alternate hypothesis points to the region of rejection in the left tail of the distribution.

Step 2: Select the Level of Significance We decided on the .01 significance level.

Step 3: Select the Test Statistic The test statistic in this situation is the t distribution. Why? First, it is reasonable to assume that the distribution of the cost per claim follows the normal distribution. However, we do not know the value of the population standard deviation. Thus, we must substitute the sample standard deviation for the population standard deviation. When the sample is large, we can make the substitution and still use the standard normal distribution. We usually define large as 30 or more. In this case there are fewer than 30 observations in the sample, so we cannot use the standard normal distribution. Instead, we use t. The value of the test statistic is computed using formula 10–3:

$$t = \frac{\bar{X} - \mu}{s/\sqrt{n}}$$

Step 4: Formulate the Decision Rule The critical values of t are given in Appendix F, a portion of which is shown in Table 10–1. Appendix F is also repeated in the back inside cover of the text. The far left column of the table is labeled "Degrees of Freedom, *df*." The number of degrees of freedom is the total number of observations in the sample minus the number of samples, written $n - 1$. In this case the number of observations in the sample is 26, so there are $26 - 1 = 25$ degrees of freedom. To find the critical value, first locate the row with the appropriate degrees of freedom. This row is shaded in Table 10–1. Next, determine whether the test is one-tailed or two-tailed. In this case, we have a one-tailed test, so find the portion of the table that is labeled "one-tailed." Locate the column with the selected significance level. In this example, the significance level is .01. Move down the column labeled "0.01" until it intersects the row with 25 degrees of freedom. The value is 2.485. Because this is a one-tailed test and the rejection region is in the left tail, the critical value is negative. The decision rule is to reject H_0 if the value of t is less than -2.485.

TABLE 10–1 A Portion of the *t* Distribution Table

	Confidence Intervals					
	80%	90%	95%	98%	99%	99.9%
	Level of Significance for One-Tailed Test					
df	0.100	0.050	0.025	0.010	0.005	0.0005
	Level of Significance for Two-Tailed Test					
	0.20	0.10	0.05	0.02	0.01	0.001
⋮	⋮	⋮	⋮	⋮	⋮	⋮
21	1.323	1.721	2.080	2.518	2.831	3.819
22	1.321	1.717	2.074	2.508	2.819	3.792
23	1.319	1.714	2.069	2.500	2.807	3.768
24	1.318	1.711	2.064	2.492	2.797	3.745
25	1.316	1.708	2.060	2.485	2.787	3.725
26	1.315	1.706	2.056	2.479	2.779	3.707
27	1.314	1.703	2.052	2.473	2.771	3.690
28	1.313	1.701	2.048	2.467	2.763	3.674
29	1.311	1.699	2.045	2.462	2.756	3.659
30	1.310	1.697	2.042	2.457	2.750	3.646

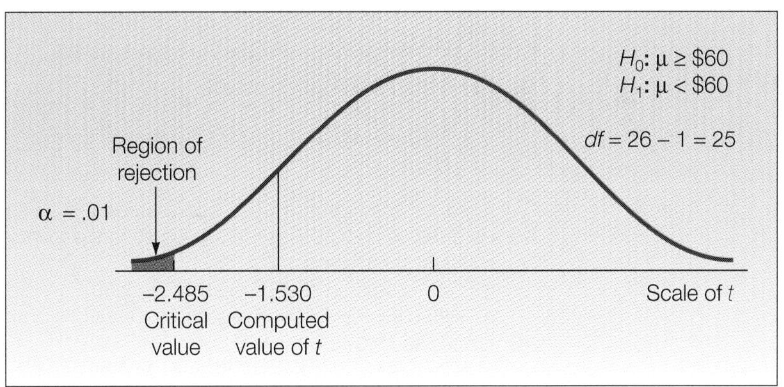

CHART 10-6 Rejection Region, *t* Distribution, .01 Significance Level

Step 5: Make a Decision In this problem:

$\bar{X}$ = \$57, the sample mean.
μ = \$60, the hypothesized population mean.
s = \$10, the sample standard deviation.
n = 26, the number of observations in the sample.

The value of *t* is −1.530, found by:

$$t - \frac{\bar{X} - \mu}{s/\sqrt{n}} = \frac{\$57 - \$60}{\$10/\sqrt{26}} = -1.530$$

Because −1.530 lies in the region to the right of the critical value of −2.485, the null hypothesis is not rejected at the .01 significance level. There is not a statistically significant difference between $\bar{X}$ and μ. This indicates that the cost-cutting measures have not reduced the mean cost per claim to less than $60. The difference of $3 between the sample mean and the population mean could be due to chance. The computed value of t is shown in Chart 10–6. It is in the region where the null hypothesis is not rejected.

SELF-REVIEW 10–3 The mean life of a battery used in a digital clock is 305 days. The lives of the batteries follow the normal distribution. The battery was recently modified to last longer. A sample of 20 of the modified batteries had a mean life of 311 days with a standard deviation of 12 days. Did the modification increase the mean life of the battery?

(a) State the null hypothesis and the alternate hypothesis.
(b) Show the decision rule graphically. Use the .05 significance level.
(c) Compute the value of *t*. What is your decision regarding the null hypothesis? Briefly summarize your results.

Exercises

9. Given the following hypothesis:

H_0: $\mu \le 10$
H_1: $\mu > 10$

For a random sample of 10 observations, the sample mean was 12 and the sample standard deviation 3. Using the .05 significance level:

a. State the decision rule.
b. Compute the value of the test statistic.
c. What is your decision regarding the null hypothesis?

10. Given the following hypothesis:

H_0: $\mu = 400$
H_1: $\mu \ne 400$

For a random sample of 12 observations, the sample mean was 407 and the sample standard deviation 6. Using the .01 significance level:

a. State the decision rule.
b. Compute the value of the test statistic.
c. What is your decision regarding the null hypothesis?

11. The Rocky Mountain district sales manager of Rath Publishing, Inc., a college textbook publishing company, claims that the sales representatives make an average of 40 sales calls per week on professors. Several reps say that this estimate is too low. To investigate, a random sample of 28 sales representatives reveals that the mean number of calls made last week was 42. The standard deviation of the sample is 2.1 calls. Using the .05 significance level, can we conclude that the mean number of calls per salesperson per week is more than 40?

12. The management of White Industries is considering a new method of assembling its golf cart. The present method requires 42.3 minutes, on the average, to assemble a cart. The mean assembly time for a random sample of 24 carts, using the new method, was 40.6 minutes, and the standard deviation of the sample was 2.7 minutes. Using the .10 level of significance, can we conclude that the assembly time using the new method is faster?

10. a. Reject if $t < -3.106$ or $t > 3.106$.
b. $t = 4.042$.
c. Reject H_0.

12. H_0: $\mu \ge 42.3$
H_1: $\mu < 42.3$
Reject if $t < -1.319$.
$t = -3.084$
Reject H_0.

13. The records of Yellowstone Trucks reveal that the mean life of a set of spark plugs is 22,100 miles. The distribution of the life of the plugs is approximately normal. A spark plug manufacturer claimed that its plugs have a mean life in excess of 22,100 miles. The fleet owner purchased a large number of sets. A sample of 18 sets revealed that the mean life was 23,400 miles and the standard deviation was 1,500 miles. Is there enough evidence to substantiate the manufacturer's claim at the .05 significance level?

14. H_0: $\mu \leq 15$ H_1: $\mu > 15$ Reject if $t > 1.725$. $t = 13.75$ Reject H_0.

14. Fast Service, a chain of automotive tune-up shops, advertises that its personnel can change the oil, replace the oil filter, and lubricate any standard automobile in 15 minutes, on the average. The National Business Bureau received complaints from customers that service takes considerably longer. To check the Fast Service claim, the Bureau had service done on 21 unmarked cars. The mean service time was 18 minutes, and the standard deviation of the sample was 1 minute. Use the .05 significance level to check the reasonableness of the Fast Service claim.

In the previous example the mean and the standard deviation were included in the problem. The following example requires this information to be computed from the sample data.

EXAMPLE

The mean length of a small counterbalance bar is 43 millimeters. The production supervisor is concerned that the adjustments of the machine producing the bars have changed. He asks the Engineering Department to investigate. Engineering selects a random sample of 12 bars and measures each. The results are reported below in millimeters.

42	39	42	45	43	40	39	41	40	42	43	42

Is it reasonable to conclude that there has been a change in the mean length of the bars? Use the .02 significance level.

SOLUTION

We begin by stating the null hypothesis and the alternate hypothesis.

H_0: $\mu = 43$
H_1: $\mu \neq 43$

The alternate hypothesis does not state a direction, so this is a two-tailed test. There are 11 degrees of freedom, found by $n - 1 = 12 - 1 = 11$. The t value is 2.718, found by referring to Appendix F for a two-tailed test, using the .02 significance level, with 11 degrees of freedom. The decision rule is: Reject the null hypothesis if the computed t is to the left of -2.718 or to the right of 2.718. This information is summarized in Chart 10–7.

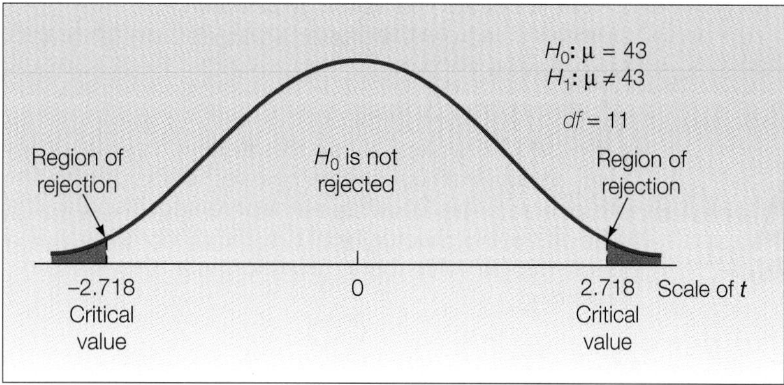

CHART 10–7 Regions of Rejection, Two-Tailed Test, Student's t Distribution, $\alpha = .02$

The standard deviation of the sample can be determined either by squaring the deviations from the mean or by an equivalent formula using the squares of the actual values. The two formulas from Chapter 4, 4–5 and 4–7, are:

Using squared deviations from mean:

$$s = \sqrt{\frac{\Sigma(X - \bar{X})^2}{n - 1}}$$

Using squares of raw data:

$$s = \sqrt{\frac{\Sigma X^2 - \frac{(\Sigma X)^2}{n}}{n - 1}}$$

The necessary calculations for these two methods are shown in Table 10-2 below. The mean, $\bar{X}$, is 41.5 millimeters, and the standard deviation, s, is 1.78 millimeters.

TABLE 10–2 Calculations of the Sample Standard Deviation

X (mm)	$X - \bar{X}$	$(X - \bar{X})^2$	X^2
42	0.5	0.25	1,764
39	−2.5	6.25	1,521
42	0.5	0.25	1,764
45	3.5	12.25	2,025
43	1.5	2.25	1,849
40	−1.5	2.25	1,600
39	−2.5	6.25	1,521
41	−0.5	0.25	1,681
40	−1.5	2.25	1,600
42	0.5	0.25	1,764
43	1.5	2.25	1,849
42	0.5	0.25	1,764
498	0	35.00	20,702

$$\bar{X} = \frac{498}{12} = 41.5 \text{ mm}$$

Squared deviation method:

$$s = \sqrt{\frac{\Sigma(X - \bar{X})^2}{n - 1}} = \sqrt{\frac{35}{12 - 1}} = 1.78$$

Squaring raw data:

$$s = \sqrt{\frac{\Sigma X^2 - \frac{(\Sigma X)^2}{n}}{n - 1}} = \sqrt{\frac{20{,}702 - \frac{(498)^2}{12}}{12 - 1}}$$

$$= 1.78$$

Now we are ready to compute the value of t, using formula 10–3.

$$t = \frac{\bar{X} - \mu}{s/\sqrt{n}} = \frac{41.5 - 43.0}{1.78/\sqrt{12}} = -2.92$$

The null hypothesis that the population mean is 43 millimeters is rejected because the computed t of −2.92 lies in the area to the left of −2.718. We accept the alternate hypothesis and conclude that the population mean is not 43 millimeters. The machine is out of control and needs adjustment.

A Computer Solution

The MINITAB statistical software system, used in earlier chapters, provides an efficient way of conducting a one-sample test of hypothesis for a population mean. The steps to generate the following output are shown in the Computer Commands section at the end of the chapter. Note that the computed value of t (−2.91) is approximately the same as the value found using formula 10–1 (−2.92). The slight difference is due to rounding.

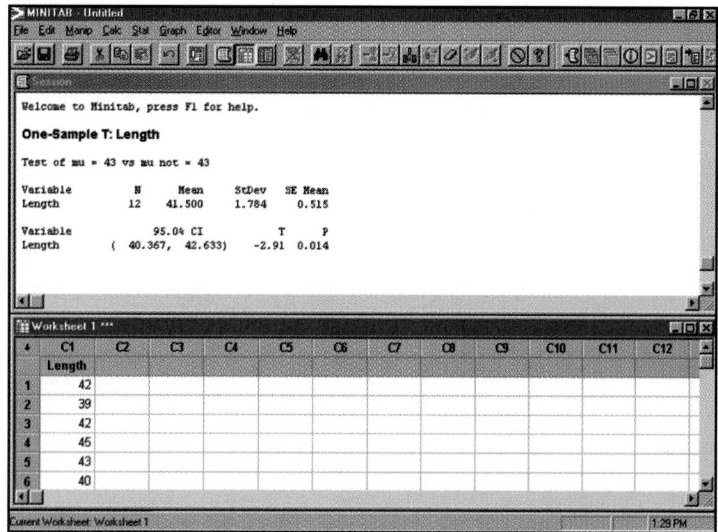

An additional feature of MINITAB, and most other statistical software packages, is to report the *p*-value, which gives additional information on the null hypothesis. The *p*-value is the probability of a *t* value as extreme as that computed, given that the null hypothesis is true. In this case, the *p*-value of .014 is the likelihood of a *t* value of −2.91 or less plus the likelihood of a *t* value of 2.91 or larger, given a population mean of 43. Thus, comparing the *p*-value to the significance level tells us whether the null hypothesis was close to being rejected, barely rejected, and so on.

To explain further, refer to the following diagram, in which the *p*-value of .014 is shown in purple and the significance level is the yellow area plus the purple area. Because the *p*-value of .014 is less than the significance level of .02, the null hypothesis is rejected. Had the *p*-value been larger than the significance level — say, .06, .19, or .57 — the null hypothesis would not be rejected. If the significance level had initially been selected as .01, the null hypothesis would not be rejected.

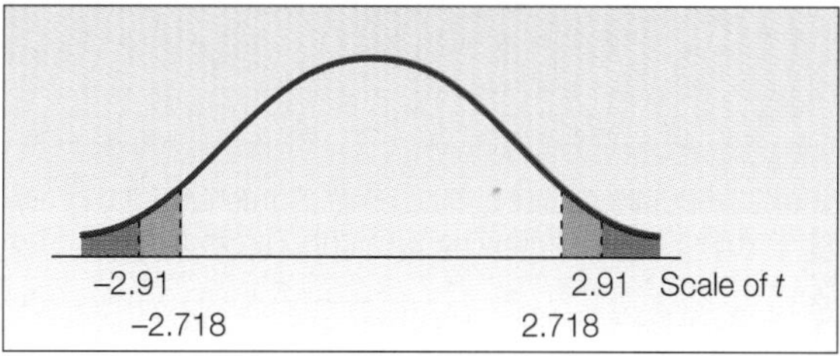

In the preceding example the alternate hypothesis was two-tailed, so there were rejection areas in both the upper and the lower tails. To determine the *p*-value, it was necessary to determine the area to the left of −2.91 for a *t* distribution with 11 degrees of freedom and add to it the value to the right of 2.91, also with 11 degrees of freedom.

What if we were conducting a one-tailed test, so that the entire rejection region would be in either the upper or the lower tail? In that case, we would report the area from only the one tail. In the counterbalance example, if H_1 were stated as $\mu < 43$, the inequality would point to the left. Thus, we would have reported the *p*-value as the area to the left of −2.91. This value is .007, found by .014/2. Thus, the *p*-value for a one-tailed test would be .007.

How can we estimate a *p*-value without a computer? To illustrate, recall that, in the example regarding the length of a counterbalance, we rejected the null hypothesis that $\mu = 43$ and accepted the alternate hypothesis that $\mu \neq 43$. The significance level was .02, so logically the *p*-value is less than .02. To estimate the *p*-value more accurately, go to Appendix F and find the row with 11 degrees of freedom. The computed *t* value of 2.91 is between 2.718 and 3.106. (A portion of Appendix F is reproduced as Table 10–3.) The two-tailed significance level corresponding to 2.718 is .02, and for 3.106 it is .01. Therefore, the *p*-value is between .01 and .02. The usual practice is to report that the *p*-value is *less* than the larger of the two significance levels. So we would report, "the *p*-value is less than .02."

TABLE 10–3 A Portion of Student's *t* Distribution

	Confidence Intervals					
	80%	90%	95%	98%	99%	99.9%
	Level of Significance for One-Tailed Test					
df	0.100	0.050	.0025	0.010	0.005	0.0005
	Level of Significance for Two-Tailed Test					
	0.20	0.10	0.05	0.02	0.01	0.001
⋮	⋮	⋮	⋮	⋮	⋮	⋮
9	1.383	1.833	2.262	2.821	3.250	4.781
10	1.372	1.812	2.228	2.764	3.169	4.587
11	1.363	1.796	2.201	2.718	3.106	4.437
12	1.356	1.782	2.179	2.681	3.055	4.318
13	1.350	1.771	2.160	2.650	3.012	4.221
14	1.345	1.761	2.145	2.624	2.977	4.140
15	1.341	1.753	2.131	2.602	2.947	4.073

SELF-REVIEW 10–4 A machine is set to fill a small bottle with 9.0 grams of medicine. A sample of eight bottles revealed the following amounts (grams) in each bottle.

9.2	8.7	8.9	8.6	8.8	8.5	8.7	9.0

At the .01 significance level, can we conclude that the mean weight is less than 9.0 grams?

(a) State the null hypothesis and the alternate hypothesis.
(b) How many degrees of freedom are there?
(c) Give the decision rule.
(d) Compute the value of *t*. What is your decision regarding the null hypothesis?
(e) Estimate the *p*-value.

Exercises

15. Given the following hypothesis:

H_0: $\mu \geq 20$
H_1: $\mu < 20$

A random sample of five resulted in the following values: 18, 15, 12, 19, and 21. Using the .01 significance level, can we conclude the population mean is less than 20?

a. State the decision rule.
b. Compute the value of the test statistic.
c. What is your decision regarding the null hypothesis?
d. Estimate the p-value.

16. Given the following hypothesis:

H_0: $\mu = 100$
H_1: $\mu \neq 100$

A random sample of six resulted in the following values: 118, 105, 112, 119, 105, and 111. Using the .05 significance level, can we conclude the mean is different from 100?

a. State the decision rule.
b. Compute the value of the test statistic.
c. What is your decision regarding the null hypothesis?
d. Estimate the p-value.

16. **a.** Reject if $t < -2.571$ or $t > 2.571$. **b.** $t = 4.72$ **c.** Reject H_0. **d.** Less than .01.

17. Experience raising New Jersey Red chickens revealed the mean weight of the chickens at five months is 4.35 pounds. The weights follow the normal distribution. In an effort to increase their weight, a special additive is added to the chicken feed. The subsequent weights of a sample of five-month-old chickens were (in pounds):

4.41	4.37	4.33	4.35	4.30	4.39	4.36	4.38	4.40	4.39

At the .01 level, has the special additive increased the mean weight of the chickens? Estimate the p-value.

18. The liquid chlorine added to swimming pools to combat algae has a relatively short shelf life before it loses its effectiveness. Records indicate that the mean shelf life of a 5-gallon jug of chlorine is 2,160 hours (90 days). As an experiment, Holdlonger was added to the chlorine to find whether it would increase the shelf life. A sample of nine jugs of chlorine had these shelf lives (in hours):

2,159	2,170	2,180	2,179	2,160	2, 167	2,171	2,181	2,185

At the .025 level, has Holdlonger increased the shelf life of the chlorine? Estimate the p-value.

18. H_0: $\mu \leq 2{,}160$ H_1: $\mu > 2{,}160$ Reject if $t > 2.306$. $t = 3.98$ Reject H_0. p-value $< .005$

19. Wyoming fisheries contend that the mean number of cutthroat trout caught during a full day of fly-fishing on the Snake, Buffalo, and other rivers and streams in the Jackson Hole area is 4.0. To make their yearly update, the fishery personnel asked a sample of fly-fishermen to keep a count of the number caught during the day. The numbers were: 4, 4, 3, 2, 6, 8, 7, 1, 9, 3, 1, and 6. At the .05 level, can we conclude that the mean number caught is greater than 4.0? Estimate the p-value.

20. Hugger Polls contends that an agent conducts a mean of 53 in-depth home surveys every week. A streamlined survey form has been introduced, and Hugger wants to evaluate its effectiveness. The number of in-depth surveys conducted during a week by a random sample of agents are:

53	57	50	55	58	54	60	52	59	62	60	60	51	59	56

At the .05 level of significance, can we conclude that the mean number of interviews conducted by the agents is more than 53 per week? Estimate the p-value.

20. H_0: $\mu \leq 53$ H_1: $\mu > 53$ Reject if $t > 1.761$. $t = 3.52$ Reject H_0. p-value less than .005.

Tests Concerning Proportions

In the previous chapter we discussed confidence intervals for proportions. We can also conduct a test of hypothesis for a proportion. Recall that a proportion is the ratio of the number of successes to the number of observations. We let X refer to the number of successes and n the number of observations, so the proportion of success in a fixed number of trials is X/n. Thus, the formula for computing a sample proportion, p, is $p = X/n$. Consider the following potential hypothesis-testing situations.

- Historically, General Motors reports that 70 percent of leased vehicles are returned with less than 36,000 miles. A recent sample of 200 vehicles returned at the end of their lease showed 158 had less than 36,000 miles. Has the proportion increased?
- The American Association of Retired Persons (AARP) reports that 60 percent of retired persons under the age of 65 would return to work on a full-time basis if a suitable job were available. A sample of 500 retirees under 65 revealed 315 would return to work. Can we conclude that more than 60 percent would return to work?
- Able Moving and Storage, Inc. advises its clients for long distance residential moves that their household goods will be delivered in 3 to 5 days from the time they are picked up. Able's records show that they are successful 90 percent of the time with this claim. A recent audit revealed they were successful 190 times out of 200. Can they conclude that their success rate has increased?

Some assumptions must be made and conditions met before testing a population proportion. To test a hypothesis about a population proportion, a random sample is chosen from the population. It is assumed that the binomial assumptions discussed in Chapter 6 are met: (1) the sample data collected are the result of counts; (2) the outcome of an experiment is classified into one of two mutually exclusive categories — a "success" or a "failure"; (3) the probability of a success is the same for each trial; and (4) the trials are independent, meaning the outcome of one trial does not affect the outcome of any other trial. The test we will conduct shortly is appropriate when both $n\pi$ and $n(1 - \pi)$ are at least 5. n is the sample size, and π is the population proportion. It takes advantage of the fact that a binomial distribution can be approximated by the normal distribution.

$n\pi$ and $n(1 - \pi)$ must be at least 5.

EXAMPLE

Suppose prior elections in a state indicated it is necessary for a candidate for governor to receive at least 80 percent of the vote in the northern section of the state to be elected. The incumbent governor is interested in assessing his chances of returning to office and plans to conduct a survey of 2,000 registered voters in the northern section of the state.

Using the hypothesis-testing procedure, assess the governor's chances of reelection.

SOLUTION

The following test of hypothesis can be conducted because both $n\pi$ and $n(1 - \pi)$ exceed 5. In this case, $n = 2{,}000$ and $\pi = .80$ (π is the proportion of the vote in the northern part of the state, or 80 percent, needed to be elected). Thus, $n\pi = 2{,}000(.80) = 1{,}600$ and $n(1 - \pi) = 2{,}000(1 - .80) = 400$. Both 1,600 and 400 are greater than 5.

Step 1: The null hypothesis, H_0, is that the population proportion π is .80 or larger. The alternate hypothesis, H_1, is that the proportion is less than .80. From a practical standpoint, the incumbent governor is concerned only when the proportion is less than .80. If it is equal to or greater than .80, he will have no problem; that is, the sample data would indicate he will probably be reelected. These hypotheses are written symbolically as:

H_0: $\pi \geq .80$
H_1: $\pi < .80$

H_1 states a direction. Thus, as noted previously, the test is one-tailed with the inequality sign pointing to the tail of the distribution containing the region of rejection.

Step 2: The level of significance is .05. This is the likelihood that a true hypothesis will be rejected.

Step 3: z is the appropriate statistic, found by:

TEST OF HYPOTHESIS, ONE PROPORTION $$z = \frac{p - \pi}{\sigma_p} \quad [10-4]$$

where :

π is the population proportion.
p is the sample proportion.
n is the sample size.
σ_π is the standard error of the population proportion. It is computed by $\sqrt{\pi(1 - \pi)/n}$, so the formula for z becomes:

TEST OF HYPOTHESIS, ONE PROPORTION $$z = \frac{p - \pi}{\sqrt{\dfrac{\pi(1 - \pi)}{n}}} \quad [10–5]$$

Finding the critical value

Step 4: The critical value or values of z form the dividing point or points between the regions where H_0 is rejected and where it is not rejected. Since the alternate hypothesis states a direction, this is a one-tailed test. The sign of the inequality points to the left, so only the left half of the curve is used. (See Chart 10–8.) The significance level was given as .05 in step 2. This probability is in the left tail and determines the region of rejection. The area between zero and the critical value is .4500, found by .5000 − .0500. Referring to Appendix D and searching for .4500, we find the critical value of z is 1.65. The decision rule is, therefore: Reject the null hypothesis and accept the alternate hypothesis if the computed value of z falls to the left of -1.65; otherwise do not reject H_0.

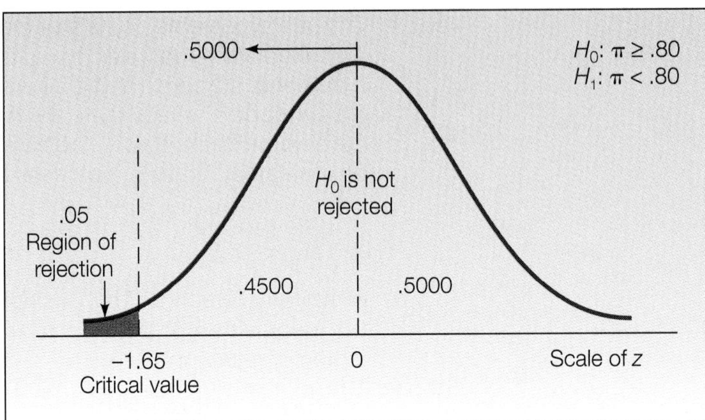

CHART 10–8 Rejection Region for the .05 Level of Significance, One-Tailed Test

Select a sample and make a decision regarding H_0.

Step 5: Select a sample and make a decision about H_0. A sample survey of 2,000 potential voters in the northern part of the state revealed that 1,550 planned to vote for the incumbent governor. Is the sample proportion of .775 (found by 1,550/2,000) close enough to .80 to conclude that the difference is due to chance? In this case:

- p is .775, the proportion in the sample who plan to vote for the governor.
- n is 2,000, the number of voters surveyed.
- π is .80, the hypothesized population proportion.
- z is a normally distributed test statistic when the hypothesis is true and the other assumptions are true.

Using formula 10–5 and computing z:

$$z = \frac{p - \pi}{\sqrt{\frac{\pi(1-\pi)}{n}}} = \frac{\frac{1{,}550}{2{,}000} - .80}{\sqrt{\frac{.80(1-.80)}{2{,}000}}} = \frac{.775 - .80}{\sqrt{.00008}} = -2.80$$

The computed value of z (−2.80) is in the rejection region, so the null hypothesis is rejected at the .05 level. The difference of 2.5 percentage points between the sample percent (77.5 percent) and the hypothesized population percent in the northern part of the state necessary to carry the state (80 percent) is statistically significant. It is probably not due to sampling variation. To put it another way, the evidence at this point does not support the claim that the incumbent governor will return to the governor's mansion for another four years.

The p-value is the probability of finding a z value less than −2.80. From Appendix D, the probability of a z value less than −2.80 is .4974. So the p-value is .0026, found by .5000 − .4974. The governor cannot be confident of reelection!

SELF-REVIEW 10–5 A recent insurance industry report indicated that 40 percent of those persons involved in minor traffic accidents this year have been involved in a least one other traffic accident in the last five years. An advisory group decided to investigate this claim, believing it was too large. A sample of 200 traffic accidents this year showed 74 persons were also involved in another accident within the last five years. Use the .01 significance level.

(a) Can we use z as the test statistics? Tell why or why not.
(b) State the null hypothesis and the alternate hypothesis.
(c) Show the decision rule graphically.
(d) Compute the value of z and state your decision regarding the null hypothesis.
(e) Determine and interpret the p-value.

Exercises

21. The following hypotheses are given.

$$H_0: \pi \leq .70$$
$$H_1: \pi > .70$$

A sample of 100 observations revealed that $p = .75$. At the .05 significance level, can the null hypothesis be rejected?

a. State the decision rule.
b. Compute the value of the test statistic.
c. What is your decision regarding the null hypothesis?

22. The following hypotheses are given.

$$H_0: \pi = .40$$
$$H_1: \pi \neq .40$$

A sample of 120 observations revealed that $p = .30$. At the .05 significance level, can the null hypothesis be rejected?

a. State the decision rule.
b. Compute the value of the test statistic.
c. What is your decision regarding the null hypothesis?

22. **a.** Reject H_0 if $z < -1.96$ or $z > 1.96$. **b.** $z = -2.24$ **c.** H_0 is rejected.

Note: It is recommended that you use the five-step hypothesis-testing procedure in solving the following problems.

23. The National Safety Council reported that 52 percent of American turnpike drivers are men. A sample of 300 cars traveling southbound on the New Jersey Turnpike yesterday revealed that 170 were driven by men. At the .01 significance level, can we conclude that a larger proportion of men were driving on the New Jersey Turnpike than the national statistics indicate?

24. A recent article in *USA Today* reported that a job awaits only one in three new college graduates. The major reasons given were an overabundance of college graduates and a weak economy. A survey of 200 recent graduates from your school revealed that 80 students had jobs. At the .02 significance level, can we conclude that a larger proportion of students at your school have jobs?

24. Do not reject H_0, $z = 2.00$

25. Chicken Delight claims that 90 percent of its orders are delivered within 10 minutes of the time the order is placed. A sample of 100 orders revealed that 82 were delivered within the promised time. At the .10 significance level, can we conclude that less than 90 percent of the orders are delivered in less than 10 minutes?

26. Research at the University of Toledo indicates that 50 percent of the students change their major area of study after their first year in a program. A random sample of 100 students in the College of Business revealed that 48 had changed their major area of study after their first year of the program. Has there been a significant decrease in the proportion of students who change their major after the first year in this program? Test at the .05 level of significance.

26. Do not reject H_0, $z = -0.40$

Type II Error

Recall that the level of significance, identified by the symbol α, is the probability that the null hypothesis is rejected when it is true. This is called a Type I error. The most common levels of significance are .05 and 01.

In a hypothesis-testing situation there is also the possibility that a null hypothesis is not rejected when it is actually false. That is, we accept a false null hypothesis. This is called a Type II error. The probability of a Type II error is identified by the Greek letter beta (β).

To illustrate the computation of beta, suppose a manufacturer purchases steel bars to make cotter pins. Past experience indicates that the mean tensile strength of all incoming shipments is 10,000 psi and that the standard deviation, σ, is 400 psi.

In order to make a decision about incoming shipments of steel bars, the manufacturer set up this rule for the quality-control inspector to follow: "Take a sample of 100 steel bars. If the sample mean ($\bar{X}$) strength falls between 9,922 psi and 10,078 psi, accept the lot. Otherwise the lot is to be rejected." Refer to Chart 10–9 and the region labeled *A.* It shows the region where each lot is rejected and where it is not rejected. The mean of this distribution is designated μ_0. The tails of the curve represent the probability of making a Type I error, that is, rejecting the incoming lot of steel bars when in fact it is a good lot, with a mean of 10,000 psi.

How is the probability of a Type II error computed? (Recall that it is the probability of accepting an incoming lot as a "good lot" when in fact the mean is not 10,000 psi.)

EXAMPLE

Suppose the unknown population mean of an incoming lot, designated μ_1, is really 9,900 psi. What is the probability that the quality-control inspector will fail to reject the shipment (a Type II error)?

SOLUTION

Computations for β (Type II error)

The probability of committing a Type II error, as represented by the green area in Chart 10–9, region *B,* can be computed by determining the area under the normal curve that lies above 9,922 pounds. The calculation of the areas under the normal curve was discussed in Chapter 7. Reviewing briefly, it is necessary first to determine the probability of the sample mean falling between 9,900 and 9,922. Then this probability is subtracted from .5000 (which represents all the area beyond the mean of 9,900) to arrive at the probability of making a Type II error in this case.

The number of standard units (z value) between the mean of the incoming lot (9,900), designated by μ_1, and $\bar{X}_c$, representing the critical value for 9,922, is computed by:

TYPE II ERROR

$$z = \frac{\bar{X}_c - \mu_1}{\sigma/\sqrt{n}} \qquad \textbf{[10–6]}$$

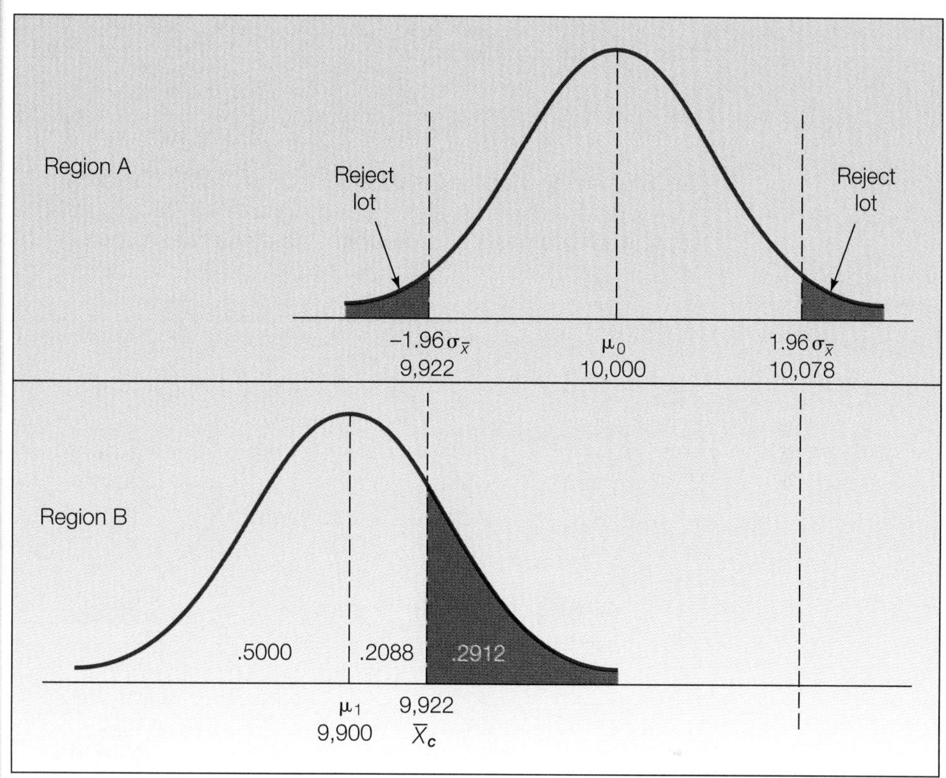

CHART 10–9 Charts Showing Type I and Type II Errors

With $n = 100$ and $\sigma = 400$, the value of z is 0.55:

$$z = \frac{\bar{X}_c - \mu_1}{\sigma/\sqrt{n}} = \frac{9{,}922 - 9{,}900}{400/\sqrt{100}} = \frac{22}{40} = 0.55$$

The area under the curve between 9,900 and 9,922 (a z value of 0.55) is .2088 (from Appendix D).

The area under the curve beyond 9,922 pounds is .5000 − .2088, or .2912; this is the probability of making a Type II error — that is, accepting an incoming lot of steel bars when the population mean is 9,900 psi.

Another illustration in Chart 10–10, region *C*, depicts the probability of accepting a lot when the population mean is 10,120. To find the probability:

$$z = \frac{\bar{X}_c - \mu_1}{\sigma/\sqrt{n}} = \frac{10{,}078 - 10{,}120}{400/\sqrt{100}} = -1.05$$

The probability that *z* is less than −1.05 is .1469, found by .5000 − .3531.

Using the methods illustrated by Charts 10–9*B* and 10–10*C,* the probability of accepting a hypothesis as true when it is actually false can be determined for any value of μ_1.

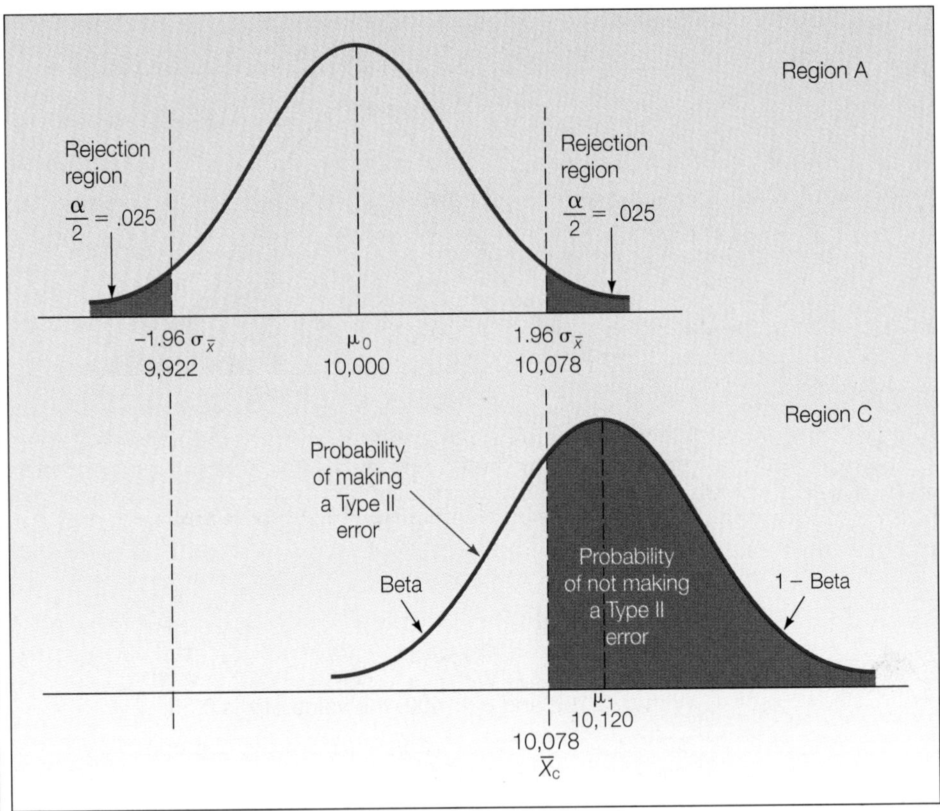

CHART 10–10 Type I and Type II Errors (Another Example)

Type II error probabilities are shown in the center column of Table 10–4 for selected values of μ, given in the left column. The right column gives the probability of not making a Type II error, which is also known as the power of a test.

TABLE 10–4 Probabilities of a Type II Error for $\mu_0 = 10{,}000$ Pounds and Selected Alternative Means, .05 Level of Significance

Selected Alternative Mean (pounds)	Probability of Type II Error (β)	Probability of Not Making a Type II Error ($1 - \beta$)
9,820	.0054	.9946
9.880	.1469	.8531
9,900	.2912	.7088
9,940	.6736	.3264
9,980	.9265	.0735
10,000	—*	—
10,020	.9265	.0735
10,060	.6736	.3264
10,100	.2912	.7088
10,120	.1469	.8531
10,180	.0054	.9946

*It is not possible to make a Type II error when $\mu = \mu_0$.

SELF-REVIEW 10–6

Suppose the true mean of an incoming lot of steel bars is 10,180 psi. What is the probability that the quality control inspector will accept the bars having a mean of 10,000 psi? (It sounds implausible that steel bars will be rejected if the tensile strength is higher than specified. However, it may be that the cotter pin has a dual function in an outboard motor. It may be designed not to shear off if the motor hits a small object, but to shear off if it hits a rock. Therefore, the steel should not be *too* strong.)

The light area in Chart 10–10C represents the probability of falsely accepting the hypothesis that the mean tensile strength of the incoming steel is 10,000 psi. What is the probability of committing a Type II error?

Exercises

28. $z = -0.45$ Type II error = .6736.

27. Refer to Table 10–4 and the example just completed. With $n = 100$, $\sigma = 400$, $\bar{X}_c = 9{,}922$, and $\mu_1 = 9{,}880$, verify that the probability of a Type II error is .1469.

28. Refer to Table 10–4 and the example just completed. With $n = 100$, $\sigma = 400$, $\bar{X}_c = 9{,}922$, and $\mu_1 = 9{,}940$, verify that the probability of a Type II error is .6736

Chapter Outline

I. The objective of hypothesis testing is to check the validity of a statement about a population parameter.

II. The steps in conducting a test of hypothesis are:

- **A.** State the null hypothesis (H_0) and the alternate hypothesis (H_1).
- **B.** Select the level of significance.
  - **1.** The level of significance is the likelihood of rejecting a true null hypothesis.
  - **2.** The most frequently used significance levels are .01, .05, and .10, but any value between 0 and 1.00 is possible.

C. Select the test statistic.
  1. A test statistic is a value calculated from sample information used to determine whether to reject the null hypothesis.
  2. Two test statistics were considered in this chapter.
    a. The standard normal distribution is used when the population follows the normal distribution and the population standard deviation is known.
    b. The standard normal distribution is used when the population follows the normal distribution, the population standard deviation is unknown, but the sample contains at least 30 observations.
    c. The *t* distribution is used when the population follows the normal distribution, the population standard deviation is unknown, and the sample contains fewer than 30 observations.

D. State the decision rule.
  1. The decision rule indicates the condition or conditions when the null hypothesis is rejected.
  2. In a two-tailed test, the rejection region is evenly split between the upper and lower tails.
  3. In a one-sample test, all of the rejection region is in either the upper or the lower tail.

E. Select a sample, compute the value of the test statistic, make a decision regarding the null hypothesis, and interpret the results.

III. A *p*-value is the probability that the value of the test statistic is as extreme as the value computed, when the null hypothesis is true.

IV. Testing a hypothesis about a population mean.
  A. If the population standard deviation, σ, is known, the test statistic is the standard normal distribution and is determined from:

$$z = \frac{\bar{X} - \mu}{\sigma/\sqrt{n}} \qquad \textbf{[10–1]}$$

  B. If the population standard deviation is not known, but there are at least 30 observations in the sample, s is substituted for σ. The test statistic is the standard normal distribution, and its value is determined from:

$$z = \frac{\bar{X} - \mu}{s/\sqrt{n}} \qquad \textbf{[10–2]}$$

  C. If the population standard deviation is not known, but there are fewer than 30 observations in the sample, s is substituted for σ. The test statistic is the *t* distribution, and its value is determined from:

$$t = \frac{\bar{X} - \mu}{s/\sqrt{n}} \qquad \textbf{[10–3]}$$

  The major characteristics of the *t* distribution are:
  1. It is a continuous distribution.
  2. It is mound-shaped and symmetrical.
  3. It is flatter, or more spread out, than the standard normal distribution.
  4. There is a family of *t* distributions, depending on the number of degrees of freedom.

V. Testing about a population proportion.
  A. Both $n\pi$ and $n(1 - \pi)$ must be at least 5.
  B. The test statistic is

$$z = \frac{p - \pi}{\sqrt{\frac{\pi(1 - \pi)}{n}}} \qquad \textbf{[10-5]}$$

VI. There are two types of errors that can occur in a test of hypothesis.
  A. A Type I error occurs when a true null hypothesis is rejected.
    1. The probability of making a Type I error is equal to the level of significance.
    2. This probability is designated by the Greek letter α.

B. A Type II error occurs when a false null hypothesis is not rejected.
   1. The probability of making a Type II error is designated by the Greek letter β.
   2. The likelihood of a Type II error is found by

$$z = \frac{\bar{X}_c - \mu_1}{\sigma/\sqrt{n}} \qquad \textbf{[10-6]}$$

Pronunciation Key

SYMBOL	MEANING	PRONUNCIATION
H_0	Null hypothesis	*H sub zero*
H_1	Alternate hypothesis	*H sub one*
$\alpha/2$	Two-tailed significance level	*Alpha over 2*
$\bar{X}_c$	Limit of the sample mean	*X bar sub c*
μ_0	Assumed population mean	*mu sub zero*

Chapter Exercises

29. A new weight-watching company, Weight Reducers International, advertises that those who join will lose, on the average, 10 pounds the first two weeks. A random sample of 50 people who joined the new weight reduction program revealed the mean loss to be 9 pounds with a standard deviation of 2.8 pounds. At the .05 level of significance, can we conclude that those joining Weight Reducers on average will lose less than 10 pounds? Determine the *p*-value.

30. $z = 11.79$ Reject H_0, *p*-value = 0.

30. Dole Pineapple, Inc. is concerned that the 16-ounce can of sliced pineapple is being overfilled. The quality-control department took a random sample of 50 cans and found that the arithmetic mean weight was 16.05 ounces, with a sample standard deviation of 0.03 ounces. At the 5 percent level of significance, can we conclude that the mean weight is greater than 16 ounces? Determine the *p*-value.

31. The Peoria Board of Education wants to consider a new academic program funded by the U.S. Department of Education. To be eligible for the federal grant, the arithmetic mean income per household must not be more than $15,000. The board hired a research firm to gather the required data. In its report the firm indicated that the arithmetic mean income in the district is $17,000. They further reported that 75 households were surveyed and that the standard deviation of the sample was $3,000. Can the board argue that the difference between the mean income resulting from the sample survey and the mean specified by the Department of Education is due to chance (sampling)? Use the .05 significance level.

32. $z = 1.82$ Reject H_0.

32. A statewide real estate sales agency, Farm Associates, specializes in selling farm property in the state of Nebraska. Their records indicate that the mean selling time of farm property is 90 days. Because of recent drought conditions, they believe that the mean selling time is now greater than 90 days. A statewide survey of 100 farms sold recently revealed that the mean selling time was 94 days, with a standard deviation of 22 days. At the .10 significance level, has there been an increase in selling time?

33. According to the local union president, the mean gross income of plumbers in the Salt Lake City area is normally distributed, with a mean of $30,000 and a standard deviation of $3,000. A recent investigative reporter for KYAK TV found, for a sample of 120 plumbers, the mean gross income was $30,500. At the .10 significance level, is it reasonable to conclude that the mean income is not equal to $30,000? Determine the *p*-value.

34. $z = -1.40$ H_0 not rejected. *p*-value = .0808

34. A recent article in *Vitality* magazine reported that the mean amount of leisure time per week for American men is 40.0 hours. You believe this figure is too large and decide to conduct your own test. In a random sample of 60 men, you find that the mean is 37.8 hours of leisure per week and that the standard deviation of the sample is 12.2 hours. Can you conclude that the information in the article is untrue? Use the .05 significance level. Determine the *p*-value and explain its meaning.

35. NBC TV news, in a segment on the price of gasoline, reported last evening that the mean price nationwide is $1.50 per gallon for self-serve regular unleaded. A random sample of 35 stations in the Milwaukee, WI, area revealed that the mean price was $1.52 per gallon and that the standard deviation was $0.05 per gallon. At the .05 significance level, can we conclude that the price of gasoline is higher in the Milwaukee area? Determine the *p*-value.

36. The Rutter Nursery Company packages their pine bark mulch in 50-pound bags. From a long history, the production department reports that the distribution of the bag weights follows the normal distribution and the standard deviation of this process is 3 pounds per bag. At the end of each day, Jeff Rutter, the production manager, weighs 10 bags and computes the mean weight of the sample. Below are the weights of 10 bags from today's production.

45.6	47.7	47.6	46.3	46.2	47.4	49.2	55.8	47.5	48.5

36. a. $z = -1.92$
b. See IM.
c. .0274

a. Can Mr. Rutter conclude that the mean weight of the bags is less than 50 pounds? Use the .01 significance level.
b. In a brief report, tell why Mr. Rutter can use the *z* distribution as the test statistic.
c. Compute the *p*-value.

37. In a recent national survey, the mean weekly allowance for a nine-year-old child from his or her parents was reported to be $3.65. A random sample of 45 nine-year-olds in central Florida revealed the mean allowance to be $3.69, with a standard deviation of $0.24. At the .05 significance level, is there a difference in the mean allowance nationally and the mean allowance in central Florida for nine-year-olds?

38. $t = -2.61$ Reject H_0.

38. The manufacturer of the Ososki motorcycle advertises that the cycle will average 87 miles per gallon of gasoline. A sample of eight bikes revealed the following mileage.

88	82	81	87	80	78	79	89

At the .05 level, is the mean mileage less than the advertised 87 miles per gallon?

39. The Myers Summer Casual Furniture Store tells customers that a special order will take six weeks (42 days). During recent months the owner has received several complaints that the special orders are taking longer than 42 days. A sample of 12 special orders delivered in the last month showed that the mean waiting time was 51 days, with a standard deviation of 8 days. At the .05 significance level, are customers waiting an average of more than 42 days? Estimate the *p*-value.

40. $t = 2.95$; do not reject. *p*-value between .01 and .025.

40. A recent article in the *Wall Street Journal* reported that the prime rate for large banks now exceeds 9 percent. A sample of eight small banks in the Midwest revealed the following prime rates (in percent):

10.1	9.3	9.2	10.2	9.3	9.6	9.4	8.8

At the .01 significance level, can we conclude that the prime rate for small banks also exceeds 9 percent? Estimate the *p*-value.

41. A typical college student drinks an average of 27 gallons of coffee each year, or 2.25 gallons per month. A sample of 12 students at Northwestern State University revealed the following amounts of coffee consumed last month.

1.75	1.96	1.57	1.82	1.85	1.82	2.43	2.65	2.60	2.24	1.69	2.66

At the .05 significance level, is there a significant difference between the average amount consumed at Northwestern State and the national average?

42. $t = 2.702$; reject H_0. *p*-value less than .025.

42. The postanesthesia care area (recovery room) at St. Luke's Hospital in Maumee, Ohio, was recently enlarged. The hope was that with the enlargement the mean number of patients per day would be more than 25. A random sample of 15 days revealed the following numbers of patients.

25	27	25	26	25	28	28	27	24	26	25	29	25	27	24

At the .01 significance level, can we conclude that the mean number of patients per day is more than 25? Estimate the p-value and interpret it.

43. egolf.com receives an average of 6.5 returns per day from online shoppers. For a sample of 12 days, they received the following number of returns.

0	4	3	4	9	4	5	9	1	6	7	10

At the .01 significance level, can we conclude the mean number of returns is less than 6.5?

44. $t = -4.013$; reject H_0.

44. During recent seasons, Major League Baseball has been criticized for the length of the games. A report indicated that the average game lasts 3 hours and 30 minutes. A sample of 17 games revealed the following times to completion. (Note that the minutes have been changed to fractions of hours, so that a game that lasted 2 hours and 24 minutes is reported at 2.40 hours.)

2.98	2.40	2.70	2.25	3.23	3.17	2.93	3.18	2.80
2.38	3.75	3.20	3.27	2.52	2.58	4.45	2.45	

Can we conclude that the mean time for a game is less than 3.50 hours? Use the .05 significance level.

45. The Watch Corporation of Switzerland claims that their watches on average will neither gain nor lose time during a week. A sample of 18 watches provided the following gains (+) or losses (−) in seconds per week.

−0.38	−0.20	−0.38	−0.32	+0.32	−0.23	+0.30	+0.25	−0.10
−0.37	−0.61	−0.48	−0.47	−0.64	−0.04	−0.20	−0.68	+0.05

Is it reasonable to conclude that the mean gain or loss in time for the watches is 0? Use the .05 significance level. Estimate the p-value.

46. $t = 1.033$; do not reject.

46. Listed below is the rate of return for one year (reported in percent) for a sample of 12 mutual funds that are classified as taxable money market funds.

4.63	4.15	4.76	4.70	4.65	4.52	4.70	5.06	4.42	4.51	4.24	4.52

Using the .05 significance level is it reasonable to conclude that the mean rate of return is more than 4.50 percent?

47. Tina Dennis is the comptroller for Meek Industries. She believes that the current cash-flow problem at Meek is due to the slow collection of accounts receivable. She believes that more than 60 percent of the accounts are in arrears more than three months. A random sample of 200 accounts showed that 140 were more than three months old. At the .01 significance level, can she conclude that more than 60 percent of the accounts are in arrears for more than three months?

48. $z = 0.841$; do not reject.

48. The policy of the Suburban Transit Authority is to add a bus route if more than 55 percent of the potential commuters indicate they would use the particular route. A sample of 70 commuters revealed that 42 would use a proposed route from Bowman Park to the downtown area. Does the Bowman-to-downtown route meet the STA criterion? Use the .05 significance level.

49. Past experience at the Crowder Travel Agency indicated that 44 percent of those persons who wanted the agency to plan a vacation for them wanted to go to Europe. During the most recent busy season, a sampling of 1,000 plans was selected at random from the files. It was found that 480 persons wanted to go to Europe on vacation. Has there been a significant shift upward in the percentage of persons who want to go to Europe? Test at the .05 significance level.

50. $z = 1.89$; H_0 is rejected.

50. From past experience a television manufacturer found that 10 percent or less of its sets needed any type of repair in the first two years of operation. In a sample of 50 sets manufactured two years ago, 9 needed repair. At the .05 significance level, has the percent of sets needing repair increased? Determine the p-value.

51. An urban planner claims that, nationally, 20 percent of all families renting condominiums move during a given year. A random sample of 200 families renting condominiums in Dallas revealed that 56 had moved during the past year. At the .01 significance level, does this evidence suggest that a larger proportion of condominium owners moved in the Dallas area? Determine the p-value.

52. One of the major U.S. automakers wishes to review its warranty. The warranty covers the engine, transmission, and drive train of all new cars for up to two years or 24,000 miles, whichever comes first. The manufacturer's quality-assurance department believes that the mean number of miles driven by owners is more than 24,000. A sample of 35 cars revealed that the mean number of miles was 24,421, with a standard deviation of 1,944 miles.

52. a. $z = 1.28$ Do not reject.
b. 24,542
c. .0823

a. Conduct the following hypothesis test. Use the .05 significance level.

$$H_0: \mu \leq 24{,}000$$
$$H_1: \mu > 24{,}000$$

b. What is the largest value for the sample mean for which H_0 is not rejected?
c. Suppose the population mean shifts to 25,000 miles. What is the probability this change will not be detected?

53. A cola-dispensing machine is set to dispense 9.00 ounces of cola per cup, with a standard deviation of 1.00 ounces. The manufacturer of the machine would like to set the control limit in such a way that for samples of 36, 5 percent of the sample means will be greater than the upper control limit, and 5 percent of the sample means will be less than the lower control limit.
a. At what value should the control limit be set?
b. What is the probability that if the population mean shifts to 8.9, this change will not be detected?
c. What is the probability that if the population mean shifts to 9.3, this change will not be detected?

54. The owners of the Franklin Park Mall wished to study customer shopping habits. From earlier studies the owners are under the impression that a typical shopper spends 0.75 hours at the mall, with a standard deviation of 0.10 hours. Recently the mall owners added some specialty restaurants designed to keep shoppers in the mall longer. The consulting firm, Brunner and Swanson Marketing Enterprises, has been hired to evaluate the effects of the restaurants. A sample of 45 shoppers by Brunner and Swanson revealed that the mean time spent in the mall had increased to 0.80 hours.

54. a. $z = 3.35$, reject H_0.
b. $\bar{X}_c = .6217$
c. Increase α.

a. Develop a test of hypothesis to determine if the mean time spent in the mall is more than 0.75 hours. Use the .05 significance level.
b. Suppose the mean shopping time actually increased from 0.75 hours to 0.77 hours. What is the probability this increase would not be detected?
c. When Brunner and Swanson reported the information in part (b) to the mall owners, the owners were upset with the statement that a survey could not detect a change from 0.75 to 0.77 hours of shopping time. How could this probability be reduced?

55. The following null and alternate hypotheses are given.

$$H_0: \mu \leq 50$$
$$H_1: \mu > 50$$

Suppose the population standard deviation is 10. The probability of a Type I error is set at .01 and the probability of a Type II error at .30. Assume that the population mean shifts from 50 to 55. How large a sample is necessary to meet these requirements?

56. $z = 2.176$ Reject H_0.

56. An insurance company, based on past experience, estimates the mean damage for a natural disaster in its area is $5,000. After introducing several plans to prevent loss, they randomly sample 200 policyholders and find the mean amount per claim was $4,800 with a standard deviation of $1,300. Does it appear the prevention plans were effective in reducing the mean amount of a claim? Use the .05 significance level.

57. A national grocer's magazine reports the typical shopper spends eight minutes in line waiting to check out. A sample of 24 shoppers at the local Farmer Jack's showed a mean of 7.5 minutes with a standard deviation of 3.2 minutes. Is the waiting time at the local Farmer Jack's less than that reported in the national magazine? Use the .05 significance level.

58. $t = 3.42$, p-value less than .005.

58. In the year 2000 the mean fare to fly from Charlotte, North Carolina, to Seattle, Washington, on a discount ticket was \$267. A random sample of round-trip discount fares on this route last month gives:

\$321	\$286	\$290	\$330	\$310	\$250	\$270	\$280	\$299	\$265	\$291	\$275	\$281

At the .01 significance level can we conclude that the mean fare has increased? What is the p-value?

59. The President's call for designing and building a missile defense system that ignores restrictions of the Anti-Ballistic Missile Defense System treaty (ABM) is supported by 483 of the respondents in a nationwide poll of 1,002 adults. Is it reasonable to conclude that the nation is evenly divided on the issue? Use the .05 significance level.

exercises.com

60. Answers will vary.

60. The *USA Today* (http://www.usatoday.com/sports/mtb.htm) and Major League Baseball (http://www.majorleaguebaseball.com) websites regularly report information on individual player salaries. Go to one of these sites and find the individual salaries for your favorite team. Compute the mean and the standard deviation. Is it reasonable to conclude that the mean salary on your favorite team is *different from* \$1.80 million? If you are more of a football, basketball, or hockey enthusiast, information is also available on their salaries.

61. The Gallup Organization in Princeton, New Jersey, is one of the best-known polling organizations in the United States. They often combine with *USA Today* or CNN to conduct polls of current interest. They also maintain a website at: http://www.gallup.com/index.html. Consult this website to find the most recent polling results on Presidential approval ratings. You may need to click on Fast Facts. Test whether the majority (more than 50 percent) approve of the President's performance. If the article does not report the number of respondents included in the survey, assume that it is 1,000, a number that is typically used.

Computer Data Exercises

62. Refer to the Real Estate data, which reports information on the homes sold in Venice, Florida, last year.

62. a. $z = 0.24$, p-value = .4052

a. A recent article in the *Tampa Times* indicated that the mean selling price of the homes on the west coast of Florida is more than \$220,000. Can we conclude that the mean selling price in the Venice area is more than \$220,000? Use the .01 significance level. What is the p-value?

b. $z = 5.10$, p-value = 0

b. The same article reported the mean size was more than 2,100 square feet. Can we conclude that the mean size of homes sold in the Venice area is more than 2,100 square feet? Use the .01 significance level. What is the p-value?

c. $z = 1.59$, p-value = .0559

c. Determine the proportion of homes that have an attached garage. At the .05 significance level can we conclude that more than 60 percent of the homes sold in the Venice area had an attached garage? What is the p-value?

d. $z = 0.80$, p-value = .2119

d. Determine the proportion of homes that have a pool. At the .05 significance level, can we conclude that more than 60 percent of the homes sold in the Venice area had a pool? What is the p-value?

63. Refer to the Baseball 2000 data, which reports information on the 30 Major League Baseball teams for the 2000 season.

a. Conduct a test of hypothesis to determine whether the mean salary of the teams was different from \$50.0 million. Use the .05 significance level.

b. Conduct a test of hypothesis to determine whether the mean attendance was more than 2,000,000 per team.

64. $t = -0.49$. Do not reject.

64. Refer to the OECD data, which reports information on census, economic, and business data for 29 countries. Conduct a test of hypothesis to determine if the mean number of people employed was less than 20,000. (Remember the data is reported in thousands, so the actual number employed is 20,000,000.) Use the .05 significance level. Estimate the p-value.

Computer Commands

1. The MINITAB commands for the one-sample *t* test on page 357 are:
   a. Enter the data into column C1 and name the variable *Length.*
   b. From the menu bar select **Stat, Basic Statistics, 1-Sample t,** and then hit Enter. The following dialog box will appear.

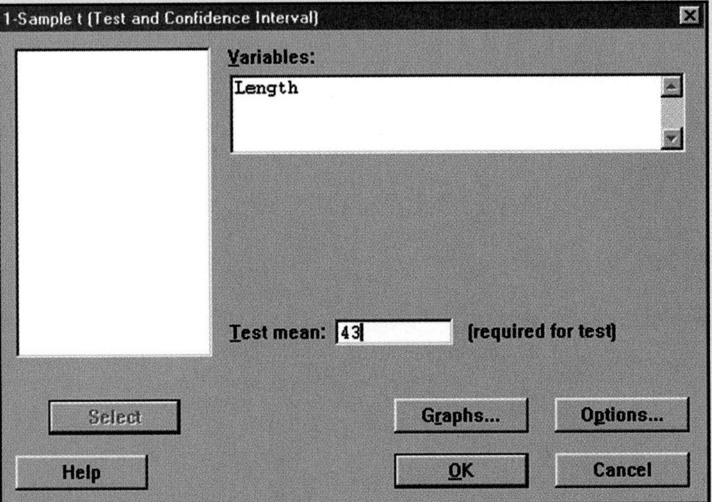

   c. Select *Length* as the variable, select **Test mean,** insert *43.* Click on **Options,** and select **Alternative** and the **not equal** option. Then click **OK** for both dialog boxes.

Chapter 10 Answers to Self-Review

10–1 (a) H_0: $\mu = 6.0$; H_1: $\mu \neq 6.0$

(b) .05.

(c) $z = \dfrac{\bar{X} - \mu}{\sigma/\sqrt{n}}$

(d) Do not reject the null hypothesis if the computed z value falls between -1.96 and $+1.96$.

(e) Yes. Computed $z = -2.56$, found by:

$$z = \frac{5.84 - 6.0}{0.5/\sqrt{64}} = \frac{-0.16}{.0625} = -2.56$$

Reject H_0 at the .05 level. Accept H_1. The mean turnover rate is not equal to 6.0.

10–2 (a) H_0: $\mu \geq 6.0$

(b) H_1: $\mu < 6.0$.

(c) Note that the inequality sign (<) in the alternate hypothesis points in the direction of the region of rejection. To determine the critical value: .5000 − .05 = .4500. z from Appendix D is about −1.65.

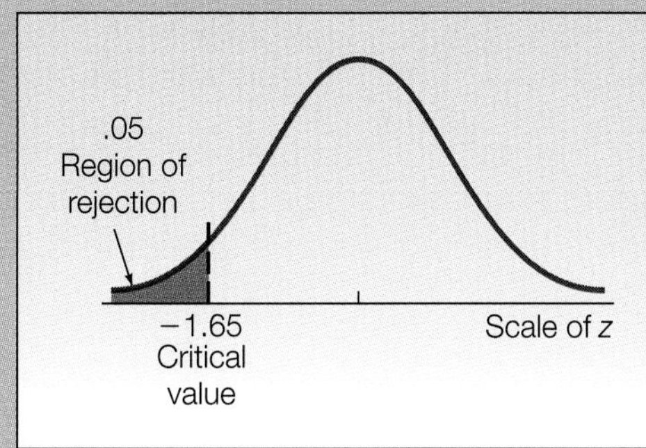

10–3 (a) H_0: $\mu \leq 305$, H_1: $\mu > 305$.

(b) $df = n - 1 = 20 - 1 = 19$

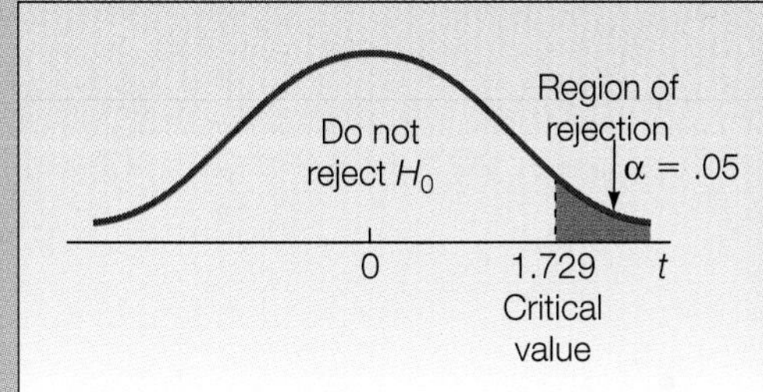

(c) $t = \dfrac{\bar{X} - \mu}{s/\sqrt{n}} = \dfrac{311 - 305}{12/\sqrt{20}} = 2.236$

Reject H_0 because $2.236 > 1.729$. The modification increased the mean battery life to more than 305 days.

10–4 (a) H_0: $\mu \geq 9.0$, H_1: $\mu < 9.0$.

(b) 7, found by $n - 1 = 8 - 1 = 7$.

(c) Reject H_0 if $t < -2.998$.

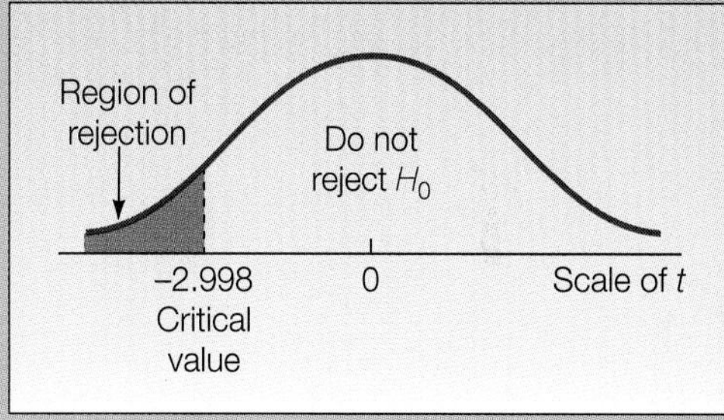

(d) $t = -2.494$, found by:

$$s = \sqrt{\frac{619.88 - \dfrac{(70.4)^2}{8}}{8 - 1}} = 0.2268$$

$$\bar{X} = \frac{70.4}{8} = 8.8$$

Then

$$t = \frac{8.8 - 9.0}{0.2268/\sqrt{8}} = -2.494$$

Since −2.494 lies to the right of −2.998, H_0 is not rejected. We have not shown that the mean is less than 9.0.

(e) The p-value is between .025 and .010.

10–5 (a) Yes, because both $n\pi$ and $n(1 - \pi)$ exceed 5: $n\pi = 200(.40) = 80$, and $n(1 - \pi) = 200(.60) = 120$.

(b) H_0: $\pi \geq .40$

H_1: $\pi < .40$

(c)

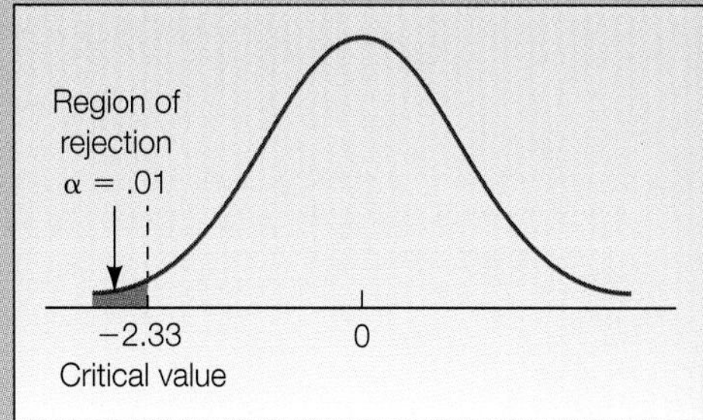

(d) $z = -0.87$, found by:

$$z = \frac{.37 - .40}{\sqrt{\frac{.40(1 - .40)}{200}}} = \frac{-.03}{\sqrt{.0012}} = -0.87$$

Do not reject H_0.

(e) The p-value is .1922, found by .5000 − .3078.

10–6 .0054, found by determining the area under the curve between 10,078 and 10,180 (Chart 10–10B).

$$z = \frac{\bar{X}_C - \mu_1}{\sigma/\sqrt{n}}$$

$$= \frac{10{,}078 - 10{,}180}{400/\sqrt{100}} = -2.55$$

The area under the curve for a z of −2.55 is .4946 (Appendix D), and .5000 − .4946 = .0054.

11

Two-Sample Tests of Hypothesis

A sample of 30 members at the Anchor Pointe Marina who have boats 10 to 20 feet in length showed an average of 11 days of use last July, with a standard deviation of 3.88 days. For a sample of 40 members with boats 21 to 40 feet in length, the average was 7.67 days of use in July, with a standard deviation of 4.42 days. At the .02 significance level, can the managers conclude that those with smaller boats used their crafts more frequently? (See Goal 2 and Exercise 29.)

GOALS

When you have completed this chapter, you will be able to:

1 Understand the difference between dependent and independent samples.

2 Conduct a test of hypothesis about the difference between two independent population means when both samples have 30 or more items.

3 Conduct a test of hypothesis about the difference between two population means when at least one sample has fewer than 30 items.

4 Conduct a test of hypothesis about the difference between two population proportions.

5 Conduct a test of hypothesis about the mean difference between paired or dependent observations.

Statistics in Action

The Election of 2000 turned out to be one of the closest in history. The news media were unable to project a winner, and the final decision, including recounts and court decisions, took more than five weeks. This was not the only election in which there was controversy. Shortly before the 1936 presidential election, the *New York Times* carried the headline: "*Digest* Poll Gives Landon 32 States: Landon Leads 4–3." However, Alfred Landon of Kansas was not elected President. In fact, Roosevelt won by more than 11 million votes and received 523 Electoral College votes. How could the headline have been so wrong?

The *Literary Digest* collected a sample of voters

Introduction

Chapter 10 began our study of hypothesis testing. We described the nature of hypothesis testing and conducted tests of hypothesis in which we compared the results of a single sample to a population value. That is, we selected a single random sample from a population and conducted a test of whether the proposed population value was reasonable. Recall, in Chapter 10 we selected a sample of the number of desks assembled per week at the Jamestown Steel Company to determine whether there was a change in the production rate. Similarly, we sampled voters in one area of a particular state to determine whether the population proportion that would support the governor for reelection was less than .80. In both of these cases, we compared the results of a *single* sample statistic to a population parameter.

In this chapter we expand the idea of hypothesis testing to two samples. That is, we select two random samples to determine whether the samples are from the same or equal populations. Some questions we might want to test are:

1. Is there a difference in the mean amount of residential real estate sold by male agents and female agents in south Florida?
2. Is there a difference in the mean number of defects produced on the day and the afternoon shifts at Kimble Products?
3. Is there a difference in the mean number of days absent between young workers (under 21 years of age) and older workers (more than 60 years of age) in the fast-food industry?

4. Is there is a difference in the proportion of Ohio State University graduates and University of Cincinnati graduates who pass the state Certified Public Accounting Examination on their first attempt?
5. Is there an increase in the production rate if music is piped into the production area?

We begin this chapter with the case in which we select random samples from two populations and wish to investigate whether these populations have the same mean.

Hypothesis Testing: Population Means

A city planner in Florida wishes to know whether there is a difference in the mean hourly wage rate of plumbers and electricians in central Florida. A financial accountant from lists of telephone numbers, automobile registrations, and *Digest* readers. In 1936 not many people could afford a telephone or an automobile. In addition those who read the *Digest* tended to be wealthier and vote Republican. Thus, the population that was sampled did not represent the population of voters. A second problem was with the nonresponses. More than 10 million people were sent surveys, and more than 2.3 million responded. However, no attempt was made to see whether those responding represented a cross-section of all the voters.

With modern computers and survey methods, samples are carefully selected and checked to ensure they are representative. What happened to the *Literary Digest*? It went out of business shortly after the 1936 election.

wishes to know whether the mean rate of return for high yield mutual funds is different from the mean rate of return on global mutual funds. In each of these cases there are two independent populations. In the first case, the plumbers represent one population and the electricians the other. In the second case, high yield mutual funds are one population and global mutual funds the other.

In each of these cases, to investigate the question, we would select a random sample from each population and compute the mean of the two samples. If the two populations are the same, that is, the mean hourly rate is the same for the plumbers and the electricians, we would expect the *difference* between the two sample means to be zero. But what if our sample results yield a difference other than zero? Is that difference due to chance or is it because there is a difference in the hourly earnings? A two-sample test of means will help to answer this question.

We do need to return to the results of Chapter 9. Recall that we showed that a distribution of sample means would tend to approximate the normal distribution when the sample size was at least 30. We need to again assume that a distribution of sample means will follow the normal distribution. It can be shown mathematically that the distribution of the differences between two normal distributions is also normal.

We can illustrate this theory in terms of the city planner in Florida. To begin, let's assume some information that is not usually available. Suppose that the population of plumbers has a mean of \$30.00 per hour and a standard deviation of \$5.00 per hour. The population of electricians has a mean of \$29.00 and a standard deviation of \$4.50. Now, from this information it is clear that the two population means are not the same. The plumbers actually earn \$1.00 per hour more than the electricians. But we cannot expect to uncover this difference each time we sample the two populations.

Suppose we select a random sample of 40 plumbers and a random sample of 35 electricians and compute the mean of each sample. Then, we determine the difference between the sample means. It is this difference between the sample means that holds our interest. If the populations have the same mean, then we would expect the difference between the two sample means to be zero. If there is a difference between the population means, then we expect to find a difference between the sample means.

To understand the theory, we need to take several pairs of samples, compute the mean of each, determine the difference between the sample means, and study the distribution of the differences in the sample means. Because of our study of the distribution of sample means in Chapter 9, we know that the distribution of the sample means follows the normal distribution (assume at least $n = 30$). If the two distributions of sample means follow the normal distribution, then we can reason that the distribution of their differences will also follow the normal distribution. This is the first hurdle.

The second hurdle refers to the mean of this distribution of differences. If we find the mean of this distribution is zero, that implies that there is no difference in the two populations. On the other hand, if the mean of the distribution of differences is equal to some value other than zero, either positive or negative, then we conclude that the two populations do not have the same mean.

To report some concrete results, let's return to the city planner in Florida. Table 11–1 shows the result of selecting 20 samples of 40 plumbers and 35 electricians, computing the mean of each sample, and finding the difference between the two sample means. In the first case the sample of 40 plumbers has a mean of \$29.80, and for the 35 electricians the mean is \$28.76. The difference between the sample means is \$1.04. This process was repeated 19 more times. Observe that in 17 of the 20 cases the mean of the plumbers is larger than the mean of the electricians.

TABLE 11–1 The Means of Random Samples of Plumbers and Electricians

Sample	Plumbers	Electricians	Difference
1	$29.80	$28.76	$ 1.04
2	30.32	29.40	0.92
3	30.57	29.94	0.63
4	30.04	28.93	1.11
5	30.09	29.78	0.31
6	30.02	28.66	1.36
7	29.60	29.13	0.47
8	29.63	29.42	0.21
9	30.17	29.29	0.88
10	30.81	29.75	1.06
11	30.09	28.05	2.04
12	29.35	29.07	0.28
13	29.42	28.79	0.63
14	29.78	29.54	0.24
15	29.60	29.60	0.00
16	30.60	30.19	0.41
17	30.79	28.65	2.14
18	29.14	29.95	−0.81
19	29.91	28.75	1.16
20	28.74	29.21	−0.47

Our final hurdle is that we need to know something about the *variability* of the distribution of differences. To put it another way, what is the standard deviation of this distribution of differences? Statistical theory shows that when we have independent populations, such as the case here, the distribution of the differences has a variance (standard deviation squared) equal to the sum of the two individual variances. This means that we can add the variances of the two sampling distributions.

VARIANCE OF THE DISTRIBUTION OF DIFFERENCES IN SAMPLE MEANS

$$s^2_{\bar{X}_1 - \bar{X}_2} = \frac{s_1^2}{n_1} + \frac{s_2^2}{n_2} \qquad [11\text{–}1]$$

The term $s^2_{\bar{X}_1 - \bar{X}_2}$ looks complex but need not be difficult to interpret. The s^2 portion reminds us that it is a sample variance, and the subscript $\bar{X}_1 - \bar{X}_2$ that it is a distribution of differences in the sample means.

We can put this equation in more usable form by taking the square root, so that we have the standard deviation of the distribution of the differences. Finally, we standardize the distribution of the differences. The result is the following equation.

TEST STATISTIC FOR THE DIFFERENCE BETWEEN TWO SAMPLE MEANS

$$z = \frac{\bar{X}_1 - \bar{X}_2}{\sqrt{\dfrac{s_1^2}{n_1} + \dfrac{s_2^2}{n_2}}} \qquad [11\text{–}2]$$

Before we present an example, let's review the assumptions necessary for using formula 11–2. First, the two populations must be unrelated, that is, independent. Second, the samples must be large enough that the distribution of the sample means follows the normal distribution. The usual practice is to require that both samples have at least 30 observations.

The following example shows the details of the two-sample test of hypothesis for means.

EXAMPLE

Each patient at Aloha Memorial Hospital is asked to evaluate the service at the time of release. Recently there have been complaints that resident physicians and nurses on the surgical wing respond too slowly to calls of senior citizens. In fact, it is claimed that the other patients receive faster service. Mr. Robert Armstrong, president of the hospital, asked the quality-assurance department (QA) to investigate. After studying the problem, the QA department collected the following sample information. At the .01 significance level, is it reasonable to conclude the mean response time is longer for the senior citizen cases? What is the *p*-value in this case?

Patient Type	Sample Mean	Sample Standard Deviation	Sample Size
Senior citizens	5.50 minutes	0.40 minutes	50
Other	5.30 minutes	0.30 minutes	100

SOLUTION

We use the five-step hypothesis testing procedure to investigate the question.

Step 1: State the null hypothesis and the alternate hypothesis. The null hypothesis is that there is no difference in the mean response times for the two groups. In other words, the difference of 0.20 minutes between the mean response time for the senior citizens and the mean response time for the other patients is due to chance. The alternate hypothesis is that the mean response time is longer for senior citizens. We will let μ_s refer to the mean response time for the population of senior citizens and μ_0 the mean response time for the other patients. The null and alternative hypotheses are:

$$H_0: \mu_s \leq \mu_0$$
$$H_1: \mu_s > \mu_0$$

Step 2: Select the level of significance. The significance level is the probability that we reject the null hypothesis when it is actually true. This likelihood is determined prior to selecting the sample or performing any calculations. The .05 and .01 significance levels are the most common, but other values, such as .02 and .10, are also used. In theory, we may select any value between 0 and 1 for the significance level. In this case the QA department selected the .01 significance level.

Step 3: Determine the test statistic. In Chapter 10 we used the standard normal distribution (that is z) and t as test statistics. In this case, because the samples are large, we use the z distribution as the test statistic. In later chapters we will employ other test statistics such as the F distribution and the χ^2 distribution.

Step 4: Formulate a decision rule. The decision rule is based on the null and the alternate hypotheses (i.e., one-tailed or two-tailed test), the level of significance, and the test statistic used. We selected the .01 significance level, the z distribution as the test statistic, and we wish to determine whether the mean response time is longer for senior citizens. We set the alternate hypothesis to indicate that the mean response time is longer for

Statistics in Action

Do you live to work or work to live? A recent poll of 802 working Americans revealed that, among those who considered their work as a career, the mean number of hours worked per day was 8.7. Among those who considered their work a job, the mean number of hours worked per day was 7.6.

the senior citizens than for the other group. Hence, the rejection region is in the upper tail of the standard normal distribution. To find the critical value, place .01 of the total area in the upper tail. This means that .4900 (.5000 − .0100) of the area is located between the z value of 0 and the critical value. Next, we search the body of Appendix D for a value located near .4900. It is 2.33, so our decision rule is to reject H_0 if the value computed from the test statistic exceeds 2.33. Chart 11–1 depicts the decision rule.

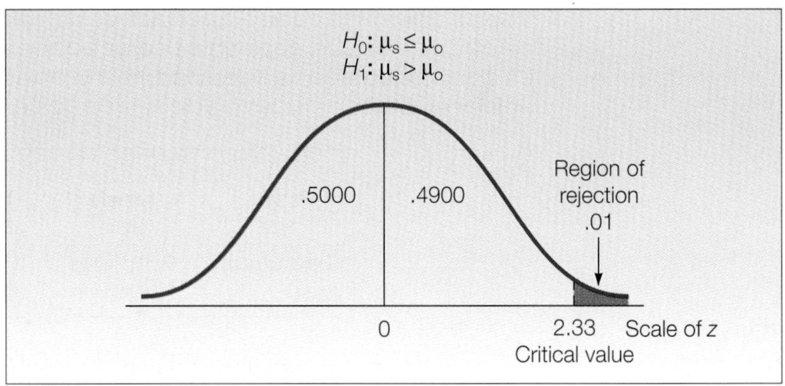

CHART 11–1 Decision Rule for One-Tailed Test at .01 Significance Level

Step 5: Make the decision regarding H_0 and interpret the result. We use formula 11–2 to compute the value of the test statistic.

$$z = \frac{\bar{X}_s - \bar{X}_o}{\sqrt{\frac{s_s^2}{n_s} + \frac{s_o^2}{n_o}}} = \frac{5.5 - 5.3}{\sqrt{\frac{0.40^2}{50} + \frac{0.30^2}{100}}} = \frac{0.2}{0.064} = 3.13$$

The computed value of 3.13 is larger than the critical value of 2.33. Our decision is to reject the null hypothesis and accept the alternate hypothesis. The difference of .20 minutes between the mean response time of the senior citizens and the other patients is too large to have occurred by chance. The QA Department can report to President Armstrong that the mean response time is longer for senior citizens than for other patients.

What is the p-value for the test statistic? Recall that the p-value is the probability of finding a value of the test statistic this extreme when the null hypothesis is true. To calculate the p-value we need the probability of a z value larger than 3.13. From Appendix D we cannot find the probability associated with 3.13. The largest value available is 3.09. The area corresponding to 3.09 is .4990. In this case we can report that the p-value is less than .0010, found by .5000 − .4990. We conclude that there is very little likelihood that the null hypothesis is true!

In summary, the criteria for using the large sample test of means are:

1. *Both samples are at least 30*. In the Aloha Hospital Example, one sample was 50 and the other 100. Because both samples are considered large, we can substitute the sample standard deviations for the population standard deviations and use formula 11–2 to find the value of the test statistic.

2. *The samples are from independent populations*. This means, for example, that the sample response time for the senior citizens is unrelated to the response time for the other patients. If Mr. Smith is a senior citizen and his response time is sampled, that does not affect the response time for any other patient.

Self-Review 11–1

Tom Sevits is the owner of the Appliance Patch. Recently Tom observed a difference in the dollar value of sales between the men and women he employs as sales associates. A sample of 40 days revealed the men sold a mean of $1,400 worth of appliances per day with a standard deviation of $200. For a sample of 50 days, the women sold a mean of $1,500 worth of appliances per day with a standard deviation of $250. At the .05 significance level can Mr. Sevits conclude that the mean amount sold per day is larger for the women?

(a) State the null hypothesis and the alternate hypothesis.
(b) What is the decision rule?
(c) What is the value of the test statistic?
(d) What is your decision regarding the null hypothesis?
(e) What is the *p*-value?
(f) Interpret the result.

Exercises

1. A sample of 40 observations is selected from one population. The sample mean is 102 and the sample standard deviation is 5. A sample of 50 observations is selected from a second population. The sample mean is 99 and the sample standard deviation is 6. Conduct the following test of hypothesis using the .04 significance level.

H_0: $\mu_1 = \mu_2$
H_1: $\mu_1 \neq \mu_2$

a. Is this a one-tailed or a two-tailed test?
b. State the decision rule.
c. Compute the value of the test statistic.
d. What is your decision regarding H_0?
e. What is the *p*-value?

2. A sample of 65 observations is selected from one population. The sample mean is 2.67 and the sample standard deviation is 0.75. A sample of 50 observations is selected from a second population. The sample mean is 2.59 and the sample standard deviation is 0.66. Conduct the following test of hypothesis using the .08 significance level.

H_0: $\mu_1 \leq \mu_2$
H_1: $\mu_1 > \mu_2$

a. Is this a one-tailed or a two-tailed test?
b. State the decision rule.
c. Compute the value of the test statistic.
d. What is your decision regarding H_0?
e. What is the *p*-value?

2. **a.** One-tailed.
b. Reject H_0 if $z > 1.41$.
c. $z = 0.61$
d. Do not reject.
e. .2709

Note: Use the five-step hypothesis testing procedure to solve the following exercises.

3. The Gibbs Baby Food Company wishes to compare the weight gain of infants using their brand versus their competitor's. A sample of 40 babies using the Gibbs products revealed a mean weight gain of 7.6 pounds in the first three months after birth. The standard deviation of the sample was 2.3 pounds. A sample of 55 babies using the competitor's brand revealed a mean increase in weight of 8.1 pounds, with a standard deviation of 2.9 pounds. At the .05 significance level, can we conclude that babies using the Gibbs brand gained less weight? Compute the *p*-value and interpret it.

4. Do not reject H_0. $z = -1.53$ p-value = .1260.

4. As part of a study of corporate employees, the Director of Human Resources for PNC, Inc. wants to compare the distance traveled to work by employees at their office in downtown Cincinnati with the distance for those in downtown Pittsburgh. A sample of 35 Cincinnati employees showed they travel a mean of 370 miles per month, with a standard deviation of 30 miles per month. A sample of 40 Pittsburgh employees showed they travel a mean of 380 miles per month, with a standard deviation of 26 miles per month. At the .05 significance level, is there a difference in the mean number of miles traveled per month between Cincinnati and Pittsburgh employees? Use the five-step hypothesis-testing procedure.

5. A financial analyst wants to compare the turnover rates, in percent, for shares of oil related stocks versus other stocks, such as GE and IBM. She selected 32 oil-related stocks and 49 other stocks. The mean turnover rate of oil-related stocks is 31.4 percent and the standard deviation 5.1 percent. For the other stocks, the mean rate was computed to be 34.9 percent and the standard deviation 6.7 percent. Is there a significant difference in the turnover rates of the two types of stock? Use the .01 significance level.

6. Reject H_0. $z = 2.09$, p-value = .0183.

6. Mary Jo Fitzpatrick is the Vice President for Nursing Services at St. Luke's Memorial Hospital. Recently she noticed in the job postings for nurses that those that are unionized seem to offer higher wages. She decided to investigate and gathered the following sample information.

Group	Mean Wage	Sample Standard Deviation	Sample Size
Union	$20.75	$2.25	40
Nonunion	$19.80	$1.90	45

Would it be reasonable for her to conclude that union nurses earn more? Use the .02 significance level. What is the p-value?

Comparing Populations with Small Samples

In the previous section we assumed that the two population standard deviations were unknown but that we selected random samples containing 30 or more observations each. In this section we consider the case in which the population standard deviations are unknown and the number of observations in at least one of the samples is less than 30. We often refer to this as a "small sample test of means." The requirements for the small sample test are more stringent. The three required assumptions are:

1. The sampled populations follow the normal distribution.
2. The two samples are from independent populations.
3 The standard deviations of the two populations are equal.

The test statistic is the t distribution. The formula for computing the value of t is similar to 11–2, but an additional calculation is necessary. The third assumption above indicates that the population standard deviations must be equal. The two sample variances are pooled to form a single estimate of the unknown population variance. In essence, we compute a weighted mean of the two sample standard deviations and use this as an estimate of the population standard deviation. The weights are the degrees of freedom that each sample provides. Why do we need to pool the standard deviations? In most cases when the samples each have fewer than 30 observations, the population standard deviations are not known. Thus, we calculate s, the sample standard deviation, and substitute it for σ, the population standard deviation. Because we assume that the two populations have equal standard deviations, the best estimate we can make of that value is to combine or pool all the information we have about the value of the population standard deviation.

The following formula is used to pool the sample variances. Notice that two factors are involved: the number of observations in each sample and the sample standard deviations themselves.

POOLED VARIANCE

$$s_p^2 = \frac{(n_1 - 1)s_1^2 + (n_2 - 1)s_2^2}{n_1 + n_2 - 2} \qquad \textbf{[11–3]}$$

where:

s_1^2 is the variance (standard deviation squared) of the first sample.
s_2^2 is the variance of the second sample.

The value of t is computed from the following equation.

TWO SAMPLE TEST OF MEANS—SMALL SAMPLES

$$t = \frac{\bar{X}_1 - \bar{X}_2}{\sqrt{s_p^2\left(\frac{1}{n_1} + \frac{1}{n_2}\right)}} \qquad \textbf{[11–4]}$$

where:

$\bar{X}_1$ is the mean of the first sample.
$\bar{X}_2$ is the mean of the second sample.
n_1 is the number of observations in the first sample.
n_2 is the number of observations in the second sample.
s_p^2 is the pooled estimate of the population variance.

The number of degrees of freedom in the test is the total number of items sampled minus the total number of samples. Because there are two samples, there are $n_1 + n_2 - 2$ degrees of freedom.

EXAMPLE

Owens Lawn Care, Inc. manufactures and assembles lawnmowers that are shipped to dealers throughout the United States and Canada. Two different procedures have been proposed for mounting the engine on the frame of the lawnmower. The question is: Is there a difference in the mean time to mount the engines on the frames of the lawnmowers? The first procedure was developed by longtime Owens employee Herb Welles (designated as procedure 1), and the other procedure was developed by Owens Vice-President of Engineering William Atkins (designated as procedure 2). To evaluate the two methods, it was decided to conduct a time and motion study. A sample of five employees was timed using procedure 1 and six using procedure 2. The results, in minutes, are shown below. Is there a difference in the mean mounting times? Use the .10 significance level.

Procedure 1 (minutes)	Procedure 2 (minutes)
2	3
4	7
9	5
3	8
2	4
	3

SOLUTION

The null hypothesis states that there is no difference in mean mounting times between the two procedures. The alternate hypothesis indicates that there is a difference.

H_0: $\mu_1 = \mu_2$
H_1: $\mu_1 \neq \mu_2$

The required assumptions are:

1. The observations in the Welles sample are *independent* of the observations in the Atkins sample and of each other.
2. The two populations follow the normal distribution.
3. The two populations have equal standard deviations.

Is there a difference between the mean assembly times using the Welles and the Atkins methods? The degrees of freedom are equal to the total number of items sampled minus the number of samples. In this case that is $n_1 + n_2 - 2$. Five assemblers used the Welles method and six the Atkins method. Thus, there are 9 degrees of freedom, found by 5 + 6 − 2. The critical values of t, from Appendix F for $df = 9$, a two-tailed test, and the .10 significance level, are −1.833 and 1.833. The decision rule is portrayed graphically in Chart 11–2. We do not reject the null hypothesis if the computed value of t falls between −1.833 and 1.833.

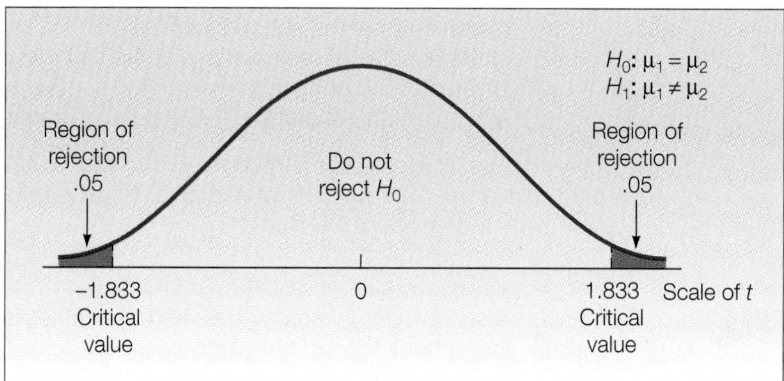

CHART 11–2 Regions of Rejection, Two-Tailed Test, $df = 9$, and .10 Significance Level

We use three steps to compute the value of t.

Step 1: Calculate the Sample Standard Deviations. See the details below.

Procedure 1		Procedure 2	
X_1	X_1^2	X_2	X_2^2
2	4	3	9
4	16	7	49
9	81	5	25
3	9	8	64
2	4	4	16
20	114	3	9
		30	172

$$s_1 = \sqrt{\frac{\Sigma X_1^2 - \frac{(\Sigma X_1)^2}{n_1}}{n_1 - 1}} = \sqrt{\frac{114 - \frac{(20)^2}{5}}{5 - 1}} = 2.9155 \qquad s_2 = \sqrt{\frac{\Sigma X_2^2 - \frac{(\Sigma X_2)^2}{n_2}}{n_2 - 1}} = \sqrt{\frac{172 - \frac{(30)^2}{6}}{6 - 1}} = 2.0976$$

Step 2: Pool the Sample Variances. We use formula 11–3 to pool the sample variances (standard deviations squared).

$$s_p^2 = \frac{(n_1 - 1)s_1^2 + (n_2 - 1)s_2^2}{n_1 + n_2 - 2} = \frac{(5 - 1)(2.9155)^2 + (6 - 1)(2.0976)^2}{5 + 6 - 2} = 6.2222$$

Step 3: Determine the value of *t*. The mean mounting time for procedure 1 is 4.00 minutes, found by $\bar{X}_1 = 20/5$. The mean mounting time for procedure 2 is 5.00 minutes, found by $\bar{X}_2 = 30/6$. We use formula 11–4 to calculate the value of *t*.

$$t = \frac{\bar{X}_1 - \bar{X}_2}{\sqrt{s_p^2\left(\frac{1}{n_1} + \frac{1}{n_2}\right)}} = \frac{4.00 - 5.00}{\sqrt{6.2222\left(\frac{1}{5} + \frac{1}{6}\right)}} = -0.662$$

The decision is not to reject the null hypothesis, because -0.662 falls in the region between -1.833 and 1.833. We conclude that there is no difference in the mean times to mount the engine on the frame using the two methods.

We can also estimate the *p*-value using Appendix F. Locate the row with 9 degrees of freedom, and use the two-tailed test column. Find the *t* value, without regard to the sign, which is closest to our computed value of 0.662. It is 1.383, corresponding to a significance level of .20. Thus, even had we used the 20 percent significance level, we would not have rejected the null hypothesis of equal means. We can report that the *p*-value is greater than .20.

A Software Example Using Excel

Excel has a procedure called "t-Test: Two Sample Assuming Equal Variances" that will perform the calculations of formulas 11–3 and 11–4 as well as find the sample means and sample variances. The data are input in the first two columns of the Excel spreadsheet. They are labeled "One" and "Two." The output follows. The value of *t*, called the "t Stat," is -0.66205, and the two-tailed *p*-value is .52453. As we would expect, the *p*-value is larger than the significance level of .10. The conclusion is not to reject the null hypothesis.

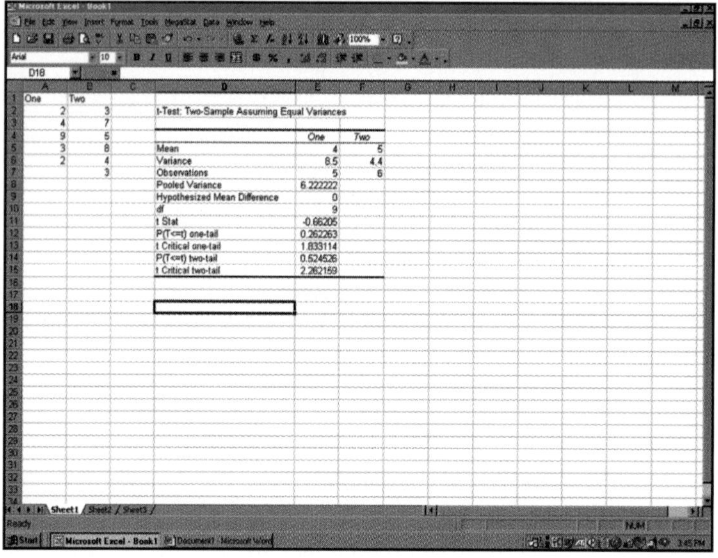

Self-Review 11–2

The production manager at Bellevue Steel, a manufacturer of wheelchairs, wants to compare the number of defective wheelchairs produced on the day shift with the number on the afternoon shift. A sample of the production from 6 day shifts and 8 afternoon shifts revealed the following number of defects.

Day	5	8	7	6	9	7		
Afternoon	8	10	7	11	9	12	14	9

At the .05 significance level, is there a difference in the mean number of defects per shift?

(a) State the null hypothesis and the alternate hypothesis.
(b) What is the decision rule?
(c) What is the value of the test statistic?
(d) What is your decision regarding the null hypothesis?
(e) What is the *p*-value?
(f) Interpret the result.

Exercises

For Exercises 7 and 8: (a) state the decision rule, (b) compute the pooled estimate of the population variance, (c) compute the test statistic, (d) state your decision about the null hypothesis, and (e) estimate the *p*-value.

7. The null and alternate hypotheses are:

$$H_0: \mu_1 = \mu_2$$
$$H_1: \mu_1 \neq \mu_2$$

A random sample of 10 observations from one population revealed a sample mean of 23 and a sample deviation of 4. A random sample of 8 observations from another population revealed a sample mean of 26 and a sample standard deviation of 5. At the .05 significance level, is there a difference between the population means?

8. a. Reject H_0 if $t = -1.697$ or $t > 1.697$.
b. $s_p^2 = 187.20$
c. $t = 1.651$
d. Do not reject.
e. $0.1 < p < 0.2$

8. The null and alternate hypotheses are:

$$H_0: \mu_1 = \mu_2$$
$$H_1: \mu_1 \neq \mu_2$$

A random sample of 15 observations from the first population revealed a sample mean of 350 and a sample standard deviation of 12. A random sample of 17 observations from the second population revealed a sample mean of 342 and a sample standard deviation of 15. At the .10 significance level, is there a difference in the population means?

Note: Use the five-step hypothesis testing procedure for the following exercises.

9. A sample of scores on an examination given in Statistics 201 are:

Men	72	69	98	66	85	76	79	80	77
Women	81	67	90	78	81	80	76		

At the .01 significance level, is the mean grade of the women higher than that of the men?

10. $s_p^2 = 278.69$
$t = 1.949$
Do not reject.

10. A recent study compared the time spent together by single- and dual-earner couples. According to the records kept by the wives during the study, the mean amount of time spent together watching television among the single-earner couples was 61 minutes per day, with a standard deviation of 15.5 minutes. For the dual-earner couples, the mean number of minutes spent watching television was 48.4 minutes, with a standard deviation of 18.1 minutes. At the .01 significance level, can we conclude that the single-earner couples on average spend more time watching television together? There were 15 single-earner and 12 dual-earner couples studied.

11. Ms. Lisa Monnin is the budget director for the New Process Company. She would like to compare the daily travel expenses for the sales staff and the audit staff. She collected the following sample information.

Sales ($)	131	135	146	165	136	142	
Audit ($)	130	102	129	143	149	120	139

At the .10 significance level, can she conclude that the mean daily expenses are greater for the sales staff than the audit staff? What is the *p*-value?

12. $s_p^2 = 777.88$
$t = 0.707$
Do not reject.

12. The Tampa Bay (Florida) Area Chamber of Commerce wanted to know whether the mean weekly salary of nurses was larger than that of school teachers. To investigate, they collected the following information on the amounts earned last week by a sample of school teachers and nurses.

School teachers ($)	845	826	827	875	784	809	802	820	829	830	842	832
Nurses ($)	841	890	821	771	850	859	825	829				

Is it reasonable to conclude that the mean weekly salary of nurses is higher? Use the .01 significance level. What is the *p*-value?

Tests about Proportions

In the previous two sections, we considered tests involving the mean. However, we are often interested also in whether two sample proportions came from populations that are equal. Here are several examples.

- The Vice President of Human Resources wishes to know whether there is a difference in the proportion of hourly employees who miss more than 5 days of work per year at the Atlanta and the Houston plants.

- General Motors is considering a new design for the Pontiac Grand Am. The design is shown to a group of potential buyers under 30 years of age and another group over 60 years of age. Pontiac wishes to know whether there is a difference in the proportion of the two groups who like the new design.
- United Airlines is investigating the fear of flying among adults. Specifically, they wish to know whether there is a difference in the proportion of men versus women who are fearful of flying.

In the above cases each sampled item or individual can be classified as a "success" or a "failure." That is, in the Grand Am example each potential buyer is classified as "liking the new design" or "not liking the new design." We then compare the proportion in the under 30 group with the proportion in the over 60 group who indicated they liked the new design. Can we conclude that the differences are due to chance? In this study there is no measurement obtained, only classifying the individuals or objects.

To conduct the test, we assume each sample is large enough that the normal distribution will serve as a good approximation of the binomial distribution. The test statistic follows the standard normal distribution. We compute the value of z from the following formula:

TWO-SAMPLE TEST OF PROPORTIONS

$$z = \frac{p_1 - p_2}{\sqrt{\dfrac{p_c(1-p_c)}{n_1} + \dfrac{p_c(1-p_c)}{n_2}}} \quad \textbf{[11–5]}$$

Formula 11–5 is formula 11–2 with the respective sample proportions replacing the sample means and $p_c(1 - p_c)$ replacing the two sample standard deviations. In addition:

n_1 is the number of observations in the first sample.
n_2 is the number of observations in the second sample.
p_1 is the proportion in the first sample possessing the trait.
p_2 is the proportion in the second sample possessing the trait.
p_c is the pooled proportion possessing the trait in the combined samples. It is called the pooled estimate of the population proportion and is computed from the following formula.

POOLED PROPORTION

$$p_c = \frac{X_1 + X_2}{n_1 + n_2} \quad \textbf{[11–6]}$$

where:

X_1 is the number possessing the trait in the first sample.
X_2 is the number possessing the trait in the second sample.

The following example will illustrate the two-sample test of proportions.

EXAMPLE

The Manelli Perfume Company recently developed a new fragrance that they plan to market under the name "Heavenly". A number of market studies indicate that Heavenly has very good market potential. The Sales Department at Manelli is particularly interested in whether there is a difference in the proportions of younger and older women who would purchase Heavenly if it were marketed. There are two independent populations, a population consisting of the younger women and a population consist-

ing of the older women. Each sampled woman will be asked to smell Heavenly and indicate whether she likes the fragrance well enough to purchase a bottle.

SOLUTION

We will use the usual five-step hypothesis-testing procedure.

Step 1: State H_0 and H_1. In this case the null hypothesis is: "There is no difference in the proportion of young women and older women who prefer Heavenly." We designate π_1 as the proportion of young women who would purchase Heavenly and π_2 as the proportion of older women who would purchase. The alternate hypothesis is that the two proportions are not equal.

$$H_0: \pi_1 = \pi_2$$
$$H_1: \pi_1 \neq \pi_2$$

Step 2: Select the level of significance. We use the .05 significance level in this example.

Step 3: Determine the test statistic. The test statistic follows the standard normal distribution. The value of the test statistic can be computed from formula 11–5.

Step 4: Formulate the decision rule. Recall that the alternate hypothesis from step 1 does not state a direction, so this is a two-tailed test. To determine the critical value, we divide the significance level in half and place this amount in each tail of the z distribution. Next, we subtract this amount from the total area to the right of zero. That is .5000 − .0250 = .4750. Finally, we search the body of the z table (Appendix D) for the closest value. It is 1.96. The critical values are −1.96 and + 1.96. As before, if the computed z value falls in the region between + 1.96 and −1.96, the null hypothesis is not rejected. If that does occur, it is assumed that any difference between the two sample proportions is due to chance variation. This information is summarized in Chart 11– 3.

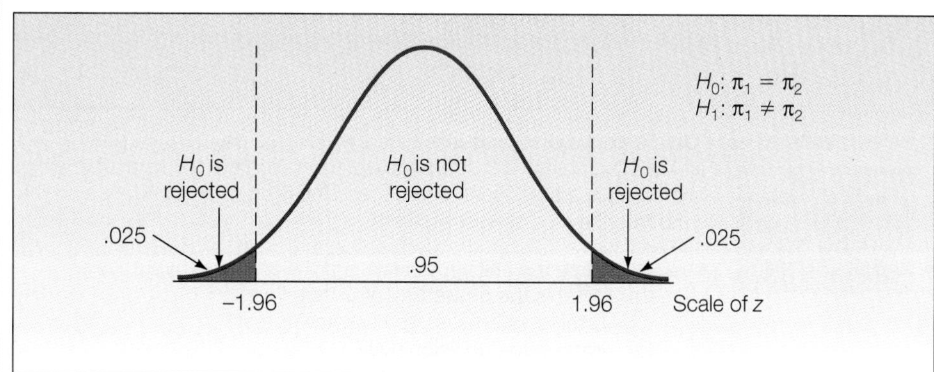

CHART 11–3 Decision Rules for Heavenly Fragrance Test, .05 Significance Level

Step 5: Select a sample and make a decision. A random sample of 100 young women revealed 20 liked the Heavenly fragrance well enough to purchase it. Similarly, a sample of 200 older women revealed 100 liked the fragrance well enough to make a purchase. We let p_1 refer to the young women and p_2 to the older women.

$$p_1 = \frac{X_1}{n_1} = \frac{20}{100} = .20 \qquad p_2 = \frac{X_2}{n_2} = \frac{100}{200} = .50$$

The research question is whether the difference of .30 in the two sample proportions is due to chance or whether there a difference in the proportion of younger and older women who like the Heavenly fragrance.

Next, we combine or pool the sample proportions. We use formula 11–6.

$$p_c = \frac{X_1 + X_2}{n_1 + n_2} = \frac{20 + 100}{100 + 200} = .40$$

Note that the pooled proportion is closer to .50 than to .20 because more older women than younger women were sampled.

We use formula 11–5 to find the value of the test statistic.

$$z = \frac{p_1 - p_2}{\sqrt{\dfrac{p_c(1-p_c)}{n_1} + \dfrac{p_c(1-p_c)}{n_2}}} = \frac{.20 - .50}{\sqrt{\dfrac{.40(1-40)}{100} + \dfrac{.40(1-.40)}{200}}} = -5.00$$

The computed value of −5.00 is in the area of rejection, that is, it is to the left of −1.96. Therefore, the null hypothesis is rejected at the .05 significance level. To put it another way, the null hypothesis that the proportion of young women who would purchase Heavenly is equal to the proportion of older women who would purchase Heavenly is rejected. It is unlikely that the difference between the two sample proportions is due to chance. To find the p-value we go to Appendix D and look for the likelihood of finding a z value less than −5.00 or greater than 5.00. The largest value of z reported is 3.09, with a corresponding probability of .4990. So the probability of finding a z value greater than 5.00 or less than −5.00 is virtually zero. So we report zero as the p-value. There is very little likelihood the null hypothesis is true. We conclude that there is a difference in the proportion of younger and older women who would purchase Heavenly.

Self-Review 11–3

Of 150 adults who tried a new peach-flavored peppermint patty, 87 rated it excellent. Of 200 children sampled, 123 rated it excellent. Using the .10 level of significance, can we conclude that there is a significant difference in the proportion of adults and the proportion of children who rate the new flavor excellent?

(a) State the null hypothesis and the alternate hypothesis.
(b) What is the probability of a Type I error?
(c) Is this a one-tailed or a two-tailed test?
(d) What is the decision rule?
(e) What is the value of the test statistic?
(f) What is your decision regarding the null hypothesis?
(g) What is the p-value? Explain what it means in terms of this problem.

Exercises

13. The null and alternate hypotheses are:

H_0: $\pi_1 \leq \pi_2$
H_1: $\pi_1 > \pi_2$

A sample of 100 observations from the first population indicated that X_1 is 70. A sample of 150 observations from the second population revealed X_2 to be 90. Use the .05 significance level to test the hypothesis.

a. State the decision rule.
b. Compute the pooled proportion.
c. Compute the value of the test statistic.
d. What is your decision regarding the null hypothesis?

14. a. Reject H_0 if $z < -1.96$ or $z > 1.96$.
b. $p_c = .80$
c. $z = 2.70$
d. Reject H_0.

14. The null and alternate hypotheses are:

H_0: $\pi_1 = \pi_2$
H_1: $\pi_1 \neq \pi_2$

A sample of 200 observations from the first population indicated that X_1 is 170. A sample of 150 observations from the second population revealed X_2 to be 110. Use the .05 significance level to test the hypothesis.

a. State the decision rule.
b. Compute the pooled proportion.
c. Compute the value of the test statistic.
d. What is your decision regarding the null hypothesis?

Note: Use the five-step hypothesis-testing procedure in solving the following exercises.

15. The Damon family owns a large grape vineyard in western New York along Lake Erie. The grapevines must be sprayed at the beginning of the growing season to protect against various insects and diseases. Two new insecticides have just been marketed: Pernod 5 and Action. To test their effectiveness, three long rows were selected and sprayed with Pernod 5, and three others were sprayed with Action. When the grapes ripened, 400 of the vines treated with Pernod 5 were checked for infestation. Likewise, a sample of 400 vines sprayed with Action were checked. The results are:

Insecticide	Number of Vines Checked (sample size)	Number of Infested Vines
Pernod 5	400	24
Action	400	40

At the .05 significance level, can we conclude that there is a difference in the proportion of vines infested using Pernod 5 as opposed to Action?

16. $z = -12.60$ Reject H_0.

16. The Roper Organization conducted identical surveys in 1990 and 2000. One question asked women was, "Are most men basically kind, gentle, and thoughtful?" The 1990 survey revealed that, of the 3,000 women surveyed, 2,010 said that they were. In 2000, 1,530 of the 3,000 women surveyed thought that men were kind, gentle, and thoughtful. At the .05 level, can we conclude that women think men are less kind, gentle, and thoughtful in 2000 compared with 1990?

17. A nationwide sample of influential Republicans and Democrats was asked as a part of a comprehensive survey whether they favored lowering environmental standards so that high-sulfur coal could be burned in coal-fired power plants. The results were:

	Republicans	Democrats
Number sampled	1,000	800
Number in favor	200	168

At the .02 level of significance, can we conclude that there is a larger proportion of Democrats in favor of lowering the standards?

18. $z = 1.74$
Do not reject.

18. The research department at the home office of New Hampshire Insurance conducts ongoing research on the causes of automobile accidents, the characteristics of the drivers, and so on. A random sample of 400 policies written on single persons revealed 120 had at least one accident in the previous three-year period. Similarly, a sample of 600 policies written on married persons revealed that 150 had been in at least one accident. At the .05 significance level, is there a significant difference in the proportions of single and married persons having an accident during a three-year period?

Dependent Samples

On page 385, we tested the difference between the means from two independent samples. We compared the mean time required to mount an engine using the Welles method to the time to mount the engine using the Atkins method. The samples were *independent,* meaning that the sample of assembly times using the Welles method was in no way related to the sample of assembly times using the Atkins method.

There are situations, however, in which the samples are not independent. To put it another way, the samples are **dependent** or related. As an example, Nickel Savings and Loan employs two firms, Schadek Appraisals and Bowyer Real Estate, to appraise the value of the real estate properties on which they make loans. It is important that these two firms be similar in their appraisal values. To review the consistency of the two appraisal firms, Nickel Savings randomly selects 10 homes and has both Schadek Appraisals and Bowyer Real Estate appraise the value of the selected homes. For each home, there will be a pair of appraisal values. That is, for each home there will be an appraised value from both Schadek Appraisals and Bowyer Real Estate. The appraised values depend on, or are related to, the home selected. This is also referred to as a **paired sample.**

For hypothesis testing, we are interested in the distribution of the *differences* in the appraised value. Hence, there is only one sample. To put it more formally, we are investigating whether the mean of the distribution of differences in the appraised values is 0. The sample is made up of the *differences* between the appraised values determined by Schadek Appraisals and the values from Bowyer Real Estate. If the two appraisal firms are reporting similar estimates, then sometimes Schadek Appraisals will be the higher value and sometimes Bowyer Real Estate will have the higher value. However, the mean of the distribution of differences will be 0. On the other hand, if one of the firms consistently reports the larger appraisal values, then the mean of the distribution of the differences will not be 0.

We will use the symbol μ_d to indicate the mean of the population of the distribution of differences. We assume the distribution of the population of differences follows the normal distribution. The test statistic follows the *t* distribution and we calculate its value from the following formula:

PAIRED *t* TEST

$$t = \frac{\bar{d}}{s_d/\sqrt{n}} \qquad [11\text{–}7]$$

There are $n - 1$ degrees of freedom and

- $\bar{d}$ is the mean of the difference between the paired or related observations.
- s_d is the standard deviation of the differences between the paired or related observations.
- n is the number of paired observations.

The standard deviation of the differences is computed using formula 4–7 except d is substituted for X. The formula is:

$$s_d = \sqrt{\frac{\Sigma d^2 - \frac{(\Sigma d)^2}{n}}{n - 1}}$$

The following example illustrates this test.

EXAMPLE

Recall that Nickel Savings and Loan wishes to compare the two companies they use to appraise the value of residential homes. Nickel Savings selected a sample of 10 residential properties and scheduled both firms for an appraisal. The results, reported in $000, are:

Home	Schadek	Bowyer
1	135	128
2	110	105
3	131	119
4	142	140
5	105	98
6	130	123
7	131	127
8	110	115
9	125	122
10	149	145

At the .05 significance level, can we conclude there is a difference in the mean appraised values of the homes?

SOLUTION

The first step is to state the null and the alternate hypotheses. In this case a two-tailed alternative is appropriate because we are interested in determining whether there is a *difference* in the appraised values. We are not interested in showing whether one particular firm appraises property at a higher value than the other. The question is whether the sample differences in the appraised values could have come from a population with a mean of 0. If the population mean of the differences is 0, then we conclude that there is no difference in the appraised values. The null and alternate hypotheses are:

$$H_0: \mu_d = 0$$
$$H_1: \mu_d \neq 0$$

There are 10 homes appraised by both firms, so $n = 10$, and $df = n - 1 = 10 - 1 = 9$. We have a two-tailed test, and the significance level is .05. To determine the critical value, go to Appendix F, move across the row with 9 degrees of freedom to the column for a two-tailed test and the .05 significance level. The value at the intersection is 2.262. The decision rule is to reject the null hypothesis if the computed value of t is less than -2.262 or greater than 2.262. Here are the computational details.

Home	Schadek	Bowyer	Difference, d	Difference Squared, d^2
1	135	128	7	49
2	110	105	5	25
3	131	119	12	144
4	142	140	2	4
5	105	98	7	49
6	130	123	7	49
7	131	127	4	16
8	110	115	−5	25
9	125	122	3	9
10	149	145	4	16
			46	386

$$\bar{d} = \frac{\Sigma d}{n} = \frac{46}{10} = 4.60$$

$$s_d = \sqrt{\frac{\Sigma d^2 - \frac{(\Sigma d)^2}{n}}{n-1}} = \sqrt{\frac{386 - \frac{(46)^2}{10}}{10-1}} = 4.402$$

Using formula 11–7, the value of t is 3.305, found by

$$t = \frac{\bar{d}}{s_d/\sqrt{n}} = \frac{4.6}{4.402/\sqrt{10}} = 3.305$$

Because the computed t falls in the rejection region, the null hypothesis is rejected. The population distribution of differences does not have a mean of 0. We conclude

TABLE 11–2 A Portion of the t Distribution from Appendix F

	Confidence Intervals					
	80%	90%	95%	98%	99%	99.9%
	Level of Significance for One-Tailed Test					
df	0.100	0.050	0.025	0.010	0.005	0.0005
	Level of Significance for Two-Tailed Test					
	0.20	0.10	0.05	0.02	0.01	0.001
1	3.078	6.314	12.706	31.821	63.657	636.619
2	1.886	2.920	4.303	6.965	9.925	31.599
3	1.638	2.353	3.182	4.541	5.841	12.924
4	1.533	2.132	2.776	3.747	4.604	8.610
5	1.476	2.015	2.571	3.365	4.032	6.869
6	1.440	1.943	2.447	3.143	3.707	5.959
7	1.415	1.895	2.365	2.998	3.499	5.408
8	1.397	1.860	2.306	2.896	3.355	5.041
9	1.383	1.833	2.262	2.821	3.250	4.781
10	1.372	1.812	2.228	2.764	3.169	4.587

that there is a difference in the mean appraised values of the homes. The largest difference of $12,000 is for Home 3. Perhaps that would be an appropriate place to begin a more detailed review.

To find the p-value, we use Appendix F and the section for a two-tailed test. Move along the row with 9 degrees of freedom and find the values of t that are closest to our calculated value. For a .01 significance level, the value of t is 3.250. The computed value is larger than this value, but smaller than the value of 4.781 corresponding to the .001 significance level. Hence, the p-value is less than .01. This information is highlighted in Table 11–2 at the bottom of the previous page.

Excel has a procedure called "t-Test: Paired Two-Sample for Means" that will perform the calculations of formula 11–7. The output from this procedure is below

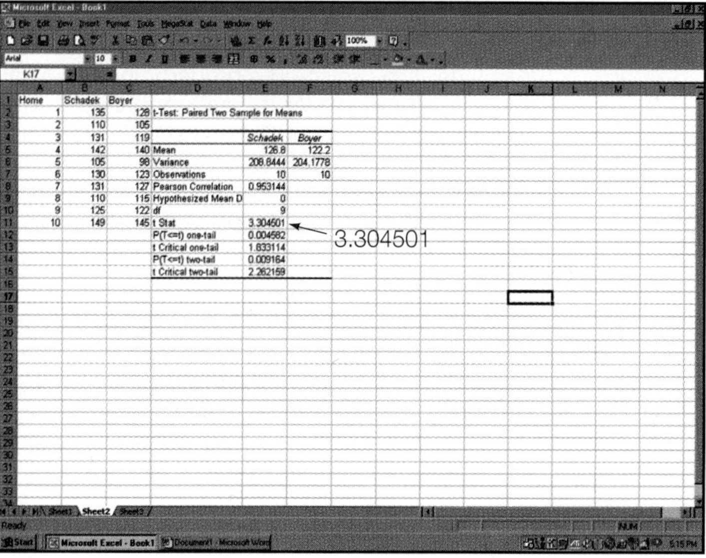

The computed value of t is 3.304501, and the two-tailed p-value is .009164. Because the p-value is less than .05, we reject the hypothesis that the mean of the distribution of the differences between the appraised values is zero. In fact, this p-value is less than 1.0%. There is very little likelihood that the null hypothesis is true.

Comparing Dependent and Independent Samples

Beginning students are often confused by the difference between tests for independent samples (formula 11–3) and tests for dependent samples (formula 11–7). How do we tell the difference between dependent and independent samples? There are two types of dependent samples: (1) those characterized by a measurement, an intervention of some type, and then another measurement; and (2) a matching or pairing of the observations. To explain further:

1. The first type of dependent sample is characterized by a measurement followed by an intervention of some kind and then another measurement. This could be called a "before" and "after" study. Two examples will help to clarify. Suppose we want to show that, by placing speakers in the production area and playing soothing music, we are able to increase production. We begin by selecting a sample of workers and measuring their output under the current conditions. The speakers

are then installed in the production area, and we again measure the output of the same workers. There are two measurements, before placing the speakers in the production area and after. The intervention is placing speakers in the production area.

A second example involves an educational firm that offers courses designed to increase test scores and reading ability. Suppose the firm wants to offer a course that will help high school juniors increase their SAT scores. To begin, each student takes the SAT in the junior year in high school. During the summer between the junior and senior year, they participate in the course that gives them tips on taking tests. Finally, during the fall of their senior year in high school, they retake the SAT. Again, the procedure is characterized by a measurement (taking the SAT as a junior), an intervention (the summer workshops), and another measurement (taking the SAT during their senior year).

2. The second type of dependent sample is characterized by matching or pairing observations. Nickel Savings in the previous example is a dependent sample of this type. They selected a property for appraisal and then had two appraisals on the same property. As a second example, suppose an industrial psychologist wishes to study the intellectual similarities of newly married couples. She selects a sample of newlyweds. Next, she administers a standard intelligence test to both the man and woman to determine the difference in the scores. Notice the matching that occurred: comparing the scores of the man and the woman.

Why do we prefer dependent samples to independent samples? By using dependent samples, we are able to reduce the variation in the sampling distribution. To illustrate, we will use the Nickel Savings and Loan example just completed. Suppose we assume that we have two independent samples of real estate property for appraisal and conduct the following test of hypothesis, using formula 11–3. The null and alternate hypotheses are:

$$H_0: \mu_1 = \mu_2$$
$$H_1: \mu_1 \neq \mu_2$$

There are now two independent samples of 10 each. So the number of degrees of freedom is 10 + 10 − 2 = 18. From Appendix D, using the .05 significance level, H_0 is rejected if t is less than −2.101 or greater than 2.101.

The mean of the appraised value of the 10 properties by Schadek is \$126,800, and the standard deviation is \$14,500. For Bowyer Real Estate the mean appraised value is \$122,200, and the standard deviation is \$14,300. To make the calculations easier, we use \$000 instead of \$. The value of the pooled estimate of the variance from formula 11–2 is

$$s_p^2 = \frac{(n_1 - 1)s_1^2 + (n_2 - 1)s_2^2}{n_1 + n_2 - 2} = \frac{(10 - 1)14.5^2 + (10 - 1)14.3^2}{10 + 10 - 2} = 207.37$$

Using formula 11–3, t is 0.714.

$$t = \frac{\bar{X}_1 - \bar{X}_2}{\sqrt{s_p^2\left(\frac{1}{n_1} + \frac{1}{n_2}\right)}} = \frac{126.8 - 122.2}{\sqrt{207.37\left(\frac{1}{10} + \frac{1}{10}\right)}} = \frac{4.6}{6.4403} = 0.714$$

The computed t (0.714) is less than 2.101, so the null hypothesis is not rejected. We cannot show that there is a difference in the mean appraisal value. That is not the same conclusion that we got before! Why does this happen? The numerator is the same in the paired observations test (4.6). However, the denominator is smaller. In the paired test the denominator is 1.3920 (see the calculations on page 396). In the case of the independent samples, the denominator is 6.4403. There is more variation or uncertainty. This accounts for the difference in the t values and the difference in the statistical decisions. The denominator measures the standard error of the statistic. When the samples are not paired, two kinds of variation are present: differences between the two appraisal firms and the difference in the value of the real estate. Properties numbered 4 and 10 have relatively high values, whereas number 5 is relatively low. These data show how different the values of the property are, but we are really interested in the difference between the two appraisal firms.

The trick is to pair the values to reduce the variation among the properties. The paired test uses only the difference between the two appraisal firms for the same property. Thus, the paired or dependent statistic focuses on the variation between Schadek Appraisals and Bowyer Real Estate. Thus, its standard error is always smaller. That, in turn, leads to a larger test statistic and a greater chance of rejecting the null hypothesis. So whenever possible you should pair the data.

There is a bit of bad news here. In the paired observations test, the degrees of freedom are half of what they are if the samples are not paired. For the real estate example, the degrees of freedom drop from 18 to 9 when the observations are paired. However, in most cases, this is a small price to pay for a better test.

Self-Review 11–4

Advertisements by Sylph Fitness Center claim that completing their course will result in losing weight. A random sample of eight recent participants showed the following weights before and after completing the course. At the .01 significance level, can we conclude the students lost weight?

Name	Before	After
Hunter	155	154
Cashman	228	207
Mervine	141	147
Massa	162	157
Creola	211	196
Perterson	164	150
Redding	184	170
Poust	172	165

(a) State the null hypothesis and the alternate hypothesis
(b) What is the critical value of t?
(c) What is the computed value of t?
(d) Interpret the result. What is the p-value?

Exercises

19. The null and alternate hypotheses are:

H_0: $\mu_d \leq 0$
H_1: $\mu_d > 0$

The following sample information shows the number of defective units produced on the day shift and the afternoon shift for a sample of four days last month.

	Day			
	1	**2**	**3**	**4**
Day shift	10	12	15	19
Afternoon shift	8	9	12	15

At the .05 significance level, can we conclude there are more defects produced on the afternoon shift?

20. a. Reject H_0 if $t < -2.776$ or $t > 2.776$.
b. $\bar{d} = 4.6$
c. $t = 6.767$
d. Reject H_0.
e. $.001 < p < .01$

20. The null and alternate hypotheses are:

$$H_0: \mu_d = 0$$
$$H_1: \mu_d \neq 0$$

The following paired observations show the number of traffic citations given for speeding by Officer Dhondt and Officer Meredith of the South Carolina Highway Patrol for the last five months.

	Day				
	May	**June**	**July**	**August**	**September**
Officer Dhondt	30	22	25	19	26
Officer Meredith	26	19	20	15	19

At the .05 significance level, is there a difference in the mean number of citations given by the two officers?

Note: Use the five-step hypothesis testing procedure to solve the following exercises.

21. A survey is conducted at North Central University to measure the effect of the change in environment on international students. One of the facets of the study is a comparison of student weights upon arrival on campus with weights one year later. It is suspected that the richer American food will cause an increase in weights. Use the .01 significance level. A random sample of 11 international students is chosen for the study. What is your conclusion?

	Weight	
Name	**Arrival**	**One Year Later**
Nassar	124	142
O'Toole	157	157
Obie	98	96
Silverman	190	212
Kim	103	116
Gross	135	134
Farouk	149	150
Thatcher	176	184
Sambul	200	209
Onassis	180	180
Pierre	256	269

22. The management of Discount Furniture, a chain of discount furniture stores in the Northeast, designed an incentive plan for salespeople. To evaluate this innovative plan, 12 salespeople were selected at random, and their weekly incomes before and after the plan were recorded.

22. H_0: $\mu_d \leq 0$
H_0: $\mu_d > 0$
Reject H_0 if $t > 1.796$.
$\bar{d} = 25.917$
$s_d = 40.791$
$t = 2.20$
Reject H_0.
p-value about .025

Salesperson	Before	After
Sid Mahone	$320	$340
Carol Quick	290	285
Tom Jackson	421	475
Andy Jones	510	510
Jean Sloan	210	210
Jack Walker	402	500
Peg Mancuso	625	631
Anita Loma	560	560
John Cuso	360	365
Carl Utz	431	431
A. S. Kushner	506	525
Fern Lawton	505	619

Was there a significant increase in the typical salesperson's weekly income due to the innovative incentive plan? Use the .05 significance level. Estimate the p-value, and interpret it.

23. Harry Hutchings is the owner of Hutchings Weightlifting Clinic. He claims that by taking a special vitamin, a weightlifter can increase his strength. Ten student athletes are randomly selected and given a test of strength using the standard bench press. After two weeks of regular training, supplemented with the vitamin, they are tested again. The results are shown below.

	Weight	
Name	**Before**	**After**
Evie Gorky	190	196
Bob Mack	250	240
Lou Brandon	345	345
Karl Unger	210	212
Sue Koontz	114	113
Pat O'Leary	126	129
Kim Dennis	186	189
Connie Kaye	116	115
Tom Dama	196	194
Maxine Sims	125	124

At the .01 level of significance, can we conclude the special vitamin increased the strength of the student athletes?

24. $\bar{d} = 3.625$
$s_d = 4.8385$
Reject if $t < -2.998$
$t = 2.12$
Do not reject H_0.

24. The federal government recently granted funds for a special program designed to reduce crime in high-crime areas. A study of the results of the program in eight high-crime areas of Miami, FL, yielded the following results.

	Number of Crimes by Area							
	A	**B**	**C**	**D**	**E**	**F**	**G**	**H**
Before	14	7	4	5	17	12	8	9
After	2	7	3	6	8	13	3	5

Has there been a decrease in the number of crimes since the inauguration of the program? Use the .01 significance level. Estimate the p-value.

Chapter Outline

I. In comparing two-sample means we wish to know whether they came from the same or equal populations.

A. We are investigating whether the distribution of the difference between the sample means could have a mean of 0.

B. The test statistic is the standard normal (z) if the two samples both contain at least 30 observations and the population standard deviations are unknown.

1. No assumption about the shape of either population is required.
2. The samples are from independent populations.
3. The formula for computing the value of z is

$$z = \frac{\bar{X}_1 - \bar{X}_2}{\sqrt{\frac{s_1^2}{n_1} + \frac{s_2^2}{n_2}}} \quad [11\text{–}2]$$

C. The test statistic is the t distribution if one or both of the samples contain fewer than 30 observations.

1. Both populations must follow the normal distribution.
2. The populations must have equal standard deviations.
3. The samples are independent.
4. Finding the value of t requires two steps.

a. The first step is to pool the standard deviations according to the following formula:

$$s_p^2 = \frac{(n_1 - 1)s_1^2 + (n_2 - 1)s_2^2}{n_1 + n_2 - 2} \quad [11\text{–}3]$$

b. The value of t is computed from the following formula:

$$t = \frac{\bar{X}_1 - \bar{X}_2}{\sqrt{s_p^2\left(\frac{1}{n_1} + \frac{1}{n_2}\right)}} \quad [11\text{–}4]$$

II. We can also test whether two samples came from populations with an equal proportion of successes.

A. The two sample proportions are pooled using the following formula:

$$p_c = \frac{X_1 + X_2}{n_1 + n_2} \quad [11\text{–}6]$$

B. We compute the value of the test statistic from the following formula:

$$z = \frac{p_1 - p_2}{\sqrt{\frac{p_c(1 - p_c)}{n_1} + \frac{p_c(1 - p_c)}{n_2}}} \quad [11\text{–}5]$$

III. For dependent samples, we assume the distribution of the differences in the populations has a mean of 0.

A. We first compute the mean and the standard deviation of the sample differences.

B. The value of the test statistic is computed from the following formula:

$$t = \frac{\bar{d}}{s_d/\sqrt{n}} \quad [11\text{–}7]$$

Pronunciation Key

SYMBOL	MEANING	PRONUNCIATION
p_c	Pooled proportion	*p sub c*
s_p^2	Pooled sample variance	*s sub p squared*

$\bar{X}_1$	Mean of the first sample	*X bar sub 1*
$\bar{X}_2$	Mean of the second sample	*X bar sub 2*
$\bar{d}$	Mean of the difference between dependent observations	*d bar*
s_d	Standard deviation of the difference between dependent observations	*s sub d*

Chapter Exercises

25. An official of the Iowa Department of Highways wants to compare the useful life, in months, of two brands of paint used for striping roads. The mean number of months Cooper Paint lasted was 36.2, with a standard deviation of 1.14 months. The official reviewed 35 road stripes. For King Paint, the mean number of months was 37.0, with a standard deviation of 1.3 months. The official reviewed 40 road stripes. At the .01 significance level, is there a difference in the useful life of the two paints? Compute the *p*-value.

26. $z = -1.30$ Do not reject H_0.

26. Clark Heter is an industrial engineer at Lyons Products. He would like to determine whether there are more units produced on the afternoon shift than on the day shift. A sample of 54 day-shift workers showed that the mean number of units produced was 345, with a standard deviation of 21. A sample of 60 afternoon-shift workers showed that the mean number of units produced was 351, with a standard deviation of 28 units. At the .05 significance level, is the number of units produced on the afternoon shift larger?
27. Fry Brothers Heating and Air Conditioning, Inc. employs Larry Clark and George Murnen to make service calls to repair furnaces and air conditioning units in homes. Tom Fry, the owner, would like to know whether there is a difference in the mean number of service calls they make per day. A random sample of 40 days last year showed that Larry Clark made an average of 4.77 calls per day, with a standard deviation of 1.05 calls per day. For a sample of 50 days George Murnen made an average of 5.02 calls per day, with a standard deviation of 1.23 calls per day. At the .05 significance level, is there a difference in the mean number of calls per day between the two employees? What is the *p*-value?

28. $z = -5.44$ Reject H_0. $p < .001$

28. A coffee manufacturer is interested in whether the mean daily consumption of regular-coffee drinkers is less than that of decaffeinated-coffee drinkers. A random sample of 50 regular-coffee drinkers showed a mean of 4.35 cups per day, with a standard deviation of 1.20 cups per day. A sample of 40 decaffeinated-coffee drinkers showed a mean of 5.84 cups per day, with a standard deviation of 1.36 cups per day. Use the .01 significance level. Compute the *p*-value.
29. The board of directors at the Anchor Pointe Marina is studying the usage of boats among its members. A sample of 30 members who have boats 10 to 20 feet in length showed that they used their boats an average of 11 days last July. The standard deviation of the sample was 3.88 days. For a sample of 40 members with boats 21 to 40 feet in length, the average number of days they used their boats in July was 7.67, with a standard deviation of 4.42 days. At the .02 significance level, can the board of directors conclude that those with the smaller boats used their crafts more frequently?

30. $z = 4.10$ Reject H_0.

30. The *fog index* is used to measure the reading difficulty of written text. Calculating the index involves the following steps: (1) Find the mean number of words per sentence. (2) Find the percent of words with three or more syllables. (3) The fog index is 40 percent of the sum of 1 and 2. The fog index for a sample of 36 articles from a scientific journal showed a sample mean of 11.0 and a standard deviation of 2.65. A sample of 40 articles from trade publications showed a mean of 8.9 and a standard deviation of 1.64. At the .01 significance level, is the fog index in the scientific journal significantly higher?
31. The manufacturer of Advil, a common headache remedy, recently developed a new formulation of the drug that is claimed to be more effective. To evaluate the new drug, a sample of 200 current users is asked to try it. After a one-month trial, 180 indicated the new drug was more effective in relieving a headache. At the same time a sample of 300 current Advil users is given the current drug but told it is the new formulation. From this group, 261 said it was an improvement. At the .05 significance level can we conclude that the new drug is more effective?

32. $p_c = .21$
$z = -1.61$
Do not reject H_0.

32. A random sample of 1,000 American-born citizens revealed that 198 favored resumption of full diplomatic relations with Cuba. Similarly, 117 of a sample of 500 foreign-born citizens favored it. At the .05 significance level, is there a difference in the proportions of American-born versus foreign-born citizens who favor restoring diplomatic relations with Cuba?

33. Is there a difference in the proportions of college men versus college women who smoke at least a pack of cigarettes a day at Northern State University? A sample of 400 women revealed 72 smoked at least one pack per day. A sample of 500 men revealed that 70 smoked at least a pack of cigarettes a day. At the .05 significance level, is there a difference between the proportion of men and the proportion of women who smoke at least a pack of cigarettes a day, or can the difference in the proportions be attributed to sampling error?

34. $z = -1.29$
Do not reject H_0.

34. Each month the National Association of Purchasing Managers publishes the NAPM index. One of the questions asked on the survey to purchasing agents is: Do you think the economy is expanding? Last month, of the 300 responses 160 answered yes to the question. This month, 170 of the 290 responses indicated they felt the economy was expanding. At the .05 significance level, can we conclude that a larger proportion of the agents believe the economy is expanding this month?

35. As part of a recent survey among dual-wage-earner couples, an industrial psychologist found that 990 men out of the 1,500 surveyed believed the division of household duties was fair. A sample of 1,600 women found 970 believed the division of household duties was fair. At the .01 significance level, is it reasonable to conclude that the proportion of men who believe the division of household duties is fair is larger? What is the *p*-value?

36. $z = 0.96$
Do not reject.

36. There are two major Internet providers in the Colorado Springs, CO, area, one called HTC and the other Mountain. We want to investigate whether there is a difference in the proportion of times a customer is able to access the Internet. During a one-week period, 500 calls were placed at random times throughout the day and night to HTC. A connection was made to the Internet on 450 occasions. A similar one-week study with Mountain showed the Internet to be available on 352 of 400 trials. At the .01 significance level, is there a difference in the percent of time that access to the Internet is successful?

37. A study of the health benefits packages for employees of large and small firms was recently completed by Pohlman Associates, a management consulting firm. Among the 15 large firms studied, the mean cost of the benefits package was 17.6 percent of salary, with a standard deviation of 2.6 percent. Among the 12 small firms studied, the mean cost of the benefits package was 16.2 percent of salary, with a standard deviation of 3.3 percent. Is there a significant difference between the mean percent of the employees' salaries spent by large firms and by small firms on health benefits? Use the .05 level of significance. What is the *p*-value?

38. $s_p^2 = 33.4767$
$t = 2.031$
Reject H_0.

38. The manager of a package courier service believes that packages shipped at the end of the month are heavier than those shipped early in the month. As an experiment, he weighed a random sample of 20 packages at the beginning of the month. He found that the mean weight was 20.25 pounds and that the standard deviation was 5.84 pounds. Ten packages randomly selected at the end of the month had a mean weight of 24.80 pounds and a standard deviation of 5.67 pounds. At the .05 significance level, can we conclude that the packages shipped at the end of the month weigh more?

39. The owner of Bun 'N' Run Hamburger wishes to compare the sales per day at two locations. The mean number sold for 10 randomly selected days at the Northside site was 83.55, and the standard deviation was 10.50. For a random sample of 12 days at the Southside location, the mean number sold was 78.80 and the standard deviation was 14.25. At the .05 significance level, is there a difference in the mean number of hamburgers sold at the two locations? What is the *p*-value?

40. $s_p^2 = 103.16$
$t = 1.07$
Do not reject H_0.

40. The Engineering Department at Sims Software, Inc., recently developed two chemical solutions designed to increase the usable life of computer disks. A sample of disks treated with the first solution lasted 86, 78, 66, 83, 84, 81, 84, 109, 65, and 102 hours. Those treated with the second solution lasted 91, 71, 75, 76, 87, 79, 73, 76, 79, 78, 87, 90, 76, and 72 hours. At the .10 significance level, can we conclude that there is a difference in the length of time the two types of treatment lasted?

41. The Willow Run Outlet Mall has two Haggar Outlet Stores, one located on Peach Street and the other on Plum Street. The two stores are laid out differently, but both store managers claim their layout maximizes the amounts customers will purchase on impulse. A sample of

10 customers at the Peach Street store revealed they spent the following amounts more than planned: \$17.58, \$19.73, \$12.61, \$17.79, \$16.22, \$15.82, \$15.40, \$15.86, \$11.82, and \$15.85. A sample of 14 customers at the Plum Street store revealed they spent the following amounts more than they planned: \$18.19, \$20.22, \$17.38, \$17.96, \$23.92, \$15.87, \$16.47, \$15.96, \$16.79, \$16.74, \$21.40, \$20.57, \$19.79, and \$14.83. At the .01 significance level, is there a difference in the mean amounts purchased on impulse at the two stores?

42. $s_p^2 = 12.8164$, $t = 1.15$, Do not reject H_0.

42. The Grand Strand Family Medical Center is specifically set up to treat minor medical emergencies for visitors to the Myrtle Beach area. There are two facilities, one in the Little River Area and the other in Murrells Inlet. The Quality Assurance Department wishes to compare the mean waiting time for patients at the two locations. Samples of the waiting times, reported in minutes, follow:

Location	Waiting Time											
Little River	31.73	28.77	29.53	22.08	29.47	18.60	32.94	25.18	29.82	26.49		
Murrells Inlet	22.93	23.92	26.92	27.20	26.44	25.62	30.61	29.44	23.09	23.10	26.69	22.31

At the .05 significance level, is there a difference in the mean waiting time?

43. The Commercial Bank and Trust Company is studying the use of its automatic teller machines (ATMs). Of particular interest is whether young adults (under 25 years) use the machines more than senior citizens. To investigate further, samples of customers under 25 years of age and customers over 60 years of age were selected. The number of ATM transactions last month was determined for each selected individual, and the results are shown below. At the .01 significance level, can bank management conclude that younger customers use the ATMs more?

Under 25	10	10	11	15	7	11	10	9			
Over 60	4	8	7	7	4	5	1	7	4	10	5

44. $s_p^2 = 3.1832$, $t = -3.541$, Reject H_0.

44. Two boats, the *Sea Hawk* and the *Sea Queen*, are competing for a spot in the upcoming *America's Cup* race. To decide which will represent the United States, they race over a part of the course several times. Below are the sample times in minutes. At the .05 significance level, can we conclude that there is a difference in their mean times?

Boat	Times (minutes)											
Sea Hawk	12.9	12.5	11.0	13.3	11.2	11.4	11.6	12.3	14.2	11.3		
Sea Queen	14.1	14.1	14.2	17.4	15.8	16.7	16.1	13.3	13.4	13.6	10.8	19.0

45. The manufacturer of a compact disc player wanted to know whether a 10 percent reduction in price is enough to increase the sales of their product. To investigate, the owner randomly selected eight outlets and sold the disc player at the reduced price. At seven randomly selected outlets, the disc player was sold at the regular price. Reported below is the number of units sold last month at the sampled outlets. At the .01 significance level, can the manufacturer conclude that the price reduction resulted in an increase in sales?

Regular price	138	121	88	115	141	125	96	
Reduced price	128	134	152	135	114	106	112	120

46. $t = -2.415$, Do not reject.

46. A number of minor automobile accidents occur at various high-risk intersections in Teton County despite traffic lights. The traffic department claims that a modification in the type of light will reduce these accidents. The county commissioners have agreed to a proposed experiment. Eight intersections were chosen at random, and the lights at those intersections were modified. The numbers of minor accidents during a six-month period before and after the modifications were:

	Number of Accidents							
	A	B	C	D	E	F	G	H
Before modification	5	7	6	4	8	9	8	10
After modification	3	7	7	0	4	6	8	2

At the .01 significance level is it reasonable to conclude that the modification reduced the number of traffic accidents?

47. Lester Hollar is Vice President for Human Resources for a large manufacturing company. In recent years he has noticed an increase in absenteeism that he thinks is related to the general health of the employees. Four years ago, in an attempt to improve the situation, he began a fitness program in which employees exercise during their lunch hour. To evaluate the program, he selected a random sample of eight participants and found the number of days each was absent in the six months before the exercise program began and in the last six months. Below are the results. At the .05 significance level, can he conclude that the number of absences has declined? Estimate the p-value.

Employee	Before	After
1	6	5
2	6	2
3	7	1
4	7	3
5	4	3
6	3	6
7	5	3
8	6	7

48. $t = 2.027$ Reject H_0. p-value = $.025 < p < .05$

48. Scott Seggity, owner of Seggity Software, Inc., recently purchased a special math co-processor chip advertised to "drastically reduce processing time." To test the chip, he selected a sample of 12 programs. The selected programs were run on two identical computers, one with the chip and the other without it. The processing times are reported below, in seconds. At the .05 significance level, can Mr. Seggity conclude that the new co-processor will reduce the processing time? Estimate the p-value.

Program	Without	With
1	1.23	0.60
2	0.69	0.93
3	1.28	0.95
4	1.19	1.37
5	0.78	0.62
6	1.02	0.99
7	1.30	0.60
8	1.37	1.35
9	1.29	0.67
10	1.17	0.89
11	1.14	1.29
12	1.09	1.00

49. Dr. Thomas Sharkey, Dean of the College of Business at Genoa University, wants to study the effect on student grade point averages (GPAs) of moving from the quarter system to the semester system. (Under the quarter system, the academic year is divided into three 10-week sessions, whereas under the semester system there are two 15-week sessions.) Genoa U. recently switched from the quarter to the semester system. To investigate, Dean

Sharkey selected a sample of 10 students enrolled in the fall quarter last year and the fall semester this year. Listed below are their GPAs for the two periods. At the .05 significance level, is there evidence that the student grades declined after the conversion?

Student	Last Fall	This Fall
Asad	2.98	3.17
Becha	2.34	2.04
Bowerman	3.68	3.62
Sweede	3.13	3.19
Davis	3.34	2.90
Volmer	2.09	2.08
Anderson	2.45	2.88
Bolger	2.96	3.15
Palmer	2.80	2.49
Weis	4.00	3.98

50. $\bar{d} = 246$
$s_d = 547$
$t = -1.742$
Do not reject H_0.

50. The president of the American Insurance Institute wants to compare the yearly costs of auto insurance offered by two leading companies. He selects a sample of 15 families, some with only a single insured driver, others with several teenage drivers, and pays each family a stipend to contact the two companies and ask for a price quote. To make the data comparable, certain features, such as the amount deductible and limits of liability, are standardized. The sample information is reported below. At the .10 significance level, can we conclude that there is a difference in the amounts quoted?

Family	American Car Insurance	St. Paul Mutual Insurance
Becker	$2,090	$1,610
Berry	1,683	1,247
Cobb	1,402	2,327
Debuck	1,830	1,367
DuBrul	930	1,461
Eckroate	697	1,789
German	1,741	1,621
Glasson	1,129	1,914
King	1,018	1,956
Kucic	1,881	1,772
Meredith	1,571	1,375
Obeid	874	1,527
Price	1,579	1,767
Phillips	1,577	1,636
Tresize	860	1,188

51. Fairfield Homes is developing two parcels near Pigeon Fork, Tennessee. In order to test different advertising approaches, they use different media to reach potential buyers. The mean annual family income for 75 people making inquiries at the first development is $150,000, with a standard deviation of $40,000. A corresponding sample of 120 people at the second development had a mean of $180,000, with a standard deviation of $30,000. At the .05 significance level, can Fairfield conclude that the population means are different?

52. $s_p^2 = 1.683$
$t = 1.50$
Do not reject H_0.

52. The following data resulted from a taste test of two different chocolate bars. The first number is a rating of the taste, which could range from 0 to 5, with a 5 indicating the person liked the taste. The second number indicates whether a "secret ingredient" was present. If the ingredient was present a code of "1" was used and a "0" otherwise. At the .05 significance level, does this data show a difference in the taste ratings?

Rating	"With/ Without"	Rating	"With/ Without"
3	1	1	1
1	1	4	0
0	0	4	0
2	1	2	1
3	1	3	0
1	1	4	0

53. An investigation of the effectiveness of an antibacterial soap in reducing operating room contamination resulted in the accompanying table. The new soap was tested in a sample of eight operating rooms in the greater Seattle area during the last year.

	Operating Room							
	A	B	C	D	E	F	G	H
Before	6.6	6.5	9.0	10.3	11.2	8.1	6.3	11.6
After	6.8	2.4	7.4	8.5	8.1	6.1	3.4	2.0

At the 0.05 significance level, can we conclude the contamination measurements are lower after use of the new soap?

54. $s_p^2 = 25.78145$
$t = 0.58$
Do not reject H_0.

54. The following data on annual rates of return were collected from five stocks listed on the New York Stock Exchange ("the big board") and five stocks listed on NASDAQ. At the .10 significance level, can we conclude that the annual rates of return are higher on the big board?

NYSE	NASDAQ
17.16	15.80
17.08	16.28
15.51	16.21
8.43	17.97
25.15	7.77

exercises.com

55. Listed on the next page are several prominent companies and their stock prices in the summer of 2000. Go to the Web and look up today's price. There are many sources to find stock prices, such as Yahoo and CNNFI. The Yahoo address is http://www.quote.yahoo.com. Enter the symbol identification to find the current price. At the .05 significance level, can we conclude that the prices have changed?

Company	Symbol	Price
Coca-Cola	KO	58.75
Walt Disney	DIS	38.0625
Eastman Kodak	EK	60.3125
Ford Motor Company	F	44.8125
General Motors	GM	60
Goodyear Tire	GT	21.4375
IBM	IBM	105
McDonald's	MCD	31.8125
McGraw-Hill Publishing	MHP	54.5625
Oracle	ORCL	72.3125
Johnson and Johnson	JNJ	90.25
General Electric	GE	52.25
Home Depot	HD	51.5

56. Answers will vary.

56. The *USA Today* (*http://www.usatoday.com/sports/mlb.htm*) and Major League Baseball's Website (*http://www.majorleaguebaseball.com*) regularly report information on individual player salaries. Go to one of these sites and find the individual salaries for your favorite team. Compute the mean and the standard deviation. Is it reasonable to conclude that your favorite (or local) team has a mean player salary different from $1,500,000?

Computer Data Exercises

57. Refer to the Real Estate data, which reports information on the homes sold in Venice, Florida, last year.

- **a.** At the .05 significance level, can we conclude that there is a difference in the mean selling price of homes with a pool and homes without a pool?
- **b.** At the .05 significance level, can we conclude that there is a difference in the mean selling price of homes with an attached garage and homes without a garage?
- **c.** At the .05 significance level, can we conclude that there is a difference in the mean selling price of homes in Township 1 and Township 2?
- **d.** Find the median selling price of the homes. Divide the homes into two groups, those that sold for more than (or equal to) the median price and those that sold for less. Is there a difference in the proportion of homes with a pool for those that sold at or above the median price versus those that sold for less than the median price? Use the .05 significance level.

58. Refer to the Baseball 2000 data, which reports information on the 30 Major League Baseball teams for the 2000 season.

58. a. $t = -0.22$

- **a.** At the .05 significance level, can we conclude that there is a difference in the mean salary of teams in the American League versus teams in the National League?

b. $t = 0.49$

- **b.** At the .05 significance level, can we conclude that there is a difference in the mean home attendance of teams in the American League versus teams in the National League?

c. $t = 2.88$

- **c.** At the .05 significance level, can we conclude that there is a difference in the mean number of wins for teams that have artificial turf home fields versus teams that have grass home fields?

d. $t = 1.56$

- **d.** At the .05 significance level, can we conclude that there is a difference in the mean number of home runs for teams that have artificial turf home fields versus teams that have grass home fields?

59. Refer to the OECD data, which reports information on census, economic, and business data for 29 countries. Conduct a test of hypothesis to determine whether the mean percent of the population that is over 65 years of age in G7 countries is different from those that are not G7 members.

60. Refer to the Schools data set, which refers to the 94 school districts in northwest Ohio. Divide the school districts into two groups. Include all schools with less than 2,000 students (small districts) in one group and those with 2,000 or more (large districts) in the other.

60. a. $z = 6.75$

b. $z = 0.11$

c. $z = -5.41$

a. Compute the mean teacher salary for the two groups. At the .05 significance level, can we conclude that the mean teacher salary is higher in the larger school districts?

b. Compute the mean amount spent per pupil for the large and the small districts. At the .05 significance level, can we conclude that there is a difference in the mean amount spent?

c. Compute the mean daily percent of students attending for the large and small districts. At the .05 significance level, can we conclude that there is a difference in the mean daily attendance?

Computer Commands

1. The Excel commands for the two-sample *t*-test on page 388 are:
   a. Enter the data into columns A and B (or any other columns) in the spreadsheet. Use the first row of each column to enter the variable name.
   b. From the menu bar select **Tools** and **Data Analysis**. Select **t-Test**: **Two-Sample Assuming Equal Variances**, then click **OK**.
   c. In the dialog box indicate that the range of **Variable 1** is from *A1* to *A6* and **Variable 2** from *B1* to *B7*, the **Hypothesized Mean Difference** is 0, the **Labels** are in the first row, **Alpha** is *0.05*, and the **Output Range** is *D2*. Click **OK**.

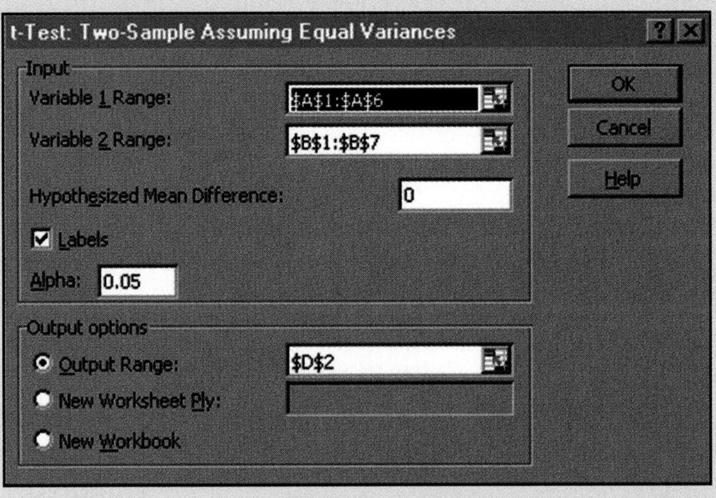

2. The Excel commands for the paired *t*-test on page 397 are:
   a. Enter the data into columns A and B (or any other two columns) in the spreadsheet, with the variable names in the first row.
   b. From the menu bar select **Tools** and **Data Analysis**. Select **t-Test**: **Paired Two Sample for Means**, then click **OK**.
   c. In the dialog box indicate that the range of **Variable 1** is from *B1* to *B11* and **Variable 2** from *C1* to *C11*, the **Hypothesized Mean Difference** is *0*, the **Labels** are in the first row, **Alpha** is *.05*, and the **Output Range** is *D2*. Click **OK**.

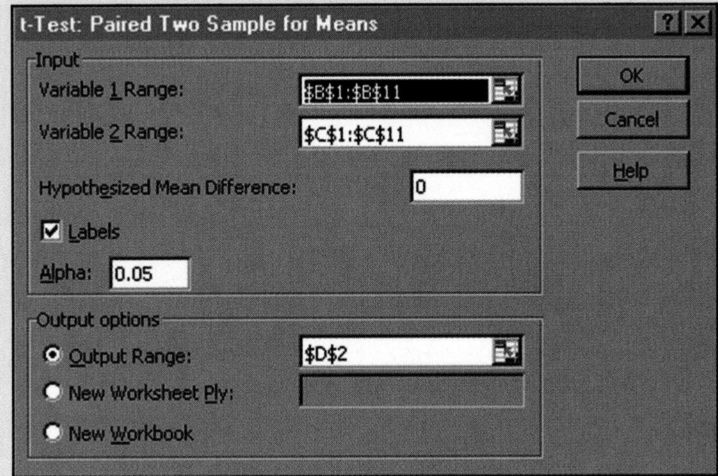

Chapter 11 Answers to Self-Review

11–1 **(a)** H_0: $\mu_W \leq \mu_M$
H_1: $\mu_W > \mu_M$
The subscript W refers to the women and M to the men.

(b) Reject H_0 if $z > 1.65$

(c) $$z = \frac{\$1{,}500 - \$1{,}400}{\sqrt{\frac{(\$250)^2}{50} + \frac{(\$200)^2}{40}}} = 2.11$$

(d) Reject the null hypothesis

(e) p-value $= .5000 - .4826 = .0174$

(f) The mean amount sold per day is larger for women.

11–2 **(a)** H_0: $\mu_d = \mu_a$
H_1: $\mu_d \neq \mu_a$

(b) $df = 6 + 8 - 2 = 12$
Reject H_0 if t is less than -2.179 or t is greater than 2.179.

(c) $$\bar{X}_1 = \frac{42}{6} = 7.00 \qquad s_1 = \sqrt{\frac{304 - \frac{42^2}{6}}{6-1}} = 1.4142$$

$$\bar{X}_2 = \frac{80}{8} = 10.00 \qquad s = \sqrt{\frac{836 - \frac{80^2}{8}}{8-1}} = 2.2678$$

$$s_p^2 = \frac{(6-1)(1.4142)^2 + (8-1)(2.2678)^2}{6+8-2}$$

$$= 3.8333$$

$$t = \frac{7.00 - 10.00}{\sqrt{3.8333\left(\frac{1}{6} + \frac{1}{8}\right)}} = -2.837$$

(d) Reject H_0 because -2.837 is less than the critical value.

(e) The p-value is less than .02.

(f) The mean number of defects is not the same on the two shifts.

11–3 **(a)** H_0: $\pi_1 = \pi_2$
H_1: $\pi_1 \neq \pi_2$

(b) .10

(c) Two-tailed

(d) Reject H_0 if z is less than -1.65 or greater than 1.65.

(e) $$p_c = \frac{87 + 123}{150 + 200} = \frac{210}{350} = .60$$

$$p_1 = \frac{87}{150} = .58 \qquad p_2 = \frac{123}{200} = .615$$

$$z = \frac{.58 - .615}{\sqrt{\frac{.60(.40)}{150} + \frac{.60(.40)}{200}}} = -0.66$$

(f) Do not reject H_0.

(g) p-value $= 2(.5000 - .2454) = .5092$
There is no difference in the proportion of adults and children that liked the proposed flavor.

11–4 **(a)** H_0: $\mu_d \leq 0$, H_1: $\mu_d > 0$.

(b) Reject H_0 if $t > 2.998$.

(c)

Name	Before	After	d	d^2
Hunter	155	154	1	1
Cashman	228	207	21	441
Mervine	141	147	−6	36
Massa	162	157	5	25
Creola	211	196	15	225
Peterson	164	150	14	196
Redding	184	170	14	196
Poust	172	165	7	49
			71	1,169

$$\bar{d} = \frac{71}{8} = 8.875$$

$$s_d = \sqrt{\frac{1{,}169 - \frac{(71)^2}{8}}{8-1}} = 8.774$$

$$t = \frac{8.875}{8.774/\sqrt{8}} = 2.861.$$

(d) Do not reject H_0. We cannot conclude that the students lost weight. The p-value is less than .025 but larger than .01.

12

Analysis of Variance

GOALS

When you have completed this chapter, you will be able to:

1. **Discuss the general idea of analysis of variance.**
2. **List the characteristics of the *F* distribution.**
3. **Conduct a test of hypothesis to determine whether the variances of two populations are equal.**
4. **Organize data into a one-way and a two-way ANOVA table.**
5. **Define and understand the terms *treatments* and *blocks.***
6. **Conduct a test of hypothesis among three or more treatment means.**
7. **Develop confidence intervals for the difference in treatment means.**
8. **Conduct a test of hypothesis to determine whether there is a difference among block means.**

An international advertising firm wants to know whether the size and color of an advertisement affect the response of customers. A random sample of customers are polled on their reactions to 3 different ad sizes and 4 different ad colors. Based on their responses of color and size combinations, determine if size and color affect an ad's effectiveness. Use the .05 level of significance. (See Goal 6 and Exercise 31.)

Introduction

In this chapter we continue our discussion of hypothesis testing. Recall that in Chapters 10 and 11 we examined the general theory of hypothesis testing. We described the case where a large sample was selected from the population. We used the z distribution (the standard normal distribution) to determine whether it was reasonable to conclude that the population mean was equal to a specified value. We tested whether two population means are the same. We also conducted both one- and two-sample tests for population proportions, again using the standard normal distribution as the distribution of the test statistic. We described methods for conducting tests of means where the populations were assumed normal but the samples were small (contained fewer than 30 observations). In that case the t distribution was used as the distribution of the test statistic. In this chapter we expand further our idea of hypothesis tests. We describe a test for variances and then a test that simultaneously compares several means to determine if they came from equal populations.

The *F* Distribution

The probability distribution used in this chapter is the F distribution. It was named to honor Sir Ronald Fisher, one of the founders of modern-day statistics. This probability distribution is used as the distribution of the test statistic for several situations. It is used to test whether two samples are from populations having equal variances, and it is also applied when we want to compare several population means simultaneously. The simultaneous comparison of several population means is called **analysis of variance (ANOVA).** In both of these situations, the populations must be normal, and the data must be at least interval-scale.

What are the characteristics of the F distribution?

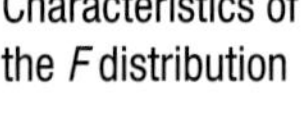
Characteristics of the *F* distribution

1. **There is a "family" of *F* distributions.** A particular member of the family is determined by two parameters: the degrees of freedom in the numerator and the degrees of freedom in the denominator. The shape of the distribution is illustrated by the following graph. There is one F distribution for the combination of 29 degrees of freedom in the numerator and 28 degrees of freedom in the denominator. There is another F distribution for 19 degrees in the numerator and 6 degrees of freedom in the denominator. Note that the shape of the curves changes as the degrees of freedom change.

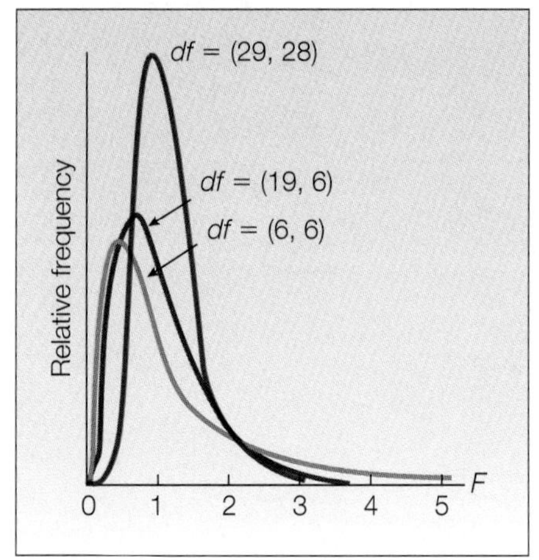

2. **The *F* distribution is continuous.** This means that it can assume an infinite number of values between 0 and plus infinity.
3. **The *F* distribution cannot be negative.** The smallest value *F* can assume is 0.
4. **It is positively skewed.** The long tail of the distribution is to the right-hand side. As the number of degrees of freedom increases in both the numerator and denominator the distribution approaches a normal distribution.
5. **It is asymptotic.** As the values of *X* increase, the *F* curve approaches the *X*-axis but never touches it. This is similar to the behavior of the normal distribution, described in Chapter 7.

Comparing Two Population Variances

The *F* distribution is used to test the hypothesis that the variance of one normal population equals the variance of another normal population. The following examples will show the use of the test:

- Two Barth shearing machines are set to produce steel bars of the same length. The bars, therefore, should have the same mean length. We want to ensure that in addition to having the same mean length they also have similar variation.

- The mean rate of return on two types of common stock may be the same, but there may be more variation in the rate of return in one than the other. A sample of 10 Internet stocks and 10 utility stocks shows the same mean rate of return, but there is likely more variation in the Internet stocks.
- A study by the marketing department for a large newspaper found that men and women spent about the same amount of time per day reading the paper. However, the same report indicated there was nearly twice as much variation among the men as the women.

The *F* distribution is also used to test assumptions for some statistical tests. Recall that in the previous chapter when small samples were assumed, we used the *t* test to investigate whether the means of two independent populations differed. To employ that test, we assume that the variances of two normal populations are the same. See this list of assumptions on page 384. The *F* distribution provides a means for conducting a test regarding the variances of two normal populations.

Regardless of whether we want to determine whether one population has more variation than another population or validate an assumption for a statistical test, we first state the null hypothesis. The null hypothesis is that the variance of one normal population, σ_1^2, equals the variance of the other normal population, σ_2^2. The alternate hypothesis could be that the variances differ. In this instance the null hypothesis and the alternate hypothesis are:

$$H_0: \sigma_1^2 = \sigma_2^2$$
$$H_1: \sigma_1^2 \neq \sigma_2^2$$

To conduct the test, we select a random sample of n_1 observations from one population, and a sample of n_2 observations from the second population. The test statistic is defined as follows.

TEST STATISTIC FOR COMPARING TWO VARIANCES

$$F = \frac{s_1^2}{s_2^2} \quad [12\text{–}1]$$

The terms s_1^2 and s_2^2 are the respective sample variances. If the null hypothesis is true, the test statistic follows the F distribution with $n_1 - 1$ and $n_2 - 1$ degrees of freedom. In order to reduce the size of the table of critical values, the *larger* sample variance is placed in the numerator; hence, the tabled F ratio is always larger than 1.00. Thus, the right-tail critical value is the only one required. The critical value of F for a two-tailed test is found by dividing the significance level in half ($\alpha/2$) and then referring to the appropriate degrees of freedom in Appendix G. An example will illustrate.

EXAMPLE

Lammers Limos offers limousine service from the city hall in Toledo, Ohio, to Metro Airport in Detroit. Sean Lammers, president of the company, is considering two routes. One is via U.S. 25 and the other via I-75. He wants to study the time it takes to drive to the airport using each route and then compare the results. He collected the following sample data, which is reported in minutes. Using the .10 significance level, is there a difference in the variation in the driving times using the two routes?

U.S. Route 25	Interstate 75
52	59
67	60
56	61
45	51
70	56
54	63
64	57
	65

SOLUTION

The mean driving times along the two routes are nearly the same. The mean time is 58.29 minutes for the U.S. 25 route and 59.0 minutes along the I-75 route. However, in evaluating travel times, Mr. Lammers is also concerned about the variation in the travel times. The first step is to compute the two sample variances. We'll use formula 4–7 to compute the sample standard deviations. To obtain the sample variances, we square the standard deviations.

U.S. Route 25

$$\bar{X} = \frac{\Sigma X}{n} = \frac{408}{7} = 58.29 \qquad s = \sqrt{\frac{\Sigma X^2 - \frac{(\Sigma X)^2}{n}}{n-1}} = \sqrt{\frac{24{,}266 - \frac{(408)^2}{7}}{7-1}} = 8.9947$$

Interstate 75

$$\bar{X} = \frac{\Sigma X}{n} = \frac{472}{8} = 59.00 \qquad s = \sqrt{\frac{\Sigma X^2 - \frac{(\Sigma X)^2}{n}}{n-1}} = \sqrt{\frac{27{,}982 - \frac{(472)^2}{8}}{8-1}} = 4.3753$$

There is more variation, as measured by the standard deviation, in the U.S. 25 route than in the I-75 route. This is somewhat consistent with his knowledge of the two routes; the U.S. 25 route contains more stoplights, whereas I-75 is a limited-access interstate highway. However, the I-75 route is several miles longer. It is important that the service offered be both timely and consistent, so he decides to conduct a statistical test to determine whether there really is a difference in the variation of the two routes.

The usual five-step hypothesis-testing procedure will be employed.

Step 1: We begin by stating the null hypothesis and the alternate hypothesis. The test is two-tailed because we are looking for a difference in the variation of the two routes. We are *not* trying to show that one route has more variation than the other.

$$H_0: \sigma_1^2 = \sigma_2^2$$
$$H_1: \sigma_1^2 \neq \sigma_2^2$$

Step 2: We selected the .10 significance level.

Step 3: The appropriate test statistic follows the F distribution.

Step 4: The critical value is obtained from Appendix G, a portion of which is reproduced as Table 12–1. Because we are conducting a two-tailed test, the tabled significance level is .05, found by $\alpha/2 = .10/2 = .05$. There are $n_1 - 1 = 7 - 1 = 6$ degrees of freedom in the numerator, and $n_2 - 1 = 8 - 1 = 7$ degrees of freedom in the denominator. To find the critical value, move horizontally across the top portion of the F table (Table 12–1 or Appendix G) for the .05 significance level to 6 degrees of freedom in the numerator. Then move down that column to the critical value opposite 7 degrees of freedom in the denominator. The critical value is 3.87. Thus, the decision rule is: Reject the null hypothesis if the ratio of the sample variances exceeds 3.87.

TABLE 12–1 Critical Values of the F Distribution, $\alpha = .05$

Degrees of Freedom for Denominator	Degrees of Freedom for Numerator			
	5	6	7	8
1	230	234	237	239
2	19.3	19.3	19.4	19.4
3	9.01	8.94	8.89	8.85
4	6.26	6.16	6.09	6.04
5	5.05	4.95	4.88	4.82
6	4.39	4.28	4.21	4.15
7	3.97	3.87	3.79	3.73
8	3.69	3.58	3.50	3.44
9	3.48	3.37	3.29	3.23
10	3.33	3.22	3.14	3.07

Step 5: The final step is to take the ratio of the two sample variances, determine the value of the test statistic, and make a decision regarding the null hypothesis. Note that formula 12–1 refers to the sample *variances* but we calculated the sample *standard deviations*. We need to square the standard deviations to determine the variances.

$$F = \frac{s_1^2}{s_2^2} = \frac{(8.9947)^2}{(4.3753)^2} = 4.23$$

The decision is to reject the null hypothesis, because the computed F value (4.23) is larger than the critical value (3.87). We conclude that there is a difference in the variation of the travel times along the two routes.

As noted, the usual practice is to determine the F ratio by putting the larger of the two sample variances in the numerator. This will force the F ratio to be at least 1.00. This allows us to always use the right tail of the F distribution, thus avoiding the need for more extensive F tables.

A logical question arises regarding one-tailed tests. For example, suppose in the previous example we suspected that the variance of the times using the U.S. 25 route is *larger* than the variance of the times along the I-75 route. We would state the null and the alternate hypothesis as

$$H_0: \sigma_1^2 \leq \sigma_2^2$$
$$H_1: \sigma_1^2 > \sigma_2^2$$

The test statistic is computed as s_1^2/s_2^2. Notice that we labeled the population with the suspected largest variance as population 1. So s_1^2 appears in the numerator. The F ratio will be larger than 1.00, so we can use the upper tail of the F distribution. Under these conditions, it is not necessary to divide the significance level in half. Because Appendix G gives us only the .05 and .01 significance levels, we are restricted to these levels for one-tailed tests and .10 and .02 for two-tailed tests unless we consult a more complete table or use the distribution function on either MINITAB or Excel.

The Excel software system has a procedure to perform a test of variances. Below is the output. The computed value of F is the same as determined using formula 12–1.

US-25	I-75		F-Test Two-Sample for Variances		
52	59				
67	60			US-25	I-75
56	61		Mean	58.28571	59
45	51		Variance	80.90476	19.14286
70	56		Observations	7	8
54	63		df	6	7
64	57		F	4.226368	
	65		P(F<=f) one-tail	0.040397	
			F Critical one-tail	3.865978	

Self-Review 12–1

Steele Electric Products, Inc. assembles electrical components for stereo equipment. For the last 10 days Mark Nagy has averaged 9 rejects, with a standard deviation of 2 rejects per day. Debbie Richmond averaged 8.5 rejects, with a standard deviation of 1.5 rejects, over the same period. At the .05 significance level, can we conclude that there is more variation in the number of rejects per day attributed to Mark?

Exercises

1. What is the critical F value for a sample of six observations in the numerator and four in the denominator? Use a two-tailed test and the .10 significance level.

2. 9.78

2. What is the critical F value for a sample of four observations in the numerator and seven in the denominator? Use a one-tailed test and the .01 significance level.
3. The following hypotheses are given.

$$H_0: \sigma_1^2 = \sigma_2^2$$
$$H_1: \sigma_1^2 \neq \sigma_2^2$$

A random sample of eight observations from the first population resulted in a standard deviation of 10. A random sample of six observations from the second population resulted in a standard deviation of 7. At the .02 significance level, is there a difference in the variation of the two populations?

4. $F = 2.94$ Do not reject.

4. The following hypotheses are given.

$$H_0: \sigma_1^2 \leq \sigma_2^2$$
$$H_1: \sigma_1^2 > \sigma_2^2$$

A random sample of five observations from the first population resulted in a standard deviation of 12. A random sample of seven observations from the second population showed a standard deviation of 7. At the .01 significance level, is there more variation in the first population?

5. Stargell Research Associates conducted a study of the radio listening habits of men and women. One facet of the study involved the mean listening time. It was discovered that the mean listening time for men was 35 minutes per day. The standard deviation of the sample of the 10 men studied was 10 minutes per day. The mean listening time for the 12 women studied was also 35 minutes, but the standard deviation of the sample was 12 minutes. At the .10 significance level, can we conclude that there is a difference in the variation in the listening times for men and women?

6. $F = 1.24$ Do not reject.

6. A stockbroker at Critical Securities reported that the mean rate of return on a sample of 10 oil stocks was 12.6 percent with a standard deviation of 3.9 percent. The mean rate of return on a sample of 8 utility stocks was 10.9 percent with a standard deviation of 3.5 percent. At the .05 significance level, can we conclude that there is more variation in the oil stocks?

ANOVA Assumptions

Another use of the F distribution is the analysis of variance (ANOVA) technique in which we compare three or more population means to determine whether they could be equal. To use ANOVA, we assume the following:

1. The populations are normally distributed.
2. The populations have equal standard deviations (σ).
3. The samples are selected independently.

When these conditions are met, F is used as the distribution of the test statistic.

Why do we need to study ANOVA? Why can't we just use the test of differences in population means discussed in the previous chapter? We could compare the treatment means two at a time. The major reason is the unsatisfactory buildup of Type I error. To explain further, suppose we have four different methods (A, B, C, and D) of training new recruits to be firefighters. We randomly assign each of the 40 recruits in this year's class to one of the four methods. At the end of the training program, we administer to the four groups a common test to measure understanding of firefighting techniques. The question to be explored is: Is there a difference in the mean test scores among the four groups? An answer to this question will allow us to compare the four training methods.

Using the *t* distribution leads to a buildup of Type I error.

Using the *t* distribution to compare the four population means, we would have to conduct six different *t* tests. That is, we would need to compare the mean scores for the four methods as follows: A versus B, A versus C, A versus D, B versus C, B versus D, and C versus D. If we set the significance level at .05, the probability of a correct statistical decision is .95, found by 1 − .05. Because we conduct six separate (independent) tests the probability that we do *not* make an incorrect decision due to sampling in any of the six independent tests is:

$$P(\text{All correct}) = (.95)(.95)(.95)(.95)(.95)(.95) = .735.$$

To find the probability of a least one error due to sampling, we subtract this result from 1. Thus, the probability of at least one incorrect decision due to sampling is 1 − .735 = .265. To summarize, if we conduct six independent tests using the *t* distribution, the likelihood of at least one sampling error is increased from .05 to an unsatisfactory level of .265. It is obvious that we need a better method than conducting six *t* tests. ANOVA will allow us to compare the treatment means simultaneously and avoid the buildup of the Type I error.

ANOVA was developed for applications in agriculture, and many of the terms related to that context remain. In particular the term *treatment* is used to identify the different populations being examined. The following illustration will clarify the term *treatment* and demonstrate an application of ANOVA.

Bruce Kuhlman, the owner of Kuhlman Farms, wants to use the brand of fertilizer that will produce the maximum yield per acre of wheat. Mr. Kuhlman can select from three different commercial brands: Wolfe, White, and Korosa. To begin, Mr. Kuhlman divides his field into 12 plots of equal size. The wheat is then planted at the same time in the same manner. The only difference in the plots is that he randomly assigns the Wolfe brand of fertilizer to four plots, the White brand to four plots, and the Korosa brand to four plots. At the end of the growing season, he records the number of bushels of wheat produced on each plot. In this illustration there are three treatments. That is, the three different brands of fertilizer are the three different treatments. The results, in bushels at the end of the growing season, are:

Wolfe	White	Korosa
55	66	47
54	76	51
59	67	46
56	71	48

Is there a difference in the mean number of bushels of wheat produced? Chart 12–1 illustrates how the populations would appear if there was a difference in the treatment means. Note that the populations are approximately normal and the variation in each population is the same, but the fertilizer (treatment) means are *not* the same.

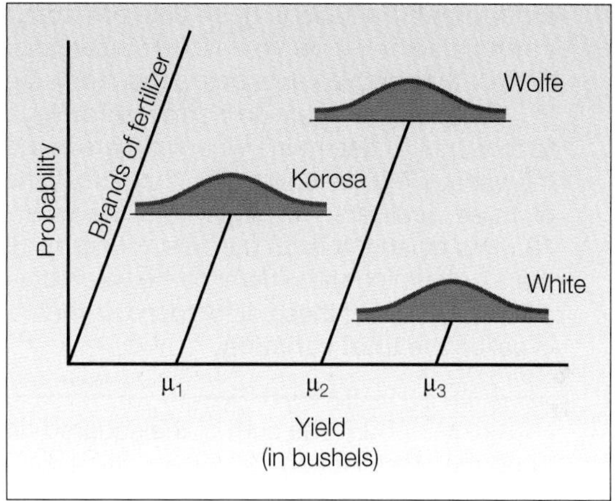

CHART 12–1 Case Where Treatment Means Are Different

Suppose the populations are the same. That is, there is no difference in the fertilizer (treatment) means. This is shown in Chart 12–2. This would indicate that the population means are the same. Note again that the populations are approximately normal and the variation in each of the populations is the same.

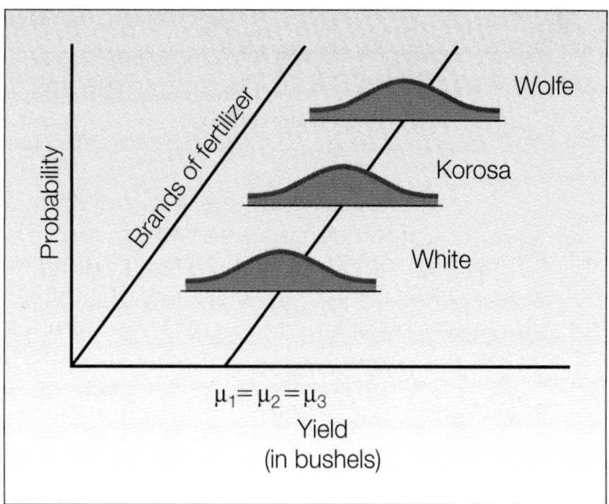

CHART 12–2 Case Where Treatment Means Are the Same

The ANOVA Test

How does the ANOVA test work? Recall that we want to determine whether the various sample means came from a single population or populations with different means. We actually compare these sample means through their variances. To explain, recall that on page 419 we listed the assumptions required for ANOVA. One of those assumptions was that the standard deviations of the various normal populations had to be the same. We take advantage of this requirement in the ANOVA test. The underlying strategy is to estimate the population variance (standard deviation squared) two ways and then find the ratio of these two estimates. If this ratio is about 1, then logically the two estimates are the same, and we conclude that the population means are the same. If the ratio is quite different from 1, then we conclude that the population means are not the same. The *F* distribution serves as a referee by indicating when the ratio of the sample variances is too much greater than 1 to have occurred by chance.

Refer to the Kuhlman Farms example in the previous section. The owner of the farm wants to determine whether there is a difference in the mean yields of wheat for the various fertilizers. He has 12 plots of land and randomly assigned 4 plots to each of three fertilizers. To begin, find the overall mean wheat yield, in bushels, of the 12 plots of land. It is 58 bushels, found by $(55 + 54 + \cdots + 48)/12$. Next, for each of the 12 plots find the difference between the yield for the particular plot and the overall mean. Each of these differences is squared and these squares summed. This term is called the **total variation.**

> **TOTAL VARIATION** The sum of the squared differences between each observation and the overall mean.

In our example the total variation is 1,082, found by $(55 - 58)^2 + (54 - 58)^2 + \cdots + (48 - 58)^2$.

Next, break this total variation into two components: that which is due to the **treatments** and that which is **random.** To find these two components, determine the mean of each of the treatments. In our Kuhlman Farms example, we calculate the mean wheat yield of the four plots that were fertilized with the Wolfe brand, the mean yield of the four plots using the White brand, and the mean yield of the four plots using the Korosa brand. The first source of variation is due to the treatments.

> **TREATMENT VARIATION** The sum of the squared differences between each treatment mean and the overall mean.

In the fertilizer example the variation due to the treatments is the sum of the squared differences between the mean of each fertilizer and the overall mean. This term is 992. To calculate it we first find the mean yield of each of the three treatments. The mean yield for the Wolfe brand is 56 bushels, found by $(55 + 54 + 59 + 56)/4$. The other means are 70 bushels and 48 bushels, respectively. The sum of the squares due to the treatments is:

$$(56 - 58)^2 + (56 - 58)^2 + \cdots + (48 - 58)^2 = 4(56 - 58)^2 + 4(70 - 58)^2 + 4(48 - 58)^2$$
$$= 992$$

If there is considerable variation among the treatment means, it is logical that this term will be large. If the treatment means are similar, this term will be a small value. The smallest possible value would be zero. This would occur when all the treatment means are the same.

The other source of variation is referred to as the **random** component, or the error component.

> **RANDOM VARIATION** The sum of the squared differences between each observation and its treatment mean.

In the fertilizer example this term is the sum of the sq
wheat yield for each plot and the mean yield for that pa
is 90.

$$(55 - 56)^2 + (54 - 56)^2 + \cdots + (4$$

We determine the test statistic, which is the
population variance, from the following equation.

$$F = \frac{\text{Estimate of the population variance based on the differences among the sample means}}{\text{Estimate of the population variance based on the variation within the samples}}$$

Our first estimate of the population variance is based on the treatments, that is, the difference *between* the means. It is 992/2. Why did we divide by 2? Recall from Chapter 4, to find a sample variance (see formula 4–5), we divide by the number of observations minus one. In this case there are three treatments, so we divide by 2. Our first estimate of the population variance is 992/2.

The variance estimate *within* the treatments is the random variation divided by the total number of observations less the number of treatments. That is 90/(12 − 3). Hence, our second estimate of the population variance is 90/9. This is actually a generalization of formula 11–3, where we pooled the sample variances from two populations.

The last step is to take the ratio of these two estimates.

$$F = \frac{992/2}{90/9} = 49.6$$

Because this ratio is quite different from 1, we can conclude that the treatment means are not the same. There is a difference in the mean yield of the three fertilizers.

The above conceptual view of ANOVA is fairly difficult to carry out. That is, the calculations can be quite tedious, particularly when the overall mean and the treatment means are not whole numbers. There are two alternatives to avoid the extensive calculations. In the following example we provide an efficient method that minimizes the calculations for solving the ANOVA problem. We could also use a spreadsheet or statistical software package. Later in the chapter we will provide such an example.

Here's another example, which shows some shortcut computational formulas and also deals with samples of different sizes.

EXAMPLE

Professor James Brunner had students in his marketing class rate his performance as Excellent, Good, Fair, or Poor. A graduate student collected the ratings and assured the students that Professor Brunner would not receive them until after course grades had been sent to the records office. The rating (i.e., the treatment) a student gave the professor was matched with his or her course grade, which could range from 0 to 100. The sample information is reported on the next page. Is there a difference in the mean score of the students in each of the four rating categories? Use the .01 significance level.

Course Grades			
Excellent	**Good**	**Fair**	**Poor**
94	75	70	68
90	68	73	70
85	77	76	72
80	83	78	65
	88	80	74
		68	65
		65	

SOLUTION

We will follow the usual five-step hypothesis-testing procedure.

Step 1: State the null hypothesis and the alternate hypothesis. The null hypothesis is that the mean scores are the same for the four ratings.

H_0: $\mu_1 = \mu_2 = \mu_3 = \mu_4$

The alternate hypothesis is that the mean scores are not all the same for the four ratings.

H_1: The mean scores are not all equal.

If the null hypothesis is not rejected, we conclude that there is no difference in the mean course grades based on the instructor ratings. If H_0 is rejected, we conclude that there is a difference in at least one pair of mean ratings, but at this point we do not know which pair or how many pairs differ.

Step 2: Select the level of significance. We selected the .01 significance level.

Step 3: Determine the test statistic. The test statistic follows the *F* distribution.

Step 4: Formulate the decision rule. To determine the decision rule, we need the critical value. The critical value for the *F* statistic is found in Appendix G. The critical values for the .05 significance level are found on the first page and the .01 significance level on the second page. To use this table we need to know the degrees of freedom in the numerator and the denominator. The degrees of freedom in the numerator equals the number of treatments, designated as *k,* minus 1. The degrees of freedom in the denominator is the total number of observations, *n,* minus the number of treatments. For this problem there are four treatments and a total of 22 observations.

Degrees of freedom in the numerator $= k - 1 = 4 - 1 = 3$

Degrees of freedom in the denominator $= n - k = 22 - 4 = 18$

Refer to Appendix G and the .01 significance level. Move horizontally across the top of the page to 3 degrees of freedom in the numerator. Then move down that column to the row with 18 degrees of freedom. The value at this intersection is 5.09. So the decision rule is to reject H_0 if the computed value of *F* exceeds 5.09.

Step 5: Select the sample, perform the calculations, and make a decision. It is convenient to summarize the calculations of the *F* statistic in an **ANOVA table.** The format for an ANOVA table is as follows.

ANOVA Table				
Source of Variation	**Sum of Squares**	**Degrees of Freedom**	**Mean Square**	***F***
Treatments	SST	$k - 1$	SST/$(k - 1)$ = MST	MST/MSE
Error	SSE	$n - k$	SSE/$(n - k)$ = MSE	
Total	SS total	$n - 1$		

There are three values, the **sum of squares,** used to compute *F*. We can determine these values by finding SS total and SST, then finding SSE by subtraction. The SS total term is the total variation, SST is the variation due to the treatments, and SSE is the variation within the treatments.

To find the value of *F*, we work our way across the table. The degrees of freedom for the numerator and the denominator are the same as those for finding the critical values of *F*. The term **mean square** is another expression for an estimate of the variance. The mean square for the treatment is SST divided by its degrees of freedom. The result is the **mean square for treatments** and is written MST. We compute the **mean square error** (MSE) similarly. We divide the SSE term by its degrees of freedom. To complete the process and find *F*, we divide MST by MSE.

We usually start the process by finding SS total. This is the sum of the squared differences between each observation and the overall mean. The formula for finding SS total is

SUM OF SQUARES TOTAL

$$\text{SS total} = \Sigma X^2 - \frac{(\Sigma X)^2}{n} \qquad [12\text{–}2]$$

where:

ΣX^2 is the X values squared and then summed.
$(\Sigma X)^2$ is the X values summed and then squared.
n is the total number of observations.

Next we determine SST, the sum of squares due to the treatments. The formula for finding SST is

SUM OF SQUARES TREATMENT

$$\text{SST} = \Sigma\left(\frac{T_c^2}{n_c}\right) - \frac{(\Sigma X)^2}{n} \qquad [12\text{–}3]$$

where:

T_c is the column total for each treatment.
n_c is the number of observations (sample size) for each treatment.

Finally we determine SSE, the sum of squares error, by subtraction. The formula is

SUM OF SQUARES ERROR

$$\text{SSE} = \text{SS total} - \text{SST} \qquad [12\text{–}4]$$

The detailed calculations for this example are shown in Table 12–2.

Statistics in Action

Have you ever waited in line for a telephone and it seemed like the person using the phone talked on and on? There is evidence that people actually talk longer on public telephones when someone is waiting. In a recent survey, researchers measured the length of time that 56 shoppers in a mall spent on the phone (1) when they were alone, (2) when a person was using the adjacent phone, and (3) when a person was using an adjacent phone and someone was waiting to use the phone. The study, using the one-way ANOVA technique, showed that the mean time using the telephone was significantly less when the person was alone.

TABLE 12–2 Calculations Necessary for Computing the Value of *F*

	Excellent		Good		Fair		Poor		Total
	X	X^2	X	X^2	X	X^2	X	X^2	
	94	8,836	75	5,625	70	4,900	68	4,624	
	90	8,100	68	4,624	73	5,329	70	4,900	
	85	7,225	77	5,929	76	5,776	72	5,184	
	80	6,400	83	6,889	78	6,084	65	4,225	
			88	7,744	80	6,400	74	5,476	
					68	4,624	65	4,225	
					65	4,225			
T_c	349		391		510		414		1,664
n_c	4		5		7		6		22
X^2		30,561		30,811		37,338		28,634	127,344

The entries for the ANOVA table are computed as follows. First, using formula 12–2, we compute the total variation:

$$\text{SS total} = \Sigma X^2 - \frac{(\Sigma X)^2}{n} = 127{,}344 - \frac{1{,}664^2}{22} = 1{,}485.09$$

Next, using formula 12–3, we compute the treatment variation.

$$\text{SST} = \Sigma\left(\frac{T_c^2}{n_c}\right) - \frac{(\Sigma X)^2}{n} = \frac{349^2}{4} + \frac{391^2}{5} + \frac{510^2}{7} + \frac{414^2}{6} - \frac{1{,}664^2}{22} = 890.68$$

Finally, by subtraction, we determine the error variation.

$$\text{SSE} = \text{SS total} - \text{SST} = 1{,}485.09 - 890.68 = 594.41$$

Inserting these values into an ANOVA table and computing the value of *F:*

Source of Variation	Sum of Squares	Degrees of Freedom	Mean Square	*F*
Treatments	890.68	3	296.89	8.99
Error	594.41	18	33.02	
Total	1,485.09	21		

The computed value of *F* is 8.99, which is greater than the critical value of 5.09, so the null hypothesis is rejected. We conclude the population means are not all equal. The mean scores are not the same in each of the four ratings groups. It is likely that the grades students earned in the course are related to the opinion they have of the overall competency and classroom performance of the instructor. At this point we can only conclude there is a difference in the treatment means. We cannot determine which treatment groups differ or how many treatment groups differ.

As you noted from the previous example, the calculations become very tedious if the number of observations in each treatment is large. Following is the MINITAB output from the student ratings example. The output is in the form of an ANOVA table.

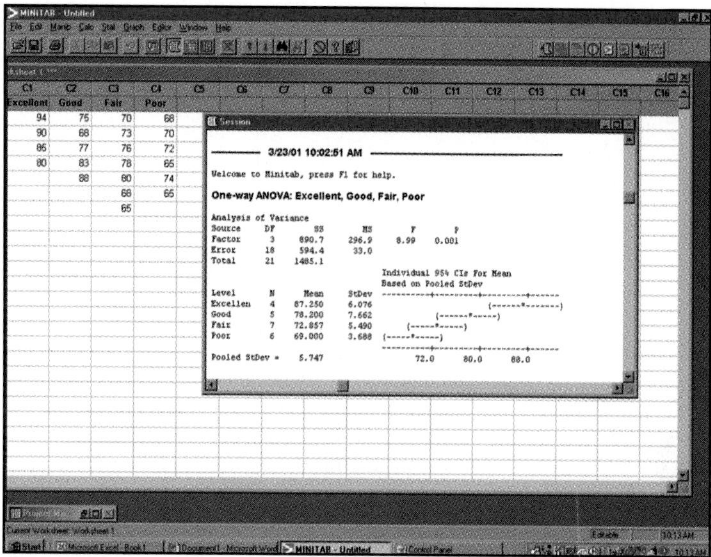

The MINITAB system uses the term *factor* instead of *treatment,* with the same intended meaning. The p-value is .001 and is located under the heading "P". How do we interpret this value? It is the probability of finding an F value to the right of 8.99 with 3 degrees of freedom in the numerator and 18 in the denominator, given that H_0 is true. So the likelihood of committing a Type I error by rejecting a true H_0 is 0.001 or .01 percent—a very small likelihood indeed!

Self-Review 12–2

Clean All is a new all-purpose cleaner being test marketed by placing displays in three different locations within various supermarkets. The number of 12-ounce bottles sold from each location within the supermarket is reported below.

Near the bread	20	15	24	18
Near the beer	12	18	10	15
With other cleaners	25	28	30	32

At the .05 significance level, is there a difference in the mean number of bottles sold at the three locations?

(a) State the null hypothesis and the alternate hypothesis.
(b) What is the decision rule?
(c) Compute the values of SS total, SST, and SSE.
(d) Develop an ANOVA table.
(e) What is your decision regarding the null hypothesis?

Exercises

7. The following is sample information. Test the hypothesis that the treatment means are equal. Use the .05 significance level.

Treatment 1	Treatment 2	Treatment 3
8	3	3
6	2	4
10	4	5
9	3	4

a. State the null hypothesis and the alternate hypotheses.
b. What is the decision rule?
c. Compute SST, SSE, and SS total.
d. Complete an ANOVA table.
e. State your decision regarding the null hypothesis.

8. The following is sample information. Test the hypothesis at the .05 significance level that the treatment means are equal.

Treatment 1	Treatment 2	Treatment 3
9	13	10
7	20	9
11	14	15
9	13	14
12		15
10		

a. State the null hypothesis and the alternate hypotheses.
b. What is the decision rule?
c. Compute SST, SSE, and SS total.
d. Complete an ANOVA table.
e. State your decision regarding the null hypothesis.

8. a. H_0: $\mu_1 = \mu_2 = \mu_3$
b. Reject if $F > 3.89$.
c. SST = 70.40 SSE = 82.53
d. $F = 5.12$
e. Reject H_0.

9. A real estate developer is considering investing in a shopping mall on the outskirts of Atlanta, Georgia. Three parcels of land are being evaluated. Of particular importance is the income in the area surrounding the proposed mall. A random sample of four families is selected near each proposed mall. Following are the sample results. At the .05 significance level, can the developer conclude there is a difference in the mean income? Use the usual five-step hypothesis testing procedure.

Southwyck Area ($000)	Franklin Park ($000)	Old Orchard ($000)
64	74	75
68	71	80
70	69	76
60	70	78

10. $F = 5.73$ Reject H_0.

10. The manager of a computer software company wishes to study the number of hours top executives spend at their computer terminals by type of industry. The manager selected a sample of five executives from each of three industries. At the .05 significance level, can she conclude there is a difference in the mean number of hours spent at a terminal per week by industry?

Banking	Retail	Insurance
12	8	10
10	8	8
10	6	6
12	8	8
10	10	10

Inferences about Pairs of Treatment Means

Suppose we carry out the ANOVA procedure and make the decision to reject the null hypothesis. This allows us to conclude that all the treatment means are not the same. Sometimes we may be satisfied with this conclusion, but in other instances we may want to know which treatment means differ. This section provides the details for such a test.

Recall that in the example regarding student opinions and grades there was a difference in the treatment means. That is, the null hypothesis was rejected and the alternate hypothesis accepted. If the student opinions do differ, the question is: Between which groups do the treatment means differ?

Several procedures are available to answer this question. The simplest is through the use of confidence intervals, that is, formula 9–2. From the computer output of the previous example (see page 427), note that the sample mean score for those students rating the instruction Excellent is 87.250, and for those rating the instruction poor it is 69.000. Thus, those students who rated the instruction Excellent seemingly earned higher grades than those who rated the instruction Poor. Is there enough disparity to justify the conclusion that there is a significant difference in the mean scores of the two groups?

The *t* distribution, described in Chapters 10 and 11, is used as the basis for this test. Recall that one of the assumptions of ANOVA is that the population variances are the same for all treatments. This common population value is the **mean square error,** or MSE, and is determined by SSE/$(n - k)$. A confidence interval for the difference between two populations is found by:

CONFIDENCE INTERVAL FOR THE DIFFERENCE IN TREATMENT MEANS	$(\bar{X}_1 - \bar{X}_2) \pm t\sqrt{\text{MSE}\left(\frac{1}{n_1} + \frac{1}{n_2}\right)}$	**[12–5]**

where:

- $\bar{X}_1$ is the mean of the first sample.
- $\bar{X}_2$ is the mean of the second sample.
- t is obtained from Appendix F. The degrees of freedom is equal to $n - k$.
- MSE is the mean square error term obtained from the ANOVA table [SSE/$(n - k)$].
- n_1 is the number of observations in the first sample.
- n_2 is the number of observations in the second sample.

How do we decide whether there is a difference in the treatment means? If the confidence interval includes zero, there is *not* a difference between the treatment means. For example, if the left endpoint of the confidence interval has a negative sign and the right endpoint has a positive sign, the two means do not differ. So if we develop a confidence interval from formula 12–5 and find the difference in the sample means was 5.00, that is, if $\bar{X}_1 - \bar{X}_2 = 5$ and $t\sqrt{\text{MSE}\left(\frac{1}{n_1} + \frac{1}{n_2}\right)} = 12$, the confidence interval would range from -7.00 up to 17.00. To put it in symbols:

$$(\bar{X}_1 - \bar{X}_2) \pm t\sqrt{\text{MSE}\left(\frac{1}{n_1} + \frac{1}{n_2}\right)} = 5.00 \pm 12.00 = -7.00 \text{ up to } 17.00$$

Note that zero is included in this interval. Therefore, we conclude that there is no significant difference in the selected treatment means.

On the other hand, if the endpoints of the confidence interval have the same sign, this indicates that the treatment means differ. For example, if $\bar{X}_1 - \bar{X}_2 = -0.35$ and $t\sqrt{\text{MSE}\left(\frac{1}{n_1} + \frac{1}{n_2}\right)} = 0.25$, the confidence interval would range from -0.60 up to -0.10.

Because −0.60 and −0.10 have the same sign, both negative, we conclude that these treatment means differ.

Using the previous student opinion example let us compute the confidence interval for the difference between the mean scores of all students who provide "Excellent" and "Poor" ratings. Assume the populations are labeled 1 and 4. With a 95 percent level of confidence, the endpoints of the confidence interval are 10.46 and 26.04.

$$(\bar{X}_1 - \bar{X}_4) \pm t\sqrt{\text{MSE}\left(\frac{1}{n_1} + \frac{1}{n_4}\right)} = (87.25 - 69.00) \pm 2.101\sqrt{33.0\left(\frac{1}{4} + \frac{1}{6}\right)}$$
$$= 18.25 \pm 7.79$$

where:

- $\bar{X}_1$ is 87.25.
- $\bar{X}_4$ is 69.00.
- t is 2.101: from Appendix F with $(n - k) = 22 - 4 = 18$ degrees of freedom.
- MSE is 33.0: from the ANOVA table with $\text{SSE}/(n - k)) = 594.4/18$.
- n_1 is 4.
- n_4 is 6.

The 95 percent confidence interval ranges from 10.46 up to 26.04. Both endpoints are positive; hence, we can conclude these treatment means differ significantly. That is, students who rated the instructor Excellent have significantly higher grades than those who rated the instructor as Poor.

Approximate results can also be obtained directly from the MINITAB output. Below is the lower portion of the output from page 427. On the left side is the number of observations, the mean, and the standard deviation for each treatment. Seven students, for example, rated the instructor as Fair. The mean course grade they earned is 72.857. The standard deviation of their scores is 5.490.

```
                                         Individual 95% CIs For Mean
                                         Based on Pooled StDev
Level       N      Mean     StDev    ---------+---------+---------+------
Excellen    4    87.250     6.076                            (------*-------)
Good        5    78.200     7.662                 (------*-----)
Fair        7    72.857     5.490          (-----*-----)
Poor        6    69.000     3.688    (-----*-----)
                                     ---------+---------+---------+------
Pooled StDev =    5.747                      72.0      80.0      88.0
```

On the right side of the printout is a confidence interval for each treatment mean. The asterisk (*) indicates the location of the treatment mean and the open parenthesis and close parenthesis, the endpoints of the confidence interval. In those instances where there is overlap (common area), the treatment means may not differ. If there is no common area in the confidence intervals, that pair of means differ.

The endpoints of a 95 percent confidence interval for the scores of students rating the instructor Fair are about 69 and 77. For students rating the instructor Poor, the endpoints of the confidence interval are about 64 and 74. There is common area in this confidence interval, so we conclude that this pair of means does not differ. In other words, there is no significant difference between the scores of students rating the instructor Fair and those rating him Poor.

There are two pairs of means that differ. The scores of students who rated the instructor Excellent differ from the scores of the students who rated the instructor Fair and those who rated the instructor Poor. There is no common area between the two pairs of confidence intervals.

We should emphasize that this investigation is a step-by-step process. The initial step is to conduct the ANOVA test. Only if the null hypothesis that the treatment means are equal is rejected should any analysis of the individual treatment means be attempted.

Self-Review 12–3

The following data are the tuition charges ($000) for a sample of private colleges in various regions of the United States. At the .05 significance level, can we conclude there is a difference in the mean tuition rates for the various regions?

Northeast ($000)	Southeast ($000)	West ($000)
10	8	7
11	9	8
12	10	6
10	8	7
12		6

(a) State the null and the alternate hypotheses.
(b) What is the decision rule?
(c) Develop an ANOVA table. What is the value of the test statistic?
(d) What is your decision regarding the null hypothesis?
(e) Could there be a significant difference between the mean tuition in the Northeast and that of the West? If so, develop a 95 percent confidence interval for that difference.

Exercises

11. Given the following sample information, test the hypothesis that the treatment means are equal at the .05 significance level.

Treatment 1	Treatment 2	Treatment 3
8	3	3
11	2	4
10	1	5
	3	4
	2	

a. State the null hypothesis and the alternate hypothesis.
b. What is the decision rule?
c. Compute SST, SSE, and SS total.
d. Complete an ANOVA table.
e. State your decision regarding the null hypothesis.
f. If H_0 is rejected, can we conclude that treatment 1 and treatment 2 differ? Use the 95 percent level of confidence.

12. Given the following sample information, test the hypothesis that the treatment means are equal at the .05 significance level.

Treatment 1	Treatment 2	Treatment 3
3	9	6
2	6	3
5	5	5
1	6	5
3	8	5
1	5	4
	4	1
	7	5
	6	
	4	

12. a. H_0: $\mu_1 = \mu_2 = \mu_3$ H_1: means not equal.
b. Reject if $F > 3.47$.
c. SST = 46.96 SSE = 53.00 SS total = 99.96
d. $F = 9.30$
e. Reject H_0.
f. 1.75 ± 1.57

a. State the null hypothesis and the alternate hypothesis.
b. What is the decision rule?
c. Compute SST, SSE, and SS total.
d. Complete an ANOVA table.
e. State your decision regarding the null hypothesis.
f. If H_0 is rejected, can we conclude that treatment 2 and treatment 3 differ? Use the 95 percent level of confidence.

13. A senior accounting major at Midsouth State University has job offers from four CPA firms. To explore the offers further, she asked a sample of recent trainees how many months each worked for the firm before receiving a raise in salary. The sample information is

Number of Months before First Raise in Salary			
CPA, Inc.	AB Intl.	Acct Ltd.	Pfisters
12	14	18	12
10	12	12	14
14	10	16	16
12	10		

At the .05 level of significance, is there a difference in the mean number of months before a raise was granted among the four CPA firms?

14. A stock analyst wants to determine whether there is a difference in the mean rate of return for three types of stock: utility, retail, and banking stocks. The following sample information is collected.

Rates of Return		
Utility	Retail	Banking
14.3	11.5	15.5
18.1	12.0	12.7
17.8	11.1	18.2
17.3	11.9	14.7
19.5	11.6	18.1
		13.2

14. a. Yes, $F = 13.09$.
b. 5.78 ± 2.48 Treatment means differ.

a. Using the .05 level of significance, is there a difference in the mean rate of return among the three types of stock?
b. Suppose the null hypothesis is rejected. Can the analyst conclude there is a difference between the mean rates of return for the utility and the retail stocks? Explain.

Two-Way Analysis of Variance

In the student ratings example, we divided the total variation into two categories: the variation between the treatments and the variation within the treatments. We also called the variation within the treatments the error or the random variation. To put it another way, we considered only two sources of variation, that due to the treatments and the random. In the student ratings example there may be other causes of variation in the student grades beside the instructor rating. These factors might include the number of hours per week the student studied, the mathematics ability of the student, or the gender of the student.

The benefit of considering other factors is that we can reduce the error variance. That is, if we can reduce the denominator of the *F* statistic (reducing the error variance or, more directly, the SSE term) the value of *F* will be larger, causing us to reject the hypothesis of equal treatment means. In other words, if we can explain more of the variation, then there is less "error." An example will clarify the reduction in the error variance.

EXAMPLE

WARTA, the Warren Area Regional Transit Authority, is expanding bus service from the suburb of Starbrick into the central business district of Warren. There are four routes being considered from Starbrick to downtown Warren: (1) via U.S. 6, (2) via the west end, (3) via the Hickory Street Bridge, and (4) via Route 59. WARTA conducted several tests to determine whether there was a difference in the mean travel times along the four routes. Because there will be many different drivers, the test was set up so each driver drove along each of the four routes. Below is the travel time, in minutes, for each driver-route combination.

	Travel Time from Starbrick to Warren (minutes)			
Driver	**U.S. 6**	**West End**	**Hickory St.**	**Rte. 59**
Deans	18	20	20	22
Snaverly	21	22	24	24
Ormson	20	23	25	23
Zollaco	25	21	28	25
Filbeck	26	24	28	25

At the .05 significance level, is there a difference in the mean travel time along the four routes? If we remove the effect of the drivers, is there a difference in the mean travel time?

SOLUTION

To begin, we conduct a test of hypothesis using a one-way ANOVA. That is, we consider only the four routes. Under this condition the variation is either due to the treatments or it is random. The null hypothesis and the alternate hypothesis for comparing the mean travel time along the four routes are:

H_0: $\mu_1 = \mu_2 = \mu_3 = \mu_4$
H_1: Not all treatment means are the same.

There are four routes, so for the numerator the degrees of freedom is $k - 1 = 4 - 1 = 3$. There are 20 observations, so the degrees of freedom in the denominator is $n - k = 20 - 4 = 16$. From Appendix G, with the .05 significance level, the critical value of F is 3.24. The decision rule is to reject the null hypothesis if the computed value of F is greater than 3.24. The details of the treatment totals and squares are reported in Table 12–3.

TABLE 12–3 Calculations Needed for a One-Way and a Two-Way ANOVA

	Travel Time from Starbrick to Warren (minutes)				
Driver	**U.S. 6**	**West End**	**Hickory St.**	**Rte. 59**	**Row Sum, B_r**
Deans	18	20	20	22	80
Snaverly	21	22	24	24	91
Ormson	20	23	25	23	91
Zollaco	25	21	28	25	99
Filbeck	26	24	28	25	103
Column total, T_c	110	110	125	119	464
Sum of squares	2,466	2,430	3,169	2,839	10,904

The entries for the ANOVA table are computed as follows. First, using formula 12–2, we determine the total variation:

$$\text{SS total} = \Sigma X^2 - \frac{(\Sigma X)^2}{n} = 10{,}904 - \frac{464^2}{20} = 139.2$$

Next, using formula 12–3, we compute the treatment variation:

$$\text{SST} = \Sigma\left(\frac{T_c^2}{n_c}\right) - \frac{(\Sigma X)^2}{n} = \frac{110^2}{5} + \frac{110^2}{5} + \frac{125^2}{5} + \frac{119^2}{5} - \frac{464^2}{20} = 32.4$$

Finally, by subtraction, we determine the error variation.

$$\text{SSE} = \text{SS total} - \text{SST} = 139.2 - 32.4 = 106.8$$

Inserting these values into an ANOVA table and computing the value of F:

Source of Variation	Sum of Squares	Degrees of Freedom	Mean Square	F
Treatments	32.4	3	10.8	1.618
Error	106.8	16	6.675	
Total	139.2	19		

Because the computed F value of 1.618 is less than the critical value of 3.24, we do not reject the null hypothesis. WARTA can conclude that there is no difference in the mean travel time along the four routes. There is no reason to select one of the routes as faster than the others.

In the above example we considered the variation due to the treatments (routes) and took all the remaining variation to be random. However, we did not set up the trials so that each of the five drivers drove along each of the four routes. If we could consider the effect of the several drivers, this would allow us to reduce the SSE term, which would lead to a larger value of *F*. The second treatment variable, the drivers in this case, is referred to as a **blocking variable.**

BLOCKING VARIABLE A second treatment variable that when included in the ANOVA analysis will have the effect of reducing the SSE term.

In this case we let the drivers be the blocking variable, and removing the effect of the drivers from the SSE term will change the *F* ratio for the treatment variable. First, we need to determine the sum of squares due to the blocks. The equation for determining the sum of squares blocks is quite similar to the equation for the sum of squares for treatments:

SUM OF SQUARES BLOCKS

$$\text{SSB} = \Sigma\left(\frac{B_t^2}{k}\right) - \frac{(\Sigma X)^2}{n} \qquad \textbf{[12–6]}$$

where B_t refers to the block total, that is, the total for the row, and k is the number of items in each block.

The same format is used in the two-way ANOVA table as in the one-way case, except there is an additional row for the blocking variable. SS total and SST are calculated as before, and SSB is found from formula 12–6. The SSE term is found by subtraction.

SUM OF SQUARES ERROR, TWO-WAY

$$\text{SSE} = \text{SS total} - \text{SST} - \text{SSB} \qquad \textbf{[12–7]}$$

The values for the various components of the ANOVA table are computed as follows.

Source of Variation	Sum of Squares	Degrees of Freedom	Mean Square	F
Treatments	SST	$k - 1$	SST/$(k - 1)$ = MST	MST/MSE
Blocks	SSB	$b - 1$	SSB/$(b - 1)$ = MSB	MSB/MSE
Error	SSE	$(k - 1)(b - 1)$	SSE/$(k - 1)(b - 1)$ = MSE	
Total	SS total	$n - 1$		

SSB is found by formula 12–6.

$$\text{SST} = \Sigma\left(\frac{B_t^2}{k}\right) - \frac{(\Sigma X)^2}{n} = \left(\frac{80^2}{4} + \frac{91^2}{4} + \frac{91^2}{4} + \frac{99^2}{4} + \frac{103^2}{4}\right) - \frac{464^2}{20} = 78.2$$

SSE is found by formula 12–7.

$$\text{SSE} = \text{SS total} - \text{SST} - \text{SSB} = 139.2 - 32.4 - 78.2 = 28.6$$

Source of Variation	(1) Sum of Squares	(2) Degrees of Freedom	(3) Mean Square (1)/(2)
Treatments	32.4	3	10.80
Blocks	78.2	4	19.550
Error	28.6	12	2.383
Total	139.2		

There is disagreement at this point. If the purpose of the blocking variable (the drivers in this example) was only to reduce the error variation, we should not conduct a test of hypothesis for the difference in block means. That is, if our goal was to reduce the MSE term, then we should not test a hypothesis regarding the blocking variable. On the other hand, we may wish to give the blocks the same status as the treatments and conduct a test of hypothesis. In the latter case, when the blocks are important enough to be considered as a second factor, we refer to this as a **two-factor experiment.** In many cases the decision is not clear. In our example we are concerned about the difference in the travel time for the different drivers, so we will conduct the test of hypothesis. The two sets of hypotheses are:

1. H_0: The treatment means are the same ($\mu_1 = \mu_2 = \mu_3 = \mu_4$).
   H_1: The treatment means are not the same.
2. H_0: The block means are the same ($\mu_1 = \mu_2 = \mu_3 = \mu_4 = \mu_5$).
   H_1: The block means are not the same.

First, we will test the hypothesis concerning the treatment means. There are $k - 1 = 4 - 1 = 3$ degrees of freedom in the numerator and $(b - 1)(k - 1) = (5 - 1)(4 - 1) = 12$ degrees of freedom in the denominator. Using the .05 significance level, the critical value of F is 3.49. The null hypothesis that the mean times for the four routes are the same is rejected if the F ratio exceeds 3.49.

$$F = \frac{\text{MST}}{\text{MSE}} = \frac{10.80}{2.383} = 4.53$$

The null hypothesis is rejected and the alternate accepted. We conclude that the mean travel time is not the same for all routes. WARTA will want to conduct some tests to determine which treatment means differ.

Next, we test to find whether the travel time is the same for the various drivers. The degrees of freedom in the numerator for blocks is $b - 1 = 5 - 1 = 4$. The degrees of freedom for the denominator are the same as before: $(b - 1)(k - 1) = (5 - 1)(4 - 1) = 12$. The null hypothesis that the block means are the same is rejected if the F ratio exceeds 3.26.

$$F = \frac{\text{MSB}}{\text{MSE}} = \frac{19.550}{2.383} = 8.20$$

The null hypothesis is rejected, and the alternate is accepted. The mean time is not the same for the various drivers. Thus, WARTA management can conclude, based on the sample results, that there is a difference in the routes and in the drivers.

The Excel spreadsheet has a two-factor ANOVA procedure. The output for the WARTA example just completed is repeated on the next page. The results are the same as reported earlier. In addition the Excel output reports the p-values. The p-value for the null hypothesis regarding the drivers is .002 and .024 for the routes. These p-values confirm the hypothesis that the null hypotheses for treatments and blocks should both be rejected using the .05 significance level.

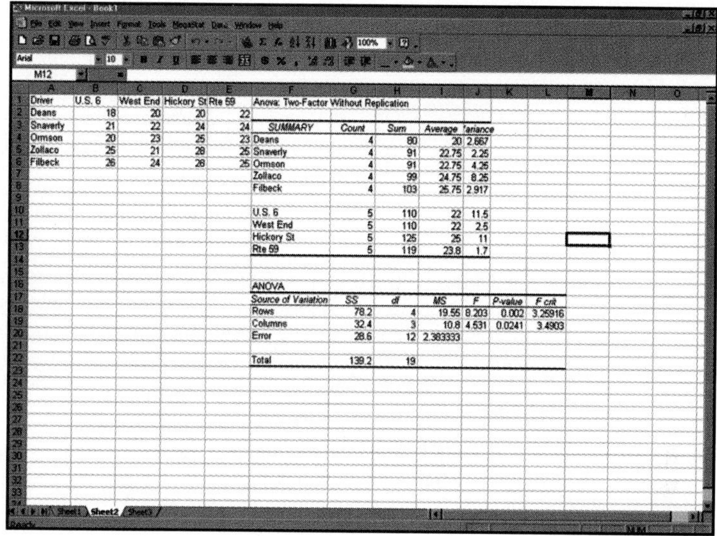

Self-Review 12–4

Rudduck Shampoo sells three shampoos, one each for dry, normal, and oily hair. Sales, in millions of dollars, for the past five months are given in the following table. Using the .05 significance level, test whether the mean sales differ for the three types of shampoo or by month.

	Sales ($ million)		
Month	**Dry**	**Normal**	**Oily**
June	7	9	12
July	11	12	14
August	13	11	8
September	8	9	7
October	9	10	13

Exercises

For exercises 15 and 16, conduct a test of hypothesis to determine whether the block and the treatment means differ. Using the .05 significance level: (a) state the null and alternate hypotheses for treatments; (b) state the decision rule for treatments; and (c) state the null and alternate hypotheses for blocks. Also, state the decision rule for blocks, then: (d) compute SST, SSB, SS total, and SSE; (e) complete an ANOVA table; and (f) give your decision regarding the two sets of hypotheses.

15. The following data are given for a two-factor ANOVA.

	Treatment	
Block	**1**	**2**
A	46	31
B	37	26
C	44	35

16. SST = 10.889
SSB = 20.222
SSE = 11.111
$F = 1.96, 3.64$
Do not reject either H_0.

16. The following data are given for a two-factor ANOVA.

Block	Treatment 1	2	3
A	12	14	8
B	9	11	9
C	7	8	8

17. The Chapin Manufacturing Company operates 24 hours a day, five days a week. The workers rotate shifts each week. Management is interested in whether there is a difference in the number of units produced when the employees work on various shifts. A sample of five workers is selected and their output recorded on each shift. At the .05 significance level, can we conclude there is a difference in the mean production rate by shift or by employee?

	Units Produced		
Employee	Day	Afternoon	Night
Skaff	31	25	35
Lum	33	26	33
Clark	28	24	30
Treece	30	29	28
Morgan	28	26	27

18. $F = 1.97$, treatments; $F = 1.29$, blocks. Do not reject either H_0.

18. There are three hospitals in the Tulsa, Oklahoma, area. The following data show the number of outpatient surgeries performed at each hospital last week. At the .05 significance level, can we conclude there is a difference in the mean number of surgeries performed by hospital or by day of the week?

	Number of Surgeries Performed		
Day	St. Luke's	St. Vincent	Mercy
Monday	14	18	24
Tuesday	20	24	14
Wednesday	16	22	14
Thursday	18	20	22
Friday	20	28	24

Chapter Outline

I. The characteristics of the *F* distribution are:
- **A.** It is continuous.
- **B.** Its values cannot be negative.
- **C.** It is positively skewed.
- **D.** There is a family of *F* distributions. Each time the degrees of freedom in either the numerator or the denominator changes, a new distribution is created.

II. The *F* distribution is used to test whether two population variances are the same.
- **A.** The sampled populations must be normal.
- **B.** The larger of the two sample variances is placed in the numerator, forcing the ratio to be at least 1.00.

C. The value of F is computed using the following equation:

$$F = \frac{s_1^2}{s_2^2} \quad \textbf{[12–1]}$$

III. A one-way ANOVA is used to compare several treatment means.

A. A treatment is a source of variation.

B. The assumptions underlying ANOVA are:

1. The samples are from populations which follow the normal distribution.
2. The populations have equal standard deviations.
3. The samples are independent.

C. The information for finding the value of F is summarized in an ANOVA table.

1. The formula for SS total, the sum of squares total, is:

$$\text{SS total} = \Sigma X^2 - \frac{(\Sigma X)^2}{n} \quad \textbf{[12–2]}$$

2. The formula for the SST, the sum of squares treatment, is:

$$\text{SST} = \Sigma\left(\frac{T_c^2}{n_c}\right) - \frac{(\Sigma X)^2}{n} \quad \textbf{[12–3]}$$

3. The SSE, the sum of squares error, is found by subtraction.

$$\text{SSE} = \text{SS total} - \text{SST} \quad \textbf{[12–4]}$$

4. This information is summarized in the following table and the value of F determined.

Source of Variation	Sum of Squares	Degrees of Freedom	Mean Square	F
Treatments	SST	$k - 1$	SST/$(k - 1)$ = MST	MST/MSE
Error	SSE	$n - k$	SSE/$(n - k)$ = MSE	
Total	SS total	$n - 1$		

IV. If a null hypothesis of equal treatment means is rejected, we can identify the pairs that differ from the following confidence interval.

$$(\bar{X}_1 - \bar{X}_2) \pm t\sqrt{\text{MSE}\left(\frac{1}{n_1} + \frac{1}{n_2}\right)} \quad \textbf{[12–5]}$$

V. In a two-way ANOVA we consider a second treatment variable.

A. The second treatment variable is called the blocking variable.

B. It is determined using the following equation:

$$\text{SSB} = \Sigma\left(\frac{B_t^2}{k}\right) - \frac{(\Sigma X)^2}{n} \quad \textbf{[12–6]}$$

C. The SSE term, or sum of squares error, is found from the following equation.

$$\text{SSE} = \text{SS total} - \text{SST} - \text{SSB} \quad \textbf{[12–7]}$$

D. The F statistics for the treatment variable and the blocking variable are determined in the following table.

Source of Variation	Sum of Squares	Degrees of Freedom	Mean Square	F
Treatments	SST	$k - 1$	SST/$(k - 1)$ = MST	MST/MSE
Blocks	SSB	$b - 1$	SSB/$(b - 1)$ = MSB	MSB/MSE
Error	SSE	$(k - 1)(b - 1)$	SSE/$(k - 1)(b - 1)$ = MSE	
Total	SS total	$n - 1$		

Pronunciation Key

SYMBOL	MEANING	PRONUNCIATION
SS total	Sum of squares total	*S S total*
SST	Sum of squares treatment	*S S T*
SSE	Sum of squares error	*S S E*
T_c^2	Column totals squared	*T sub c squared*
n_c	Number of observations in each treatment	*n sub c*
MSE	Mean square error	*M S E*
SSB	Block sum of squares	*S S B*

Chapter Exercises

19. A real estate agent in the coastal area of the Carolinas wants to compare the variation in the selling price of homes on the oceanfront with those one to three blocks from the ocean. A sample of 21 oceanfront homes sold within the last year revealed the standard deviation of the selling prices was $45,600. A sample of 18 homes, also sold within the last year, that were one to three blocks from the ocean revealed that the standard deviation was $21,330. At the .01 significance level, can we conclude that there is more variation in the selling prices of the oceanfront homes?

20. $F = 3.36$ Reject H_0.

20. A computer manufacturer is about to unveil a new, faster personal computer. The new machine clearly is faster, but initial tests indicate there is more variation in the processing time. The processing time depends on the particular program being run, the amount of input data, and the amount of output. A sample of 16 computer runs, covering a range of production jobs, showed that the standard deviation of the processing time was 22 (hundredths of a second) for the new machine and 12 (hundredths of a second) for the current machine. At the .05 significance level can we conclude that there is more variation in the processing time of the new machine?

21. There are two Chevrolet dealers in Jamestown, New York. The mean weekly sales at Sharkey Chevy and Dave White Chevrolet are about the same. However, Tom Sharkey, the owner of Sharkey Chevy, believes his sales are more consistent. Below is the number of new cars sold at Sharkey in the last seven months and for the last eight months at Dave White. Do you agree with Mr. Sharkey? Use the .01 significance level.

Sharkey	98	78	54	57	68	64	70	
Dave White	75	81	81	30	82	46	58	101

22. a. See IM. b. $F > 3.89$ c. $F = 4.0$ d. Reject H_0.

22. Random samples of five were selected from each of three populations. The sum of squares total was 100. The sum of squares due to the treatments was 40.
a. Set up the null hypothesis and the alternate hypothesis.
b. What is the decision rule? Use the .05 significance level.
c. Complete the ANOVA table. What is the value of F?
d. What is your decision regarding the null hypothesis?

23. In an ANOVA table MSE was equal to 10. Random samples of six were selected from each of four populations, where the sum of squares total was 250.
a. Set up the null hypothesis and the alternate hypothesis.
b. What is the decision rule? Use the .05 significance level.
c. Complete the ANOVA table. What is the value of F?
d. What is your decision regarding the null hypothesis?

24. The following is a partial ANOVA table.

Source	Sum of Squares	*df*	Mean Square	*F*
Treatment		2		
Error			20	
Total	500	11		

24. **a.** 3
b. 12
c. 4.26
d. See IM.
e. Reject H_0.

Complete the table and answer the following questions. Use the .05 significance level.

a. How many treatments are there?
b. What is the total sample size?
c. What is the critical value of F?
d. Write out the null and alternate hypotheses.
e. What is your conclusion regarding the null hypothesis?

25. A consumer organization wants to know whether there is a difference in the price of a particular toy at three different types of stores. The price of the toy was checked in a sample of five discount stores, five variety stores, and five department stores. The results are shown below. Use the .05 significance level.

Discount	Variety	Department
$12	$15	$19
13	17	17
14	14	16
12	18	20
15	17	19

26. H_0: $\mu_1 = \mu_2 = \mu_3$
H_1: Not all means are equal.
Reject H_0 if $F > 3.89$.
SS total = 37.73.
SST = 26.13
SSE = 11.60
$F = 13.52$
Reject H_0.

26. A physician who specializes in weight control has three different diets she recommends. As an experiment, she randomly selected 15 patients and then assigned 5 to each diet. After three weeks the following weight losses, in pounds, were noted. At the .05 significance level, can she conclude that there is a difference in the mean amount of weight loss among the three diets?

Plan A	Plan B	Plan C
5	6	7
7	7	8
4	7	9
5	5	8
4	6	9

27. The City of Maumee comprises four districts. Chief of police Andy North wants to determine whether there is a difference in the mean number of crimes committed among the four districts. He recorded the number of crimes reported in each district for a sample of six days. At the .05 significance level, can the chief of police conclude there is a difference in the mean number of crimes?

Number of Crimes			
Rec Center	Key Street	Monclova	Whitehouse
13	21	12	16
15	13	14	17
14	18	15	18
15	19	13	15
14	18	12	20
15	19	15	18

28. a. $F = 5.09$ Reject H_0.
b. Limits are 0.68 and 9.10; means differ.

28. The personnel director of Cander Machine Products is investigating "perfectionism" on the job. A test designed to measure perfectionism was administered to a random sample of 18 employees. The scores ranged from 20 to about 40. One of the facets of the study involved the early background of each employee. Did the employee come from a rural background, a small city, or a large city? The scores are:

Rural Area	Small Urban Area	Large Urban Area
35	28	24
30	24	28
36	25	26
38	30	30
29	32	34
34	28	
31		

a. At the .05 level, can it be concluded that there is a difference in the three mean scores?
b. If the null hypothesis is rejected, can you state that the mean score of those with a rural background is different from the score of those with a large-city background?

29. It can be shown that when only two treatments are involved, ANOVA and the Student t test (Chapter 10) result in the same conclusions. Also, $t^2 = F$. As an example, suppose that 14 randomly selected students were divided into two groups, one consisting of 6 students and the other of 8. One group was taught using a combination of lecture and programmed instruction, the other using a combination of lecture and television. At the end of the course, each group was given a 50-item test. The following is a list of the number correct for each of the two groups.

Lecture and Programmed Instruction	Lecture and Television
19	32
17	28
23	31
22	26
17	23
16	24
	27
	25

a. Using analysis of variance techniques, test H_0 that the two mean test scores are equal; $\alpha = .05$.
b. Using the t test from Chapter 10, compute t.
c. Interpret the results.

30. $F = 10.18$ Reject H_0. See IM.

30. One reads that a business school graduate with an undergraduate degree earns more than a high school graduate with no additional education, and a person with a master's degree or a doctorate earns even more. To test this, a random sample of 25 executives from companies with assets over $1 million was selected. Their incomes, classified by highest level of education, follow.

Income ($ thousands)		
High School or Less	**Undergraduate Degree**	**Master's Degree or More**
45	49	51
47	57	73
53	85	82
62	73	59
39	81	94
43	84	89
54	89	89
	92	95
	62	73

Test at the .05 level of significance that there is no difference in the arithmetic mean salaries of the three groups. If the null hypothesis is rejected, conduct further tests to determine which groups differ.

31. Shank's, Inc., a nationwide advertising firm, wants to know whether the size of an advertisement and the color of the advertisement make a difference in the response of magazine readers. A random sample of readers is shown ads of four different colors and three different sizes. Each reader is asked to give the particular combination of size and color a rating between 1 and 10. Assume that the ratings are approximately normally distributed. The rating for each combination is shown in the following table (for example, the rating for a small red ad is 2).

	Color of Ad			
Size of Ad	**Red**	**Blue**	**Orange**	**Green**
Small	2	3	3	8
Medium	3	5	6	7
Large	6	7	8	8

Is there a difference in the effectiveness of an advertisement by color and by size? Use the .05 level of significance.

32. There are four McBurger restaurants in the Columbus, Georgia, area. The numbers of burgers sold at the respective restaurants for each of the last six weeks are shown below. At the .05 significance level, is there a difference in the mean number sold among the four restaurants, when the factor of week is considered?

	Restaurant			
Week	**Metro**	**Interstate**	**University**	**River**
1	124	160	320	190
2	234	220	340	230
3	430	290	290	240
4	105	245	310	170
5	240	205	280	180
6	310	260	270	205

a. Is there a difference in the treatment means?
b. Is there a difference in the block means?

32. a. Fail to reject H_0. $F = 2.865$.
b. Fail to reject H_0. $F = 1.93$.

33. The city of Tucson, Arizona, employs people to assess the value of homes for the purpose of establishing real estate tax. The city manager routinely sends each assessor to five homes and then compares the results. The information is given below, in thousands of dollars. Can we conclude that there is a difference in the assessors, at $\alpha = .05$?

	Assessor			
Home	**Zawodny**	**Norman**	**Cingle**	**Holiday**
A	$53.0	$55.0	$49.0	$45.0
B	50.0	51.0	52.0	53.0
C	48.0	52.0	47.0	53.0
D	70.0	68.0	65.0	64.0
E	84.0	89.0	92.0	86.0

a. Is there a difference in the treatment means?
b. Is there a difference in the block means?

34. Martin Motors has in stock three cars of the same make and model. The president would like to compare the gas consumption of the three cars (labeled car A, car B, and car C) using four different types of gasoline. For each trial, a gallon of gasoline was added to an empty tank, and the car was driven until it ran out of gas. The following table shows the number of miles driven in each trial.

	Distance (miles)		
Types of Gasoline	**Car A**	**Car B**	**Car C**
Regular	22.4	20.8	21.5
Super regular	17.0	19.4	20.7
Unleaded	19.2	20.2	21.2
Premium unleaded	20.3	18.6	20.4

34. a. $F = 2.41$, no difference.
b. $F = 1.39$, no difference.

Using the .05 level of significance:
a. Is there a difference among types of gasoline?
b. Is there a difference in the cars?

35. A research firm wants to compare the miles per gallon of unleaded regular, mid-grade, and super premium gasolines. Because of differences in the performance of different automobiles, seven different automobiles were selected and treated as blocks. Therefore, each brand of gasoline was tested with each type of automobile. The results of the trials, in miles per gallon, are shown in the following table. At the .05 significance level, is there a difference in the gasolines and automobiles?

Automobile	Regular	Mid-grade	Super Premium
1	21	23	26
2	23	22	25
3	24	25	27
4	24	24	26
5	26	26	30
6	26	24	27
7	28	27	32

36. H_0 is rejected for items, $F = 405.62$. H_0 is not rejected for store, $F = 3.10$.

36. Three supermarket chains in the Denver area each claim to have the lowest overall prices. As part of an investigative study on supermarket advertising, the *Denver Daily News* conducted a study. First, a random sample of nine grocery items was selected. Next, the price of each selected item was checked at each of the three chains on the same day. At the .05 significance level, is there a difference in the mean prices at the supermarkets and for the items?

Item	Super$	Ralph's	Lowblaws
1	$1.12	$1.02	$1.07
2	1.14	1.10	1.21
3	1.72	1.97	2.08
4	2.22	2.09	2.32
5	2.40	2.10	2.30
6	4.04	4.32	4.15
7	5.05	4.95	5.05
8	4.68	4.13	4.67
9	5.52	5.46	5.86

37. Listed below are the weights (in grams) of a sample of M&M's Plain candies, classified according to color. Use a statistical software system to determine whether there is a difference in the mean weights of candies of different colors. Use the .05 significance level.

Red	Orange	Yellow	Brown	Tan	Green
0.946	0.902	0.929	0.896	0.845	0.935
1.107	0.943	0.960	0.888	0.909	0.903
0.913	0.916	0.938	0.906	0.873	0.865
0.904	0.910	0.933	0.941	0.902	0.822
0.926	0.903	0.932	0.838	0.956	0.871
0.926	0.901	0.899	0.892	0.959	0.905
1.006	0.919	0.907	0.905	0.916	0.905
0.914	0.901	0.906	0.824	0.822	0.852
0.922	0.930	0.930	0.908		0.965
1.052	0.883	0.952	0.833		0.898
0.903		0.939			
0.895		0.940			
		0.882			
		0.906			

38. There are four radio stations in Midland. The stations have different formats (hard rock, classical, country/western, and easy listening), but each is concerned with the number of minutes of music played per hour. From a sample of 10 hours from each station, the following sample means were offered.

$$\bar{X}_1 = 51.43 \quad \bar{X}_2 = 44.64 \quad \bar{X}_3 = 47.2 \quad \bar{X}_4 = 50.85$$

$$\text{SS total} = 650.75$$

a. Determine SST.
b. Determine SSE.
c. Complete an ANOVA table.
d. At the .05 significance level, is there a difference in the treatment means?
e. Is there a difference in the mean amount of music time between station 1 and station 4? Use the .05 significance level.

38. a. SST = 300.645
b. SSE = 350.105
c. $F = 10.304$
d. Reject H_0.
e. Means do not differ.

exercises.com

WWW

39. Many real estate companies and rental agencies now publish their listings on the Web. One example is the Dunes Realty Company, located in Garden City Beach, South Carolina. Go to their Website, http://www.dunes.com, select **Cottage Search,** then indicate 5 bedroom, accommodations for 14 people, second row (this means it is across the street from the beach), no pool or floating dock, select a period in July and August, indicate that you are willing to spend $5,000 per week, and then click on **Search the Cottages.** The output should include details on the cottages that met your criteria. At the .05 significance level, is there a difference in the mean rental prices for the different number of bedrooms? (You may want to combine some of the larger homes, such as 8 or more bedrooms.) Which pairs of means differ?

40. Answers will vary.

40. The percentages of quarterly changes in the gross domestic product for 20 countries are available at the following site: http://www.oecd.org/std/qnagdp/qnagdp.htm. Copy the data for Germany, Japan, and the United States into three columns in MINITAB or Excel. Perform an ANOVA to see whether there is a difference in the means. What can you conclude?

Computer Data Exercises

41. Refer to the Real Estate data, which reports information on the homes sold in the Venice, Florida, area last year.

a. At the .02 significance level, is there a difference in the variability of the selling prices of the homes that have a pool versus those that do not have a pool?

b. At the .02 significance level, is there a difference in the variability of the selling prices of the homes with an attached garage versus those that do not have an attached garage?

c. At the .05 significance level, is there a difference in the mean selling price of the homes among the five townships?

42. a. $F = 1.074$ Do not reject. b. $F = 3.67$ Reject H_0. c. $F = 1.55$ Do not reject. d. $F = 14.73$ Reject H_0.

42. Refer to the Baseball 2000 data, which reports information on the 30 Major League Baseball teams for the 2000 season.

a. At the .10 significance level, is there a difference in the variation of the number of stolen bases among the teams that play their home games on natural grass versus on artificial turf?

b. Create a variable that classifies a team's total attendance into three groups: less than 2.0 (million), 2.0 up to 3.0, and 3.0 or more. At the .05 significance level, is there a difference in the mean number of games won among the three groups?

c. Using the same attendance variable developed in part (b), is there a difference in the mean team batting average?

d. Using the same attendance variable developed in part (b), is there a difference in the mean salary of the three groups?

43. Refer to OECD data, which reports information on census, economic, and business data for 29 countries.

a. Categorize the 29 countries, indicating whether they are in Europe, North America, or the Far East. At the .05 significance level, is there a difference in the mean percent of the population over 65 years of age?

b. Use the same three categories developed in part (a). Divide the gross national product by the population to create a new variable. This variable shows the per capita GNP. At the .05 significance level, is there a difference in the mean of this variable by geographic region?

44. Refer to Schools data, which reports information on 94 school districts in northwest Ohio.

44. a. $F = 0.98$ Do not reject.

a. Create a variable related to the size of the school district. The three groups are: (1) small (less than 1,000 students), (2) medium (1,000 up to 3,000 students), and (3) large (more than 3,000 students). Is there a difference in the mean amount spent on instruction for these three groups? If the null hypothesis is rejected, determine which pair or pairs of means differ.

b. $F = 25.10$ Reject H_0.

b. Using the size variable created in part (a), is there a difference in the means of the salaries of the three groups? Use the .05 significance level. If the null hypothesis is rejected, determine which pair or pairs of means differ.

Computer Commands

1. The Excel commands for the test of variances on page 418 are:
   a. Enter the data for U.S. 25 in column A and for I-75 in column B. Label the two columns.
   b. Click on **Tools**, **Data Analysis**, select **F-Test: Two-Sample for Variances,** and click **OK**.
   c. The range of the first variable is *A1:A8* and *B1:B9* for the second, click on **Labels,** select *D1* for the output range, and click **OK.**

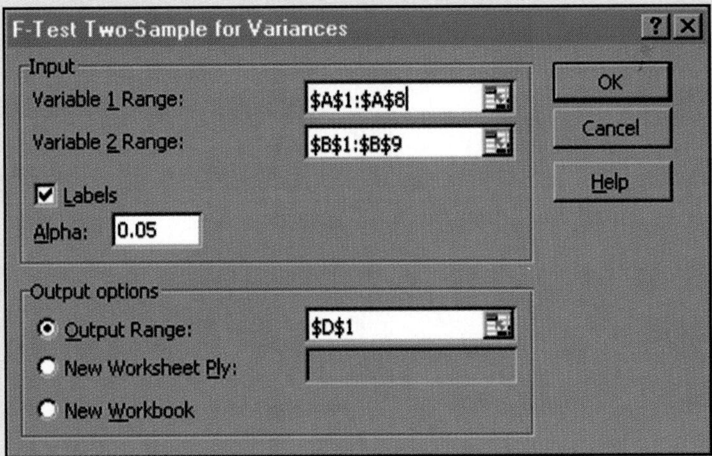

2. The MINITAB commands for the one-way ANOVA on page 427 are:
   a. Input the data into four columns and identify the columns as *Excellent, Good, Fair,* and *Poor.*
   b. Select **Stat**, **ANOVA**, and **Oneway (Unstacked)** and click **OK.**

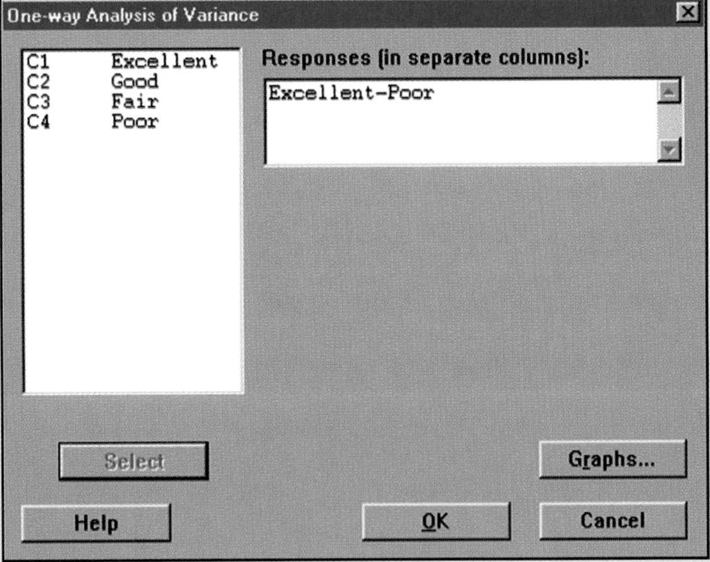

3. The Excel commands for the two-way ANOVA on page 437 are:
   a. In the first row of the first column write the word *Drivers,* then list the five drivers in the first column. In the first row of the next four columns enter the name of the routes. Enter the data under each route name.
   b. Select **Tools**, **Data Analysis**, and **ANOVA: Two-Factor Without Replication,** and then click **OK**.
   c. In the dialog box the **Input Range** is *A1:E6*, click on **Labels**, select *A10* for **Output Range**, and then click **OK**.

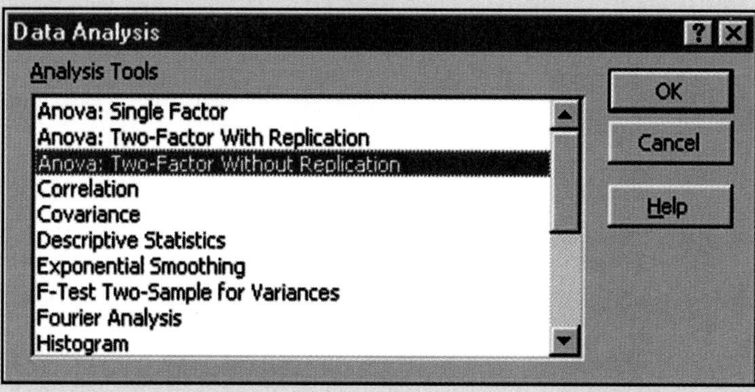

Chapter 12 Answers to Self-Review

12–1 Let Mark's assemblies be population 1, then H_0: $\sigma_1^2 \leq \sigma_2^2$; H_1: $\sigma_1^2 > \sigma_2^2$; $df_1 = 10 - 1 = 9$; and df_2 also equals 9. H_0 is rejected if $F > 3.18$.

$$F = \frac{(2.0)^2}{(1.5)^2} = 1.78$$

H_0 is not rejected. The variation is the same for both employees.

12–2 **(a)** H_0: $\mu_1 = \mu_2 = \mu_3$
H_1: At least one treatment mean is different.

(b) Reject H_0 if $F > 4.26$

(c) $\text{SS total} = 5{,}651 - \frac{(247)^2}{12} = 566.92$

$$\text{SST} = \frac{(77)^2}{4} + \frac{(55)^2}{4} + \frac{(115)^2}{4} - \frac{(247)^2}{12}$$

$$= 460.67$$

$$\text{SSE} = 566.92 - 460.67 = 106.25$$

(d)

Source	Sum of Squares	Degrees of Freedom	Mean Square	*F*
Treatment	460.67	2	230.335	19.510
Error	106.25	9	11.806	

(e) H_0 is rejected. There is a difference in the mean number of bottles sold at the various locations.

12–3 **(a)** H_0: $\mu_1 = \mu_2 = \mu_3$
H_1: Not all means are equal.

(b) H_0 is rejected if $F > 3.98$.

(c) $\text{SS total} = 1{,}152 - \frac{(124)^2}{14} = 53.71$

$$\text{SST} = \frac{(55)^2}{5} + \frac{(35)^2}{4} + \frac{(34)^2}{5} - \frac{(124)^2}{14} = 44.16$$

$$\text{SSE} = 53.71 - 44.16 = 9.55$$

Source	Sum of Squares	*df*	Mean Square	*F*
Treatment	44.16	2	22.08	25.43
Error	9.55	11	0.8682	
Total	53.71	13		

(d) H_0 is rejected. The treatment means differ.

(e) $(11.0 - 6.8) \pm 2.201\sqrt{0.8682(\frac{1}{5} + \frac{1}{5})} =$
$4.2 \pm 1.30 = 2.90$ and 5.50

These treatment means differ because both endpoints of the confidence interval are of the same sign — positive in this problem.

12–4 For types:

H_0: $\mu_1 = \mu_2 = \mu_3$
H_1: The treatment means are not equal.

Reject H_0 if $F > 4.46$.
For months:

H_0: $\mu_1 = \mu_2 = \mu_3 = \mu_4 = \mu_5$
H_1: The block means are not equal.

Reject H_0 if $F > 3.84$.

The analysis of variance table is as follows:

Source:	*df*	SS	MS	*F*
Types	2	3.60	1.80	0.39
Months	4	31.73	7.93	1.71
Error	8	37.07	4.63	
Total	14	72.40		

The null hypotheses cannot be rejected for either types or months. There is no difference in the mean sales among types or months.

A Review of Chapters 10–12

This section is a review of the major concepts and terms introduced in Chapters 10, 11, and 12. Chapter 10 began our study of hypothesis testing. A hypothesis is a statement about the value of a population parameter. In statistical hypothesis testing, we begin by making a statement about the value of the population parameter in the null hypothesis. We establish the null hypothesis for the purpose of testing. When we complete the testing, our decision is either to reject or fail to reject the null hypothesis. If we reject the null hypothesis, we conclude that the alternate hypothesis is true. The alternate hypothesis is accepted only if we show that the null hypothesis is false. We also refer to the alternate hypothesis as the research hypothesis. Most of the time we want to prove the alternate hypothesis.

In Chapter 10 we selected random samples from a single population and tested whether it was reasonable that the population parameter under study equals a given value. For example, we wish to investigate whether the mean tenure time of those holding the position of CEO in large firms is 12 years. We select a sample of CEOs, compute the sample mean, and compare the mean of the sample to the population. The single population under consideration is the CEOs of large firms. We described methods for conducting the test when the population standard deviation was available, when the sample was large (usually 30 or more), and when the sample was small. Also, in Chapter 10 we conducted tests of hypothesis about a population proportion. A proportion is the fraction of individuals or objects possessing a certain characteristic. For example, industry records indicate that 70 percent of gasoline sales for automobiles are for the regular grade of gasoline. A sample of the 100 sales from last month at the Pantry in Conway revealed 76 were for the regular grade. Can the owners conclude that more than 70 percent of their customers purchase the regular grade?

In Chapter 11 we extended the idea of hypothesis testing to comparing whether two independent random samples came from the same or equal populations. For example, St. Mathews Hospital operates an urgent care facility on both the north and south sides of Ft. Wayne, Indiana. The research question is: Is the mean waiting time for patients visiting the two facilities the same? To investigate, we select a random sample from each of the facilities and compute the sample means. We test the null hypothesis that the mean waiting time is the same at the two facilities. The alternate hypothesis is that the mean waiting time is not the same for the two facilities. If both samples are at least 30, then we use the z distribution as the distribution of the test statistic. If one of the samples is less than 30, the test statistic follows the t.

Our discussion in Chapter 11 also concerned dependent samples. For *dependent* samples, we applied the *paired difference test.* The test statistic is the t distribution. One typical paired sample problem calls for recording an individual's blood pressure before administering medication and then again afterward in order to evaluate the effectiveness of the medication. We also considered the case of testing two population proportions. For example, the production manager wished to compare the proportion of defects on the day shift with that of the second shift.

Chapter 11 dealt with the difference between two population means. Chapter 12 presented tests for variances and a procedure called the *analysis of variance,* or *ANOVA,* used to simultaneously determine whether several independent normal populations have the same mean. This is accomplished by comparing the variances of the random samples selected from these populations. We apply the usual hypothesis-testing procedure, but we use the F distribution as the test statistic. Often the calculations are tedious, so a software package is recommended.

As an example of the analysis of variance, a test could be conducted to find whether there is any difference in effectiveness among five fertilizers on the weight of popcorn ears. This type of analysis is referred to as *one-factor ANOVA* because we are able to draw conclusions about only one factor, called a *treatment.* If we want to draw conclusions about the simultaneous effects of more than one factor or variable, the *two-factor ANOVA* technique is applied. Both the one-factor and two-factor tests use the *F distribution* as the distribution of the test statistic. The F distribution is also the distribution of the test statistic used to find whether one normal population has more variation than another.

Glossary

Chapter 10

Alpha The probability of a Type I error. Its symbol is the Greek letter α.

Alternate hypothesis The conclusion we accept when we demonstrate that the null hypothesis is false. It is also called the research hypothesis.

Critical value A value that is the dividing point between the region where the null hypothesis is not rejected and the region where it is rejected. For a one-tailed test, there is only one critical value, such as 1.65. For a two-tailed test, there are two critical values, one in each tail, such as −1.96 and +1.96.
Degrees of freedom The number of items in a sample that are free to vary. Suppose there are two items in a sample, and we know the mean. We are free to specify only one of the two values, because the other value is automatically determined (since the two values total twice the mean). Example: If the mean is $6, we are free to choose only one value. Choosing $4 makes the other value $8 because $4 + $8 = 2($6). So there is 1 degree of freedom in this illustration. We can determine the degrees of freedom by $n - 1 = 2 - 1 = 1$. If n is 4, then there are 3 degrees of freedom, found by $n - 1 = 4 - 1 = 3$.
Hypothesis A statement about the value of a population parameter. Examples: 40.7 percent of all persons 65 years old and older live alone. The mean number of people in a car is 1.33.
Hypothesis testing A statistical procedure, based on sample evidence and probability theory, used to determine whether the statement about the population parameter is a reasonable statement.
One-tailed test Used when the alternate hypothesis states a direction, such as H_1: $\mu > 40$. Here the rejection region is only in one tail (the right tail).
Proportion A fraction or percentage of a sample or a population having a particular trait. If 5 out of 50 in a sample liked a new cereal, the proportion is 5/50, or .10.
***p*-value** The probability of computing a value of the test statistic at least as extreme as the one found in the sample data when the null hypothesis is true.
Two-tailed test Used when the alternate hypothesis does not state a direction, such H_1: $\mu \neq 75$, read "the population mean is not equal to 75." There is a region of rejection in each tail.
Type I error Occurs when a true H_0 is rejected.
Type II error Occurs when a false H_0 is accepted.

Chapter 11

Dependent samples Dependent samples are characterized by a measurement, then some type of intervention, followed by another measurement. Paired samples are also dependent because the same individual or item is a member of both samples. Example: Ten participants in a marathon were weighed prior to and after competing in the race. We wish to study the mean amount of weight loss.
Independent samples The samples chosen at random are not related to each other. We wish to study the mean age of the inmates at the Auburn and Allegheny prisons. We select a random sample of 28 inmates from the Auburn prison and a sample of 19 inmates at Allegheny prison. A person cannot be an inmate in both prisons. The samples are independent, that is, unrelated.
Pooled estimate of the population variance A weighted average of s_1^2 and s_2^2 used to estimate the common variance, σ^2, when using small samples to test the difference between two population means.
***t* distribution** Investigated and reported by William S. Gossett in 1908 and published under the pseudonym *Student.* It is similar to the standard normal distribution presented in Chapter 7. The major characteristics of *t* are:

1. It is a continuous distribution.
2. It can assume values between minus infinity and plus infinity.
3. It is symmetrical about its mean of zero. However, it is more spread out and flatter at the apex than the standard normal distribution.
4. It approaches the standard normal distribution as *n* gets larger.
5. There is a family of *t* distributions. One *t* distribution exists for a sample of 15 observations, another for 25, and so on.

Chapter 12

Analysis of variance (ANOVA) A technique used to test simultaneously whether the means of several populations are equal. It uses the *F* distribution as the distribution of the test statistic.
Block A second source of variation, in addition to treatments.
***F* distribution** It is used as the test statistic for ANOVA problems, as well as others. The major characteristics of the *F* distribution are:

1. It is never negative.
2. It is a continuous distribution approaching the *X*-axis but never touching it.
3. It is positively skewed.
4. It is based on two sets of degrees of freedom.
5. Like the *t* distribution, there is a "family" of *F* distributions. There is one distribution for 17 degrees of freedom in the numerator and 9 degrees of freedom in the denominator, there is another *F* distribution for 7 degrees of freedom in the numerator and 12 degrees of freedom in the denominator, and so on.

Exercises

Part I Multiple Choice

1. In a one-tailed test using the *z* distribution as the test statistic and the .01 significance level, the critical value is either
   a. −1.96 or +1.96.
   b. −1.65 or +1.65.
   c. −2.58 or +2.58.
   d. 0 or 1.
   e. None of these is correct.

2. e

2. A Type II error is committed if we:
   a. Reject a true null hypothesis.
   b. Accept a true alternate hypothesis.
   c. Reject a true alternate hypothesis.
   d. Accept both the null and alternate hypotheses at the same time.
   e. None of these is correct.

3. The hypotheses are H_0: $\mu = 240$ pounds of pressure and H_1: $\mu \neq 240$ pounds of pressure.
   a. A one-tailed test is being applied.
   b. A two-tailed test is being applied.
   c. A three-tailed test is being applied.
   d. The wrong test is being applied.
   e. None of these is correct.

4. a

4. The .01 significance level is used in an experiment, and a one-tailed test with the rejection region in the lower tail is applied. Computed *z* is −1.8. This indicates:
   a. H_0 should not be rejected.
   b. We should reject H_0 and accept H_1
   c. We should take a larger sample.
   d. We should have used the .05 level of significance.
   e. None of these is correct.

5. b

5. The test statistic for testing a hypothesis for small sample means when the population standard deviation is not known is:
   a. *z*. **b.** *t*. **c.** *F*. **d.** χ^2.

6. We want to test a hypothesis for the difference between two population means. The null and alternate hypotheses are stated as

$$H_0: \mu_1 = \mu_2$$
$$H_1: \mu_1 \neq \mu_2$$

   a. A left-tailed test should be applied.
   b. A two-tailed test should be applied.
   c. A right-tailed test should be applied.
   d. We cannot determine whether a left-, right-, or two-tailed test should be applied based on the information given.
   e. None of these is correct.

7. a

7. The *F* distribution:
   a. Cannot be negative.
   b. Cannot be positive.
   c. Is the same as the *t* distribution.
   d. Is the same as the *z* distribution.
   e. None of these is correct.

8. As the sample size increases, the *t* distribution approaches:
   a. ANOVA.
   b. The standard normal or z distribution.

c. The Poisson distribution.
d. Zero.
e. None of these is correct.

9. d

9. To conduct a paired difference test, the samples must be:
a. Infinitely large.
b. Equal to ANOVA.
c. Independent.
d. Dependent.
e. None of these is correct.

10. c

10. An ANOVA test was conducted with respect to the population mean. The null hypothesis was rejected. This indicates
a. There were too many degrees of freedom.
b. There is no difference between the population means.
c. There is a difference between at least two population means.
d. A larger sample should be selected.
e. None of these is correct.

Part II Problems

For each of the following problems, state: (a) the null and the alternate hypothesis, (b) the decision rule, and (c) the decision regarding the null hypothesis, (d) then interpret the result.

11. A machine is set to produce tennis balls so the mean bounce is 36 inches when the ball is dropped from a platform of a certain height. The supervisor suspects that the mean bounce has changed and is less than 36 inches. As an experiment 42 balls were dropped from the platform and the mean height of the bounce was 35.5 inches, with a standard deviation of 0.9 inches. At the .05 significance level, can the supervisor conclude that the mean bounce height is less than 36 inches?

12. $z = 0.737$
Do not reject.

12. Research by the Illinois Banking Company revealed that only 8 percent of their customers wait more than five minutes to do their banking. Management considers this reasonable and will not add more tellers unless the proportion becomes larger than 8 percent. The branch manager at the Litchfield Branch believes that the wait is longer than the standard at her branch and requested additional part-time tellers. To support her request the branch manager reported that in a sample of 100 customers, 10 waited more than five minutes. At the .01 significance level, is it reasonable to conclude that more than 8 percent of the customers wait more than five minutes?

13. It was hypothesized that university clerical employees did not engage in productive work 20 minutes on the average out of every hour. Some claimed the time lost was greater than 20 minutes. An actual study was conducted at a midwestern university using a stopwatch and other ways of checking the work habits of the clerical employees. A random check of the employees revealed the following unproductive times, in minutes, during a one-hour period (exclusive of regularly scheduled breaks):

10	25	17	20	28	30	18	23	18

Using the .05 significance level, is it reasonable to conclude the mean unproductive time is greater than 20 minutes?

14. A test is to be conducted involving the mean holding power of two glues designed for plastic. First, a small plastic hook was coated at one end with Epox glue and fastened to a sheet of plastic. After it dried, weight was added to the hook until it separated from the sheet of plastic. The weight was then recorded. This was repeated until 12 hooks were tested. The same procedure was followed for Holdtite glue, but only 10 hooks were used. The sample results, in pounds, were:

	Epox	Holdtite
Sample mean	250	252
Sample standard deviation	5	8
Sample size	12	10

14. $t = -0.716$

At the .01 significance level, is there a difference between the mean holding power of Epox and that of Holdtite?

15. An additive formulated to add to the life of paints used in the South is to be tested. The top half of a piece of wood was painted using the regular paint. The bottom half was painted with the paint including the additive. The same procedure was followed for a total of 10 pieces. Then each piece was subjected to high-pressure water and brilliant light. The data, the number of hours each piece lasted before it faded beyond a certain point, follow:

	Number of Hours by Sample									
	A	B	C	D	E	F	G	H	I	J
Without additive	325	313	320	340	318	312	319	330	333	319
With additive	323	313	326	343	310	320	313	340	330	315

Using the .05 significance level, determine whether the additive is effective in prolonging the life of the paint.

16. The Buffalo, New York, cola distributor is featuring a super-special sale on 12-packs. She wonders where in the grocery store to place the cola for maximum attention. Should it be near the front door of the grocery stores, in the cola section, at the checkout registers, or near the milk and other dairy products? Four stores with similar total sales cooperated in an experiment. In one store the 12-packs were stacked near the front door, in another they were placed near the checkout registers, and so on. Sales were checked at specified times in each store for exactly four minutes. The results were:

Cola at the Door	In Soft Drink Section	Near Registers	Dairy Section
$6	$ 5	$ 7	$10
8	10	10	9
3	12	9	6
7	4	4	11
	9	5	
		7	

16. $F = 1.04$
Do not reject.

The Buffalo distributor wants to find out whether there is a difference in the mean sales for cola stacked at the four locations in the store. Use the .05 significance level.

Cases

A. Century National Bank

Refer to the description of Century National Bank at the end of the Review of Chapters 1–4 on page 147. The bank has branch offices in four different cities: Cincinnati, Ohio; Atlanta, Georgia; Louisville, Kentucky; and Erie, Pennsylvania. Mr. Selig would like to know whether there is a difference in the mean checking account balance among the four branches. If there are differences, between which branches do these differences occur?

Mr. Selig is also interested in the ATMs. Is there a difference in the ATM use among the branches? Also, do customers who have debit cards tend to use the ATMs differently from those who do not have debit cards? Is there a difference in ATM use by those with checking accounts that pay interest versus those that do not? Prepare a report for Mr. Selig answering these questions.

B. Bell Grove Medical Center

Ms. Gene Dempsey manages the emergency care center at the Bell Grove Medical Center. One of her responsibilities is to have enough nurses so that incoming patients needing service can be handled promptly. It is stressful for patients to wait a long time for emergency care even when their care needs are not life threatening. Ms. Dempsey gathered the following information regarding the number of patients over the last several weeks. The center is not open on weekends. Does it appear that there are any differences in the number of patients served by the day of the week? If there are differences, which days seem to be the busiest?

Date	Day	Patients
9-29-00	Monday	38
9-30-00	Tuesday	28
10-1-00	Wednesday	28
10-2-00	Thursday	30
10-3-00	Friday	35
10-6-00	Monday	35
10-7-00	Tuesday	25
10-8-00	Wednesday	22
10-9-00	Thursday	21
10-10-00	Friday	32
10-13-00	Monday	37
10-14-00	Tuesday	29
10-15-00	Wednesday	27
10-16-00	Thursday	28
10-17-00	Friday	35
10-20-00	Monday	37
10-21-00	Tuesday	26
10-22-00	Wednesday	28
10-23-00	Thursday	23
10-24-00	Friday	33

13 Linear Regression and Correlation

GOALS

When you have completed this chapter, you will be able to:

1 **Draw a scatter diagram.**

2 **Understand and interpret the terms *dependent variable* and *independent variable.***

3 **Calculate and interpret the coefficient of correlation, the coefficient of determination, and the standard error of estimate.**

4 **Conduct a test of hypothesis to determine whether the coefficient of correlation in the population is zero.**

5 **Calculate the least squares regression line.**

6 **Construct and interpret confidence intervals and prediction intervals for the dependent variable.**

7 **Set up and interpret an ANOVA table.**

A study of college soccer games revealed the correlation between the number of shots attempted and the number of goals scored to be 0.21 for a sample of 20 games. Is it reasonable to conclude that there is a positive correlation between the two variables? Use the .05 significance level. (See Goal 4 and Exercise 36.)

Introduction

Chapters 2 through 4 dealt with *descriptive statistics.* We organized raw data into a frequency distribution, and computed several measures of central tendency and measures of dispersion to describe the major characteristics of the data. Chapter 5 started the study of *statistical inference.* The main emphasis was on inferring something about a population parameter, such as the population mean, based on a sample. We tested for the reasonableness of a population mean or a population proportion, the difference between two population means, or whether several population means were equal. All of these tests involved just *one* interval- or ratio-level variable, such as the weight of a plastic soft drink bottle, the income of bank presidents, or the number of patients admitted to a particular hospital.

We shift our emphasis in this chapter. Here we study the *relationship* between *two variables* and *develop an equation that allows us to estimate one variable based on another.* Is there a relationship between the amount Healthtex spends on advertising and its sales? Can we estimate the cost to heat a home in January in the upper Midwest based on the number of square feet in the home? Is there a relationship between the advertising rate per line in a newspaper and the circulation of the paper? Is there a relationship between the number of years a production worker has been on the job and the number of units produced? Note in each of these instances there are two variables—for example, the number of years on the job and the number of units produced.

We begin this chapter by examining the meaning and purpose of **correlation analysis.** Then we look at a chart designed to portray the relationship between two variables: a **scatter diagram.** We continue our study by developing a mathematical equation that will allow us to estimate the value of one variable based on the value of another. This is called **regression analysis.** We will (1) determine the equation of the line that best fits the data, (2) estimate the value of one variable based on another, (3) measure the error in our estimate, and (4) establish confidence and prediction intervals for our estimate.

What Is Correlation Analysis?

Correlation analysis is the study of the relationship between variables. To explain, suppose the sales manager of Copier Sales of America, which has a large sales force throughout the United States and Canada, wants to determine whether there is a relationship between the number of sales calls made in a month and the number of copiers sold that month. The manager selects a random sample of 10 representatives and determines the number of sales calls each representative made last month and the number of copiers sold. The sample information is shown in Table 13–1.

TABLE 13–1 Sales Calls and Copiers Sold for Ten Salespeople

Sales Representative	Number of Sales Calls	Number of Copiers Sold
Tom Keller	20	30
Jeff Hall	40	60
Brian Virost	20	40
Greg Fish	30	60
Susan Welch	10	30
Carlos Ramirez	10	40
Rich Niles	20	40
Mike Kiel	20	50
Mark Reynolds	20	30
Soni Jones	30	70

There does seem to be some relationship between the number of sales calls and the number of units sold. That is, the salespeople who made the most sales calls sold the most units. The relationship is not "perfect" or exact, however. For example, Soni Jones made fewer sales calls than Jeff Hall, but she sold more units.

Instead of talking in generalities, as we have been doing up to this point, we will develop some statistical measures to portray more precisely the relationship between the two variables, sales calls and copiers sold. This group of statistical techniques is called **correlation analysis.**

CORRELATION ANALYSIS A group of techniques to measure the strength of the association between two variables.

The basic idea of correlation analysis is to report the strength of the association between two variables. The usual first step is to plot the data in a **scatter diagram.**

SCATTER DIAGRAM A chart that portrays the relationship between two variables.

An example will show how a scatter diagram is used.

EXAMPLE

Copier Sales of America, Inc., sells copiers to businesses of all sizes throughout the United States and Canada. Ms. Marcy Bancer was recently promoted to the position of national sales manager. At the upcoming sales meeting, the sales representatives from all over the country will be in attendance. She would like to impress upon them the importance of making that extra sales call each day. She decides to gather some information on the relationship between the number of sales calls and the number of copiers sold. She selected a random sample of 10 sales representatives and determined the number of sales calls they made last month and the number of copiers they sold. The sample information is reported in Table 13–1. What observations can you make about the relationship between the number of sales calls and the number of copiers sold? Develop a scatter diagram to display the information.

SOLUTION

Based on the information in Table 13–1, Ms. Bancer suspects there is a relationship between the number of sales calls made in a month and the number of copiers sold. Soni Jones sold the most copiers last month, and she was one of three representatives making 30 or more sales calls. On the other hand, Susan Welch and Carlos Ramirez made only 10 sales calls last month. Ms. Welch had the lowest number of copiers sold among the sampled representatives.

The implication is that the number of copiers sold is related to the number of sales calls made. As the number of sales calls increases, the number of copiers sold also increases. We refer to number of sales calls as the *independent variable* and number of copiers sold as the *dependent variable.*

DEPENDENT VARIABLE The variable that is being predicted or estimated.

INDEPENDENT VARIABLE A variable that provides the basis for estimation. It is the predictor variable.

It is common practice to scale the dependent variable (copiers sold) on the vertical or *Y*-axis and the independent variable (number of sales calls) on the horizontal or *X*-axis. To develop the scatter diagram of the Copier Sales of America sales information, we begin with the first sales representative, Tom Keller. Tom made 20 sales calls last month and sold 30 copiers, so $X = 20$ and $Y = 30$. To plot this point, move along the horizontal axis to $X = 20$, then go vertically to $Y = 30$ and place a dot at the intersection. This process is continued until all the paired data are plotted, as shown in Chart 13–1.

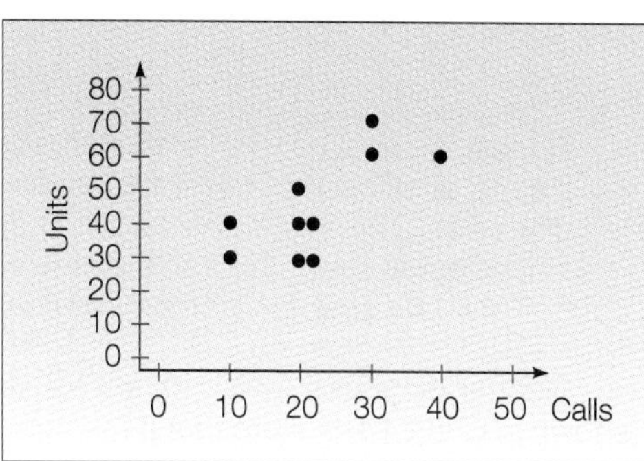

CHART 13–1 Scatter Diagram Showing Sales Calls and Copiers Sold

The scatter diagram shows graphically that the sales representatives who make more calls tend to sell more copiers. It is reasonable for Ms. Bancer, the national sales manager at Copier Sales of America, to tell her salespeople that the more sales calls they make the more copiers they can expect to sell. Note that while there appears to be a positive relationship between the two variables, all the points do not fall on a line. In the following section you will measure the strength and direction of this relationship between two variables by determining the coefficient of correlation.

The Coefficient of Correlation

Interval- or ratio-level data is required.

Originated by Karl Pearson about 1900, the **coefficient of correlation** describes the strength of the relationship between two sets of interval-scaled or ratio-scaled variables. Designated *r,* it is often referred to as *Pearson's r* and as the *Pearson product-moment correlation coefficient.* It can assume any value from -1.00 to $+1.00$ inclusive. A correlation coefficient of -1.00 or $+1.00$ indicates *perfect correlation.* For example, a correlation coefficient for the preceding example computed to be $+1.00$ would indicate that the number of sales calls and the number of copiers sold are perfectly related in a positive linear sense. A computed value of -1.00 reveals that sales calls and the number of copiers sold are perfectly related in a negative linear sense. How the scatter diagram would appear if the relationship between the two sets of data were linear and perfect is shown in Chart 13–2.

Characteristics of *r*

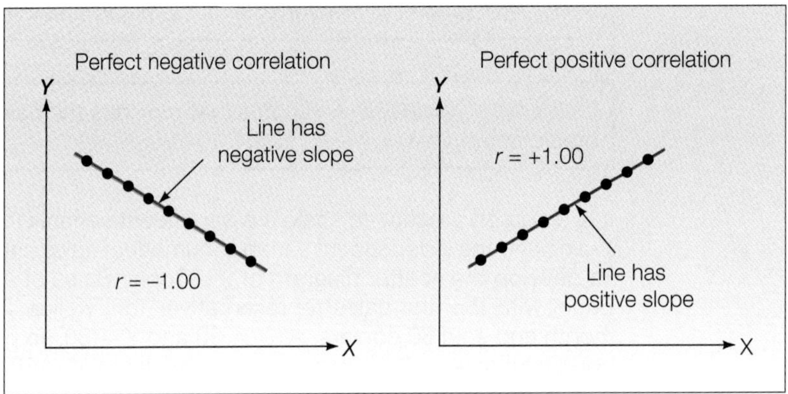

CHART 13–2 Scatter Diagrams Showing Perfect Negative Correlation and Perfect Positive Correlation

If there is absolutely no relationship between the two sets of variables, Pearson's *r* is zero. A coefficient of correlation *r* close to 0 (say, .08) shows that the relationship is quite weak. The same conclusion is drawn if $r = -.08$. Coefficients of $-.91$ and $+.91$ have equal strength; both indicate very strong correlation between the two variables. Thus, *the strength of the correlation does not depend on the direction (either − or +).*

Scatter diagrams for $r = 0$, a weak *r* (say, − .23), and a strong *r* (say, + .87) are shown in Chart 13–3. Note that if the correlation is weak, there is considerable scatter about a line drawn through the center of the data. For the scatter diagram representing a strong relationship, there is very little scatter about the line. This indicates, in the example shown on the chart, that high school GPA is a good predictor of performance in college.

Examples of degrees of correlation

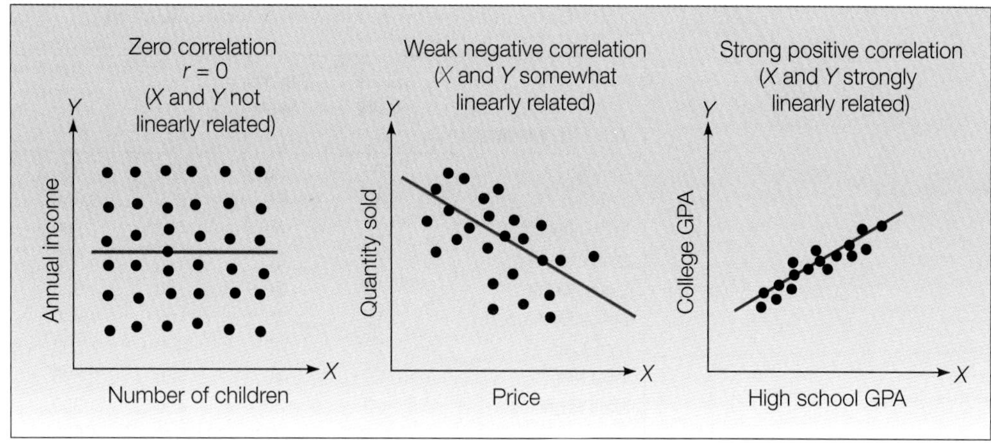

CHART 13–3 Scatter Diagrams Depicting Zero, Weak, and Strong Correlation

The following drawing summarizes the strength and direction of the coefficient of correlation.

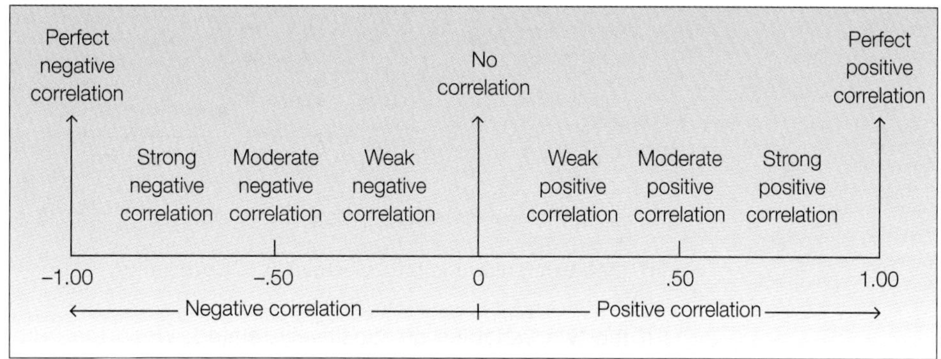

COEFFICIENT OF CORRELATION A measure of the strength of the linear relationship between two variables.

How is the value of the coefficient of correlation determined? We will use the Copier Sales of America data, which are reported in Table 13–2, as an example. We begin with a scatter diagram, similar to Chart 13–2. Draw a vertical line through the data values at the mean of the X-values and a horizontal line at the mean of the Y-values. In Chart 13–4 we've added a vertical line at 22.0 calls ($\bar{X} = \Sigma X/n = 220/10 = 22$) and a horizontal line at 45.0 copies ($\bar{Y} = \Sigma Y/n = 450/10 = 45.0$). These lines pass through the "center" of the data and divide the scatter diagram into four quadrants. Think of moving the origin from (0,0) to (22,45).

TABLE 13–2 Sales Calls and Copiers Sold for 10 Salespeople

Sales Representative	Sales Calls (X)	Copiers Sold (Y)	X^2	Y^2	XY
Tom Keller	20	30	400	900	600
Jeff Hall	40	60	1,600	3,600	2,400
Brian Virost	20	40	400	1,600	800
Greg Fish	30	60	900	3,600	1,800
Susan Welch	10	30	100	900	300
Carlos Ramirez	10	40	100	1,600	400
Rich Niles	20	40	400	1,600	800
Mike Kiel	20	50	400	2,500	1,000
Mark Reynolds	20	30	400	900	600
Soni Jones	30	70	900	4,900	2,100
Total	220	450	5,600	22,100	10,800

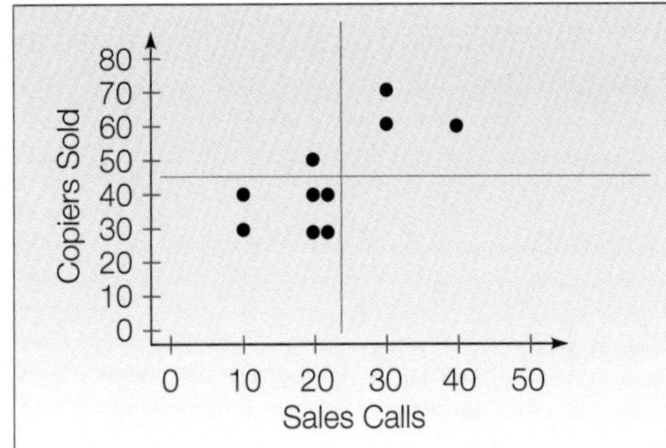

CHART 13–4 Computation of the Coefficient of Correlation

If the two variables are positively related, when the number of copiers sold is above the mean the number of sales calls will also be above the mean. These points appear in the upper-right quadrant of Chart 13–4. Similarly, when the number of copiers sold is less than the mean, so is the number of sales calls; these points fall in the lower-left quadrant. For example, the last person on the list in Table 13–2, Soni Jones, made 30 sales calls and sold 70 copiers. These values are above their respective means, so this point is located in the upper-right quadrant. She made 8 ($X - \bar{X} = 30 - 22$) more sales calls than the mean and sold 25 ($Y - \bar{Y} = 70 - 45$) more copiers than the mean. Tom Keller, the first name on the list in Table 13–2, made 20 sales calls and sold 30 copiers. Both of these values are less than their respective mean; hence this point is in the lower-left quadrant. Tom made 2 less sales calls and sold 15 less copiers than the respective means. The deviations from the mean number of sales calls and for the mean number of copiers sold are summarized in Table 13–3 for the 10 sales representatives. The sum of the products of the deviations from the respective means is 900. That is, the term $\Sigma(X - \bar{X})(Y - \bar{Y}) = 900$.

TABLE 13–3 Deviations from the Mean and Their Products

Sales Representative	Calls Y	Sales X	$X - \bar{X}$	$Y - \bar{Y}$	$(X - \bar{X})(Y - \bar{Y})$
Tom Keller	20	30	−2	−15	30
Jeff Hall	40	60	18	15	270
Brian Virost	20	40	−2	−5	10
Greg Fish	30	60	8	15	120
Susan Welch	10	30	−12	−15	180
Carlos Ramirez	10	40	−12	−5	60
Rich Niles	20	40	−2	−5	10
Mike Kiel	20	50	−2	5	−10
Mark Reynolds	20	30	−2	−15	30
Soni Jones	30	70	8	25	200
					900

In both the upper-right and the lower-left quadrants, the product of $(X - \bar{X})(Y - \bar{Y})$ is positive because both of the factors have the same sign. In our example this happens for all sales representatives except Mike Kiel. We can therefore expect the coefficient of correlation to have a positive value.

If the two variables are inversely related, one variable will be above the mean and the other below the mean. Most of the points in this case occur in the upper-left and lower-right quadrants. Now $(X - \bar{X})$ and $(Y - \bar{Y})$ will have opposite signs, so their product is negative. The resulting correlation coefficient is negative.

What happens if there is no linear relationship between the two variables? The points in the scatter diagram will appear in all four quadrants. The negative products of $(X - \bar{X})(Y - \bar{Y})$ offset the positive products, so the sum is near zero. This leads to a correlation coefficient near zero.

Pearson also wanted the correlation coefficient to be unaffected by the units of the two variables. For example, if we had used hundreds of copiers sold instead of the number sold, the coefficient of correlation would be the same. The coefficient of correlation is independent of the scale used if we divide the term $\Sigma(X - \bar{X})(Y - \bar{Y})$ by the sample standard deviations. It is also made independent of the sample size and bounded by the values $+1.00$ and -1.00 if we divide by $(n - 1)$.

This reasoning leads to the following formula:

CORRELATION COEFFICIENT — CONCEPTUAL FORM

$$r = \frac{\Sigma(X - \bar{X})(Y - \bar{Y})}{(n - 1)\, s_x\, s_y} \qquad [13\text{–}1]$$

To compute the coefficient of correlation, we use the standard deviations of the sample of 10 sales calls and 10 copiers sold. We could use formula 4–7 to calculate the sample standard deviations or we could use one of the software packages. The following is the Excel output. The standard deviation of the number of sales calls is 9.189 and of the number of copiers sold 14.337.

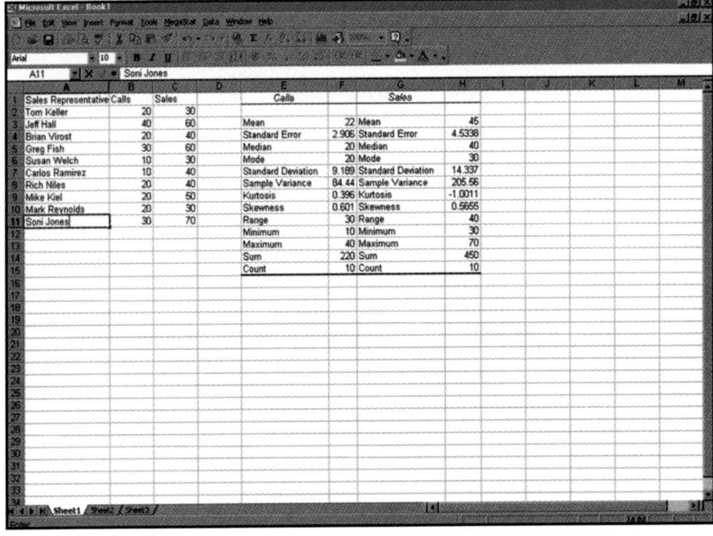

Sales Representative	Calls	Sales		Calls		Sales	
Tom Keller	20	30					
Jeff Hall	40	60		Mean	22	Mean	45
Brian Virost	20	40		Standard Error	2.906	Standard Error	4.5336
Greg Fish	30	60		Median	20	Median	40
Susan Welch	10	30		Mode	20	Mode	30
Carlos Ramirez	10	40		Standard Deviation	9.189	Standard Deviation	14.337
Rich Niles	20	40		Sample Variance	84.44	Sample Variance	205.56
Mike Kiel	20	50		Kurtosis	0.396	Kurtosis	-1.0011
Mark Reynolds	20	30		Skewness	0.601	Skewness	0.5655
Soni Jones	30	70		Range	30	Range	40
				Minimum	10	Minimum	30
				Maximum	40	Maximum	70
				Sum	220	Sum	450
				Count	10	Count	10

We now insert these values into formula 13–1 to determine the coefficient of correlation:

$$r = \frac{\Sigma(X - \bar{X})(Y - \bar{Y})}{(n - 1)\, s_y\, s_y} = \frac{900}{(10 - 1)(9.189)(14.337)} = 0.759$$

The coefficient of correlation can also be computed from a computational formula based on the actual values of X and Y. The formula is:

CORRELATION COEFFICIENT

$$r = \frac{n(\Sigma XY) - (\Sigma X)(\Sigma Y)}{\sqrt{[n(\Sigma X^2) - (\Sigma X)^2][n(\Sigma Y^2) - (\Sigma Y)^2]}} \qquad \textbf{[13–2]}$$

where:

- n is the number of paired observations.
- ΣX is the X variable summed.
- ΣY is the Y variable summed.
- (ΣX^2) is the X variable squared and the squares summed.
- $(\Sigma X)^2$ is the X variable summed and the sum squared.
- (ΣY^2) is the Y variable squared and the squares summed.
- $(\Sigma Y)^2$ is the Y variable summed and the sum squared.
- ΣXY is the sum of the products of X and Y.

EXAMPLE

Refer to the previous example where we developed a scatter diagram depicting the relationship between the number of sales calls and the number of copiers sold. Determine the coefficient of correlation and interpret its value.

SOLUTION

Table 13–2 repeats the information on the number of sales calls and the number of copiers sold. Also included are additional totals necessary to determine the coefficient of correlation.

The coefficient of correlation is 0.759, found by using formula 13–2.

$$r = \frac{n\Sigma XY - \Sigma X\Sigma Y}{\sqrt{[n(\Sigma X^2) - (\Sigma X)^2][n(\Sigma Y^2) - (\Sigma Y)^2]}}$$

$$= \frac{10(10{,}800) - (220)(450)}{\sqrt{[10(5{,}600) - (220)^2][(10(22{,}100) - (450)^2]}}$$

$$= 0.759$$

How do we interpret a correlation of 0.759? First, it is positive, so we see there is a direct relationship between the number of sales calls and the number of copiers sold. This confirms our reasoning based on the scatter diagram, Chart 13–4. The value of 0.759 is fairly close to 1.00, so we conclude that the association is strong. To put it another way, a 25 percent increase in calls will likely lead to 25 percent more sales.

The Coefficient of Determination

In the previous Example regarding the relationship between the number of sales calls and the units sold, the coefficient of correlation, 0.759, was interpreted as being "strong." Terms such as *weak, moderate,* and *strong,* however, do not have precise meaning. A measure that has a more easily interpreted meaning is the **coefficient of determination.** It is computed by squaring the coefficient of correlation. In the example, the coefficient of determination, r^2, is 0.576, found by $(0.759)^2$. This is a proportion or a percent; we can say that 57.6 percent of the variation in the number of copiers sold is explained, or accounted for, by the variation in the number of sales calls.

COEFFICIENT OF DETERMINATION The proportion of the total variation in the dependent variable Y that is explained, or accounted for, by the variation in the independent variable X.

Further discussion of the coefficient of determination is found later in the chapter.

A Word of Caution

If there is a strong relationship (say, .91) between two variables, we are tempted to assume that an increase or decrease in one variable *causes* a change in the other variable. For example, it can be shown that the consumption of Georgia peanuts and the consumption of aspirin have a strong correlation. However, this does not indicate that an increase in the consumption of peanuts *caused* the consumption of aspirin to increase. Likewise, the incomes of professors and the number of inmates in mental institutions have increased proportionately. Further, as the population of donkeys has decreased, there has been an increase in the number of doctoral degrees granted. Relationships such as these are called **spurious correlations.** What we can conclude when we find two variables with a strong correlation is that there is a relationship between the two variables, not that a change in one causes a change in the other.

Self-Review 13–1

Reliable Furniture is a family business that has been selling to retail customers in the Chicago area for many years. They advertise extensively on radio and TV, emphasizing their low prices and easy credit terms. The owner would like to review the relationship between sales and the amount spent on advertising. Below is information on sales and advertising expense for the last four months.

Month	Advertising Expense ($ million)	Sales Revenue ($ million)
July	2	7
August	1	3
September	3	8
October	4	10

(a) The owner wants to forecast sales based on advertising expense. Which variable is the dependent variable? Which variable is the independent variable?
(b) Draw a scatter diagram.
(c) Determine the coefficient of correlation.
(d) Interpret the strength of the correlation coefficient.
(e) Determine the coefficient of determination. Interpret.

Exercises

1. The following sample observations were randomly selected.

X:	4	5	3	6	10
Y:	4	6	5	7	7

Determine the coefficient of correlation and the coefficient of determination. Interpret.

2. $r = -0.89$
$r^2 = 0.7921$

2. The following sample observations were randomly selected.

X:	5	3	6	3	4	4	6	8
Y:	13	15	7	12	13	11	9	5

Determine the coefficient of correlation and the coefficient of determination. Interpret.

3. Bi-lo Appliance Stores has outlets in several large metropolitan areas. The general sales manager plans to air a commercial for a digital camera on selected local TV stations prior to a sale starting on Saturday and ending Sunday. She plans to get the information for Saturday–Sunday digital camera sales at the various outlets and pair them with the number of times the advertisement was shown on the local TV stations. The purpose is to find whether there is any relationship between the number of times the advertisement was aired and digital camera sales. The pairings are:

Location of TV Station	Number of Airings	Saturday–Sunday Sales ($ thousands)
Buffalo	4	15
Albany	2	8
Erie	5	21
Syracuse	6	24
Rochester	3	17

a. What is the dependent variable?
b. Draw a scatter diagram.
c. Determine the coefficient of correlation.
d. Determine the coefficient of determination.
e. Interpret these statistical measures.

4. The production department of NDB Electronics wants to explore the relationship between the number of employees who assemble a subassembly and the number produced. As an experiment, two employees were assigned to assemble the subassemblies. They produced 15 during a one-hour period. Then four employees assembled them. They produced 25 during a one-hour period. The complete set of paired observations follows.

Number of Assemblers	One-Hour Production (units)
2	15
4	25
1	10
5	40
3	30

4. a. See IM.
b. Yes, positive.
c. $r = 0.927$
d. Strong, $r^2 = .8593$

The dependent variable is production; that is, it is assumed that the level of production depends upon the number of employees.
a. Draw a scatter diagram.
b. Based on the scatter diagram, does there appear to be any relationship between the number of assemblers and production? Explain.
c. Compute the coefficient of correlation.
d. Evaluate the strength of the relationship by computing the coefficient of determination.

5. The city council of Pine Bluffs is considering increasing the number of police in an effort to reduce crime. Before making a final decision, the council asks the Chief of Police to survey other cities of similar size to determine the relationship between the number of police and the number of crimes reported. The Chief gathered the following sample information.

City	Police	Number of Crimes	City	Police	Number of Crimes
Oxford	15	17	Holgate	17	7
Starksville	17	13	Carey	12	21
Danville	25	5	Whistler	11	19
Athens	27	7	Woodville	22	6

a. If we want to estimate crimes based on the number of police, which variable is the dependent variable and which is the independent variable?
b. Draw a scatter diagram.
c. Determine the coefficient of correlation.
d. Determine the coefficient of determination.
e. Interpret these statistical measures. Does it surprise you that the relationship is inverse?

6. The owner of Maumee Motors wants to study the relationship between the age of a car and its selling price. Listed below is a random sample of 12 used cars sold at Maumee Motors during the last year.

Car	Age (years)	Selling Price ($000)	Car	Age (years)	Selling Price ($000)
1	9	8.1	7	8	7.6
2	7	6.0	8	11	8.0
3	11	3.6	9	10	8.0
4	12	4.0	10	12	6.0
5	8	5.0	11	6	8.6
6	7	10.0	12	6	8.0

6. a. Age is independent, price dependent
b. See IM.
c. $r = -0.544$
d. $r^2 = 0.296$
e. Moderate correlation.

a. If we want to estimate selling price based on the age of the car, which variable is the dependent variable and which is the independent variable?
b. Draw a scatter diagram.
c. Determine the coefficient of correlation.
d. Determine the coefficient of determination.
e. Interpret these statistical measures. Does it surprise you that the relationship is inverse?

Testing the Significance of the Correlation Coefficient

Recall the sales manager of Copier Sales of America found the correlation between the number of sales calls and the number of copiers sold was 0.759. This indicated a strong association between the two variables. However, only 10 salespeople were sampled. Could it be that the correlation in the population is actually 0? This would mean the correlation of 0.759 was due to chance. The population in this example is all the salespeople employed by the firm.

Could the correlation in the population be zero?

Resolving this dilemma requires a test to answer the obvious question: Could there be zero correlation in the population from which the sample was selected? To put it another way, did the computed r come from a population of paired observations with zero correlation? To continue our convention of allowing Greek letters to represent a population parameter, we will let ρ represent the correlation in the population. It is pronounced "rho."

We will continue with the illustration involving sales calls and copiers sold. The null hypothesis and the alternate hypothesis are:

H_0: $\rho = 0$ (The correlation in the population is zero.)
H_1: $\rho \neq 0$ (The correlation in the population is different from zero.)

From the way H_1 is stated, we know that the test is two-tailed.

The formula for t is:

t TEST FOR THE COEFFICIENT OF CORRELATION

$$t = \frac{r\sqrt{n-2}}{\sqrt{1-r^2}} \quad \text{with } n - 2 \text{ degrees of freedom} \qquad [13\text{–}3]$$

Using the .05 level of significance, the decision rule states that if the computed t falls in the area between plus 2.306 and minus 2.306, the null hypothesis is not rejected. To locate the critical value of 2.306, refer to Appendix F for $df = n - 2 = 10 - 2 = 8$. See Chart 13–5.

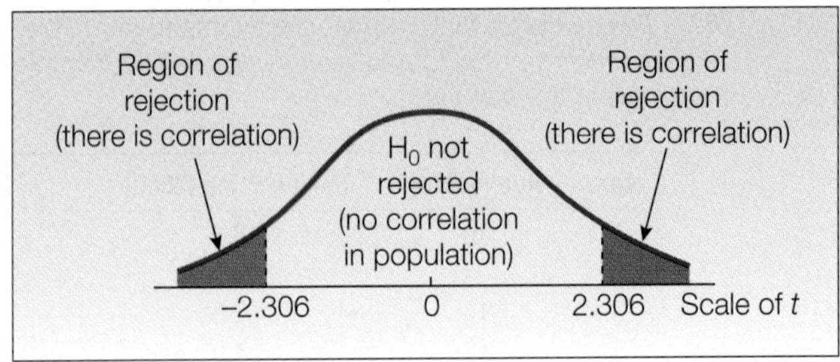

CHART 13–5 Decision Rule for Test of Hypothesis at .05 Significance Level and 8 *df*

Applying formula 13–3 to the example regarding the number of sales calls and units sold:

$$t = \frac{r\sqrt{n-2}}{\sqrt{1-r^2}} = \frac{.759\sqrt{10-2}}{\sqrt{1-.759^2}} = 3.297$$

The computed t is in the rejection region. Thus, H_0 is rejected at the .05 significance level. This means the correlation in the population is not zero. From a practical standpoint, it indicates to the sales manager that there is correlation in the population of salespeople with respect to the number of sales calls made and the number of copiers sold.

We can also interpret the test of hypothesis in terms of p-values. A p-value is the likelihood of finding a value of the test statistic more extreme than the one computed, when H_0 is true. To determine the p-value, go to the t distribution in Appendix F and find the row for 8 degrees of freedom. The value of the test statistic is 3.297, so in the row for 8 degrees of freedom and a two-tailed test, find the value closest to 3.297. For a two-tailed test at the .02 significance level, the critical value is 2.896, and the critical value at the .01 significance level is 3.355. Because 3.297 is between 2.896 and 3.355 we conclude that the p-value is less than .02.

Both MINITAB and Excel will report the correlation between two variables. In addition to the correlation, MINITAB reports the p-value for the test of hypothesis that the correlation in the population between the two variables is 0. The MINITAB output showing the results is below. They are the same as those calculated earlier.

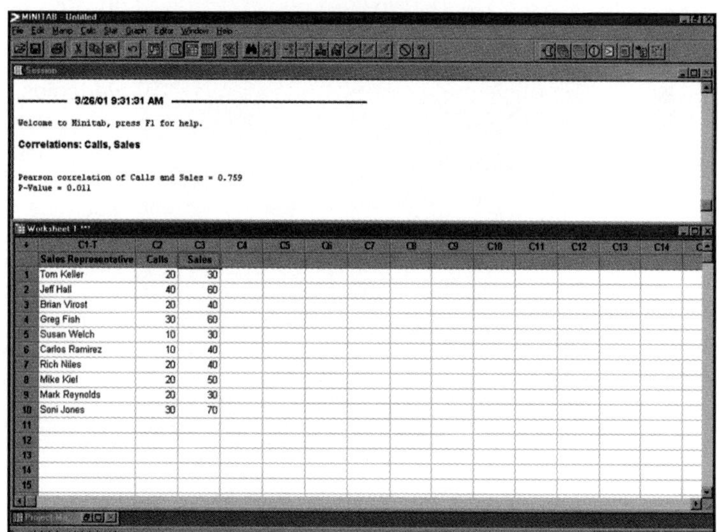

Self-Review 13–2

A sample of 25 mayoral campaigns in cities with populations larger than 50,000 showed that the correlation between the percent of the vote received and the amount spent on the campaign by the candidate was .43. At the .05 significance level, is there a positive association between the variables?

Exercises

7. The following hypotheses are given.

$$H_0: \rho \leq 0$$
$$H_1: \rho > 0$$

A random sample of 12 paired observations indicated a correlation of .32. Can we conclude that the correlation in the population is greater than zero? Use the .05 significance level.

8. $t = -1.868$ Reject H_0.

8. The following hypotheses are given.

$$H_0: \rho \geq 0$$
$$H_1: \rho < 0$$

A random sample of 15 paired observations have a correlation of −.46. Can we conclude that the correlation in the population is less than zero? Use the .05 significance level.

9. The Pennsylvania Refining Company is studying the relationship between the pump price of gasoline and the number of gallons sold. For a sample of 20 stations last Tuesday, the correlation was .78. At the .01 significance level, is the correlation in the population greater than zero?

10. $t = 7.15$ Reject H_0.

10. A study of 20 worldwide financial institutions showed the correlation between their assets and pretax profit to be .86. At the .05 significance level, can we conclude that there is positive correlation in the population?

Regression Analysis

In the previous section we developed measures to express the strength and the direction of the relationship between two variables. In this section we wish to develop next an equation to express the *linear* (straight line) relationship between two variables. In addition we want to be able to estimate the value of the dependent variable Y based on a selected value of the independent variable X. The technique used to develop the equation and provide the estimates is called **regression analysis.**

In Table 13–1 we reported the number of sales calls and the number of units sold for a sample of 10 sales representatives employed by Copier Sales of America. Chart 13–1 portrayed this information in a scatter diagram. Now we want to develop a linear equation that expresses the relationship between the number of sales calls and the number of units sold. The equation for the line used to estimate Y based on X is referred to as the **regression equation.**

> **REGRESSION EQUATION** An equation that defines the linear relationship between two variables.

The scatter diagram in Chart 13–1 is reproduced in Chart 13–6, with a line drawn with a ruler through the dots to illustrate that a straight line would probably fit the data. However, the line drawn using a straight edge has one disadvantage: Its position is based in part on the judgment of the person drawing the line. The hand-drawn lines in Chart 13–7 represent the judgments of four people. All the lines except line A seem to be reasonable. However, each would result in a different estimate of units sold for a particular number of sales calls.

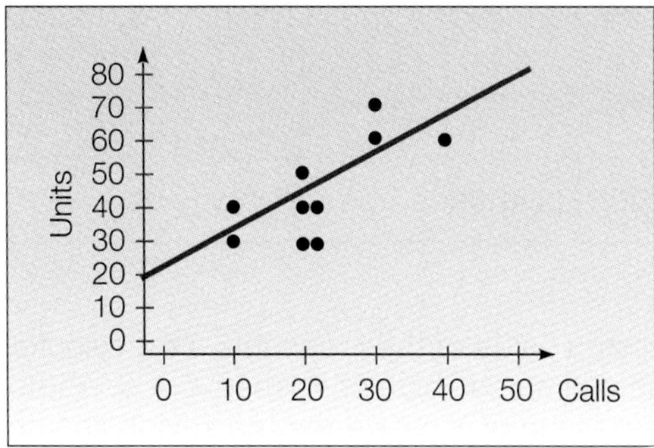

CHART 13–6 Sales Calls and Copiers Sold for 10 Sales Representatives

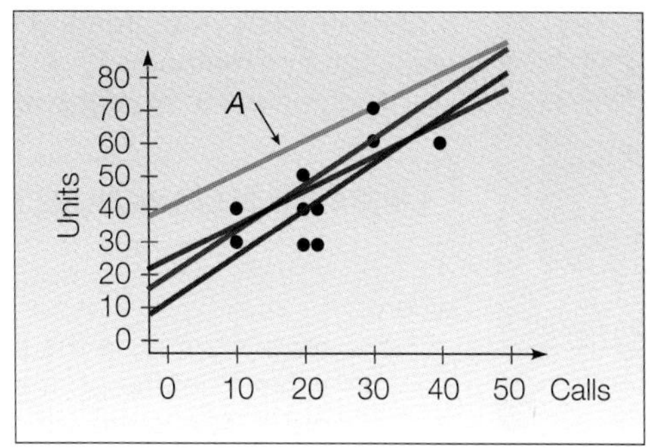

CHART 13–7 Four Lines Superimposed on the Scatter Diagram

Least Squares Principle

Least squares line gives "best" fit; subjective method is unreliable

Judgment is eliminated by determining the regression line using a mathematical method called the **least squares principle.** This method gives what is commonly referred to as the "best-fitting" line.

> **LEAST SQUARES PRINCIPLE** Determining a regression equation by minimizing the sum of the squares of the vertical distances between the actual Y values and the predicted values of Y.

To illustrate this concept, the same data are plotted in the three charts that follow. The regression line in Chart 13–8 was determined using the least squares method. It is the best-fitting line because the sum of the squares of the vertical deviations about it is at a minimum. The first plot ($X = 3$, $Y = 8$) deviates by 2 from the line, found by $10 - 8$. The deviation squared is 4. The squared deviation for the plot $X = 4$, $Y = 18$ is 16. The squared deviation for the plot $X = 5$, $Y = 16$ is 4. The sum of the squared deviations is 24, found by $4 + 16 + 4$.

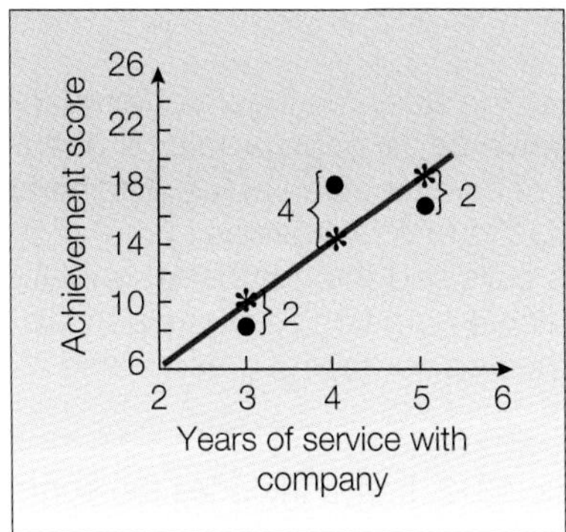

CHART 13–8 The Least Squares Line

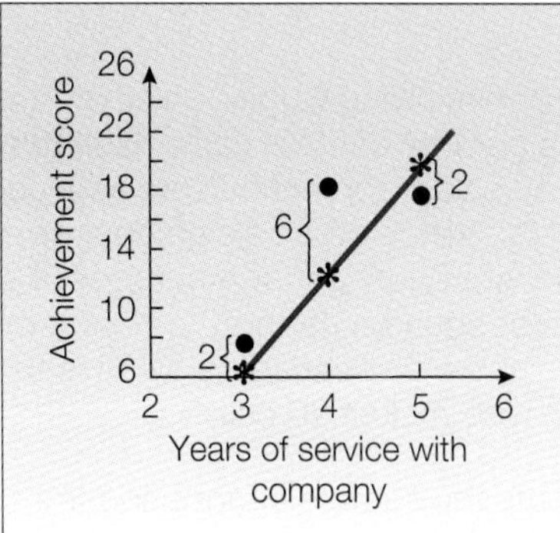

CHART 13–9 Line Drawn Using a Straight Edge

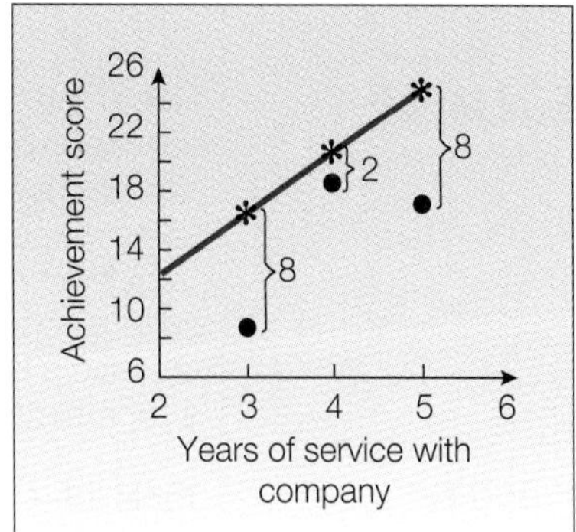

CHART 13–10 Line Drawn Using a a Straight Edge

Assume that the lines in Charts 13–9 and 13–10 were drawn using a straight edge. The sum of the squared vertical deviations in Chart 13–9 is 44. For Chart 13–10 it is

Statistics in Action

Sir Francis Galton compared the heights of parents with the heights of their children. He converted the heights of parents and their children to z-values and noted that the children's z-value deviated less from the mean than did the value for their parents. He called this "regression" toward the mean. This discovery formed the basis of regression analysis.

132. Both sums are greater than the sum for the line in Chart 13–8, found using the least squares method.

The general form of the regression equation is:

GENERAL FORM OF LINEAR REGRESSION EQUATION $$Y' = a + bX \qquad [13\text{–}4]$$

where:

- Y' read Y prime, is the predicted value of the Y variable for a selected X value.
- a is the Y-intercept. It is the estimated value of Y when $X = 0$. Another way to put it is: a is the estimated value of Y where the regression line crosses the Y-axis when X is zero.
- b is the slope of the line, or the average change in Y' for each change of one unit (either increase or decrease) in the independent variable X.
- X is any value of the independent variable that is selected.

It should be noted that the linear regression equation for the sample of salespeople is just an estimate of the relationship between the two variables in the population. Thus, the values of a and b in the regression equation are usually referred to as the **estimated regression coefficients,** or simply the **regression coefficients.**

The formulas for b and a are:

SLOPE OF THE REGRESSION LINE $$b = \frac{n(\Sigma XY) - (\Sigma X)(\Sigma Y)}{n(\Sigma X^2) - (\Sigma X)^2} \qquad [13\text{–}5]$$

***Y*-INTERCEPT** $$a = \frac{\Sigma Y}{n} - b\frac{\Sigma X}{n} \qquad [13\text{–}6]$$

where:

- X is a value of the independent variable.
- Y is a value of the dependent variable.
- n is the number of items in the sample.

EXAMPLE

Recall the example involving Copier Sales of America. The sales manager gathered information on the number of sales calls made and the number of copiers sold for a random sample of 10 sales representatives. As a part of her presentation at the upcoming sales meeting, Ms. Bancer, the sales manager, would like to offer specific information about the relationship between the number of sales calls and the number of copiers sold. Use the least squares method to determine a linear equation to express the relationship between the two variables. What is the expected number of copiers sold by a representative who makes 20 calls?

SOLUTION

Table 13–4 repeats the sample information from Table 13–2. It also includes the sums needed in formulas (13–5) and (13–6) to calculate the regression equation.

The calculations necessary to determine the regression equation are as follows:

$$b = \frac{n(\Sigma XY) - \Sigma X \Sigma Y}{n\Sigma X^2 - (\Sigma X)^2} = \frac{10(10{,}800) - (220)(450)}{10(5{,}600) - (220)^2} = 1.1842$$

$$a = \frac{\Sigma Y}{n} - b\frac{\Sigma X}{n} = \frac{450}{10} - (1.1842)\frac{220}{10} = 18.9476$$

TABLE 13–4 Calculations Needed for Determining the Least Squares Regression Equation

Sales Representative	Sales Calls (X)	Copiers Sold (Y)	X^2	Y^2	XY
Tom Keller	20	30	400	900	600
Jeff Hall	40	60	1,600	3,600	2,400
Brian Virost	20	40	400	1,600	800
Greg Fish	30	60	900	3,600	1,800
Susan Welch	10	30	100	900	300
Carlos Ramirez	10	40	100	1,600	400
Rich Niles	20	40	400	1,600	800
Mike Kiel	20	50	400	2,500	1,000
Mark Reynolds	20	30	400	900	600
Soni Jones	30	70	900	4,900	2,100
Total	220	450	5,600	22,100	10,800

Thus, the regression equation is $Y' = 18.9476 + 1.1842X$. So if a salesperson makes 20 calls, they can expect to sell 42.6316 copiers, found by $Y' = 18.9476 + 1.1842X = 18.9476 + 1.1842(20)$. The b value of 1.1842 means that for each additional sales call made the sales representative can expect to increase the number of copiers sold by about 1.2. To put it another way, five additional sales calls in a month will result in about six more copiers being sold [$1.1842(5) = 5.921$].

The a value of 18.9476 is the point where the equation crosses the Y-axis. A literal translation is that if no sales calls are made, that is, $X = 0$, 18.9476 copiers will be sold. Note that $X = 0$ is outside the range of values included in the sample and, therefore, should not be used to estimate the number of copiers sold. The sales calls ranged from 10 to 40, so estimates should be made within that range.

Drawing the Line of Regression

The least squares equation, $Y' = 18.9476 + 1.1842X$, can be drawn on the scatter diagram. The first sales representative in the sample is Tom Keller. He made 20 calls. His estimated number of copiers sold is $Y' = 18.9476 + 1.1842(20) = 42.6316$. The plot $X = 20$ and $Y = 42.6316$ is located by moving to 20 on the X-axis and then going vertically to 42.6316. The other points on the regression equation can be determined by substituting the particular value of X into the regression equation.

Sales Representative	Sales Calls (X)	Estimated Sales (Y')	Sales Representative	Sales Calls (X)	Estimated Sales (Y')
Tom Keller	20	42.6316	Carlos Ramirez	10	30.7896
Jeff Hall	40	66.3156	Rich Niles	20	42.6316
Brian Virost	20	42.6316	Mike Kiel	20	42.6316
Greg Fish	30	54.4736	Mark Reynolds	20	42.6316
Susan Welch	10	30.7896	Soni Jones	30	54.4736

All the other points are connected to give the line. See Chart 13–11.

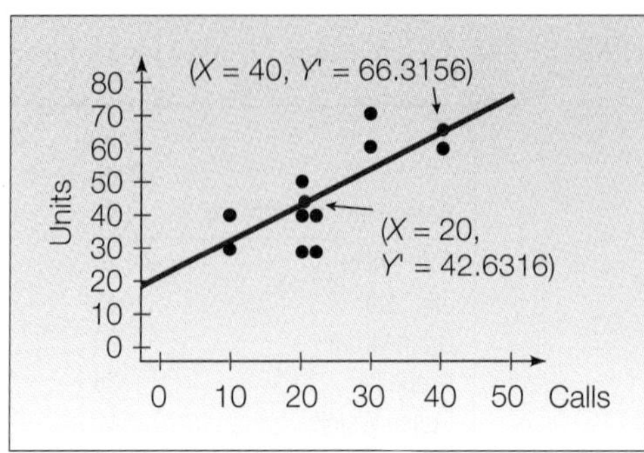

CHART 13–11 The Line of Regression Drawn on the Scatter Diagram

This line has some interesting features. As we have discussed, there is no other line through the data for which the sum of the squared deviations is less. In addition, this line will pass through the points represented by the mean of the X values and the mean of the Y values, that is, $\bar{X}$ and $\bar{Y}$. In this example $\bar{X} = 22.0$ and $\bar{Y} = 45.0$.

Self-Review 13–3

Refer to Self-Review 13–1, where the owner of the Reliable Furniture Company was studying the relationship between sales and the amount spent on advertising. The sales information for the last four months is repeated below.

Month	Advertising Expense ($ million)	Sales Revenue ($ million)
July	2	7
August	1	3
September	3	8
October	4	10

(a) Determine the regression equation.
(b) Interpret the values of *a* and *b*.
(c) Estimate sales when $3 million is spent on advertising.

Exercises

Note: It is suggested that you save your values for ΣX, ΣX^2, ΣXY, ΣY, and ΣY^2, as these exercises will be referred to later in the chapter.

11. The following sample observations were randomly selected.

X:	4	5	3	6	10
Y:	4	6	5	7	7

a. Determine the regression equation.
b. Determine the value of Y' when X is 7.

12. The following sample observations were randomly selected.

X:	5	3	6	3	4	4	6	8
Y:	13	15	7	12	13	11	9	5

12. a. $Y' = 19.1198 - 1.7425X$
b. 6.9223

a. Determine the regression equation.
b. Determine the value of Y' when X is 7.

13. The Bradford Electric Illuminating Company is studying the relationship between kilowatt-hours (thousands) used and the number of rooms in a private single-family residence. A random sample of 10 homes yielded the following.

Number of Rooms	Kilowatt-Hours (thousands)	Number of Rooms	Kilowatt-Hours (thousands)
12	9	8	6
9	7	10	8
14	10	10	10
6	5	5	4
10	8	7	7

a. Determine the regression equation.
b. Determine the number of kilowatt-hours, in thousands, for a six-room house.

14. Mr. James McWhinney, president of Daniel-James Financial Services, believes there is a relationship between the number of client contacts and the dollar amount of sales. To document this assertion, Mr. McWhinney gathered the following sample information. The X column indicates the number of client contacts last month, and the Y column shows the value of sales ($ thousands) last month for each client sampled.

Number of Contacts, X	Sales ($ thousands), Y	Number of Contacts, X	Sales ($ thousands), Y
14	24	23	30
12	14	48	90
20	28	50	85
16	30	55	120
46	80	50	110

14. a. $Y' = -12.201 + 2.1946X$
b. 75.583

a. Determine the regression equation.
b. Determine the estimated sales if 40 contacts are made.

15. A recent article in *Business Week* listed the "Best Small Companies." We are interested in the current results of the companies' sales and earnings. A random sample of 12 companies was selected and the sales and earnings, in millions of dollars, are reported below.

Company	Sales ($ millions)	Earnings ($ millions)	Company	Sales ($ millions)	Earnings ($ millions)
Papa John's International	$89.2	$4.9	Checkmate Electronics	$17.5	$ 2.6
Applied Innovation	18.6	4.4	Royal Grip	11.9	1.7
Integracare	18.2	1.3	M-Wave	19.6	3.5
Wall Data	71.7	8.0	Serving-N-Slide	51.2	8.2
Davidson Associates	58.6	6.6	Daig	28.6	6.0
Chico's Fas	46.8	4.1	Cobra Golf	69.2	12.8

Let sales be the independent variable and earnings be the dependent variable.
a. Draw a scatter diagram.
b. Compute the coefficient of correlation.
c. Compute the coefficient of determination.
d. Interpret your findings in parts b and c.
e. Determine the regression equation.
f. For a small company with $50.0 million in sales, estimate the earnings.

16. We are studying mutual bond funds for the purpose of investing in several funds. For this particular study, we want to focus on the assets of a fund and its five-year performance. The question is: Can the five-year rate of return be estimated based on the assets of the fund? Nine mutual funds were selected at random, and their assets and rates of return are shown below.

Fund	Assets ($ millions)	Return (%)	Fund	Assets ($ millions)	Return (%)
AARP High Quality Bond	$622.2	10.8	MFS Bond A	$494.5	11.6
Babson Bond L	160.4	11.3	Nichols Income	158.3	9.5
Compass Capital Fixed Income	275.7	11.4	T. Raive Price Short-term	681.0	8.2
Galaxy Bond Retail	433.2	9.1	Thompson Income B	241.3	6.8
Keystone Custodian B-1	437.9	9.2			

16. a. See IM.
b. −.046
c. .002
d. See IM.
e. $Y' = 9.9197 - 0.000393X$
f. 9.7625

a. Draw a scatter diagram.
b. Compute the coefficient of correlation.
c. Compute the coefficient of determination.
d. Write a brief report of your findings for parts b and c.
e. Determine the regression equation. Use assets as the independent variable.
f. For a fund with $400.0 million in sales, determine the five-year rate of return (in percent).

17. Refer to Exercise 5.
a. Determine the regression equation.
b. Estimate the number of crimes for a city with 20 police.
c. Interpret the regression equation.

18. a. $Y' = 11.179 - 0.479X$
b. 6.389
c. Decrease $479 per year.

18. Refer to Exercise 6.
a. Determine the regression equation.
b. Estimate the selling price of a 10-year-old car.
c. Interpret the regression equation.

The Standard Error of Estimate

Note in the preceding scatter diagram (Chart 13–11) that all of the points do not lie exactly on the regression line. If they all were on the line, and if the number of observations were sufficiently large, there would be no error in estimating the number of units sold. To put it another way, if all the points were on the regression line, units sold could be predicted with 100 percent accuracy. Thus, there would be no error in predicting the Y variable based on an X variable. This is true in the following hypothetical case (see Chart 13–12). Theoretically, if $X = 4$, then an exact Y of 100 could be predicted with 100 percent confidence. Or if $X = 12$, then $Y = 300$. Because there is no difference between the observed values and the predicted values, there is no error in this estimate.

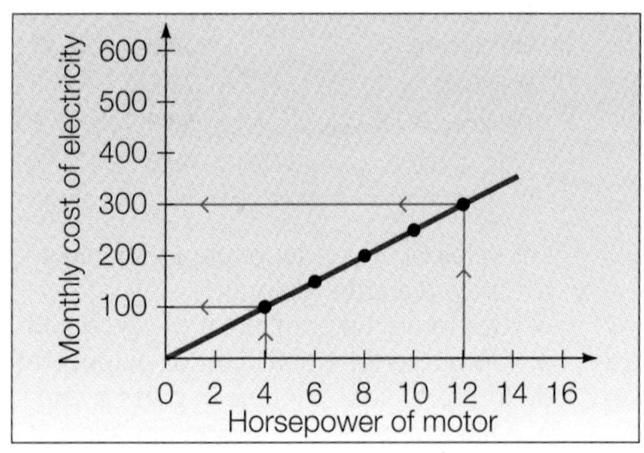

CHART 13–12 Example of Perfect Prediction: Horsepower and Cost of Electricity

Perfect prediction unrealistic in business

Perfect prediction in economics and business is practically impossible. For example, the revenue for the year from gasoline sales (Y) based on the number of automobile registrations (X) as of a certain date could no doubt be approximated fairly closely, but the prediction would not be exact to the nearest dollar, or probably even to the nearest thousand dollars. Even predictions of tensile strength of steel wires based on the outside diameters of the wires are not always exact due to slight differences in the composition of the steel.

What is needed, then, is a measure that describes how precise the prediction of Y is based on X or, conversely, how inaccurate the estimate might be. This measure is called the **standard error of estimate.** The standard error of estimate, symbolized by $s_{y \cdot x}$, is the same concept as the standard deviation discussed in Chapter 4. The standard deviation measures the dispersion around the mean. The standard error of estimate measures the dispersion about the regression line.

STANDARD ERROR OF ESTIMATE A measure of the scatter, or dispersion, of the observed values around the line of regression.

The standard error of estimate is found by the following equation. Note that the equation is quite similar to the one for the standard deviation of a sample.

STANDARD ERROR OF ESTIMATE

$$s_{y \cdot x} = \sqrt{\frac{\Sigma(Y - Y')^2}{n - 2}} \qquad [13\text{–}7]$$

The standard deviation is based on squared deviations from the mean, whereas the standard error of estimate is based on squared deviations from the regression line. If the squared deviations result in a small total, this means that the regression line is representative of the data. If the squared deviations are a large value, then the regression line may not represent the data.

EXAMPLE

Recall the example involving Copier Sales of America. The sales manager determined the least squares regression equation to be $Y' = 18.9476 + 1.1842X$, where Y refers to the number of copiers sold and X the number of sales calls made. Determine the standard error of estimate as a measure of how well the values fit the regression line.

SOLUTION

To find the standard error, we begin by finding the difference between the value, Y, and the value estimated from the regression equation, Y'. Next we square this difference, that is, $(Y - Y')^2$. We do this for each of the n observations and sum the results. That is, we compute $\Sigma(Y - Y')^2$, which is the numerator of formula 13–7. Finally, we divide by the number of observations minus 2. Why minus 2? We lose a degree of freedom each for estimating the intercept value, a, and the slope value, b. The details of the calculations are summarized in Table 13–5.

Statistics in Action

Studies indicate that for both men and women, those who are considered good looking earn higher wages than those who are not. In addition, for men there is a correlation between height and salary. For each additional inch of height, a man can expect to earn an additional \$250 per year. So a man 6′6″ tall receives a \$3,000 "stature" bonus over his 5′6″ counterpart. Being overweight or underweight is also related to earnings, particularly among women. A study of young women showed the heaviest 10 percent earned about 6 percent less than their lighter counterparts.

TABLE 13–5 Computations Needed for the Standard Error of Estimate

Sales Representative	Actual Sales (Y)	Estimated Sales (Y')	Deviation ($Y - Y'$)	Deviation Squared ($(Y - Y')^2$)
Tom Keller	30	42.6316	−12.6316	159.557
Jeff Hall	60	66.3156	−6.3156	39.887
Brian Virost	40	42.6316	−2.6316	6.925
Greg Fish	60	54.4736	5.5264	30.541
Susan Welch	30	30.7896	−0.7896	0.623
Carlos Ramirez	40	30.7896	9.2104	84.831
Rich Niles	40	42.6316	−2.6316	6.925
Mike Kiel	50	42.6316	7.3684	54.293
Mark Reynolds	30	42.6316	−12.6316	159.557
Soni Jones	70	54.4736	15.5264	241.069
			0.0000	784.208

The standard error of estimate is 9.901, found by using formula 13–7.

$$s_{y \cdot x} = \sqrt{\frac{\Sigma(Y - Y')^2}{n - 2}} = \sqrt{\frac{784.208}{10 - 2}} = 9.901$$

The deviations $(Y - Y')$ are the vertical deviations from the regression line. To illustrate, the 10 deviations from Table 13–5 are shown in Chart 13–13. Note in Table 13–5 that the sum of the signed deviations is zero. This indicates that the positive deviations (above the regression line) are offset by the negative deviations (below the regression line).

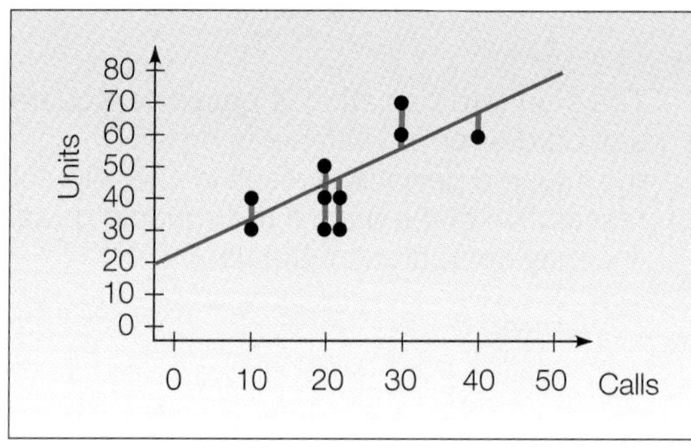

CHART 13–13 Sales Calls and Copiers Sold for 10 Salespeople

Formula 13–7 for the standard error of estimate was applied to show the similarity in concept and computation between the standard deviation and the standard error of estimate. Suppose a large number of observations are being studied, and the numbers are large. Computing each Y' point on the regression line and then squaring the differences—that is, $(Y - Y')^2$—would be rather tedious. The following formula is algebraically equivalent to formula 13–7 but is much easier to use.

COMPUTATION FORMULA FOR THE STANDARD ERROR OF ESTIMATE	$s_{y \cdot x} = \sqrt{\dfrac{\Sigma Y^2 - a(\Sigma Y) - b(\Sigma XY)}{n-2}}$	**[13–8]**

The squares, sums, and other numbers for the Copier Sales of America example were calculated in Table 13–4. Inserting these values into the formula:

$$s_{y \cdot x} = \sqrt{\frac{22{,}100 - 18.9476(450) - 1.1842(10{,}800)}{10 - 2}}$$

$$= 9.901$$

This is the same standard error of estimate as computed previously.

Assumptions Underlying Linear Regression

To properly apply liner regression, several assumptions must be met. Chart 13–14 illustrates these assumptions.

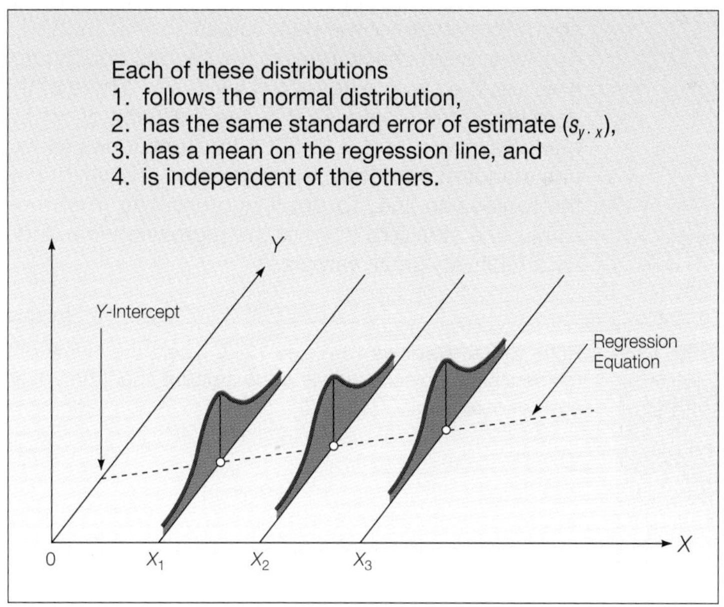

CHART 13–14 Regression Assumptions Shown Graphically

1. For each value of X, there is a group of Y values. These Y values follow the normal distribution.
2. The means of these normal distributions lie on the regression line.
3. The standard deviations of these normal distributions are all the same. The best estimate we have of this common standard deviation is the standard error of estimate ($s_{y \cdot x}$).
4. The Y values are statistically independent. This means that in selecting a sample a particular X does not depend on any other value of X. This assumption is particularly important when data are collected over a period of time. In such

situations, the errors for a particular time period are often correlated with those of other time periods.

Recall from Chapter 7 that if the values follow a normal distribution, then the mean plus or minus one standard deviation will encompass 68 percent of the observations, the mean plus or minus two standard deviations will encompass 95 percent of the observations, and the mean plus or minus three standard deviations will encompass virtually all of the observations. The same relationship exists between the predicted values Y' and the standard error of estimate ($s_{y \cdot x}$).

1. $Y' \pm s_{y \cdot x}$ will include the middle 68 percent of the observations.
2. $Y' \pm 2s_{y \cdot x}$ will include the middle 95 percent of the observations.
3. $Y' \pm 3s_{y \cdot x}$ will include virtually all the observations.

We can now relate these assumptions to Copier Sales of America, where we studied the relationship between the number of sales calls and the number of copiers sold. Assume that we took a much larger sample than $n = 10$, but that the standard error of estimate was still 9.901. If we drew a parallel line 9.901 units above the regression line and another 9.901 units below the regression line, about 68 percent of the points would fall between the two lines. Similarly, a line 19.862 [$2s_{y \cdot x} = 2(9.901)$] units above the regression line and another 19.802 units below the regression line should include about 95 percent of the data values.

As a rough check, refer to the second column from the right in Table 13–5 on page 478, i.e., the column headed "Deviation." Three of the 10 deviations exceed one standard error of estimate. That is, the deviation of −12.6316 for Tom Keller, −12.6316 for Mark Reynolds, and +15.5264 for Soni Jones all exceed the value of 9.901, which is one standard error from the regression line. All of the values are within 19.802 units of the regression line. To put it another way, 7 of the 10 deviations in the sample are within one standard error of the regression line and all are within two—a good result for a relatively small sample.

Self-Review 13–4

Refer to Self-Reviews 13–1 and 13–3, where the owner of Reliable Furniture was studying the relationship between sales and the amount spent on advertising. Determine the standard error of estimate.

Exercises

19. Refer to Exercise 11.
 a. Determine the standard error of estimate.
 b. Suppose a large sample is selected (instead of just five). About 68 percent of the predictions would be between what two values?

20. Refer to Exercise 12.
 a. Determine the standard error of estimate.
 b. Suppose a large sample is selected (instead of just eight). About 95 percent of the predictions would be between what two values?

20. a. 1.6578
 b. ±2(1.6578)

21. Refer to Exercise 13.
 a. Determine the standard error of estimate.
 b. Suppose a large sample is selected (instead of just 10). About 95 percent of the predictions regarding kilowatt-hours would occur between what two values?

22. Refer to Exercise 14.
 a. Determine the standard error of estimate.

22. a. 9.3178

b. ± 18.636

b. Suppose a large sample is selected (instead of just 10). About 95 percent of the predictions regarding sales would occur between what two values?

23. Refer to Exercise 5. Determine the standard error of estimate.

24. 1.733

24. Refer to Exercise 6. Determine the standard error of estimate.

Confidence Intervals and Prediction Intervals

The standard error of estimate is also used to establish confidence intervals when the sample size is large and the scatter around the regression line approximates the normal distribution. In our example involving the number of sales calls and the number of copiers sold, the sample size is small; hence, we need a correction factor to account for the size of the sample. In addition, when we move away from the mean of the independent variable, our estimates are subject to more variation, and we also need to adjust for this.

We are interested in providing interval estimates of two types. The first, which is called a **confidence interval,** reports the *mean* value of Y for a given X. The second type of estimate is called a **prediction interval,** and it reports the *range of values* of Y for a *particular* value of X. To explain further, suppose we estimate the salary of executives in the retail industry based on their years of experience. If we want an interval estimate of the mean salary of *all* retail executives with 20 years of experience, we calculate a confidence interval. If we want an estimate of the salary of Curtis Bender, a particular retail executive with 20 years of experience, we calculate a prediction interval.

To determine the confidence interval for the mean value of Y for a given X, the formula is:

CONFIDENCE INTERVAL FOR THE MEAN OF Y, GIVEN X.

$$Y' \pm t(s_{y \cdot x})\sqrt{\frac{1}{n} + \frac{(X - \bar{X})^2}{\Sigma X^2 - \frac{(\Sigma X)^2}{n}}} \qquad \textbf{[13–9]}$$

where:

- Y' is the predicted value for any selected X value.
- X is any selected value of X.
- $\bar{X}$ is the mean of the Xs, found by $\Sigma X/n$.
- n is the number of observations.
- $s_{y \cdot x}$ is the standard error of estimate.
- t is the value of t from Appendix F with $n - 2$ degrees of freedom.

It is sufficient to again note that the concept of t was developed by William Gossett in the early 1900s. He noticed that $\bar{X} \pm z(s)$ was not precisely correct for small samples. He observed, for example, for samples of size 120, that 95 percent of the items fell within $\bar{X} \pm 1.98s$ instead of $\bar{X} \pm 1.96s$. This difference is not too critical, but note what happens as the sample size becomes smaller:

df	*t*
120	1.980
60	2.000
21	2.080
10	2.228
3	3.182

This is logical. The smaller the sample, the larger the possible error. The increase in the t value compensates for this possibility.

EXAMPLE

We return to the Copier Sales of America illustration. Determine a 95 percent confidence interval for all sales representatives who make 25 calls and for Sheila Baker, a West Coast sales representative who made 25 calls.

SOLUTION

We use formula 13–9 to determine a confidence interval. Table 13–6 includes the necessary totals and a repeat of the information of Table 13–2 on page 462.

TABLE 13–6 Calculations Needed for Determining the Confidence Interval and Prediction Interval

Sales Representative	Sales Calls (X)	Copiers Sold (Y)	X^2	Y^2	XY
Tom Keller	20	30	400	900	600
Jeff Hall	40	60	1,600	3,600	2,400
Brian Virost	20	40	400	1,600	800
Greg Fish	30	60	900	3,600	1,800
Susan Welch	10	30	100	900	300
Carlos Ramirez	10	40	100	1,600	400
Rich Niles	20	40	400	1,600	800
Mike Kiel	20	50	400	2,500	1,000
Mark Reynolds	20	30	400	900	600
Soni Jones	30	70	900	4,900	2,100
Total	220	450	5,600	22,100	10,800

The first step is to determine the number of copiers we expect a sales representative to sell if he or she makes 25 calls. It is 48.5526, found by $Y' = 18.9476 + 1.1842X = 18.9476 + 1.1842(25)$.

To find the t value, we need to first know the number of degrees of freedom. In this case the degrees of freedom is $n - 2 = 10 - 2 = 8$. We set the confidence level at 95 percent. To find the value of t, move down the left-hand column to 8 degrees of freedom, then move across to the column with the 95 percent level of confidence. The value of t is 2.306.

In the previous section we calculated the standard error of estimate to be 9.901, $X = 25$, and from Table 13–6 $\Sigma X = 220$ and $\Sigma X^2 = 5{,}600$. In addition $\bar{X} = \Sigma X/n = 220/10 = 22$. Inserting these values in formula 13–9, we can determine the confidence interval.

$$\text{Confidence interval} = Y' \pm ts_{y \cdot x}\sqrt{\frac{1}{n} + \frac{(X - \bar{X})^2}{\Sigma X^2 - \frac{(\Sigma X)^2}{n}}}$$

$$= 48.5526 \pm 2.306(9.901)\sqrt{\frac{1}{10} + \frac{(25 - 22)^2}{5{,}600 - \frac{(220)^2}{10}}}$$

$$= 48.5526 \pm 7.6356$$

Thus, the 95 percent confidence interval for all sales representatives who make 25 calls is from 40.9170 up to 56.1882. To interpret, let's round the values. If a sales representative makes 25 calls, he or she can expect to sell 48.6 copiers. It is likely those sales will range from 40.9 to 56.2 copiers.

To determine the prediction interval for a particular value of Y for a given X, formula 13–9 is modified slightly: A "1" is added under the radical. The formula becomes:

PREDICTION INTERVAL FOR *Y*, GIVEN *X*

$$Y' \pm ts_{y \cdot x}\sqrt{1 + \frac{1}{n} + \frac{(X - \bar{X})^2}{\Sigma X^2 - \frac{(\Sigma X)^2}{n}}} \qquad \textbf{[13–10]}$$

Suppose we want to estimate the number of copiers sold by Sheila Baker, who made 25 sales calls. The 95 percent prediction interval is determined as follows:

$$\text{Prediction Interval} = Y' \pm ts_{y \cdot x}\sqrt{1 + \frac{1}{n} + \frac{(X - \bar{X})^2}{\Sigma X^2 - \frac{(\Sigma X)^2}{n}}}$$

$$= 48.5526 \pm 2.306(9.901)\sqrt{1 + \frac{1}{10} + \frac{(25 - 22)^2}{5{,}600 - \frac{(220)^2}{10}}}$$

$$= 48.5526 \pm 24.0746$$

Thus, the interval is from 24.478 up to 72.627 copiers. We conclude that the number of copiers sold will be between about 24 and 73 for a particular sales representative. This interval is quite large. It is much larger than the confidence interval for all sales representatives who made 25 calls. It is logical, however, that there should be more variation in the sales estimate for an individual than for a group.

The following MINITAB graph shows the relationship between the regression line (shown in green), the confidence interval (shown in crimson), and the prediction interval (shown in yellow). The bands for the prediction interval are always further from the regression line than for the confidence interval. Also, as the values of X move away from the mean number of calls (22) in either the positive or the negative direction the confidence interval and prediction interval bands widen. This is caused by the numerator of the right-hand term under the radical in formulas 13–9 and 13–10. That is, as the term $(X - \bar{X})^2$ increases, the widths of the confidence interval and the prediction interval also increase. To put it another way, there is less precision in our estimates as we move away, in either direction, from the mean of the independent variable.

Confidence and Prediction Intervals for Copier Sales of America Data

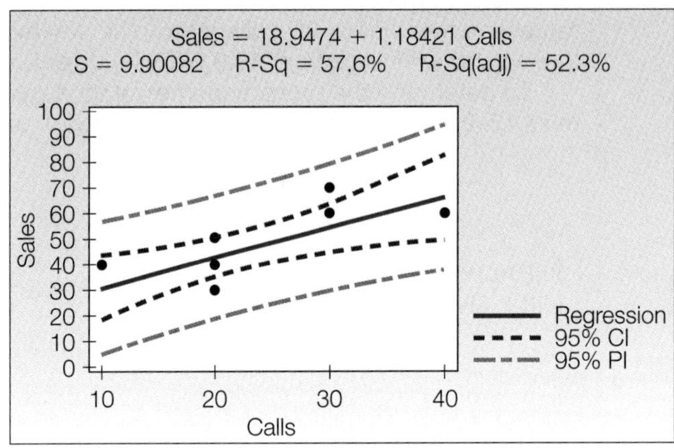

We wish to emphasize again the distinction between a confidence interval and a prediction interval. A confidence interval refers to all cases with a given value of X and is computed using formula 13–9. A prediction interval refers to a particular case for a given value of X and is computed using formula 13–10. The prediction interval will always be wider because of the extra "1" under the radical in the second equation.

Self-Review 13–5

Refer to the sample data in Self-Reviews 13–1, 13–3, and 13–4, where the owner of Reliable Furniture was studying the relationship between sales and the amount spent on advertising. The sales information for the last four months is repeated below.

Month	Advertising Expense ($ millions)	Sales Revenue ($ millions)
July	2	7
August	1	3
September	3	8
October	4	10

The regression equation was computed to be $Y' = 1.5 + 2.2X$, and the standard error is 0.9487. Both variables are reported in millions of dollars. Determine the 90 percent confidence interval for the typical month in which $3 million was spent on advertising.

Exercises

25. Refer to Exercise 11.
   a. Determine the .95 confidence interval for the mean predicted when $X = 7$.
   b. Determine the .95 prediction interval for an individual predicted when $X = 7$.

26. a. 4.5522, 9.2923
    b. 2.2238, 11.6208

26. Refer to Exercise 12.
   a. Determine the .95 confidence interval for the mean predicted when $X = 7$.
   b. Determine the .95 prediction interval for an individual predicted when $X = 7$.

27. Refer to Exercise 13.
   a. Determine the .95 confidence interval, in thousands of kilowatt-hours, for the mean of all six-room homes.

b. Determine the .95 prediction interval, in thousands of kilowatt-hours, for a particular six-room home.

28. Refer to Exercise 14.

28. a. [68.29, 82.88] **a.** Determine the .95 confidence interval, in thousands of dollars, for the mean of all sales personnel who make 40 contacts.

b. [52.91, 98.26] **b.** Determine the .95 prediction interval, in thousands of dollars, for a particular salesperson who makes 40 contacts.

More on the Coefficient of Determination

Formula 13–2 is a convenient computational formula to determine the coefficient of correlation, *r.* The coefficient of determination is found by squaring the coefficient of correlation.

To further examine the basic concept of the coefficient of determination, suppose there is interest in the relationship between years on the job, *X,* and weekly production, *Y.* Sample data revealed:

Employee	Years on Job, *X*	Weekly Production, *Y*
Gordon	14	6
James	7	5
Ford	3	3
Salter	15	9
Artes	11	7

The sample data were plotted in a scatter diagram. Since the relationship between *X* and *Y* appears to be linear, a line was drawn through the plots (see Chart 13–15). The equation is $Y' = 2 + 0.4X$.

Note in Chart 13–15 that if we were to use that line to predict weekly production for an employee, in no case would our prediction be exact. That is, there would be some error in each of our predictions. As an example, for Gordon, who has been with the company 14 years, we would predict weekly production to be 7.6 units; however, he produces only 6 units.

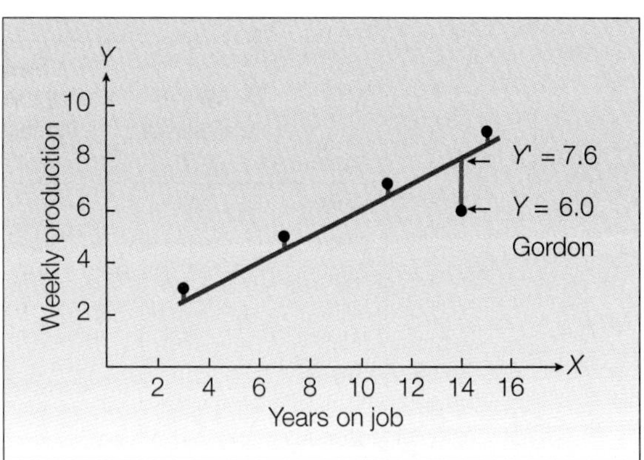

CHART 13–15 Observed Data and the Least Squares Line

To measure the overall error in our prediction, every deviation from the line is squared and the squares summed. The predicted point on the line is designated Y', read Y prime, and the observed point is designated Y. For Gordon, $(Y - Y')^2 = (6 - 7.6)^2 = (-1.6)^2 = 2.56$. Logically, this variation cannot be explained by the independent variable, so it is referred to as the *unexplained variation.* Specifically, we cannot explain why Gordon's production of 6 units is 1.6 units below his predicted production of 7.6 units, based on the number of years he has been on the job.

Unexplained variation

The sum of the squared deviations, $\Sigma(Y - Y')^2$, is 4.00. (See Table 13–7.) The term $\Sigma(Y - Y')^2 = 4.00$ is the variation in Y (production) that cannot be predicted from X. It is the "unexplained" variation in Y.

TABLE 13–7 Computations Needed for the Unexplained Variation

	X	Y	Y'	$Y - Y'$	$(Y - Y')^2$
Gordon	14	6	7.6	−1.6	2.56
James	7	5	4.8	0.2	0.04
Ford	3	3	3.2	−0.2	0.04
Salter	15	9	8.0	1.0	1.00
Artes	11	7	6.4	0.6	0.36
Total	50	30		0.0*	4.00

*Must be 0.

Now suppose *only* the Y values (weekly production, in this problem) are known and we want to predict production for every employee. The actual production figures for the employees are 6, 5, 3, 9, and 7 (from Table 13–7). To make these predictions, we could assign the mean weekly production (6 units, found by $\Sigma Y/n = 30/5 = 6$) to each employee. This would keep the sum of the squared prediction errors at a minimum. (Recall from Chapter 3 that the sum of the squared deviations from the arithmetic mean for a set of numbers is smaller than the sum of the squared deviations from any other value, such as the median.) Table 13–8 shows the necessary calculations. The sum of the squared deviations is 20, as shown in Table 13–8. The value 20 is referred to as the *total variation in* Y.

Total variation in Y

TABLE 13–8 Calculations Needed for the Total Variation in Y

Name	Weekly Production, Y	Mean Weekly Production, $\bar{Y}$	$Y - \bar{Y}$	$(Y - \bar{Y})^2$
Gordon	6	6	0	0
James	5	6	−1	1
Ford	3	6	−3	9
Salter	9	6	3	9
Artes	7	6	1	1
Total			0*	20

*Must be 0.

What we did to arrive at the total variation in Y is shown diagrammatically in Chart 13–16.

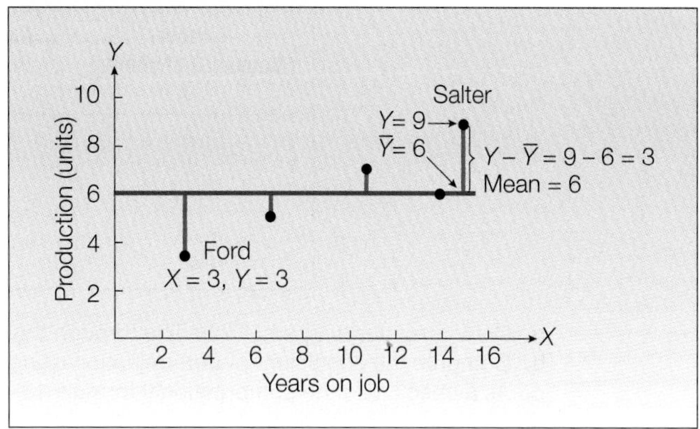

CHART 13–16 Plots Showing Deviations from the Mean of Y

Logically, the total variation in Y can be subdivided into unexplained variation and explained variation. To arrive at the explained variation, since we know the total variation and unexplained variation, we simply subtract: Explained variation = Total variation − Unexplained variation. Dividing the explained variation by the total variation gives the coefficient of determination, r^2, which is a proportion. In terms of a formula:

COEFFICIENT OF DETERMINATION

$$r^2 = \frac{\text{Total variation} - \text{Unexplained variation}}{\text{Total variation}} = \frac{\Sigma(Y - \bar{Y})^2 - \Sigma(Y - Y')^2}{\Sigma(Y - \bar{Y})^2} \quad \textbf{[13–11]}$$

In this problem:

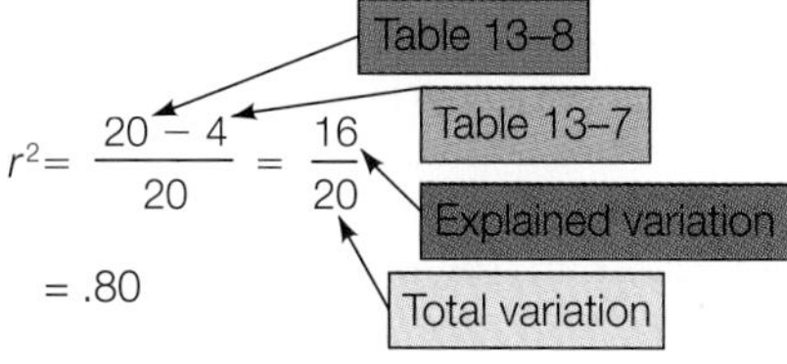

$$r^2 = \frac{20 - 4}{20} = \frac{16}{20} = .80$$

As mentioned, .80 is a proportion. We say that 80 percent of the variation in weekly production, Y, is determined, or accounted for, by its linear relationship with X (years on the job).

As a check, the computational formula (13–1) for the coefficient of correlation could be used. Squaring r gives the coefficient of determination. Exercise 29 offers a check on the preceding problem.

Exercises

29. Using the preceding problem, involving years on the job and weekly production, verify that the coefficient of determination is in fact .80.

30. The number of shares of Icom, Inc., turned over during a month, and the price at the end of the month, are listed in the following table. Also, the Y' plots on the line going through observed data are given.

Turnover (thousands of shares), X	Actual Price, Y	Estimated Price, Y'
4	\$2	\$2.7
1	1	0.6
5	4	3.4
3	2	2.0
2	1	1.3

30. a. See IM.
b. .8167
c. .8167
d. See IM.

a. Draw a scatter diagram. Plot a line through the dots.
b. Compute the coefficient of determination using formula 12–10.
c. As a check, use the computational formula 13–2 for *r.*
d. Interpret the coefficient of determination.

The Relationships among the Coefficient of Correlation, the Coefficient of Determination, and the Standard Error of Estimate

In an earlier section, we discussed the standard error of estimate, which measures how close the actual values are to the regression line. When the standard error is small, it indicates that the two variables are closely related. In the calculation of the standard error, the key term is $\Sigma(Y - Y')^2$. If the value of this term is small, then the standard error will also be small.

The correlation coefficient measures the strength of the association between two variables. When the points on the scatter diagram appear close to the line, we note that the correlation coefficient tends to be large. Thus, the standard error of estimate and the coefficient of correlation relate the same information but use a different scale to report the strength of the association. However, both measures involve the term $\Sigma(Y - Y')^2$.

We also noted that the square of the correlation coefficient is the coefficient of determination. The coefficient of determination measures the percent of the variation in *Y* that is explained by the variation in *X.*

A convenient vehicle for showing the relationship among these three measures is an ANOVA table. This table is similar to the analysis of variance table developed in Chapter 12. In that chapter, the total variation was divided into two components: that due to the *treatments* and that due to *random error.* The concept is similar in regression analysis. The total variation, $\Sigma(Y - \bar{Y})^2$, is divided into two components: (1) that explained by the *regression* (explained by the independent variable) and (2) the *error,* or unexplained variation. These two categories are identified in the first column of the ANOVA table that follows. The column headed "df" refers to the degrees of freedom associated with each category. The total number of degrees of freedom is $n - 1$. The number of degrees of freedom in the regression is 1, since there is only one independent variable. The number of degrees of freedom associated with the error term is $n - 2$. The term "SS" located in the middle of the ANOVA table refers to the sum of squares—the variation. The terms are computed as follows:

$$\text{Regression} = \text{SSR} = \Sigma(Y' - \bar{Y})^2$$
$$\text{Error variation} = \text{SSE} = \Sigma(Y - Y')^2$$
$$\text{Total variation} = \text{SS total} = \Sigma(Y - \bar{Y})^2$$

The format for the ANOVA table is:

Source	df	SS	MS
Regression	1	SSR	SSR/1
Error	$n - 2$	SSE	SSE/$(n - 2)$
Total	$n - 1$	SS total*	

*SS total = SSR + SSE.

The coefficient of determination, r^2, can be obtained directly from the ANOVA table by:

COEFFICIENT OF DETERMINATION

$$r^2 = \frac{\text{SSR}}{\text{SS total}} = 1 - \frac{\text{SSE}}{\text{SS total}} \quad \textbf{[13–12]}$$

The term "SSR/SS total" is the proportion of the variation in Y *explained* by the independent variable, X. Note the effect of the SSE term on r^2. As SSE decreases, r^2 will increase. Conversely, as the standard error decreases, the r^2 term increases.

The standard error of estimate can also be obtained from the ANOVA table using the following equation:

STANDARD ERROR OF ESTIMATE

$$s_{y \cdot x} = \sqrt{\frac{\text{SSE}}{n - 2}} \quad \textbf{[13–13]}$$

The Copier Sales of America example is used to illustrate the computations of the coefficient of determination and the standard error of estimate from an ANOVA table.

EXAMPLE

In the Copier Sales of America example we studied the relationship between the number of sales calls made and the number of copiers sold. Use a computer software package to determine the least squares regression equation and the ANOVA table. Identify the regression equation, the standard error of estimate, and the coefficient of determination on the computer output. From the ANOVA table on the computer output, determine the coefficient of determination and the standard error of estimate using formulas 13–12 and 13–13.

SOLUTION

Following is the output from Excel.

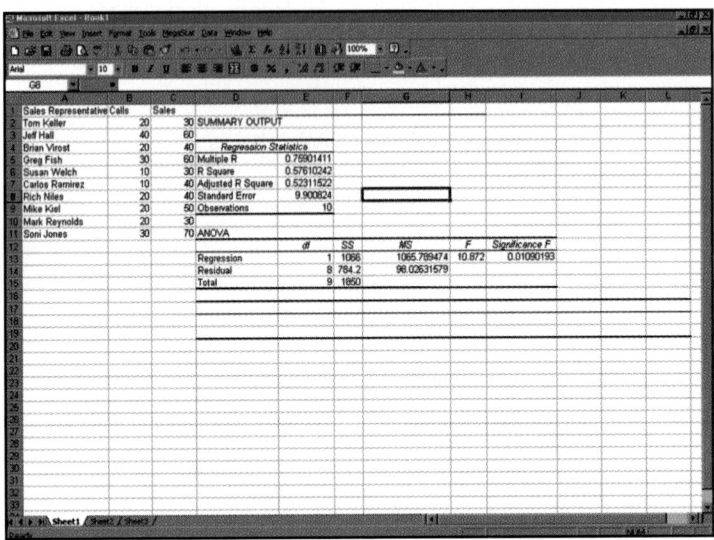

Using formula 13–12 the coefficient of determination is .576, found by

$$r^2 = \frac{\text{SSR}}{\text{SS total}} = \frac{1066}{1850} = .576$$

This is the same value we computed earlier in the chapter, when we found the coefficient of determination by squaring the coefficient of correlation. Again, the interpretation is that the independent variable, *Calls,* explains 57.6 percent of the variation in the number of copiers sold. If we needed the coefficient of correlation, we could find it by taking the square root of the coefficient of determination:

$$r = \sqrt{r^2} = \sqrt{.576} = .759$$

A problem does remain, and that involves the sign for the coefficient of correlation. Recall that the square root of a value could have either a positive or a negative sign. The sign of the coefficient of correlation will always be the same as that of the slope. That is, *b* and *r* will always have the same sign. In this case the sign is positive, so the coefficient of correlation is .759.

To find the standard error of estimate, we use formula 13–13:

$$s_{y \cdot x} = \sqrt{\frac{\text{SSE}}{n-2}} = \sqrt{\frac{784.2}{10-2}} = 9.901$$

Again, this is the same value calculated earlier in the chapter. These values are identified on the Excel computer output.

Exercises

31. Given the following ANOVA table:

SOURCE	DF	SS	MS	F
Regression	1	1000.0	1000.00	26.00
Error	13	500.0	38.46	
Total	14	1500.0		

a. Determine the coefficient of determination.
b. Assuming a direct relationship between the variables, what is the coefficient of correlation?
c. Determine the standard error of estimate.

32. See IM.

32. On the first statistics exam the coefficient of determination between the hours studied and the grade earned was 80 percent. The standard error of estimate was 10. There were 20 students in the class. Develop an ANOVA table.

Chapter Outline

I. A scatter diagram is a graphic tool to portray the relationship between two variables.
- **A.** The dependent variable is scaled on the *Y*-axis and is the variable being estimated.
- **B.** The independent variable is scaled on the *X*-axis and is the variable used as the estimator.

II. The coefficient of correlation measures the strength of the association between two variables.
- **A.** Both variables must be at least the interval scale of measurement.
- **B.** The coefficient of correlation can range from −1.00 up to 1.00.
- **C.** If the correlation between two variables is 0, there is no association between them.
- **D.** A value of 1.00 indicates perfect positive correlation, and −1.00 perfect negative correlation.
- **E.** A positive sign means there is a direct relationship between the variables, and a negative sign means there is an inverse relationship.
- **F.** It is designated by the letter r and found by the following equations:

$$r = \frac{\Sigma(X - \bar{X})(Y - \bar{Y})}{(n - 1)\, s_x s_y} = \frac{n\Sigma XY - \Sigma X \Sigma Y}{\sqrt{[n\Sigma X^2 - (\Sigma X)^2][n\Sigma Y^2 - (\Sigma Y)^2]}} \qquad \textbf{[13–1, 13–2]}$$

- **G.** The following equation is used to determine whether the correlation in the population is different from 0.

$$t = \frac{r\sqrt{n-2}}{\sqrt{1-r^2}} \qquad \textbf{[13–3]}$$

III. The coefficient of determination is the fraction of the variation in one variable that is explained by the variation in the other variable.
- **A.** It ranges from 0 to 1.0.
- **B.** It is the square of the coefficient of correlation.

IV. In regression analysis we estimate one variable based on another variable.
- **A.** The variable being estimated is the dependent variable.
- **B.** The variable used to make the estimate is the independent variable.
  1. The relationship between the variables must be linear.
  2. Both the independent and the dependent variable must be interval or ratio scale.
  3. The least squares criterion is used to determine the regression equation.

V. The least squares regression line is of the form $Y' = a + bX$.
- **A.** Y' is the estimated value of Y for a selected value of X.
- **B.** a is the constant or intercept.
  1. It is the value of Y' when $X = 0$.
  2. a is computed using the following equation.

$$a = \frac{\Sigma Y}{n} - b\frac{\Sigma X}{n} \qquad \textbf{[13–6]}$$

- **C.** b is the slope of the line.
  1. It shows the amount of change in Y' for a change of 1 in X.
  2. A positive value for b indicates a direct relationship between the two variables, and a negative value an inverse relationship.

3. The sign of b and the sign of r, the coefficient of correlation, are always the same.
4. b is computed using the following equation.

$$b = \frac{n(\Sigma XY) - (\Sigma X)(\Sigma Y)}{n(\Sigma X^2) - (\Sigma X)^2} \qquad [13\text{–}5]$$

D. X is the value of the independent variable.

VI. The standard error of estimate measures the variation around the regression line.

A. It is in the same units as the dependent variable.
B. It is based on squared deviations from the regression line.
C. Small values indicate that the points cluster closely about the regression line.
D. It is computed using the following formula.

$$s_{y \cdot x} = \sqrt{\frac{\Sigma(Y - Y')^2}{n-2}} = \sqrt{\frac{\Sigma Y^2 - a(\Sigma Y) - b(\Sigma XY)}{n-2}} \qquad [13\text{–}7, 13\text{–}8]$$

VII. Inference about linear regression is based on the following assumptions.

A. For a given value of X, the values of Y are normally distributed about the line of regression.
B. The standard deviation of each of the normal distributions is the same for all values of X and is estimated by the standard error of estimate.
C. The deviations from the regression line are independent, with no pattern to the size or direction.

VIII. There are two types of interval estimates.

A. In a confidence interval the mean value of Y is estimated for a given value of X.

1. It is computed from the following formula.

$$Y' \pm t s_{y \cdot x} \sqrt{\frac{1}{n} + \frac{(X - \bar{X})^2}{\Sigma X^2 - \frac{(\Sigma X)^2}{n}}} \qquad [13\text{–}9]$$

2. The width of the interval is affected by the level of confidence, the size of the standard error of estimate, and the size of the sample, as well as the value of the independent variable.

B. In a prediction interval the individual value of Y is estimated for a given value of X.

1. It is computed from the following formula.

$$Y' \pm t s_{y \cdot x} \sqrt{1 + \frac{1}{n} + \frac{(X - \bar{X})^2}{\Sigma X^2 - \frac{(\Sigma X)^2}{n}}} \qquad [13\text{–}10]$$

2. The difference between formulas 13–9 and 13–10 is the 1 under the radical.
   a. The prediction interval will be wider than the confidence interval.
   b. The prediction interval is also based on the level of confidence, the size of the standard error of estimate, the size of the sample, and the value of the independent variable.

Pronunciation Key

SYMBOL	MEANING	PRONUNCIATION
ΣXY	Sum of the products of X and Y	*Sum X Y*
ρ	Coefficient of correlation in the population	*Rho*
Y'	Estimated value of Y	*Y prime*
$s_{y \cdot x}$	Standard error of estimate	*s sub y dot x*
r^2	Coefficient of determination	*r square*

Chapter Exercises

33. A major airline selected a random sample of 25 flights and found that the correlation between the number of passengers and the total weight, in pounds, of luggage stored in the luggage compartment is 0.94. Using the .05 significance level, can we conclude that there is a positive association between the two variables?

34. $t = 1.852$ Do not reject H_0.

34. A sociologist claims that the success of students in college (measured by their GPA) is related to their family's income. For a sample of 20 students, the coefficient of correlation is 0.40. Using the 0.01 significance level, can we conclude that there is a positive correlation between the variables?

35. An Environmental Protection Agency study of 12 automobiles revealed a correlation of 0.47 between the engine size and performance. At the .01 significance level, can we conclude that there is a positive association between these variables? What is the p-value? Interpret.

36. $t = 0.911$ Do not reject H_0.

36. A study of college soccer games revealed the correlation between the number of shots attempted and the number of goals scored to be 0.21 for a sample of 20 games. Is it reasonable to conclude that there is a positive correlation between the two variables? Use the .05 significance level. Determine the p-value.

37. A sample of 30 used cars sold by Northcut Motors in 2000 revealed that the correlation between the selling price and the number of miles driven was −.45. At the .05 significance level, can we conclude that there is a negative association in the population between the two variables?

38. $t = -2.13$ Reject H_0.

38. For a sample of 32 large U.S. cities, the correlation between the mean number of square feet per office worker and the mean monthly rental rate in the central business district is −.363. At the .05 significance level, can we conclude that there is a negative association in the population between the two variables?

39. What is the relationship between the amount spent per week on food and the size of the family? Do larger families spend more on food? A sample of 10 families in the Chicago area revealed the following figures for family size and the amount spent on food per week.

Family Size	Amount Spent on Food	Family Size	Amount Spent on Food
3	$ 99	3	$111
6	104	4	74
5	151	4	91
6	129	5	119
6	142	3	91

a. Compute the coefficient of correlation.
b. Determine the coefficient of determination.
c. Can we conclude that there is a positive association between the amount spent on food and the family size? Use the .05 significance level.

40. A sample of 12 homes sold last week in St. Paul, Minnesota, is selected. Can we conclude that as the size of the home (reported below in thousands of square feet) increases, the selling price (reported in $ thousands) also increases?

Home Size (thousands of square feet)	Selling Price ($ thousands)	Home Size (thousands of square feet)	Selling Price ($ thousands)
1.4	100	1.3	110
1.3	110	0.8	85
1.2	105	1.2	105
1.1	120	0.9	75
1.4	80	1.1	70
1.0	105	1.1	95

40. a. 0.307
b. 0.0942
c. $t = 1.02$
Do not reject H_0.

a. Compute the coefficient of correlation.
b. Determine the coefficient of determination.
c. Can we conclude that there is a positive association between the size of the home and the selling price? Use the .05 significance level.

41. The manufacturer of Cardio Glide exercise equipment wants to study the relationship between the number of months since the glide was purchased and the length of time the equipment was used last week.

Person	Months Owned	Hours Exercised	Person	Months Owned	Hours Exercised
Rupple	12	4	Massa	2	8
Hall	2	10	Sass	8	3
Bennett	6	8	Karl	4	8
Longnecker	9	5	Malrooney	10	2
Phillips	7	5	Veights	5	5

a. Plot the information on a scatter diagram. Let hours of exercise be the dependent variable. Comment on the graph.
b. Determine the coefficient of correlation. Interpret.
c. At the .01 significance level, can we conclude that there is a negative association between the variables?

42. The following regression equation was computed from a sample of 20 observations:

$$Y' = 15 - 5X$$

42. a. 2.357
b. 0.75
c. −0.866

SSE was found to be 100 and SS total 400.
a. Determine the standard error of estimate.
b. Determine the coefficient of determination.
c. Determine the coefficient of correlation. (Caution: Watch the sign!)

43. An ANOVA table is:

SOURCE	DF	SS	MS	F
Regression	1	50		
Error				
Total	24	500		

a. Complete the ANOVA table.
b. How large was the sample?
c. Determine the standard error of estimate.
d. Determine the coefficient of determination.

44. Following is a regression equation.

$$Y' = 17.08 + 0.16X$$

44. a. 25.08
b. [10.60, 39.56]

This information is also available: $s_{y \cdot x} = 4.05$, $\Sigma X = 210$, $\Sigma X^2 = 9{,}850$, and $n = 5$.
a. Estimate the value of Y' when $X = 50$.
b. Develop a 95 percent prediction interval for an individual value of Y for $X = 50$.

45. The National Highway Association is studying the relationship between the number of bidders on a highway project and the winning (lowest) bid for the project. Of particular interest is whether the number of bidders increases or decreases the amount of the winning bid.

Project	Number of Bidders, X	Winning Bid ($ millions), Y	Project	Number of Bidders, X	Winning Bid ($ millions), Y
1	9	5.1	9	6	10.3
2	9	8.0	10	6	8.0
3	3	9.7	11	4	8.8
4	10	7.8	12	7	9.4
5	5	7.7	13	7	8.6
6	10	5.5	14	7	8.1
7	7	8.3	15	6	7.8
8	11	5.5			

a. Determine the regression equation. Interpret the equation. Do more bidders tend to increase or decrease the amount of the winning bid?
b. Estimate the amount of the winning bid if there were seven bidders.
c. A new entrance is to be constructed on the Ohio Turnpike. There are seven bidders on the project. Develop a 95 percent prediction interval for the winning bid.
d. Determine the coefficient of determination. Interpret its value.

46. Mr. William Profit is studying companies going public for the first time. He is particularly interested in the relationship between the size of the offering and the price per share. A sample of 15 companies that recently went public revealed the following information.

Company	Size ($ millions), X	Price per Share, Y	Company	Size ($ millions), X	Price per Share, Y
1	9.0	10.8	9	160.7	11.3
2	94.4	11.3	10	96.5	10.6
3	27.3	11.2	11	83.0	10.5
4	179.2	11.1	12	23.5	10.3
5	71.9	11.1	13	58.7	10.7
6	97.9	11.2	14	93.8	11.0
7	93.5	11.0	15	34.4	10.8
8	70.0	10.7			

46. a. $Y' = 10.6678 + 0.003X$
b. 0.2172

a. Determine the regression equation.
b. Determine the coefficient of determination. Do you think Mr. Profit should be satisfied with using the size of the offering as the independent variable?

47. The Bardi Trucking Co., located in Cleveland, Ohio, makes deliveries in the Great Lakes region, the Southeast, and the Northeast. Jim Bardi, the president, is studying the relationship between the distance a shipment must travel and the length of time, in days, it takes the shipment to arrive at its destination. To investigate, Mr. Bardi selected a random sample of 20 shipments made last month. Shipping distance is the independent variable, and shipping time is the dependent variable. The results are as follows:

Shipment	Distance (miles)	Shipping Time (days)	Shipment	Distance (miles)	Shipping Time (days)
1	656	5	11	862	7
2	853	14	12	679	5
3	646	6	13	835	13
4	783	11	14	607	3
5	610	8	15	665	8
6	841	10	16	647	7
7	785	9	17	685	10
8	639	9	18	720	8
9	762	10	19	652	6
10	762	9	20	828	10

a. Draw a scatter diagram. Based on these data, does it appear that there is a relationship between how many miles a shipment has to go and the time it takes to arrive at its destination?

b. Determine the coefficient of correlation. Can we conclude that there is a positive correlation between distance and time? Use the .05 significance level.

c. Determine and interpret the coefficient of determination.

d. Determine the standard error of estimate.

48. $uper Markets, Inc. is considering expanding into the Scottsdale, Arizona, area. Ms. Luann Miller, Director of Planning, must present an analysis of the proposed expansion to the operating committee of the board of directors. As a part of her proposal, she needs to include information on the amount people in the region spend per month for grocery items. She would also like to include information on the relationship between the amount spent for grocery items and income. She gathered the following sample information.

Household	Monthly Amount	Monthly Income	Household	Monthly Amount	Monthly Income
1	$555	$4,388	21	$ 913	$6,688
2	489	4,558	22	918	6,752
3	458	4,793	23	710	6,837
4	613	4,856	24	1,083	7,242
5	647	4,856	25	937	7,263
6	661	4,899	26	839	7,540
7	662	4,899	27	1,030	8,009
8	675	5,091	28	1,065	8,094
9	549	5,133	29	1,069	8,264
10	606	5,304	30	1,064	8,392
11	668	5,304	31	1,015	8,414
12	740	5,304	32	1,148	8,882
13	592	5,346	33	1,125	8,925
14	720	5,495	34	1,090	8,989
15	680	5,581	35	1,208	9,053
16	540	5,730	36	1,217	9,138
17	693	5,943	37	1,140	9,329
18	541	5,943	38	1,265	9,649
19	673	6,156	39	1,206	9,862
20	676	6,603	40	1,145	9,883

48. a. See IM.
b. $Y' = -74.37 + 0.1339X$
c. $r = 0.945$, $t = 17.811$ Correlation greater than 0.

a. Let the amount spent be the dependent variable and monthly income the independent variable. Create a scatter diagram, using a software package.

b. Determine the regression equation. Interpret the slope value.

c. Determine the coefficient of correlation. Can you conclude that it is greater than 0?

49. Below is information on the price per share and the dividend for a sample of 30 companies.

Company	Price per share	Dividend	Company	Price per share	Dividend
1	$20.00	$ 3.14	16	$57.06	$ 9.53
2	22.01	3.36	17	57.40	12.60
3	31.39	0.46	18	58.30	10.43
4	33.57	7.99	19	59.51	7.97
5	35.86	0.77	20	60.60	9.19
6	36.12	8.46	21	64.01	16.50
7	36.16	7.62	22	64.66	16.10
8	37.99	8.03	23	64.74	13.76
9	38.85	6.33	24	64.95	10.54
10	39.65	7.96	25	66.43	21.15
11	43.44	8.95	26	68.18	14.30
12	49.08	9.61	27	69.56	24.42
13	53.73	11.11	28	74.90	11.54
14	54.41	13.28	29	77.91	17.65
15	55.10	10.22	30	80.00	17.36

a. Calculate the regression equation using selling price based on the annual dividend. Interpret the slope value.
b. Determine the coefficient of determination. Interpret its value.
c. Determine the coefficient of correlation. Can you conclude that it is greater than 0 using the .05 significance level?

exercises.com

50. Suppose you want to study the association between the literacy rate in a country, the population, and the country's gross domestic product (GDP). Go to the Web site of *Information Please Almanac* (http://www.infoplease.com). Select the category **World,** and then select **Countries.** A list of 195 countries starting with Afghanistan and ending with Zimbabwe will appear. Randomly select a sample of about 20 countries. It may be convenient to use a systematic sample. In other words, randomly select 1 of the first 10 countries and then select every tenth country thereafter. Click on each country name and scan the information to find the literacy rate, the population, and the GDP. Compute the correlation among the variables. In other words, find the correlation between: literacy and population, literacy and GDP, and population and GDP. *Warning:* Be careful of the units. Sometimes population is reported in millions, other times in thousands. At the .05 significance level, can we conclude that the correlation is different from 0?

50. Answers will vary.

51. Many real estate companies and rental agencies now publish their listings on the Web. One example is the Dunes Realty Company, located in Garden City and Surfside Beaches in South Carolina. Go to the Web site http://www.dunes.com and select **Cottage Search.** Then indicate 5 bedroom, accommodations for 14 people, second row (this means it is across the street from the beach), and no pool or floating dock; select a period in July or August; indicate that you are willing to spend $5,000 per week; and then click on **Search the Cottages.** The output should include details on the cottages that met your criteria.
a. Determine the correlation between the number of baths in each cottage and the weekly rental price. Can you conclude that the correlation is greater than zero at the .05 significance level? Determine the coefficient of determination.
b. Determine the regression equation using the number of bathrooms as the independent variable and the price per week as the dependent variable. Interpret the regression equation.
c. Calculate the correlation between the number of people the cottage will accommodate and the weekly rental price. At the .05 significance level can you conclude that it is different from zero?

Computer Data Exercises

52. a. $Y' = 64.79 + 0.070X$ See IM for intervals.
b. $Y' = 270.17 - 3.354X$ See IM for intervals.
c. $r = -0.347$ $t = -3.755$ p-value = .000 $r = 0.371$ $t = 4.05$ p-value = .000

52. Refer to the Real Estate data, which reports information on homes sold in Venice, Florida, last year.

a. Let selling price be the dependent variable and size of the home the independent variable. Determine the regression equation. Estimate the selling price for a home with an area of 2,200 square feet. Determine the 95 percent confidence interval and the 95 percent prediction interval for the selling price of a home with 2,200 square feet.

b. Let selling price be the dependent variable and distance from the center of the city the independent variable. Determine the regression equation. Estimate the selling price of a home 20 miles from the center of the city. Determine the 95 percent confidence interval and the 95 percent prediction interval for homes 20 miles from the center of the city.

c. Can you conclude that the independent variables "distance from the center of the city" and "selling price" are negatively correlated and that the area of the home and the selling price are positively correlated? Use the .05 significance level. Report the *p*-value of the test.

53. Refer to the Baseball 2000 data, which reports information on the 2000 Major League Baseball season.

a. Let the games won be the dependent variable and total team salary, in millions of dollars, be the independent variable. Can you conclude that there is a positive association between the two variables? Determine the regression equation. Interpret the slope, that is the value of *b*. How many additional wins will an additional $5 million in salary bring?

b. Determine the correlation between games won and ERA and between games won and team batting average. Which has the stronger correlation? Can we conclude that there is a positive correlation between wins and team batting and a negative correlation between wins and ERA? Use the .05 significance level.

c. Assume the number of games won is the dependent variable and attendance the independent variable. Can we conclude that the correlation between these two variables is greater than 0? Use the .05 significance level.

54. a. $Y' = -1{,}141 + .496X$
b. $r = .482$ $t = 2.859$
c. No. $r = -0.031$ $t = -0.161$

54. Refer to the OECD data that reports information on 29 countries.

a. Suppose you wish to use the population as the independent variable to predict the number of people employed (the dependent variable). Develop the appropriate linear regression equation. Use the equation to predict employment in Mexico, where the population is 96,582.

b. Find the correlation coefficient between land area and domestic production. Use the .05 significance level to test whether there is a positive correlation between these two variables.

c. Does there appear to be a relationship between the level of manufacturing and energy consumption? Support your answer with statistical evidence.

55. Refer to the Schools data, which includes information on the 94 school districts in northwestern Ohio.

a. Let the independent variable be the percent of families on welfare in the school district and the number of students in the district be the dependent variable.

1. Determine the regression equation. Comment on the values you found for the slope and the intercept. Are they reasonable?
2. Estimate the number of students in a school district in which 10 percent of the families are on welfare.
3. Develop a 95 percent confidence interval and a 95 percent prediction interval for all schools that have 10 percent of families on welfare.

b. Let the independent variable be the attendance rate and the dependent variable be the percent passing the proficiency examination.

1. Determine the regression equation. Comment on the values you found for *a* and *b*. Are they reasonable?

2. Estimate the percent of students passing the proficiency examination if the attendance rate is 90 percent.
3. Develop a 95 percent confidence interval and a 95 percent prediction interval for the percentage passing the proficiency examination if the attendance rate is 90 percent.

c. At the .01 significance level can we conclude that there is a positive association between the variables "attendance rate" and "percent passing the proficiency examination"?

Computer Commands

1. The MINITAB commands for the output showing the coefficient of correlation on page 469 are:
   a. Enter the data in columns C1 and C2. Use the **Name** command to identify the variables. We've used the names *Calls* and *Sales.*
   b. Select **Stat, Basic Statistics,** and **Correlation.**
   c. Select *Calls* and *Sales* as the variables, click on **Display p-values,** and then click **OK.**

2. The computer commands for the Excel output on page 490 are:
   a. Enter the variable names in row 1 of columns A and B. Enter the data in rows 2 through 11 in the same columns.
   b. Select **Tools, Data Analysis,** and then select **Regression.**
   c. For our spreadsheet we have *Calls* in column B and *Sales* in column C. The **Input Y-Range** is *C1:C11* and the **Input X-Range** is *B1:B11,* click on **Labels,** select *D2* as the **Output Range,** and click **OK.**

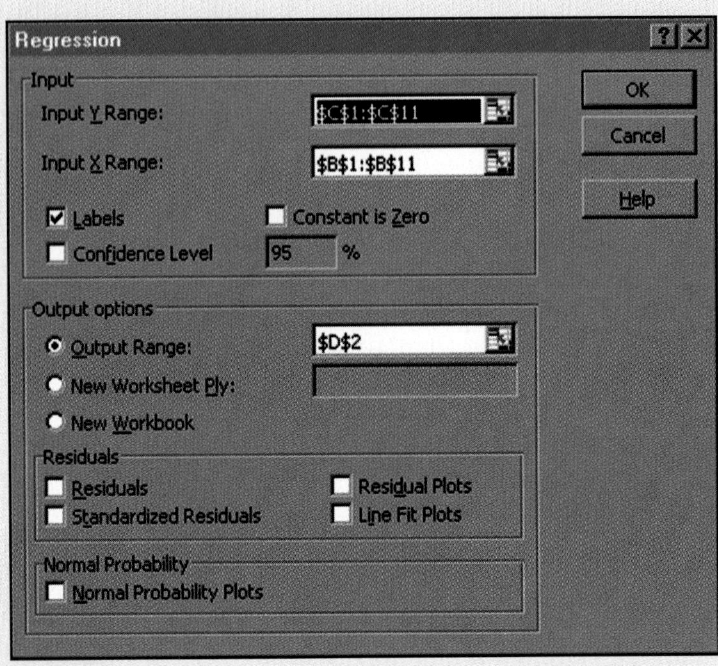

Regression
Input
Input Y Range:
$C$1:$C$11
Input X Range:
$B$1:$B$11
Labels
Constant is Zero
Confidence Level
95
%
OK
Cancel
Help
Output options
Output Range:
$D$2
New Worksheet Ply:
New Workbook
Residuals
Residuals
Residual Plots
Standardized Residuals
Line Fit Plots
Normal Probability
Normal Probability Plots

Chapter 13 Answers to Self-Review

13–1 (a) Advertising expense is the independent variable and sales revenue is the dependent variable.

(b)

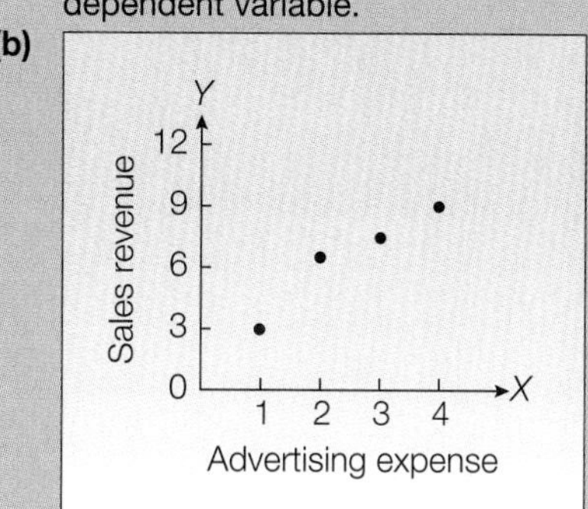

(c)

X	Y	XY	X^2	Y^2
2	7	14	4	49
1	3	3	1	9
3	8	24	9	64
4	10	40	16	100
10	28	81	30	222

$r = .96$, found by

$$r = \frac{4(81) - (10)(28)}{\sqrt{[4(30) - (10)^2][4(222) - (28)^2]}}$$

$$= \frac{44}{\sqrt{2{,}080}} = \frac{44}{45.607017} = .9648$$

(d) There is a strong correlation between the advertising expense and sales.

(e) $r^2 = .93$, 93% of the variation in sales is "explained" by variation in advertising.

13–2 $H_0: \rho \leq 0$, $H_1: \rho > 0$. H_0 is rejected if $t > 1.714$.

$$t = \frac{.43\sqrt{25 - 2}}{\sqrt{1 - (.43)^2}} = 2.284$$

H_0 is rejected. There is a positive correlation between the percent of the vote received and the amount spent on the campaign.

13–3 (a) See the calculations in Self-Review 13–1, part (c).

$$b = \frac{4(81) - (10)(28)}{4(30) - (10)^2}$$

$$= \frac{324 - 280}{120 - 100} = 2.2$$

$$a = \frac{28}{4} - 2.2\left(\frac{10}{4}\right)$$

$$= 7 - 5.5 = 1.5$$

(b) The slope is 2.2. This indicates that an increase of \$1 million in advertising will result in an increase of \$2.2 million in sales. The intercept is 1.5. If there was no expenditure for advertising, sales would be \$1.5 million.

(c) $Y' = 1.5 + 2.2(3) = 8.1$

13–4 0.9487, found by:

$$s_{y \cdot x} = \sqrt{\frac{\Sigma Y^2 - a(\Sigma Y) - b(\Sigma XY)}{n - 2}}$$

$$= \sqrt{\frac{222 - 1.5(28) - 2.2(81)}{4 - 2}}$$

$$= \sqrt{\frac{1.8}{2}} = 0.9487$$

13–5 6.58 and 9.62, since Y' for an X of 3 is 8.1, found by $Y' = 1.5 + 2.2(3) = 8.1$, then $\bar{X} = 2.5$ and $\Sigma X^2 = 30$ and $\Sigma X = 10$.

t from Appendix F for $4 - 2 = 2$ degrees of freedom at the .10 level is 2.920.

$$Y' \pm t(s_{y \cdot x})\sqrt{\frac{1}{n} + \frac{(X - \bar{X})^2}{\Sigma X^2 - \frac{(\Sigma X)^2}{n}}}$$

$$= 8.1 \pm 2.920(0.9487)\sqrt{\frac{1}{4} + \frac{(3 - 2.5)^2}{30 - \frac{(10)^2}{4}}}$$

$$= 8.1 \pm 2.920(0.9487)(0.5477)$$

$$= 6.58 \text{ and } 9.62 \text{ (in \$ millions)}$$

14 Multiple Regression and Correlation Analysis

GOALS

When you have completed this chapter, you will be able to:

1. Describe the relationship between several independent variables and a dependent variable using a multiple regression equation.
2. Compute and interpret the multiple standard error of estimate and the coefficient of determination.
3. Interpret a correlation matrix.
4. Set up and interpret an ANOVA table.
5. Conduct a test of hypothesis to determine whether regression coefficients differ from zero.
6. Conduct a test of hypothesis on each of the regression coefficients.

In working with those who work on sophisticated machinery, the production department needed to know if age, length of service, mechanical aptitude, or prior on-the-job rating as a machine operator are important to determine performance on the machines. How many dependent and independent variables are there? (See Goal 1 and Exercise 2.)

Introduction

In the previous chapter we described the relationship between two sets of interval or ratio-scaled measurements. One was designated the independent variable and the other the dependent variable. We noted that if the relationship between the two variables is linear, the regression equation $Y' = a + bX$ can predict the dependent variable, Y, based on the independent variable, X. Further, the coefficient of correlation is one measure that reveals whether the relationship is strong, moderate, or weak. A coefficient near plus or minus 1.00 ($-.88$ or $.88$, for example) indicates a very strong linear relationship between X and Y. A coefficient near 0 ($-.12$ or $+.12$, for example) means that the relationship is weak.

Use of only one independent variable to predict the dependent variable ignores the relationship of other variables to the dependent variable. This chapter expands our study of correlation and regression by examining the influence of *two or more* independent variables on the dependent variable. We refer to this approach as multiple regression and correlation analysis. We present multiple regression analysis first by developing and explaining the use of the multiple regression equation and the multiple standard error of estimate. Then we measure the strength of the relationship between the independent variables and the dependent variable.

Multiple Regression Analysis

Recall from Chapter 13 that the linear regression equation using one independent variable has the form $Y' = a + bX$. The multiple regression case extends the equation to include additional independent variables. For two independent variables, the general form of the multiple regression equation is:

MULTIPLE REGRESSION EQUATION WITH TWO INDEPENDENT VARIABLES

$$Y' = a + b_1X_1 + b_2X_2 \qquad \textbf{[14–1]}$$

where:

- X_1 and X_2 are the two independent variables.
- a is the Y-intercept. This is the point where the equation crosses the Y-axis.
- b_1 is the net change in Y for each unit change in X_1, while holding X_2 constant. It is called a **partial regression coefficient**, a **net regression coefficient**, or just a **regression coefficient**.
- b_2 is the net change in Y for each unit change in X_2, while holding X_1 constant. It is also called a **partial regression coefficient**, a **net regression coefficient**, or just a **regression coefficient**.

When we have two independent variables and a single dependent variable, the geometric interpretation is a regression plane because we are considering three dimensions. Chart 14–1 is an example of how a sample of 10 observations might appear.

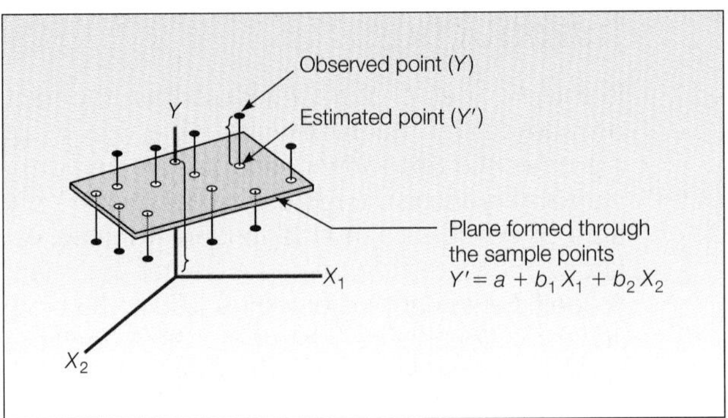

CHART 14–1 Regression Plane with Ten Sample Points

To illustrate the interpretation of the intercept and the two regression coefficients, suppose a vehicle's mileage per gallon of gasoline is directly related to the octane rating of the gasoline being used (X_1) and inversely related to the weight of the automobile (X_2). Assume that the regression equation, calculated using statistical software, is:

$$Y' = 6.3 + 0.2X_1 - 0.001X_2$$

The intercept value of 6.3 indicates the regression equation intersects the Y-axis at 6.3 when both X_1 and X_2 are zero. Of course, this does not make any physical sense to own an automobile that has no (zero) weight and to use gasoline with no octane. It is important to keep in mind that a regression equation is not generally used outside the range of the sample values.

The b_1 of 0.2 indicates that for each increase of 1 in the octane rating of the gasoline, the automobile would travel 2/10 of a mile more per gallon, *regardless of the weight of the vehicle.* That is, the vehicle's weight is held constant. The b_2 value of -0.001 reveals that for each increase of one pound in the vehicle's weight, the number of miles traveled per gallon decreases by 0.001, *regardless of the octane of the gasoline being used.*

As an example, an automobile with 92-octane gasoline in the tank and weighing 2,000 pounds would travel an average 22.7 miles per gallon, found by:

$$Y' = a + b_1X_1 + b_2X_2 = 6.3 + 0.2(92) - 0.001(2{,}000) = 22.7$$

The value of 22.7 is in miles per gallon.

We can expand the number of independent variables. For three independent variables designated X_1, X_2, and X_3, the general multiple regression equation is:

MULTIPLE REGRESSION EQUATION WITH THREE INDEPENDENT VARIABLES

$$Y' = a + b_1X_1 + b_2X_2 + b_3X_3 \qquad \textbf{[14–2]}$$

This can be extended to any number of independent variables *(k),* with the general multiple regression equation being:

MULTIPLE REGRESSION EQUATION WITH *k* INDEPENDENT VARIABLES

$$Y' = a + b_1X_1 + b_2X_2 + b_3X_3 + \cdots + b_kX_k \qquad \textbf{[14–3]}$$

As in Chapter 13, the least squares method of estimating a, b_1, b_2, and so forth minimizes the sum of the squares of the vertical deviations from the regression plane. The same applies to multiple regression. To arrive at a, b_1, and b_2 in the multiple regression equation, however, the many calculations are very tedious, even using a hand calculator. As an example, for two independent variables, three equations must be solved simultaneously, namely:

$$\Sigma Y = na + b_1 \Sigma X_1 + b_2 \Sigma X_2$$

$$\Sigma X_1 Y = a \Sigma X_1 + b_1 \Sigma X_1^2 + b_2 \Sigma X_1 X_2$$

$$\Sigma X_2 Y = a \Sigma X_2 + b_1 \Sigma X_1 X_2 + b_2 \Sigma X_2^2$$

There are many software packages available to perform the calculations and output the results. MINITAB, SAS, Excel, and SPSS are four of the most widely used packages. The format of the output is fairly standard. We begin the discussion of multiple regression by describing a situation involving three independent variables.

EXAMPLE

Salsberry Realty sells homes along the east coast of the United States. One of the questions most frequently asked by prospective buyers is: If we purchase this home, how much can we expect to pay to heat it during the winter? The research department at Salsberry has been asked to develop some guidelines regarding heating costs for single-family homes. Three variables are thought to relate to the heating costs: (1) the mean daily outside temperature, (2) the number of inches of insulation in the attic, and (3) the age of the furnace. To investigate, Salsberry's research department selected a random sample of 20 recently sold homes. They determined the cost to heat the home last January, as well as the January outside temperature in the region, the number of inches of insulation in the attic, and the age of the furnace. The sample information is reported in Table 14–1.

TABLE 14–1 Factors in January Heating Cost for a Sample of 20 Homes

Home	Heating Cost ($)	Mean Outside Temperature (°F)	Attic Insulation (inches)	Age of Furnace (years)
1	$250	35	3	6
2	360	29	4	10
3	165	36	7	3
4	43	60	6	9
5	92	65	5	6
6	200	30	5	5
7	355	10	6	7
8	290	7	10	10
9	230	21	9	11
10	120	55	2	5
11	73	54	12	4
12	205	48	5	1
13	400	20	5	15
14	320	39	4	7
15	72	60	8	6
16	272	20	5	8
17	94	58	7	3
18	190	40	8	11
19	235	27	9	8
20	139	30	7	5

Determine the multiple regression equation. Which variables are the independent variables? Which variable is the dependent variable? Discuss the regression coefficients. What does it indicate that some are positive and some are negative? What is the intercept value? What is the estimated heating cost for a home if the mean outside temperature is 30 degrees, there are 5 inches of insulation in the attic, and the furnace is 10 years old?

SOLUTION

The MINITAB statistical software system generates the output shown below.

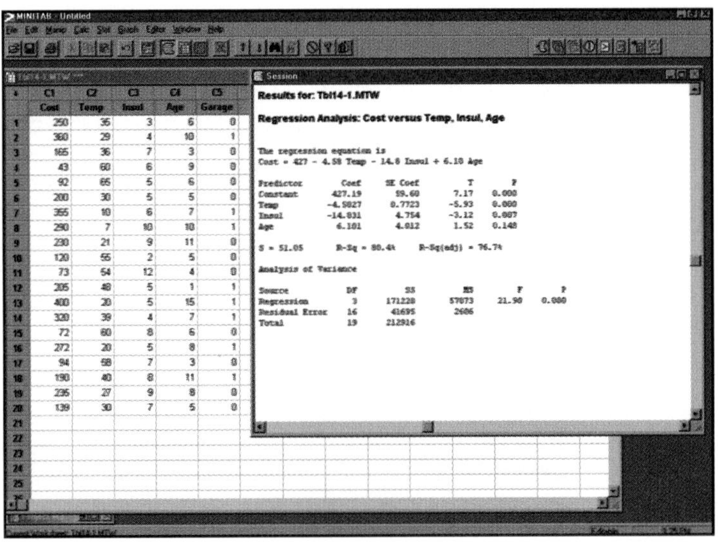

The dependent variable is the January heating cost. There are three independent variables, the mean outside temperature, the number of inches of insulation in the attic, and the age of the furnace.

The general form of a multiple regression equation with three independent variables is:

$$Y' = a + b_1X_1 + b_2X_2 + b_3X_3$$

In this case the multiple regression equation is $Y' = 427 - 4.58X_1 - 14.8X_2 + 6.10X_3$. The intercept value is 427. This is the point where the regression equation crosses the Y-axis. The regression coefficients for the mean outside temperature and the amount of attic insulation are both negative. This is not surprising. As the outside temperature increases, the cost to heat the home will go down. Hence, we would expect an inverse relationship. For each degree the mean temperature increases, we expect the heating cost to decrease \$4.58 per month. So if the mean temperature in Boston is 25 degrees and it is 35 degrees in Philadelphia, all other things being the same, we expect the heating cost would be \$45.80 less in Philadelphia.

The variable "attic insulation" also shows an inverse relationship: the more insulation in the attic the less the cost to heat the home. So the negative sign for this coefficient is logical. For each additional inch of insulation, we expect the cost to heat the home to decline \$14.80 per month, regardless of the outside temperature or the age of the furnace.

Statistics in Action

Many studies indicate a woman will earn about 70 percent of what a man would for the same work. Researchers at the University of Michigan Institute for Social Research found that about one-third of the difference can be explained by such social factors as differences in education, seniority, and work interruptions. The remaining two-thirds is not explained by these social factors.

The furnace variable shows a direct relationship. With an older furnace, the cost to heat the home increases. Specifically, for each additional year old the furnace is, we expect the cost to increase $6.10 per month.

The estimated heating cost for the month is $276.60 if the mean outside temperature for the month is 30 degrees, there are 5 inches of insulation in the attic, and the furnace is 10 years old.

$$Y' = a + b_1X_1 + b_2X_2 + b_3X_3 = 427 - 4.58(30) - 14.8(5) + 6.10(10) = 276.60$$

Self-Review 14–1

The quality control engineer at Palmer Industries is interested in estimating the tensile strength of steel wire based on its outside diameter and the amount of molybdenum in the steel. As an experiment, she selected twenty-five pieces of wire, measured the outside diameters, and determined the molybdenum content. Then she measured the tensile strength of each piece. The results of the first four were:

Piece	Tensile Strength, (psi), Y	Outside Diameter (mm), X_1	Amount of Molybdenum (units), X_2
A	11	.3	6
B	9	.2	5
C	16	.4	8
D	12	.3	7

Using a statistical software package, the QC engineer determined the multiple regression equation to be $Y' = -0.5 + 20X_1 + 1X_2$.

(a) Based on the equation, what is the estimated tensile strength of a steel wire having an outside diameter of .35 mm and 6.4 units of molybdenum?

(b) Interpret the value of b_1 in the equation.

Exercises

1. The director of marketing at Reeves Wholesale Products is studying the monthly sales. Three independent variables were selected as estimators of sales: regional population, per-capita income, and regional unemployment rate. The regression equation was computed to be (in dollars):

$$Y' = 64{,}100 + 0.394X_1 + 9.6X_1 - 11{,}600X_3$$

a. What is the full name of the equation?

b. Interpret the number 64,100.

c. What are the estimated monthly sales for a particular region with a population of 796,000, per-capita income of $6,940, and an unemployment rate of 6.0 percent?

2. Thompson Machine Works purchased several new, highly sophisticated machines. The production department needed some guidance with respect to qualifications needed by an operator. Is age a factor? Is the length of service as a machine operator important? In order to explore further the factors needed to estimate performance on the new machines, four variables were listed:

X_1 = Length of time employee was a machinist.
X_2 = Mechanical aptitude test score.
X_3 = Prior on-the-job rating.
X_4 = Age.

Performance on the new machine is designated Y.

Thirty machinists were selected at random. Data were collected for each, and their performances on the new machines were recorded. A few results are:

Name	Performance on New Machine, Y	Length of Time as a Machinist, X_1	Mechanical Aptitude Score, X_2	Prior On-the-Job Performance, X_3	Age, X_4
Andy Kosin	112	12	312	121	52
Sue Annis	113	2	380	123	27

The equation is:

$$Y' = 11.6 + 0.4X_1 + 0.286X_2 + 0.112X_3 + 0.002X_4$$

2. a. Multiple regression.
   b. 1, 4
   c. Regression coefficient.
   d. .002
   e. 105.014

a. What is the full designation of the equation?
b. How many dependent variables are there? Independent variables?
c. What is the number 0.286 called?
d. As age increases by one year, how much does estimated performance on the new machine increase?
e. Carl Knox applied for a job on a new machine. He has been a machinist for six years, and scored 280 on the mechanical aptitude test. Carl's prior on-the-job performance rating is 97, and he is 35 years old. Estimate Carl's performance on the new machine.

3. A sample of widowed senior citizens was studied to determine their degree of satisfaction with their present life. A special index, called the index of satisfaction, was used to measure satisfaction. Six factors were studied, namely, age at the time of first marriage (X_1), annual income (X_2), number of children living (X_3), value of all assets (X_4), status of health in the form of an index (X_5), and the average number of social activities per week—such as bowling and dancing (X_6). Suppose the multiple regression equation is:

$$Y' = 16.24 + 0.017X_1 + 0.0028X_2 + 42X_3 + 0.0012X_4 + 0.19X_5 + 26.8X_6$$

a. What is the estimated index of satisfaction for a person who first married at 18, has an annual income of $26,500, has three children living, has assets of $156,000, has an index of health status of 141, and has 2.5 social activities a week on the average?
b. Which would add more to satisfaction, an additional income of $10,000 a year or two more social activities a week?

4. Cellulon, a manufacturer of a new type of home insulation, wants to develop guidelines for builders and consumers regarding the effects on natural gas consumption (1) of the thickness of the insulation in the attic of a home and (2) of the outdoor temperature. In the laboratory they varied the insulation thickness and temperature. A few of the findings are:

Monthly Natural Gas Consumption (cubic feet), Y	Thickness of Insulation (inches), X_1	Outdoor Temperature (°F), X_2
30.3	6	40
26.9	12	40
22.1	8	49

Based on the sample results, the regression equation is:

$$Y' = 62.65 - 1.86X_1 - 0.52X_2$$

4. a. 30.69

a. How much natural gas can homeowners expect to use per month if they install 6 inches of insulation and the outdoor temperature is 40 degrees F?

b. −1.86

c. See IM.

b. What effect would installing 7 inches of insulation instead of 6 have on the monthly natural gas consumption (assuming the outdoor temperature remains at 40 degrees F)?

c. Why are the regression coefficients b_1 and b_2 negative? Is this logical?

Multiple Standard Error of Estimate

In the Salsberry Realty example we estimated the cost to heat a home during the month of January when the mean outside temperature was 30 degrees, there were 5 inches of attic insulation, and the furnace was 10 years old to be $276.60. We would expect to find some random error in this estimate. Sometimes a home with these statistics would cost more than $276.60 to heat and other times less. The error in this estimate is measured by the **multiple standard error of estimate.** The standard error, as it is usually called, is denoted $s_{y \cdot 123}$. The subscripts indicate that three independent variables are being used to estimate the value of Y.

Recall from Chapter 13 the standard error of estimate described the variation around the regression line. A small standard error indicates the points are close to the regression line, whereas a large value indicates the points are scattered about the regression line. The same concept is true in multiple regression. If we have two independent variables, then we can think of the variation around a regression plane. See Chart 14–1 on page 504. If there are more than two independent variables, we do not have a geometric interpretation of the equation, but the standard error is still a measure of the "error" or variability in the prediction.

The formula to compute the standard error is similar to that used in the previous chapter. See formula 13–7 on page 477. The numerator is the sum of the squared differences between the estimated and the actual values of the dependent variable. In the denominator, we adjust for the fact that we are considering several, that is, k, independent variables.

MULTIPLE STANDARD ERROR OF ESTIMATE

$$s_{y \cdot 12 \cdots k} = \sqrt{\frac{\Sigma(Y - Y')^2}{n - (k + 1)}} \qquad [14\text{–}4]$$

where:

Y is the observation.
Y' is the value estimated from the regression equation.
n is the number of observations in the sample.
k is the number of independent variables.

In the Salsberry Realty example, $k = 3$.

Again, we use the Salsberry Realty problem to illustrate. The first home had a mean outside temperature of 35 degrees, 3 inches of attic insulation, and a 6-year-old furnace. Substituting these values into the regression equation, the estimated heating cost is $258.90, determined by $427 - 4.58(35) - 14.80(3) + 6.10(6)$. The Y' values for the other homes are found similarly and are reported in Table 14–2.

The actual heating cost for the first home is $250, in contrast to the estimated cost of $258.90. That is, the error in the prediction is −$8.90, found by ($250 − $258.90). This difference between the actual heating cost and the estimated heating cost is called the **residual.** To find the multiple standard error of estimate, we determine the residual for each of the sampled homes, square the residual, and then total the squared residuals. The total is reported in the lower right corner of Table 14–2.

TABLE 14–2 Calculations Needed for the Multiple Standard Error of Estimate

Home	Temperature (°F)	Insulation (inches)	Age (years)	Cost, Y	Y'	$(Y - Y')$	$(Y - Y')^2$
1	35	3	6	$250	258.90	−8.90	79.21
2	29	4	10	360	295.98	64.02	4,098.56
3	36	7	3	165	176.82	−11.82	139.71
4	60	6	9	43	118.30	−75.30	5,670.09
5	65	5	6	92	91.90	0.10	0.01
6	30	5	5	200	246.10	−46.10	2,125.21
7	10	6	7	355	335.10	19.90	396.01
8	7	10	10	290	307.94	−17.94	321.84
9	21	9	11	230	264.72	−34.72	1,205.48
10	55	2	5	120	176.00	−56.00	3,136.00
11	54	12	4	73	26.48	46.52	2,164.11
12	48	5	1	205	139.26	65.74	4,321.75
13	20	5	15	400	352.90	47.10	2,218.41
14	39	4	7	320	231.88	88.12	7,765.13
15	60	8	6	72	70.40	1.60	2.56
16	20	5	8	272	310.20	−38.20	1,459.24
17	58	7	3	94	76.06	17.94	321.84
18	40	8	11	190	192.50	−2.50	6.25
19	27	9	8	235	218.94	16.06	257.92
20	30	7	5	139	216.50	−77.50	6,006.25
Total							41,695.58

In this example $n = 20$ and $k = 3$ (three independent variables), so the multiple standard error of estimate is:

$$s_{y \cdot 123} = \sqrt{\frac{\Sigma(Y - Y')^2}{n - (k + 1)}} = \sqrt{\frac{41{,}695.58}{20 - (3 + 1)}} = 51.05$$

How do we interpret the 51.05? It is the typical "error" we make when we use this equation to predict the cost. First, the units are the same as the dependent variable, so the standard error is in dollars. Second, if the errors are normally distributed, about 68 percent of the residuals should be less than ± 51.05 and about 95 percent should be less than $\pm 2(51.05)$ or ± 102.10. Refer to the second column from the right in Table 14–2, the column headed $(Y - Y')$. Of the 20 residuals reported in this column, 14 are less than ± 51.05 and all are less than ± 102.10, which is quite close to the guidelines of 68 percent and 95 percent.

In Chapter 13 we used the standard error of estimate to construct confidence intervals and prediction intervals. We will not detail these procedures for multiple regression, but they are available on statistical software systems, such as MINITAB.

Assumptions about Multiple Regression and Correlation

Before continuing our discussion of multiple correlation, we list the assumptions underlying both multiple regression and multiple correlation. As noted in several previous

chapters, we identify the assumptions because if they are not fully met, the results might be biased. For instance, in selecting a sample, we assume that all the items in the population have a chance of being selected. If our research involves surveying all those who ski, but we ignore those over 40 because we believe they are "too old," we would be biasing the responses toward the younger skiers. It should be mentioned, however, that in practice strict adherence to the following assumptions is not always possible in multiple regression and correlation problems involving the ever-changing business climate. But the statistical techniques discussed in this chapter appear to work well even when one or more of the assumptions are violated. Even if the values in the multiple regression equation are "off" slightly, our estimates based on the equation will be closer than any that could otherwise be made.

Each of the following assumptions will be discussed in more detail as we progress through the chapter.

1. The independent variables and the dependent variable have a linear relationship.
2. The dependent variable is continuous and at least interval scale.
3. The variation in the difference between the actual and the predicted values is the same for all fitted values of Y. That is, $(Y - Y')$ must be approximately the same for all values of Y'. When this is the case, differences exhibit **homoscedasticity.**

Homoscedasticity

4. The residuals, computed by $Y - Y'$, are normally distributed with a mean of 0.
5. Successive observations of the dependent variable are uncorrelated. Violation of this assumption is called **autocorrelation.** Autocorrelation often happens when data are collected successively over periods of time.

Autocorrelation

Statistical tests are available to detect homoscedasticity and autocorrelation. For those interested, these tests are covered in more advanced textbooks such as *Applied Linear Statistical Models* by Neter, Kutner, Nachtscheim, and Wasserman (4th ed., 1996, published by Richard D. Irwin, Inc.).

The ANOVA Table

As mentioned previously, the multiple regression calculations are lengthy. Fortunately, many software systems are available to perform the calculations. Most of the systems report the results in a fairly standard format. The output from the MINITAB system shown on page 506 is typical. It includes the regression equation, the standard error of estimate, the coefficient of determination, as well as an analysis of variance table. We have already described the meaning of the regression coefficients in the equation $Y' = 427 - 4.58X_1 - 14.8X_2 + 6.10X_3$. We will discuss the "Coef," "StDev," and "T" (i.e., t ratio) columns later in the chapter. A portion of the output from MINITAB is repeated here.

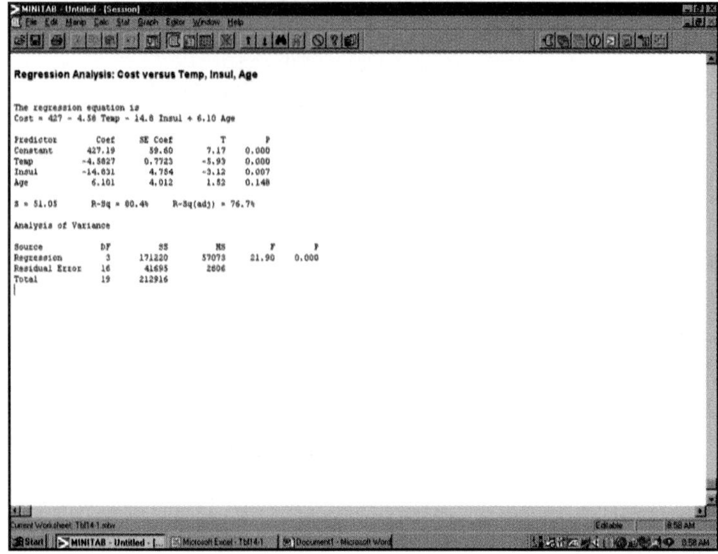

First, let's focus on the analysis of variance table. It is similar to the ANOVA table described in Chapter 12. In that chapter the variation was divided into two components: that due to the *treatments* and that due to random *error.* Here the total is also divided into two components: that explained by the **regression,** that is, the independent variables, and the **error,** or unexplained variation. These two categories are identified in the "Source" column of the analysis of variance table. In the example there are 20 observations, so $n = 20$. The *total* number of degrees of freedom is $n - 1$, or $20 - 1 = 19$. The number of degrees of freedom in the "Regression" row is the number of independent variables. We let k represent the number of independent variables, so $k = 3$. The number of degrees of freedom in the "Error" row is $n - (k + 1) = 20 - (3 + 1) = 16$ degrees of freedom.

The heading "SS" in the middle of the ANOVA table refers to the sum of squares, or the variation.

$$\text{Total variation} = \text{SS total} = \Sigma(Y - \bar{Y})^2 = 212{,}916$$

$$\text{Error variation} = \text{SSE} = \Sigma(Y - Y')^2 = 41{,}695$$

$$\text{Regression variation} = \text{SSR} = \text{SS total} - \text{SSE} = 212{,}916 - 41{,}695 = 171{,}220$$

The column headed "MS" (mean square) is determined by dividing the SS term by the *df* term. Thus, MSR, the mean square regression, is equal to SSR/k, and MSE equals SSE/$[n - (k + 1)]$. The general format of the ANOVA table is:

Source	*df*	SS	MS	*F*
Regression	k	SSR	MSR = SSR/k	MSR/MSE
Error	$n - (k + 1)$	SSE	MSE = SSE/$[n - (k + 1)]$	
Total	$n - 1$	SS total		

The **coefficient of multiple determination,** written as R^2, is the percent of the variation explained by the regression. It is the sum of squares due to the regression, divided by the sum of squares total.

COEFFICIENT OF MULTIPLE DETERMINATION $$R^2 = \frac{\text{SSR}}{\text{SS total}} \quad [14\text{–}5]$$

$$R^2 = \frac{\text{SSR}}{\text{SS total}} = \frac{171{,}220}{212{,}916} = .804$$

The multiple standard error of estimate may also be found directly from the ANOVA table.

$$s_{y \cdot 123} = \sqrt{\frac{\text{SSE}}{n - (k + 1)}} = \sqrt{\frac{41{,}695}{[(20 - (3 + 1)]}} = 51.05$$

These values, $R^2 = .804$ and $s_{y \cdot 123} = 51.05$, are included in the MINITAB output.

Self-Review 14–2 Refer to the following ANOVA table.

SOURCE	DF	SS	MS	F
Regression	4	10	2.50	10.0
Error	20	5	0.25	
Total	24	15		

(a) How large was the sample?
(b) How many independent variables are there?
(c) Compute the coefficient of multiple determination.
(d) Compute the multiple standard error of estimate.

Exercises

5. Refer to the following ANOVA table.

SOURCE	DF	SS	MS	F
Regression	3	21	7.0	2.33
Error	15	45	3.0	
Total	18	66		

a. How large was the sample?
b. How many independent variables are there?
c. Compute the coefficient of multiple determination.
d. Compute the multiple standard error of estimate.

6. Refer to the following ANOVA table.

SOURCE	DF	SS	MS	F
Regression	5	60	12	1.714
Error	20	140	7	
Total	25	200		

a. How large was the sample?
b. How many independent variables are there?
c. Compute the coefficient of multiple determination.
d. Compute the multiple standard error of estimate.

6. **a.** 26
b. 5
c. .3
d. 2.65

Evaluating the Regression Equation

Earlier in the chapter we described an example in which Salsberry Realty developed, using multiple regression techniques, an equation to express the cost to heat a home during the month of January based on the mean outside temperature, the number of inches of attic insulation, and the age of the furnace. The equation seemed reasonable, but we wish to verify that the multiple coefficient of determination is significantly larger than zero, evaluate the regression coefficients to see which are not equal to zero, and verify that the regression assumptions are met.

Using a Scatter Diagram

There are three independent variables, designated X_1, X_2, and X_3. The dependent variable, the heating cost, is designated Y. In order to visualize the relationships between the dependent variable and each of the independent variables, we drew the following scatter diagrams.

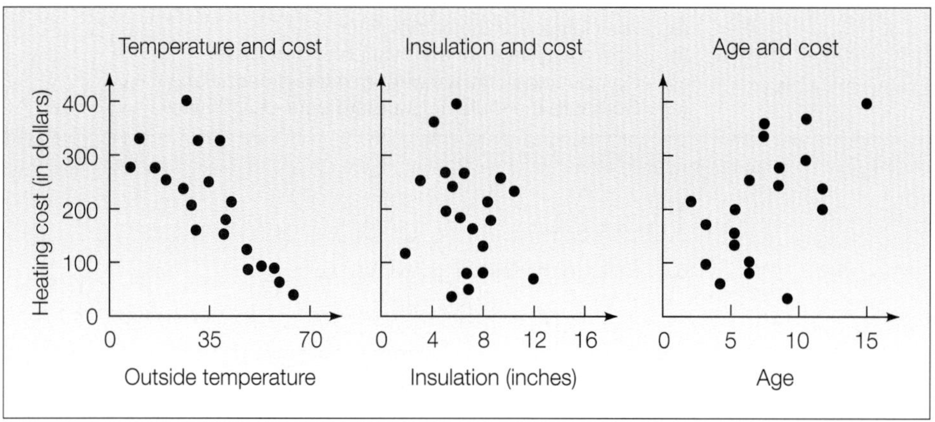

Of the three independent variables, the strongest association is between heating cost and the mean outside temperature. The relationships between cost and temperature and cost and insulation both are inverse. That is, as the independent variable increases, the dependent variable decreases. The relationship between the heating cost and the age of the furnace is direct. As the furnace gets older, it costs more to heat the home.

Correlation Matrix

A correlation matrix is also useful in analyzing the factors involved in the cost to heat a home.

CORRELATION MATRIX A matrix showing the coefficients of correlation between all pairs of variables.

The correlation matrix of the Salsberry Realty example follows. The matrix, which appears on the right-hand side of the output, was developed using the Excel software.

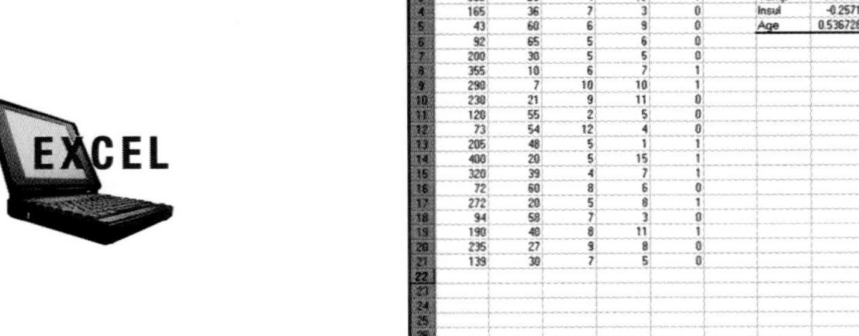

Cost	Temp	Insul	Age	Garage
250	35	3	6	0
360	29	4	10	1
165	36	7	3	0
43	60	6	9	0
92	65	5	6	0
200	30	5	5	0
355	10	6	7	1
290	7	10	10	1
230	21	9	11	0
120	55	2	5	0
73	54	12	4	0
205	48	5	1	1
400	20	5	15	1
320	39	4	7	1
72	60	8	6	0
272	20	5	8	1
94	58	7	3	0
190	40	8	11	1
235	27	9	8	0
139	30	7	5	0

	Cost	Temp	Insul	Age
Cost	1			
Temp	-0.81151	1		
Insul	-0.2571	-0.10302	1	
Age	0.536728	-0.48599	0.063617	1

Cost is the dependent variable, Y. We are particularly interested in independent variables that have a strong correlation with the dependent variable. We may wish to develop a simpler multiple regression equation using fewer independent variables and the correlation matrix helps us identify which may be relatively more important. As indicated in the output, temperature has the strongest correlation with cost, −0.81151. The negative sign indicates the inverse relationship we were expecting. Age has a stronger correlation with cost than insulation and, again as we expected, the correlation between cost and the age of the furnace is direct. It is 0.536728.

A second use of the correlation matrix is to check for **multicollinearity.**

> **MULTICOLLINEARITY** Correlation among the independent variables.

Multicollinearity can distort the standard error of estimate and may, therefore, lead to incorrect conclusions as to which independent variables are statistically significant. In this case, the correlation between the age of the furnace and the temperature is the strongest, but it is not large enough to cause a problem. A common rule of thumb is that correlations among the independent variables between −.70 and .70 do not cause difficulties. The usual remedy for multicollinearity is to drop one of the independent variables that are strongly correlated and recompute the regression equation.

Global Test: Testing Whether the Multiple Regression Model Is Valid

The ability of the independent variables $X_1, X_2, \dots, X_k$ to explain the behavior of the dependent variable Y can be tested. To put this in question form: Can the dependent variable be estimated without relying on the independent variables? The test used is referred to as the **global test.** Basically, it investigates whether it is possible all the independent variables have zero net regression coefficients. To put it another way, could the amount of explained variation, R^2, occur by chance?

To relate this question to the heating cost example, we will test whether the independent variables (amount of insulation in the attic, mean daily outside temperature, and age of furnace) are capable of effectively estimating home heating costs.

Recall that in testing a hypothesis, we first state the null hypothesis and the alternate hypothesis. In the heating cost example, there are three independent variables. Recall that b_1, b_2, and b_3 are sample net regression coefficients. The corresponding coefficients in the population are given the symbols β_1, β_2, and β_3. We now test whether the net regression coefficients in the population are zero. The null hypothesis is:

$$H_0: \beta_1 = \beta_2 = \beta_3 = 0$$

The alternate hypothesis is:

H_1: Not all the βs are 0.

If the null hypothesis is true, it implies the regression coefficients are all zero and, logically, are of no use in estimating the dependent variable (heating cost). Should that be the case, we would have to search for some other independent variables—or take a different approach—to predict home heating costs.

To test the null hypothesis that the multiple regression coefficients are all zero, we employ the F distribution introduced in Chapter 12. We will use the .05 level of significance. Recall these characteristics of the F distribution:

Characteristics of the F distribution

1. It is positively skewed, with the critical value located in the right tail. The critical value is the point that separates the region where H_0 is not rejected from the region of rejection.
2. It is constructed by knowing the number of degrees of freedom in the numerator and the number of degrees of freedom in the denominator.

The degrees of freedom for the numerator and the denominator may be found in the software summary in the analysis of variance table. That portion of the table is included below. The top number in the column marked "DF" is 3, indicating that there are 3 degrees of freedom in the numerator. The middle number in the "DF" column (16) indicates that there are 16 degrees of freedom in the denominator. The number 16 is found by $n - (k + 1) = 20 - (3 + 1) = 16$. The number 3 corresponds to the number of independent variables.

MINITAB - Untitled

Session

Analysis of Variance

Source	DF	SS	MS	F	P
Regression	3	171220	57073	21.90	0.000
Residual Error	16	41695	2606		
Total	19	212916			

Tbl12-1.MTW

	C2 Temp	C3 Insul	C4 Age	C5 Garage
1	35	3	6	0
2	29	4	10	1
3	36	7	3	0
4	60	6	9	0
5	65	5	6	0
6	30	5	5	0

Current Worksheet: Tbl12-1.MTW

The value of F is found from the following equation.

GLOBAL TEST	$F = \dfrac{\text{SSR}/k}{\text{SSE}/[n - (k + 1)]}$	**[14–6]**

SSR is the sum of the squares "explained by" the regression, SSE the sum of squares error, n the number of observations, and k the number of independent variables. Inserting these values in formula 14–6:

$$F = \frac{\text{SSR}/k}{\text{SSE}/[n - (k + 1)]} = \frac{171{,}220/3}{41{,}695/[20 - (3 + 1)]} = 21.90$$

The critical value of F is found in Appendix G. Using the table for the .05 level, move horizontally to 3 degrees of freedom in the numerator, then down to 16 degrees of freedom in the denominator, and read the critical value. It is 3.24. The region where H_0 is not rejected and the region where H_0 is rejected are shown in the following diagram.

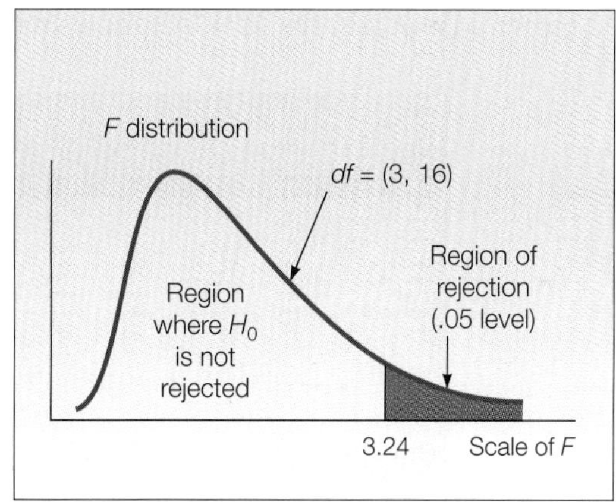

Continuing with the global test, the decision rule is: Do not reject the null hypothesis that all the regression coefficients are 0 if the computed value of F is less than or equal to 3.24. If the computed F is greater than 3.24, reject H_0 and accept the alternate hypothesis, H_1.

The computed value of F is 21.90, which is in the rejection region. The null hypothesis that all the multiple regression coefficients are zero is therefore rejected. The p-value is 0.000 from the above analysis of variance table, so it is quite unlikely that H_0 is true. The alternate hypothesis is accepted, indicating that not all the regression coefficients are zero. From a practical standpoint, this means that the independent variables (amount of insulation, etc.) do have the ability to explain the variation in the dependent variable (heating cost). We expected this decision. Logically, the outside temperature, the amount of insulation, and age of the furnace have a great bearing on heating costs. The global test assures us that they do.

Evaluating Individual Regression Coefficients

So far we have shown that some, but not necessarily all, of the regression coefficients are not equal to zero and thus useful for predictions. The next step is to test the variables *individually* to determine which regression coefficients may be 0 and which are not.

Why is it important to find whether it is possible that any of the βs equal 0? If a β could equal 0, it implies that this particular independent variable is of no value in explaining any variation in the dependent value. If there are coefficients for which H_0 cannot be rejected, we may want to eliminate them from the regression equation.

We will now conduct three separate tests of hypothesis—for temperature, for insulation, and for the age of the furnace.

For temperature:	For insulation:	For furnace age:
H_0: $\beta_1 = 0$	H_0: $\beta_2 = 0$	H_0: $\beta_3 = 0$
H_1: $\beta_1 \neq 0$	H_1: $\beta_2 \neq 0$	H_1: $\beta_3 \neq 0$

We will test the hypotheses at the .05 level. The way the alternate hypothesis is stated indicates that the test is two-tailed.

The test statistic is the Student t distribution with $n - (k + 1)$ degrees of freedom. The number of sample observations is n. There are 20 homes in the study, so $n = 20$. The number of independent variables is k, which is 3. Thus, there are $n - (k + 1) = 20 - (3 + 1) = 16$ degrees of freedom.

The critical value for t is in Appendix F. For a two-tailed test with 16 degrees of freedom using the .05 significance level, H_0 is rejected if t is less than -2.120 or greater than 2.120. The MINITAB software produced the following output.

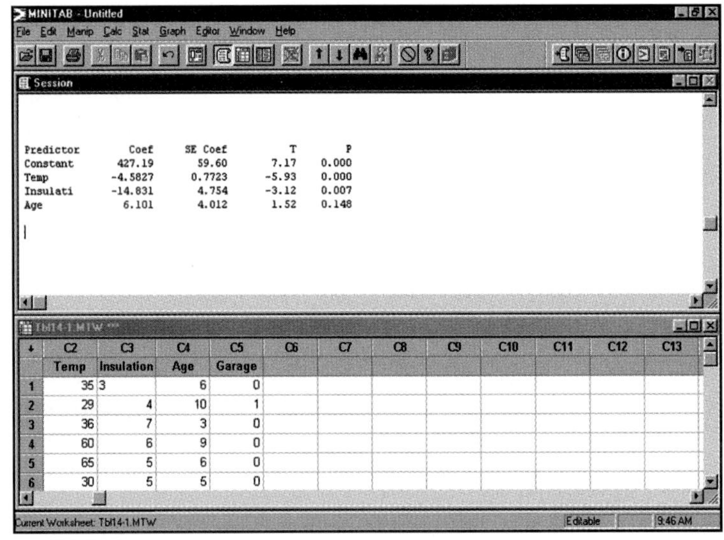

The column headed "Coef" gives the multiple regression equation:

$$Y' = 427.19 - 4.5827X_1 - 14.831X_2 + 6.101X_3$$

Interpreting the term $-4.5827X_1$ in the equation: For each degree the temperature increases, it is expected that the heating cost will decrease about $4.58, holding the two other variables constant.

The column on the MINITAB output labeled "SE Coef" indicates the standard error of the sample regression coefficient. Recall that Salsberry Realty selected a sample of 20 homes along the east coast of the United States. If they were to select a second sample at random and compute the regression coefficients of that sample, the values would not be exactly the same. If they repeated the sampling process many times, however, we could design a sampling distribution of the regression coefficients. The column labeled "SE Coef" estimates the variability of these regression coefficients. The sampling distribution of Coef/SE Coef follows the t distribution with $n - (k + 1)$ degrees of freedom. Hence, we are able to test the independent variables individually to determine whether the net regression coefficients differ from zero. The computed t ratio is -5.93 for temperature and -3.12 for insulation. Both of these t values are in the rejection region to the left of -2.120. Thus, we conclude that the regression coefficients for the temperature and insulation variables are *not* zero. The computed t for age of the furnace is 1.52, so we conclude that β_3 could equal 0. The independent variable "age of the furnace" is not a significant predictor of heating cost. It can be dropped from the analysis. We can test individual regression coefficients using the t distribution. The formula is:

$$t = \frac{b_1 - 0}{s_{b_1}} \quad \textbf{[14–7]}$$

The b_1 refers to any one of the net regression coefficients and s_{b_1} refers to standard deviation of that distribution of the net regression coefficient. We include 0 in the equation because the null hypothesis is $\beta_1 = 0$.

To illustrate this formula, refer to the test of the regression coefficient for the independent variable Temperature. We let b_1 refer to the net regression coefficient. From the computer output on page 518 it is -4.5827. s_{b_1} is the standard deviation of the sampling distribution of the net regression coefficient for the independent variable Temperature. Again, from the computer output on page 518, it is 0.7723. Inserting these values in formula (14–7):

$$t = \frac{b_1 - 0}{s_{b_1}} = \frac{-4.5827 - 0}{0.7723} - -5.93$$

This is the value found in the "T" column of the output.

In Self-Review 14–3, we run the multiple regression example again using MINITAB, but only two variables—"temperature" and "insulation"—are included. These two variables explained 77.6 percent of the variation in heating cost. Using all three variables—temperature, insulation, and furnace age—a total of 80.4 percent of the variation is explained. The additional variable increased R^2 by only 2.8 percent—a rather small increase for the addition of an independent variable.

At this point we should also develop a strategy for deleting independent variables. In the Salsberry Realty case there were three independent variables and one (age) had a regression coefficient that did not differ from 0. It is clear that we should drop that variable. So we delete that variable and rerun the regression equation. However, in some instances it may not be as clear-cut which variable to delete.

To explain, suppose we developed a multiple regression equation based on five independent variables. We conducted the global test and found that some of the regression coefficients were different from zero. Next, we tested the regression coefficients individually and found that three were significant and two were not. The preferred procedure is to drop the single independent variable with the *smallest absolute* t *value* or *largest* p-*value* and rerun the regression equation with the four remaining variables. Then, on the new regression equation with four independent variables, conduct the individual tests. If there are still regression coefficients that are not significant, again drop the variable with the smallest absolute t value. To describe the process in another way, we should delete only one variable at a time. Each time we delete a variable, we need to rerun the regression equation and check the remaining variables.

Self-Review 14–3

The multiple regression and correlation data for the preceding heating cost example were rerun using only the first two significant independent variables—temperature and insulation. (See the following MINITAB output.)

(a) What is the new multiple regression equation? (Temperature is X_1 and insulation X_2.)
(b) What is the coefficient of multiple determination? Interpret.
(c) How can you tell that these two independent variables are of value in predicting heating costs?
(d) What is the *p*-value of insulation? Interpret.

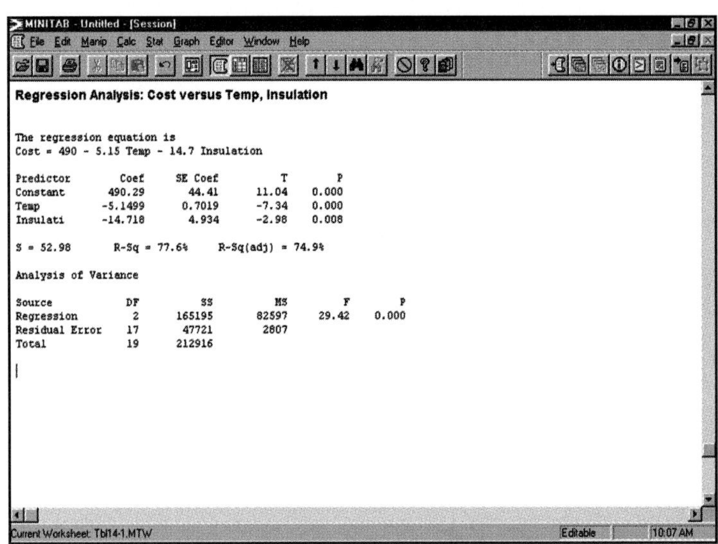

Regression Analysis: Cost versus Temp, Insulation

The regression equation is
Cost = 490 - 5.15 Temp - 14.7 Insulation

Predictor	Coef	SE Coef	T	P
Constant	490.29	44.41	11.04	0.000
Temp	-5.1499	0.7019	-7.34	0.000
Insulati	-14.718	4.934	-2.98	0.008

S = 52.98 R-Sq = 77.6% R-Sq(adj) = 74.9%

Analysis of Variance

Source	DF	SS	MS	F	P
Regression	2	165195	82597	29.42	0.000
Residual Error	17	47721	2807		
Total	19	212916			

Qualitative Independent Variables

The three variables used in the Salsberry Realty example were all quantitative; that is, numerical in nature. Frequently we wish to use nominal-scale variables—such as gender, whether the home has a swimming pool, or whether the sports team was the home or the visiting team—in our analysis. These are called *qualitative variables* because they describe a particular quality, such as male or female. To use a qualitative variable in regression analysis, we use a scheme of **dummy variables** in which one of the two possible conditions is coded 0 and the other 1.

DUMMY VARIABLE A variable in which there are only two possible outcomes. For analysis, one of the outcomes is coded a 1 and the other a 0.

For example, we might be interested in estimating an executive's salary based on years of job experience and whether he or she graduated from college. "Graduation from college" can take on only one of two conditions: yes or no. Thus, it is considered a qualitative variable.

Suppose in the Salsberry Realty example that the independent variable "garage" is added. For those homes without an attached garage, 0 is used; for homes with an

Statistics in Action

In recent years, multiple regression has been used in a variety of legal proceedings. It is particularly useful in cases alleging discrimination by gender or race. As an example, suppose that a woman alleges that Company X's wage rates are unfair to women. To support the claim, the plaintiff produces data showing that, on the average, women earn less than men. In response, Company X argues that its wage rates are based on experience, training, and skill and that its female employees, on the average, are younger and less experienced than the male employees. In fact, the company might further argue that the current situation is actually due to its recent successful efforts to hire more women.

attached garage, a 1 is used. We will refer to the "garage" variable as X_4. The data from Table 14–3 are entered into the MINITAB system.

TABLE 14–3 Home Heating Costs, Temperature, Insulation, and Presence of a Garage for a Sample of 20 Homes

Cost, Y	Temperature, X_1	Insulation, X_2	Garage, X_4
$250	35	3	0
360	29	4	1
165	36	7	0
43	60	6	0
92	65	5	0
200	30	5	0
355	10	6	1
290	7	10	1
230	21	9	0
120	55	2	0
73	54	12	0
205	48	5	1
400	20	5	1
320	39	4	1
72	60	8	0
272	20	5	1
94	58	7	0
190	40	8	1
235	27	9	0
139	30	7	0

The output from MINITAB is:

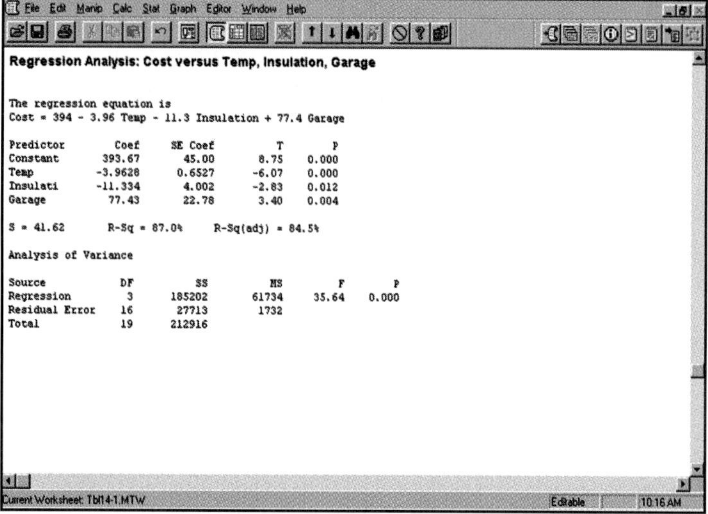
```
MINITAB - Untitled - [Session]
File Edit Manip Calc Stat Graph Editor Window Help

Regression Analysis: Cost versus Temp, Insulation, Garage

The regression equation is
Cost = 394 - 3.96 Temp - 11.3 Insulation + 77.4 Garage

Predictor       Coef     SE Coef        T        P
Constant      393.67       45.00     8.75    0.000
Temp         -3.9628      0.6527    -6.07    0.000
Insulati     -11.334       4.002    -2.83    0.012
Garage         77.43       22.78     3.40    0.004

S = 41.62     R-Sq = 87.0%     R-Sq(adj) = 84.5%

Analysis of Variance

Source           DF        SS        MS        F        P
Regression        3    185202     61734    35.64    0.000
Residual Error   16     27713      1732
Total            19    212916

Current Worksheet: Tbl14-1.MTW                    Editable    10:16 AM
```

What is the effect of the variable "garage"? Should it be included in the analysis? To show the effect of the variable, suppose we have two houses exactly alike next to each other in Buffalo, New York; one has an attached garage, and the other does not. Both homes have 3 inches of insulation, and the mean January temperature in Buffalo is 20 degrees. For the house without an attached garage, a 0 is substituted for X_4 in the regression equation. The estimated heating cost is \$280.90, found by:

$$\begin{aligned} Y' &= 394 - 3.96X_1 - 11.3X_2 + 77.4X_4 \\ &= 394 - 3.96(20) - 11.3(3) + 77.4(0) = 280.90 \end{aligned}$$

For the house with an attached garage, a 1 is substituted for X_4 in the regression equation. The estimated heating cost is \$358.30, found by:

$$\begin{aligned} Y' &= 394 - 3.96X_1 - 11.3X_2 + 77.4X_4 \\ &= 394 - 3.96(20) - 11.3(3) + 77.4(1) = 358.30 \end{aligned}$$

The difference between the estimated heating costs is \$77.40 (\$358.30 − \$280.90). Hence, we can expect the cost to heat a house with an attached garage to be \$77.40 more than the cost for an equivalent house without a garage.

We have shown the difference between the two types of homes to be \$77.40, but is the difference significant? We conduct the following test of hypothesis.

$$H_0\colon \beta_4 = 0$$
$$H_1\colon \beta_4 \neq 0$$

The information necessary to answer this question is on the MINITAB output above. The net regression coefficient for the independent variable Garage is 77.43, the standard deviation of the distribution of sampling distribution is 22.78. We identify this as the fourth independent variable, so we use a subscript of 4. Finally, we insert these values in formula 14–7.

$$t = \frac{b_4 - 0}{s_{b_4}} = \frac{77.43 - 0}{22.78} = 3.40$$

There are three independent variables in the analysis, so there are $n - (k + 1) = 20 - (3 + 1) = 16$ degrees of freedom. The critical value from Appendix F is 2.120. The decision rule, using a two-tailed test and the .05 significance level, is to reject H_0 if the computed t is to the left of −2.120 or to the right of 2.120. Since the computed value of 3.40 is to the right of 2.120, the null hypothesis is rejected. It is concluded that the regression coefficient is not zero. The independent variable "garage" should be included in the analysis.

Is it possible to use a qualitative variable with more than two possible outcomes? Yes, but the coding scheme becomes more complex and will require a series of dummy variables. To explain, suppose a company is studying its sales as they relate to advertising expense by quarter for the last 5 years. Let sales be the dependent variable and advertising expense be the first independent variable, X_1. To include the qualitative information regarding the quarter, we use three additional independent variables. For the variable X_2, the five observations referring to the first quarter of each of the 5 years are coded 1 and the other quarters 0. Similarly, for X_3 the five observations referring to the second quarter are coded 1 and the other quarters 0. For X_4 the five observations referring to the third quarter are coded 1 and the other quarters 0. An observation that does not refer to any of the first three quarters must refer to the fourth quarter, so a distinct independent variable referring to this quarter is not necessary.

Exercises

7. Refer to the following information:

Predictor	Coef	StDev		
Constant	20.00	10.00		
X_1	−1.00	0.25		
X_2	12.00	8.00		
X_3	−15.00	5.00		
SOURCE	DF	SS	MS	F
Regression	3	7,500.00		
Error	18			
Total	21	10,000.0		

a. Complete the ANOVA table.
b. Conduct a global test of hypothesis, using the .05 significance level. Can you conclude that any of the net regression coefficients are different from zero?
c. Conduct a test of hypothesis on each of the regression coefficients. Could you delete any of the variables?

8. Refer to the following information:

Predictor	Coef	StDev		
Constant	−150	90		
X_1	2000	500		
X_2	−25	30		
X_3	5	5		
X_4	−300	100		
X_5	0.60	0.15		
SOURCE	DF	SS	MS	F
Regression	5	1,500.0		
Error	15			
Total	20	2,000.0		

8. **a.** $F = 9.00$ **b.** Reject if $F > 2.90$. **c.** Delete X_3 then retest, perhaps X_2.

a. Complete the ANOVA table.
b. Conduct a global test of hypothesis, using the .05 significance level. Can you conclude that any of the net regression coefficients are different from zero?
c. Conduct a test of hypothesis on each of the regression coefficients. Could you delete any of the variables?

Analysis of Residuals

In an earlier section we describe the assumptions required for regression and correlation analysis. These assumptions are:

1. There is a linear relationship between the dependent variable and the independent variables.
2. The dependent variable is of interval- or ratio-scale.
3. Successive observations of the dependent variable are not correlated.
4. The differences between the actual values and estimated values, that is, the residuals, are normally distributed.
5. The variation in the residuals is the same for all fitted values of Y'. That is, the distribution of $(Y - Y')$ is the same for all values of Y'.

The last two assumptions can be verified by plotting the residuals. That is, we want to confirm that the residuals follow a normal distribution and that residuals have the same variation whether the Y' value is large or small. We present the necessary data in Table 14–4. The column headed "Actual Cost" is the original heating cost, first presented in Table 14–1. The next column, labeled "Estimated Cost," is the cost to heat the home as estimated from the regression equation. This is also referred to as the fitted value and is Y'. The value for the first home is found by substituting the actual values of the three variables into the regression equation. For example, from Table 14–3, for the first home the mean outside temperature was 35 degrees, it had 3 inches of attic insulation, and did not have an attached garage. The actual heating cost was $250, and the estimated heating cost is $221.08, found by

$$Y' = 393.67 - 3.96(35) - 11.33(3) + 77.43(0) = 221.08$$

The residual is in the last column. It is 28.92, found by 250 − 221.08. The residuals for the 19 other values are computed similarly.

TABLE 14–4 Summary of Actual Costs, Estimated Costs, and Residuals for Salsberry Realty Problem

Home	Actual Cost, Y	Estimated Cost, Y'	Residual, $Y - Y'$
1	250	221.08	28.92
2	360	310.94	49.06
3	165	171.80	−6.80
4	43	88.09	−45.09
5	92	79.62	12.38
6	200	218.22	−18.22
7	355	363.52	−8.52
8	290	330.08	−40.08
9	230	208.54	21.46
10	120	153.21	−33.21
11	73	43.87	29.13
12	205	224.37	−19.37
13	400	335.25	64.75
14	320	271.34	48.66
15	72	65.43	6.57
16	272	335.25	−63.25
17	94	84.68	9.32
18	190	222.06	−32.06
19	235	184.78	50.22
20	139	195.56	−56.56

We can use the last column, the residuals, to verify the normality assumption. The following MINITAB output shows a stem-and-leaf display and a histogram of the residuals. Both charts indicate that the distribution of the residuals is somewhat normal, as required in the assumptions. To interpret the output, note that the residuals are tallied into classes with a class interval of 20: −70 up to −50, with a midpoint of −60; −50 up to −30, with a midpoint of −40; and so on. The details of the first three classes are:

Class	Midpoint	Residuals	Count
−70 up to −50	−60	−63.25, −56.56	2
−50 up to −30	−40	−45.09, −40.08, −33.21, −32.06	4
−30 up to −10	−20	−19.37, −18.22	2

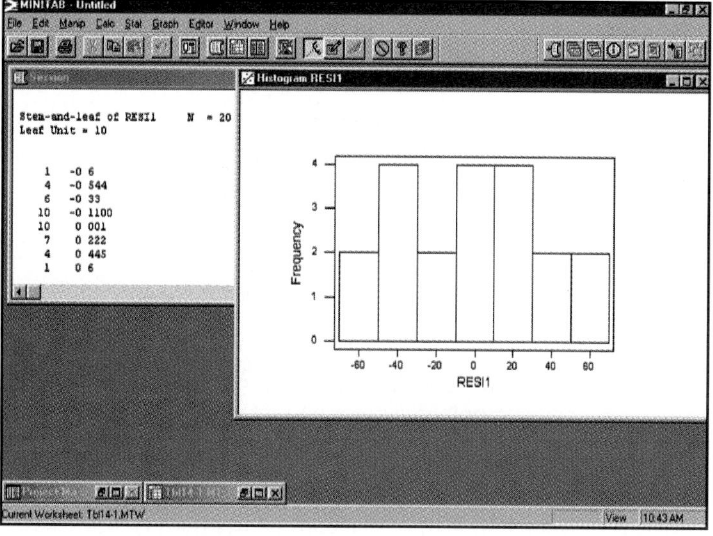

Homoscedasticity

The assumptions for regression analysis also require that the residuals remain constant for all values of Y'. Recall that this condition is called **homoscedasticity**. To check for homoscedasticity, the residuals are plotted against the fitted values of Y. That is, we develop a scatter plot with the values in the Estimated Cost column of Table 14–4 plotted on the horizontal axis and the residuals on the vertical axis. The first plot is 221.08 for X and 28.92 for Y. Because there is no more variation around the large Y' values than the small Y', we conclude that this assumption has not been violated.

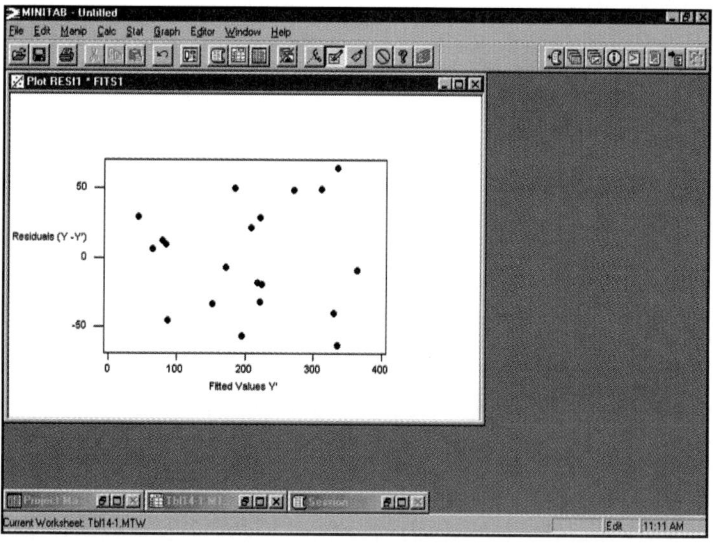

Following are two examples in which the homoscedasticity requirement is not met. Note in the first example, the plot of residuals is funnel-shaped. That is, as the fitted Y values increase, so does the variation in the residuals. In the second example, there is a pattern to the residuals. The residuals seem to take the shape of a polynomial, or a second-degree equation.

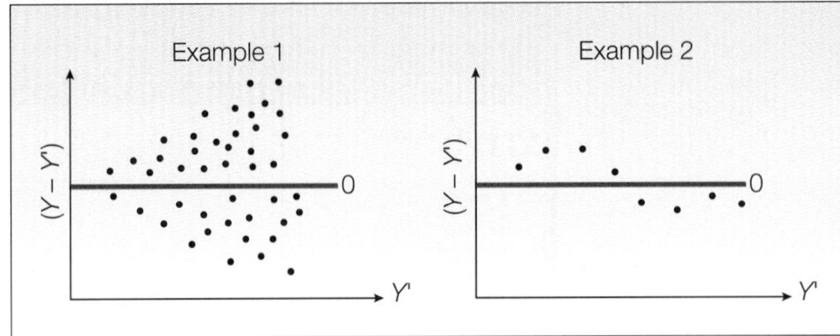

What problems are caused by residuals that fail to show homoscedasticity? The standard deviations of the regression coefficients will be understated (too small), causing potential independent variables to appear to be significant when they may not be. The remedy for this condition is to select other independent variables or to transform some of the variables. For a more detailed discussion of residual analysis, refer to an advanced text, such as *Applied Linear Statistical Models* by Neter, Kutner, Nachtsheim, and Wasserman (Richard D. Irwin, 1996).

Chapter Outline

I. Multiple regression and correlation analysis is based on these assumptions.

- **A.** There is a linear relationship between the independent variables and the dependent variable.
- **B.** The dependent variable is continuous and of interval scale.
- **C.** The residual variation is the same for all fitted values of Y.
- **D.** The residuals are normally distributed.
- **E.** Successive observations of the dependent variable are uncorrelated.

II. The general form of the multiple regression equation is:

$$Y' = a + b_1X_1 + b_2X_2 + \cdots + b_kX_k \quad \textbf{[14–3]}$$

where Y' is the estimated value, a is the Y-intercept, the bs are the sample regression coefficients, and the Xs represent the values of the various independent variables.

- **A.** There can be any number of independent variables.
- **B.** The least squares criterion is used to develop the equation.
- **C.** A computer is needed to determine a and the various b values.

III. There are two measures of the effectiveness of the regression equation.

- **A.** The multiple standard error of estimate is similar to the standard deviation.
  1. It is measured in the same units as the dependent variable.
  2. It is difficult to determine what is a large value and what is a small value of the standard error.
- **B.** The coefficient of determination may range from 0 to 1.
  1. It shows the fraction of the variation in Y that is explained by the set of independent variables.
  2. It does not reveal the direction of the relationship.

IV. The ANOVA table gives the variation in the dependent variable explained by the regression equation.

V. A correlation matrix shows all possible simple correlation coefficients between pairs of variables.

VI. A global test is used to investigate whether any of the independent variables have significant regression coefficients.

- **A.** The null hypothesis is: All the regression coefficients are zero.
- **B.** The alternate hypothesis is: At least one regression coefficient is not zero.

C. The test statistic is the *F* distribution with *k* (the number of independent variables) degrees of freedom in the numerator and $n - (k + 1)$ degrees of freedom in the denominator, where *n* is the sample size.
D. The formula to calculate the value of the test statistic for the global test is:

$$F = \frac{\text{SSR}/k}{\text{SSE}/[n - (k + 1)]} \quad \textbf{[14–6]}$$

VII. The test for individual variables determines which independent variables have nonzero regression coefficients.
A. The variables that have zero regression coefficients are usually dropped from the analysis.
B. The test statistic is the *t* distribution with $n - (k + 1)$ degrees of freedom.
C. The formula to calculate the value of the test statistic for the individual test is:

$$t = \frac{b_i - 0}{s_{b_i}} \quad \textbf{[14–7]}$$

VIII. Dummy variables are used to represent qualitative variables and can assume only one of two possible conditions.
IX. A residual is the difference between the actual value of *Y* and the predicted value of *Y*.
A. Residuals should be approximately normally distributed. Histograms and stem-and-leaf charts are useful in checking this requirement.
B. A plot of the residuals and their corresponding Y' values is useful for showing that there are no trends or patterns in the residuals.

Pronunciation Key

SYMBOL	MEANING	PRONUNCIATION
b_1	Regression coefficient for the first independent variable	*b sub 1*
b_k	Regression coefficient for any independent variable	*b sub k*
$s_{y \cdot 12 \cdots k}$	Multiple standard error of estimate	*s sub y dot 1, 2 . . . k*

Chapter Exercises

9. A multiple regression equation yields the following partial results.

Source	Sum of Squares	*df*
Regression	750	4
Error	500	35

a. What is the total sample size?
b. How many independent variables are being considered?
c. Compute the coefficient of determination.
d. Compute the standard error of estimate.
e. Test the hypothesis that none of the regression coefficients is equal to zero. Let $\alpha = .05$.

10. In a multiple regression equation two independent variables are considered, and the sample size is 25. The regression coefficients and the standard errors are as follows.

$$b_1 = 2.676 \qquad s_{b_1} = 0.56$$

$$b_2 = -0.880 \qquad s_{b_2} = 0.71$$

Conduct a test of hypothesis to determine whether either independent variable has a coefficient equal to zero. Would you consider deleting either variable from the regression equation? Use the .05 significance level.

10. $t_1 = 4.78$, no. $t_2 = -1.24$, yes.

11. The following output was obtained.

Analysis of variance

SOURCE	DF	SS	MS
Regression	5	100	20
Error	20	40	2
Total	25	140	

Predictor	Coef	StDev	t-ratio
Constant	3.00	1.50	2.00
X_1	4.00	3.00	1.33
X_2	3.00	0.20	15.00
X_3	0.20	0.05	4.00
X_4	−2.50	1.00	−2.50
X_5	3.00	4.00	0.75

a. What is the sample size?
b. Compute the value of R^2.
c. Compute the multiple standard error of estimate.
d. Conduct a global test of hypothesis to determine whether any of the regression coefficients are significant. Use the .05 significance level.
e. Test the regression coefficients individually. Would you consider omitting any variable(s)? If so, which one(s)? Use the .05 significance level.

12. Yes, $F = 17.58$.

12. In a multiple regression equation $k = 5$ and $n = 20$, the MSE value is 5.10, and SS total is 519.68. At the .05 significance level, can we conclude that any of the regression coefficients are not equal to 0?

13. The district manager of Jasons, a large discount retail chain, is investigating why certain stores in her region are performing better than others. She believes that three factors are related to total sales: the number of competitors in the region, the population in the surrounding area, and the amount spent on advertising. From her district, consisting of several hundred stores, she selects a random sample of 30 stores. For each store she gathered the following information.

Y = total sales last year (in $ thousands).
X_1 = number of competitors in the region.
X_2 = population of the region (in millions).
X_3 = advertising expense (in $ thousands).

The sample data were run on MINITAB, with the following results.

Analysis of variance

SOURCE	DF	SS	MS
Regression	3	3050.00	1016.67
Error	26	2200.00	84.62
Total	29	5250.00	

Predictor	Coef	StDev	t-ratio
Constant	14.00	7.00	2.00
X_1	−1.00	0.70	−1.43
X_2	30.00	5.20	5.77
X_3	0.20	0.08	2.50

a. What are the estimated sales for the Bryne Store, which has four competitors, a regional population of 0.4 (400,000), and advertising expense of 30 ($30,000)?
b. Compute the R^2 value.

c. Compute the multiple standard error of estimate.

d. Conduct a global test of hypothesis to determine whether any of the regression coefficients are not equal to zero. Use the .05 level of significance.

e. Conduct tests of hypotheses to determine which of the independent variables have significant regression coefficients. Which variables would you consider eliminating? Use the .05 significance level.

14. Suppose that the sales manager of a large automotive parts distributor wants to estimate as early as April the total annual sales of a region. Based on regional sales, the total sales for the company can also be estimated. If, based on past experience, it is found that the April estimates of annual sales are reasonably accurate, then in future years the April forecast could be used to revise production schedules and maintain the correct inventory at the retail outlets.

Several factors appear to be related to sales, including the number of retail outlets in the region stocking the company's parts, the number of automobiles in the region registered as of April 1, and the total personal income for the first quarter of the year. Five independent variables were finally selected as being the most important (according to the sales manager). Then the data were gathered for a recent year. The total annual sales for that year for each region were also recorded. Note in the following table that for region 1 there were 1,739 retail outlets stocking the company's automotive parts, there were 9,270,000 registered automobiles in the region as of April 1, and sales for that year were $37,702,000.

Annual Sales ($ millions), Y	Number of Retail Outlets, X_1	Number of Automobiles Registered (millions), X_2	Personal Income ($ billions), X_3	Average Age of Automobiles (years), X_4	Number of Supervisors, X_5
37.702	1,739	9.27	85.4	3.5	9.0
24.196	1,221	5.86	60.7	5.0	5.0
32.055	1,846	8.81	68.1	4.4	7.0
3.611	120	3.81	20.2	4.0	5.0
17.625	1,096	10.31	33.8	3.5	7.0
45.919	2,290	11.62	95.1	4.1	13.0
29.600	1,687	8.96	69.3	4.1	15.0
8.114	241	6.28	16.3	5.9	11.0
20.116	649	7.77	34.9	5.5	16.0
12.994	1,427	10.92	15.1	4.1	10.0

14. a. Income has the strongest correlation with sales. Possible problems with multicollinearity.

a. Consider the following correlation matrix. Which single variable has the strongest correlation with the dependent variable? The correlations between the independent variables "outlets" and "income" and between "cars" and "outlets" are fairly strong. Could this be a problem? What is this condition called?

	sales	outlets	cars	income	age
outlets	0.899				
cars	0.605	0.775			
income	0.964	0.825	0.409		
age	−0.323	−0.489	−0.447	−0.349	
bosses	0.286	0.183	0.395	0.155	0.291

b. $R^2 = .994$

b. The following regression equation was obtained using the five independent variables. What percent of the variation is explained by the regression equation?

```
The regression equation is
sales = -19.7 - 0.00063 outlets + 1.74 cars + 0.410 income
        + 2.04 age - 0.034 bosses

          Predictor          Coef          StDev       t-ratio
          Constant        -19.672          5.422         -3.63
          outlets       -0.000629       0.002638         -0.24
          cars             1.7399         0.5530          3.15
          income          0.40994        0.04385          9.35
          age              2.0357         0.8779          2.32
          bosses          -0.0344         0.1880         -0.18

Analysis of Variance
          SOURCE          DF           SS         MS
          Regression       5      1593.81     318.76
          Error            4         9.08       2.27
          Total            9      1602.89
```

c. $F = 140.42$

c. Conduct a global test of hypothesis to determine whether any of the regression coefficients are not zero. Use the .05 significance level.

d. Delete both.

d. Conduct a test of hypothesis on each of the independent variables. Would you consider eliminating "outlets" and "bosses"? Use the .05 significance level.

e. Almost no change

e. The regression has been rerun below with "outlets" and "bosses" eliminated. Compute the coefficient of determination. How much has R^2 changed from the previous analysis?

```
The regression equation is
        sales = -18.9 + 1.61 cars + 0.400 income + 1.96 age

          Predictor          Coef          StDev       t-ratio
          Constant        -18.924          3.636         -5.20
          Cars             1.6129         0.1979          8.15
          Income          0.40031        0.01569         25.52
          Age              1.9637         0.5846          3.36

Analysis of Variance
          SOURCE          DF           SS         MS
          Regression       3      1593.66     531.22
          Error            6         9.23       1.54
          Total            9      1602.89
```

f. Yes.

f. Following is a histogram and a stem-and-leaf chart of the residuals. Does the normality assumption appear reasonable?

```
Histogram of residual N = 10        Stem-and-leaf of residual N = 10
                                    Leaf Unit = 0.10

Midpoint  Count
   -1.5      1   *                  1  -1  7
   -1.0      1   *                  2  -1  2
   -0.5      2   **                 2  -0
   -0.0      2   **                 5  -0  440
    0.5      2   **                 5   0  24
    1.0      1   *                  3   0  68
    1.5      1   *                  1   1
                                    1   1  7
```

g. No.

g. Following is a plot of the fitted values of Y (i.e., Y') and the residuals. Do you see any violations of the assumptions?

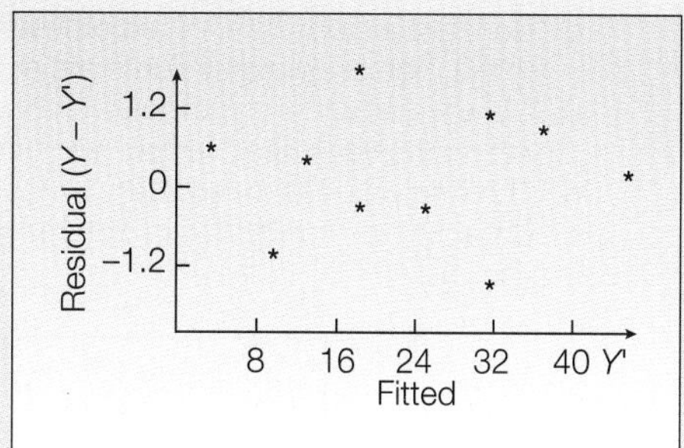

15. The administrator of a new paralegal program at Seagate Technical College wants to estimate the grade point average in the new program. He thought that high school GPA, the verbal score on the Scholastic Aptitude Test (SAT), and the mathematics score on the SAT would be good predictors of paralegal GPA. The data on nine students are:

Student	High School GPA	SAT Verbal	SAT Math	Paralegal GPA
1	3.25	480	410	3.21
2	1.80	290	270	1.68
3	2.89	420	410	3.58
4	3.81	500	600	3.92
5	3.13	500	490	3.00
6	2.81	430	460	2.82
7	2.20	320	490	1.65
8	2.14	530	480	2.30
9	2.63	469	440	2.33

a. Consider the following correlation matrix. Which variable has the strongest correlation with the dependent variable? Some of the correlations among the independent variables are strong. Does this appear to be a problem?

```
            legal      gpa    verbal
gpa         0.911
verbal      0.616    0.609
math        0.487    0.636     0.599
```

b. Consider the following output. Compute the coefficient of multiple determination.

```
The regression equation is
legal = −0.411 + 1.20 gpa + 0.00163 verbal − 0.00194 math

Predictor            Coef              StDev          t-ratio
Constant          −0.4111             0.7823            −0.53
gpa                1.2014             0.2955             4.07
verbal           0.001629           0.002147             0.76
math            −0.001939           0.002074            −0.94

Analysis of Variance
SOURCE           DF        SS         MS
Regression        3    4.3595     1.4532
Error             5    0.7036     0.1407
Total             8    5.0631
```

c. Conduct a global test of hypothesis from the preceding output. Does it appear that any of the regression coefficients are not equal to zero?

d. Conduct a test of hypothesis on each independent variable. Would you consider eliminating the variables "verbal" and "math"? Let $\alpha = .05$.

e. The analysis has been rerun without "verbal" and "math." See the following output. Compute the coefficient of determination. How much has R^2 changed from the previous analysis?

```
The regression equation is
legal = −0.454 + 1.16 gpa

  Predictor          Coef       StDev     t-ratio
  Constant        −0.4542      0.5542       −0.82
  gpa              1.1589      0.1977        5.86

Analysis of Variance

SOURCE        DF        SS          MS
Regression     1    4.2061      4.2061
Error          7    0.8570      0.1224
Total          8    5.0631
```

f. Following are a histogram and a stem-and-leaf diagram of the residuals. Does the normality assumption for the residuals seem reasonable?

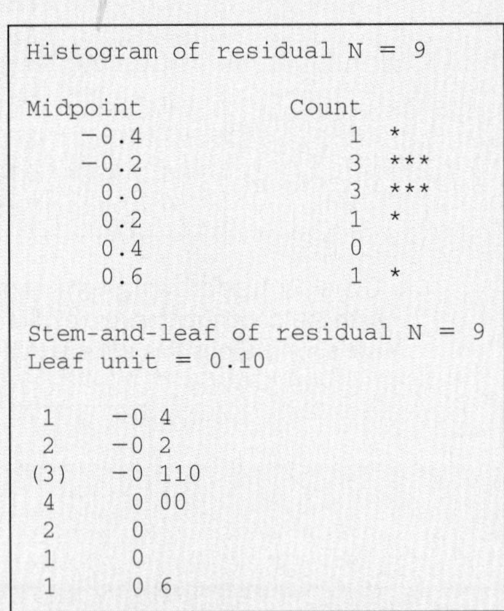

```
Histogram of residual N = 9

Midpoint            Count
   −0.4                 1  *
   −0.2                 3  ***
    0.0                 3  ***
    0.2                 1  *
    0.4                 0
    0.6                 1  *

Stem-and-leaf of residual N = 9
Leaf unit = 0.10

  1      −0 4
  2      −0 2
 (3)     −0 110
  4       0 00
  2       0
  1       0
  1       0 6
```

g. Following is a plot of the residuals and the Y' values. Do you see any violation of the assumptions?

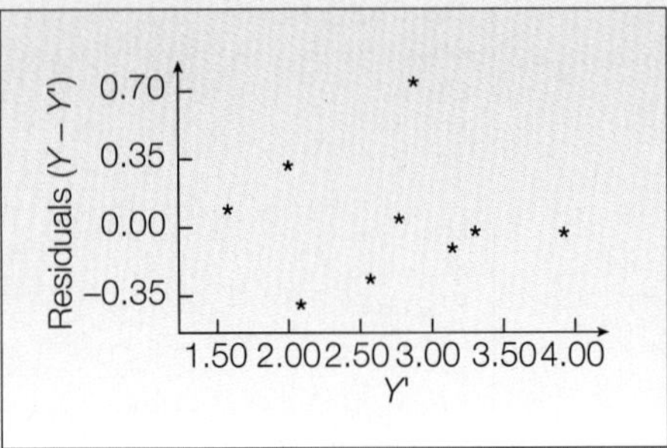

The following problems require a software package.

16. Mike Wilde is president of the teachers' union for Otsego School District. In preparing for upcoming negotiations, he would like to investigate the salary structure of classroom teachers in the district. He believes there are three factors that affect a teacher's salary: years of experience, a rating of teaching effectiveness given by the principal, and whether the teacher has a master's degree. A random sample of 20 teachers resulted in the following data.

Salary ($ thousands), Y	Years of Experience, X_1	Principal's Rating, X_2	Master's Degree,* Y_3
21.1	8	35	0
23.6	5	43	0
19.3	2	51	1
33.0	15	60	1
28.6	11	73	0
35.0	14	80	1
32.0	9	76	0
26.8	7	54	1
38.6	22	55	1
21.7	3	90	1
15.7	1	30	0
20.6	5	44	0
41.8	23	84	1
36.7	17	76	0
28.4	12	68	1
23.6	14	25	0
31.8	8	90	1
20.7	4	62	0
22.8	2	80	1
32.8	8	72	0

*1 = yes, 0 = no.

16. a. Years. No.
b. $Y' = \$23,655$
c. $F = 52.72$
d. Drop X_3.
e. $Y' = 10.1 + 0.893X_1 + 0.146X_2$
f. Meets normality assumption, see IM.
g. No pattern, see IM.

a. Develop a correlation matrix. Which independent variable has the strongest correlation with the dependent variable? Does it appear there will be any problems with multicollinearity?
b. Determine the regression equation. What salary would you estimate for a teacher with five years' experience, a rating by the principal of 60, and no master's degree?
c. Conduct a global test of hypothesis to determine whether any of the net regression coefficients differ from zero. Use the .05 significance level.
d. Conduct a test of hypothesis for the individual regression coefficients. Would you consider deleting any of the independent variables? Use the .05 significance level.
e. If your conclusion in part (d) was to delete one or more independent variables, run the analysis again without those variables.
f. Determine the residuals for the equation of part (e). Use a stem-and-leaf chart or a histogram to verify that the distribution of the residuals is approximately normal.
g. Plot the residuals computed in part (f) in a scatter diagram with the residuals on the Y-axis and the Y' values on the X-axis. Does the plot reveal any violations of the assumptions of regression?

17. The district sales manager for a major automobile manufacturer is studying car sales. Specifically, he would like to determine what factors affect the number of cars sold at a dealership. To investigate, he randomly selects 12 dealers. From these dealers he obtains the number of cars sold last month, the minutes of radio advertising purchased last month, the number of full-time salespeople employed in the dealership, and whether the dealer is located in the city. The information is as follows:

Cars Sold Last Month, Y	Advertising, X_1	Sales Force, X_2	City, X_3	Cars Sold Last Month, Y	Advertising, X_1	Sales Force, X_2	City, X_3
127	18	10	Yes	161	25	14	Yes
138	15	15	No	180	26	17	Yes
159	22	14	Yes	102	15	7	No
144	23	12	Yes	163	24	16	Yes
139	17	12	No	106	18	10	No
128	16	12	Yes	149	25	11	Yes

a. Develop a correlation matrix. Which independent variable has the strongest correlation with the dependent variable? Does it appear there will be any problems with multicollinearity?

b. Determine the regression equation. How many cars would you expect to be sold by a dealership employing 20 salespeople, purchasing 15 minutes of advertising, and located in a city?

c. Conduct a global test of hypothesis to determine whether any of the net regression coefficients differ from zero. Let $\alpha = .05$.

d. Conduct a test of hypothesis for the individual regression coefficients. Would you consider deleting any of the independent variables? Let $\alpha = .05$.

e. If your conclusion in part (d) was to delete one or more independent variables, run the analysis again without those variables.

f. Determine the residuals for the equation of part (e). Use a stem-and-leaf chart or a histogram to verify that the distribution of the residuals is approximately normal.

g. Plot the residuals computed in part (f) in a scatter diagram with the residuals on the Y-axis and the Y' values on the X-axis. Does the plot reveal any violations of the assumptions of regression?

18. Fran's Convenience Marts are located throughout metropolitan Erie, Pennsylvania. Fran, the owner, would like to expand into other communities in northwestern Pennsylvania and southwestern New York, such as Jamestown, Corry, Meadville, and Warren. As part of her presentation to the local bank, she would like to better understand the factors that make a particular outlet profitable. She must do all the work herself, so she will not be able to study all her outlets. She selects a random sample of 15 marts and records the average daily sales (Y), the floor space (area), the number of parking spaces, and the median income of families in that ZIP code region for each. The sample information is reported below.

Sampled Mart	Daily Sales	Store Area	Parking Spaces	Income ($ thousands)
1	$1,840	532	6	44
2	1,746	478	4	51
3	1,812	530	7	45
4	1,806	508	7	46
5	1,792	514	5	44
6	1,825	556	6	46
7	1,811	541	4	49
8	1,803	513	6	52
9	1,830	532	5	46
10	1,827	537	5	46
11	1,764	499	3	48
12	1,825	510	8	47
13	1,763	490	4	48
14	1,846	516	8	45
15	1,815	482	7	43

18. a. $Y' = 1480.7 + 0.7315X_1 + 9.991X_2 - 2.308X_3$
b. .835
c. 18.60
d. Delete income.
e. $R^2 = 0.804$, $Y' = 1342.49 + 0.7727X_1 + 11.634X_2$

a. Determine the regression equation.
b. What is the value of R^2? Comment on the value.
c. Conduct a global hypothesis test to determine if any of the independent variables are different from zero.
d. Conduct individual hypothesis tests to determine if any of the independent variables can be dropped.
e. If variables are dropped, recompute the regression equation and R^2.

19. Steve Douglas has been hired as a management trainee by a large brokerage firm. As his first project, he is asked to study the gross profit of firms in the chemical industry. What factors affect profitability in that industry? Steve selects a random sample of 16 firms and obtains data on the number of employees, number of consecutive common stock dividends paid, the total value of inventory at the start of the current year, and the gross profit for each firm. His findings are:

Company	Gross Profit ($ thousands), Y	Number of Employees, X_1	Consecutive Dividends, X_2	Beginning Inventory ($ thousands), X_3
1	2,800	140	12	1,800
2	1,300	65	21	320
3	1,230	130	42	820
4	1,600	115	80	76
5	4,500	390	120	3,600
6	5,700	670	64	8,400
7	3,150	205	43	508
8	640	40	14	870
9	3,400	480	88	5,500
10	6,700	810	98	9,875
11	3,700	120	44	6,500
12	6,440	590	110	9,130
13	1,280	440	38	1,200
14	4,160	280	24	890
15	3,870	650	60	1,200
16	980	150	24	1,300

a. Determine the regression equation. The Master Chemical Company employs 220 people, has paid 64 consecutive common stock dividends, and has an inventory valued at $1,500,000 at the start of the year. What is the estimate of the gross profit?
b. Conduct a global test of hypothesis to determine whether any of the net regression coefficients differ from zero.
c. Conduct a test of hypothesis for the individual regression coefficients. Would you consider deleting any of the independent variables?
d. If your conclusion in part (c) was to delete one or more independent variables, run the analysis again, deleting those variables.
e. Determine the residuals for the equation of part (d). Use a stem-and-leaf chart or a histogram to verify that the distribution of the residuals is approximately normal.
f. Plot the residuals computed in part (e) in a scatter diagram with the residuals on the Y-axis and the Y' values on the X-axis. Does the plot reveal any violations of the assumptions of regression?

20. The *Times-Observer* is a daily newspaper in Metro City. Like many city newspapers, the *Times-Observer* is suffering through difficult financial times. The circulation manager is studying other papers in similar cities in the United States and Canada. She is particularly interested in what variables relate to the number of subscriptions to the paper. She is able to obtain the following sample information on 25 newspapers in similar cities. The following notation is used:

Sub = Number of subscriptions (in thousands).
Popul = The metropolitan population (in thousands).
Adv = The advertising budget of the paper (in $ hundreds).
Income = The median family income in the metropolitan area (in $ thousands).

Paper	Sub	Popul	Adv	Income	Paper	Sub	Popul	Adv	Income
1	37.95	588.9	13.2	35.1	14	38.39	586.5	15.4	35.5
2	37.66	585.3	13.2	34.7	15	37.29	544.0	11.0	34.9
3	37.55	566.3	19.8	34.8	16	39.15	611.1	24.2	35.0
4	38.78	642.9	17.6	35.1	17	38.29	643.3	17.6	35.3
5	37.67	624.2	17.6	34.6	18	38.09	635.6	19.8	34.8
6	38.23	603.9	15.4	34.8	19	37.83	598.9	15.4	35.1
7	36.90	571.9	11.0	34.7	20	39.37	657.0	22.0	35.3
8	38.28	584.3	28.6	35.3	21	37.81	595.2	15.4	35.1
9	38.95	605.0	28.6	35.1	22	37.42	520.0	19.8	35.1
10	39.27	676.3	17.6	35.6	23	38.83	629.6	22.0	35.3
11	38.30	587.4	17.6	34.9	24	38.33	680.0	24.2	34.7
12	38.84	576.4	22.0	35.4	25	40.24	651.2	33.0	35.8
13	38.14	570.8	17.6	35.0					

20. a. $Y' = -5.7328 + 0.00754X_1 + 0.0509X_2 + 1.0974X_3$
b. $F = 35.38$
c. Keep all 3.
d. See IM.
e. See IM.

a. Determine the regression equation.
b. Conduct a global test of hypothesis to determine whether any of the net regression coefficients are not equal to zero.
c. Conduct a test for the individual coefficients. Would you consider deleting any coefficients?
d. Determine the residuals and plot them against the fitted values. Do you see any problems?
e. Develop a histogram of the residuals. Do you see any problems with the normality assumption?

21. How important is GPA in determining the starting salary of recent business school graduates? Does graduating from a business school increase the starting salary? The Director of Undergraduate Studies at a major university wanted to study these questions. She gathered the following sample information on 15 graduates last spring to investigate these questions.

Student	Salary	GPA	Business
1	$31.5	3.245	0
2	33.0	3.278	0
3	34.1	3.520	1
4	35.4	3.740	1
5	34.2	3.520	1
6	34.0	3.421	1
7	34.5	3.410	1
8	35.0	3.630	1
9	34.7	3.355	1
10	32.5	3.080	0
11	31.5	3.025	0
12	32.2	3.146	0
13	34.0	3.465	1
14	32.8	3.245	0
15	31.8	3.025	0

The salary is reported in $000, GPA on the traditional 4-point scale. A 1 indicates the student graduated from a school of business; a 0 indicates that the student graduated from one of the other schools.

a. Develop a correlation matrix. Do you see any problems with multicollinearity?
b. Determine the regression equation. Discuss the regression equation. How much does graduating from a college of business add to a starting salary? What starting salary would you estimate for a student with a GPA of 3.00 who graduated from a college of business?
c. What is the value of R^2? Can we conclude that this value is greater than 0?
d. Would you consider deleting either of the independent variables?
e. Plot the residuals in a histogram. Is there any problem with the normality assumption?
f. Plot the fitted values against the residuals. Does this plot indicate any problems with homoscedasticity?

22. A mortgage department of a large bank is studying its recent loans. Of particular interest is how such factors as the value of the home (in thousands of dollars), education level of the head of the household, age of the head of the household, current monthly mortgage payment (in dollars), and sex of the head of the household (male = 1, female = 0) relate to the family income. Are these variables effective predictors of the income of the household? A random sample of 25 recent loans is obtained.

Income ($ thousands)	Value ($ thousands)	Years of Education	Age	Mortgage Payment	Sex
$40.3	$190	14	53	$230	1
39.6	121	15	49	370	1
40.8	161	14	44	397	1
40.3	161	14	39	181	1
40.0	179	14	53	378	0
38.1	99	14	46	304	0
40.4	114	15	42	285	1
40.7	202	14	49	551	0
40.8	184	13	37	370	0
37.1	90	14	43	135	0
39.9	181	14	48	332	1
40.4	143	15	54	217	1
38.0	132	14	44	490	0
39.0	127	14	37	220	0
39.5	153	14	50	270	1
40.6	145	14	50	279	1
40.3	174	15	52	329	1
40.1	177	15	47	274	0
41.7	188	15	49	433	1
40.1	153	15	53	333	1
40.6	150	16	58	148	0
40.4	173	13	42	390	1
40.9	163	14	46	142	1
40.1	150	15	50	343	0
38.5	139	14	45	373	0

22. a. $Y' = 28.2 + 0.0287X_1 + 0.650X_2 - 0.049X_3 - 0.0004X_4$
b. .750
c. $F = 11.39$
d. Drop age and mortgage payment.
e. See IM.

a. Determine the regression equation.
b. What is the value of R^2? Comment on the value.
c. Conduct a global hypothesis test to determine whether any of the independent variables are different from zero.
d. Conduct individual hypothesis tests to determine whether any of the independent variables can be dropped.
e. If variables are dropped, recompute the regression equation and R^2.

23. Fred G. Hire is the manager of human resources at St. Luke's Medical Center. As part of his yearly report to the president of the medical center, he is required to present an analysis of the salaried employees. Because there are over 1,000 employees, he does not have the staff to gather information on each salaried employee, so he selects a random sample of

30. For each employee, he records monthly salary; service at St. Luke's, in months; sex (1 = male, 0 = female); and whether the employee has a technical or clerical job. Those working technical jobs are coded 1, and those who are clerical 0.

Sampled Employee	Monthly Salary	Length of Service	Age	Sex	Job
1	$1,769	93	42	1	0
2	1,740	104	33	1	0
3	1,941	104	42	1	1
4	2,367	126	57	1	1
5	2,467	98	30	1	1
6	1,640	99	49	1	1
7	1,756	94	35	1	0
8	1,706	96	46	0	1
9	1,767	124	56	0	0
10	1,200	73	23	0	1
11	1,706	110	67	0	1
12	1,985	90	36	0	1
13	1,555	104	53	0	0
14	1,749	81	29	0	0
15	2,056	106	45	1	0
16	1,729	113	55	0	1
17	2,186	129	46	1	1
18	1,858	97	39	0	1
19	1,819	101	43	1	1
20	1,350	91	35	1	1
21	2,030	100	40	1	0
22	2,550	123	59	1	0
23	1,544	88	30	0	0
24	1,766	117	60	1	1
25	1,937	107	45	1	1
26	1,691	105	32	0	1
27	1,623	86	33	0	0
28	1,791	131	56	0	1
29	2,001	95	30	1	1
30	1,874	98	47	1	0

a. Determine the regression equation, using salary as the dependent variable and the other four variables as independent variables.
b. What is the value of R^2? Comment on this value.
c. Conduct a global test of hypothesis to determine whether any of the independent variables are different from 0.
d. Conduct an individual test to determine whether any of the independent variables can be dropped.
e. Rerun the regression equation, using only the independent variables that are significant. How much more does a man earn per month than a woman? Does it make a difference whether the employee has a technical or a clerical job?

24. Many regions along the coast in North and South Carolina and Georgia have experienced rapid population growth over the last 10 years. It is expected that the growth will continue over the next 10 years. This has resulted in many of the large grocery store chains building new stores in the region. The Kelley's Super Grocery Stores, Inc. chain is no exception. The director of planning for Kelley's Super Grocery Stores wants to study adding more stores in this region. He believes there are two main factors that indicate the amount families spend on groceries. The first is their income and the other is the number of people in the family. The director gathered the following sample information.

Family	Food	Income	Size
1	$5.04	$ 73.98	4
2	4.08	54.90	2
3	5.76	94.14	4
4	3.48	52.02	1
5	4.20	65.70	2
6	4.80	53.64	4
7	4.32	79.74	3
8	5.04	68.58	4
9	6.12	165.60	5
10	3.24	64.80	1
11	4.80	138.42	3
12	3.24	125.82	1
13	6.60	77.58	7
14	4.92	171.36	2
15	6.60	82.08	9
16	5.40	141.30	3
17	6.00	36.90	5
18	5.40	56.88	4
19	3.36	71.82	1
20	4.68	69.48	3
21	4.32	54.36	2
22	5.52	87.66	5
23	4.56	38.16	3
24	5.40	43.74	7
25	4.80	48.42	5

Food and income are reported in thousands of dollars per year, and the variable "size" refers to the number of people in the household.

a. Develop a correlation matrix. Do you see any problems with multicollinearity?
b. Determine the regression equation. Discuss the regression equation. How much does an additional family member add to the amount spent on food?
c. What is the value of R^2? Can we conclude that this value is greater than 0?
d. Would you consider deleting either of the independent variables?
e. Plot the residuals in a histogram. Is there any problem with the normality assumption?
f. Plot the fitted values against the residuals. Does this plot indicate any problems with homoscedasticity?

24. a. See IM.
b. $Y' = 2.84 + .00613X_1 + 0.425X_2$
c. $R^2 = 82.6\%$
d. No.
e. See IM.
f. See IM.

exercises.com

25. The National Institute of Standards and Technology provides several datasets to allow any user to test the accuracy of their statistical software. Go to the Web site: *http://www.itl.nist.gov/div898/strd*. Select the "Dataset Archives" section and, within that, the "Linear Regression" section. You will find the names of 11 small datasets stored in ASCII format on this page. Select one and run the data through your statistical software. Compare your results with the "official" results of the federal government.

26. As described in the examples in Chapters 12 and 13, many real estate companies and rental agencies now publish their listings on the Web. One example is the Dunes Realty Company, located in Garden City and Surfside Beaches in South Carolina. Go to the Web site *http://www.dunes.com,* select Cottage Search, then indicate 5 bedroom, accommodations for 14 people, oceanfront, and no pool or floating dock, select a period in July and August, indicate that you are willing to spend $5,000 per week, and then click on Search the Cottages. The output should include details on the cottages that met your criteria. Develop a multiple linear regression equation using the rental price per week as the dependent

26. Answers will vary.

variable and number of bedrooms, number of bathrooms, and how many people the cottage will accommodate as independent variables. Analyze the regression equations. Would you consider deleting any independent variables? What is the coefficient of determination? If you delete any of the variables, rerun the regression equation and discuss the new equation.

Computer Data Exercises

27. Refer to the Real Estate data which reports information on homes sold in the Venice, Florida, area during the last year. Use the selling price of the home as the dependent variable and determine the regression equation with number of bedrooms, size of the house, whether there is a pool, whether there is an attached garage, distance from the center of the city, and number of bathrooms as independent variables.

- **a.** Write out the regression equation. Discuss each of the variables. For example, are you surprised that the regression coefficient for distance from the center of the city is negative? How much does a garage or a swimming pool add to the selling price of a home?
- **b.** Determine the value of R^2. Interpret.
- **c.** Develop a correlation matrix. Which independent variables have strong or weak correlations with the dependent variable? Do you see any problems with multicollinearity?
- **d.** Conduct the global test on the set of independent variables. Interpret.
- **e.** Conduct a test of hypothesis on each of the independent variables. Would you consider deleting any of the variables? If so, which ones?
- **f.** Rerun the analysis until only significant net regression coefficients remain in the analysis. Identify these variables.
- **g.** Develop a histogram or a stem-and-leaf display of the residuals from the final regression equation developed in part (f). Is it reasonable to conclude that the normality assumption has been met?
- **h.** Plot the residuals against the fitted values from the final regression equation developed in part (f) against the fitted values of Y. Plot the residuals on the vertical axis and the fitted values on the horizontal axis.

28. Refer to the Baseball 2000 data, which reports information on the 30 Major League Baseball teams for the 2000 season. Let the number of games won be the dependent variable and the following variables be independent variables: team batting average, number of stolen bases, number of errors committed, team ERA, and whether the team's home field is natural grass or artificial turf.

- **a.** Write out the regression equation. Discuss each of the variables. For example, are you surprised that the regression coefficient for ERA is negative? How many wins does playing on natural grass for a home field add to or subtract from the total wins for the season?
- **b.** Determine the value of R^2. Interpret.
- **c.** Develop a correlation matrix. Which independent variables have strong or weak correlations with the dependent variable? Do you see any problems with multicollinearity?
- **d.** Conduct a global test on the set of independent variables. Interpret.
- **e.** Conduct a test of hypothesis on each of the independent variables. Would you consider deleting any of the variables? If so, which ones?
- **f.** Rerun the analysis until only significant net regression coefficients remain in the analysis. Identify these variables.
- **g.** Develop a histogram or a stem-and-leaf display of the residuals from the final regression equation developed in part (f). Is it reasonable to conclude that the normality assumption has been met?
- **h.** Plot the residuals against the fitted values from the final regression equation developed in part (f) against the fitted values of Y. Plot the residuals on the vertical axis and the fitted values on the horizontal axis.

28. a. See IM.
b. $R^2 = .875$
c. ERA strongest, $-.660$.
d. See IM.
e. Drop stolen bases and errors.
f. $Y' = 29.5 + 537X_1 - 19.5X_4 - 4.35X_5$
g. See IM.
h. See IM.

29. Refer to the OECD data, which reports information on 29 countries. Let employment be the dependent variable and use land area, population, domestic production, G7 membership, and energy consumption as independent variables.

- **a.** Write out the regression equation and interpret the coefficients.
- **b.** What is the value of the coefficient of determination?

c. Check the independent variables for multicollinearity.
d. Conduct the global test on the regression equation. Is anything significant occurring?
e. Test each of the individual coefficients for significance.
f. Rerun the regression analysis with only the significant independent variables in the equation.
g. Make a histogram of the residuals from your answer in part (f). Do they appear to be normally distributed?
h. Plot the residuals versus the fitted values and check whether the usual assumptions are satisfied.

30. Refer to Schools data, which reports information on the 94 school districts in northwest Ohio. Let the dependent variable be the percent passing the state proficiency test. The independent variables are the average teacher's salary, the percent on welfare in the district, the instructional cost per student in the district, and the percent attendance in the district.
a. Write out the regression equation. Discuss each of the variables.
b. Determine the value of R^2. Interpret.
c. Develop a correlation matrix. Which independent variables have strong or weak correlations with the dependent variable? Do you see any problems with multicollinearity?
d. Conduct a global test on the set of independent variables. Interpret.
e. Conduct a test of hypothesis on each of the independent variables. Would you consider deleting any of the variables? If so, which ones?
f. Rerun the analysis until only significant net regression coefficients remain in the analysis. Identify these variables.
g. Develop a histogram or a stem-and-leaf display of the residuals from the final regression equation developed in part (f). Is it reasonable to conclude that the normality assumption has been met?
h. Plot the residuals against the fitted values from the final regression equation developed in part (f) against the fitted values of *Y*. Plot the residuals on the vertical axis and the fitted values on the horizontal axis.

30. a. See IM.
b. $R^2 = .475$
c. Attendance.
d. See IM.
e. See IM.
f. See IM.
g. Residuals not normally distributed.
h. See IM.

Computer Commands

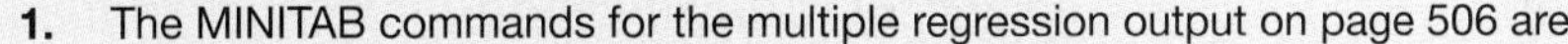

1. The MINITAB commands for the multiple regression output on page 506 are:
a. Import the data from the CD. The file name is Tbl14-1.
b. Select **Stat**, **Regression,** and then click on **Regression**.
c. Select *Cost* as the **Response** variable, and *Temp, Insulation,* and *Age* as the **Predictors**, then click on **OK.**

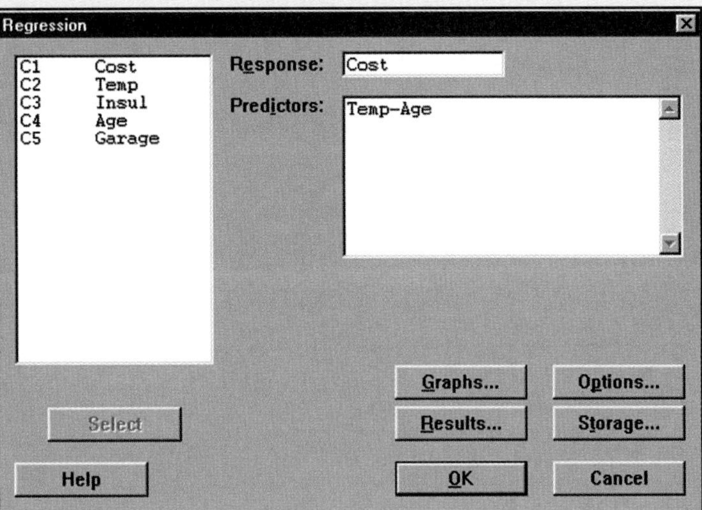

2. The Excel commands to develop the correlation matrix on page 515 are:
   a. Import the data from the CD. The file name is Tbl14-1.
   b. Select **Tools**, **Data Analysis**, then hit **Enter**. Select the command **Correlation** and then hit **OK**.
   c. The **Input Range** is *A1:D21,* grouped by **Columns**, check the **Labels** box, select the **Output Range** as *G1,* and click **OK**.

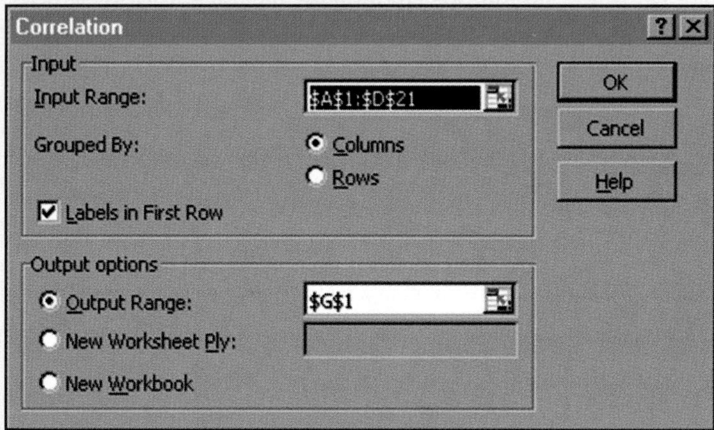

3. The MINITAB commands for the multiple regression output on page 525 are:
   a. Import the data from the CD. The file name is Tbl14-1.
   b. Select **Stat**, **Regression,** and then click on **Regression**.
   c. Select *Cost* as the **Response** variable, and *Temp, Insulation,* and *Age* as the **Predictors**, then click on **OK.**
   d. Click on **Storage,** then check **Residuals** and **Fits,** and click **OK** in both dialog boxes.

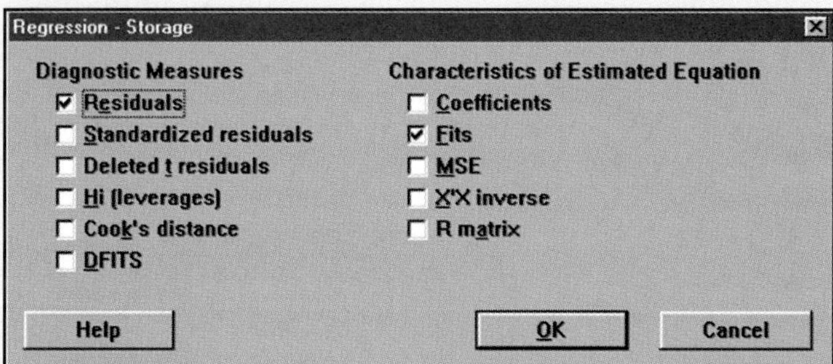

Chapter 14 Answers to Self-Review

14–1 (a) 12.9 psi, found by $Y' = -0.5 + 20(.35) + 1(6.4)$.

(b) The b_1 of 20 indicates that the tensile strength of the wire will increase 20 psi for each increase of 1 mm in outside diameter, with the amount of molybdenum held constant. That is, tensile strength will increase 20 psi regardless of the amount of molybdenum in the wire.

14–2 (a) $n = 25$

(b) 4

(c) $R^2 = \frac{10}{15} = 0.667$

(d) $s_{y \cdot 1234} = \sqrt{\frac{5}{20}} = 0.50$

14–3 (a) $Y' = 490 - 5.15X_1 - 14.7X_2$

(b) .776. A total of 77.6% of the variation in heating cost is explained by temperature and insulation.

(c) The results of the global test indicate that at least one of the regression coefficients is not zero. To arrive at that conclusion, we first stated the null hypothesis as H_0: $\beta_1 = \beta_2 = 0$. The critical value of F is 3.59, and the computed value 29.4, found by 82,597/2,807. Since 29.4 lies in the region of rejection beyond 3.59, we reject H_0.

(d) The p-value is .008. The probability of a t-value less than -2.98 or greater than 2.98, with 17 degrees of freedom, is .008.

A Review of Chapters 13 and 14

Simple regression and correlation examine the relationship between two variables.

This section is a review of the major concepts and terms introduced in Chapters 13 and 14. Chapter 13 noted that the strength of the relationship between the independent variable and the dependent variable can be measured by the *coefficient of correlation.* Developed by Karl Pearson, Pearson's r can assume any value between -1.00 and $+1.00$ inclusive. Coefficients of -1.00 and $+1.00$ indicate perfect relationship, and 0 indicates no relationship. A value near 0, such as $-.14$ or .14, indicates a weak relationship. A value near -1 or $+1$, such as $-.90$ or $+.90$, indicates a strong relationship. Squaring r gives the *coefficient of determination,* also called r^2. It indicates the proportion of the total variation in the dependent variable explained by the independent variable.

Multiple regression and correlation is concerned with relationship between two or more independent variables and the dependent variable.

Likewise, the strength of the relationship between several independent variables and a dependent variable is measured by the *coefficient of multiple determination,* R^2. It measures the proportion of the variation in Y explained by two or more independent variables.

The linear relationship in the simple case involving one independent variable and one dependent variable is described by the equation $Y' = a + bX$. For three independent variables, X_1, X_2, and X_3, the same multiple regression equation is

$$Y' = a + b_1X_1 + b_2X_2 + b_3X_3$$

Computer invaluable in multiple regression and correlation.

Solving for $b_1, b_2, b_3, \ldots, b_k$ would involve tedious calculations. Fortunately, this type of problem can be quickly solved using one of the many statistical packages and spreadsheet packages available for the computer. Various measures, such as the coefficient of determination, the multiple standard error of estimate, the results of the global test, and the test of the individual variables are reported in the output of most computer software programs.

Glossary

Chapter 13

Coefficient of correlation A measure of the strength of association between two variables. It is computed by:

$$r = \frac{n(\Sigma XY) - (\Sigma X)(\Sigma Y)}{\sqrt{[n(\Sigma X^2) - (\Sigma X)^2][n(\Sigma Y^2) - (\Sigma Y)^2]}} \quad \textbf{[13–1]}$$

Coefficient of determination The proportion of the total variation in the dependent variable that is explained by the independent variable. It can assume any value between 0 and $+1.00$ inclusive. A coefficient of .82 indicates that 82 percent of the variation in Y is accounted for by X. This coefficient is computed by squaring the coefficient of correlation, r.

Correlation analysis A group of statistical techniques used to measure the strength of the relationship between two variables.

Least squares method A technique used to arrive at the regression equation by minimizing the sum of the squares of the vertical distances between the actual Y values and the predicted Y values.

Linear regression equation A mathematical equation that defines the relationship between two variables. It has the form $Y' = a + bX$. It is used to predict Y based on a selected X value. Y is the dependent variable and X the independent variable.

Scatter diagram A chart that visually depicts the relationship between two variables.

Standard error of estimate Measures the dispersion of the actual Y values about the regression line. It is reported in the same units as the dependent variable.

Test of significance of r A formula to answer the question: Is the correlation in the population from which the sample was selected zero? The test statistic is t, and the number of degrees of freedom is $n - 2$.

$$t = \frac{r\sqrt{n-2}}{\sqrt{1-r^2}} \quad \textbf{[13–2]}$$

Chapter 14

Autocorrelation Correlation of successive residuals. This condition frequently occurs when time is involved in the analysis.

Correlation matrix A listing of all possible simple coefficients of correlation. A correlation matrix includes the correlations between each of the independent variables and the dependent variable, as well as those among all the independent variables.

Homoscedasticity The standard error of estimate is the same for all fitted values of the dependent variable.

Multicollinearity A condition that occurs in multiple regression analysis if the independent variables are themselves correlated.

Multiple regression equation The relationship in the form of a mathematical equation between

several independent variables and a dependent variable. The general form is $Y' = a + b_1X_1 + b_2X_2 + b_3X_3 + \cdots + b_kX_k$. It is used to estimate Y given selected X values and k independent variables.
Qualitative variables A nominal-scale variable that can assume only one of two possible outcomes. For example, a person is considered either employed or unemployed.
Residual The difference between the actual value of the dependent variable and the estimated value of the dependent variable, that is $Y - Y'$.

Exercises

Part I — Fill in the Blanks and Discussion

1. The strength of the relationship between a set of independent variables X and a dependent variable Y is measured by the ________.
2. A coefficient of correlation was computed to be −.90. Comment.
3. Pearson's r for a problem involving 60 pairs of data was computed to be .40. Comment. Is the correlation in the population zero? Give evidence.
4. The coefficient of determination was computed to be .38 in a problem involving one independent and one dependent variable. What does this mean?
5. What is the relationship between the coefficient of correlation and the coefficient of determination?

Exercises 6 through 10 are based on the following table. The accounting division for a large chain of department stores is trying to predict the net profit for each of the chain's many stores based on the number of employees in the store, overhead cost, and so on. A few statistics from some of the stores are:

Store	Net Profit ($ thousands)	Number of Employees	Overhead Cost ($ thousands)	Average Markup (percent)	Theft Loss ($ thousands)
1	$846	143	$79	69	$52
2	513	110	64	50	45

6. The dependent variable is ________.
7. The general equation for this problem is ________.
8. The multiple regression equation was computed to be $Y' = 67 + 8X_1 - 10X_2 + 0.004X_3 - 3X_4$. What is predicted sales for a store with 112 employees, an overhead cost of $65,000, a markup rate of 50 percent, and a loss from theft of $50,000?
9. Suppose R^2 was computed to be .86. Explain.
10. Suppose that the multiple standard error of estimate was 3 (in $ thousands). Explain what this means in this problem.

Part II — Problems

11. Quick-print firms in a large downtown business area spend most of their advertising dollars on advertisements on bus benches. A research project involves predicting monthly sales based on the annual amount spent on placing ads on bus benches. A sample of quick-print firms revealed these advertising expenses and sales:

Firm	Annual Bus Bench Advertising ($ thousands)	Monthly Sales ($ thousands)
A	2	10
B	4	40
C	5	30
D	7	50
E	3	20

a. Draw a scatter diagram.
b. Determine the coefficient of correlation.
c. What is the coefficient of determination?
d. Compute the regression equation.
e. Estimate the monthly sales of a quick-print firm that spends $4,500 on bus bench advertisements.
f. Summarize your findings.

12. The following ANOVA output is given.

SOURCE	Sum of Squares	DF	MS
Regression	1050.8	4	262.70
Error	83.8	20	4.19
Total	1134.6	24	

Predictor	Coef	St.Dev.	t-ratio
Constant	70.06	2.13	32.89
X_1	0.42	0.17	2.47
X_2	0.27	0.21	1.29
X_3	0.75	0.30	2.50
X_4	0.42	0.07	6.00

a. Compute the coefficient of determination.
b. Compute the multiple standard error of estimate.
c. Conduct a test of hypothesis to determine whether any of the net regression coefficients are different from zero.
d. Conduct a test of hypothesis on the individual regression coefficients. Can any of the variables be detected?

Cases

A. The Century National Bank

Refer to the Century National Bank data. Using checking account balance as the dependent variable and using the number of ATM transactions, the number of other services used, whether the individual has a debit card, and whether interest is paid on the particular account as independent variables, write a report indicating which of the variables seem related to the account balance and how well they explain the variation in account balances. Should all of the independent variables proposed be used in the analysis or can some be dropped?

B. Terry and Associates: The Time to Deliver Medical Kits

Terry and Associates is a specialized medical testing center in Denver, Colorado. One of their major sources of revenue is a kit used to test for elevated amounts of lead in the blood. Workers in auto body shops, those in the lawn care industry, and commercial house painters are exposed to large amounts of lead and thus must be randomly tested. It is expensive to conduct the test, so the kits are delivered on demand to a variety of locations throughout the Denver area.

Kathleen Terry, the owner, is concerned about appropriate costing of each delivery. To investigate, Ms. Terry gathered information on a random sample of 50 recent deliveries. Factors thought to be related to the cost of delivering a kit are:

Prep The time between when the customized order is phoned into the company and when it is ready for delivery.

Delivery The actual travel time from Terry's plant to the customer.

Mileage The distance in miles from Terry's plant to the customer.

Sample Number	Cost	Prep	Delivery	Mileage
1	$32.60	10	51	20
2	23.37	11	33	12
3	31.49	6	47	19
4	19.31	9	18	8
5	28.35	8	88	17
6	22.63	9	20	11
7	22.63	9	39	11
8	21.53	10	23	10
9	21.16	13	20	8
10	21.53	10	32	10
11	28.17	5	35	16
12	20.42	7	23	9
13	21.53	9	21	10
14	27.55	7	37	16
15	23.37	9	25	12
16	17.10	15	15	6
17	27.06	13	34	15
18	15.99	8	13	4
19	17.96	12	12	4
20	25.22	6	41	14
21	24.29	3	28	13
22	22.76	4	26	10
23	28.17	9	54	16
24	19.68	7	18	8
25	25.15	6	50	13
26	20.36	9	19	7

Sample Number	Cost	Prep	Delivery	Mileage
27	21.16	3	19	8
28	25.95	10	45	14
29	18.76	12	12	5
30	18.76	8	16	5
31	24.29	7	35	13
32	19.56	2	12	6
33	22.63	8	30	11
34	21.16	5	13	8
35	21.16	11	20	8
36	19.68	5	19	8
37	18.76	5	14	7
38	17.96	5	11	4
39	23.37	10	25	12
40	25.22	6	32	14
41	27.06	8	44	16
42	21.96	9	28	9
43	22.63	8	31	11
44	19.68	7	19	8
45	22.76	8	28	10
46	21.96	13	18	9
47	25.95	10	32	14
48	26.14	8	44	15
49	24.29	8	34	13
50	24.35	3	33	12

1. Develop a multiple linear regression equation that describes the relationship between the cost of delivery and the other variables. Do these three variables explain a reasonable amount of the variation in the dependent variable? Estimate the delivery cost for a kit that takes 10 minutes for preparation, takes 30 minutes to deliver, and must cover a distance of 14 miles.
2. Test to determine that some of the set of net regression coefficients differ from zero. Also test to see whether any of the variables can be dropped from the analysis. If some of the variables can be dropped, rerun the regression equation until only significant variables are included. Write a brief report interpreting the final regression equation.

15

Nonparametric Methods

Chi-Square Applications

GOALS

When you have completed this chapter, you will be able to:

1 List the characteristics of the chi-square distribution.

2 Conduct a test of hypothesis comparing an observed set of frequencies to an expected distribution.

3 Conduct a test of hypothesis for normality using the chi-square distribution.

4 Conduct a test of hypothesis to determine whether two classification criteria are related.

There are four entrances to the Government Center Building in downtown Philadelphia. To investigate if the entrances are equally utilized, 400 people were observed entering the building. At the .01 significance level, is there a difference in the use of the four entrances based on the data provided? (See Goal 2 and Exercise 22.)

Introduction

Chapters 9 through 12 deal with data of at least interval scale, such as weights, incomes, and ages. We conduct tests of hypothesis about a single population mean, two population means, and three or more population means. For these tests we assume the populations follow the normal distribution. There are tests available in which no assumption regarding the shape of the population is necessary. There are also tests exclusively for data of nominal or ordinal scale. Recall from Chapter 1 that nominal data is the "lowest" or most primitive. For this type of measurement, data are classified into categories where there is no natural order. Examples include gender, state of birth, or brand of peanut butter purchased. Ordinal data assumes that one category is ranked higher than the next one. For example, a sample of joggers is asked by a marketing research firm to rate a newly developed shoe as outstanding, good, fair, or unsatisfactory. The rank of outstanding is higher than good, good is higher than fair, and so on. However, we are unsure if the amount by which outstanding exceeds good is the same as the amount by which good exceeds fair.

Nonparametric or **distribution-free** tests of hypothesis use nominal and ordinal data. The latter name implies that these tests are free of assumptions regarding the shape of the population. That is, it is not necessary that we assume the population follows the normal distribution. Generally, these tests are easy to apply and the computations minimal.

Goodness-of-Fit Test: Equal Expected Frequencies

The goodness-of-fit test is one of the most commonly used of the family of nonparametric tests. Karl Pearson, the same person who developed the coefficient of correlation, first described the test in the early 1900s. It is actually appropriate for any level of data. The first illustration of this test involves the case in which the expected cell frequencies are equal.

As the full name implies, the purpose of the goodness-of-fit test is to compare an observed set of frequencies to an expected set of frequencies. An example will describe the hypothesis-testing situation.

EXAMPLE

Ms. Jan Kilpatrick is the marketing manager for a manufacturer of sports cards. She plans to begin a series of cards with pictures and playing statistics of former Major League Baseball players. One of the problems is the selection of the former players. At the baseball card show at the Southwyck Mall last weekend, she set up a booth and offered cards of the following six Hall of Fame baseball players: Tom Seaver, Nolan Ryan, Ty Cobb, George Brett, Hank Aaron, and Johnny Bench. At the end of the day she sold a total of 120 cards. The number of cards sold for each old-time player is shown in Table 15–1. Can she conclude the sales are not the same for each player?

TABLE 15–1 Number of Cards Sold for Each Player

Player	Cards Sold
Tom Seaver	13
Nolan Ryan	33
Ty Cobb	14
George Brett	7
Hank Aaron	36
Johnny Bench	17
Total	120

If there is no significant difference in the popularity of the players, we would expect that the observed frequencies (f_o) would be equal — or nearly equal. That is, we would expect to sell as many cards for Tom Seaver as for Nolan Ryan. Thus, any discrepancy in the observed and expected frequencies could be attributed to sampling (chance).

Because there are 120 cards in the sample, we expect that 20 cards will fall in each of the six categories. These categories are called **cells.** An examination of the set of observed frequencies in Table 15–1 indicates that the card for George Brett is sold rather infrequently, whereas the cards for Hank Aaron and Nolan Ryan are sold more often. Is the difference in sales due to chance, or can we conclude that there is a preference for the cards of certain players?

TABLE 15–2 Observed and Expected Frequencies for the 120 Cards Sold

Player	Cards Sold, f_o	Expected Number Sold, f_e
Tom Seaver	13	20
Nolan Ryan	33	20
Ty Cobb	14	20
George Brett	7	20
Hank Aaron	36	20
Johnny Bench	17	20
Total	120	120

SOLUTION

We will use the same systematic five-step hypothesis-testing procedure followed in previous chapters.

Step 1: State the null hypothesis and the alternate hypothesis. The null hypothesis, H_0, is that there is no difference between the set of observed frequencies and the set of expected frequencies; that is, any difference between the two sets of frequencies can be attributed to sampling (chance). The alternate hypothesis, H_1, is that there is a difference between the observed and expected sets of frequencies. If H_0 is rejected and H_1 is accepted, it means that sales are not equally distributed among the six categories (cells).

Step 2: Select the level of significance. We selected the .05 level, which is the same as the Type I error probability. Thus, the probability is .05 that a true null hypothesis will be rejected.

Step 3: Select the test statistic. It is the chi-square distribution, designated as χ^2:

CHI-SQUARE TEST STATISTIC

$$\chi^2 = \Sigma\left[\frac{(f_o - f_e)^2}{f_e}\right] \quad \textbf{[15–1]}$$

with $k - 1$ degrees of freedom, where:

k is the number of categories.
f_o is an observed frequency in a particular category.
f_e is an expected frequency in a particular category.

We will examine the characteristics of the chi-square distribution in more detail shortly.

Step 4: Formulate the decision rule. Recall the decision rule in hypothesis testing requires finding a number that separates the region where we do not reject H_0 from the region of rejection. This number is called the *critical value.* As we will soon see, the chi-square distribution is really a family of distributions. Each distribution has a slightly different shape, depending on the number of degrees of freedom. The number of degrees of freedom in this type of problem is found by $k - 1$, where k is the number of categories. In this particular problem there are six. Since there are six categories, there are $k - 1 = 6 - 1 = 5$ degrees of freedom. As noted, a category is called a *cell,* so there are six cells. The critical value for 5 degrees of freedom and the .05 level of significance is found in Appendix H. A portion of that table is shown in Table 15–3. The critical value is 11.070, found by locating 5 degrees of freedom in the left margin and then moving horizontally (to the right) and reading the critical value in the .05 column.

TABLE 15–3 A Portion of the Chi-Square Table

Degrees of Freedom, *df*	Right-Tail Area .10	.05	.02	.01
1	2.706	3.841	5.412	6.635
2	4.605	5.991	7.824	9.210
3	6.251	7.815	9.837	11.345
4	7.779	9.488	11.668	13.277
5	9.236	11.070	13.388	15.086

The decision rule is to reject H_0 if the computed value of chi-square is greater than 11.070. If it is less than or equal to 11.070, do not reject H_0. Chart 15–1 shows the decision rule.

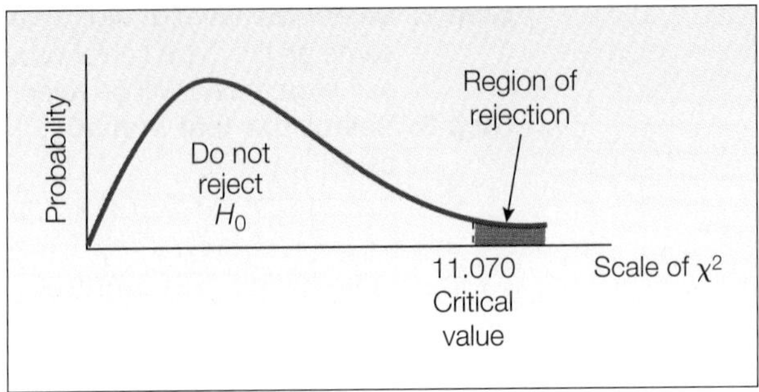

CHART 15–1 Chi-Square Probability Distribution for 5 Degrees of Freedom, Showing the Region of Rejection, .05 Level of Significance

The decision rule indicates that if there are large differences between the observed and expected frequencies, resulting in a computed χ^2 of more than 11.070, the null hypothesis should be rejected. However, if the differences between f_o and f_e are small, the computed χ^2 value will be 11.070 or less, and the null hypothesis should not be rejected. The reasoning is that such small differences between the observed and expected frequencies are probably due to chance.

Step 5: Compute the value of chi-square and make a decision. Of the 120 cards sold in the sample, we counted the number of times Tom Seaver and Nolan Ryan, and each of the others were sold. The counts were reported in Table 15–1. The calculations for chi-square follow. (Note again that the expected frequencies are the same for each cell.)

Column 1: Determine the differences between each f_o and f_e. That is, $(f_o - f_e)$. The sum of these differences is zero.

Column 2: Square the difference between each observed and expected frequency. That is, $(f_o - f_e)^2$.

Column 3: Divide the result for each observation by the expected frequency. That is, $\frac{(f_o - f_e)^2}{f_e}$. Finally, sum these values. The result is the value of χ^2, which is 34.40.

Baseball Player	f_o	f_e	(1) $(f_o - f_e)$	(2) $(f_o - f_e)^2$	(3) $\frac{(f_o - f_e)^2}{f_e}$
Tom Seaver	13	20	−7	49	49/20 = 2.45
Nolan Ryan	33	20	13	169	169/20 = 8.45
Ty Cobb	14	20	−6	36	36/20 = 1.80
George Brett	7	20	−13	169	169/20 = 8.45
Hank Aaron	36	20	16	256	256/20 = 12.80
Johnny Bench	17	20	−3	9	9/20 = 0.45
		Must be	0	χ^2	34.40

The computed χ^2 of 34.40 is in the rejection region beyond the critical value of 11.070. The decision, therefore, is to reject H_0 at the .05 level and to accept H_1. The difference between the observed and the expected frequencies is not due to chance. Rather, the differences between f_o and f_e are large enough to be considered significant. The chance of these differences being due to sampling is very small. So we conclude that it is unlikely that card sales are the same among the six players.

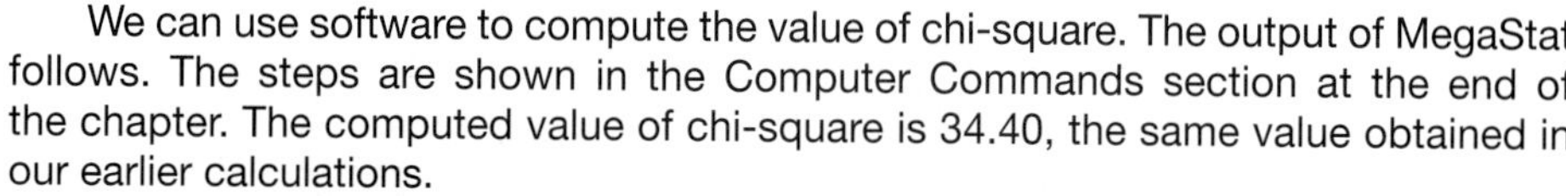

We can use software to compute the value of chi-square. The output of MegaStat follows. The steps are shown in the Computer Commands section at the end of the chapter. The computed value of chi-square is 34.40, the same value obtained in our earlier calculations.

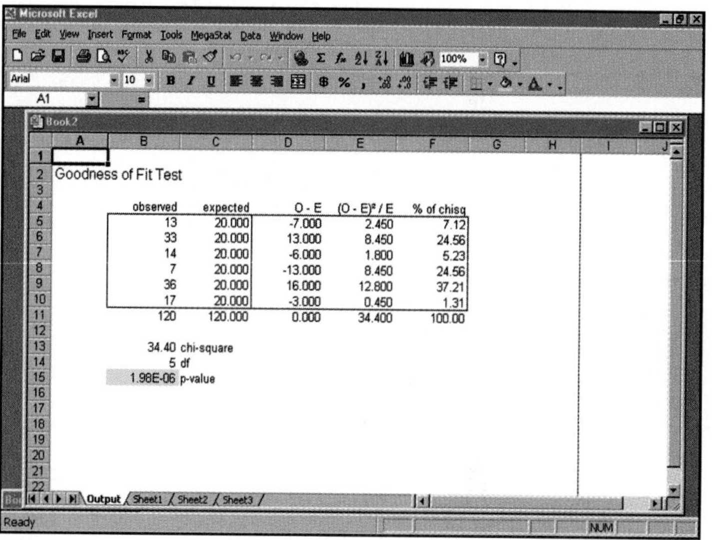

Goodness of Fit Test

observed	expected	O - E	(O - E)²/E	% of chisq
13	20.000	-7.000	2.450	7.12
33	20.000	13.000	8.450	24.56
14	20.000	-6.000	1.800	5.23
7	20.000	-13.000	8.450	24.56
36	20.000	16.000	12.800	37.21
17	20.000	-3.000	0.450	1.31
120	120.000	0.000	34.400	100.00

34.40 chi-square
5 df
1.98E-06 p-value

The chi-square distribution, which is used as the test statistic in this chapter, has the following characteristics.

1. **Chi-square is never negative.** This is because the difference between f_o and f_e is squared, that is, $(f_o - f_e)^2$.
2. **There is a family of chi-square distributions.** There is a chi-square distribution for 1 degree of freedom, another for 2 degrees of freedom, another for 3 degrees of freedom, and so on. In this type of problem the number of degrees of freedom is determined by $k - 1$, where k is the number of categories. Therefore, the shape of the chi-square distribution does *not* depend on the size of the sample, but on the number of categories used. For example, if 200 employees of an airline were classified into one of three categories—flight personnel, ground support, and administrative personnel—there would be $k - 1 = 3 - 1 = 2$ degrees of freedom.
3. **The chi-square distribution is positively skewed.** However, as the number of degrees of freedom increases, the distribution begins to approximate the normal distribution. Chart 15–2 shows the distributions for selected degrees of freedom. Notice that for 10 degrees of freedom the curve is approaching a normal distribution.

Shape of χ^2 distribution approaches normal distribution as *df* becomes larger

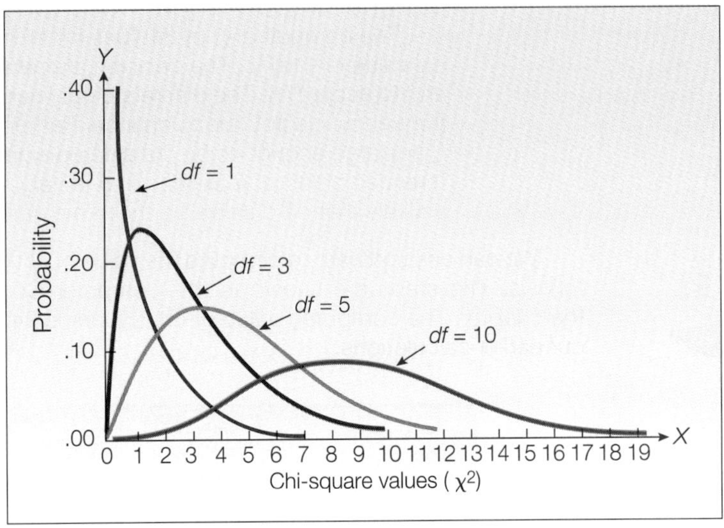

CHART 15–2 Chi-Square Distributions for Selected Degrees of Freedom

Self-Review 15–1

The human resources director at Georgetown Paper, Inc. is concerned about absenteeism among hourly workers. She decides to sample the records to determine whether absenteeism is distributed evenly throughout the six-day workweek. The null hypothesis to be tested is: Absenteeism is distributed evenly throughout the week. The .01 level is to be used. The sample results are:

	Number Absent		Number Absent
Monday	12	Thursday	10
Tuesday	9	Friday	9
Wednesday	11	Saturday	9

(a) What are the numbers 12, 9, 11, 10, 9, and 9 called?
(b) How many categories (cells) are there?
(c) What is the *expected* frequency for each day?
(d) How many degrees of freedom are there?
(e) What is the chi-square critical value at the 1 percent significance level?
(f) Compute the χ^2 test statistic.
(g) What is the decision regarding the null hypothesis?
(h) Specifically, what does this indicate to the human resources director?

Exercises

1. In a particular chi-square goodness-of-fit test there are four categories and 200 observations. Use the .05 significance level.
   a. How many degrees of freedom are there?
   b. What is the critical value of chi-square?
2. In a particular chi-square goodness-of-fit test there are six categories and 500 observations. Use the .01 significance level.

2. **a.** 5
b. 15.086

a. How many degrees of freedom are there?
b. What is the critical value of chi-square?

3. The null hypothesis and the alternate are:

H_0: The cell categories are equal.
H_1: The cell categories are not equal.

Category	f_o
A	10
B	20
C	30

a. State the decision rule, using the .05 significance level.
b. Compute the value of chi-square.
c. What is your decision regarding H_0?

4. The null hypothesis and the alternate are:

H_0: The cell categories are equal.
H_1: The cell categories are not equal.

Category	f_o
A	10
B	20
C	30
D	20

4. **a.** Reject H_o if $\chi^2 > 7.815$.
b. 10
c. Reject H_o.

a. State the decision rule, using the .05 significance level.
b. Compute the value of chi-square.
c. What is your decision regarding H_0?

5. A six-sided die is rolled 30 times and the numbers 1 through 6 appear as shown in the following frequency distribution. At the .10 significance level, can we conclude that the die is fair?

Outcome	Frequency	Outcome	Frequency
1	3	4	3
2	6	5	9
3	2	6	7

6. $\chi^2 = 15.308$
Reject H_o.

6. The Director of Golf for the Links Group wishes to study the number of rounds of golf played by members on weekdays. He gathered the following sample information for 520 rounds.

Day	Rounds
Monday	124
Tuesday	74
Wednesday	104
Thursday	98
Friday	120

At the .05 significance level, is there a difference in the number of rounds played by day of the week?

7. A group of department store buyers viewed a new line of dresses and gave their opinions of them. The results were:

Opinion	Number of Buyers	Opinion	Number of Buyers
Outstanding	47	Good	39
Excellent	45	Fair	35
Very good	40	Undesirable	34

Because the largest number (47) indicated the new line is outstanding, the head designer thinks that this is a mandate to go into mass production of the dresses. The head sweeper (who somehow became involved in this) believes that there is not a clear mandate and claims that the opinions are evenly distributed among the six categories. He further states that the slight differences among the various counts are probably due to chance. Test the null hypothesis that there is no significant difference among the opinions of the buyers. Test at the .01 level of risk. Follow a formal approach; that is, state the null hypothesis, the alternate hypothesis, and so on.

8. $\chi^2 = 24.600$ Reject H_o.

8. The safety director of Honda USA took samples at random from the file of minor accidents and classified them according to the time the accident took place.

Time	Number of Accidents	Time	Number of Accidents
8 up to 9 A.M.	6	1 up to 2 P.M.	7
9 up to 10 A.M.	6	2 up to 3 P.M.	8
10 up to 11 A.M.	20	3 up to 4 P.M.	19
11 up to 12 P.M.	8	4 up to 5 P.M.	6

Using the goodness-of-fit test and the .01 level of significance, determine whether the accidents are evenly distributed throughout the day. Write a brief explanation of your conclusion.

Goodness-of-Fit Test: Unequal Expected Frequencies

The expected frequencies (f_e) in the previous example involving baseball cards were all equal (20). According to the null hypothesis, it was expected that a picture of Tom Seaver would appear 20 times at random, a picture of Johnny Bench would appear 20 times out of 120 trials, and so on. The chi-square test can also be used if the expected frequencies are not equal.

Expected frequencies not equal in this problem

The following example illustrates the case of unequal frequencies and also gives a practical use of chi-square—namely, to find whether a local experience differs from the national experience.

EXAMPLE

A national study of hospital admissions during a two-year period revealed these statistics concerning senior citizens who resided in care centers and who were hospitalized anytime during the period: Forty percent were admitted only once in the two-year period. Twenty percent were admitted twice. Fourteen percent were admitted three times, and so on. The complete distribution is given in Table 15–4.

TABLE 15–4 National Study: Admissions of Senior Citizens to Hospitals in a Two-Year Period

Number of Times Admitted	Percent of Total
1	40
2	20
3	14
4	10
5	8
6	6
7	2
	100

TABLE 15–5 Local Study: Admissions to the Bartow County Hospital during a Two-Year Period

Number of Times Admitted	Number of Senior Citizens, f_o
1	165
2	79
3	50
4	44
5	32
6	20
7	10
	400

The administrator of the local hospital is anxious to compare her Bartow County Hospital experience with the national pattern or distribution. She selected 400 senior citizens in local care centers who needed hospitalization and determined the number of times during a two-year period each was admitted to her hospital. The observed frequencies are listed in Table 15–5.

The chi-square statistic is used to compare this local experience with the national experience. The question is: How can the locally observed frequencies in Table 15–5 be compared with the national percentages in Table 15–4? We will use the .05 level of significance.

SOLUTION

Determining expected frequencies

Obviously, the *number* of observed frequencies of local senior citizens cannot be compared directly with the *percentages* given for the nation's hospitals. However, the percentages for the nation in Table 15–4 can be converted to expected frequencies, f_e. Table 15–4 shows that 40 percent of the senior citizens who required hospitalization went only once in a two-year period. Thus, if there is *no* difference between the experience at Bartow County Hospital and the national experience, then 40 percent of the 400 sampled by the hospital administrator (160 senior citizens) would have been admitted just once in the period. Further, 20 percent of the 400 sampled (80 people) would have been admitted twice, and so on. The observed local frequencies and the expected local frequencies based on the percents in the national study are given in Table 15–6.

TABLE 15–6 Observed and Expected Frequencies for Bartow County Hospital

Number of Times Admitted	Observed Number of Admissions, f_o	Expected Number of Admissions, f_e	
1	165	160 ←	40% × 400
2	79	80 ←	20% × 400
3	50	56 ←	14% × 400
4	44	40 ←	10% × 400
5	32	32 ←	8% × 400
6	20	24 ←	6% × 400
7	10	8 ←	2% × 400
	400	400	

Must be equal

The null and alternate hypotheses are:

H_0: There is no difference between the local experience and the national experience.

H_1: There is a difference between the local experience and the national experience.

To find the decision rule we use Appendix I. There are seven admitting categories, so the degrees of freedom are $df = k - 1 = 7 - 1 = 6$. The critical value is 12.592. Therefore, the decision rule is to reject H_0 if $\chi^2 > 12.592$. The decision rule is portrayed graphically in Chart 15–3.

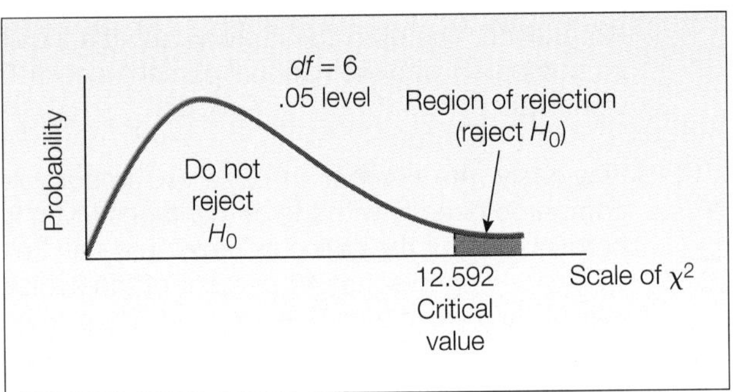

CHART 15–3 Decision Criteria for the Bartow County Hospital Research Study

Now to compute the chi-square test statistic:

Number of Times Admitted	f_o	f_e	$f_o - f_e$	$(f_o - f_e)^2$	$\frac{(f_o - f_e)^2}{f_e}$
1	165	160	5	25	0.156
2	79	80	−1	1	0.013
3	50	56	−6	36	0.643
4	44	40	4	16	0.400
5	32	32	0	0	0.000
6	20	24	−4	16	0.667
7	10	8	2	4	0.500
			0		$\chi^2 = 2.379$

The computed value of chi-square (2.379) lies to the left of 12.592 and is, therefore, in the region where we cannot reject H_0. The null hypothesis, that there is no difference between the local experience at Bartow County Hospital and the national experience, is therefore not rejected. The hospital administrator would conclude that the local situation with respect to the hospitalization of senior citizens in care centers is like that in other parts of the country.

Limitations of Chi-Square

Be careful in applying χ^2 to some problems.

If there is an unusually small expected frequency in a cell, chi-square (if applied) might result in an erroneous conclusion. This can happen because f_e appears in the denominator, and dividing by a very small number makes the quotient quite large! Two generally accepted rules regarding small cell frequencies are:

1. If there are only two cells, the *expected* frequency in each cell should be 5 or more. The computation of chi-square would be permissible in the following problem, involving a minimum f_e of 6.

Individual	f_o	f_e
Literate	643	642
Illiterate	7	6

2. For more than two cells, chi-square should *not* be used if more than 20 percent of the f_e cells have expected frequencies less than 5. According to this rule, it would not be appropriate to use the goodness-of-fit test on the following data. Three of the seven cells, or 43 percent, contain less than 5 observations.

Level of Management	f_o	f_e
Foreman	30	32
Supervisor	110	113
Manager	86	87
Middle management	23	24
Assistant vice president	5	2
Vice president	5	4
Senior vice president	4	1
Total	263	263

To show the reason for the 5 percent policy, we conducted the goodness-of-fit test on the above data on the levels of management. The MegaStat output follows.

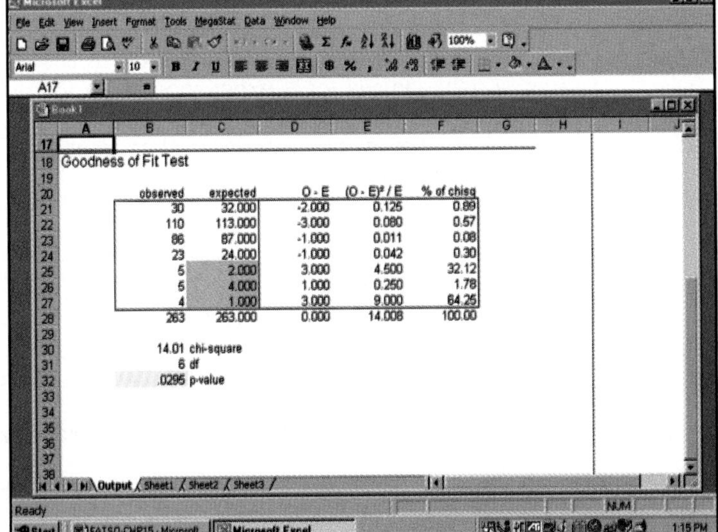

For this test at the .05 significance level, H_0 is rejected if the computed value of chi-square is greater than 12.592. The computed value is 14.01, so we reject the null hypothesis that the observed frequencies represent a random sample from the population of the expected values. Examine the MegaStat output. More than 98 percent of the computed chi-square value is accounted for by the three vice president categories ([4.500 + .250 + 9.000]/14.008 = 0.9815). Logically, too much weight is being given to these categories.

The dilemma can be resolved by combining categories. In the above example we combine the three vice-presidential categories, which satisfies the 20 percent rule.

Level of Management	f_o	f_e
Foreman	30	32
Supervisor	110	113
Manager	86	87
Middle management	23	24
Vice president	14	7
Total	263	263

The computed value of chi-square with the revised categories is 7.26. See the following output. This value is less than the critical value of 9.488 for the .05 significance level. The null hypothesis is, therefore, not rejected at the .05 significance level. This indicates there is no significant difference between the observed distribution and the expected distribution.

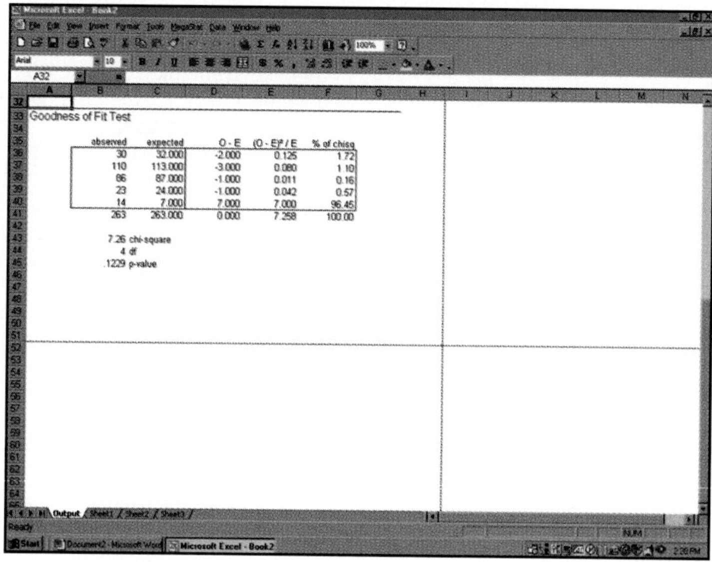

Goodness of Fit Test

observed	expected	O - E	(O - E)² / E	% of chisq
30	32.000	-2.000	0.125	1.72
110	113.000	-3.000	0.080	1.10
86	87.000	-1.000	0.011	0.16
23	24.000	-1.000	0.042	0.57
14	7.000	7.000	7.000	96.45
263	263.000	0.000	7.258	100.00

7.26 chi-square
4 df
.1229 p-value

Self-Review 15–2

The American Accounting Association classifies accounts receivable as "current," "late," and "not collectible." Industry figures show that 60 percent of accounts receivable are current, 30 percent are late, and 10 percent are not collectible. Massa and Barr, attorneys in Greenville, Ohio, has 500 accounts receivable: 320 are current, 120 are late, and 60 are not collectible. Are these numbers in agreement with the industry distribution? Use the .05 significance level.

Exercises

9. The following hypotheses are given:

H_0: Forty percent of the observations are in category A, 40 percent are in B, and 20 percent are in C.
H_1: The observations are not as described in H_0.

We took a sample of 60, with the following results.

Category	f_o
A	30
B	20
C	10

a. State the decision rule using the .01 significance level.
b. Compute the value of chi-square.
c. What is your decision regarding H_0?

10. $\chi^2 = 12.00$ Reject H_0.

10. The chief of security for the Mall of the Dakotas was directed to study the problem of missing goods. He selected a sample of 100 boxes that had been tampered with and ascertained that for 60 of the boxes, the missing pants, shoes, and so on were attributed to shoplifting. For 30 other boxes employees had stolen the goods, and for the remaining 10 boxes he blamed poor inventory control.

    In his report to the mall management, can he say that shoplifting is *twice* as likely to be the cause of the loss as compared with either employee theft or poor inventory control and that employee theft and poor inventory control are equally likely? Use the .02 level.
11. The bank credit card department of Carolina Bank knows from experience that 5 percent of the card holders have had some high school, 15 percent have completed high school, 25 percent have had some college, and 55 percent have completed college. Of the 500 card holders whose cards have been called in for failure to pay their charges this month, 50 had some high school, 100 had completed high school, 190 had some college, and 160 had completed college. Can we conclude that the distribution of card holders who do not pay their charges is different from all others? Use the .01 significance level.

12. $\chi^2 = 14.333$. Reject H_0.

12. For many years TV executives used the guideline that 30 percent of the audience were watching each of the prime-time networks and 10 percent cable stations on a weekday night. A random sample of 500 viewers in the Tampa–St. Petersburg, Florida, area last Monday night showed that 165 homes were tuned in to the ABC affiliate, 140 to the CBS affiliate, 125 to the NBC affiliate, and the remainder were viewing a cable station. At the .05 significance level, can we conclude that the guideline is still reasonable?

Using the Goodness-of-Fit Test to Test for Normality

The goodness-of-fit test is one of several ways to determine whether a set of observed frequencies matches a set of expected frequencies that conforms to a normal distribution. To put it another way, do the observed values in a frequency distribution coincide with the expected values based on a normal distribution? Recall in earlier chapters we often assumed that the sampled populations followed the normal distribution. This test offers a way to check that assumption.

EXAMPLE

Dr. Beth McPherson, president of Duval University, collected data on the annual salaries of full professors at 160 colleges. Using a statistical software package, she determined that the mean salary was $54.03 (in thousands) and that the standard deviation was $13.76 (in thousands). The frequency distribution for these annual salaries is shown in Table 15–7.

TABLE 15–7 Average Annual Salaries of Professors at 160 Colleges

Salary ($ thousands)	Number of Colleges
20 up to 30	4
30 up to 40	20
40 up to 50	41
50 up to 60	44
60 up to 70	29
70 up to 80	16
80 up to 90	2
90 up to 100	4
Total	160

Do the observed frequencies coincide with the expected frequencies based on the normal probability distribution?

SOLUTION

The mean and standard deviation are inserted into formula 7–1 (the formula for finding z). X in the formula is the lower or the upper class limit. To illustrate the computation of the z values, we selected the "70 up to 80" class.

$$z = \frac{X - \mu}{\sigma}$$

where X is the particular salary class limit, such as \$70 (thousand), μ is the mean (54.03), and σ is the standard deviation (13.76).

The z value for 70, the lower limit of the "70 up to 80" class, is 1.16, found by

$$z = \frac{X - \mu}{\sigma} = \frac{70 - 54.03}{13.76} = 1.16$$

This indicates that 70 is 1.16 standard deviations above the mean of 54.03.

For the upper limit of the "70 up to 80" class, $z = 1.89$, found by

$$z = \frac{X - \mu}{\sigma} = \frac{80 - 54.03}{13.76} = 1.89$$

Thus, 80 is 1.89 standard deviations above the mean of 54.03.

To determine the area in the standard normal distribution from 0 to 1.16, refer to Appendix D or the standard normal distribution on the back inside cover of this book. Go down the left margin to 1.1, then horizontally to 0.06, and read the area. It is .3770. This is also the area under the curve between the mean of 54.03 and 70.00.

Next, the area between 54.03 (the mean) and 80 is .4706. To find the area under the curve between 1.16 and 1.89, we subtract .4706 − .3770 = .0936. Thus we expect .0936 or 9.36 percent of the salaries to be between 1.16 and 1.89 standard deviations above the mean. Thus, the expected number of salaries between \$70 and \$80 (thousand) is 14.976, found by 160(.0936). This information is summarized in the following drawing. The expected frequencies for all the other categories are listed in Table 15–8.

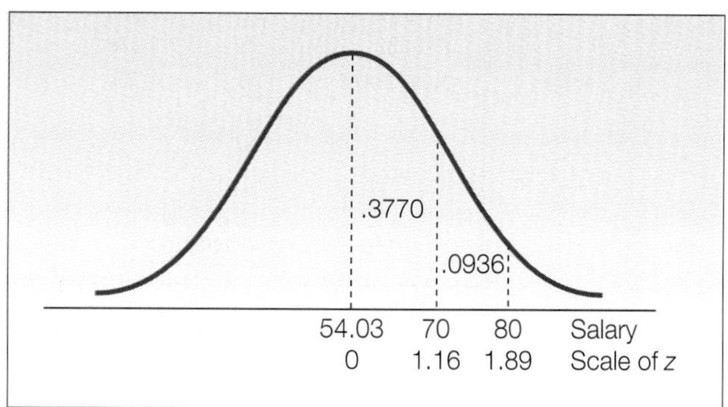

Before continuing, we should emphasize one of the limitations of tests using chi-square as the test statistic. The second limitation on page 559 indicates that if more than 20 percent of the cells have *expected frequencies* of less than 5, some of the categories should be combined. In Table 15–7 there are three cases where the *observed frequencies* are less than 5. To avoid the possibility that there will be too many cells with expected frequencies less than 5, the two highest salary categories are combined in Table 15–8. So the groups "80 up to 90" and "90 up to 100" are combined into a single group of "80 or more." The details for determining the expected frequency (f_e) for each of the categories are shown in Table 15–8.

TABLE 15–8 Salaries, z Values, Normal Areas, and f_e

Salary ($ thousands)	z Value	Area	Expected Frequency, f_e
Under 30	Under −1.75	.0401	6.416 ← .0401 × 160
30 to 40	−1.75 to −1.02	.1138	18.208 ← .1138 × 160
40 to 50	−1.02 to −0.29	.2320	37.120 ← .2320 × 160
50 to 60	−0.29 to 0.43	.2805	44.880 ← .2805 × 160
60 to 70	0.43 to 1.16	.2106	33.696 ← .2106 × 160
70 to 80	1.16 to 1.89	.0936	14.976 ← .0936 × 160
80 or more	Over 1.89	.0294	4.704 ← .0294 × 160
		1.0000	160.000

Now to compute the value of chi-square: (See Table 15–9.) Column 2 shows the observed frequency and column 3 the expected frequency for each of the salary categories. Columns 4, 5, and 6 show the computations for the chi-square value. Computed chi-square is 2.590.

TABLE 15–9 Calculations for Chi-Square

(1) Salary ($ thousands)	(2) f_o	(3) f_e	(4) $f_o - f_e$	(5) $(f_o - f_e)^2$	(6) $\frac{(f_o - f_e)^2}{f_e}$
Under 30	4	6.416	−2.416	5.837	0.910
30 to 40	20	18.208	1.792	3.211	0.176
40 to 50	41	37.120	3.880	15.054	0.406
50 to 60	44	44.880	−0.880	0.774	0.017
60 to 70	29	33.696	−4.696	22.052	0.654
70 to 80	16	14.976	1.024	1.049	0.070
80 and over	6	4.704	1.296	1.680	0.357
	160	160			2.590

Must be equal

χ^2

As usual, the null and the alternate hypotheses are stated:

H_0: The population follows the normal distribution.
H_1: The population does not follow the normal distribution.

To locate the critical value of chi-square, we need to know the degrees of freedom. In this case there are 7 categories (see Table 15–9), so the degrees of freedom are $7 - 1 = 6$. In addition, the values $54.03, the mean salary, and $13.76, the standard deviation of the salaries of full professors, were computed from this sample data. When we estimate population parameters from sample data, we lose a degree of freedom for each estimate. So we lose two more degrees of freedom for estimating the population mean and the population standard deviation. Thus, the number of degrees of freedom in this problem is 4, found by $k - 2 - 1 = 7 - 2 - 1 = 4$.

From Appendix I, using the .05 significance level, the critical value of χ^2 is 9.488. H_0 is rejected if the computed value of chi-square is greater than 9.488. In this case we computed χ^2 to be 2.590, so the null hypothesis is not rejected. We conclude that the distribution of full professors' salaries follows the normal distribution.

To expand on the calculation of the number of degrees of freedom, suppose we knew the mean and standard deviation of a population but wished to find whether some sample information conformed to the normal distribution. In this case the degrees of freedom is *k*, the number of categories minus 1. On the other hand, suppose we have sample data grouped into a frequency distribution, but we do not know the population mean or the population standard deviation. We wish to test whether the sample data follow the normal distribution. Because we are estimating the population mean and the population standard deviation from the sample data, the number of degrees of freedom is $k - 2 - 1$. In general, when we use sample statistics to estimate population parameters, the number of degrees of freedom is found by $k - p - 1$, where *p* represents the number of population parameters being estimated from the sample data.

Self-Review 15–3 Refer to the example of salaries of full professors. Verify the expected number of salaries between \$60 and \$70 (thousand).

Exercises

13. The manufacturer of a computer terminal reports in its advertising that the mean life of the terminal, under normal use, is 6 years, with a standard deviation of 1.4 years. (Assume these are population values.) A sample of 90 units sold 10 years ago revealed the following distribution of the lengths of life. At the .05 significance level, can the manufacturer conclude that the terminal lives are normally distributed?

Length of Life (years)	Frequency
Up to 4	7
4 up to 5	14
5 up to 6	25
6 up to 7	22
7 up to 8	16
8 or more	6

14. $\chi^2 = 1.74$ Do not reject H_0.

14. The commissions for sales of new cars are reported to average \$1,500 per month with a standard deviation of \$300. A sample of 500 sales representatives in the Northwest revealed the following distribution of commissions. At the .01 significance level, can we conclude that the population is normally distributed, with a mean of \$1,500 and a standard deviation of \$300?

Commission ($)	Frequency
Less than 900	9
900 up to 1,200	63
1,200 up to 1,500	165
1,500 up to 1,800	180
1,800 up to 2,100	71
2,100 or more	12
Total	500

Contingency Table Analysis

The goodness-of-fit tests applied in the previous sections were concerned with only a single variable or a single trait. The chi-square test can also be used for a research project involving *two* traits. As examples:

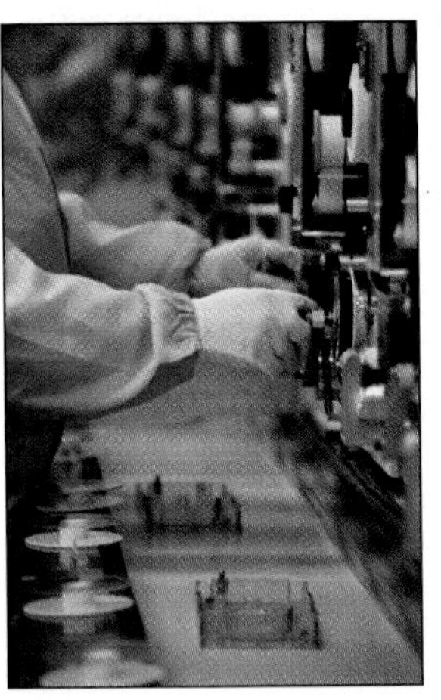

- Is there any relationship between the grade point average students earn in college and their income 10 years after graduation? The two traits measured for each individual are grade point average and income.
- The quality control manager of a company that operates three shifts (24 hours a day) wishes to know if there is a difference in quality on the three shifts. To investigate he selects a sample of 500 parts from yesterday's production. Each part is classified according to two criteria: whether the part is acceptable or not and on which of the shifts it was manufactured.
- Does a male released from federal prison make a different adjustment to civilian life if he returns to his hometown or if he goes elsewhere to live? The two traits are adjustment to civilian life and place of residence. Note that both traits are measured on the nominal scale.

EXAMPLE

Suppose the Federal Correction Agency wants to investigate the last question cited above: Does a male released from federal prison make a different adjustment to civilian life if he returns to his hometown or if he goes elsewhere to live? To put it another way, is there a relationship between adjustment to civilian life and place of residence after release from prison?

SOLUTION

As before, the first step in hypothesis testing is to state the null and alternate hypotheses.

H_0: There is no relationship between adjustment to civilian life and where the individual lives after being released from prison.

H_1: There is a relationship between adjustment to civilian life and where the individual lives after being released from prison.

The .01 level of significance will be used to test the hypothesis. Recall that this is the probability of a Type I error (i.e., the probability is .01 that a true null hypothesis is rejected).

The agency's psychologists interviewed 200 randomly selected former prisoners. Using a series of questions, the psychologists classified the adjustment of each individual to civilian life as outstanding, good, fair, or unsatisfactory. The classifications for the 200 former prisoners were tallied as follows. Joseph Camden, for example, returned to his hometown and has shown outstanding adjustment to civilian life. His case is one of the 27 tallies in the upper left box.

Residence after Release from Prison	**Adjustment to Civilian Life**			
	Outstanding	**Good**	**Fair**	**Unsatisfactory**
Hometown	𝍸 𝍸 𝍸 𝍸 𝍸 II	𝍸 𝍸 𝍸 𝍸 𝍸 𝍸 𝍸	𝍸 𝍸 𝍸 𝍸 𝍸 𝍸 III	𝍸 𝍸 𝍸 𝍸 𝍸
Not hometown	𝍸 𝍸 III	𝍸 𝍸 𝍸	𝍸 𝍸 𝍸 𝍸 𝍸 II	𝍸 𝍸 𝍸 𝍸 𝍸

Contingency table consists of count data

The tallies in each box, or *cell,* were counted. The counts are given in the following **contingency table.** (See Table 15–10.) In this case, the Federal Correction Agency wondered whether adjustment to civilian life is *contingent on* where the prisoner goes after release from prison.

TABLE 15–10 Adjustment to Civilian Life and Place of Residence

Residence after Release from Prison	**Adjustment to Civilian Life**				
	Outstanding	**Good**	**Fair**	**Unsatisfactory**	**Total**
Hometown	27	35	33	25	120
Not hometown	13	15	27	25	80
Total	40	50	60	50	200

Once we know how many rows (2) and columns (4) there are in the contingency table, we can determine the critical value and the decision rule. For a chi-square test of significance where two traits are classified in a contingency table, the degrees of freedom are found by:

$$df = (\text{number of rows} - 1)(\text{number of columns} - 1) = (r - 1)(c - 1)$$

In this problem:

$$df = (r - 1)(c - 1) = (2 - 1)(4 - 1) = 3$$

To find the critical value for 3 degrees of freedom and the .01 level (selected earlier), refer to Appendix I. It is 11.345. The decision rule is to reject the null hypothesis if the computed value of χ^2 is greater than 11.345. The decision rule is portrayed graphically in Chart 15–4.

Statistics in Action

A study of 1,000 Americans over the age of 24 showed that 28 percent never married. Of those, 22 percent completed college. Twenty-three percent of the 1,000 married and completed college. Can we conclude for the information given that being married is related to completing college? The study indicated that the two variables were related, that the computed value of the chi-square statistic was 11.525, and that the *p*-value was less than .0001. Can you duplicate these results?

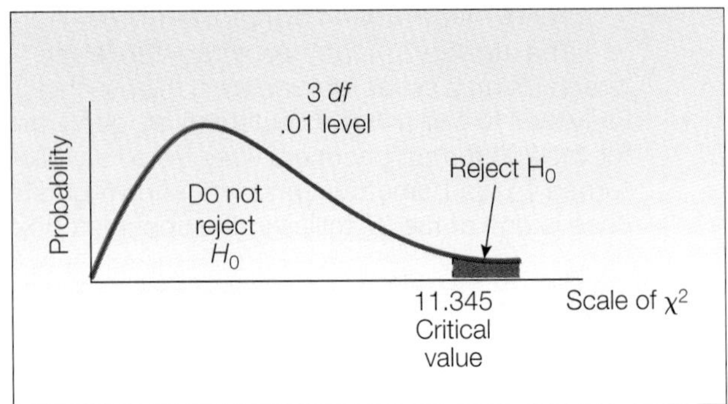

CHART 15–4 Chi-Square Distribution for 3 Degrees of Freedom

Now to find the computed value of χ^2: The observed frequencies, f_o, are shown in Table 15–10. How are the corresponding expected frequencies, f_e, determined? Note in the "Total" column of Table 15–10 that 120 of the 200 former prisoners (60 percent) returned to their hometowns. *If there were no relationship* between adjustment and residency after release from prison, we would expect 60 percent of the 40 ex-prisoners who made outstanding adjustment to civilian life to reside in their hometowns. Thus, the expected frequency f_e for the upper left cell is $.60 \times 40 = 24$. Likewise, if there were no relationship between adjustment and present residence, we would expect 60 percent of the 50 ex-prisoners (30) who had "good" adjustment to civilian life to reside in their hometowns.

Further, notice that 80 of the 200 ex-prisoners studied (40 percent) did not return to their hometowns to live. Thus, of the 60 considered by the psychologists to have made "fair" adjustment to civilian life, $.40 \times 60$, or 24, would be expected not to return to their hometowns.

The expected frequency for any cell can be determined by

EXPECTED FREQUENCY

$$\text{Expected frequency for a cell} = \frac{\text{(Row total)(Column total)}}{\text{Grand total}} \qquad \textbf{[15–2]}$$

Using this formula, the expected frequency for the upper left cell in Table 15–10 is:

$$\text{Expected frequency} = \frac{\text{(Row total)(Column total)}}{\text{Grand total}} = \frac{(120)(40)}{200} = 24$$

The observed frequencies, f_o, and the expected frequencies, f_e, for all of the cells in the contingency table are listed in Table 15–11.

TABLE 15–11 Observed and Expected Frequencies

Residence after Release from Prison	Adjustment to Civilian Life								Total	
	Outstanding		Good		Fair		Unsatisfactory			
	f_o	f_e	f_o	f_e	f_o	f_e	f_o	f_e	f_o	f_e
Hometown	27	24	35	30	33	36	25	30	120	120
Not hometown	13	16	15	20	27	24	25	20	80	80
Total	40	40	50	50	60	60	50	50	200	200

Must be equal (40 and 40) ; $\frac{(80)(50)}{200}$ (expected frequency 20) ; Must be equal (200 and 200)

Recall that the computed value of chi-square using formula (15–1) is found by:

$$\chi^2 = \sum \left[\frac{(f_o - f_e)^2}{f_e}\right]$$

Starting with the upper left cell:

$$\chi^2 = \frac{(27-24)^2}{24} + \frac{(35-30)^2}{30} + \frac{(33-36)^2}{36} + \frac{(25-30)^2}{30}$$

$$+ \frac{(13-16)^2}{16} + \frac{(15-20)^2}{20} + \frac{(27-24)^2}{24} + \frac{(25-20)^2}{20}$$

$$= 0.375 + 0.833 + 0.250 + 0.833 + 0.563 + 1.250 + 0.375 + 1.250$$

$$= 5.729$$

Because the computed value of chi-square (5.729) lies in the region to the left of 11.345, the null hypothesis is not rejected at the .01 level. We conclude there is no relationship between adjustment to civilian life and where the prisoner resides after being released from prison. For the Federal Correction Agency's advisement program, adjustment to civilian life is not related to where the ex-prisoner lives.

The following output is from the MINITAB system.

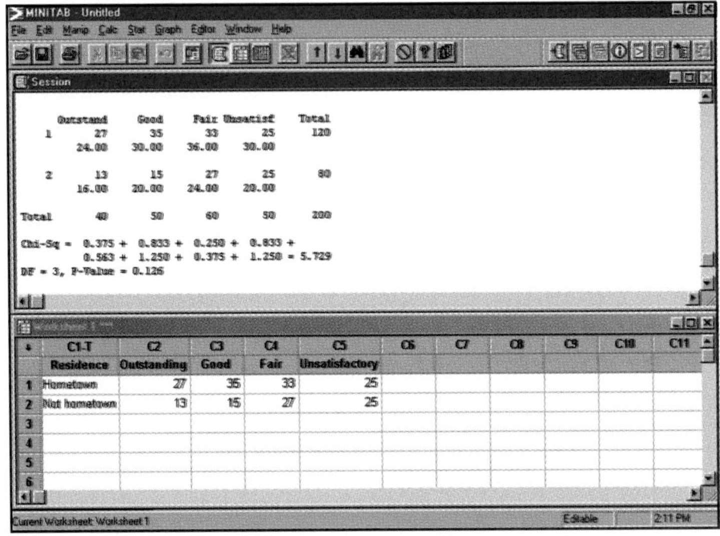

Observe that the value of chi-square is the same as that computed earlier. In addition, the p-value is reported, .126. So the probability of finding a value of the test statistic as large or larger is .126 when the null hypothesis is true.

Self-Review 15–4

Current projections suggest, with the current strong economy, the federal government will be generating budget surpluses for the next ten years. How to spend this money is an issue being debated. The major options are reduce taxes, pay down the debt, or improve Social Security benefits. A sample of 135 voters was classified according to political affiliation and which of the major options should be paid first. The results follow. Use .05 significance level.

Budget Surplus Option	Democrat	Republican	Independent	Total
Reduce taxes	18	12	10	40
Pay down debt	17	15	13	45
Improve social security	9	9	22	40
Total	44	36	45	125

(a) What is this table called?
(b) State the null hypothesis.
(c) Determine the value of chi-square. What is your decision regarding the null hypothesis?
(d) Interpret the results.

Exercises

15. The director of advertising for the *Carolina Sun Times,* the largest newspaper in the Carolinas, is studying the relationship between the type of community in which a subscriber resides and the portion of the newspaper he or she reads first. For a sample of readers, she collected the following sample information.

	National News	Sports	Comics
City	170	124	90
Suburb	120	112	100
Rural	130	90	88

At the .05 significance level, can we conclude there is a relationship between the type of community where the person resides and the portion of the paper read first?

16. $\chi^2 = 3.663$ Do not reject H_0.

16. Four brands of light bulbs are being considered for use in a large manufacturing plant. The director of purchasing asked for samples of 100 from each manufacturer. The numbers of acceptable and unacceptable bulbs from each manufacturer are shown below. At the .05 significance level, is there a difference in the quality of the bulbs?

	Manufacturer			
	A	B	C	D
Unacceptable	12	8	5	11
Acceptable	88	92	95	89
Total	100	100	100	100

17. The Quality Control Department at Food Town, Inc., a grocery chain in upstate New York, conducts a monthly check on the comparison of scanned prices to posted prices. The chart below summarizes the results of a sample of 500 items last month. Company management would like to know whether there is any relationship between error rates on regular priced items and specially priced items. Use the .01 significance level.

	Regular Price	Advertised Special Price
Undercharge	20	10
Overcharge	15	30
Correct price	200	225

18. $\chi^2 = 2.523$ Do not reject H_0.

18. The use of cellular phones in automobiles has increased dramatically in the last few years. Of concern to traffic experts, as well as manufacturers of cellular phones, is the effect on accident rates. Is someone who is using a cellular phone more likely to be involved in a traffic accident? What is your conclusion from the following sample information? Use the .05 significance level.

	Had Accident in the Last Year	Did Not Have an Accident in the Last Year
Cellular phone in use	25	300
Cellular phone not in use	50	400

Chapter Outline

I. The characteristics of the chi-square distribution are:

A. The value of chi-square is never negative.

B. The chi-square distribution is positively skewed.

C. There is a family of chi-square distributions.

1. Each time the degrees of freedom change, a new distribution is formed.
2. As the degrees of freedom increase, the distribution approaches a normal distribution.

II. A goodness-of-fit test will show whether an observed set of frequencies could have come from a hypothesized population distribution.
  A. The degrees of freedom are $k - 1$, where k is the number of categories.
  B. The formula for computing the value of chi-square is

$$\chi^2 = \sum \frac{(f_o - f_e)^2}{f_e} \quad \textbf{[15–1]}$$

III. A goodness-of-fit test can also be used to determine whether the sample observations came from a particular distribution such as the normal distribution.
  A. To conduct the test for a normal distribution, find the mean and standard deviation of the distribution.
  B. Group the data into a frequency distribution.
  C. Convert the class limits to z values.
  D. Multiply the probability for finding a value in each class by the total number of observations to find the expected frequency.
  E. Use formula 15–1 to determine the value of chi-square.
  F. The degrees of freedom are equal to $k - 3$ if the mean and the standard deviation are estimated from the data.

IV. A contingency table is used to test whether two traits or characteristics are related.
  A. Each observation is classified according to two traits.
  B. The expected frequency is determined as follows:

$$f_e = \frac{\text{(Row total)(Column total)}}{\text{(Grand total)}} \quad \textbf{[15–2]}$$

  C. The degrees of freedom are found by:

$$df = (\text{Rows} - 1)(\text{Columns} - 1)$$

  D. The usual hypothesis testing procedure is used.

Pronunciation Key

SYMBOL	MEANING	PRONUNCIATION
χ^2	Probability distribution	*ki square*
f_o	Observed frequency	*f sub oh*
f_e	Expected frequency	*f sub e*

Chapter Exercises

19. Vehicles heading west on Front Street may turn right, left, or go straight ahead at Elm Street. The city traffic engineer believes that half of the vehicles will continue straight through the intersection. Of the remaining half, equal proportions will turn right and left. Two hundred vehicles were observed, with the following results. Use the .10 significance level. Can we conclude that the traffic engineer is correct?

	Straight	Right Turn	Left Turn
Frequency	112	48	40

20. $\chi^2 = 5.67$ Do not reject H_0.

20. The publisher of a sports magazine plans to offer new subscribers one of three gifts: a sweatshirt with the logo of their favorite team, a coffee cup with the logo of their favorite team, or a pair of earrings also with the logo of their favorite team. In a sample of 500 new subscribers, the number selecting each gift is reported on the next page. At the .05 significance level, is there a preference for the gifts or should we conclude that the gifts are equally well liked?

Gift	Frequency
Sweatshirt	183
Coffee cup	175
Earrings	142

21. In a particular market there are three commercial television stations, each with its own evening news program from 6:00 to 6:30 P.M. According to a report in this morning's local newspaper, a random sample of 150 viewers last night revealed 53 watched the news on WNAE (channel 5), 64 watched on WRRN (channel 11), and 33 on WSPD (channel 13). At the .05 significance level, is there a difference in the proportion of viewers watching the three channels?

22. Reject if $\chi^2 >$ 11.345. $\chi^2 = 46.0$ Reject H_0.

22. There are four entrances to the Government Center Building in downtown Philadelphia. The building maintenance supervisor would like to know if the entrances are equally utilized. To investigate, 400 people were observed entering the building. The number using each entrance is reported below. At the .01 significance level, is there a difference in the use of the four entrances?

Entrance	Frequency
Main Street	140
Broad Street	120
Cherry Street	90
Walnut Street	50
Total	400

23. The owner of a mail-order catalog would like to compare her sales with the geographic distribution of the population. According to the United States Bureau of the Census, 21 percent of the population lives in the Northeast, 24 percent in the Midwest, 35 percent in the South, and 20 percent in the West. Listed below is a breakdown of a sample of 400 orders randomly selected from those shipped last month.

At the .01 significance level, does the distribution of the orders reflect the population?

Region	Frequency
Northeast	68
Midwest	104
South	155
West	73
Total	400

24. Reject if $\chi^2 >$ 9.488. Do not reject. $\chi^2 = 4.1558$

24. The Banner Mattress and Furniture Company wishes to study the number of credit applications received per day for the last 300 days. The information is reported below.

Number of Credit Applications	Frequency (Number of Days)
0	50
1	77
2	81
3	48
4	31
5 or more	13

To interpret, there were 50 days on which no credit applications were received, 77 days on which only one application was received, and so on. Would it be reasonable to conclude that the population distribution is Poisson with a mean of 2.0? Use the .05 significance level. *Hint:* To find the expected frequencies use the Poisson distribution with a mean of 2.0. Find the probability of exactly one success given a Poisson distribution with a mean 2.0. Multiply this probability by 300 to find the expected frequency for the number of days in which there was exactly one application. Determine the expected frequency for the other days in a similar manner.

25. In the 1990s the Deep Down Mining Company implemented new safety guidelines. Prior to these new guidelines, management expected there to be no accidents in 40 percent of the months, one accident in 30 percent of the months, two accidents in 20 percent of the months, and three accidents in 10 percent of the months. Over the last 10 years, or 120 months, there have been 46 months in which there were no accidents, 40 months in which there was one accident, 22 months in which there were two accidents, and 12 months in which there were 3 accidents. At the .05 significance level can the management at Deep Down conclude that there has been a change in the monthly accident distribution?

26. $\chi^2 = 9.733$ Do not reject H_0.

26. The American Association of Television Broadcasters recently reported the mean number of television sets per household in the United States is 2.30 sets and that the standard deviation is 1.474 sets. A sample of 100 homes in Boise, Idaho, revealed the following number of sets per household:

Number of Television Sets	Number of Households	Number of Television Sets	Number of Households
0	7	3	18
1	27	4	10
2	28	5 or more	10

At the .05 significance level, is it reasonable to conclude that the number of television sets per household follows the normal distribution? (*Hint:* Use limits such as 0.50, 1.5, etc.)

27. Eckel Manufacturing believes that their hourly wages follow a normal probability distribution. To confirm this, 300 workers were sampled and the results organized into the following frequency distribution. Find the mean and the standard deviation of these data grouped into a frequency distribution. At the .10 significance level, is it reasonable to conclude that the distribution of hourly wages approximates the normal distribution?

Hourly Wage ($)	Frequency
5.50 up to 6.50	20
6.50 up to 7.50	54
7.50 up to 8.50	130
8.50 up to 9.50	68
9.50 up to 10.50	28
Total	300

28. $\chi^2 = 18.177$ Reject H_0.

28. A recent study by a large retailer designed to determine whether there was a relationship between the importance a store manager placed on advertising and the size of the store revealed the following sample information:

	Important	Not Important
Small	40	52
Medium	106	47
Large	67	32

What is your conclusion? Use the .05 significance level.

29. Two hundred managers from various levels were randomly selected and interviewed regarding their concern about environmental issues. The response of each person was tallied into one of three categories: no concern, some concern, and great concern. The results were:

Level of Management	No Concern	Some Concern	Great Concern
Top management	15	13	12
Middle management	20	19	21
Supervisor	7	7	6
Group leader	28	21	31

Use the .01 significance level to determine whether there is a relationship between management level and environmental concern.

30. $\chi^2 = 2.191$ Do not reject H_0.

30. A study regarding the relationship between age and the amount of pressure sales personnel feel in relation to their jobs revealed the following sample information. At the .01 significance level, is there a relationship between job pressure and age?

	Degree of Job Pressure		
Age (years)	**Low**	**Medium**	**High**
Less than 25	20	18	22
25 up to 40	50	46	44
40 up to 60	58	63	59
60 and older	34	43	43

31. The claims department at the Wise Insurance Company believes that younger drivers have more accidents and, therefore, should be charged higher insurance rates. Investigating a sample of 1,200 Wise policyholders revealed the following breakdown on whether a claim had been filed in the last three years and the age of the policyholder. Is it reasonable to conclude that there is a relationship between the age of the policyholder and whether or not the person filed a claim? Use the .05 significance level.

Age Group	No Claim	Claim
16 up to 25	170	74
25 up to 40	240	58
40 up to 55	400	44
55 or older	190	24
Total	1,000	200

32. $\chi^2 = 84.04$ Reject H_0.

32. A sample of employees at a large chemical plant was asked to indicate a preference for one of three pension plans. The results are given in the following table. Does it seem that there is a relationship between the pension plan selected and the job classification of the employees? Use the .01 significance level.

	Pension Plan		
Job Class	**Plan A**	**Plan B**	**Plan C**
Supervisor	10	13	29
Clerical	19	80	19
Labor	81	57	22

exercises.com

33. Did you ever purchase a bag of M&M candies and wonder about the distribution of colors? You can go to the Web site www.baking.m-ms.com and click on Frequently Asked Questions or just go to the site www.baking.m-ms.com/faq and find the percentage breakdown according to the manufacturer, as well as a brief history of the product. Did you know in the beginning they were all brown? For M&M peanuts 20 percent are blue, 20 percent brown, 20 percent yellow, 20 percent red, 10 percent green, and 10 percent orange. A 6 oz. bag purchased at the Book Store at Coastal Carolina University on June 1, 2001 had 13 blue, 17 brown, 20 yellow, 7 red, 9 orange, and 6 green. Is it reasonable to conclude that actual distribution agrees with the expected distribution? Use the .05 significance level. Conduct your own trial. Be sure to share with your instructor.

34. Answers will vary.

34. As described in earlier chapters, many real estate companies and rental agencies now publish their listings on the World Wide Web. One example is the Dunes Realty Company, located in Garden City and Surfside Beaches in South Carolina. Go to the Web site www.dunes.com, select **Cottage Search,** then indicate 5 bedroom, accommodations for 14 people, oceanfront, and no pool or floating dock; select a period in July and August; indicate that you are willing to spend $5,000 per week; and then click on **Search the Cottages.** The output should include details on the cottages that met your criteria. Organize the rental rates into a frequency distribution. Is it reasonable to conclude that the distribution is normal with a population mean of $3,000 and standard deviation of $900?

Computer Data Exercises

35. Refer to the Real Estate data, which reports information on homes sold in the Venice, Florida, area last year.

a. Develop a contingency table that shows whether a home has a pool and the township in which the house is located. Is there an association between the variables "pool" and "township"? Use the .05 significance level.

b. Develop a contingency table that shows whether a home has an attached garage and the township in which the home is located. Is there an association between the variables "attached garage" and "township"? Use the .05 significance level.

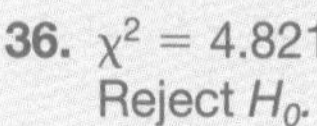

36. $\chi^2 = 4.821$ Reject H_0.

36. Refer to the Baseball 2000 data, which reports information on the 30 Major League Baseball teams for the 2000 season. Set up a variable that divides the teams into two groups, those that had a winning season and those that did not. There are 162 games in the season, so define a winning season as having won 81 or more games. Next, divide the teams into two salary groups. Let the 15 teams with the largest salaries be in one group and the 15 teams with the smallest salaries in the other. At the .05 significance level is there a relationship between salaries and winning?

37. Refer to the Schools data, which reports information on 94 school districts in northwest Ohio.

a. Group the districts based on the percent of students on welfare: "low" (less than 5 percent), "moderate" (5 up to 10 percent), and "high" (10 percent or more). Conduct a test of hypothesis to determine whether the three categories are equally represented in the sample. Use the .05 significance level.

b. Identify each district as "small" (less than 1,000 students), "medium" (1,000 up to 3,000), or "large" (more than 3,000 students). Create a table that shows the districts classified by both percent of students on welfare and the size of the district. At the .05 significance level, can we conclude that the two characteristics are related?

Computer Commands

1. The MegaStat commands to create the chi-square goodness-of-fit test on page 553 are:

a. Enter the information from Table 15–1 into a worksheet as shown on the next page.

b. Select **MegaStat, Chi-Square/Crosstabs,** and **Goodness-of-fit** and hit **Enter.**

c. In the dialog box select *B2:B7* as the **Observed values,** *C2:C7* as the **Expected values,** and enter *0* as the **Number of parameters estimated from the data.** Click on **OK.**

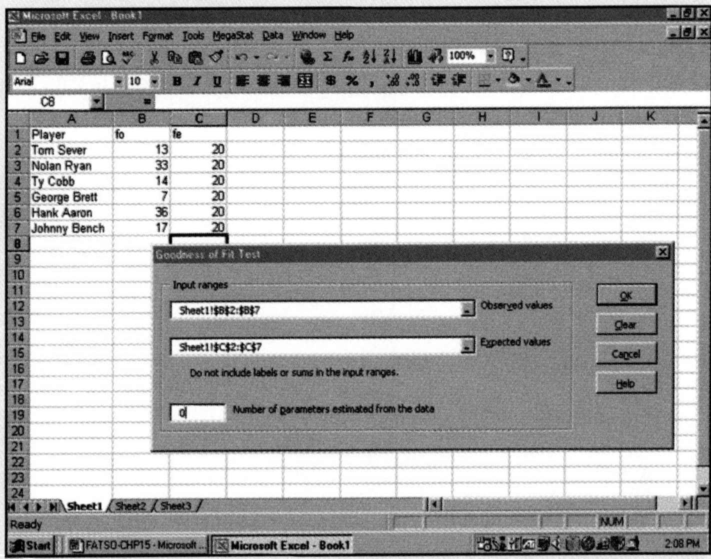

2. The MegaStat commands to create the chi-square goodness-of-fit tests on pages 560 and 561 are the same except for the number of items in the observed and expected frequency columns. Only one dialog box is shown.
   a. Enter the Levels of Management information shown on page 560.
   b. Select **MegaStat, Chi-Square/Crosstabs,** and **Goodness-of-fit** and hit **Enter.**
   c. In the dialog box select *B2:B8* as the **Observed values,** *C2:C8* as the **Expected values,** and enter *0* as the **Number of parameters estimated from the data.** Click on **OK.**

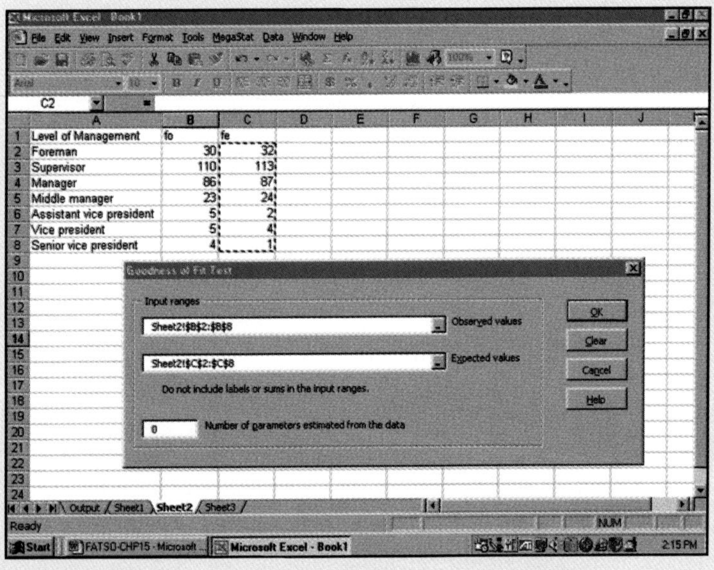

3. The MINITAB commands for the chi-square analysis on page 570 are:
   a. Enter the names of the variables in the first row and the data in the next two rows as shown on the next page.
   b. Select **Stat, Table,** and then click on **Chi-square test** and hit **Enter.**
   c. In the dialog box select the columns labeled *Outstanding* to *Unsatisfactory* and click **OK.**

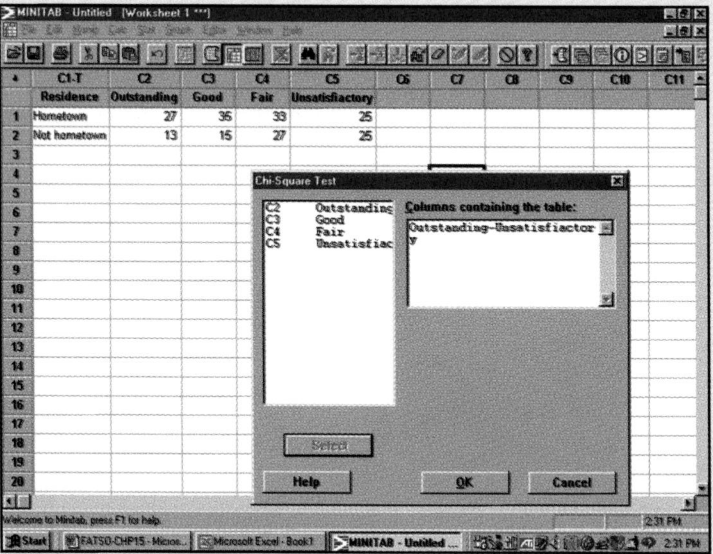
MINITAB - Untitled [Worksheet 1 ***]
C1-T
C2
C3
C4
C5
C6
C7
C8
C9
C10
C11
Residence
Outstanding
Good
Fair
Unsatisfiactory
Hometown
27
36
33
25
Not hometown
13
15
27
25
Chi-Square Test
C2 Outstanding
C3 Good
C4 Fair
C5 Unsatisfiac
Columns containing the table:
Outstanding-Unsatisfiactory
Select
Help
OK
Cancel
Welcome to Minitab, press F1 for help.
Start
Microsoft Excel - Book1
MINITAB - Untitled ...
2:31 PM

Chapter 15 Answers to Self-Review

15–1 **(a)** Observed frequencies.
(b) Six (six days of the week).
(c) 10. Total observed frequencies ÷ 6 = 60/6 = 10.
(d) 5; $k - 1 = 6 - 1 = 5$.
(e) 15.086 (from the chi-square table in Appendix I).
(f)

$$\chi^2 = \sum \left[\frac{(f_o - f_e)^2}{f_e}\right] = \frac{(12 - 10)^2}{10} + \cdots + \frac{(9 - 10)^2}{10} = 0.8$$

(g) No. We do not reject H_0.
(h) Absenteeism is distributed evenly throughout the week. The observed differences are due to sampling variation.

15–2 H_0: $P_C = .60$, $P_L = .30$, and $P_U = .10$.

H_1: Distribution is not as above.

Reject H_0 if $\chi^2 > 5.991$.

Category	f_o	f_e	$\frac{(f_o - f_e)^2}{f_e}$
Current	320	300	1.33
Late	120	150	6.00
Uncollectible	60	50	2.00
	500	500	9.33

Reject H_0. The accounts receivable data does not reflect the national average.

15–3 33.696, found by $z = (60 - 54.03)/13.76 = 0.43$ and $z = (70 - 54.03)/13.76 = 1.16$. Then $.3770 - .1664 = .2106$ and $.2106 \times 160 = 33.696$.

15–4 **(a)** Contingency table
(b) There is no relationship between political affiliation and budget surplus option.
(c) The value of chi-square is computed from the following table.

	Democrat		Republican		Independent		
Option	f_o	f_e	f_o	f_e	f_o	f_e	**Total**
Reduce taxes	18	14.08	12	11.52	10	14.40	40
Pay down debt	17	15.84	15	12.96	13	16.20	45
Improve Social Security	9	14.08	9	11.52	22	14.40	40
	44	44.00	36	36.00	45	45.00	125

$$\chi^2 = \frac{(18 - 14.08)^2}{14.08} + \frac{(12 - 11.52)^2}{11.52} + \cdots + \frac{(22 - 14.40)^2}{14.40}$$

$$= 9.889$$

The critical value of chi-square is 9.488, so H_0 is rejected.

(d) There is a relationship between the political affiliation and the preferred option.

16

Nonparametric Methods

Analysis of Ranked Data

GOALS

When you have completed this chapter, you will be able to:

1 Conduct the sign test for dependent samples using the binomial and standard normal distributions as the test statistics.

2 Conduct a test of hypothesis for dependent samples using the Wilcoxon signed-rank test.

3 Conduct and interpret the Wilcoxon rank-sum test for independent samples.

4 Conduct and interpret the Kruskal-Wallis test for several independent samples.

5 Compute and interpret Spearman's coefficient of rank correlation.

6 Conduct a test of hypothesis to determine whether the correlation among the ranks in the population is different from zero.

A department store wants to handle one brand of high-quality compact disc player. A panel of 16 audio experts met to test CD passages played on each system to indicate preference. Based on their responses, conduct a test of hypothesis at the .10 significance level to determine if there is a preference between the players. (See Goal 2 and Exercise 31.)

Introduction

Chapter 15 introduced nonparametric, or distribution-free, tests of hypotheses. We stressed that the goodness-of-fit test is especially useful for the *nominal* level of measurement. Recall from Chapter 1 that nominal level of measurement implies that the data can only be classified into categories, and there is no particular order to the categories. The purpose of these tests is to determine whether an observed set of frequencies, f_o, is significantly different from a corresponding set of expected frequencies, f_e. Likewise, if you are interested in the relationship between two characteristics — such as the age of an individual and his or her music preference — you would tally the data into a contingency table and use the chi-square distribution as the test statistic. For both these types of problems, no assumptions need to be made about the shape of the population. We do not have to assume, for example, that the population of interest follows the normal distribution, as was done with tests of hypotheses in Chapters 10 through 12.

This chapter is a continuation of tests of hypotheses designed especially for nonparametric data. However, instead of being applicable to nominal-level data, these tests require that the responses be at least *ordinal* level. That is, the responses can be ranked from low to high. An example of ranking is the executive title. Executives are ranked assistant vice president, vice president, senior vice president, and president. A vice president is ranked higher than an assistant vice president, a senior vice president is ranked higher than a vice president, and so on.

Five distribution-free tests and the Spearman coefficient of rank correlation are considered in this chapter. The tests are: the sign test, the median test, the Wilcoxon signed-rank test, the Wilcoxon rank-sum test, the Kruskal-Wallis analysis of variance by ranks.

The Sign Test

The **sign test** is based on the sign of a difference between two related observations. We usually designate a plus sign for a positive difference and a minus sign for a negative difference. If, for example, sales increased from $34,698 in October to $51,276 in November, we record the $16,578 difference as a plus sign. If production dropped from 98,000 computers in the first quarter to 51,000 in the second quarter, a minus sign is recorded. For a sign test, we are not concerned with the magnitude of the difference, only the direction of the difference.

The sign test has many applications. One is for "before/after" experiments. To illustrate, suppose an evaluation is to be made on a new tune-up program for automobiles. We record the number of miles traveled per gallon of gasoline before the tune-up and again after the tune-up. If the tune-up is not effective, that is, had no effect on performance, then about half of the automobiles tested would show an increase in miles per gallon and the other half a decrease. A "+" sign is assigned to an increase, a "−" sign to a decrease.

A product-preference experiment illustrates another use of the sign test. Taster's Choice markets two kinds of coffee in a 4-ounce jar: decaffeinated and regular. Their market research department wants to determine whether coffee drinkers prefer decaffeinated or regular coffee. Coffee drinkers are given two small, unmarked cups of coffee, and each is asked his or her preference. Preference for decaffeinated could be coded "+" and preference for regular "−." In a sense the data are ordinal level because the coffee drinkers give their preferred coffee the higher rank; they rank the other kind below it. Here again, if the population of consumers do not have a preference, we would expect half of the sample of coffee drinkers to prefer decaffeinated and the other half regular coffee.

We can best show the application of the sign test by an example. We will use a "before/after" experiment.

EXAMPLE

The director of information technology at Samuelson Chemicals recommended that an in-plant computer training program be instituted for managers. The objective is to improve the knowledge of computer usage in accounting, procurement, production, and so on. Some managers thought it would be a worthwhile program; others resisted it, saying it would be of no value. Despite these objections, it was announced that the computer sessions would commence the first of the month.

A sample of 15 managers was selected at random. The general level of competence of each manager with respect to the computer was determined by a panel of experts before the program started. Their competence and understanding were rated as being either outstanding, excellent, good, fair, or poor. (See Table 16–1.) After the three-month training program, the same panel of computer experts rated each manager again. The two ratings (before and after) are shown along with the sign of the difference. A "+" sign indicates improvement, and a "−" sign indicates that the manager's competence on the computer had declined after the training program.

TABLE 16–1 Competence before and after the Computer Training Program

	Name	Before	After	Sign of Difference
	T. J. Bowers	Good	Outstanding	+
	Sue Jenkins	Fair	Excellent	+
	James Brown	Excellent	Good	−
	Tad Jackson	Poor	Good	+
Dropped from analysis	~~Andy Love~~	~~Excellent~~	~~Excellent~~	~~0~~
	Sarah Truett	Good	Outstanding	+
	John Sinshi	Poor	Fair	+
	Jean Unger	Excellent	Outstanding	+
	Coy Farmer	Good	Poor	−
	Troy Archer	Poor	Good	+
	V. A. Jones	Good	Outstanding	+
	Coley Casper	Fair	Excellent	+
	Candy Fry	Good	Fair	−
	Arthur Seiple	Good	Outstanding	+
	Sandy Gumpp	Poor	Good	+

We are interested in whether the in-plant computer training program was effective in increasing the competence of the managers on the computer. That is, are the managers more competent after the training program than before?

SOLUTION

We will use the five-step hypothesis-testing procedure.

Step 1: State the null hypothesis and the alternate hypothesis.

Statistics in Action

A recent study of undergraduate students at the University of Michigan revealed the students with the worst attendance records also tended to earn the lowest grades. Does that surprise you? Students who were absent less than 10 percent of the time tended to earn a B or better. The same study also found that students who sit in the front of the class earn higher grades than those who sit in the back.

Hypothesis	Meaning
H_0: $\pi \leq .50$	There is no increase in competence as a result of the in-plant computer training program.
H_1: $\pi > .50$	The computer competence of the managers has increased.

The symbol π refers to the proportion in the population with a particular characteristic. If we *do not reject* the null hypothesis, it will indicate the training program has produced no change in the level of computer competence, or competence actually decreased. If we *reject* the null hypothesis, it will indicate that the computer competence of the managers has increased as a result of the training program.

The binomial distribution discussed in Chapter 6 is used as the test statistic. It is appropriate because the sign test meets all the binomial assumptions, namely:

1. There are only two outcomes: a "success" and a "failure." A manager either increased in computer competence (a success) or did not.
2. For each trial the probability of success is assumed to be .50. Thus, the probability of a success is the same for all trials (managers in this case).
3. The total number of trials is fixed (15 in this experiment).
4. Each trial is independent. This means, for example, that Arthur Seiple's performance in the three-month course is unrelated to Sandy Gumpp's performance.

Step 2: Select a level of significance. We chose the .10 level.

Step 3: Decide on the test statistic. It is the *number of plus signs* resulting from the experiment.

Step 4: Formulate a decision rule. Fifteen managers were enrolled in the computer course, but Andy Love showed no increase or decrease in competence. (See Table 16–1.) He was, therefore, eliminated from the study, so $n = 14$. From the binomial probability distribution table in Appendix A, for an n of 14 and a probability of .50, we copied the binomial probability distribution in Table 16–2. The number of successes is in column 1, the probability of success in column 2, and the cumulative probabilities in column 3. To arrive at the cumulative probabilities, we *add* the probabilities of success in column 2 from the bottom. For illustration, to get the cumulative probability of 11 or more successes, we add .000 + .001 + .006 + 022 = .029.

This is a one-tailed test because the alternate hypothesis gives a direction. The inequality (>) points to the right. Thus, the region of rejection is in the upper tail. If the inequality sign pointed toward the left tail (<), the region of rejection would be in the lower tail. If that were the case, we would add the probabilities in column 2 *down* to get the cumulative probabilities in column 3.

Recall that we selected the .10 level of significance. To arrive at the decision rule for this problem, we go to the cumulative probabilities in Table 16–2, column 3. We read up from the bottom until we come to the *cumulative probability nearest to but not exceeding the level of significance (.10).* That cumulative probability is .090. The number of successes (plus signs) corresponding to .090 in column 1 is 10. Therefore, the decision rule is: If the number of pluses in the sample is 10 or more, the null hypothesis is rejected and the alternate hypothesis accepted.

TABLE 16–2 Binomial Probability Distribution for $n = 14$, $\pi = .50$

(1) Number of Successes	(2) Probability of Success		(3) Cumulative Probability	
0	.000		1.000	
1	.001		.999	
2	.006		.998	
3	.022		.992	
4	.061		.970	
5	.122		.909	
6	.183		.787	
7	.209		.604	
8	.183		.395	
9	.122		.212	
10	.061	↑	.090	
11	.022		.029	← .000 + .001 +
12	.006		.007	.006 + .022
13	.001	Add	.001	
14	.000	up	.000	

To repeat: We add the probabilities up from the bottom because the direction of the inequality (>) is toward the right, indicating that the region of rejection is in the upper tail. If the number of plus signs in the sample is 10 or more, we reject the null hypothesis; otherwise, we do not reject H_0. The region of rejection is portrayed in Chart 16–1.

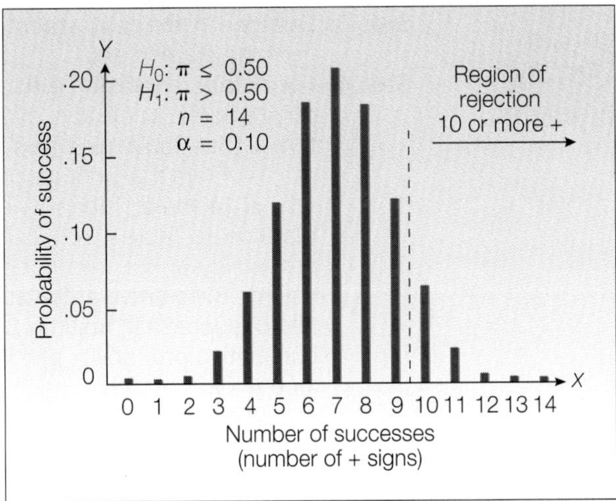

CHART 16–1 Region of Rejection, $n = 14$, $\pi = .50$

What procedure is followed for a two-tailed test? We combine (add) the probabilities of success in the two tails until we come as close to α as possible without exceeding it. In this example α is .10. The probability of 3 or fewer successes is .029, found by .000 + .001 + .006 + .022. The probability of 11 or more successes is also .029. Adding the two probabilities gives .058. This is the closest we can come to .10 without exceeding it. Had we included the probabilities of 4 and 10 successes, the total would be .180, which exceeds .10. Hence, the decision rule for a two-tailed test would be to reject the null hypothesis if there are 3 or fewer plus signs, or 11 or more plus signs.

Step 5: Make a decision regarding the null hypothesis. Eleven out of the 14 managers in the computer course increased their computer competency. The number 11 is in the rejection region, which starts at 10, so H_0 is rejected. The three-month computer course was effective. It increased the computer competency of the managers.

It should be noted again that if the alternate hypothesis does not give a direction — for example, H_0: $\pi = .50$ and H_1: $\pi \neq .50$ — the test of hypothesis is *two-tailed.* In such cases there will be two rejection regions — one in the lower tail and one in the upper tail. If $\alpha = .10$ and the test is two-tailed, the area in each tail is .05 ($\alpha/2 = .10/2 = .05$). Self-Review 16–1 illustrates this.

Self-Review 16–1

Recall the Taster's Choice example described on page 581, involving a consumer test to determine the preference for decaffeinated versus regular coffee. The null and alternate hypotheses are:

H_0: $\pi = .50$ $\quad n = 12 \quad \alpha = .10$
H_1: $\pi \neq .50$

(a) Is this a one-tailed or a two-tailed test of hypothesis?
(b) Show the decision rule in a chart.
(c) Letting consumer preference for decaffeinated coffee be a "+" and preference for regular coffee a "−," it was found that two customers preferred decaffeinated. What is your decision? Explain.

Exercises

1. The following hypothesis-testing situation is given: H_0: $\pi \leq .50$ and H_1: $\pi > .50$. The significance level is .10, and the sample size is 12.
   a. What is the decision rule?
   b. There were nine successes. What is your decision regarding the null hypothesis? Explain.
2. The following hypothesis-testing situation is given: H_0: $\pi = .50$ and H_1: $\pi \neq .50$. The significance level is .05, and the sample size is 9.
   a. What is the decision rule?
   b. There were five successes. What is your decision regarding the null hypothesis?

   2. **a.** Reject 0, 1, 8, 9. **b.** H_0 is not rejected.
3. Calorie Watchers has low-calorie breakfasts, lunches, and dinners. If you join the club, you receive two packaged meals a day. CW claims that you can eat anything you want for the third meal and still lose at least five pounds the first month. Members of the club are weighed before commencing the program and again at the end of the first month. The experiences of a random sample of 11 enrollees are:

Name	Weight Change	Name	Weight Change
Foster	Lost	Hercher	Lost
Taoka	Lost	Camder	Lost
Lange	Gained	Hinckle	Lost
Rousos	Lost	Hinkley	Lost
Stephens	No change	Justin	Lost
Cantrell	Lost		

We are interested in whether there has been a weight loss as a result of the Calorie Watchers program.

a. State H_0 and H_1.

b. Using the .05 level of significance, what is the decision rule?

c. What is your conclusion about the Calorie Watchers program?

4. **a.** H_0: $\pi \leq .50$, H_1: $\pi > .50$ **b.** Reject if 10 or more +. **c.** Increased self-confidence.

4. Many new stockbrokers resist giving presentations to bankers and certain other groups. Sensing this lack of self-confidence, management arranged to have a confidence-building seminar for a sample of new stockbrokers and enlisted Career Boosters for a three-week course. Before the first session, Career Boosters measured the level of confidence of each participant. It was measured again after the three-week seminar. The before and after levels of self-confidence for the 14 in the course are shown below. Self-confidence was classified as being either negative, low, high, or very high.

Stockbroker	Before Seminar	After Seminar	Stockbroker	Before Seminar	After Seminar
J. M. Martin	Negative	Low	F. M. Orphey	Low	Very high
T. D. Jagger	Negative	Negative	C. C. Ford	Low	High
A. D. Hammer	Low	High	A. R. Utz	Negative	Low
T. A. Jones, Jr.	Very high	Low	M. R. Murphy	Low	High
J. J. Cornwall	Low	High	P. A. Arms	Negative	Low
D. A. Skeen	Low	High	B. K. Pierre	Low	High
C. B. Simmer	Negative	High	N. S. Walker	Low	Very high

The purpose of this study is to find whether Career Boosters was effective in raising the self-confidence of the new stockbrokers. That is, was the level of self-confidence higher after the seminar than before it? Use the .05 significance level.

a. State the null and alternate hypotheses.

b. Using the .05 level of significance, state the decision rule — either in words or in chart form.

c. Draw conclusions about the seminar offered by Career Boosters.

Using the Normal Approximation to the Binomial

If the number of observations in the sample is larger than 10, the normal distribution can be used to approximate the binomial. Recall in Chapter 6, we computed the mean of the binomial distribution from $\mu = \pi n$ and the standard deviation from $\sigma = \sqrt{n\pi(1 - \pi)}$. In this case $\pi = .50$, so the equations reduce to $\mu = .50n$ and $\sigma = .50\sqrt{n}$, respectively.

The test statistic z is

SIGN TEST, LARGE SAMPLE

$$z = \frac{(X \pm .50) - \mu}{\sigma} \qquad \textbf{[16–1]}$$

If the number of pluses or minuses is *more than n/2*, we use the following form as the test statistic:

SIGN TEST, LARGE SAMPLE, + SIGNS MORE THAN $n/2$

$$z = \frac{(X - .50) - \mu}{\sigma} = \frac{(X - .50) - .50n}{.50\sqrt{n}} \quad [16\text{–}2]$$

If the number of pluses or minuses is *less than n/2,* the test statistic z is

SIGN TEST, LARGE SAMPLE, + SIGNS LESS THAN $n/2$

$$z = \frac{(X + .50) - \mu}{\sigma} = \frac{(X + .50) - .50n}{.50\sqrt{n}} \quad [16\text{–}3]$$

In the preceding formulas, X is the number of plus (or minus) signs. The value $+.50$ or $-.50$ is the *continuity correction factor,* discussed in Chapter 7. Briefly, it is applied when a continuous distribution such as the normal distribution (which we are using) is used to approximate a discrete distribution (the binomial).

EXAMPLE

The market research department of Cola, Inc. has been given the assignment of testing a new soft drink. Two versions of the drink are considered — a rather sweet drink and a somewhat bitter one. A preference test is to be conducted consisting of a sample of 64 consumers. Each will taste both the sweet cola (labeled A) and the bitter one (labeled B) and indicate a preference. How will the test of hypothesis be conducted, and what cola, if any, is preferred?

SOLUTION

Step 1: State the null and alternate hypotheses.

H_0: $\pi = .50$ There is no preference.
H_1: $\pi \neq .50$ There is a preference.

Step 2: Select a level of significance. It is the .05 level.

Step 3: Select the test statistic. It is z, given in formula 16–1.

$$z = \frac{(X \pm .50) - \mu}{\sigma}$$

where $\mu = .50n$ and $\sigma = .50\sqrt{n}$.

Step 4: Formulate the decision rule. Referring to Appendix D, Areas under the Normal Curve, for a two-tailed test (because H_1 states that $\pi \neq .50$) and the .05 significance level, the critical values are $+1.96$ and -1.96. Recall from Chapter 10 that for a two-tailed test we split the rejection probability in half and place one half in each tail. That is, $\alpha/2 = .05/2 = .025$. Continuing, $.5000 - .0250 = .4750$. Searching for .4750 in the body of the table and reading the z value in the left margin gives 1.96, the critical value. Therefore, do not reject H_0 if the computed z value is between $+1.96$ and -1.96. Otherwise, reject H_0 and accept H_1.

Step 5: Compute z, compare the computed value with the critical value, and make a decision regarding H_0. Preference for cola A was given a "+" sign and preference for B a "−" sign. Out of the 64 in the sample, 42 preferred the sweet cola, A. Therefore, there are 42 pluses. Since 42 is *more than* $n/2 = 64/2 = 32$, we use formula 16–2 for z:

$$z = \frac{(X - .50) - .50n}{.50\sqrt{n}} = \frac{(42 - .50) - .50(64)}{.50\sqrt{64}} = 2.38$$

The computed z of 2.38 is beyond the critical value of 1.96. Therefore, the null hypothesis of no difference is rejected at the .05 significance level.

There is a difference in consumer preference. That is, we conclude consumers prefer one cola over another.

The *p*-value is the probability of finding a *z* value larger than 2.38 or smaller than −2.38. From Appendix D, the probability of finding a *z* value greater than 2.38 is .5000 − .4913 = .0087. Thus, the two-tailed *p*-value is .0174. So the probability that the null hypothesis is true is less than 2 percent.

Self-Review 16–2

The Human Resources Department in a large automobile assembly plant began blood pressure screening and education for the 100 employees in the Paint Department the first of the year. As a follow-up in July the same 100 employees were again screened for blood pressure and 80 showed a reduction. Can we conclude the screening was effective in reducing blood pressure readings?

(a) State the null hypothesis and the alternate hypothesis.
(b) What is the decision rule for a significance level of .05?
(c) Compute the value of the test statistic.
(d) What is your decision regarding the null hypothesis?
(e) Interpret your decision.

Exercises

5. A sample of 45 overweight men participated in an exercise program. At the conclusion of the program 32 had lost weight. At the .05 significance level, can we conclude the program is effective?
   a. State the null hypothesis and the alternate hypothesis.
   b. State the decision rule.
   c. Compute the value of the test statistic.
   d. What is your decision regarding the null hypothesis?
6. A sample of 60 college students was given a special training program designed to improve their study and time management skills. One month after completing the course the students were contacted and asked whether the skills learned in the program were effective. A total of 42 responded yes. At the .05 significance level, can we conclude the program is effective?
   a. State the null hypothesis and the alternate hypothesis.
   b. State the decision rule.
   c. Compute the value of the test statistic.
   d. What is your decision regarding the null hypothesis?

6. **a.** H_0: $\pi \leq .50$, H_1: $\pi > .50$ **b.** Reject if $z > 1.65$ **c.** $z = 2.97$ **d.** Reject H_0.

7. Pierre's Restaurant announced that on Thursday night the menu would consist of unusual gourmet items, such as squid, rabbit, snails from Scotland, and dandelion greens. As part of a larger survey, a sample of 81 regular customers was asked whether they preferred the regular menu or the gourmet menu. Forty-three preferred the gourmet menu. Using the sign test and the .02 level, test whether the customers liked the gourmet menu better than the regular menu. Justify your conclusion.
8. Assembly workers at Computer Associates assemble just one or two subassemblies and insert them in a frame. The executives at CA think that the employees would have more pride in their work if they assembled all of the subassemblies and tested the complete computer. A sample of 25 employees was selected to experiment with the idea. The null hypothesis is that the employees have no preference. After a training program, each was asked his or her preference. Twenty liked assembling the entire unit and testing it. At the .05 level, use the sign test to arrive at a decision regarding employee preference. Explain the steps you used to arrive at your decision.

8. **a.** H_0: $\pi \leq .50$, H_1: $\pi > .50$ $z = 2.80$ Reject H_0.

Testing a Hypothesis about a Median

Most of the tests of hypothesis we have conducted so far involved the population mean or a proportion. The sign test is one of the few tests that can be used to test the value of a median. Recall from Chapter 3 that the median is the value above which half of the observations lie and below which the other half lie. For hourly wages of $7, $9, $11, and $18, the median is $10. Half of the wages are above $10 an hour and the other half below $10.

To conduct a test of hypothesis, a value above the median is assigned a plus sign, and a value below the median is assigned a minus sign. If a value is the same as the median, it is dropped from further analysis. The procedure is identical to that followed in the small-sample and large-sample sign tests just discussed.

EXAMPLE

A study several years ago by the Customer Research Department of Superior Grocers found the median weekly amount spent on grocery items by young married couples was $123. The CEO would like to repeat the research to determine whether the median amount spent has changed. Customer Research's new sample information showed that, in a random sample of 102 young adult married couples, 60 spent more than $123 last week on grocery items, 40 spent less, and 2 spent exactly $123. At the .10 significance level, is it reasonable to conclude that the median amount spent is not equal to $123?

SOLUTION

If the population median is $123, then we expect about half the sampled couples to have spent more than $123 last week and about half less than $123. After discarding the two customers who spent exactly $123, we would expect 50 to be above the median and 50 to be below the median. Is this difference attributable to chance, or is the median some value other than $123? The statistical test for the median will help answer that question.

The null and the alternate hypotheses are:

H_0: Median $= \$123$
H_1: Median $\neq \$123$

This is a two-tailed test because the alternate hypothesis does not indicate a direction. That is, we are not interested in whether the median is less than or greater than $123, only that it is different from $123. The test statistic meets the binomial assumptions. That is:

1. An observation is either larger or smaller than the proposed median, so there are only two possible outcomes.
2. The probability of a success remains constant at .50. That is, $\pi = .50$.
3. The couples selected as part of the sample represent independent trials.
4. We count the number of successes in a fixed number of trials. In this case we consider 100 couples and count the number who spend more than $123 per week on grocery items.

However, the sample size is 100 and π is .50, so $n\pi = 100(.50) = 50$ and $n(1 - \pi) = 100(1 - .50) = 50$, which are both larger than 5, so we use the normal distribution to approximate the binomial. That is, we actually use the standard normal distribution as the test statistic. The significance level is .10, so $\alpha/2 = .10/2 = .05$ of the area is in each tail of a normal distribution. From Appendix D, which shows the areas under a normal curve, the critical values are -1.65 and 1.65. The decision rule is to reject H_0 if z is less than -1.65 or greater than 1.65.

We use formula 16–2 for z because 60 is greater than $n/2$ ($100/2 = 50$).

$$z = \frac{(X - .50) - .50n}{.50\sqrt{n}} = \frac{(60 - .5) - .50(100)}{.50\sqrt{100}} = 1.90$$

The null hypothesis is rejected because the computed value of 1.90 is greater than the critical value of 1.65. The median amount spent per week on grocery items by young couples is *not* \$123. The p-value for this test is .0574, found by 2(.5000 − .4713).

Self-Review 16–3

After receiving the results regarding the weekly amount spent on grocery items for young couples from the Consumer Research Department, the CEO of Superior Grocers wondered whether the same was true for senior citizen couples. In this case the CEO wants the Customer Research Department to investigate whether the median weekly amount spent per week by senior citizens is *greater than* \$123. A sample of 64 senior citizen couples revealed 42 spent more than \$123 per week on grocery items. Use the .05 significance level.

Exercises

9. A trade journal reported that the median starting salary for systems engineers is \$80,000. A group of recent graduates believe this amount is too low. In a random sample of 205 systems engineers who recently graduated from engineering school, 170 began with a salary of more than \$80,000 and five earned a salary of exactly \$80,000.
- **a.** State the null and alternate hypotheses.
- **b.** State the decision rule. Use the .05 significance level.
- **c.** Do the necessary computations and interpret the results.

10. Central Airlines claims that the median price of a round-trip ticket to Jackson Hole, Wyoming, is \$503. This claim is being challenged by the Association of Travel Agents, who believe the median price is less than \$503. To resolve the issue, a random sample of 400 round-trip tickets was selected. Of these, 160 tickets were below \$503. None of the tickets were exactly \$503. Let $\alpha = .05$.
- **a.** State the null and alternate hypotheses.
- **b.** Reach a decision regarding the controversy.

10. a. H_1: Median $< \$503$
b. Reject if $z < -1.65$
$z = -3.95$

Wilcoxon Signed-Rank Test

The paired t test, described in Chapter 11, had two requirements. First, the samples must be dependent. Recall that dependent samples are characterized by a measurement, some type of intervention, and then another measurement. For example, a large company began a "wellness" program at the start of the year. Suppose 20 workers enrolled in the weight reduction portion of the program. To begin, all participants were weighed. Next they dieted, did the exercise, and so forth in an attempt to lose weight. At the end of the program, which lasted six months, all participants were weighed again. The difference in their weight between the start and the end of the program is the variable of interest. Note that there is a measurement, an intervention, and then another measurement.

The second requirement for the paired t test is that the distribution of the differences follow a normal distribution. In the company wellness example in the previous paragraph, this would require that the differences in the weights of the 20 participants

follow the normal distribution. In that case this assumption is reasonable. However, there are instances when we want to study the differences between dependent observations where we cannot assume that the distribution of the differences approximates a normal distribution. Frequently we encounter a problem with the normality assumption when the level of measurement in the samples is ordinal, rather than interval or ratio. For example, suppose there are 10 surgical patients on 3 East today. The nursing supervisor asks Nurse Benner and Nurse Jurris to rate each of the 10 patients on a scale of 1 to 10, based on the difficulty of patient care. The distribution of the differences probably would not approximate the normal distribution, and, therefore, the paired *t* test would not be appropriate.

In 1945, Frank Wilcoxon developed a nonparametric test, based on the differences in dependent samples, where the normality assumption is not required. This test is called the **Wilcoxon signed-rank test.** The following example details its application.

EXAMPLE

Fricker's is a family restaurant chain located primarily in the southeastern part of the United States. They offer a full dinner menu, but their specialty is chicken. Recently, Bernie Frick, the owner and founder, developed a new spicy flavor for the batter in which the chicken is cooked. Before replacing the current flavor, he wants to conduct some tests to be sure that patrons will like the spicy flavor better.

To begin, Bernie selects a random sample of 15 customers. Each member of the sample is given a small sample of the current chicken and asked to rate its overall taste on a scale of 1 to 20. A value near 20 indicates the participant liked the flavor, whereas a score near 0 indicates they did not like the flavor. Next, the same 15 participants are given a sample of the new chicken with the spicier flavor and again asked to rate its taste on a scale of 1 to 20. The results are reported below. Is it reasonable to conclude that the spicy flavor is preferred? Use the .05 significance level.

Participant	Spicy Flavor Score	Current Flavor Score	Participant	Spicy Flavor Score	Current Flavor Score
Arquette	14	12	Garcia	19	10
Jones	8	16	Sundar	18	10
Fish	6	2	Miller	16	13
Wagner	18	4	Peterson	18	2
Badenhop	20	12	Boggart	4	13
Hall	16	16	Hein	7	14
Fowler	14	5	Whitten	16	4
Virost	6	16			

SOLUTION

The samples are dependent or related. That is, the participants are asked to rate both flavors of chicken. Thus, if we compute the difference between the rating for the spicy flavor and the current flavor, the resulting value shows the amount the participants favor one flavor over the other. If we choose to subtract the current flavor score from the spicy flavor score, a positive result is the "amount" the participant favors the spicy flavor. Negative difference scores indicate the participant favored the current flavor. Because of the somewhat subjective nature of the scores, we are not sure the distribution of the differences follows the normal distribution. We decide to use the nonparametric Wilcoxon signed-rank test.

As usual, we will use the five-step hypothesis-testing procedure. The null hypothesis is that there is no difference in the rating of the chicken flavors by the participants. That is, as many participants in the study rated the spicy flavor higher as rated the regular flavor higher. The alternate hypothesis is that the ratings are higher for the spicy flavor. More formally:

H_0: There is no difference in the ratings of the two flavors.
H_1: The spicy ratings are higher.

This is a one-tailed test. Why? Because Bernie Frick, the owner of Fricker's, will want to change his chicken flavor only if the sample participants show that the population of customers like the new flavor better. The significance level is .05, as stated in the problem above.

The steps to conduct the Wilcoxon signed-rank test are as follows.

1. Compute the difference between the spicy flavor score and the current flavor score for each participant. For example, Arquette's spicy flavor score was 14 and current flavor score was 12, so the amount of the difference is 2. For Jones, the difference is -8, found by $8 - 16$, and for Fish it is 4, found by $6 - 2$. The differences for all participants are shown in column 4 of Table 16–3.
2. Only the positive and negative differences are considered further. That is, if the difference in flavor scores is 0, that participant is dropped from further analysis and the number in the sample reduced. From Table 16–3, Hall, the sixth participant, scored both the spicy and the current flavor a 16. Hence, Hall is dropped from the study and the usable sample size reduced from 15 to 14.
3. Determine the absolute differences for the values computed in column 4. Recall that in an absolute difference we ignore the sign of the difference. The absolute differences are shown in column 5.
4. Next, rank the absolute differences from smallest to largest. Arquette, the first participant scored the spicy chicken a 14 and the current a 12. The difference of 2 in the two scores is the smallest absolute difference, so it is given a ranking of 1. The next largest difference is 3, given by Miller, so it is given a rank of 2. The other differences are ranked in a similar manner. There are three participants who rated the difference in the flavor as 8. That is, Jones, Badenhop, and Sundar each had a difference of 8 between their rating of the spicy flavor and the current flavor. To resolve this problem, we average the ranks involved and report the average rank for each. This situation involves the ranks 5, 6, and 7, so all three participants are assigned the rank of 6. The same situation occurs for those participants with a

TABLE 16–3 Flavor Rating for Current and Spicy Flavors

(1) Participant	(2) Spicy Score	(3) Current Score	(4) Difference in Score	(5) Absolute Difference	(6) Rank	(7) Signed Rank R^+	R^-
Arquette	14	12	2	2	1	1	
Jones	8	16	−8	8	6		6
Fish	6	2	4	4	3	3	
Wagner	18	4	14	14	13	13	
Badenhop	20	12	8	8	6	6	
Hall	16	16	*	*	*	*	
Fowler	14	5	9	9	9	9	
Virost	6	16	−10	10	11		11
Garcia	19	10	9	9	9	9	
Sunder	18	10	8	8	6	6	
Miller	16	13	3	3	2	2	
Peterson	18	2	16	16	14	14	
Boggart	4	13	−9	9	9		9
Hein	7	14	−7	7	4		4
Whitten	16	4	12	12	12	12	
Total						75	30

difference of 9. The ranks involved are 8, 9, and 10, so those participants are assigned a rank of 9.

5. Each assigned rank in column 6 is then given the same sign as the original difference, and the results are reported in column 7. For example, the second participant has a difference score of −8 and a rank of 6. This value is located in the R^- section of column 7.
6. The R^+ and R^- columns are totaled. The sum of the positive ranks is 75 and the sum of the negative ranks is 30. The smaller of the two rank sums is used as the test statistic and referred to as T.

The critical values for the Wilcoxon signed-rank test are located in Appendix H. A portion of that table is repeated on the following page. The α row is used for one-tailed tests and the 2α row for two-tailed tests. In this case we want to show that customers like the spicy taste better, which is a one-tailed test, so we select the α row. We chose the .05 significance level, so move to the right to the column headed .05. Go down that column to the row where n is 14. (Recall that one person in the study rated the chicken flavors the same and was dropped from the study, making the usable sample size 14.) The value at the intersection is 25, so the critical value is 25. The decision rule is to reject the null hypothesis if the *smaller* of the rank sums is 25 or less. The value obtained from Appendix H is the *largest value in the rejection region.* In this case the smaller rank sum is 30, so the decision is not to reject the null hypothesis. We cannot conclude there is a difference in the flavor ratings between the current and the spicy. Mr. Frick has not shown that customers prefer the new flavor.

n	2α .15 α .075	.10 .050	.05 .025	.04 .020	.03 .015	.02 .010	.01 .005
4	0						
5	1	0					
6	2	2	0	0			
7	4	3	2	1	0	0	
8	7	5	3	3	2	1	0
9	9	8	5	5	4	3	1
10	12	10	8	7	6	5	3
11	16	13	10	9	8	7	5
12	19	17	13	12	11	9	7
13	24	21	17	16	14	12	9
14	28	25	21	19	18	15	12
15	33	30	25	23	21	19	15

Self-Review 16–4

A record of the production for each machine operator was kept over a period of time. Certain changes in the production procedure were suggested, and 11 operators were picked as an experimental test group to determine whether the new procedures were worthwhile. Their production rates before and after the new procedures were established are as follows:

Operator	Production Before	Production After	Operator	Production Before	Production After
S. M.	17	18	U. Z.	10	22
D. J.	21	23	Y. U.	20	19
M. D.	25	22	U. T.	17	20
B. B.	15	25	Y. H.	24	30
M. F.	10	28	Y. Y.	23	26
A. A.	16	16			

(a) How many usable pairs are there? That is, what is n?
(b) Using the Wilcoxon signed-rank test, determine whether the new procedures actually increased production. Use the .05 level and a one-tailed test.

Exercises

11. An industrial psychologist selected a random sample of seven young urban professional couples who own their homes. The size of their home (square feet) is compared with that of their parents. At the .05 significance level, can we conclude that the yuppies live in larger homes?

Couple Name	Professional	Parent	Couple Name	Professional	Parent
Gordon	1,725	1,175	Kuhlman	1,290	1,360
Sharkey	1,310	1,120	Welch	1,880	1,750
Uselding	1,670	1,420	Anderson	1,530	1,440
Bell	1,520	1,640			

12. $T = 11$, do not reject.

12. One of the major car manufacturers is studying the effect of regular versus high-octane gasoline in its economy cars. Ten executives are selected and asked to maintain records on the number of miles traveled per gallon of gas. The results are:

	Miles per Gallon			Miles per Gallon	
Executive	**Regular**	**High-Octane**	**Executive**	**Regular**	**High-Octane**
Bowers	25	28	Rau	38	40
Demars	33	31	Greolke	29	29
Grasser	31	35	Burns	42	37
DeToto	45	44	Snow	41	44
Kleg	42	47	Lawless	30	44

At the .05 significance level, is there a difference in the number of miles traveled per gallon between regular and high-octane gasoline?

13. A new assembly-line procedure has been suggested by Mr. Mump. To test whether the new procedure is superior to the old procedure, a sample group of 15 men was selected at random. First their production under the old system was determined. Then the new Mump procedure was introduced. After an appropriate break-in period, their production was measured again. The results were:

	Production			Production	
Employee	**Old System**	**Mump Method**	**Employee**	**Old System**	**Mump Method**
A	60	64	I	87	84
B	40	52	J	80	80
C	59	58	K	56	57
D	30	37	L	21	21
E	70	71	M	99	108
F	78	83	N	50	56
G	43	46	0	56	62
H	40	52			

At the .05 significance level can we conclude the production is greater using the Mump method?

a. State the null and alternate hypotheses.
b. State the decision rule.
c. Arrive at a decision regarding the null hypothesis.

14. It has been suggested that daily production of a subassembly would be increased if better portable lighting were installed and background music and free coffee and doughnuts were provided during the day. Management agreed to try the scheme for a limited time. The number of subassemblies produced per week by a sample of employees follows.

Employee	Past Production Record	Production after Installing Lighting, Music, etc.	Employee	Past Production Record	Production after Installing Lighting, Music, etc.
JD	23	33	WWJ	21	25
SB	26	26	OP	25	22
MD	24	30	CD	21	23
RCF	17	25	PA	16	17
MF	20	19	RRT	20	15
UHH	24	22	AT	17	9
IB	30	29	QQ	23	30

14. a. H_0: Production has not changed.
b. H_1: Production has increased.
c. We selected .05.
d. Reject if $T \leq 21$.
e. $T = 34$, H_0 is not rejected.

Using the Wilcoxon signed-rank test, determine whether the suggested changes are worthwhile.

a. State the null hypothesis.
b. You decide on the alternate hypothesis.
c. You decide on the level of significance.
d. State the decision rule.
e. Compute T and arrive at a decision.

Wilcoxon Rank-Sum Test

Test using independent samples

One test specifically designed to determine whether two independent samples came from equal populations is the **Wilcoxon rank-sum test.** This test is an alternative to the two-sample t test described in Chapter 11. Recall that the t test requires that the two populations follow the normal distribution and have equal population variances. These conditions are not required for the Wilcoxon rank-sum test.

The Wilcoxon rank-sum test is based on the average of ranks. The data are ranked as if the observations were part of a single sample. If the null hypothesis is true, then the ranks will be about evenly distributed between the two samples, and the average of the ranks for the two samples will be about the same. That is, the low, medium, and high ranks should be about equally divided between the two samples. If the alternate hypothesis is true, one of the samples will have more of the lower ranks and, thus, a smaller rank average. The other sample will have more of the higher ranks and, therefore, a larger average. If each of the samples contains *at least eight observations,* the standard normal distribution is used as the test statistic. The formula is:

WILCOXON RANK-SUM TEST

$$z = \frac{W - \dfrac{n_1(n_1 + n_2 + 1)}{2}}{\sqrt{\dfrac{n_1 n_2(n_1 + n_2 + 1)}{12}}} \qquad [16\text{–}4]$$

where:

n_1 is the number of observations from the first population.
n_2 is the number of observations from the second population.
W is the sum of the ranks from the first population.

EXAMPLE

Dan Thompson, the president of CEO Airlines, recently noted an increase in the number of no-shows for flights out of Atlanta. He is particularly interested in determining whether there are more no-shows for flights that originate from Atlanta compared with flights leaving Chicago. A sample of nine flights from Atlanta and eight from Chicago are reported in Table 16–4. At the .05 significance level, can we conclude that there are more no-shows for the flights originating in Atlanta?

TABLE 16–4 Number of No-Shows for Scheduled Flights

Atlanta	Chicago	Atlanta	Chicago
11	13	20	9
15	14	24	17
10	10	22	21
18	8	25	
11	16		

SOLUTION

If the populations of no-shows followed the normal distribution and had equal variances, the two-sample t test, discussed in Chapter 11, would be appropriate. In this case Mr. Thompson believes these two conditions cannot be met. Therefore, a nonparametric test, the Wilcoxon rank-sum test, is appropriate.

If the number of no-shows is the same for Atlanta and Chicago, then we expect the means of the two ranks to be about the same. If the number of no-shows is not the same, we expect the two sums of ranks to be quite different.

Mr. Thompson believes there are more no-shows for Atlanta flights. Thus, a one-tailed test is appropriate, with the rejection region located in the upper tail. The null and alternate hypotheses are:

H_0: The distribution of no-shows is the same for Atlanta and Chicago.
H_1: The distribution of no-shows is larger for Atlanta than for Chicago.

The test statistic follows the standard normal distribution. At the .05 significance level, we find from Appendix D the critical value of z is 1.65. The null hypothesis is rejected if the computed value of z is greater than 1.65.

The alternate hypothesis is that there are more no-shows in Atlanta, which means that distribution is larger and is located to the right of the Chicago distribution. The value of W is calculated for the Atlanta group and is found to be 96.5, which is the sum of the ranks for the no-shows for the Atlanta flights. The details of rank assignment are shown in Table 16–5. We rank the observations from *both* samples as if they were a single group. The Chicago flight with only 8 no-shows had the fewest, so it is assigned a rank of 1. The Chicago flight with 9 no-shows is ranked 2, and so on. The Atlanta flight with 25 no-shows is the highest, so it is assigned the largest rank, 17. There are also two instances of tied ranks. There are an Atlanta and a Chicago flight that each had 10 no-shows and two Atlanta flights with 11 no-shows. How do we handle these ties? The solution is to average the ranks involved and assign the average rank to both flights. In the case involving 10 no-shows the ranks involved are 3 and 4. The mean of these ranks is 3.5, so a rank of 3.5 is assigned to both the Atlanta and the Chicago flights with 10 no-shows.

TABLE 16–5 Ranked Number of No-Shows for Scheduled Flights

Atlanta		Chicago	
No-Shows	Rank	No-Shows	Rank
11	5.5	13	7
15	9	14	8
10	3.5	10	3.5
18	12	8	1
11	5.5	16	10
20	13	9	2
24	16	17	11
22	15	21	14
25	17		
	96.5		56.5

Note from Table 16–5 that there are nine flights originating in Atlanta and eight in Chicago, so $n_1 = 9$ and $n_2 = 8$. Computing z from formula 16–4 gives:

$$z = \frac{W - \frac{n_1(n_1 + n_2 + 1)}{2}}{\sqrt{\frac{n_1 n_2(n_1 + n_2 + 1)}{12}}} = \frac{96.5 - \frac{9(9 + 8 + 1)}{2}}{\sqrt{\frac{9(8)(9 + 8 + 1)}{12}}} = 1.49$$

Because the computed z value (1.49) is less than 1.65, the null hypothesis is not rejected. The evidence does not show a difference in the typical number of no-shows. That is, it appears that the number of no-shows is the same in Atlanta as in Chicago. The p-value is .0681, found by determining the area to the right of 1.49 (.5000 − .4319).

The MegaStat software can produce the same results. The MegaStat p-value is .0677, which is close to the value we calculated. The difference is due to rounding in the system and correcting for ties.

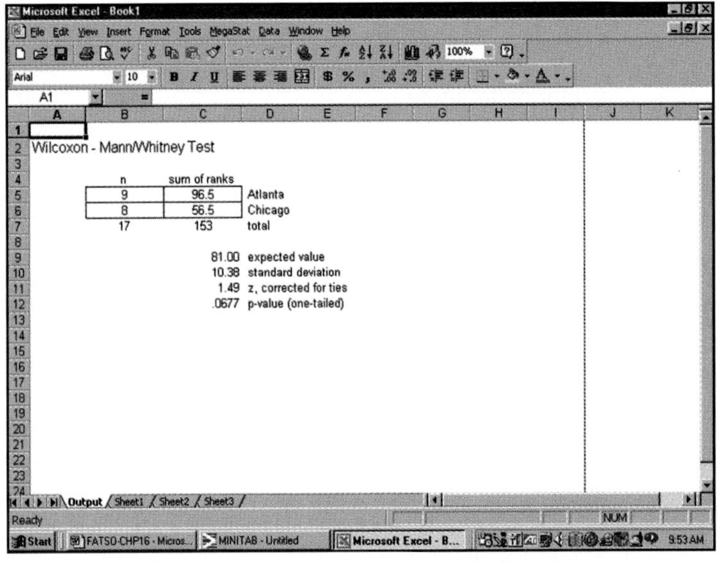

In using the Wilcoxon rank-sum test, you may number the two populations in either order. However, once you have made a choice, W must be the sum of the ranks identified as population 1. If, in the no-show example, the population of Chicago was identified as number 1, the direction of the alternate hypothesis would be changed, but the *absolute value of z* would remain the same.

H_0: The distribution of no-shows is the same for Chicago and Atlanta.
H_1: The distribution of no-shows is smaller for Chicago than for Atlanta.

The computed value of z is −1.49, found by:

$$z = \frac{W - \frac{n_1(n_1 + n_2 + 1)}{2}}{\sqrt{\frac{n_1 n_2(n_1 + n_2 + 1)}{12}}} = \frac{56.5 - \frac{8(8 + 9 + 1)}{2}}{\sqrt{\frac{8(9)(8 + 9 + 1)}{12}}} = -1.49$$

Self-Review 16–5

The research director for a golf ball manufacturer wants to know whether there is a difference in the distribution of the distances traveled by two of the company's golf balls. Eight of their Dino brand and eight of their Maxi brand balls were hit by an automatic driver. The distances (in yards) were as follows:

Dino:	252, 263, 279, 273, 271, 265, 257, 280
Maxi:	262, 242, 256, 260, 258, 243, 239, 265

Assume the distributions are not normally distributed. At the .05 significance level, is there a difference between the two distributions?

Exercises

15. The following observations were randomly selected from populations that were not necessarily normally distributed. Use the .05 significance level, a two-tailed test, and the Wilcoxon rank-sum test to determine whether there is a difference between the two populations.

Population A:	38, 45, 56, 57, 61, 69, 70, 79
Population B:	26, 31, 35, 42, 51, 52, 57, 62

16. $W = 80$, $z = -0.096$, Do not reject H_0.

16. The following observations were randomly selected from populations that are not necessarily normally distributed. Use the .05 significance level, a two-tailed test, and the Wilcoxon rank-sum test to determine whether there is a difference between the two populations.

Population A:	12, 14, 15, 19, 23, 29, 33, 40, 51
Population B:	13, 16, 19, 21, 22, 33, 35, 43

17. Two groups of professional musicians — rock and country-western — are being studied. One facet of the study involves the age of those in the two groups. Assume the populations of ages do not follow the normal distribution. A sample of 10 rock and 12 country-western musicians revealed the following ages, in years.

Rock:	28, 16, 42, 29, 31, 22, 50, 42, 23, 25
Country-western:	26, 42, 65, 38, 29, 32, 59, 42, 27, 41, 46, 18

At the .05 significance level, can we conclude the country-western singers are older?

18. $W = 49.5$, $z = -3.031$, Reject H_0.

18. One group was taught an assembly procedure using a standard sequence of steps and another group was taught a new experimental technique. The time to complete the assembly, in seconds, for a sample of workers is shown below.

Current method:	41, 36, 42, 39, 36, 48, 49, 38
Experimental:	21, 27, 36, 20, 19, 21, 39, 24, 22

At the .05 significance level, can we conclude the experimental method is faster? Assume that the distribution of assembly lines is not normal.

Kruskal-Wallis Test: Analysis of Variance by Ranks

Kruskal-Wallis test less restrictive than ANOVA

The analysis of variance (ANOVA) procedure discussed in Chapter 12 was concerned with whether several population means are equal. The data were interval or ratio level. Also, it was assumed the populations follow the normal distribution and their standard deviations were equal. What if the data are ordinal scale and/or the populations do not follow a normal distribution? W. H. Kruskal and W. A. Wallis reported a nonparametric test in 1952 requiring only ordinal-level (ranked) data. No assumptions about the shape of the populations are required. The test is referred to as the **Kruskal-Wallis one-way analysis of variance by ranks.**

For the Kruskal-Wallis test to be applied, the samples selected from the populations must be *independent.* For example, if samples from three groups — executives, staff, and supervisors — are to be selected and interviewed, the responses of one group (say, the executives) must in no way influence the responses of the others.

To compute the Kruskal-Wallis test statistic, (1) all the samples are combined, (2) the combined values are ordered from low to high, and (3) the ordered values are *replaced by ranks, starting with 1 for the smallest value.* An example will clarify the procedure.

EXAMPLE

A management seminar consists of executives from manufacturing, finance, and the trades. Before scheduling the seminar sessions, the seminar leader is interested in whether the three groups are equally knowledgeable about management principles. Plans are to take samples of the executives in manufacturing, in finance, and in trade and to administer a test to each executive. If there is no difference in the scores for the three distributions, the seminar leader will conduct just one session. However, if there is a difference in the scores, separate sessions will be given.

We will use the Kruskal-Wallis test instead of ANOVA because the seminar leader is unwilling to assume that (1) the populations of management scores follow the normal distribution or (2) the population standard deviations are the same.

SOLUTION

The usual first step in hypothesis testing is to state the null and the alternate hypotheses.

H_0: The distributions of the management scores for the populations of executives in manufacturing, finance, and trade are equal.
H_1: The distributions are not all equal.

The seminar leader selected the .05 level of risk.

The test statistic used for the Kruskal-Wallis test is designated H. Its formula is:

KRUSKAL-WALLIS TEST

$$H = \frac{12}{n(n+1)}\left[\frac{(\Sigma R_1)^2}{n_1} + \frac{(\Sigma R_2)^2}{n_2} + \cdots + \frac{(\Sigma R_k)^2}{n_k}\right] - 3(n+1) \qquad \textbf{[16–5]}$$

with $k - 1$ degrees of freedom (k is the number of populations), where:

$\Sigma R_1, \Sigma R_2, \ldots, \Sigma R_k$ are the sums of the ranks of samples $1, 2, \ldots, k$, respectively.
$n_1, n_2, \ldots, n_k$ are the sizes of samples $1, 2, \ldots, k$, respectively.
n is the combined number of observations for all samples.

Chi-square used if every sample is at least 5

The distribution of the sample H statistic is very close to the chi-square distribution with $k - 1$ degrees of freedom *if every sample size is at least 5.* Therefore, we will use chi-square in formulating the decision rule. In this example there are three populations — a population of executives in manufacturing, another for executives in finance, and a third population of trade executives. Thus, there are $k - 1$, or $3 - 1 = 2$ degrees of freedom. Refer to the chi-square table of critical values in Appendix I. The critical value for 2 degrees of freedom and the .05 level of risk is 5.991. Do not reject H_0 if the computed value of the test statistic H is less than or equal to 5.991. Reject H_0 if the computed value of H is greater than 5.991, and accept H_1.

The next step is to select random samples from the three populations. A sample of seven manufacturing, eight finance, and six trade executives was selected. Their scores on the test are recorded in Table 16–6.

TABLE 16–6 Management Test Scores for Manufacturing, Finance, and Trade Executives

Manufacturing Executives	Finance Executives	Trade Executives
56	103	42
39	87	38 ← tie for next lowest
48	51	89
38 ← tie for next lowest	95	75
73	68	35 ← lowest
50	42	61
62	107 ← highest score	
	89	

Considering the scores as a single population, the trade executive with a score of 35 is the lowest, so it is ranked 1. There are two scores of 38. To resolve this tie, each score is given a rank of 2.5, found by $(2 + 3)/2$. This process is continued for all scores. The highest score is 107, and that finance executive is given a rank of 21. The scores, the ranks, and the sum of the ranks for each of the three samples are given in Table 16–7.

TABLE 16–7 Scores, Ranks, and Sums of Ranks for Management Test Scores

Manufacturing Executives		Finance Executives		Trade Executives	
Scores	Ranks (R_1)	Scores	Ranks (R_2)	Scores	Ranks (R_3)
56	10.0	103	20.0	42	5.5
39	4.0	87	16.0	38	2.5
48	7.0	51	9.0	89	17.5
38	2.5	95	19.0	75	15.0
73	14.0	68	13.0	35	1.0
50	8.0	42	5.5	61	11.0
62	12.0	107	21.0		
		89	17.5		
	$\Sigma R_1 = 57.5$		$\Sigma R_2 = 121.0$		$\Sigma R_3 = 52.5$

Solving for H:

$$H = \frac{12}{n(n+1)}\left[\frac{(\Sigma R_1)^2}{n_1} + \frac{(\Sigma R_2)^2}{n_2} + \frac{(\Sigma R_3)^2}{n_3}\right] - 3(n+1)$$

$$= \frac{12}{21(21+1)}\left[\frac{57.5^2}{7} + \frac{121^2}{8} + \frac{52.5^2}{6}\right] - 3(21+1) = 5.736$$

Because the computed value of H (5.736) is not beyond 5.991, the null hypothesis is not rejected. There is no difference among the executives from manufacturing, finance, and trade with respect to their typical knowledge of management principles. From a practical standpoint, the seminar leader should consider offering only one session including executives from all areas.

The Kruskal-Wallis procedure is available on the MINITAB system. Output for the example regarding the knowledge of management principles of executives from several industries follows. The computed value of H is 5.74 and the p-value reported on the output is .057. This agrees with our earlier calculations.

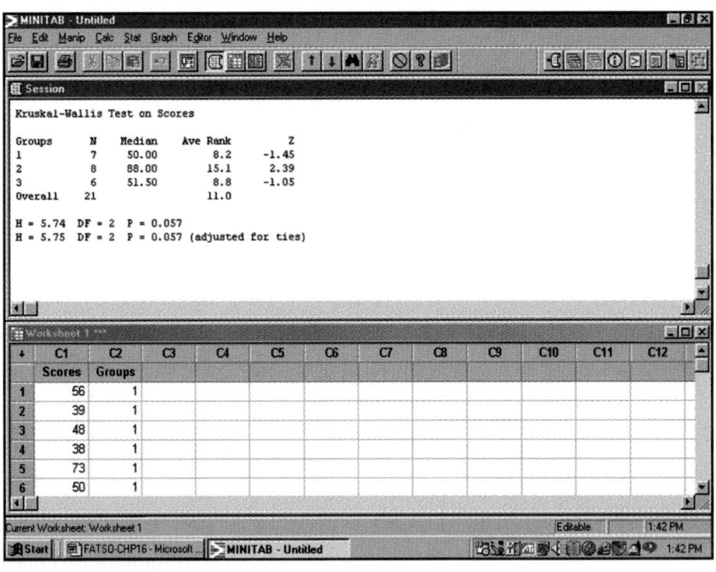

Recall from Chapter 12 that for the analysis of variance technique to apply, we assume that: (1) the populations are normally distributed, (2) these populations have equal standard deviations, and (3) the samples are selected independently. If these assumptions are met, we use the F distribution as the test statistic. If these assumptions cannot be met, we apply the distribution-free test by Kruskal-Wallis. To highlight the similarities between the two approaches, we will solve the example regarding executive knowledge of management principles using the ANOVA technique.

To begin, we state the null and the alternate hypotheses for the three groups.

H_0: $\mu_1 = \mu_2 = \mu_3$
H_1: The treatment means are not all the same.

Using the .05 significance level, with $k - 1 = 3 - 1 = 2$ degrees of freedom in the numerator and $n - k = 21 - 3 = 18$ degrees of freedom in the denominator, the critical value of F is 3.55. The decision rule is to reject the null hypothesis if the computed value of F is greater than 3.55. The output from the Excel system follows.

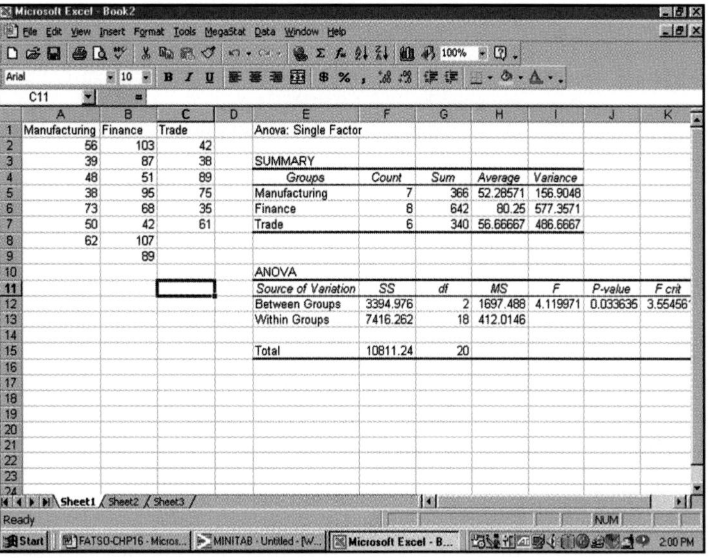

Manufacturing	Finance	Trade
56	103	42
39	87	38
48	51	89
38	95	75
73	68	35
50	42	61
62	107	
	89	

Anova: Single Factor

SUMMARY

Groups	Count	Sum	Average	Variance
Manufacturing	7	366	52.28571	156.9048
Finance	8	642	80.25	577.3571
Trade	6	340	56.66667	486.6667

ANOVA

Source of Variation	SS	df	MS	F	P-value	F crit
Between Groups	3394.976	2	1697.488	4.119971	0.033635	3.55456
Within Groups	7416.262	18	412.0146			
Total	10811.24	20				

From the above output, the computed value of F is 4.12 (rounded) and the p-value is .034 (also rounded). Our decision is to reject the null hypothesis and accept the alternate hypothesis. Using this test we conclude that the treatment means are not the same. That is, the knowledge of management principles is different among the three executive groups.

We have contradictory conclusions on the same data. How can this happen? If we compare the results using p-values, the answers are similar. For the Kruskal-Wallis test the p-value was .057, which is only slightly more than the significance level of .05, but our decision was not to reject H_0. The p-value using ANOVA is .034, which is not far beyond the critical value into the rejection region. So, to summarize, we just missed rejecting H_0 with the Kruskal-Wallis test, and we were just in the rejection region using ANOVA. The difference in the p-values is .023. Thus, the results are actually quite close in terms of the p-values.

Self-Review 16–6

The regional bank manager of Statewide Financial is interested in the turnover rate of personal checking accounts in four of the large branch banks. (Turnover rate is the speed at which the money in an account is deposited and withdrawn. An extremely active account may have a rate of 300; if only one or two checks were written, the rate could be about 30.) The turnover rates of the samples selected from the four branch banks are shown. Using the .01 level and the Kruskal-Wallis test, determine whether there is a difference in the turnover rates of the personal checking accounts among the four branches.

Englewood Branch	West Side Branch	Great Northern Branch	Sylvania Branch
208	91	302	99
307	62	103	116
199	86	319	189
142	91	340	103
91	80	180	100
296			131

Exercises

19. Under what conditions should the Kruskal-Wallis test be used instead of analysis of variance?

20. More than two populations.

20. Under what conditions should the Kruskal-Wallis test be used instead of the Wilcoxon rank-sum test?

21. The following sample data were obtained from three populations that were not necessarily normal.

Sample 1	Sample 2	Sample 3
50	48	39
54	49	41
59	49	44
59	52	47
65	56	51
	57	

a. State the null hypothesis.
b. Using the .05 level of risk, state the decision rule.
c. Compute the value of the test statistic.
d. What is your decision on the null hypothesis?

22. The following sample data were obtained from three populations where the variances were not equal, and you wish to compare the populations.

Sample 1	Sample 2	Sample 3
21	15	38
29	17	40
35	22	44
45	27	51
56	31	53
71		

22. a. H_0: Distributions the same. H_1: Distributions not the same.
b. Reject if $\chi^2 > 9.210$.
c. $H = 7.324$
d. H_0 is not rejected.

a. State the null hypothesis.
b. Using the .01 level of risk, state the decision rule.
c. Compute the value of the test statistic.
d. What is your decision on the null hypothesis?

23. Davis Outboard Motors, Inc. recently developed an epoxy painting process for corrosion protection on exhaust components. Bill Davis, the owner, wishes to determine whether the distributions of the length of life for the paint are equal for three different conditions: salt water, fresh water without weeds, and fresh water with a heavy concentration of weeds. Accelerated-life tests were conducted in the laboratory, and the number of hours the paint lasted before peeling was recorded.

Salt Water	Fresh Water	Fresh Water with Weeds
167.3	160.6	182.7
189.6	177.6	165.4
177.2	185.3	172.9
169.4	168.6	169.2
180.3	176.6	174.7

Use the Kruskal-Wallis test and the .01 level to determine whether the lasting quality of the paint is the same for the three water conditions.

24. $H = 0.31$
H_0 is not rejected.

Statistics in Action

Manatees are large mammals that like to float just below the water's surface. Because they float just below the surface, they are in danger from powerboat propellers. A study of the correlation between the number of powerboat registrations in coastal Florida counties and the number of accidental manatee deaths revealed a strong positive correlation. As a result, Florida created regions where powerboats are prohibited, so that manatees could thrive.

24. The National Turkey Association wants to experiment with three different food mixtures for very young turkeys. Since no experience exists regarding the three food mixtures, no assumptions can be made about the distribution of weights. The Kruskal-Wallis test must be used to test whether the turkeys are equal in weight after eating the food for a specified length of time. Five young turkeys were given food A, six were given food B, and five were given food C. Test at the .05 level whether the mean weights of the turkeys who ate food A, food B, and food C are equal.

Weight (in pounds)		
Food Mixture A	**Food Mixture B**	**Food Mixture C**
11.2	12.6	11.3
12.1	10.8	11.9
10.9	11.3	12.4
11.3	11.0	10.6
12.0	12.0	12.0
	10.7	

Rank-Order Correlation

In Chapter 13, we discussed r, the coefficient of correlation, which measures the association between two interval- or ratio-scaled variables. For example, the coefficient of correlation reports the association between the salary of executives and their years of experience, or the association between the number of miles a shipment had to travel and the number of days it took to arrive at its destination.

Charles Spearman, a British statistician, introduced a measure of correlation for ordinal-level data. This measure allows us to describe the relationship between sets of ranked data. For example, two staff members in the Office of Research at the University of the Valley are asked to rank 10 faculty research proposals. We want to study the association between the ratings of the two staff members. That is, do the two staff members rate the same proposals as the most worthy and the least worthy of funding? Spearman's coefficient of rank correlation, denoted r_s, provides a measure of the association.

The coefficient of rank correlation is computed using the following formula.

SPEARMAN'S COEFFICIENT OF RANK CORRELATION
$$r_s = 1 - \frac{6\Sigma d^2}{n(n^2 - 1)} \qquad \textbf{[16–6]}$$

where:

d is the difference between the ranks for each pair.

n is the number of paired observations.

Like the coefficient of correlation, the coefficient of rank correlation can assume any value from -1.00 up to 1.00. A value of -1.00 indicates perfect negative correlation and a value of 1.00 perfect positive correlation among the ranks. A rank correlation of 0 indicates that there is no strong association among the ranks. Rank correlations of $-.84$ and .84 indicate a strong association, but the former indicates an inverse relationship between the ranks and the latter a direct relationship.

EXAMPLE

A composite rating is given by executives to each college graduate joining a plastics manufacturing firm. The executive rating is an expression of the future potential of the college graduate. The ratings represent, of course, the ordinal level of measurement. The recent college graduate then enters an in-plant training program and is given another composite rating based on tests, opinions of group leaders, training officers, and so on. The executive ratings and the in-plant training ratings are given in Table 16–8.

TABLE 16–8 Executive Ratings and In-Plant Training Ratings for a Sample of Recent College Graduates

Graduate	Executive Rating, X	Training Rating, Y	Graduate	Executive Rating, X	Training Rating, Y
A	8	4	G	11	9
B	10	4	H	7	6
C	9	4	I	8	6
D	4	3	J	13	9
E	12	6	K	10	5
F	11	9	L	12	9

Calculate the coefficient of rank correlation. Interpret its value.

SOLUTION

It was decided to rank the variables from low to high. The lowest rating given by the executives was a 4 to graduate D, so it was ranked 1. The next lowest was a 7 to graduate H, so it was ranked 2. There were two graduates rated 8. The tie is resolved by giving each a rank of 3.5, which is the average of ranks 3 and 4. The same procedure is followed when there are more than two ratings tied. For example, note that the lowest training rating is 3, and it is given a rank of 1. Then there are three ratings of 4. The average of the three tied ranks is 3, found by $(2 + 3 + 4)/3$. This is illustrated along with the necessary calculations for r_s in Table 16–9.

TABLE 16–9 Calculations Needed for r_s

Graduate	Executive Rating, X	Training Rating, Y	Rank		Difference between Ranks, d	Difference Squared, d^2
			Executive	Training		
A	8	4	3.5	3.0	0.5	0.25
B	10	4	6.5	3.0	3.5	12.25
C	9	4	5.0	3.0	2.0	4.00
D	4	3	1.0	1.0	0	0
E	12	6	10.5	7.0	3.5	12.25
F	11	9	8.5	10.5	−2.0	4.00
G	11	9	8.5	10.5	−2.0	4.00
H	7	6	2.0	7.0	−5.0	25.00
I	8	6	3.5	7.0	−3.5	12.25
J	13	9	12.0	10.5	1.5	2.25
K	10	5	6.5	5.0	1.5	2.25
L	12	9	10.5	10.5	0	0
					0.0	78.50

r_s is .726, found by:

$$r_s = 1 - \frac{6\Sigma d^2}{n(n^2 - 1)} = 1 - \frac{6(78.50)}{12(143)} = .726$$

The value of .726 indicates a strong positive association between the ratings of the executives and the ratings of the training staff. The graduates that received high ratings from the executives also tended to be the ones that received high ratings from the training staff.

Testing the Significance of r_s

Testing whether correlation in the population is zero

In Chapter 13 we tested the significance of Pearson's *r*. For ranked data the question also arises whether the correlation in the population is actually zero. For instance, there were only 12 graduates sampled in the preceding example. In the solution to the example, the rank correlation coefficient of .726 indicates a rather strong relationship between the two sets of ranks. Is it possible that the correlation of .726 is due to chance and that the correlation among the ranks in the population is really 0? We will now conduct a test of significance to answer that question.

"Large" samples — 10 or more

For a sample of 10 or more, the significance of r_s is determined by computing *t* using the following formula. The sampling distribution of r_s follows the *t* distribution with $n - 2$ degrees of freedom.

HYPOTHESES TEST, RANK CORRELATION

$$t = r_s \sqrt{\frac{n - 2}{1 - r_s^2}} \quad \textbf{[16–7]}$$

The null and the alternate hypotheses are:

H_0: The rank correlation in the population is zero.
H_1: There is a positive association among the ranks.

The decision rule is to reject H_0 if the computed value of *t* is greater than 1.812 (from Appendix F, .05 significance level, one-tailed test, and 10 degrees of freedom, found by $n - 2 = 12 - 2 = 10$).

The computed value of *t* is 3.338:

$$t = r_s \sqrt{\frac{n - 2}{1 - r_s^2}} = .726 \sqrt{\frac{12 - 2}{1 - (.726)^2}} = 3.338$$

H_0 is rejected because the computed *t* of 3.338 is greater than 1.812. H_1 is accepted. There is positive correlation between the ranks given by the executives and the ranks assigned during training.

Self-Review 16–7

A sample of individuals applying for factory positions at Davis Enterprises revealed the following scores on an eye perception test (X) and a mechanical aptitude test (Y):

Subject	Eye Perception	Mechanical Aptitude	Subject	Eye Perception	Mechanical Aptitude
001	805	23	006	810	28
002	777	62	007	805	30
003	820	60	008	840	42
004	682	40	009	777	55
005	777	70	010	820	51

(a) Compute the coefficient of rank correlation.
(b) At the .05 significance level, can we conclude that the correlation in the population is different from 0?

Exercises

25. The ABC network television research staff wants to pretest a questionnaire to be mailed to several thousand viewers. One question involves the ranking of male and female senior citizens with respect to the popularity of certain prime-time programs. The composite rankings of a small group of senior citizens are:

Program	Ranking by Males	Ranking by Females
"Monday Night Football"	1	5
"Robin Crest"	4	1
"Simon and Sandor"	3	2
Evening News	2	4
"Our Hero"	5	3

a. Draw a scatter diagram. Let the rankings by males be X.
b. Compute Spearman's rank-order correlation coefficient. Interpret.

26. $r = -0.857$

26. Far West University offers both day and evening classes in business administration. One question in a survey of students inquires how they perceive the prestige associated with certain careers. Each student was asked to rank the careers from 1 to 8, with 1 having the most prestige and 8 the least prestige. The results were:

Career	Ranking by Day Students	Ranking by Evening Students	Career	Ranking by Day Students	Ranking by Evening Students
Accountant	6	3	Statistician	1	7
Computer programmer	7	2	Marketing researcher	4	8
Branch bank manager	2	6	Stock analyst	3	5
Hospital administrator	5	4	Production manager	8	1

Find the coefficient of rank correlation.

27. New representatives for the John Ford Metal and Wheel Company attend a brief training program before being assigned to a regional office. At the end of such a program, each representative was ranked with respect to future sales potential. At the end of the first sales year, their rankings were paired with their annual sales:

Representative	Annual Sales ($ thousands)	Ranking in Training Program	Representative	Annual Sales ($ thousands)	Ranking in Training Program
Kitchen	319	3	Arden	300	10
Bond	150	9	Crane	280	5
Gross	175	6	Arthur	200	2
Arbuckle	460	1	Keene	190	7
Greene	348	4	Knopf	300	8

a. Compute and interpret Spearman's rank correlation coefficient.
b. At the .05 significance level, can we conclude that there is a positive association among the ranks?

28. The University of Winston has five scholarships available for the women's basketball team. The coach provided two scouts with the names of 10 high school players with potential. Each scout attended three games and then ranked the 10 players with respect to potential. To explain, the first scout ranked Norma Tidwell as the best player among the 10 scouted and Jeannie Black the worst.

	Rank, by Scout			Rank, by Scout	
Player	Jean Cann	John Cannelli	Player	Jean Cann	John Cannelli
Cora Jean Seiple	7	5	Candy Jenkins	3	1
Bette Jones	2	4	Rita Rosinski	5	7
Jeannie Black	10	10	Anita Lockes	4	2
Norma Tidwell	1	3	Brenda Towne	8	9
Kathy Marchal	6	6	Denise Ober	9	8

28. a. .8424
b. $t = 4.422$

a. Determine Spearman's rank correlation coefficient.
b. At the .05 significance level, can we conclude there is a positive association between the ranks?

Chapter Outline

I. The sign test.
  A. No assumptions need be made about the shape of the two populations.
  B. It is based on paired or dependent samples.
  C. For small samples find the number of + or − signs and refer to the binomial distribution for the critical value.
  D. For large samples (more than 10) use the standard normal distribution and the following formula.

$$z = \frac{(X \pm .50) - .50n}{.50\sqrt{n}} \qquad \textbf{[16–2] [16–3]}$$

II. The median test is used to test a hypothesis about a population median.
  A. Find μ and σ for a binomial distribution.
  B. The z distribution is used as the test statistic.
  C. The value of z is computed from the following formula, where X is the number of observations above or below the median.

$$z = \frac{(X \pm .50) - \mu}{\sigma} \qquad \textbf{[16–1]}$$

III. The Wilcoxon signed-rank test.
  A. Data must be at least ordinal scale, and the samples must be dependent.
  B. The steps to conduct the test are:

1. Rank absolute differences between the related observations.
2. Apply the sign of the differences to the ranks.
3. Sum negative ranks and positive ranks.
4. The smaller of the two sums is the computed T value.
5. Refer to Appendix H for the critical value, and make a decision regarding H_0.

IV. The Wilcoxon rank-sum test is used to test whether two independent samples came from equal populations.

A. No assumption about the shape of the population is required.
B. To apply the test, the data must be at least ordinal scale.
C. Each sample must contain at least eight observations.
D. To determine the value of the test statistic W, all data values are ranked from low to high as if they were from a single population.
E. The sum of ranks for each of the two samples is determined.
F. W is used to compute z, where W is the sum of the ranks for population 1, from

$$z = \frac{W - \dfrac{n_1(n_1 + n_2 + 1)}{2}}{\sqrt{\dfrac{n_1 n_2(n_1 + n_2 + 1)}{12}}} \qquad \text{[16–4]}$$

G. The z distribution is used as the test statistic.

V. The Kruskal-Wallis one-way ANOVA by ranks.

A. No assumptions regarding the shape of the populations are required.
B. The samples must be independent and at least ordinal scale.
C. It is used to test whether several populations are the same.
D. The sample observations are ranked from smallest to largest as though they were a single group.
E. The chi-square distribution can be used as the test statistic, provided there are at least 5 observations in each sample.
G. The value of the test statistic is computed from the following:

$$H = \frac{12}{n(n+1)}\left[\frac{(\Sigma R_1)^2}{n_1} + \frac{(\Sigma R_2)^2}{n_2} + \cdots + \frac{(\Sigma R_k)^2}{n_k}\right] - 3(n+1) \qquad \text{[16–5]}$$

VI. Spearman's coefficient of rank correlation is a measure of the association between two ordinal-scale variables.

A. It can range from −1 up to 1.
1. A value of 0 indicates there is no association between the variables.
2. A value of −1 indicates perfect negative correlation, and 1 is perfect positive correlation.

B. The value of r_s is computed from the following formula.

$$r_s = 1 - \frac{6\Sigma d^2}{n(n^2 - 1)} \qquad \text{[16–6]}$$

C. Provided the sample size is at least 10, we can conduct a test of hypothesis using the following formula:

$$t = r_s\sqrt{\frac{n-2}{1-r_s^2}} \qquad \text{[16–7]}$$

1. The test statistic is the t distribution.
2. There are $n - 2$ degrees of freedom.

Pronunciation Key

SYMBOL	MEANING	PRONUNCIATION
$(\Sigma R_1)^2$	Square of the total of the first column ranks	*Sigma R sub 1 squared*
r_s	Coefficient of rank correlation	*r sub s*

Chapter Exercises

29. The program director at NBC is finalizing the prime-time schedule for next fall. She has decided to include a Western but is unsure which of two possibilities to select. She has a pilot called "The Loner" and another called "Cattleman." To help her make a final decision, a sample of 20 viewers from throughout the United States were asked to watch the two pilots and indicate which show they prefer. The results were that 12 liked "The Loner," 7 liked "Cattleman," and one had no preference. Is there a preference for one of the two shows? Use the .10 significance level.

30. Suppose Merrill Lynch wants to award a substantial contract for fine-line pens to be used nationally in their offices. Two suppliers, Bic and Pilot, have submitted the lowest bids. To determine the preference of office employees, brokers, and others, a personal preference test is to be conducted using a randomly selected sample of 20 employees. The .05 level of significance is to be used.
   a. If the alternate hypothesis states that Bic is preferred over Pilot, is the sign test to be conducted as a one-tailed or a two-tailed test? Explain.
   b. As each of the sample members told the researchers his or her preference, a "+" was recorded if it was Bic and a "−" if it was the Pilot fine-line pen. A count of the pluses revealed that 12 employees preferred Bic, 5 preferred Pilot, and 3 were undecided. What is n?
   c. What is the decision rule in words?
   d. What conclusion did you reach regarding pen preference? Explain.

30. a. One-tailed
b. $n = 17$
c. Reject H_0 with 13 or more +.
d. Do not reject.

31. Cornwall and Hudson, a large department store chain, wants to handle just one brand of high-quality compact disc player. The list has been narrowed to two brands: Sony and Pioneer. To help make a decision, a panel of 16 audio experts met. A passage using Sony components (labeled A) was played. Then the same passage was played using Pioneer components (labeled B). A "+" in the following table indicates an individual's preference for the Sony components, a "−" indicates preference for Pioneer, and a 0 signifies no preference.

Expert															
1	2	3	4	5	6	7	8	9	10	11	12	13	14	15	16
+	−	+	−	+	+	−	0	−	+	−	+	+	−	+	−

Conduct a test of hypothesis at the .10 significance level to determine whether there is a difference in preference between the two brands.

32. The South Carolina Real Estate Association claims that the median rental for three-bedroom condominiums in a metropolitan area is more than $1,200 a month. To check this, a random sample of 149 units was selected. Of the 149, 5 rented for exactly $1,200 a month, and 75 rented for more than $1,200. At the .05 level can we conclude that the median rental is more than $1,200?
   a. State H_0 and H_1.
   b. Give the decision rule.
   c. Do the necessary calculations, and arrive at a decision.

32. a. H_0: Median $\leq$ \$1,200; H_1: Median $>$ \$1,200
b. H_0 is rejected if $z > 1.65$.
c. H_1 is not rejected. $z = 0.42$.

33. The Citrus Council wants to find whether consumers prefer plain orange juice or juice with some orange pulp in it. A random sample of 212 consumers was selected. Each member of the sample tasted a small, unlabeled cup of one kind and then tasted the other kind. Twelve consumers said they had no preference, 40 preferred plain juice, and the remainder liked the juice with pulp better. Test at the .05 level that the preferences for plain juice and for orange juice with pulp are equal.

34. A research project involving community responsibility is to be conducted. The objective is to find whether women are more community conscious before marriage or after five years of marriage. A test to measure community consciousness was administered to a sample of women before marriage, and the same test was given to them five years after marriage. The test scores are:

Name	Before Marriage	After Marriage	Name	Before Marriage	After Marriage
Beth	110	114	Carol	186	196
Jean	157	159	Lisa	116	116
Sue	121	120	Sandy	160	140
Cathy	96	103	Petra	149	142
Mary	130	139			

34. H_0 is rejected if $T \leq 3, N = 8$. H_0 is not rejected. $T = 13.5$

Test at the .05 level. H_0 is: There is no difference in community consciousness before and after marriage. H_1 is: There is a difference.

35. Is there a difference in the annual divorce rates in predominantly rural counties among three geographic regions, namely, the Southwest, the Southeast, and the Northwest? Test at the .05 level. Annual divorce rates per 1,000 population for randomly selected counties are:

Southwest:	5.9, 6.2, 7.9, 8.6, 4.6
Southeast:	5.0, 6.4, 7.3, 6.2, 8.1, 5.1
Northwest:	6.7, 6.2, 4.9, 8.0, 5.5

36. $z = 0.73$ H_0 is not rejected.

36. The idle times during the eight-hour day shift and the night shift are to be compared. A time study revealed the following numbers of minutes of idle time for eight-hour periods.

Day shift:	92, 103, 116, 81, 89
Night shift:	96, 114, 80, 82, 88, 91

Is there a difference in the idle time between the two shifts? Test at the .05 level.

37. The mobility of executives in stock exchanges, in service, in heavy construction, and in air transportation is to be researched. Samples from each of these industries were selected, and the number of times an executive moved during a 10-year period was converted to an index. An index of 0 would indicate no movement, whereas 100 would indicate almost constant movement from one location to another or one firm to another. The indexes for the four groups are:

Stock Exchange	Service	Heavy Construction	Air Transportation
4	3	62	30
17	12	40	38
8	40	81	46
20	17	96	40
16	31	76	21
	19		

We cannot assume that the indexes follow the normal distribution. Thus, we must use a nonparametric test. Using the .05 level, determine whether the four populations of mobility indexes are identical.

38. A series of questions on sports and world events was asked of a randomly selected group of male senior citizens. The results were translated into a "knowledge" score. The scores were:

Citizen	Sports	World Events	Citizen	Sports	World Events
J. C. McCarthy	47	49	L. M. Zaugg	87	75
A. N. Baker	12	10	J. B. Simon	59	86
B. B. Beebe	62	76	J. Goulden	40	61
L. D. Gaucet	81	92	A. A. Davis	87	18
C. A. Jones	90	86	A. M. Carbo	16	75
J. N. Narko	35	42	A. O. Smithy	50	51
A. F. Nissen	61	61	J. J. Pascal	60	61

38. a. $r_s = .486$
b. $t = 1.926$
H_0 is rejected.

a. Determine the degree of association between how the senior citizens ranked with respect to knowledge of sports and how they ranked on world events.

b. At the .05 significance level, is the rank correlation in the population greater than zero?

39. Early in the basketball season, 12 teams appeared to be outstanding. A panel of sportswriters and a panel of college basketball coaches were asked to rank the 12 teams. Their composite rankings were as follows.

Team	Coaches	Sportswriters	Team	Coaches	Sportswriters
Duke	1	1	Syracuse	7	10
UNLV	2	5	Georgetown	8	11
Indiana	3	4	Villanova	9	7
North Carolina	4	6	LSU	10	12
Louisville	5	3	St. Johns	11	8
Ohio State	6	2	Michigan	12	9

Determine the correlation between the rankings of the coaches and the sportswriters. At the .05 significance level, can we conclude it is different from zero?

40. Professor Bert Forman believes the students who complete his examinations in the shortest time receive the highest grades and those who take the longest to complete them receive the lowest grades. To verify his suspicion, he assigns a rank to the order of finish and then grades the examinations. The results are shown below:

Student	Order of Completion	Score (50 possible)	Student	Order of Completion	Score (50 possible)
Gromney	1	48	Smythe	7	39
Bates	2	48	Arquette	8	30
MacDonald	3	43	Govito	9	37
White	4	49	Gankowski	10	35
Harris	5	50	Bonfigilo	11	36
Cribb	6	47	Hineman	12	33

40. $r_s = .788$
$t = 4.047$.
H_0 is rejected.

Convert the test scores to a rank and find the coefficient of rank correlation. At the .05 significance level, can Professor Forman conclude there is a positive association between the order of finish and the test scores?

exercises.com

41. Is there a correlation between the starting position in an auto race and the order of finish? To investigate, use the results of one of the major races, such as the Daytona 500 or the Indianapolis 500. You can access the results of the Indianapolis 500 by going to *http://www.indy500.com*. Click on **Stats,** then select **Grids and Race Results,** and click on the most recent year. You will need to download the data into either Excel or MINITAB.

a. Compute the coefficient of rank correlation between the starting position and the order of finish. Both of these are ordinal scale variables. Interpret this value.
b. Conduct a test of hypothesis to determine whether the rank correlation computed in part (a) is greater than zero. Interpret the result.

42. See IM.

42. There is lot of information available in the online edition of the *Information Please Almanac.* For example, go to http://infoplease.com, click on **Tabulated Data on State Governments,** and click on **Governor's salary.** There is data on the salary for the governor and the highest court for each state. You will need to download the data into Excel or MINITAB.
a. Compute the coefficient of correlation between the two variables using the Pearson and Spearman methods. Comment on the amount of the difference between the two values. (Hint: to find the coefficient of rank correlation, you will need to first rank the two variables and then use the statistical software to find the Pearson coefficient of correlation *using the ranked data.*)
b. Conduct a test of hypothesis to determine whether the coefficient of rank correlation is different from zero.

Computer Data Exercises

43. Refer to the Real Estate data which reports information on homes sold in the Venice, Florida, area during the last year.
a. Use an appropriate nonparametric test to determine whether there is a difference in the typical selling price of the homes in the several townships. Assume the selling prices are not normally distributed. Use the .05 significance level.
b. Combine the homes with 6 or more bedrooms into one group and determine whether there is a difference according to the number of bedrooms in the typical selling prices of the homes. Use the .05 significance level and assume the distribution of selling prices is not normally distributed.
c. Assume that the distribution of the distance from the center of the city is positively skewed. That is, the normality assumption is not reasonable. Compare the distribution of the distance from the center of the city of the homes that have a pool with those that do not have a pool. Can we conclude there is a difference in the distributions? Use the .05 significance level.

44. Refer to the Baseball 2000 data, which reports information on the 2000 Major League Baseball season.
a. Rank the teams by the number of wins and their total team salary. Compute the coefficient of rank correlation between the two variables. At the .01 significance level, can you conclude that it is greater than zero?
b. Assume that the distributions of team salaries for the American League and National League do not follow the normal distribution. Conduct a test of hypothesis to see if there is a difference in the two distributions.

44. a. $r_s = .512$, $t = 3.154$
b. $z = 0.54$ Do not reject.

45. Refer to the OECD data, which reports information on census, economic, and business data for 29 countries. Categorize the countries, indicating whether they are in Europe, North America, or the Far East. Divide the gross national product by the population to determine the per capita GNP. Without assuming normality, test at the .05 significance level whether there is a difference in the distributions for the three regions. Compare the results to those of Exercise 43b in Chapter 12.

46. Refer to the Schools data, which reports information on 94 school districts in northwest Ohio.
a. Group the data by size of the school district: "large" is 3,000 or more students, "medium" is 1,000 up to 3,000 students, and "small" is less than 1,000 students. Now compare the distributions of amount spent on instruction for the three groups. At the .05 significance level, is there a difference? Assume that the distributions of amount spent on instruction do not follow the normal distribution.
b. Use the same grouping regarding size and compare the distributions of salary. Use the .05 significance level.
c. Compute the coefficient of rank correlation between the number of students in the district and mean salary of the teachers in the district. Can you conclude there is a positive association? Use the .01 significance level.

46. a. $H = 10.95$, reject.
b. $H = 39.99$, reject.
c. $r_s = .72$, $t = 9{,}95$, reject H_0.

Computer Commands

1. The Excel MegaStat commands necessary for the Wilcoxon rank-sum test on page 598 are:
   a. Enter the number of no-shows for Atlanta in column A and for Chicago in column B.
   b. Select **MegaStat, Nonparametric Tests,** and **Wilcoxon-Mann/Whitney Test,** then hit **Enter.**
   c. For Group 1 use the data on Atlanta flights (*A2:A10*) and for Group 2 use the data on Chicago flights (*B2:B9*). Click on **Correct for ties** and **one-tailed,** then click on **OK.**

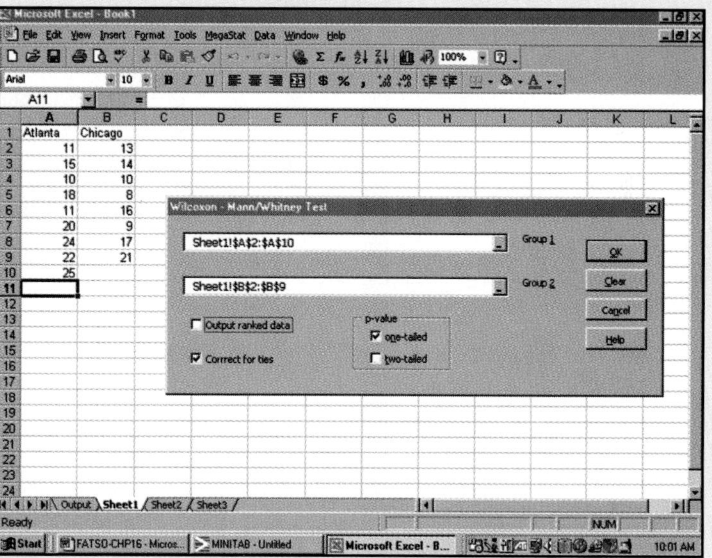

2. The MINITAB commands for the Kruskal-Wallis test on page 602 are:
   a. Enter the scores in column 1 and a code corresponding to their group in column 2. Name the variable in C1 *Scores* and the variable in C2 *Groups.*
   b. From the menu bar select **Stat, Nonparametric,** and **Kruskal-Wallis,** and hit **Enter.**
   c. Select the variables *Scores* as the **Response** variable and *Groups* as the **Factor.**

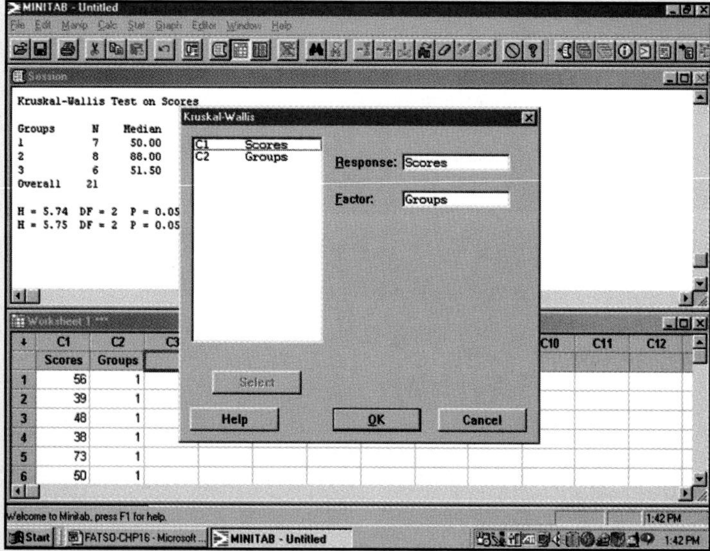

3. The Excel commands for the one-way ANOVA on page 603 are:
   a. Enter the names *Manufacturing, Finance,* and *Trade* in the first row and the data in the columns under them.
   b. Select **Tools, Data Analysis,** and **ANOVA: Single Factor,** and then click **OK.**
   c. In the Dialog box the Input Range is *A1:C9,* click on **Labels in First Row,** and enter *E1* as the **Output Range,** then click **OK.**

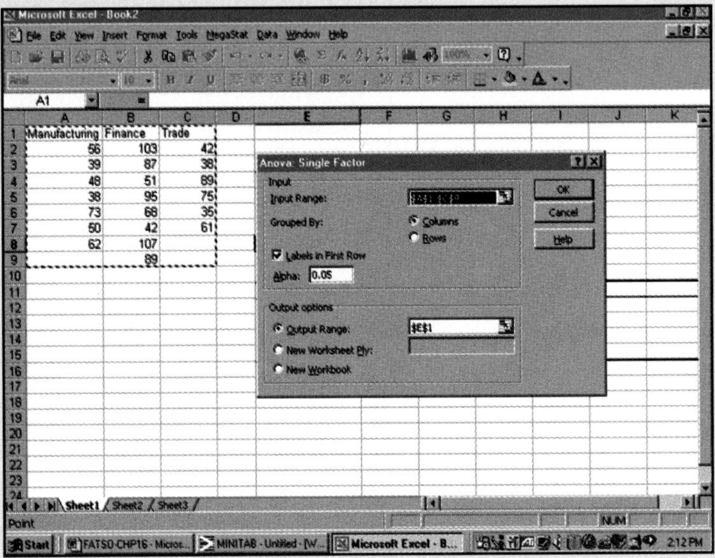

Chapter 16 Answers to Self-Review

16–1 (a) Two-tailed because H_1 does not state a direction.

(b)

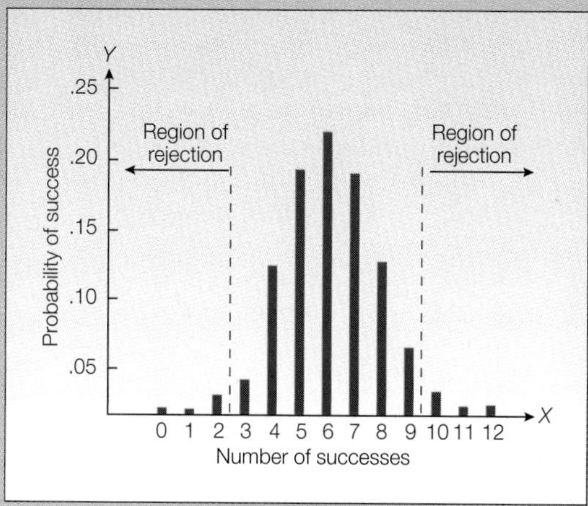

Adding down, .000 + .003 + .016 = .019. This is the largest cumulative probability up to but not exceeding .050, which is half the level of significance.

(c) Reject H_0; accept H_1. There is a preference.

16–2 (a) H_0: $\pi \leq 0.50$, H_1: $\pi > 0.50$.

(b) Reject H_0 if $z > 1.65$.

(c) Since 80 is more than $n/2 = 100/2 = 50$, we use:

$$z = \frac{(80 - .50) - .50(100)}{.50\sqrt{100}} = \frac{29.5}{5} = 5.9$$

(d) H_0 is rejected.

(e) The screening was effective.

16–3 (a) H_0: The median $\leq$ \$123, H_1: The median is more than \$123.

(b) Reject H_0 if $z > 1.65$.

(c) $z = \dfrac{(42 - .50) - 32}{.50\sqrt{64}} = \dfrac{9.5}{4} = 2.38$

(d) Reject H_0.

(e) The median amount spent is more than \$123.

16–4 (a) $n = 10$ (because there was no change for A.A.)

(b)

Before	After	Difference	Absolute Difference	Rank of Absolute Difference	Negative Ranks	Positive Ranks
17	18	−1	1	1.5	1.5	
21	23	−2	2	3.0	3.0	
25	22	3	3	5.0		5.0
15	25	−10	10	8.0	8.0	
10	28	−18	18	10.0	10.0	
16	16	—	—	—	—	—
10	22	−12	12	9.0	9.0	
20	19	1	1	1.5		1.5
17	20	−3	3	5.0	5.0	
24	30	−6	6	7.0	7.0	
23	26	−3	3	5.0	5.0	
					48.5	6.5

H_0: Production is the same.
H_1: Production has increased.

The sum of the positive signed ranks is 6.5; the negative sum is 48.5. From Appendix J, one-tailed test, $n = 10$, the critical value is 10. Since 6.5 is less than 10, reject the null hypothesis and accept the alternate. New procedures did increase production.

16–5 H_0: There is no difference in the distances traveled by Dino and by Maxi.

H_1: There is a difference in the distances traveled by Dino and by Maxi.

Do not reject H_0 if the computed z is between 1.96 and −1.96 (from Appendix D); otherwise, reject H_0 and accept H_1. $n_1 = 8$, the number of observations in the first sample.

Dino		Maxi	
Distance	Rank	Distance	Rank
252	4	262	9
263	10	242	2
279	15	256	5
273	14	260	8
271	13	258	7
265	11.5	243	3
257	6	239	1
280	16	265	11.5
Total	89.5		46.5

$W = 89.5$

$$z = \frac{89.5 - \frac{8(8 + 8 + 1)}{2}}{\sqrt{\frac{(8)(8)(8 + 8 + 1)}{12}}}$$

$$= \frac{21.5}{9.52} = 2.26$$

Reject H_0: accept H_1. There is a difference in the distances traveled by the two golf balls.

16–6

Ranks			
Englewood	**West Side**	**Great Northern**	**Sylvania**
17	5	19	7
20	1	9.5	11
16	3	21	15
13	5	22	9.5
5	2	14	8
18			12

$\Sigma R_1 = 89$ $\Sigma R_2 = 16$ $\Sigma R_3 = 85.5$ $\Sigma R_4 = 62.5$

$n_1 = 6$ $n_2 = 5$ $n_3 = 5$ $n_4 = 6$

H_0: The distributions are the same.
H_1: The distributions are not the same.

$$H = \frac{12}{22(22 + 1)}\left[\frac{(89)^2}{6} + \frac{(16)^2}{5} + \frac{(85.5)^2}{5} + \frac{(62.5)^2}{6}\right] - 3(22 + 1)$$

$$= 13.635$$

The critical value of chi-square for $k - 1 = 4 - 1 = 3$ degrees of freedom is 11.345. Since the computed value of 13.635 is greater than 11.345, the null hypothesis is rejected. We conclude that the distributions are not the same.

16–7 (a)

		Rank			
X	Y	X	Y	d	d^2
805	23	5.5	1	4.5	20.25
777	62	3.0	9	−6.0	36.00
820	60	8.5	8	0.5	0.25
682	40	1.0	4	−3.0	9.00
777	70	3.0	10	−7.0	49.00
810	28	7.0	2	5.0	25.00
805	30	5.5	3	2.5	6.25
840	42	10.0	5	5.0	25.00
777	55	3.0	7	−4.0	16.00
820	51	8.5	6	2.5	6.25
				0	193.00

$$r_s = 1 - \frac{6(193)}{10(99)} = -.170$$

(b) H_0: $\rho = 0$; H_1: $\rho \neq 0$. Reject H_0 if $t < -2.306$ or $t > 2.306$.

$$t = -0.170\sqrt{\frac{10 - 2}{1 - (-0.170)^2}} = -0.488$$

H_0 is not rejected. We have not shown a relationship between the two tests.

A Review of Chapters 15 and 16

Goodness-of-fit test and contingency table analysis applicable to nominal-level data

This section is a review of the major concepts and terms introduced in Chapters 15 and 16. Chapter 15 began the study of *nonparametric,* or *distribution-free,* tests by discussing the *chi-square goodness-of-fit* test. This test compares a set of observed frequencies, f_o, and the corresponding set of expected frequencies, f_e. It involves only one characteristic possessed by an individual, such as education. If we are interested in two characteristics, such as a relationship between education level and income, the data are cross-classified into a contingency table, and the chi-square test for independence is applied. For these two tests, no assumption about the shape of the population is needed; they require only that the data be nominal level. The chi-square goodness-of-fit test is also used to determine whether a set of observed frequencies is normally distributed.

Five tests for ordinal-level data

Chapter 16 presented five nonparametric tests of hypothesis and the coefficient of rank correlation, all of which require the ordinal level of measurement. That is, the data must be ranked from low to high. The tests discussed were the *sign test,* the *median test,* the *Wilcoxon rank-sum test,* the *Kruskal-Wallis analysis of variance test,* and the *Wilcoxon signed-rank test.*

Glossary

Chapter 15

Chi-square distribution A distribution with these characteristics: (1) Its value can only be positive. (2) There is a family of chi-square distributions, a different one for each different degree of freedom. (3) The distributions are positively skewed, but as the number of degrees of freedom increases, the distribution approaches the normal distribution.

Chi-square goodness-of-fit test A test with the objective of determining how well an observed set of frequencies fits an expected set of frequencies. It is concerned with one nominal-scale variable, such as the color of a car.

Contingency table If two characteristics, such as education and income, are cross-classified into a table, the result is called a contingency table. The chi-square test statistic is used to investigate whether the two characteristics are related.

Nominal level of measurement The "lowest" level of measurement. Such data can only be classified into categories, and there is no particular order for the categories. For example, it makes no difference whether the categories "male" and "female" are listed in that order, or female first and male second. The categories are mutually exclusive — meaning, in this illustration, that a person cannot be a male and a female at the same time.

Nonparametric or distribution-free tests Hypothesis tests involving nominal- and ordinal-level data. No assumptions need be made about the shape of the population; that is, we do not assume the population is normally distributed.

Chapter 16

Kruskal-Wallis one-way analysis of variance by ranks A test used when the assumptions for the parametric analysis of variance (ANOVA) cannot be met. Its purpose is to test whether several populations are equal. Again, the data must be at least ordinal scale.

Sign test A test used for dependent samples. The sign test is used to find whether there is a brand preference for two products or to determine whether performance after an experiment is greater than before the experiment. Also, the sign test is used to test a hypothesis about the median.

Spearman's coefficient of rank correlation A measure of the association between the ranks of two variables. It can range from −1.00 to 1.00. A value of −1.00 indicates a perfect negative association among the ranks and a value of 1.00 a perfect positive association among the ranks. A value of 0 indicates no association among the ranks.

Wilcoxon matched-pair signed-rank test A nonparametric test requiring at least ordinal-level data. Its purpose is to find whether there is any difference between two sets of paired (related) observations. It is used if the assumptions required for the paired *t* test cannot be met.

Wilcoxon rank-sum test A nonparametric test requiring independent samples. The data must be at least ordinal level. That is, the data must be capable of being ranked. The test is used when the assumptions for the parametric Student *t* test cannot be met. The objective of the test is to find whether two independent samples can be considered as coming from the same population.

Exercises

1. For a chi-square test, what do f_o and f_e stand for?

2. Contingency table.

2. The following is an example of what?

Political Affiliation	Amount Contributed to Campaign		
	$1–$99	$100–$999	$1,000 and More
Republican	42	87	342
Democrat	596	302	116
Socialist	42	49	36
All others	19	17	11

3. Refer to Exercise 2. What test statistic would be used to find whether there is any relationship between political affiliation and the amount contributed?

4. 6

4. Refer to Exercise 2. How many degrees of freedom are there?
5. Refer to Exercise 2. Suppose the computed value of χ^2 is 11.248, and the .05 level is being used. Should the null hypothesis be rejected?

6. Reject H_0.

6. For a goodness-of-fit test, the computed value of chi-square is 8.403, and the critical value is 5.991. The .05 level is being used. Is the null hypothesis rejected?
7. Refer to Exercise 6. What is the null hypothesis?

8. At least interval.

8. What level of measurement is required for the parametric tests of hypotheses discussed in Chapters 11 and 12?
9. What level of measurement is required for the goodness-of-fit test?

10. Ordinal.

10. What level of measurement is required for the Wilcoxon rank-sum test?
11. What is the purpose of the Wilcoxon rank-sum test?

12. None.

12. What assumptions are made about the shape of the populations in using the Kruskal-Wallis test?
13. What is the objective of the Kruskal-Wallis test?

14. Median = 0.

14. What is the objective of the Wilcoxon signed-rank test?
15. Of the following nonparametric tests (sign test, Wilcoxon rank-sum, Kruskal-Wallis, and Wilcoxon signed-rank), which one deals with three or more samples?

16. Sign test or Wilcoxon signed-rank.

16. Refer to Exercise 15. Which test deals with paired data?
17. Refer to Exercise 15. Can these tests be applied to interval- and ratio-level data?

18. One-tailed.

18. For a Wilcoxon rank-sum test, the alternate hypothesis is: The women have better eye perception than the men. Would a one-tailed or a two-tailed test be applied?
19. The chi-square distribution for 5 degrees of freedom is approximately normally distributed. Is that statement true?

20. Categories − 1

20. How are the degrees of freedom for a goodness-of-fit test determined?
21. Describe the steps followed, using a simple example, to test a hypothesis involving the median.

Cases

A. Century National Bank

Is there a relationship between the location of the branch bank and whether the customer has a debit card? Based on the information available, develop a table that shows the relationship between these two variables. At the .05 significance level, can we conclude there is a relationship between the branch location and whether the customer uses a debit card?

B. Thomas Testing Labs

John Thomas, the owner of Thomas Testing, has for some time done contract work for insurance companies regarding drunk driving. To improve his research capabilities, he recently purchased the Rupple Driving Simulator. This device will allow a subject to take a "road test" and provide a score indicating the number of driving errors committed during the test drive. Higher scores indicate more driving errors. Driving errors would include: not coming to a complete stop at a stop sign, not using turning signals, not exercising caution on wet or snowy pavement, and so on. During the road test, problems appear at random and not all problems appear in each road test. These are major advantages to the Rupple Driving Simulator because subjects do not gain any advantage by taking the test several times.

With the new driving simulator, Mr. Thomas would like to study in detail the problem of drunk driving. He begins by selecting a random sample of 25 drivers. He asks each of the selected individuals to take the test drive on the Rupple Driving Simulator. The number of errors for each driver is recorded. Next, he has each of the individuals in the group drink 3 16-ounce cans of beer in a 60-minute period and return to the Rupple Driving Simulator for another test drive. The number of driving errors after drinking the beer is also shown. The research question is: Does alcohol impair the driver's ability and, therefore, increase the number of driving errors?

Mr. Thomas believes the distribution of scores on the test drive does not follow a normal distribution and, therefore, a nonparametric test should be used. Because the observations are paired, he decides to use both the sign test and the Wilcoxon signed-rank test. Compare the results using these two procedures. Which statistical test would you suggest? What conclusion would you make regarding the effects of drunk driving? Write a brief report summarizing your findings.

	Driving Errors			Driving Errors	
Subject	Without Alcohol	With Alcohol	Subject	Without Alcohol	With Alcohol
1	75	89	14	72	106
2	78	83	15	83	89
3	89	80	16	99	89
4	100	90	17	75	77
5	85	84	18	58	78
6	70	68	19	93	108
7	64	84	20	69	69
8	79	104	21	86	84
9	83	81	22	97	86
10	82	88	23	65	92
11	83	93	24	96	97
12	84	92	25	85	94
13	80	103			

17

Statistical Quality Control

GOALS

When you have completed this chapter, you will be able to:

1 Discuss the role of quality control in production and service operations.

2 Define and understand the terms *chance cause, assignable cause, in control, out of control, attribute,* and *variable.*

3 Construct and interpret a *Pareto chart.*

4 Construct and interpret a *fishbone diagram.*

5 Construct and interpret a *mean* and *range chart.*

6 Construct and interpret a *percent defective* and a *c-bar chart.*

7 Discuss *acceptance sampling.*

8 Construct an *operating characteristic curve* for various sampling plans.

Every hour a quality control inspector measures the outside diameter of four parts. Based on the results of the measurements, are the measurements within the control limit? (See Self-Review 17-2 and Goal 5.)

Introduction

Throughout this text we have presented many applications of hypothesis testing. In Chapter 10 we described methods for testing a hypothesis regarding a single population value. In Chapter 11 we described methods for testing a hypothesis about two populations. In this chapter we present another, somewhat different application of hypothesis testing, called **statistical process control** or **SPC.**

Statistical process control is a collection of strategies, techniques, and actions taken by an organization to ensure they are producing a quality product or providing a quality service. It begins at the product planning stage, when we specify the attributes of the product or service. It continues through the production stage. Each attribute throughout the process contributes to the overall quality of the product. To effectively use quality control, measurable attributes and specifications must be developed against which the actual attributes of the product or service can be compared.

A Brief History of Quality Control

Prior to the 1900s U.S. industry was largely characterized by small shops making relatively simple products, such as candles or furniture. In these small shops the individual worker was generally a craftsman who was completely responsible for the quality of the work. The worker could ensure the quality through the personal selection of the materials, skillful manufacturing, and selective fitting and adjustment.

In the early 1900s factories sprang up, where people with limited training were formed into large assembly lines. Products became much more complex. The individual worker no longer had complete control over the quality of the product. A semiprofessional staff, usually called the Inspection Department, became responsible for the quality of the product. The quality responsibility was usually fulfilled by a 100 percent inspection of all the important characteristics. If there were any discrepancies noted, these problems were handled by the manufacturing department supervisor. In essence, quality was attained by "inspecting the quality into the product."

During the 1920s Dr. Walter A. Shewhart, of the Bell Telephone Laboratories, developed the concepts of statistical quality control. He introduced the concept of "controlling" the quality of a product as it was being manufactured, rather than inspecting the quality into the product after it was manufactured. For the purpose of controlling quality, Shewhart developed charting techniques for controlling in-process manufacturing operations. In addition, he introduced the concept of statistical sample inspection to estimate the quality of a product as it was being manufactured. This replaced the old method of inspecting each part after it was completed in the production operation.

Statistical quality control really came into its own during World War II. The need for mass-produced war related items, such as bomb sights, accurate radar, and other electronic equipment, at the lowest possible cost hastened the use of statistical sampling and quality control charts. Since World War II these statistical techniques have been refined and sharpened. The use of computers in the last decade has also widened the use of these techniques.

World War II virtually destroyed the Japanese production capability. Rather than retool their old production methods, the Japanese enlisted the aid of the late Dr. W. Edwards Deming, of the United States Department of Agriculture, to help them develop an overall plan. In a series of seminars with Japanese planners he stressed a philosophy that is known today as Deming's 14 points. These 14 points are listed on the following page. He emphasized that quality originates from improving the process, not from inspection, and that quality is determined by the customers. The manufacturer must be able, via market research, to anticipate the needs of customers. Upper management has the responsibility for long-term improvement. Another of his points, and one that the Japanese strongly endorsed, is that every member of the company must contribute to the long-term improvement. To achieve this improvement, ongoing education and training are necessary.

Deming had some ideas that did not mesh with contemporary management philosophies in the United States. Two areas where Deming's ideas differed from U.S. management philosophy were with production quotas and merit ratings. He claimed these two practices, which are both common in the United States, are not productive and should be eliminated. He also pointed out that U.S. managers are mostly interested in good news. Good news, however, does not provide an opportunity for improvement. On the other hand, bad news opens the door for new products and allows for company improvement.

Listed below, in a condensed form, are Dr. Deming's 14 points. He was adamant that the 14 points needed to be adopted as a package in order to be successful. The underlying theme is cooperation, teamwork, and the belief that workers want to do their jobs in a quality fashion.

1. Create constancy of purpose for the continual improvement of products and service to society.
2. Adopt a philosophy that we can no longer live with commonly accepted levels of delays, mistakes, defective materials, and defective workmanship.
3. Eliminate the need for mass inspection as the way to achieve quality. Instead achieve quality by building the product correctly in the first place.
4. End the practice of awarding business solely on the basis of price. Instead, require meaningful measures of quality along with the price.
5. Improve constantly and forever every process for planning, production, and service.
6. Institute modern methods of training on the job for all employees, including managers. This will lead to better utilization of each employee.
7. Adopt and institute leadership aimed at helping people do a better job.
8. Encourage effective two-way communication and other means to drive out fear throughout the organization so that everyone may work more effectively and more productively for the company.
9. Break down barriers between departments and staff areas.
10. Eliminate the use of slogans, posters, and exhortations demanding zero defects and new levels of productivity without providing methods.
11. Eliminate work standards that prescribe quotas for the workforce and numerical goals for people in management. Substitute aids and helpful leadership in order to achieve continual improvement in quality and productivity.
12. Remove the barriers that rob hourly workers and the people in management of their right to pride of workmanship.
13. Institute a vigorous program of education and encourage self-improvement for everyone. What an organization needs is good people and people who are improving with education. Advancement to a competitive position will have its roots in knowledge.
14. Define clearly management's permanent commitment to ever-improving quality and productivity to implement all of these principles.

Deming's 14 points did not ignore statistical quality control, which is often abbreviated as SQC, TQC, or just QC. The objective of statistical quality control is to monitor production through many stages of manufacturing. We use the tools of statistical quality control, such as X-bar and R charts, to monitor the quality of many processes and services. Control charts allow us to identify when a process or service is "out of control," that is, when the point is reached where an excessive number of defective units are being produced.

Interest in quality has accelerated dramatically in the United States since the late 1980s. Turn on the television and watch the commercials sponsored by Ford, Nissan, and GM to verify the emphasis on quality control on the assembly line. It is now one of the "in" topics in all facets of business. V. Daniel Hunt, president of Technology Research Corporation, wrote in his book *Quality in America* that in the United States, 20 to 25 percent of the cost of production is currently spent finding and correcting mistakes. And, he added, the additional cost incurred in repairing or replacing faulty products in the field drives the total cost of poor quality to nearly 30 percent. In Japan, he indicates, this cost is about 3 percent!

In recent years companies have been motivated to improve quality by the challenge of being recognized for their quality achievements. The Malcolm Baldrige National Quality Award, established in 1988, is awarded annually to U.S. companies that demonstrate excellence in quality achievement and management. The award categories include manufacturing, service, and small business. Past winners include Motorola, Xerox, IBM, Federal Express, and Cadillac. The 2000 award winners were Dana Corporation–Spicer Driveshaft Division of Toledo, Ohio; Karalee Company of Garland, Texas; Operations Management International of Greenwood Village, Colorado; and Los Alamos National Bank of Los Alamos, New Mexico. The Dana Corporation and Karalee were the recipients in the manufacturing sector, Operations Management International, a wastewater and water treatment facility, in the service sector, and Los Alamos Bank in the small business sector. Los Alamos Bank employs about 170; the award is not limited to large companies. You can obtain more information on the 2000 winners and subsequent winners by visiting the website*: http://www.quality.nist.gov.*

What is quality? There is no commonly agreed upon definition of quality. To cite a few diverse definitions: From Westinghouse, "Total quality is performance leadership in meeting the customer requirements by doing the right things right the first time." From AT&T, "Quality is meeting customer expectations." Historian Barbara W. Tuchman says, "Quality is achieving or reaching the highest standard as against being satisfied with the sloppy or fraudulent."

Causes of Variation

No two parts are *exactly* the same. There is always some variation. The weight of each McDonald's Quarter Pounder is not exactly 0.25 pounds. Some will weigh more than 0.25 pounds, others less. The standard time for the TARTA (Toledo Area Regional Transit Authority) bus run from downtown Toledo, Ohio, to Perrysburg is 25 minutes. However, each run does not take *exactly* 25 minutes. Some runs take longer. Other times the TARTA driver must wait in Perrysburg before returning to Toledo. In some cases there is a reason for the bus being late, an accident on the expressway or a snowstorm, for example. In other cases the driver may not "hit" the green lights or the traffic is unusually heavy and slow for no apparent reason. There are two general causes of variation in a process—chance and assignable.

CHANCE VARIATION Variation that is random in nature. This type of variation cannot be completely eliminated unless there is a major change in the equipment or material used in the process.

Internal machine friction, slight variations in material or process conditions (such as the temperature of the mold being used to make glass bottles), atmospheric conditions (such as temperature, humidity, and the dust content of the air), and vibrations transmitted to a machine from a passing forklift are a few examples of sources of chance variation.

If the hole drilled in a piece of steel is too large due to a dull drill, the drill may be sharpened or a new drill inserted. An operator who continually sets up the machine incorrectly can be replaced or retrained. If the roll of steel to be used in the process does not have the correct tensile strength, it can be rejected. These are examples of assignable variation.

ASSIGNABLE VARIATION Variation that is not random. It can be eliminated or reduced by investigating the problem and finding the cause.

There are several reasons we should be concerned with variation.

1. It will change the shape, dispersion, and central tendency of the distribution of the product characteristic being measured.
2. Assignable variation is usually correctable, whereas chance variation usually cannot be corrected or stabilized economically.

Diagnostic Charts

There are a variety of diagnostic techniques available to investigate quality problems. Two of the more prominent of these techniques are *Pareto charts* and *fishbone diagrams.*

Pareto Charts

Pareto analysis is a technique for tallying the number and type of defects that happen within a product or service. The chart is named after a 19th-century Italian scientist, Vilfredo Pareto. He noted that most of the "activity" in a process is caused by relatively few of the "factors." His concept, often called the 80–20 rule, is that 80 percent of the activity is caused by 20 percent of the factors. By concentrating on 20 percent of the factors, managers can attack 80 percent of the problem. For example, Emily's Family Restaurant, located at the junction of Interstates 75 and 70, is investigating "customer complaints." The five complaints heard most frequently are: discourteous service, cold food, long wait for seating, few menu choices, and unruly young children. Suppose discourteous service was mentioned most frequently and cold food second. These two factors total more than 85 percent of the complaints and hence are the two that should be addressed first because this will yield the largest reduction in complaints.

To develop a Pareto chart, we begin by tallying the type of defects. Next, we rank the defects in terms of frequency of occurrence from largest to smallest. Finally, we produce a vertical bar chart, with the height of the bars corresponding to the frequency of each defect. The following example illustrates these ideas.

EXAMPLE

The city manager of Grove City, Utah, is concerned with water usage, particularly in single family homes. She would like to develop a plan to reduce the water usage in Grove City. To investigate, she selects a sample of 100 homes and determines the typical daily water usage for various purposes. These sample results are as follows.

Reasons for Water Usage	Gallons per Day	Reasons for Water Usage	Gallons per Day
Laundering	24.9	Swimming pool	28.3
Watering lawn	143.7	Dishwashing	12.3
Personal bathing	106.7	Car washing	10.4
Cooking	5.1	Drinking	7.9

What is the area of greatest usage? Where should she concentrate her efforts to reduce the water usage?

SOLUTION

A Pareto chart is useful for identifying the major areas of water usage and focusing on those areas where the greatest reduction can be achieved. The first step is to convert each of the activities to a percent and then to order them from largest to smallest. The total water usage per day is 339.3 gallons, found by totaling the gallons used in the eight activities. The activity with the largest use is watering lawns. It accounts for 143.7 gallons of water per day, or 42.4 percent of the amount of water used. The next largest category is personal bathing, which accounts for 31.4 percent of the water used. These two activities account for 73.8 percent of the water usage.

Reasons for Water Usage	Gallons per Day	Percent
Laundering	24.9	7.3
Watering lawn	143.7	42.4
Personal bathing	106.7	31.4
Cooking	5.1	1.5
Swimming pool usage	28.3	8.3
Dishwashing	12.3	3.6
Car washing	10.4	3.1
Drinking	7.9	2.3
Total	339.3	100.0

To draw the Pareto chart, we begin by scaling the number of gallons used on the left vertical axis and the corresponding percent on the right vertical axis. Next we draw a vertical bar with the height of the bar corresponding to the activity with the largest number of occurrences. In the Grove City example, we draw a vertical bar for the activity watering lawns to a height of 143.7 gallons. (We call this the count.) We continue this procedure for the other activities, as shown in the MINITAB output in Chart 17–1.

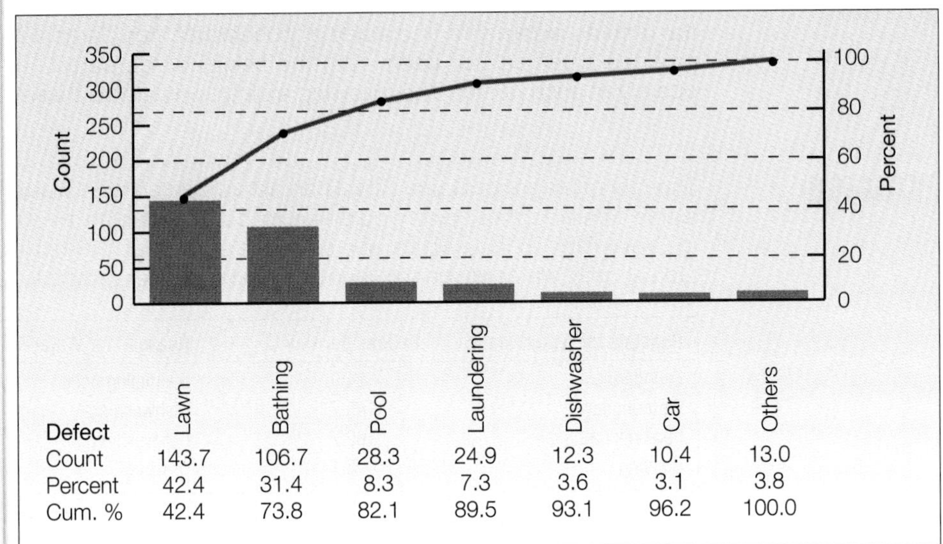

CHART 17–1 Pareto Chart for Water Usage in Grove City, Utah

Below the chart we list the activities, their frequency of occurrence, and the percent of the time each activity occurs. In the last row we list the cumulative percentage. This cumulative row will allow us to quickly determine which set of activities account for most of the activity. These cumulative percents are plotted above the vertical bars. In the Grove City example, the activities of watering lawn, personal bathing, and pools account for 82.1 percent of the water usage. The city manager can attain the greatest gain by looking to reduce the water usage in these three areas.

Fishbone Diagram

Another diagnostic chart is a **cause-and-effect diagram** or a **fishbone diagram.** It is called a cause-and-effect diagram to emphasize the relationship between an effect and a set of possible causes that produce the particular effect. This diagram is useful to help organize ideas and to identify relationships. It is a tool that encourages open "brainstorming" for ideas. By identifying these relationships we can determine factors that are the cause of variability in our process. The name *fishbone* comes from the manner in which the various causes and effects are organized on the diagram. The effect is usually a particular problem, or perhaps a goal, and it is shown on the right-hand side of the diagram. The major causes are listed on the left-hand side of the diagram.

The usual approach to a fishbone diagram is to consider four problem areas, namely, methods, materials, equipment, and personnel. The problem, or the effect, is the head of the fish. See Chart 17–2.

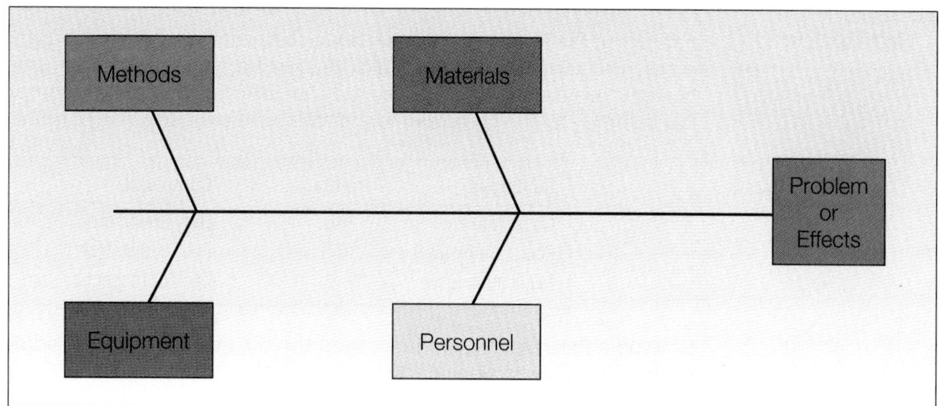

CHART 17–2 Fishbone Diagram

Under each of the possible causes are subcauses that are identified and investigated. The subcauses are factors that may be producing the particular effect. Information is gathered about the problem and used to fill in the fishbone diagram. Each of the subcauses is investigated and those that are not important eliminated, until the real cause of the problem is identified.

Chart 17–3 illustrates the details of a fishbone diagram. Suppose a family restaurant, such as those found along an interstate highway, has recently been experiencing complaints from customers that the food being served is cold. Notice each of the subcauses are listed as assumptions. Each of these subcauses must be investigated to find the real problem regarding the cold food. In a fishbone diagram there is no weighting of the subcauses.

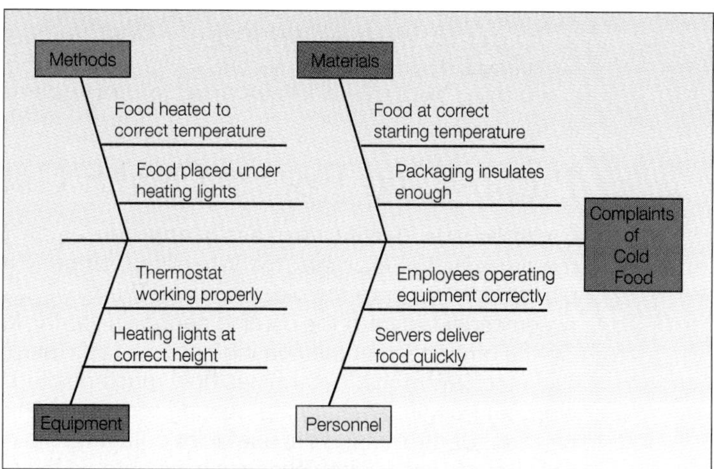

CHART 17–3 Fishbone Diagram for a Restaurant Investigation of Cold Food Complaints

SOURCE: Adapted from M. A. Vonderembse and G. P. White, *Operations Management*, 3rd Ed. (South Western College Publishing, 1996), p. 489.

Self-Review 17–1

Patients at the Rouse Home have been complaining recently about the conditions at the home. The administrator would like to use a Pareto chart to investigate. When a patient or patient's relative has a complaint, they are asked to complete a complaint form. Listed below is a summary of the complaint forms received during the last 12 months.

Complaint	Number	Complaint	Number
Nothing to do	45	Dirty conditions	63
Poor care by staff	71	Poor quality food	84
Medication error	2	Lack of respect by staff	35

Develop a Pareto chart. What complaints would you suggest the administrator work on first to achieve the most significant improvement?

Exercises

1. Tom Sharkey is the owner of Sharkey Chevy. At the start of the year Tom instituted a customer opinion program to find ways to improve service. One week after the service is performed, Tom's administrative assistant calls the customer to find out whether the service was performed satisfactorily and how the service might be improved. Listed below is a summary of the complaints for the first six months. Develop a Pareto chart. What complaints would you suggest that Tom work on to improve the quality of service?

Complaint	Frequency	Complaint	Frequency
Problem not corrected	38	Price too high	23
Error on invoice	8	Wait too long for service	10
Unfriendly atmosphere	12		

2. See IM.

2. Out of 110 diesel engines tested, a rework and repair facility found 9 had leaky water pumps, 15 had faulty cylinders, 4 had ignition problems, 52 had oil leaks, and 30 had cracked blocks. Draw a Pareto chart to identify the key problem in the engines.

Purpose and Types of Quality Control Charts

Control charts identify when assignable causes of variation or changes have entered the process. For example, the Wheeling Company makes vinyl-coated aluminum replacement windows for older homes. The vinyl coating must have a thickness between certain limits. If the coating becomes too thick, it will cause the windows to jam. On the other hand, if the coating becomes too thin, the window will not seal properly. The mechanism that determines how much coating is put on each window becomes worn and begins making the coating too thick. Thus, a change has occurred in the process. Control charts are useful for detecting the change in process conditions. It is important to know when changes have entered the process, so that the cause may be identified and corrected before a large number of unacceptable items are produced.

Control charts may be compared to the scoreboard in a baseball game. By looking at the scoreboard, the fans, coaches, and players can tell which team is winning the game. However, the scoreboard can do nothing to win or lose the game. Control charts provide a similar function. These charts indicate to the workers, group leaders, quality control engineers, production supervisor, and management whether the production of the part or service is "in control" or "out of control." If the production is "out of control," the control chart will not fix the situation; it is just a piece of paper with figures and dots on it. Instead, the person responsible will adjust the machine manufacturing the part or do what is necessary to return production to "in control."

There are two types of control charts. A **variable control chart** portrays measurements, such as the amount of cola in a two liter bottle or the time it takes a nurse at Mt. Carmel Hospital to respond to a patient's call. A variable control chart requires the interval or the ratio scale of measurement. An **attribute control chart** classifies a product or service as either acceptable or unacceptable. It is based on the nominal scale of measurement. Patients in a hospital are asked to rate the meals served as acceptable or unacceptable; bank loans are either repaid or they are defaulted.

Control Charts for Variables

To develop control charts for variables, we rely on the sampling theory discussed in connection with the central limit theorem in Chapter 8. Suppose a sample of five pieces is selected each hour from the production process and the mean of each sample computed. The sample means are $\bar{X}_1$, $\bar{X}_2$, $\bar{X}_3$, and so on. The mean of these sample means is denoted as $\bar{\bar{X}}$. We use k to indicate the number of sample means. The overall or grand mean is found by:

GRAND MEAN

$$\bar{\bar{X}} = \frac{\Sigma \text{ of the means of the subgroups}}{\text{Number of sample means}} = \frac{\Sigma\bar{X}}{k} \qquad [17\text{–}1]$$

The standard error of the distribution of the sample means is designated by $s_{\bar{X}}$. It is found by:

STANDARD ERROR OF THE MEAN

$$s_{\bar{X}} = \frac{s}{\sqrt{n}} \qquad [17\text{–}2]$$

These relationships allow limits to be set up around the sample means to show how much variation can be expected for a given sample size. These expected limits are called the **upper control limit** (*UCL*) and the **lower control limit** (*LCL*). An example will illustrate the use of control limits and how the limits are determined.

EXAMPLE

Statistical Software, Inc., offers a toll-free number where customers can call with problems involving the use of their products from 7 A.M. until 11 P.M. daily. It is impossible to have every call answered immediately by a technical representative, but it is important customers do not wait too long for a person to come on the line. Customers become upset when they hear the message "Your call is important to us. The next available representative will be with you shortly" too many times. To understand their process, Statistical Software decides to develop a control chart describing the total time from when a call is received until the representative answers the caller's question. Yesterday, for the 16 hours of operation, five calls were sampled each hour. This information is reported on the next page, in minutes until a call was answered.

Time	Sample Number 1	2	3	4	5
A.M. 7	8	9	15	4	11
8	7	10	7	6	8
9	11	12	10	9	10
10	12	8	6	9	12
11	11	10	6	14	11
P.M. 12	7	7	10	4	11
1	10	7	4	10	10
2	8	11	11	7	7
3	8	11	8	14	12
4	12	9	12	17	11
5	7	7	9	17	13
6	9	9	4	4	11
7	10	12	12	12	12
8	8	11	9	6	8
9	10	13	9	4	9
10	9	11	8	5	11

Based on this information, develop a control chart for the mean duration of the call. Does there appear to be a trend in the calling times? Is there any period in which it appears that customers wait longer than others?

SOLUTION

A mean chart has two limits, an upper control limit (*UCL*) and a lower control limit (*LCL*). These upper and lower control limits are computed by:

CONTROL LIMITS FOR THE MEAN

$$UCL = \bar{\bar{X}} + 3\frac{s}{\sqrt{n}} \quad \text{and} \quad LCL = \bar{\bar{X}} - 3\frac{s}{\sqrt{n}} \qquad [17\text{–}3]$$

where s is an estimate of the standard deviation of the population, σ. Notice that in the calculation of the upper and lower control limits the number 3 appears. It represents the 99.74 percent confidence limits. The limits are often called the 3-sigma limits. However, other levels of confidence (such as 90 or 95 percent) can be used.

This application developed before computers were widely available and computing standard deviations was difficult. Rather than calculate the standard deviation from each sample as a measure of variation, it is easier to use the range. For fixed sized samples there is a constant relationship between the range and the standard deviation, so we can use the following formulas to determine the 99.74 percent control limits for the mean. It can be demonstrated that the term $3(s/\sqrt{n})$ from formula 17–3 is equivalent to $A_2\bar{R}$ in the following formula.

CONTROL LIMITS FOR THE MEAN

$$UCL = \bar{\bar{X}} + A_2\bar{R} \qquad LCL = \bar{\bar{X}} - A_2\bar{R} \qquad [17\text{–}4]$$

where:

A_2 is a constant used in computing the upper and the lower control limits. It is based on the average range, $\bar{R}$. The factors for various sample sizes can be found in Appendix B. (Note: n in this table refers to the number in the sample.) A portion of Appendix B is shown below. To locate the A_2 factor for this problem, find the sample size for n in the left margin. It is 5. Then move horizontally to the A_2 column, and read the factor. It is 0.577.

n	A_2	D_2	D_3	D_4
2	1.880	1.128	0	3.267
3	1.023	1.693	0	2.575
4	0.729	2.059	0	2.282
5	0.577	2.326	0	2.115
6	0.483	2.534	0	2.004

$\bar{\bar{X}}$ is the mean of the sample means, computed by $\Sigma\bar{X}/k$, where k is the number of samples selected. In this problem a sample of 5 observations is taken each hour for 16 hours, so $k = 16$.

$\bar{R}$ is the mean of the ranges of the sample. It is $\Sigma R/k$. Remember the range is the difference between the largest and the smallest value in each sample. It describes the variability occurring in that particular sample. (See Table 17–1.)

TABLE 17–1 Duration of 16 Samples of Five Help Sessions

Time	1	2	3	4	5	Mean	Range
A.M. 7	8	9	15	4	11	9.4	11
8	7	10	7	6	8	7.6	4
9	11	12	10	9	10	10.4	3
10	12	8	6	9	12	9.4	6
11	11	10	6	14	11	10.4	8
P.M. 12	7	7	10	4	11	7.8	7
1	10	7	4	10	10	8.2	6
2	8	11	11	7	7	8.8	4
3	8	11	8	14	12	10.6	6
4	12	9	12	17	11	12.2	8
5	7	7	9	17	13	10.6	10
6	9	9	4	4	11	7.4	7
7	10	12	12	12	12	11.6	2
8	8	11	9	6	8	8.4	5
9	10	13	9	4	9	9.0	9
10	9	11	8	5	11	8.8	6
Total						150.60	102

The centerline for the chart is $\bar{\bar{X}}$. It is 9.4125 minutes, found by 150.60/16. The mean of the ranges ($\bar{R}$) is 6.375 minutes, found by 102/16. Thus, the upper control limit of the X bar chart is:

$$UCL = \bar{\bar{X}} + A_2\bar{R} = 9.4125 + 0.577(6.375) = 13.0909$$

The lower control limit of the X bar chart is:

$$LCL = \bar{\bar{X}} - A_2\bar{R} = 9.4125 - 0.577(6.375) = 5.7341$$

$\bar{\bar{X}}$, UCL, and LCL, and the sample means are portrayed in Chart 17–4. The mean, $\bar{\bar{X}}$, is 9.4125 minutes, the upper control limit is located at 13.0909 minutes, and the lower control limit is located at 5.7341. There is some variation in the duration of the calls, but all sample means are within the control limits. Thus, based on 16 samples of five calls, we conclude that 99.74 percent of the time the mean length of a sample of 5 calls will be between 5.7341 minutes and 13.0909 minutes.

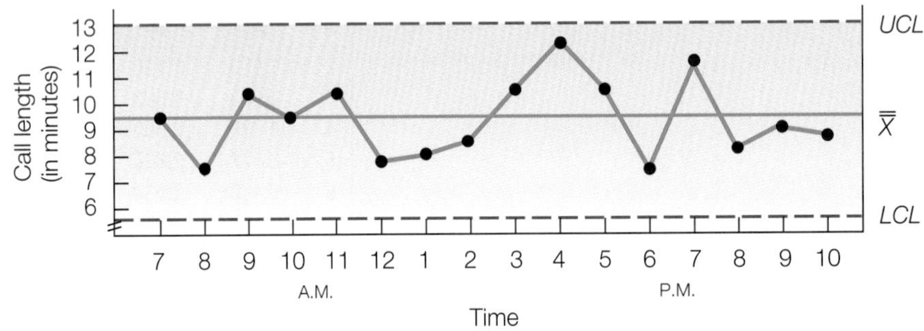

CHART 17–4 Control Chart for Mean Length of Customer Calls to Statistical Software, Inc.

Statistics in Action

Control charts were used to help convict a person who bribed jai alai players to lose. $\bar{X}$ and R charts showed unusual betting patterns and that some contestants did not win as much as expected when they made certain bets. A quality control expert was able to identify times when assignable variation stopped, and prosecutors were able to tie those times to the arrest of the suspect.

Because the statistical theory is based on the normality of large samples, control charts should be based on a stable process, that is, a fairly large sample, taken over a long period of time. One rule of thumb is to design the chart after at least 25 samples have been selected.

Range Chart

In addition to the central tendency in a sample, we must also monitor the amount of variation from sample to sample. A **range chart** shows the variation in the sample ranges. If the points representing the ranges fall between the upper and the lower limits, it is concluded that the operation is in control. According to chance, about 997 times out of 1,000 the range of the samples will fall within the limits. If the range should fall above the limits, we conclude that an assignable cause affected the operation and an adjustment to the process is needed. Why are we not as concerned about the lower control limit of the range? For small samples the lower limit is often zero. Actually, for any sample of six or less, the lower control limit is 0. If the range is zero, then logically all the parts are the same and there is not a problem with the variability of the operation.

The upper and lower control limits of the range chart are determined from the following equations.

CONTROL CHART FOR RANGES $UCL = D_4\bar{R} \qquad LCL = D_3\bar{R}$ **[17–5]**

The values for D_3 and D_4, which reflect the usual three σ (sigma) limits for various sample sizes, are found in Appendix B or in the table on page 633.

EXAMPLE

The length of time customers of Statistical Software, Inc. waited from the time their call was answered until a technical representative answered their question or solved their problem is recorded in Table 17–1. Develop a control chart for the range. Does it appear that there is any time when there is too much variation in the operation?

SOLUTION

The first step is to find the mean of the sample ranges. The range for the five calls sampled in the 7 A.M. hour is 11 minutes. The longest call selected from that hour was 15 minutes and the shortest 4 minutes; the difference in the lengths is 11 minutes. In the 8 A.M. hour the range is 4 minutes. The total of the 16 ranges is 102 minutes, so the average range is 6.375 minutes, found by $\bar{R} = 102/16$. Referring to Appendix B or the partial table on page 633, D_3 and D_4 are 0 and 2.115, respectively. The lower and upper control limits are 0 and 13.4831.

$$UCL = D_4\bar{R} = 2.115(6.375) = 13.4831$$
$$LCL = D_3\bar{R} = 0(6.375) = 0$$

The range chart with the 16 sample ranges plotted is shown in Chart 17–5. This chart shows all the ranges are well within the control limits. Hence, we conclude the variation in the time to service the customer's calls is within normal limits, that is, "in control." Of course, we should be determining the control limits based on one set of data and then applying them to evaluate future data, not the data we already know.

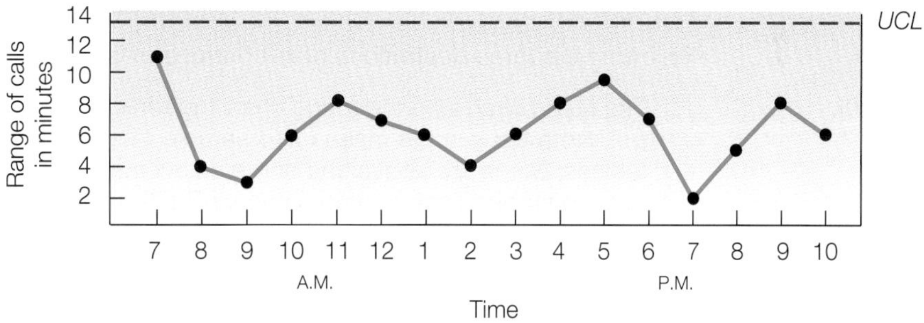

CHART 17–5 Control Chart for Ranges of Length of Customer Calls to Statistical Software, Inc.

MINITAB will draw a control chart for the mean and the range. Following is the output for the Statistical Software example. The data is in Table 17–1. The minor differences in the control limits are due to rounding.

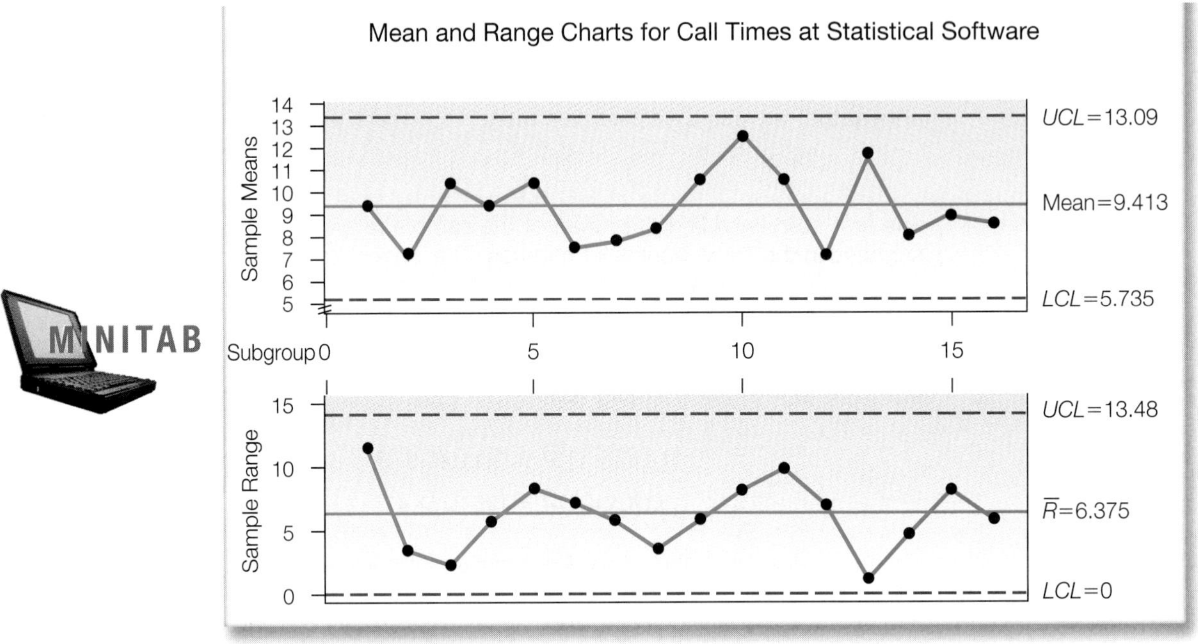

Some In-Control and Out-of-Control Situations

Following are three illustrations of in-control and out-of-control processes.

Everything OK

1. The mean chart and the range chart together indicate that the process is in control. Note the sample means and sample ranges are clustered close to the centerlines. Some are above and some below the centerlines, indicating the process is quite stable. That is, there is no visible tendency for the means and ranges to move toward the "out of control" areas.

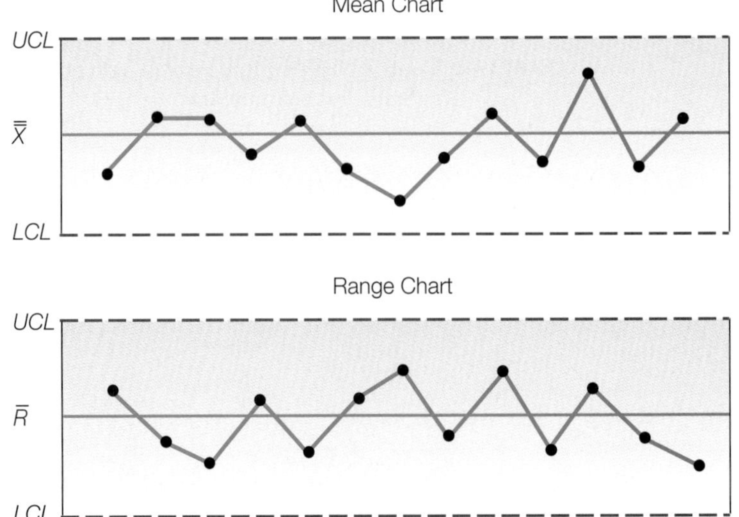

Considerable variation in ranges

2. The sample means are in control, but the ranges of the last two samples are out of control. This indicates there is considerable variation from piece to piece. Some pieces are large; others are small. An adjustment in the process is probably necessary.

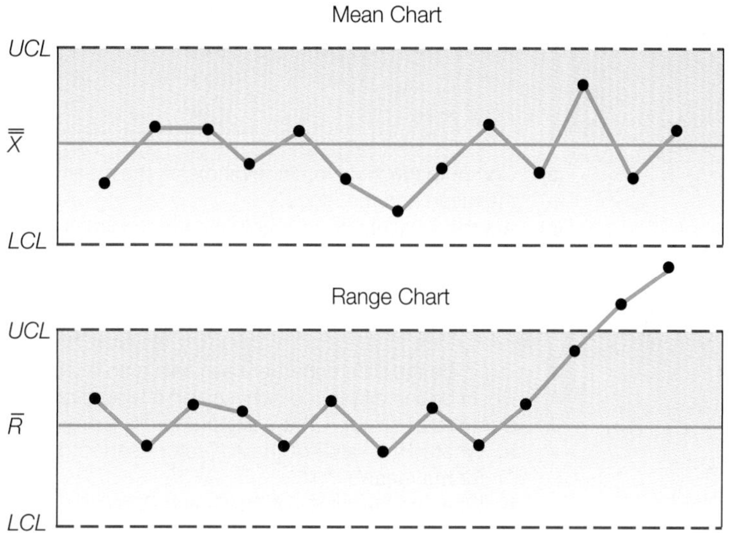

3. The mean was in control for the first samples, but there is an upward trend toward *UCL*. The last two sample means were out of control. An adjustment in the process is indicated.

Mean out of control

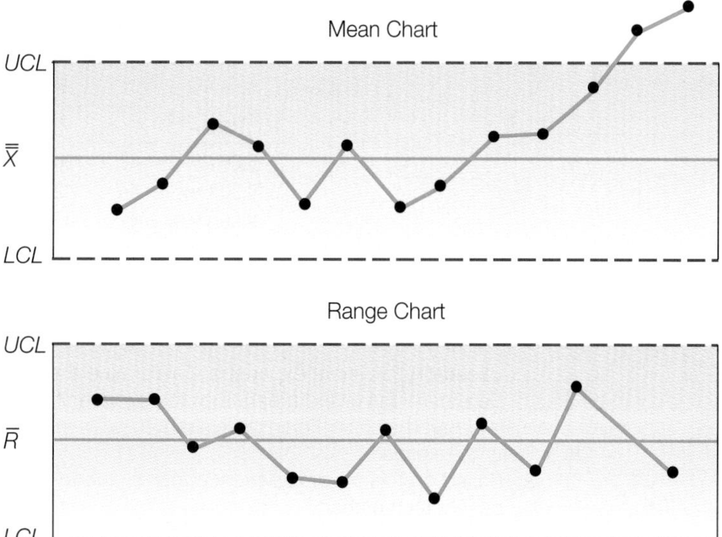

The above chart for the mean is an example in which the control chart offers some additional information. Note the direction of the last five observations of the mean. They are all above $\overline{\overline{X}}$ and increasing, and, in fact, the last two observations are out of control. The fact that the sample means were increasing for seven consecutive observations is very improbable and another indication that the process is out of control.

Self-Review 17–2

Every hour a quality control inspector measures the outside diameter of four parts. The results of the measurements are shown below.

	Sample Piece			
Time	1	2	3	4
9 A.M.	1	4	5	2
10 A.M.	2	3	2	1
11 A.M.	1	7	3	5

(a) Compute the mean outside diameter, the mean range, and determine the control limits for the mean and the range.
(b) Are the measurements within the control limits? Interpret the chart.

Exercises

3. Describe the difference between assignable variation and chance variation.
4. Describe the difference between an attribute control chart and a variable control chart.
5. Samples of size $n = 4$ are selected from a production line.
   a. What is the value of the A_2 factor used to determine the upper and lower control limits for the mean?
   b. What are the values of the D_3 and D_4 factors used to determine the upper and lower control limits for the range?
6. Samples of size 5 are selected from a manufacturing process. The mean of the sample ranges is .50. What is the estimate of the standard deviation of the population?
7. A new industrial oven has just been installed at the Piatt Bakery. To develop experience regarding the oven temperature, an inspector reads the temperature at four different places inside the oven each half hour. The first reading, taken at 8:00 A.M., was 340 degrees Fahrenheit. (Only the last two digits are given in the following table to make the computations easier.)

	Reading			
Time	1	2	3	4
8:00 A.M.	40	50	55	39
8:30 A.M.	44	42	38	38
9:00 A.M.	41	45	47	43
9:30 A.M.	39	39	41	41
10:00 A.M.	37	42	46	41
10:30 A.M.	39	40	39	40

   a. Based on this initial experience, determine the control limits for the mean temperature. Determine the grand mean. Plot the experience on a chart.
   b. Interpret the chart. Does there seem to be a time when the temperature is out of control?
8. Refer to exercise 7.
   a. Based on this initial experience, determine the control limits for the range. Plot the experience on a chart.
   b. Does there seem to be a time when there is too much variation in the temperature?

4. Variable: actual reading. Attribute: good, no good.

6. 0. 215

8. a. 15.22, 0
   b. First range is outside limit.

Attribute Control Charts

Often the data we collect are the result of counting rather than measuring. That is, we observe the presence or absence of some attribute. For example, the screw top on a bottle of shampoo either fits onto the bottle and does not leak (an "acceptable" condition) or does not seal and a leak results (an "unacceptable" condition), or a bank makes a loan to a customer and the loan is either repaid or it is not repaid. In other cases we are interested in the number of defects in a sample. British Airways might count the number of its flights arriving late per day at Gatwick Airport in London. In this section we discuss two types of attribute charts: the p (percent defective) and the c (number of defectives).

Percent Defective Chart

If the item recorded is the fraction of unacceptable parts made in a larger batch of parts, the appropriate control chart is the percent defective chart. This chart is based on the binomial distribution, discussed in Chapter 6, and proportions, discussed in Chapter 9. The centerline is at p, the mean proportion defective. The p replaces the $\bar{\bar{X}}$ of the variable control chart. The mean proportion defective is found by:

MEAN PROPORTION DEFECTIVE
$$p = \frac{\text{Total number defective}}{\text{Total number of items sampled}} \qquad [17\text{–}6]$$

The variation in the sample proportion is described by the standard error of a proportion. It is found by:

STANDARD ERROR OF THE PROPORTION
$$s_p = \sqrt{\frac{p(1-p)}{n}} \qquad [17\text{–}7]$$

Hence, the upper control limit (UCL) and the lower control limit (LCL) are computed as the mean percent defective plus or minus three times the standard error of the percents (proportions). The formula for the control limits is:

CONTROL LIMITS FOR PROPORTIONS
$$LCL, UCL = p \pm 3\sqrt{\frac{p(1-p)}{n}} \qquad [17\text{–}8]$$

An example will show the details of the calculations and the conclusions.

EXAMPLE

The Credit Department at Global National Bank is responsible for entering each transaction charged to the customer's monthly statement. Of course, accuracy is critical and errors will make the customer very unhappy! To guard against errors, each data entry clerk rekeys a sample of 1,500 of their batch of work a second time and a computer program checks that the numbers match. The program also prints a report of the number and size of any discrepancy. Seven people were working last hour and here are their results:

Inspector	Number Inspected	Number Mismatched
Mullins	1,500	4
Rider	1,500	6
Gankowski	1,500	6
Smith	1,500	2
Reed	1,500	15
White	1,500	4
Reading	1,500	4

Construct the percent defective chart for this process. What are the upper and the lower control limits? Interpret the results. Does it appear any of the data entry clerks are "out of control"?

SOLUTION

The first step is to determine the mean proportion defective p, using formula 17–6. It is .0039, found by 41/10,500.

Inspector	Number Inspected	Number Mismatched	Proportion Defective
Mullins	1,500	4	.00267
Rider	1,500	6	.00400
Gankowski	1,500	6	.00400
Smith	1,500	2	.00133
Reed	1,500	15	.01000
White	1,500	4	.00267
Reading	1,500	4	.00267
Total	10,500	41	

The upper and lower control limits are computed using formula (17–8).

$$LCL, UCL = p \pm 3\sqrt{\frac{p(1-p)}{n}}$$

$$= \frac{41}{10{,}500} \pm 3\sqrt{\frac{.0039(1-.0039)}{1{,}500}} = .0039 \pm .0048$$

From the above calculations, the upper control limit is .0087, found by .0039 + .0048. The lower control limit is 0. Why? The lower limit by formula is determined by .0039 − .0048, which is equal to −0.0009. A negative proportion defective is not possible, so the smallest value is 0. We set the control limit at 0. Thus, any data entry clerk whose proportion defective is between 0 and .0087 is "in control." Clerk number 5, whose name is Reed, is out of control. Her proportion defective is .01, or 1.0 percent, which is outside the upper control limit. Perhaps she should receive additional training or be transferred to another position. This information is summarized in Chart 17–6, which is output from the MINITAB system.

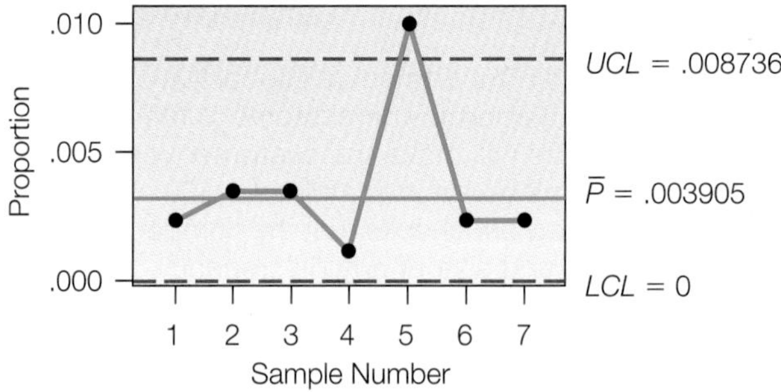

CHART 17–6 Control Chart for Proportion of Entries Defective among Data Entry Clerks at Global National Bank

c-Bar Chart

The c-bar chart plots the number of defects or failures per unit. It is based on the Poisson distribution discussed in Chapter 6. The number of bags mishandled on a flight by Southwest Airlines might be monitored by a c-bar chart. The "unit" under consideration is the flight. On most flights there are no bags mishandled. On others there may be only one, on others two, and so on. The Internal Revenue Service might count and develop a control chart for the number of errors in arithmetic per tax return. Most returns will not have any errors, some returns will have a single error, others will have two, and so on. We let $\bar{c}$ be the mean number of defects per unit. Thus, $\bar{c}$ is the mean number of bags mishandled by Southwest Airlines per flight or the mean number of arithmetic errors per tax return. Recall from Chapter 6 that the standard deviation of a Poisson distribution is the square root of the mean. Thus, we can determine the 3-sigma, or 99.74 percent limits on a c-bar chart by:

CONTROL LIMITS FOR THE NUMBER OF DEFECTS PER UNIT

$$LCL, UCL = \bar{c} \pm 3\sqrt{\bar{c}} \quad \textbf{[17–9]}$$

EXAMPLE

The publisher of the *Oak Harbor Daily Telegraph* is concerned about the number of misspelled words in the daily newspaper. They do not print a paper on Saturday or Sunday. In an effort to control the problem and promote the need for correct spelling, a control chart is to be instituted. The number of misspelled words found in the final edition of the paper for the last 10 days is: 5, 6, 3, 0, 4, 5, 1, 2, 7, and 4. Determine the appropriate control limits and interpret the chart. Were there any days during the period that the number of misspelled words was out of control?

SOLUTION

The sum of the number of misspelled words over the 10-day period is 37. So the mean number of defects, $\bar{c}$, is 3.7. The square root of this number is 1.924. So the upper control limit is:

$$UCL = \bar{c} + 3\sqrt{\bar{c}} = 3.7 + 3\sqrt{3.7} = 3.7 + 5.77 = 9.47$$

The computed lower control limit would be $3.7 - 3(1.924) = -2.07$. However, the number of misspelled words cannot be less than 0, so we use 0 as the lower limit. The lower control limit is 0 and the upper limit is 9.47. When we compare each of the data points to the value of 9.47, we see they are all less than the upper control limit; the number of misspelled words is "in control." Of course, newspapers are going to strive to eliminate all misspelled words, but control charting techniques offer a means of tracking daily results and determining whether there has been a change. For example, if a new proofreader was hired, her work could be compared with others. These results are summarized in Chart 17–7, which is output from the MINITAB system.

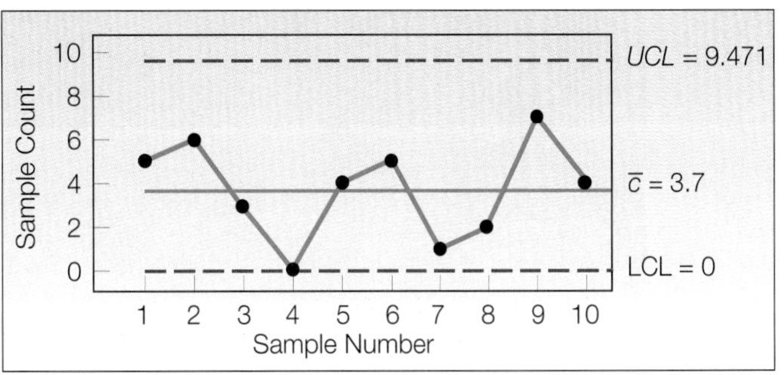

CHART 17–7 c-Bar Chart for Number of Misspelled Words per Edition of the *Oak Harbor Daily Telegraph*

Self-Review 17–3

The Auto-Lite Company manufactures car batteries. At the end of each shift the Quality Assurance Department selects a sample of batteries and tests them. The number of defective batteries found over the last 12 shifts is 2, 1, 0, 2, 1, 1, 7, 1, 1, 2, 6, and 1. Construct a control chart for the process and comment on whether the process is in control.

Exercises

9. A bicycle manufacturer randomly selects 10 frames each day and tests for defects. The number of defective frames found over the last 14 days is 3, 2, 1, 3, 2, 2, 8, 2, 0, 3, 5, 2, 0, 4. Construct a control chart for this process and comment on whether the process is "in control."

10. 1.6 ± 3.79

10. Scott Paper tests its toilet paper by subjecting 15 rolls to a wet stress test to see whether and how often the paper tears during the test. Following are the number of defectives found over the last 15 days: 2, 3, 1, 2, 2, 1, 3, 2, 2, 1, 2, 2, 1, 0, and 0. Construct a control chart for the process and comment on whether the process is "in control."

11. Sam's Supermarkets tests its checkout clerks by randomly examining the printout receipts for scanning errors. The following numbers are the number of errors on each receipt for October 27: 0, 1, 1, 0, 0, 1, 1, 0, 1, 1, 0. Construct a control chart for this process and comment on whether the process is "in control."

12. 3.6 ± 5.69

12. Dave Christi runs a car wash chain scattered throughout Chicago. He is concerned that some local managers are giving away free washes to their friends. He decides to collect data on the number of "voided" sales receipts. Of course, some of them are legitimate voids. Would the following data indicate a reasonable number of "voids" at his facilities: 3, 8, 3, 4, 6, 5, 0, 1, 2, 4? Construct a control chart for this process and comment on whether the process is "in control."

Statistics in Action

It was reported during the late 1980s that a Canadian firm ordered some parts from a Japanese company with instructions that there should be "no more than three defective parts per one thousand." When the parts arrived, there was a note attached that said, "Your three defective parts are wrapped separately in the upper left compartment of the shipment." This is a far cry from the days when "Made in Japan" meant cheap.

Acceptance Sampling

The previous section was concerned with maintaining the *quality of the product as it is being produced.* In many business situations we are also concerned with the *quality of the incoming finished product.* What do the following cases have in common?

- Sims Software, Inc., purchases CDs from CDs International. The normal purchase order is for 100,000 CDs, packaged in lots of 1,000. Todd Sims, president, does not expect each CD to be perfect. In fact, he has agreed to accept lots of 1,000 with up to 10 percent defective. He would like to develop a plan to inspect incoming lots, to ensure that the quality standard is met. The purpose of the inspection procedure is to separate the acceptable from the unacceptable lots.
- Zenith Electric purchases magnetron tubes from Bono Electronics for use in their new microwave oven. The tubes are shipped to Zenith in lots of 10,000. Zenith

allows the incoming lots to contain up to 5 percent defective tubes. They would like to develop a sampling plan to determine which lots meet the criterion and which do not.

- General Motors purchases windshields from many suppliers. GM insists that the windshields be in lots of 1,000. They are willing to accept 50 or fewer defects in each lot, that is, 5 percent defective. They would like to develop a sampling procedure to verify that incoming shipments meet the criterion.

The common thread in these cases is a need to verify that an incoming product meets the stipulated requirements. The situation can be likened to a screen door, which allows the warm summer air to enter the room while keeping the bugs out. Acceptance sampling lets the lots of acceptable quality into the manufacturing area and screens out lots that are not acceptable.

Of course, the situation in modern business is more complex. The buyer wants protection against accepting lots that are below the quality standard. The best protection against inferior quality is 100 percent inspection. Unfortunately, the cost of 100 percent inspection is often prohibitive. Another problem with checking each item is that the test may be destructive. If all light bulbs were tested until burning out before they were shipped, there would be none left to sell. Also, 100 percent inspection may not lead to the identification of all defects, because boredom might cause a loss of perception on the part of the inspectors. Thus, complete inspection is rarely employed in practical situations.

Acceptance sampling

Acceptance number

The usual procedure is to screen the quality of incoming parts by using a statistical sampling plan. According to this plan, a sample of n units is randomly selected from the lots of N units (the population). This is called **acceptance sampling.** The inspection will determine the number of defects in the sample. This number is compared with a predetermined number called the **critical number** or the **acceptance number.** The acceptance number is usually designated c. If the number of defects in the sample of size n is less than or equal to c, the lot is accepted. If the number of defects exceeds c, the lot is rejected and returned to the supplier, or perhaps submitted to 100 percent inspection.

Consumer's risk

Producer's risk

Acceptance sampling is a decision-making process. There are two possible decisions: accept or reject the lot. In addition, there are two situations under which the decision is made: the lot is good or the lot is bad. These are the states of nature. If the lot is good and the sample inspection reveals the lot to be good, or if the lot is bad and the sample inspection indicates it is bad, then a correct decision is made. However, there are two other possibilities. The lot may actually contain more defects than it should, but it is accepted. This is called **consumer's risk.** Similarly, the lot may be within the agreed-upon limits, but it is rejected during the sample inspection. This is called the **producer's risk.** The following summary table for acceptance decisions shows these possibilities. Notice how this discussion is very similar to the ideas of Type I and Type II errors presented at the beginning of Chapter 10. (See page 339.)

	States of Nature	
Decision	**Good Lot**	**Bad Lot**
Accept lot	Correct	Consumer's risk
Reject lot	Producer's risk	Correct

OC curve

To evaluate a sampling plan and determine that it is fair to both the producer and the consumer, the usual procedure is to develop an **operating characteristic curve,** or an **OC curve** as it is usually called. An OC curve reports the percent defective along the horizontal axis and the probability of accepting that percent defective along the vertical axis. A smooth curve is usually drawn connecting all the possible levels of quality. The binomial distribution is used to develop the probabilities for an OC curve.

EXAMPLE

Sims Software, as mentioned earlier, purchases CDs from CDs International. The CDs are packaged in lots of 1,000 each. Todd Sims, president of Sims Software, has agreed to accept lots with 10 percent or fewer defective CDs. Todd has directed his inspection department to select a random sample of 20 CDs and examine them carefully. He will accept the lot if it has two or fewer defectives in the sample. Develop an OC curve for this inspection plan. What is the probability of accepting a lot that is 10 percent defective?

SOLUTION

Attribute sampling

This type of sampling is called **attribute sampling** because the sampled item, a CD in this case, is classified as acceptable or unacceptable. No "reading" or "measurement" is obtained on the CD. Let's structure the problem in terms of the states of nature. Let π represent the actual proportion defective in the population.

The lot is good if $\pi \leq .10$.
The lot is bad if $\pi > .10$.

Decision rule

Let X be the number of defects in the sample. The decision rule is:

Reject the lot if $X \geq 3$.
Accept the lot if $X \leq 2$.

Here the acceptable lot is one with 10 percent or fewer defective CDs. If the lot is acceptable when it has exactly 10 percent defectives, it would be even more acceptable if it contained fewer than 10 percent defectives. Hence, it is the usual practice to work with the upper limit of the percent of defectives.

The binomial distribution is used to compute the various values on the OC curve. Recall that for us to use the binomial there are four requirements:

1. There are only two possible outcomes. Here the CD is either acceptable or unacceptable.
2. There is a fixed number of trials. In this instance the number of trials is the sample size of 20.
3. There is a constant probability of success. A success is the probability of finding a defective CD. It is assumed to be .10.
4. The trials are independent. The probability of obtaining a defective CD on the third one selected is not related to the likelihood of finding a defect on the fourth CD selected.

Appendix A gives the various binomial probabilities. We need to convert the acceptance sampling vocabulary to that used in Chapter 6 for discrete probability distributions. Let $\pi = .10$, the probability of a success, and $n = 20$, the number of trials. c is the number of defects allowed—two in this case. We will now determine the probability of accepting an incoming lot that is 10 percent defective using a sample size of 20 and allowing zero, one, or two defects. First, locate within Appendix A the case where $n = 20$ and $\pi = .10$. Find the row where X, the number of defects, is 0. The probability is .122. Next find the probability of one defect, that is, where $X = 1$. It is .270. Similarly, the probability of $X = 2$ is .285. To find the probability of two or fewer defects, we need to add these three probabilities. The total is .677. Hence, the probability of accepting a lot that is 10 percent defective is .677. The probability of rejecting this lot is .323, found by $1 - .677$. This result is usually written in shorthand notation as follows (the bar, |, means "given that"):

$$P(X \leq 2 \mid \pi = .10 \text{ and } n = 20) = .677$$

The OC curve in Chart 17–8 shows various values of π and the corresponding probabilities of accepting a lot of that quality. Management of Sims Software will be able to quickly evaluate the probabilities of various quality levels.

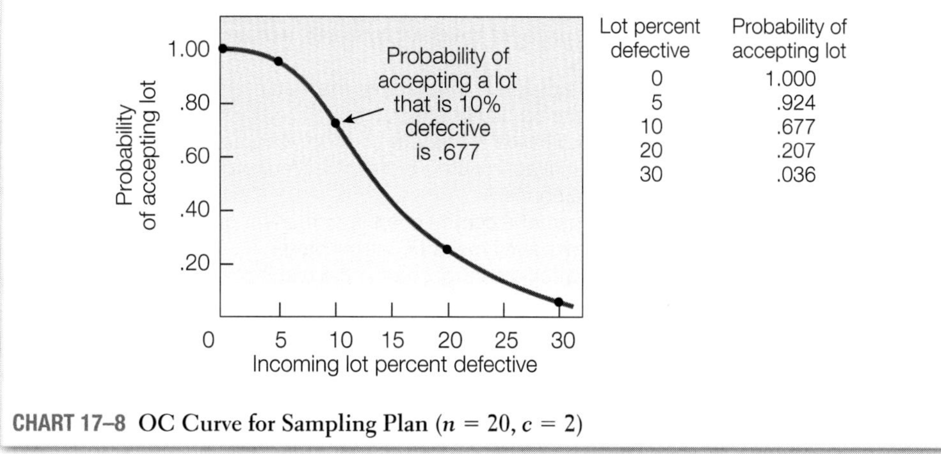

Lot percent defective	Probability of accepting lot
0	1.000
5	.924
10	.677
20	.207
30	.036

CHART 17–8 OC Curve for Sampling Plan ($n = 20, c = 2$)

Self-Review 17–4

Compute the probability of accepting a lot of CDs that is actually 30 percent defective, using the sampling plan for Sims Software.

Exercises

13. Determine the probability of accepting lots that are 10 percent, 20 percent, 30 percent, and 40 percent defective using a sample of size 12 and an acceptance number of 2.

14. .956, .698, .355, .125

14. Determine the probability of accepting lots that are 10 percent, 20 percent, 30 percent, and 40 percent defective using a sample of size 14 and an acceptance number of 3.

15. Warren Electric manufactures fuses for many customers. To ensure the quality of the outgoing product, they test 10 fuses each hour. If no more than one fuse is defective, they package the fuses and prepare them for shipment. Develop an OC curve for this sampling plan. Compute the probabilities of accepting lots that are 10 percent, 20 percent, 30 percent, and 40 percent defective. Draw the OC curve for this sampling plan using the four quality levels.

16. .763, .235, .032, .002

16. Grills Radio Products purchases transistors from Mira Electronics. According to his sampling plan, Art Grills, owner of Grills Radio, will accept a shipment of transistors if three or fewer are defective in a sample of 25. Develop an OC curve for these percents defective: 10 percent, 20 percent, 30 percent, and 40 percent.

Chapter Outline

I. The objective of statistical quality control is to control the quality of the product or service as it is being developed.

II. A Pareto chart is a technique for tallying the number and type of defects that happen within a product or service.

A. This chart was named after an Italian scientist, Vilfredo Pareto.
B. The concept of the chart is that 80 percent of the activity is caused by 20 percent of the factors.

III. A fishbone diagram emphasizes the relationship between a possible problem cause that will produce the particular effect.
A. It is also called a cause-and-effect diagram.
B. The usual approach is to consider four problem areas: methods, materials, equipment, and personnel.

IV. The purpose of a control chart is to monitor graphically the quality of a product or service.
A. There are two types of control charts.
1. A variable control chart is the result of a measurement.
2. An attribute chart shows whether the product or service is acceptable or not acceptable.
B. There are two sources of variation in the quality of a product or service.
1. Chance variation is random in nature and cannot be controlled or eliminated.
2. Assignable variation is not due to random causes and can be eliminated.
C. Four control charts were considered in this chapter.
1. A mean chart shows the mean of a variable, and a range chart shows the range of the variable.
a. The upper and lower control limits are set at plus or minus 3 standard errors from the mean.
b. The formulas for the upper and lower control limits for the mean are:

$$UCL = \bar{\bar{X}} + A_2\bar{R} \qquad LCL = \bar{\bar{X}} - A_2\bar{R} \qquad \textbf{[17–4]}$$

c. The formulas for the upper and lower control limits for the range are:

$$UCL = D_4\bar{R} \qquad LCL = D_3\bar{R} \qquad \textbf{[17–5]}$$

2. A percent defective chart is an attribute chart that shows the proportion of the product or service that does not conform to the standard.
a. The mean percent defective is found by

$$p = \frac{\text{Total number defective}}{\text{Total number of items sampled}} \qquad \textbf{[17–6]}$$

b. The control limits for the proportion defective are determined from the equation

$$LCL, UCL = p \pm 3\sqrt{\frac{p(1-p)}{n}} \qquad \textbf{[17–8]}$$

3. A *c*-bar chart refers to the number of defects per unit.
a. It is based on the Poisson distribution.
b. The mean number of defects per unit is $\bar{c}$.
c. The control limits are determined from the following equation.

$$LCL, UCL = \bar{c} \pm 3\sqrt{\bar{c}} \qquad \textbf{[17–9]}$$

V. Acceptance sampling is a method to determine whether an incoming lot of a product meets specified standards.
A. It is based on random sampling techniques.
B. A random sample of n units is selected from a population of N units.
C. c is the maximum number of defective units that may be found in the sample of n and the lot still considered acceptable.
D. An OC (operating characteristic) curve is developed using the binomial probability distribution to determine the probability of accepting lots of various quality levels.

Pronunciation Key

SYMBOL	MEANING	PRONUNCIATION
$\bar{\bar{X}}$	Mean of the sample means	*X double bar*
$s_{\bar{X}}$	Standard error of the mean	*s sub X bar*

A_2	Constant used to determine the upper and lower control limit for the mean	*A sub 2*
$\bar{R}$	Mean of the sample ranges	*R bar*
D_4	Constant used to determine the upper control limit for the range	*D sub 4*
$\bar{c}$	Mean number of defects per unit	*c bar*

Chapter Exercises

17. The production supervisor at Westburg Electric, Inc., noted an increase in the number of electric motors rejected at the time of final inspection. Of the last 200 motors rejected, 80 of the defects were due to poor wiring, 60 contained a short in the coil, 50 involved a defective plug, and 10 involved other defects. Develop a Pareto chart to show the major problem areas.

18. See IM.

18. The manufacturer of athletic shoes conducted a study on their newly developed jogging shoe. Listed below are the type and frequency of the nonconformities and failures found. Develop a Pareto chart to show the major problem areas.

Type of Nonconformity	Frequency	Type of Nonconformity	Frequency
Sole separation	34	Lace breakage	14
Heel separation	98	Eyelet failure	10
Sole penetration	62	Other	16

19. Wendy's fills their soft drinks with an automatic machine that operates based on the weight of the soft drink. When the process is in control, the machine fills each cup so that the grand mean is 10.0 ounces and the mean range is 0.25 for samples of 5.

a. Determine the upper and lower control limits for the process for both the mean and the range.

b. The manager of the I-280 store tested five soft drinks served last hour and found that the mean was 10.16 ounces and the range was 0.35 ounces. Is the process in control? Should other action be taken?

20. A new machine has just been installed to cut and rough-shape large slugs. The slugs are then transferred to a precision grinder. One of the critical measurements is the outside diameter. The quality control inspector randomly selected five slugs each hour, measured the outside diameter, and recorded the results. The measurements (in millimeters) for the period 8:00 A.M. to 10:30 A.M. follow.

	Outside Diameter (millimeters)				
Time	1	2	3	4	5
8:00	87.1	87.3	87.9	87.0	87.0
8:30	86.9	88.5	87.6	87.5	87.4
9:00	87.5	88.4	86.9	87.6	88.2
9:30	86.0	88.0	87.2	87.6	87.1
10:00	87.1	87.1	87.1	87.1	87.1
10:30	88.0	86.2	87.4	87.3	87.8

20. a. *UCL* = 88.11
LCL = 86.61
b. See IM.
c. No points out of control.

a. Determine the control limits for the mean and the range.

b. Plot the control limits for the mean outside diameter and the range.

c. Are there any points on the mean or the range chart that are out of control? Comment on the chart.

21. The Long Last Tire Company, as part of its inspection process, tests its tires for tread wear under simulated road conditions. Twenty samples of three tires each were selected from different shifts over the last month of operation. The tread wear is reported below in hundredths of an inch.

Sample	Tread Wear			Sample	Tread Wear		
1	44	41	19	11	11	33	34
2	39	31	21	12	51	34	39
3	38	16	25	13	30	16	30
4	20	33	26	14	22	21	35
5	34	33	36	15	11	28	38
6	28	23	39	16	49	25	36
7	40	15	34	17	20	31	33
8	36	36	34	18	26	18	36
9	32	29	30	19	26	47	26
10	29	38	34	20	34	29	32

a. Determine the control limits for the mean and the range.
b. Plot the control limits for the mean outside diameter and the range.
c. Are there any points on the mean or the range chart that are "out of control"? Comment on the chart.

22. 55.14 ± 20.48
0, 75.08

22. The Charter National Bank has a staff of loan officers located in its branch offices throughout the Southwest. The vice president in charge of the loan officers would like some information on the typical amount of loans and the range in the amount of the loans. A staff analyst of the vice president selected a sample of 10 loan officers and from each officer selected a sample of five loans he or she made last month. The data are reported below. Develop a control chart for the mean and the range. Do any of the officers appear to be "out of control"? Comment on your findings.

	Loan Amount ($000)						Loan Amount ($000)				
Officer	**1**	**2**	**3**	**4**	**5**	**Officer**	**1**	**2**	**3**	**4**	**5**
Weinraub	59	74	53	48	65	Bowyer	66	80	54	68	52
Visser	42	51	70	47	67	Kuhlman	74	43	45	65	49
Moore	52	42	53	87	85	Ludwig	75	53	68	50	31
Brunner	36	70	62	44	79	Longnecker	42	65	70	41	52
Wolf	34	59	39	78	61	Simonetti	43	38	10	19	47

23. The producer of a candy bar, called the "A Rod" Bar, reports on the package that the calorie content is 420 per 2-ounce bar. A sample of 5 bars from each of the last 10 days is sent for a chemical analysis of the calorie content. The results are shown below. Does it appear that there are any days where the calorie count is out of control? Develop an appropriate control chart and analyze your findings.

	Calorie Count						Calorie Count				
Sample	**1**	**2**	**3**	**4**	**5**	**Sample**	**1**	**2**	**3**	**4**	**5**
1	426	406	418	431	432	6	427	417	408	418	422
2	421	422	415	412	411	7	422	417	426	435	426
3	425	420	406	409	414	8	419	417	412	415	417
4	424	419	402	400	417	9	417	432	417	416	422
5	421	408	423	410	421	10	420	422	421	415	422

24. The Early Morning Delivery Service guarantees delivery of small packages by 10:30 A.M. Of course, some of the packages are not delivered by 10:30 A.M. For a sample of 200 packages delivered each of the last 15 working days, the following number of packages were delivered after the deadline: 9, 14, 2, 13, 9, 5, 9, 3, 4, 3, 4, 3, 3, 8, and 4.

24. a. .031
b. 0, .068
c. .05

a. Determine the mean proportion of packages delivered after 10:30 A.M.
b. Determine the control limits for the proportion of packages delivered after 10:30 A.M. Were any of the sampled days out of control?
c. If 10 packages out of 200 in the sample were delivered after 10:30 A.M. today, is this sample within the control limits?

25. An automatic machine produces 5.0 millimeter bolts at a high rate of speed. A quality control program has been started to control the number of defectives. The quality control inspector selects 50 bolts at random and determines how many are defective. The number of defectives in the first 10 samples is 3, 5, 0, 4, 1, 2, 6, 5, 7, and 7.
a. Design a percent defective chart. Insert the mean percent defective, *UCL*, and *LCL*.
b. Plot the percent defective for the first 10 samples on the chart.
c. Interpret the chart.

26. $\bar{X} = 24.972$
$LCL = 23.62$,
$UCL = 26.33$
$\bar{R} = 1.86$
$UCL = 4.243$

26. Steele Breakfast Foods, Inc. produces a popular brand of raisin brand cereal. The package indicates it contains 25.0 ounces of cereal. To ensure the product quality, the Steele Inspection Department makes hourly checks on the production process. As a part of the hourly check, 4 boxes are selected and their contents weighed. The results are reported below.

Sample	Weights			
1	26.1	24.4	25.6	25.2
2	25.2	25.9	25.1	24.8
3	25.6	24.5	25.7	25.1
4	25.5	26.8	25.1	25.0
5	25.2	25.2	26.3	25.7
6	26.6	24.1	25.5	24.0
7	27.6	26.0	24.9	25.3
8	24.5	23.1	23.9	24.7
9	24.1	25.0	23.5	24.9
10	25.8	25.7	24.3	27.3
11	22.5	23.0	23.7	24.0
12	24.5	24.8	23.2	24.2
13	24.4	24.5	25.9	25.5
14	23.1	23.3	24.4	24.7
15	24.6	25.1	24.0	25.3
16	24.4	24.4	22.8	23.4
17	25.1	24.1	23.9	26.2
18	24.5	24.5	26.0	26.2
19	25.3	27.5	24.3	25.5
20	24.6	25.3	25.5	24.3
21	24.9	24.4	25.4	24.8
22	25.7	24.6	26.8	26.9
23	24.8	24.3	25.0	27.2
24	25.4	25.9	26.6	24.8
25	26.2	23.5	23.7	25.0

Develop an appropriate control chart. What are the limits? Is the process out of control at any time?

27. An investor believes there is a 50-50 chance that a stock will increase or decrease on a particular day. To investigate this idea, for 30 consecutive trading days the investor selects a random sample of 50 stocks and counts the number that increase. The number of stocks in the sample that increased is reported below.

14	12	13	17	10	18	10	13	13	14
13	10	12	11	9	13	14	11	12	11
15	13	10	16	10	11	12	15	13	10

Develop a percent defective chart and write a brief report summarizing your findings. Based on these sample results, is it reasonable that the odds are 50-50 that a stock will increase? What percent of the stocks would need to increase in a day for the process to be "out of control?"

28. $\bar{c} = 9.417$
$UCL = 18.62$

28. Lahey Motors specializes in selling cars to buyers with a poor credit history. Listed below is the number of cars that were repossessed from Lahey customers because they did not meet the payment obligations over the last 36 months.

6	5	8	20	11	10	9	3	9	9
15	12	4	11	9	9	6	18	6	8
9	7	13	7	11	8	11	13	6	14
13	5	5	8	10	11				

Develop a *c*-bar chart for the number repossessed. Were there any months when the number was out of control? Write a brief report summarizing your findings.

29. A process engineer is considering two sampling plans. In the first a sample of 10 will be selected and the lot accepted if 3 or fewer are found defective. In the second the sample size is 20 and the acceptance number is 5. Develop an OC curve for each. Compare the probability of acceptance for lots that are 5, 10, 20, and 30 percent defective. Which of the plans would you recommend if you were the supplier?

30. $.14 \pm .15$

30. The Inter State Moving and Storage Company is setting up a control chart to monitor the proportion of residential moves that result in written complaints due to late delivery, lost items, or damaged items. A sample of 50 moves is selected for each of the last 12 months. The number of written complaints in each sample is 8, 7, 4, 8, 2, 7, 11, 6, 7, 6, 8, and 12.

a. Design a percent defective chart. Insert the mean percent defective, *UCL*, and *LCL*.
b. Plot the proportion of written complaints in the last 12 months.
c. Interpret the chart. Does it appear that the number of complaints is out of control for any of the months?

31. Eric's Cookie House sells chocolate chip cookies in shopping malls. Of concern is the number of chocolate chips in each cookie. Eric, the owner and president, would like to establish a control chart for the number of chocolate chips per cookie. He selects a sample of 15 cookies from today's production and counts the number of chocolate chips in each. The results are as follows: 6, 8, 20, 12, 20, 19, 11, 23, 12, 14, 15, 16, 12, 13, and 12.

a. Determine the centerline and the control limits.
b. Develop a control chart and plot the number of chocolate chips per cookie.
c. Interpret the chart. Does it appear that the number of chocolate chips is out of control in any of the cookies sampled?

32. 3.0 ± 5.20

32. The number of "near misses" recorded for the last 20 months at the Lima International Airport is 3, 2, 3, 2, 2, 3, 5, 1, 2, 2, 4, 4, 2, 6, 3, 5, 2, 5, 1, and 3. Develop an appropriate control chart. Determine the mean number of misses per month and the limits on the number of misses per month. Are there any months where the number of near misses is out of control?

33. The following number of robberies were reported during the last 10 days to the Robbery Division of the Metro City Police: 10, 8, 8, 7, 8, 5, 8, 5, 4, and 7. Develop an appropriate control chart. Determine the mean number of robberies reported per day and determine the control limits. Are there any days when the number of robberies reported is out of control?

34. Seiko purchases watch stems for their watches in lots of 10,000. Seiko's sampling plan calls for checking 20 stems, and if 3 or fewer stems are defective, the lot is accepted.

34. a. .015
b. 1.00, .867, .412, .108, .015

a. Based on their sampling plan, what is the probability that a lot of 40 percent defective will be accepted?
b. Design an OC curve for incoming lots that have zero, 10 percent, 20 percent, 30 percent, and 40 percent defective stems.

35. Automatic Screen Door Manufacturing Company purchases door latches from a number of vendors. The purchasing department is responsible for inspecting the incoming latches. Automatic purchases 10,000 door latches per month and inspects 20 latches selected at random. Develop an OC curve for the sampling plan if three latches can be defective and the incoming lot is still accepted.

36. At the beginning of each football season Team Sports, the local sporting goods store, purchases 5,000 footballs. A sample of 25 balls is selected, and they are inflated, tested, and then deflated. If more than two balls are found defective, the lot of 5,000 is returned to the manufacturer. Develop an OC curve for this sampling plan.

36. a. .537, .099, .008
b. .2538
c. .8729

a. What are the probabilities of accepting lots that are 10 percent, 20 percent, and 30 percent defective?

b. Estimate the probability of accepting a lot that is 15 percent defective.

c. John Brennen, owner of Team Sports, would like the probability of accepting a lot that is 5 percent defective to be more than 90 percent. Does this appear to be the case with this sampling plan?

Computer Commands

1. The MINITAB commands for the Pareto chart on page 628 are:

a. Enter the reasons for water usage in column C1 and the gallons used in C2. Give the columns appropriate names.

b. Click on **Stat, Quality Tools, Pareto Chart,** and then hit **Enter.**

c. Select **Chart defects table,** indicate the location of the labels and frequencies, type a chart title, and click on **OK.**

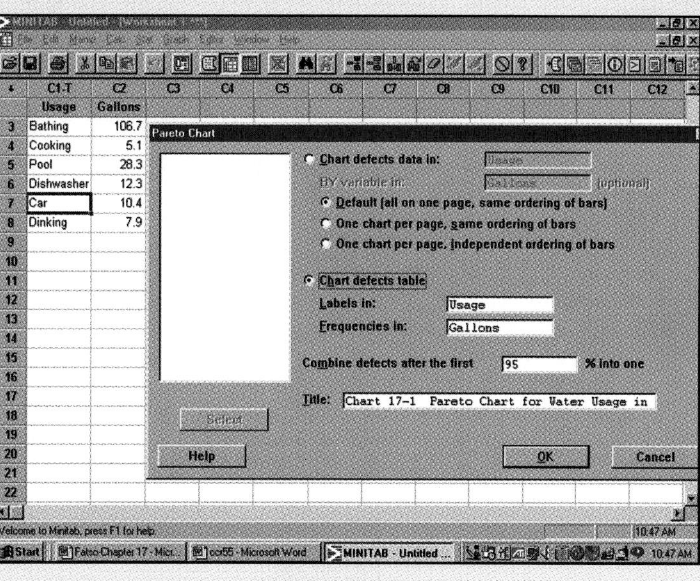

2. The MINITAB commands for the *X*-bar and *R* charts on page 636 are:

a. Enter the information in Table 17–1 or from the CD. The file name is *tbl17-1.*

b. Click on **Stat, Control charts, Xbar-R,** and hit **Enter.**

c. Click on the **Single column** option and enter the variable by name of column. The **Subgroup size** is *5.* Click on **Options,** enter the name of the chart, and then click **OK** twice.

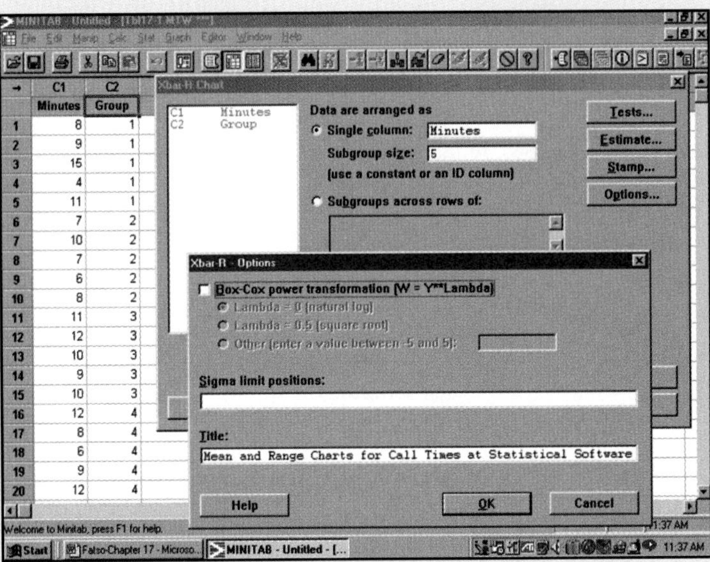

3. The MINITAB commands for the percent defective chart on page 640 are:
   a. Enter the data on the number of mismatches from page 639.
   b. Click on **Stat, Control charts, P,** and hit **Enter.**
   c. Select the **Variable** indicating the number of mismatches, click on **Subgroup size,** and enter *1500.* In the lower right click on **Annotation, Title,** type the title in the space provided, and click **OK** twice.

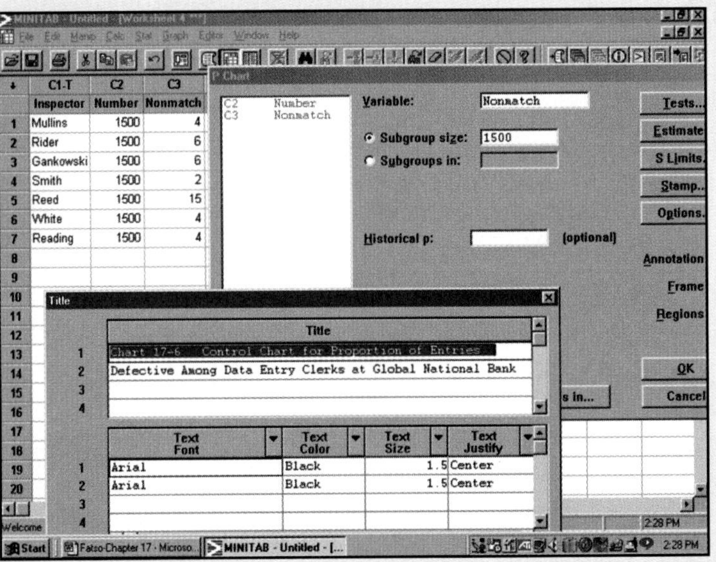

4. The MINITAB commands for the *c*-chart on page 641 are:
   a. Enter the data on the number of misspelled words from page 641.
   b. Click on **Stat, Control charts, C Chart,** and hit **Enter.**
   c. Select the **Variable** indicating the number of misspelled words. In the lower right click on **Annotation, Title,** type the title in the space provided, and click **OK** twice.

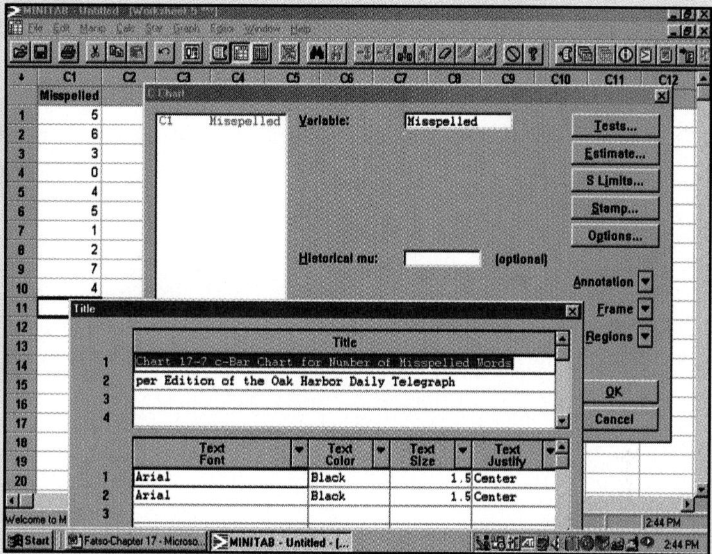
MINITAB - Untitled - [Worksheet 5 ***]
C Chart
C1 Misspelled
Variable: Misspelled
Tests...
Estimate...
S Limits...
Stamp...
Options...
Historical mu: (optional)
Annotation
Frame
Regions
OK
Cancel
Title
Chart 17-7 c-Bar Chart for Number of Misspelled Words
per Edition of the Oak Harbor Daily Telegraph
Text Font
Text Color
Text Size
Text Justify
Arial Black 1.5 Center
Arial Black 1.5 Center
Misspelled
5
6
3
0
4
5
1
2
7
4
Start
Fatso-Chapter 17 - Microso...
MINITAB - Untitled - [...
2:44 PM

Chapter 17 Answers to Self-Review

17–1

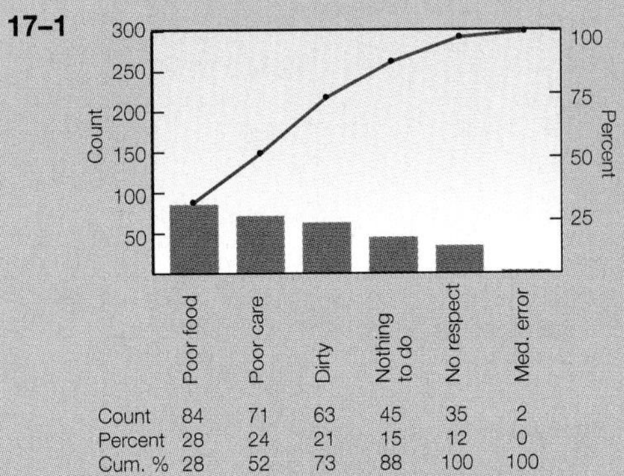

Seventy-three percent of the complaints involve poor food, poor care, or dirty conditions. These are the factors the administrator should address.

17–2 (a)

Sample Piece						
1	**2**	**3**	**4**	**Total**	**Average**	**Range**
1	4	5	2	12	3	4
2	3	2	1	8	2	2
1	7	3	5	16	4	6
					9	12

$$\bar{\bar{X}} = \frac{9}{3} = 3 \qquad \bar{R} = \frac{12}{3} = 4$$

$$UCL \text{ and } LCL = \bar{\bar{X}} \pm A_2\bar{R}$$

$$= 3 \pm 0.729(4)$$

$$UCL = 5.916 \qquad LCL = 0.084$$

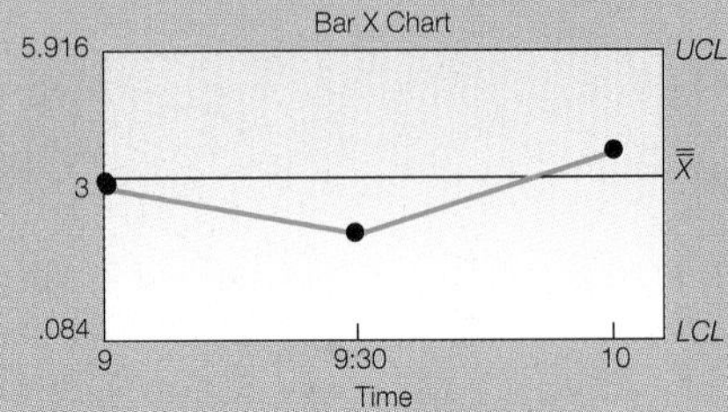

$$LCL = D_3\bar{R} = 0(4) = 0$$

$$UCL = D_4\bar{R} = 2.282(4) = 9.128$$

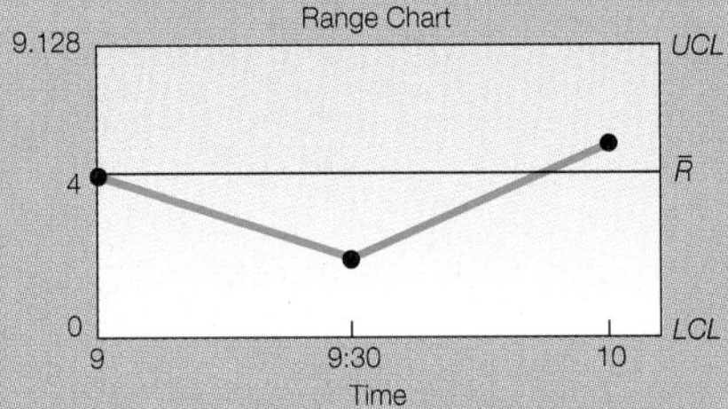

(b) Yes. Both the mean chart and the range chart indicate that the process is in control.

17–3 $\bar{c} = \frac{25}{12} = 2.083$

$$UCL = 2.083 + 3\sqrt{2.083} = 6.413$$

$$LCL = 2.083 - 3\sqrt{2.083} = 0$$

The shift with 7 defects is out of control.

17–4 $P(X \leq 2 \mid \pi = .30 \text{ and } n = 20) = .036$

18

Index Numbers

Johnson and Johnson's common stock is listed on the New York Stock Exchange using the symbol JNJ. This stock information is reported in their annual reports. Use the data provided to compute a simple index for domestic sales. (See Goal 1 and Exercise 17.)

GOALS

When you have completed this chapter, you will be able to:

1 **Describe the term *index*.**

2 **Understand the difference between a weighted and an unweighted index.**

3 **Construct and interpret a *Laspeyers price index*.**

4 **Construct and interpret a *Paasche price index*.**

5 **Construct and interpret a *value index*.**

6 **Explain how the Consumer Price Index is constructed and interpreted.**

Introduction

In this chapter we will examine a useful descriptive tool called an **index**. No doubt you are familiar with indexes such as the **Consumer Price Index**, which is released monthly. There are many other indexes, such as the **Dow Jones Industrial Average** and **Standard & Poor's 500 Stock Average**. Indexes are published on a regular basis by the federal government, by business publications such as *Business Week* and *Forbes,* and in most daily newspapers.

Of what importance is an index? Why is the Consumer Price Index so important and so widely reported? As the name implies, it measures the change in the price of a large group of items consumers purchase. The Federal Reserve Board, consumer groups, unions, management, senior citizens organizations, and others in business and economics are very concerned about changes in prices. These groups closely monitor the Consumer Price Index as well as the **Producer Price Index**, which measures price fluctuations at all stages of production. To combat sharp price increases, the Federal Reserve often raises the interest rate to "cool down" the economy. Likewise, the Dow Jones Industrial Average, which is published daily, describes the overall change in common stock prices of 30 large companies during the day.

A few stock market indexes appear daily in the financial section of most newspapers. They are updated at least every 15 minutes on many Web sites, such as the business section of *USA Today* (*http://www.usatoday.com/money/mfront.htm*). Shown below are the Dow Jones Industrial Average, New York Stock Exchange Index, Nasdaq, and S&P 500 from the *USA Today* Web site.

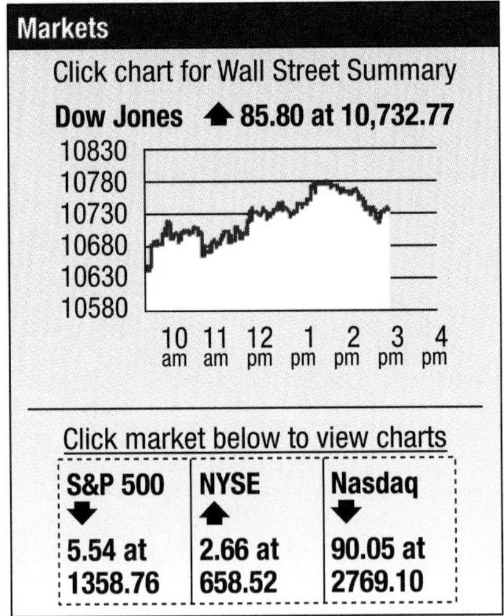

Simple Index Numbers

What is an index number?

> **INDEX NUMBER** A number that expresses the relative change in price, quantity, or value compared to a base period.

If the index number is used to measure the relative change in just one variable, such as hourly wages in manufacturing, we refer to this as a simple index. It is the ratio of two variables and that ratio converted to a percentage. The following four examples will serve to illustrate the use of index numbers. As noted in the definition, the main use of an index number in business is to show the percent change in one or more items from one time period to another.

EXAMPLE

According to the Bureau of Labor Statistics, in January 1987 the average hourly earnings of production workers was \$8.90. In December 2000 it was \$14.02. What is the index of hourly earnings of production workers for December 2000 based on January 1987?

SOLUTION

It is 157.5, found by:

$$P = \frac{\text{Average hourly earnings of production workers in December 2000}}{\text{Average hourly earnings of production workers in January 1987}}(100)$$

$$= \frac{\$14.02}{\$8.90}(100) = 157.5$$

Thus, the hourly earnings in December 2000 compared to January 1987 were 157.5 percent. This means there was a 57.5 percent increase in hourly earnings during the period, found by 157.5 − 100.0 = 57.5.

You can check the latest information on wages, the Consumer Price Indexes, and other business related values at the Bureau of Labor Statistics (BLS) website: *http://www.bls.gov/datahome.htm.* The following chart shows some statistics from the BLS.

Latest Numbers
CPI: +0.2% in December 2000
Unemployment Rate: 4.0% in December 2000
Payroll Employment: +105,000 in December 2000
Average Hourly Earnings: +\$0.05 in December 2000
PPI: unchanged in December 2000
ECI: +0.8% in 4th Quarter of 2000
Productivity: +3.3% in 3rd Quarter of 2000
U.S. Import Price Index: −0.5% in December 2000

EXAMPLE

The Bureau of the Census reported the number of farms in the United States dropped from 3,157,857 in 1964 to an estimated 1,200,000 in 2000. What is the index for the number of farms in 2000 based on the number in 1964?

SOLUTION

The index is 38.0, found by:

$$P = \frac{\text{Number of farms in 2000}}{\text{Number of farms in 1964}}(100) = \frac{1{,}200{,}000}{3{,}157{,}857}(100) = 38.0$$

This indicates that the number of farms in 2000 compared with 1964 was 38.0 percent. To put it another way, the number of farms in the United States decreased by 62.0 percent (100 − 38) during the period.

EXAMPLE

An index can also compare one item with another. The population of the Canadian province of British Columbia in 1999, the latest data available, was 4,023,100 and for Ontario it was 11,513,800. What is the population of British Columbia compared to Ontario?

SOLUTION

The index of population for British Columbia is 34.9, found by:

$$P = \frac{\text{Population of British Columbia}}{\text{Population of Ontario}}(100) = \frac{4{,}023{,}100}{11{,}513{,}800}(100) = 34.9$$

This indicates that the population of British Columbia is 34.9 percent (about one third) of the population of Ontario, or the population of British Columbia is 65.1 percent less than the population of Ontario (100 − 34.9 = 65.1).

EXAMPLE

The following graph shows the number of revenue passenger miles, reported in millions, for the four largest airline carriers in the United States in 1999. What is the index of revenue passenger miles for United, American, and Delta compared to Northwest?

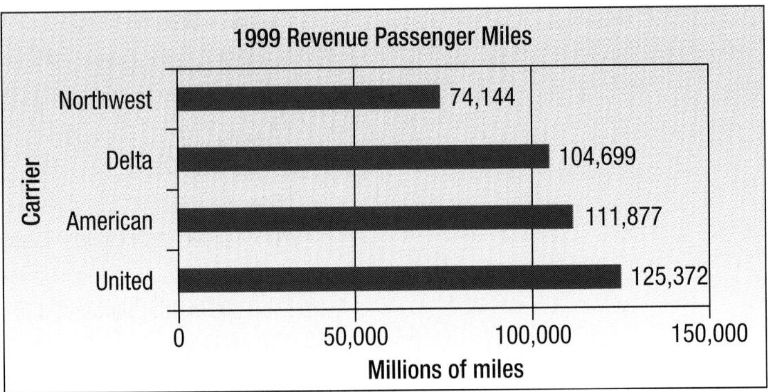

SOLUTION

To find the three indexes, we divide the revenue passenger miles for United, American, and Delta by those generated by Northwest. We conclude that United generated 69.1

percent more revenue passenger miles than Northwest, 50.9 for American, and 41.2 for Delta.

Air Carrier	Miles	Index	Found by
United	125,372	169.1	(125,372/74,144) × 100
American	111,877	150.9	(111,877/74,144) × 100
Delta	104,699	141.2	(104,699/74,144) × 100
Northwest	74,144	100.0	(74,144/74,144) × 100

Note from the previous discussion that:

1. The index of average hourly earnings of production workers (157.5) and the index of the number of farms (38.0) are actually percentages because they are based on the number 100. However, the percent symbol is usually omitted.
2. Each index has a **base period**. In the example regarding the average hourly earnings of production workers, we used January 1987 as the base period. The base period for the Consumer Price Index is 1993–95. The parity ratio, which is the ratio of the prices received by farmers to the prices paid by farmers, still has 1910–14 as the base period.
3. Most business and economic indexes are computed to the nearest whole number, such as 214 or 96, or to the nearest tenth of a percent, such as 83.4 or 118.7.

Why Convert Data to Indexes?

Indexes allow us to express a change in price, quantity, or value as a percent

Compiling index numbers is not a recent innovation. An Italian, G. R. Carli, is credited with originating index numbers in 1764. They were incorporated in a report he made regarding price fluctuations in Europe from 1500 to 1750. No systematic approach to collecting and reporting data in index form was evident in the United States until about 1900. The cost-of-living index (now called the Consumer Price Index) was introduced in 1913, and a long list of indexes has been compiled since then.

Why convert data to indexes? An index is a convenient way to express a change in a diverse group of items. The Consumer Price Index (CPI), for example, encompasses about 400 items—including golf balls, lawn mowers, hamburgers, funeral services, and dentists' fees. Prices are expressed in dollars per pound, box, yard, and many other different units. Only by converting the prices of these many diverse goods and services to one index number can the federal government and others concerned with inflation keep informed of the overall movement of consumer prices.

Converting data to indexes also makes it easier to assess the trend in a series composed of exceptionally large numbers. For example, suppose retail sales for the first six months of 2001 were $185,679,432,621.87 and 2000 six-month sales were $185,500,000,000.00. The increase of $179,432,621.87 appears significant. Yet if the 2001 sales total were expressed as an index based on 2000 sales, the increase would be less than one tenth of 1 percent!

$$\frac{\text{Retail sales in 2001}}{\text{Retail sales in 2000}} = \frac{\$185{,}679{,}432{,}621.87}{\$185{,}500{,}000{,}000.00} \times 100 = 100.09$$

Construction of Index Numbers

We already discussed the construction of a simple price index. The price in a selected year (such as 2001) is divided by the price in the base year. The base-period price is designated as p_0, and a price other than the base period is often referred to as the *given period* or *selected period* and designated p_t. To calculate the simple price index P using 100 as the base value for any given period use the formula:

SIMPLE INDEX
$$P = \frac{p_t}{p_0} \times 100 \qquad [18\text{–}1]$$

Suppose that the price of a standard lot at the Shady Rest Cemetery in 1995 was \$450. The price rose to \$795 in 2001. What is the price index for 2001 using 1995 as the base period and 100 as the base value? It is 176.7, found by:

$$P = \frac{p_t}{p_0}(100) = \frac{\$795}{\$450}(100) = 176.7$$

Interpreting this result, the price of a cemetery lot increased 76.7 percent from 1995 to 2001.

The base period need not be a single year. Note in Table 18–1 that if we use 1990–91 = 100, the base price for the stapler would be \$21 [found by determining the mean price of 1990 and 1991, (\$20 + \$22)/2 = \$21]. The prices \$20, \$22, and \$23 is averaged if 1990–92 had been selected as the base. The mean price would be \$21.67. The indexes constructed using the three different base periods are presented in Table 18–1. (Note that when 1990–92 = 100, the index numbers for 1990, 1991, and 1992 average 100.0, as we would expect.) Logically, the index numbers for 2001 using the three different bases are not the same.

TABLE 18–1 Prices of a Benson Automatic Stapler, Model 3, Converted to Indexes Using Three Different Base Periods

Year	Price of Stapler	Price Index (1990 = 100)	Price index (1990–91 = 100)	Price index (1990–92 = 100)
1985	\$18	90.0	$\frac{18}{21} \times 100 = 85.7$	$\frac{18}{21.67} \times 100 = 83.1$
1990	20	100.0	$\frac{20}{21} \times 100 = 95.2$	$\frac{20}{21.67} \times 100 = 92.3$
1991	22	110.0	$\frac{22}{21} \times 100 = 104.8$	$\frac{22}{21.67} \times 100 = 101.5$
1992	23	115.0	$\frac{23}{21} \times 100 = 109.5$	$\frac{23}{21.67} \times 100 = 106.1$
2001	38	190.0	$\frac{38}{21} \times 100 = 181.0$	$\frac{38}{21.67} \times 100 = 175.4$

Self-Review 18–1

1. The annual incomes in 2000 for a few selected companies are:

Company	Sales ($ millions)
Schering-Plough	2,110
Boeing	2,309
Exxon-Mobil	7,910
Johnson and Johnson	4,167
PepsiCo, Inc.	2,050

Express the annual income of Schering-Plough, Boeing, Exxon-Mobil, and Johnson and Johnson as an index, using the sales of PepsiCo, Inc. as the base (denominator) and 100 as the base value. Interpret.

2. The average hourly earnings of production workers for selected periods are given below.

Year	Average Hourly Earnings
1991	$10.32
1992	10.57
1993	10.83
1995	11.43
1997	12.28
1999	13.24
2000	13.74*

*preliminary estimate

(a) Using 1991 as the base period and 100 as the base value, determine the indexes for 1999 and for the preliminary 2000 data. Interpret the index.
(b) Use the average of 1991, 1992, and 1993 as the base and determine indexes for 1999 and the preliminary 2000 data using 100 as the base value. Interpret the index.
(c) What is the index for the preliminary 2000 data using 1995 as the base?

Exercises

1. PNC Bank, Inc., which has their headquarters in Pittsburgh, Pennsylvania, reported $17,446 (million) in commercial loans in 1995, $19,989 in 1997, and $21,468 in 1999. Using 1995 as the base, develop a simple index for the change in the amount of commercial loans for the years 1997 and 1999, based on 1995.

2. The table below reports the split adjusted stock prices for Home Depot for recent years. Develop an index, with 1995 as the base, for the change in stock price over the period.

2. 109.7, 201.1, 402.1, 554.6

Year	Year-end Stock Price
1995	$10.03
1996	11.00
1997	20.17
1998	40.33
1999	55.63

3. Listed below are the net sales for Blair Corporation, a mail-order retailer located in Warren, Pennsylvania, for the years 1995 to 1999. Their website is *www.blair.com.* Use the mean sales for the earliest three years to determine a base and then find the index for 1998 and 1999. By how much have net sales increased from the base period?

Year	Sales (millions)
1995	$560.9
1996	544.1
1997	486.6
1998	506.8
1999	522.2
2000	574.6

4. 114.8, 14.8%

4. In January 1994 the price for a whole fresh chicken was $0.899 per pound. In September 2000 the price for the same chicken was $1.032. Use the January 1994 price as the base period and 100 as the base value to develop a simple index. By what percent has the cost of chicken increased?

Unweighted Indexes

In many situations we wish to combine several items and develop an index to compare the cost of this aggregation of items in two different time periods. For example, we might be interested in an index for items that relate to the expense of running and maintaining an automobile. The items in the index might include tires, oil changes, and gasoline prices. Or we might be interested in a college student index. This index might include the cost of books, tuition, housing, meals, and entertainment. There are several ways we can combine the items to determine the index.

Simple Average of the Price Indexes

Table 18–2 reports the prices for several food items for the years 1995 and 2001. We would like to develop an index for this group of food items for 2001, using 1995 as the base. This is written in the abbreviated code 1995 = 100.

TABLE 18–2 Computation of Index for Food Price 2001, 1995 = 100

Item	1995 Price	2001 Price	Simple Index
Bread, white, cost per pound	$ 0.77	$ 0.89	115.6
Eggs, dozen	1.85	1.84	99.5
Milk, gallon, white	.88	1.01	114.8
Apples, Red Delicious, 1 pound	1.46	1.56	106.8
Orange Juice, 12 oz concentrate	1.58	1.70	107.6
Coffee, 100% ground roast, 1 pound	4.40	4.62	105.0
Total	$10.94	$11.62	

We could begin by computing a **simple average of the price indexes** for each item, using 1995 as the base year and 2001 as the given year. The simple index for bread is 115.6, found by using formula (18–1).

$$P = \frac{p_t}{p_0}(100) = \frac{\$0.89}{\$0.77}(100) = 115.6$$

We compute the simple index for the other items in Table 18–2 similarly. The largest price increase was for bread, 15.6 percent, and milk was a close second with 14.8

percent. The price of eggs dropped by a half a percent in the period, found by 100.0 − 99.5 = 0.5. Then it would be natural to average the simple indexes. The formula is:

SIMPLE AVERAGE OF THE PRICE RELATIVES $$P = \frac{\Sigma P_i}{n}$$ **[18–2]**

where P_i refers to the simple index for each of the items and n the number of items. In our example the index is 108.2, found by:

$$P = \frac{\Sigma P_i}{n} = \frac{115.6 + \cdots + 105.0}{6} = \frac{649.3}{6} = 108.2$$

This indicates that the mean of the group of indexes increased 8.2 percent from 1995 to 2001.

A positive feature of the simple average of price indexes is that we would obtain the same value for the index regardless of the units of measure. In the above index, if apples were priced in tons, instead of pounds, the impact of apples on the combined index would not change. That is, the commodity "apples" represents one of six items in the index, so the impact of the item is not related to the units. A negative feature of this index is that it fails to consider the relative importance of the items included in the index. For example, milk and eggs receive the same weight, even though a typical family might spend far more over the year on milk than on eggs.

Simple Aggregate Index

A second possibility is to sum the prices (rather than the indexes) for the two periods and then determine the index based on the totals. The formula is

SIMPLE AGGREGATE INDEX $$P = \frac{\Sigma p_t}{\Sigma p_0} \times 100$$ **[18–3]**

This is called a **simple aggregate index.** The index for the above food items is found by summing the prices in 1995 and 2001. The sum of the prices for the base period is $10.94 and for the given period it is $11.62. The simple aggregate index is 106.2. This means that the aggregate group of prices had increased 6.2 percent in the six-year period.

$$P = \frac{\Sigma p_t}{\Sigma p_0}(100) = \frac{\$11.62}{\$10.94}(100) = 106.2$$

Because the value of a simple aggregate index can be influenced by the units of measurement, it is not used frequently. In our example the value of the index would differ significantly if we were to report the price of apples in tons rather than pounds. Also, note the effect of coffee on the total index. For both the current year and the base year, the value of coffee is about 40 percent of the total index, so a change in the price of coffee will drive the index much more than any other item. So we need a way to appropriately "weight" the items according to their relative importance.

Weighted Indexes

Two methods of computing a **weighted price index** are the **Laspeyres** method and the **Paasche** method. They differ only in the period used for weighting. The

Laspeyres method uses *base-period weights*; that is, the original prices and quantities of the items bought are used to find the percent change over a period of time in either price or quantity consumed, depending on the problem. The Paasche method uses *current-year weights* for the denominator of the weighted index.

Laspeyres' Price Index

Etienne Laspeyres developed a method in the latter part of the 18th century to determine a weighted index using base-period weights. Applying his method, a weighted price index is computed by:

LASPEYRES' PRICE INDEX

$$P = \frac{\Sigma p_t q_0}{\Sigma p_0 q_0} \times 100 \qquad [18\text{–}4]$$

where:

P is the price index.
p_t is the current price.
p_0 is the price in the base period.
q_0 is the quantity used in the base period.

EXAMPLE

The prices for the six food items from Table 18–2 are repeated below in Table 18–3. Also included is the number of units of each consumed by a typical family in 1995 and 2001.

TABLE 18–3 Computation of Laspeyres and Paasche Indexes of Food Price, 1995 = 100

Item	1995 Price	1995 Quantity	2001 Price	2001 Quantity
Bread, white, cost per pound	$0.77	50	$0.89	55
Eggs, dozen	1.85	26	1.84	20
Milk, gallon, white	.88	102	1.01	130
Apples, Red Delicious, 1 pound	1.46	30	1.56	40
Orange Juice, 12 oz concentrate	1.58	40	1.70	41
Coffee, 100% ground roast, 1 pound	4.40	12	4.62	12

Determine a weighted price index using the Laspeyres method. Interpret the result.

SOLUTION

First we determine the total amount spent for the six items in the base period, 1995. To find this value we multiply the base period price for bread ($0.77) by the base period quantity of 50. The result is $38.50. This indicates that a total of $38.50 was spent in the base period on bread. We continue that for all items and total the results. The base period total is $336.16. The current period total is computed in a similar fashion. For the first item, bread, we multiply the quantity in 1995 by the price of bread in 2001, that is, $0.89(50). The result is $44.50. We make the same calculation for each item and total the result. The total is $365.60. Because of the repetitive nature of these calculations, a spreadsheet is effective for carrying out the calculations. Following is a copy of the Excel output.

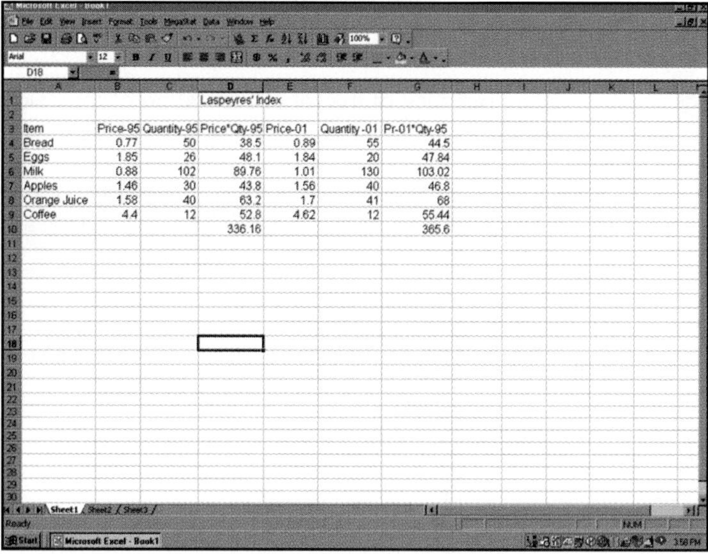

Laspeyres' Index

Item	Price-95	Quantity-95	Price*Qty-95	Price-01	Quantity -01	Pr-01*Qty-95
Bread	0.77	50	38.5	0.89	55	44.5
Eggs	1.85	26	48.1	1.84	20	47.84
Milk	0.88	102	89.76	1.01	130	103.02
Apples	1.46	30	43.8	1.56	40	46.8
Orange Juice	1.58	40	63.2	1.7	41	68
Coffee	4.4	12	52.8	4.62	12	55.44
			336.16			365.6

The weighted price index for 2001 is 108.8, found by

$$P = \frac{\Sigma p_t q_0}{\Sigma p_0 q_0}(100) = \frac{\$365.60}{\$336.16}(100) = 108.8$$

Based on this analysis we conclude that the price of this group of items has increased 8.8 percent in the six year period. The advantage of this method over the simple aggregate index is that the weight of each of the items is considered. In the simple aggregate index coffee had about 40 percent of the weight in determining the index. In the Laspeyres index the item with the most weight is milk, because the product of the price and the units sold is the largest.

Paasche's Price Index

The major disadvantage of the Laspeyres index is it assumes that the base-period quantities are still realistic in the given period. That is, the quantities used for the six items are about the same in 1995 as 2001. In this case notice that the quantity of eggs purchased declined by 23 percent, the quantity of milk increased by nearly 28 percent, and the number of apples increased by 33 percent.

The Paasche index is an alternative. The procedure is similar, but instead of using base period weights, we use current period weights. We use the sum of the products of the 1995 prices and the 2001 quantities. This has the advantage of using the more recent quantities. If there has been a change in the quantities consumed since the base period, such a change is reflected in the Paasche index.

PAASCHE'S PRICE INDEX

$$P = \frac{\Sigma p_t q_t}{\Sigma p_0 q_t} \times 100 \qquad \textbf{[18–5]}$$

EXAMPLE

Use the information from Table 18–3 to determine the Paasche index. Discuss which of the indexes should be used.

SOLUTION

Again, because of the repetitive nature of the calculations, Excel is used to perform the calculations. The results are shown in the following output.

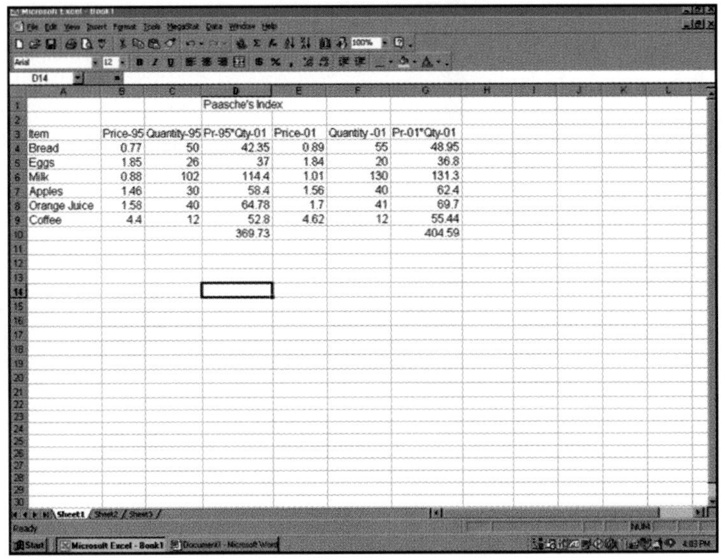

Paasche's Index

Item	Price-95	Quantity-95	Pr-95*Qty-01	Price-01	Quantity -01	Pr-01*Qty-01
Bread	0.77	50	42.35	0.89	55	48.95
Eggs	1.85	26	37	1.84	20	36.8
Milk	0.88	102	114.4	1.01	130	131.3
Apples	1.46	30	58.4	1.56	40	62.4
Orange Juice	1.58	40	64.78	1.7	41	69.7
Coffee	4.4	12	52.8	4.62	12	55.44
			369.73			404.59

The Paasche index is 109.4, found by

$$P = \frac{\Sigma p_t q_0}{\Sigma p_0 q_0}(100) = \frac{\$404.59}{\$369.73}(100) = 109.4$$

This result indicates that there has been an increase of 9.4 percent in the price of this market basket of goods between 1995 and 2001. That is, it costs 9.4 percent more to purchase these items in 2001 than it did in 1995. All things considered, because of the change in the quantities purchased between 1995 and 2001, the Paasche index is more reflective of the current situation. It should be noted that the Laspeyres index is more widely used. The Consumer Price Index, the most widely reported index, is an example of a Laspeyres index.

How do we decide which index to use? When is Laspeyres' most appropriate and when is Paasche's the better choice?

Laspeyres'

Advantages	Requires quantity data from only the base period. This allows a more meaningful comparison over time. The changes in the index can be attributed to changes in the price.
Disadvantages	Does not reflect changes in buying patterns over time. Also, it may overweight goods whose prices increase.

Paasche's

Advantages	Because it uses quantities from the current period, it reflects current buying habits.

Disadvantages It requires quantity data for each year, which may be difficult to obtain. Because different quantities are used each year, it is impossible to attribute changes in the index to changes in price alone. It tends to overweight the goods whose prices have declined. It requires the prices to be recomputed each year.

Fisher's Ideal Index

As noted above, Laspeyres' index tends to overweight goods whose prices have increased. Paasche's index, on the other hand, tends to overweight goods whose prices have gone down. In an attempt to offset these shortcomings, Irving Fisher, in his book *The Making of Index Numbers,* published in 1922, proposed an index called **Fisher's ideal index.** It is the geometric mean of the Laspeyres and Paasche indexes. We described the geometric mean in Chapter 3. It is determined by taking the *k*th root of the product of *k* positive numbers.

$$\text{Fisher's ideal index} = \sqrt{(\text{Laspeyres' index})(\text{Paasche's index})} \qquad \textbf{[18–6]}$$

Fisher's index seems to be theoretically ideal because it combines the best features of both Laspeyres and Paasche. That is, it balances the effects of the two indexes. However, it is rarely used in practice because it has the same basic set of problems as the Paasche index. It requires that a new set of quantities be determined for each year.

EXAMPLE

Determine Fisher's ideal index for the data in Table 18–3.

SOLUTION

Fisher's ideal index is 109.1.

$$\begin{aligned}\text{Fisher's ideal index} &= \sqrt{(\text{Laspeyres' index})(\text{Paasche's index})}\\ &= \sqrt{(108.8)(109.4)} = 109.1\end{aligned}$$

Self-Review 18–2

An index of clothing prices for 2002 based on 1995 is to be constructed. The clothing items considered are shoes and dresses. The information for prices and quantities for both years is given below. Use 1995 as the base period and 100 as the base value.

	1995		2002	
Item	**Price**	**Quantity**	**Price**	**Quantity**
Dress (each)	$75	500	$85	520
Shoes (pair)	40	1,200	45	1,300

(a) Determine the simple average of the price indexes.
(b) Determine the aggregate price indexes for the two years.
(c) Determine Laspeyres' price index.
(d) Determine the Paasche price index.
(e) Determine Fisher's ideal index.

Exercises

For exercises 5–8:

a. Determine the simple price indexes.
b. Determine the simple aggregate price indexes for the two years.
c. Determine Laspeyres' price index.
d. Determine the Paasche price index.
e. Determine Fisher's ideal index.

5. Below are the prices of toothpaste (9 oz), shampoo (7 oz), cough tablets (package of 100), and antiperspirant (2 oz) for August 1998 and August 2001. Also included are the quantity purchased. Use August 1998 as the base.

	August 1998		August 2001	
Item	**Price**	**Quantity**	**Price**	**Quantity**
Toothpaste	$2.49	6	$2.69	6
Shampoo	3.29	4	3.59	5
Cough tablets	1.59	2	1.79	3
Antiperspirant	1.79	3	2.29	4

6. a. 152.17, 93.10, 100.0, 137.26, 111.24
b. 120.86
c. 118.1
d. 119.8
e. 118.95

6. Fruit prices and the amounts consumed for 1995 and 2001 are below. Use 1995 as the base.

	1995		2001	
Fruit	**Price**	**Quantity**	**Price**	**Quantity**
Bananas (pound)	$0.23	100	$0.35	120
Grapefruit (each)	0.29	50	0.27	55
Apples (pound)	0.35	85	0.35	85
Strawberries (basket)	1.02	8	1.40	10
Oranges (bag)	0.89	6	0.99	8

7. The prices and the numbers of various items produced by a small machine and stamping plant are reported below. Use 1995 as the base.

	1995		2001	
Item	**Price**	**Quantity**	**Price**	**Quantity**
Washer	$0.07	17,000	$0.10	20,000
Cotter pin	0.04	125,000	0.03	130,000
Stove bolt	0.15	40,000	0.15	42,000
Hex nut	0.08	62,000	0.10	65,000

8. a. 109.9, 110.0, 108.3, 108.3, 106.6
b. 108.6
c. 107.5
d. 107.3
e. 107.4

8. Following are the quantities and prices for the years 1995 and 2001 for Kinzua Valley Geriatrics. Use 1995 as the base period.

	1995		2001	
Item	**Price**	**Quantity**	**Price**	**Quantity**
Syringes (dozen)	$ 6.10	1,500	$ 6.50	2,000
Thermometers	8.10	10	8.90	12
Advil (bottle)	4.00	250	4.40	250
Patient record forms (box)	6.00	1,000	6.50	900
Computer paper (box)	12.00	30	13.00	40

Value Index

Value index measures percent change in value

A **value index** measures changes in both the price and quantities involved. A value index, such as the index of department store sales, needs the original base-year prices, the original base-year quantities, the present-year prices, and the present-year quantities for its construction. Its formula is:

VALUE INDEX
$$V = \frac{\Sigma p_t q_t}{\Sigma p_0 q_0} \times 100 \quad [18\text{–}7]$$

EXAMPLE

The prices and quantities sold at the Waleska Department Store for various items of apparel for May 1995 and May 2001 are:

Item	1995 Price, p_0	1995 Quantity Sold (thousands), q_0	2001 Price, p_t	2001 Quantity Sold (thousands), q_t
Ties (each)	$ 1	1,000	$ 2	900
Suits (each)	30	100	40	120
Shoes (pair)	10	500	8	500

What is the index of value for May 2001 using May 1995 as the base period?

SOLUTION

Total sales in May 2001 were $10,600,000, and the comparable figure for 1995 is $9,000,000. (See Table 18–4.) Thus, the index of value for May 2001 using 1995 = 100 is 117.8. The value of apparel sales in 2001 was 117.8 percent of the 1995 sales. To put it another way, the value of apparel sales increased 17.8 percent from May 1995 to May 2001.

$$V = \frac{\Sigma p_t q_t}{\Sigma p_0 q_0}(100) = \frac{\$10{,}600{,}000}{\$9{,}000{,}000}(100) = 117.8$$

TABLE 18–4 Construction of a Value Index for 2001 (1992 = 100)

Item	1995 Price, p_0	1995 Quantity Sold (thousands), q_0	p_0q_0 ($ thousands)	2001 Price, p_t	2001 Quantity Sold (thousands), q_t	p_tq_t ($ thousands)
Ties (each)	$ 1	1,000	$1,000	$ 2	900	$ 1,800
Suits (each)	30	100	3,000	40	120	4,800
Shoes (pair)	10	500	5,000	8	500	4,000
			$9,000			$10,600

Self-Review 18–3 The number of items produced by Houghton Products for 1996 and 2002 and the wholesale prices for the two periods are:

	Price		Number Produced	
Item Produced	**1996**	**2002**	**1996**	**2002**
Shear pins (box)	$ 3	$4	10,000	9,000
Cutting compound (pound)	1	5	600	200
Tie rods (each)	10	8	3,000	5,000

(a) Find the index of the value of production for 2002 using 1996 as the base period.
(b) Interpret the index.

Exercises

9. The prices and production of grains for August 1995 and August 2001 are:

Grain	1995 Price	1995 Quantity Produced (millions of bushels)	2001 Price	2001 Quantity Produced (millions of bushels)
Oats	$1.52	200	$1.87	214
Wheat	2.10	565	2.05	489
Corn	1.48	291	1.48	203
Barley	3.05	87	3.29	106

Using 1995 as the base period, find the value index of grains produced for August 2001.

10. 108.7

10. The Johnson Wholesale Company manufactures a variety of products. The prices and quantities produced for April 1994 and April 2001 are:

Product	1994 Price	2001 Price	1994 Quantity Produced	2001 Quantity Produced
Small motor (each)	$23.60	$28.80	1,760	4,259
Scrubbing compound (gallon)	2.96	3.08	86,450	62,949
Nails (pound)	0.40	0.48	9,460	22,370

Using April 1994 as the base period, find the index of the value of goods produced for April 2001.

Special-Purpose Indexes

Many important indexes are prepared and published by private organizations. J. D. Power & Associates surveys automobile purchasers to determine how satisfied customers are with their vehicle after one year of ownership. This special index is called the *Consumer Satisfaction Index.* Financial institutions, utility companies, and university bureaus of research often prepare indexes on employment, factory hours and wages, and retail sales for the regions they serve. Many trade associations prepare indexes of price and quantity that are vital to their particular area of interest. How are these special indexes prepared? An example, simplified of course, will help to explain some of the details.

EXAMPLE

The Seattle Chamber of Commerce wants to develop a measure of general business activity for the northwest portion of the United States. The Director of Economic Development has been assigned to develop the index. It will be called the *General Business Activity Index of the Northwest.*

SOLUTION

After considerable thought and research, the director has concluded that four factors should be considered: the regional department store sales (which are reported in $ millions), the regional employment index (which has a 1990 base and is reported by the Commonwealth of Washington), the freight car loadings (reported in millions), and exports for the Seattle Harbor (reported in thousands of tons). Recent information on these variables is reported in Table 18–5.

TABLE 18–5 Data for the Computation of the General Business Activity Index of the Northwest

Year	Department Store Sales	Index of Employment	Freight Car Loadings	Exports
1990	20	100	50	500
1995	41	110	30	900
2001	44	125	18	700

After review and consultation the director assigned weights of 40 percent to department store sales, 30 percent to employment, 10 percent to freight car loadings, and 20 percent to exports.

To develop the General Business Activity Index of the Northwest for 2001 using 1990 = 100, each 2001 value is expressed as a percentage, with the base-period value as the denominator. For illustration, department store sales for 2001 are converted to a percentage by ($44/$20)(100) = 220. This means that department store sales have increased 120 percent in the period. This percentage is then adjusted by the appropriate weight. For the department store sales this is (220)(.40) = 88.0. The details of the calculations for the years 1995 and 2001 are shown below.

	1995		2001	
Department store sales	($41/$20)(100)(.40) =	82.0	($44/$20)(100)(.40) =	88.0
Employment	(110/100)(100)(.30) =	33.0	(125/100)(100)(.30) =	37.5
Freight car loadings	(30/50)(100)(.10) =	6.0	(18/50)(100)(.10) =	3.6
Exports	(900/500)(100)(.20) =	36.0	(700/500)(100)(.20) =	28.0
Total		157.0		157.1

The General Business Activity Index of the Northwest for 1995 is 157.0 and for 2001 it is 157.1. Interpreting, business activity has increased 57.0 percent from 1990 to 1995 and 57.1 percent from the base period of 1990 to 2001.

As we stated at the start of the section, there are many special-purpose indexes. Here are a few examples.

The Consumer Price Index The U.S. Bureau of Labor Statistics reports this index monthly. It describes the changes in prices from one period to another for a "market basket" of goods and services. We discuss its history in detail and present some applications in the next section. You can access this information by going to *www.bls.gov/datahome.htm,* click on **Prices**, and select **Consumer Price Index—All Urban Consumers**. You may elect to include different periods. Following is a recent summary report.

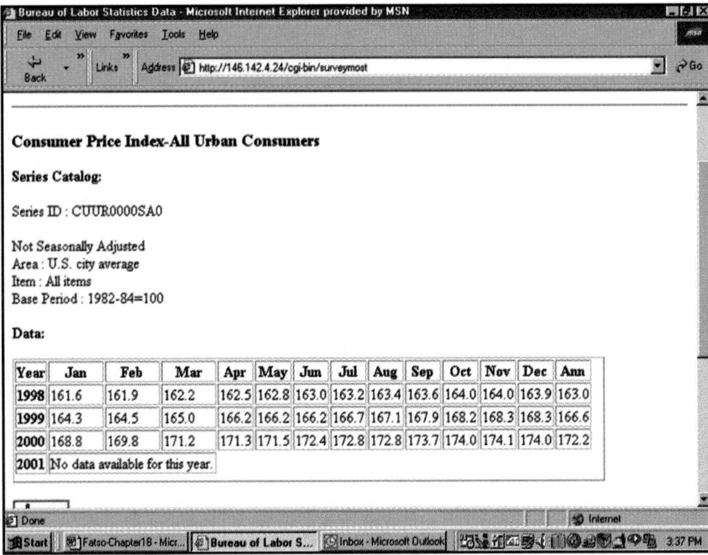

Consumer Price Index-All Urban Consumers

Series Catalog:

Series ID : CUUR0000SA0

Not Seasonally Adjusted
Area : U.S. city average
Item : All items
Base Period : 1982-84=100

Data:

Year	Jan	Feb	Mar	Apr	May	Jun	Jul	Aug	Sep	Oct	Nov	Dec	Ann
1998	161.6	161.9	162.2	162.5	162.8	163.0	163.2	163.4	163.6	164.0	164.0	163.9	163.0
1999	164.3	164.5	165.0	166.2	166.2	166.2	166.7	167.1	167.9	168.2	168.3	168.3	166.6
2000	168.8	169.8	171.2	171.3	171.5	172.4	172.8	172.8	173.7	174.0	174.1	174.0	172.2
2001	No data available for this year.												

The Producer Price Index Formerly called the Wholesale Price Index, it dates back to 1890 and is also published by the U.S. Bureau of Labor Statistics. It reflects the prices of over 3,400 commodities. Price data are collected from the sellers of the commodities, and it usually refers to the first large-volume transaction for each commodity. It is a Laspeyres-type index. You can access this information by going to *www.bls.gov/datahome.htm,* click on **Prices**, and select **Producer Price Index—Commodities**, then select **Finished Goods.** You may select to include different periods. Below is a recent output.

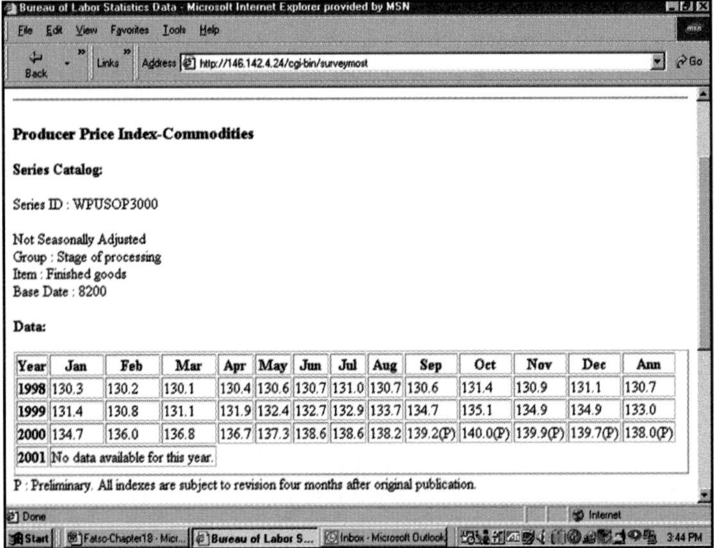

Producer Price Index-Commodities

Series Catalog:

Series ID : WPUSOP3000

Not Seasonally Adjusted
Group : Stage of processing
Item : Finished goods
Base Date : 8200

Data:

Year	Jan	Feb	Mar	Apr	May	Jun	Jul	Aug	Sep	Oct	Nov	Dec	Ann
1998	130.3	130.2	130.1	130.4	130.6	130.7	131.0	130.7	130.6	131.4	130.9	131.1	130.7
1999	131.4	130.8	131.1	131.9	132.4	132.7	132.9	133.7	134.7	135.1	134.9	134.9	133.0
2000	134.7	136.0	136.8	136.7	137.3	138.6	138.6	138.2	139.2(P)	140.0(P)	139.9(P)	139.7(P)	138.0(P)
2001	No data available for this year.												

P : Preliminary. All indexes are subject to revision four months after original publication.

Dow Jones Industrial Average (DJIA) This is an index of stock prices, but perhaps it would be better to say it is an "indicator" rather than an index. It is supposed to be the mean price of 30 specific industrial stocks. However, summing the 30 stocks and dividing by 30 does not calculate its value. This is because of stock splits, mergers, and stocks being added or dropped. When changes occur, adjustments are made in the denominator used with the average. Today the DJIA is more of a psychological indicator than a representation of the general price movement on the New York Stock Exchange. The lack of representativeness of the stocks on the DJIA is one of the reasons for the development of the **New York Stock Exchange Index.** This index was developed as an average price of *all* stocks on the New York Stock Exchange. You can find more information about the DJIA by going to the website: *www.dowjones.com.* You can find its current value as well as the 30 stocks that are now a part of its calculation. A history of the DJIA is available at *www.dowjones.com/corp/index_average.html.* Below is a recent summary.

S&P 500 Index

The full name of this index is the Standard and Poor's Composite Index of Stock Prices. It is an aggregate price index of 500 common stocks. It, too, is probably a better reflection of the market than is the DJIA. You can access information about the S&P 500 from the Dow Jones website. Below is a recent summary.

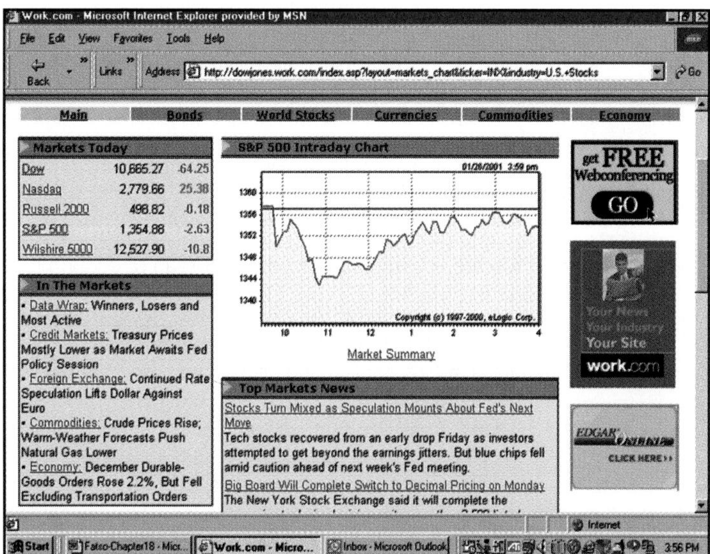

There are many other indices that track business and economic behavior, such as the Nasdaq, the Russell 2000, and the Wilshire 5000.

Self-Review 18–4

As an intern in the Fulton County Economic Development Office, you have been asked to develop a special-purpose index for your county. Three economic series seem to hold promise as the basis of an index. These data are the price of cotton (per pound), the number of new automobiles sold in the county, and the rate of money turnover (published by the local bank). After discussing the project with your supervisor and the director, you decide that money turnover should have a weight of .60, the number of new automobiles sold a weight of .30, and the cotton price .10. The base period is 1992.

Year	Cotton Price	Automobiles Sold	Money Turnover
1992	$0.20	1,000	80
1998	0.25	1,200	90
2000	0.50	900	75

(a) Construct the index for 1998 and 2000.
(b) Interpret the index for 1998 and 2000.

Exercises

11. The index of leading economic indicators, compiled and published by the U.S. National Bureau of Economic Research, is composed of 12 time series, such as the average work hours of production in manufacturing, manufacturers' new orders, and money supply. This index and similar indexes are designed to move up or down before the economy begins to move the same way. Thus, an economist has statistical evidence to forecast future trends.

You want to construct a leading indicator for Erie County in upstate New York. The index is to be based on 1995 data. Because of the time and work involved, you decide to use only four time series. As an experiment, you select these four series: unemployment in the county, a composite index of county stock prices, County Price Index, and retail sales. Here are the figures for 1995 and 2001.

	1995	2001
Unemployment rate (percent)	5.3	6.8
Composite county stocks	265.88	362.26
County Price Index (1982 = 100)	109.6	125.0
Retail sales ($ millions)	529,917.0	622,864.0

The weights you assigned are: unemployment rate 20 percent, stock prices 40 percent, County Price Index 25 percent, and retail sales 15 percent.

a. Using 1995 as the base period, construct a leading economic indicator for 2001.
b. Interpret your leading index.

12. You are employed by the state bureau of economic development. There is a demand for a leading economic index to review past economic activity and to forecast future economic trends in the state. You decide that several key factors should be included in the index: number of new businesses started during the year, number of business failures, state income tax receipts, college enrollment, and the state sales tax receipts. Here are the data for 1997 and 2001.

12. Answers will vary.

	1997	2001
New businesses	1,088	1,162
Business failures	627	520
State income tax receipts ($ millions)	191.7	162.6
College student enrollment	242,119	290,841
State sales tax ($ millions)	41.6	39.9

a. Decide on the weights to be applied to each item in the leading index.
b. Compute the leading economic indicator for 2001.
c. Interpret the indexes.

Consumer Price Index

There are two consumer price indexes.

Frequent mention has been made of the Consumer Price Index (CPI) in the preceding pages. It measures the change in price of a fixed market basket of goods and services from one period to another. In January 1978 the Bureau of Labor Statistics began publishing CPIs for two groups of the population. One index, called the Consumer Price Index—All Urban Consumers covers about 80 percent of the total population. The other index is for urban wage earners and clerical workers and covers about 32 percent of the population.

In brief, the CPI serves several major functions. It allows consumers to determine the degree to which their purchasing power is being eroded by price increases. In that respect, it is a yardstick for revising wages, pensions, and other income payments to keep pace with changes in price. Equally important, it is an economic indicator of the rate of inflation in the United States.

The index includes about 400 items, and about 250 agents collect price data monthly. Prices are collected from more than 21,000 retail establishments and 60,000 housing units in 91 urban areas across the country. The prices of baby cribs, bread, beer, cigars, gasoline, haircuts, mortgage interest rates, physicians' fees, taxes, and operating-room charges are just a few of the items included in what is often termed a typical "market basket" of goods and services that you purchase.

The CPI originated in 1913 and has been published regularly since 1921. The standard reference period (the base period) has been updated periodically. Beginning with the release of the CPI for January 1999, the base period was changed to 1993–95 = 100. The earlier base periods were: 1982–84, 1967, 1957–59, 1947–49, 1935–39, and 1925–29. Why is it necessary to change the base? Our expenditure patterns change dramatically, and these changes must be reflected in the index. The most recent revision includes consumer items, such as VCRs, home computers, and cell phones. Earlier versions of the CPI did not include these items. By changing the base, the CPI captures the most recent expenditure patterns.

The CPI is actually not just one index. There are Consumer Price Indexes for New York, Chicago, Seattle, and Atlanta, as well as a number of other large cities. There are also price indexes for food, apparel, medical care, and other items. A few of them are shown on the next page, 1982–84 = 100, for 2000.

Item	CPI-U
All items	172.2
Food and beverage	168.4
Apparel and upkeep	129.6
Transportation	153.3
Medical care	260.8
Housing	169.6

A perusal of this listing shows that a weighted index of all items has increased 72.2 percent since 1982–84; medical care has increased the most, 260.8 percent; and apparel and upkeep went up the least, 29.6 percent. You can find the latest information on the CPI by going to the U.S. Bureau of Labor Statistics Web site at: *http://stats.bls.gov/cpihome.htm.*

Special Uses of the Consumer Price Index

In addition to measuring changes in the prices of goods and services, both consumer price indexes have a number of other applications. The CPI is used to determine real disposable personal income, to deflate sales or other series, to find the purchasing power of the dollar, and to establish cost-of-living increases. We first discuss the use of the CPI in determining **real income.**

Real income

Money income

Real Income As an example of the meaning and computation of *real income,* assume the Consumer Price Index is presently 200 with 1982–84 = 100. Also, assume that Ms. Watts earned $20,000 in the base period of 1982, 1983, and 1984. She has a current income of $40,000. Note that although her *money income* has doubled since the base period of 1982–84, the prices she paid for food, gasoline, clothing, and other items have also doubled. Thus, Ms. Watts's standard of living has remained the same from the base period to the present time. Price increases have exactly offset an increase in income, so her present buying power (real income) is still $20,000. (See Table 18–6 for computations.) In general:

REAL INCOME

$$\text{Real income} = \frac{\text{Money income}}{\text{CPI}} \times 100 \qquad \textbf{[18–8]}$$

TABLE 18–6 Computation of Real Income for 1982–84 and Present Year

Year	Money Income	Consumer Price Index (1982–84 = 100)	Real Income	Computation of Real Income
1982–84	$20,000	100	$20,000	$\frac{\$20{,}000}{100}(100)$
Present year	40,000	200	20,000	$\frac{\$40{,}000}{200}(100)$

Deflated income and real income are the same

The concept of real income is sometimes called *deflated income,* and the CPI is called the *deflator.* Also, a popular term for deflated income is *income expressed in constant dollars.* Thus, in Table 18–6, to determine whether Ms. Watts's standard of living changed, her money income was converted to constant dollars. We found that her purchasing power, expressed in 1982–84 dollars (constant dollars), remained at $20,000.

Self-Review 18–5

The take-home pay of Jon Greene and the CPI for 1995 and 2000 are:

Year	Take-Home Pay	CPI (1982–84 = 100)
1995	$25,000	152.4
2000	41,200	172.2

(a) What was Jon's real income in 1995?
(b) What was his real income in 2000?
(c) Interpret your findings.

Deflated sales important for showing the trend in "real" sales

Deflating Sales A price index can also be used to "deflate" sales or similar money series. Deflated sales are determined by

USING AN INDEX AS A DEFLATOR

$$\text{Deflated sales} = \frac{\text{Actual sales}}{\text{An appropriate index}} \times 100 \qquad \textbf{[18–9]}$$

EXAMPLE

The sales of Hill Enterprises, a small injection molding company in upstate New York, increased from $875,000 in 1982, to $1,482,000 in 1995, $1,491,000 in 1998, and $1,502,000 in 2000. The owner, Harry Hill, realizes that the price of raw materials used in the process has also increased over the period, so Mr. Hill wants to deflate sales to account for the increase in raw material prices. What are the deflated sales for 1995, 1998, and 2000 based on 1982 dollars? That is, what are sales for 1995, 1998, and 2000 expressed in constant 1982 dollars?

SOLUTION

The Producer Price Index (PPI) is an index released every month and published in the *Monthly Labor Review* and is also available at the Bureau of Labor Statistics website. The prices included in the PPI reflect the prices charged the manufacturer for the metals, rubber, and other items purchased. So the PPI seems an appropriate index to use to deflate the manufacturer's sales. The manufacturer's sales are listed in the second column of Table 18–7, and the PPI is in the third column. The next column shows sales divided by the PPI. The right-hand column details the calculations. The results are shown in the following Excel output.

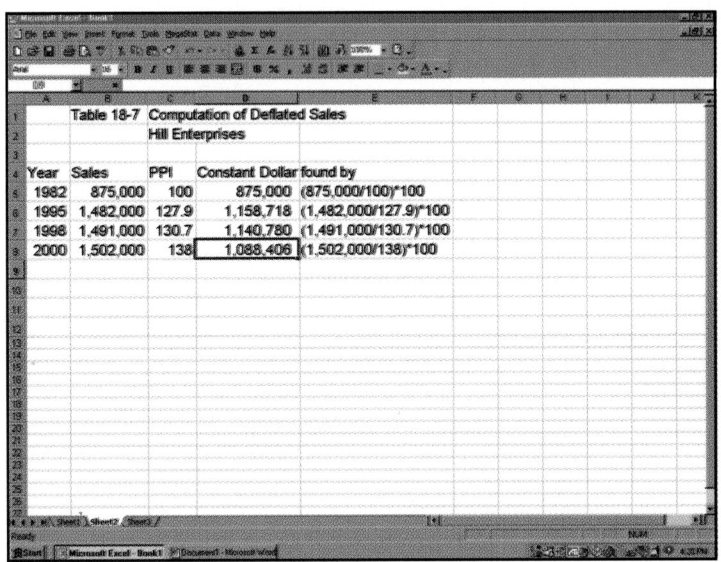

Table 18-7 Computation of Deflated Sales
Hill Enterprises

Year	Sales	PPI	Constant Dollar	found by
1982	875,000	100	875,000	(875,000/100)*100
1995	1,482,000	127.9	1,158,718	(1,482,000/127.9)*100
1998	1,491,000	130.7	1,140,780	(1,491,000/130.7)*100
2000	1,502,000	138	1,088,406	(1,502,000/138)*100

Actual sales have increased from 1995 through 2000, but if we compare the sales in constant dollars, sales declined during the period. That is, deflated sales were \$1,158,718 in 1995 but declined to \$1,088,406 in 2000. This is so because the prices Hill Enterprises paid for raw materials grew more rapidly than sales.

What has happened to the purchasing power of your dollar?

Purchasing Power of the Dollar The Consumer Price Index is also used to determine the *purchasing power of the dollar.*

USING AN INDEX TO FIND PURCHASING POWER

$$\text{Purchasing power of dollar} = \frac{\$1}{\text{CPI}} \times 100 \qquad \textbf{[18–10]}$$

EXAMPLE

Suppose the Consumer Price Index this month is 200.0 (1982–84 = 100). What is the purchasing power of the dollar?

SOLUTION

Using formula 18–10, it is 50 cents, found by:

$$\text{Purchasing power of dollar} = \frac{\$1}{200.0}(100) = \$0.50$$

The CPI of 200.0 indicates that prices have doubled from the years 1982–84 to this month. Thus, the purchasing power of a dollar has been cut in half. That is, a 1982–84 dollar is worth only 50 cents this month. To put it another way, if you lost \$1,000 in the period 1982–84 and just found it, the \$1,000 could only buy half of what it could have bought in the years 1982, 1983, and 1984.

CPI used to adjust wages, pensions, and so on

Cost-of-Living Adjustments The Consumer Price Index is also the basis for cost-of-living adjustments in many management-union contracts. The specific clause in the contract is often referred to as the "escalator clause" or COLA. About 31 million Social Security beneficiaries, 2.5 million retired military and federal civil service employees and survivors, and 600,000 postal workers have their incomes or pensions pegged to the Consumer Price Index.

The CPI is also used to adjust alimony and child support payments; attorneys' fees; workers' compensation payments; rentals on apartments, homes, and office buildings; welfare payments; and so on. In brief, say a retiree receives a pension of \$500 a month and the Consumer Price Index increases 5 points from 165 to 170. Suppose for each point that the CPI increases the pension benefits increase 1.0 percent, so the monthly increase in benefits will be \$25, found by \$500 (5 points)(.01). Now the retiree will receive \$525 per month.

Self-Review 18–6 Suppose the Consumer Price Index for the latest month is 174.0 (1982–84 = 100). What is the purchasing power of the dollar? Interpret.

Shifting the Base

If two or more time series have the same base period, they can be compared directly. As an example, suppose we are interested in the trend in the prices of food and beverages, housing, medical care, and so on since the base period, 1982–84. Note in Table 18–8 that all of the consumer price indexes use the same base. Thus, it can be said that the price of all consumer items combined increased 72.2 percent from the base period (1982–84) to the year 2000. Likewise, housing prices increased 69.4 percent, medical care 160.8 percent, and so on.

TABLE 18–8 Trend in Consumer Prices to 2000 (1982–84 = 100)

Year	All Items	Food and Beverages	Housing	Apparel and Upkeep	Medical Care
1982–84	100.0	100.0	100.0	100.0	100.0
1990	130.7	132.1	128.5	124.1	162.8
1995	152.4	148.9	148.5	132.0	220.5
2000	172.2	168.4	169.6	129.6	260.8

A problem arises, however, when two or more series being compared do not have the same base period. The following example compares the two most widely reported business indexes, the DJIA and Nasdaq.

EXAMPLE

We want to compare the price changes on the Dow Jones Industrial Average with the Nasdaq. The two indexes for selected periods are as follows.

	Year			
Index	**1995**	**1998**	**1999**	**2000**
Dow Jones	5,117.10	9,181.40	11,497.10	10,797.99
Nasdaq	1,059.79	2,192.69	4,069.69	2,470.51

SOLUTION

From the information given, we are not sure the base periods are the same, so a direct comparison is not appropriate. Because we want to compare the changes in the two business indexes, the logical thing to do is to let a particular year, say 1995, be the base for both periods. For the Dow Jones, 5,117.10 becomes the base, and for the Nasdaq the base is 1,059.79.

The calculations for the 2000 Nasdaq using 1995 = 100 are:

$$\text{Index} = \frac{2{,}470.51}{1{,}059.79}(100) = 233.1$$

The following Excel output reports the complete set of indexes.

Comparison of Dow Jones and Nasdaq

Index	1995	1998	1999	2000
Dow Jones	5,117.10	9181.4	11,497.10	10,797.99
Index	100.00	179.43	224.68	211.02
Nasdaq	1,059.79	2,192.69	4,069.69	2,470.52
Index	100.00	206.90	384.01	233.11

We conclude that both indexes have increased over the period. The Nasdaq has increased more, 133.1 percent versus 111.0 percent. Both indexes declined from 1999 to 2000, with the decline in the Nasdaq much steeper.

The following chart, obtained from the financial section of Yahoo!, shows a visual comparison of the Dow Jones and the Nasdaq. The vertical axis shows the change from the base year of 1995 for both. From this graph we conclude that both measures have increased over the five-year period, but that the Nasdaq has grown more. Also, note the decline from 1999 to 2000.

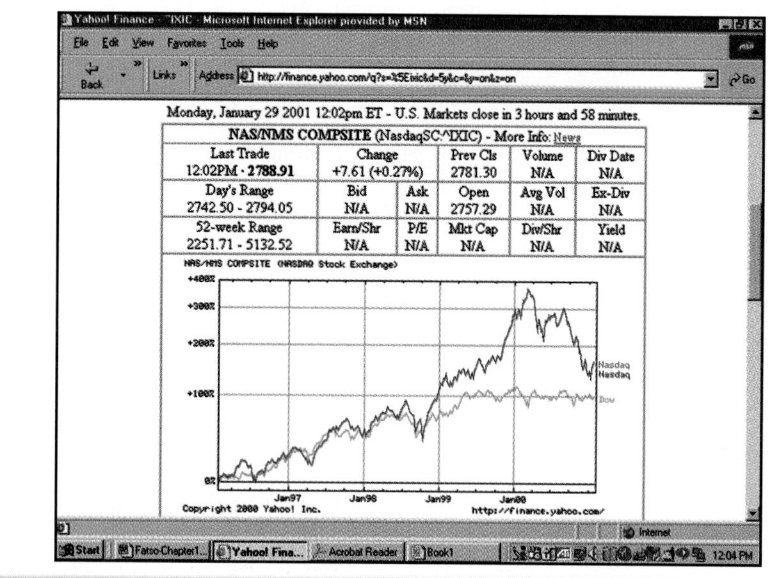

Self-Review 18–7

1. In the preceding example, verify that the Dow Jones price index for 1998, using 1995 as the base period, is 179.43.
2. The changes in industrial production and in the prices manufacturers have paid for raw materials since 1982 are to be compared. Unfortunately, the index of industrial production, which measures changes in production, and the Producer Price Index, which measures the change in the prices of raw materials, have different base periods. The production index has a 1977 base period, and the Producer Price Index uses 1982 as the base period. Shift the base to 1982 and make the two series comparable. Interpret.

Year	Industrial Production Index (1977 = 100)	Producer Price Index (1982 = 100)
1982	115.3	100.0
1987	129.8	105.4
1994	142.8	119.2
1997	172.3	131.2
2000	185.6	138.0

Exercises

13. In December 2000 the mean salary for an experienced registered nurse with a bachelor's degree was \$42,000. The Consumer Price Index for December 2000 was 174.0 (1982–84 = 100). The mean annual salary for a nurse in the base period of 1982–84 was \$19,800. What was the real income of the nurse in 2000? How much had the mean salary increased?

14. 119.1, 126.0

14. The Trade Union Association of Orlando, Florida, maintains indexes on the hourly wages for a number of the trades. Unfortunately, the indexes do not all have the same base periods. Listed below is information on plumbers and electricians. Shift the base periods to 1995 and compare the hourly wage increases.

Year	Plumbers (1990 = 100)	Electricians (1992 = 100)
1995	133.8	126.0
2000	159.4	158.7

15. In 1990 the mean salary of classroom teachers in the Tinora School District was $23,650. By 1995 the mean salary increased to $28,972, and further increased in 2000 to $32,382. The American Federation of Classroom Teachers maintains information on the trends throughout the United States in classroom teacher salaries. Their index, which has a base of 1990, was 122.5 for 1995 and 136.9 for 2000. Compare the Tinora teachers to the national trends.

16. Increased $1,600

16. Sam Steward is a freelance computer programmer. Listed below are his yearly wages for the years 1995 through 2000. Also included is an industry index for computer programmers that reports the rate of wage inflation in the industry. This index has a base of 1990.

Year	Wage ($000)	Index (1990 = 100)
1995	125.0	148.3
1996	134.8	160.6
1997	145.2	173.6
1998	156.6	187.9
1999	168.8	203.3
2000	179.6	210.4

Compute Sam's real income for the period. Did his wages keep up with inflation, or did he lose ground?

Chapter Outline

I. An index number measures the relative change from one period to another.
  A. The major characteristics of an index are:
    1. It is a percentage, but the percent sign is usually omitted.
    2. It has a base period.
    3. Most indexes are reported to the nearest tenth of a percent, such as 153.1.
    4. The base of most indexes is 100.
  B. The reasons for computing an index are:
    1. It facilitates the comparison of unlike series.
    2. If the numbers are very large, often it is easier to comprehend the change of the index than the actual numbers.

II. There are two types of price indexes, unweighted and weighted.
  A. In an unweighted index we do not consider the quantities.
    1. In a simple index we compare the base period to the given period.

$$P = \frac{p_t}{p_0} \times 100 \qquad \textbf{[18–1]}$$

where p_t refers to the price in the current period, and p_0 is the price in the base period.

    2. In the simple average of price indexes, we add the simple indexes for each item and divide by the number of items.

$$P = \frac{\Sigma P_i}{n} \qquad \textbf{[18–2]}$$

3. In a simple aggregate price index the price of the items in the group are totaled for both periods and compared.

$$P = \frac{\Sigma p_t}{\Sigma p_0} \times 100 \qquad [18\text{–}3]$$

B. In a weighted index the quantities are considered.
1. In the Laspeyres method the base period quantities are used in both the base period and the given period.

$$P = \frac{\Sigma p_t q_0}{\Sigma p_0 q_0} \times 100 \qquad [18\text{–}4]$$

2. In the Paasche method current period quantities are used.

$$P = \frac{\Sigma p_t q_t}{\Sigma p_0 q_t} \times 100 \qquad [18\text{–}5]$$

3. Fisher's ideal index is the geometric mean of Laspeyres' index and Paasche's index.

$$\text{Fisher's ideal index} = \sqrt{(\text{Laspeyres' index})(\text{Paasche's index})} \qquad [18\text{–}6]$$

C. A value index uses both base period and current period prices and quantities.

$$V = \frac{\Sigma p_t q_t}{\Sigma p_0 q_0} \qquad [18\text{–}7]$$

III. The most widely reported index is the Consumer Price Index (CPI).
A. It is often used to show the rate of inflation in the United States.
B. It is reported monthly by the U.S. Bureau of Labor Statistics.
C. Through 1998 the base period is 1982–84, but starting with the reports in 1999, the base changed to 1993–95.
D. It is used by the Social Security system, so when the CPI changes, retirement benefits also change.

Statistics in Action

In the 1920s wholesale prices in Germany increased dramatically. In 1920 wholesale prices increased about 80 percent, in 1921 the rate of increase was 140 percent, and in 1922 it was a whopping 4,100 percent! Between December 1922 and November 1923 wholesale prices increased another 4,100 percent. By that time government printing presses could not keep up, even by printing notes as large as 500 million marks. Stories are told that workers were paid daily, then twice daily, so their wives could shop for necessities before the wages became too devalued.

Chapter Exercises

The following information was taken from Johnson and Johnson annual reports. The principal office of Johnson and Johnson is in New Brunswick, New Jersey. Their common stock is listed on the New York Stock Exchange, using the symbol JNJ.

	Sales		
Year	Domestic ($ million)	International ($ million)	Employees (000)
1990	5,427	5,805	82.2
1991	6,248	6,199	82.7
1992	6,903	6,850	84.9
1993	7,203	6,935	81.6
1994	7,812	7,922	81.5
1995	9,190	9,652	82.3
1996	10,899	10,721	89.3
1997	11,895	10,935	91.1
1998	12,848	11,147	94.3
1999	15,385	12,086	97.8

17. Refer to the Johnson and Johnson data. Use 1990 as the base period and compute a simple index of domestic sales for each year from 1996 until 1999. Interpret the trend in domestic sales.

18. 248.4 for 1999.

18. Refer to the Johnson and Johnson data. Use the period 1990–92 as the base period and compute a simple index of domestic sales for each year from 1996 to 1999.

19. Refer to the Johnson and Johnson data. Use 1990 as the base period and compute a simple index of international sales for each year from 1996 until 1999. Interpret the trend in international sales.

20. 192.3 for 1999.

20. Refer to the Johnson and Johnson data. Use the period 1990–92 as the base period and compute a simple index of international sales for each year from 1996 to 1999.

21. Refer to the Johnson and Johnson data. Use 1990 as the base period and compute a simple index of the number of employees for each year from 1996 until 1999. Interpret the trend in the number of employees.

22. 117.5 for 1999.

22. Refer to the Johnson and Johnson data. Use the period 1990–92 as the base period and compute a simple index of the number of employees for each year from 1996 to 1999.

The following information is from the General Electric Corporation annual report for 1999.

Year	Revenue ($ millions)	Earnings (per share)
1995	70,028	1.95
1996	79,179	2.20
1997	90,840	2.50
1998	100,469	2.84
1999	111,630	3.22

23. Compute a simple index for the revenue of GE. Use 1995 as the base period. What can you conclude about the change in revenue over the period?

24. 139.5 for 1999.

24. Compute a simple index for the revenue of GE using the period 1995–97 as the base. What can you conclude about the change in revenue over the period?

25. Compute a simple index for earnings per share for GE. Use 1995 as the base period. What can you conclude about the change in earnings per share over the period?

26. 145.3 for 1999.

26. Compute a simple index for earnings for GE using the period 1995–97 as the base. What can you conclude about the change in earnings per share over the period?

The U.S. Department of Labor reported the following information on food items for the years 1995 and 2001.

	1995		2001	
Item	Price	Quantity	Price	Quantity
Margarine (pound)	$0.81	18	$0.89	27
Shortening (pound)	.84	5	.94	9
Milk (½ gallon)	1.44	70	1.43	65
Potato chips	2.91	27	3.07	33

27. Compute a simple price index for each of the four items. Use 1995 as the base period.

28. 105.5

28. Compute a simple aggregate price index. Use 1995 as the base period.

29. Compute Laspeyres' price index for 2001 using 1995 as the base period.

30. 103.51

30. Compute Paasche's index for 2001 using 1995 as the base period.

31. Determine Fisher's ideal index using the values for the Laspeyres and Paasche indexes computed in the two previous problems.

32. 114.43

32. Determine a value index for 2001 using 1995 as the base period.

Betts Electronics purchases three replacement parts for robotic machines used in their manufacturing process. Information on the price of the replacement parts and the quantity purchased is given below.

	Price		Quantity	
Part	1995	2001	1995	2001
RC-33	$0.50	$0.60	320	340
SM-14	1.20	0.90	110	130
WC50	0.85	1.00	230	250

33. Compute a simple price index for each of the three items. Use 1995 as the base period.

34. 98.04

34. Compute a simple aggregate price index for 2001. Use 1995 as the base period.
35. Compute Laspeyres' price index for 2001 using 1995 as the base period.

36. 106.04

36. Compute Paasche's index for 2001 using 1995 as the base period.
37. Determine Fisher's ideal index using the values for the Laspeyres and Paasche indexes computed in the two previous problems.

38. 117.13

38. Determine a value index for 2001 using 1995 as the base period.

Prices for selected foods for 1995 and 2001 are given in the following table.

	Price		Quantity	
Item	**1995**	**2001**	**1995**	**2001**
Cabbage (pound)	$0.06	$0.05	2,000	1,500
Carrots (bunch)	0.10	0.12	200	200
Peas (quart)	0.20	0.18	400	500
Endive (bunch)	0.15	0.15	100	200

39. Compute a simple price index for each of the four items. Use 1995 as the base period.

40. 98.04

40. Compute a simple aggregate price index. Use 1995 as the base period.
41. Compute Laspeyres' price index for 2001 using 1995 as the base period.

42. 91.25

42. Compute Paasche's index for 2001 using 1995 as the base period.
43. Determine Fisher's ideal index using the values for the Laspeyres and Paasche indexes computed in the two previous problems.

44. 93.19

44. Determine a value index for 2001 using 1995 as the base period.

The prices of selected items for 1980 and 2001 follow. Production figures for those two periods are also given.

	Price		Quantity	
Item	**1980**	**2001**	**1980**	**2001**
Aluminum (cents per pound)	$ 0.287	$ 0.76	1,000	1,200
Natural gas (1,000 cu. ft.)	0.17	2.50	5,000	4,000
Petroleum (barrel)	3.18	26.00	60,000	60,000
Platinum (troy ounce)	133.00	490.00	500	600

45. Compute a simple price index for each of the four items. Use 1980 as the base period.

46. 380.03

46. Compute a simple aggregate price index. Use 1980 as the base period.
47. Compute Laspeyres' price index for 2001 using 1980 as the base period.

48. 686.58

48. Compute Paasche's index for 2001 using 1980 as the base period.
49. Determine Fisher's ideal index using the values for the Laspeyres and Paasche indexes computed in the two previous problems.

50. 721.61

50. Determine a value index for 2001 using 1980 as the base period.
51. A special-purpose index is to be designed to monitor the overall economy of the Southwest. Four key series were selected. After considerable deliberation it was decided to weight retail sales 20 percent, total bank deposits 10 percent, industrial production in the area 40 percent, and nonagricultural employment 30 percent. The data for 1996 and 2001 are:

Year	Retail Sales ($ millions)	Bank Deposits ($ billions)	Industrial Production (1990 = 100)	Employment
1996	1,159.0	87	110.6	1,214,000
2001	1,971.0	91	114.7	1,501,000

Construct a special-purpose index for 2001 using 1996 as the base period and interpret.

52. a. See IM.

b. See IM.

52. We are making a historical study of the American economy from 1950 to 1980. Data on prices, the labor force, productivity, and the GNP were collected. Note in the following table that the CPI is on a 1967 base, employment is in millions of persons, and so on. A direct comparison, therefore, is not feasible.

a. Make whatever calculations are necessary to compare the trend in the four series from 1950 to 1980.

b. Interpret.

Year	Consumer Price Index (1967 = 100)	Total Labor Force (millions)	Index of Productivity in Manufacturing (1967 = 100)	Gross National Product ($ billions)
1950	72.1	64	64.9	286.2
1967	100.0	81	100.0	789.6
1971	121.3	87	110.3	1,063.4
1975	161.2	95	114.9	1,516.3
1980	246.8	107	146.6	2,626.0

53. The management of Ingalls Super Discount stores, with several stores in the Oklahoma City area, wants to construct an index of economic activity for the metropolitan area. Management contends that if the index reveals that the economy is slowing down, inventory should be kept at a low level.

Three series seem to hold promise as predictors of economic activity—area retail sales, bank deposits, and employment. All of these data can be secured monthly from the U.S. government. Retail sales is to be weighted 40 percent, bank deposits 35 percent, and employment 25 percent. Seasonally adjusted data for the first three months of the year are:

Month	Retail Sales ($ millions)	Bank Deposits ($ billions)	Employment (thousands)
January	8.0	20	300
February	6.8	23	303
March	6.4	21	297

Construct an index of economic activity for each of the three months, using January as the base period.

54. The following table gives information on the Consumer Price Index and the monthly take-home pay of Bill Martin, an employee at the Jeep Corporation.

Year	Consumer Price Index (1982–84 = 100)	Mr. Martin's Monthly Take-Home Pay
1982–84	100.0	$ 600
2000 (Dec.)	174.0	2,000

54. a. $0.58

b. $1,149.43

a. What is the purchasing power of the dollar for December 2000 based on the period 1982–84?

b. Determine Mr. Martin's "real" monthly income for December 2000.

55. Suppose that the Producer Price Index and the sales of Hoskin's Wholesale Distributors for 1991 and 2000 are:

Year	Producer Price Index	Sales
1991	121.7	$2,400,000
2000	138.0	3,500,000

What are Hoskin's real sales (also called deflated sales) for the two years?

exercises.com

www

56. Answers will vary.

56. The Super Bowl is usually the TV program with the largest viewing audience each year; therefore, many companies use the Super Bowl to launch major advertising campaigns. The cost for a 30-second spot, as reported below, has increased dramatically since the first game in 1967. Also shown is the face value of a ticket to the game for the selected years.

Year	TV Commercial	Game Ticket
1967	$ 42,000	$ 8.00
1988	525,000	100.00
1999	1,600,000	325.00
2001	2,300,000	420.00

Go to the Bureau of Labor Statistics Web site, click on **Most Requested Series,** and find the **Consumer Price Index—All Urban Consumers.** Select the base as *1967,* and find the CPI for the above years. Compare the rate of change in the Consumer Price Index to the cost of TV commercials and the cost of a game ticket. Write a brief report summarizing your findings.

57. Listed below are the monthly sales for the Master Chemical Company for 2000 and the first six months of 2001. Go to the U.S. Bureau of Labor Statistics (*http://stats.bls.gov/datahome.htm*). Select **Most Requested Series,** and find the **Consumer Price Index—All Urban Consumers** (CPI-U) for the corresponding period. Select all items with the 1982–84 base and a period that includes 2000 and 2001. Adjust the CPI-U to a base of January 2000. Adjust the sales values to the same base. Write a brief report detailing the change in sales during the 18-month period in terms of constant dollars.

Month	Year	Sales ($ million)	Month	Year	Sales ($ million)	Month	Year	Sales ($ million)
Jan	2000	28.3	Jul	2000	44.0	Jan	2001	48.2
Feb	2000	38.1	Aug	2000	42.6	Feb	2001	53.5
Mar	2000	37.5	Sep	2000	48.3	Mar	2001	55.6
Apr	2000	39.0	Oct	2000	46.7	Apr	2001	54.7
May	2000	40.1	Nov	2000	51.3	May	2001	64.2
Jun	2000	41.9	Dec	2000	52.1	Jun	2001	58.3

Computer Commands

1. The Excel commands for the spreadsheet on page 665 are:

a. Enter the data for the prices and quantities. We entered the label *Item* in cell A3, and the item names in cells A4 through A9. The label *Price-95* was entered in B3, and the price data for 1995 in cells B4 through B9. The label *Quantity-95* was entered in cell C3, with the 1995 quantities in cells C4 through C9. Cell D3 was labeled *Price*Qty-95.*

b. To determine the product of the 1995 prices and quantities, highlight the cells from D4 to D9. With this group of cells still highlighted, type *=B4*C4* in cell D4 and hit **Enter.** The value 38.5 should appear. This is the product of the price of bread ($0.77) and the quantity of bread (50) sold in 1995.

c. With cells D4 through D9 still highlighted, select **Edit,** then **Fill,** then **Down,** and hit **Enter.** The remaining products should appear.

d. Move to cell D10, click on Σ on the toolbar, and hit **Enter.** The value 336.16 will appear. This is the denominator for the Laspeyres price index. The other products and column totals are determined in a similar manner. The other Excel output in the chapter is computed similarly.

Chapter 18 Answers to Self-Review

18–1 **1.** For Schering-Plough
$P = (\$2{,}110/\$2{,}050)(100) = 102.9$
For Boeing
$P = (\$2{,}309/\$2{,}050)(100) = 112.6$
For Exxon-Mobil
$P = (\$7{,}910/\$2{,}050)(100) = 385.9$
For Johnson and Johnson
$P = (\$4{,}167/\$2{,}050)(100) = 203.3$
Sales of Exxon-Mobil are 285.9 percent greater than PepsiCo.
Sales for Schering-Plough are only 2.9 percent greater than PepsiCo.

2. **(a)** $P = (\$13.24/\$10.32)(100) = 128.3$
$P = (\$13.74/\$10.32)(100) = 133.1$

(b) $X = (\$10.32 + \$10.57 + \$10.83)/3 = \$10.57$
$P = (\$13.24/\$10.57)(100) = 125.3$
$P = (\$13.74/\$10.57)(100) = 130.0$

(c) $P = (\$13.74/\$11.43)(100) = 120.2$

18–2 **(a)** $P_1 = (\$85/\$75)(100) = 113.3$
$P_2 = (\$45/\$40)(100) = 112.5$
$P = (113.3 + 112.5)/2 = 112.9$

(b) $P = (\$130/\$115)(100) = 113.0$

(c)
$$P = \frac{\$85(500) + \$45(1{,}200)}{\$75(500) + \$40(1{,}200)}(100)$$
$$= \frac{\$96{,}500}{85{,}500}(100) = 112.9$$

(d)
$$P = \frac{\$85(520) + \$45(1{,}300)}{\$75(520) + \$40(1{,}300)}(100)$$
$$= \frac{\$102{,}700}{\$91{,}000}(100) = 112.9$$

(e) $P = \sqrt{(112.9)(112.9)} = 112.9$

18–3 **(a)**
$$P = \frac{\$4(9{,}000) + \$5(200) + \$8(5{,}000)}{\$3(10{,}000) + \$1(600) + \$10(3{,}000)}(100)$$
$$= \frac{\$77{,}000}{60{,}600}(100) = 127.1$$

(b) The value of sales has gone up 27.1 percent from 1996 to 2002.

18–4 **(a)**

For 2000

Item	Weight	
Cotton	(\$0.50/\$0.20)(100)(.10) =	25.00
Autos	(900/1,000)(100)(.30) =	27.00
Money turnover	(75/80)(100)(.60) =	56.25
		108.25

For 1998

Item	Weight	
Cotton	(\$0.25/\$0.20)(100)(.10) =	12.5
Autos	(1,200/1,000)(100)(.30) =	36.0
Money turnover	(90/80)(100)(.60) =	67.5
		116.0

(b) Business activity increased 16 percent from 1992 to 1998. It increased 8.25 percent from 1992 to 2000.

18–5 **(a)** \$16,404, found by (\$25,000/152.4)(100).

(b) \$23,926, found by (\$41,200/172.2)(100).

(c) In terms of the base period, Jon's salary was \$16,404 in 1995 and \$23,926 in 2000. This indicates his take-home pay increased at a faster rate than the price paid for food, transportation, etc.

18–6 \$0.57, found by (\$1.00/174.0)(100).

18–7 **1.** 179.4, found by (9,181.40/5,117.10)(100).

2. **(a)** Using 1982 as the base period for both series:

	Industrial Production Index	Producer Price Index
1982	100.0	100.0
1987	112.6	105.4
1994	123.9	119.2
1997	149.4	131.2
2000	161.0	138.2

(b) From the base of 1982 to 2000, industrial production increased at a faster rate (61.0 percent) than prices (38.2 percent).

19

Time Series and Forecasting

Look at the selling price for a share of PepsiCo, Inc. at the close of the year. Estimate the selling price in 2003. Does this seem like a reasonable estimate based on the historical data? (See Goal 5 and Exercise 18.)

GOALS

When you have completed this chapter, you will be able to:

1. Define the four components of a time series.
2. Determine a linear trend equation.
3. Compute a moving average.
4. Compute a trend equation for a nonlinear trend.
5. Use a trend equation to forecast future time periods and to develop seasonally adjusted forecasts.
6. Determine and interpret a set of seasonal indexes.
7. Deseasonalize data using a seasonal index.

Introduction

What is a time series?

The emphasis in this chapter is on time series analysis and forecasting. A **time series** is a collection of data recorded over a period of time — weekly, monthly, quarterly, or yearly. Two examples of time series are the sales by quarter of the Microsoft Corporation since 1985 and the annual production of sulfuric acid since 1970. The computer image in the photo shows the volume of data traveling into the National Science Foundation network in one month. The colors represent traffic volume from zero bytes (purple) to 100 billion bytes (white).

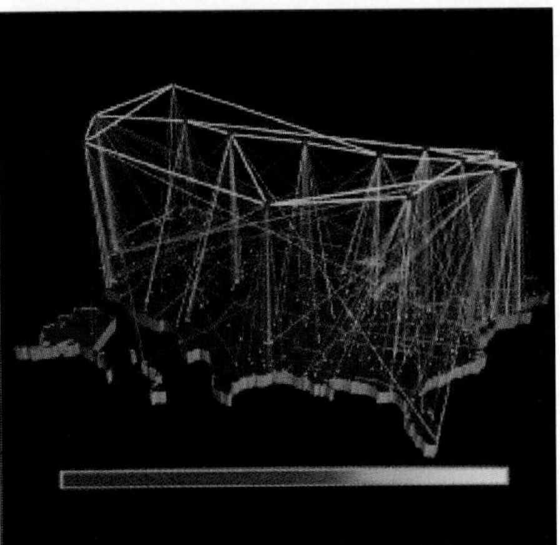

An analysis of history — a time series — can be used by management to make current decisions and for long-term forecasting and planning. We usually assume past patterns will continue into the future. Long-term forecasts extend more than 1 year into the future; 5-, 10-, 15-, and 20-year projections are common. Long-range predictions are essential to allow sufficient time for the procurement, manufacturing, sales, finance, and other departments of a company to develop plans for possible new plants, financing, development of new products, and new methods of assembling.

Forecasting the level of sales, both short-term and long-term, is practically dictated by the very nature of business organizations in the United States. Competition for the consumer's dollar, stress on earning a profit for the stockholders, a desire to procure a larger share of the market, and the ambitions of executives are some of the prime motivating forces in business. Thus, a forecast (a statement of the goals of management) is necessary to have the raw materials, production facilities, and staff available to meet the projected demand.

This chapter deals with the use of data to forecast future events. First, we look at the components of a time series. Then, we examine some of the techniques used in analyzing data. Finally, we project future events.

Components of a Time Series

There are four components to a time series: the trend, the cyclical variation, the seasonal variation, and the irregular variation.

Secular Trend

The long-term trends of sales, employment, stock prices, and other business and economic series follow various patterns. Some move steadily upward, others decline, and still others stay the same over time.

SECULAR TREND The smooth long-term direction of a time series.

The following are several examples of a secular trend.

- The following chart shows the number of subscribers to America Online from the second quarter of 1995 until the third quarter of 2000. The number of subscribers increased from 3.0 million to 24.6 million. This is an increase of 21.6 million subscribers, or 720 percent. The long-run direction of the time series is increasing.

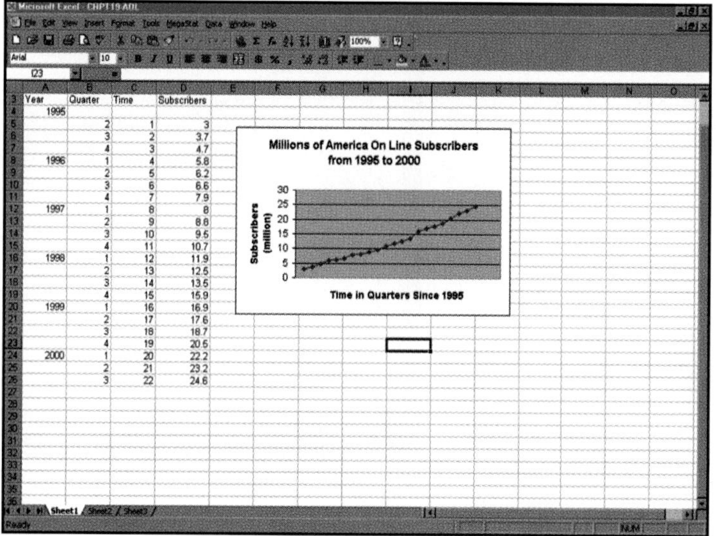

EXCEL

- The following chart shows the mean selling price of single-family homes in Horry County in South Carolina from 1993 until 2000. In 1993 the mean selling price was $96,577. By 1997 it increased to $141,232, and by 2000 to $169,527. Again, the long-run direction of the time series is increasing.

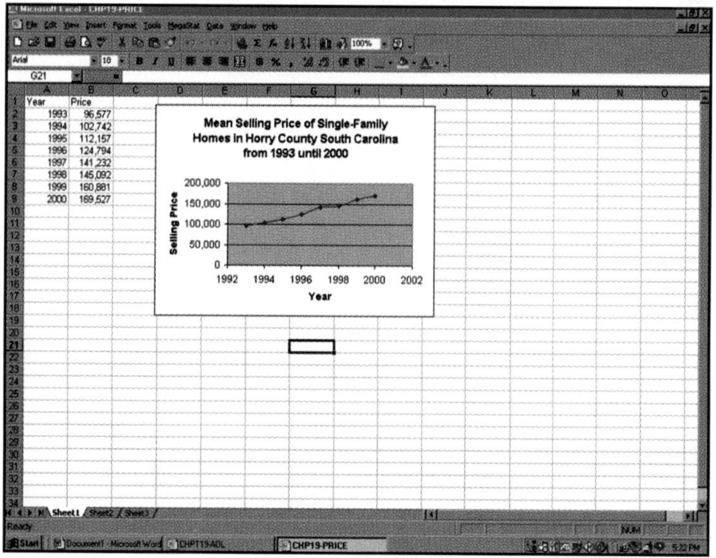

- The next chart is an example of a declining long-run trend. In 1988, 36 new outlet shopping malls opened in the United States. In 1989 the number increased to 43, but since 1990 there has been a steady decline. In 1999, which is the latest information available, only 5 new outlet malls opened.

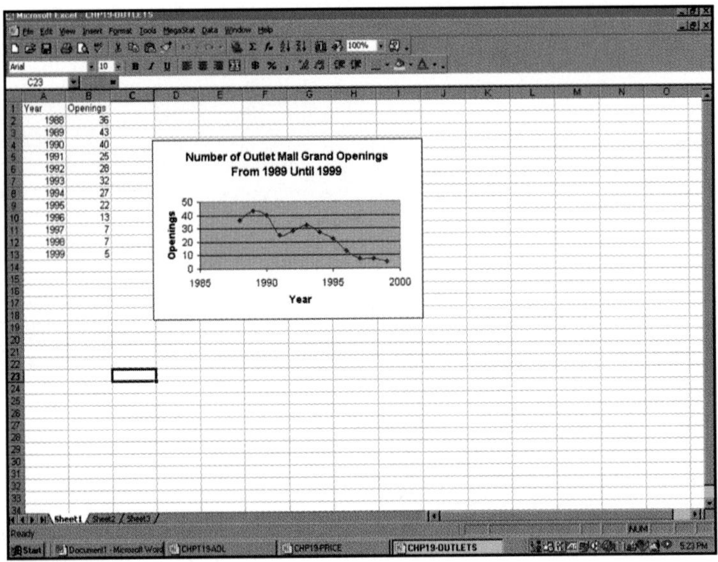

Cyclical Variation

The second component of a time series is cyclical variation. A typical business cycle consists of a period of prosperity followed by periods of recession, depression, and then recovery. There are sizable fluctuations unfolding over more than one year in time above and below the secular trend. In a recession, for example, employment, production, the Dow Jones Industrial Average, and many other business and economic series are below the long-term trend lines. Conversely, in periods of prosperity they are above their long-term trend lines.

> **CYCLICAL VARIATION** The rise and fall of a time series over periods longer than one year.

Chart 19–1 shows the number of batteries sold by National Battery Sales, Inc. from 1984 through 2001. The cyclical nature of business is highlighted. There are periods of recovery, followed by prosperity, then recession, and finally the cycle bottoms out with depression.

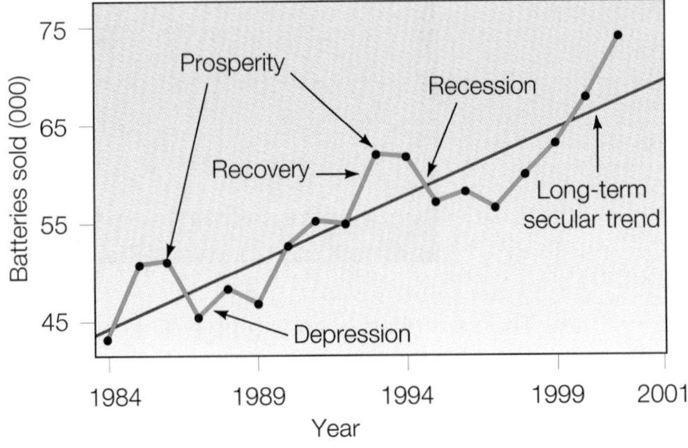

CHART 19–1 Battery Sales by National Battery Sales, Inc., 1984–2001.

Seasonal Variation

The third component of a time series is the seasonal component. Many sales, production, and other series fluctuate with the seasons. The unit of time reported is either quarterly or monthly.

SEASONAL VARIATION Patterns of change in a time series within a year. These patterns tend to repeat themselves each year.

Statistics in Action

Statisticians, economists, and business executives are constantly looking for variables that will forecast the country's economy. The production of crude oil, price of gold on world markets, the Dow Jones average, as well as many published government indexes are variables that have been used with some success. Variables such as the length of hemlines and the winner of the Super Bowl have also been tried. The variable that seems overall to be the most successful is the price of scrap metal. Why? Scrap metal is the beginning of the manufacturing chain. When its demand increases, this is an indication that manufacturing is also increasing.

Almost all businesses tend to have recurring seasonal patterns. Men's and boys' clothing, for example, have extremely high sales just prior to Christmas and relatively low sales just after Christmas and during the summer. Toy sales is another example with an extreme seasonal pattern. More than half of the business for the year is usually done in the months of November and December. The lawn care business is seasonal in the northeast and north-central states. Many businesses try to even out the seasonal effects by engaging in an offsetting seasonal business. In the Northeast you will see the operator of a lawn care business with a snowplow on the front of the truck in an effort to earn income in the off-season. In northern Michigan and other ski areas, you will often find golf courses nearby. The owners of the lodges try to rent to skiers in the winter and golfers in the summer. This is an effective method of spreading their fixed costs over the entire year rather than a few months.

Chart 19–2 shows the quarterly sales, in millions of dollars, of Hercher Sporting Goods, Inc. They are a Chicago area sporting goods company that specializes in selling baseball and softball equipment to high schools, colleges, and youth leagues. They also have several retail outlets in some of the larger shopping malls. There is a distinct seasonal pattern to their business. Most of their sales are in the first and second quarters of the year, when schools and organizations are purchasing equipment for the upcoming season. During the early summer, they keep busy by selling replacement equipment. They do some business during the holidays (fourth quarter). The late summer (third quarter) is their slow season.

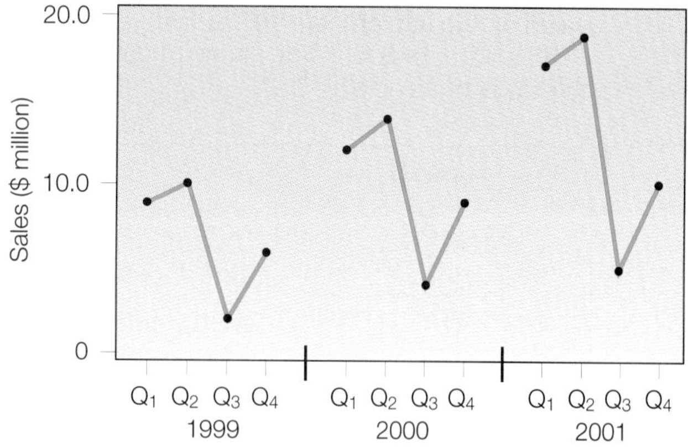

CHART 19–2 Sales of Baseball and Softball Equipment, Hercher Sporting Goods, 1999–2001 by Quarter

Irregular Variation

Many analysts prefer to subdivide the **irregular variation** into *episodic* and *residual* variations. Episodic fluctuations are unpredictable, but they can be identified. The initial impact on the economy of a major strike or a war can be identified, but a strike or war cannot be predicted. After the episodic fluctuations have been removed, the remaining variation is called the residual variation. The residual fluctuations, often called chance fluctuations, are unpredictable, and they cannot be identified. Of course, neither episodic nor residual variation can be projected into the future.

Linear Trend

The long-term trend of many business series, such as sales, exports, and production, often approximates a straight line. If so, the equation to describe this growth is:

LINEAR TREND EQUATION	$Y' = a + bt$	**[19–1]**

where:

- Y' read Y prime, is the projected value of the Y variable for a selected value of t.
- a is the Y-intercept. It is the estimated value of Y when $t = 0$. Another way to put it is: a is the estimated value of Y where the line crosses the Y-axis when t is zero.
- b is the slope of the line, or the average change in Y' for each change of one unit in t.
- t is any value of time that is selected.

Slope of trend line is *b*

To illustrate the meaning of Y', a, b, and t in a time-series problem, a line has been drawn in Chart 19–3 to represent the typical trend of sales. Assume that this company started in business in 1993. This beginning year (1993) has been arbitrarily designated as year 1. Note that sales increased $2 million on the average every year; that is, based on the straight line drawn through the sales data, sales increased from $3 million in 1993 to $5 million in 1994, to $7 million in 1995, to $9 million in 1996, and so on. The slope, or b, is therefore 2. Note too that the line intercepts the Y-axis (when $t = 0$) at $1 million. This point is a. Another way of determining b is to locate the starting place of the straight line in year (1). It is 3 for 1993 in this problem. Then locate the value on the straight line for the last year. It is 19 for 2001. Sales went up $19 million − $3 million, or $16 million, in eight years (1993 to 2001). Thus, $16 \div 8 = 2$, which is the slope of the line, or b.

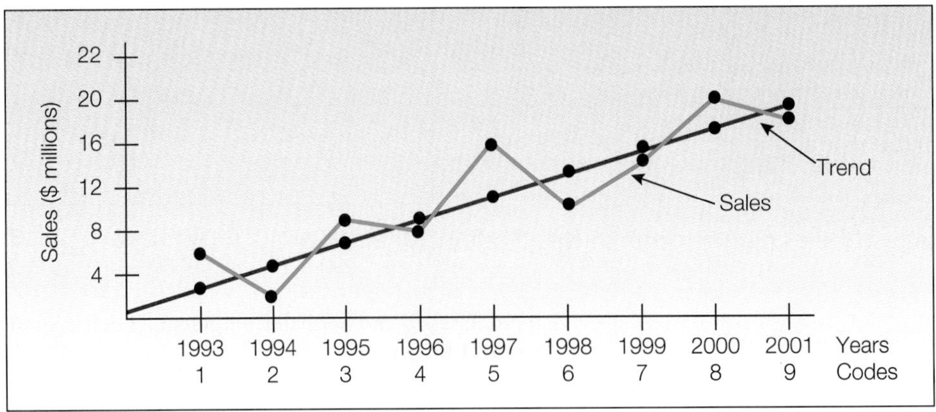

CHART 19–3 A Straight Line Fitted to Sales Data

Statistics in Action

Investors frequently use regression analysis to study the relationship between a particular stock and the general condition of the market. The dependent variable is the monthly percentage change in the value of the stock, and the independent variable is the monthly percentage change in a market index, such as the Standard & Poor's 500 Composite Index. The value of b in the regression equation is the particular stock's *beta coefficient* or just the *beta*. If b is greater than 1, the implication is that the stock is sensitive to market changes. If b is between 0 and 1, the implication is that the stock is not sensitive to market changes. This is the same concept that economists refer to as *elasticity*.

The equation for the line in Chart 19–3 is:

$$Y' = 1 + 2t \text{ (in millions)}$$

where:

Sales are in millions of dollars. The origin, or year 0, is 1992.
t increases by one unit for each year.

In Chapter 13 we drew a line through points on a scatter diagram to approximate the regression line. We stressed, however, that this method for determining the regression equation has a serious drawback — namely, the position of the line depends on the judgment of the individual who drew the line. Three people would probably draw three different lines through the scatter plots. Likewise, the line we drew through the sales data in Chart 19–3 might not be the "best-fitting" line. Because of the subjective judgment involved, this method should be used only when a quick approximation of the straight-line equation is needed, or to check the reasonableness of the least squares line, which is discussed next.

Least Squares Method

The **least squares method** of computing the equation for a line through the data of interest gave the "best-fitting" line. Two equations may be solved simultaneously to arrive at the least squares trend equation. They are:

EQUATIONS FOR THE TREND LINE

$$\Sigma Y = na + b\Sigma t$$
$$\Sigma tY = a\Sigma t + b\Sigma t^2 \qquad \textbf{[19–2]}$$

You may recognize these as the normal equations discussed in Chapter 13, with t replacing X in the equations. As we described in Chapter 13, using the normal equations to determine a and b can be tedious. A better approach is to use the following computational equations.

THE SLOPE

$$b = \frac{n\Sigma tY - (\Sigma Y)(\Sigma t)}{n\Sigma t^2 - (\Sigma t)^2} \qquad \textbf{[19–3]}$$

THE INTERCEPT

$$a = \frac{\Sigma Y}{n} - b\left(\frac{\Sigma t}{n}\right) \qquad \textbf{[19–4]}$$

If the number of years is large — say, 15 or more — and the magnitude of the numbers is also large, a computer software package is recommended.

EXAMPLE

The sales of Jensen Foods, a small grocery chain, since 1997 are:

Year	Sales ($ millions)
1997	7
1998	10
1999	9
2000	11
2001	13

Determine the least squares trend-line equation.

SOLUTION

To simplify the calculations, the years are replaced by *coded* values. That is, we let 1997 be 1, 1998 be 2, and so forth. This reduces the size of the values of Σt, Σt^2, and ΣtY. (See Table 19–1.) This is often referred to as the **coded method.**

Determining a and b using formulas 19–3 and 19–4:

$$b = \frac{n\Sigma tY - (\Sigma Y)(\Sigma t)}{n\Sigma t^2 - (\Sigma t)^2} = \frac{5(163) - 50(15)}{5(55) - (15)^2} = 1.3$$

$$a = \frac{\Sigma Y}{n} - b\left(\frac{\Sigma t}{n}\right) = \frac{50}{5} - 1.3\left(\frac{15}{5}\right) = 6.1$$

TABLE 19–1 Computations Needed for Determining the Trend Equation

Year	Sales ($ millions), Y	t	tY	t^2
1997	7	1	7	1
1998	10	2	20	4
1999	9	3	27	9
2000	11	4	44	16
2001	13	5	65	25
	50	15	163	55

The trend equation is, therefore, $Y' = 6.1 + 1.3t$, where:

Sales are in millions of dollars.
The origin, or year 0, is 1996, and t increases by one unit for each year.

How do we interpret the equation? The value of 1.3 indicates sales increased at a rate of $1.3 million per year. The value 6.1 is the estimated sales when $t = 0$. That is, the estimated sales amount for 1996 (the base year) is $6.1 million.

Plotting the Line

The least squares equation can be used to find points on the line through the data. The sales data from Table 19–1 are repeated in Table 19–2 to show the procedure. The equation determined earlier is $Y' = 6.1 + 1.3t$. To get the coordinates of the point on the line for 2000, for example, insert the t value of 4 in the equation. Then $Y' = 6.1 + 1.3(4) = 11.3$.

TABLE 19–2 Calculations Needed for Determining the Points on the Straight Line Using the Coded Method

Year	Sales ($ millions), Y	t	Y'		Found by
1997	$ 7	1	7.4	⟵	6.1 + 1.3(1)
1998	10	2	8.7	⟵	6.1 + 1.3(2)
1999	9	3	10.0	⟵	6.1 + 1.3(3)
2000	11	4	11.3	⟵	6.1 + 1.3(4)
2001	13	5	12.6	⟵	6.1 + 1.3(5)

The actual sales and the trend in sales as represented by the line are shown in the MINITAB output Chart 19–4. The first point on the line has the coordinates $t = 1$, $Y' = 7.4$. Another point is $t = 3$, $Y' = 10$.

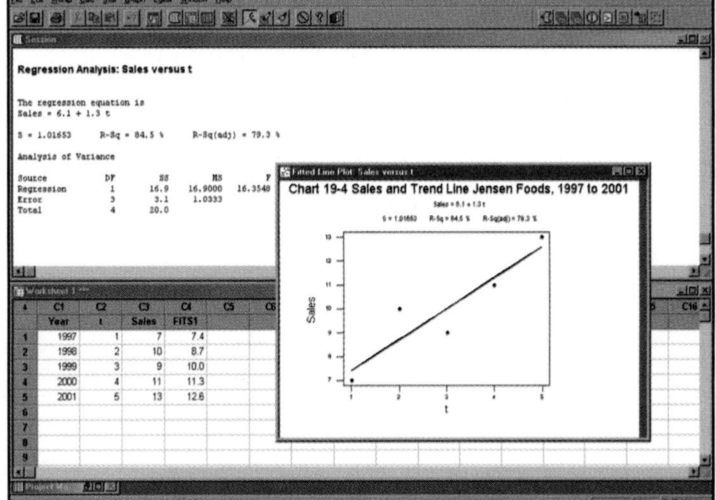

Estimation

If the sales, production, or other data approximate a linear trend, the equation developed by the least squares method can be used to estimate sales for some future period.

EXAMPLE

Refer to the sales data in Table 19–1. The year 1997 is coded 1, and 1998 is coded 2. What is the sales forecast for 2004?

SOLUTION

The year 1999 is coded 3, 2000 is coded 4, 2001 is coded 5, 2002 is coded 6, 2003 is coded 7, and 2004 is logically coded 8. Thus, in 2004 $t = 8$. Substituting the period 8 in the equation (formula 19–1):

$$Y' = a + bt = 6.1 + 1.3(8) = 16.5$$

Thus, based on past sales, the estimate for 2004 is $16.5 million.

In this time series example, there were five years of sales data. Based on those five sales figures, we estimated sales for 2004. Many researchers suggest that we do not project sales, production, and other business and economic series more than $n/2$ time periods into the future where n is the number of data points. If, for example, there are 10 years of data, we would make estimates only up to 5 years into the future ($n/2 = 10/2 = 5$). Others suggest the forecast may be for no longer than 2 years, especially in rapidly changing economic times.

Self-Review 19–1 Annual production of king-size rockers by Wood Products, Inc. since 1994 follows.

Year	Production (thousands)	Year	Production (thousands)
1994	4	1998	11
1995	8	1999	9
1996	5	2000	11
1997	8	2001	14

(a) Plot the production data.
(b) Determine the least squares equation.
(c) Determine the points on the line for 1994 and 2000. Connect the two points to arrive at the line.
(d) Based on the linear trend equation, what is the estimated production for 2004?

Exercises

1. The numbers of bank failures for the years 1997 through 2001 are given below. Determine the least squares equation and estimate the number of failures in 2003.

Year	Code	Number of Failures
1997	1	79
1998	2	120
1999	3	138
2000	4	184
2001	5	200

2. $Y' = 35.880 + 1.7486t$
$Y' = 51.62$
($ billions)

2. The personal consumption expenditures for telephone, in billions of dollars, in the United States for the years 1996 to 2001 are given below. Determine the least squares equation, and estimate the expenditure for 2004.

Year	Code	Expenditures ($ billions)
1996	1	37.9
1997	2	39.8
1998	3	40.4
1999	4	42.7
2000	5	44.1
2001	6	47.1

3. The following table gives the annual amount of scrap produced by Machine Products, Inc.

Year	Code	Scrap (tons)
1997	1	2.0
1998	2	4.0
1999	3	3.0
2000	4	5.0
2001	5	6.0

Determine the least squares trend equation. Estimate the amount of scrap for the year 2003.

4. The amounts spent in vending machines in the United States, in billions of dollars, for the years 1997 through 2001 are given below. Determine the least squares trend equation, and estimate vending sales for 2003.

4. $Y' = 15.63 + 1.77t$
$Y' = 28.02$ ($ billions)

Year	Code	Vending Machine Sales ($ billions)
1997	1	17.5
1998	2	19.0
1999	3	21.0
2000	4	22.7
2001	5	24.5

The Moving-Average Method

Moving-average method smooths out fluctuations

The **moving-average method** is not only useful in smoothing a time series to see its trend; it is the basic method used in measuring the seasonal fluctuation, described later in the chapter. In contrast to the least squares method, which expresses the trend in terms of a mathematical equation ($Y' = a + bt$), the moving-average method merely smooths the fluctuations in the data. This is accomplished by "moving" the arithmetic mean values through the time series.

To apply the moving-average method to a time series, the data should follow a fairly linear trend and have a definite rhythmic pattern of fluctuations (repeating, say, every three years). The data in the following example have three components — trend, cycle, and irregular, abbreviated *T, C,* and *I.* There is no seasonal variation, because the data are recorded annually. What the moving-average method does, in effect, is average out *C* and *I*. The residual is trend.

If the duration of the cycles is constant, and if the amplitudes of the cycles are equal, the cyclical and irregular fluctuations can be removed entirely using the moving-average method. The result is a line. For example, in the following time series the cycle repeats itself every seven years, and the amplitude of each cycle is 4; that is, there are exactly four units from the trough (lowest time period) to the peak. The seven-year moving average, therefore, averages out the cyclical and irregular fluctuations perfectly, and the residual is a linear trend.

Compute mean of first seven years

The first step in computing the seven-year moving average is to determine the seven-year moving totals. The total sales for the first seven years (1976–82 inclusive) are $22 million, found by $1 + 2 + 3 + 4 + 5 + 4 + 3$. (See Table 19–3.) The total of $22 million is divided by 7 to determine the arithmetic mean sales per year. The seven-year total (22) and the seven-year mean (3.143) are positioned opposite the middle year for that group of seven, namely, 1979, as shown in Table 19–3. Then the total sales for the next seven years (1977–83 inclusive) are determined. (A convenient way of doing this is to subtract the sales for 1976 [$1 million] from the first seven-year total [$22 million] and add the sales for 1983 [$2 million], to give the new total of $23 million.) The mean of this total, $3.286 million, is positioned opposite the middle year, 1980. The sales data and seven-year moving average are shown graphically in Chart 19–5.

TABLE 19–3 The Computations for the Seven-Year Moving Average

Year	Sales ($ millions)	Seven-Year Moving Total	Seven-Year Moving Average
1976	$1		
1977	2		
1978	3		
1979	4	22	3.143
1980	5	23	3.286
1981	4	24	3.429
1982	3	25	3.571
1983	2	26	3.714
1984	3	27	3.857
1985	4	28	4.000
1986	5	29	4.143
1987	6	30	4.286
1988	5	31	4.429
1989	4	32	4.571
1990	3	33	4.714
1991	4	34	4.857
1992	5	35	5.000
1993	6	36	5.143
1994	7	37	5.286
1995	6	38	5.429
1996	5	39	5.571
1997	4	40	5.714
1998	5	41	5.857
1999	6		
2000	7		
2001	8		

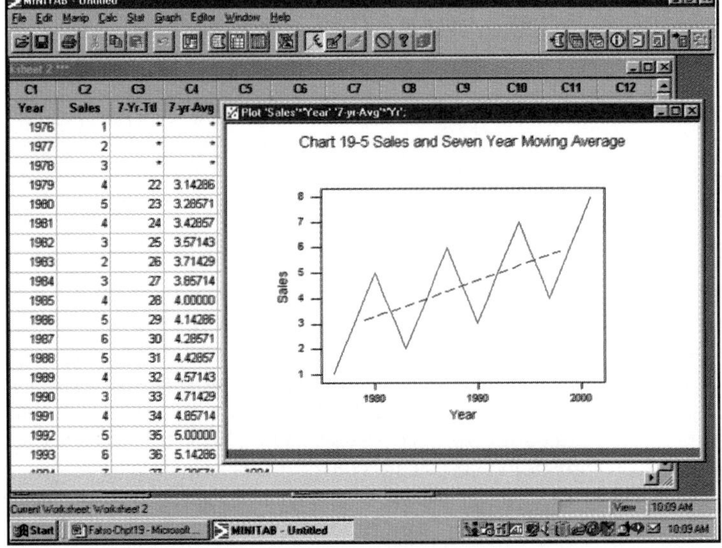

A three-year and a five-year moving average for some production data are shown in Table 19–4 and depicted in Chart 19–6.

TABLE 19–4 A Three-Year Moving Average and a Five-Year Moving Average

Year	Production, *Y*	Three-Year Moving Total	Three-Year Moving Average	Five-Year Moving Total	Five-Year Moving Average
1983	5				
1984	6	19	6.3		
1985	8	24	8.0	34	6.8
1986	10	23	7.7	32	6.4
1987	5	18	6.0	33	6.6
1988	3	15	5.0	35	7.0
1989	7	20	6.7	37	7.4
1990	10	29	9.7	43	8.6
1991	12	33	11.0	49	9.8
1992	11	32	10.7	55	11.0
1993	9	33	11.0	60	12.0
1994	13	37	12.3	66	13.2
1995	15	46	15.3	70	14.0
1996	18	48	16.0	72	14.4
1997	15	44	14.7	73	14.6
1998	11	40	13.3	75	15.0
1999	14	42	14.0	79	15.8
2000	17	53	17.7		
2001	22				

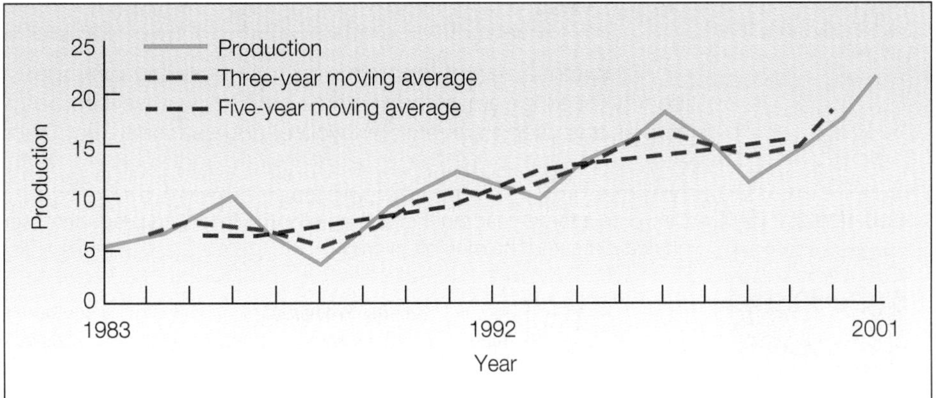

CHART 19–6 A Three-Year Moving Average and a Five-Year Moving Average

Sales, production, and other economic and business series usually do not have (1) periods of oscillation that are of equal length or (2) oscillations that have identical amplitudes. Thus, in actual practice, the application of the moving-average method to data does not result precisely in a line. For example, the production series in Table 19–4 repeats about every five years, but the amplitude of the data varies from one oscillation to another. The trend appears to be upward and somewhat linear. Both moving averages — the three-year and the five-year — seem to adequately describe the trend in production since 1983.

Determining a moving average for an even-numbered period, such as four years

Four-year, six-year, and other even-numbered-year moving averages present one minor problem regarding the centering of the moving totals and moving averages. Note in Table 19–5 that there is no center time period, so the moving totals are positioned *between* two time periods. The total for the first four years ($42) is positioned between 1994 and 1995. The total for the next four years is $43. The averages of the first four years and the second four years ($10.50 and $10.75, respectively) are averaged, and the resulting figure is centered on 1995. This procedure is repeated until all possible four-year averages are computed.

TABLE 19–5 A Four-Year Moving Average

Year	Sales, Y	Four-Year Moving Total	Four-Year Moving Average	Centered Four-Year Moving Average
1993	$ 8			
1994	11			
		$42 (8 + 11 + 9 + 14)	$10.50 ($42 ÷ 4)	
1995	9			10.625
		43 (11 + 9 + 14 + 9)	10.75 ($43 ÷ 4)	
1996	14			10.625
		42	10.50	
1997	9			10.625
		43	10.75	
1998	10			10.000
		37	9.25	
1999	10			9.625
		40	10.00	
2000	8			
2001	12			

To summarize the technique of using moving averages, its purpose is to help identify the long-term trend in a time series (because it smooths out short-term fluctuations). It is used to reveal any cyclical and seasonal fluctuations.

Self-Review 19–2

Compute a three-year moving average for the following production series. Plot both the original data and the moving average.

Year	Number Produced (thousands)	Year	Number Produced (thousands)
1996	2	1999	5
1997	6	2000	3
1998	4	2001	10

Nonlinear Trends

The emphasis in the previous discussion was on a time series whose growth or decline approximated a line. A linear trend equation is used to represent the time series when it is believed that the data are increasing (or decreasing) by *equal amounts,* on the average, from one period to another.

Data that increase (or decrease) by *increasing amounts* over a period of time appear *curvilinear* when plotted on paper having an arithmetic scale. To put it another way, data that increase (or decrease) by *equal percents or proportions* over a period of time appear curvilinear on arithmetic paper. (See Chart 19–7.)

The trend equation for a time series that does approximate a curvilinear trend, such as the one portrayed in Chart 19–7, may be computed by using the logarithms of the data and the least squares method. The general equation for the logarithmic trend equation is:

LOG TREND EQUATION $\log Y' = \log a + \log b(t)$ **[19–5]**

The logarithmic trend equation can be determined for the import data in Chart 19–7 using Excel. The first step is to enter the data, then find the log base 10 of each year's imports. Finally, use the regression procedure to find the least squares equation. To put it another way, we take the log of each year's data then use the logs as the dependent variable and the coded year as the independent variable.

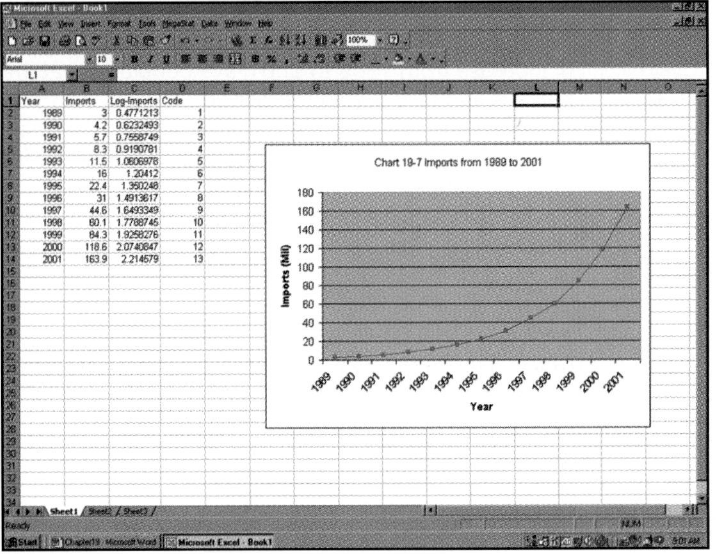

Year	Imports	Log-Imports	Code
1989	3	0.4771213	1
1990	4.2	0.6232493	2
1991	5.7	0.7558749	3
1992	8.3	0.9190781	4
1993	11.5	1.0606978	5
1994	16	1.20412	6
1995	22.4	1.350248	7
1996	31	1.4913617	8
1997	44.6	1.6493349	9
1998	60.1	1.7788745	10
1999	84.3	1.9258276	11
2000	118.6	2.0740847	12
2001	163.9	2.214579	13

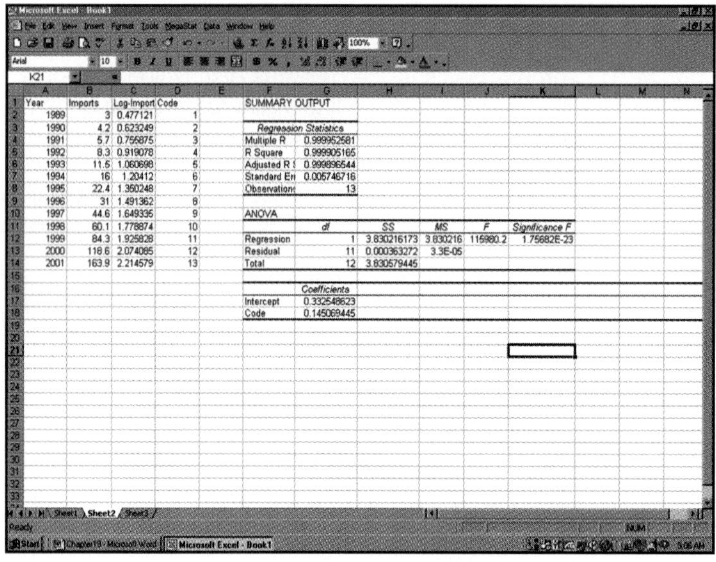

Year	Imports	Log-Import	Code
1989	3	0.477121	1
1990	4.2	0.623249	2
1991	5.7	0.755875	3
1992	8.3	0.919078	4
1993	11.5	1.060698	5
1994	16	1.20412	6
1995	22.4	1.350248	7
1996	31	1.491362	8
1997	44.6	1.649335	9
1998	60.1	1.778874	10
1999	84.3	1.925828	11
2000	118.6	2.074085	12
2001	163.9	2.214579	13

SUMMARY OUTPUT

Regression Statistics	
Multiple R	0.999952581
R Square	0.999905165
Adjusted R S	0.999896544
Standard Err	0.005746716
Observations	13

ANOVA

	df	*SS*	*MS*	*F*	*Significance F*
Regression	1	3.830216173	3.830216	115980.2	1.75682E-23
Residual	11	0.000363272	3.3E-05		
Total	12	3.830579445			

	Coefficients
Intercept	0.332548623
Code	0.145069445

The regression equation is $Y' = 0.332549 + 0.145069X$, which is the log form. We now have a trend equation in terms of percent change. That is, the value 0.145069 is the percent change in Y' for each unit change in t. This value is similar to the geometric mean described in Chapter 3.

The log of b is 0.145069 and its antilog or inverse is 1.3966. If we subtract 1 from this value, as we did in Chapter 3, the value .3966 indicates the geometric mean rate of increase from 1989 to 2001. We conclude that imports increased at a rate of 39.66 percent annually during the period.

We can also use the logarithmic trend equation to make estimates of future values. Suppose we want to estimate the imports in the year 2006. The first step is to determine the code for the year 2006, which is 18. How did we get 18? The year 2001 has a code of 13 and the year 2006 is five years later, so 13 + 5 = 18. The log of imports for the year 2006 is

$$Y' = .332549 + .145069(t) = .332549 + .145069(18) = 2.943791$$

To find the estimated imports for the year 2006, we need the antilog of 2.943791. It is 878.6. This is our estimate of the number of imports for 2006. Recall that the data were in thousands of dollars, so the estimate is $878,600.

Self-Review 19–3

Sales at Tomlin Manufacturing since 1997 are:

Year	Sales ($ millions)
1997	2.13
1998	18.10
1999	39.80
2000	81.40
2001	112.00

(a) Determine the logarithmic trend equation for the sales data.
(b) Sales increased by what percent annually?
(c) What is the projected sales amount for 2002?

Exercises

5. Sally's Software, Inc. is a rapidly growing supplier of computer software to the Sarasota area. Sales for the last five years are given below.

Year	Sales ($ millions)
1996	1.1
1997	1.5
1998	2.0
1999	2.4
2000	3.1

a. Determine the logarithmic trend equation.
b. By what percent did sales increase, on the average, during the period?
c. Estimates sales for the year 2003.

6. It appears that the imports of carbon black have been increasing by about 10 percent annually.

Year	Imports of Carbon Black (thousands of tons)	Year	Imports of Carbon Black (thousands of tons)
1993	92.0	1997	135.0
1994	101.0	1998	149.0
1995	112.0	1999	163.0
1996	124.0	2000	180.0

6. a. $Y' = 1.92333 + 0.0415302t$
b. 10.03%
c. 239.97

a. Determine the logarithmic trend equation.
b. By what percent did imports increase, on the average, during the period?
c. Estimate imports for the year 2003.

Seasonal Variation

We mentioned that *seasonal variation* is another of the components of a time series. Business series, such as automobile sales, shipments of soft-drink bottles, and residential construction, have periods of above-average and below-average activity each year.

In the area of production, one of the reasons for analyzing seasonal fluctuations is to have a sufficient supply of raw materials on hand to meet the varying seasonal demand. The glass container division of a large glass company, for example, manufactures nonreturnable beer bottles, iodine bottles, aspirin bottles, bottles for rubber cement, and so on. The production scheduling department must know how many bottles to produce and when to produce each kind. A run of too many bottles of one kind may cause a serious storage problem. Production cannot be based entirely on orders on hand, because many orders are telephoned in for immediate shipment. Since the demand for many of the bottles varies according to the season, a forecast a year or two in advance, by month, is essential to good scheduling.

An analysis of seasonal fluctuations over a period of years can also help in evaluating current sales. The typical sales of department stores in the United States, excluding mail-order sales, are expressed as indexes in Table 19–6. Each index represents the average sales for a period of several years. The actual sales for some months were above average (which is represented by an index over 100.0), and the sales for other months were below average. The index of 126.8 for December indicates that, typically, sales for December are 26.8 percent above an average month;

the index of 86.0 for July indicates that department store sales for July are typically 14 percent below an average month.

TABLE 19–6 Typical Seasonal Indexes for U.S. Department Store Sales, Excluding Mail-Order Sales

January	87.0	July	86.0
February	83.2	August	99.7
March	100.5	September	101.4
April	106.5	October	105.8
May	101.6	November	111.9
June	89.6	December	126.8

Suppose an enterprising store manager, in an effort to stimulate sales during December, introduced a number of unique promotions, including bands of carolers strolling through the store singing holiday songs, large mechanical exhibits, and clerks dressed in Santa Claus costumes. When the index of sales was computed for that December, it was 150.0. Compared with the typical sales of 126.8, it was concluded that the promotional program was a huge success.

Determining a Seasonal Index

Objective: To determine a set of "typical" seasonal indexes

A typical set of monthly indexes consists of 12 indexes that are representative of the data for a 12-month period. Logically, there are four typical seasonal indexes for data reported quarterly. Each index is a percent, with the average for the year equal to 100.0; that is, each monthly index indicates the level of sales, production, or another variable in relation to the annual average of 100.0. A typical index of 96.0 for January indicates that sales (or whatever the variable is) are usually 4 percent below the average for the year. An index of 107.2 for October means that the variable is typically 7.2 percent above the annual average.

Several methods have been developed to measure the typical seasonal fluctuation in a time series. The method most commonly used to compute the typical seasonal pattern is called the **ratio-to-moving-average method.** It eliminates the trend, cyclical, and irregular components from the original data (Y). In the following discussion, T refers to trend, C to cyclical, S to seasonal, and I to irregular variation. The numbers that result are called the *typical seasonal index.*

We will discuss in detail the steps followed in arriving at typical seasonal indexes using the ratio-to-moving-average method. The data of interest might be monthly or quarterly. To illustrate, we have chosen the quarterly sales of Toys International. First, we will show the steps needed to arrive at a set of typical quarterly indexes. Then we use the MegaStat Excel and MINITAB software to calculate the seasonal indexes.

EXAMPLE

Table 19–7 shows the quarterly sales for Toys International for the years 1996 through 2001. The sales are reported in millions of dollars. Determine a quarterly seasonal index using the ratio-to-moving-average method.

TABLE 19–7 Quarterly Sales of Toys International ($ millions)

Year	Winter	Spring	Summer	Fall
1996	6.7	4.6	10.0	12.7
1997	6.5	4.6	9.8	13.6
1998	6.9	5.0	10.4	14.1
1999	7.0	5.5	10.8	15.0
2000	7.1	5.7	11.1	14.5
2001	8.0	6.2	11.4	14.9

SOLUTION

Chart 19–8 depicts the quarterly sales for Toys International over the six-year period. Notice the seasonal nature of the sales. For each year, the fourth-quarter sales are the largest and the second-quarter sales are the smallest. Also, there is a moderate increase in the sales from one year to the next. To observe this feature, look only at the six fourth-quarter sales values. Over the six-year period, the sales in the fourth quarter increased. If you connect these points in your mind, you can visualize fourth-quarter sales increasing for 2002.

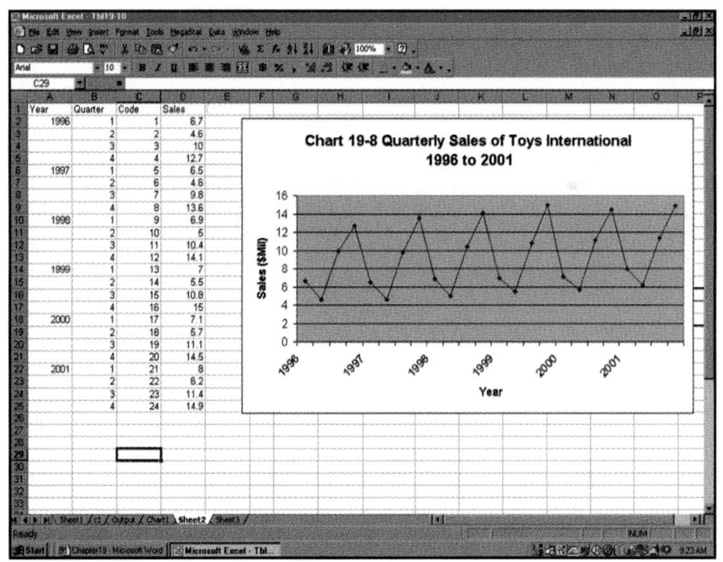

There are six steps to determining the quarterly seasonal indexes.

Step 1 For the following discussion, refer to Table 19–8. The first step is to determine the four-quarter moving total for 1996. Starting with the winter quarter of 1996, we add $6.7, $4.6, $10.0, and $12.7. The total is $34.0 (million). The four-quarter total is "moved along" by adding the spring, summer, and fall sales of 1996 to the winter sales of 1997. The total is $33.8 (million), found by 4.6 + 10.0 + 12.7 + 6.5. This procedure is continued for the quarterly sales for each of the six years. Column 2 of Table 19–8 shows all of the moving totals. Note that the moving total 34.0 is positioned between the spring and summer sales of 1996. The next moving total, 33.8, is positioned between sales for summer and fall of 1996, and so on. Check the totals frequently to avoid arithmetic errors.

TABLE 19–8 Computations Needed for the Specific Seasonal Indexes

Year	Quarter	(1) Sales ($ millions)	(2) Four-Quarter Total	(3) Four-Quarter Moving Average	(4) Centered Moving Average	(5) Specific Seasonal
1996	Winter	6.7				
	Spring	4.6				
			34.0	8.500		
	Summer	10.0			8.475	1.180
			33.8	8.450		
	Fall	12.7			8.450	1.503
			33.8	8.450		
1997	Winter	6.5			8.425	0.772
			33.6	8.400		
	Spring	4.6			8.513	0.540
			34.5	8.625		
	Summer	9.8			8.675	1.130
			34.9	8.725		
	Fall	13.6			8.775	1.550
			35.3	8.825		
1998	Winter	6.9			8.900	0.775
			35.9	8.975		
	Spring	5.0			9.038	0.553
			36.4	9.100		
	Summer	10.4			9.113	1.141
			36.5	9.125		
	Fall	14.1			9.188	1.535
			37.0	9.250		
1999	Winter	7.0			9.300	0.753
			37.4	9.350		
	Spring	5.5			9.463	0.581
			38.3	9.575		
	Summer	10.8			9.588	1.126
			38.4	9.600		
	Fall	15.0			9.625	1.558
			38.6	9.650		
2000	Winter	7.1			9.688	0.733
			38.9	9.725		
	Spring	5.7			9.663	0.590
			38.4	9.600		
	Summer	11.1			9.713	1.143
			39.3	9.825		
	Fall	14.5			9.888	1.466
			39.8	9.950		
2001	Winter	8.0			9.888	0.801
			40.1	10.025		
	Spring	6.2			10.075	0.615
			40.5	10.125		
	Summer	11.4				
	Fall	14.9				

Step 2 Each quarterly moving total in column 2 is divided by 4 to give the four-quarter moving average. (See column 3.) All the moving averages are still positioned between the quarters. For example, the first moving average (8.500) is positioned between spring and summer of 1996.

Step 3 The moving averages are then centered. The first centered moving average is found by (8.500 + 8.450)/2 = 8.475 and centered opposite summer 1996. The second moving average is found by (8.450 + 8.450)/2 = 8.45. The others are found similarly. Note in column 4 that a centered moving average is positioned on a particular quarter.

Step 4 The **specific seasonal** for each quarter is then computed by dividing the sales in column 1 by the centered moving average in column 4. The specific seasonal reports the ratio of the original time series value to the moving average. To explain further, if the time series is represented by *TSCI* and the moving average by *TCI,* then, algebraically, if we compute *TSCI/TCI,* the result is the seasonal component. The specific seasonal for the summer quarter of 1996 is 1.180, found by 10.0/8.475.

Step 5 The specific seasonals are organized in a table. (See Table 19–9.) This table will help us locate the specific seasonals for the corresponding quarters. The values 1.180, 1.130, 1.141, 1.126, and 1.143 all represent estimates of the typical seasonal index for the summer quarter. A reasonable method to find a typical seasonal index is to average these values. So we find the typical index for the summer quarter by (1.180 + 1.130 + 1.141 + 1.126 + 1.143)/5 = 1.144. We used the arithmetic mean, but the median or a modified mean can also be used.

TABLE 19–9 Calculations Needed for Typical Quarterly Indexes

Year	Winter	Spring	Summer	Fall	
1996			1.180	1.503	
1997	0.772	0.540	1.130	1.550	
1998	0.775	0.553	1.141	1.535	
1999	0.753	0.581	1.126	1.558	
2000	0.733	0.590	1.143	1.466	
2001	0.801	0.615			
Total	3.834	2.879	5.720	7.612	
Mean	0.767	0.576	1.144	1.522	4.009
Adjusted	0.765	0.575	1.141	1.519	4.000
Index	76.5	57.5	114.1	151.9	

Step 6 The four quarterly means (0.767, 0.576, 1.144, and 1.522) should theoretically total 4.00 because the average is set at 1.0. The total of the four quarterly means may not exactly equal 4.00 due to rounding. In this problem the total of the means is 4.009. A *correction factor* is therefore applied to each of the four means to force them to total 4.00.

CORRECTION FACTOR FOR ADJUSTING QUARTERLY MEANS

$$\text{Correction factor} = \frac{4.00}{\text{Total of four means}} \quad \textbf{[19–6]}$$

In this example,

$$\text{Correction factor} = \frac{4.00}{4.009} = 0.997755$$

The adjusted winter quarterly index is, therefore, .767(.997755) = .765. Each of the means is adjusted downward so that the total of the four quarterly means is 4.00. Usually indexes are reported as percentages, so each value in the last row of Table 19–9 has been multiplied by 100. So the index for the winter quarter is 76.5 and for the fall it is 151.9. How are these values interpreted? Sales for the fall quarter are 51.9 percent above the typical quarter, and for winter they are 23.5 below the typical quarter (100.0 − 76.5). These findings should not surprise you. The period prior to Christmas (the fall quarter) is when toy sales are brisk. After Christmas (the winter quarter) sales of the toys decline drastically.

As we noted earlier there is software that will perform the calculations and output the results. The MegaStat Excel output is shown below. Use of software will greatly reduce the computational time and the chance of an error in arithmetic, but you should understand the steps in the process, as outlined earlier. There can be slight differences in the answers, due to the number of digits carried in the calculations.

Centered Moving Average and Deseasonalization

t	Year	Quarter	Sales	Centered Moving Average	Ratio to CMA	Seasonal Indexes	Sales Deseasonalized
1	1	1	6.7			0.765	8.76
2	1	2	4.6			0.575	8.00
3	1	3	10.0	8.475	1.180	1.141	8.76
4	1	4	12.7	8.450	1.503	1.519	8.36
5	2	1	6.5	8.425	0.772	0.765	8.50
6	2	2	4.6	8.513	0.540	0.575	8.00
7	2	3	9.8	8.675	1.130	1.141	8.59
8	2	4	13.6	8.775	1.550	1.519	8.95
9	3	1	6.9	8.900	0.775	0.765	9.02
10	3	2	5.0	9.038	0.553	0.575	8.70
11	3	3	10.4	9.113	1.141	1.141	9.11
12	3	4	14.1	9.188	1.535	1.519	9.28
13	4	1	7.0	9.300	0.753	0.765	9.15
14	4	2	5.5	9.463	0.581	0.575	9.57
15	4	3	10.8	9.588	1.126	1.141	9.46
16	4	4	15.0	9.625	1.558	1.519	9.88
17	5	1	7.1	9.688	0.733	0.765	9.28
18	5	2	5.7	9.663	0.590	0.575	9.92
19	5	3	11.1	9.713	1.143	1.141	9.72
20	5	4	14.5	9.888	1.466	1.519	9.55
21	6	1	8.0	9.988	0.801	0.765	10.46
22	6	2	6.2	10.075	0.615	0.575	10.79
23	6	3	11.4			1.141	9.99
24	6	4	14.9			1.519	9.81

Calculation of Seasonal Indexes

	1	2	3	4	
1			1.180	1.503	
2	0.772	0.540	1.130	1.550	
3	0.775	0.553	1.141	1.535	
4	0.753	0.581	1.126	1.558	
5	0.733	0.590	1.143	1.466	
6	0.801	0.615			
mean:	0.767	0.576	1.144	1.522	4.009
adjusted:	0.765	0.575	1.141	1.519	4.000

Now to briefly summarize the reasoning underlying the preceding calculations. The original data in column 1 of Table 19–8 contain trend (*T*), cyclic (*C*), seasonal (*S*), and irregular (*I*) components. The ultimate objective is to remove seasonal (*S*) from the original sales valuation.

Columns 2 and 3 in Table 19–8 are concerned with deriving the centered moving average given in column 4. Basically, we "average out" the seasonal and irregular fluctuations from the original data in column 1. Thus, in column 4 we have only trend and cyclic (*TC*).

Next, we divide the sales data in column 1 (*TCSI*) by the centered fourth-quarter moving average in column 4 (*TC*) to arrive at the specific seasonals in column 5 (*SI*). In terms of letters, *TCSI*/*TC* = *SI*. We multiply *SI* by 100.0 to express the typical seasonal in index form.

Finally, we take the mean of all the winter typical indexes, all the spring indexes, and so on. This averaging eliminates most of the irregular fluctuations from the seasonals, and the resulting four indexes indicate the typical seasonal sales pattern.

Self-Review 19–4

Teton Village, Wyoming, near Grand Teton Park and Yellowstone Park, contains shops, restaurants, and motels. They have two peak seasons — winter, for skiing on the 10,000-foot slopes, and summer, for tourists visiting the parks. The specific seasonals with respect to the total sales volume for recent years are:

	Quarter			
Year	**Winter**	**Spring**	**Summer**	**Fall**
1997	117.0	80.7	129.6	76.1
1998	118.6	82.5	121.4	77.0
1999	114.0	84.3	119.9	75.0
2000	120.7	79.6	130.7	69.6
2001	125.2	80.2	127.6	72.0

(a) Develop the typical seasonal pattern for Teton Village using the ratio-to-moving-average method.
(b) Explain the typical index for the winter season.

Exercises

7. Victor Anderson, the owner of Anderson Belts, Inc., is studying absenteeism among his employees. His workforce is small, consisting of only five employees. For the last three years he recorded the following number of employee absences, in days, for each quarter.

	Quarter			
Year	**I**	**II**	**III**	**IV**
1999	4	10	7	3
2000	5	12	9	4
2001	6	16	12	4

Determine a typical seasonal index for each of the four quarters.

8. 0.9077
0.7609
1.1261
1.2098

8. The Appliance Center sells a variety of electronic equipment and home appliances. For the last four years the following quarterly sales (in $ millions) were reported.

	Quarter			
Year	I	II	III	IV
1998	5.3	4.1	6.8	6.7
1999	4.8	3.8	5.6	6.8
2000	4.3	3.8	5.7	6.0
2001	5.6	4.6	6.4	5.9

Determine a typical seasonal index for each of the four quarters.

Deseasonalizing Data

A set of typical indexes is very useful in adjusting a sales series, for example, for seasonal fluctuations. The resulting sales series is called **deseasonalized sales** or **seasonally adjusted sales.** The reason for deseasonalizing the sales series is to remove the seasonal fluctuations so that the trend and cycle can be studied. To illustrate the procedure, the quarterly sales totals of Toys International from Table 19–7 are repeated in column 1 of Table 19–10.

TABLE 19–10 Actual and Deseasonalized Sales for Toys International

Year	Quarter	(1) Sales	(2) Seasonal Index	(3) Deseasonalized Sales
1996	Winter	6.7	0.765	8.76
	Spring	4.6	0.575	8.00
	Summer	10.0	1.141	8.76
	Fall	12.7	1.519	8.36
1997	Winter	6.5	0.765	8.50
	Spring	4.6	0.575	8.00
	Summer	9.8	1.141	8.59
	Fall	13.6	1.519	8.95
1998	Winter	6.9	0.765	9.02
	Spring	5.0	0.575	8.70
	Summer	10.4	1.141	9.11
	Fall	14.1	1.519	9.28
1999	Winter	7.0	0.765	9.15
	Spring	5.5	0.575	9.57
	Summer	10.8	1.141	9.46
	Fall	15.0	1.519	9.88
2000	Winter	7.1	0.765	9.28
	Spring	5.7	0.575	9.92
	Summer	11.1	1.141	9.72
	Fall	14.5	1.519	9.55
2001	Winter	8.0	0.765	10.46
	Spring	6.2	0.575	10.79
	Summer	11.4	1.141	9.99
	Fall	14.9	1.519	9.81

To remove the effect of seasonal variation, the sales amount for each quarter (which contains trend, cyclical, irregular, and seasonal effects) is divided by the seasonal index for that quarter, that is, *TSCI/S.* For example, the actual sales for the first quarter of 1996 were \$6.7 million. The seasonal index for the winter quarter is 76.5, using the MegaStat results on page 710. The index of 76.5 indicates that sales for the first quarter are typically 23.5 percent below the average for a typical quarter. By dividing the actual sales of \$6.7 million by 76.5 and multiplying the result by 100, we find the *deseasonalized sales* value for the first quarter of 1996. It is \$8,758,170, found by (\$6,700,000/76.5)100. We continue this process for the other quarters in column 3 of Table 19–10, with the results reported in millions of dollars. Because the seasonal component has been removed (divided out) from the quarterly sales, the deseasonalized sales figure contains only the trend (T), cyclical (C), and irregular (I) components. Scanning the deseasonalized sales in column 3 of Table 19–10, we see that the sales of toys showed a moderate increase over the six-year period. Chart 19–9 shows both the actual sales and the deseasonalized sales. It is clear that removing the seasonal factor allows us to focus on the overall long-term trend of sales. We will also be able to determine the regression equation of the trend data and use it to forecast future sales.

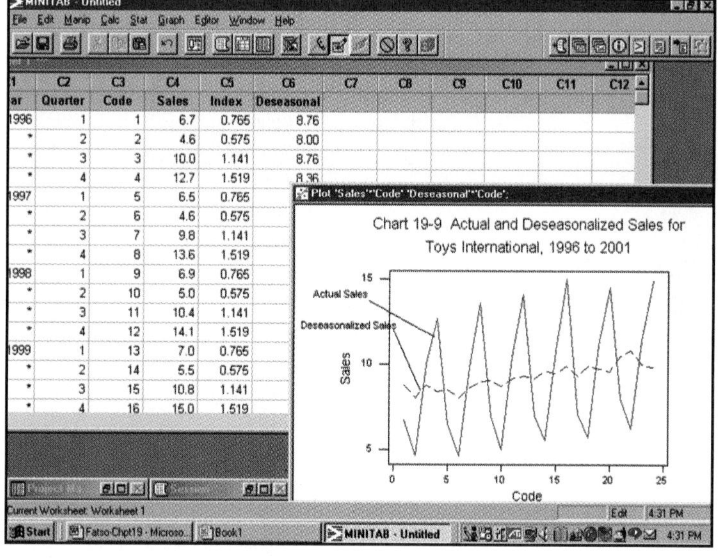

ar	C2 Quarter	C3 Code	C4 Sales	C5 Index	C6 Deseasonal
1996	1	1	6.7	0.765	8.76
*	2	2	4.6	0.575	8.00
*	3	3	10.0	1.141	8.76
*	4	4	12.7	1.519	8.36
1997	1	5	6.5	0.765	
*	2	6	4.6	0.575	
*	3	7	9.8	1.141	
*	4	8	13.6	1.519	
1998	1	9	6.9	0.765	
*	2	10	5.0	0.575	
*	3	11	10.4	1.141	
*	4	12	14.1	1.519	
1999	1	13	7.0	0.765	
*	2	14	5.5	0.575	
*	3	15	10.8	1.141	
*	4	16	15.0	1.519	

Using Deseasonalized Data to Forecast

The procedure for identifying trend and the seasonal adjustments can be combined to yield seasonally adjusted forecasts. To identify the trend, we determine the least squares trend equation on the deseasonalized historical data. Then we project this trend into future periods, and finally we adjust these trend values to account for the seasonal factors. The following example will help to clarify.

EXAMPLE

Toys International would like to forecast their sales for each quarter of 2002. Use the information in Table 19–10 to determine the forecast.

SOLUTION

The first step is to use the deseasonalized data in column 3 of Table 19–10 to determine the least squares trend equation. The deseasonalized trend equation is:

$$Y' = a + bt$$

Statistics in Action

Forecasts are not always correct. The reality is that a forecast may just be a best guess as to what will happen. What are the reasons forecasts are not correct? One expert lists eight common errors: (1) failure to carefully examine the assumptions, (2) limited expertise, (3) lack of imagination, (4) neglect of constraints, (5) excessive optimism, (6) reliance on mechanical extrapolation, (7) premature closure, and (8) overspecification.

where:

Y' is the estimated trend for Toys International sales for period t.
a is the intercept of the trend line at time 0.
b is the slope of the trend line.

The winter quarter of 1996 is the period $t = 1$, and $t = 24$ corresponds to the fall quarter of 2001. (See column 1 in Table 19–11.) The sums needed to compute a and b are also shown in Table 19–11.

$$b = \frac{n\Sigma tY - (\Sigma Y)(\Sigma t)}{n\Sigma t^2 - (\Sigma t)^2} = \frac{24(2{,}873.4) - (221.60)(300)}{24(4{,}900) - (300)^2} = \frac{2{,}481.6}{27{,}600.0} = 0.0899$$

$$a = \frac{\Sigma Y}{n} - b\left(\frac{\Sigma t}{n}\right) = \frac{221.60}{24} - 0.0899\left(\frac{300}{24}\right) = 8.1096$$

TABLE 19–11 Deseasonalized Sales for Toys International: Data Needed for Determining Trend Line

Year	Quarter	(1) t	(2) Y	(3) tY	(4) t^2
1996	Winter	1	8.76	8.76	1
	Spring	2	8.00	16.00	4
	Summer	3	8.76	26.28	9
	Fall	4	8.36	33.44	16
1997	Winter	5	8.50	42.50	25
	Spring	6	8.00	48.00	36
	Summer	7	8.59	60.13	49
	Fall	8	8.95	71.60	64
1998	Winter	9	9.02	81.18	81
	Spring	10	8.70	87.00	100
	Summer	11	9.11	100.21	121
	Fall	12	9.28	111.36	144
1999	Winter	13	9.15	118.95	169
	Spring	14	9.57	133.98	196
	Summer	15	9.47	142.05	225
	Fall	16	9.87	157.92	256
2000	Winter	17	9.28	157.76	289
	Spring	18	9.91	178.38	324
	Summer	19	9.73	184.87	361
	Fall	20	9.55	191.00	400
2001	Winter	21	10.46	219.66	441
	Spring	22	10.78	237.16	484
	Summer	23	9.99	229.77	529
	Fall	24	9.81	235.44	576
Total		300	221.60	2,873.40	4,900

The trend equation is:

$$Y' = 8.1096 + 0.0899t$$

The slope of the trend line is 0.0899. This shows that over the 24 quarters the deseasonalized sales increased at a rate of 0.0899 ($ millions) per quarter, or $89,900 per quarter. The value of 8.1096 is the intercept of the trend line on the Y-axis (i.e., for $t = 0$).

Of course, we can use a statistical software package to determine the regression equation. The following output is from the MINITAB system. Using a software package will reduce the possibility of an error in arithmetic. In addition, we can use the value of R^2 to give an indication of the fit of the data. Because this is *not* sample information, technically, we should not use R^2 for judging a regression equation. It will serve, however, to quickly evaluate the fit of the deseasonalized data. In this instance the R^2 value is 78.6 percent, which indicates that time does a good job of explaining the variation in the deseasonalized data.

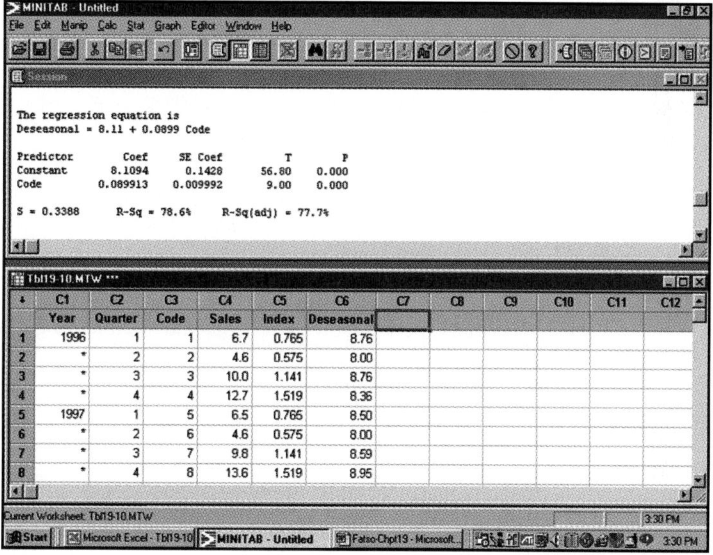

If we assume that the past 24 periods are a good indicator of future sales, we can use the trend equation to estimate future sales. For example, for the winter quarter of 2002, the value of t is 25. The estimated sales total for that period is $10,357,100, found by

$$Y' = 8.1096 + 0.0899(25) = 10.3571$$

Using the trend equation, we can forecast sales at Toys International for the four quarters of 2002. These estimates are shown in Table 19–12.

TABLE 19–12 Quarterly Forecast for Toys International for 2002

Quarter	t	Estimated Sales	Seasonal Index	Quarterly Forecast
Winter	25	10.3571	.765	7.923
Spring	26	10.4770	.575	6.024
Summer	27	10.5369	1.141	12.03
Fall	28	10.6268	1.519	16.142

Now that we have the forecasts for the four quarters of 2002, we can seasonally adjust them. The index for the winter quarter is 0.765 (see Table 19–9 earlier in the chapter), so we can estimate the sales in this quarter by 10.3571(0.765) = 7.923. The estimates for the four quarters of 2002 are shown in the last column of Table 19–12. Notice how the seasonal adjustments drastically increase the sales estimates for the last two quarters of the year.

Self-Review 19–5

The Westberg Electric Company sells electric motors to customers in the Jamestown, New York, area. The monthly trend equation, based on five years of monthly data, is

$$Y' = 4.4 + 0.5t$$

The seasonal factor for the month of January is 120, and it is 95 for February. Determine the seasonally adjusted forecast for January and February of the sixth year.

Exercises

9. The planning department of Padget and Kure Shoes, the manufacturer of an exclusive brand of women's shoes, developed the following trend equation, in millions of pairs, based on five years of quarterly data.

$$Y' = 3.30 + 1.75t$$

The following table gives the seasonal factors for each quarter.

	Quarter			
	I	II	III	IV
Index	110.0	120.0	80.0	90.0

Determine the seasonally adjusted forecast for each of the four quarters of the sixth year.

10. 725

10. Team Sports, Inc. sells sporting goods to high schools and colleges via a nationally distributed catalog. Management at Team Sports estimates they will sell 2,000 Wilson Model A2000 catcher's mitts next year. The deseasonalized sales are projected to be the same for each of the four quarters next year. The seasonal factor for the second quarter is 145. Determine the seasonally adjusted sales for the second quarter of next year.

11. Refer to Exercise 7, regarding the absences at Anderson Belts, Inc. Use the seasonal indexes you computed to determine the deseasonalized absences. Determine the linear trend equation based on the quarterly data for the three years. Forecast the seasonally adjusted absences for 2002.

12. $Y' = 5.48 - 0.0112t$

12. Refer to Exercise 8, regarding sales at the Appliance Center. Use the seasonal indexes you computed to determine the deseasonalized sales. Determine the linear trend equation based on the quarterly data for the four years. Forecast the seasonally adjusted sales for 2002.

Chapter Outline

I. A time series is a collection of data over a period of time.
   - **A.** The trend is the long-run direction of the time series.
   - **B.** The cyclical component is the fluctuation above and below the long-term trend line.
   - **C.** The seasonal variation is the pattern in a time series within a year. These patterns tend to repeat themselves from year to year for most businesses.

D. The irregular variation is divided into two components.
  1. The episodic variations are unpredictable, but they can usually be identified. A flood is an example.
  2. The residual variations are random in nature.

II. The linear trend equation is $Y' = a + bt$, where a is the Y-intercept, b is the slope of the line, and t is the coded time.
  A. The trend equation is determined using the least squares principle.
  B. If the trend is not linear, but rather the increases tend to be a constant percent, the Y values are converted to logarithms, and a least squares equation is determined using the logarithms.

III. A moving average is used to smooth the trend in a time series.

IV. A seasonal factor can be estimated using the ratio-to-moving-average method.
  A. The six-step procedure yields a seasonal index for each period.
    1. Seasonal factors are usually computed on a monthly or a quarterly basis.
    2. The seasonal factor is used to adjust forecasts, taking into account the effects of the season.

Chapter Exercises

13. Refer to the following diagram.
  a. Estimate the linear trend equation for the production series by drawing a line through the data.
  b. What is the average annual decrease in production?
  c. Based on the trend equation, what is the forecast for the year 2005?

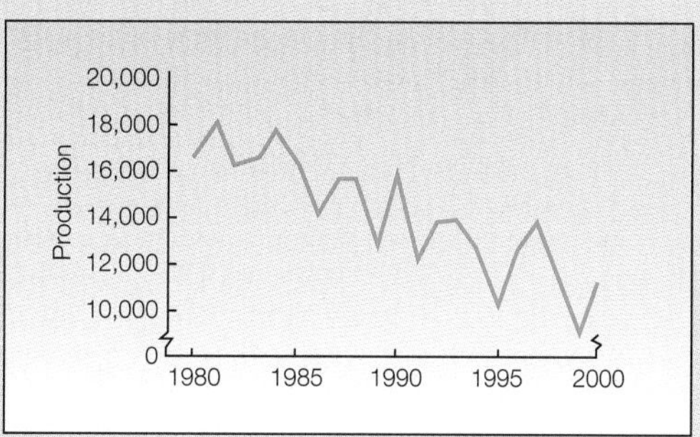

14. a. $Y' = 4{,}000 + 933t$
b. \$933

14. Refer to the following diagram.
  a. Estimate the linear trend equation for the personal income series.
  b. What is the average annual increase in personal income?

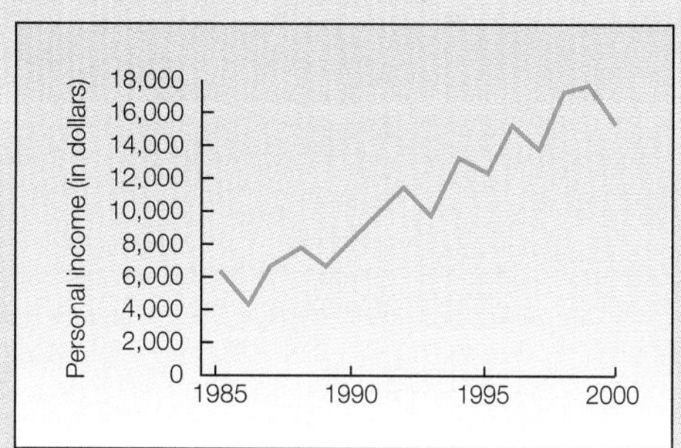

15. The asset turnovers, excluding cash and short-term investments, for the RNC Company from 1990 to 2000 are:

1990	1991	1992	1993	1994	1995	1996	1997	1998	1999	2000
1.11	1.28	1.17	1.10	1.06	1.14	1.24	1.33	1.38	1.50	1.65

a. Plot the data.
b. Determine the least squares trend equation.
c. Calculate the points on the trend line for 1993 and 1998, and plot the line on the graph.
d. Estimate the asset turnover for 2005.
e. How much did the asset turnover increase per year, on the average, from 1990 to 2000?

16. The sales, in billions of dollars, of Keller Overhead Door, Inc. for 1995 to 2000 are:

Year	Sales	Year	Sales
1995	7.45	1998	7.94
1996	7.83	1999	7.76
1997	8.07	2000	7.90

16. a. See IM.
b. $Y' = 7.6340 + 0.05457t$
c. 7.79771, 7.90685
d. 8.12513
e. 0.05457

a. Plot the data.
b. Determine the least squares trend equation.
c. Use the trend equation to calculate the points for 1997 and 1999. Plot them on the graph and draw the regression line.
d. Estimate the net sales for 2003.
e. By how much have sales increased (or decreased) per year on the average during the period?

17. The number of employees, in thousands, of Keller Overhead Door, Inc. for the years 1995 to 2000 are:

Year	Employees	Year	Employees
1995	45.6	1998	39.3
1996	42.2	1999	34.0
1997	41.1	2000	30.0

a. Plot the data.
b. Determine the least squares trend equation.
c. Use the trend equation to calculate the points for 1997 and 1999. Plot them on the graph and draw the regression line.
d. Estimate the number of employees in 2003.
e. By how much has the number of employees increased (or decreased) per year on the average during the period?

18. Listed below is the selling price for a share of PepsiCo, Inc. at the close of the year.

Year	Price	Year	Price	Year	Price
1990	12.9135	1994	18.3160	1998	40.6111
1991	16.8250	1995	27.7538	1999	35.0230
1992	20.6125	1996	29.0581	2000	49.5625
1993	20.3024	1997	36.0155		

18. a. See IM.
b. $Y' = 8.370 + 3.256t$
c. \$21.394, \$37.674

a. Plot the data.
b. Determine the least squares trend equation.
c. Calculate the points for the years 1993 and 1998.

d. $53.954. Yes, R^2 = 0.898.
e. $3.26 per year.

d. Estimate the selling price in 2003. Does this seem like a reasonable estimate based on the historical data?
e. By how much has the stock price increased or decreased (per year) on average during the period?

19. If plotted on arithmetic paper, the following sales series would appear curvilinear. This indicates that sales are increasing at a somewhat constant annual rate (percent). To fit the sales, therefore, a logarithmic straight-line equation should be used.

Year	Sales ($ millions)	Year	Sales ($ millions)
1991	8.0	1997	39.4
1992	10.4	1998	50.5
1993	13.5	1999	65.0
1994	17.6	2000	84.1
1995	22.8	2001	109.0
1996	29.3		

a. Determine the logarithmic equation.
b. Determine the coordinates of the points on the logarithmic straight line for 1994 and 1999.
c. By what percent did sales increase per year, on the average, during the period from 1991 to 2001?
d. Based on the equation, what are the estimated sales for 2002?

20. Reported below are the amounts spent on advertising ($ millions) by a large firm from 1990 to 2000.

Year	Amount	Year	Amount
1990	88.1	1996	132.6
1991	94.7	1997	141.9
1992	102.1	1998	150.9
1993	109.8	1999	157.9
1994	118.1	2000	162.6
1995	125.6		

20. a. Log Y = 1.92767 + 0.0272809t
b. 204.0
c. 6.48%

a. Determine the logarithmic trend equation.
b. Estimate the advertising expenses for 2003.
c. By what percent per year did advertising expense increase during the period?

21. Listed below is the selling price for a share of Oracle, Inc. stock at the close of the year.

Year	Price	Year	Price	Year	Price
1990	0.1944	1994	2.1790	1998	7.1875
1991	0.3580	1995	3.1389	1999	28.0156
1992	0.7006	1996	4.6388	2000	29.0625
1993	1.4197	1997	3.7188		

a. Plot the data.
b. Determine the least squares trend equation. Use both the actual stock price and the logarithm of the price. Which seems to yield a more accurate forecast?
c. Calculate the points for the years 1993 and 1998.
d. Estimate the selling price in 2003. Does this seem like a reasonable estimate based on the historical data?
e. By how much has the stock price increased or decreased (per year) on average during the period? Use your best answer from part (b).

22. The production of the Reliable Manufacturing Company for 1997 and part of 1998 follows.

Month	1997 Production (thousands)	1998 Production (thousands)	Month	1997 Production (thousands)	1998 Production (thousands)
January	6	7	July	3	4
February	7	9	August	5	
March	12	14	September	14	
April	8	9	October	6	
May	4	5	November	7	
June	3	4	December	6	

22. a. 44.2, 72.3, 197.5
b. See IM.

a. Using the ratio-to-moving-average method, determine the specific seasonals for July, August, and September 1997.

b. Assume that the specific seasonal indexes in the following table are correct. Insert in the table the specific seasonals you computed in part (a) for July, August, and September 1997, and determine the 12 typical seasonal indexes.

Year	Jan.	Feb.	Mar.	Apr.	May	June	July	Aug.	Sept.	Oct.	Nov.	Dec.
1997							?	?	?	92.1	106.5	92.9
1998	88.9	102.9	178.9	118.2	60.1	43.1	44.0	74.0	200.9	90.0	101.9	90.9
1999	87.6	103.7	170.2	125.9	59.4	48.6	44.2	77.2	196.5	89.6	113.2	80.6
2000	79.8	105.6	165.8	124.7	62.1	41.7	48.2	72.1	203.6	80.2	103.0	94.2
2001	89.0	112.1	182.9	115.1	57.6	56.9						

c. Interpret the typical seasonal index.

23. The sales of Andre's Boutique for 1996 and part of 1997 are:

Month	1996 Sales (thousands)	1997 Sales (thousands)	Month	1996 Sales (thousands)	1997 Sales (thousands)
January	78	65	July	81	65
February	72	60	August	85	61
March	80	72	September	90	75
April	110	97	October	98	
May	92	86	November	115	
June	86	72	December	130	

a. Using the ratio-to-moving-average method, determine the specific seasonals for July, August, September, and October 1996.

b. Assume that the specific seasonals in the following table are correct. Insert in the table the specific seasonals you computed in part (a) for July, August, September, and October 1996, and determine the 12 typical seasonal indexes.

Year	Jan.	Feb.	Mar.	Apr.	May	June	July	Aug.	Sept.	Oct.	Nov.	Dec.
1996							?	?	?	?	123.6	150.9
1997	83.9	77.6	86.1	118.7	99.7	92.0	87.0	91.4	97.3	105.4	124.9	140.1
1998	86.7	72.9	86.2	121.3	96.6	92.0	85.5	93.6	98.2	103.2	126.1	141.7
1999	85.6	65.8	89.2	125.6	99.6	94.4	88.9	90.2	100.2	102.7	121.6	139.6
2000	77.3	81.2	85.8	115.7	100.3	89.7						

c. Interpret the typical seasonal index.

24. The quarterly production of pine lumber, in millions of board feet, by Northwest Lumber since 1996 is:

24. a. 0.7558, 0.9924, 1.4060, 0.8505.
b. See IM.
c. $Y' = 10.0989 + 0.14213t$.
d. 9.889, 13.125, 18.795, 11.490.

Year	Quarter			
	Winter	Spring	Summer	Fall
1996	7.8	10.2	14.7	9.3
1997	6.9	11.6	17.5	9.3
1998	8.9	9.7	15.3	10.1
1999	10.7	12.4	16.8	10.7
2000	9.2	13.6	17.1	10.3

a. Determine the typical seasonal pattern for the production data using the ratio-to-moving-average method.
b. Interpret the pattern.
c. Deseasonalize the data and determine the linear trend equation.
d. Project the seasonally adjusted production for the four quarters of 2001.

25. Work Gloves Corp. is reviewing its quarterly sales of Toughie, the most durable glove they produce. The numbers of pairs produced (in thousands) by quarter are:

Year	Quarter			
	I Jan.–Mar.	II Apr.–June	III July–Sept.	IV Oct.–Dec.
1995	142	312	488	208
1996	146	318	512	212
1997	160	330	602	187
1998	158	338	572	176
1999	162	380	563	200
2000	162	362	587	205

a. Using the ratio-to-moving-average method, determine the four typical quarterly indexes.
b. Interpret the typical seasonal pattern.

26. Sales of roof material, by quarter, since 1994 for Carolina Home Construction, Inc. are shown below (in $000).

Year	Quarter			
	I	II	III	IV
1994	210	180	60	246
1995	214	216	82	230
1996	246	228	91	280
1997	258	250	113	298
1998	279	267	116	304
1999	302	290	114	310
2000	321	291	120	320

26. a. 1.1939, 1.1243, 0.4361, 1.2548.
b. $Y' = 163.208 + 4.1253t$.
c. 337.7, 322.6, 126.9, 370.4.

a. Determine the typical seasonal patterns for sales using the ratio-to-moving-average method.
b. Deseasonalize the data and determine the trend equation.
c. Project the sales for 2001, and then seasonally adjust each quarter.

27. The inventory turnover rates for Bassett Wholesale Enterprises, by quarter, are:

Year	Quarter I	II	III	IV
1996	4.4	6.1	11.7	7.2
1997	4.1	6.6	11.1	8.6
1998	3.9	6.8	12.0	9.7
1999	5.0	7.1	12.7	9.0
2000	4.3	5.2	10.8	7.6

a. Arrive at the four typical quarterly turnover rates for the Bassett company using the ratio-to-moving-average method.
b. Deseasonalize the data and determine the trend equation.
c. Project the turnover rates for 2001, and seasonally adjust each quarter of 2001.

28. The following is the number of retirees receiving benefits from the State Teachers Retirement System of Ohio from 1991 until 2000.

Year	Service	Year	Service	Year	Service
1991	58,436	1995	67,989	1999	78,341
1992	59,994	1996	70,448	2000	81,111
1993	61,515	1997	72,601		
1994	63,182	1998	75,482		

28. a. See IM.
b. $Y' = 54{,}475 + 2{,}625t$
c. 62,350, 75,475
d. 88,600. Yes, R^2 is nearly 1.0.
e. 2,625 increase per year.

a. Plot the data.
b. Determine the least squares trend equation. Use a linear equation.
c. Calculate the points for the years 1993 and 1998.
d. Estimate the number of retirees that will be receiving benefits in 2003. Does this seem like a reasonable estimate based on the historical data?
e. By how much has the number of retirees increased or decreased (per year) on average during the period?

29. Ray Anderson, owner of the Anderson Ski Lodge in upstate New York, is interested in forecasting the number of visitors for the upcoming year. The following data are available, by quarter, since 1994. Develop a seasonal index for each quarter. How many visitors would you expect for each quarter of 2001, if Ray projects that there will be a 10 percent increase from the total number of visitors in 2000? Determine the trend equation, project the number of visitors for 2001, and seasonally adjust the forecast. Which forecast would you choose?

Year	Quarter	Visitors	Year	Quarter	Visitors
1994	I	86	1998	I	188
	II	62		II	172
	III	28		III	128
	IV	94		IV	198
1995	I	106	1999	I	208
	II	82		II	202
	III	48		III	154
	IV	114		IV	220
1996	I	140	2000	I	246
	II	120		II	240
	III	82		III	190
	IV	154		IV	252
1997	I	162			
	II	140			
	III	100			
	IV	174			

30. The enrollment in the College of Business at Midwestern University by quarter since 1996 is:

Year	Quarter			
	Winter	Spring	Summer	Fall
1996	2,033	1,871	714	2,318
1997	2,174	2,069	840	2,413
1998	2,370	2,254	927	2,704
1999	2,625	2,478	1,136	3,001
2000	2,803	2,668	—	—

30. a. 1.1896, 1.1040, .4447, 1.2617
b. See IM.
c. See IM.

Using the ratio-to-moving-average method:

a. Determine the four quarterly indexes.

b. Interpret the quarterly pattern of enrollment. Does the seasonal variation surprise you?

c. Compute the trend equation, and forecast the 2001 enrollment by quarter.

31. The Jamie Farr Kroger Classic is an LPGA (Women's Professional Golf) tournament played in Toledo, Ohio, each year. Listed below are the total purse and the prize for winner for the 15 years from 1987 through 2001. Develop a trend equation for both variables. Which variable is increasing at a faster rate? Project both the amount of the purse and the prize for the winner in 2005. Find the ratio of the winner's prize to the total purse. What do you find? Which variable can we estimate more accurately, the size of the purse or the winner's prize?

Year	Purse	Prize	Year	Purse	Prize
1987	$225,000	$33,750	1995	$ 500,000	$ 75,000
1988	275,000	41,250	1996	575,000	86,250
1989	275,000	41,250	1997	700,000	105,000
1990	325,000	48,750	1998	800,000	120,000
1991	350,000	52,500	1999	800,000	120,000
1992	400,000	60,000	2000	1,000,000	150,000
1993	450,000	67,500	2001	1,000,000	150,000
1994	500,000	75,000			

exercises.com

W W W

32. See IM.

32. Go to the Bureau of Labor Statistics website, which is www.bls.gov, click on the **Consumer Price Index** option, select **Most Requested Series, Prices and Living Conditions,** and then **Consumer Price Index — All Urban Consumers (Current Series).** Ask for the yearly output for the last 10 to 20 years. Develop a regression equation for the annual Consumer Price Index for the selected period. Use both the linear and the log approach. Which do you think is best?

33. Develop a trend line for a large or well-known company, such as GM, General Electric, or Microsoft, for the last 10 years. You could go to the company website. Most companies have a section called "Financial Information." Go to that location and look for sales over the last 10 years. If you do not know the website of the company, go to the financial section of Yahoo or *USA Today,* where there is a location for "symbol look up." Type in the company name, which should then give you the symbol. Look up the company via the symbol, and you should find the information. The symbol for GM is just *GM,* the symbol for General Electric is *GE.* Comment on the trend line of the company you selected over the period. Is the trend increasing or decreasing? Does the trend follow a linear or log equation?

34. See IM.

34. Select one of the major economic indicators, such as the Dow Jones Average, Nasdaq, or the S&P 500. Develop a trend line for the index over the last 10 years by using the value of the index at the end of the year, or for the last 30 days by selecting the closing value of the index for the last 30 days. You can locate this information many places. For example, go to http://finance.yahoo.com, click on **Nasdaq** in the lower right corner, select **historical quotes,** and a period of time, perhaps the last 30 days, and you will find the information.

You should be able to download it directly to Excel to create your trend equation. Comment on the trend line you created. Is it increasing or decreasing? Does the trend line follow a linear or log equation?

Computer Data Exercises

35. Refer to the Baseball 2000 data, which includes information on the 2000 Major League Baseball season. The data include the average player salary since 1976 and the median player salary since 1983. Plot the information and develop a linear trend equation for each. Compare the rate of increase in the median with the rate of increase for the average. Write a brief report on your findings.

Computer Commands

1. The MINITAB commands to determine the graph for Chart 19–4 on page 697 is:
   a. Enter the year or time periods and the data in two columns.
   b. Select **Stat**, **Regression**, and **Fitted Line Plots**, and hit **Enter.**
   c. In **Response (Y)** select the time series variable and select the time period as the **Predictor (X)**. Click on **Linear** as the **Type of Regression**. If you wish to include a chart title or do a transformation, click on **Options** and make the selections. Click **OK**.
2. The MegaStat commands for creating the seasonal indexes on page 710 are:
   a. Enter the coded time period and the value of the time series in two columns. You may also want to include information on the years and quarters.
   b. Select **MegaStat, Time Series/Forecasting,** and **Deseasonalization,** and hit **Enter.**
   c. Input the range of the data, indicate the data is in the first quarter, and click **OK.**

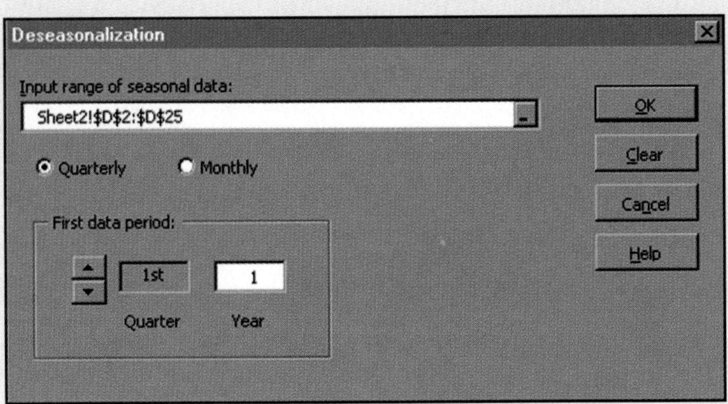

Chapter 19 Answers to Self-Review

19–1 (a)

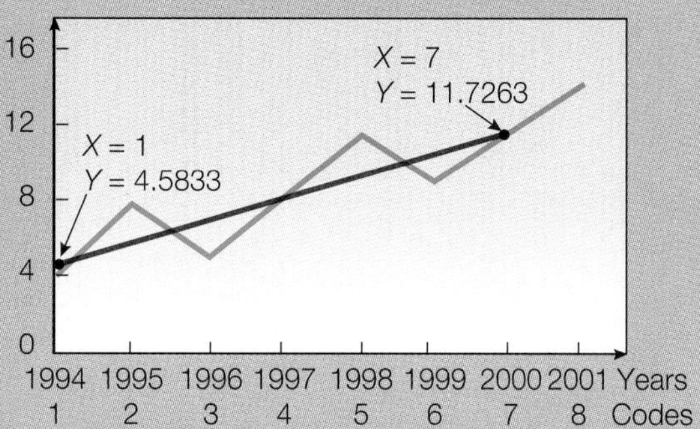

(b) $Y' = a + bt = 3.3928 + 1.1905t$ (in thousands)

$$b = \frac{8(365) - 36(70)}{8(204) - (36)^2} = \frac{50}{42} = 1.1905$$

$$a = \frac{70}{8} - 1.1905\left(\frac{36}{8}\right) = 3.3928$$

(c) For 1994:

$$Y' = 3.3928 + 1.1905(1) = 4.5833$$

for 2000:

$$Y' = 3.3928 + 1.1905(7) = 11.7263$$

(d) For 2004, $t = 11$, so

$$Y' = 3.3928 + 1.1905(11) = 16.4883$$

or 16,488 king-size rockers.

19–2

Year	Production (thousands)	Three-Year Moving Total	Three-Year Moving Average
1996	2	—	—
1997	6	12	4
1998	4	15	5
1999	5	12	4
2000	3	18	6
2001	10	—	—

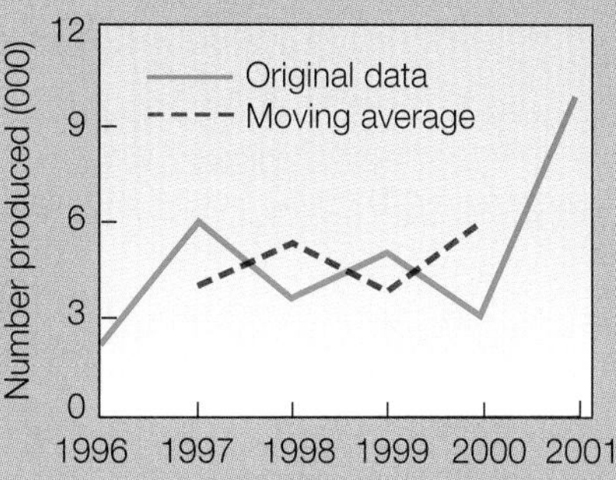

19–3 (a)

Year	Y	log Y	t	t log Y	t^2
1997	2.13	0.3284	1	0.3284	1
1998	18.10	1.2577	2	2.5154	4
1999	39.80	1.5999	3	4.7997	9
2000	81.40	1.9106	4	7.6424	16
2001	112.00	2.0492	5	10.2460	25
		7.1458	15	25.5319	55

$$b = \frac{5(25.5319) - (7.1458)(15)}{5(55) - (15)^2} = \frac{20.4725}{50} = 0.40945$$

$$a = \frac{7.1458}{5} - 0.40945\left(\frac{15}{5}\right) = 0.20081$$

(b) About 156.7 percent. The antilog of 0.40945 is 2.567. Subtracting 1 yields 1.567.

(c) About 454.5, found by $Y' = 0.20081 + .40945(6) = 2.65751$. The antilog of 2.64751 is 454.5.

19–4 (a) The following values are from a software package. Due to rounding, your figures might be slightly different.

	Winter	Spring	Summer	Fall
Mean	119.35	81.66	125.31	74.24
Typical seasonal	119.35	81.66	125.31	74.24

No correction is needed.

(b) Total sales at Teton Village for the winter season are typically 19.35 percent above the annual average.

19–5 The forecast value for January of the sixth year is 34.9, found by

$$Y' = 4.40 + 0.5(61) = 34.9$$

Seasonally adjusting the forecast, $34.9(120)/100 = 41.88$. For February, $Y' = 4.40 + 0.50(62) = 35.4$. Then $(35.4)95/100 = 33.63$.

20

An Introduction to Decision Theory

GOALS

When you have completed this chapter, you will be able to:

1 Define the terms *state of nature*, *event*, *decision alternative*, and *payoff*.

2 Organize information in a payoff table or a decision tree.

3 Find the expected payoff of a decision alternative.

4 Compute opportunity loss and expected opportunity loss.

5 Assess the expected value of information.

The proprietor of the newly built Ski and Swim Lodge has been considering purchasing or leasing several snowmobiles for guest use. After investigating lease prices and the records of other resort owners, the lodge proprietor compiled data on the number of snowmobiles demanded by guests with the number of weeks the vehicles need to be available. Compute the expected profits for leasing 7, 8, 9, and 10 snowmobiles based on the cost of leasing of $20 per week, the rental charge of $25 per week, and the data compiled on the other lodges. (See Goal 3 and Exercise 16.)

Introduction

A branch of statistics called **statistical decision theory** has developed rapidly since the early 1950s. The term **Bayesian statistics** is also used to indicate this branch of statistics. As the name implies, the focus is on the process of making decisions and explicitly includes the payoffs that may result. In contrast, classical statistics focuses on estimating a parameter, such as the population mean, constructing a confidence interval, or conducting a hypothesis test. Classical statistics does not address the financial consequences.

Statistical decision theory is concerned with determining which decision, from a set of possible alternatives, is optimal for a particular set of conditions. Consider the following examples of decision-theory problems.

- Ford Motor Company must decide whether to purchase assembled door locks for the new model Ford F-150 truck or to manufacture and assemble the parts at their Sandusky, Ohio, plant. If sales of the F-150 truck continue to increase, it will be more profitable to manufacture and assemble the parts. If sales level off or decline, it will be more profitable to purchase the door locks assembled. Which decision should be made?

- Banana Republic developed a new line of jackets that are very popular in the cold-weather regions of the country. They would like to purchase commercial television time during the upcoming NCAA basketball final. If both teams that play in the game are from warm parts of the country, they estimate that only a small proportion of the viewers will be interested in the jackets. However, a match-up between two teams who come from cold climates would reach a large proportion of viewers who wear jackets. What decision should they make?
- General Electric is considering three options regarding the prices of stereos for next year. GE could (1) raise the prices 5 percent, (2) raise the prices 2.5 percent, or (3) leave the prices as they are. The final decision will be based on sales estimates and on GE's knowledge of what other stereo manufacturers might do.

In each of these cases the decision is characterized by several alternative courses of action and several factors not under the control of the decision maker. For example, Banana Republic has no control over which teams reach the final. These cases characterize the nature of decision making. Possible decision alternatives can be listed, possible future events determined, and even probabilities established, but *the decisions are made in the face of uncertainty.*

Elements of a Decision

There are three components to any decision: (1) the choices available, or alternatives; (2) the states of nature, which are not under the control of the decision maker; and (3) the payoffs. These concepts will be explained in the following paragraphs.

The **alternatives,** or **acts,** are the choices available to the decision maker. Ford can decide to manufacture and assemble the door locks in Sandusky, or they can decide to purchase them. To simplify our presentation, we assume the decision maker can select from a rather small number of outcomes. With the help of computers, however, the decision alternatives can be expanded to a large number of possibilities.

The **states of nature** are the uncontrollable future events. The state of nature that actually happens is outside the control of the decision maker. Ford does not know whether demand will remain high for the F-150. Banana Republic cannot determine whether warm-weather or cold-weather teams will play in the NCAA basketball final.

A **payoff** is needed to compare each combination of decision alternative and state of nature. Ford may estimate that if they assemble door locks at their Sandusky plant and the demand for F-150 trucks is low, the payoff will be $40,000. Conversely, if they purchase the door locks assembled and the demand is high, the payoff is estimated to be $22,000.

The main elements of the decision under conditions of uncertainty are identified schematically:

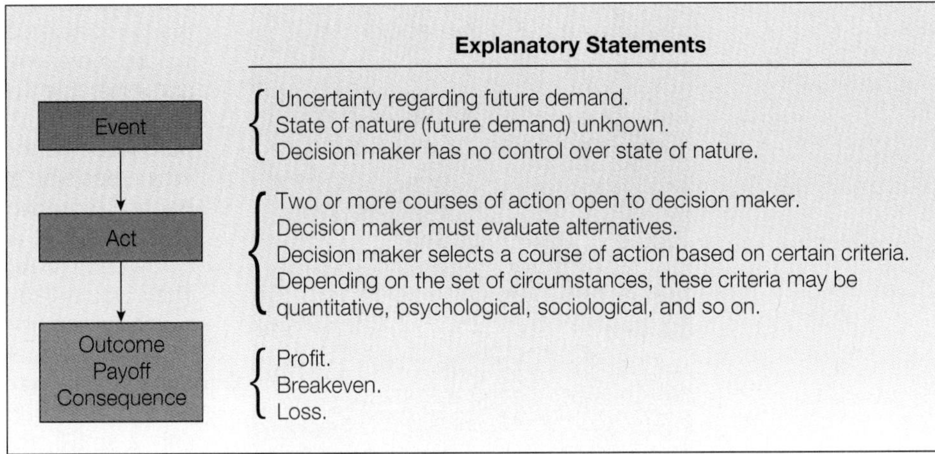

In many cases we can make better decisions if we establish probabilities for the states of nature. These probabilities may be based on historical data or subjective estimates. Ford may estimate the probability of continued high demand as .70. GE may estimate the probability to be .25 that Sears and other manufacturers will raise the prices of their stereos.

A Case Involving Decision Making under Conditions of Uncertainty

At the outset it should be emphasized that this case description includes only the fundamental concepts found in decision-making. The purpose of examining the case is to explain the logical procedure followed. In many cases there are other variables to consider.

The first step is to set up a payoff table.

Payoff Table

Bob Hill, a small investor, has $1,100 to invest. He has studied several common stocks and narrowed his choices to three, namely, Kayser Chemicals, Rim Homes, and Texas Electronics. He estimated that if his $1,100 were invested in Kayser

Chemicals and a strong bull market developed by the end of the year (that is, stock prices increased drastically), the value of his Kayser stock would more than double, to $2,400. However, if there were a bear market (i.e., stock prices declined), the value of his Kayser stock could conceivably drop to $1,000 by the end of the year. His predictions regarding the value of his $1,100 investment for the three stocks for a bull market and for a bear market are shown in Table 20–1. This table is a **payoff table.**

TABLE 20–1 Payoff Table for Three Common Stocks under Two Market Conditions

Purchase	Bull Market, S_1	Bear Market, S_2
Kayser Chemicals (A_1)	$2,400	$1,000
Rim Homes (A_2)	2,200	1,100
Texas Electronics (A_3)	1,900	1,150

The various choices are called the **decision alternatives** or the **acts.** There are three in this situation. Let A_1 be the purchase of Kayser Chemicals, A_2 the purchase of Rim Homes, and A_3 the purchase of Texas Electronics. Whether the market turns out to be bear or bull is not under the control of Bob Hill. These uncontrolled future events are the states of nature. Let the bull market be represented by S_1 and the bear market by S_2.

Expected Payoff

If the payoff table were the only information available, the investor might take a conservative action and buy Texas Electronics in order to be assured of at least $1,150 at the end of the year (a slight profit). A speculative venture, however, might be to buy Kayser Chemicals, with the possibility of more than doubling the $1,100 investment.

Any decision regarding the purchase of one of the three common stocks made solely on the information in the payoff table would ignore the valuable historical records kept by Moody's, Value Line, and other investment services relative to stock price movements over a long period. A study of these records, for example, revealed that during the past 10 years stock market prices increased six times and declined only four times. Thus, it can be said that the probability of a market rise is .60 and the probability of a market decline is .40.

Assuming these historical frequencies are somewhat typical, we see that the payoff table and the probability estimates (.60 and .40) can be combined to arrive at the **expected payoff** of buying each of the three stocks. Expected payoff is also called **expected monetary value,** shortened to EMV. It can also be described as the **mean payoff.** The calculations needed to arrive at the expected payoff for the act of purchasing Kayser Chemicals are shown in Table 20–2.

TABLE 20–2 Expected Payoff for the Act of Buying Kayser Chemicals, EMV (A_1)

State of Nature	Payoff	Probability of State of Nature	Expected Value
Market rise, S_1	$2,400	.60	$1,440
Market decline, S_2	1,000	.40	400
			$1,840

To explain one expected monetary value calculation, note that if the investor had purchased Kayser Chemicals and the market prices declined, the value of the stock would be only $1,000 at the end of the year (from Table 20–1). Past experience, however, revealed that this event (a market decline) occurred only 40 percent of the time. In the long run, therefore, a market decline would contribute $400 to the total expected payoff from the stock, found by $1,000 × .40. Adding the $400 to the $1,440 expected under rising market conditions gives $1,840, the "expected" payoff in the long run.

These calculations are summarized as follows.

EXPECTED MONETARY VALUE $$EMV(A_i) = \Sigma [P(S_j) \times V(A_i, S_j)] \qquad [20\text{–}1]$$

where:

- $EMV(A_i)$ refers to the expected monetary value of decision alternative i. There may be many decisions possible. We will let 1 stand for the first decision, 2 for the second, and so on. The lower-case letter i represents the entire set of decisions.
- $P(S_j)$ refers to the probability of the states of nature. There can be an unlimited number, so we will let j represent this possible outcome.
- $V(A_i, S_j)$ refers to the value of the payoffs. Note that each payoff is the result of a combination of a decision alternative and a state of nature.

$EMV(A_1)$, the expected monetary value for the decision alternative of purchasing Kayser Chemicals stock, is computed by:

$$\begin{aligned} EMV(A_1) &= P(S_1) \times V(A_1, S_1) + P(S_2) \times V(A_1, S_2) \\ &= .60(\$2,400) + .40(\$1,000) = \$1,840 \end{aligned}$$

Purchasing Kayser Chemicals stock is only one possible choice. The expected payoffs for the acts of buying Kayser Chemicals, Rim Homes, and Texas Electronics are given in Table 20–3.

TABLE 20–3 Expected Payoffs for Three Stocks

Purchase	Expected Payoff
Kayser Chemicals	$1,840
Rim Homes	1,760
Texas Electronics	1,600

An analysis of the expected payoffs in Table 20–3 indicates that purchasing Kayser Chemicals would yield the greatest expected profit. This outcome is based on (1) the investor's estimated future value of the stocks and (2) historical experience with respect to the rise and decline of stock prices. It should be emphasized that although purchasing Kayser stock represents the best action under the expected-value criterion, the investor still might decide to buy Texas Electronics stock in order to minimize the risk of losing some of the $1,100 investment.

Self-Review 20–1

Verify the conclusion, shown in Table 20–3, that the expected payoff for the act of purchasing Rim Homes stock is $1,760.

Exercises

1. The following payoff table was developed. Let $P(S_1) = .30$, $P(S_2) = .50$, and $P(S_3) = .20$. Compute the expected monetary value for each of the alternatives. What decision would you recommend?

Alternative	State of Nature S_1	S_2	S_3
A_1	\$50	\$70	\$100
A_2	90	40	80
A_3	70	60	90

2. EMV (Ret) = \$68.0 EMV (No-ret) = \$35.5 Use returnable.

2. The Wilhelms Cola Company plans to market a new pineapple-flavored cola this summer. The decision is whether to package the cola in returnable or in no-return bottles. Currently, the state legislature is considering eliminating no-return bottles. Tybo Wilhelms, president of Wilhelms Cola Company, has discussed the problem with his state representative and established the probability to be .70 that no-return bottles will be eliminated. The following table shows the estimated monthly profits (in thousands of dollars) if the pineapple cola is bottled in returnable versus no-return bottles. Of course, if the law is passed and the decision is to bottle the cola in no-return bottles, all profits would be from out-of-state sales. Compute the expected profit for both bottling decisions. Which decision do you recommend?

Alternative	Law Is Passed (\$000), S_1	Law Is Not Passed (\$000), S_2
Returnable bottle	80	40
No-return bottle	25	60

Opportunity Loss

Another method to analyze a decision regarding which common stock to purchase is to determine the profit that might be lost because the state of nature (the market behavior) was not known at the time the investor bought the stock. This potential loss is called **opportunity loss** or **regret.** To illustrate, suppose the investor had purchased the common stock of Rim Homes, and a bull market developed. Further, suppose the value of his Rim Homes stock increased from \$1,100 to \$2,200, as anticipated. But had the investor bought Kayser Chemicals stock and market values increased, the value of his Kayser stock would be \$2,400 (from Table 20–1). Thus, the investor missed making an extra profit of \$200 by buying Rim Homes instead of Kayser Chemicals. To put it another way, the \$200 represents the opportunity loss for not knowing the correct state of nature. If market prices did increase, the investor would have *regretted* buying Rim Homes. However, had the investor bought Kayser Chemicals and market prices increased, he would have had no regret, that is, no opportunity loss.

The opportunity losses corresponding to this example are given in Table 20–4. Each amount is the outcome (opportunity loss) of a particular combination of acts and a state of nature, that is, stock purchase and market reaction.

Notice that the stock of Kayser Chemicals would be a good investment choice in a rising (bull) market, Texas Electronics would be the best buy in a declining (bear) market, and Rim Homes is somewhat of a compromise.

TABLE 20–4 Opportunity Losses for Various Combinations of Stock Purchase and Market Movement

	Opportunity Loss	
Purchase	**Market Rise**	**Market Decline**
Kayser Chemicals	$ 0	$150
Rim Homes	200	50
Texas Electronics	500	0

Self-Review 20–2

Refer to Table 20–4. Verify that the opportunity loss for:

(a) Rim Homes given a market decline is $50.
(b) Texas Electronics given a market rise is $500.

Exercises

3. Refer to Exercise 1. Develop an opportunity loss table. Determine the opportunity loss for each decision.

4. Refer to Exercise 2, involving the Wilhelms Cola Company. Develop an opportunity loss table, and determine the opportunity loss for each decision.

4.

	Passed	Not Passed
Returnable	$ 0	$20
Not-returnable	55	0

Expected Opportunity Loss

The opportunity losses in Table 20–4 again ignore the historical experience of market movements. Recall that the probability of a market rise is .60 and that of a market decline .40. These probabilities and the opportunity losses can be combined to determine the **expected opportunity loss.** These calculations are shown in Table 20–5 for the decision to purchase Rim Homes. The expected opportunity loss is $140.

Interpreting, the expected opportunity loss of $140 means that, in the long run, the investor would lose the opportunity to make an additional profit of $140 if he decided to buy Rim Homes stock. This expected loss would be incurred because the investor was unable to accurately predict the trend of the stock market. In a bull market, he could earn an additional $200 by purchasing the common stock of Kayser Chemicals, but in a bear market an investor could earn an additional $50 by buying Texas Electronics stock. When weighted by the probability of the event, the expected opportunity loss is $140.

TABLE 20–5 Expected Opportunity Loss for the Act of Buying Rim Homes Stock

State of Nature	Opportunity Loss	Probability of State of Nature	Expected Opportunity Loss
Market rise, S_1	$200	.60	$120
Market decline, S_2	50	.40	20
			$140

These calculations are summarized as follows:

EXPECTED OPPORTUNITY LOSS $$EOL(A_i) = \Sigma [P(S_j) \times R(A_i, S_j)]$$ **[20–2]**

where:

$EOL(A_i)$ refers to the expected opportunity loss for a particular decision alternative.

$P(S_j)$ refers to the probability associated with the states of nature j.

$R(A_i, S_j)$ refers to the regret or loss for a particular combination of a state of nature and a decision alternative.

$EOL(A_2)$, the regret, or expected opportunity loss, for selecting Rim Homes, is computed as follows:

$$
\begin{aligned}
EOL(A_2) &= P(S_1) \times R(A_2, S_1) + P(S_2) \times R(A_2, S_2) \\
&= .60(\$200) + .40(\$50) = \$140
\end{aligned}
$$

The expected opportunity losses for the three decision alternatives are given in Table 20–6. The lowest expected opportunity loss is $60, meaning that the investor would experience the least regret on average if he purchased Kayser Chemicals.

TABLE 20–6 Expected Opportunity Losses for the Three Stocks

Purchase	Expected Opportunity Loss
Kayser Chemicals	$ 60
Rim Homes	140
Texas Electronics	300

Incidentally, note that the decision to purchase Kayser Chemicals stock because it offers the lowest expected opportunity loss reinforces the decision made previously, that Kayser stock would ultimately result in the highest expected payoff ($1,840). These two approaches (lowest expected opportunity loss and highest expected payoff) will always lead to the same decision concerning which course of action to follow.

Self-Review 20–3

Referring to Table 20–6, verify that the expected opportunity loss for the act of purchasing Texas Electronics is $300.

Exercises

5. Refer to Exercises 1 and 3. Compute the expected opportunity losses.
6. Refer to Exercises 2 and 4. Compute the expected opportunity losses.

6. EOL (Ret) = $6.0
EOL (No-ret) = $38.5

Maximin, Maximax, and Minimax Regret Strategies

Maximin strategy

Several financial advisors consider the purchase of Kayser Chemicals stock too risky. They note that the payoff might not be $1,840, but only $1,000 (from Table 20–1). Arguing that the stock market is too unpredictable, they urge the investor to take a more conservative position and buy Texas Electronics. This is called a **maximin strategy:** it maximizes the minimum gain. Based on the payoff table (Table 20–1), they reason that the investor would be assured of at least a $1,150 return, that is, a small profit. Those who subscribe to this somewhat pessimistic strategy are sometimes called **maximiners.**

Maximax strategy

At the other extreme are the optimistic *maximaxers,* who would select the stock that maximizes the maximum gain. If their **maximax strategy** were followed, the investor would purchase Kayser Chemicals stock. These optimists stress that there is a possibility of selling the stock in the future for $2,400 instead of only $1,150, as advocated by the maximiners.

Minimax strategy

Another strategy is the **minimax regret strategy.** Advisors advocating this approach would scan the opportunity losses in Table 20–4 and select the stock that minimizes the maximum regret. In this example it would be Kayser Chemicals stock, with a maximum opportunity loss of $150. Recall that you wish to *avoid* opportunity losses! The maximum regrets were $200 for Rim Homes and $500 for Texas Electronics.

Value of Perfect Information

How much is "perfect" information worth?

Before deciding on a stock, the investor might want to consider ways of predicting the movement of the stock market. If he knew precisely what the market would do, he could maximize profit by always purchasing the correct stock. The question is: What is this advance information worth? The dollar value of this information is called the **expected value of perfect information,** written EVPI. In this example, it would mean that Bob Hill knew beforehand whether the stock market would rise or decline in the near future.

An acquaintance who is an analyst with a large brokerage firm said that he would be willing to supply Bob with information that he might find valuable in predicting market rises and declines. Of course, there would be a fee, as yet undetermined, for this information, regardless of whether the investor used it. What is the maximum amount that Bob should pay for this special service? $10? $100? $500?

The value of the information from the analyst is, in essence, the expected value of perfect information, because the investor would then be assured of buying the most profitable stock.

VALUE OF PERFECT INFORMATION The difference between the maximum payoff under conditions of certainty and the maximum payoff under uncertainty.

In this example it is the difference between the maximum value of the stock at the end of the year under conditions of certainty and the value associated with the optimum decision using the expected-value criterion.

From a practical standpoint, the maximum expected value under conditions of certainty means that the investor would buy Kayser Chemicals if a market rise were predicted and Texas Electronics if a market decline were imminent. The expected payoff under conditions of certainty is $1,900. (See Table 20–7.)

TABLE 20–7 Calculations for the Expected Payoff under Conditions of Certainty

State of Nature	Payoff	Probability of State of Nature	Expected Payoff
Market rise, S_1	$2,400	.60	$1,440
Market decline, S_2	1,150	.40	460
			$1,900

Recall that if the actual behavior of the stock market were unknown (conditions of uncertainty), the stock to buy would be Kayser Chemicals; its expected value at the end of the period was computed to be $1,840 (from Table 20–3). The value of perfect information is, therefore, $60, found by:

$1,900	Expected value of stock purchased under conditions of certainty
−1,840	Expected value of purchase (Kayser) under conditions of uncertainty
$ 60	Expected value of perfect information

In general, the expected value of perfect information is computed as follows:

EXPECTED VALUE OF PERFECT INFORMATION

$$\text{EVPI} = \text{Expected value under conditions of certainty} - \text{Optimal decision under conditions of uncertainty} \quad \textbf{[20–3]}$$

It would be worth up to $60 for the information the stock analyst might supply. In essence, the analyst would be "guaranteeing" a selling price on average of $1,900, and if the analyst asked $40 for the information, the investor would be assured of a $1,860 payoff, found by $1,900 − $40. Thus, it would be worthwhile for the investor to agree to this fee ($40) because the expected outcome ($1,860) would be greater than the expected value under conditions of uncertainty ($1,840). However, if his acquaintance wanted a fee of $100 for the service, the investor would realize only $1,800 on average, found by $1,900 − $100. Logically, the service would not be worth $100, because the investor could expect $1,840 on average without agreeing to this financial arrangement. Notice that the expected value of perfect information ($60) is the same as the minimum of the expected regrets (Table 20–6). That is not an accident.

The output for the investment example using the Excel system is shown below. The expected payoff and the expected opportunity loss are the same as reported in Table 20–3 and Table 20–6. The calculations in the preceding investment example were kept at a minimum to emphasize the new terms and the decision-making procedures. When the number of decision alternatives and the number of states of nature become large, a computer package or spreadsheet is recommended.

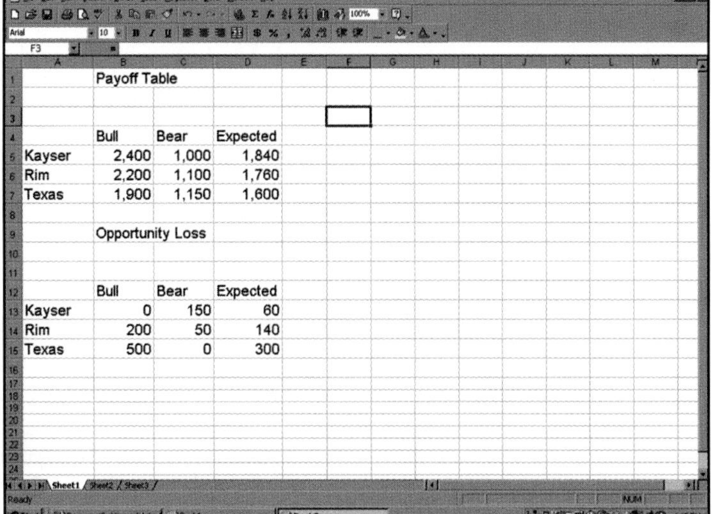

Payoff Table

	Bull	Bear	Expected
Kayser	2,400	1,000	1,840
Rim	2,200	1,100	1,760
Texas	1,900	1,150	1,600

Opportunity Loss

	Bull	Bear	Expected
Kayser	0	150	60
Rim	200	50	140
Texas	500	0	300

Sensitivity Analysis

Expected payoffs are not highly sensitive.

In the foregoing stock selection situation, the set of probabilities applied to the payoff values was derived from historical experience with similar market conditions. Objections may be voiced, however, that future market behavior may be different from past experiences. Despite these differences, *the rankings of the decision alternatives are frequently not highly sensitive to changes within a plausible range.* As an example, suppose the investor's brother believes that instead of a 60 percent chance of a market rise and a 40 percent chance of a decline, the reverse is true — that is, there is a .40 probability that the stock market will rise and a .60 probability of a decline. Further, the investor's cousin thinks the probability of a market rise is .50 and that of a decline is .50. A comparison of the original expected payoffs (left column), the expected payoffs for the set of probabilities suggested by the investor's brother (center column), and those cited by the cousin (right column) is shown in Table 20–8. The decision is the same in all three cases — purchase Kayser Chemicals.

TABLE 20–8 Expected Payoffs for Three Sets of Probabilities

	Expected Payoffs		
Purchase	**Historical Experience (probability of .60 rise, .40 decline)**	**Brother's Estimate (probability of .40 rise, .60 decline)**	**Cousin's Estimate (probability of .50 rise, .50 decline)**
Kayser Chemicals	$1,840	$1,560	$1,700
Rim Homes	1,760	1,540	1,650
Texas Electronics	1,600	1,450	1,525

Self-Review 20–4

Referring to Table 20–8, verify that:

(a) The expected payoff for Texas Electronics for the brother's set of probabilities is $1,450.
(b) The expected payoff for Kayser Chemicals for the cousin's set of probabilities is $1,700.

A comparison of the three sets of expected payoffs in Table 20–8 reveals the best alternative would still be to purchase Kayser Chemicals. As might be expected, there are some differences in the expected future values for each of the three stocks.

If there are drastic changes in the assigned probabilities, the expected values and the optimal decision may change. As an example, suppose the prognostication for a market rise was .20 and for a market decline .80. The expected payoffs would be as shown in Table 20–9. In the long run, the best alternative would be to buy Rim Homes stock. Thus, sensitivity analysis lets you see how accurate the probability estimates need to be in order to feel comfortable with your choice.

TABLE 20–9 Expected Values for Purchasing the Three Stocks

Purchase	Expected Payoff
Kayser Chemicals	$1,280
Rim Homes	1,320
Texas Electronics	1,300

Self-Review 20–5

Is there any choice of probabilities for which the best alternative would be to purchase Texas Electronics stock? (*Hint:* This can be arrived at algebraically or using a trial-and-error method. Try a somewhat extreme probability for a market rise.)

Exercises

8. EVPI = $6.0

10. $52.0, $49.5 No.

7. Refer to Exercises 1, 3, and 5. Compute the expected value of perfect information.
8. Refer to Exercises 2, 4, and 6. Compute the expected value of perfect information.
9. Refer to Exercise 1. Revise the probabilities as follows: $P(S_1) = .50$, $P(S_2) = .20$, and $P(S_3) = .30$. Does this change the decision?
10. Refer to Exercise 2. Reverse the probabilities; that is, let $P(S_1) = .30$ and $P(S_2) = .70$. Does this alter your decision?

Decision Trees

Decision tree: A picture of all possible outcomes

Decision tree shows Kayser Chemicals best buy

An analytic tool introduced in Chapter 5 that is also useful for studying a decision situation is a *decision tree.* Basically, it is a picture of all the possible courses of action and the consequent possible outcomes. A box is used to indicate the point at which a decision must be made, and the branches going out from the box indicate the alternatives under consideration. Referring to Chart 20–1, on the left is the box with three branches radiating from it, representing the acts of purchasing Kayser Chemicals, Rim Homes, or Texas Electronics.

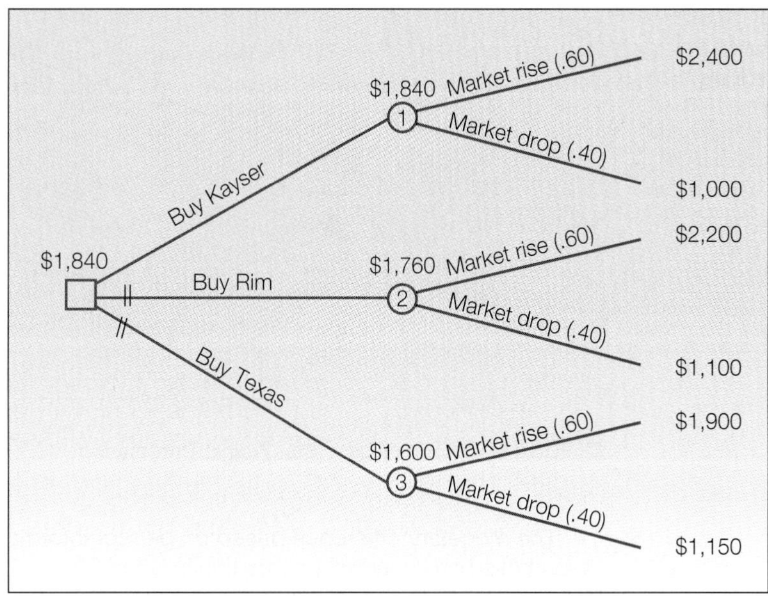

CHART 20–1 Decision Tree for the Investor's Decision

The three nodes, or circles, numbered 1, 2, and 3, represent the expected payoff of each of the three stocks. The branches going out to the right of the nodes show the chance events (market rise or decline) and their corresponding probabilities in parentheses. The numbers at the extreme ends of the branches are the estimated future values of ending the decision process at those points. This is sometimes called the *conditional payoff* to denote that the payoff depends on a particular choice of action and a particular chance outcome. Thus, if the investor purchased Rim Homes stock and the market rose, the conditional value of the stock would be $2,200.

After the decision tree has been constructed, the best decision strategy can be found by what is termed *backward induction.* For example, suppose the investor is considering the act of purchasing Texas Electronics. Starting at the lower right in Chart 20–1 with the anticipated payoff given a market rise ($1,900) versus a market decline ($1,150) and going backward (moving left), the appropriate probabilities are applied to give the expected payoff of $1,600 [found by .60($1,900) + .40($1,150)]. The investor would mark the expected value of $1,600 above circled node 3 as shown in Chart 20–1. Similarly, the investor would determine the expected values for Rim Homes and Kayser Chemicals.

Assuming the investor wants to maximize the expected value of his stock purchase, $1,840 would be preferred over $1,760 or $1,600. Continuing to the left toward the box, the investor would draw a double bar across branches representing the two alternatives he rejected (numbers 2 and 3, representing Rim Homes and Texas Electronics). The unmarked branch that leads to the box is clearly the best action to follow, namely, buy Kayser Chemicals stock.

The expected value under *conditions of certainty* can also be portrayed via a decision tree analysis (see Chart 20–2). Recall that under conditions of certainty the investor would know *before the stock is purchased* whether the stock market will rise or decline. Hence, he would purchase Kayser Chemicals in a rising market and Texas Electronics in a falling market, and the expected payoff would be $1,900. Again, backward induction would be used to arrive at the expected payoff of $1,900.

If perfect information is available: Buy Kayser in rising market; buy Texas in declining market.

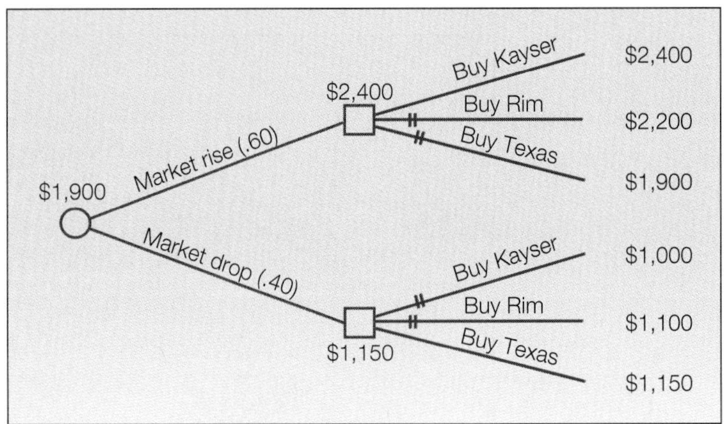

CHART 20–2 Decision Tree Given Perfect Information

The monetary difference based on perfect information in Chart 20–2 and the decision based on imperfect information in Chart 20–1 is $60, found by $1,900 − $1,840. Recall that the $60 is the value of perfect information.

Decision tree analysis provides an alternative way to perform the calculations presented earlier in the chapter. Some managers find these graphic sketches help them in following the decision logic.

Chapter Outline

I. Statistical decision theory is concerned with making decisions from a set of alternatives.
  A. The various courses of action are called the acts or alternatives.
  B. The uncontrollable future events are called the states of nature. Probabilities are usually assigned to the states of nature.
  C. The consequence of a particular decision alternative and state of nature is called the payoff.
  D. All possible combinations of decision alternatives and states of nature result in a payoff table.

II. There are several criteria for selecting the best decision alternative.
  A. In the expected monetary value (EMV) criterion, the expected value for each decision alternative is computed, and the optimal (largest if profits, smallest if cost) is selected.
  B. An opportunity loss table can be developed.
    1. An opportunity loss table is constructed by taking the difference between the optimal decision for each state of nature and the other decision alternatives.
    2. The difference between the optimal decision and any other decision is the opportunity loss or regret due to making a decision other than the optimum.
    3. The expected opportunity loss (EOL) is similar to the expected monetary value. The opportunity loss is combined with the probabilities of the various states of nature for each decision alternative to determine the expected opportunity loss.
  C. The strategy of maximizing the minimum gain is referred to as maximin.
  D. The strategy of maximizing the maximum gain is called maximax.
  E. The strategy that minimizes the maximum regret is designated minimax regret.

III. The expected value of perfect information (EVPI) is the difference between the best expected payoff under certainty and the best expected payoff under uncertainty.

IV. Sensitivity analysis examines the effects of various probabilities for the states of nature on the expected values.

V. Decision trees are useful for structuring the various alternatives. They present a picture of the various courses of action and the possible states of nature.

Chapter Exercises

11. The Twenge Manufacturing Company is considering introducing two new products. The company can add both to the current line, neither, or just one of the two. The success of these products depends on the general economy and on consumers' reactions to the products. These reactions can be summarized as "good," $P(S_1) = .30$; "fair," $P(S_2) = .50$; or "poor," $P(S_3) = .20$. The company's revenues, in thousands of dollars, are estimated in the following payoff table.

	State of Nature		
Decision	S_1	S_2	S_3
Neither	0	0	0
Product 1 only	125	65	30
Product 2 only	105	60	30
Both	220	110	40

a. Compute the expected monetary value for each decision.
b. What decision would you recommend?
c. Develop an opportunity loss table.
d. Compute the expected opportunity loss for each decision.
e. Compute the expected value of perfect information.

12. EMV(Train) = $98. EVPI = 0

12. A financial executive lives in Boston but frequently must travel to New York. She can go to New York by car, train, or plane. The cost for a plane ticket from Boston to New York is $100, and it is estimated that the trip takes 30 minutes in good weather and 45 minutes in bad weather. The cost for a train ticket is $50, and the trip takes an hour in good weather and two hours in bad weather. The cost to drive her own car from Boston to New York is $20, and this trip takes three hours in good weather and four in bad weather. The executive places a value of $30 per hour on her time. The weather forecast is for a 60 percent chance of bad weather tomorrow.

What decision would you recommend? (*Hint:* Set up a payoff table, and remember that you want to minimize costs.) What is the expected value of perfect information?

13. The Thomas Manufacturing Company has $100,000 available to invest. Doctor Thomas, the president and CEO of the company, would like to either expand his production, invest the money in stocks, or purchase a certificate of deposit from the bank. Of course, the unknown is whether the economy will continue at a high level or there will be a recession. He estimates the likelihood of a recession at .20. Whether there is a recession or not, the certificate of deposit will result in a gain of 6 percent. If there is a recession, he predicts a 10 percent loss if he expands his production and a 5 percent loss if he invests in stocks. If there is not a recession, an expansion of production will result in a 15 percent gain, and stock investment will produce a 12 percent gain.
   a. What decision should he make if he uses the maximin strategy?
   b. What decision should Doctor Thomas make if the maximax strategy is used?
   c. What decision would be made if he uses the expected-monetary-value criterion?
   d. What is the expected value of perfect information?

14. The quality-assurance department at Malcomb Products must either inspect each part in a lot or not inspect any of the parts. That is, there are two decision alternatives: inspect all the parts or inspect none of the parts. The proportion of parts defective in the lot, S_j, is known from historical data to assume the following probability distribution.

State of Nature, S_j	Probability, $P(S_j)$
.02	.70
.04	.20
.06	.10

For the decision not to inspect any parts, the cost of quality is $C = NS_jK$. For inspecting all the items in the lot, it is $C = Nk$, where:

$N = 20$ (lot size)
$K = \$18.00$ (the cost of finding a defect)
$k = \$0.50$ (the cost of sampling one item)

14. a. See IM. b. 10.08, 10.0 Inspect. c. EVPI = $-1.96

   a. Develop a payoff table.
   b. What decision should be made if the expected-value criterion is used?
   c. What is the expected value of perfect information?

15. Dude Ranches Incorporated was founded on the idea that many families in the eastern and southern areas of the United States do not have a sufficient amount of vacation time to drive to the dude ranches in the Southwest and Rocky Mountain areas for their vacations. Various surveys indicated, however, that there was a considerable interest in this type of family vacation, which includes horseback riding, cattle drives, swimming, fishing, and the like. Dude Ranches Incorporated bought a large farm near several eastern cities and constructed a lake, a swimming pool, and other facilities. However, to build a number of family cottages on the ranch would have required a considerable investment. Further, they reasoned that most of this investment would be lost should the ranch-farm complex be a financial failure. Instead, they decided to enter into an agreement with the Mobile Homes Manufacturing Company to supply a very attractive authentic ranch-type mobile home. Mobile Homes agreed to deliver a mobile home on Saturday for $300 a week. Mobile Homes must know early Saturday morning how many mobile homes Dude Ranches Incorporated wants for the forthcoming week. They have other customers to supply and can only deliver

the homes on Saturday. This presents a problem. Dude Ranches will have some reservations by Saturday, but indications are that many families do not make them. Instead, they prefer to examine the facilities before making a decision. An analysis of the various costs involved indicated that $350 a week should be charged for a ranch home, including all privileges. The basic problem is how many mobile ranch homes to order from Mobile Homes each week. Should Dude Ranches Incorporated order 10 (considered the minimum), 11, 12, 13, or 14 (considered the maximum)?

Any decision made solely on the information in the payoff table would ignore, however, the valuable experience that Dude Ranches Incorporated has acquired in the past four years (about 200 weeks) actually operating a dude ranch in the Southwest. Their records showed that they always had nine advance reservations. Also, they never had a demand for 15 or more cottages. The occupancy of 10, 11, 12, 13, or 14 ranch cottages, in part, represented families who drove in and inspected the facilities before renting. A frequency distribution showing the number of weeks in which 10, 11, . . . , 14 ranch cottages were rented during the 200-week period is found in the following table.

Number of Cottages Rented	Number of Weeks
10	26
11	50
12	60
13	44
14	20
	200

a. Construct a payoff table.
b. Determine the expected payoffs, and arrive at a decision.
c. Set up an opportunity loss table.
d. Compute the expected opportunity losses, and arrive at a decision.
e. Determine the value of perfect information.

16. The proprietor of the newly built Ski and Swim Lodge has been considering purchasing or leasing several snowmobiles for the use of guests. The owner found that other financial obligations made it impossible to purchase the machines. Snowmobiles Incorporated (SI) will lease a machine for $20 a week, including any needed maintenance. According to SI, the usual rental charge to the guests of the lodge is $25 a week. Gasoline and oil are extra. Snowmobiles Incorporated only leases a machine for the full season. The proprietor of Ski and Swim, knowing that leasing an excessive number of snowmobiles might cause a net loss for the lodge, investigated the records of other resort owners. The combined experience at several other lodges was found to be:

Number of Snowmobiles Demanded by Guests	Number of Weeks
7	10
8	25
9	45
10	20

a. Design a payoff table.
b. Compute the expected profits for leasing 7, 8, 9, and 10 snowmobiles based on the cost of leasing of $20, the rental charge of $25, and the experience of other lodges.
c. Which alternative is the most profitable?
d. Design an opportunity loss table.
e. Find the expected opportunity losses for leasing 7, 8, 9, and 10 snowmobiles.
f. Which act would give the least expected opportunity loss?

16. a. See IM.
b. $35.00, $37.50, $33.75, $18.75
c. Lease 8.
d. See IM.
e. $8.75, $6.25, $10.00, $25.00
f. Lease 8.

g. EVPI = $6.25
h. Lease 8.

g. Determine the expected value of perfect information.
h. Suggest a course of action to the proprietor of the Ski and Swim Lodge. Include in your explanation the various figures, such as expected profit.

17. A furniture store has had numerous inquiries regarding the availability of furniture and equipment that could be rented for large outdoor summer parties. This includes such items as folding chairs and tables, a deluxe grill, propane gas, and lights. No rental equipment of this nature is available locally, and the management of the furniture store is considering forming a subsidiary to handle rentals.

An investigation revealed that most people interested in renting wanted a complete group of party essentials (about 12 chairs, four tables, a deluxe grill, a bottle of propane gas, tongs, etc.). Management decided not to buy a large number of complete sets because of the financial risk involved. That is, if the demand for the rental groups was not as large as anticipated, a large financial loss might be incurred. Further, outright purchase would mean that the equipment would have to be stored during the off-season.

It was then discovered that a firm in Boston leased a complete party set for $560 for the summer season. This amounts to about $5 a day. In the promotional literature from the Boston firm, a rental fee of $15 was suggested. For each set rented, a profit of $10 would thus be earned. It was then decided to lease from the Boston firm, at least for the first season.

The Boston firm suggested that, based on the combined experience of similar rental firms in other cities, either 41, 42, 43, 44, 45, or 46 complete sets be leased for the season. Based on this suggestion, management must now decide on the most profitable number of complete sets to lease for the season.

The leasing firm in Boston also made available some additional information gathered from several rental firms similar to the newly formed subsidiary. Note in the following table (which is based on the experience of the other rental firms) that for 360 days of the total of 6,000 days' experience — or about 6 percent of the days — these rental firms rented out 41 complete party sets. On 10 percent of the days during a typical summer, they rented 42 complete sets, and so on.

Number of Sets Rented	Number of Days	Number of Sets Rented	Number of Days
40	0	44	2,400
41	360	45	1,500
42	600	46	300
43	840	47	0

a. Construct a payoff table. (As a check figure, for the act of having 41 complete sets available and the event of renting 41, the payoff is $410.)
b. The expected daily profit for leasing 43 complete sets from the Boston firm is $426.70; for 45 sets, $431.70; and for 46 sets, $427.45. Organize these expected daily profits into a table, and complete the table by finding the expected daily profit for leasing 41, 42, and 44 sets from the Boston firm.
c. Based on the expected daily profit, what is the most profitable action to take?
d. The expected opportunity loss for leasing 43 party sets from the Boston firm is $11.60; for 45 sets, $6.60; for 46 sets, $10.85. Organize these into an expected opportunity loss table, and complete the table by computing the expected opportunity loss for 41, 42, and 44.
e. Based on the expected opportunity loss table, what is the most profitable course of action to take? Does this agree with your decision for part (c)?
f. Determine the value of perfect information. Explain what it indicates in this problem.

18. Tim Waltzer owns and operates Waltzer's Wrecks, a discount car rental agency near the Cleveland Hopkins International Airport. He rents a wreck for $20 a day. He has an arrangement with Landrum Leasing to purchase used cars at $6,000 each. His cars receive only needed maintenance and, as a result, are worth only $2,000 at the end of the year of operation. Tim has decided to sell all his wrecks every year and purchase a complete set of used cars from Landrum Leasing.

His clerk-accountant provided him with a probability distribution with respect to the number of cars rented per day.

	Numbers of Cars Rented per Day			
	20	**21**	**22**	**23**
Probability	.10	.20	.50	.20

Tim is an avid golfer and tennis player. He is either on the golf course on weekends or playing tennis indoors. Thus, his car rental agency is only open weekdays. Also, he closes for two weeks during the summer and goes on a golfing tour.

The clerk-accountant estimated that it cost $1.50 per car rental for minimal maintenance and cleaning.

18. a. 21 cars.
b. $962.50

a. How many cars should he purchase to maximize profit?
b. What is the expected value of perfect information?

Chapter 20 Answers to Self-Review

20–1

Event	Payoff	Probability of Event	Expected Value
Market rise	$2,200	.60	$1,320
Market decline	1,100	.40	440
			$1,760

20–2 **(a)** Suppose the investor purchased Rim Homes stock, and the value of the stock in a bear market dropped to $1,100 as anticipated (Table 20–1). Instead, had the investor purchased Texas Electronics and the market declined, the value of the Texas Electronics stock would be $1,150. The difference of $50, found by $1,150 − $1,100, represents the investor's regret for buying Rim Homes stock.

(b) Suppose the investor purchased Texas Electronics stock, and then a bull market developed. The stock rose to $1,900, as anticipated (Table 20–1). However, had the investor bought Kayser Chemicals stock and the market value increased to $2,400 as anticipated, the difference of $500 represents the extra profit the investor could have made by purchasing Kayser Chemicals stock.

20–3

Event	Payoff	Probability of Event	Expected Opportunity Loss
Market rise	$500	.60	$300
Market decline	0	.40	0
			$300

20–4 **(a)**

Event	Payoff	Probability of Event	Expected Value
Market rise	$1,900	.40	$ 760
Market decline	1,150	.60	690
			$1,450

(b)

Event	Payoff	Probability of Event	Expected Value
Market rise	$2,400	.50	$1,200
Market decline	1,000	.50	500
			$1,700

20–5 For probabilities of a market rise (or decline) down to .333, Kayser Chemicals stock would provide the largest expected profit. For probabilities .333 to .143, Rim Homes would be the best buy. For .143 and below, Texas Electronics would give the largest expected profit. Algebraic solutions:

Kayser: $2{,}400p + (1 - p)1{,}000$
Rim: $2{,}200p + (1 - p)1{,}100$

$$1{,}400p + 1{,}000 = 1{,}100p + 1{,}100$$
$$p = .333$$

Rim: $2{,}200p + (1 - p)1{,}100$
Texas: $1{,}900p + (1 - p)1{,}150$

$$1{,}100p + 1{,}100 = 750p + 1{,}150$$
$$p = .143$$

Appendixes

TABLES AND DATA SETS

Appendix A

Binomial Probability Distribution

$n = 1$

Probability

x	0.05	0.10	0.20	0.30	0.40	0.50	0.60	0.70	0.80	0.90	0.95
0	0.950	0.900	0.800	0.700	0.600	0.500	0.400	0.300	0.200	0.100	0.050
1	0.050	0.100	0.200	0.300	0.400	0.500	0.600	0.700	0.800	0.900	0.950

$n = 2$

Probability

x	0.05	0.10	0.20	0.30	0.40	0.50	0.60	0.70	0.80	0.90	0.95
0	0.903	0.810	0.640	0.490	0.360	0.250	0.160	0.090	0.040	0.010	0.003
1	0.095	0.180	0.320	0.420	0.480	0.500	0.480	0.420	0.320	0.180	0.095
2	0.003	0.010	0.040	0.090	0.160	0.250	0.360	0.490	0.640	0.810	0.903

$n = 3$

Probability

x	0.05	0.10	0.20	0.30	0.40	0.50	0.60	0.70	0.80	0.90	0.95
0	0.857	0.729	0.512	0.343	0.216	0.125	0.064	0.027	0.008	0.001	0.000
1	0.135	0.243	0.384	0.441	0.432	0.375	0.288	0.189	0.096	0.027	0.007
2	0.007	0.027	0.096	0.189	0.288	0.375	0.432	0.441	0.384	0.243	0.135
3	0.000	0.001	0.008	0.027	0.064	0.125	0.216	0.343	0.512	0.729	0.857

$n = 4$

Probability

x	0.05	0.10	0.20	0.30	0.40	0.50	0.60	0.70	0.80	0.90	0.95
0	0.815	0.656	0.410	0.240	0.130	0.063	0.026	0.008	0.002	0.000	0.000
1	0.171	0.292	0.410	0.412	0.346	0.250	0.154	0.076	0.026	0.004	0.000
2	0.014	0.049	0.154	0.265	0.346	0.375	0.346	0.265	0.154	0.049	0.014
3	0.000	0.004	0.026	0.076	0.154	0.250	0.346	0.412	0.410	0.292	0.171
4	0.000	0.000	0.002	0.008	0.026	0.063	0.130	0.240	0.410	0.656	0.815

$n = 5$

Probability

x	0.05	0.10	0.20	0.30	0.40	0.50	0.60	0.70	0.80	0.90	0.95
0	0.774	0.590	0.328	0.168	0.078	0.031	0.010	0.002	0.000	0.000	0.000
1	0.204	0.328	0.410	0.360	0.259	0.156	0.077	0.028	0.006	0.000	0.000
2	0.021	0.073	0.205	0.309	0.346	0.313	0.230	0.132	0.051	0.008	0.001
3	0.001	0.008	0.051	0.132	0.230	0.313	0.346	0.309	0.205	0.073	0.021
4	0.000	0.000	0.006	0.028	0.077	0.156	0.259	0.360	0.410	0.328	0.204
5	0.000	0.000	0.000	0.002	0.010	0.031	0.078	0.168	0.328	0.590	0.774

Binomial Probability Distribution *(continued)*

$n = 6$
Probability

x	0.05	0.10	0.20	0.30	0.40	0.50	0.60	0.70	0.80	0.90	0.95
0	0.735	0.531	0.262	0.118	0.047	0.016	0.004	0.001	0.000	0.000	0.000
1	0.232	0.354	0.393	0.303	0.187	0.094	0.037	0.010	0.002	0.000	0.000
2	0.031	0.098	0.246	0.324	0.311	0.234	0.138	0.060	0.015	0.001	0.000
3	0.002	0.015	0.082	0.185	0.276	0.313	0.276	0.185	0.082	0.015	0.002
4	0.000	0.001	0.015	0.060	0.138	0.234	0.311	0.324	0.246	0.098	0.031
5	0.000	0.000	0.002	0.010	0.037	0.094	0.187	0.303	0.393	0.354	0.232
6	0.000	0.000	0.000	0.001	0.004	0.016	0.047	0.118	0.262	0.531	0.735

$n = 7$
Probability

x	0.05	0.10	0.20	0.30	0.40	0.50	0.60	0.70	0.80	0.90	0.95
0	0.698	0.478	0.210	0.082	0.028	0.008	0.002	0.000	0.000	0.000	0.000
1	0.257	0.372	0.367	0.247	0.131	0.055	0.017	0.004	0.000	0.000	0.000
2	0.041	0.124	0.275	0.318	0.261	0.164	0.077	0.025	0.004	0.000	0.000
3	0.004	0.023	0.115	0.227	0.290	0.273	0.194	0.097	0.029	0.003	0.000
4	0.000	0.003	0.029	0.097	0.194	0.273	0.290	0.227	0.115	0.023	0.004
5	0.000	0.000	0.004	0.025	0.077	0.164	0.261	0.318	0.275	0.124	0.041
6	0.000	0.000	0.000	0.004	0.017	0.055	0.131	0.247	0.367	0.372	0.257
7	0.000	0.000	0.000	0.000	0.002	0.008	0.028	0.082	0.210	0.478	0.698

$n = 8$
Probability

x	0.05	0.10	0.20	0.30	0.40	0.50	0.60	0.70	0.80	0.90	0.95
0	0.663	0.430	0.168	0.058	0.017	0.004	0.001	0.000	0.000	0.000	0.000
1	0.279	0.383	0.336	0.198	0.090	0.031	0.008	0.001	0.000	0.000	0.000
2	0.051	0.149	0.294	0.296	0.209	0.109	0.041	0.010	0.001	0.000	0.000
3	0.005	0.033	0.147	0.254	0.279	0.219	0.124	0.047	0.009	0.000	0.000
4	0.000	0.005	0.046	0.136	0.232	0.273	0.232	0.136	0.046	0.005	0.000
5	0.000	0.000	0.009	0.047	0.124	0.219	0.279	0.254	0.147	0.033	0.005
6	0.000	0.000	0.001	0.010	0.041	0.109	0.209	0.296	0.294	0.149	0.051
7	0.000	0.000	0.000	0.001	0.008	0.031	0.090	0.198	0.336	0.383	0.279
8	0.000	0.000	0.000	0.000	0.001	0.004	0.017	0.058	0.168	0.430	0.663

Appendix A

Binomial Probability Distribution *(continued)*

$n = 9$

Probability

x	0.05	0.10	0.20	0.30	0.40	0.50	0.60	0.70	0.80	0.90	0.95
0	0.630	0.387	0.134	0.040	0.010	0.002	0.000	0.000	0.000	0.000	0.000
1	0.299	0.387	0.302	0.156	0.060	0.018	0.004	0.000	0.000	0.000	0.000
2	0.063	0.172	0.302	0.267	0.161	0.070	0.021	0.004	0.000	0.000	0.000
3	0.008	0.045	0.176	0.267	0.251	0.164	0.074	0.021	0.003	0.000	0.000
4	0.001	0.007	0.066	0.172	0.251	0.246	0.167	0.074	0.017	0.001	0.000
5	0.000	0.001	0.017	0.074	0.167	0.246	0.251	0.172	0.066	0.007	0.001
6	0.000	0.000	0.003	0.021	0.074	0.164	0.251	0.267	0.176	0.045	0.008
7	0.000	0.000	0.000	0.004	0.021	0.070	0.161	0.267	0.302	0.172	0.063
8	0.000	0.000	0.000	0.000	0.004	0.018	0.060	0.156	0.302	0.387	0.299
9	0.000	0.000	0.000	0.000	0.000	0.002	0.010	0.040	0.134	0.387	0.630

$n = 10$

Probability

x	0.05	0.10	0.20	0.30	0.40	0.50	0.60	0.70	0.80	0.90	0.95
0	0.599	0.349	0.107	0.028	0.006	0.001	0.000	0.000	0.000	0.000	0.000
1	0.315	0.387	0.268	0.121	0.040	0.010	0.002	0.000	0.000	0.000	0.000
2	0.075	0.194	0.302	0.233	0.121	0.044	0.011	0.001	0.000	0.000	0.000
3	0.010	0.057	0.201	0.267	0.215	0.117	0.042	0.009	0.001	0.000	0.000
4	0.001	0.011	0.088	0.200	0.251	0.205	0.111	0.037	0.006	0.000	0.000
5	0.000	0.001	0.026	0.103	0.201	0.246	0.201	0.103	0.026	0.001	0.000
6	0.000	0.000	0.006	0.037	0.111	0.205	0.251	0.200	0.088	0.011	0.001
7	0.000	0.000	0.001	0.009	0.042	0.117	0.215	0.267	0.201	0.057	0.010
8	0.000	0.000	0.000	0.001	0.011	0.044	0.121	0.233	0.302	0.194	0.075
9	0.000	0.000	0.000	0.000	0.002	0.010	0.040	0.121	0.268	0.387	0.315
10	0.000	0.000	0.000	0.000	0.000	0.001	0.006	0.028	0.107	0.349	0.599

Binomial Probability Distribution *(continued)*

$n = 11$
Probability

x	0.05	0.10	0.20	0.30	0.40	0.50	0.60	0.70	0.80	0.90	0.95
0	0.569	0.314	0.086	0.020	0.004	0.000	0.000	0.000	0.000	0.000	0.000
1	0.329	0.384	0.236	0.093	0.027	0.005	0.001	0.000	0.000	0.000	0.000
2	0.087	0.213	0.295	0.200	0.089	0.027	0.005	0.001	0.000	0.000	0.000
3	0.014	0.071	0.221	0.257	0.177	0.081	0.023	0.004	0.000	0.000	0.000
4	0.001	0.016	0.111	0.220	0.236	0.161	0.070	0.017	0.002	0.000	0.000
5	0.000	0.002	0.039	0.132	0.221	0.226	0.147	0.057	0.010	0.000	0.000
6	0.000	0.000	0.010	0.057	0.147	0.226	0.221	0.132	0.039	0.002	0.000
7	0.000	0.000	0.002	0.017	0.070	0.161	0.236	0.220	0.111	0.016	0.001
8	0.000	0.000	0.000	0.004	0.023	0.081	0.177	0.257	0.221	0.071	0.014
9	0.000	0.000	0.000	0.001	0.005	0.027	0.089	0.200	0.295	0.213	0.087
10	0.000	0.000	0.000	0.000	0.001	0.005	0.027	0.093	0.236	0.384	0.329
11	0.000	0.000	0.000	0.000	0.000	0.000	0.004	0.020	0.086	0.314	0.569

$n = 12$
Probability

x	0.05	0.10	0.20	0.30	0.40	0.50	0.60	0.70	0.80	0.90	0.95
0	0.540	0.282	0.069	0.014	0.002	0.000	0.000	0.000	0.000	0.000	0.000
1	0.341	0.377	0.206	0.071	0.017	0.003	0.000	0.000	0.000	0.000	0.000
2	0.099	0.230	0.283	0.168	0.064	0.016	0.002	0.000	0.000	0.000	0.000
3	0.017	0.085	0.236	0.240	0.142	0.054	0.012	0.001	0.000	0.000	0.000
4	0.002	0.021	0.133	0.231	0.213	0.121	0.042	0.008	0.001	0.000	0.000
5	0.000	0.004	0.053	0.158	0.227	0.193	0.101	0.029	0.003	0.000	0.000
6	0.000	0.000	0.016	0.079	0.177	0.226	0.177	0.079	0.016	0.000	0.000
7	0.000	0.000	0.003	0.029	0.101	0.193	0.227	0.158	0.053	0.004	0.000
8	0.000	0.000	0.001	0.008	0.042	0.121	0.213	0.231	0.133	0.021	0.002
9	0.000	0.000	0.000	0.001	0.012	0.054	0.142	0.240	0.236	0.085	0.017
10	0.000	0.000	0.000	0.000	0.002	0.016	0.064	0.168	0.283	0.230	0.099
11	0.000	0.000	0.000	0.000	0.000	0.003	0.017	0.071	0.206	0.377	0.341
12	0.000	0.000	0.000	0.000	0.000	0.000	0.002	0.014	0.069	0.282	0.540

Appendix A

Binomial Probability Distribution *(continued)*

$n = 13$

Probability

x	0.05	0.10	0.20	0.30	0.40	0.50	0.60	0.70	0.80	0.90	0.95
0	0.513	0.254	0.055	0.010	0.001	0.000	0.000	0.000	0.000	0.000	0.000
1	0.351	0.367	0.179	0.054	0.011	0.002	0.000	0.000	0.000	0.000	0.000
2	0.111	0.245	0.268	0.139	0.045	0.010	0.001	0.000	0.000	0.000	0.000
3	0.021	0.100	0.246	0.218	0.111	0.035	0.006	0.001	0.000	0.000	0.000
4	0.003	0.028	0.154	0.234	0.184	0.087	0.024	0.003	0.000	0.000	0.000
5	0.000	0.006	0.069	0.180	0.221	0.157	0.066	0.014	0.001	0.000	0.000
6	0.000	0.001	0.023	0.103	0.197	0.209	0.131	0.044	0.006	0.000	0.000
7	0.000	0.000	0.006	0.044	0.131	0.209	0.197	0.103	0.023	0.001	0.000
8	0.000	0.000	0.001	0.014	0.066	0.157	0.221	0.180	0.069	0.006	0.000
9	0.000	0.000	0.000	0.003	0.024	0.087	0.184	0.234	0.154	0.028	0.003
10	0.000	0.000	0.000	0.001	0.006	0.035	0.111	0.218	0.246	0.100	0.021
11	0.000	0.000	0.000	0.000	0.001	0.010	0.045	0.139	0.268	0.245	0.111
12	0.000	0.000	0.000	0.000	0.000	0.002	0.011	0.054	0.179	0.367	0.351
13	0.000	0.000	0.000	0.000	0.000	0.000	0.001	0.010	0.055	0.254	0.513

$n = 14$

Probability

x	0.05	0.10	0.20	0.30	0.40	0.50	0.60	0.70	0.80	0.90	0.95
0	0.488	0.229	0.044	0.007	0.001	0.000	0.000	0.000	0.000	0.000	0.000
1	0.359	0.356	0.154	0.041	0.007	0.001	0.000	0.000	0.000	0.000	0.000
2	0.123	0.257	0.250	0.113	0.032	0.006	0.001	0.000	0.000	0.000	0.000
3	0.026	0.114	0.250	0.194	0.085	0.022	0.003	0.000	0.000	0.000	0.000
4	0.004	0.035	0.172	0.229	0.155	0.061	0.014	0.001	0.000	0.000	0.000
5	0.000	0.008	0.086	0.196	0.207	0.122	0.041	0.007	0.000	0.000	0.000
6	0.000	0.001	0.032	0.126	0.207	0.183	0.092	0.023	0.002	0.000	0.000
7	0.000	0.000	0.009	0.062	0.157	0.209	0.157	0.062	0.009	0.000	0.000
8	0.000	0.000	0.002	0.023	0.092	0.183	0.207	0.126	0.032	0.001	0.000
9	0.000	0.000	0.000	0.007	0.041	0.122	0.207	0.196	0.086	0.008	0.000
10	0.000	0.000	0.000	0.001	0.014	0.061	0.155	0.229	0.172	0.035	0.004
11	0.000	0.000	0.000	0.000	0.003	0.022	0.085	0.194	0.250	0.114	0.026
12	0.000	0.000	0.000	0.000	0.001	0.006	0.032	0.113	0.250	0.257	0.123
13	0.000	0.000	0.000	0.000	0.000	0.001	0.007	0.041	0.154	0.356	0.359
14	0.000	0.000	0.000	0.000	0.000	0.000	0.001	0.007	0.044	0.229	0.488

Appendix A

Binomial Probability Distribution *(continued)*

$n = 15$
Probability

x	0.05	0.10	0.20	0.30	0.40	0.50	0.60	0.70	0.80	0.90	0.95
0	0.463	0.206	0.035	0.005	0.000	0.000	0.000	0.000	0.000	0.000	0.000
1	0.366	0.343	0.132	0.031	0.005	0.000	0.000	0.000	0.000	0.000	0.000
2	0.135	0.267	0.231	0.092	0.022	0.003	0.000	0.000	0.000	0.000	0.000
3	0.031	0.129	0.250	0.170	0.063	0.014	0.002	0.000	0.000	0.000	0.000
4	0.005	0.043	0.188	0.219	0.127	0.042	0.007	0.001	0.000	0.000	0.000
5	0.001	0.010	0.103	0.206	0.186	0.092	0.024	0.003	0.000	0.000	0.000
6	0.000	0.002	0.043	0.147	0.207	0.153	0.061	0.012	0.001	0.000	0.000
7	0.000	0.000	0.014	0.081	0.177	0.196	0.118	0.035	0.003	0.000	0.000
8	0.000	0.000	0.003	0.035	0.118	0.196	0.177	0.081	0.014	0.000	0.000
9	0.000	0.000	0.001	0.012	0.061	0.153	0.207	0.147	0.043	0.002	0.000
10	0.000	0.000	0.000	0.003	0.024	0.092	0.186	0.206	0.103	0.010	0.001
11	0.000	0.000	0.000	0.001	0.007	0.042	0.127	0.219	0.188	0.043	0.005
12	0.000	0.000	0.000	0.000	0.002	0.014	0.063	0.170	0.250	0.129	0.031
13	0.000	0.000	0.000	0.000	0.000	0.003	0.022	0.092	0.231	0.267	0.135
14	0.000	0.000	0.000	0.000	0.000	0.000	0.005	0.031	0.132	0.343	0.366
15	0.000	0.000	0.000	0.000	0.000	0.000	0.000	0.005	0.035	0.206	0.463

$n = 16$
Probability

x	0.05	0.10	0.20	0.30	0.40	0.50	0.60	0.70	0.80	0.90	0.95
0	0.440	0.185	0.028	0.003	0.000	0.000	0.000	0.000	0.000	0.000	0.000
1	0.371	0.329	0.113	0.023	0.003	0.000	0.000	0.000	0.000	0.000	0.000
2	0.146	0.275	0.211	0.073	0.015	0.002	0.000	0.000	0.000	0.000	0.000
3	0.036	0.142	0.246	0.146	0.047	0.009	0.001	0.000	0.000	0.000	0.000
4	0.006	0.051	0.200	0.204	0.101	0.028	0.004	0.000	0.000	0.000	0.000
5	0.001	0.014	0.120	0.210	0.162	0.067	0.014	0.001	0.000	0.000	0.000
6	0.000	0.003	0.055	0.165	0.198	0.122	0.039	0.006	0.000	0.000	0.000
7	0.000	0.000	0.020	0.101	0.189	0.175	0.084	0.019	0.001	0.000	0.000
8	0.000	0.000	0.006	0.049	0.142	0.196	0.142	0.049	0.006	0.000	0.000
9	0.000	0.000	0.001	0.019	0.084	0.175	0.189	0.101	0.020	0.000	0.000
10	0.000	0.000	0.000	0.006	0.039	0.122	0.198	0.165	0.055	0.003	0.000
11	0.000	0.000	0.000	0.001	0.014	0.067	0.162	0.210	0.120	0.014	0.001
12	0.000	0.000	0.000	0.000	0.004	0.028	0.101	0.204	0.200	0.051	0.006
13	0.000	0.000	0.000	0.000	0.001	0.009	0.047	0.146	0.246	0.142	0.036
14	0.000	0.000	0.000	0.000	0.000	0.002	0.015	0.073	0.211	0.275	0.146
15	0.000	0.000	0.000	0.000	0.000	0.000	0.003	0.023	0.113	0.329	0.371
16	0.000	0.000	0.000	0.000	0.000	0.000	0.000	0.003	0.028	0.185	0.440

Appendix A

Binomial Probability Distribution *(continued)*

$n = 17$

Probability

x	0.05	0.10	0.20	0.30	0.40	0.50	0.60	0.70	0.80	0.90	0.95
0	0.418	0.167	0.023	0.002	0.000	0.000	0.000	0.000	0.000	0.000	0.000
1	0.374	0.315	0.096	0.017	0.002	0.000	0.000	0.000	0.000	0.000	0.000
2	0.158	0.280	0.191	0.058	0.010	0.001	0.000	0.000	0.000	0.000	0.000
3	0.041	0.156	0.239	0.125	0.034	0.005	0.000	0.000	0.000	0.000	0.000
4	0.008	0.060	0.209	0.187	0.080	0.018	0.002	0.000	0.000	0.000	0.000
5	0.001	0.017	0.136	0.208	0.138	0.047	0.008	0.001	0.000	0.000	0.000
6	0.000	0.004	0.068	0.178	0.184	0.094	0.024	0.003	0.000	0.000	0.000
7	0.000	0.001	0.027	0.120	0.193	0.148	0.057	0.009	0.000	0.000	0.000
8	0.000	0.000	0.008	0.064	0.161	0.185	0.107	0.028	0.002	0.000	0.000
9	0.000	0.000	0.002	0.028	0.107	0.185	0.161	0.064	0.008	0.000	0.000
10	0.000	0.000	0.000	0.009	0.057	0.148	0.193	0.120	0.027	0.001	0.000
11	0.000	0.000	0.000	0.003	0.024	0.094	0.184	0.178	0.068	0.004	0.000
12	0.000	0.000	0.000	0.001	0.008	0.047	0.138	0.208	0.136	0.017	0.001
13	0.000	0.000	0.000	0.000	0.002	0.018	0.080	0.187	0.209	0.060	0.008
14	0.000	0.000	0.000	0.000	0.000	0.005	0.034	0.125	0.239	0.156	0.041
15	0.000	0.000	0.000	0.000	0.000	0.001	0.010	0.058	0.191	0.280	0.158
16	0.000	0.000	0.000	0.000	0.000	0.000	0.002	0.017	0.096	0.315	0.374
17	0.000	0.000	0.000	0.000	0.000	0.000	0.000	0.002	0.023	0.167	0.418

$n = 18$

Probability

x	0.05	0.10	0.20	0.30	0.40	0.50	0.60	0.70	0.80	0.90	0.95
0	0.397	0.150	0.018	0.002	0.000	0.000	0.000	0.000	0.000	0.000	0.000
1	0.376	0.300	0.081	0.013	0.001	0.000	0.000	0.000	0.000	0.000	0.000
2	0.168	0.284	0.172	0.046	0.007	0.001	0.000	0.000	0.000	0.000	0.000
3	0.047	0.168	0.230	0.105	0.025	0.003	0.000	0.000	0.000	0.000	0.000
4	0.009	0.070	0.215	0.168	0.061	0.012	0.001	0.000	0.000	0.000	0.000
5	0.001	0.022	0.151	0.202	0.115	0.033	0.004	0.000	0.000	0.000	0.000
6	0.000	0.005	0.082	0.187	0.166	0.071	0.015	0.001	0.000	0.000	0.000
7	0.000	0.001	0.035	0.138	0.189	0.121	0.037	0.005	0.000	0.000	0.000
8	0.000	0.000	0.012	0.081	0.173	0.167	0.077	0.015	0.001	0.000	0.000
9	0.000	0.000	0.003	0.039	0.128	0.185	0.128	0.039	0.003	0.000	0.000
10	0.000	0.000	0.001	0.015	0.077	0.167	0.173	0.081	0.012	0.000	0.000
11	0.000	0.000	0.000	0.005	0.037	0.121	0.189	0.138	0.035	0.001	0.000
12	0.000	0.000	0.000	0.001	0.015	0.071	0.166	0.187	0.082	0.005	0.000
13	0.000	0.000	0.000	0.000	0.004	0.033	0.115	0.202	0.151	0.022	0.001
14	0.000	0.000	0.000	0.000	0.001	0.012	0.061	0.168	0.215	0.070	0.009
15	0.000	0.000	0.000	0.000	0.000	0.003	0.025	0.105	0.230	0.168	0.047
16	0.000	0.000	0.000	0.000	0.000	0.001	0.007	0.046	0.172	0.284	0.168
17	0.000	0.000	0.000	0.000	0.000	0.000	0.001	0.013	0.081	0.300	0.376
18	0.000	0.000	0.000	0.000	0.000	0.000	0.000	0.002	0.018	0.150	0.397

Binomial Probability Distribution *(continued)*

n = 19
Probability

x	0.05	0.10	0.20	0.30	0.40	0.50	0.60	0.70	0.80	0.90	0.95
0	0.377	0.135	0.014	0.001	0.000	0.000	0.000	0.000	0.000	0.000	0.000
1	0.377	0.285	0.068	0.009	0.001	0.000	0.000	0.000	0.000	0.000	0.000
2	0.179	0.285	0.154	0.036	0.005	0.000	0.000	0.000	0.000	0.000	0.000
3	0.053	0.180	0.218	0.087	0.017	0.002	0.000	0.000	0.000	0.000	0.000
4	0.011	0.080	0.218	0.149	0.047	0.007	0.001	0.000	0.000	0.000	0.000
5	0.002	0.027	0.164	0.192	0.093	0.022	0.002	0.000	0.000	0.000	0.000
6	0.000	0.007	0.095	0.192	0.145	0.052	0.008	0.001	0.000	0.000	0.000
7	0.000	0.001	0.044	0.153	0.180	0.096	0.024	0.002	0.000	0.000	0.000
8	0.000	0.000	0.017	0.098	0.180	0.144	0.053	0.008	0.000	0.000	0.000
9	0.000	0.000	0.005	0.051	0.146	0.176	0.098	0.022	0.001	0.000	0.000
10	0.000	0.000	0.001	0.022	0.098	0.176	0.146	0.051	0.005	0.000	0.000
11	0.000	0.000	0.000	0.008	0.053	0.144	0.180	0.098	0.017	0.000	0.000
12	0.000	0.000	0.000	0.002	0.024	0.096	0.180	0.153	0.044	0.001	0.000
13	0.000	0.000	0.000	0.001	0.008	0.052	0.145	0.192	0.095	0.007	0.000
14	0.000	0.000	0.000	0.000	0.002	0.022	0.093	0.192	0.164	0.027	0.002
15	0.000	0.000	0.000	0.000	0.001	0.007	0.047	0.149	0.218	0.080	0.011
16	0.000	0.000	0.000	0.000	0.000	0.002	0.017	0.087	0.218	0.180	0.053
17	0.000	0.000	0.000	0.000	0.000	0.000	0.005	0.036	0.154	0.285	0.179
18	0.000	0.000	0.000	0.000	0.000	0.000	0.001	0.009	0.068	0.285	0.377
19	0.000	0.000	0.000	0.000	0.000	0.000	0.000	0.001	0.014	0.135	0.377

Appendix A

Binomial Probability Distribution *(continued)*

$n = 20$

Probability

x	0.05	0.10	0.20	0.30	0.40	0.50	0.60	0.70	0.80	0.90	0.95
0	0.358	0.122	0.012	0.001	0.000	0.000	0.000	0.000	0.000	0.000	0.000
1	0.377	0.270	0.058	0.007	0.000	0.000	0.000	0.000	0.000	0.000	0.000
2	0.189	0.285	0.137	0.028	0.003	0.000	0.000	0.000	0.000	0.000	0.000
3	0.060	0.190	0.205	0.072	0.012	0.001	0.000	0.000	0.000	0.000	0.000
4	0.013	0.090	0.218	0.130	0.035	0.005	0.000	0.000	0.000	0.000	0.000
5	0.002	0.032	0.175	0.179	0.075	0.015	0.001	0.000	0.000	0.000	0.000
6	0.000	0.009	0.109	0.192	0.124	0.037	0.005	0.000	0.000	0.000	0.000
7	0.000	0.002	0.055	0.164	0.166	0.074	0.015	0.001	0.000	0.000	0.000
8	0.000	0.000	0.022	0.114	0.180	0.120	0.035	0.004	0.000	0.000	0.000
9	0.000	0.000	0.007	0.065	0.160	0.160	0.071	0.012	0.000	0.000	0.000
10	0.000	0.000	0.002	0.031	0.117	0.176	0.117	0.031	0.002	0.000	0.000
11	0.000	0.000	0.000	0.012	0.071	0.160	0.160	0.065	0.007	0.000	0.000
12	0.000	0.000	0.000	0.004	0.035	0.120	0.180	0.114	0.022	0.000	0.000
13	0.000	0.000	0.000	0.001	0.015	0.074	0.166	0.164	0.055	0.002	0.000
14	0.000	0.000	0.000	0.000	0.005	0.037	0.124	0.192	0.109	0.009	0.000
15	0.000	0.000	0.000	0.000	0.001	0.015	0.075	0.179	0.175	0.032	0.002
16	0.000	0.000	0.000	0.000	0.000	0.005	0.035	0.130	0.218	0.090	0.013
17	0.000	0.000	0.000	0.000	0.000	0.001	0.012	0.072	0.205	0.190	0.060
18	0.000	0.000	0.000	0.000	0.000	0.000	0.003	0.028	0.137	0.285	0.189
19	0.000	0.000	0.000	0.000	0.000	0.000	0.000	0.007	0.058	0.270	0.377
20	0.000	0.000	0.000	0.000	0.000	0.000	0.000	0.001	0.012	0.122	0.358

Binomial Probability Distribution *(concluded)*

n = 25
Probability

x	0.05	0.10	0.20	0.30	0.40	0.50	0.60	0.70	0.80	0.90	0.95
0	0.277	0.072	0.004	0.000	0.000	0.000	0.000	0.000	0.000	0.000	0.000
1	0.365	0.199	0.024	0.001	0.000	0.000	0.000	0.000	0.000	0.000	0.000
2	0.231	0.266	0.071	0.007	0.000	0.000	0.000	0.000	0.000	0.000	0.000
3	0.093	0.226	0.136	0.024	0.002	0.000	0.000	0.000	0.000	0.000	0.000
4	0.027	0.138	0.187	0.057	0.007	0.000	0.000	0.000	0.000	0.000	0.000
5	0.006	0.065	0.196	0.103	0.020	0.002	0.000	0.000	0.000	0.000	0.000
6	0.001	0.024	0.163	0.147	0.044	0.005	0.000	0.000	0.000	0.000	0.000
7	0.000	0.007	0.111	0.171	0.080	0.014	0.001	0.000	0.000	0.000	0.000
8	0.000	0.002	0.062	0.165	0.120	0.032	0.003	0.000	0.000	0.000	0.000
9	0.000	0.000	0.029	0.134	0.151	0.061	0.009	0.000	0.000	0.000	0.000
10	0.000	0.000	0.012	0.092	0.161	0.097	0.021	0.001	0.000	0.000	0.000
11	0.000	0.000	0.004	0.054	0.147	0.133	0.043	0.004	0.000	0.000	0.000
12	0.000	0.000	0.001	0.027	0.114	0.155	0.076	0.011	0.000	0.000	0.000
13	0.000	0.000	0.000	0.011	0.076	0.155	0.114	0.027	0.001	0.000	0.000
14	0.000	0.000	0.000	0.004	0.043	0.133	0.147	0.054	0.004	0.000	0.000
15	0.000	0.000	0.000	0.001	0.021	0.097	0.161	0.092	0.012	0.000	0.000
16	0.000	0.000	0.000	0.000	0.009	0.061	0.151	0.134	0.029	0.000	0.000
17	0.000	0.000	0.000	0.000	0.003	0.032	0.120	0.165	0.062	0.002	0.000
18	0.000	0.000	0.000	0.000	0.001	0.014	0.080	0.171	0.111	0.007	0.000
19	0.000	0.000	0.000	0.000	0.000	0.005	0.044	0.147	0.163	0.024	0.001
20	0.000	0.000	0.000	0.000	0.000	0.002	0.020	0.103	0.196	0.065	0.006
21	0.000	0.000	0.000	0.000	0.000	0.000	0.007	0.057	0.187	0.138	0.027
22	0.000	0.000	0.000	0.000	0.000	0.000	0.002	0.024	0.136	0.226	0.093
23	0.000	0.000	0.000	0.000	0.000	0.000	0.000	0.007	0.071	0.266	0.231
24	0.000	0.000	0.000	0.000	0.000	0.000	0.000	0.001	0.024	0.199	0.365
25	0.000	0.000	0.000	0.000	0.000	0.000	0.000	0.000	0.004	0.072	0.277

Appendix B

Factors for Control Charts

Number of Items in Sample, n	Chart for Averages	Chart for Ranges		
	Factors for Control Limits	Factors for Central Line	Factors for Control Limits	
	A_2	d_2	D_3	D_4
2	1.880	1.128	0	3.267
3	1.023	1.693	0	2.575
4	.729	2.059	0	2.282
5	.577	2.326	0	2.115
6	.483	2.534	0	2.004
7	.419	2.704	.076	1.924
8	.373	2.847	.136	1.864
9	.337	2.970	.184	1.816
10	.308	3.078	.223	1.777
11	.285	3.173	.256	1.744
12	.266	3.258	.284	1.716
13	.249	3.336	.308	1.692
14	.235	3.407	.329	1.671
15	.223	3.472	.348	1.652

SOURCE: Adapted from American Society for Testing and Materials, *Manual on Quality Control of Materials,* 1951, Table B2, p. 115. For a more detailed table and explanation, see Acheson, J. Duncan, *Quality Control and Industrial Statistics,* 3d ed. (Homewood, Ill.: Richard D. Irwin, 1974), Table M, p. 927.

Appendix C

Poisson Distribution

	μ								
x	0.1	0.2	0.3	0.4	0.5	0.6	0.7	0.8	0.9
0	0.9048	0.8187	0.7408	0.6703	0.6065	0.5488	0.4966	0.4493	0.4066
1	0.0905	0.1637	0.2222	0.2681	0.3033	0.3293	0.3476	0.3595	0.3659
2	0.0045	0.0164	0.0333	0.0536	0.0758	0.0988	0.1217	0.1438	0.1647
3	0.0002	0.0011	0.0033	0.0072	0.0126	0.0198	0.0284	0.0383	0.0494
4	0.0000	0.0001	0.0003	0.0007	0.0016	0.0030	0.0050	0.0077	0.0111
5	0.0000	0.0000	0.0000	0.0001	0.0002	0.0004	0.0007	0.0012	0.0020
6	0.0000	0.0000	0.0000	0.0000	0.0000	0.0000	0.0001	0.0002	0.0003
7	0.0000	0.0000	0.0000	0.0000	0.0000	0.0000	0.0000	0.0000	0.0000

	μ								
x	1.0	2.0	3.0	4.0	5.0	6.0	7.0	8.0	9.0
0	0.3679	0.1353	0.0498	0.0183	0.0067	0.0025	0.0009	0.0003	0.0001
1	0.3679	0.2707	0.1494	0.0733	0.0337	0.0149	0.0064	0.0027	0.0011
2	0.1839	0.2707	0.2240	0.1465	0.0842	0.0446	0.0223	0.0107	0.0050
3	0.0613	0.1804	0.2240	0.1954	0.1404	0.0892	0.0521	0.0286	0.0150
4	0.0153	0.0902	0.1680	0.1954	0.1755	0.1339	0.0912	0.0573	0.0337
5	0.0031	0.0361	0.1008	0.1563	0.1755	0.1606	0.1277	0.0916	0.0607
6	0.0005	0.0120	0.0504	0.1042	0.1462	0.1606	0.1490	0.1221	0.0911
7	0.0001	0.0034	0.0216	0.0595	0.1044	0.1377	0.1490	0.1396	0.1171
8	0.0000	0.0009	0.0081	0.0298	0.0653	0.1033	0.1304	0.1396	0.1318
9	0.0000	0.0002	0.0027	0.0132	0.0363	0.0688	0.1014	0.1241	0.1318
10	0.0000	0.0000	0.0008	0.0053	0.0181	0.0413	0.0710	0.0993	0.1186
11	0.0000	0.0000	0.0002	0.0019	0.0082	0.0225	0.0452	0.0722	0.0970
12	0.0000	0.0000	0.0001	0.0006	0.0034	0.0113	0.0263	0.0481	0.0728
13	0.0000	0.0000	0.0000	0.0002	0.0013	0.0052	0.0142	0.0296	0.0504
14	0.0000	0.0000	0.0000	0.0001	0.0005	0.0022	0.0071	0.0169	0.0324
15	0.0000	0.0000	0.0000	0.0000	0.0002	0.0009	0.0033	0.0090	0.0194
16	0.0000	0.0000	0.0000	0.0000	0.0000	0.0003	0.0014	0.0045	0.0109
17	0.0000	0.0000	0.0000	0.0000	0.0000	0.0001	0.0006	0.0021	0.0058
18	0.0000	0.0000	0.0000	0.0000	0.0000	0.0000	0.0002	0.0009	0.0029
19	0.0000	0.0000	0.0000	0.0000	0.0000	0.0000	0.0001	0.0004	0.0014
20	0.0000	0.0000	0.0000	0.0000	0.0000	0.0000	0.0000	0.0002	0.0006
21	0.0000	0.0000	0.0000	0.0000	0.0000	0.0000	0.0000	0.0001	0.0003
22	0.0000	0.0000	0.0000	0.0000	0.0000	0.0000	0.0000	0.0000	0.0001

Appendix D

Areas under the Normal Curve

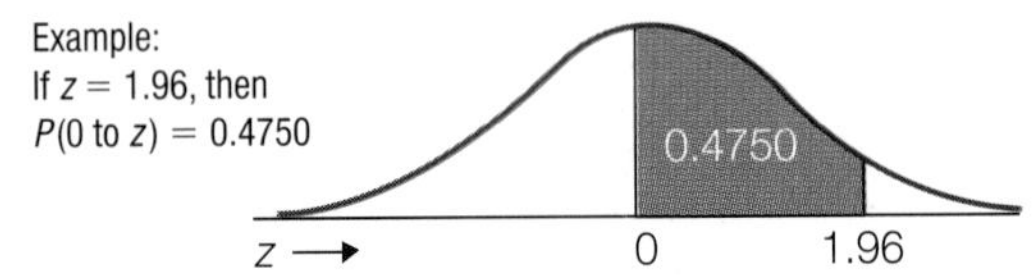

z	0.00	0.01	0.02	0.03	0.04	0.05	0.06	0.07	0.08	0.09
0.0	0.0000	0.0040	0.0080	0.0120	0.0160	0.0199	0.0239	0.0279	0.0319	0.0359
0.1	0.0398	0.0438	0.0478	0.0517	0.0557	0.0596	0.0636	0.0675	0.0714	0.0753
0.2	0.0793	0.0832	0.0871	0.0910	0.0948	0.0987	0.1026	0.1064	0.1103	0.1141
0.3	0.1179	0.1217	0.1255	0.1293	0.1331	0.1368	0.1406	0.1443	0.1480	0.1517
0.4	0.1554	0.1591	0.1628	0.1664	0.1700	0.1736	0.1772	0.1808	0.1844	0.1879
0.5	0.1915	0.1950	0.1985	0.2019	0.2054	0.2088	0.2123	0.2157	0.2190	0.2224
0.6	0.2257	0.2291	0.2324	0.2357	0.2389	0.2422	0.2454	0.2486	0.2517	0.2549
0.7	0.2580	0.2611	0.2642	0.2673	0.2704	0.2734	0.2764	0.2794	0.2823	0.2852
0.8	0.2881	0.2910	0.2939	0.2967	0.2995	0.3023	0.3051	0.3078	0.3106	0.3133
0.9	0.3159	0.3186	0.3212	0.3238	0.3264	0.3289	0.3315	0.3340	0.3365	0.3389
1.0	0.3413	0.3438	0.3461	0.3485	0.3508	0.3531	0.3554	0.3577	0.3599	0.3621
1.1	0.3643	0.3665	0.3686	0.3708	0.3729	0.3749	0.3770	0.3790	0.3810	0.3830
1.2	0.3849	0.3869	0.3888	0.3907	0.3925	0.3944	0.3962	0.3980	0.3997	0.4015
1.3	0.4032	0.4049	0.4066	0.4082	0.4099	0.4115	0.4131	0.4147	0.4162	0.4177
1.4	0.4192	0.4207	0.4222	0.4236	0.4251	0.4265	0.4279	0.4292	0.4306	0.4319
1.5	0.4332	0.4345	0.4357	0.4370	0.4382	0.4394	0.4406	0.4418	0.4429	0.4441
1.6	0.4452	0.4463	0.4474	0.4484	0.4495	0.4505	0.4515	0.4525	0.4535	0.4545
1.7	0.4554	0.4564	0.4573	0.4582	0.4591	0.4599	0.4608	0.4616	0.4625	0.4633
1.8	0.4641	0.4649	0.4656	0.4664	0.4671	0.4678	0.4686	0.4693	0.4699	0.4706
1.9	0.4713	0.4719	0.4726	0.4732	0.4738	0.4744	0.4750	0.4756	0.4761	0.4767
2.0	0.4772	0.4778	0.4783	0.4788	0.4793	0.4798	0.4803	0.4808	0.4812	0.4817
2.1	0.4821	0.4826	0.4830	0.4834	0.4838	0.4842	0.4846	0.4850	0.4854	0.4857
2.2	0.4861	0.4864	0.4868	0.4871	0.4875	0.4878	0.4881	0.4884	0.4887	0.4890
2.3	0.4893	0.4896	0.4898	0.4901	0.4904	0.4906	0.4909	0.4911	0.4913	0.4916
2.4	0.4918	0.4920	0.4922	0.4925	0.4927	0.4929	0.4931	0.4932	0.4934	0.4936
2.5	0.4938	0.4940	0.4941	0.4943	0.4945	0.4946	0.4948	0.4949	0.4951	0.4952
2.6	0.4953	0.4955	0.4956	0.4957	0.4959	0.4960	0.4961	0.4962	0.4963	0.4964
2.7	0.4965	0.4966	0.4967	0.4968	0.4969	0.4970	0.4971	0.4972	0.4973	0.4974
2.8	0.4974	0.4975	0.4976	0.4977	0.4977	0.4978	0.4979	0.4979	0.4980	0.4981
2.9	0.4981	0.4982	0.4982	0.4983	0.4984	0.4984	0.4985	0.4985	0.4986	0.4986
3.0	0.4987	0.4987	0.4987	0.4988	0.4988	0.4989	0.4989	0.4989	0.4990	0.4990

Appendix E

Table of Random Numbers

02711	08182	75997	79866	58095	83319	80295	79741	74599	84379
94873	90935	31684	63952	09865	14491	99518	93394	34691	14985
54921	78680	06635	98689	17306	25170	65928	87709	30533	89736
77640	97636	37397	93379	56454	59818	45827	74164	71666	46977
61545	00835	93251	87203	36759	49197	85967	01704	19634	21898
17147	19519	22497	16857	42426	84822	92598	49186	88247	39967
13748	04742	92460	85801	53444	65626	58710	55406	17173	69776
87455	14813	50373	28037	91182	32786	65261	11173	34376	36408
08999	57409	91185	10200	61411	23392	47797	56377	71635	08601
78804	81333	53809	32471	46034	36306	22498	19239	85428	55721
82173	26921	28472	98958	07960	66124	89731	95069	18625	92405
97594	25168	89178	68190	05043	17407	48201	83917	11413	72920
73881	67176	93504	42636	38233	16154	96451	57925	29667	30859
46071	22912	90326	42453	88108	72064	58601	32357	90610	32921
44492	19686	12495	93135	95185	77799	52441	88272	22024	80631
31864	72170	37722	55794	14636	05148	54505	50113	21119	25228
51574	90692	43339	65689	76539	27909	05467	21727	51141	72949
35350	76132	92925	92124	92634	35681	43690	89136	35599	84138
46943	36502	01172	46045	46991	33804	80006	35542	61056	75666
22665	87226	33304	57975	03985	21566	65796	72915	81466	89205
39437	97957	11838	10433	21564	51570	73558	27495	34533	57808
77082	47784	40098	97962	89845	28392	78187	06112	08169	11261
24544	25649	43370	28007	06779	72402	62632	53956	24709	06978
27503	15558	37738	24849	70722	71859	83736	06016	94397	12529
24590	24545	06435	52758	45685	90151	46516	49644	92686	84870
48155	86226	40359	28723	15364	69125	12609	57171	86857	31702
20226	53752	90648	24362	83314	00014	19207	69413	97016	86290
70178	73444	38790	53626	93780	18629	68766	24371	74639	30782
10169	41465	51935	05711	09799	79077	88159	33437	68519	03040
81084	03701	28598	70013	63794	53169	97054	60303	23259	96196
69202	20777	21727	81511	51887	16175	53746	46516	70339	62727
80561	95787	89426	93325	86412	57479	54194	52153	19197	81877
08199	26703	95128	48599	09333	12584	24374	31232	61782	44032
98883	28220	39358	53720	80161	83371	15181	11131	12219	55920
84568	69286	76054	21615	80883	36797	82845	39139	90900	18172
04269	35173	95745	53893	86022	77722	52498	84193	22448	22571
10538	13124	36099	13140	37706	44562	57179	44693	67877	01549
77843	24955	25900	63843	95029	93859	93634	20205	66294	41218
12034	94636	49455	76362	83532	31062	69903	91186	65768	55949
10524	72829	47641	93315	80875	28090	97728	52560	34937	79548
68935	76632	46984	61772	92786	22651	07086	89754	44143	97687
89450	65665	29190	43709	11172	34481	95977	47535	25658	73898
90696	20451	24211	97310	60446	73530	62865	96574	13829	72226
49006	32047	93086	00112	20470	17136	28255	86328	07293	38809
74591	87025	52368	59416	34417	70557	86746	55809	53628	12000
06315	17012	77103	00968	07235	10728	42189	33292	51487	64443
62386	09184	62092	46617	99419	64230	95034	85481	07857	42510
86848	82122	04028	36959	87827	12813	08627	80699	13345	51695
65643	69480	46598	04501	40403	91408	32343	48130	49303	90689
11084	46534	78957	77353	39578	77868	22970	84349	09184	70603

Appendix F

Student's *t* Distribution

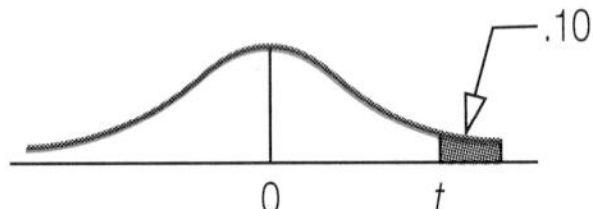

Example: With *df*=9 and .10 area in the upper tail, *t*=1.383

	Confidence Intervals					
	80%	90%	95%	98%	99%	99.9%
	Level of Significance for One-Tailed Test					
df	0.100	0.050	0.025	0.010	0.005	0.0005
	Level of Significance for Two-Tailed Test					
	0.20	0.10	0.05	0.02	0.01	0.001
1	3.078	6.314	12.706	31.821	63.657	636.619
2	1.886	2.920	4.303	6.965	9.925	31.599
3	1.638	2.353	3.182	4.541	5.841	12.924
4	1.533	2.132	2.776	3.747	4.604	8.610
5	1.476	2.015	2.571	3.365	4.032	6.869
6	1.440	1.943	2.447	3.143	3.707	5.959
7	1.415	1.895	2.365	2.998	3.499	5.408
8	1.397	1.860	2.306	2.896	3.355	5.041
9	1.383	1.833	2.262	2.821	3.250	4.781
10	1.372	1.812	2.228	2.764	3.169	4.587
11	1.363	1.796	2.201	2.718	3.106	4.437
12	1.356	1.782	2.179	2.681	3.055	4.318
13	1.350	1.771	2.160	2.650	3.012	4.221
14	1.345	1.761	2.145	2.624	2.977	4.140
15	1.341	1.753	2.131	2.602	2.947	4.073
16	1.337	1.746	2.120	2.583	2.921	4.015
17	1.333	1.740	2.110	2.567	2.898	3.965
18	1.330	1.734	2.101	2.552	2.878	3.922
19	1.328	1.729	2.093	2.539	2.861	3.883
20	1.325	1.725	2.086	2.528	2.845	3.850
21	1.323	1.721	2.080	2.518	2.831	3.819
22	1.321	1.717	2.074	2.508	2.819	3.792
23	1.319	1.714	2.069	2.500	2.807	3.768
24	1.318	1.711	2.064	2.492	2.797	3.745
25	1.316	1.708	2.060	2.485	2.787	3.725
26	1.315	1.706	2.056	2.479	2.779	3.707
27	1.314	1.703	2.052	2.473	2.771	3.690
28	1.313	1.701	2.048	2.467	2.763	3.674
29	1.311	1.699	2.045	2.462	2.756	3.659
30	1.310	1.697	2.042	2.457	2.750	3.646
40	1.303	1.684	2.021	2.423	2.704	3.551
60	1.296	1.671	2.000	2.390	2.660	3.460
120	1.289	1.658	1.980	2.358	2.617	3.373
∞	1.282	1.645	1.960	2.326	2.576	3.291

Appendix G

Critical Values of the *F* Distribution at a 5 Percent Level of Significance

Degrees of Freedom for the Denominator	Degrees of Freedom for the Numerator															
	1	2	3	4	5	6	7	8	9	10	12	15	20	24	30	40
1	161	200	216	225	230	234	237	239	241	242	244	246	248	249	250	251
2	18.5	19.0	19.2	19.2	19.3	19.3	19.4	19.4	19.4	19.4	19.4	19.4	19.4	19.5	19.5	19.5
3	10.1	9.55	9.28	9.12	9.01	8.94	8.89	8.85	8.81	8.79	8.74	8.70	8.66	8.64	8.62	8.59
4	7.71	6.94	6.59	6.39	6.26	6.16	6.09	6.04	6.00	5.96	5.91	5.86	5.80	5.77	5.75	5.72
5	6.61	5.79	5.41	5.19	5.05	4.95	4.88	4.82	4.77	4.74	4.68	4.62	4.56	4.53	4.50	4.46
6	5.99	5.14	4.76	4.53	4.39	4.28	4.21	4.15	4.10	4.06	4.00	3.94	3.87	3.84	3.81	3.77
7	5.59	4.74	4.35	4.12	3.97	3.87	3.79	3.73	3.68	3.64	3.57	3.51	3.44	3.41	3.38	3.34
8	5.32	4.46	4.07	3.84	3.69	3.58	3.50	3.44	3.39	3.35	3.28	3.22	3.15	3.12	3.08	3.04
9	5.12	4.26	3.86	3.63	3.48	3.37	3.29	3.23	3.18	3.14	3.07	3.01	2.94	2.90	2.86	2.83
10	4.96	4.10	3.71	3.48	3.33	3.22	3.14	3.07	3.02	2.98	2.91	2.85	2.77	2.74	2.70	2.66
11	4.84	3.98	3.59	3.36	3.20	3.09	3.01	2.95	2.90	2.85	2.79	2.72	2.65	2.61	2.57	2.53
12	4.75	3.89	3.49	3.26	3.11	3.00	2.91	2.85	2.80	2.75	2.69	2.62	2.54	2.51	2.47	2.43
13	4.67	3.81	3.41	3.18	3.03	2.92	2.83	2.77	2.71	2.67	2.60	2.53	2.46	2.42	2.38	2.34
14	4.60	3.74	3.34	3.11	2.96	2.85	2.76	2.70	2.65	2.60	2.53	2.46	2.39	2.35	2.31	2.27
15	4.54	3.68	3.29	3.06	2.90	2.79	2.71	2.64	2.59	2.54	2.48	2.40	2.33	2.29	2.25	2.20
16	4.49	3.63	3.24	3.01	2.85	2.74	2.66	2.59	2.54	2.49	2.42	2.35	2.28	2.24	2.19	2.15
17	4.45	3.59	3.20	2.96	2.81	2.70	2.61	2.55	2.49	2.45	2.38	2.31	2.23	2.19	2.15	2.10
18	4.41	3.55	3.16	2.93	2.77	2.66	2.58	2.51	2.46	2.41	2.34	2.27	2.19	2.15	2.11	2.06
19	4.38	3.52	3.13	2.90	2.74	2.63	2.54	2.48	2.42	2.38	2.31	2.23	2.16	2.11	2.07	2.03
20	4.35	3.49	3.10	2.87	2.71	2.60	2.51	2.45	2.39	2.35	2.28	2.20	2.12	2.08	2.04	1.99
21	4.32	3.47	3.07	2.84	2.68	2.57	2.49	2.42	2.37	2.32	2.25	2.18	2.10	2.05	2.01	1.96
22	4.30	3.44	3.05	2.82	2.66	2.55	2.46	2.40	2.34	2.30	2.23	2.15	2.07	2.03	1.98	1.94
23	4.28	3.42	3.03	2.80	2.64	2.53	2.44	2.37	2.32	2.27	2.20	2.13	2.05	2.01	1.96	1.91
24	4.26	3.40	3.01	2.78	2.62	2.51	2.42	2.36	2.30	2.25	2.18	2.11	2.03	1.98	1.94	1.89
25	4.24	3.39	2.99	2.76	2.60	2.49	2.40	2.34	2.28	2.24	2.16	2.09	2.01	1.96	1.92	1.87
30	4.17	3.32	2.92	2.69	2.53	2.42	2.33	2.27	2.21	2.16	2.09	2.01	1.93	1.89	1.84	1.79
40	4.08	3.23	2.84	2.61	2.45	2.34	2.25	2.18	2.12	2.08	2.00	1.92	1.84	1.79	1.74	1.69
60	4.00	3.15	2.76	2.53	2.37	2.25	2.17	2.10	2.04	1.99	1.92	1.84	1.75	1.70	1.65	1.59
120	3.92	3.07	2.68	2.45	2.29	2.18	2.09	2.02	1.96	1.91	1.83	1.75	1.66	1.61	1.55	1.50
∞	3.84	3.00	2.60	2.37	2.21	2.10	2.01	1.94	1.88	1.83	1.75	1.67	1.57	1.52	1.46	1.39

Appendix G

Critical Values of the *F* Distribution at a 1 Percent Level of Significance

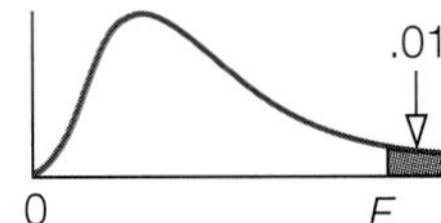

Degrees of Freedom for the Denominator	Degrees of Freedom for the Numerator															
	1	2	3	4	5	6	7	8	9	10	12	15	20	24	30	40
1	4052	5000	5403	5625	5764	5859	5928	5981	6022	6056	6106	6157	6209	6235	6261	6287
2	98.5	99.0	99.2	99.2	99.3	99.3	99.4	99.4	99.4	99.4	99.4	99.4	99.4	99.5	99.5	99.5
3	34.1	30.8	29.5	28.7	28.2	27.9	27.7	27.5	27.3	27.2	27.1	26.9	26.7	26.6	26.5	26.4
4	21.2	18.0	16.7	16.0	15.5	15.2	15.0	14.8	14.7	14.5	14.4	14.2	14.0	13.9	13.8	13.7
5	16.3	13.3	12.1	11.4	11.0	10.7	10.5	10.3	10.2	10.1	9.89	9.72	9.55	9.47	9.38	9.29
6	13.7	10.9	9.78	9.15	8.75	8.47	8.26	8.10	7.98	7.87	7.72	7.56	7.40	7.31	7.23	7.14
7	12.2	9.55	8.45	7.85	7.46	7.19	6.99	6.84	6.72	6.62	6.47	6.31	6.16	6.07	5.99	5.91
8	11.3	8.65	7.59	7.01	6.63	6.37	6.18	6.03	5.91	5.81	5.67	5.52	5.36	5.28	5.20	5.12
9	10.6	8.02	6.99	6.42	6.06	5.80	5.61	5.47	5.35	5.26	5.11	4.96	4.81	4.73	4.65	4.57
10	10.0	7.56	6.55	5.99	5.64	5.39	5.20	5.06	4.94	4.85	4.71	4.56	4.41	4.33	4.25	4.17
11	9.65	7.21	6.22	5.67	5.32	5.07	4.89	4.74	4.63	4.54	4.40	4.25	4.10	4.02	3.94	3.86
12	9.33	6.93	5.95	5.41	5.06	4.82	4.64	4.50	4.39	4.30	4.16	4.01	3.86	3.78	3.70	3.62
13	9.07	6.70	5.74	5.21	4.86	4.62	4.44	4.30	4.19	4.10	3.96	3.82	3.66	3.59	3.51	3.43
14	8.86	6.51	5.56	5.04	4.69	4.46	4.28	4.14	4.03	3.94	3.80	3.66	3.51	3.43	3.35	3.27
15	8.68	6.36	5.42	4.89	4.56	4.32	4.14	4.00	3.89	3.80	3.67	3.52	3.37	3.29	3.21	3.13
16	8.53	6.23	5.29	4.77	4.44	4.20	4.03	3.89	3.78	3.69	3.55	3.41	3.26	3.18	3.10	3.02
17	8.40	6.11	5.18	4.67	4.34	4.10	3.93	3.79	3.68	3.59	3.46	3.31	3.16	3.08	3.00	2.92
18	8.29	6.01	5.09	4.58	4.25	4.01	3.84	3.71	3.60	3.51	3.37	3.23	3.08	3.00	2.92	2.84
19	8.18	5.93	5.01	4.50	4.17	3.94	3.77	3.63	3.52	3.43	3.30	3.15	3.00	2.92	2.84	2.76
20	8.10	5.85	4.94	4.43	4.10	3.87	3.70	3.56	3.46	3.37	3.23	3.09	2.94	2.86	2.78	2.69
21	8.02	5.78	4.87	4.37	4.04	3.81	3.64	3.51	3.40	3.31	3.17	3.03	2.88	2.80	2.72	2.64
22	7.95	5.72	4.82	4.31	3.99	3.76	3.59	3.45	3.35	3.26	3.12	2.98	2.83	2.75	2.67	2.58
23	7.88	5.66	4.76	4.26	3.94	3.71	3.54	3.41	3.30	3.21	3.07	2.93	2.78	2.70	2.62	2.54
24	7.82	5.61	4.72	4.22	3.90	3.67	3.50	3.36	3.26	3.17	3.03	2.89	2.74	2.66	2.58	2.49
25	7.77	5.57	4.68	4.18	3.85	3.63	3.46	3.32	3.22	3.13	2.99	2.85	2.70	2.62	2.54	2.45
30	7.56	5.39	4.51	4.02	3.70	3.47	3.30	3.17	3.07	2.98	2.84	2.70	2.55	2.47	2.39	2.30
40	7.31	5.18	4.31	3.83	3.51	3.29	3.12	2.99	2.89	2.80	2.66	2.52	2.37	2.29	2.20	2.11
60	7.08	4.98	4.13	3.65	3.34	3.12	2.95	2.82	2.72	2.63	2.50	2.35	2.20	2.12	2.03	1.94
120	6.85	4.79	3.95	3.48	3.17	2.96	2.79	2.66	2.56	2.47	2.34	2.19	2.03	1.95	1.86	1.76
∞	6.63	4.61	3.78	3.32	3.02	2.80	2.64	2.51	2.41	2.32	2.18	2.04	1.88	1.79	1.70	1.59

Appendix H

Wilcoxon *T* Values

	2α						
	.15	.10	.05	.04	.03	.02	.01
	α						
n	.075	.050	.025	.020	.015	.010	.005
4	0						
5	1	0					
6	2	2	0	0			
7	4	3	2	1	0	0	
8	7	5	3	3	2	1	0
9	9	8	5	5	4	3	1
10	12	10	8	7	6	5	3
11	16	13	10	9	8	7	5
12	19	17	13	12	11	9	7
13	24	21	17	16	14	12	9
14	28	25	21	19	18	15	12
15	33	30	25	23	21	19	15
16	39	35	29	28	26	23	19
17	45	41	34	33	30	27	23
18	51	47	40	38	35	32	27
19	58	53	46	43	41	37	32
20	65	60	52	50	47	43	37
21	73	67	58	56	53	49	42
22	81	75	65	63	59	55	48
23	89	83	73	70	66	62	54
24	98	91	81	78	74	69	61
25	108	100	89	86	82	76	68
26	118	110	98	94	90	84	75
27	128	119	107	103	99	92	83
28	138	130	116	112	108	101	91
29	150	140	126	122	117	110	100
30	161	151	137	132	127	120	109
31	173	163	147	143	137	130	118
32	186	175	159	154	148	140	128
33	199	187	170	165	159	151	138
34	212	200	182	177	171	162	148
35	226	213	195	189	182	173	159
40	302	286	264	257	249	238	220
50	487	466	434	425	413	397	373
60	718	690	648	636	620	600	567
70	995	960	907	891	872	846	805
80	1,318	1,276	1,211	1,192	1,168	1,136	1,086
90	1,688	1,638	1,560	1,537	1,509	1,471	1,410
100	2,105	2,045	1,955	1,928	1,894	1,850	1,779

SOURCE: Abridged from Robert L. McCormack, "Extended Tables of the Wilcoxon Matched-Pair Signed Rank Statistic," *Journal of the American Statistical Association,* September 1965, pp. 866–67.

Appendix I

Critical Values of Chi-Square

This table contains the values of χ^2 that correspond to a specific right-tail area and specific number of degrees of freedom.

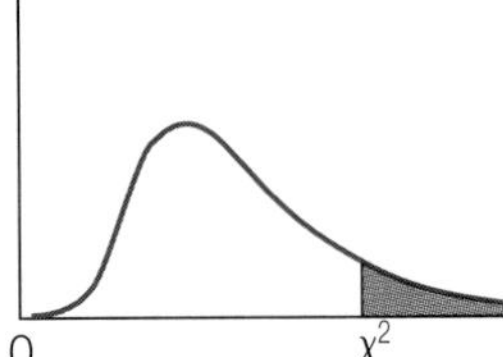

Example: With 17 *df* and a .02 area in the upper tail, χ^2=30.995

Degrees of Freedom, *df*	Right-Tail Area			
	0.10	**0.05**	**0.02**	**0.01**
1	2.706	3.841	5.412	6.635
2	4.605	5.991	7.824	9.210
3	6.251	7.815	9.837	11.345
4	7.779	9.488	11.668	13.277
5	9.236	11.070	13.388	15.086
6	10.645	12.592	15.033	16.812
7	12.017	14.067	16.622	18.475
8	13.362	15.507	18.168	20.090
9	14.684	16.919	19.679	21.666
10	15.987	18.307	21.161	23.209
11	17.275	19.675	22.618	24.725
12	18.549	21.026	24.054	26.217
13	19.812	22.362	25.472	27.688
14	21.064	23.685	26.873	29.141
15	22.307	24.996	28.259	30.578
16	23.542	26.296	29.633	32.000
17	24.769	27.587	30.995	33.409
18	25.989	28.869	32.346	34.805
19	27.204	30.144	33.687	36.191
20	28.412	31.410	35.020	37.566
21	29.615	32.671	36.343	38.932
22	30.813	33.924	37.659	40.289
23	32.007	35.172	38.968	41.638
24	33.196	36.415	40.270	42.980
25	34.382	37.652	41.566	44.314
26	35.563	38.885	42.856	45.642
27	36.741	40.113	44.140	46.963
28	37.916	41.337	45.419	48.278
29	39.087	42.557	46.693	49.588
30	40.256	43.773	47.962	50.892

Appendix J

Data Set 1 — Real Estate

x_1 = Selling price in \$000
x_2 = Number of bedrooms
x_3 = Size of the home in square feet
x_4 = Pool (1 = yes, 0 = no)
x_5 = Distance from the center of the city
x_6 = Township
x_7 = Garage attached (1 = yes, 0 = no)
x_8 = Number of bathrooms

x_1	x_2	x_3	x_4	x_5	x_6	x_7	x_8
263.1	4	2,300	0	17	5	1	2
182.4	4	2,100	1	19	4	0	2
242.1	3	2,300	1	12	3	0	2
213.6	2	2,200	1	16	2	0	2.5
139.9	2	2,100	1	28	1	0	1.5
245.4	2	2,100	0	12	1	1	2
327.2	6	2,500	1	15	3	1	2
271.8	2	2,100	1	9	2	1	2.5
221.1	3	2,300	0	18	1	0	1.5
266.6	4	2,400	1	13	4	1	2
292.4	4	2,100	1	14	3	1	2
209	2	1,700	1	8	4	1	1.5
270.8	6	2,500	1	7	4	1	2
246.1	4	2,100	1	18	3	1	2
194.4	2	2,300	1	11	3	0	2
281.3	3	2,100	1	16	2	1	2
172.7	4	2,200	0	16	3	0	2
207.5	5	2,300	0	21	4	0	2.5
198.9	3	2,200	0	10	4	1	2
209.3	6	1,900	0	15	4	1	2
252.3	4	2,600	1	8	4	1	2
192.9	4	1,900	0	14	2	1	2.5
209.3	5	2,100	1	20	5	0	1.5
345.3	8	2,600	1	9	4	1	2
326.3	6	2,100	1	11	5	1	3
173.1	2	2,200	0	21	5	1	1.5
187	2	1,900	1	26	4	0	2
257.2	2	2,100	1	9	4	1	2
233	3	2,200	1	14	3	1	1.5
180.4	2	2,000	1	11	5	0	2
234	2	1,700	1	19	3	1	2
207.1	2	2,000	1	11	5	1	2
247.7	5	2,400	1	16	2	1	2
166.2	3	2,000	0	16	2	1	2
177.1	2	1,900	1	10	5	1	2

Appendix J

Data Set 1 — Real Estate *(continued)*

X_1	X_2	X_3	X_4	X_5	X_6	X_7	X_8
182.7	4	2,000	0	14	4	0	2.5
216	4	2,300	1	19	2	0	2
312.1	6	2,600	1	7	5	1	2.5
199.8	3	2,100	1	19	3	1	2
273.2	5	2,200	1	16	2	1	3
206	3	2,100	0	9	3	0	1.5
232.2	3	1,900	0	16	1	1	1.5
198.3	4	2,100	0	19	1	1	1.5
205.1	3	2,000	0	20	4	0	2
175.6	4	2,300	0	24	4	1	2
307.8	3	2,400	0	21	2	1	3
269.2	5	2,200	1	8	5	1	3
224.8	3	2,200	1	17	1	1	2.5
171.6	3	2,000	0	16	4	0	2
216.8	3	2,200	1	15	1	1	2
192.6	6	2,200	0	14	1	0	2
236.4	5	2,200	1	20	3	1	2
172.4	3	2,200	1	23	3	0	2
251.4	3	1,900	1	12	2	1	2
246	6	2,300	1	7	3	1	3
147.4	6	1,700	0	12	1	0	2
176	4	2,200	1	15	1	1	2
228.4	3	2,300	1	17	5	1	1.5
166.5	3	1,600	0	19	3	0	2.5
189.4	4	2,200	1	24	1	1	2
312.1	7	2,400	1	13	3	1	3
289.8	6	2,000	1	21	3	1	3
269.9	5	2,200	0	11	4	1	2.5
154.3	2	2,000	1	13	2	0	2
222.1	2	2,100	1	9	5	1	2
209.7	5	2,200	0	13	2	1	2
190.9	3	2,200	0	18	3	1	2
254.3	4	2,500	0	15	3	1	2
207.5	3	2,100	0	10	2	0	2
209.7	4	2,200	0	19	2	1	2
294	2	2,100	1	13	2	1	2.5
176.3	2	2,000	0	17	3	0	2
294.3	7	2,400	1	8	4	1	2
224	3	1,900	0	6	1	1	2
125	2	1,900	1	18	4	0	1.5
236.8	4	2,600	0	17	5	1	2
164.1	4	2,300	1	19	4	0	2
217.8	3	2,500	1	12	3	0	2
192.2	2	2,400	1	16	2	0	2.5
125.9	2	2,400	1	28	1	0	1.5
220.9	2	2,300	0	12	1	1	2
294.5	6	2,700	1	15	3	1	2
244.6	2	2,300	1	9	2	1	2.5

Data Set 1 — Real Estate *(concluded)*

X_1	X_2	X_3	X_4	X_5	X_6	X_7	X_8
199	3	2,500	0	18	1	0	1.5
240	4	2,600	1	13	4	1	2
263.2	4	2,300	1	14	3	1	2
188.1	2	1,900	1	8	4	1	1.5
243.7	6	2,700	1	7	4	1	2
221.5	4	2,300	1	18	3	1	2
175	2	2,500	1	11	3	0	2
253.2	3	2,300	1	16	2	1	2
155.4	4	2,400	0	16	3	0	2
186.7	5	2,500	0	21	4	0	2.5
179	3	2,400	0	10	4	1	2
188.3	6	2,100	0	15	4	1	2
227.1	4	2,900	1	8	4	1	2
173.6	4	2,100	0	14	2	1	2.5
188.3	5	2,300	1	20	5	0	1.5
310.8	8	2,900	1	9	4	1	2
293.7	6	2,400	1	11	5	1	3
179	3	2,400	1	8	4	1	2
188.3	6	2,100	0	14	2	1	2.5
227.1	4	2,900	1	20	5	0	1.5
173.6	4	2,100	1	9	4	1	2
188.3	5	2,300	1	11	5	1	3

Appendix K

Data Set 2 — Major League Baseball

x_1 = Team
x_2 = League (American = 1, National = 0)
x_3 = Built (Year Stadium Was Built)
x_4 = Size (Stadium Capacity)
x_5 = Salary (Total 2000 Team Salary $ Mil)
x_6 = Attendance (Total 2000 Team Attendance)
x_7 = Wins (Number of Wins in 2000)
x_8 = ERA (Earned Run Average)
x_9 = Batting (Team Batting Average)
x_{10} = HR (Number of Home Runs for the Team)
x_{11} = Surface (Natural = 0, Artificial = 1)
x_{12} = Stolen (Stolen Bases)
x_{13} = Errors (Team Errors)
x_{14} = Year
x_{15} = Average (Average Player Salary)
x_{16} = Median (Median Player Salary)

	x_1	x_2	x_3	x_4	x_5	x_6	x_7
Row	**Team**	**League**	**Built**	**Size**	**Salary**	**Attendance**	**Wins**
1	Boston	1	1912	33,871	93.9	2,585,895	85
2	New York Yankees	1	1923	57,746	113.4	3,227,657	87
3	Oakland	1	1966	43,662	33.0	1,728,885	91
4	Baltimore	1	1992	48,262	59.2	3,297,031	74
5	Anaheim	1	1966	45,050	58.7	2,066,982	82
6	Cleveland	1	1994	43,368	78.7	3,456,278	90
7	Chicago	1	1991	44,321	36.9	1,947,799	95
8	Toronto	1	1989	50,516	54.6	1,819,919	83
9	Minnesota	1	1982	48,678	15.8	1,059,415	69
10	Tampa Bay	1	1990	44,027	55.2	1,479,782	69
11	Texas	1	1994	52,000	61.4	2,800,075	71
12	Detroit	1	2000	40,000	60.6	2,533,753	79
13	Seattle	1	1999	45,611	62.6	3,148,317	91
14	Kansas City	1	1973	40,529	24.5	1,677,915	77
15	Atlanta	0	1993	50,062	95.0	3,234,304	95
16	Arizona	0	1998	49,075	80.8	2,819,539	85
17	Houston	0	2000	42,000	52	3,056,139	72
18	Cincinnati	0	1970	52,953	35.1	2,577,371	85
19	New York Mets	0	1964	55,775	89.7	2,820,530	94
20	Pittsburgh	0	1970	47,972	31.9	1,748,908	69
21	Los Angeles	0	1962	56,000	94.2	3,011,539	86
22	San Diego	0	1967	53,166	54.7	2,423,149	76
23	Montreal	0	1976	46,500	28	926,272	67
24	San Francisco	0	1900	40,800	54.2	3,318,800	97
25	St. Louis	0	1966	49,625	72.4	3,336,493	95
26	Florida	0	1987	42,531	25.9	1,218,326	79
27	Philadelphia	0	1971	62,411	36.7	1,612,769	65
28	Milwaukee	0	1953	43,000	33.8	1,573,621	73
29	Chicago Cubs	0	1914	38,957	51.1	2,789,511	65
30	Colorado	0	1995	50,381	56	3,295,129	82

Data Set 2 — Major League Baseball *(c*

	x_1	x_7	x_8					
Row	**Team**	**Wins**	**ERA**					
1	Boston	85	4.23					
2	New York Yankees	87	4.76					
3	Oakland	91	4.58					
4	Baltimore	74	5.37					
5	Anaheim	82	5.00					
6	Cleveland	90	4.84					
7	Chicago	95	4.66					
8	Toronto	83	5.14	0.275	244	1	198	100
9	Minnesota	69	5.14	0.270	116	1	128	102
10	Tampa Bay	69	4.86	0.257	162	1	228	118
11	Texas	71	5.52	0.283	173	0	130	135
12	Detroit	79	4.71	0.275	177	0	110	105
13	Seattle	91	4.49	0.269	198	0	164	99
14	Kansas City	77	5.48	0.288	150	0	236	102
15	Atlanta	95	4.05	0.271	179	0	198	129
16	Arizona	85	4.35	0.265	179	0	204	107
17	Houston	72	5.42	0.278	249	0	222	133
18	Cincinnati	85	4.33	0.274	200	1	162	111
19	New York Mets	94	4.16	0.263	198	0	266	118
20	Pittsburgh	69	4.94	0.267	168	1	202	132
21	Los Angeles	86	4.10	0.257	211	0	212	135
22	San Diego	76	4.52	0.254	157	0	212	141
23	Montreal	67	5.13	0.266	178	1	246	132
24	San Francisco	97	4.21	0.278	226	0	194	93
25	St. Louis	95	4.38	0.270	235	0	138	111
26	Florida	79	4.59	0.262	160	0	208	125
27	Philadelphia	65	4.77	0.251	144	1	154	100
28	Milwaukee	73	4.63	0.246	177	0	172	118
29	Chicago Cubs	65	5.25	0.256	183	0	188	100
30	Colorado	82	5.26	0.294	161	0	204	94

— Major League Baseball *(concluded)*

	x_{14}	x_{15}	x_{16}
Row	Year	Average	Median
1	1976	52,300	*
2	1977	74,000	*
3	1978	97,800	*
4	1979	121,900	*
5	1980	146,500	*
6	1981	196,500	*
7	1982	245,000	*
8	1983	289,000	207,500
9	1984	325,900	229,750
10	1985	368,998	265,833
11	1986	410,517	275,000
12	1987	402,579	235,000
13	1988	430,688	235,000
14	1989	489,539	280,000
15	1990	589,483	350,000
16	1991	845,383	412,000
17	1992	1,012,424	392,500
18	1993	1,062,780	371,500
19	1994	1,154,486	450,000
20	1995	1,094,440	275,000
21	1996	1,101,455	300,000
22	1997	1,314,420	400,000
23	1998	1,384,530	427,500
24	1999	1,567,873	495,000
25	2000	1,983,849	700,000

Appendix L

Data Set 3 — OECD

x_1 = Country
x_2 = G7 Member (1 = Yes, 0 = No)
x_3 = Total area of country in thousand square kilometers
x_4 = Population in thousands
x_5 = Percent of population over 65 years of age
x_6 = Exchange rate per U.S. dollar
x_7 = Gross Domestic Product at current exchange rate in billions of dollars
x_8 = Energy use in millions of tons of oil equivalent
x_9 = Index of total manufacturing (1900 = 100)
x_{10} = Total labor force
x_{11} = Region (1 = Far East, 2 = Europe, 3 = North America)

x_1	x_2	x_3	x_4	x_5	x_6	x_7	x_8	x_9	x_{10}	x_{11}
Australia	0	7,687	18,289	12.1	1.509	390.9	100.61	109	9,184	1
Austria	0	84	8,060	15	12.51	228.7	27.19	111	3,876	2
Belgium	0	31	10,157	16.1	36.61	268.2	56.4	108	4,297	2
Canada	1	9,976	29,964	12.2	1.426	579.2	236.17	112	15,209	3
Czech Republic	0	79	10,316	13.4	34.73	56.2	40.4		5,175	2
Denmark	0	43	5,262	15.1	6.771	174.9	22.87	117	2,822	2
Finland	0	338	5,125	14.4	5.369	125.1	31.48	121	2,531	2
France	1	549	58,380	15.3	5.955	1,536.6	254.2	98	25,613	2
Germany	1	357	81,877	15.8	1.777	235.35	349.55	97	39,294	2
Greece	0	132	10,465	15.8	279.6	122.4	24.39	98	4,249	2
Hungary	0	93	10,193	14.2	201.3	44	25.47		4,048	2
Iceland	0	103	270	11.4	71.71	7.3	2.27		148	2
Ireland	0	70	3,621	11.5	0.687	70.7	11.96	175	1,494	2
Italy	1	301	57,473	15.8	1743	1,243.2	161.14	104	23,385	2
Japan	1	378	125,864	14.5	129.4	4,595.2	510.36	98	67,110	1
Korea	0	98	45,545	6.1	1477	484.8	162.87	163	21,188	1
Luxembourg	0	3	418	14.2		17	3.45	100	218	2
Mexico	0	1,973	96,582	4.8	8.123	329.4	141.38	118	34,325	3
Netherlands	0	41	15,494	13.3	2.004	396	75.8	109	7,516	2
New Zealand	0	269	3,640	11.6	1.689	65.9	16.3	119	1,797	1
Norway	0	324	4,370	15.9	7.25	157.8	23.15	115	2,246	2
Poland	0	313	38,618	11.3	3.532	134.4	108.41		17,203	2
Portugal	0	92	9,935	14.8	181.5	103.6	19.15	97	4,885	2
Spain	0	505	39,270	15.6	150.3	584.9	101.41	103	16,159	2
Sweden	0	450	8,901	17.3	7.785	251.7	52.57	121	4,310	2
Switzerland	0	41	7,085	14.9	1.44	294.3	25.62	103	3,967	2
Turkey	0	781	62,695	4.8	199,026	181.5	65.52	129	22,736	2
United Kingdom	1	245	58,782	15.7	0.603	1,153.4	234.72	102	28,552	2
United States	1	9,373	265,557	12.8	1	7,388.1	2,134.96	118	135,231	3

Appendix M

Data Set 4 — Northwest Ohio School Districts

x_1 = Name of district
x_2 = Number of students
x_3 = Mean family income in the district ($)
x_4 = Mean property value in the district ($)
x_5 = Percent of families receiving welfare
x_6 = Mean salary of classroom teachers ($)
x_7 = Amount spent per pupil ($)
x_8 = Mean daily attendance
x_9 = Percent passing 12th grade proficiency exam

x_1	x_2	x_3	x_4	x_5	x_6	x_7	x_8	x_9
Bluffton	1,132	24,487	62,678	1.8	31,221	2,130	95.7	85
Shawnee	2,472	29,777	130,910	2.6	34,860	2,570	94.7	73
Spencerville	1,026	23,161	51,645	5.4	30,155	2,262	95.5	68
Delphos	1,104	21,792	88,453	6.2	32,273	2,506	96.5	65
Elida	3,204	24,446	65,550	8.9	32,876	2,250	94.1	62
Lima	5,963	18,394	44,138	33.8	33,142	2,657	92.3	40
Northeastern	1,194	26,428	88,789	1.7	30,919	2,431	96.1	72
Ayersville	921	28,228	82,707	3.9	32,850	2,693	95.6	68
Defiance	3,046	23,812	56,333	11.2	34,750	2,438	94.2	63
Hicksville	990	22,448	56,411	7	34,224	2,351	95.7	59
Central	1,216	24,189	53,923	4.6	34,430	2,496	94.8	56
Berlin-Milan	1,593	25,223	76,878	4	32,166	2,564	96.1	77
Perkins	2,038	25,586	117,545	3.3	39,352	2,861	95.8	74
Huron	1,494	27,135	105,588	4.6	33,433	2,968	95.4	74
Margaretta	1,560	23,849	74,601	2.8	37,084	2,464	95.5	66
Sandusky	4,426	19,529	72,425	25.2	36,042	2,766	93	37
Kelleys Island	20	19,854	802,081	11.4	27,144	11,226	95	100
Pettisville	503	25,079	53,948	3.9	31,159	2,834	96.1	78
Wauseon	1,864	23,408	60,896	4.9	32,499	2,252	95.3	75
Evergreen	1,238	23,826	69,432	5.2	32,353	2,250	95	72
Archbold-Area	1,401	26,706	107,547	4.1	35,982	2,837	96.2	69
Pike-Delta-York	1,559	23,396	48,638	6.1	31,310	2,309	94.8	66
Gorham-Fayette	487	22,405	57,221	6.9	33,166	2,492	94.6	51
Swanton	1,725	24,596	69,320	6.3	33,690	2,615	94.9	50
Arlington	685	26,175	55,478	2.7	31,821	2,205	96.5	84
Vanlue	346	24,709	49,606	4.1	28,411	2,420	96.2	83
Liberty-Benton	954	28,718	77,503	1.5	30,330	2,063	96.7	78
Van Buren	840	28,964	151,992	1.8	33,447	2,584	96.4	75
Cory-Rawson	794	23,904	69,242	2.4	31,241	2,416	96.4	73
Arcadia	597	24,305	78,102	2.5	30,738	2,752	95.9	64
McComb	805	23,754	69,347	5.7	28,986	2,321	95.9	61
Findlay	5,758	24,269	92,648	7.6	35,879	2,860	94.9	60

Appendix M

Data Set 4 — Northwest Ohio School Districts *(continued)*

X_1	X_2	X_3	X_4	X_5	X_6	X_7	X_8	X_9
Ada	855	23,029	52,655	5.3	28,479	2,380	95.9	69
Kenton	2,228	20,418	61,155	13.8	30,907	2,512	93.7	54
Liberty Center	1,009	24,723	57,685	4.1	30,904	2,431	95.8	82
Patrick Henry	1,176	23,061	63,134	5.2	31,895	2,552	95.9	75
Napoleon Area	2,331	25,304	84,245	6.6	32,773	2,422	94.6	73
Holgate	605	23,962	49,709	6	31,324	2,454	94.9	71
Monroeville	686	22,942	63,103	4.3	30,838	2,474	95.8	64
Bellevue	2,276	24,025	66,912	6.9	32,164	2,374	95.1	55
Willard	2,300	23,304	58,832	14.3	35,042	2,347	94.6	53
Norwalk	2,650	21,551	72,266	12.2	37,145	2,384	94	50
Ottawa Hills	933	45,723	122,356	0.2	43,256	4,150	95.7	95
Anthony Wayne	3,178	29,215	88,004	3.1	35,617	2,844	95.3	75
Sylvania	7,822	32,114	101,503	3.8	39,684	2,943	95.5	72
Maumee	3,009	27,604	117,921	3.9	41,634	3,933	95	69
Oregon	3,594	24,525	123,599	8.7	35,848	2,941	94.7	52
Washington	7,154	23,507	102,485	11.8	39,155	2,997	93.7	51
Springfield	3,575	26,048	98,346	12.2	34,437	2,774	93.8	49
Toledo	36,790	21,079	62,668	42.8	36,190	2,611	90.7	28
Benton Carroll Salem	2,063	23,899	237,206	4.7	42,734	3,444	95.6	81
Danbury	635	21,325	182,360	3.2	34,971	3,158	95.3	65
Genoa	1,584	25,321	53,120	4.8	34,661	2,845	95.9	65
Port Clinton	2,238	20,941	129,961	10.5	39,542	2,926	94.5	50
Put-in-Bay	70	19,266	426,419	1.4	30,242	7,824	94.5	33
Paulding	1,993	22,677	46,163	8.6	32,928	2,560	94.5	59
Ottoville	610	24,128	46,582	0.2	26,125	2,588	99.8	86
Columbus Grove	866	23,562	55,568	8.4	30,476	2,174	96.2	84
Kalida	775	24,456	44,267	0.7	28,962	2,274	96.8	81
Continental	792	23,625	37,277	10	28,945	2,225	95.5	79
Ottawa-Glandorf	1,749	25,363	64,288	6.5	31,185	2,154	96.5	77
Pandora-Gilboa	632	23,806	55,446	1.2	27,693	2,078	96.5	67
Leipsic	748	20,941	62,648	16.1	30,282	2,811	93.9	47
Gibsonburg	983	23,312	46,098	17.8	31,244	2,242	94.4	71
Lakota	1,332	22,678	55,933	10.5	30,765	2,306	95.2	66
Fremont	5,156	22,327	74,874	16.2	37,759	2,616	94.7	57
Woodmore	1,141	26,460	90,484	10.9	32,296	2,227	96.5	56
Clyde–Green Springs	2,368	23,854	55,724	7	33,998	2,383	94.6	47
Bettsville	347	22,103	37,269	6.1	27,466	2,394	95.8	83
Seneca East	1,183	22,656	50,895	4.8	29,940	2,435	95.9	80
Old Fort	540	23,208	50,712	19.3	28,195	2,743	96	78
Hopewell-Loudon	870	22,103	72,201	4.7	30,644	2,564	94.6	74
New Riegel	459	23,314	41,376	2.7	29,099	2,501	97	73
Tiffin	3,632	21,246	65,291	9	35,513	2,506	94.7	67
Fostoria	2,742	20,809	62,268	20.4	34,241	2,455	92.7	34
Van Wert	2,504	22,728	67,932	7.1	33,885	2,511	95.3	61
Edon-Northwest	744	23,035	38,462	2.7	30,833	1,916	95.1	73
Milcreek–West Unity	788	21,302	40,239	3.2	31,582	2,382	95.9	71
Bryan	2,266	22,607	81,152	4.2	32,643	2,706	95.2	69
North Central	757	21,871	59,396	2.9	31,978	2,349	95.6	68

Appendix M

Data Set 4 — Northwest Ohio School Districts *(concluded)*

X_1	X_2	X_3	X_4	X_5	X_6	X_7	X_8	X_9
Montpelier	1,172	20,787	44,383	8.2	33,243	2,654	94.8	67
Edgerton	767	22,429	54,040	4.1	28,975	2,470	95.9	61
Stryker	579	24,084	65,532	3.4	33,855	2,617	95.7	47
Perrysburg	3,839	32,773	97,888	2.6	40,320	3,011	96.1	98
Elmwood	1,237	22,179	47,644	7.5	30,434	2,643	95.2	68
Bowling Green	3,534	21,307	84,682	7.5	37,983	2,849	94.7	68
Otsego	1,643	24,614	57,601	5	36,065	2,539	95.4	64
Northwood	1,091	25,905	77,077	7.9	35,536	2,979	94.9	61
Eastwood	1,739	25,043	67,929	4.7	35,742	2,499	95.9	60
Lake	1,665	23,559	95,859	6.2	38,046	2,820	95.2	55
Rossford	2,087	25,360	123,725	7.2	39,476	3,258	94.9	54
North Baltimore	839	22,075	58,383	10.6	29,579	2,331	94.5	50
Upper Sandusky	1,801	21,063	68,348	3.9	32,778	2,267	95.6	62
Carey	915	21,658	51,497	6	30,968	2,513	95.5	59

Appendix N

Banking Data Set — Case

x_1 = Account balance in \$
x_2 = Number of ATM transactions in the month
x_3 = Number of other bank services used
x_4 = Has a debit card (1 = yes, 0 = no)
x_5 = Receives interest on the account
x_6 = City where banking is done

x_1	x_2	x_3	x_4	x_5	x_6
1,756	13	4	0	1	2
748	9	2	1	0	1
1,501	10	1	0	0	1
1,831	10	4	0	1	3
1,622	14	6	0	1	4
1,886	17	3	0	1	1
740	6	3	0	0	3
1,593	10	8	1	0	1
1,169	6	4	0	0	4
2,125	18	6	0	0	2
1,554	12	6	1	0	3
1,474	12	7	1	0	1
1,913	6	5	0	0	1
1,218	10	3	1	0	1
1,006	12	4	0	0	1
2,215	20	3	1	0	4
137	7	2	0	0	3
167	5	4	0	0	4
343	7	2	0	0	1
2,557	20	7	1	0	4
2,276	15	4	1	0	3
1,494	11	2	0	1	1
2,144	17	3	0	0	3
1,995	10	7	0	0	2
1,053	8	4	1	0	3
1,526	8	4	0	1	2
1,120	8	6	1	0	3
1,838	7	5	1	1	3
1,746	11	2	0	0	2
1,616	10	4	1	1	2
1,958	6	2	1	0	2
634	2	7	1	0	4
580	4	1	0	0	1
1,320	4	5	1	0	1
1,675	6	7	1	0	2

Appendix N

Banking Data Set — Case *(concluded)*

X_1	X_2	X_3	X_4	X_5	X_6
789	8	4	0	0	4
1,735	12	7	0	1	3
1,784	11	5	0	0	1
1,326	16	8	0	0	3
2,051	14	4	1	0	4
1,044	7	5	1	0	1
1,885	10	6	1	1	2
1,790	11	4	0	1	3
765	4	3	0	0	4
1,645	6	9	0	1	4
32	2	0	0	0	3
1,266	11	7	0	0	4
890	7	1	0	1	1
2,204	14	5	0	0	2
2,409	16	8	0	0	2
1,338	14	4	1	0	2
2,076	12	5	1	0	2
1,708	13	3	1	0	1
2,138	18	5	0	1	4
2,375	12	4	0	0	2
1,455	9	5	1	1	3
1,487	8	4	1	0	4
1,125	6	4	1	0	2
1,989	12	3	0	1	2
2,156	14	5	1	0	2

Appendix O

MegaStat Quick Reference Guide

What Is MegaStat?

MegaStat is an Excel add-in that performs statistical analysis within an Excel workbook. After it is installed it appears on the Excel menu and works like **Edit, View,** or any of the other Excel options. MegaStat contains options to perform most of the calculations described in an introductory business statistics course.

When you click on **MegaStat** its main menu appears. Most of the options contain submenus. If the menu item is followed by the periods, i.e., ". . . ," clicking on that item will display a dialog box. If the menu item contains the symbol "►" additional submenu items are available. Below is the screen if you select **MegaStat** and then **Frequency Distributions.**

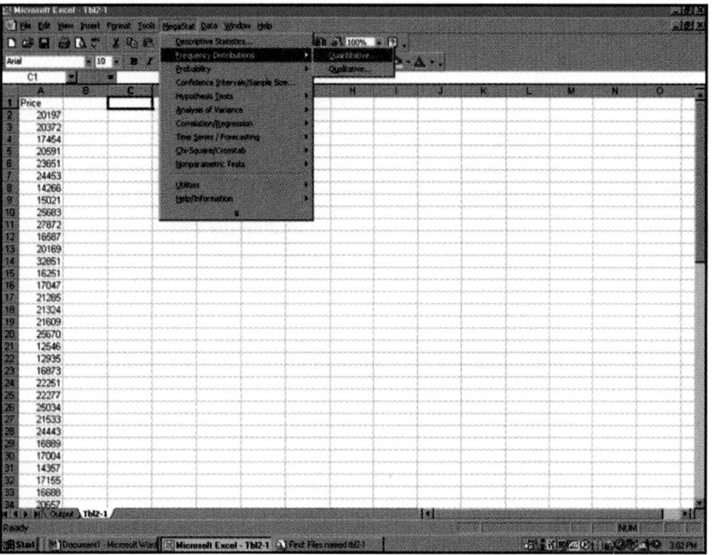

How MegaStat Works

Most MegaStat input is from dialog boxes. For example, if you selected **MegaStat, Frequency Distributions,** and **Quantitative** you will see the following dialog box. The dialog boxes allow you to specify the data cells for the procedure and to specify options. All dialog boxes have a **Help** button that will provide more information about the procedure. When the required information has been provided, click **OK** to perform the procedure.

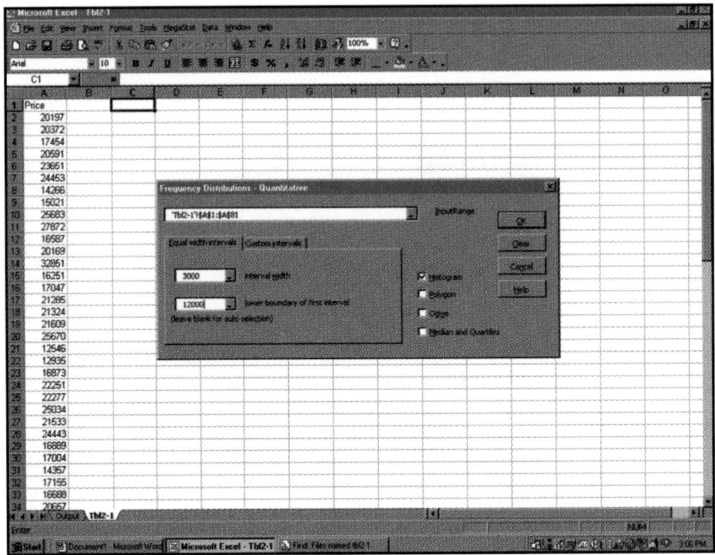

Most dialog boxes require you to specify the data for the procedure. This can be done in one of several ways:

1. Pointing and dragging with the mouse. This is the easiest and most common method.
2. Typing the name of the named data range.
3. Typing the range address.
4. Using **Ctrl, Shift,** and **Arrow** keystroke combinations.

For most procedures the first cell in each input range is the label. If the first cell in a range is text, it is considered a label, if it is a numeric value, it is considered data.

MegaStat Output

MegaStat output is placed in a worksheet titled "Output." If there is an existing Output sheet, the new output is placed at the end. The MegaStat output is in the standard Excel format, so you may insert, modify, or delete any cells. You can copy all or part of the output to another worksheet or to a word processing application.

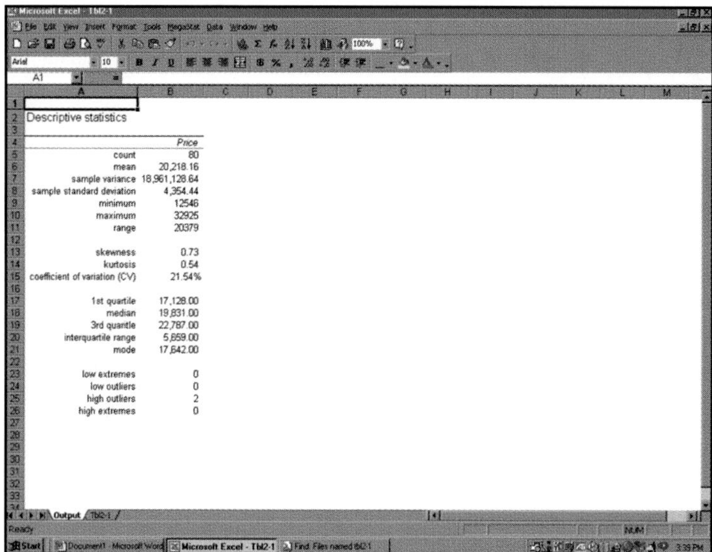

Help Is Always Available

Most of the dialog boxes are self-explanatory, but if you need more information, click on **Help** and browse the Help contents.

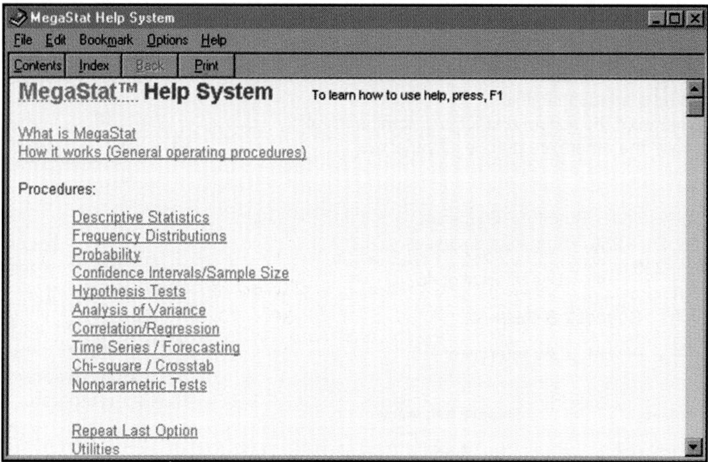

Answers

to Odd-Numbered Chapter Exercises

CHAPTER 1

1. a. Interval
   b. Ratio
   c. Interval
   d. Nominal
   e. Ordinal
   f. Ratio
3. Answers will vary.
5. Qualitative data is not numerical, whereas quantitative data is numerical. Examples will vary by student.
7. Nominal, ordinal, interval, and ratio. Examples will vary.
9. A categorization is exhaustive if every object appears in some category.
11. Based on these sample findings, we can infer that 270/300, or 90 percent, of the executives would move.
13. Discrete variables can assume only certain values, but continuous variables can assume any values within some range. Examples will vary.
15. Answers will vary.
17. a. Grass or artificial turf field is a qualitative variable, the others are quantitative.
    b. Grass or artificial turf field is a nominal level variable, the others are ratio level variables.
19. a. The name of the school district is a qualitative variable, the others are quantitative.
    b. The name of the school district is a nominal level variable, the others are ratio level variables.

CHAPTER 2

1. $2^5 = 32, 2^6 = 64$ Therefore, 6 classes.
3. $2^7 = 128, 2^8 = 256$ Suggests 8 classes.
   $i \geq \frac{567 - 235}{8} = 41$ Use interval of 45.
5. a. $2^4 = 16$ Suggests 5 classes.
   b. $i \geq \frac{31 - 25}{5} = 1$ Use interval of 1.5.
   c. 24
   d.

Patients	f	Relative frequency
24.0 up to 25.5	2	0.125
25.5 up to 27.0	4	0.250
27.0 up to 28.5	8	0.500
28.5 up to 30.0	0	0.000
30.0 up to 31.5	2	0.125
Total	16	1.000

   e. The largest concentration is in the 27 up to 28.5 class (8).
7. a.

Number of Shoppers	f
0 up to 3	9
3 up to 6	21
6 up to 9	13
9 up to 12	4
12 up to 15	3
15 up to 18	1
Total	51

   b. The largest group of shoppers (21) shop at Food Queen 3, 4 or 5 times during a two-week period. Some customers visit the store only 1 time during the two weeks, but others shop as many as 15 times.
   c.

Number of Visits	Percent of Total
0 up to 3	17.65
3 up to 6	41.18
6 up to 9	25.49
9 up to 12	7.84
12 up to 15	5.88
15 up to 18	1.96
Total	100.00

9. a. 620 to 629
   b. 5
   c. 621, 623, 623, 627, 629
11. a. 25
    b. One
    c. 38, 106
    d. 60, 61, 63, 63, 65, 65, 69
    e. No values.
    f. 9
    g. 9
    h. 76
    i. 16
13.

Stem	Leaves
0	5
1	28
2	
3	0024789
4	12366
5	2

There were a total of 16 subscribers studied. The number of calls ranged from 5 to 52 received. Seven of the 16 subscribers received between 30 and 39 calls.

15. a. Histogram
    b. 100
    c. 5
    d. 28
    e. 0.28
    f. 12.5
    g. 13
17. a. 50
    b. 1.5 days
    c. Using lower limits on the X-axis:

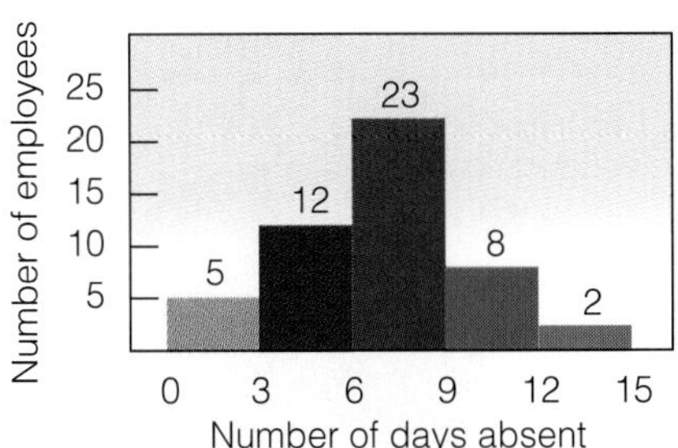

d. $X = 1.5$, $Y = 5$

e.

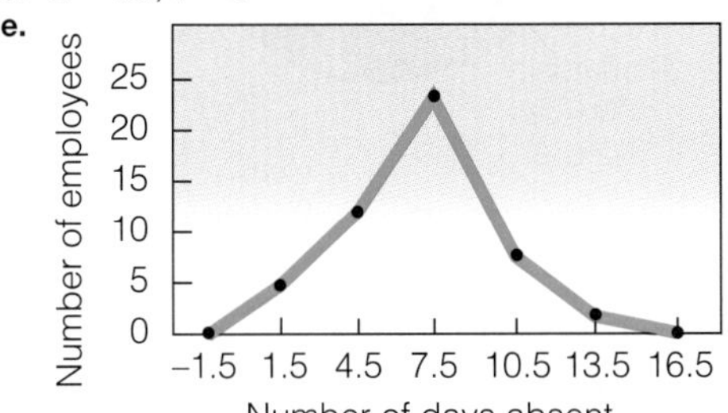

f. For the 50 employees about half were absent between 6 and 9 days. Five employees were absent less than 3 days, and two were absent 12 or more days.

19. **a.** 40
b. 5
c. 11 or 12
d. About $18/hr
e. About $9/hr
f. About 75%

21. **a.** 5, 17
b.

Days Absent	f	CF
0 up to 3	5	5
3 up to 6	12	17
6 up to 9	23	40
9 up to 12	8	48
12 up to 15	2	50

c.

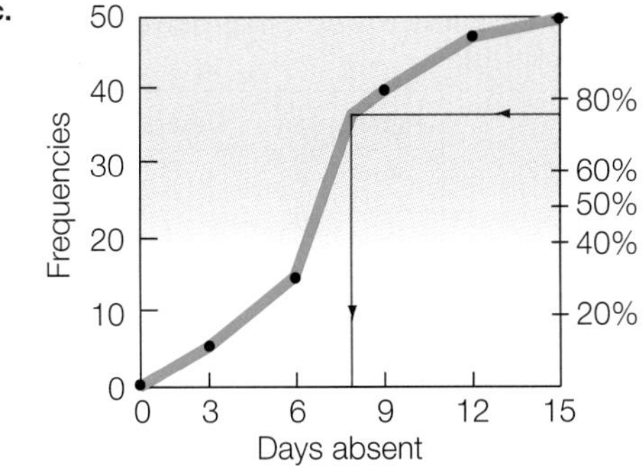

d. About 8.7 days

23. Maxwell Heating & Air Conditioning far exceeds the other corporations in sales. Mancell Electric & Plumbing and Mizelle Roofing & Sheet Metal are the two corporations with the least amount of fourth quarter sales.

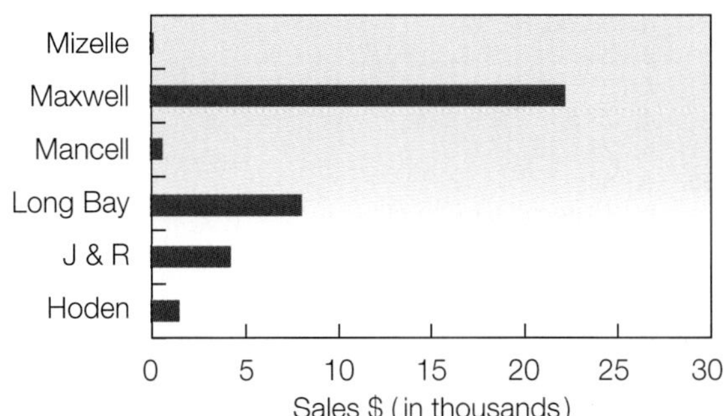

25. Homicides reached the highest number in 1993. They decreased steadily since 1993.

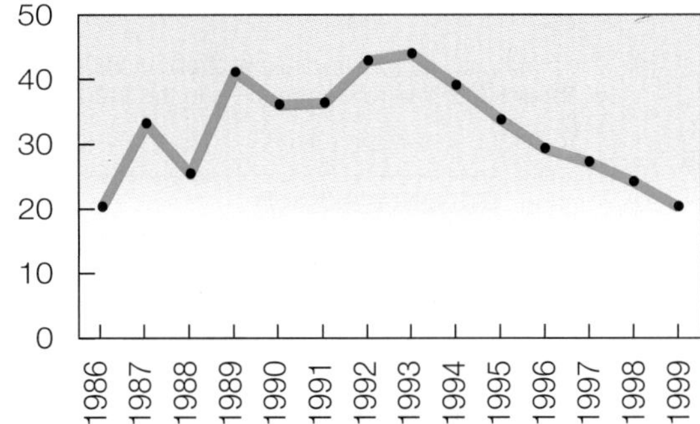

27. Population Growth in the United States

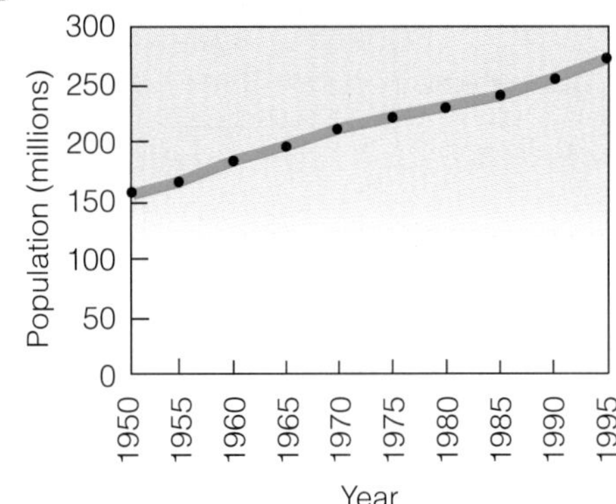

Population in the United States has increased steadily since 1950.

29. $2^6 = 64$ and $2^7 = 128$. Suggest 7 classes.

31. **a.** 5, because $2^4 = 16 < 25$ and $2^5 = 32 > 25$.
b. $i > \frac{48 - 16}{5} = 6.4$ Use interval of 7.
c. 15
d.

Class	Frequency	
15 up to 22	III	3
22 up to 29	~~IIII~~ III	8
29 up to 36	~~IIII~~ II	7
36 up to 43	~~IIII~~	5
43 up to 50	II	2
		25

e. It is fairly symmetrical, with most of the values between 22 and 36.

33. **a.** 70
b. one
c. 0, 145

d. 30, 30, 32, 39
e. 24
f. 21
g. 77.5
h. 25

35. a. 56
b. 10 (found by 60 − 50)
c. 55
d. 17

37. a. $36.60, found by ($265 − $82)/5.
b. $40.
c.

$ 80 up to $120	8
120 up to 160	19
160 up to 200	10
200 up to 240	6
240 up to 280	1
Total	44

d. The purchases ranged from a low of about $80 to a high of about $280. The concentration is in the $120 up to $160 class.

39.

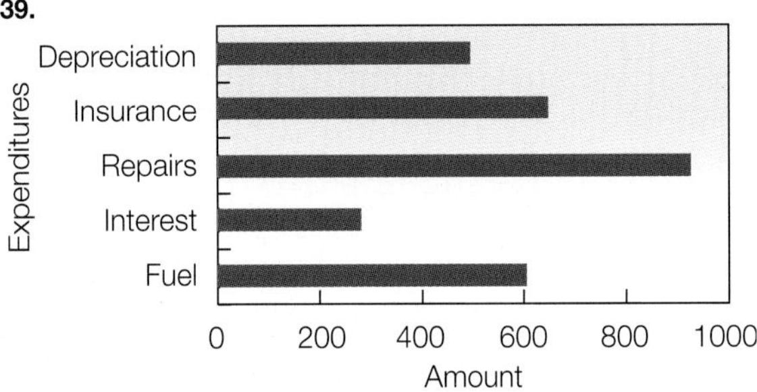

41. Unit = 0.10

3	76	149
3	77	
4	78	1
(2)	79	77
6	80	14
4	81	04
2	82	77

The lowest percent of on time is 76.1%, the largest is 82.7%. The typical airline is on time 79.7% of the time.

43. a. Since $2^6 = 64 < 70 < 128 = 2^7$, 7 classes are recommended. The interval should be at least $(1{,}002.2 - 3.3)/7 = 142.7$. Use 150 as a convenient value.
b.

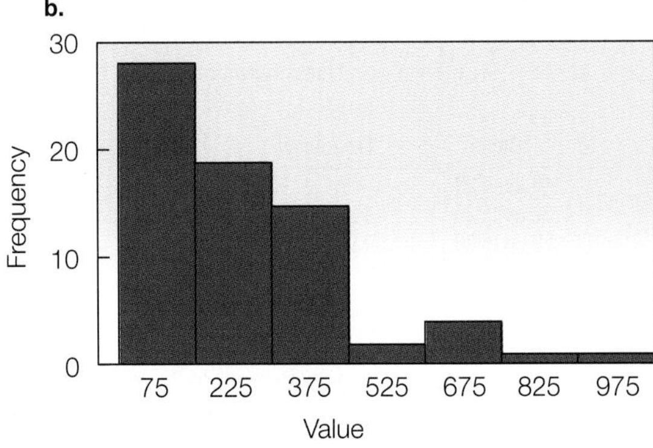

45.

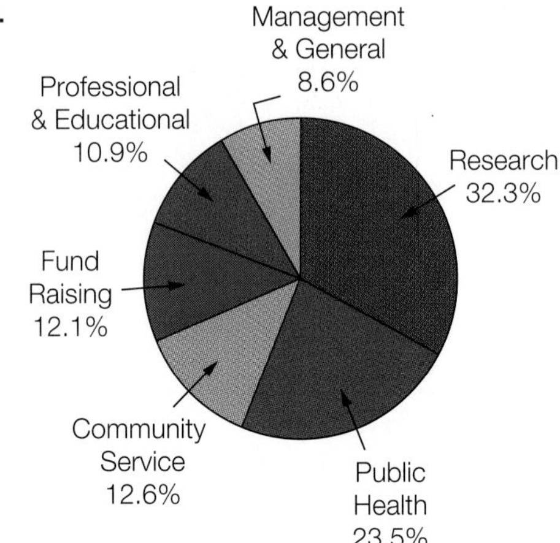

More than half of the expenses are concentrated in the categories Research and Public Health Education.

47.

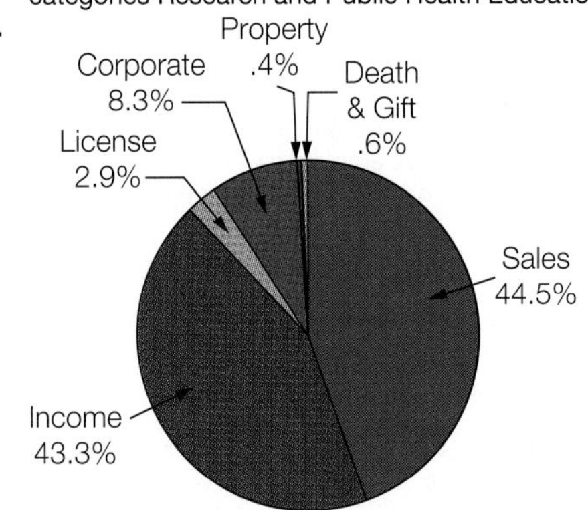

Sales tax and income tax dominate the total revenues for the state of Georgia.

49. There are 50 observations, so the recommended number of classes is 6. However, there are several states that have many more farms than the others, so it may be useful to have an open-ended class. One possible frequency distribution is:

Farms in USA	Frequency
0 up to 20	16
20 up to 40	13
40 up to 60	8
60 up to 80	6
80 up to 100	4
100 or more	3
Total	50

Twenty-nine of the 50 states, or 58 percent, have fewer than 40,000 farms. There are three states that have more than 100,000 farms.

51. In 1993 the price for a Toyota Camry and a Ford Taurus was about the same, a little more than $11,000 each. Since that time the price of both cars has increased, but the rate of increase of the Camry has been larger than the Taurus. The difference in the selling price between the two cars was the largest in 1999, about \$6,500. From 1999 to 2000 the selling price of the Camry decreased about \$500, the only price decrease for either car during the 9-year period.

53. Answers will vary depending on when you collect the data.

55. **a.** Since $2^4 = 16 < 30 < 32 = 2^5$, use 5 classes. The interval should be at least (113.4 − 15.8)/5 = 19.52. Use 20. The resulting frequency distribution is:

Class	f
15 up to 35	7
35 up to 55	8
55 up to 75	8
75 up to 95	5
95 up to 115	2

1. The typical team salary is 55. It ranges from 15.8 to 113.4.
2. The distribution is positively skewed. The higher salary teams are further from the center than the lower salary teams. The Yankees appear to be quite unusual.

b.

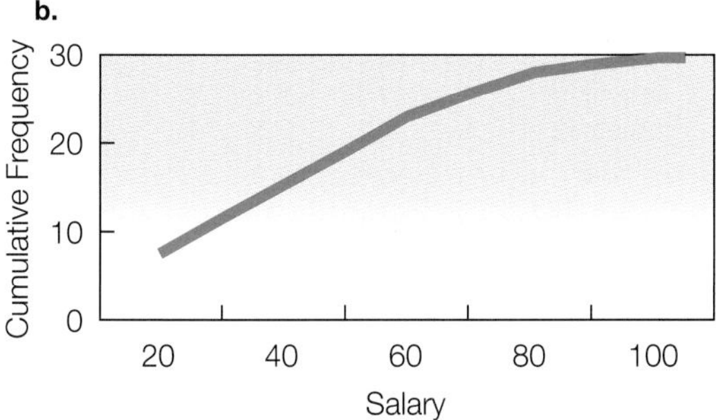

1. Forty percent of the teams have salaries less than \$53,000,000.
2. Ten teams pay less than \$50,000,000.
3. The lowest five teams pay less than \$32,000,000.

c. Use 5 classes here also. The interval should be at least (62,411 − 33,871)/5 = 5,708. Use 6,000 for convenience. The resulting frequency distribution is:

Class	f
33,000 up to 39,000	2
39,000 up to 45,000	10
45,000 up to 51,000	11
51,000 up to 57,000	5
57,000 up to 63,000	2

1. A typical stadium seats 47,000. The sizes cluster between 39,000 and 51,000.
2. The distribution is well balanced. No stadium is out of line with the others.

d. Use 5 classes here also. The interval should be at least (2,000 − 1,900)/5 = 20. Use 25 for convenience and to include extreme values. The resulting frequency distribution is below.

Class	f
1900 up to 1925	4
1925 up to 1950	0
1950 up to 1975	11
1975 up to 2000	13
2000 up to 2025	2

1. There are two clusters: 4 "old" stadiums built around 1910 and 26 "new" stadiums built around 1980.
2. The distribution is bimodal, or has two peaks. The four "old" stadiums are about 70 years older than the rest.

57. **a.** The salaries are in \$000.

1	26	1
4	27	146
11	28	1449999
14	29	059
29	30	122344677889999
40	31	11222335889
(12)	32	112234677889
42	33	112446889
33	34	22446789
25	35	05567889
17	36	001
14	37	0179
10	38	0
9	39	13456
4	40	3
3	41	6
2	42	7
1	43	2

a. The lowest salary(\$000) is \$26.1 and the largest is \$43.2.
b. A typical salary is about \$32.6.
c. Fourteen districts have salaries of less than \$30, so 80 have salaries of \$30.0 or more.
d. The teacher salaries (in \$000) ranged from a low of \$26.1 to a high of \$43.2. The typical salary is about \$32,000. There were 14 districts where the average salary was less than \$30,000 and 4 where the salary was more than \$40,000.

CHAPTER 3

1. $\mu = 5.4$, found by 27/5.

3. **a.** Mean = 7.0, found by 28/4.
b. (5 − 7) + (9 − 7) + (4 − 7) + (10 − 7) = 0

5. 14.58, found by 43.74/3.

7. **a.** 15.4, found by 154/10.
b. Population parameter, since it includes all the salespersons at Midtown Ford.

9. **a.** \$54.55, found by \$1,091/20.
b. A sample statistic—assuming that the power company serves more than 20 customers.

11. \$22.91, found by $\dfrac{300(\$20) + 400(\$25) + 400(\$23)}{300 + 400 + 400}$.

13. \$11.50, found by (\$400 + \$500 + \$1,400)/200 = \$2,300/200.

15. **a.** No mode
b. The given value would be the mode.
c. 3 and 4 bimodal.

17. Median = 5, Mode = 5

19. **a.** Median = 2.9
b. 2.9

21. 11.18, found by $\sqrt[5]{(8)(12)(14)(26)(5)}$.

23. 12.16, found by $\sqrt[5]{(9.4)(13.8)(11.7)(11.9)(14.7)}$.

25. 10.33%, found by $\sqrt[13]{\dfrac{14.0}{3.9}} - 1$.

27. 10.76%, found by $\sqrt[5]{\dfrac{70}{42}} - 1$.

29. Because the exact values in a frequency distribution are not known, the midpoint of the class is used for every member of that class.

31.

Class	f	X	fX
20 up to 30	7	25	175
30 up to 40	12	35	420
40 up to 50	21	45	945
50 up to 60	18	55	990
60 up to 70	12	65	780
	70		3,310

$$\bar{X} = \frac{3{,}310}{70} = 47.2857$$

33.

Age	f	X	fX
20 up to 30	1	25	25
30 up to 40	15	35	525
40 up to 50	22	45	990
50 up to 60	8	55	440
60 up to 70	4	65	260
	50		2,240

$$\bar{X} = \frac{2{,}240}{50} = 44.8$$

35.

Class	f	CF
0 up to 5	2	2
5 up to 10	7	9
10 up to 15	12	21
15 up to 20	6	27
20 up to 25	3	30
	30	

$$\text{Median} = 10 + \frac{\frac{30}{2} - 9}{12}(5) = 12.5$$

Mode = 12.5

37.

Amount	f	CF
\$ 0 up to \$ 2,000	4	4
\$ 2,000 up to \$ 4,000	15	19
\$ 4,000 up to \$ 6,000	18	37
\$ 6,000 up to \$ 8,000	10	47
\$ 8,000 up to \$10,000	4	51
\$10,000 up to \$12,000	3	54

a. $\text{Median} = \$4{,}000 + \frac{\frac{54}{2} - 19}{18}(\$2{,}000)$

$= \$4{,}889$

b. Mode = \$5,000

39. 13.95, found by $10 + \frac{(50 - 40)}{38}(15)$.

41. **a.** Mean = 5, found by (6 + 4 + 3 + 7 + 5)/5. Median is 5, found by rearranging the values and selecting the middle value.

b. Population, because all partners were included.

c. $\Sigma(X - \mu) = (6 - 5) + (4 - 5) + (3 - 5) + (7 - 5) + (5 - 5) = 0$.

43. $\bar{X} = \frac{545}{16} = 34.06$

Median = 37.50

45. 370.08, found by 18,504/50.

47. $\bar{X}_w = \frac{\$5(270) + \$6.50(300) + \$8.00(100)}{270 + 300 + 100} = \$6.12$

49. $\bar{X}_w = \frac{[15{,}300(4.5) + 10{,}400(3.0) + 150{,}600(10.2)]}{176{,}300}$

$= 9.28$

51. 3.38%, found by (3.25 + 3.51)/2.

53. Earthquake mean size = 7.0, found by 168.2/24.

Median size = 7.05.

Earthquake deaths: mean = 5,607.79; median = 1,100.

Mean for the size and the median for deaths because of all the extreme values listed.

55. 61.68%

57. 83.215%

59.

Monthly Mortgage	f	X	fX	CF
\$ 100 up to \$ 500	1	300	300	1
500 up to 900	9	700	6,300	10
900 up to 1,300	11	1,100	12,100	21
1,300 up to 1,700	23	1,500	34,500	44
1,700 up to 2,100	11	1,900	20,900	55
2,100 up to 2,500	4	2,300	9,200	59
2,500 up to 2,900	1	2,700	2,700	60
	60		86,000	

a. $\bar{X} = \frac{\$86{,}000}{60} = \$1{,}433.33$

b. $\text{Median} = \$1{,}300 + \frac{30 - 21}{23}(\$400) = \$1{,}456.52$

61.

Days Missed	f	X	fX	CF
0 up to 3	17	1.5	25.5	17
3 up to 6	13	4.5	58.5	30
6 up to 9	7	7.5	52.5	37
9 up to 12	3	10.5	31.5	40
Total	40		168.0	

a. $\bar{X} = \frac{168}{40} = 4.2$

b. $\text{Median} = 3.0 + \frac{(20 - 17)}{13}(3) = 3.69$

63.

Cost	f	X	fX	CF
\$100 up to \$200	1	150	150	1
200 up to 300	9	250	2,250	10
300 up to 400	20	350	7,000	30
400 up to 500	15	450	6,750	45
500 up to 600	5	550	2,750	50
Total	50		18,900	

a. $\frac{\$18{,}900}{50} = \$378$

b. $\$300 + \frac{(25 - 10)(100)}{20} = \$375$

65. Answers will vary. The paragraph should discuss issues such as: The average is higher for part-time nurses compared to full-time nurses. This may be because there are not as many part-time nurses. Therefore, when you calculate the mean it will be higher. Also, as the number of beds increases, the average hourly wage increases. Again this could be because there are not many hospitals with 500 or more beds. On the other hand, the lowest average is the hospital located in the rural setting. The type of hospital dictates the average. The private, non-profit hospital has a greater hourly wage compared to the public hospital.

67. Answers will vary.

69. **a.** $\bar{X} = \$221.1$, and the median is \$213.57 (answers in 000). Either measure is acceptable.

b. $\bar{X} = 3.8$, median = 4.

c. $\bar{X} = 2.08$, median = 2.

d. $\bar{X} = 14.6$ miles, and the median is 15.0 miles

71. **a.** The mean for the employment variable is 17,544, and the median is 5,175. Since every value is different, there is no mode. The distribution is quite skewed. Thus, the median is most representative.

b. The mean for the over 65 variable is 13.3, the median is 14.4, and the mode is 15.8. Again there is enough skewness that the median is most representative.

CHAPTER 4

1. **a.** 7, found by 10 − 3.
b. 6, found by 30/5.
c. 2.4, found by 12/5.
d. The difference between the highest number sold (10) and the smallest number sold (3) is 7. On average, the number of service reps on duty deviates by 2.4 from the mean of 6.

3. **a.** 30, found by 54 − 24.
b. 38, found by 380/10.
c. 7.2, found by 72/10.
d. The difference of 54 and 24 is 30. On average, the number of minutes required to install a door deviates 7.2 minutes from the mean of 38 minutes.

5. **a.** 15, found by 41 − 26.
b. 33.9, found by 339/10.
c. 4.12, found by 41.2/10.
d. The ratings deviate 4.12 from the mean of 33.9 on average.

7. **a.** 5
b. 4.4, found by

$$\frac{(8-5)^2+(3-5)^2+(7-5)^2+(3-5)^2+(4-5)^2}{5}.$$

9. **a.** \$2.77
b. 1.26, found by

$$\frac{(2.68-2.77)^2+(1.03-2.77)^2+(2.26-2.77)^2+(4.30-2.77)^2+(3.58-2.77)^2}{5}.$$

11. **a.** Range: 7.3, found by 11.6 − 4.3. Arithmetic mean: 6.94, found by 34.7/5. Variance: 6.5944, found by 32.972/5. Standard deviation: 2.568, found by $\sqrt{6.5944}$.
b. Dennis has a higher mean return (11.76 > 6.94). However, Dennis has greater spread in their returns on equity (16.89 > 6.59).

13. **a.** $\bar{X} = 4$

$$s^2 = \frac{(7-4)^2+\cdots+(3-4)^2}{5-1} = 5.5$$

b. $$s^2 = \frac{102 - \frac{(20)^2}{5}}{5-1} = 5.50$$

c. $s = 2.3452$

15. **a.** $\bar{X} = 38$

$$s^2 = \frac{(28-38)^2+\cdots+(42-38)^2}{10-1} = 82.6667$$

b. $$s^2 = \frac{15{,}184 - \frac{(380)^2}{10}}{10-1} = 82.6667$$

c. $s = 9.0921$

17. **a.** $\bar{X} = 124$

$$s^2 = \frac{(124-124)^2+\cdots+(121-124)^2}{10-1} = 4.6667$$

b. $$s^2 = \frac{153{,}802 - \frac{(1240)^2}{10}}{10-1} = 4.6667$$

c. $s = \sqrt{4.6667} = 2.1602$

19. **a.** 25, found by 25 − 0.
b. 5.331, found by

$$\sqrt{\frac{5{,}637.50 - \frac{(380)^2}{30}}{30-1}}.$$

c. 28.42, found by 5.331^2.

21. **a.** 12 minutes, found by 14 − 2.
b. 2.5959 minutes, found by:

$$\sqrt{\frac{2{,}594 - \frac{(312)^2}{42}}{42-1}}.$$

c. 6.7387, found by $(2.5959)^2$.

23. About 69%, found by $1 - 1/(1.8)^2$.

25. **a.** About 95%.
b. 47.5%, 2.5%.

27. 8.06%, found by (.25/3.10)(100).

29. **a.** Because the two series are in different units of measurement.
b. P.E. ratio is 16.51%. ROI 20.8%. Less spread in the P.E. ratios.

31. **a.** The mean is 30.8, found by 154/5. The median is 31.0, and the standard deviation is 3.96, found by

$$\sqrt{\frac{4{,}806 - \frac{154^2}{5}}{4}}.$$

b. −0.15, found by $\frac{3(30.8-31.0)}{3.96}$.

c.

Salary	$\frac{(X-\bar{X})}{s}$	$\left(\frac{(X-\bar{X})}{s}\right)^3$
36	1.313131	2.264250504
26	−1.21212	−1.780894343
33	0.555556	0.171467764
28	−0.70707	−0.353499282
31	0.050505	0.000128826
		0.301453469

0.125, found by $[5/(4 \times 3)] \times 0.301$.

33. **a.** The mean is 21.93, found by 328.9/15. The median is 15.8, and the standard deviation is 21.18, found by

$$\sqrt{\frac{13{,}494.676 - \frac{328.9^2}{15}}{14}}.$$

b. 0.868, found by [3(21.93 − 15.8)]/21.18.
c. 2.444, found by $[15/(14 \times 13)] \times 29.658$.

35. Median = 53, found by $(11+1)(\frac{1}{2}) \therefore$ 6 value in from lowest.
$Q_1 = 49$, found by $(11+1)(\frac{1}{4}) \therefore$ 3 value in from lowest.
$Q_3 = 55$, found by $(11+1)(\frac{3}{4}) \therefore$ 9 value in from lowest.

37. **a.** $Q_1 = 33.25$, $Q_3 = 50.25$
b. $D_2 = 27.8$, $D_8 = 52.6$
c. $P_{67} = 47$

39. **a.** 350
b. $Q_1 = 175$, $Q_3 = 930$
c. 930 − 175 = 755
d. Less than 0, or more than about 2060.
e. There are no outliers.
f. The distribution is positively skewed.

41.

The distribution is somewhat positively skewed. Note that the dashed line above 35 is longer than below 18.

43. Line 2

45. 239.2 and 240.8

47. 239.9, 240.1

49. 1.60%, found by $\frac{3.9}{242.9}(100)$.

51. 9, found by 3^2.

53. Negatively skewed. The mean is smaller than the median. The longer tail is to the left.

55. **a.** 55, found by 72 − 17.
b. 14.4, found by 144/10, where $\bar{X} = 43.2$.
c. 17.6245.

57. **a.** Population.
b. 183.47.
c. 94.92%.

59. Range is 25 − 0 = 25.

$$s = \sqrt{\frac{13{,}637.50 - \frac{(910)^2}{70}}{69}} = 5.118$$

61. $Q_1 = 44.25$, $Q_3 = 68.5$, and the median is 55.50. The distribution is approximately symmetric. The box plot is as follows.

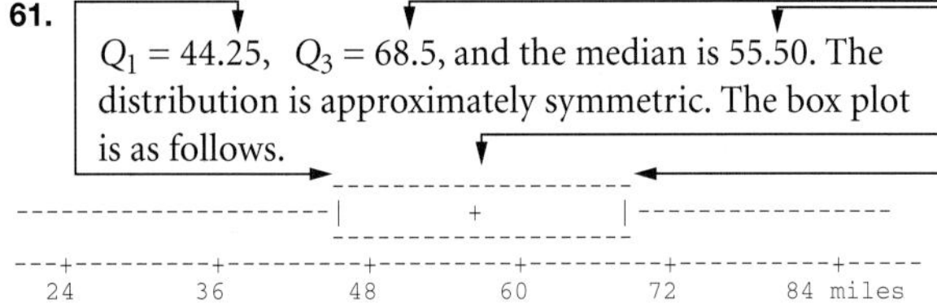

The above results are found using MINITAB.

63. The distribution is positively skewed. The first quartile is approx. \$20 and the third quartile is approx. \$90. There is one outlier located at \$255. The median is about \$50.

65. **a.** −18.6434, 78.76104, found by 30.05882 ± 2(24.35111).
b. 81%, found by $\frac{24.35111}{30.05882}(100)$.
The standard deviation is 81% of the mean.
c. Positive skewness because the mean is greater than the median.

67. **a.** $\bar{X} = \frac{857.90}{50} = 17.158$, median = 16.35

b. $s = \sqrt{\frac{20{,}206.73 - \frac{(857.90)^2}{50}}{50 - 1}} = 10.58$

c. 17.158 ± (1.5)(10.58) = 1.288 up to 33.028
d. 17.158 ± (2)(10.58) = 17.158 ± 21.16 = −4.002, 38.318
e. $CV = \frac{10.58}{17.158}(100) = 61.66\%$
f. $sk = \frac{3(17.158 - 16.35)}{10.58} = 0.23$
g. $L_{25} = (50 + 1)\frac{25}{100} = 12.75 \qquad Q_1 = 7.825$

$L_{75} = (50 + 1)\frac{75}{100} = 38.25 \qquad Q_3 = 27.400$

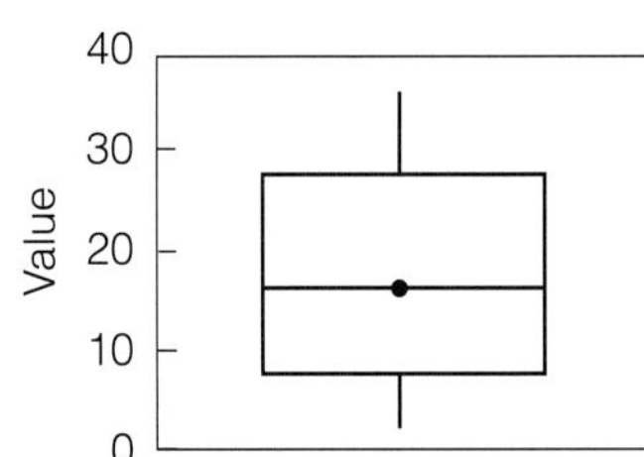

h. The distribution is nearly symmetrical. The mean is 17.158, the median is 16.35 and the standard deviation is 10.58. About 75 percent of the companies have a value less than 27.4, and 25 percent have a value less than 7.825.

69. **a.** The mean is 173.77 hours, found by 2,259/13. The median is 195 hours.

$s = 105.61$ hours, found by $\sqrt{\frac{526{,}391 - \frac{2{,}259^2}{13}}{12}}$.

b. $CV = 60.78\%$, found by $\frac{105.61}{173.77}(100)$.
Coefficient of skewness is −0.697.
c. $L_{45} = 14 \times .45 = 6.3$. So the 45th percentile is 192 + 0.3(195 − 192) = 192.9.
$L_{82} = 14 \times .82 = 11.48$. So the 82nd percentile is 260 + 0.48(295 − 260) = 276.8.
d.

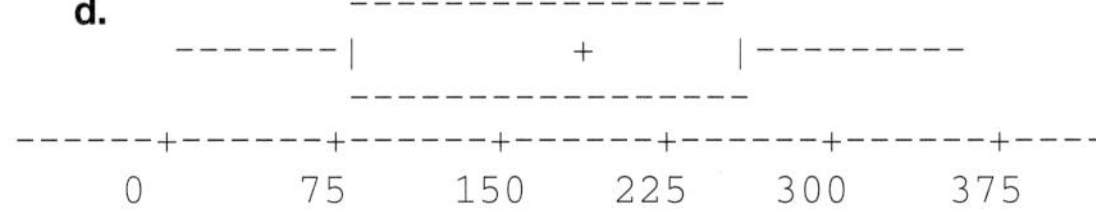

There is a slight negative skewness visible, but no outliers.

71. **a.** A software package gave the output:

```
Variable N   Mean     Median  TrMean  StDev   SE Mean
Pop      50  5913436  4008479 4891780 6624974 936913

Variable   Minimum   Maximum    Q1        Q3
Pop        479602    33145121   1562781   7067381
```

b. $L_{15} = 51 \times 0.15 = 7.65$. So the 15th percentile is 882,779 + 0.65 (990,819 − 882,779) = 953,005.
$L_{90} = 51 \times 0.90 = 45.9$. So the 90th percentile is 12,128,370 + 0.9 (15,111,244 − 12,128,370) = 14,812,957.
c. The coefficient of skewness is 2.32984, which indicates a long tail in the positive direction.
d.

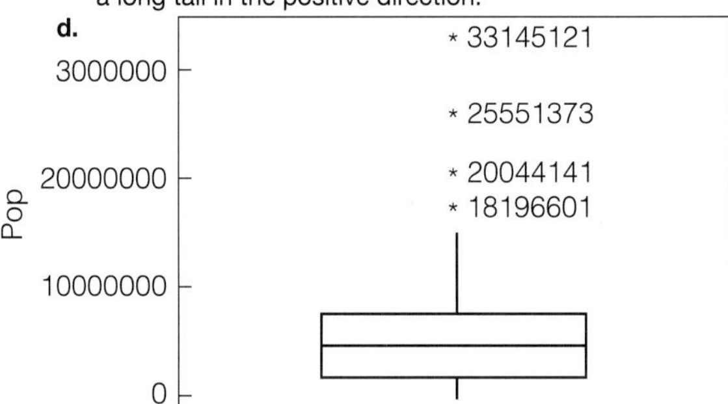

The plot shows four states (California, Arkansas, Texas, and New York) with populations much greater than the others. Perhaps the data for Arkansas has been typed incorrectly.

73. **a.**

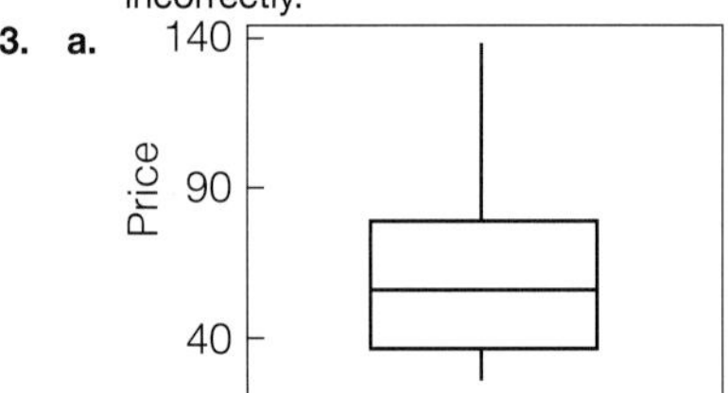

The distribution is positively skewed. The first quartile is near 37; the third quartile about 79; and the median near 57. There don't appear to be any outliers.
b. The standard deviation is 29.52, which is 47 percent of the mean. So there is a relatively large amount of variation.
c. Answers will vary.

75. **a.** :

Descriptive Statistics: Salary

Variable	N	Mean	Median	TrMean	StDev	SE Mean
Salary	30	56.67	54.95	55.82	24.54	4.48

Variable	Minimum	Maximum	Q1	Q3
Salary	15.80	113.40	34.78	73.98

2. The coefficient of skewness is 0.470, which indicates a positive tail.

3.

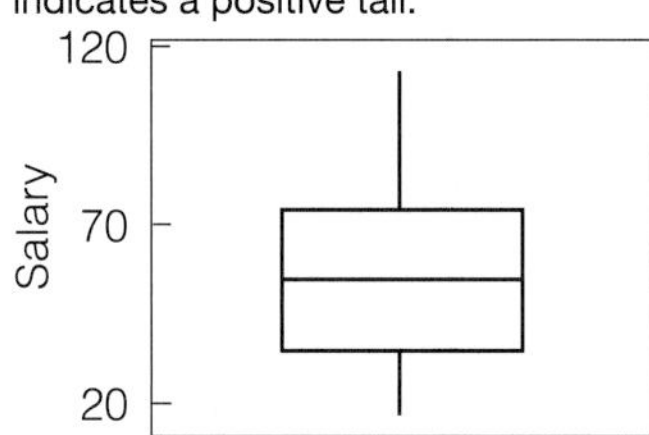

There are no outliers. The first quartile is about 35 and the third about 75.

4. The distribution is centered at 55 with most values within 20 on either side. However, there are a few positive values that are much further away from the mean.

b. **1.** A software package gave the output:

Descriptive Statistics: age (2001-built)

Variable	N	Mean	Median	TrMean	StDev	SE Mean
Age	30	29.10	26.50	26.19	27.44	5.01

Variable	Minimum	Maximum	Q1	Q3
Age	1.00	101.00	7.75	35.50

2. The coefficient of skewness is 1.342, which indicates a very long positive tail.

3.

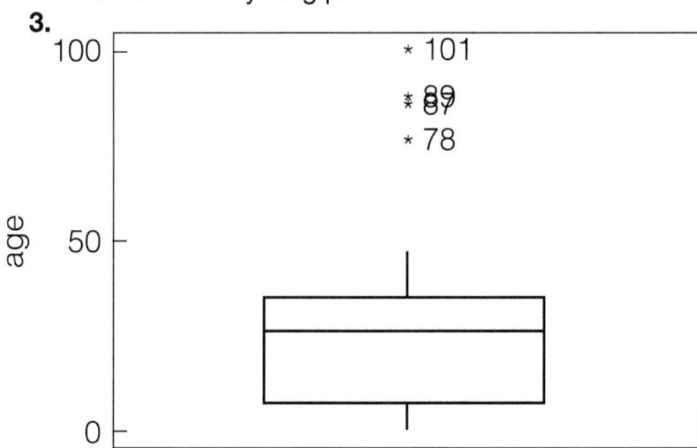

There are four outliers between 78 and 101 years old. The first quartile is about 8, the third about 35.

4. The distribution is centered about 20 years with most ages within 15 years of that value. However, there are a few very old stadiums.

77. **a.** **1.** A software package gave the output:

Descriptive Statistics: Salary

Variable	N	Mean	Median	TrMean	StDev	SE Mean
Salary	94	33181	32708	33033	3549	366

Variable	Minimum	Maximum	Q1	Q3
Salary	26125	43256	30816	35519

2. The coefficient of skewness is 0.670, which indicates a slight positive tail.

3.

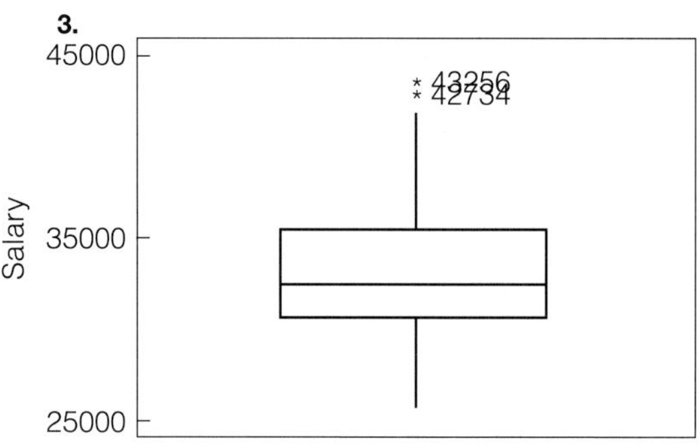

There are two salaries which are unusually high. The first quartile is about 30,000, the third about 35,000.

4. The distribution is symmetric around $33,000, and most values are within $2,500 of the center.

b. **1.** A software package gave the output:

Descriptive Statistics: Students

Variable	N	Mean	Median	TrMean	StDev	SE Mean
Students	94	2134	1227	1618	3895	402

Variable	Minimum	Maximum	Q1	Q3
Students	20	36790	794	2282

2. The coefficient of skewness is 7.802, which indicates a very long positive tail.

3.

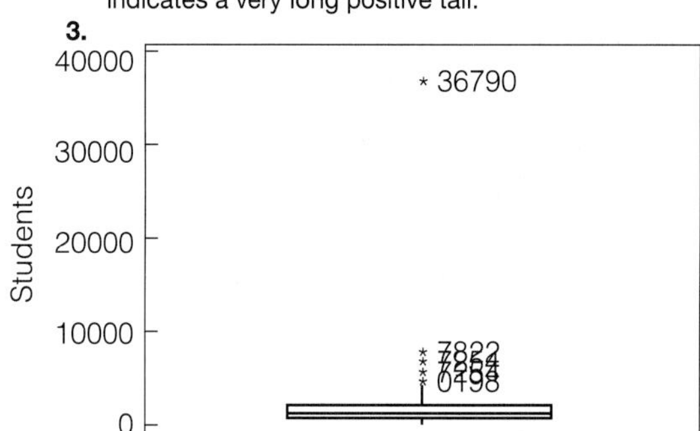

There are several outliers on the high or positive side, including one at 36,790! The first quartile is about 1,000; the third, about 2,000.

4. The distribution is positively skewed, as six schools have more than 5,000 students. However, most schools have between 1,000 and 2,000 students.

CHAPTER 5

1.

	Person	
Outcome	**1**	**2**
1	A	A
2	A	F
3	F	A
4	F	F

3. **a.** .176, found by $\frac{6}{34}$.

b. Empirical.

5. **a.** The experiment is asking the 500 citizens whether they favor or oppose widening Indiana Avenue to three lanes.

b. Possible outcomes include 321 favor the widening, 387 favor the widening, 444 favor the widening, and so on.

- **c.** Answers will vary, but two possibilities are: a majority favor the widening, which would be 251 or more, and more than 300 favor the widening.

7. **a.** Empirical.
b. Classical.
c. Classical.
d. Empirical, based on seismological data.

9. **a.** 13/52 = .25
b. 1/52 = .019
c. Classical.

11. **a.** The survey of 40 people about environmental issues.
b. 26 or more respond yes, for example.
c. 10/40 = .25
d. Empirical.
e. The events are not equally likely, but they are mutually exclusive.

13. **a.** Answers will vary. Here are some possibilities: 123, 124, 125, 999.
b. $(1/10)^3$
c. Classical.

15. $P(A \text{ or } B) = P(A) + P(B) = .30 + .20 = .50$
$P(\text{neither}) = 1 - .50 = .50$.

17. **a.** 102/200 = .51
b. .49, found by 61/200 + 37/200 = .305 + .185. Special rule of addition.

19. **a.** 80%, found by 50% + 30%.
b. 80%, found by 100% − 20%.

21. Events *A* and *C*; *B* and *C* are mutually exclusive. Events *B* and *C* are complements.

23. $P(A \text{ or } B) = P(A) + P(B) - P(A \text{ and } B) = .20 + .30 - .15 = .35$

25. When two events are mutually exclusive, it means that if one occurs the other event cannot occur. Therefore, the probability of their joint occurrence is zero.

27. **a.** .65, found by .35 + .40 − .10.
b. A joint probability.
c. No, an executive might read more than one magazine.

29. $P(A \text{ and } B) = P(A) \times P(B|A) = .40 \times .30 = .12$

31. .90, found by (.80 + .60) − .5.
.10, found by (1 − .90).

33. **a.** $P(A_1) = 3/10 = .30$
b. $P(B_1|A_2) = 1/3 = .33$
c. $P(B_2 \text{ and } A_3) = 1/10 = .10$

35. **a.** A contingency table.
b. .27, found by 300/500 × 135/300.
c. The tree diagram would appear as:

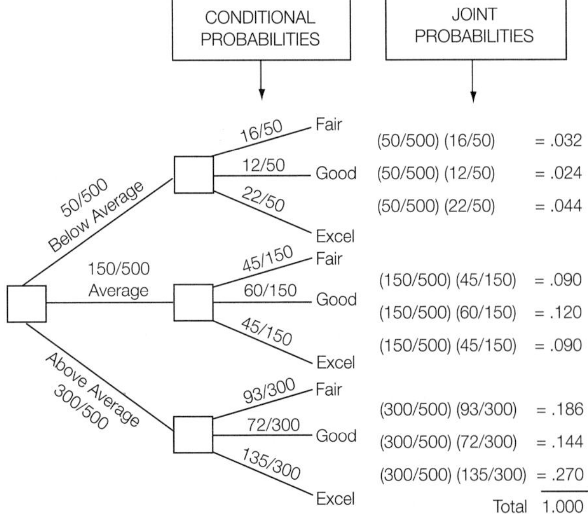

37. Probability the first presentation wins = 3/5 = .60.
Probability the second presentation wins = 2/5 (3/4) = .30.
Probability the third presentation wins = (2/5)(1/4)(3/3) = .10.

39.
$$P(A_1 \mid B_1) = \frac{P(A_1) \times P(B_1 \mid A_1)}{P(A_1) \times P(B_1 \mid A_1) + P(A_2) \times P(B_1 \mid A_2)} = \frac{.60 \times .05}{(.60 \times .05) + (.40 \times .10)} = .4286$$

41.
$$P(\text{night}|\text{win}) = \frac{P(\text{night})P(\text{win}|\text{night})}{P(\text{night})P(\text{win}|\text{night}) + P(\text{day})P(\text{win}|\text{day})} = \frac{(.70)(.50)}{[(.70)(.50)] + [(.30)(.90)]} = .5645$$

43.
$$P(\text{cash})| > \$50) = \frac{P(\text{cash})\ P(> \$50|\text{cash})}{P(\text{cash})\ P(> \$50|\text{cash}) + P(\text{check})\ P(> \$50|\text{check}) + P(\text{charge})\ P(> \$50|\text{charge})} = \frac{(.30)(.20)}{(.30)(.20) + (.30)(.90) + (.40)(.60)} = .1053$$

45. **a.** 78,960,960
b. 840, found by (7)(6)(5)(4). That is 7!/3!.
c. 10, found by 5!/3!2!.

47. 210, found by (10)(9)(8)(7)/(4)(3)(2).

49. 120, found by 5!.

51. 10,897,286,400, found by
${}_{15}P_{10} = (15)(14)(13)(12)\ (11)(10)(9)(8)(7)(6)$.

53. **a.** Asking teenagers to compare their reactions to a newly developed soft drink.
b. Answers will vary. One possibility is more than half of the respondents like it.

55. Subjective.

57. 3/6 or 1/2, found by 1/6 + 1/6 + 1/6. Classical.

59. **a.** The likelihood an event will occur, assuming that another event has already occurred.
b. The collection of one or more outcomes of an experiment.
c. A measure of the likelihood that two or more events will happen concurrently.

61. **a.** .8145, found by $(.95)^4$.
b. Special rule of multiplication.
c. $P(A \text{ and } B \text{ and } C \text{ and } D) = P(A) \times P(B) \times P(C) \times P(D)$.

63. **a.** .08, found by .80 × .10.
b.

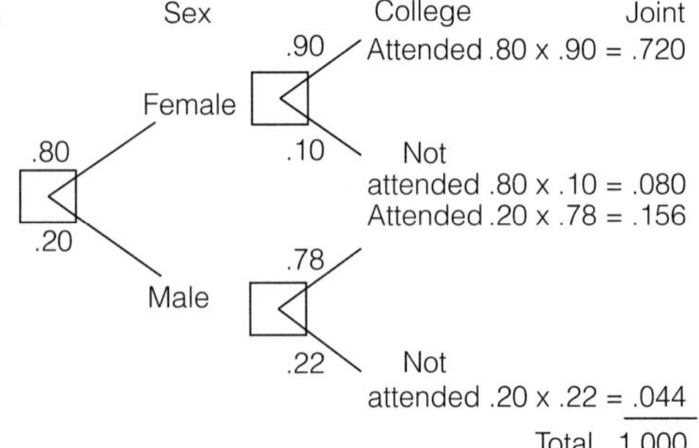

c. Yes, because all the possible outcomes are shown on the tree diagram.

65. **a.** 0.57, found by 57/100.
b. 0.97, found by (57/100) + (40/100).
c. Yes, because an employee cannot be both.
d. 0.03, found by 1 − 0.97.

67. **a.** 0.4096, found by $(0.8)^4$.
b. 0.0016, found by $(0.2)^4$.
c. 0.9984, found by 1 − 0.0016.
69. **a.** 0.9039, found by $(0.98)^5$.
b. 0.0961, found by 1 − 0.9039.
71. **a.** 0.0333, found by (4/10)(3/9)(2/8).
b. 0.1667, found by (6/10)(5/9)(4/8).
c. 0.8333, found by 1 − 0.1667.
d. Dependent
73. **a.** 0.3818, found by (9/12)(8/11)(7/10).
b. 0.6182, found by 1 − 0.3818.
75. **a.** 0.5467, found by 82/150.
b. 0.76, found by (39/150) + (75/150).
c. 0.6267, found by 82/150 + 39/150 − 27/150. General rule of addition.
d. 0.3293, found by 27/82.
e. 0.2972, found by (82/150)(81/149).
77. $P(\text{poor|profit}) = \dfrac{(0.10)(0.20)}{(0.10)(0.20) + (0.60)(0.80) + (0.30)(0.60)} = 0.0294$
79. **a.** $P(\text{P or D}) = (1/50)(9/10) + (49/50)(1/10) = 0.116$
b. $P(\text{No}) = (49/50)(9/10) = 0.882$
c. $P(\text{No on 3}) = (0.882)^3 = 0.686$
d. $P(\text{at least one prize}) = 1 - 0.686 = 0.314$
81. 24, found by 4!.
83. .4545, found by $\dfrac{(.50)(.625)}{(.50)(.625) + (.50)(.75)} = \dfrac{.3125}{.6875}$
85. Yes. 256 is found by 2^8.
87. ${}_7P_5 = \dfrac{7!}{(7-5)!} = 2{,}520$
89. .9744, found by $1 - (.40)^4$.
91. **a.** .185, found by (.15)(.95) + (.05)(.85).
b. .0075, found by (.15)(.05).
93. **a.** $P(\text{F and} >60) = .25$, found by solving with the general rule of multiplication:
$P(F) \cdot P(>60|F) = (.5)(.5)$
b. 0
c. .3333, found by 1/3.
95. $26^4 = 456{,}976$
97. For the system to operate, both components in the series must work. The probability they both work is 0.81, found by $P(A) \times P(B) = (.90)(.90)$.
99. 1/3,628,800
101. See diagram below.
a. $P(\text{Buys}) = P(S)P(\text{Buy}|S) + P(NS)P(\text{Buy}|NS)$

$$= (.05)(.01) + (.95)(.005) = .00525$$

b. $P(S|\text{Buy}) = \dfrac{(.05)(.01)}{(.05)(.01) + (.95)(.005)} = .0952$

c. $P(S|\text{Not Buy}) = \dfrac{(.05)(.99)}{(.05)(.99) + (.95)(.995)} = .0498$

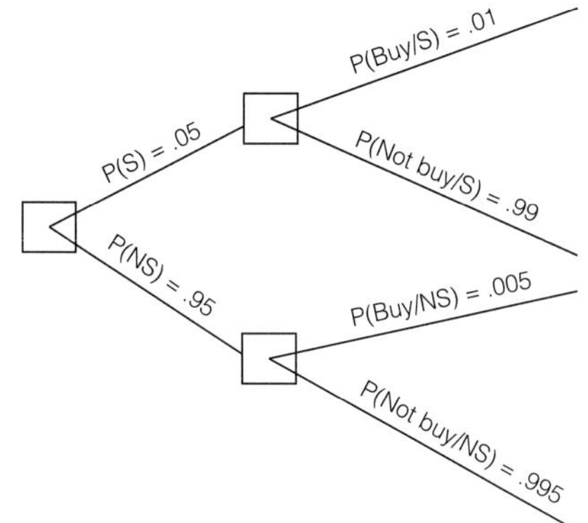

103. Answer depends on the game show host.
105. **a.**

Winning Season	Low Attendance	Moderate Attendance	High Attendance	Total
No	4	5	5	14
Yes	0	4	12	16
Total	4	9	17	30

1. 0.533, found by 16/30.
2. 0.7, found by 16/30 + 17/30 − 12/30 = 21/30.
3. 0.706, found by 12/17.
4. 0.133, found by 4/30.

b.

Turf	Losing Season	Winning Season	Total
Grass	9	14	23
Artificial	5	2	7
Total	14	16	30

1. 0.767, found by 23/30.
2. Grass: 0.609, found by 14/23. Artificial: 0.286, found by 2/7. So grass appears better.
3. 0.7, found by 16/30 + 7/30 − 2/30 = 21/30.

CHAPTER 6

1. Mean = 1.3, variance = .81, found by:

$$\mu = 0(.20) + 1(.40) + 2(.30) + 3(.10) = 1.3$$
$$\sigma^2 = (0-1.3)^2(.2) + (1-1.3)^2(.4) + (2-1.3)^2(.3) + (3-1.3)^2(.1) = .81$$

3. **a.** The second, or middle, one.
b. .2, .4, .9
c. $\mu = 14.5$, variance = 27.25, found by:

$$\mu = 5(.1) + 10(.3) + 15(.2) + 20(.4) = 14.5$$
$$\sigma^2 = (5-14.5)^2(.1) + (10-14.5)^2(.3) + (15-14.5)^2(.2) + (20-14.5)^2(.4) = 27.25$$
$$\sigma = 5.22, \text{ found by } \sqrt{27.25}$$

5.
$$\mu = 0(.3) + 1(.4) + 2(.2) + 3(.1) = 1.1$$
$$\sigma^2 = (0-1.1)^2(.3) + (1-1.1)^2(.4) + (2-1.1)^2(.2) + (3-1.1)^2(.1) = 0.89$$
$$\sigma = .943.$$

7. **a.** .20
b. .55
c. .95
d. $\mu = 0(.45) + 10(.30) + 100(.20) + 500(.05) = 48.0$

$$\sigma^2 = (0-48)^2(.45) + (10-48)^2(.3) + (100-48)^2(.2) + (500-48)^2(.05) = 12{,}226$$
$$\sigma = 110.57, \text{ found by } \sqrt{12{,}226}$$

9. **a.** $P(2) = \dfrac{4!}{2!(4-2)!}(.25)^2(.75)^{4-2} = .2109$

b. $P(3) = \dfrac{4!}{3!(4-3)!}(.25)^3(.75)^{4-3} = .0469$

11. **a.**

X	P(X)
0	.064
1	.288
2	.432
3	.216

b. $\mu = 1.8$

$\sigma^2 = 0.72$

$\sigma = \sqrt{0.72} = .8485$

13. a. .2668, found by $P(2) = \frac{9!}{(9-2)!2!}(.3)^2(.7)^7$.

b. .1715, found by $P(4) = \frac{9!}{(9-4)!4!}(.3)^4(.7)^5$.

c. .0404, found by $P(0) = \frac{9!}{(9-0)!0!}(.3)^0(.7)^9$.

15. a. .2824, found by $P(0) = \frac{12!}{(12-0)!0!}(.10)^0(.9)^{12}$.

b. .3765, found by $P(1) = \frac{12!}{(12-1)!1!}(.10)^1(.9)^{11}$.

c. .2301, found by $P(2) = \frac{12!}{(12-2)!2!}(.10)^2(.9)^{10}$.

d. $\mu = 1.2$, found by 12(.10).

$\sigma = 1.0392$, found by $\sqrt{1.08}$.

17. a. 0.1858, found by $\frac{15!}{2!13!}(0.23)^2(0.77)^{13}$.

b. 0.1416, found by $\frac{15!}{5!10!}(0.23)^5(0.77)^{10}$.

c. 3.45, found by (0.23)(15).

19. a. 0.296, found by using Appendix A with n of 8, π of 0.30, and x of 2.

b. $P(x \le 2) = 0.058 + 0.198 + 0.296 = 0.552$

c. 0.448, found by $P(x \ge 3) = 1 - P(x \le 2) = 1 - 0.552$.

21. a. 0.387, found from Appendix A with n of 9, π of 0.90, and x of 9.

b. $P(x < 5) = 0.001$

c. 0.992, found by 1 − 0.008.

d. 0.947, found by 1 − 0.053.

23. a. $\mu = 10.5$, found by 15(0.7) and $\sigma = \sqrt{15(0.7)(0.3)} = 1.7748$.

b. 0.2061, found by $\frac{15!}{10!5!}(0.7)^{10}(0.3)^5$.

c. 0.4247, found by 0.2061 + 0.2186.

d. 0.5154, found by 0.2186 + 0.1700 + 0.0916 + 0.0305 + 0.0047.

25. $P(2) = \frac{[_6C_2][_4C_1]}{_{10}C_3} = \frac{15(4)}{120} = .50$

27. $P(0) = \frac{[_7C_2][_3C_0]}{[_{10}C_2]} = \frac{21(1)}{45} = .4667$

29. $P(2) = \frac{[_9C_3][_6C_2]}{[_{15}C_5]} = \frac{84(15)}{3003} = .4196$

31. a. .6703

b. .3297

33. a. .0613

b. .0803

35. $\mu = 6$

$P(X \ge 5) = .7149 = 1 - (.0025 + .0149 + .0446 + .0892 + .1339)$

37. A random variable is a quantitative or qualitative outcome that results from a chance experiment. A probability distribution also includes the likelihood of each possible outcome.

39. The binomial distribution is a discrete probability distribution for which there are only two possible outcomes. A second important part is that data collected are a result of counts. Additionally, one trial is independent from the next, and the chance for success remains the same from one trial to the next.

41. $\mu = 0(.1) + 1(.2) + 2(.3) + 3(.4) = 2.00$

$\sigma^2 = (0-2)^2(.1) + \cdots + (3-2)^2(.40) = 1.0$

$\sigma = 1$

43. $\mu = 0(.4) + 1(.2) + 2(.2) + 3(.1) + 4(.1) = 1.3$

$\sigma^2 = (0-1.30)^2(.4) + \cdots + (4-1.30)^2(.1) = 1.81$

$\sigma = 1.3454$

45. a. 0.001

b. 0.001

47. a. 6, found by 0.4 × 15.

b. 0.0245, found by $\frac{15!}{10!5!}(0.4)^{10}(0.6)^5$

c. 0.0338, found by 0.0245 + 0.0074 + 0.0016 + 0.0003 + 0.0000.

d. 0.0093, found by 0.0338 − 0.0245.

49. a. $\mu = 20(0.075) = 1.5$

$\sigma = \sqrt{20(0.075)(0.925)} = 1.1779$

b. 0.2103, found by $\frac{20!}{0!20!}(0.075)^0(0.925)^{20}$.

c. 0.7897, found by 1 − 0.2103.

51. a. 0.1311, found by $\frac{16!}{4!12!}(0.15)^4(0.85)^{12}$.

b. 2.4, found by (0.15)(16).

c. 0.2100, found by 1 − 0.0743 − 0.2097 − 0.2775 − 0.2285.

53. $P(2) = \frac{[_6C_2][_4C_2]}{[_{10}C_4]} = \frac{(15)(6)}{210} = 0.4286$

55. a.

0	0.0001
1	0.0019
2	0.0116
3	0.0418
4	0.1020
5	0.1768
6	0.2234
7	0.2075
8	0.1405
9	0.0676
10	0.0220
11	0.0043
12	0.0004

b. $\mu = 12(0.52) = 6.24$

$\sigma = \sqrt{12(0.52)(0.48)} = 1.7307$

c. 0.1768

d. 0.3343, found by 0.0002 + 0.0019 + 0.0116 + 0.0418 + 0.1020 + 0.1768.

57. a. $P(1) = \frac{[_7C_2][_3C_1]}{[_{10}C_3]} = \frac{(21)(3)}{120} = .5250$

b. $P(0) = \frac{[_7C_3][_3C_0]}{[_{10}C_3]} = \frac{(35)(1)}{120} = .2917$

$P(X \ge 1) = 1 - P(0) = 1 - .2917 = .7083$

59. $P(X = 0) = \frac{[_8C_4][_4C_0]}{[_{12}C_4]} = \frac{70}{495} = .141$

61. a. .0498

b. .7746, found by $(1 - .0498)^5$.

63. $\mu = 4.0$, from Appendix C.
 a. .0183
 b. .1954
 c. .6289
 d. .5665

65. a. 0.1733, found by $\frac{(3.1)^4 e^{-3.1}}{4!}$.
 b. 0.0450, found by $\frac{(3.1)^0 e^{-3.1}}{0!}$.
 c. 0.9550, found by $1 - 0.0450$.

67. For NASA, $\mu = n\pi = 25(1/60{,}000) = 0.0004$

$$P(0) = \frac{0.0004^0 e^{-0.0004}}{0!} = 0.9996$$

$P(X \geq 1) = 1 - 0.9996 = 0.0004$
For Air Force, $\mu = 25(1/35) = .7143$

$$P(0) = \frac{0.7143^0 e^{-0.7143}}{0!} = 0.4895$$

$P(X \geq 1) = 1 - .4895 = 0.5105$

Summarizing, Air Force estimate is .5105 and NASA estimate is 0.0004.

69. Let $\mu = n\pi = 155(1/3709) = 0.042$

$$P(5) = \frac{0.042^5 e^{-0.042}}{5!} = 0.000000001$$

Very unlikely!

71. $$P(2) = \frac{({}_7C_2)({}_{23}C_3)}{{}_{30}C_5} = \frac{(21)(1771)}{142{,}506} = 0.2610$$

CHAPTER 7

1. The actual shape of a normal distribution depends on its mean and standard deviation. Thus, there is a normal distribution, and an accompanying normal curve, for a mean of 7 and a standard deviation of 2. There is another normal curve for a mean of \$25,000 and a standard deviation of \$1,742, and so on.

3. a. 490 and 510, found by $500 \pm 1(10)$.
 b. 480 and 520, found by $500 \pm 2(10)$.
 c. 470 and 530, found by $500 \pm 3(10)$.

5. $$Z_{Rob} = \frac{\$50{,}000 - \$60{,}000}{\$5000} = -2$$

$$Z_{Rachel} = \frac{\$50{,}000 - \$35{,}000}{\$8000} = 1.875$$

Adjusting for their industries, Rob is well below average and Rachel well above.

7. a. 1.25, found by $z = \frac{25 - 20}{4.0} = 1.25$.
 b. 0.3944, found in Appendix D.
 c. 0.3085, found by $z = \frac{18 - 20}{2.5} = -0.5$.

 Find 0.1915 in Appendix D for $z = -0.5$. Then $0.5000 - 0.1915 = 0.3085$.

9. a. 0.3413, found by $z = \frac{\$20 - \$16.50}{\$3.50} = 1.00$. Then find 0.3413 in Appendix D for $z = 1$.
 b. 0.1587, found by $0.5000 - 0.3413 = 0.1587$.
 c. 0.3336, found by $z = \frac{\$15.00 - \$16.50}{\$3.50} = -0.43$.

 Find 0.1664 in Appendix D, for $z = -0.43$, then $0.5000 - 0.1664 = 0.3336$.

11. a. 0.8276: First find $z = -1.5$, found by $(44 - 50)/4$ and $z = 1.25 = (55 - 50)/4$. The area between -1.5 and 0 is 0.4332 and the area between 0 and 1.25 is 0.3944, both from Appendix D. Then adding the two areas we find that $0.4332 + 0.3944 = 0.8276$.
 b. 0.1056, found by $0.5000 - 0.3994$, where $z = 1.25$.
 c. 0.2029: Recall that the area for $z = 1.25$ is 0.3944, and the area for $z = 0.5$, found by $(52 - 50)/4$, is 0.1915. Then subtract $0.3944 - 0.1915$ and find 0.2029.

13. a. 0.1525, found by subtracting $0.4938 - 0.3413$, which are the areas associated with z values of 2.5 and 1, respectively.
 b. 0.0062, found by $0.5000 - 0.4938$.
 c. 0.9710, found by recalling that the area of the z value of 2.5 is 0.4938. Then find $z = -2.00$, found by $(6.8 - 7.0)/0.1$. Thus, $0.4938 + 0.4772 = 0.9710$.

15. a. 0.0764, found by $z = (20 - 15)/3.5 = 1.43$, then $0.5000 - 0.4236 = 0.0764$.
 b. 0.9236, found by $0.5000 + 0.4236$, where $z = 1.43$.
 c. 0.1185, found by $z = (12 - 15)/3.5 = -0.86$. The area under the curve is 0.3051, then $z = (10 - 15/3.5) = -1.43$. The area is 0.4236. Finally, $0.4236 - 0.3051 = 0.1185$.

17. $X = 56.60$, found by adding 0.5000 (the area left of the mean) and then finding a z value that forces 45 percent of the data to fall inside the curve. Solving for X: $1.65 = (X - 50)/4 = 56.60$.

19. 7.233: Find a z value where 0.4900 of area is between 0 and z. That value is $z = 2.33$. Then solve for X: $(X - 7)/0.1$, so $X = 7.233$.

21. \$1,630, found by \$2,100 − 1.88(\$250).

23. a. $\mu = n\pi = 50(0.25) = 12.5$
 $\sigma^2 = n\pi(1 - \pi) = 12.5(1 - 0.25) = 9.375$
 $\sigma^2 = \sqrt{9.375} = 3.0619$
 b. 0.2578, found by $(14.5 - 12.5)/3.0619 = 0.65$. The area is 0.2422. Then $0.5000 - 0.2422 = 0.2578$.
 c. 0.2578, found by $(10.5 - 12.5)/3.0619 = -0.65$. The area is 0.2422. Then $0.5000 - 0.2422 = 0.2578$.

25. a. 0.0192, found by $0.500 - 0.4808$.
 b. 0.0694, found by $0.500 - 0.4306$.
 c. 0.0502, found by $0.0694 - 0.0192$.

27. a. Yes. (1) There are two mutually exclusive outcomes: overweight and not overweight. (2) It is the result of counting the number of successes (overweight members). (3) Each trial is independent. (4) The probability of 0.30 remains the same for each trial.
 b. 0.0084, found by
 $\mu = 500(0.30) = 150.$

 $\sigma^2 = 500(.30)(.70) = 105$

 $\sigma = \sqrt{105} = 10.24695$

$$z = \frac{X - \mu}{\sigma} = \frac{174.5 - 150}{10.24695} = 2.39$$

 The area under the curve for 2.39 is 0.4916. Then $0.5000 - 0.4916 = 0.0084$.
 c. 0.8461, found by $z = \frac{139.5 - 150}{10.24695} - 1.02$

 The area between 139.5 and 150 is 0.3461. Adding $0.3461 + 0.5000 = 0.8461$.

29. a. −0.4 for net sales, found by $(170 - 180)/25$. 2.92 for employees, found by $(1{,}850 - 1{,}500)/120$.
 b. Net sales are 0.4 standard deviations below the mean. Employees is 2.92 standard deviations above the mean.

c. 65.54 percent of the aluminum fabricators have greater net sales compared with Clarion, found by 0.1554 + 0.5000. Only 0.18 percent have more employees than Clarion, found by 0.5000 − 0.4982.

31. **a.** 0.5000, because $z = \frac{30 - 490}{90} = -5.11$.
b. 0.2514, found by 0.5000 − 0.2486.
c. 0.6374, found by 0.2486 + 0.3888.
d. 0.3450, found by 0.3888 − 0.0438.

33. **a.** 0.3015, found by 0.5000 − 0.1985.
b. 0.2579, found by 0.4564 − 0.1985.
c. 0.0011, found by 0.5000 − 0.4989.
d. 1,818, found by 1,280 + 1.28(420).

35. **a.** 0.1587, found by 0.5000 − 0.3413.
b. 0.0548, found by 0.5000 − 0.4452.
c. 0.7865, found by 0.3413 + 0.4452.
d. 0.0047, found by 0.5000 − 0.4953.

37. **a.** 0.0026, found by 0.5000 − 0.4974.
b. 0.1129, found by 0.4772 − 0.3643.
c. 0.8617, found by 0.4974 + 0.3643.

39. About 4,099 units, found by solving for X.
$1.65 = (X - 4000)/60$

41. **a.** $z = \frac{50{,}400 - 48{,}000}{1{,}200} = 2$ He makes more than 98% of the others.
b. $z = \frac{10 - 20}{5} = -2$ Only 2 percent have been there for less time than he has.
c. 46,308, found by 48,000 − 1.41(1,200).

43. **a.** 15.39%, found by (8 − 10.3)/2.25 = −1.02, then 0.5000 − 0.3461 = 0.1539.
b. 17.31%, found by:
$z = (12 - 10.3)/2.25 = 0.76$. Area is 0.2764.
$z = (14 - 10.3)/2.25 = 1.64$. Area is 0.4495.
The area between 12 and 14 is 0.1731, found by 0.4495 − 0.2764.
c. Yes, but it is rather remote. Reasoning: On 99.73 percent of the days, returns are between 3.55 and 17.03, found by 10.3 ± 3(2.25). Thus, the chance of less than 3.55 returns is rather remote.

45. **a.** 0.9678, found by:

$$\mu = 60(0.64) = 38.4.$$

$$\sigma^2 = 60(0.64)(0.36) = 13.824$$

$$\sigma = \sqrt{13.824} = 3.72$$

Then (31.5 − 38.4)/3.72 = −1.85, for which the area is 0.4678.
Then 0.5000 + 0.4678 = 0.9678.
b. 0.0853, found by (43.5 − 38.4)/3.72 = 1.37, for which the area is 0.4147. Then 0.5000 − 0.4147 =.0853.
c. 0.8084, found by 0.4441 + 0.3643.
d. 0.0348, found by 0.4495 − 0.4147.

47. **a.** $\mu = 50(0.2) = 10$ and $\sigma = \sqrt{50(0.2)(0.8)} = 2.83$
b. A student either drops or not. Each has a 20 percent chance of dropping independent of the others. You are counting the number who drop.
c. 0.8106, found by 0.5000 + 0.3106.
d. 0.2981, found by 0.5000 − 0.2019.
e. 0.1087, found by 0.3106 − 0.2019.

49. 0.0968, found by:
$\mu = 50(0.40) = 20$
$\sigma^2 = 50(0.40)(0.60) = 12$
$\sigma = \sqrt{12} = 3.4641$
$z = (24.5 - 20)/3.4641 = 1.30$.
The area is 0.4032. Then, for 25 or more, 0.5000 − 0.4032 = 0.0968.

51. **a.** $1.65 = (45 - \mu)/5$ $\mu = 36.75$
b. $1.65 = (45 - \mu)/10$ $\mu = 28.5$
c. $z = (30 - 28.5)/10 = 0.15$, then 0.5000 + 0.0596 = 0.5596.

53. **a.** $\frac{2 - 3.1}{0.3} = -3.67$ $\frac{3 - 3.1}{0.3} = -0.33$
0.3707, found by 0.5000 − 0.1293.
b. None.
c. 0.0228, found by 0.5000 − 0.4772; leads to 228 students, found by 10000(.0228).
d. 3.484, found by 3.1 + 1.28(0.3).

55. **a.** 21.19 percent found by $z = (9.00 - 9.20)/0.25 = -0.80$; so 0.5000 − 0.2881 = 0.2119.
b. Increase the mean. $z = (9.00 - 9.25)/0.25 = -1.00$; $P = 0.5000 - 0.3413 = 0.1587$.
Reduce the standard deviation. $\sigma = (9.00 - 9.20)/0.15 = -1.33$; $P = 0.500 - 0.4082 = 0.0918$.
Reducing the standard deviation is better because a smaller percent of the hams will be below the limit.

57. **a.** $z = (52 - 60)/5 = 1.60$, so 0.5000 − 0.4452 = 0.0548.
b. Let $z = 0.67$, so $0.67 = (X - 52)/5$ and $X = 55.35$.
Set mileage at 55,350.
c. $z = (45 - 52)/5 = -1.40$, so 0.5000 − 0.4192 = 0.0808.

59. $\frac{470 - \mu}{\sigma} = 0.25$ $\frac{500 - \mu}{\sigma} = 1.28$
$\sigma = 29.126$ and $\mu = 462.719$

61. $\mu = 150(0.15) = 22.5$ $\sigma \sqrt{150(0.15)(0.85)} = 4.3732$
$z = (30.5 - 22.5)/4.3732 = 1.83$
$P(z > 1.83) = 0.5000 - 0.4664 = 0.0336$

63. **a.** 0.0823, found by 0.5000 − 0.4177; leads to 2.5 teams, found by 30(0.0823). No team actually had attendance of more than 3.5 million, but three teams were above 3.3 million.
b. 0.6064, found by 0.5000 + 0.1064; leads to 18.2 teams, found by 30(0.6064). Twenty teams actually had salaries of more than $50 million, so the estimate is fairly accurate.

CHAPTER 8

1. **a.** 303 Louisiana, 5155 S. Main, 3501 Monroe, 2652 W. Central
b. Answers will vary.
c. 630 Dixie Hwy, 835 S. McCord Rd, 4624 Woodville Rd
d. Answers will vary.

3. **a.** Bob Schmidt Chevrolet
Great Lakes Ford Nissan
Grogan Towne Chrysler
Southside Lincoln Mercury
Rouen Chrysler Plymouth Jeep Eagle
b. Answers will vary.
c. York Automotive
Thayer Chevrolet Geo Toyota
Franklin Park Lincoln Mercury
Mathews Ford Oregon Inc
Valiton Chrysler Plymouth

5. **a.**

Sample	Values	Sum	Mean
1	12, 12	24	12
2	12, 14	26	13
3	12, 16	28	14
4	12, 14	26	13
5	12, 16	28	14
6	14, 16	30	15

b. $\mu_{\bar{X}} = (12 + 13 + 14 + 13 + 14 + 15)/6 = 13.5$
$\mu = (12 + 12 + 14 + 16)/4 = 13.5$
c. More dispersion with population data compared to the sample means. The sample means vary from 12 to 15, whereas the population varies from 12 to 16.

7. a.

Sample	Values	Sum	Mean
1	12, 12, 14	38	12.66
2	12, 12, 15	39	13.00
3	12, 12, 20	44	14.66
4	14, 15, 20	49	16.33
5	12, 14, 15	41	13.66
6	12, 14, 15	41	13.66
7	12, 15, 20	47	15.66
8	12, 15, 20	47	15.66
9	12, 14, 20	46	15.33
10	12, 14, 20	46	15.33

b. $\mu_{\bar{X}} = \dfrac{(12.66 + \cdots + 15.33 + 15.33)}{10} = 14.6$

$\mu = (12 + 12 + 14 + 15 + 20)/5 = 14.6$

c. The dispersion of the population is greater than that of the sample means. The sample means vary from 12.66 to 16.33, whereas the population varies from 12 to 20.

9. a. 20, found by ${}_6C_3$

b.

Sample	Cases	Sum	Mean
Ruud, Austin, Sass	3, 6, 3	12	4.00
Ruud, Sass, Palmer	3, 3, 3	9	3.00
⋮	⋮	⋮	⋮
Sass, Palmer, Schueller	3, 3, 1	7	2.33

c. $\mu_{\bar{X}} = 2.63$, found by $\dfrac{52.63}{20}$.

$\mu = 2.66$, found by $(3 + 6 + 3 + 3 + 0 + 1)/6$.

They are equal.

d.

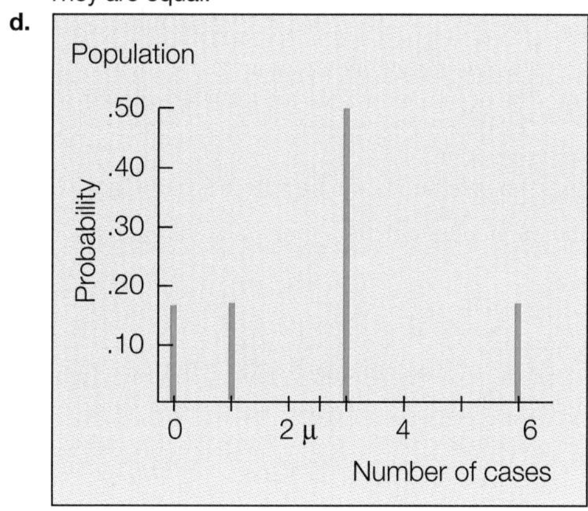

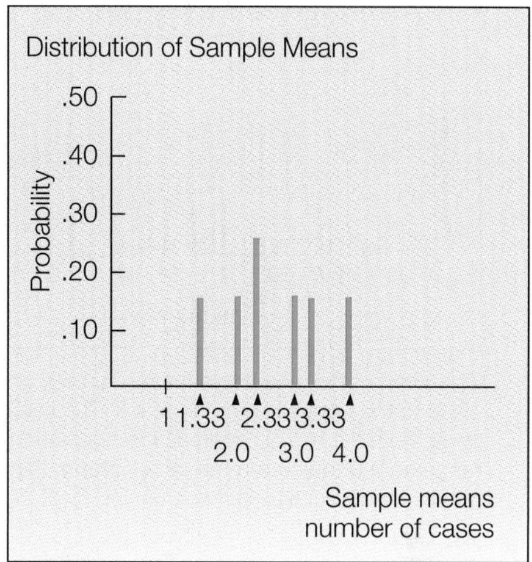

Sample Mean	Number of Means	Probability
1.33	3	.1500
2.00	3	.1500
2.33	5	.2500
3.00	3	.1500
3.33	3	.1500
4.00	3	.1500
	20	1.0000

The population has more dispersion than the sample means. The sample means vary from 1.33 to 4.0. The population varies from 0 to 6.

11. a.

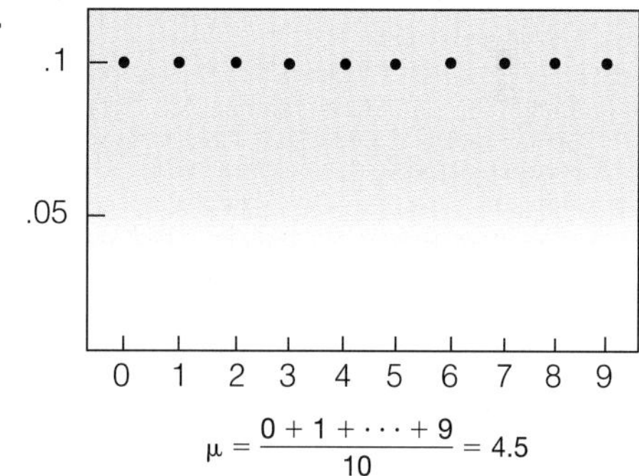

$\mu = \dfrac{0 + 1 + \cdots + 9}{10} = 4.5$

b.

Sample	Sum	$\bar{X}$
1	11	2.2
2	31	6.2
3	21	4.2
4	24	4.8
5	21	4.2
6	20	4.0
7	23	4.6
8	29	5.8
9	35	7.0
10	27	5.4

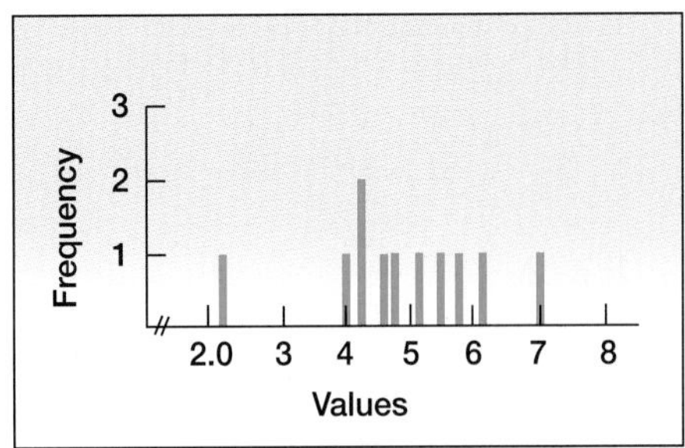

The mean of the 10 sample means is 4.84, which is close to the population mean of 4.5. The sample means range from 2.2 to 7.0, whereas the population values range from 0 to 9. From the above graph, the sample means tend to cluster between 4 and 5.

13. **a.** $z = \dfrac{63 - 60}{12/\sqrt{9}} = 0.75$

$P = .2266$, found by $.5000 - .2734$.

b. $z = \dfrac{56 - 60}{12/\sqrt{9}} = -1.00$

$P = .1587$, found by $.5000 - .3413$.

c. $P = .6147$, found by $.0.3413 + 0.2734$.

15. $z = \dfrac{950 - 1200}{250/\sqrt{50}} = -7.07$ $P = 1$, or virtually certain.

17. **a.** Formal Man, Summit Stationers, Bootleggers, Leather Ltd, Petries.
b. Answers may vary.
c. Elder-Beerman, Frederick's of Hollywood, Summit Stationers, Lion Store, Leather Ltd., Things Remembered, County Seat, Coach House Gifts, Regis Hairstylists

19. The difference between a sample statistic and the population parameter. Yes, the difference could be zero. The sample mean and the population parameter are equal.

21. Use of either a proportional or nonproportional stratified random sample would be appropriate. For example, suppose the number of banks in Region III were as follows:

Assets	Number	Percent of Total
$500 million and more	20	2.0
$100–$499 million	324	32.4
Less than $100 million	656	65.6
	1,000	100.0

For a proportional stratified sample, if the sample size is 100, then two banks with assets of $500 million would be selected, 32 medium-size banks, and 66 small banks. For a nonproportional sample, 10 or even all 20 large banks could be selected and fewer medium- and small-size banks and the sample results weighted by the appropriate percents of the total.

23. **a.** We selected 60, 104, 75, 72, and 48. Answers will vary.
b. We selected the third observation. So the sample consists of 75, 72, 68, 82, 48. Answers will vary.
c. Number the first 20 motels from 00 to 19. Randomly select three numbers. Then number the last five numbers 20 to 24. Randomly select two numbers from that group.

25. **a.** 15, found by ${}_6C_2$.
b.

Sample	Value	Sum	Mean
1	79, 64	143	71.5
2	79, 84	163	81.5
⋮	⋮	⋮	⋮
15	92, 77	169	84.5
			1,195.0

c. $\mu_{\bar{X}} = 79.67$, found by 1,195/15.
$\mu = 79.67$, found by 478/6.
They are equal.
d. No. The student is not graded on all available information. He/she is as likely to get a lower grade based on the sample as a higher grade.

27. **a.** 10, found by ${}_5C_2$.
b.

Number of Shutdowns	Mean	Number of Shutdowns	Mean
4, 3	3.5	3, 3	3.0
4, 5	4.5	3, 2	2.5
4, 3	3.5	5, 3	4.0
4, 2	3.0	5, 2	3.5
3, 5	4.0	3, 2	2.5

Sample Mean	Frequency	Probability
2.5	2	.20
3.0	2	.20
3.5	3	.30
4.0	2	.20
4.5	1	.10
	10	1.00

c. $\mu_{\bar{X}} = (3.5 + 4.5 + \cdots + 2.5)/10 = 3.4$
$\mu = (4 + 3 + 5 + 3 + 2)/5 = 3.4$
The two means are equal.
d. The population values are relatively uniform in shape. The distribution of sample means tends toward normality.

29. **a.** The distribution will be normal.
b. $\sigma_{\bar{X}} = \dfrac{5.5}{\sqrt{25}} = 1.1$
c. $z = \dfrac{35 - 36}{5.5/\sqrt{25}} = 0.91$

$P = 0.1814$, found by $0.5000 - 0.3186$.

d. $z = \dfrac{34.5 - 35}{5.5/\sqrt{25}} = -0.45$

$P = 0.6736$, found by $0.5000 + 0.1736$.

e. 0.4922, found by $0.3186 + 0.1736$.

31. $z = \dfrac{\$335 - \$350}{\$45/\sqrt{40}} = -2.11$

$P = 0.9826$, found by $0.5000 + 0.4826$.

33. $z = \dfrac{25.1 - 24.8}{2.5/\sqrt{60}} = 0.93$

$P = 0.8238$, found by $0.5000 + 0.3238$.

35. Between 5,954 and 6,046, found by $6{,}000 \pm 1.96(150/\sqrt{40})$.

37. $z = \dfrac{900 - 947}{205/\sqrt{60}} = -1.78$

$P = 0.0375$, found by $0.5000 - 0.4625$.

39. **a.** Alaska, Ohio, New Jersey, Texas, Utah, Florida, Vermont, and Connecticut.

b. Maine, Maryland, Michigan, Missouri, Florida, South Carolina, Oklahoma, Wyoming, and Washington.
c. Answers will vary depending on random numbers selected.

41. Answers will vary.

CHAPTER 9

1. 51.314 and 58.686, found by $55 \pm 2.58(10/\sqrt{49})$.

3. **a.** 1.581, found by $\sigma_{\overline{X}} = 5/\sqrt{10}$.
b. The population is normally distributed and the population variance is known.
c. 16.901 and 23.099, found by 20 ± 3.099.

5. **a.** $20. It is our best estimate of the population mean.
b. $18.60 and $21.40, found by $\$20 \pm 1.96(\$5/\sqrt{49})$. About 95 percent of the intervals similarly constructed will include the population mean.

7. **a.** 8.60 gallons.
b. 7.83 and 9.37, found by $8.60 \pm 2.58(2.30/\sqrt{60})$.
c. If 100 such intervals were determined, the population mean would be included in about 99 intervals.

9. **a.** 2.201
b. 1.729
c. 3.499

11. **a.** The population mean is unknown, but the best estimate is 20, the sample mean.
b. Use the *t* distribution as the standard deviation is unknown and the sample size is small. However, assume the population is normally distributed.
c. 2.093
d. Between 19.06 and 20.94, found by $20 \pm 2.093(2/\sqrt{20})$.
e. Neither value is reasonable, because they are not inside the interval.

13. Between 95.39 and 101.81, found by $98.6 \pm 1.833(5.54/\sqrt{10})$.

15. **a.** 0.8, found by 80/100.
b. 0.04, found by $\sqrt{\dfrac{0.8(1-0.8)}{100}}$.
c. Between 0.72 and 0.88, found by $0.8 \pm 1.96\left(\sqrt{\dfrac{0.8(1-0.8)}{100}}\right)$.
d. We are reasonably sure the population proportion is between 72 and 88 percent.

17. **a.** 0.625, found by 250/400.
b. 0.0242, found by $\sqrt{\dfrac{0.625(1-0.625)}{400}}$.
c. Between 0.563 and 0.687, found by $0.625 \pm 2.58\left(\sqrt{\dfrac{0.625(1-0.625)}{400}}\right)$.
d. We are reasonably sure the population proportion is between 56 and 69 percent.

19. 33.465 and 36.535, found by $35 \pm 1.96\left(\dfrac{5}{\sqrt{36}}\right)\sqrt{\dfrac{300-36}{300-1}}$.

21. 1.689 up to 2.031, found by $1.86 \pm 2.58\left(\dfrac{0.50}{\sqrt{50}}\right)\sqrt{\dfrac{400-50}{400-1}}$.

23. 97, found by $n = \left[\dfrac{1.96 \times 10}{2}\right]^2 = 96.04$.

25. 196, found by $n = 0.15(0.85)\left(\dfrac{1.96}{0.05}\right)^2 = 195.9216$.

27. 554, found by $n = \left(\dfrac{1.96 \times 3}{0.25}\right)^2 = 553.19$.

29. **a.** 577, found by $n = 0.60(0.40)\left(\dfrac{1.96}{0.04}\right)^2 = 576.24$.
b. 601, found by $n = 0.50(0.50)\left(\dfrac{1.96}{0.04}\right)^2 = 600.25$.

31. 6.14 years to 6.86 years, found by $6.5 \pm 1.96(1.7/\sqrt{85})$.

33. **a.** Between $1.168 and 1.190, found by $1.179 \pm 2.68\left(\dfrac{0.03}{\sqrt{50}}\right)$.
b. $1.20 is not reasonable, because it is outside of the confidence interval. A *z* value of 2.58 leads to the same answer.

35. **a.** Between 7.22 and 8.78, found by $8 \pm 1.68(3/\sqrt{40})$.
b. 9 is not reasonable because it is outside of the confidence interval. A *z* value of 1.65 leads to the same answer.

37. **a.** 65.61 up to 71.59 hours, found by $68.6 \pm 2.58(8.2/\sqrt{50})$.
b. The value suggested by the NCAA is included in the confidence interval. Therefore, it is reasonable.
c. Changing the confidence interval to 95 would reduce the width of the interval. The value of 2.58 would change to 1.96.

39. 61, found by $1.96(16/\sqrt{n}) = 4$.

41. Between $13,734 up to $15,028, found by $14{,}381 \pm 1.711(1{,}892/\sqrt{25})$. 15,000 is reasonable because it is inside of the confidence interval.

43. **a.** $62.583, found by $751/12.
b. Between $60.54 and $64.63, found by $62.583 \pm 1.796(3.94/\sqrt{12})$.
c. $60 is not reasonable, because it is outside of the confidence interval.

45. **a.** 89.4667, found by 1,342/15.
b. Between 84.99 and 93.94, found by $89.4667 \pm 2.145(8.08/\sqrt{15})$.
c. Yes, because even the lower limit of the confidence interval is above 80.

47. Between 0.648 and 0.752, found by $.7 \pm 2.58\left(\sqrt{\dfrac{0.7(1-0.7)}{500}}\right)\left(\sqrt{\dfrac{20{,}000-500}{20{,}000-1}}\right)$. Yes, because even the lower limit of the confidence interval is above 0.500.

49. $52.56 and $55.44, found by $\$54.00 \pm 1.96\dfrac{\$4.50}{\sqrt{35}}\sqrt{\dfrac{(500-35)}{500-1}}$.

51. 369, found by $n = 0.60(1 - 0.60)(1.96/0.05)^2$.

53. 97, found by $[(1.96 \times 500)/100]^2$.

55. **a.** 708.13, rounded up to 709, found by $0.21(1 - 0.21)[1.96/0.03]^2$.
b. 1,068, found by $0.50(0.50)(1.96/0.03)^2$.

57. Between 0.573 and 0.653, found by $.613 \pm 2.58\left(\sqrt{\dfrac{0.613(1-0.613)}{1{,}000}}\right)$. Yes, because even the lower limit of the confidence interval is above 0.500.

59. Between 12.69 and 14.11, found by $13.4 \pm 1.96(6.8/\sqrt{352})$.

61. Answers will vary.

63. **a.** For selling price: 212.09 up to 230.11, found by $221.1 \pm (1.96)(47.11/\sqrt{105}) = 221.1 \pm 9.01$.
b. For distance: 13.697 up to 15.561, found by $14.629 \pm (1.96)(4.874/\sqrt{105}) = 14.629 \pm 0.932$.
c. For garage: 0.5867 up to 0.7657, found by $0.6762 \pm (1.96)\sqrt{\dfrac{0.6762(1-0.6762)}{105}} = 0.6762 \pm 0.0895$.

65. **a.** Between 12.279 and 14.321, found by 13.3 ± 1.701 $(3.233/\sqrt{29})$.
b. Between 48.24 and 297.96, found by 173.1 ± 1.701 $(395.3/\sqrt{29})$.

CHAPTER 10

1. **a.** Two-tailed.
b. Reject H_0 and accept H_1 when z does not fall in the region from −1.96 and 1.96.
c. −1.2, found by $z = (49 - 50)/(5/\sqrt{36}) = -1.2$
d. Fail to reject H_0.
e. $p = .2302$, found by 2(.5000 − .3849). A 23.02 percent chance of finding a z value this large when H_0 is true.

3. **a.** One-tailed.
b. Reject H_0 and accept H_1 where $z > 1.65$.
c. 1.2, found by $z = (21 - 20)/(5/\sqrt{36}) = 1.2$
d. Fail to reject H_0 at the .05 significance level.
e. $p = .1151$, found by .5000 − .3849. An 11.51 percent chance of finding a z-value this large or larger.

5. **a.** H_0: $\mu = 60{,}000$ H_1: $\mu \neq 60{,}000$
b. Reject H_0 if $z < -1.96$ or $z > 1.96$.
c. −0.69, found by:

$$z = \frac{59{,}500 - 60{,}000}{(5{,}000/\sqrt{48})} = -0.69$$

d. Do not reject H_0.
e. $p = .4902$, found by 2(.5000 − .2549). Crosset's experience is not different from that claimed by the manufacturer. If H_0 is true, the probability of finding a value more extreme than this is .4902.

7. **a.** H_0: $\mu \geq 6.8$ H_1: $\mu < 6.8$
b. Reject H_0 if $z < -1.65$
c. $z = \dfrac{6.2 - 6.8}{0.5/\sqrt{36}} = -7.2$
d. H_0 is rejected.
e. $p = 0$. The mean number of videos watched is less than 6.8 per month. If H_0 is true, there is virtually no chance of getting a statistic this small.

9. **a.** Reject H_0 where $t > 1.833$.
b. $t = \dfrac{12 - 10}{(3/\sqrt{10})} = 2.108$
c. Reject H_0. The mean is greater than 10.

11. H_0: $\mu \leq 40$ H_1: $\mu > 40$
Reject H_0 if $t > 1.703$.

$$t = \frac{42 - 40}{(2.1/\sqrt{28})} = 5.040$$

Reject H_0 and conclude that the mean number of calls is greater than 40 per week.

13. H_0: $\mu \leq 22{,}100$ H_1: $\mu > 22{,}100$
Reject H_0 if $t > 1.740$.

$$t = \frac{23{,}400 - 22{,}100}{(1{,}500/\sqrt{18})} = 3.680$$

Reject H_0 and conclude that the mean life of the spark plugs is greater than 22,100 miles.

15. **a.** Reject H_0 if $t < -3.747$.
b. $\bar{X} = 17$ and $s = \sqrt{\dfrac{1495 - (85)^2/5}{5 - 1}} = 3.536$

$$t = \frac{17 - 20}{(3.536/\sqrt{5})} = -1.90$$

c. Do not reject H_0. We cannot conclude the population mean is less than 20.
d. Between .05 and .10, about .065.

17. H_0: $\mu \leq 4.35$ H_1: $\mu > 4.35$
Reject H_0 if $t > 2.821$.

$$t = \frac{4.368 - 4.35}{(0.0339/\sqrt{10})} = 1.68$$

Do not reject H_0. The additive did not increase the mean weight of the chickens. The p-value is between 0.10 and 0.05.

19. H_0: $\mu \leq 4.0$ H_1: $\mu > 4.0$
Reject H_0 if $t > 1.796$.

$$t = \frac{4.50 - 4.0}{(2.68/\sqrt{12})} = 0.65$$

Do not reject H_0. The mean number of fish caught has not been shown to be greater than 4.0. The p-value is greater than 0.10.

21. **a.** H_0 is rejected if $z > 1.65$.
b. 1.09, found by $z = \sqrt{(0.70) \times 0.30)/100}$.
c. H_0 is not rejected.

23. **a.** H_0: $\pi \leq 0.52$ H_1: $\pi > 0.52$
b. H_0 is rejected if $z > 2.33$.

$$z = \frac{.5667 - .52}{\sqrt{\dfrac{.52(.48)}{300}}}$$

c. 1.62, found by $z = \sqrt{(0.52 \times 0.48)/300}$.
d. H_0 is not rejected. We cannot conclude that the proportion of men driving on the Ohio Turnpike is larger than 0.52.

25. **a.** H_0: $\pi \geq 0.90$ H_1: $\pi < 0.90$
b. H_0 is rejected if $z < -1.28$.

$$z = \frac{.82 - .80}{\sqrt{\dfrac{.90(.10)}{100}}}$$

c. −2.67, found by $z = \sqrt{(0.90 \times 0.10)/100}$
d. H_0 is rejected. Fewer than 90 percent of the customers receive their orders in less than 10 minutes.

27. 1.05, found by $z = (9{,}922 - 9{,}880)/(400/\sqrt{100})$. Then 0.5000 − 0.3531 = 0.1469, which is the probability of a Type II error.

29. H_0: $\mu \geq 10$ H_1: $\mu < 10$
Reject H_0 if $z < -1.65$.

$$z = \frac{9.0 - 10.0}{2.8/\sqrt{50}} = -2.53$$

Reject H_0. The mean weight loss is less than 10 pounds. p-value = 0.5000 − 0.4943 = 0.0057

31. H_0: $\mu \leq \$15{,}000$ H_1: $\mu > \$15{,}000$
Reject H_0 if $z > 1.65$.

$$z = \frac{\$17{,}000 - \$15{,}000}{\$3000/\sqrt{75}} = 5.77$$

Reject H_0. At the 0.05 level we can conclude that the mean household income is greater than $15,000.

33. H_0: $\mu = \$30{,}000$ H_1: $\mu \neq \$30{,}000$
Reject H_0 if $z < 1.65$ or $z > 1.65$.

$$z = \frac{\$30{,}500 - \$30{,}000}{\$3000/\sqrt{120}} = 1.83$$

Reject H_0. We can conclude that the mean salary is not $30,000. p-value = 0.0672, found by 2(0.5000 − 0.4664).

35. H_0: $\mu \leq 1.50$ H_1: $\mu > 1.50$
Reject H_0 if $z > 1.65$.

$$z = \frac{\$1.52 - \$1.50}{\$0.05/\sqrt{35}} = 2.37$$

Reject H_0. The mean price of gasoline is greater than $1.50. The p-value = 0.5000 − 0.4911 = 0.0089.

37. H_0: $\mu = \$3.65$ H_1: $\mu \neq \$3.65$
Reject H_0 where z does not fall in the range between −1.96 and 1.96.

$$z = \frac{\$3.69 - \$3.65}{\$0.24/\sqrt{45}} = 1.12$$

c. $H_0: \mu_1 = \mu_2$ $H_1: \mu_1 \neq \mu_2$
Reject H_0 if $t > 2.036$ or $t < -2.036$.
$\bar{X}_1 = 196.91$ $s_1 = 35.78$ $n_1 = 15$
$\bar{X}_2 = 227.45$ $s_2 = 44.19$ $n_2 = 20$

$$s_p^2 = \frac{(15-1)(35.78)^2 + (20-1)(44.19)^2}{15+20-2} = 1{,}667.43$$

$$t = \frac{196.92 - 227.45}{\sqrt{1{,}667.43\left(\frac{1}{15}+\frac{1}{20}\right)}} = -2.19$$

Reject H_0. There is a difference in mean selling price for homes in Township 1 and Township 2.

d. $H_0: \pi_1 = \pi_2$ $H_1: \pi_1 \neq \pi_2$
If z is not between −1.96 and 1.96, reject H_0.

$$p_c = \frac{24+43}{52+53} = 0.64$$

$$z = \frac{0.462 - 0.811}{\sqrt{0.64 \times 0.36/52 + 0.64 \times 0.36/53}} = -3.73$$

Reject the null hypothesis. There is a difference.

59. $H_0: \mu_1 = \mu_2$ $H_1: \mu_1 \neq \mu_2$
If t is not between −2.052 and 2.052, reject H_0.

$$s_p^2 = \frac{(22-1)(3.54)^2 + (7-1)(1.50)^2}{22+7-2} = 10.25$$

$$t = \frac{12.89 - 14.59}{\sqrt{10.25\left(\frac{1}{22}+\frac{1}{7}\right)}} = -1.22$$

Do not reject H_0.

CHAPTER 12

1. 9.01, from Appendix G.
3. Reject H_0 if $F > 10.5$, where degrees of freedom in the numerator are 7 and 5 in the denominator. Computed $F = 2.04$, found by:

$$F = \frac{s_1^2}{s_2^2} = \frac{(10)^2}{(7)^2} = 2.04$$

Do not reject H_0. There is no difference in the variations of the two populations.

5. $H_0: \sigma_1^2 = \sigma_2^2$ $H_1: \sigma_1^2 \neq \sigma_2^2$
Reject H_0 where $F > 3.10$. (3.10 is about halfway between 3.14 and 3.07.) Computed $F = 1.44$, found by:

$$F = \frac{(12)^2}{(10)^2} = 1.44$$

Do not reject H_0. There is no difference in the variations of the two populations.

7. a. $H_0: \mu_1 = \mu_2 = \mu_3$; H_1: Treatment means are not all the same.
b. Reject H_0 if $F > 4.26$.
c. & d.

Source	SS	df	MS	F
Treatment	62.17	2	31.08	21.94
Error	12.75	9	1.42	
Total	74.92	11		

e. Reject H_0. The treatment means are not all the same.

9. $H_0: \mu_1 = \mu_2 = \mu_3$; H_1: Treatment means are not all the same. Reject H_0 if $F > 4.26$.

Source	SS	df	MS	F
Treatment	276.50	2	138.25	14.18
Error	87.75	9	9.75	

Reject H_0. The treatment means are not all the sa

11. a. $H_0: \mu_1 = \mu_2 = \mu_3$; H_1: Not all means are the same.
b. Reject H_0 if $F > 4.26$.
c. SST = 107.20, SSE = 9.47, SS total = 116.67.
d.

Source	SS	df	MS	F
Treatment	107.20	2	53.600	50.96
Error	9.47	9	1.052	
Total	116.67	11		

e. Since 50.96 > 4.26, H_0 is rejected. At least one of the means differs.
f. $(\bar{X}_1 - \bar{X}_2) \pm t\sqrt{MSE(1/n_1 + 1/n_2)}$
$= (9.667 - 2.20) \pm 2.262\sqrt{1.052(1/3 + 1/5)}$
$= 7.467 \pm 1.69$
$= [5.777, 9.157]$

Yes, we can conclude that treatments 1 and 2 have different means.

13. $H_0: \mu_1 = \mu_2 = \mu_3 = \mu_4$; H_1: Not all means are equal. H_0 is rejected if $F > 3.71$.

Source	SS	df	MS	F
Treatment	32.33	3	10.77	2.36
Error	45.67	10	4.567	
Total	78.00	13		

Because 2.36 is less than 3.71, H_0 is not rejected. There is no difference in the mean number of weeks.

15. a. $H_0: \mu_1 = \mu_2$; H_1: Not all treatment means are equal.
b. Reject H_0 if $F > 18.5$.
c. $H_0: \mu_1 = \mu_2 = \mu_3$; H_1: Not all block means are equal. H_0 is rejected if $F > 19.0$.
d. $$SST = \frac{(127)^2}{3} + \frac{(92)^2}{3} - \frac{(219)^2}{6} = 204.167$$

$$SSB = \frac{(77)^2}{2} + \frac{(63)^2}{2} + \frac{(79)^2}{2} - \frac{(219)^2}{6} = 76$$

SS total = 8,283 − $(219)^2/6$ = 289.5
SSE = 289.5 − 204.167 − 76 = 9.333

e.

Source	SS	df	MS	F
Treatment	204.167	1	204.167	43.75
Blocks	76.000	2	38.000	8.14
Error	9.333	2	4.667	
Total	289.5000	5		

f. 43.75 > 18.5, so reject H_0. There is a difference in the treatments. 8.14 < 19.0, so do not reject H_0 for blocks. There is no difference among blocks.

17. For treatment:
$H_0: \mu_1 = \mu_2 = \mu_3$
H_1: Not all means equal
Reject if $F > 4.46$

For blocks:
$H_0: \mu_1 = \mu_2 = \mu_3 = \mu_4 = \mu_5$
H_1: Not all means equal
Reject if $F > 3.84$

Source	SS	df	MS	F
Treatment	62.53	2	31.2650	5.75
Blocks	33.73	4	8.4325	1.55
Error	43.47	8	5.4338	
Total	138.73			

There is a difference in shifts, but not by employee.

19. $H_0: \sigma_1^2 \leq \sigma_2^2$; $H_1: \sigma_1^2 > \sigma_2^2$. $df_1 = 21 - 1 = 20$; $df_2 = 18 - 1 = 17$. H_0 is rejected if $F > 3.16$.

$$F = \frac{(45{,}600)^2}{(21{,}330)^2} = 4.57$$

Fail to reject H_0. There is no difference in the mean allowance for 9-year-olds in the Tampa area and the rest of the United States.

39. $H_0: \mu \leq 42$ $H_1: \mu > 42$
Reject H_0 if $t > 1.796$.

$$t = \frac{51 - 42}{8/\sqrt{12}} = 3.90$$

Reject H_0. The mean time for delivery is more than 42 days. The p-value is less than 0.005.

41. $H_0: \mu = 2.25$ $H_1: \mu \neq 2.25$
Reject H_0 if $t < -2.201$ or $t > 2.201$.
$\bar{X} = 2.087$ $s_s = 0.4048$

$$t = \frac{2.087 - 2.25}{0.4048/\sqrt{12}} = -1.395$$

Do not reject H_0. There is not a difference in the mean amount of coffee consumed by students at Northwestern State and other college students.

42. $H_0: \mu \leq 25$ $H_1: \mu > 25$
Reject H_0 if $t > 2.624$.
$\bar{X} = 26.07$ $s = 1.5337$

$$t = \frac{26.07 - 25.00}{1.5337/\sqrt{15}} = 2.702$$

Reject H_0. The mean number of patients per day is more than 25. The p-value is less than 0.01.

43. $H_0: \mu \geq 6.5$ $H_1: \mu < 6.5$
Reject H_0 if $t < -2.718$.
$\bar{X} = 5.1667$ $s = 3.1575$

$$t = \frac{5.1667 - 6.5}{3.1575/\sqrt{12}} = -1.463$$

Do not reject H_0. The p-value is greater than 0.05.

45. $H_0: \mu = 0$ $H_1: \mu \neq 0$
Reject H_0 if $t < -2.110$ or $t > 2.110$.
$\bar{X} = -0.2322$ $s = 0.3120$

$$t = \frac{-0.2322 - 0}{0.3120/\sqrt{18}} = -3.158$$

Reject H_0. The mean gain or loss does not equal 0. The p-value is less than 0.01, but greater than 0.001.

47. $H_0: \pi \leq 0.60$ $H_1: \pi > 0.60$
H_0 is rejected if $z > 2.33$.

$$z = \frac{0.70 - 0.60}{\sqrt{(0.60 \times 0.40)/200}} = 2.89$$

H_0 is rejected. Ms. Dennis is correct. More than 60 percent of the accounts are more than 3 months old.

49. $H_0: \pi \leq 0.44$ $H_1: \pi > 0.44$
H_0 is rejected if $z > 1.65$.

$$z = \frac{0.480 - 0.44}{\sqrt{(0.44 \times 0.56)/1{,}000}} = 2.55$$

H_0 is rejected. We conclude that there has been an increase in the proportion of people wanting to go to Europe.

51. $H_0: \pi \leq 0.20$ $H_1: \pi > 0.20$
H_0 is rejected if $z > 2.33$.

$$z = \frac{(56/200) - 0.20}{\sqrt{(0.20 \times 0.80)/200}} = 2.83$$

H_0 is rejected. More than 20 percent of the owners move during a particular year. p-value = 0.5000 − 0.4977 = 0.0023.

53. a. $9.00 \pm 1.65(1/\sqrt{36}) = 9.00 \pm 0.275$
So the limits are 8.725 and 9.275.
b. $z = (8.725 - 8.900)/(1/\sqrt{36}) = -1.05$
$P(z > -1.05) = 0.5000 + 0.3531 = 0.8531$
c. $z = (9.275 - 9.300)/(1/\sqrt{36}) = -0.15$
$P(z < -0.15) = 0.5000 - 0.0596 = 0.4404$
$50 + 2.33(10/\sqrt{n}) = 55 - 0.525(10/\sqrt{n})$.

55. $$50 + 2.33\frac{10}{\sqrt{n}} = 55 - .525\frac{10}{\sqrt{n}} \qquad n = (5.71)^2 = 32.6$$
Let $n = 33$.

57. $H_0: \mu \geq 8$ $H_1: \mu < 8$
Reject H_0 if $t < -1.714$.

$$t = \frac{7.5 - 8}{3.2/\sqrt{24}} = -0.77$$

Do not reject the null hypothesis. The time is not less.

59. $H_0: \pi = 0.50$ $H_1: \pi \neq 0.50$
Reject H_0 if z is not between −1.96 and 1.96.

$$z = \frac{0.482 - 0.500}{\sqrt{(0.5)(0.5)/1{,}002}} = -1.14$$

Do not reject the null. The nation may be evenly divided.

61. Answers will vary.
63. a. $H_0: \mu = 50$ $H_1: \mu \neq 50$
Reject H_0 if t is not between −2.045 and 2.045.

$$t = \frac{56.67 - 50}{24.54/\sqrt{30}} = 1.49$$

Do not reject the null.
b. $H_0: \mu \leq 2{,}000{,}000$ $H_1: \mu > 2{,}000{,}000$
Reject H_0 if t is > 1.699.

$$t = \frac{2{,}419{,}737 - 2{,}000{,}000}{776{,}558/\sqrt{30}} = 2.96$$

Reject the null.

CHAPTER 11

1. a. Two-tailed test.
b. Reject H_0 if $z < -2.05$ or $z > 2.05$.
c. $$z = \frac{102 - 99}{\sqrt{\frac{5^2}{40} + \frac{6^2}{50}}} = 2.59$$
d. Reject H_0 and accept H_1.
e. $p = .0096$, found by 2(.5000 − .4952).

3. **Step 1** $H_0: \mu_1 \geq \mu_2$ $H_1: \mu_1 < \mu_2$
Step 2 The .05 significance level was chosen.
Step 3 Reject H_0 and accept H_1 if $z < -1.65$.
Step 4 −0.94, found by:

$$z = \frac{7.6 - 8.1}{\sqrt{\frac{(2.3)^2}{40} + \frac{(2.9)^2}{55}}} = -0.94$$

Step 5 Fail to reject H_0. Babies using the Gibbs brand did not gain less weight. $p = .1736$, found by .5000 − .3264.

5. Two-tailed test, because we are trying to show that a difference exists between the two means.
Reject H_0 if $z < -2.58$ or $z > 2.58$.

$$z = \frac{31.4 - 34.9}{\sqrt{\frac{(5.1)^2}{32} + \frac{(6.7)^2}{49}}} = -2.66$$

Reject H_0 at the .01 level. There is a difference in the mean turnover rate. P-value = 2(.5000 − .4961) = .0078

7. a. Reject H_0 if $t > 2.120$ or $t < -2.120$.
$df = 10 + 8 - 2 = 16$
b. $$s_p^2 = \frac{(10-1)(4)^2 + (8-1)(5)^2}{10+8-2} = 19.9375$$

c. $t = \dfrac{23 - 26}{\sqrt{19.9375\left(\frac{1}{10} + \frac{1}{8}\right)}} = -1.416$

d. Do not reject H_0.

e. *p*-value is greater than 0.10 and less than 0.20.

9. $H_0: \mu_f \leq \mu_m$ $H_1: \mu_f > \mu_m$
$df = 9 + 7 - 2 = 14$
Reject H_0 if $t > 2.624$.

$$s_p^2 = \frac{(7-1)(6.88)^2 + (9-1)(9.49)^2}{7 + 9 - 2} = 71.749$$

$$t = \frac{79 - 78}{\sqrt{71.749\left(\frac{1}{7} + \frac{1}{9}\right)}} = 0.234$$

Do not reject H_0. There is no difference in the mean grades.

11. $H_0: \mu_s \leq \mu_a$ $H_1: \mu_s > \mu_a$
$df = 6 + 7 - 2 = 11$
Reject H_0 if $t > 1.363$.

$$s_p^2 = \frac{(6-1)(12.2)^2 + (7-1)(15.8)^2}{6 + 7 - 2} = 203.82$$

$$t = \frac{142.5 - 130.3}{\sqrt{203.82\left(\frac{1}{6} + \frac{1}{7}\right)}} = 1.536$$

Reject H_0. The mean daily expenses are greater for the sales staff. The *p*-value is between 0.05 and 0.10.

13. a. H_0 is rejected if $z > 1.65$.

b. 0.64, found by $p_c = \dfrac{70 + 90}{100 + 150}$.

c. 1.61, found by

$$z = \frac{0.70 - 0.60}{\sqrt{(0.64 \times 0.36)/100] + [(0.64 \times 0.36)/150]}}.$$

d. H_0 is not rejected.

15. a. $H_0: \pi_1 = \pi_2$ $H_1: \pi_1 \neq \pi_2$

b. H_0 is rejected if $z < -1.96$ or $z > 1.96$.

c. $p_c = \dfrac{24 + 40}{400 + 400} = 0.08$

d. -2.09, found by

$$z = \frac{0.06 - 0.10}{\sqrt{[(0.08 \times 0.92)/400] + [(0.08 \times 0.92)/400]}}.$$

e. H_0 is rejected. The proportion infested is not the same in the two fields.

17. $H_0: \pi_d \leq \pi_r$ $H_1: \pi_d > \pi_r$
H_0 is rejected if $z > 2.05$.

$$p_c = \frac{168 + 200}{800 + 1000} = 0.2044$$

$$z = \frac{0.21 - 0.20}{\sqrt{\frac{(0.2044)(0.7956)}{800} + \frac{(0.2044)(0.7956)}{1000}}} = 0.52$$

H_0 is not rejected. There is no difference in the proportion of Democrats and Republicans who favor lowering the standards.

19. a. Reject H_0 if $t > 2.353$.

b. $\bar{d} = \dfrac{12}{4} = 3.00$ $s_d = \sqrt{\dfrac{38 - 12^2/4}{3}} = 0.816$

c. $t = \dfrac{3.00}{0.816/\sqrt{4}} = 7.35$

d. Reject H_0. There are more defective parts produced on the day shift.

e. *p*-value is less than 0.005, but greater than 0.0005.

21. $H_0: \mu_d \leq 0$ $H_d: \mu_d > 0$
Reject H_0 if $t > 2.764$.
$\bar{d} = 7.3636$ $s_d = 8.3699$

$$t = \frac{7.3636}{8.3699/\sqrt{11}} = 2.92$$

Reject H_0. The weights have increased.

23. $H_0: \mu_d \leq 0$ $H_d: \mu_d > 0$
Reject H_0 if $t > 2.821$.
$\bar{d} = 0.10$ $s_d = 4.28$

$$t = \frac{0.10}{4.28/\sqrt{10}} = 0.07$$

Fail to reject H_0. There has been no reduction.

25. $H_0: \mu_1 = \mu_2$ $H_1: \mu_1 \neq \mu_2$
Reject H_0 if $z < -2.58$ or $z > 2.58$.

$$z = \frac{36.2 - 37.0}{\sqrt{\frac{(1.14)^2}{35} + \frac{(1.30)^2}{40}}} = -2.84$$

Reject H_0. There is a difference in the useful life of the two brands of paint. The *p*-value is 0.0046, found by 2(0.5000 - 0.4977).

27. $H_0: \mu_1 = \mu_2$ $H_1: \mu_1 \neq \mu_2$
Reject H_0 if $z < -1.96$ or $z > 1.96$.

$$z = \frac{4.77 - 5.02}{\sqrt{\frac{(1.05)^2}{40} + \frac{(1.23)^2}{50}}} = -1.04$$

H_0 is not rejected. There is no difference in the mean number of calls. *p*-value = 2(0.5000 - 0.3508) = 0.2984.

29. $H_0: \mu_1 \leq \mu_2$ $H_1: \mu_1 > \mu_2$
Reject H_0 if $z > 2.05$.

$$z = \frac{11.00 - 7.67}{\sqrt{\frac{(3.88)^2}{30} + \frac{(4.42)^2}{40}}} = 3.35$$

H_0 is rejected. Those with smaller boats use their boats more often. The *p*-value is less than 0.0001.

31. $H_0: \pi_1 \leq \pi_2$ $H_1: \pi_1 > \pi_2$
Reject H_0 if $z > 1.65$.

$$p_c = \frac{180 + 261}{200 + 300} = 0.882$$

$$z = \frac{0.90 - 0.87}{\sqrt{\frac{0.882(0.118)}{200} + \frac{0.882(0.118)}{300}}} = 1.019$$

H_0 is not rejected. There is no difference in the proportions that found relief with the new and the old drugs.

33. $H_0: \pi_m = \pi_w$ $H_1: \pi_m \neq \pi_w$
Reject H_0 if $z < -1.96$ or $z > 1.96$.

$$p_c = \frac{70 + 72}{500 + 400} = 0.1578$$

$$z = \frac{0.14 - 0.18}{\sqrt{\frac{0.1578(0.8422)}{500} + \frac{0.1578(0.8422)}{400}}} = -1.636$$

H_0 is not rejected. There is no difference in the proportion of smokers.

35. $H_0: \pi_1 \leq \pi_2$ $H_1: \pi_1 > \pi_2$
If $z > 2.33$, reject H_0.

$$p_c = \frac{990 + 970}{1{,}500 + 1{,}600} = 0.63$$

$$z = \frac{.6600 - .60625}{\sqrt{\frac{.63(.37)}{1{,}500} + \frac{.63(.37)}{1{,}600}}} = 3.10$$

Do not reject the null hypothesis. We can conclude the proportion of men who believe the division is fair is greater.

37. $H_0: \mu_1 = \mu_2$ $H_1: \mu_1 \neq \mu_2$
Reject H_0 if $t < -2.060$ or $t > 2.060$.

$$s_p^2 = \frac{(15-1)(2.6)^2 + (12-1)(3.3)^2}{15 + 12 - 2} = 8.5772$$

$$t = \frac{17.6 - 16.2}{\sqrt{8.5772\left(\frac{1}{15} + \frac{1}{12}\right)}} = 1.23$$

Do not reject H_0. There is no difference in the mean percent of salaries spent by employees on the two health packages.

39. $H_0: \mu_n = \mu_s$ $H_1: \mu_n \neq \mu_s$
Reject H_0 if $t < -2.086$ or $t > 2.086$.

$$s_p^2 = \frac{(10-1)(10.5)^2 + (12-1)(14.25)^2}{10 + 12 - 2} = 161.2969$$

$$t = \frac{83.55 - 78.8}{\sqrt{161.2969\left(\frac{1}{10} + \frac{1}{12}\right)}} = 0.874$$

Do not reject H_0. There is no difference in the mean number of hamburgers sold at the two locations.

41. $H_0: \mu_1 = \mu_2$ $H_1: \mu_1 \neq \mu_2$
Reject H_0 if $t > 2.819$ or $t < -2.819$.

$$s_p^2 = \frac{(10-1)(2.33)^2 + (14-1)(2.55)^2}{10 + 14 - 2} = 6.06$$

$$t = \frac{15.87 - 18.29}{\sqrt{6.06\left(\frac{1}{10} + \frac{1}{14}\right)}} = -2.374$$

Do not reject H_0. There is no difference in the mean amount purchased.

43. $H_0: \mu_1 \leq \mu_2$ $H_1: \mu_1 > \mu_2$
Reject H_0 if $t > 2.567$.

$$s_p^2 = \frac{(8-1)(2.2638)^2 + (11-1)(2.4606)^2}{8 + 11 - 2} = 5.672$$

$$t = \frac{10.375 - 5.636}{\sqrt{5.672\left(\frac{1}{8} + \frac{1}{11}\right)}} = 4.28$$

Reject H_0.. The mean number of transactions by the young adults is more than for the senior citizens.

45. $H_0: \mu_1 \leq \mu_2$ $H_1: \mu_1 > \mu_2$
Reject H_0 if $t > 2.650$.
$\bar{X}_1 = 125.125$ $s_1 = 15.094$
$\bar{X}_2 = 117.714$ $s_2 = 19.914$

$$s_p^2 = \frac{(8-1)(15.094)^2 + (7-1)(19.914)^2}{8 + 7 - 2} = 305.708$$

$$t = \frac{125.125 - 117.714}{\sqrt{305.708\left(\frac{1}{8} + \frac{1}{7}\right)}} = 0.819$$

H_0 is not rejected. There is no difference in the me
number sold at the regular price and the mean nu
sold at reduced price.

47. $H_0: \mu_d \leq 0$ $H_1: \mu_d > 0$
Reject H_0 if $t > 1.895$.
$\bar{d} = 1.75$ $s_d = 2.9155$

$$t = \frac{1.75}{2.9155/\sqrt{8}} = 1.698$$

Do not reject H_0. There is no difference in the mea
of absences. The *p*-value is greater than 0.05.

49. $H_0: \mu_d \leq 0$ $H_1: \mu_d > 0$
Reject H_0 if $t > 1.833$.
$\bar{d} = 0.027$ $s_d = 0.2661$

$$t = \frac{0.027}{0.2661/\sqrt{10}} = 0.321$$

Do not reject H_0. We have not shown a decline in

51. $H_0: \mu_1 = \mu_2$ $H_1: \mu_1 \neq \mu_2$
If z is not between -1.96 and 1.96, reject H_0.

$$z = \frac{150 - 180}{\sqrt{\frac{(40)^2}{75} + \frac{(30)^2}{120}}} = -5.59$$

Reject the null hypothesis. The population means are different.

53. $H_0: \mu_d \leq 0$ $H_1: \mu_d > 0$
Reject H_0 if $t > 1.895$.
$\bar{d} = 3.11$ $s_d = 2.91$

$$t = \frac{3.11}{2.91/\sqrt{8}} = 3.02$$

Reject H_0. The mean is lower.

55. Answers will vary.

57. a. μ_1 = without pool μ_2 = with pool
$H_0: \mu_1 = \mu_2$ $H_1: \mu_1 \neq \mu_2$
Reject H_0 if $t > 2.000$ or $t < -2.000$.
$\bar{X}_1 = 202.8$ $s_1 = 33.7$ $n_1 = 38$
$\bar{X}_2 = 231.5$ $s_2 = 50.6$ $n_2 = 67$

$$s_p^2 = \frac{(38-1)(33.7)^2 + (67-1)(50.6)^2}{38 + 67 - 2} = 2{,}0$$

$$t = \frac{202.8 - 231.5}{\sqrt{2048.6\left(\frac{1}{38} + \frac{1}{67}\right)}} = -3.12$$

Reject H_0. There is a difference in mean selling p
homes with and without a pool.

b. μ_1 = without garage μ_2 = with garage
$H_0: \mu_1 = \mu_2$ $H_1: \mu_1 \neq \mu_2$
Reject H_0 if $t > 2.000$ or $t < -2.000$.
$\alpha = 0.05$ $df = 34 + 71 - 2 = 103$
$\bar{X}_1 = 185.44$ $s_1 = 28.01$
$\bar{X}_2 = 238.18$ $s_2 = 44.88$

$$s_p^2 = \frac{(34-1)(28.01)^2 + (71-1)(44.88)^2}{103} = 1{,}62$$

$$t = \frac{185.44 - 238.18}{\sqrt{1{,}620.25\left(\frac{1}{34} + \frac{1}{71}\right)}} = -6.28$$

Reject H_0. There is a difference in mean selling pri
homes with and without a garage.

Fail to reject H_0. There is no difference in the mean allowance for 9-year-olds in the Tampa area and the rest of the United States.

39. $H_0: \mu \leq 42 \quad H_1: \mu > 42$
Reject H_0 if $t > 1.796$.

$$t = \frac{51 - 42}{8/\sqrt{12}} = 3.90$$

Reject H_0. The mean time for delivery is more than 42 days. The p-value is less than 0.005.

41. $H_0: \mu = 2.25 \quad H_1: \mu \neq 2.25$
Reject H_0 if $t < -2.201$ or $t > 2.201$.
$\bar{X} = 2.087 \quad s_s = 0.4048$

$$t = \frac{2.087 - 2.25}{0.4048/\sqrt{12}} = -1.395$$

Do not reject H_0. There is not a difference in the mean amount of coffee consumed by students at Northwestern State and other college students.

42. $H_0: \mu \leq 25 \quad H_1: \mu > 25$
Reject H_0 if $t > 2.624$.
$\bar{X} = 26.07 \quad s = 1.5337$

$$t = \frac{26.07 - 25.00}{1.5337/\sqrt{15}} = 2.702$$

Reject H_0. The mean number of patients per day is more than 25. The p-value is less than 0.01.

43. $H_0: \mu \geq 6.5 \quad H_1: \mu < 6.5$
Reject H_0 if $t < -2.718$.
$\bar{X} = 5.1667 \quad s = 3.1575$

$$t = \frac{5.1667 - 6.5}{3.1575/\sqrt{12}} = -1.463$$

Do not reject H_0. The p-value is greater than 0.05.

45. $H_0: \mu = 0 \quad H_1: \mu \neq 0$
Reject H_0 if $t < -2.110$ or $t > 2.110$.
$\bar{X} = -0.2322 \quad s = 0.3120$

$$t = \frac{-0.2322 - 0}{0.3120/\sqrt{18}} = -3.158$$

Reject H_0. The mean gain or loss does not equal 0. The p-value is less than 0.01, but greater than 0.001.

47. $H_0: \pi \leq 0.60 \quad H_1: \pi > 0.60$
H_0 is rejected if $z > 2.33$.

$$z = \frac{0.70 - 0.60}{\sqrt{(0.60 \times 0.40)/200}} = 2.89$$

H_0 is rejected. Ms. Dennis is correct. More than 60 percent of the accounts are more than 3 months old.

49. $H_0: \pi \leq 0.44 \quad H_1: \pi > 0.44$
H_0 is rejected if $z > 1.65$.

$$z = \frac{0.480 - 0.44}{\sqrt{(0.44 \times 0.56)/1{,}000}} = 2.55$$

H_0 is rejected. We conclude that there has been an increase in the proportion of people wanting to go to Europe.

51. $H_0: \pi \leq 0.20 \quad H_1: \pi > 0.20$
H_0 is rejected if $z > 2.33$.

$$z = \frac{(56/200) - 0.20}{\sqrt{(0.20 \times 0.80)/200}} = 2.83$$

H_0 is rejected. More than 20 percent of the owners move during a particular year. p-value $= 0.5000 - 0.4977 = 0.0023$.

53. **a.** $9.00 \pm 1.65(1/\sqrt{36}) = 9.00 \pm 0.275$
So the limits are 8.725 and 9.275.
b. $z = (8.725 - 8.900)/(1/\sqrt{36}) = -1.05$
$P(z > -1.05) = 0.5000 + 0.3531 = 0.8531$
c. $z = (9.275 - 9.300)/(1/\sqrt{36}) = -0.15$
$P(z < -0.15) = 0.5000 - 0.0596 = 0.4404$
$50 + 2.33(10/\sqrt{n}) = 55 - 0.525\,(10/\sqrt{n})$.

55. $50 + 2.33\frac{10}{\sqrt{n}} = 55 - .525\frac{10}{\sqrt{n}} \qquad n = (5.71)^2 = 32.6$
Let $n = 33$.

57. $H_0: \mu \geq 8 \quad H_1: \mu < 8$
Reject H_0 if $t < -1.714$.

$$t = \frac{7.5 - 8}{3.2/\sqrt{24}} = -0.77$$

Do not reject the null hypothesis. The time is not less.

59. $H_0: \pi = 0.50 \quad H_1: \pi \neq 0.50$
Reject H_0 if z is not between –1.96 and 1.96.

$$z = \frac{0.482 - 0.500}{\sqrt{(0.5)(0.5)/1{,}002}} = -1.14$$

Do not reject the null. The nation may be evenly divided.

61. Answers will vary.

63. **a.** $H_0: \mu = 50 \quad H_1: \mu \neq 50$
Reject H_0 if t is not between -2.045 and 2.045.

$$t = \frac{56.67 - 50}{24.54/\sqrt{30}} = 1.49$$

Do not reject the null.
b. $H_0: \mu \leq 2{,}000{,}000 \quad H_1: \mu > 2{,}000{,}000$
Reject H_0 if t is > 1.699.

$$t = \frac{2{,}419{,}737 - 2{,}000{,}000}{776{,}558/\sqrt{30}} = 2.96$$

Reject the null.

CHAPTER 11

1. **a.** Two-tailed test.
b. Reject H_0 if $z < -2.05$ or $z > 2.05$.
c. $z = \dfrac{102 - 99}{\sqrt{\dfrac{5^2}{40} + \dfrac{6^2}{50}}} = 2.59$
d. Reject H_0 and accept H_1.
e. $p = .0096$, found by $2(.5000 - .4952)$.

3. **Step 1** $H_0: \mu_1 \geq \mu_2 \quad H_1: \mu_1 < \mu_2$
Step 2 The .05 significance level was chosen.
Step 3 Reject H_0 and accept H_1 if $z < -1.65$.
Step 4 -0.94, found by:

$$z = \frac{7.6 - 8.1}{\sqrt{\dfrac{(2.3)^2}{40} + \dfrac{(2.9)^2}{55}}} = -0.94$$

Step 5 Fail to reject H_0. Babies using the Gibbs brand did not gain less weight. $p = .1736$, found by $.5000 - .3264$.

5. Two-tailed test, because we are trying to show that a difference exists between the two means.
Reject H_0 if $z < -2.58$ or $z > 2.58$.

$$z = \frac{31.4 - 34.9}{\sqrt{\dfrac{(5.1)^2}{32} + \dfrac{(6.7)^2}{49}}} = -2.66$$

Reject H_0 at the .01 level. There is a difference in the mean turnover rate. P-value $= 2(.5000 - .4961) = .0078$

7. **a.** Reject H_0 if $t > 2.120$ or $t < -2.120$.
$df = 10 + 8 - 2 = 16$
b. $s_p^2 = \dfrac{(10 - 1)(4)^2 + (8 - 1)(5)^2}{10 + 8 - 2} = 19.9375$

c. $t = \dfrac{23 - 26}{\sqrt{19.9375\left(\dfrac{1}{10} + \dfrac{1}{8}\right)}} = -1.416$

d. Do not reject H_0.

e. p-value is greater than 0.10 and less than 0.20.

9. H_0: $\mu_f \leq \mu_m$ H_1: $\mu_f > \mu_m$

$df = 9 + 7 - 2 = 14$

Reject H_0 if $t > 2.624$.

$$s_p^2 = \frac{(7-1)(6.88)^2 + (9-1)(9.49)^2}{7 + 9 - 2} = 71.749$$

$$t = \frac{79 - 78}{\sqrt{71.749\left(\frac{1}{7} + \frac{1}{9}\right)}} = 0.234$$

Do not reject H_0. There is no difference in the mean grades.

11. H_0: $\mu_s \leq \mu_a$ H_1: $\mu_s > \mu_a$

$df = 6 + 7 - 2 = 11$

Reject H_0 if $t > 1.363$.

$$s_p^2 = \frac{(6-1)(12.2)^2 + (7-1)(15.8)^2}{6 + 7 - 2} = 203.82$$

$$t = \frac{142.5 - 130.3}{\sqrt{203.82\left(\frac{1}{6} + \frac{1}{7}\right)}} = 1.536$$

Reject H_0. The mean daily expenses are greater for the sales staff. The p-value is between 0.05 and 0.10.

13. a. H_0 is rejected if $z > 1.65$.

b. 0.64, found by $p_c = \dfrac{70 + 90}{100 + 150}$.

c. 1.61, found by

$$z = \frac{0.70 - 0.60}{\sqrt{(0.64 \times 0.36)/100] + [(0.64 \times 0.36)/150]}}.$$

d. H_0 is not rejected.

15. a. H_0: $\pi_1 = \pi_2$ H_1: $\pi_1 \neq \pi_2$

b. H_0 is rejected if $z < -1.96$ or $z > 1.96$.

c. $p_c = \dfrac{24 + 40}{400 + 400} = 0.08$

d. -2.09, found by

$$z = \frac{0.06 - 0.10}{\sqrt{[(0.08 \times 0.92)/400] + [(0.08 \times 0.92)/400]}}.$$

e. H_0 is rejected. The proportion infested is not the same in the two fields.

17. H_0: $\pi_d \leq \pi_r$ H_1: $\pi_d > \pi_r$

H_0 is rejected if $z > 2.05$.

$$p_c = \frac{168 + 200}{800 + 1000} = 0.2044$$

$$z = \frac{0.21 - 0.20}{\sqrt{\dfrac{(0.2044)(0.7956)}{800} + \dfrac{(0.2044)(0.7956)}{1000}}} = 0.52$$

H_0 is not rejected. There is no difference in the proportion of Democrats and Republicans who favor lowering the standards.

19. a. Reject H_0 if $t > 2.353$.

b. $\bar{d} = \dfrac{12}{4} = 3.00$ $s_d = \sqrt{\dfrac{38 - 12^2/4}{3}} = 0.816$

c. $t = \dfrac{3.00}{0.816/\sqrt{4}} = 7.35$

d. Reject H_0. There are more defective parts produced on the day shift.

e. p-value is less than 0.005, but greater than 0.0005.

21. H_0: $\mu_d \leq 0$ H_a: $\mu_d > 0$

Reject H_0 if $t > 2.764$.

$\bar{d} = 7.3636$ $s_d = 8.3699$

$$t = \frac{7.3636}{8.3699/\sqrt{11}} = 2.92$$

Reject H_0. The weights have increased.

23. H_0: $\mu_d \leq 0$ H_a: $\mu_d > 0$

Reject H_0 if $t > 2.821$.

$\bar{d} = 0.10$ $s_d = 4.28$

$$t = \frac{0.10}{4.28/\sqrt{10}} = 0.07$$

Fail to reject H_0. There has been no reduction.

25. H_0: $\mu_1 = \mu_2$ H_1: $\mu_1 \neq \mu_2$

Reject H_0 if $z < -2.58$ or $z > 2.58$.

$$z = \frac{36.2 - 37.0}{\sqrt{\dfrac{(1.14)^2}{35} + \dfrac{(1.30)^2}{40}}} = -2.84$$

Reject H_0. There is a difference in the useful life of the two brands of paint. The p-value is 0.0046, found by 2(0.5000 – 0.4977).

27. H_0: $\mu_1 = \mu_2$ H_1: $\mu_1 \neq \mu_2$

Reject H_0 if $z < -1.96$ or $z > 1.96$.

$$z = \frac{4.77 - 5.02}{\sqrt{\dfrac{(1.05)^2}{40} + \dfrac{(1.23)^2}{50}}} = -1.04$$

H_0 is not rejected. There is no difference in the mean number of calls. p-value = 2(0.5000 – 0.3508) = 0.2984.

29. H_0: $\mu_1 \leq \mu_2$ H_1: $\mu_1 > \mu_2$

Reject H_0 if $z > 2.05$.

$$z = \frac{11.00 - 7.67}{\sqrt{\dfrac{(3.88)^2}{30} + \dfrac{(4.42)^2}{40}}} = 3.35$$

H_0 is rejected. Those with smaller boats use their boats more often. The p-value is less than 0.0001.

31. H_0: $\pi_1 \leq \pi_2$ H_1: $\pi_1 > \pi_2$

Reject H_0 if $z > 1.65$.

$$p_c = \frac{180 + 261}{200 + 300} = 0.882$$

$$z = \frac{0.90 - 0.87}{\sqrt{\dfrac{0.882(0.118)}{200} + \dfrac{0.882(0.118)}{300}}} = 1.019$$

H_0 is not rejected. There is no difference in the proportions that found relief with the new and the old drugs.

33. H_0: $\pi_m = \pi_w$ H_1: $\pi_m \neq \pi_w$

Reject H_0 if $z < -1.96$ or $z > 1.96$.

$$p_c = \frac{70 + 72}{500 + 400} = 0.1578$$

$$z = \frac{0.14 - 0.18}{\sqrt{\dfrac{0.1578(0.8422)}{500} + \dfrac{0.1578(0.8422)}{400}}} = -1.636$$

H_0 is not rejected. There is no difference in the proportion of smokers.

35. $H_0: \pi_1 \leq \pi_2 \quad H_1: \pi_1 > \pi_2$
If $z > 2.33$, reject H_0.

$$p_c = \frac{990 + 970}{1{,}500 + 1{,}600} = 0.63$$

$$z = \frac{.6600 - .60625}{\sqrt{\frac{.63(.37)}{1{,}500} + \frac{.63(.37)}{1{,}600}}} = 3.10$$

Do not reject the null hypothesis. We can conclude the proportion of men who believe the division is fair is greater.

37. $H_0: \mu_1 = \mu_2 \quad H_1: \mu_1 \neq \mu_2$
Reject H_0 if $t < -2.060$ or $t > 2.060$.

$$s_p^2 = \frac{(15 - 1)(2.6)^2 + (12 - 1)(3.3)^2}{15 + 12 - 2} = 8.5772$$

$$t = \frac{17.6 - 16.2}{\sqrt{8.5772\left(\frac{1}{15} + \frac{1}{12}\right)}} = 1.23$$

Do not reject H_0. There is no difference in the mean percent of salaries spent by employees on the two health packages.

39. $H_0: \mu_n = \mu_s \quad H_1: \mu_n \neq \mu_s$
Reject H_0 if $t < -2.086$ or $t > 2.086$.

$$s_p^2 = \frac{(10 - 1)(10.5)^2 + (12 - 1)(14.25)^2}{10 + 12 - 2} = 161.2969$$

$$t = \frac{83.55 - 78.8}{\sqrt{161.2969\left(\frac{1}{10} + \frac{1}{12}\right)}} = 0.874$$

Do not reject H_0. There is no difference in the mean number of hamburgers sold at the two locations.

41. $H_0: \mu_1 = \mu_2 \quad H_1: \mu_1 \neq \mu_2$
Reject H_0 if $t > 2.819$ or $t < -2.819$.

$$s_p^2 = \frac{(10 - 1)(2.33)^2 + (14 - 1)(2.55)^2}{10 + 14 - 2} = 6.06$$

$$t = \frac{15.87 - 18.29}{\sqrt{6.06\left(\frac{1}{10} + \frac{1}{14}\right)}} = -2.374$$

Do not reject H_0. There is no difference in the mean amount purchased.

43. $H_0: \mu_1 \leq \mu_2 \quad H_1: \mu_1 > \mu_2$
Reject H_0 if $t > 2.567$.

$$s_p^2 = \frac{(8 - 1)(2.2638)^2 + (11 - 1)(2.4606)^2}{8 + 11 - 2} = 5.672$$

$$t = \frac{10.375 - 5.636}{\sqrt{5.672\left(\frac{1}{8} + \frac{1}{11}\right)}} = 4.28$$

Reject H_0. The mean number of transactions by the young adults is more than for the senior citizens.

45. $H_0: \mu_1 \leq \mu_2 \quad H_1: \mu_1 > \mu_2$
Reject H_0 if $t > 2.650$.
$\bar{X}_1 = 125.125 \quad s_1 = 15.094$
$\bar{X}_2 = 117.714 \quad s_2 = 19.914$

$$s_p^2 = \frac{(8 - 1)(15.094)^2 + (7 - 1)(19.914)^2}{8 + 7 - 2} = 305.708$$

$$t = \frac{125.125 - 117.714}{\sqrt{305.708\left(\frac{1}{8} + \frac{1}{7}\right)}} = 0.819$$

H_0 is not rejected. There is no difference in the mean number sold at the regular price and the mean number sold at reduced price.

47. $H_0: \mu_d \leq 0 \quad H_1: \mu_d > 0$
Reject H_0 if $t > 1.895$.
$\bar{d} = 1.75 \quad s_d = 2.9155$

$$t = \frac{1.75}{2.9155/\sqrt{8}} = 1.698$$

Do not reject H_0. There is no difference in the mean number of absences. The p-value is greater than 0.05.

49. $H_0: \mu_d \leq 0 \quad H_1: \mu_d > 0$
Reject H_0 if $t > 1.833$.
$\bar{d} = 0.027 \quad s_d = 0.2661$

$$t = \frac{0.027}{0.2661/\sqrt{10}} = 0.321$$

Do not reject H_0. We have not shown a decline in grades.

51. $H_0: \mu_1 = \mu_2 \quad H_1: \mu_1 \neq \mu_2$
If z is not between -1.96 and 1.96, reject H_0.

$$z = \frac{150 - 180}{\sqrt{\frac{(40)^2}{75} + \frac{(30)^2}{120}}} = -5.59$$

Reject the null hypothesis. The population means are different.

53. $H_0: \mu_d \leq 0 \quad H_1: \mu_d > 0$
Reject H_0 if $t > 1.895$.
$\bar{d} = 3.11 \quad s_d = 2.91$

$$t = \frac{3.11}{2.91/\sqrt{8}} = 3.02$$

Reject H_0. The mean is lower.

55. Answers will vary.

57. **a.** μ_1 = without pool $\quad \mu_2$ = with pool
$H_0: \mu_1 = \mu_2 \quad H_1: \mu_1 \neq \mu_2$
Reject H_0 if $t > 2.000$ or $t < -2.000$.
$\bar{X}_1 = 202.8 \quad s_1 = 33.7 \quad n_1 = 38$
$\bar{X}_2 = 231.5 \quad s_2 = 50.6 \quad n_2 = 67$

$$s_p^2 = \frac{(38 - 1)(33.7)^2 + (67 - 1)(50.6)^2}{38 + 67 - 2} = 2{,}048.6$$

$$t = \frac{202.8 - 231.5}{\sqrt{2048.6\left(\frac{1}{38} + \frac{1}{67}\right)}} = -3.12$$

Reject H_0. There is a difference in mean selling price for homes with and without a pool.

b. μ_1 = without garage $\quad \mu_2$ = with garage
$H_0: \mu_1 = \mu_2 \quad H_1: \mu_1 \neq \mu_2$
Reject H_0 if $t > 2.000$ or $t < -2.000$.
$\alpha = 0.05 \quad df = 34 + 71 - 2 = 103$
$\bar{X}_1 = 185.44 \quad s_1 = 28.01$
$\bar{X}_2 = 238.18 \quad s_2 = 44.88$

$$s_p^2 = \frac{(34 - 1)(28.01)^2 + (71 - 1)(44.88)^2}{103} = 1{,}620.25$$

$$t = \frac{185.44 - 238.18}{\sqrt{1{,}620.25\left(\frac{1}{34} + \frac{1}{71}\right)}} = -6.28$$

Reject H_0. There is a difference in mean selling price for homes with and without a garage.

c. $H_0: \mu_1 = \mu_2 \quad H_1: \mu_1 \neq \mu_2$
Reject H_0 if $t > 2.036$ or $t < -2.036$.
$\bar{X}_1 = 196.91 \quad s_1 = 35.78 \quad n_1 = 15$
$\bar{X}_2 = 227.45 \quad s_2 = 44.19 \quad n_2 = 20$

$$s_p^2 = \frac{(15-1)(35.78)^2 + (20-1)(44.19)^2}{15+20-2} = 1{,}667.43$$

$$t = \frac{196.92 - 227.45}{\sqrt{1{,}667.43\left(\frac{1}{15} + \frac{1}{20}\right)}} = -2.19$$

Reject H_0. There is a difference in mean selling price for homes in Township 1 and Township 2.

d. $H_0: \pi_1 = \pi_2 \quad H_1: \pi_1 \neq \pi_2$
If z is not between -1.96 and 1.96, reject H_0.

$$p_c = \frac{24+43}{52+53} = 0.64$$

$$z = \frac{0.462 - 0.811}{\sqrt{0.64 \times 0.36/52 + 0.64 \times 0.36/53}} = -3.73$$

Reject the null hypothesis. There is a difference.

59. $H_0: \mu_1 = \mu_2 \quad H_1: \mu_1 \neq \mu_2$
If t is not between -2.052 and 2.052, reject H_0.

$$s_p^2 = \frac{(22-1)(3.54)^2 + (7-1)(1.50)^2}{22+7-2} = 10.25$$

$$t = \frac{12.89 - 14.59}{\sqrt{10.25\left(\frac{1}{22} + \frac{1}{7}\right)}} = -1.22$$

Do not reject H_0.

CHAPTER 12

1. 9.01, from Appendix G.
3. Reject H_0 if $F > 10.5$, where degrees of freedom in the numerator are 7 and 5 in the denominator. Computed $F = 2.04$, found by:

$$F = \frac{s_1^2}{s_2^2} = \frac{(10)^2}{(7)^2} = 2.04$$

Do not reject H_0. There is no difference in the variations of the two populations.

5. $H_0: \sigma_1^2 = \sigma_2^2 \quad H_1: \sigma_1^2 \neq \sigma_2^2$
Reject H_0 where $F > 3.10$. (3.10 is about halfway between 3.14 and 3.07.) Computed $F = 1.44$, found by:

$$F = \frac{(12)^2}{(10)^2} = 1.44$$

Do not reject H_0. There is no difference in the variations of the two populations.

7. a. $H_0: \mu_1 = \mu_2 = \mu_3$; H_1: Treatment means are not all the same.
b. Reject H_0 if $F > 4.26$.
c. & d.

Source	SS	df	MS	F
Treatment	62.17	2	31.08	21.94
Error	12.75	9	1.42	
Total	74.92	11		

e. Reject H_0. The treatment means are not all the same.

9. $H_0: \mu_1 = \mu_2 = \mu_3$; H_1: Treatment means are not all the same. Reject H_0 if $F > 4.26$.

Source	SS	df	MS	F
Treatment	276.50	2	138.25	14.18
Error	87.75	9	9.75	

Reject H_0. The treatment means are not all the same.

11. a. $H_0: \mu_1 = \mu_2 = \mu_3$; H_1: Not all means are the same.
b. Reject H_0 if $F > 4.26$.
c. SST = 107.20, SSE = 9.47, SS total = 116.67.
d.

Source	SS	df	MS	F
Treatment	107.20	2	53.600	50.96
Error	9.47	9	1.052	
Total	116.67	11		

e. Since $50.96 > 4.26$, H_0 is rejected. At least one of the means differs.
f. $(\bar{X}_1 - \bar{X}_2) \pm t\sqrt{MSE(1/n_1 + 1/n_2)}$
$= (9.667 - 2.20) \pm 2.262\sqrt{1.052(1/3 + 1/5)}$
$= 7.467 \pm 1.69$
$= [5.777, 9.157]$

Yes, we can conclude that treatments 1 and 2 have different means.

13. $H_0: \mu_1 = \mu_2 = \mu_3 = \mu_4$; H_1: Not all means are equal. H_0 is rejected if $F > 3.71$.

Source	SS	df	MS	F
Treatment	32.33	3	10.77	2.36
Error	45.67	10	4.567	
Total	78.00	13		

Because 2.36 is less than 3.71, H_0 is not rejected. There is no difference in the mean number of weeks.

15. a. $H_0: \mu_1 = \mu_2$; H_1: Not all treatment means are equal.
b. Reject H_0 if $F > 18.5$.
c. $H_0: \mu_1 = \mu_2 = \mu_3$; H_1: Not all block means are equal. H_0 is rejected if $F > 19.0$.
d. $$SST = \frac{(127)^2}{3} + \frac{(92)^2}{3} - \frac{(219)^2}{6} = 204.167$$

$$SSB = \frac{(77)^2}{2} + \frac{(63)^2}{2} + \frac{(79)^2}{2} - \frac{(219)^2}{6} = 76$$

SS total $= 8{,}283 - (219)^2/6 = 289.5$
SSE $= 289.5 - 204.167 - 76 = 9.333$

e.

Source	SS	df	MS	F
Treatment	204.167	1	204.167	43.75
Blocks	76.000	2	38.000	8.14
Error	9.333	2	4.667	
Total	289.5000	5		

f. $43.75 > 18.5$, so reject H_0. There is a difference in the treatments. $8.14 < 19.0$, so do not reject H_0 for blocks. There is no difference among blocks.

17. For treatment:
$H_0: \mu_1 = \mu_2 = \mu_3$
H_1: Not all means equal
Reject if $F > 4.46$

For blocks:
$H_0: \mu_1 = \mu_2 = \mu_3 = \mu_4 = \mu_5$
H_1: Not all means equal
Reject if $F > 3.84$

Source	SS	df	MS	F
Treatment	62.53	2	31.2650	5.75
Blocks	33.73	4	8.4325	1.55
Error	43.47	8	5.4338	
Total	138.73			

There is a difference in shifts, but not by employee.

19. $H_0: \sigma_1^2 \leq \sigma_2^2$; $H_1: \sigma_1^2 > \sigma_2^2$. $df_1 = 21 - 1 = 20$; $df_2 = 18 - 1 = 17$. H_0 is rejected if $F > 3.16$.

$$F = \frac{(45{,}600)^2}{(21{,}330)^2} = 4.57$$

Reject H_0. There is more variation in the selling price of oceanfront homes.

21. Sharkey: $n = 7$ $s_s = 14.79$
White: $n = 8$ $s_w = 22.95$

H_0: $\sigma_w^2 \leq \sigma_s^2$; H_1: $\sigma_w^2 > \sigma_s^2$. $df_s = 7 - 1 = 6$; $df_w = 8 - 1 = 7$. Reject H_0 if $F > 8.26$.

$$F = \frac{(22.95)^2}{(14.79)^2} = 2.41$$

Cannot reject H_0. There is no difference in the variation of the weekly sales.

23. **a.** H_0: $\mu_1 = \mu_2 = \mu_3 = \mu_4$
H_1: Treatment means are not all equal.
b. $\alpha = .05$ Reject H_0 if $F > 3.10$.
c.

Source	SS	df	MS	F
Treatment	50	$4 - 1 = 3$	50/3	$\frac{50/3}{10} = 1.67$
Error	200	$24 - 4 = 20$	10	
Total	250	$24 - 1 = 23$		

d. Do not reject H_0.

25. H_0: $\mu_1 = \mu_2 = \mu_3$; H_1: Not all treatment means are equal. H_0 is rejected if $F > 3.89$.

Source	df	SS	MS	F
Treatment	2	63.33	31.667	13.38
Error	12	28.40	2.367	
Total	14	91.73		

H_0 is rejected. There is a difference in the treatment means.

27. H_0: $\mu_1 = \mu_2 = \mu_3 = \mu_4$; H_1: Not all means are equal. H_0 is rejected if $F > 3.10$

Source	df	SS	MS	F
Factor	3	87.79	29.26	9.12
Error	20	64.17	3.21	
Total	23	151.96		

Because computed F of $9.12 > 3.10$, the null hypothesis of no difference is rejected at the .05 level.

29. **a.** H_0: $\mu_1 = \mu_2$; H_1: $\mu_1 \neq \mu_2$. Critical value of $F = 4.75$.

Source	SS	df	MS	F
Treatment	219.43	1	219.43	23.10
Error	114.00	12	9.5	
Total	333.43	13		

b. $$t = \frac{19 - 27}{\sqrt{9.5\left(\frac{1}{6} + \frac{1}{8}\right)}} = -4.81$$

Then $t^2 = F$. That is $(-4.81)^2 \approx 23.10$ (actually 23.14. Difference due to rounding)

c. H_0 is rejected. There is a difference in the mean scores.

31. For color, the critical value of F is 4.76; for size, it is 5.14.

Source	SS	df	MS	F
Treatment	25.0	3	8.3333	5.88
Blocks	21.5	2	10.75	7.59
Error	8.5	6	1.4167	
Total	55.0	11		

H_0s for both treatment and blocks (color and size) are rejected. At least one mean differs for color and at least one mean differs for size.

33. **a.** Critical value of F is 3.49. Computed F is .668. Do not reject H_0.
b. Critical value of F is 3.26. Computed F value is 100.204. Reject H_0 for block means.

35. For gasoline:
H_0: $\mu_1 = \mu_2 = \mu_3$; H_1: Mean mileage is not the same.
Reject H_0 if $F > 3.89$.
For automobile:
H_0: $\mu_1 = \mu_2 = \cdots \mu_7$; H_1: Mean mileage is not the same.
Reject H_0 if $F > 3.00$.

ANOVA Table

Source	df	SS	MS	F
Gasoline	2	44.095	22.048	26.71
Autos	6	77.238	12.873	15.60
Error	12	9.905	0.825	
Total	20			

There is a difference in both autos and gasoline.

37. **a.** H_0: $\mu_1 = \mu_2 = \mu_3 = \mu_4 = \mu_5 = \mu_6$; H_1: The treatment means are not equal. Reject H_0 if $F > 2.37$.

Source	df	SS	MS	F
Treatment	5	0.03478	0.00696	3.86
Error	58	0.10439	0.0018	
Total	63	0.13917		

H_0 is rejected. There is a difference in the mean weight of the colors.

39. Answers will vary.

41. **a.** H_0: $\sigma_P^2 = \sigma_{NP}^2$; H_1: $\sigma_P^2 \neq \sigma_{NP}^2$. Reject H_0 if $F > 1.88$ (estimated).
$df_1 = 67 - 1 = 66$; $df_2 = 38 - 1 = 37$.

$$F = \frac{(50.58)^2}{(33.71)^2} = 2.25$$

Reject H_0. There is a difference in the variance of the two selling prices.

b. H_0: $\sigma_g^2 = \sigma_{ng}^2$; H_1: $\sigma_g^2 \neq \sigma_{ng}^2$. Reject H_0 if $F > 1.93$ (estimated).

$$F = \frac{(44.88)^2}{(28.00)^2} = 2.57$$

Reject H_0. There is a difference in the variance of the two selling prices.

c. H_0: $\mu_1 = \mu_2 = \mu_3 = \mu_4 = \mu_5$; H_1: Not all treatment means are equal. Reject H_0 if $F > 2.50$.

Source	SS	df	MS	F
Township	13,263	4	3,316	1.52
Error	217,505	100	2,175	
Total	230,768	104		

Do not reject H_0. There is no difference in the mean selling prices in the five townships.

43. **a.** H_0: $\mu_1 = \mu_2 = \mu_2$; H_1: Not all treatment means are equal. Reject H_0 if $F > 3.39$.

Source	SS	df	MS	F
Treatment	70.21	2	35.11	4.10
Error	222.39	26	8.55	
Total	292.60	28		

Reject H_0. The mean percentages are different in the regions.

b. H_0: $\mu_1 = \mu_2 = \mu_3$; H_1: Not all treatment means are equal. Reject H_0 if $F > 3.39$.

Source	SS	*df*	MS	*F*
Treatment	0.000046	2	0.000023	0.16
Error	0.003803	26	0.000146	
Total	0.003849	28		

Do not reject H_0. The per capita GNP is the same in the regions.

CHAPTER 13

1. $\Sigma X = 28$, $\Sigma Y = 29$, $\Sigma X^2 = 186$, $\Sigma XY = 173$, $\Sigma Y^2 = 175$

$$r = \frac{5(173) - (28)(29)}{\sqrt{[5(186) - (28)^2][5(175) - (29)^2]}} = 0.75$$

The 0.75 coefficient indicates a rather strong positive correlation between X and Y. The coefficient of determination is 0.5625, found by $(0.75)^2$. More than 56 percent of the variation in Y is accounted for by X.

3. **a.** Sales.

b.

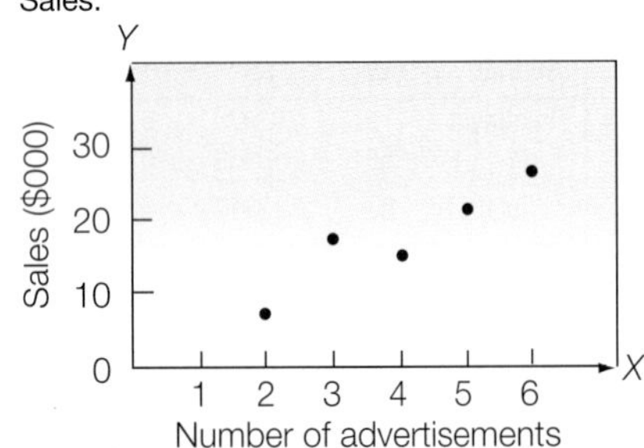

c. $n = 5$, $\Sigma X = 20$, $\Sigma X^2 = 90$, $\Sigma Y = 85$, $\Sigma Y^2 = 1595$, and $\Sigma XY = 376$, so:

$$r = \frac{5(376) - (20)(85)}{\sqrt{[5(90) - (20)^2][5(1595) - (85)^2]}} = 0.93$$

d. The coefficient of determination is 0.8649, found by $(0.93)^2$.

e. There is a strong positive association between the variables. About 86 percent of the variation in sales is explained by the number of airings.

5. **a.** Police is the independent variable, and crime is the dependent variable.

b.

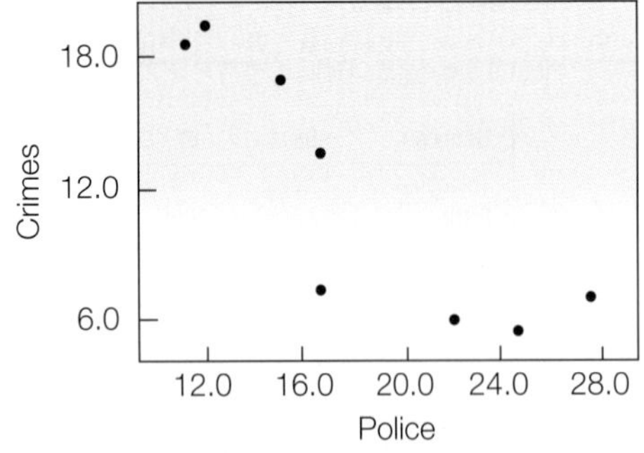

c. $n = 8$, $\Sigma X = 146$, $\Sigma X^2 = 2906$, $\Sigma Y = 95$, $\Sigma Y^2 = 1{,}419$, and $\Sigma XY = 1{,}502$

$$r = \frac{8(1{,}502) - 146(95)}{\sqrt{[8(2{,}906) - (146)^2][8(1{,}419) - (95)^2]}}$$

$= -.874$

d. 0.76, found by $(-.874)^2$

e. Strong inverse relationship. As the number of police increases, the crime decreases.

7. Reject H_0 if $t > 1.812$.

$$t = \frac{.32\sqrt{12 - 2}}{\sqrt{1 - (.32)^2}} = 1.07$$

Do not reject H_0.

9. H_0: $\rho \le 0$; H_1: $\rho > 0$. Reject H_0 if $t > 2.552$. $df = 18$.

$$t = \frac{.78\sqrt{20 - 2}}{\sqrt{1 - (.78)^2}} = 5.288$$

Reject H_0. There is a positive correlation between gallons sold and the pump price.

11. **a.** $Y' = 3.7671 + .3630X$

$$b = \frac{5(173) - (28)(29)}{5(186) - (28)^2} = 0.3630$$

$$a = \frac{29}{5} - (0.363)\frac{28}{5} = 3.7671$$

b. 6.3081, found by $Y' = 3.7671 + 0.3630(7)$

13. **a.** $b = \dfrac{10(718) - (91)(74)}{10(895) - (91)^2} = 0.667$

$$a = \frac{74}{10} - .667\left(\frac{91}{10}\right) = 1.333$$

b. $Y' = 1.333 + .667(6) = 5.335$

15. **a.**

Earnings
10
5
0
0 10 20 30 40 50 60 70 80 90
Sales

b. $r = \dfrac{12(3{,}306.35) - (501.10)(64.1)}{\sqrt{[12(28{,}459) - (501.10)^2][12(458.41) - (64.1)^2]}}$

$= 0.673$

c. $r^2 = (0.673)^2 = 0.4529$

d. A strong positive association between the variables. About 45 percent of the variation in earnings is accounted for by sales.

e. $b = \dfrac{12(3{,}306.35) - (501.1)(64.1)}{12(28{,}459) - (501.1)^2} = 0.0836$

$$a = \frac{64.1}{12} - 0.0836\left(\frac{501.10}{12}\right) = 1.8507$$

f. $Y' = 1.8507 + 0.0836(50.0) = 6.0307$ ($ millions)

17. **a.** $b = \dfrac{8(1502) - (146)(95)}{8(2906) - (146)^2} = -0.9596$

$$a = \frac{95}{8} - (-0.9596)\left(\frac{146}{8}\right) = 29.3877$$

b. 10.1957, found by $29.3877 - 0.9596(20)$

c. For each policeman added, crime goes down by almost one.

19. **a.** $\sqrt{\dfrac{175 - 3.767(29) - 0.363(173)}{5-2}} = .993$

b. $Y' \pm .993$

21. **a.** $\sqrt{\dfrac{584 - 1.333(74) - 0.667(718)}{10-2}} = .898$

b. $Y' \pm 1.796$

23. $\sqrt{\dfrac{1419 - 29.3877(95) - (-.9596)(1{,}502)}{8-2}} = 3.379$

25. **a.** $6.308 \pm (3.182)(.993)\sqrt{.2 + \dfrac{(7-5.6)^2}{186 - (784/5)}}$
$= 6.308 \pm 1.633$
$= [4.675, 7.941]$

b. $6.308 \pm (3.182)(.993)\sqrt{1 + 1/5 + .0671}$
$= [2.751, 9.865]$

27. **a.** [4.2939, 6.3721]

b. [2.9854, 7.6806]

29. $r = \dfrac{(5)(340) - (50)(30)}{\sqrt{[(5)(600) - (50)^2][(5)(200) - (30)^2]}} = .8944$

Then, $(.8944)^2 = .80$, the coefficient of determination.

31. **a.** $r^2 = 1000/1500 = .667$

b. .82, found by $\sqrt{.667}$

c. 6.20, found by $s_{y \cdot x} = \sqrt{\dfrac{500}{15-2}}$

33. H_0: $\rho \le 0$; H_1: $\rho > 0$. Reject H_0 if $t > 1.714$.

$$t = \frac{.94\sqrt{25-2}}{\sqrt{1-(.94)^2}} = 13.213$$

Reject H_0. There is a positive correlation between passengers and weight of luggage.

35. H_0: $\rho \le 0$; H_1: $\rho > 0$. Reject H_0 if $t > 2.764$.

$$t = \frac{.47\sqrt{12-2}}{\sqrt{1-(.47)^2}} = 1.684$$

Do not reject H_0. There is not a positive correlation between engine size and performance. *p*-value is greater than .05, but less than .10.

37. H_0: $\rho \ge 0$; H_1: $\rho < 0$. Reject H_0 if $t < -1.701$, $df = 28$.

$$t = \frac{-.45\sqrt{30-2}}{\sqrt{1-.2025}} = -2.67$$

Reject H_0. There is a negative correlation between the selling price and the number of miles driven.

39. **a.** $r = 0.589$

b. $r^2 = (0.589)^2 = 0.3469$

c. H_0: $\rho \le 0$; H_1: $\rho > 0$. Reject H_0 if $t > 1.860$.

$$t = \frac{0.589\sqrt{10-2}}{\sqrt{1-(.589)^2}} = 2.062$$

H_0 is rejected. There is a positive association between family size and the amount spent on food.

41. **a.**

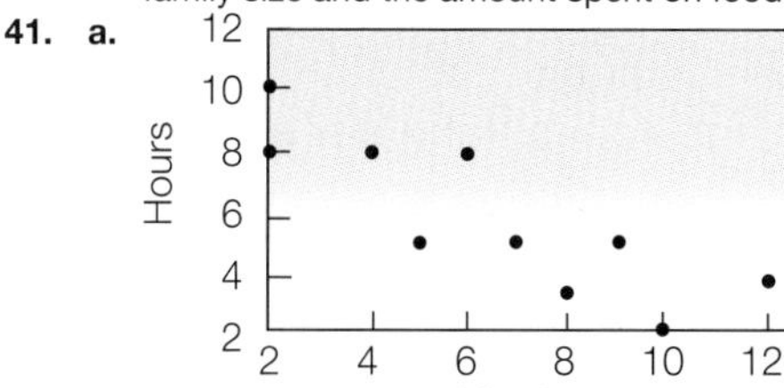

There is an inverse relationship between the variables. As the months owned increase, the number of hours exercised decreases.

b. $r = \dfrac{10(313) - (65)(58)}{\sqrt{[10(523) - (65)^2][10(396) - (58)^2]}}$
$= -0.827$

c. H_0: $\rho \ge 0$; H_1: $\rho < 0$. Reject H_0 if $t < -2.896$.

$$t = \frac{-0.827\sqrt{10-2}}{\sqrt{1-(-0.827)^2}} = -4.16$$

Reject H_0. There is a negative association between months owned and hours exercised.

43. **a.**

Source	SS	df	MS	F
Regression	50	1	50	2.5556
Error	450	23	19.5652	
Total	500	24		

b. $n = 25$

c. $s_{y \cdot x} = \sqrt{19.5652} = 4.4233$

d. $r^2 = \dfrac{50}{500} = 0.10$

45. **a.** $n = 15$, $\Sigma X = 107$, $\Sigma X^2 = 837$, $\Sigma Y = 118.6$, $\Sigma Y^2 = 969.92$, $\Sigma XY = 811.60$, $s_{y \cdot x} = 1.114$

$$b = \frac{15(811.60) - (107)(118.6)}{15(837.0) - (107)^2} = -0.4667$$

$$a = \frac{118.6}{15} - (-0.4667)\left(\frac{107}{15}\right) = 11.2358$$

b. $Y' = 11.2358 - 0.4667(7.0) = 7.9689$

c. $7.9689 \pm (2.160)(1.114)\sqrt{1 + \dfrac{1}{15} + \dfrac{(7-7.1333)^2}{837 - \dfrac{(107)^2}{15}}}$
$= 7.9689 \pm 2.4854$
$= [5.4835, 10.4543]$

d. $r^2 = 0.499$. Nearly 50 percent of the variation in the amount of the bid is explained by the number of bidders.

47. **a.**

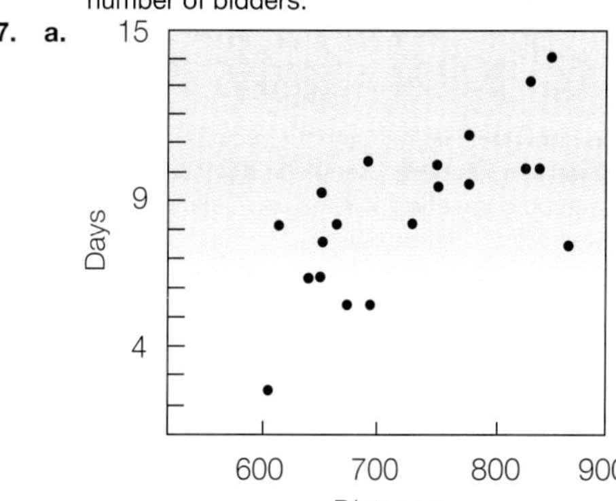

There appears to be a relationship between the two variables. As the distance increases, so does the shipping time.

b. $r = 0.692$

H_0: $\rho \le 0$; H_1: $\rho > 0$. Reject H_0 if $t > 1.734$.

$$t = \frac{0.692\sqrt{20-2}}{\sqrt{1-(0.692)^2}} = 4.067$$

H_0 is rejected. There is a positive association between shipping distance and shipping time.

c. $r^2 = 0.479$. Nearly half of the variation in shipping time is explained by shipping distance.

d. $s_{y \cdot x} = \sqrt{\dfrac{1550 - (-7.126)(168) - .0214(125{,}051)}{20-2}}$
$= 1.987$

49. **a.** $b = \dfrac{30(18{,}924) - (320.33)(1575.6)}{30(4292.5) - (320.33)^2} = 2.41$

$a = \dfrac{1575.6}{30} - 2.41\left(\dfrac{320.33}{30}\right) = 26.8$

The regression equation is: Price = 26.8 + 2.41 × dividend. For each additional dollar of dividend, the price increases by $2.41.

b. $r^2 = \dfrac{5057.6}{7682.7} = 0.658$ Thus, 65.8 percent of the variation in price is explained by the dividend.

c. $r = \sqrt{.658} = 0.811$ $H_0: \rho \le 0$ $H_1: \rho > 0$
At the 5 percent level, reject H_0 when $t > 1.701$.

$$t = \frac{0.811\sqrt{30-2}}{\sqrt{1-(0.811)^2}} = 7.34$$

Thus H_0 is rejected. The population correlation is positive.

51. **a.** Answers will vary as the number of cottages available and their prices change. At this time there are 14 cottages that meet the criteria. The correlation between the number of baths and rental price is 0.668.
$H_0: \rho \le 0$ $H_1: \rho > 0$
Reject H_0 if $t > 1.782$.

$$t = \frac{0.668\sqrt{14-2}}{\sqrt{1-(0.668)^2}} = 3.11$$

Reject H_0. There is a positive correlation between baths and cottage price.

b. The regression equation is $Y' = 758 + 347X$. The weekly price increases almost $350 for each bathroom.

c. $H_0: \rho \le 0$ $H_1: \rho > 0$
Reject H_0 if $t > 1.782$.

$$t = \frac{0.085\sqrt{14-2}}{\sqrt{1-(0.085)^2}} = .296$$

Do not reject H_0. We cannot conclude that there is an association between people and price.

53. **a.** Pearson correlation of Wins and Salary = 0.498
$H_0: \rho \le 0$ $H_1: \rho > 0$
At the 5% level, reject H_0 if $t > 1.701$.

$$t = \frac{0.498\sqrt{30-2}}{\sqrt{1-(0.498)^2}} = 3.04$$

Reject H_0. The population correlation is positive. The regression equation is Wins = 69.4 + 0.203 × Salary. An additional $5 million would increase the wins by 1.015, found by 0.203(5).

b. The correlation between games won and ERA is −0.66; and between games won and batting average 0.357. ERA has a stronger correlation. Critical values of t are −1.701 for ERA and 1.701 for batting average.

$$t_{ERA} = \frac{-0.66\sqrt{30-2}}{\sqrt{1-(-0.66)^2}} = -4.65$$

$$t_{batting} = \frac{0.357\sqrt{30-2}}{\sqrt{1-(-0.357)^2}} = 2.02$$

So both conclusions are supported.

c. The correlation between wins and attendance is .519.
$H_0: \rho \le 0$ $H_1: \rho > 0$
At the 5 percent level, reject H_0 if $t > 1.701$.

$$t = \frac{0.519\sqrt{30-2}}{\sqrt{1-(0.519)^2}} = 3.21$$

Reject H_0. The population correlation is positive.

55. **a.** The regression equation is $Y' = -699.2 + 391.71X$. Forty-three percent of the variation in the number of students in the system is explained by the variation in percent of families on welfare. For an increase of one percent in the percent on welfare, the number of students in the system can be expected to increase by about 392 students. The larger school systems have the higher percent of students on welfare. A system with 10 percent of the students on welfare can expect to have 3,218 students. The 95 percent confidence interval is from 2,559 up to 3,876. The 95 percent prediction interval is from −2,691 students up to 9,127 students. Logically, the end point of the prediction interval cannot be less than zero.

b. The independent variable regarding attendance rate explains 44.6 percent of the variation in the percent of students passing the comprehensive exam. The regression equation is $Y' = -718.7 + 8.235X$. An increase of one percent in the percent attending will result in an increase of 8.235 in the percent passing the exam. A school system with a 90 percent attendance rate can be expected to have a passing rate of 22.45 percent. The 95 percent confidence interval is from 12.22 up to 32.68 percent and the 95 percent prediction interval is from −0.22 up to 45.12 percent.

c. $H_0: \rho \le 0$ $H_1: \rho > 0$
Reject H_0 if $t > 2.326$.

$$t = \frac{0.668\sqrt{94-2}}{\sqrt{1-(0.668)^2}} = 8.61$$

Reject H_0. There is a significant positive correlation between attendance and passing.

CHAPTER 14

1. **a.** Multiple regression equation.
b. The Y-intercept.
c. $Y' = 64{,}100 + 0.394(796{,}000) + 9.6(6{,}940) - 11{,}600(6.0) = \$374{,}748$

3. **a.** 497.736, found by
$Y' = 16.24 + 0.017(18) + 0.0028(26{,}500) + 42(3) + 0.0012(156{,}000) + 0.19(141) + 26.8(2.5)$
b. Two more social activities. Income added only 28 to the index; social activities added 53.6.

5. **a.** 19
b. 3
c. .318, found by 21/66.
d. 1.732, found by $\sqrt{\dfrac{45}{[19-(3+1)]}}$.

7. **a.**

Source	SS	df	MS	F
Regression	7,500.0	3	2,500	18
Error	2,500.0	18	138.89	
Total	10,000.0	21		

b. $H_0: \beta_1 = \beta_2 = \beta_3 = 0$; H_1: Not all βs are 0. Reject H_0 if $F > 3.16$.
Reject H_0. Not all net regression coefficients equal zero.

c.

For X_1:	For X_2:	For X_3:
$H_0: \beta_1 = 0$	$H_0: \beta_2 = 0$	$H_0: \beta_3 = 0$
$H_1: \beta_1 \ne 0$	$H_1: \beta_2 \ne 0$	$H_1: \beta_3 \ne 0$
$t = -4.00$	$t = 1.50$	$t = -3.00$

Reject H_0 if $t > 2.101$ or $t < -2.101$.
Delete variable 2, keep 1 and 3.

9. **a.** $n = 40$
b. 4

c. $R^2 = \frac{750}{1250} = .60$
d. $s_{y \cdot 1234} = \sqrt{500/35} = 3.7796$
e. $H_0: \beta_1 = \beta_2 = \beta_3 = \beta_4 = 0$
H_1: Not all the βs equal zero.
H_0 is rejected if $F > 2.65$.

$$F = \frac{750/4}{500/35} = 13.125$$

H_0 is rejected. At least one β_i does not equal zero.

11. a. $n = 26$.
b. $R^2 = 100/140 = .7143$
c. 1.4142, found by $\sqrt{2}$.
d. $H_0: \beta_1 = \beta_2 = \beta_3 = \beta_4 = \beta_5 = 0$
H_1: Not all the βs are 0.
H_0 is rejected if $F > 2.71$.
Computed $F = 10.0$. Reject H_0. At least one regression coefficient is not zero.
e. H_0 is rejected in each case if $t < -2.086$ or $t > 2.086$. X_1 and X_5 should be dropped.

13. a. $28,000
b. $R^2 = \frac{\text{SSR}}{\text{SStotal}} = \frac{3,050}{5,250} = .5809$
c. 9.199, found by $\sqrt{84.62}$.
d. H_0 is rejected if $F > 2.97$ (approximately).

$$\text{Computed } F = \frac{1016.67}{84.62} = 12.01$$

H_0 is rejected. At least one regression coefficient is not zero.
e. If computed t is to the left of -2.056 or to the right of 2.056, the null hypothesis in each of these cases is rejected. Computed t for X_2 and X_3 exceed the critical value. Thus, "population" and "advertising expenses" should be retained and "number of competitors," X_1, dropped.

15. a. The strongest correlation is between GPA and legal. No problem with multicollinearity.
b. $R^2 = \frac{4.3595}{5.0631} = .8610$
c. H_0 is rejected if $F > 5.41$.

$$F = \frac{1.4532}{0.1407} = 10.328.$$

At least one coefficient is not zero.
d. Any H_0 is rejected if $t < -2.571$ or $t > 2.571$. It appears that only GPA is significant. Verbal and math could be eliminated.
e. $R^2 = \frac{4.2061}{5.0631} = .8307$.
R^2 has only been reduced .0303.
f. The residuals appear slightly skewed (positive), but acceptable.
g. There does not seem to be a problem with the plot.

17. a. The correlation matrix is:

	cars	*adv*	*sales*
adv	0.808		
sales	0.872	0.537	
city	0.639	0.713	0.389

Size of sales force (0.872) has the strongest correlation with cars sold. Fairly strong relationship between location of dealership and advertising (0.713). Could be a problem.

b. The regression equation is:
$Y' = 31.1328 + 2.1516adv + 5.0140sales + 5.6651city$
$Y' = 31.1328 + 2.1516(15) + 5.0140(20) + 5.6651(1) = 169.352$.
c. $H_0: \beta_1 = \beta_2 = \beta_3 = 0$; H_1: Not all βs are 0. Reject H_0 if computed $F > 4.07$.

Analysis of Variance			
Source	**SS**	***df***	**MS**
Regression	5504.4	3	1834.8
Error	420.2	8	52.5
Total	5924.7	11	

$F = 1,834.8/52.5 = 34.95$.
Reject H_0. At least one regression coefficient is not 0.
d. H_0 is rejected in all cases if $t < -2.306$ or if $t > 2.306$. Advertising and sales force should be retained, city dropped. (Note that dropping city removes the problem with multicollinearity.)

Predictor	Coef	StDev	*t*-ratio	*P*
Constant	31.13	13.40	2.32	0.049
adv	2.1516	0.8049	2.67	0.028
sales	5.0140	0.9105	5.51	0.000
city	5.665	6.332	0.89	0.397

e. The new output is

$$Y' = 25.2952 + 2.6187adv + 5.0233sales$$

Predictor	Coef	StDev	*t*-ratio
Constant	25.30	11.57	2.19
adv	2.6187	0.6057	4.32
sales	5.0233	0.9003	5.58

Analysis of Variance			
Source	**SS**	***df***	**MS**
Regression	5462.4	2	2731.2
Error	462.3	9	51.4
Total	5924.7	11	

f. Stem-and-leaf
Leaf unit = 1.0

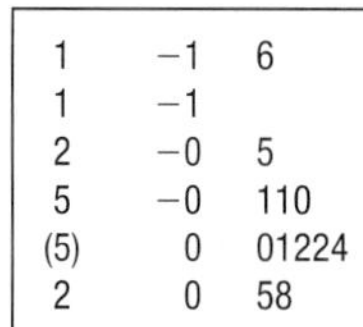

1	−1	6
1	−1	
2	−0	5
5	−0	110
(5)	0	01224
2	0	58

The normality assumption is reasonable.

g.

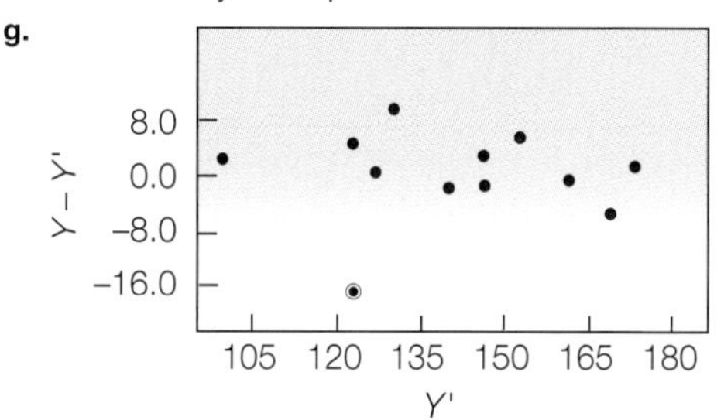

For this small sample the residual plot is acceptable.

19. **a.** The regression equation is:

$Y' = 965.3 + 2.865X_1 + 6.75X_2 + 0.2873X_3$

$Y' = \$2{,}458{,}780$

b. **Analysis of Variance**

Source	SS	df	MS
Regression	45510096	3	15170032
Error	12215892	12	1017991
Total	57725984	15	

$$F = \frac{15170032}{1017991} = 14.902$$

H_0 is rejected because computed F of 14.9 is greater than the critical value of 3.49. At least one of the regression coefficients is not zero.

c. $H_0\colon \beta_1 = 0$ $\quad H_0\colon \beta_2 = 0$ $\quad H_0\colon \beta_3 = 0$

$H_1\colon \beta_1 \neq 0$ $\quad H_1\colon \beta_2 \neq 0$ $\quad H_1\colon \beta_3 \neq 0$

The H_0s are rejected if $t < -2.179$ or $t > 2.179$. Both workers and dividends are not significant variables. Inventory is significant. Delete dividends and rerurn analysis.

d. The regression equation (if we used X_1 and X_3)

$$Y' = 1134.8 + 3.258X_1 + 0.3099X_3$$

Predictor	Coef	StDev	t-ratio
Constant	1134.8	418.6	2.71
Workers	3.258	1.434	2.27
Inv	0.3099	0.1033	3.00

Analysis of Variance

Source	SS	df	MS	F
Regression	45,070,624	2	22,535,312	23.15
Error	12,655,356	13	973,489	
Total	57,725,968	15		

e.

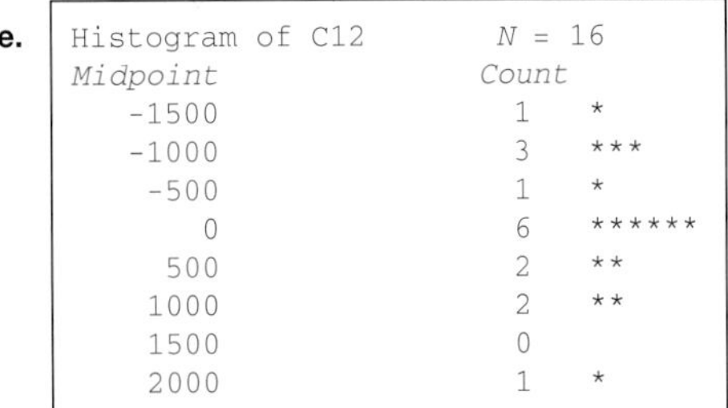

```
Histogram of C12          N = 16
Midpoint                  Count
  -1500                     1   *
  -1000                     3   ***
   -500                     1   *
      0                     6   ******
    500                     2   **
   1000                     2   **
   1500                     0
   2000                     1   *
```

The normality assumption is reasonable.

f.

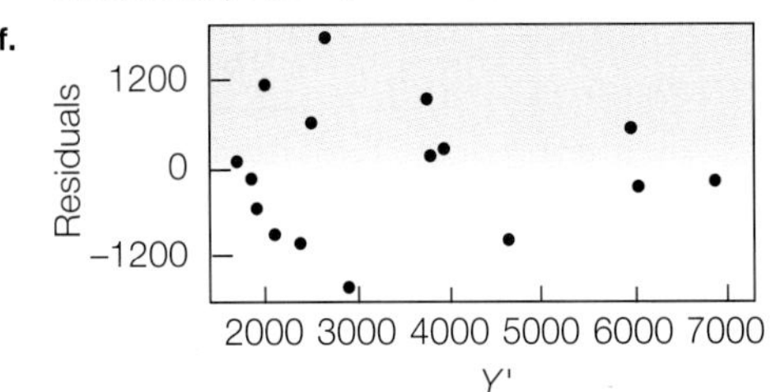

21. **a.** The correlation matrix is:

	Salary	GPA
GPA	0.902	
Business	0.911	0.851

The two independent variables are related. There may be multicollinearity.

b. The regression equation is: Salary = 23.447 + 2.775 GPA + 1.307 Business. As GPA increases by one point, salary increases by \$2,775. The average business school graduate makes \$1,307 more than a corresponding nonbusiness graduate. Estimated salary is \$33,079; found by \$23,447 + 2,775(3.00) + 1,307(1).

c. $R^2 = \dfrac{21.182}{23.857} = 0.888$

To conduct the global test: $H_0\colon = \beta_1 = \beta_2 = 0$:

H_1: Not all β_i's = 0

At the 0.05 significance level, H_0 is rejected if $F > 3.89$.

Source	DF	SS	MS	F	p
Regression	2	21.182	10.591	47.50	0.000
Error	12	2.676	0.223		
Total	14	23.857			

The computed value of F is 47.50, so H_0 is rejected. Some of the regression coefficients and R^2 are not zero.

d. Since the p-values are less than 0.05, there is no need to delete variables.

Predictor	Coef	SE Coef	T	P
Constant	23.447	3.490	6.72	0.000
GPA	2.775	1.107	2.51	0.028
Business	1.3071	0.4660	2.80	0.016

e. The residuals appear normally distributed.

Histogram of the Residuals
(response is Salary)

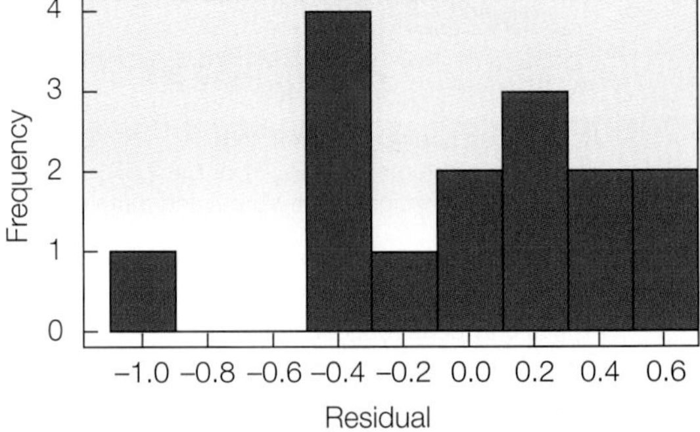

f. The variance is the same as we move from small values to large. So there is no homoscedasticity problem.

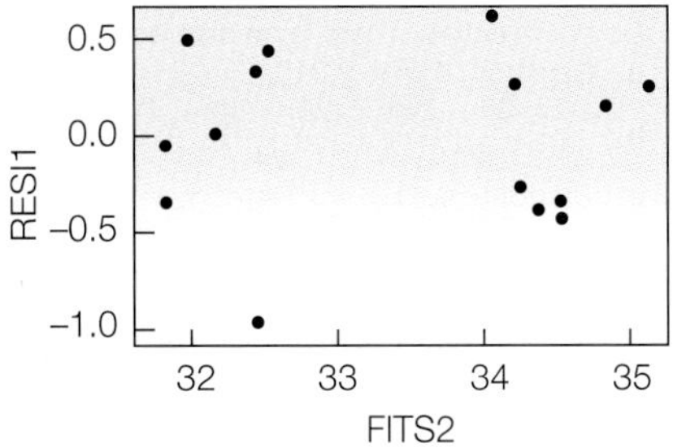

23. The computer output is:

Predictor	*Coef*	*Stdev*	*t-ratio*	*p*
Constant	651.9	345.3	1.89	0.071
Service	13.422	5.125	2.62	0.015
Age	-6.710	6.349	-1.06	0.301
Gender	205.65	90.27	2.28	0.032
Job	-33.45	89.55	-0.37	0.712

Analysis of Variance

SOURCE	*DF*	*SS*	*MS*	*F*	*p*
Regression	4	1066830	266708	4.77	0.005
Error	25	1398651	55946		
Total	29	2465481			

a. $Y' = 651.9 + 13.422X_1 - 6.710X_2 + 205.65X_3 - 33.45X_4$

b. $R^2 = .433$, which is somewhat low for this type of study.

c. H_0: $\beta_1 = \beta_2 = \beta_3 = \beta_4 = 0$; H_1: not all βs equal zero. Reject H_0 if $F > 2.76$.

$$F = \frac{1{,}066{,}830/4}{1{,}398{,}651/25} = 4.77$$

H_0 is rejected. Not all the β_is equal 0.

d. Using the .05 significance level, reject the hypothesis that the regression coefficient is 0 if $t < -2.060$ or $t > 2.060$. Service and gender should remain in the analyses, age and job should be dropped.

e. Following is the computer output using the independent variables service and gender.

Predictor	*Coef*	*Stdev*	*t-ratio*	*p*
Constant	784.2	316.8	2.48	0.020
Service	9.021	3.106	2.90	0.007
Gender	224.41	87.35	2.57	0.016

Analysis of Variance

SOURCE	*DF*	*SS*	*MS*	*F*	*p*
Regression	2	998779	499389	9.19	0.001
Error	27	1466703	54322		
Total	29	2465481			

A man earns $224 more per month than a woman. The difference between technical and clerical jobs is not significant.

25. Answers will vary as the rental prices change.

27. The computer output is as follows:

Predictor	*Coef*	*SE Coef*	*T*	*P*
Constant	38.71	39.02	0.99	0.324
Bedrooms	7.118	2.551	2.79	0.006
Size	0.03800	0.01468	2.59	0.011
Pool	18.321	6.999	2.62	0.010
Distance	-0.9295	0.7279	-1.28	0.205
Garage	35.810	7.638	4.69	0.000
Baths	23.315	9.025	2.58	0.011

S = 33.21 R-Sq = 53.2% R-Sq (adj) = 50.3%

Analysis of Variance

Source	*DF*	*SS*	*MS*	*F*	*P*
Regression	6	122676	20446	18.54	0.000
Residual Error	98	108092	1103		
Total	104	230768			

a. Each additional bedroom adds about $7,000 to the selling price, a pool adds $18,300, an attached garage $35,800, and each mile the home is from the center of the city reduces the selling price by $929.

b. The *R*-square value is 0.532.

c. The correlation matrix is as follows:

	Price	Bedrooms	Size	Pool	Distance	Garage
Bedrooms	0.467					
Size	0.371	0.383				
Pool	0.294	0.005	0.201			
Distance	−0.347	−0.153	−0.117	−0.139		
Garage	0.526	0.234	0.083	0.114	−0.359	
Baths	0.382	0.329	0.024	0.055	−0.195	0.221

The independent variable *garage* has the strongest correlation with price. Distance is inversely related, as expected, and there does not seem to be a problem with correlation among the independent variables.

d. The results of the global test suggest that some of the independent variables have net regression coefficients different from zero.

e. We can delete *distance*.

f. The new regression output follows.

Predictor	*Coef*	*SE Coef*	*T*	*P*
Constant	17.01	35.24	0.48	0.630
Bedrooms	7.169	2.559	2.80	0.006
Size	0.03919	0.01470	2.67	0.009
Pool	19.110	6.994	2.73	0.007
Garage	38.847	7.281	5.34	0.000
Baths	24.624	8.995	2.74	0.007

S = 33.32 R-Sq = 52.4% R-Sq (adj) = 50.0%

Analysis of Variance

Source	*DF*	*SS*	*MS*	*F*	*P*
Regression	5	120877	24175	21.78	0.000
Residual Error	99	109890	1110		
Total	104	230768			

In reviewing the *p*-values for the various regression coefficients, all are less than .05. We leave all the independent variables.

g. & h. Analysis of the residuals, not shown, indicates the normality assumption is reasonable. In addition, there is no pattern to the plots of the residuals and the fitted values of *Y*.

29. **a.** The regression equation is: Employment = 248 − 0.144 Area + 0.356 Population + 2.63 Domestic + 1,555 G7 + 10.2 Energy. Employment increases as both domestic product and energy use increase. In addition, employment is higher in G7 than in other countries. Employment declines as land area increases.

b. $R^2 = 0.996$ These five independent variables explain nearly all the variation in employment.

c. The correlation matrix is as follows:

	Employ	Area	Population	Domestic	G7
Area	0.506				
Population	0.992	0.491			
Domestic	0.938	0.482	0.902		
G7	0.639	0.382	0.625	0.614	
Energy	0.949	0.599	0.923	0.925	0.554

There are problems with multicollinearity. Energy, population, and domestic production are all strongly correlated.

d. To conduct the global test: H_0: $\beta_1 = \beta_2 = \beta_3 = \beta_4 = \beta_5 = 0$; H_1: Not all β_i's = 0.
At the 0.05 significance level, H_0 is rejected if $F > 2.64$.

Source	DF	SS	MS	F	P
Regression	5	20,605,387,329	4,121,077,466	1,292.75	0.000
Error	23	73,320,535	3,187,849		
Total	28	20,678,707,864			

The computed value of F is 1,292.75, so H_0 is rejected. Some of the regression coefficients are not zero.

e. *Area* and *G7* would be deleted because of their large *p*-values.

Predictor	Coef	SE Coef	T	P
Constant	247.7	460.3	0.54	0.596
Area	−0.1438	0.1630	−0.88	0.387
Population	0.35594	0.01808	19.69	0.000
Domestic	2.6316	0.6436	4.09	0.000
G7	1555	1047	1.49	0.151
Energy	10.178	3.110	3.27	0.003

f. The regression equation is:
Employment = 207 + 0.365 Population + 2.96 Domestic + 8.14 Energy

g. The residuals do not appear normally distributed.

h. The variance is larger as we move from small values to large. So there is a homoscedasticity problem.

CHAPTER 15

1. **a.** 3
b. 7.815

3. **a.** Reject H_0 if $\chi^2 > 5.991$.

b. $$\chi^2 = \frac{(10-20)^2}{20} + \frac{(20-20)^2}{20} + \frac{(30-20)^2}{20} = 10.0$$

c. Reject H_0. The proportions are not equal.

5. H_0: The outcomes are the same; H_1: The outcomes are not the same. Reject H_0 if $\chi^2 > 9.236$

$$\chi^2 = \frac{(3-5)^2}{5} + \cdots + \frac{(7-5)^2}{5} = 7.60$$

Do not reject H_0. Cannot reject H_0 that outcomes are the same.

7. H_0: There is no difference in the proportions.
H_1: There is a difference in the proportions.
Reject H_0 if $\chi^2 > 15.086$.

$$\chi^2 = \frac{(47-40)^2}{40} + \cdots + \frac{(34-40)^2}{40} = 3.400$$

Do not reject H_0. There is no difference in the proportions.

9. **a.** Reject H_0 if $\chi^2 > 9.210$.

b. $$\chi^2 = \frac{(30-24)^2}{24} + \frac{(20-24)^2}{24} + \frac{(10-12)^2}{12} = 2.50$$

c. Do not reject H_0.

11. H_0: Proportions are as stated; H_1: Proportions are not as stated. Reject H_0 if $\chi^2 > 11.345$.

$$\chi^2 = \frac{(50-25)^2}{25} + \cdots + \frac{(160-275)^2}{275} = 115.22$$

Reject H_0. The proportions are not as stated.

13. H_0: Distribution is normally distributed. H_1: It is not normally distributed. Reject H_0 if $\chi^2 > 11.070$.

Time	z Areas	f_o	f_e	$\frac{(f_o - f_e)^2}{f_e}$
Up to 4	.0764	7	6.9	.001
4 to 5	.1625	14	14.6	.025
5 to 6	.2611	25	23.5	.096
6 to 7	.2611	22	23.5	.096
7 to 8	.1625	16	14.6	.134
8 or more	.0764	6	6.9	.117
Total	1.000	90	90	.469

Computed $\chi^2 = .469$. Do not reject H_0 that the distribution is normal.

15. H_0: There is no relationship between community size and section read. H_1: There is a relationship. Reject H_0 if $\chi^2 > 9.488$.

$$\chi^2 = \frac{(170-157.50)^2}{157.50} + \cdots + \frac{(88-83.62)^2}{83.62} = 7.340$$

Do not reject H_0. There is no relationship between community size and section read.

17. H_0: No relationship between error rates and item type. H_1: There is a relationship between error rates and item type. Reject H_0 if $\chi^2 > 9.21$.

$$\chi^2 = \frac{(20-14.1)^2}{14.1} + \cdots + \frac{(225-225.25)^2}{225.25} = 8.033$$

Do not reject H_0. There is not a relationship between error rates and item type.

19. H_0: $\pi_s = 0.50$, $\pi_r = \pi_e = 0.25$
H_1: Distribution is not as given above.
$df = 2$. Reject H_0 if $\chi^2 > 4.605$.

Turn	f_o	f_e	$f_o - f_e$	$(f_o - f_e)^2/f_e$
Straight	112	100	12	1.44
Right	48	50	−2	0.08
Left	40	50	−10	2.00
Total	200	200		3.52

H_0 is not rejected. The proportions are as given in the null hypothesis.

21. H_0: There is no preference with respect to TV stations.
H_1: There is a preference with respect to TV stations.
$df = 3 - 1 = 2$. H_0 is rejected if $\chi^2 > 5.991$.

TV Station	f_o	f_e	$f_o - f_e$	$(f_o - f_e)^2$	$(f_o - f_e)^2/f_e$
WNAE	53	50	3	9	0.18
WRRN	64	50	14	196	3.92
WSPD	33	50	−17	289	5.78
	150	150	0		9.88

H_0 is rejected. There is a preference for TV stations.

23. H_0: $\pi_n = 0.21$, $\pi_m = 0.24$, $\pi_s = 0.35$, $\pi_w = 0.20$.
H_1: The distribution is not as given.
Reject H_0 if $\chi^2 > 11.345$.

Region	f_o	f_e	$f_o - f_e$	$(f_o - f_e)^2/f_e$
Northeast	68	84	−16	3.0476
Midwest	104	96	8	0.6667
South	155	140	15	1.6071
West	73	80	−7	0.6125
Total	400	400	0	5.9339

H_0 is not rejected. The distribution of order destinations reflects the population.

25. H_0: $\pi_0 = 0.40$, $\pi_1 = 0.30$, $\pi_2 = 0.20$, $\pi_3 = 0.1$
H_1: The proportions are not as given. Reject H_0 if $\chi^2 > 7.815$.

Accidents	f_o	f_e	$(f_o - f_e)^2/f_e$
0	46	48	0.083
1	40	36	0.444
2	22	24	0.167
3	12	12	0.000
Total	120		0.694

Do not reject H_0. Evidence does not show a change in the accident distribution.

27. H_0: The distribution is normal; H_1: The distribution is not normal. Reject H_0 if $\chi^2 > 4.605$.

$$\bar{X} = \frac{2430}{300} = 8.10$$

$$s = \sqrt{\frac{19{,}994 - \frac{(2430)^2}{300}}{300 - 1}} = 1.02$$

Wage	f_o	Area	f_e	$\frac{(f_o - f_e)^2}{f_e}$
\$5.50 up to \$ 6.50	20	.0582	17.46	0.370
6.50 up to 7.50	54	.2194	65.82	2.123
7.50 up to 8.50	130	.3741	112.23	2.814
8.50 up to 9.50	68	.2630	78.90	1.506
9.50 up to 10.50	28	.0853	25.59	0.227
Total	300			7.040

Reject H_0. We conclude that the distribution is normal.

29. H_0: Levels of management and concern regarding the environment are not related. H_1: Levels of management and concern regarding the environment are related. Reject H_0 if $\chi^2 > 16.812$.

$$\chi^2 = \frac{(15 - 14)^2}{14} + \cdots + \frac{(31 - 28)^2}{28} = 1.550$$

Do not reject H_0. Levels of management and environmental concern are not related.

31. H_0: Whether a claim is filed and age are not related.
H_1: Whether a claim is filed and age are related.
Reject H_0 if $\chi^2 > 7.815$.

$$\chi^2 = \frac{(170 - 203.33)^2}{203.33} + \cdots + \frac{(24 - 35.67)^2}{35.67} = 53.639$$

Reject H_0. Age is related to whether a claim is filed.

33. H_0: $\pi_{BL} = \pi_{BR} = \pi_Y = \pi_R = 0.2$, $\pi_G = \pi_O = 0.1$
H_1: The proportions are not as given.
Reject H_0 if $\chi^2 > 11.070$.

Color f_o		f_e	$(f_o - f_e)^2/f_e$
Blue	13	14.4	0.136
Brown	17	14.4	0.469
Yellow	20	14.4	2.178
Red	7	14.4	3.803
Green	9	7.2	0.450
Orange	6	7.2	0.200
Total	72		7.236

Do not reject H_0. The color distribution agrees with the manufacturer's information.

35. **a.** H_0: There is no relationship between pool and township.
H_1: There is a relationship between pool and township.
Reject H_0 if $\chi^2 > 9.488$.

	Township					
Pool	1	2	3	4	5	Total
No	9	8	7	11	3	38
Yes	6	12	18	18	13	67
Total	15	20	25	29	16	105

$$\chi^2 = \frac{(9 - 5.43)^2}{5.43} + \cdots + \frac{(13 - 10.21)^2}{10.21} = 6.680$$

Do not reject H_0. There is no relationship between pool and township.

b. H_0: There is no relationship between attached garage and township. H_1: There is a relationship between attached garage and township. Reject H_0 if $\chi^2 > 9.488$.

	Township					
Garage	1	2	3	4	5	Total
No	6	5	10	9	4	34
Yes	9	15	15	20	12	71
Total	15	20	25	29	16	105

$$\chi^2 = \frac{(6 - 4.86)^2}{4.86} + \cdots + \frac{(12 - 10.82)^2}{10.82} = 1.980$$

Do not reject H_0. There is no relationship between attached garage and township.

37. **a.** H_0: The proportions are the same.
H_1: The proportions are not the same.
Reject H_0 if $\chi^2 > 5.991$.

$$\chi^2 = \frac{(43 - 31.33)^2}{31.33} + \frac{(31 - 31.33)^2}{31.33} + \frac{(20 - 31.33)^2}{31.33} = 8.448$$

Reject H_0, the proportions on welfare are not the same.

b. H_0: Welfare and size are not related.
H_1: Welfare and size are related.
Reject H_0 if $\chi^2 > 5.991$.

	Size			
Welfare	Small	Medium	Large	Total
Low	22	17	4	43
Medium	8	18	5	31
High	6	7	7	20
Total	36	42	16	94

$$\chi^2 = \frac{(22 - 16.468)^2}{16.468} + \cdots + \frac{(7 - 3.404)^2}{3.404} = 10.716$$

Reject H_0; conclude that welfare and size are related.

CHAPTER 16

1. **a.** If the number of pluses (successes) in the sample is 9 or more, reject H_0.

b. Reject H_0 because the cumulative probability associated with nine or more successes (.073) does not exceed the significance level (.10).

3. **a.** H_0: $\pi \leq .50$; H_1: $\pi > .50$; $n = 10$.

b. H_0 is rejected if there are nine or more plus signs. A "+" represents a loss.

c. Reject H_0. It is an effective program, because there were 9 people who lost weight.

5. **a.** H_0: $\pi \leq .50$ (There is no change in weight.)
H_0: $\pi > .50$ (There is a loss of weight.)

b. Reject H_0 if $z > 1.65$.

c. $z = \dfrac{(32 - .50) - .50(45)}{.50\sqrt{45}} = 2.68$

d. Reject H_0. The weight loss program is effective.

7. **a.** H_0: $\pi \leq .50$, H_1: $\pi > .50$. H_0 is rejected if $z > 2.05$.

$$z = \frac{42.5 - 40.5}{4.5} = .44$$

Because $.44 < 2.05$, do not reject H_0. No preference.

9. **a.** H_0: Median $\leq$ \$80,000; H_1: Median $>$ \$80,000.

b. H_0 is rejected if $z > 1.65$.

c. $z = \dfrac{170 - .5 - 100}{7.07} = 9.83$

H_0 is rejected. The median income is greater than \$80,000.

11.

Couple	Difference	Rank
1	550	7
2	190	5
3	250	6
4	−120	3
5	−70	1
6	130	4
7	90	2

Sums: −4, +24. So $T = 4$ (the smaller of the two sums). From Appendix J, .05 level, one-tailed test, $n = 7$, the critical value is 3. Since the T of $4 > 3$, do not reject H_0 (one-tailed test). There is no difference in square footage. Yuppies do not live in larger homes.

13. **a.** H_0: The production is the same for the two systems.
H_1: Production using the Mump method is greater.

b. H_0 is rejected if $T \leq 21$, $n = 13$.

c. The calculations for the first three employees are:

Employee	Old	Mump	d	Rank	R^+	R^-
A	60	64	4	6	6	
B	40	52	12	12.5	12.5	
C	59	58	−1	2		2

The sum of the negative ranks is 6.5. Since 6.5 is less than 21, H_0 is rejected. Production using the Mump method is greater.

15. H_0: The distributions are the same. H_1: The distributions are not the same. Reject H_0 if $z < -1.96$ or $z > 1.96$.

A		B	
Score	Rank	Score	Rank
38	4	26	1
45	6	31	2
56	9	35	3
57	10.5	42	5
61	12	51	7
69	14	52	8
70	15	57	10.5
79	16	62	13
	86.5		49.5

$$z = \frac{86.5 - \dfrac{8(8+8+1)}{2}}{\sqrt{\dfrac{8(8)(8+8+1)}{12}}} = 1.943$$

H_0 is not rejected. There is no difference in the two populations.

17. H_0: The distributions are the same. H_1: The distribution of Country is to the right. Reject H_0 if $z > 1.65$.

Country		Rock	
Age	Rank	Age	Rank
26	6	28	8
42	16.5	16	1
65	22	42	16.5
38	13	29	9.5
29	9.5	31	11
32	12	22	3
59	21	50	20
42	16.5	42	16.5
27	7	23	4
41	14	25	5
46	19		94.5
18	2		
	158.5		

$$z = \frac{158.5 - \dfrac{12(12+10+1)}{2}}{\sqrt{\dfrac{12(10)(12+10+1)}{12}}} = 1.35$$

H_0 is not rejected. There is no difference in the distributions.

19. ANOVA requires that we have two or more populations, the data are interval or ratio-level, the populations are normally distributed, and the population standard deviations are equal. Kruskal-Wallis requires only ordinal-level data, and no assumptions are made regarding the shape of the populations.

21. **a.** H_0: The three population distributions are equal. H_1: Not all of the distributions are the same.

b. Reject H_0 if $H > 5.991$.

c.

Rank	Rank	Rank
8	5	1
11	6.5	2
14.5	6.5	3
14.5	10	4
16	12	9
64	13	19
	53	

$$H = \frac{12}{16(16+1)}\left[\frac{(64)^2}{5} + \frac{(53)^2}{6} + \frac{(19)^2}{5}\right] - 3(16+1)$$

$$= 59.98 - 51 = 8.98$$

d. Reject H_0 because $8.98 > 5.991$. The three distributions are not equal.

23. H_0: The distributions of the lengths of life are the same.
H_1: The distributions of the lengths of life are not the same.
H_0 is rejected if $H > 9.210$.

Salt		Fresh		Others	
Hours	Rank	Hours	Rank	Hours	Rank
167.3	3	160.6	1	182.7	13
189.6	15	177.6	11	165.4	2
177.2	10	185.3	14	172.9	7
169.4	6	168.6	4	169.2	5
180.3	12	176.6	9	174.7	8
	46		39		35

$$H = \frac{12}{15(16)}\left[\frac{(46)^2}{5} + \frac{(39)^2}{5} + \frac{(35)^2}{5}\right] - 3(16) = 0.62$$

H_0 is not rejected. There is no difference in the three distributions.

25. a.

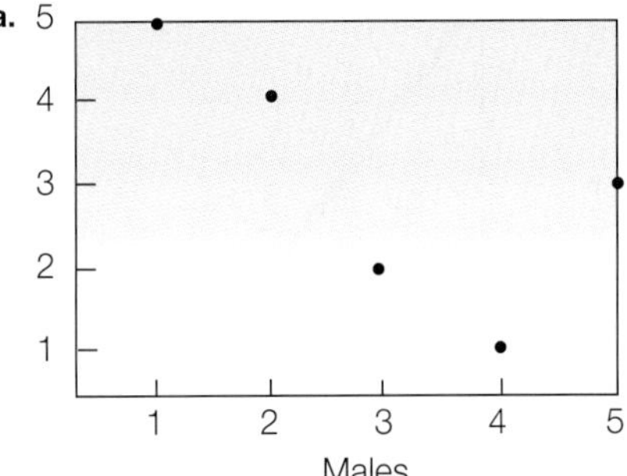

b.

Rank Males	Rank Females	d	d^2
1	5	−4	16
4	1	3	9
3	2	1	1
2	4	−2	4
5	3	2	4
			34

$$r_s = 1 - \frac{6(34)}{5(5^2 - 1)} = -0.7$$

Fairly strong negative correlation among the ranks.

27.

Representative	Sales	Rank	Training Rank	d	d^2
1	319	3	3	0	0
2	150	10	9	1	1
3	175	9	6	3	9
4	460	1	1	0	0
5	348	2	4	−2	4
6	300	4.5	10	−5.5	30.25
7	280	6	5	1	1
8	200	7	2	5	25
9	190	8	7	1	1
10	300	4.5	8	−3.5	12.25
					83.50

a. $$r_s = 1 - \frac{6(83.5)}{10(10^2 - 1)} = 0.494$$

A moderate positive correlation.

b. H_0: No correlation among the ranks. H_1: A positive correlation among the ranks. Reject H_0 if $t > 1.860$.

$$t = 0.494\sqrt{\frac{10 - 2}{1 - (0.494)^2}} = 1.607$$

H_0 is not rejected. The correlation in population among the ranks could be 0.

29. H_0: $\pi = .50$; H_1: $\pi \neq .50$; $n = 19$. H_0 is rejected if there are either 5 or fewer "+" signs, or 14 or more. The total of 12 "+" signs falls in the acceptance region. H_0 is not rejected. There is no preference between the two shows.

31. H_0: $\pi = .50$ H_1: $\pi \neq .50$
H_0 is rejected if there are 12 or more or 3 or fewer plus signs. Because there are only 8 plus signs, H_0 is not rejected. There is no preference with respect to the two brands of components.

33. H_0: $\pi = .50$; H_1: $\pi \neq .50$. Reject H_0 if $z > 1.96$ or $z < -1.96$.

$$z = \frac{159.5 - 100}{7.071} = 8.415$$

Reject H_0. There is a difference in the preference for the two types of orange juice.

35. H_0: Rates are the same; H_1: The rates are not the same. H_0 is rejected if $H > 5.991$. $H = .082$. Do not reject H_0.

37. H_0: The populations are the same. H_1: The populations differ. Reject H_0 if $H > 7.815$. $H = 14.30$. Reject H_0, accept H_1.

39. $$r_s = 1 - \frac{6(78)}{12(12^2 - 1)} = 0.727$$

H_0: There is no correlation between the rankings of the coaches and of the sportswriters.
H_1: There is a positive correlation between the rankings of the coaches and of the sportswriters.
Reject H_0 if $t > 1.812$.

$$t = 0.727\sqrt{\frac{12 - 2}{1 - (.727)^2}} = 3.348$$

H_0 is rejected. There is a positive correlation between the sportswriters and the coaches.

41. Answers will vary.

43. a. H_0: There is no difference in the distributions of the selling prices in the five townships. H_1: There is a difference in the distributions of the selling prices of the five townships. H_0 is rejected if H is greater than 9.488. The computed value of H is 4.70, so the null hypothesis is not rejected. The sample data does not suggest a difference in the distributions of selling prices.

b. H_0: There is no difference in the distributions of the selling prices depending on the number of bedrooms. H_1: There is a difference in the distributions of the selling prices depending on the number of bedrooms. H_0 is rejected if H is greater than 9.448. The computed value of H is 16.34, so the null hypothesis is rejected. The sample data indicate there is a difference in the distributions of selling prices based on the number of bedrooms.

c. H_0: There is no difference in the distributions of the distance from the center of the city depending on whether the home had a pool or not. H_1: There is a difference in the distributions of the distances from the center of the city depending on whether the home has a pool or not. H_0 is rejected if H is greater than 3.84. The computed value of H is 3.37, so the null hypothesis is not rejected. The sample data does not suggest a difference in the distributions of the distances.

45. Notice the sample sizes are smaller than 5, but we show the calculations anyway. H_0: The distributions are the same. H_1: The distributions are not the same. Reject H_0 if $H > 5.991$.

$$H = \frac{12}{29(29+1)}\left[\frac{(337)^2}{22} + \frac{(37)^2}{3} + \frac{(61)^2}{4}\right] - 3(29+1) = 0.328$$

Do not reject H_0. The distributions are the same..

CHAPTER 17

1.

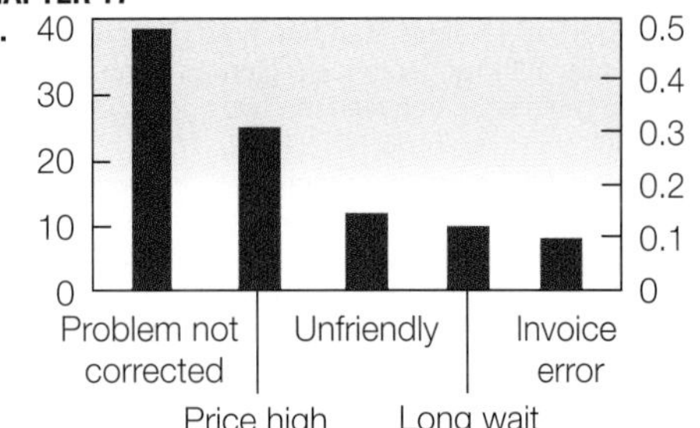

Count	38	23	12	10	8
Percent	42	25	13	11	9
Cum %	42	67	80	91	100

About 67% of the complaints concern the problem not being corrected and the price being too high.

3. Chance variation is random in nature; because the cause is a variety of factors, it cannot be entirely eliminated. Assignable variation is not random; it is usually due to a specific cause and can be eliminated.

5. **a.** The A_2 factor is 0.729.
 b. The value for D_3 is 0, and for D_4 it is 2.282.

7. **a.** UCL 46.78

$\bar{X}$ 41.92

LCL 37.06

8 8:30 9 9:30 10 10:30

Time	$\bar{X}$, Arithmetic Means	R, Range
8:00 A.M.	46	16
8:30 A.M.	40.5	6
9:00 A.M.	44	6
9:30 A.M.	40	2
10:00 A.M.	41.5	9
10:30 A.M.	39.5	1
	251.5	40

$$\bar{\bar{X}} = \frac{251.5}{6} = 41.92 \qquad \bar{R} = \frac{40}{6} = 6.67$$

$$\text{UCL} = 41.92 + 0.729(6.67) = 46.78$$

$$\text{LCL} = 41.92 - 0.729(6.67) = 37.06$$

 b. Interpreting, the mean reading was 341.92 degrees Fahrenheit. If the oven continues operating as evidenced by the first six hourly readings, about 99.7 percent of the mean readings will lie between 337.06 degrees and 346.78 degrees.

9. $p = \frac{37}{140} = .26$

$$.26 \pm 3\sqrt{\frac{.26(.74)}{10}} = .26 \pm .42$$

The control limits are from 0 to .68. The process is out of control on the seventh day.

11. $\bar{c} = \frac{6}{11} = 0.545$

$0.545 \pm 3\sqrt{0.545} = 0.545 \pm 2.215$

The control limits are from 0 to 2.760, so there are no receipts out of control.

13.

Percent Defective	Probability of Accepting Lot
10	.889
20	.558
30	.253
40	.083

15. $P(X \le 1 \mid n = 10, \pi = .10) = .736$
$P(X \le 1 \mid n = 10, \pi = .20) = .375$
$P(X \le 1 \mid n = 10, \pi = .30) = .149$
$P(X \le 1 \mid n = 10, \pi = .40) = .046$

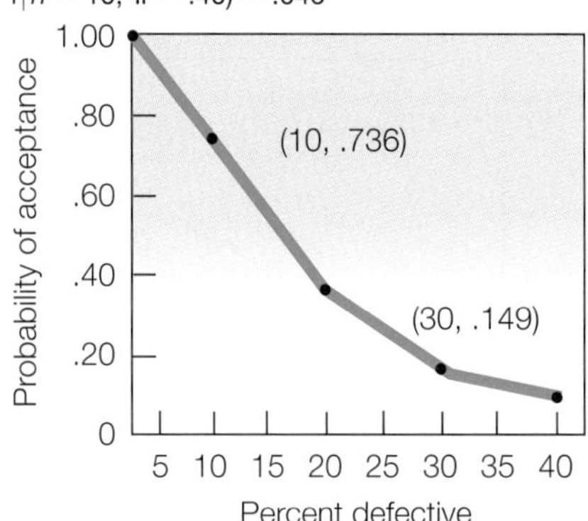

17.

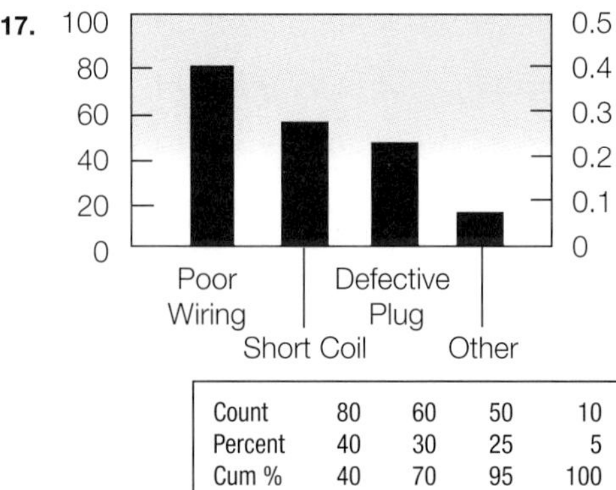

Count	80	60	50	10
Percent	40	30	25	5
Cum %	40	70	95	100

19. **a.** $\text{UCL} = 10.0 + 0.577(0.25) = 10.0 + 0.14425$
$= 10.14425$
$\text{LCL} = 10.0 - 0.577(0.25) = 10.0 - 0.14425$
$= 9.85575$
$\text{UCL} = 2.115(0.25) = 0.52875$
$\text{LCL} = 0(0.25) = 0$

 b. The mean is 10.16, which is above the upper control limit and is out of control. There is too much cola in the soft drinks. The process is in control for variation; an adjustment is needed.

21. **a.** $\bar{\bar{X}} = \frac{611.23}{20} = 30.5665$

$\bar{R} = \frac{312}{20} = 15.6$

UCL = 30.5665 + (1.023)(15.6) = 46.53

LCL = 30.5665 − (1.023)(15.6) = 14.61

UCL = 2.575(15.6) = 40.17

b.

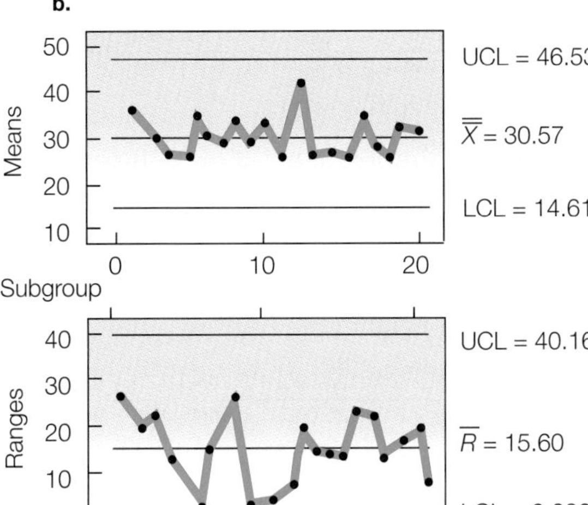

c. The points all seem to be within the control limits. No adjustments are necessary.

23. $\bar{\bar{X}} = \frac{4183}{10} = 418.3$

$\bar{R} = \frac{162}{10} = 16.2$

UCL = 418.3 + (0.577)(16.2) = 427.65

LCL = 418.3 − (0.577)(16.2) = 408.95

UCL = 2.115(16.2) = 34.26

All the points are in control for both the mean and the range.

25. **a.** $p = \frac{40}{10(50)}) = 0.08$

$3\sqrt{\frac{0.08(0.92)}{50}} = 0.115$

UCL = 0.08 + 0.115 = 0.195

LCL = 0.08 − 0.115 = 0

b.

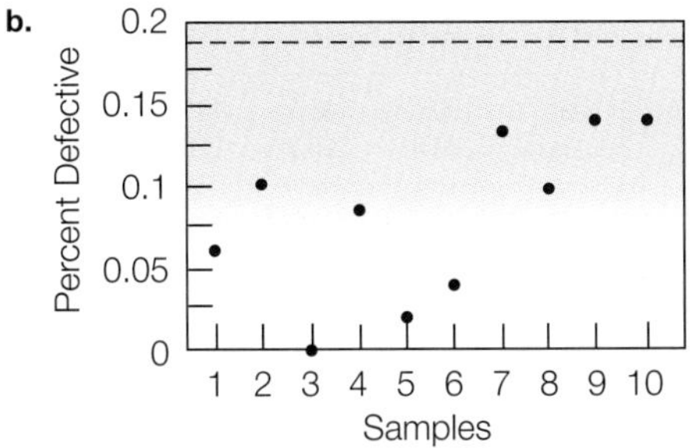

c. There are no points that exceed the limits.

27.

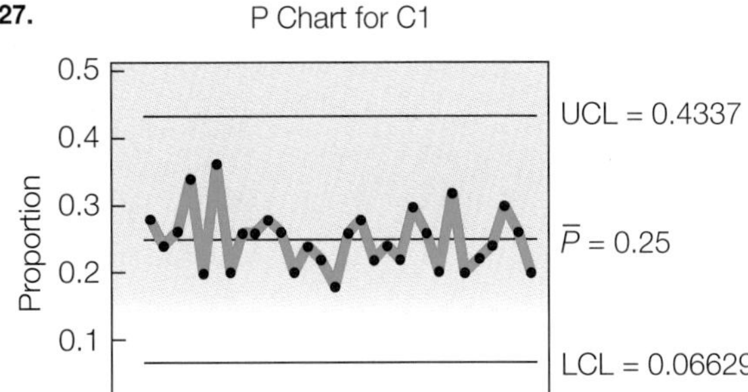

These sample results indicate that the odds are much less than 50-50 for an increase. The percent of stocks that increase is "in control" around 0.25 or 25 percent. The control limits are 0.06629 and 0.4337.

29. $P(X \le 3|n = 10, \pi = 0.05) = 0.999$
$P(X \le 3|n = 10, \pi = 0.10) = 0.987$
$P(X \le 3|n = 10, \pi = 0.20) = 0.878$
$P(X \le 3|n = 10, \pi = 0.30) = 0.649$

$P(X \le 5|n = 20, \pi = 0.05) = 0.999$
$P(X \le 5|n = 20, \pi = 0.10) = 0.989$
$P(X \le 5|n = 20, \pi = 0.20) = 0.805$
$P(X \le 5|n = 20, \pi = 0.30) = 0.417$

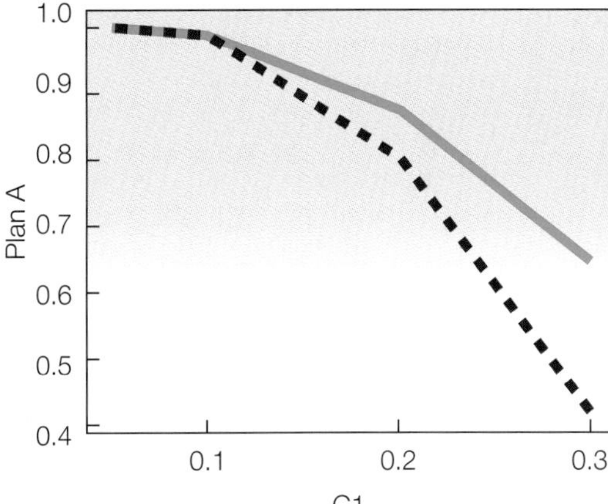

The solid line is the operating characteristic curve for the first plan, and the dashed line, the second. The supplier would prefer the first because the probability of acceptance is higher (above). However, if he is really sure of his quality, the second plan seems higher at the very low range of defect percentages and might be preferred.

31. **a.** $\bar{c} = \frac{213}{15} = 14.2; 3\sqrt{14.2} = 11.30$

UCL = 14.2 + 11.3 = 25.5

LCL = 14.2 - 11.3 = 2.9

b.

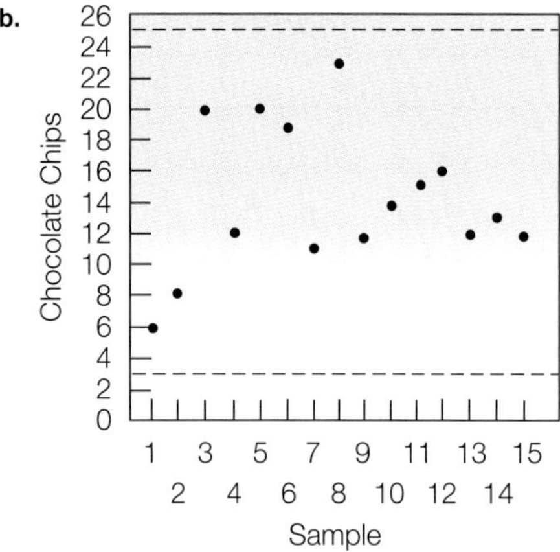

c. All the points are in control.

33. $\bar{c} = \frac{70}{10} = 7.0$

UCL $= 7.0 + 3\sqrt{7} = 14.9$

LCL $= 7.0 - 3\sqrt{7} = 0$

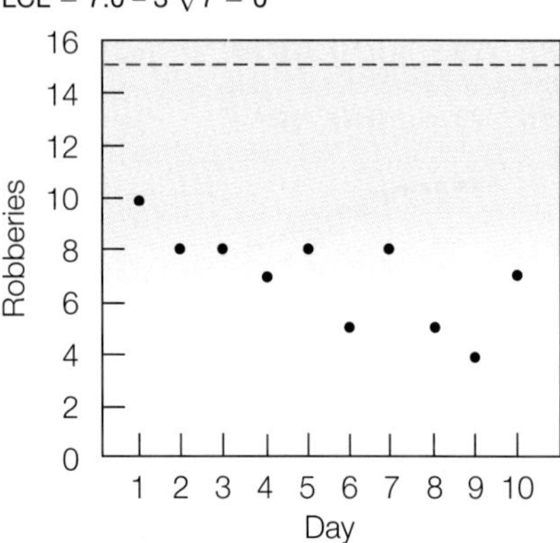

35. $P(X \leq 3 | n = 20, \pi = .10) = .867$
$P(X \leq 3 | n = 20, \pi = .20) = .412$
$P(X \leq 3 | n = 20, \pi = .30) = .108$

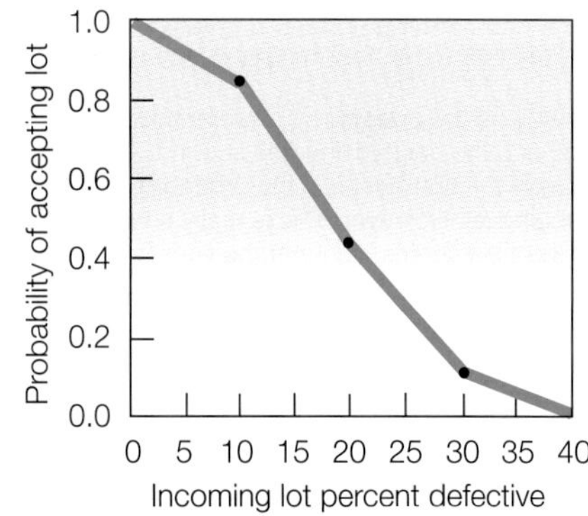

CHAPTER 18

1. 114.6, found by ($19,989/$17,446)(100).
123.1, found by ($21,468/$17,446)(100).

3. 1998: 95.5, found by (506.8/530.53)(100).
1999: 98.4, found by (522.2/530.53)(100).

5. **a.** $P_t = \frac{2.69}{2.49}(100) = 108.03$ $\quad P_s = \frac{3.59}{3.29}(100) = 109.12$

$P_c = \frac{1.79}{1.59}(100) = 112.58$ $\quad P_a = \frac{2.29}{1.79}(100) = 127.93$

b. $P = \frac{10.36}{9.16}(100) = 113.1$

c. $P = \frac{\$2.69(6) + 3.59(4) + 1.79(2) + 2.29(3)}{\$2.49(6) + 3.29(4) + 1.59(2) + 1.79(3)}(100) = 111.7$

d. $P = \frac{\$2.69(6) + 3.59(5) + 1.79(3) + 2.29(4)}{\$2.49(6) + 3.29(5) + 1.59(3) + 1.79(4)}(100) = 112.2$

e. $I = \sqrt{112.2(111.7)} = 111.95$

7. **a.** $P_W = \frac{0.10}{0.07}(100) = 142.9$ $\quad P_C = \frac{0.03}{0.04}(100) = 75.0$

$P_S = \frac{0.15}{0.15}(100) = 100$ $\quad P_H = \frac{0.10}{0.08}(100) = 125.0$

b. $P = \frac{0.38}{0.34}(100) = 111.8$

c.

$$P = \frac{0.10(17{,}000) + 0.03(125{,}000) + 0.15(40{,}000) + 0.10(62{,}000)}{0.07(17{,}000) + 0.04(125{,}000) + 0.15(40{,}000) + 0.08(62{,}000)}$$

$(100) = 102.92$

d.

$$P = \frac{0.10(20{,}000) + 0.03(130{,}000) + 0.15(42{,}000) + 0.10(65{,}000)}{0.07(20{,}000) + 0.04(130{,}000) + 0.15(42{,}000) + 0.08(65{,}000)}$$

$(100) = 103.32$

e. $P = \sqrt{102.92(103.32)} = 103.12$

9. $V = \frac{1.87(214) + 2.05(489) + 1.48(203) + 3.29(106)}{1.52(200) + 2.10(565) + 1.48(291) + 3.05(87)}(100)$

$= 93.8$

11. **a.** $I = \frac{6.8}{5.3}(0.20) + \frac{362.26}{265.88}(0.40) + \frac{125.0}{109.6}(0.25) + \frac{622{,}864}{529{,}917}$
$(0.15) = 1.263.$
Index is 126.3.

b. Business activity increased 26.3 percent from 1995 to 2001.

13. $X = (\$42{,}000)/1.74 = \$24{,}138$
Salary increased $24,138 − $19,800 = $4,338

15.

Year	Tinora	Tinora	National Index
1990	$23,650	100.0	100
1995	$28,972	122.5	122.5
2000	$32,382	136.9	136.9

The Tinora teachers received the same increase as the national average.

17. The index for selected years is:

Year	1996	1997	1998	1999
Index	200.8	219.2	236.7	283.5

The domestic sales almost tripled between 1990 and 1999.

19. The index for selected years is:

Year	1996	1997	1998	1999
Index	184.7	188.4	192.0	208.2

International sales doubled between 1990 and 1999.

21. The index for selected years is:

Year	1996	1997	1998	1999
Index	108.6	110.8	114.7	119.0

The number of employees increased almost 20 percent between 1990 and 1999.

23. The index for selected years is:

Year	1995	1996	1997	1998	1999
Index	100.00	113.1	129.7	143.5	159.4

Revenue increased about 60 percent over the period.

25. The index for selected years is:

Year	1995	1996	1997	1998	1999
Index	100.00	112.8	128.2	145.6	165.1

Earnings per share increased 65 percent between 1990 and 1999.

27. $P_M = \frac{\$0.89}{\$0.81}(100) = 109.88 \qquad P_S = \frac{\$0.94}{\$0.84}(100) = 111.90$

$P_M = \frac{1.43}{1.44}(100) = 99.31 \qquad P_P = \frac{3.07}{2.91}(100) = 105.50$

29. $P = \frac{0.89(18) + 0.94(5) + 1.43(70) + 3.07(27)}{0.81(18) + 0.84(5) + 1.44(70) + 2.91(27)}(100) = 102.81$

31. $P = \sqrt{(102.81)(103.51)} = 103.16$

33. $P_R = \frac{0.60}{0.50}(100) = 120 \qquad P_S = \frac{0.90}{1.20}(100) = 75.0$

$P_W = \frac{1.00}{0.85}(100) = 117.65$

35. $P = \frac{0.60(320) + 0.90(110) + 1.00(230)}{0.50(320) + 1.20(110) + 0.85(230)}(100) = 106.87$

37. $P = \sqrt{(106.87)(106.04)} = 106.45$

39. $P_C = \frac{0.05}{0.06}(100) = 83.33 \qquad P_C = \frac{0.12}{0.10}(100) = 120$

$P_P = \frac{0.18}{0.20}(100) = 90 \qquad P_E = \frac{.015}{0.15}(100) = 100$

41. $P = \frac{0.05(2{,}000) + 0.12(200) + 1.18(400) + 0.15(100)}{0.06(2{,}000) + 0.10(200) + 0.20(400) + 0.15(100)}(100)$

$= 89.79$

43. $P = \sqrt{(89.79)(91.25)} = 90.52$

45. $P_A = \frac{0.76}{0.287}(100) = 264.8 \qquad P_N = \frac{2.50}{0.17}(100) = 1{,}470.59$

$P_P = \frac{26.00}{3.18}(100) = 817.61 \qquad P_P = \frac{490}{133}(100) = 368.42$

47. $P = \frac{0.76(1{,}000) + 2.50(5{,}000) + 26(60{,}000) + 490(500)}{0.287(1{,}000) + 0.17(5{,}000) + 3.18(60{,}000) + 133(500)}$

$(100) = 703.56$

49. $P = \sqrt{(703.56)(686.58)} = 695.02$

51. $I = 100\frac{1{,}971.0}{1{,}159.0}(0.20) + \frac{91}{87}(0.10) + \frac{114.7}{110.6}(0.40)$

$+ \frac{1{,}501}{1{,}214}(0.30) = 123.05$

The economy is up 23.05 percent from 1996 to 2001.

53. February: $I = 100\frac{6.8}{8.0}(0.40) + \frac{23}{20}(0.35) + \frac{303}{300}(0.25)$

$= 99.50$

March: $I = 100\frac{6.4}{8.0}(0.40) + \frac{21}{20}(0.35) + \frac{297}{300}(0.25)$

$= 93.5$

55. For 1991: \$1,972,062, found by \$2,400,000/1.217.
For 2000: \$2,536,232, found by \$3,500,000/1.38.

57. Answers will vary.

CHAPTER 19

1. $b = \frac{5(2{,}469) - 721(15)}{5(55) - 15^2} = 30.6$

$a = \frac{721}{5} - 30.6\left(\frac{15}{5}\right) = 52.4 \qquad$ for 2003, $t = 7$

$Y' = 52.4 + 30.6t = 52.4 + 30.6(7) = 266.6$

3. $b = \frac{5(69) - 20(15)}{5(55) - 15^2} = 0.90$

$a = \frac{20}{5} - 0.90\left(\frac{15}{5}\right) = 1.30$

$Y' = 1.30 + 0.90t = 1.30 + 0.90(7) = 7.6$(tons)

5. **a.** $b = \frac{5(5.274318) - 1.390087(15)}{5(55) - 15^2}$

$= 0.1104057$

$a = \frac{1.390087}{5} - 0.1104057\left(\frac{15}{5}\right) = -0.0531997$

b. 28.95%, found by 1.28945 − 1.0.

c. $Y' = -0.0531997 + 0.1104057t$
$Y' = -0.0531997 + 0.1104057(8) = 0.8300459$
Antilog of 0.8300459 = 6.76

7.

Quarter	Average SI Component	Seasonal Index
1	0.6859	0.6911
2	1.6557	1.6682
3	1.1616	1.1704
4	0.4732	0.4768

9.

t	Estimated Pairs (millions)	Seasonal Index	Quarterly Forecast (millions)
21	40.05	110.0	44.055
22	41.80	120.0	50.160
23	43.55	80.0	34.840
24	45.30	90.0	40.770

11. $Y' = 5.1658 + .37805t$. The following are the sales estimates.

Estimate	Index	Seasonally Adjusted
10.080	0.6911	6.966
10.458	1.6682	17.446
10.837	1.1704	12.684
11.215	0.4768	5.343

13. **a.** $Y' = 18{,}000 - 400t$, assuming the line starts at 18,000 in 1980 and goes down to 10,000 in 2000.

b. 400

c. 8,000, found by 18,000 − 400(25).

15. a.

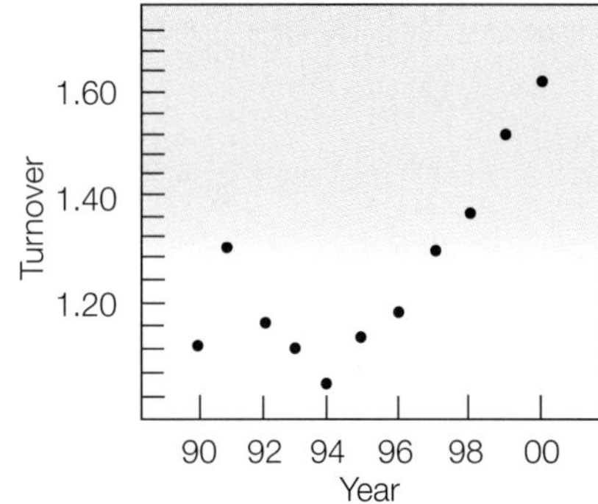

b. $Y' = 1.0045 + 0.04409t$, using $t = 1$ for 1990.
c. For 1993, $Y' = 1.18091$. For 1998 $Y' = 1.40136$.
d. For 2005, $Y' = 1.70999$.
e. Each asset turned over .044 times.

17. a.

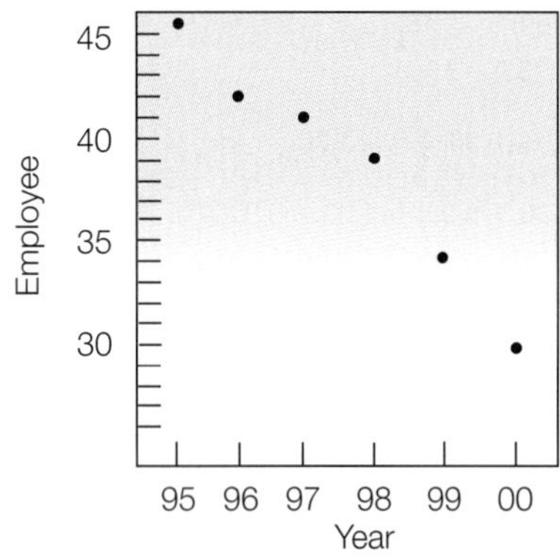

b. $Y' = 49.140 - 2.9829t$
c. For 1997, $Y' = 40.1913$. For 1999 $Y' = 34.2255$.
d. For 2003, $Y' = 22.2939$.
e. The number of employees decreases at a rate of 2,983 per year.

19. a. Log $Y' = 0.790231 + 0.113669t$
b. Log $Y' = 1.244907$, antilog is 17.575
Log $Y' = 1.813252$, antilog is 65.05
c. 29.92, which is the antilog of .113669 minus 1.
d. Log $Y' = 2.154258$, antilog is 142.65

21. a.

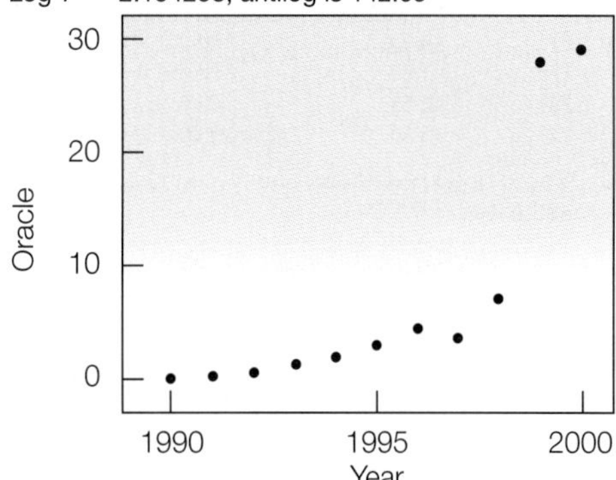

b. The equations are $Y' = -8.03 + 2.56t$ and/or Log $Y' = -0.810 + 0.206t$. The equation using the logarithm of the price seems more accurate because the R^2 term is larger.
c. Log $Y' = -0.810 + 0.206(4) = 0.014$, antilog is 1.0328
Log $Y' = -0.810 + 0.206(9) = 1.044$, antilog is 11.0662
d. Log $Y' = -0.810 + 0.206(14) = 2.074$, antilog is 118.5769. It is reasonable *if* the price rises at the historical rate!
e. The annual rate of increase is 60.7 percent, found by antilog of 0.206 minus 1.

23. a. July 87.5; August 92.9; September 99.3; October 109.1.
b.

Month	Total	Mean	Corrected
July	348.9	87.225	86.777
Aug.	368.1	92.025	91.552
Sept.	395.0	98.750	98.242
Oct.	420.4	105.100	104.560
Nov.	496.2	124.050	123.412
Dec.	572.3	143.075	142.340
Jan.	333.5	83.375	82.946
Feb.	297.5	74.375	73.993
March	347.3	86.825	86.379
April	481.3	120.325	119.707
May	396.2	99.050	98.541
June	368.1	92.025	91.552
		1,206.200	

Correction = 1,200/1,206.2 = 0.99486
c. April, November, and December are periods of high sales, while February's sales are lowest.

25. a. **Seasonal Index by Quarter**

Quarter	Average SI Component	Seasonal Index
1	0.5014	0.5027
2	1.0909	1.0936
3	1.7709	1.7753
4	0.6354	0.6370

b. Production is the largest in the third quarter. It is 77.5 percent above the average quarter. The second quarter is also above average. The first and fourth quarters are well below average, with the first quarter at about 50 percent of a typical quarter.

27. a. **Seasonal Index by Quarter**

Quarter	Average SI Component	Seasonal Index
1	0.5549	0.5577
2	0.8254	0.8296
3	1.5102	1.5178
4	1.0973	1.1029

b. $Y' = 7.667 + 0.0023t$
c.

Period	Production	Index	Forecast
21	7.7153	0.5577	4.3028
22	7.7176	0.8296	6.4025
23	7.7199	1.5178	11.7173
24	7.7222	1.1029	8.5168

29. **Seasonal Index by Quarter**

Quarter	Average SI Component	Seasonal Index
1	1.1962	1.2053
2	1.0135	1.0212
3	0.6253	0.6301
4	1.1371	1.1457

The regression equation is: $Y' = 43.611 + 7.2153t$

Period	Visitors	Index	Forecast
29	252.86	1.2053	304.77
30	260.07	1.0212	265.58
31	267.29	0.6301	168.42
32	274.50	1.1457	314.50

In 2000 there were 928 visitors. A 10 percent increase in 2001 means there will be 1,021 visitors. The quarterly estimates are 1,021/4 = 255.25 visitors per quarter.

Period	Visitors	Index	Forecast
Winter	255.25	1.2053	307.65
Spring	255.25	1.0212	260.66
Summer	255.25	0.6301	160.83
Fall	255.25	1.1457	292.44

The regression approach is probably superior because the trend is considered.

31. Purse: Log $Y' = 2.32 + 0.0466t$
Prize: Log $Y' = 1.49 + 0.0466t$
The "slopes" are identical because the prize is always 15 percent of the purse. The projected purse for 2005 is \$1.6 million, found as the antilog of $2.32 + 0.0466(19) = 3.2054$.

33. Answers will vary.

35.

Trend Analysis for Average
Linear Trend Model
$Yt = -240330 + 70063.3*t$

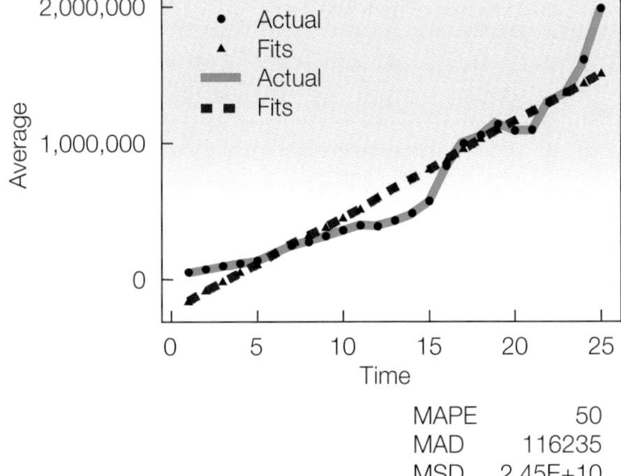

Trend Analysis for Median
Linear Trend Model
$Yt = 50603.2 + 18150.6*t$

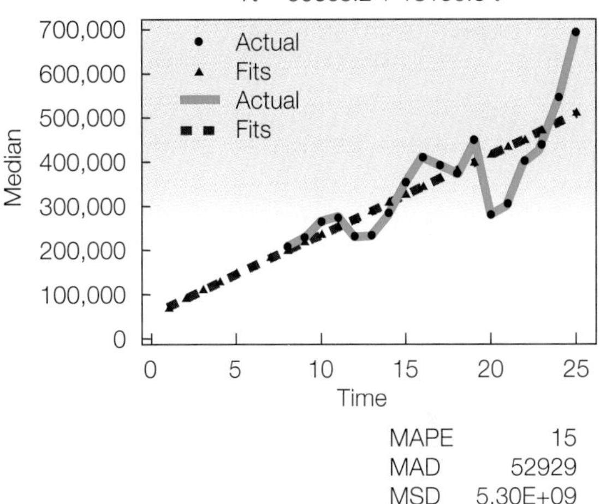

The median is increasing \$18,150 per year, while the average is increasing much more rapidly (\$70,000 per year).

CHAPTER 20

1. EMV(A_1) = .30(\$50) + .50(\$70) + .20(\$100) = \$70

EMV(A_2) = .30(\$90) + .50(\$40) + .20(\$80) = \$63

EMV(A_3) = .30(\$70) + .50(\$60) + .20(\$90) = \$69

Decision: Choose alternative 1.

3. **Opportunity Loss**

	S_1	S_2	S_3
A_1	\$40	\$ 0	\$ 0
A_2	0	30	20
A_3	20	10	10

5. (Answers in \$000)

EOL(A_1) = .30(\$40) + 50(\$0) + .20(\$0) = \$12

EOL(A_2) = .30(\$0) + .50(\$30) + .20(\$20) = \$19

EOL(A_3) = .30(\$20) + .50(\$10) + .20(\$10) = \$13

7. Expected value under conditions of certainty is \$82, found by .30(\$90) + .50(\$70) + .20(\$100) = \$82.

EVPI = \$82 − \$70 = \$12

9. Yes, it changes the decision. Choose alternative 2. (Answers in \$000).

EMV(A_1) = .50(\$50) + .20(\$70) + .30(\$100) = \$69

EMV(A_2) = .50(\$90) + .20(\$40) + .30(\$80) = \$77

EMV(A_3) = .50(\$70) + .20(\$60) + .30(\$90) = \$74

11. **a.** (Answers in \$000)

EMV(neither) = .30(\$0) + .50(\$0) + .20(\$0) = \$0

EMV(1) = .30(\$125) + .50(\$65) + .20(\$30) = \$76.00

EMV(2) = .30(\$105) + .50(\$60) + .20(\$30) = \$67.50

EMV(both) = .30(\$220) + .50(\$110) + .20(\$40) = \$129.00

b. Choose both.

c. **Opportunity Loss**

	S_1	S_2	S_3
Neither	$220	$110	$40
1	95	45	10
2	115	50	10
Both	0	0	0

d. EOL(neither) = $129.00

EOL(1) = $53.00

EOL(2) = $61.50

EOL(both) = $0

e. EVPI = $0, found by $129 − $129.

Certainty = .30($220) + .50($110) + .20($40)

= $129

13. The payoff table is as follows in $000.

	Recession, S_1	No Recession, S_2
Production	$−10.0	$15.0
Stock	−5.0	12.0
CD	6.0	6.0

a. Purchase a CD

b. Increase production.

c. (Answers in $000)

EMV(Prod.) = .2(−10) + .8(15.0) = 10.0

EMV(Stock) = .2(−5) + .8(12.0) = 8.6

EMV(CD) = .2(6) + .8(6) = 6.0

Expand production.

d. EVPI = [.2(6) + .8(15)] − [10.0] = 3.2

15. a. **Event**

Act	10	11	12	13	14
10	$500	$500	$500	$500	$500
11	200	550	550	550	550
12	−100	250	600	600	600
13	−400	−50	300	650	650
14	−700	−350	0	350	700

b.

Act	Expected Profit
10	$500.00
11	504.50
12	421.50
13	233.50
14	−31.50

Order 11 mobile homes because expected profit of $504.50 is the highest.

c. **Opportunity Loss**

Supply	10	11	12	13	14
10	$ 0	$ 50	$100	$150	$200
11	300	0	50	100	150
12	600	300	0	50	100
13	900	600	300	0	50
14	1,200	900	600	300	0

d. **Act**

	10	11	12	13	14
EOL	$95.50	$91	$174	$362	$627

Decision: Order 11 homes because the opportunity loss of $91 is the smallest.

e. $91, found by:

$595.50	profit under certainty
−504.50	profit under uncertainty
$ 91.00	value of perfect information

17. a. **Event**

Act	41	42	43	44	45	46
41	$410	$410	$410	$410	$410	$410
42	405	420	420	420	420	420
43	400	415	430	430	430	430
44	395	410	425	440	440	440
45	390	405	420	435	450	450
46	385	400	415	430	445	460

b.

Act	Expected Profit
41	$410.00
42	419.10
43	426.70
44	432.20
45	431.70
46	427.45

c. Order 44 because $432.20 is the largest expected profit.

d. Expected opportunity loss:

41	42	43	44	45	46
$28.30	$19.20	$11.60	$6.10	$6.60	$10.85

e. Order 44 because the opportunity loss of $6.10 is the smallest. Yes, it agrees.

f. $6.10, found by:

$438.30	profit under certainty
−432.20	profit under uncertainty
$ 6.10	value of perfect information

The maximum we should pay for perfect information is $6.10.

Answers

to Odd-Numbered Review Exercises

REVIEW OF CHAPTERS 1–4

1. **a.** Sample.
   b. Ratio.
   c. \$11.60, found by \$58/5.
   d. \$11.70. Half of the employees earn below \$11.70 an hour and the other half earn above \$11.70 an hour.
   e. $s^2 = \dfrac{696.18 - \dfrac{(58)^2}{5}}{5 - 1} = 5.845$
   f. $sk = \dfrac{3(11.60 - 11.70)}{2.42} = -0.124$

3. **a.**

Rolls		Frequency
3 up to 6	II	2
6 up to 9	~~IIII~~ I	6
9 up to 12	~~IIII~~ III	8
12 up to 15	III	3
15 up to 18	I	1

   b.

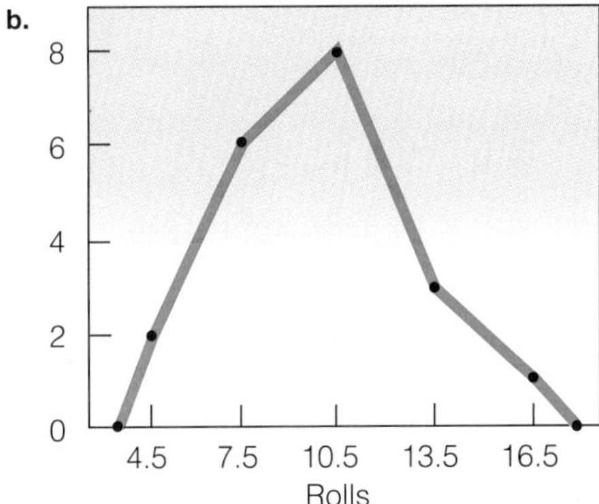

   c. $\overline{X} = \dfrac{186}{20} = 9.3$
   d. median = 9
   e. 8 and 9, each occurs 4 times
   f. 15 using the frequency distribution, 13 using the actual data.
   g. $s^2 = \dfrac{1906 - \dfrac{(186)^2}{20}}{20 - 1} = 9.2736$
   h. $s = \sqrt{9.2736} = 3.045$
   i. $9.30 \pm 2(3.045)$. The limits are 3.21 up to 15.39.

5. **a.** 8.82%, found by 44.1/5.
   b. 7.479%.
   c. Geometric mean, because it is not highly influenced by the 19.5 percent.

7.

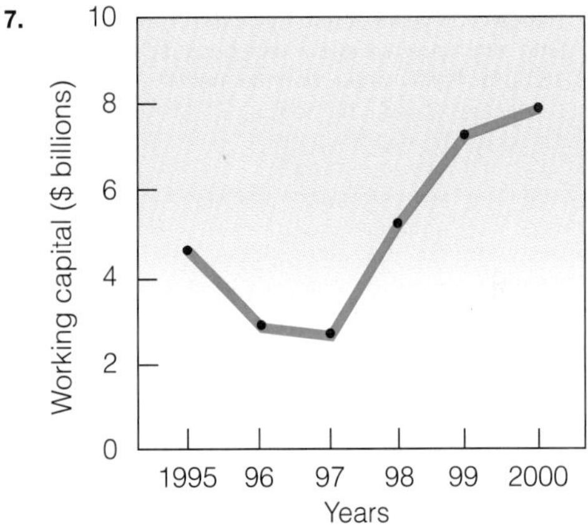

9. Ordinal.
11. Cumulative frequency polygon. About 45; about 35; 10; 35, found by 55 − 20.
13. 9.375%.
15. Coefficient of variation.
17. 92 and 108, found by $100 \pm 2(4)$.
19. **a.** The following histogram is from MINITAB.

```
Histogram of C1   N = 50
Midpoint       Count
       0           1 *
      40           7 *******
      80           3 ***
     120           8 ********
     160          15 ***************
     200          10 **********
     240           3 ***
     280           3 ***
```

   b. and c.

N	MEAN	MEDIAN	TRMEAN	STDEV	SEMEAN
50	147.90	148.50	146.11	69.24	9.79

MIN	MAX	Q1	Q3
14.00	299.00	106.00	186.25

The distribution is fairly symmetrical because the mean (\$147.90) and the median (\$148.50) are quite close. The mean ± 2*s* indicates that the middle 95 percent of the deposits are between \$147.90 ± 2(\$69.24) = \$9.42 and \$286.38. Range = \$299.00 − \$14.00 = \$285.00.

21. **a.** From MINITAB:

```
Variable      N   Mean Median Tr mean  Stdev Se mean
years        85  15.06  15.00   14.79   9.63    1.04

Variable   Min    Max     Q1      Q3
years     0.00  36.00   6.00   22.50
```

Typical length of service is about 15 years (mean or median).

b. Range is 36 years, found by 36 (MAX) − 0 (MIN).

c. Only slight positive skewness, because the mean of 15.06 is slightly larger than the median (15.00).

d.
```
Stem-and-leaf of years      N = 85
Leaf Unit = 1.0
 12    0 011222333444
 30    0 555555566677788999
 42    1 000133334444
(16)   1 5555566666788899
 27    2 00001233333
 16    2 6667889
  9    3 00123344
  1    3 6
```

23. The typical age is 55 years. The range is 27 years.

```
Variable        N   Mean Median Tr Mean StDev SE Mean
years          43 54.674 55.000  54.590 6.383   0.973

Variable     Min     Max     Q1      Q3
years     42.000  69.000 50.000  58.000

Stem-and-leaf of years      N = 43
Leaf Unit = 1.0
      2    4 23              18     5 6667777
      2    4                 11     5 8
      6    4 6677            10     6 0111
      9    4 899              6     6 2
     15    5 001111           5     6 455
     17    5 22               2     6
    (8)    5 44445555         2     6 89
```

REVIEW OF CHAPTERS 5–7

1. Subjective.
3. An outcome.
5. Complement rule. $1 - P(X) = .999$.
7. Discrete.
9. Discrete.
11. Bell-shaped, symmetrical, asymptotic.
13. **a.** .10, found by 20/200.
    b. .725, found by 145/200.
    c. .925, found by $1 - 15/200$.
15. **a.** .1353, found from Appendix C, where $\mu = 2.0$.
    b. 398, found by $400 - 2$.
    c. .3233, found by $1 - (.1353 + .2707 + .2707)$.
17. **a.** .510, found by 273/535.
    b. .513, found by 223/435.
    c. .907, found by $\frac{260 + 435 - 210}{535}$.
19. **a.** \$1.84 million, found by $0 + .64 + 1.2$.
    b. .98.
    c. .20, found by .004/.02.
    d. Yes. The \$2 million premium is greater than the expected loss of \$1.84 million. Thus, the expected profit is \$0.16 million.

REVIEW OF CHAPTERS 8 AND 9

1. B
3. D
5. D
7. A
9. B
11. $z = \frac{8.8 - 8.6}{2.0/\sqrt{35}} = 0.59$, $.5000 - .2224 = .2776$
13. $160 \pm 1.75 \frac{20}{\sqrt{40}}$, 154.47 up to 165.53
15. $985.5 \pm 2.571 \frac{115.5}{\sqrt{6}}$, 864.27 up to 1106.73
17. $240 \pm 2.131 \frac{35}{\sqrt{16}}$, 221.35 up to 258.65

    Because 250 is in the interval, the evidence does *not* indicate an increase in production.
19. $n = \left[\frac{1.96(25)}{4}\right]^2 = 150$
21. $n = .08(.92)\left(\frac{2.33}{0.02}\right)^2 = 999$
23. $n = .4(.6)\left(\frac{2.33}{0.03}\right)^2 = 1{,}448$

REVIEW OF CHAPTERS 10–12

1. E
3. B
5. B
7. A
9. D
11. H_0: $\mu \geq 36$; H_1: $\mu < 36$. Reject H_0 if $z < -1.65$.

$$z = \frac{35.5 - 36.0}{0.9/\sqrt{42}} = -3.60$$

    Reject H_0. The mean height is less than 36 inches.
13. H_0: $\mu \leq 20$, H_1: $\mu > 20$. Reject H_0 if $t > 1.860$.

$$t = \frac{21 - 20}{6.185/\sqrt{9}} = 0.485$$

    H_0 is not rejected. The mean amount of break time is not more than 20 minutes.
15. H_0: $\mu_d \leq 0$; H_1: $\mu_d > 0$. Repeat H_0 if $t > 1.883$.

$$\bar{d} = 0.4 \qquad s_d = 6.11 \qquad t = \frac{0.4}{6.11/\sqrt{10}} = 0.21$$

    H_0 is not rejected. There is no difference in the life of the paints.

REVIEW OF CHAPTERS 13 AND 14

1. Coefficient of correlation or the coefficient of determination.
3. H_0: $\rho \leq 0$; H_1: $\rho > 0$. Critical value of t is 1.671; computed $t = 3.324$. H_0 rejected. There is positive correlation.
5. The square of the coefficient of correlation is the coefficient of determination.
7. $Y' = a + b_1X_1 + b_2X_2 + b_3X_3 + b_4X_4$
9. About 86% of the variation in net profit is explained by the four variables.

11. a.

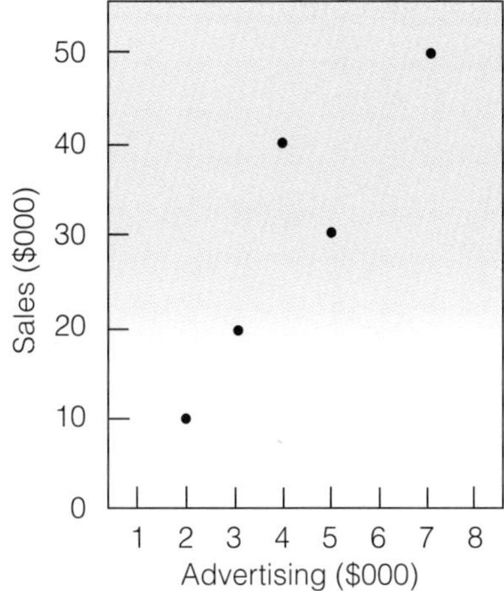

b. $r = \dfrac{5(740) - 21(150)}{\sqrt{[5(103) - (21)^2][5(5500) - (150)^2]}} = .9042$

c. $r^2 = (0.9042)^2 = 0.8176$

d. $b = \dfrac{5(740) - 21(150)}{5(103) - (21)^2} = \dfrac{550}{74} = 7.4324$

$a = \dfrac{150}{5} - (7.4324)\left(\dfrac{21}{5}\right) = -1.2161$

$Y' = -1.2161 + 7.4324X$

e. $Y' = -1.2161 + 7.4324(4.5) = \$32.23$ (in thousands).

f. Strong positive association between amount spent on advertising and monthly sales. For each additional $1,000 spent on advertising, sales increase $7,432.40.

REVIEW OF CHAPTERS 15 AND 16

1. Frequency observed and frequency expected.

3. Chi-square distribution.

5. Not rejected, because 11.248 is less than 12.592.

7. There is no difference between the observed and the expected set of frequencies.

9. Nominal level.

11. To determine whether two independent populations are the same.

13. To determine whether three or more populations are the same.

15. Kruskal-Wallis

17. Yes.

19. No. It is positively skewed.

21. H_0: Median = \$27,000; H_1: Median ≠ \$27,000. Use .05 significance level and the sign test. The critical values are −1.96 and 1.96. Count the number of values above the median, compute *z*, assuming a large sample, and make a decision.

Photo Credits

Chapter 1
p. 1: © David Burnett / Contact Press Images / PictureQuest; p. 2: © PhotoDisc; p. 4: © elektra Vision AG / Picture Quest; p. 10: © elektra Vision AG / Picture Quest.

Chapter 2
p. 21: Courtesy of Merrill Lynch; p. 22: © PhotoDisc; p. 41: © PhotoDisc; p. 50: Author provided.

Chapter 3
p. 64: © Corbis; p. 72: © Neil Beer / PhotoDisc / Picture Quest; p. 73: © PhotoDisc.

Chapter 4
p. 99: © PhotoDisc; p. 102: Photo courtesy of Hewlett-Packard Company; p. 115: Science Photo Library / Photo Researchers, Inc.

Chapter 5
p. 149: © PhotoDisc; p. 150: Mitch Kezar / Tony Stone Images; p. 158: Courtesy Dean Foods; p. 161: © 2001 Busch Entertainment Corporation. All rights reserved; p. 172: Photo courtesy of Hewlett-Packard Company.

Chapter 6
p. 191: © elektra Vision AG / Picture Quest; p. 196: © Corbis; p. 200: Jeff Zaruba / Tony Stone Images.

Chapter 7
p. 226: © Digital Vision / Picture Quest; p. 227: Courtesy of ALCOA; p. 241: Chip Henderson / Tony Stone Images.

Chapter 8
p. 263: © Digital Vision / Picture Quest; p. 264: © Corbis Images / Picture Quest; p. 265: © PhotoDisc; p. 270: Doug Plummer / Photo Researchers, Inc.

Chapter 9
p. 297: © Corbis Images; p. 299: © PhotoDisc; p. 310: © PhotoDisc; p. 313: © Corbis Images.

Chapter 10
p. 334: © PhotoDisc; p. 335: © Russell Illig / PhotoDisc / Picture Quest; p. 338: © PhotoDisc; p. 349: © PhotoDisc.

Chapter 11
p. 377: © PhotoDisc; p. 378: © Corbis Images; p. 391: © Corbis Images / Picture Quest.

Chapter 12
p. 413: © Corbis Images / Picture Quest; p. 415: © PhotoDisc; p. 420: © Corbis Images / Picture Quest; p. 433: © PhotoDisc.

Chapter 13
p. 456: © PhotoDisc; p. 457: Courtesy of VF Playwear, Healthtex Brand; p. 470: © PhotoDisc.

Chapter 14
p. 502: © PhotoDisc; p. 505: © PhotoDisc; p. 511: © PhotoDisc.

Chapter 15
p. 548: Solum / PhotoLink / PhotoDisc / Picture Quest; p. 549: Jose Azel / Aurora / Picture Quest; p. 566: © PhotoLink / PhotoDisc / Picture Quest; p. 571: © Image Ideas, Inc. / Picture Quest.

Chapter 16
p. 580: © PhotoDisc; p. 581: Courtesy of Nestlé USA—Beverage Division; p. 585: © RubberBall Productions / Picture Quest / p. 591: © PhotoDisc.

Chapter 17
p. 622: Courtesy of GE Lighting; p. 625: Courtesy of the National Institute of Standards & Technology, Office of Quality Programs, Gaithersburg, Maryland 20899. Photograph by Steuben; p. 642: Courtesy of ALCOA.

Chapter 18
p. 655: © Image Ideas, Inc. / PictureQuest.

Chapter 19
p. 689: Courtesy of Pepsi Company; p. 690: NCSA, University of Illinois / Science Photo Library / Photo Researchers, Inc.

Chapter 20
p. 726: © Corbis Images / Picture Quest; p. 727: Courtesy of Banana Republic.

Index

Areas under the Normal Curve

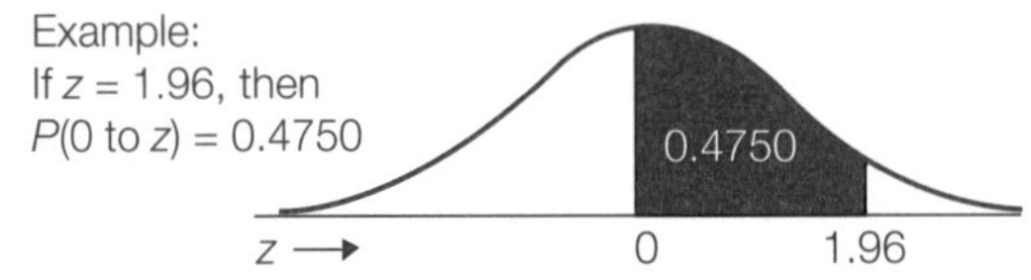

z	0.00	0.01	0.02	0.03	0.04	0.05	0.06	0.07	0.08	0.09
0.0	0.0000	0.0040	0.0080	0.0120	0.0160	0.0199	0.0239	0.0279	0.0319	0.0359
0.1	0.0398	0.0438	0.0478	0.0517	0.0557	0.0596	0.0636	0.0675	0.0714	0.0753
0.2	0.0793	0.0832	0.0871	0.0910	0.0948	0.0987	0.1026	0.1064	0.1103	0.1141
0.3	0.1179	0.1217	0.1255	0.1293	0.1331	0.1368	0.1406	0.1443	0.1480	0.1517
0.4	0.1554	0.1591	0.1628	0.1664	0.1700	0.1736	0.1772	0.1808	0.1844	0.1879
0.5	0.1915	0.1950	0.1985	0.2019	0.2054	0.2088	0.2123	0.2157	0.2190	0.2224
0.6	0.2257	0.2291	0.2324	0.2357	0.2389	0.2422	0.2454	0.2486	0.2517	0.2549
0.7	0.2580	0.2611	0.2642	0.2673	0.2704	0.2734	0.2764	0.2794	0.2823	0.2852
0.8	0.2881	0.2910	0.2939	0.2967	0.2995	0.3023	0.3051	0.3078	0.3106	0.3133
0.9	0.3159	0.3186	0.3212	0.3238	0.3264	0.3289	0.3315	0.3340	0.3365	0.3389
1.0	0.3413	0.3438	0.3461	0.3485	0.3508	0.3531	0.3554	0.3577	0.3599	0.3621
1.1	0.3643	0.3665	0.3686	0.3708	0.3729	0.3749	0.3770	0.3790	0.3810	0.3830
1.2	0.3849	0.3869	0.3888	0.3907	0.3925	0.3944	0.3962	0.3980	0.3997	0.4015
1.3	0.4032	0.4049	0.4066	0.4082	0.4099	0.4115	0.4131	0.4147	0.4162	0.4177
1.4	0.4192	0.4207	0.4222	0.4236	0.4251	0.4265	0.4279	0.4292	0.4306	0.4319
1.5	0.4332	0.4345	0.4357	0.4370	0.4382	0.4394	0.4406	0.4418	0.4429	0.4441
1.6	0.4452	0.4463	0.4474	0.4484	0.4495	0.4505	0.4515	0.4525	0.4535	0.4545
1.7	0.4554	0.4564	0.4573	0.4582	0.4591	0.4599	0.4608	0.4616	0.4625	0.4633
1.8	0.4641	0.4649	0.4656	0.4664	0.4671	0.4678	0.4686	0.4693	0.4699	0.4706
1.9	0.4713	0.4719	0.4726	0.4732	0.4738	0.4744	0.4750	0.4756	0.4761	0.4767
2.0	0.4772	0.4778	0.4783	0.4788	0.4793	0.4798	0.4803	0.4808	0.4812	0.4817
2.1	0.4821	0.4826	0.4830	0.4834	0.4838	0.4842	0.4846	0.4850	0.4854	0.4857
2.2	0.4861	0.4864	0.4868	0.4871	0.4875	0.4878	0.4881	0.4884	0.4887	0.4890
2.3	0.4893	0.4896	0.4898	0.4901	0.4904	0.4906	0.4909	0.4911	0.4913	0.4916
2.4	0.4918	0.4920	0.4922	0.4925	0.4927	0.4929	0.4931	0.4932	0.4934	0.4936
2.5	0.4938	0.4940	0.4941	0.4943	0.4945	0.4946	0.4948	0.4949	0.4951	0.4952
2.6	0.4953	0.4955	0.4956	0.4957	0.4959	0.4960	0.4961	0.4962	0.4963	0.4964
2.7	0.4965	0.4966	0.4967	0.4968	0.4969	0.4970	0.4971	0.4972	0.4973	0.4974
2.8	0.4974	0.4975	0.4976	0.4977	0.4977	0.4978	0.4979	0.4979	0.4980	0.4981
2.9	0.4981	0.4982	0.4982	0.4983	0.4984	0.4984	0.4985	0.4985	0.4986	0.4986
3.0	0.4987	0.4987	0.4987	0.4988	0.4988	0.4989	0.4989	0.4989	0.4990	0.4990